A HISTORY OF
ACADEMICAL DRESS
IN EUROPE
UNTIL THE END OF
THE EIGHTEENTH CENTURY

D.D. Chapel Dress

D.C.L. Festal Dress

D.Mus. Festal Dress

Nobleman

OXFORD ACADEMICAL DRESSES, 1792

A HISTORY OF
ACADEMICAL DRESS
IN EUROPE
UNTIL THE END OF
THE EIGHTEENTH CENTURY

BY

W. N. HARGREAVES-MAWDSLEY
M.A., D.Phil., F.S.A.

GREENWOOD PRESS, PUBLISHERS
WESTPORT, CONNECTICUT

Library of Congress Cataloging in Publication Data

Hargreaves-Mawdsley, W. N.
  A history of academical dress in Europe until the end
of the eighteenth century.

  Reprint of the ed. published by the Clarendon, Press,
Oxford.
  Bibliography: p.
  Includes index.
  1. Academic costume. I. Title.
[LB2389.H26 1978]   378'.28   77-28438
ISBN 0-313-20250-8

© Oxford University Press 1963

Reprinted with the permission of Professor W. N. Hargreaves-
Mawdsley

Reprinted in 1978 by Greenwood Press, Inc.
51 Riverside Avenue, Westport, CT. 06880

Printed in the United States of America

10 9 8 7 6 5 4 3 2 1

TO MY MOTHER
OLGA HARGREAVES-MAWDSLEY

PREFACE

THIS history is detailed, and contains all the facts gathered together during more than eight years of work. Supplementary information could be collected, but this would increase the size of the book for no commensurate gain. I trust that the essentials and all the necessary implications are here.

I have not pursued my history beyond the eighteenth century, for by that time not only was the formative period of academical dress over, but the forces which had since the Middle Ages bound all the institutions of Europe together had vanished. Nationalism entered the academical world; states made and unmade universities; in a moment the effects of the slow process of time were swept away; and the new universities founded in the iconoclastic nineteenth century gave scope for robe-makers to use their ingenuity in creating new robes for institutions without a past, sometimes borrowing freely and without true knowledge of the manner whereby the old universities had gradually acquired their costume through the years. What was devised in an age which ignored its inheritance is alien to a study which illustrates the historical continuity of the intellectual harmony of the Western world. This is also the reason why the Empires of Russia and Turkey find no place here. The Church, which inherited what Rome bestowed, is naturally the corner-stone of our Western civilization. Russia and Turkey lay beyond its bounds.

It may be asked why I have placed countries in the order they stand here. I have taken Italy first because the earliest true university in Europe was Italian and, as Spain and Portugal are naturally associated with Italy, they are included in the same chapter. France comes next, for the University of Paris is second in seniority. England follows, and the German-speaking and other nations come finally because universities were founded in those countries last of all.

It may appear that while Great Britain is very fully treated, some of the continental countries have not been similarly dealt with, but in fact this is not so, for Oxford and Cambridge have a longer and more elaborate sartorial history than any other

European universities. As is explained in the course of my book the use of academical dress in many countries was greatly curtailed during the first half of the seventeenth century, if not earlier. Such dress as remained in use, generally only on important occasions, did not alter, but the dress of the English universities continued to evolve until the end of the eighteenth century, as dress will if worn from day to day. Furthermore, in the case of certain countries, after lengthy researches, sometimes made in person, sometimes by correspondence, no more material could be found, though some may possibly exist.

In order to shorten footnotes I have omitted 'op. cit.' wherever possible, that is, when the same book is mentioned more than once in the same chapter. When there are references to more than one book by the same author in a chapter I have used a short title to distinguish one from the other. I have only in one case shortened the reference to mere letters, and that is B.M. for British Museum.

The use of the terms 'amess' and 'amice' has caused confusion among some who have read my manuscript, and the distinction between the words has not been made in the *Oxford English Dictionary*. The amice, which is an article of liturgical dress, a square of white linen, is not referred to in my book, but the amess (almuce) was the fur scarf used by men of dignity, and in later times by canons; and to this I refer. This point of difference is mentioned by W. B. Marriott in his *Vestiarium Christianum*.

Many scholars have aided me in several ways and know how much I have appreciated their help. In the course of my work I have corresponded with or met literary men of all European countries, and it is pleasant to realize that in this distracted age, when the bane of nationalism lies so heavily on us, in the Republic of Letters there are no barriers. I regret that I must refrain from naming all who have so kindly helped me, and those not mentioned individually will, I am sure, understand my confining myself to those who have given me exceptional assistance, whom I name as: Dr. A. B. Emden, F.B.A., and Dr. Czismadia Andor, to both of whom I am especially indebted, Dr. F. Brittain, Dr. C. A. H. Franklyn, F.S.A. Scot., Professor V. H. Galbraith, F.B.A., Dr. W. O. Hassall, F.S.A., Mr. W. A. Pantin, F.B.A., F.S.A., Dr. August Roth, and Mr. P. S. Spokes, F.S.A.   W. N. H.-M.

CONTENTS

LIST OF PLATES

INTRODUCTION

The Origin of Universities—The Origin of Academical Degrees—The Origin of Academical Dress—Examples of the Influence of Lay Fashion on Academical Dress—The Influence of Forms of Association on Academical Dress

1. *The Origin of Universities*

By the twelfth century there had emerged two outstanding seats of learning in Europe, Bologna and Paris. At the first the jurist Irnerius between 1116 and 1140 introduced the *Corpus juris civilis* to Europe,[1] and at the second a group of masters with the blessing of the Church occupied themselves with the liberal arts and theology. At Paris, by 1150, the theologians occupied the cathedral area and the masters and students of the liberal arts the left bank of the Seine.

The teachers in these two cities attracted audiences from all over Europe, and both teachers and students, in different ways in the two centres, formed voluntary associations for the purpose of organization and protection. These recognized groups in these two cities were known as *studia*, that is, schools of general repute, but elsewhere, in fact wherever a cathedral chapter had a school whose fame extended beyond its own locality, *studia* existed.[2]

Only the *studia* of Bologna and Paris, and a little later Oxford, reached the next stage in their development. As they grew in size and scope faculties were organized and officers appointed. The seal of their success was set upon them when they were recognized by the Holy See, for they were then accepted everywhere. They were, as *studia generalia*, free of the threat of royal or civic interference, or from the undue influence of the chancellor of the neighbouring cathedral. Paris gained this distinction before Bologna, which the Emperor Frederick Barbarossa had in 1158 taken under his wing in opposition to

---

[1] In this section and in Section 5 on the occasions when no other reference is given I have relied on H. Rashdall, *The Universities of Europe in the Middle Ages*, ed. F. M. Powicke and A. B. Emden, 3 vols., 1936, and S. d'Irsay, *L'Histoire des universités françaises et étrangères à nos jours*, 2 vols., 1933–5.

[2] There is a general account of the development of the schools of cathedral chapters in A. F. Leach, *The Schools of Medieval England*, chap. viii.

B

the pope's Paris. In this case the power of the emperor was almost equal to the prestige of the pope, and under his patronage Bologna flourished as it never did again.[1] In the course of the thirteenth century the term *universitas*, a word used in Roman law for any kind of corporation,[2] supplanted that of *studium generale* and acquired its modern sense of *universitas litterarum*.

The universities of Paris, famed for theology and the liberal arts and patronized by the papacy, and Bologna, notable for law and with a development under imperial auspices, were the models for the systems which were adopted by the other universities of Europe when they came into being. Paris, whose government was carried out by the masters, the masters constituting the university, was the prototype of the majority of the universities of northern Europe. Bologna, on the other hand, was rather a guild of students, who as a body possessed the supreme active power, while the professors formed themselves into a college of masters isolated from the students, and so outside the great university corporation which the students formed. This system was followed in general by the universities of southern Europe. The third great university of the Middle Ages was Oxford, which followed Paris. These three universities were the only ones founded *ex consuetudine*, that is they were already in existence as *studia generalia* in all but name when recognized by the pope. All the rest that followed were either founded by potentates and recognized in time by the papacy, or were founded by the papacy for the furtherance of its own influence, and as their origin was *ex privilegio* they never enjoyed the same glory.

2. *The Origin of Academical Degrees*

During the thirteenth century a system of degrees seems to have come into being at the universities then in existence. The three grades common to all were those of Scholar, Bachelor, and Master (sometimes called Doctor or Professor). The scholar attended lectures and argued on set questions in the schools, the bachelor was a student-teacher who was seeking to obtain a licence to teach in his own right. The mastership was

---

[1] C. H. Haskins, *The Rise of Universities*, as for instance on p. 13, deals with the rise of the *studia generalia*.

[2] F. K. von Savigny, *Histoire du droit romain au moyen âge*, iii. 295, § 154.

the highest grade in any faculty, and carried with it the obligation to lecture in the university for two years after inception.[1]

'Doctor', like 'Master' and 'Professor', originally meant no
more than 'teacher' or 'learned man'.[2] All three terms were
thus at first synonymous, but during the fourteenth century the
title 'Doctor' began, particularly in southern Europe, to be
used instead of 'Master' for the chief degree in the Faculties of
Canon Law, Civil Law, and Medicine, but not in those of
Theology and Arts.[3] Masters of Theology later became known
as doctors except in France where as late as 1584 they were still
called masters.[4]

The system of degrees in the three original universities was
accepted in more or less the same form by all universities subsequently founded. As time passed differences occurred in various
countries, a few of which are worth mentioning. Thus in France
the degree of Bachelor of Arts came to be little more than a
first public examination, and the Mastership of Arts was gained
after a mere two years study of philosophy.[5] In England the
Mastership of Arts became all-important and without it
membership of Convocation or Senate was impossible. In Italy
a doctorate became almost a necessity for success in the
academical world.[6] In Germany the Bachelor of Arts degree
vanished in the sixteenth century[7] and the Mastership of Arts
was incorporated in the new title of Doctor of Philosophy
which took its place.[8] Quite early the licentiateship became an
actual degree in the Faculty of Law at French universities.[9]

In all universities a distinction existed between Regents and
Non-Regents, that is those actively engaged in the teaching
work of their university and those who, having satisfied the
requirements of necessary regency, were no longer employed

[1] On the *licentia docendi* which, as at Paris, had originally always been sought from
the chancellor of the cathedral, since he had been the *magister scholarium* of the
cathedral school, see K. Edwards, *The English Secular Cathedrals in the Middle Ages*,
chap. iii. 3. The licentiate was one who had fulfilled the requirements of the course
for the mastership, but who had not yet qualified for it by necessary regency.

[2] F. K. von Savigny, iii. 151, § 77.

[3] J. Launoy, *Epistolae Omnes*, p. 801.

[4] P. Lénaudière, *De Privilegiis Doctorum*, p. 8, § xx (25–27).

[5] For example, J. C. Nadal, *Histoire de l'Université de Valence*, p. 228.

[6] G. Panzirolus, *De claris legum interpretatibus*, p. 77.

[7] F. Paulsen, *The German Universities*, p. 39.

[8] J. von Aschbach, *Geschichte der Wiener Universität*, i. 76.

[9] See Chap. II.

in public lecturing, either because they did not wish to or were considered unsuitable. Although non-regents had the right of the *ius suffragii*, the regents gained greater rights and wider powers.

Gradually a rule of precedence for faculties and degrees came into being and was practically the same in every university. An Act of the University of Vienna of 1389 gives orders for the precedence to be observed in processions. The banner of the university is to be carried first, then are to come Bachelors of Arts, then Bachelors of Medicine, followed by Bachelors of Law, then Bachelors of Theology, then Masters of Arts, Doctors of Medicine, Doctors of Law, and Doctors of Theology, Nobles walking with the Doctors. With Bachelors are to walk their group of Scholars, and with Masters of Arts and Doctors their Licentiates. This is a very clear example, and is particularly interesting as showing the position of licentiates.[1] Among the students the separate status of noblemen, scholars, and commoners was commonly recognized at all universities.[2]

3. *The Origin of Academical Dress*

The evolution of academical costume is complicated by the secular and ecclesiastical contacts which characterized the universities at the time of their earliest development.

In the early days of the *studia generalia*, which owed their beginnings to the chapter schools, the masters and scholars, being at least in minor Orders, wore, as befitting secular clerks, some sober form of dress, loosely termed a *vestimentum clausum*, something closed.[3] Even in those countries such as Italy in which scholars were not necessarily regarded as clerks,[4] they were forced in the interests of discipline to use a uniform of some kind, which in fact would be much the same as that of the secular clerks.[5]

---

[1] *Conspectus Historiae universitatis Viennensis*, i. 49. For precedence at Oxford in 1432 see S. Gibson, *Statuta Antiqua*, p. 239, and for that at Paris in 1491 see J. Launoy, op. cit., p. 62.

[2] For the distinction at Paris between undergraduates who were scholars (*Boursiers*) and so lived on the foundation of a college, and commoners (*Pension-naires*) who paid their own way see A. Franklin, *La Vie privée d'autrefois*, x. 30.

[3] A. Renan, *Le Costume en France*, p. 30.

[4] H. Rashdall, iii. 386, n. 1.

[5] See the reconstruction of students' dress in D. R. Hartley, *Mediaeval Costume and Life*, p. 15, pls. A and B, and p. 17.

The dress which the secular clergy wore was in general character no different from that worn by the laity of all classes of the community. Everyone from highest to lowest wore, as did the clergy, a hood to protect the head in bad weather.[1] If priests wore their *pluvial*, a loose cape with a hood and with a hole for the head to pass through and a slit in front for the passage of the arms,[2] it was no different from the outer garment worn by any citizen.[3] There was only one exclusively clerical non-liturgical garment, the *cappa clausa*, and even this was really no more than a development of the *pluvial*. In 1222 at the Council of Oxford Stephen Langton, Archbishop of Canterbury, ordered clerks to wear the *cappa clausa*,[4] and he thus introduced into England the clerical outdoor dress already in use on the Continent. The result of this was that at Bologna, Paris, and Oxford and at subsequent universities the *cappa clausa* came to be regarded as the academical dress, at least for formal occasions, for Doctors of Theology and Masters of Arts, who as priests—nearly all Masters were in Orders—wore this garment before any particular form of academical dress had come to be established. Further, when in due course Langton's rule about the use of the *cappa clausa* was more and more neglected by the clergy in general, the garment came to be regarded as an exclusively academical one.

As regards clerical head-dress also, its origin is to be found in lay fashion. Thus the *pileus*, which became the typical clerical head-gear and, by the same process as that of the *cappa clausa*, the head-dress of the universities, was simply adopted by the Church at the Synod of Bergamo (1311), on which occasion clergy were ordered to wear it 'after the manner of laymen'.[5]

At first the lay minority at the universities, found for the most part in the Faculties of Civil Law and Medicine, must be supposed to have worn some dignified form of dress according to the lay fashion of the time. It is noticeable that the earliest statutes of universities concerning dress are rather sumptuary

---

[1] R. A. S. Macalister, *Ecclesiastical Vestments*, pp. 254–5.

[2] F. Cabrol and H. Leclercq, *Dictionnaire d'archéologie chrétienne et de liturgie*, iii, cols. 370 and 376.

[3] W. B. Marriott, *Vestiarium Christianum*, p. 167; C. D. Du Cange, *Glossarium*, s.v. Pallium pluviale.

[4] D. Wilkins, *Concilia Magnae Britanniae et Hiberniae*, i. 589, 'Council of Oxford', § xxviii.   [5] H. Norris, *Church Vestments*, p. 161.

regulations than anything else. In time, however, the authorities succeeded in obliging members of these faculties to wear
a form of *cappa*, the *cappa manicata*, at least on formal occasions.

After the first stage during which the statutes concerning
costume were somewhat vague, we find the authorities of all
universities beginning to adopt a new and deliberate policy,
that of accepting lay fashions in a modified and particularized
form into the canon of academical requirement, thereby creating a true 'academical dress'. A special *shape* and *cut* was what
by the fourteenth century had become the essential feature of
academical dress, but the significance of *colour* in such dress
was not recognized until later.

From the late fifteenth century onwards the whole movement
of everyday fashion was towards a shorter, less cumbersome
dress in keeping with an active age, and the wide modifications
of academical and legal costume were a mirror of that age.
More than ever before the universities were open to outside
influences. The *Epistolae Obscurorum Virorum* (1516) well illustrate the change in the intellectual climate in the universities
of the day.

Then came the Reformation, resulting in upheavals which
lasted for a hundred years, during which period the discipline
of collegiate life broke down everywhere except in England,
France, Portugal, and Spain, and in a few universities in south
Germany and Austria where the Old Church was more secure.
In all other countries legislation about dress occurred less and
less, and even when orders were published they were less than
half-heartedly observed; until by the eighteenth century, when
France was beginning to fall a victim to the anti-clericalism of
the *Philosophes*, only in England, Spain, and Portugal was a
recognized academical dress worn by members of universities
on all occasions. An insular conservatism was the cause of its
preservation in England as well as a determination to keep the
strongholds of the Establishment in Oxford and Cambridge
intact, while in the other two countries a powerful church
discipline, which had scarcely been questioned, preserved it.

4. *Examples of the Influence of Lay Fashion on Academical Dress*

The hood was originally merely a useful head-covering.
Long before it had been given up in ordinary dress, that is by

about 1450,[1] it had become a recognized feature of the dress of academical persons. It is typical of the growth of specialized costume that a fashion abandoned in everyday life is appropriated by institutions, themselves strongholds of conservatism. The hood thus worn was small and close to the neck, and was joined to its 'shoulder piece' which covered the shoulders and the upper part of the arms, the two together in reality forming one article. For the most part in continental and English legal dress it remained unchanged, but in academical dress both in this country and elsewhere it was greatly modified during the sixteenth century. In England the academical 'shoulder piece' was abandoned during this period and the hood was worn alone, greatly elongated by 1592 as can be seen in an oil-painting of that year by an anonymous artist of the founding of the Vicars' Close at Wells.[2] The liripipe on the English hood, which first appears in the reign of Henry III,[3] was an appendage of it, and originally served a useful purpose, being used both to pull the hood on and off the head and to hold the hood in position by binding it round it and fastening it under the chin.[4]

On the Continent both hood and 'shoulder piece' were generally abandoned during the sixteenth century except in rectorial dress, but an equivalent of the English hood had by this time appeared. This was the scarf worn on the shoulder, variously called *chausse*, *chaperon*, and *Sendelbinde*, and was in fact a liripipe. It originated in an everyday fashion for head-dress which was in vogue between 1420 and 1470, and which consisted of three parts, the roundlet, a ring of thick rolled material which fitted the head, the *gorget*, a piece of stuff sewn on to the inside of the *roundlet* and which hung down from it, and a liripipe (later to become the *chaperon* when the other parts of the dress were given up) like a long scarf to which *roundlet* and *gorget* were attached.[5] Originally worn on the head the *roundlet* and *gorget* after the middle of the fifteenth century were usually cast on either of the shoulders and hung down behind from the liripipe.[6]

---

[1] C. W. and P. Cunnington, *Handbook of Mediaeval Costume*, p. 111.
[2] H. Parnell, *The College of Vicars Choral, Wells*, pp. 6–8, and ill., p. 7.
[3] C. H. Ashdown, p. 56, fig. 72.   [4] C. H. Ashdown, p. 143, fig. 175.
[5] W. M. Webb, *The Heritage of Dress*, pp. 114, figs. 122–3, and 115, fig. 125; C. W. and P. Cunnington, pp. 113 and 115.
[6] For example, the citizen of Bruges who appears in an illumination in the

When in the later fifteenth century this fashion began to disappear from ordinary dress, it was retained by men of official standing and particularly by professional and learned men.[1] Thus in France legal and court officials and academical persons wore the *chaperon*, the *gorget* sometimes being cut up so that several ends appeared hanging down, in which case it was known as the *cornette*.[2] The *chaperon* was also used in Germany where it was known as the *Sendelbinde*. In England, since the use of the hood was well established as part of academical costume long before the fifteenth century, the shoulder-scarf was not employed as a symbol of degree at the universities.[3] It was, however, used by great officials of the Crown.[4] Survivals of it are to be found in the little gathered piece of cloth on the lower left-hand corner of the 'bridge' yoke of the barrister's gown, attached to which is a streamer coming over the left shoulder and hanging down in front,[5] and in the little tippet of Oxford and Cambridge proctors. The latter seems to have been worn by them in their capacity as officials.

The use of the *pileus* in the early Middle Ages has already been mentioned. Other varieties of head-dress for academical use were the result of fifteenth-century lay fashions. Thus the academical bonnet, much more full and looser than the original *pileus*, was derived from an ordinary fashion which first appeared in France in 1449.[6] Another variety, rigid and somewhat square with a tump, known in later times as a biretta, appears as early as the middle of the fifteenth century worn by a figure on a choir stall in Ulm Cathedral.[7] The introduction about 1520 of a square cap at the University of Paris, which seems to have originated in Italy,[8] was a development of the true *pileus*, but

manuscript (1475–1500) of Vasco de Lucena's edition of Quintus Curtius executed at Bruges in the von Essen Collection, Skokloster, Sweden (illustrated in *Gyllena Böcker, Nationalmuseum*, Stockholm, pl. xxii).   [1] D. R. Hartley, p. 91.

[2] E. Pasquier, *Les Recherches de la France*, pp. 382D–383B; J. Malliot and P. Martin, *Recherches sur les costumes*, iii. 88.

[3] It appears on certain English brasses, but is worn by laymen, or clergy in ecclesiastical and not academical costume. For examples see H. Haines, *A Manual of Monumental Brasses*, pp. lxxviii and cciii.

[4] See the portrait of Lord Burghley (d. 1598) in the National Portrait Gallery, London, No. 362.

[5] W. M. Webb, op. cit., pp. 163, fig. 141, and 164.

[6] D. Diderot and J. le R. D'Alembert, *Encyclopédie*, ii. 324 a–b, s.v. Bonnet.

[7] W. Lübke, *Ecclesiastical Art in Germany during the Middle Ages*, p. 218, fig. 157.

[8] C. D. Du Cange, s.v. Birretum.

the results of this development were very different. It was known as the *pileus quadratus* or *bonnet carré*, and our own square cap is a particular form of it.

By 1500 the general tendency in academical dress was to become more simple and comfortable, with the result that the heavy outer, closed dress being left off, the sleeved or sleeveless tabard, or some form of sleeved *tunica*, or other such dress, now the outer garment, assumed a new significance.

At the same time as this was happening, lay fashion was rapidly changing. There were two main features of this change; one was the opening of dress in front from about 1470 onwards, the other the elaboration and increase in size of the sleeves. After 1490, not only was the over-garment open in front, but it was thrown widely open, so that the lining of fur, which was afterwards placed in front in the form of two facings, could be seen.[1]

Various forms of sleeve appeared in lay fashions during the fifteenth century. There was the bag-sleeve, a tube of material through which the arm passed, sometimes called the glove-sleeve. This tube increased in length during the sixteenth century.

An example of the bag-sleeve showing embroidery in two places on the lower part of the thigh-length sleeve is to be seen in the brass of one not connected with a university, Lawrence Colston (1550), at Colston, Staffs.[2] A bag-sleeved gown is worn in his portrait by Cardinal Granvella (1517–86), minister of the Emperor Charles V.[3] Such is the origin of the England Master of Arts gown's sleeve.

On the Continent the bell-sleeved gown, with a flap collar joined to the facings, from the sixteenth century onwards worn in nearly all countries by doctors, was derived from a late fifteenth-century Italian lay fashion.[4] The same gown, worn academically, appears in the monument of the great Italian humanist Ficino (d. 1499), in the church of Sta. Maria del Fiore, Florence.[5]

[1] H. Haines, pp. cciv and ccxxxix, e.g. brass of John Colman (1506) at Little Waldingfield, Suffolk. [2] C. H. Ashdown, p. 231, fig. 318.
[3] W. von Seidlitz, *Allgemeines historisches Porträtwerk*, portrait of Granvella in pt. 3–4.
[4] For an example of this gown worn by a rich Italian gentleman of 1494 see I. Brooke, *Western European Costume*, i, coloured plate opp. p. 102.
[5] M. Z. Boxhornius, *Monumenta illustrium virorum, et Elogia*, p. 45.

From a fashion of the later fifteenth century is also derived the winged-sleeved gown, which appeared as a feature of academical dress in England and elsewhere during the sixteenth century. It was an elaboration of a popular lay fashion of 1483.[1] It covered the upper part of the arm, and was used greatly in Germany and the Low Countries, and by graduates of the lay faculties at Oxford and Cambridge. The panel-sleeved (or false-sleeved) gown was a degenerate form of the winged-sleeved gown. This type, familiar to us from the Oxford commoner's gown, was used also by continental students from the later sixteenth century, as can be seen from a print of a student of one of the theological colleges of Rome, which were founded as a result of the Counter-Reformation.[2] No more clear example of the lay character of this form of gown could be given than the brass of a gentleman of 1607 at Dersingham, Norfolk.[3] The winged-sleeve seems to have reached England later than elsewhere, for it does not appear to have become fashionable until the reign of Elizabeth.[4]

Lastly there is the cloak-gown, allied to the gown with 'streamers', but originating in a Spanish fashion of the sixteenth century. It did not reach England directly, but the flap-collar on the English academical lay gown and undergraduate gown may have been influenced by it *via* Italian fashions. It was the last proper academical dress used by German students.[5]

5. *The Influence of Forms of Association on Academical Dress*

Three forms of association grew up in universities. The first of these was the Faculty, less strong in the English universities than elsewhere, the second the College, strong at first at all universities, but later only really so in France, England, Spain,

---

[1] C. Martin, *Civil Costume*, no. 28.

[2] P. Bonanni, *Ordinum religiosorum in ecclesia militanti catalogus*, iii, no. xxxvi, 'Student of the College of Fuccioli', and see also nos. xxxiv, xxxv, and xlii.

[3] J. S. Cotman, *Sepulchral Brasses*, ii, p. 88. John Aubrey proves the lay character of this gown when he writes: 'When about 1632 I learnt to read of John Brome the Clark of Kingston St. Michael, his old father (above eighty)... daily wore a gown like an undergraduate's at Oxford, with sleeves pinned behind, etc.' (A. Powell, *John Aubrey*, p. 31).

[4] See, for example, the portrait at Emmanuel College, Cambridge, of Sir Walter Mildmay (d. 1589) in court dress.

[5] It was even used by clergy, both Roman Catholic and Protestant, as an out-of-door dress.

and the Austrian Netherlands, and the third the Nation, strong at first in France and Italy, and in due course in Germany.

The first of these kinds of association was a result of the gathering together of those who taught the same subject and who found that only by a united effort could their common aims be made known to their university at large. It also secured them against the unqualified, who might try to set up for themselves at the university. The second was a corporate body, which enjoyed the benefits of an endowment; and the third was an association based on nationality to defend the rights of an alien in a foreign land.

The faculties, which developed at Paris in the course of the thirteenth century, played a more or less conspicuous part in the affairs of subsequent universities, particularly that of Arts, membership of which at Oxford and Cambridge as well as abroad was necessary to full membership. The other faculties were those of Theology, Canon Law, Civil Law, and Medicine.

Although the first Paris college, the *Collège de Dix-Huit*, was founded as early as 1180, it was not until the foundation of the *Collège Sorbonne* in 1257 that a college became an organization independent of an ecclesiastical corporation other than the university. Of this latter type were all the colleges of Oxford and Cambridge and those of Paris which were founded after this time.[1] In Spain and Italy the college system, though in being, played a much less important part in the life of universities.

Nations appeared at Bologna at the beginning of the thirteenth century as subdivisions of the *Collegia*,[2] but at Paris they emerged at the same period as masters' associations within the large Faculty of Arts.[3]

It is natural in view of the practice of the great guild movement, the movement towards association in every trade and profession, which affected town-life in Europe at this time, to

---

[1] Thirty-seven Paris colleges are named in a list of those existing in the fifteenth century (Oxford, Bodl. Libr. MS. Twyne 2, fo. 101). One Oxford college, University College, is known to have been in existence in 1249, but it does not appear as a true corporation until after the *Collège Sorbonne*.

[2] Not to be confused with colleges. They were more like halls (hostels) for foreign law students.

[3] For a full account of the nations see P. Kibre, *The Nations in the Mediaeval Universities*.

expect that members of faculties, colleges, and nations, as the case might be, should wear some particular dress of uniform shape and colour betokening the group to which they belonged.

Some examples of faculty colours will show that no exact code of colours was observed at all universities, but there were certain tendencies. Thus black at Paris, Oxford, and Cambridge, and white at Salamanca, Coimbra, and Perpignan were the colours of the Faculty of Theology. Green, yellow, or sanguine were at various universities the colours of the Faculty of Medicine, while blue of various shades very often denoted the Faculty of Philosophy, and in such differently placed universities as those at Perpignan, Coimbra, and Ingolstadt. The most constant of the colours was scarlet for Canon Law, but even this by no means always held good. Indeed, as can be seen from inventories[1] such as those of Oxford regents, all kinds of colour were used by academical persons as late as the middle of the fifteenth century.[2] Yet it was in the course of this century that faculty colours appeared, a significant symbolism of association.

In some countries, in England and Spain especially, founders of colleges ordered certain kinds of dress to be worn by members of their foundations.

As far as the nations were concerned a special dress was discouraged by the authorities, who with good reason feared that sartorial distinctions might encourage the rivalries and antagonisms which these divisions tended to promote. It was, however, worn by the various nations at the University of Prague until the sixteenth century at the appropriate national festivals.

[1] For example, H. E. Salter, *Registrum Cancellarii* (O.H.S.), i. 44 and 70.

[2] That it was still cut rather than colour which was significant even in 1434 as betokening the wearer's degree can be understood from a papal letter of that year in which a regular priest, an Augustinian, was allowed to wear the habit or costume wont to be worn by secular Masters of Arts and Doctors of Divinity of Oxford provided that it was of the colour of the habit of the priest's Order (*Calendar of Papal Registers*, ed. J. A. Twemlow, *Papal Letters*, viii. 504).

1

I. ITALY

1. BOLOGNA (twelfth century)

THIS ancient university had originally only a Law School with the students by the first part of the thirteenth century divided into two nations, the *Citramontani* (the Italians) and the *Ultramontani* (the rest).[1] It was not until long afterwards that Schools of Medicine and the Liberal Arts appeared, and when they did appear their members desired to form a special university of their own with their own rector. In 1295, not wishing to see the university thus divided, the magistrates of Bologna condemned this pretension of the students, who as was general in Italy had their full say in affairs. Thus for the time these two bodies were forced to remain simply as appendages of the old Law School; but having had a taste of independence the new schools still clamoured for at least partial recognition. In 1316 this was granted and the Faculties of Medicine and the Arts were at last recognized. In the second half of the fourteenth century a School of Theology was founded by Pope Innocent VI and was placed by him under the authority of the Bishop of Bologna. The theological students had no rights of their own, and as the artists were not satisfied with their privileges the two joined forces in their discontent.

The various schools were so loosely attached to one another that in reality under the title of the University of Bologna there was indeed more than one university.[2] As time went on these differences of foundation and the resultant rivalry between the schools which formed the university threatened to destroy its unity, and it was not until 1584 that the authorities, finally bowing before the arbitration of the Church when ancient civic

[1] F. K. von Savigny, *Histoire du droit romain au moyen âge*, iii. 132, § 67.
[2] F. K. von Savigny, iii. 133.

liberties had been brought low by the power of Spain and the
Counter-Reformation, put all quarrels to an end by an enactment fortified by a papal decree of 1570.[1]

The foundation of the Law School in the twelfth century by
the Emperor Frederick Barbarossa gave it an enviable and
royal character. It has been suggested that from its very beginning Doctors of Civil Law took to scarlet cloth robes dressed
with ermine as if they were nobles, and from what remains in
the university library of the frescoes depicting the pupils of
Irnerius this seems to have been the case.[2]

Doctors of Canon Law out of regard to their sacred calling
did not wear scarlet, but had by the middle of the fourteenth
century a blue *cappa manicata* reaching to the ankles with elbow-
length sleeves. Their head-dress was sometimes a small 'turban'
cap lined with miniver,[3] but there is also an example of their
wearing a round *pileus* over a small coif.[4] Doctors of Civil Law
at the same period continued to wear their scarlet, and Boccaccio in a letter of 1348 describes their robes as of scarlet cloth,
full, dressed with miniver, and with large hanging sleeves. This
was exactly the same as the dress of nobles.[5] In a Bologna
manuscript of 1354, the *Speculum Juridicae* of G. Duranti, the
author, a Doctor of Civil Law, appears in a miniature kneeling
on a light green floor wearing a vermilion gown with a red
hood and a long red fur-lined mantle with a fur collar (Pl. 1*a*).[6]
In another Bolognese manuscript of 1378, *Novella de Regulis
Juris* by J. Andreae, the author in the initial N wears the same
dress as Duranti.[7]

In 1432 the rector was ordered to wear a black cloth *cappa
manicata* or a sleeveless tabard. In either case this dress was to
be buttoned up close to the neck. In his public capacity he was
to wear no other fur but miniver on his head-dress, which is

[1] F. K. von Savigny, iii. 137, § 70.
[2] E. D. Glasson, art. 'Les Origines du costume de la magistrature' in *Nouvelle
Revue historique de Droit français et étranger* (1884), p. 114.
[3] R. Bruck, *Die Malereien in den Handschriften des Königreichs Sachsen*, pl. 210,
no. 66—Leipzig, Stadtbibliothek MS. CCXLIII (*Decretum Gratiani*, Bl. 81′).
[4] *Studia Gratiani*, ii, tav. xxviii—*Decretum Gratiani. Causa Prima. Cesenae* (Bibl.
Malatestianae, Cod. 3. 207, fo. 76, figure in foreground with hand on boy's head).
[5] C. Meiners, art. 'Geschichte der Trachten' in *Göttingische akademische Annalen*
(1804), pp. 217, 218, and 250–1; E. D. Glasson, art. cit., p. 113.
[6] H. J. Hermann, *Italienische Handschriften*, ii, Taf. lxxv, text p. 186.
[7] H. J. Hermann, op. cit. ii, Taf. lxxvii, 2, text p. 190.

PLATE I

a. Two Doctors of Civil Law of Bologna (kneeling), 1354

b. Rector of the University of Padua, 1576

mentioned as being generally a hood, but he might wear an unfurred hood on informal occasions. If, however, he chose to wear a *birretum* (*pileus*) this was not to have on it any miniver, which was to be confined to the hood. In summer he might substitute a thin cloth (*sindon*)[1] lining for that of miniver if he so wished. Later he was allowed a silk *cappa* instead of a cloth one.[2]

An excellent example of the dress of a Doctor of Both Laws of the first half of the fifteenth century is to be found in a Bolognese miniature in Antonius da Butrio's *Commentariorum super Libro II Decretalium.*[3] Da Butrio, who became a Doctor of Civil Law in 1384 and a Doctor of Canon Law in 1387, both of Bologna, wears over a blue *supertunica* a scarlet *cappa clausa* with a scarlet 'shoulder piece', the hood of which is on his head. His outer dress including the 'shoulder piece' is lined with miniver.

In spite of the fact that officially the university still demanded that Doctors of Both Laws or of Canon Law or Civil Law separately should wear a *cappa*, and a 'shoulder piece' and hood,[4] the tendency among Doctors of the Faculty of Law towards the end of the fifteenth century was to give up such dress and so allow the *supertunica* to become the outside garment. Thus on his monumental effigy in San Benedetto, Bologna, Pietro Ancharano, Doctor of Both Laws (d. 1493), wears over a *subtunica*, a loose full gown, which is what by development the *supertunica* had already become. This is the *vestis togata*, which is called the dress of Bolognese doctors in Rawlinson's transcript of the *Constitutions of the College of Civil Law, Bologna*, and is described as having very full tapering bell sleeves.[5] Ancharano has a miniver 'shoulder piece', but its hood, which he wears on his head,[6] is of cloth or silk and is not furred. The back part of the hood with its liripipe can be seen falling over his shoulders behind.[7]

---

[1] Martial, the Latin poet, uses the word.

[2] C. Malagola, *Statuti delle Università e dei Collegi dello Studio bolognese*, p. 55— Stats. of 1432, Univ. of Jurists, rubric viii; *Statuta et privilegia . . . universitatis . . . Bononiensis*, p. 5; Oxford, Bodl. Libr. MS. Rawlinson D413, fo. 68.

[3] Rome, Biblioteca Angelica MS. 569, fo. 1; M. Salmi, *La Miniatura Italiana*, tav. xi.

[4] C. Malagola, p. 196—Stats. 1459-98, rubric xxv; *Statuta et privilegia . . . universitatis . . . Bononiensis*, p. 93.

[5] Oxford, Bodl. Libr. MS. Rawlinson D 413, fo. 7[b].

[6] Cf. the wearing of the hood as a head-dress by the rector according to the statute of 1432.   [7] M. Z. Boxhornius, *Monumenta illustrium virorum, et Elogia*, p. 137.

When in the fourteenth century the Medical School began to
stand on its own, Doctors of Medicine took to the dress of
Doctors of Civil Law as they did at Oxford. Thus Boccaccio in
1348 describes Doctors of Medicine as also wearing a full
scarlet cloth robe dressed with miniver, and with large hanging
sleeves.[1] In 1378 they were ordered to wear with a dress that
was decent and befitting their standing either a furred hood or
a miniver *pileus*.[2] By 1410 they appear to have been allowed silk
(*sirichus*) hoods, perhaps as a substitute for fur in hot weather,
as at Oxford twenty-two years later.[3] The *biretta* (*pileus*) was by
this time common to all doctors.[4]

Thus we may say that as early as the fourteenth century the
dress of Bolognese doctors and those of other Italian universities,
except of Theology, had come to consist of a round scarlet
pileus and a long *supertunica* of the same colour.[5] Such a bright
dress trimmed with miniver and even ermine was worn by
doctors of Bologna as late as 1595 as can be seen from the two
figures at the bottom of the fresco-memorial to Camillo Baldo
in the *Biblioteca Comunale dell' Archiginnasio* at Bologna. Their
round *pilei* with a border of miniver are the same as that worn
by a doctor of Bologna in a miniature, *Il maestro e gli scolari* in a
fifteenth-century manuscript, *Libro dell' Università dei Notai*.[6]
But during the latter sixteenth century Italian doctors gave up
scarlet dress and took to black, and to square caps instead of
round ones.[7]

In 1347 all the university statutes promulgated from 1317
onwards were collected, and what is mentioned in them of dress
makes it clear that the costume of non-doctors and undergraduates was strictly regulated. Whatever their dress, whether
some form of *cappa* in the case of masters for formal occasions;
whether as bachelors they wore a tabard; or whether as
students they wore a cloak (*gabanus*), all were to be made of
black 'statute cloth'. In each case an under-dress (*subtunica*)

---

[1] C. Meiners, art. cit., p. 217.
[2] C. Malagola, p. 432, rubric v.
[3] C. Malagola, p. 505, rubric vi.
[4] *Chartularium Studii Bononiensis*, i. 337.
[5] A. Scappus, *De Biretto Rubeo*, p. 5; G. Panzirolus, *De claris legum interpretatibus*,
p. 95.
[6] Bologna, Museo Civico, n. 95, reproduced in D. Fava, *Tesori delle Bibliotheche
d'Italia: Emilia e Romagna*, p. 360, fig. 208.
[7] G. Péries, *La Faculté de droit dans l'ancienne Université de Paris*, p. 47.

was also to be worn, and was to be closed at the sides and buttoned up in front right to the neck. Hoods were to be worn by all.[1] In 1372 scholars of the Gregorian college were to be provided each year with two of these cloaks.[2] Members of the Faculty of Medicine not doctors were in 1378 and 1395 forbidden the use of miniver.[3]

By the end of the fifteenth century certain changes had occurred in these habits. Thus in a marginal drawing of 1491 appearing at the end of the *Acta Nationis Germanicae Universitatis Bononiensis* of that year a master, who is holding back a student from attacking the rector, wears a sleeveless tabard, while his head-dress—no head-dress for the masters is mentioned earlier —is an apexed *pileus*, and the student on the right wears an open *supertunica* reaching only to the knees with short glove-sleeves, a recent innovation. As in other universities of Europe at this time he had assumed a form of head-dress, in this case a tight skull-cap with a 'stalk' apex.[4] In 1514 students wore a *pallium*, a much longer dress than that worn earlier; it is referred to as the *toghe lunghe*.[4] Bachelors in the later fifteenth century began to wear a small plain bonnet.[6]

It seems certain that by 1491 the rector never wore the *cappa manicata* mentioned as one form of his dress in 1432, but always its alternative, the sleeveless tabard, together with a long broad *chaperon* which hung over his right shoulder.[7]

By the latter part of the sixteenth century the rector's dress had become magnificent. The scholar Ulisse Aldrovandi (1522–1605) in his *Diario* writes of the rectorial robe as being stiff with gold braid and worked with gold and silver thread.[8]

The dress of the proctor of the German nation in 1497, according to a striking picture in the Act Book of this nation,

---

[1] H. Denifle and F. Ehrle, *Archiv für Litteratur- und Kirchen-Geschichte des Mittelalters*, bd. iii, p. 366, rubric lxxxv.

[2] F. K. von Savigny, op. cit. iv. 481 ff. *De Vestibus Scholarium: Chartularium Studii Bononiensis*, ii. 291; D. Fava, p. 360, fig. 208.

[3] C. Malagola, pp. 446, 460, and 473.

[4] E. Friedlaender and C. Malagola, *Acta Nationis Germanicae Universitatis Bononiensis*, p. 425.

[5] *Statuta et privilegia . . . universitatis . . . Bononiensis*, p. 15.

[6] D. Fava, p. 360, fig. 208.

[7] E. Friedlaender and C. Malagola, p. 425; C. Malagola, *Statuti*, p. 55—Stats. of 1432, Univ. of Jurists, rubric viii.

[8] C. Malagola, *Storiche sullo Studio Bolognese*, p. 62.

in which a group of students are being sworn in by their proctor, consisted of a scarlet sleeveless tabard and a crimson 'turban' bonnet.[1]

As early as 1400 the wearing of academical dress by students at Bologna does not seem to have been strictly observed if we are to judge from Laurentius de Voltalina's miniature of a university lecture at Bologna which appears in the fragmentary *Liber Ethicorum* in the *Kupferstichkabinett* in the Berlin Museum.[2] The students wear hats of ordinary lay fashion and their other dress is of the same character. The lecturer, Henry of Germany, wears no recognizably academical costume; but this is perhaps because he was a visitor and was not a member of the university.

Although it seems that for a long time after this the tendency of students to wear lay costume was checked, during the sixteenth century they gave up all pretence of wearing academical dress.[3] The rector and the regents continued to wear their proper habits on ceremonial occasions.

The Spanish College of Bologna, dedicated to St. Clement, was founded in 1377, but its full statutes were codified only in 1536–8. At this time all members were ordered to wear over black cassocks black cloth gowns reaching to the ankles with sleeves. This is said to have been the original dress of the college and was the same in shape as that worn in the past by doctors of the University of Bologna. Besides this gown they were to wear a purple cloth hood (*exhyacinthus*, *morellus*) gathered close at the shoulders.[4] The open gown (*pallium*) was absolutely forbidden. The rector's dress was on all occasions to consist of a long, ankle-length gown and a silk hood,[5] but by 1564 he had come to wear a silk gown as well as hood.[6] In 1570 Doctors of Theology were ordered to wear the 'priestly *pileus*', that is the horned cap.[7]

In the statutes of 1660 it was ordered that candidates for

[1] E. Friedlaender and C. Malagola, col. pl. between pp. 4 and 5; D. Fava, p. 360, fig. 208.

[2] P. d'Ancona and E. Aeschlimann, *Dictionnaire des Miniaturistes*, pl. lxx.

[3] C. Meiners, art. cit., op. cit.

[4] *Statuta almi et perinsignis Collegii maioris Sancti Clementis Hispanorum Bononiae conditi*, pp. 29, 30, and 70; on p. 30 it is said to be of silk.

[5] Op. cit., *Tertia Distinctio*, Stat. 12.

[6] Op. cit., Extra Stats. XL.

[7] Op. cit., Extra Stats. XLIII.

admittance to the college should wear a long dark cloak of baize or flannel with a plain collar and facings, together with a hat with a simple cord round it.[1] The collegian when accepted was to substitute a gown for the cloak.[2] The rector was allowed a cloak and a gown of smooth black velvet. In summer he might wear a tawny-coloured cloak.[3] When important personages visited the college all the members were to wear a gown and *beca*.[4] At mass in the chapel *becas* were not to be worn, and gowns were to be worn closed.[5] The rector's *beca* was to be of velvet or stuff like velvet.[6] This is the only reference to the wearing of a *beca* by a Spanish rector and was probably used by him in this case in order to distinguish him from the other heads of colleges in Bologna.

II. PADUA (1222)

All that we learn of dress at Padua before the fifteenth century is in a stray reference which occurs in 1331, the date of the earliest surviving statutes. In that year all members of the university except canons and priests regular were told that they might spend only a certain amount on the cloth used for their dress.[7]

The most important university statutes referring to dress are those of 1465 and 1531 and concern the Faculties of Medicine and Arts. In the first of these the rector is ordered to obtain in time for his May installation a hooded robe, as *caputeum* in this case means, and if he fails to do so he is to incur the penalty of a fine of £50.[8] This robe is to be of silk on the occasion of his installation, but otherwise of cloth, thin for summer and thick for winter.[9]

All members of the university of whatever nation or degree were in the statutes of 1531 ordered to wear on all occasions a long black silk gown fastened at the neck with a band (some

---

[1] *Ceremonias y costumbres usadas y guardadas en colegio mayor de S. Clemente, Bolonia,* p. 9.
[2] Op. cit., p. 12.   [3] Op. cit., pp. 16–17.
[4] A sash, op. cit., p. 21. For *beca* see below under Salamanca.
[5] Op. cit., p. 27.   [6] Op. cit., p. 30.
[7] H. Denifle and F. Ehrle, op. cit., p. 497—Lib. 5, § 12 (*De vestibus scholarium*).
[8] *Statuta almae universitatis Patavini,* p. 9a [Bk. I, § xviii].
[9] Op. cit., p. 9a [Bk. I, § xix].

form of morse), closed in front, and having wide sleeves, which is presumably the *clericalis habitus* enjoined upon all members in 1486.[1] Members of religious Orders did not wear this, but their own habit.[2]

Doctors were distinguished from non-doctors in the fifteenth century by the Doctors of Theology wearing a violet amess (*almutium violaceum*) and by doctors of other faculties having a gold collar (*torque aurea*) and using miniver on their dress.[3]

By the middle of the sixteenth century two forms of dress for summer and for winter had developed for the dress of the rector. This is illustrated in C. Vecellio's collection of woodcuts first published in 1590, a new edition of which, sometimes better than the original, was produced in 1598. The rector's summer dress was a brocaded robe reaching to the ground with tapering bell sleeves, the lining and facings being of silk. The collar had a square flap, which was joined to the facings, and was edged with fur. In a water-colour of 1576 in an album a furred *chaperon* hangs on the rector's right shoulder[4] (Pl. 1*b*). His black cap is rigid, of the Tudor type with side pieces in the Vecellio woodcut, but is small and soft in the album. The rest of his dress was ordinary lay garb including a ruff, and he wore a double chain with a medallion suspended from it. The winter dress consisted of a soft black velvet square biretta, and a robe of gold brocade with full-hanging bell sleeves. The robe was worn closed and the whole of it was lined with miniver, while the hood which fell on the shoulders and down the back was of marten's fur.[5] According to another woodcut in the same collection, the reproduction of which appears to most advantage in the 1598 edition, Doctors of Law and Medicine from the sixteenth century, if not before, shared the same dress. This was a full robe with an upright collar and ample bell sleeves, the whole robe richly braided and with the device of a pineapple on the mid back, and a round bonnet bound with a cord.[6] Marco Bevilacqua, rector in 1595, during his term of office seems to have been zealous to preserve the dignity of doctoral dress. In

[1] J. Facciolati, *Fasti Gymnasii Patavini*, p. xx.
[2] Op. cit., p. 57*b*, Bk. IV (*De Scholarium habitu*).
[3] F. M. Colle, *Storia scientifico-letteraria dello Studio di Padova*, i. 104.
[4] B.M., MS. Eg. 1191, fo. 72ᵛ.
[5] C. Vecellio, *Habiti Antichi e Moderni* (1590), p. 156ᵇ.
[6] C. Vecellio, *Habiti Antichi* (1598), pl. op. p. 122.

that year he ordered Doctors of Medicine and Doctors of Philosophy to wear the proper dress, as described above, even if they were members of a religious Order. It was to be full-length, and short cloaks were not to be used. At the same time he ordered members of the Faculty of Theology to wear a black clerical biretta with the ridges forming a cross.[1]

Our information during the seventeenth century is particularly interesting as there is some excellent illustrative material.

First, there is a well executed woodcut of the dress of the rector and pro-rector which appears in J. P. Tomasini's *Gymnasium Patavinum*, a laudatory description of the university published in 1654. The rector wears a full and open bell-sleeved robe of damasked silk, with over the left shoulder a gold brocaded *chaperon* reaching almost to the bottom of the robe. The robe was scarlet in summer and purple in winter. His head-dress consists of a very tall cap like a *mortier*[2] with piping running along the bottom of it in the form of two snake-heads intertwined. He wears red sandals. The pro-rector has no head-dress. He wears a small turned-down white collar, a girded cassock, and over this a flap-collared, sleeveless full-length gown with very long 'streamers' running from behind the shoulders, like that of the gown of an Oxford commoner.[3]

Then there is the print of Quintilio Carbo which is pasted at the end of his diploma of the Doctorate of Law granted to him in 1627. This print, which has been coloured with water-colour paint, is of a date later than 1627 and was probably executed after he had become famous.[4] Carbo as a Doctor of Law wears an open gown with a broad flap collar and under it a cassock. The gown and cassock have been coloured dull plum-blue or dull violet. Unfortunately, since the print is only bust size the type of sleeves cannot be seen, but no doubt they were, as in 1590, of the bell-sleeved variety. He wears white bands with band-strings decorated with large pompons.[5]

[1] J. Facciolati, pt. 2, p. 221.
[2] This was tall and cylindrical.
[3] J. P. Tomasini, *Gymnasium Patavinum*, pp. 55–56, and pl. p. 57.
[4] London, Victoria and Albert Museum, MS. Drawer 53.
[5] It is interesting to notice the following extract: 'The maroon-coloured gown of the President of the Royal Society of Medicine is said to have been copied from the robe of a Doctor of Medicine of Padua of the eighteenth century' (W. J. Bishop, art. 'Notes on the History of Medical Costume', in *Annals of Medical History*, n.s. vi, No. 3 (1934), p. 205ª).

Lastly there are the series of portrait engravings illustrating a biographical account of contemporary professors of Padua, C. Patinus's *Lyceum Patavinum* (1682). According to these, three kinds of gown were at this time worn by regents. The first, which was probably the festal dress, is glove-sleeved, the arms appearing through a gash in the sleeves, and has a square flap-collar. The facings of the gown, the collar, and the gash in the sleeves are furred.[1] It would appear from the fact that these gowns are lightly engraved that they are intended to be represented as scarlet. The next type is voluminous, slightly gathered at the shoulders, with ample sleeves, a square collar, and narrow facings of fur.[2] This seems to have been the black undress gown worn for all formal occasions except when the festal robe was worn. But the most generally worn garment in this collection is a simple cloak, which was merely an informal garb for men of learning.[3] Sometimes a skull-cap is worn, but this is of no particular significance. Clerical professors wear a narrow white turned-down clerical collar, lay professors white bands. Sometimes braid or silk is used on the first two kinds of dress instead of fur, and this was very likely for summer use.[4]

At the beginning of the eighteenth century this cloak seems to have become so popular that professors wore it more and more instead of the formal full-sleeved gown; for in 1703 it was ordered that they must overcome their dislike of the gown (*toga*) and must wear it and not the cloak (*penula*) when lecturing and when taking part in university functions.[5]

Evidence for the dress of a professor in the eighteenth century is furnished by T. Viero in his collection of coloured prints issued in 1783–5. The costume consists of long white bands, a black court suit with a black apron (short cassock) over it reaching to the knees, and an open, ankle-length black gown with full, pointed bell sleeves. The sleeves are doubled back, and the gown has lapels and a collar with a flap.[6] With this was worn on formal occasions a full miniver 'shoulder piece'

---

[1] C. Patinus, *Lyceum Patavinum*, portraits of Montagnana and Scotus.
[2] C. Patinus, portraits of Scarabicius and Calliachius.
[3] C. Patinus, portrait of Pighius.
[4] C. Patinus, portraits of Frigiomelica, Albanensis, and Calafatti.
[5] J. Facciolati, pt. 2, p. 63.
[6] T. Viero, *Raccolta*, i, No. 45; G. Morazzoni, *La moda a Venezia*, tav. xviii.

open in front.[1] The head-dress was a rigid round *pileus*, the upper part of it wider than the lower.[2]

In the sixteenth century students ceased altogether to wear academical dress in spite of the order of 1531 mentioned above. In the late sixteenth century they wore ordinary lay dress of Spanish style, the latest fashion in Italy,[3] and in the seventeenth century they aped the dress of courtiers.[4]

III. THE SAPIENZA, ROME (1303; refounded 1431)

No early records dealing with the Sapienza, founded by Pope Boniface VIII in 1303, have been preserved, and not even after its real life began with its refoundation by Pope Eugenius IV in 1431 is there any mention of dress for a long time. This university is not to be confused with the university of the Roman Curia, directly governed by the papal court.

In 1552 *Punctators*[5] in the exercise of their office were to use a violet robe and a biretta of clerical shape.[6]

Not until the eighteenth century is anything more mentioned about dress. By this time the ceremonial of the university as well as many of its institutions had fallen into decay, and in 1751 Pope Benedict XIV introduced reforms, in the course of which he ordered professors to resume in the schools and at lectures the traditional biretta and black gown,[7] or rather a chimere (*zimarra*), which was long and sleeveless.[8]

Collegio de San Pietro. In the eighteenth century the dress of students at this College of Theology consisted of a cassock and over it a blue sleeveless gown with a streamer hanging from each shoulder, the left-hand streamer being adorned with filigree

[1] Oxford, Ashmolean Museum (Hope Collection)—Print of J. B. Morgagni, dated 1719.
[2] Oxford, Ashmolean Museum (Hope Collection)—Print of J. Capivacci, 18th cent.
[3] A. Rosenberg and M. Tilke, *The Design and Development of Costume*, ii, pl. clvii, fig. 10.
[4] C. Meiners, art. cit., p. 247; J. P. Tomasini, op. cit., p. 212.
[5] Examiners (H. Rashdall, *Universities*, i. 226, n. 1, and 482, n. 1).
[6] F. M. Renazzi, *Storia dell' Università di Roma*, ii. 253.
[7] F. M. Renazzi, iv. 247–8.
[8] G. Moróni, *Dizionario dell' erudizione*, ciii, s.v. Zimarra, where this dress is mentioned as being the recognized dress of the professors at Rome. Cf. M. von Boehn, *Modes and Manners*, ii. 160, where the '*Venetian zimarra*' is described as a wide-open gown of black silk.

work, a tiara, two keys, and the bees from the arms of the Barberini family, all done in braid.[1]

IV. PISA (1342)

The University of Pisa after entirely perishing was set up again by Florence when the latter city conquered Pisa in 1472, after which time it became famous.[2] Records about dress are scanty, and we know nothing of it before the university's resuscitation.

In the statutes of Cosimo I Medici of 1543 and again in those of Juliannus Lupius of 1621–2 the rector's dress was mentioned as consisting of a brocaded silk robe interlaced with gold and a hood to match. The shape of the robe was the same as that of doctors, which appears to have been closed and with full hanging bell sleeves.[3] In the Lupius statutes of 1621–2 the vice-rector's dress was described as of the same shape as that of the rector, but it was plain and was made of fine cloth instead of silk. With it he was to wear a red silk hood.[4]

V. FLORENCE (1349)

In 1397, as was the case at Bologna and Padua, only plain black cloth was to be used for the outer dress of members of the university whether as doctors they wore the *cappa* or as bachelors and students the *gabanus* (cloak).[5] Even the rector was to have the same cloth for his dress, although he was to be distinguished by having a special head-dress, a *pileus* lined in winter with miniver or squirrel and in summer with silk.[6]

If we are to believe that this is not the artist's exaggeration it would seem that the dress of professors in the fifteenth century became very rich indeed. Guarino da Verona (1374–1460), the great humanist and Professor of Greek at Florence,

---

[1] P. Bonanni, *Ordinum religiosorum in ecclesia militanti catalogus*, iii, no. li. The great Barberini family, of which Pope Urban VIII was a member, was in the seventeenth century the leading family in the papal domains. One of its members, Taddeo, founded this college and the Barberini Library.

[2] S. d'Irsay, i. 239–40 and 245.

[3] *Statuta almi Pisani studii* (*Annali delle Università toscane*, tom. 30), cap. xi, p. 12; A. Fabronius, *Historiae Academiae Pisanae*, ii. 8.

[4] *Statuta almi Pisani studii*, cap. xi, p. 13.

[5] A. Gherardi and C. Morelli, *Statuti della Università Fiorentina*, i. 97, ann. mccclxxxvii, rubrica cviii; C. Meiners, art. cit., pp. 234–5.

[6] A. Gherardi and C. Morelli, i. 15, ann. mccclxxxvii, rubric v; A. Corsini, *Il Costume del medico nelle pitture fiorentine del Rinascimento*, p. 6.

in the illumination in which he is depicted presenting his translation of Strabo to his patron Antonio Marcello, wears a full-sleeved scarlet *roba* and a light violet *chaperon* over both shoulders. He is bareheaded. The man standing behind him, no doubt an academical person, perhaps a Master of Arts, wears over a black *tunica* a silk plum-coloured *roba* with short sleeves hanging a little and doubled back, edged down the front with a narrow facing of red. His head-dress is a black *pileus* with a loose top, and slung over the shoulders is a red *chaperon*.[1]

VI. PAVIA (1361)

Originally a Law School, later of university status, Pavia had collapsed by 1421, in which year the Milanese, having conquered the city, rehabilitated its university.[2]

There is no information whatever about dress in the short statutes, but thanks to the *Memoirs* of Carlo Goldoni, the famous eighteenth-century dramatist, who was at one time a student at the *Collegio de Ghislieri*, one of the constituent parts of the university, we know what the costume was like there.

Clerical dress and the tonsure were required of all foundation scholars and exhibitioners, this being a papal college, whether the students were preparing to become priests or not, and in fact by this time few were. Their dress consisted of an abbé's court dress, i.e. a black cloth suit faced with black silk, and over it a short cape-gown with a flap-collar. On the left shoulder of the suit, not of the cape-gown, was worn a *chaperon* called at Pavia *sovrana*, of black velvet embroidered with the Ghislieri arms in gold and silver, surmounted by the pontifical tiara and the keys of St. Peter.[3]

VII. FERRARA (1389)

This university never flourished and was notorious for selling degrees. There are no records of it to be found which deal with its dress. There is, however, an interesting detached miniature belonging to a lost manuscript of the school of Ferrara painters which very likely shows the kind of dress worn by regent-

[1] P. Neveux and E. Dacier, *Les Richesses des Bibliothèques provinciales de France*, i, pl. vii, left (Albi MS. 77—*Strabo, de Situ orbis geographia* (fifteenth cent.)).

[2] N. Schachner, *Mediaeval Universities*, p. 286.

[3] C. Goldoni, *Memoirs*, pp. 30–33. The Ghislieri family had been patrons of the college. It was founded by Pope Pius V in 1569.

doctors of this university shortly after its foundation. Two Doctors of Medicine are talking together in a portico. One wears a crimson lake tight-sleeved *roba*, a red *chaperon*, and a rigid 'pill-box' *pileus* with a 'stalk' apex. The other wears a red *roba*, a violet *chaperon*, a black tabard over the *roba*, and a red Ulysses cap.[1]

The other medieval universities of Italy had only an ephemeral existence.[2]

II. SPAIN

I. SALAMANCA (1254)

In default of information about dress in the early days of Salamanca, for the statutes before the sixteenth century do not aid us in this way, we are dependent upon two stray illustrative sources.

Of these the most outstanding is the bust-portrait of a Doctor of Canon Law which appears in the first initial of an Orosius's *History*, a manuscript executed in Spain in 1442.[3] The doctor wears a crimson skull-cap which covers his ears except the lobes,[4] and a crimson lake *cappa clausa* with side slits lined with green. He has a blue 'shoulder piece' lined with ermine, and a flat blunt-ended blue hood which can be seen hanging down a little way behind. Under the *cappa* he wears a plum-coloured *tunica* (Pl. 2*b*).

In view of the fact that in 1442 Salamanca was by far the greatest of the few Spanish universities existing, and of what H. Rashdall[5] and N. F. Robinson[6] say about the colours of the Faculty of Canon Law at Salamanca at this date being red or crimson and green, there seems little doubt that a Doctor of Canon Law of this university is intended in this initial.

[1] M. Salmi, tav. lvii (*b*) (Turin, Biblioteca Nazionale MS. i. i. 22–23, fo. 22).
[2] S. d'Irsay, i. 129, 242, and 243.
[3] Cambridge, Fitzw. Mus. Maclean MS. 180. For the colours of the Faculty of Canon Law here depicted see H. Rashdall, op. cit. iii. 389, n. 3.
[4] Such a cap had been worn by some doctors who attended the Council of Constance (1414–18) (*Concilium Constantiense*, pp. 48–49).
[5] Op. cit., loc. cit.
[6] Art. 'The *Pileus Quadratus*' in *Transactions of the St. Paul's Ecclesiological Society*, v, pt. 1 (1901), p. 9, n. 3.

PLATE 2

a. Doctor of Salamanca, 1497

b. Doctor of Canon Law of
Salamanca, 1442

c. Tail-piece showing Round Bonnet,
Biretta, and *Bonnet carré*, 1666

The 'shoulder piece' can be seen, together with other dress of the same character as that worn in the *Orosius* initial, in the recumbent statue in the cloister near the entrance to the chapel of Sta. Barbara in Salamanca Cathedral, of the canon treasurer Don García de Medina, Doctor of Canon Law, and a professor of the university (d. 1474).[1]

As for other dresses, before the sixteenth century we have no definite information, for although Constitution VII of the University of Salamanca forbids the admission to an Act of anyone not in the dress of a master, we are not told what this was.[2] Students as yet had no specified garb, but wore whatever they chose provided it was not too rich.[3]

By the earlier part of the sixteenth century, however, a certain amount of information begins to accumulate and enables us to form an idea of a full system of academical dress which had come into being.

First of all, on the panels painted by Gallegos preserved as part of a retable in the cloisters of the Old Cathedral of Salamanca appear Saints Cosmas and Damian dressed as Doctors of Medicine, wearing black bell-sleeved gowns and skull-caps each with a small yellow tassel.[4] Yellow was the colour of the Faculty of Medicine at Salamanca,[5] and throughout the Middle Ages these two saints were often depicted in the dress of doctors of this faculty.

Then there are the statutes of 1538, which although they are silent about the dress of graduates, probably because the question of their costume was as yet left to ecclesiastical authority, contain much information about the dress of students. They had the choice of either a short pleated cassock (*loba sotana*) or a long cloak with a flap collar (*manteo*), but they were not to be worn together.[6] They were also to wear a particular academical cap (*bonete*) of the square type like a biretta as opposed to such a lay head-dress as the *gorra*. Only servitors (*Capigorristas*) were to wear the *gorra*. If they were in mourning, students might wear cloaks with hoods with long liripipes attached drawn over the head.[7] Students were as yet allowed

---

[1] V. de la Fuente, *Historia de las Universidades de Enseñanza en España*, i. 177.
[2] V. de la Fuente, i. 178.   [3] V. de la Fuente, i. 177.
[4] V. de la Fuente, i. 178.   [5] N. F. Robinson, loc. cit.
[6] A. Vidal y Diaz, *Memoria Histórica de la Universidad de Salamanca*, p. 94 (Stats. of 1538, Tit. LXII).   [7] A. Vidal y Diaz, loc. cit.

only short cassocks in order to distinguish them from the clergy,[1] but in 1587 at the request of the university Philip II revoked this clause and allowed all students to wear the full cassock,[2] as they do in the woodcut frontispiece to the *Estatutos hechos por lo muy ensigne Universidad de Salamanca* (1625).

By the end of the sixteenth century the dress of all students except *Capigorristas*, who wore a black cloth cassock, a small cape, and a round cap (*gorra*), had become more elaborate.[3] This elaboration was due to the necessity of distinguishing between the members of the many colleges which had recently arisen. All except *Capigorristas* wore a long brown cassock and a long brown cloak (*manteo*), but members of the College of Santa María de Burgos wore a yellow cloak instead of the brown one.[4] The distinguishing mark of the various colleges was the *beca* which was of a different colour for each. The *beca* was a strip of cloth 11 ft. 3 in. long. It was worn doubled over the chest, passed over the shoulders and fell behind in two strands which reached the heels. Students received their *beca* at the ceremony of their matriculation. It was brown for the College of San Bartolomé, blue for that of Oviedo, violet for that of Cuenca, and violet also for the College of Santa María de Burgos, but in that case it was worn with the yellow cloak.[5] The use of the *beca* was not confined to Salamanca. A blue *beca* of cloth was worn at Seville.[6]

In 1643 students were ordered to wear their caps (*bonetes*) on all occasions, not only in the schools, but outside them also.[7] Doctors at this time wore the same whether secular priests or laymen except that the clerics wore an upright, rigid variety of the *bonete*, but the laymen wore an ordinary bonnet or hat in accordance with contemporary fashion. All doctors wore a tuft of the colour of their faculty on their head-gear of whatever

[1] A. Vidal y Diaz, p. 96. [2] A. Vidal y Diaz, p. 111.
[3] G. Reynier, *La Vie universitaire dans l'ancienne Espagne*, pp. 41–42.
[4] G. Reynier, p. 19. [5] G. Reynier, pp. 17, 18, and 19.
[6] In his correspondence Joseph Blanco White, writing in 1796, describes the *beca* in full. 'This slip of cloth,' he writes, 'is about 1 ft. in breadth, and between 8 and 9 ft. in length. Folding it in the middle, so as to form an angle, and holding the fold on the breast, the two halves are thrown over the shoulder so as to fall on the back nearly reaching the heels.' At Seville a white kid glove was worn in the fold of the *beca*. The *beca* was held in position by a circular rim of wood (*The Life of the Rev. Joseph Blanco White written by himself*, i. 61).
[7] V. de la Fuente, iii. 93.

variety it might be.[1] An excellent example of the dress of a clerical regent appears in the woodcut frontispiece of 1625 mentioned above. The lecturer wears a hard horned biretta and has a cloak over his cassock.

The faculty colours on the tuft of the caps of doctors of Salamanca were for Theology, white; for Canon Law, red; for Civil Law, green; and for Medicine, yellow.[2] In 1592 this tuft reached its greatest size at Salamanca and also at Coimbra, for the birettas of Doctors of Theology were in that year covered by an enormous bush of white silk fleece which issued from the apex.[3] This was called the *floccus*, and appears to have been worn at Salamanca as early as 1497 if we are to judge from a woodcut executed in the city in that year. A doctor seated at a table writing wears a tall *pileus* with a button-apex, and from this rise many long pieces of material to form a bush[4] (Pl. 2a).

II. LÉRIDA (1300)

The University of Lérida had a short life.[5] The only reference to dress is to be seen in the statutes formulated at the time of its foundation, and is simply a collection of sumptuary rules to be observed by students.[6]

III. VALLADOLID (1346)

Valladolid, although important during the Spanish Renaissance of the sixteenth century, soon afterwards fell away and was refounded in 1773.

In the statutes of 1505 students were ordered to wear the short, pleated cassock (*loba sotana*) or the flap-collared cloak (*manteo*) and a 'Castilian cap'. No other dress was allowed. Servitors, however, might by special permission of the rector wear pointed caps (*caperuza*), which appear to have been in shape like fishermen's stocking-caps.[7]

By 1547 the colours of the faculties as used on the tassels of

---

[1] V. de la Fuente, iii. 237.   [2] N. F. Robinson, loc. cit.

[3] A. Scappus, p. 64.

[4] J. P. R. Lyell, *Early Book Illustration in Spain*, p. 71, fig. 55 (Livy, *Las Decadas*, Salamanca (Segundo grupo gótico), 1497).

[5] S. d'Irsay, i. 174.

[6] J. Villanueva, *Viage Literario a las Iglesias de España*, t. xvi, p. 230.

[7] *Estatutos de la Universidad de Valladolid* (1651), § 30, p. 91; *Historia de la Universidad de Valladolid*, i, pp. xcvii and xcviii (Stats. 1505, § 30).

the head-dress of doctors and masters were as follows: for Theology, white; for Canon Law, green; for Civil Law, red; for Medicine, yellow; and for Arts, blue.[1]

The Colegio de Santa Cruz was closely connected with the university. From the fifteenth century onwards collegians wore a dark red *beca*, a drab-coloured cloak fastened at the neck with buttons, and a black cap.[2]

IV. HUESCA (1354)

The early history of the University of Huesca is obscure, and such records as remain before the sixteenth century contain no mention of dress. During this century and later, in spite of the fact that it had declined so much that it had become no more than an academy with a local reputation, there is much information about dress.

In 1569 the *pileus flosculus*, a round cap with a broad, vertically ridged edging of wool, is described as the doctoral head-dress.[3] This head-gear, which later spread to other Spanish universities except Salamanca, was originally an Italian lay fashion of the fourteenth century as can be seen from an example in a Bolognese manuscript of Petrarch's *Canzone*, in which in a miniature an old man wears such a cap.[4]

Until the end of the seventeenth century all students, whether in orders or not, seem to have worn the clerical collar (i.e. a small white turn-down collar with a division in the middle) and a cassock or buttoned cloak (*loba cerrada*), but about this time the authorities of Huesca ordered lay students to wear, as they had done earlier, a circular ruff and a long cloak (*manteo*) with a flap-collar and with an opening down the front but held closed by a belt, while only those students who held ecclesiastical office or benefice were to wear the clerical collar

---

[1] V. Velázquez de Figueroa, *Anales universitarios*, i. 150.

[2] *Constitutiones et statuta collegii majoris Sanctae Crucis oppidi Vallisoletani*, p. 8A, Const. xxx.

[3] R. del Arco, *Memorial de la Universidad de Huesca*, ii. 309.

[4] Cambridge, Fitzw. Museum, Maclean MS. 173 (Petrarch, *Canzone*), fo. 51. It was also worn in Germany in the seventeenth century (F. Hottenroth, *Handbuch der Deutschen Tracht*, p. 763, fig. 218, No. 6). A cap with sloping sides and decorated with large tufts is worn by Canon Bonaventura who is depicted as a doctor in the seventeenth-century oil-painting by J. de Valdés Leal of Seville (1622-91) formerly in the Cook Collection, Richmond. I cannot find any other example of such Spanish doctoral head-dress.

and the cassock. These last might wear the cassock open or closed as they wished, but were forbidden to have loose tails hanging behind from the cincture.[1]

Clerical doctors wore in the seventeenth century a *bonete* (a biretta of Italian style), while secular doctors wore a wide-brimmed hat, which from the sixteenth century onwards was worn indiscriminately by clerics and laymen, professors and students. The tassel of the appropriate faculty colour was worn on both kinds of head-dress.[2]

In the early eighteenth century it was enacted by royal decree that the brims of these hats should be turned up at the edge, and this was half-heartedly enforced among the students of Huesca, Alcalá, Valladolid, Toledo, and Salamanca. It was not long, however, before these hats were superseded at Huesca and elsewhere by a new fashion, the Schomberg hat, which had a downcurving brim.[3] The authorities of Huesca seem to have taken a particular dislike to it, and in 1770 at a Convocation of the university it was forbidden, and surprisingly enough it was ordered that a three-cornered lay hat should be worn by all members of the university except clergy. The clerical members were to wear hats covered with black gummed taffeta, with the brim rising on both sides.[4] Such a hat can be seen in Goya's oil-painting 'The Bewitched' in the Spanish Room in the National Gallery, London.

At the *Colegio de Santiago*, Huesca, which was incorporated in the university in the sixteenth century, the same dress was worn as at the Colegio de Santa Cruz, Valladolid, with the addition of the cross of St. James worked on the breast of their cloaks. The cross of the rector was larger than that of others. The Inquisitor of Aragon in 1561 ordered that these crosses should be removed.[5]

v. BARCELONA (1430)

The only collection of statutes of the University of Barcelona, that made in 1629 by P. Lacavalleria and entitled *Constituciones de la Universitate de Barcelona*, contains no mention of dress.

[1] R. del Arco, i. 21.   [2] R. del Arco, i. 22.
[3] It is to this form of hat that Joseph Baretti refers when describing his amusing encounter with the students of Cervera in 1760. He mentions at the same time their 'ample black cloak' (J. Baretti, *A Journey from London to Genoa*, iv. 52-53. Letter LXXII, 26 Oct. 1760).   [4] R. del Arco, i. 41-43.   [5] R. del Arco, i. 22-23.

VI. ALCALÁ (1499)

According to the reformed statutes of 1665, the first systematic collection of Alcalá's statutes, the academical dress for all members of the university was fixed as a cloth gown (*ropa de paño*), also known as a *balandran*.[1] In 1716 gifts of biretta and gloves during the doctoral ceremony are mentioned.[2] There is in the Old Cathedral at Madrid a picture of about 1640 in which the Rector of Alcalá bestows a *pileus quadratus* upon a new doctor. Doctors seated beside the Rector wear silk 'shoulder pieces' coloured according to their faculty.

VII. MALLORCA (1698)

Although for long a college, Mallorca did not become a university until the seventeenth century. In its statutes for 1698 the dress of all, both doctors and collegians, was ordered to consist of gown and hood (*borla*).[3]

III. PORTUGAL

The University of Coimbra, founded in 1288, was moved backwards and forwards between that place and Lisbon, until in 1537 Coimbra became its permanent home.[4] It remained the only Portuguese university until the twentieth century.

Although it is said[5] that the doctoral *pileus* (*barrete*, *biretta*) and ceremonial dress is as old as the university it is not until the fourteenth century that we have any definite information about the academical costume worn here.

In 1321 graduates were ordered to wear *tunicas* reaching to the heels, and undergraduates to wear them reaching to the middle of the thigh.[6] This is repeated in the statutes of 1431, and is then particularly directed at the Faculty of Theology.[7]

In the statutes of Don Manuel (1504) the dress of bachelors is considered to be a gown (*pello*), a development of the *supertunica*, a hood (*borla*), and a round cap (*cabeça*).[8] This *cabeça* was lower and softer than the doctoral *barrete*. At the time of

---

[1] *Reformacion en la Universidad de Alcalá de Henares*, p. 13, Tit. VIII, § 4.

[2] *Constitutiones Collegii Ildephonsi ac per inde totius almae Complutensis academia*, pp. 67, § xlii and 76, § xlviii.

[3] *Constituciones, Estatutos, Privilegios de la Universidad Luliana de Mallorca*, pp. 114–15.   [4] S. d'Irsay, i. 140.

[5] T. Braga, *Historia da Universidade de Coimbra*, i. 66.   [6] H. Rashdall, ii. 113.

[7] M. E. da Motta Veiga, *Esboço Historico-Litterario da Faculdade de Theologia da Universidade de Coimbra*, p. 41.   [8] T. Braga, i. 299.

taking their degree bachelors were to make presents of a *barrete* and gloves (*luvas*) to the 'Father' (*padrinho*; praelector) who presented them, and to the rector.[1] In the same statutes the doctoral ceremony is mentioned as a well established tradition. Doctors are to wear on this occasion, and at other times when festal dress is required, a trailing cloth robe (*hũa roupa roçagante*) with a little cape (*capello*; 'shoulder piece') over it, a hood (*borla*), a biretta (*barrete*), and a ring (*anel*).[2]

In later times the everyday dress for graduates and under-graduates alike was a long plain sleeveless cloak decorated at the back with bands of stuff of the same material and colour as the main cloak. On the sides at the front ran from neck to foot two rows of buttons descending vertically and set on very thickly. The distinction between graduate and undergraduate lay in the fact that only graduates had a head-dress. This was a square black cap, whose upper part was stuffed in such a way as to form two small domes. Between these domes was a tassel.[3]

From the later sixteenth century onwards the full dress of doctors was a black silk gown with close sleeves, with for Theology a white hood and white tassel on the cap and a ring with a white stone; for Canon Law a green hood and tassel and a ring with a green stone; for Civil Law a red-crimson hood and tassel and a ring with a stone of the same colour; for Medicine, yellow hood, tassel and stone; and for Philosophy, dark blue hood, tassel and stone.[4]

In the Marqués de Pombal's statutes of 1772 Doctors of Canon Law were ordered to continue to use green and Doctors of Civil Law red.[5] Pombal in this year created a new faculty, that of Mathematics, the dress of doctors of which subject was to be a black cap with a light blue tassel, a light blue hood with white loops, and a black silk gown with an armillary sphere embroidered in white on the left breast of the gown. Doctors of other faculties who were also Doctors of Mathematics might wear the device of the armillary sphere in white embroidery on their respective gowns.[6]

---

[1] T. Braga, loc. cit.   [2] T. Braga, i. 301–2.
[3] W. Bradford, *Sketches . . . in Portugal*, ill.—'Bishop of Guarda'; W. M. Kinsey, *Portugal*, p. 397.
[4] D. J. Cunningham, *The Evolution of the Graduation Ceremony*, p. 46; A. Steger, *Dissertatio de purpura*, p. 31.   [5] *Estatutos da Universidade de Coimbra*, ii. 629.
[6] *Estatutos da Universidade de Coimbra*, iii. 147.

Later elaborations were made in the dress of doctors. Not only the tassel but the whole cap came to be of the colour of the faculty to which the doctor belonged, and doctors of two faculties wore rings with stones of the two colours. The velvet of which the hood was made was of the colour of the superior faculty, and the loops of the hood which lay above the velvet was of that colour also, but the satin lining of the hood and the lower loops were of the colour of the inferior faculty. Further, the cap of a doctor of two faculties had the two faculty colours alternating on it.

The Faculty of Theology was the exception, for if the Doctor of Theology were a doctor of another faculty also, the ring and hood were of the colour of that other faculty, but the cap was plain white. With these insignia a black silk gown with close sleeves was always worn.[1]

IV. MALTA

THE ROYAL UNIVERSITY (1769)

In the original statutes (1769) of the Royal University of Malta various costumes were prescribed. The rector, who was an ecclesiastic, was to wear a rochet and a short purple gown with an eight-pointed Maltese cross of white stuff embroidered on it. To this gown a small hood was seemingly attached. Professors, if ecclesiastics, wore from the same period a surplice and biretta at all solemn academical functions, while lay professors wore a black academical gown, but the shape is not specified.[2] No official distinction in academical costume for the various degrees appears to have been laid down in the nineteenth-century statutes, but there is preserved in the university archives a manuscript of the 1830's to the effect that at that time Masters of Arts wore a woollen gown, bachelors of higher faculties a woollen gown with a silk stole, doctors a silk gown with a biretta,

---

[1] D. J. Cunningham, p. 46.
[2] *Costituzioni per i nuovi Studi dell' Università e per il Collegio de Educazione di Malta*— Malta. Valletta, Royal University Libr. MS. 1343, Tit. XVIII, § x; Tit. XXII, § iv; Tit. XXIII, § v.

and doctors of seven years' standing a black silk gown with black velvet sleeves 'like that of Councillors'. Graduates who were ecclesiastics were allowed to wear their religious habit if they preferred.[1] These costumes may well have been worn in the latter part of the eighteenth century.

[1] Correspondence with the University of Malta, 12/9/55, Reg. No. 389/54.

2

FRANCE

1. PARIS (twelfth century)

The Thirteenth Century

THE earliest mention of academical dress at Paris is that to be found in the order of Pope Innocent III in 1215. This papal order and others of a disciplinary character were carried out by Cardinal Robert de Courçon in that year.[1] According to this Regent Masters of Theology and Regent Masters of Arts are both to wear a *cappa rotunda*, black and ankle-length, while as a less formal garment they are allowed the *pallium*, that is, a loose *supertunica*.[2] The less formal dress is worn by Pierre de Carville, Maître-ès-Arts (d. 1307) in the full-length figure of him, taken from a missing statue, to be found among the Gaignières drawings in the *Bibliothèque nationale*. Over a *tunica* he wears a shorter *supertunica* or *pallium* which has short sleeves. A hood rests on his shoulders.[3]

The next reference we have to academical dress appears in the statutes for the English nation (1251/2). Determining Bachelors of Arts were to wear the cloth *cappa* with an absolutely plain hood of the same material. A hood was always to be worn with the *cappa*, but it was not to be worn on the head, for it is expressly stated that they must go bareheaded. As admitted bachelors, however, they were to lecture in a *pallium* with a *cappa rotunda* over it, in other words the same full dress as masters except that they had no head-dress. The masters

[1] C. Meiners, art. 'Kurze Geschichte der Trachten' in *Göttingische akademische Annalen*, i (1804), 206.
[2] H. Denifle and E. Chatelain, *Chartularium Universitatis Parisiensis*, i, no. 20, p. 79; C. E. Du Boulay, *Historia Universitatis Parisiensis*, ii. 672 and iii. 82; J. B. L. Crévier, *Histoire de l'Université de Paris*, i. 300–1 and ii. 423.
[3] Paris, Bibl. Nat. Dépt. des Estampes Oa 10, J. Gaignières, *Recueil des portraits* fo. 83.

wore a *mitra* (skull-cap) which served to distinguish them from others.[1] The same dress for admitted Bachelors of Arts is again mentioned in 1280 and in 1341.[2]

Although as early as this there does not seem to have been any definite dress for undergraduates,[3] certain colleges ordered a special uniform dress for all their members, such as appears in the foundation statutes of the Sorbonne College (1274). All members of this college were to wear an entirely plain closed *supertunica*.[4] Such a dress with a hood falling back on the shoulders appears on a thirteenth-century Paris seal,[5] now lost.

As to head-dress, by 1272 the *pileus* was worn by Masters of Medicine,[6] and by incepting Bachelors of Medicine.[7]

The Fourteenth Century

In 1336 (not 1334 as is usually given) Pope Benedict XII, who as Jacques Fournier had been educated at Paris, allowed all regents in the Faculty of Canon Law to wear red 'shoulder pieces'.[8] In 1377 we find further mention of the red *cappa* (i.e. 'shoulder piece') furred with miniver worn by Doctors of Canon Law,[9] and again in 1386[10] and in 1388.[11] During this period the head-dress of Doctors of Canon Law had become a doubled scarlet *pileus*, called *birettum* to distinguish it from the lower *pileus*.[12]

The colour red seems soon after the enactment of the pope in 1336 to have spread to other parts of the dress of Doctors of Canon Law, for in an illumination in a manuscript of the *Psalterium cum Canticis* of about 1340[13] are to be seen at the

---

[1] H. Denifle and E. Chatelain, i, no. 201, p. 228, and i, no. 202, p. 230.

[2] H. Denifle and E. Chatelain, i, no. 501, p. 586; C. E. Du Boulay, iv. 273.

[3] V. de Viriville, *Histoire de l'Instruction publique*, p. 176.

[4] H. Denifle and E. Chatelain, i, no. 448, p. 506.

[5] V. de Viriville, p. 129.   [6] C. E. Du Boulay, iii. 402.

[7] H. Denifle and E. Chatelain, i, no. 444, p. 502.

[8] In the chartularies they are termed *cappa*, but with the meaning which the word sometimes has in early times of 'cape', H. Denifle and E. Chatelain, op. cit. ii, no. 1002, pp. 464–5; G. Péries, *La Faculté de droit dans l'ancienne Université de Paris* pp. 47 and 248; E. Dubarle, *Histoire de l'Université de Paris*, i. 143; J. B. L. Crévier, ii. 325.   [9] H. Denifle and E. Chatelain, iii, no. 1414, p. 233.

[10] H. Denifle and E. Chatelain, iii, no. 1531, p. 434.

[11] H. Denifle and E. Chatelain, iii, no. 1546, p. 473.

[12] H. Denifle and E. Chatelain, iii, no. 1708, §§ 20 and 24, p. 653.

[13] Cambridge, Sidney Sussex Coll. Libr. MS. James 76, fo. 56 (see Ps. lii (liii), Dixit insipiens').

bottom of the border six figures of seated doctors on benches reading books, the third, fourth, and fifth wearing blue or pink robes over red *supertunicas*, the group, if we may trust the artist, consisting probably of Doctors of Canon Law and of Civil Law, those in the pink robes being perhaps those of Both Laws.

Regents in the Faculty of Medicine were in 1350 instructed to wear a *cappa rotunda* of good cloth of a violet-brown colour.[1] According to an illuminated manuscript, a Life of Raymond Lull, their head-dress about 1320 was a white coif, with a chin-strap.[2]

The dress of regents in the Faculty of Theology would appear to have been simpler if we are to form any judgement of it from the figure of Aristotle dressed as such a regent in a miniature in a manuscript of the year 1372; for he wears a skull-cap with an 'apex', a plain *supertunica*, and a furred hood hanging down the back with two fur 'labels' on the chest[3] (Pl. 3).

It was during this century that the dress of Masters of Arts of Paris was regulated. In 1339 the Masters of the Four Nations of France met together and decided that for the future masters who took part in academical acts and ceremonies should wear a *cappa* and a furred 'shoulder piece' (*épitoge*) and *not* merely a tabard.[4] This regulation was repeated in 1363.[5] The displaced stone effigy of Jean Perdrier (d. 1376), who was a Master of Arts, shows him wearing over a *subtunica* a closed *supertunica*, moderately full, with small 'bell' sleeves reaching only just below the elbows. He has a close hood falling on the upper part of the shoulders, but no 'shoulder piece'.[6]

In the statutes of the Navarre College (1315) Bachelors of Arts were ordered to wear, before they had 'determined', tabards of a brown-black colour, but when they had 'determined', a blue *cappa rotunda*.[7] This dress for full bachelors is more clearly mentioned in 1341 when their costume is de-

---

[1] A. Franklin, *La Vie privée d'autrefois*, xi. 42.

[2] Karlsruhe, Badische Landesbibliothek, Cod. St. Peter MS. 92, fo. 11ᵛ.

[3] C. Gaspar and F. Lyna, *Bibliothèque Royale de Belgique—Principaux Manuscrits à Peintures*, i, pl. lxxviii, text pp. 354 ff. (Aristote, Éthiques, trad. de Nicole Oresme), MS. 9505–9, fo. 2ᵛ (3rd compartment).

[4] M. Félibien and G. A. Lobineau, *Histoire de la ville de Paris*, tom. i, pp. 593–4.

[5] J. B. L. Crévier, ii. 423.

[6] B. de Montfaucon, *Les Monumens de la Monarchie françoise*, iii, pl. xvii, p. 68, fig. 5; J. Malliot and P. Martin, *Recherches sur les costumes*, iii, pl. l.

[7] J. Launoy, *Regii Navarraei Gymnasii Parisiensis Historia*, i. 32.

PLATE 3

Regent Master of Theology of Paris lecturing, 1372

scribed as a *pallium* (loose *supertunica*) or *cappa rotunda* of brown-black, blue (*parsicus*) black, or full black cloth. The hood was long and full, and furred with miniver or similar fur.[1]

The first reference to the dress of students appears during this century. In 1346 students of Ave Maria College were ordered to wear the *subtunica* for ordinary occasions and for feasts a *supertunica* as well.[2]

The Fifteenth Century

By the beginning of this century if not before the dress of the rector consisted of a scarlet closed pleated and girded *supertunica* with a close hood and a 'shoulder piece' of the same colour.[3] The proctors had the same dress,[4] but it was purple.[5] The dress of the proctor of the Picardy nation about 1477 consisted of a tall rigid hat of the *mortier* type, a close miniver hood falling on the neck, a cassock, and over this a closed gown with large bell-shaped sleeves, the gown being shorter than the cassock.[6]

It was during this century that the *chaperon* or *chausse* (also called in the particular square form used by men of law, *cornette*),[7] abandoned as a lay fashion, became associated in certain instances with the dress of the universities and men of law.[8] In Paris by 1498 it had become an indispensable part of the dress of regents,[9] and of all Licentiates of Law.[10] Other lay influences which affected the academical dress of the time were the head-dress and the use of fur and embroidery on garments. The *mortier*, originally associated with the head-dress of kings, princes, and knights, by 1449 began to be worn by persons of academical dignity, while the fashion for large hats and bonnets which appeared as a general fashion about the same time also came to have a profound effect on academical head-gear.[11] The

---

[1] C. E. Du Boulay, iv. 274.

[2] A. L. Gabriel, *Student Life in Ave Maria College*, pp. 227 and 357–8.

[3] C. E. Du Boulay, *Remarques sur la dignité. . . . du recteur de l'Université de Paris*, p. 24; V. de Viriville, p. 177, ill.

[4] V. de Viriville, p. 179; C. E. Du Boulay, *Remarques*, pp. 24–26.

[5] H. Rashdall, *Universities*, iii. 389, n. 3.

[6] V. de Viriville, p. 126.

[7] J. B. Thiers, *Histoire des Perruques*, p. 89.

[8] A. de Caumont, *Cours d'antiquités monumentales*, vi, pt. 6, pp. 382–3, n.

[9] G. Péries, p. 48.   [10] C. Loyseau, *Traité des ordres*, p. 6.

[11] D. Diderot and J. le R. D'Alembert, *Encyclopédie*, ii. 324 a–b, s.v. Bonnet.

use of three rows of fur on the *chaperon* of doctors was, like the *mortier*, originally a sign of royalty.[1]

Masters of Theology were in 1452, according to the reforms of Cardinal d'Estouteville, ordered to wear an unspecified ankle-length, closed dress without a girdle, and were to have a short 'shoulder piece' with a hood.[2] In 1436 they had been allowed the *birettum*.[3] They wore a round violet *pileus* in 1478;[4] and this last form of head-dress is again mentioned in 1485.[5] The colour of the robe, which was perhaps a *cappa manicata*,[6] was sombre, such colours as grey, dull blue, dark green, and emerald-black being much used at this time.[7]

Doctors of Canon Law were also ordered in 1452 to wear a sombre dress, a *cappa* and a 'shoulder piece',[8] but whether or not this means that they had to give up their scarlet, they certainly wore it not long afterwards, and at the time of the second marriage of Francis I in the following century they wore their *chapes rouges* as a matter of course.[9]

A Doctor of Both Laws, who appears in an illumination in a late fifteenth-century French *Book of Hours*, wears a grey *mortier*, a closed pink gown with full hanging sleeves, and a large white 'bib' or 'label' without a division in it.[10] By 1491 doctors of this degree were wearing a red *birettum*.[11]

A doctor of the Faculty of Medicine of the early fifteenth century, in a miniature in a French translation by Jean Corbechon of *De Proprietatibus Rerum*, wears a violet skull-cap, a violet *supertunica*, and over this a scarlet *cappa manicata* lined with miniver. In addition he wears a 'shoulder piece' with a small hood attached, both lined with miniver[12] (Pl. 4 a). In the middle

---

[1] B. de Montfaucon, iii, pl. lvii, figs. 4 and 8, p. 276 (portraits of Charles, duc de Bourbon, and Louis III, King of Sicily); and cf. J. Quicherat, *Histoire du costume en France*, p. 324.   [2] C. E. Du Boulay, *Histoire*, v. 564.

[3] H. Denifle and E. Chatelain, iv, no. 2489, p. 591.

[4] J. Launoy, i. 195.   [5] J. B. L. Crévier, iv. 419.

[6] Cf. R. Goulet, *Compendium on the Magnificence of the University of Paris*, pp. 38 and 78.

[7] J. Quicherat, p. 323.   [8] C. E. Du Boulay, *Histoire*, v. 567.

[9] G. Péries, p. 48.

[10] B.M. MS. Add. 25695, fo. 165.   [11] J. Launoy, i. 199.

[12] Cambridge, Fitzwilliam Museum, MS. 251 (Bartholomaeus Anglicus, *De Proprietatibus Rerum*), miniature No. 9, fo. 106, lib. vii. Another example of this dress with the addition of a 'bib', the same as that worn by the Doctor of Both Laws mentioned above, is given in R. Bruck, *Die Malereien in den Handschriften des Königreichs Sachsen*, pl. no. 113, p. 299 (Galen, at Dresden).

of the century, according to the contemporary treatise, *The Commendation of the Clerk*, the red *cappa* was the particular mark of the medical man,[1] but by the latter part of the century the faculty colour for medicine appears to have been regarded as green if we are to judge from another illumination in the *Book of Hours* referred to above.[2]

In the Estouteville statutes (1452) Bachelors of Theology and Bachelors of Canon Law were apparently expected to use the same modest dress as Doctors of Canon Law.[3]

Masters of Arts were at the same time forbidden to use short garments and lay 'bourrelet' caps.[4] At this time they wore a black *cappa rotunda* of the best material, lined with fur.[5] Their proper head-dress was before about 1460 a tall rigid *pileus* 'after the fashion of a Turkish fez',[6] but by the end of the century they had exchanged this for a round bonnet (*birettum*), and were distinguished by having a *chaperon* on the left shoulder.[7] In 1447 the particular insignia of all regent masters were the *birettum* and gloves.[8]

Bachelors of Arts remained with the same dress they had had in the previous century, and no definite dress seems to have been prescribed for students as such, nor was it for a long time to come. We learn only that students of the law faculty of noble birth had no right to any particular dress differing from that of other students.[9] If they needed fur for warmth students were permitted the use of otter-fur.[10]

The Sixteenth Century

It was about the middle of the sixteenth century that the rector gave up his scarlet dress, for in the reign of Henri III

[1] L. Thorndike, *University Records in the Middle Ages*, p. 214.
[2] B.M. MS. Add. 25695, fo. 15ᵛ. There is a good German example which is worth comparing with this. It appears in an illumination in a fifteenth-century manuscript of the first part of Ludolphus of Saxony's *Vita Christi*. In it is a Doctor of Medicine wearing a green robe, a miniver 'shoulder piece', and a red *mortier*. B.M. MS. Add. 25885, fo. 72.
[3] C. E. Du Boulay, *Histoire*, v. 567.
[4] C. E. Du Boulay, *Histoire*, v. 576.
[5] L. Thorndike, p. 213. [6] J. Quicherat, p. 322.
[7] A. de Caumont, vi, pt. 6, pp. 382–3; J. B. Thiers, op. cit., p. 88.
[8] C. E. Du Boulay, *Histoire*, v. 542.
[9] G. Péries, pp. 23–24; cf. for the different dresses allowed them at Montpellier, M. Fournier, *Universités françaises: Les statuts et privilèges*, ii. 50 and 156.
[10] G. Péries, p. 48.

(1575-89) he wore a soft violet bonnet, a white ruff, a pleated tight violet *supertunica* worn closed, and a full 'shoulder piece' of white fur on a violet foundation. Some of the white fur lining of a hood fell in front. With this dress was worn a gold belt and a gold purse hanging down from it on the right side.[1]

Proctors then wore scarlet robes and had their miniver 'shoulder piece' until the latter part of the sixteenth century when the 'shoulder piece' was given up and a fur flap collar was substituted for it.[2]

Masters of Theology were in 1517 described as wearing if seculars a full grey-brown *cappa*, if regulars the habit of their Order.[3] Their head-dress was a bell-shaped black silk *pileus*.[4] In 1587 on the reform of the Faculty of Theology the *cappa* was again insisted on and cloaks were particularly condemned.[5]

In the miniature of Christ with the Doctors in an illuminated manuscript, 'Le Chappelet de Jhesus et de la Vierge Marie', of early in this century, the second of the three doctors appears dressed as a Doctor of Both Laws.[6] He wears a scarlet robe, closed, with tight sleeves. If we notice the opening in the breast of the robe we shall realize that this is the same type of *supertunica* such as may be seen in the later dress of English judges. The head-dress of this doctor is a blue-grey Ulysses cap, this part of his dress representing the Canon Law half of his double degree.

By 1540 the dress of this degree had changed in that the tight sleeves had become 'bell' sleeves, while the head-dress varied between a low *pileus* and a *mortier*. This is to be seen in a cartoon satirizing the court of King Francis I.[7] However, in the stone effigy of Pierre Rabuf (Professor of Law, 1487-1557) at the Collège d'Autun, Paris, his hands pass through the slit on the breast of what is the *cappa clausa* in its original character, and the dress is decorated with miniver.[8]

---

[1] G. Ferrario, *Le Costume*, v, pt. 2 (Europe), pl. 42; C. E. Du Boulay, *Dignité*, pp. 24-25.

[2] C. E. Du Boulay, *Dignité*, p. 25.

[3] R. Goulet, p. 38.

[4] E. E. Viollet-le-Duc, *Dictionnaire Raisonné du Mobilier français*, iv. 280-2 and fig. 41.

[5] C. E. Du Boulay, *Histoire*, vi. 791-2 and 794-5.

[6] B.M. MS. Add. 25693, fo. 15.

[7] B. de Montfaucon, iv, pl. xxxv, pp. 319-20.

[8] G. Péries, p. 168.

A Doctor of Medicine, in an illumination in 'Le Chappelet' referred to above, wears a light green, tight-sleeved robe with an opening in the breast, a pale orange 'shoulder piece', and a mid-blue 'turban' bonnet.[1] By the latter part of the century there had been a revolution in fashion, and such doctors wore a black *bonnet carré*, a white ruff, a red 'shoulder piece' trimmed with miniver with a 'roller' hood close round the neck, a scarlet sleeveless *pallium* or *tabard* edged at the bottom with miniver and reaching only to the knee, and under this a closed black *tunica*, with glove sleeves.[2]

In 1517 at the *Signita*, that is the ceremony taking place the day before the granting of the degree, the *Paranymphus* or legate of the chancellor, who was the chief state officer responsible for the granting of degrees, appeared in a scarlet *cappa* and a velvet cap.[3]

Bachelors of Theology wore *cappas* in 1517,[4] and this dress was still enforced in 1587.[5] Bachelors of the other faculties wore the same, and later in the century a black *chaperon* (*chausse*) is mentioned as being worn by them on formal occasions.[6] Bachelors of Theology at public disputations were ordered in 1561 to wear *calottes* (skull-caps).[7]

Masters of Arts wore about 1520 a round bonnet, a closed gown with a 'shoulder piece', a hood close round the neck, and a *chaperon* like a sash running over the right shoulder and under the left arm.[8] By 1593 their hood, which was attached to the 'shoulder piece', had become much enlarged, and they still wore the round bonnet,[9] which E. Pasquier writing in 1596 says were the special features of a master's dress,[10] but in 1598 they were told to wear the square cap (*pileus quadratus; bonnet carré*) instead of the round one.[11]

---

[1] B.M. MS. Add. 25693, fo. 15.

[2] C. Piton, *Costume civil en France*, p. 150 (bottom right a drawing of 1581 by the antiquary Gaignières); G. Ferrario, v, pt. 2 (Europe), pl. 42, no. 8; E. D. Glasson, art. 'Les Origines du costume de la magistrature', in *Nouvelle Revue historique de droit français et étranger* (1884), pp. 117–18.

[3] R. Goulet, p. 89.

[4] R. Goulet, p. 78.

[5] C. E. Du Boulay, *Histoire*, vi. 791–2 and 794–5.

[6] C. Jourdain, *Histoire de l'Université de Paris*, i. 43.

[7] J. B. Thiers, p. 121.

[8] V. de Viriville, p. 136.

[9] E. Dubarle, ii, 144.

[10] D. Diderot and J. le R. D'Alembert, iii. 178ᵃ.

[11] N. F. Robinson, art. 'The *Pileus Quadratus*' in *Transactions of St. Paul's Ecclesiological Society* (1901), v, pt. 1, p. 9.

In 1600 all regents were ordered to wear the square but not rigid bonnet, the *bonnet carré*.[1] As early as 1554 they had been collectively ordered to wear a full sleeved robe and 'shoulder piece',[2] but seem usually to have preferred the dress of their particular degree, and the enactment became a dead letter.

By this time we have reached the stage when besides the *mortier*, latterly confined to the legal profession, three types of head-dress had developed. There was the round bonnet, the square but not rigid bonnet (*bonnet carré*), and the stiff biretta, worn only by ecclesiastics (Pl. 2 *c*), a dress which arose in the later sixteenth century before which time they had worn the round bonnet.[3] The *bonnet carré* became rigid in the early years of the seventeenth century.[4] The ecclesiastical biretta was in the course of the seventeenth century given ridges, such as the academical *bonnet carré* never had.[5]

The Seventeenth and Eighteenth Centuries

The rector. There is a fine water-colour made by the German traveller Friedrich Rhetinger of Ingolstadt in 1605 of the Rector of the University of Paris wearing a black *bonnet carré*, a large miniver 'shoulder piece' reaching right over his chest and almost to his elbows, a closed violet robe with tight sleeves, and a violet girdle and violet purse[6] (Pl. 4 *b*). In 1668 the particular features of the rectorial dress are described as being a very large violet 'shoulder piece' lined and edged with miniver, and a great violet purse at the girdle. At this date the rector seems to have worn a *bonnet carré* and continued to do so in the eighteenth century. The 'shoulder piece' had since the sixteenth century been worn without hood and liripipe.[7]

Throughout the eighteenth century the rectorial dress consisted of the violet robe with the miniver and violet 'shoulder piece', a silk violet belt decorated with gold tassels, a violet

[1] C. Jourdain, i. 32; D. Diderot and J. le R. D'Alembert, op. cit. xvi. 420[b], s.v. Toque; N. F. Robinson, art. cit., op. cit. v, pt. 1, p. 9.

[2] A. Franklin, x. 45.

[3] E. Pasquier, *Les Recherches de la France*, pp. 382D—383B; illustrations of these kinds of head-dress are given in J. B. Thiers, p. 107, and the three appear in a tail-piece in C. Du Molinet, *Figures des different habits des Chanoines*, p. 23.

[4] J. B. Thiers, p. 110; C. Du Molinet, pp. 22–23; J. Quicherat, p. 366.

[5] J. B. Thiers, pp. 110–11; G. Burius, *Onomasticon Etymologicum*, p. 34, s.v. Birettum.   [6] Oxford, Bodl. Libr. MS. Douce 244, fo. 31.

[7] C. E. Du Boulay, *Dignité*, pp. 24–26.

PLATE 4

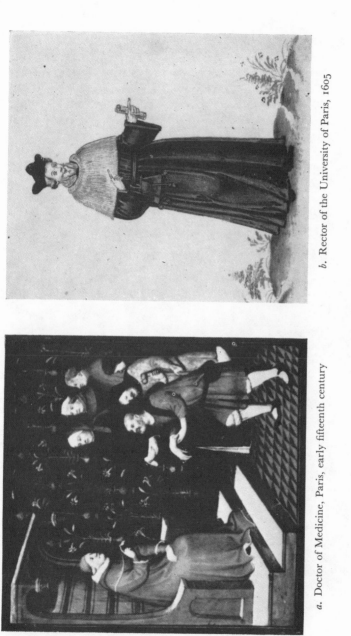

b. Rector of the University of Paris, 1605

a. Doctor of Medicine, Paris, early fifteenth century

PLATE 5

N. Edelinck's 'L'Assemblée de la Faculté de Théologie', 1717

stole (*baudrier*), really a form of *chaperon* which passed from left to right across the chest, and a violet velvet purse (*escarcelle*) decorated with gold tassels and buttons. The *bonnet carré* changed in colour in the course of the century, for in 1719 it was black, but in 1779 violet.[1]

The proctors of the four nations composing the Faculty of Arts. Throughout this period proctors wore red robes, open and faced and lined with miniver, with miniver flap collars, such as they had done since the latter sixteenth century.[2]

Deans and other administrative officers. Deans and other officials wore the same dress as the proctors.[3] The Dean of the Faculty of Medicine had formerly worn as distinct from the other deans, a light blue purse edged with miniver.[4]

The Faculty of Theology. Doctors on important occasions wore until the eighteenth century a violet bonnet, and during nearly the whole of both centuries a violet gown and a violet *chaperon* dressed with miniver.[5] For ordinary occasions all the above-mentioned dress was black. The gown worn in either case was open, and either bell-sleeved, the sleeves being edged with black braid, or else narrow-sleeved and had buttons by which the sleeves could be held close to the arms. It had a flap-collar and broad black cloth facings down the front. A *chaperon* consisting of a doubled straight section of black silk edged and lined with miniver was worn with the undress.[6] By 1779 the use of violet seems to have been abandoned and only black was used.[7]

By 1717, the date of N. Edelinck's engraving, 'L'Assemblée de la Faculté de Théologie' in the Louvre,[8] Doctors of Theology were wearing a *bonnet carré* instead of a round bonnet[9] (Pl. 5).

[1] P. T. N. Hurtaut and –. Magny, *Dictionnaire historique de la ville de Paris*, iv. 160 s.v. Procession, and iv. 742, s.v. Université; A. Franklin, x. 250.

[2] C. E. Du Boulay, *Dignité*, p. 25; D. Diderot and J. le R. D'Alembert, xiv. 309a, s.v. Robe.

[3] P. T. N. Hurtaut and –. Magny, iv. 159–60, s.v. Procession; D. Diderot and J. le R. D'Alembert, xiv. 309a, s.v. Robe.

[4] G. Ferrario, v, pt. 2 (Europe), pl. 42, no. 8.

[5] P. T. N. Hurtaut and –. Magny, iv. 160; A. Franklin, x. 250.

[6] D. Diderot and J. le R. D'Alembert, op. cit. xiv. 309a, s.v. Robe; P. T. N. Hurtaut and –. Magny, iv. 160; A. Franklin, x. 250; P. Pic, *Guy Patin*, pl. opp. p. 142 (Portrait of Antoine Arnauld, D.Th. of the Sorbonne); C. Perrault, *Les Hommes illustres qui ont paru en France*, i, ill. p. 15 (same portrait).

[7] P. T. N. Hurtaut and –. Magny, iv. 160.

[8] Reproduced in J. Bonnerot, *L'Université de Paris du moyen âge à nos jours*, p. 36.

[9] D. Diderot and J. le R. D'Alembert, ii. 324 a–b, s.v. Bonnet.

They continued throughout the century to wear a cassock underneath their gown even when outside.[1] There is a story of Voltaire's adopting the disguise in his favourite *Café de Procope* of a Doctor of the Sorbonne (i.e. of Theology), on which occasion he wore a cassock, a gown, black stockings, cincture, bands, and a large unpowdered wig.[2]

Bachelors of Theology wore throughout the period a black cassock, with a long black gown lined and dressed with white fur, and a black silk bonnet lined with miniver.[3]

The Faculty of Law. The dress of full professors (*antécesseurs*) at their investiture consisted of a purple robe (*chlamys sive toga*), a scarlet 'shoulder piece' edged with wool, a girdle of black watered silk fastened on the left side, and a black *bonnet carré*,[4] in virtue of their being professors, not doctors. But after this ceremony they always wore for formal occasions a full and long open red-scarlet robe of wool with full bell-sleeves, lined with black silk, a scarlet 'shoulder piece' dressed with miniver, and a scarlet *bonnet carré*.[5] For informal occasions they wore an open black gown lined with red and a red *chaperon*.[6]

Those Doctors of Law who were assistant professors (*agrégés*) only wore the full scarlet dress of the *antécesseurs* if they deputized for them, but whenever (and this was usually the case) they took second place to the *antécesseurs*, they wore an open black bell-sleeved gown and a red *chaperon*.[7]

During the eighteenth century the *agrégés* became more and more discontented that the *antécesseurs*, even if they were *Licenciés* only, should wear the scarlet robe, while they (the *agrégés*), who were generally doctors and had undisputed right to scarlet, should have to wear black, except when they acted as deputies of the *antécesseurs*. When it was pointed out that the *antécesseurs* wore scarlet in virtue of their being professors, the

[1] P. Lacroix, *The Eighteenth Century*, p. 243, fig. 141.
[2] T. Carlyle, *Miscellaneous Essays*, ii (1888 edn.), p. 141.
[3] P. T. N. Hurtaut and –. Magny, iv. 159; D. Diderot and J. le R. D'Alembert, ii. 7[b]; A. Franklin, x. 249.   [4] G. Péries, pp. 248 and 318, n. 2.
[5] P. T. N. Hurtaut and –. Magny, ii. 674 and iv. 159; A. Franklin, x. 249–50; D. Diderot and J. le R. D'Alembert, ii. 324 a–b, s.v. Bonnet and v. 5b, s.v. Docteur en Droit; G. Péries, p. 248. For a literary allusion to this dress see Boileau's Eighth Satire, ll. 171–2. This satire was composed in 1667.
[6] G. Péries, p. 248.
[7] G. Péries, p. 248; D. Diderot and J. le R. D'Alembert, v. 8a, s.v. Docteur en droit.

agrégés replied by wearing the scarlet robe and scarlet and miniver 'shoulder piece' on all occasions that the *antécesseurs* wore them.[1] In 1766 affairs came to a head, the *antécesseurs* accusing the *agrégés* of always wearing scarlet robes when they did, but when the parties appealed to the Paris Parliament that body decided in favour of the latter, and they were allowed to wear the scarlet robe on the same occasions as the *antécesseurs*.[2]

Other Licentiates of Law on special occasions wore as full dress an open scarlet robe with a scarlet 'shoulder piece' trimmed with miniver, but the robe was not as full as that of doctors.[3] Ordinarily their dress consisted of an open black gown and a red *chaperon* decorated with miniver.[4]

Bachelors of Law wore open black gowns and black *chausses* trimmed with miniver.[5]

The *bonnet carré*, red for those who had the right to the red robe on formal occasions, black otherwise, was worn by all, and the black cassock and white bands.[6] All gowns were bell-sleeved.[7]

The Faculty of Medicine. The dress of Regent Doctors of Medicine remained the same during this period. For full dress it consisted of an open scarlet robe with wide bell-sleeves and a scarlet and miniver 'shoulder piece' completely covering the shoulders, a black cassock with many small buttons running vertically down the front, white bands, and a scarlet *bonnet carré*.[8] A cincture round the cassock was worn until about the middle of the seventeenth century.[9]

The undress garments of Regent Doctors of Medicine were the black gown of the same shape as the scarlet one, a scarlet *chaperon*, a black cassock, and a black *bonnet carré*.[10]

Bachelors of Medicine wore a black bell-sleeved gown and a black *chaperon* trimmed with miniver.[11]

[1] G. Péries, p. 318, n. 2.   [2] G. Péries, p. 256.
[3] D. Diderot and J. le R. D'Alembert, v. 8a.
[4] G. Péries, p. 318, n. 2.
[5] P. T. N. Hurtaut and –. Magny, iv. 159.
[6] D. Diderot and J. le R. D'Alembert, ii. 324 a–b, s.v. Bonnet.
[7] Cf. A. Franklin, x. 249.   [8] G. Patin, *Lettres choisies*, frontispiece.
[9] G. Patin, pl. opp. p. 22.   [10] G. Patin, *Nouvelles lettres*, i. 167.
[11] A. Franklin, x. 249. In their professional as opposed to their academical capacity, doctors in the seventeenth century wore high pointed bonnets in shape like candle-extinguishers which appeared ludicrous on top of large wigs, and did not fail to amuse Molière (A. Franklin, xi. 146) who makes play of them in *Le Médecin malgré lui* (1666). The head-dress was derived from the *mortier*.

The Faculty of Arts. The dress of a Master of Arts at the Collège de Clermont in 1644 consisted of a violet cassock, a black sleeveless gown, and a black *chaperon*.[1] By 1719 the dress of Masters of Arts throughout the university had come to be a black bell-sleeved open gown with a plain black *chaperon* (*chausse*) and a black *bonnet carré*.[2] In 1766 on appealing to the Paris Parliament, regent masters obtained the right to wear as full dress the scarlet robe and scarlet and miniver 'shoulder piece' like that of other regents.[3] Bachelors of Arts probably wore the same dress as Bachelors of Law and Medicine. No particular mention is made of them.

Undergraduates. It was not until the beginning of the seventeenth century that a definite dress for undergraduates came into being. Throughout this century they wore an open sleeveless gown with a flap collar of black stuff, and a round bonnet.[4] They had worn this bonnet since 1600.[5] In the eighteenth century they continued to wear the same gown, but gave up the round bonnet, and wore instead a rigid variety of *toque*,[6] a flat bonnet. They wore bands in common with all other members of the university.[7]

Séminaristes were theological students at a college associated with the university run by the Church. They wore a short cassock reaching some way below the knees with numerous small buttons down the front, bands, and round felt hats.[8]

But during the eighteenth century more and more members of the University of Paris were leaving off their academical dress except on formal occasions, and were wearing lay dress which was far from being 'modest and fitting'.[9] Academical dress vanished in 1792 when the university ceased to function. By a law of the National Convention of 15 September 1793 all the universities of France were abolished.

[1] P. Lacroix, *XVIIe Siècle: Institutions, usages et costumes*, pl. p. 470.
[2] P. T. N. Hurtaut and –. Magny, ii. 790, s.v. Examinateurs; A. Franklin, x. 248. [3] P. T. N. Hurtaut and –. Magny, iv. 159.
[4] F. Hottenroth, *Handbuch*, p. 762, and fig. 217, no. 4.
[5] C. Jourdain, i. 32; D. Diderot and J. le R. D'Alembert, xvi. 420b, s.v. Toque; N. F. Robinson, art. cit., pt. 1, p. 9.
[6] D. Diderot and J. le R. D'Alembert, xvi, 420b, s.v. Toque; G. Dupont Ferrier, *Du Collège de Clermont au Lycée Louis-le-Grand*, p. 430; R. Somerset Ward, *Robespierre*, pp. 29–30.
[7] P. T. N. Hurtaut and –. Magny, iv. 159–60; A. Franklin, x. 248, and xi. 145.
[8] P. Lacroix, *XVIIe Siècle*, p. 358, fig. 156. [9] J. B. L. Crévier, vii. 73.

II. TOULOUSE (1229)

In the 'Grands statuts de l'Université et des Facultés de droit et de decret' (1314), Doctors and Masters of Law are forbidden to lecture or to take part in any public act unless wearing a *cappa manicata* or *cappa rotunda*. Licentiates and Bachelors of Law are likewise at their own lectures or when taking part in disputations or other acts bound to wear either of the two forms of *cappa* above mentioned unless with some reasonable excuse, having obtained leave of the rector. Masters of Arts were to wear a black *cappa clausa* or *cappa rotunda* for lecturing. Doctors of Law only wore the *pileus*; the rest were bareheaded.[1] Students were to use on formal occasions a closed *tunica*, but on informal occasions they might wear open ones with hoods, or other more comfortable dress, but they might never wear sleeveless dress, nor might they have mittens, boots, and caps.[2]

In 1407[3] the ordinary dress of students was regularized. They were to wear ankle-length costume of sufficient fullness, and their shoes were to be plain.

Nothing more is heard of dress until 1572 when it was forbidden to all members of the university to wear in churches, at the palace, and in courts of justice any dress whatever of a red, yellow, green, or blue colour.[4]

III. MONTPELLIER (1289)

Already a School of Medicine, Montpellier did not become a *studium generale* until so created by Pope Nicholas IV in 1289,[5] and after this fifty years passed before any enactments regarding dress appeared.

In 1339 Regent Doctors of Law and Bachelors of Law were required to wear the *cappa clausa* if in orders, but if laymen they might have the choice of wearing at all times the *cappa rotunda*, the *cappa manicata*, or a long *tabard*, which dress was always to be worn, even when walking in the town. Laymen Regent Doctors of Law (*doctores decretorum*) were to lecture in red *cappas*. No miniver was to be worn in the dress except by the rector, regent

---

[1] M. Fournier, i. 484–5 (Order no. 545, ¶ x, Year 1314).
[2] M. Fournier, i. 484–5 (Order no. 545, ¶ xl, § 3, Year 1314).
[3] M. Fournier, i. 727, §§ 2–7.
[4] R. Gadave, *Les Documents sur l'histoire de l'Université de Toulouse*, p. 179, § 500.
[5] E. Dubarle, i. 122.

doctors, those of noble blood, and those clergy who were of cathedral or ecclesiastical collegiate bodies, and even in these cases they were allowed miniver only on their hoods. At the same time students were ordered to wear a long and sufficiently full costume of the *supertunica* variety, and this dress was to be plain and without a hood.[1] By 1391 it had become necessary to forbid the wearing of any but cheap fur or lamb's wool by any but the rector, doctors, nobles, and licentiates. Regents in orders were still forced to wear a *cappa clausa*, or at least some form of *cappa*, but laymen regents might wear simply a cloak and at any rate nothing more formal than a tabard.[2]

From a title of 1462—all but the title is wanting—it is learnt that a *pileus* was bestowed on licentiates.[3] After this there is no more information about dress for more than a century.

In 1628 all professors were ordered to lecture in a gown (*toga*) and a *bonnet carré*.[4]

Until the seventeenth century the newly created Doctor of Laws, dressed in his doctoral robe and bonnet, was conducted to his house on horseback to the music of fiddles and hautboys.[5] As late as 1711 a Professor of Medicine is described as wearing at a ceremony white boots with gilt spurs.[6] This was a survival of the medieval idea of the doctor being a nobleman in the realm of learning.

At a visit of some members of the royal family to the Faculty of Medicine in 1701, the Professors of Medicine wore red damask robes with a doubled miniver *chaperon* (*chausse*), while *agrégés* wore the same *chaperon*, but a black damask robe. At a

---

[1] M. Fournier, ii. 50 (Order no. 947, ¶ iv); F. K. von Savigny, *Histoire du droit romain au moyen âge*, tom. iv, p. 494; A. Germain, art. 'L'École de Droit de Montpellier' in *Académie des Sciences et Lettres de Montpellier* (*Sect. des Lettres*, vi), p. 257ᵇ.

[2] M. Fournier, ii. 156–7 (Order no. 1040, Year 1391).

[3] M. Fournier, ii. 237 (Order no. 1163).

[4] A. Germain, art. 'La Faculté des Arts et l'Ancien Collège de Montpellier' in *Académie des Sciences et Lettres de Montpellier* (*Sect. des Lettres*, vii), p. 220, § iii; see the water-colour and pen and ink drawing dated 1579 of Laurence Joubert, M.D. and Chancellor of the University (d. 1582), in the Hope Collection in the Ashmolean, Oxford, for a good illustration of the *bonnet carré*.

[5] A. Germain, art. 'L'École de Droit de Montpellier' in *Académie des Sciences et Lettres de Montpellier* (*Sect. des Lettres*, vi), p. 245. This dress, an open bell-sleeved robe with facings, and a cassock, is to be seen in the print of François Gibieuf, M.D. (d. 1634), in the Hope Collection.

[6] A. Germain, art. 'Notice sur le cérémonial de l'Université de Médecine de Montpellier' in *Académie des Sciences et Lettres de Montpellier* (*Sect. des Lettres*, vi), p. 433.

funeral in 1711 all professors wore a plain black gown and no *chaperon*.[1] This plain black gown was the undress gown for all, the red damask being the full dress of *antécesseurs* and the black damask of *agrégés*. A black gown called at the present day the 'Robe de Rabelais' is said to be still preserved and to have belonged to the satirist. In the seventeenth century it is certain that his actual bonnet and gown were used at Montpellier on certain occasions.[2]

At the funeral of a Professor of French Law at Montpellier in 1738 the body of the dead was dressed in a red robe, a black cassock, a miniver-furred *chaperon*, white bands, a full wig, a *bonnet carré* with a tuft of red and green,[3] gloves, a sword, and boots with gilt spurs.[4] Those who attended wore the plain black gown and the *bonnet carré*.[5]

Bachelors and undergraduates at this time wore plain black gowns and round bonnet.[6]

In 1755 at a ceremony of the Faculty of Medicine, the professors wore the black gown only, bands, and an ordinary hat, except for M. Lamure, the professor who presided, who alone wore the *bonnet carré*.[7]

As late as January 1791 academical dress was still used at Montpellier.[8]

IV. AVIGNON (1303)

Not until 1503 were the statutes of the University of Avignon published, and in them is some mention of dress. No one but doctors were to wear the *birretum rotundum*.[9] Apparently of late years licentiates and even bachelors had presumed to wear this important part of the doctoral *insignia*. Licentiates and bachelors were not allowed a biretta at all. They had apparently been

---

[1] A. Germain, art. 'Le Cérémonial', pp. 421 and 433–4.
[2] D. J. Cunningham, *The Evolution of the Graduation Ceremony*, p. 31.
[3] Cf. B.M. MS. Ar. 484, fos. 61 and 105 (a German *Justiniani Digestum* with miniatures of 1399) for these two-coloured tufts used in the Middle Ages by Doctors of Both Laws, red representing Civil and green Canon Law.
[4] A. Germain, art. 'L'École de Droit', p. 244.
[5] Ibid., loc. cit., and cf. A. Germain, art. 'Le Cérémonial', pp. 433–4.
[6] A. Germain, art. 'L'École de Droit, p. 244.
[7] A. Germain, art. 'Le Cérémonial', p. 427.
[8] A. Germain, art. cit., p. 416.
[9] Cf. M. Fournier, ii. 703.

in the habit of wearing hoods lined with silk or rich furs, for they are forbidden such decoration.[1]

The doctoral *birretum* was made of two pieces and was scarlet. Doctors wore also gloves, which together with the *birretum* were presented to them on their creation. Those below the rank of doctor, such as Masters of Arts and licentiates of the various faculties, were presented with gloves but naturally not the *birretum*. Strangely enough the so strictly guarded doctoral head-dress was worn by those licentiates and bachelors, four in all, who actively took part in the ceremony of a doctor's creation.[2]

V. ORLÉANS (1312)

An order of 1336 informs us that the doctoral dress shall be made of good cloth, and that doctors are to wear a miniver-furred *mantellum*.[3] In 1363 a *supertunica* dressed with miniver might be used instead of the *mantellum*, and a miniver hood was to be used with it.[4]

In 1365 students of two or more years' standing were to wear the *cappa manicata*, but those of less standing were to continue as before to use the short *tabard*. Senior students were only allowed the *tabard* when riding.[5]

Not a word more is heard about dress until in a royal edict of 1679 it is ordered that the old ceremonial should be revived. Processions should again take place, the rector should use his red robe, the *Docteur-régents* (*antécesseurs*) should also use their red robes, and *agrégés* a black gown and a red *chaperon* (*chausse*).[6]

VI. PERPIGNAN (1349)

In 1426 students in the Faculty of Arts were ordered to wear a dress neither too long nor too short but keeping the mean.

The *pilei* of Masters of Medicine and Masters of Arts were to be the same, that is of blood-red wool.[7]

---

[1] M. Fournier, ii. 527 (Order no. 1421, § 36).
[2] M. Fournier, ii. 528 (Order no. 1421, § 38).
[3] M. Fournier, i. 100 (Order no. 117).
[4] M. Fournier, i. 120 (Order no. 161).
[5] M. Fournier, i. 122 (Order no. 167).
[6] J. Loiseleur, art. 'L'Université d'Orléans' in *Mém. de la Soc. d'Agriculture d'Orléans*, t. xxv, no. 3, p. 208.
[7] M. Fournier, ii. 703 (Order no. 1505).

VII. ANGERS (1364)

Certainly as early as about 1396 the rector has as his ceremonial dress a red robe furred with ermine, and wore as head-
dress a very large and long hood of the same colour and similarly furred.[1]

In the reformed statutes (1398) the full dress of Regent
Doctors of Canon and of Civil Law is ordered to be the *cappa*
and 'shoulder piece', or other suitable becoming dress,[2] and
in a new title[3] added to these statutes in 1410, bachelors of all
faculties were told to wear a *cappa* both going to and returning
from their lectures.

In 1431 it was found necessary to legislate against the wearing of miniver on their hoods by bachelors and licentiates.
They were to wear black lamb's wool according to the original
statutes of the university. A hood lined with miniver was really
only for the rector's wear, but by this time doctors and masters
were allowed this fur.[4]

In 1484 Bachelors of Medicine taking part in any public
scholastic act were to use the *cappa cathegorica* (i.e. a large
round-shaped *cappa* closed in front, having a large hood attached
to it), but candidates for the Licence of Medicine taking part
in the Act of Licence were to wear a short straight *tabard* unfurred, not reaching farther than the knees, and a hood.[5]

In 1494 regents in the Faculty of Arts lecturing or attending
any scholastic act are simply ordered to wear a decent habit,
but they must have a hood or 'shoulder piece'.[6]

VIII. AIX (1409)

In the fifteenth-century seal of the University of Aix the rector
wears a long closed robe with fairly full sleeves and a large
round *pileus* like a tam-o'-shanter.[7]

Among the voluminous statutes of this university (1420–40)
are a few references to dress. Doctors were to wear a gold

---

[1] L. de Lens, *Université d'Angers*, i. 49.
[2] M. Fournier, i. 324 (Order no. 434, ¶ xxxviii, § 17).
[3] Ibid. ¶ cxxxvii, § 15.
[4] M. Fournier, i. 390 (Order no. 470).
[5] C. Port, *Statuts des Quatre Facultés de l'Université d'Angers, 1464–94*, p. 33, § 33.
[6] C. Port, p. 49, § 21.
[7] R. Gandilhon, *Sigillographie des Universités de France*, p. 43 and ill. pl. i, no. 2.

cincture.[1] Masters of Theology and doctors of the other faculties wore a *pileus* of the colour of their faculty; for Theology, white; for Canon Law, green; for Civil Law, red; for Medicine, violet; and for Both Laws, red and green.

At the same time it was enjoined that candidates for the doctorate should obtain *pilei* and gloves of good quality before the ceremony of creation.[2]

IX. DÔLE (1424)

In the statutes of about 1424 the rector was ordered to wear a pleated (*rigatus*, i.e. *rugatus*) *cappa* with a cloth hood decorated with miniver.[3] At this university noblemen-students were admitted as a privileged class as at Montpellier. They were allowed special seats in university assemblies on festal occasions and were also allowed servants; but they were given no latitude as regards dress, which had to be of cloth and conformable with their standing as scholars.[4]

No one beneath the degree of doctor was allowed to wear the *birretum rotundum*.[5]

At the same time students were ordered to wear the *cappa manicata*, or at any rate a seemly dress, which was to reach *ad cavillam pedis*, to the heel, or at least to the top of the boots. Apparently this dress might be lined with fur, for students were warned that no fur must be seen at the edges of it. They were not to wear girdles unless very plain, nor were they to have convex-shaped wallets (*gibosserius*), purses, or large knives hanging from their girdles. Their dress was to be conformable to their standing and faculty, and they were to wear hoods in a modest manner and not twisted up round their heads.[6]

X. POITIERS (1431)

In 1438 Licentiates and Bachelors of Law were ordered to attend the schools in a long and ankle-length dress without a

[1] M. Fournier, iii. 23 (Order no. 1582, § 110).
[2] M. Fournier, iii. 24 (Order no. 1582, § 116).
[3] M. Fournier, iii. 107 (Order no. 1616, §xxiii); H. Beaune and J. d'Arbaumont, *Les Universités de Franche-Compté*, p. xlix, n. 2.
[4] M. Fournier, loc. cit., § xxxviii.
[5] M. Fournier, iii. 112 (Order no. 1616, § xlii).
[6] M. Fournier, iii. 114–15 (Order no. 1616, § xlix).

PLATE 6

Rector and Doctor of the University of Bourges, 1624

girdle.[1] No more information about the dress of this not very important university is to be found.

XI. CAEN (1432)

In 1439, by the statutes of King Henry VI of England, it was ordered that the dress of a Licentiate of Medicine who was to be created master was to be of good new cloth of a violet-brown colour with a close-fitting *pileus* of the same colour. This dress was to be worn by these masters, as all other Masters of Medicine, on all academical occasions.[2] The new master was to present a *pileus* and gloves to all already existing Masters of Medicine.[3] At the same time it was desired that all doctors, masters, and bachelors of the various faculties should use the *cappa clausa*, or some other decent and pleated form of *cappa* at all academical acts as at Paris.[4]

In 1457 the dress of the rector was ordered to consist of a cloth *tunica*, a pleated *cappa* (*capa rigata*, i.e. *rugata*), and a cloth hood lined with miniver.[5]

The statutes of the Faculty of Medicine (1478) contain a clause directing Doctors of Medicine to wear a violet *cappa* and a round bonnet of the same colour.[6]

XII. BORDEAUX (1441)

In 1443 doctors and masters of all faculties of the University of Bordeaux were ordered to wear a *cappa* when lecturing,[7] and at the same time students were ordered to wear ankle-length dress of such colour as befitted their station.[8]

The next mention of dress is in 1558 when regent doctors and stipendiary doctors (*agrégés*) were ordered to wear long robes to accord with their standing.[9]

---

[1] M. Fournier, iii. 303 (Order no. 1723, § vi).

[2] M. Fournier, iii. 168. (Order no. 1652, ¶ III, § 18).

[3] M. Fournier, iii. 168 (Order no. 1652, ¶ III, § 19); M. Fournier, iii. 398–9 (Order no. 1842, § xxviii).

[4] A. de Bourmont, art. 'La Fondation de l'Université de Caen' in *Bulletin de la Société des Antiquaires de Normandie*, t. xii, pp. 500 and 504–5.

[5] M. Fournier, iii. 209 (Order no. 1680, § 7); A. de Bourmont, art. cit., t. xii, p. 581.

[6] A. de Bourmont, art. cit., t. xii, p. 421.

[7] M. Fournier, iii. 342–3 (Order no. 1771, § 49).

[8] M. Fournier, loc. cit., § 54; H. Barckhausen, *Statuts et règlements de l'ancienne Université de Bordeaux*, p. 14.   [9] H. Barckhausen, p. 56.

In 1793, when the affairs of the university were wound up, an inventory was made of goods in the university's possession. Only two articles of dress are mentioned, and they no doubt formed the rector's official dress. They were an old crimson satin robe dressed with ermine, and a new gold-braided *chaperon* with tassels on it. The latter had been made in 1784.[1]

XIII. NANTES (1460)

In 1462 it was ordered that the rector's dress was to be, at scholastic acts of a solemn nature and in congregation, a *capa aperta* (probably open at the side from shoulder to hem as was sometimes the medieval practice) lined and trimmed with miniver; but in the schools at the hearing of lectures and at other less formal acts he was to use the *caputium* (i.e. the 'shoulder piece' with a hood attached) lined and trimmed with miniver in winter, but in summer lined with silk (*sandat*, i.e. 'sendal').[2]

In the same statutes of this year it was ordered that in processions and at ordinary lectures regent doctors and masters should wear a *cappa* with a furred hood or a silk one according to the season. The *cappa* itself was similarly to be worn either lined with fur or with silk.[3]

At the same time Masters and Bachelors of Theology were ordered at all acts to wear a *cappa clausa* and a hood of a becoming colour, the shape of these garments and the quality of fur used in them being suitable to their dignity. At the ceremony of licentiates becoming Masters of Theology they were to give a *birretum* (here called *birra*) to the already existing masters present.[4]

In the law faculty all nobles, licentiates, bachelors, holders of benefices, and the rest of the scholars were to appear in the schools and at all public acts of the university in a fitting ordinary dress, and over this ankle-length academical dress with a hood.[5] Regent Doctors of Law were to wear a hooded dress, furred in winter, and lined with silk in summer;[6] while

---

[1] H. Barckhausen, p. 146.   [2] M. Fournier, iii. 46 (Order no. 1595, § 8).
[3] M. Fournier, iii. 49 (Order no. 1595, § 29).
[4] M. Fournier, loc. cit., § 18.
[5] M. Fournier, iii. 64 (Order no. 1595, § 3).
[6] M. Fournier, iii. 69 (Order no. 1595, § 28).

Licentiates of Law on full ceremonial occasions at least were to use a black *cappa* and a hood, the hood only being lined and trimmed with miniver. The dress of Bachelors of Law was to be the same, except that probably the fur of the hood was to be of less expensive fur than miniver.

Students of the law faculty were to wear ankle-length dress, probably of black cloth, with a plain cloth hood. They were not to have any form of head-dress.

Proctors were to be distinguished by their 'shoulder pieces'.[1]

XIV. BOURGES (1465)

From what we read of the presentations to be made by newly created Doctors of Law who were noblemen or of other dignity, the dress of Regent Doctors of Law during the period 1470–80 consisted of a scarlet mantle with a miniver-furred hood, a scarlet *tunica*, and a scarlet *birretum duplex*. Masters of Laws (i.e. including Canon Law), Regents of the Faculties of Theology and Medicine, and the Dean of Arts also wore the scarlet *birretum duplex*.[2] In an album (Pl. 6) once owned by a member of the university are two figures in miniature dated 1624. The left-hand figure is a rector of the university, and wears a biretta, an open scarlet robe with moderately hanging sleeves, the facings in front and the cuffs of the sleeves being of black velvet, and on his left shoulder rests a scarlet *chaperon* edged with fur. The figure on the right is a doctor in undress. Over a black silk cassock he wears a black sleeveless cloak with a flap-collar. His black hat is of everyday fashion.[3]

XV. PONT-À-MOUSSON (1572), afterwards NANCY (1769)

The rector, from the time of the foundation of the university, wore a *cappa* or some kind of closed robe, and an *épitoge* ('shoulder piece'), both garments of a violet colour edged with red.[4]

All graduates wore a gown, either black or near-black, and a *bonnet carré*, but there is no mention of there having been a particular dress for students, and students of theology, about

[1] M. Fournier, loc. cit., §§ 29–31.
[2] M. Fournier, iii. 431–2 (Order no. 1862, § 14).
[3] B.M. Eg. MS. 1264, fo. 150ᵛ.
[4] E. Martin, *L'Université de Pont-à-Mousson*, p. 272.

whose dress we have information, must have been, according to the practice at all universities, already graduates of the Faculty of Philosophy (Arts).

Bachelors of Philosophy wore the gown and *bonnet carré* alone, Masters of Arts wore with the gown a black *chaperon* edged with violet, and on their black *bonnet carré* was a violet tump.[1] Professors (Doctors) of Philosophy wore under a cloak a cassock fastened at the waist, and above the cloak was a 'shoulder piece', but there is no information about the colour.[2] This dress is well illustrated in a sixteenth-century woodcut depicting four figures, one being the rector.[3]

Students of Theology, Bachelors of Theology, and licentiates of the same faculty wore a black gown, a black *bonnet carré*, and a *chaperon (chausse)* edged with white silk, but the size of the *chaperon* indicated the status, the largest indicating the licentiate. Doctors of Theology wore the same dress as licentiates except that they had a white tump on their *bonnet carré*.

Full professors of the Faculty of Law wore a black gown, over it a short knee-length *tunica* of scarlet satin, a scarlet satin *chaperon*, and a black *bonnet carré* with a red and violet tump. In 1693 they found it necessary to add to the *chaperon* a border of white fur to distinguish them from the mayor of the town. The dean of the Faculty of Law was dressed the same as the professors but the bottom of his *bonnet* was bordered with ermine.

The dress of the full professors of the Faculty of Medicine consisted of the black gown, above it a purple cloth cloak, and over both an ermine-furred 'shoulder piece'. On their *bonnet carré* they had a white and violet silk tump.[4]

The eighteenth-century seal of the Faculty of Medicine of the University of Nancy is the most useful of all French university seals for evidence of academical dress, for it is large and clear. Saints Cosmas and Damian are depicted as full Professors of Medicine (*Docteurs antécesseurs*) and wear full closed gowns with miniver-faced sleeves, miniver 'shoulder pieces', bands, and *bonnets carrés*. Below them kneels a *Docteur agrégé* wearing a long closed gown with tight sleeves, bands, and a *toque*.[5]

[1] E. Martin, p. 271.
[2] E. Martin, p. 272.
[3] V. de Viriville, p. 125.
[4] E. Martin, p. 272.
[5] R. Gandilhon, pp. 77–78 and pl. xi, no. 84.

XVI. PAU (1726)

The statutes of 1725 ordered full professors (*Docteurs antecésseurs*) to wear a black gown with a red *chaperon* bordered with ermine and a *bonnet carré* for ordinary academical occasions, and a red robe with the same *chaperon* for outstanding ceremonies.[1] *Docteurs agrégés* were to use on ordinary occasions a black gown with a black *chaperon* bordered with ermine, and a *bonnet carré*, and on the occasions when the professors wore the red robe, a black gown, and an ermine-bordered red *chaperon*.[2]

In 1777 the rector was ordered to wear a *bonnet carré* with a red silk tump if an ecclesiastic, but if a layman a hat with a gold and red silk hat-band with red silk tassels hanging off it. Rectors, whether ecclesiastics or laymen, wore a 'shoulder piece' (*épitoge*) of crimson satin bordered with ermine over presumably an open robe, and a cassock, but an ecclesiastic had the distinction of wearing a red cincture with tassels of gold and red silk on the ends of it.[3]

The prestige of a Professor of Law at Pau is indicated by the fact that for his funeral the dead professor's body was dressed in the red robe and was adorned with sword, boots, and spurs.[4]

There is no mention of any other faculty besides that of Law.

XVII. OTHER UNIVERSITIES

The records of the other French universities are defective except for Gray and Valence, whose documents are fairly complete. None of them contain any reference to academical costume.

[1] J. Maisonnier, *Le Faculté de Droit de l'Université de Pau*, p. 331 (Stat. § ix).
[2] J. Maissonier, p. 333 (Stat. § xvii).
[3] J. Maisonnier, p. 95.
[4] J. Maisonnier, p. 299, as at Montpellier.

3

GREAT BRITAIN AND IRELAND

I. OXFORD

(a) *The Chancellor*

THE first example which we possess of a chancellor is the main figure on the chancellor's first seal, an impression of which is attached to a deed of 1238.[1] The figure, which appears as half-length with the face in profile, wears a *pileus* and a loose *supertunica*.[2]

In the early fourteenth-century stained glass in Merton College Chapel given by Henry de Mannesfield (or Mamesfield), the donor's portrait is depicted twenty-four times. He was a Master of Theology and is described as *Magister*, but the dress he wears, a wide-sleeved *supertunica* and an amess (almuce), is not the costume of that degree. As he was chancellor it seems likely that he wears the dress of that office. In addition he has a *pileus*.[3] The *supertunica* and *pileus* vary in colour in nearly every miniature portrait, but this is simply according to the artist's fancy.

A remarkable miniature of 1375 in *Registrum A* in the university archives shows a chancellor kneeling before Edward III and receiving a charter from him.[4] The kneeling figure is bareheaded and tonsured, and is clad in a scarlet *supertunica* with great hanging sleeves,[5] which are lined with grey fur and edged with it. Over this can be seen what is almost certainly an amess, worn no doubt in virtue of the chancellor's ecclesiastical standing.[6]

---

[1] At Magdalen.

[2] E. T. Beaumont, *Academical Habit illustrated by Ancient Memorial Brasses*, p. 63.

[3] L. B. Saint and H. Arnold, *Stained Glass*, pp. 157–8.

[4] Registrum A, fo. 13.

[5] J. E. Sandys (art. 'Ancient University Ceremonies' in *Fasciculus Ioanni Willis Clark dicatus*, p. 238) wrongly states that it is sleeveless.

[6] N. F. Robinson, art. 'The Black Chimere of Anglican Prelates', in *Transactions of St. Paul's Ecclesiological Society*, iv (1898), 182, n. 2.

From the chancellor's fourth seal of 1429 it can be seen that the chancellor's costume has not changed. A long loose *super-tunica* with large sleeves and an amess again appear, and in addition there is a head-dress, a *pileus* with a small brim.[1]

There are no more examples of the chancellor's dress until it had been completely changed to a robe such as was worn by great officers of the Crown. Before this time there is the portrait of Sir Christopher Hatton painted at the time of his appointment to this office in 1588, but its value as evidence is very small owing to the darkening of the picture, and we are left in doubt as to whether or not he is wearing a distinctive dress or, as seems more likely, merely the dress of his degree, which was Master of Arts.[2]

The chancellor's gold-brocaded black robe of the winged-sleeved variety, the same as that of lord chancellors of England, except that the Oxford robe has a gold rosette on each sleeve and in the middle of the train,[3] was a development of a late Elizabethan fashion. A good example of this dress is to be found in one of James Roberts's water-colours of 1792, in which we see worn over ordinary dress a black brocaded robe with panel sleeves. It is braided with gold lace on the facings, the hem, on the sides, and on the sleeves.[4] The head-dress was a round black velvet cap.[5]

(b) The Vice-Chancellor

At no time did the vice-chancellor have any special dress. He wore the dress of his degree which was usually Doctor of Divinity. Thus on the occasion of Queen Elizabeth's departure after her visit to Oxford in 1566 the vice-chancellor and three other doctors, who rode before her, wore their full-dress scarlet.[6] In 1588 it was decreed that all Bachelors of Civil Law on their presentation should give the vice-chancellor gloves,[7]

---

[1] E. T. Beaumont, loc. cit.

[2] E. St. J. Brooks, *Life of Sir Christopher Hatton*, pl. opp. p. 234.

[3] L. H. D. Buxton and S. Gibson, *Oxford University Ceremonies*, p. 43.

[4] Oxf. Bodl. Libr. MS. Top. Oxon. d. 58, 8–9.

[5] Cf. T. Uwins's plate (1815). W. Combe and T. Uwins, *History of the University of Oxford*, ii. 17–18.

[6] Oxf. Bodl. Libr. MS. Twyne 17, fos. 157ᵛ and 159.

[7] A. Clark, *Register of the University of Oxford* (O.H.S., 1887), ii, pt. 1, p. 115.

and as late as the third quarter of the seventeenth century they wore them.[1]

(c) Proctors and Collectors

There are no early records of proctors' dress, nor is there any illustrative material in which they are depicted.

It is not until the first half of the seventeenth century that the dress which they still wear is mentioned.

This costume, consisting of a black bell-sleeved gown with black velvet facings, a rudimentary tippet on the shoulder, reminiscent of the fifteenth-century liripipe, and a large miniver hood, is representative of the late medieval dress of Masters of Arts. When a lay fashion of Tudor times altered the character of the masters' dress, proctors continued to use the old form. As late as the seventeenth century, however, the wide-sleeved gown was worn with a miniver hood by masters as a formal dress on special occasions such as at the time of Charles I's visit to Oxford in 1636.[2] The white furred hood in imitation of the original miniver, always worn by Masters of Arts before the introduction of silk in 1432 as an alternative for summer wear, was technically allowed to masters as full dress even as late as the statutes of 1770.[3] Proctors continued to wear this dress—the velvet facings were a Jacobean addition—as the spokesmen of Masters of Arts.[4]

As with all other Oxford dresses of modern times the seal of the Laudian statutes is set upon them. During the Civil War and Commonwealth period when the use of academical dress was to a large extent discontinued, and the wearing of hoods especially became more and more curtailed, proctors continually wore theirs.[5]

The dress of proctors and pro-proctors was at this date laid down for proctors as a bell-sleeved gown with black velvet laid on the sleeves and facings down the front, and for pro-proctors

---

[1] Oxf. Bodl. Libr. MS. Wood 276b, xix, 2.

[2] Oxf. Bodl. Libr. MS. Twyne 17, fo. 187.

[3] G. R. M. Ward, *Oxford University Statutes*, ii. 11.

[4] J. Wells, *Degree Ceremony*, p. 59. As late as 1873 a Master of Arts gown faced with velvet was worn by the senior of the two fellows of New College who went to Winchester to conduct the examination for scholarships, but its use on this occasion was thereafter discontinued (A. Clark, *The Life and Times of Anthony à Wood* (O.H.S.), iii. 226–7, n.).

[5] J. Walker, *Oxoniana*, iv. 210–11.

the ordinary Master of Arts gown with black velvet on the facings down the front only. A good example of the first of these gowns of the year 1675 is to be seen in one of Loggan's figures.[1] From this we see that as yet the tippet was much larger than it subsequently became. In No. 18 the miniver hood is shown, very full and completely covering the shoulders. Proctors still wore gloves which were presented to them by the Oxford City companies, but by the end of the century they had ceased to have any academical significance.[2] A square cap was worn with this dress.

In 1792 in a water-colour showing a proctor back-view he wears a square cap with a tassel, a full black gown with bell-sleeves, the upper part faced with black velvet, a 'bridge' yoke like those on masters' gowns, and from the lower left side of this yoke hangs a small pyramidal tippet from two buttons. The full miniver hood has all the fur showing.[3]

In 1792 the pro-proctor wore the black square cap with a tassel, and an ordinary master's gown faced on both sides down the front with black velvet, down the outside edge of which facings ran a thin line of alternating orange and yellow thread, which was simply the selvage of the velvet, and appeared also on proctors' gowns in the same place.[4] Pro-proctors wore with this gown a master's hood, although it is not shown in this Roberts water-colour, and on the gown was a tippet fastened to the lower left side of the yoke. After the expiry of their office proctors wore a tippet on their ordinary master's gown; not so pro-proctors.[5]

Collectors were representatives of Bachelors of Arts as proctors were of masters. Their gowns were exactly the same as those of bachelors with long and pointed sleeves, except that they had a broad piece of black velvet on the sleeves reaching half-way up them.[6] This proves that their dress was originally what we should call a full Bachelor of Arts dress and not a full Master of Arts dress of the old type, for at the time of Loggan's plates

[1] D. Loggan, *Oxonia Illustrata*, no. 17.
[2] L. H. D. Buxton and S. Gibson, op. cit., p. 35; cf. W. Dugdale, *Origines juridiciales*, p. 137.
[3] Oxf. Bodl. Libr. MS. Top. Oxon. d. 58, 38–39.
[4] Oxf. Bodl. Libr. MS. Top. Oxon. d. 58, 41–42.
[5] J. Woodforde, *Diary*, i. 171 (year 1775).
[6] D. Loggan, no. 10.

(1675) their sleeves were more pendulous than those of proctors, though afterwards owing to a misunderstanding of their origin the two gowns became identical. In Loggan's time they had no tippet, but the authorities of the eighteenth century, careless of tradition in many ways, allowed them to assume one and shorten the sleeves to the proctors' size, as is to be seen in the official engravings executed to illustrate the statutes of 1770 which contained clauses about academical dress (Pl. 11A)[1]. There is a pencil drawing by T. Uwins (1813–14) of the collector's gown, showing the yoke and the velvet on the sleeves which ends a little way below the shoulders. The pyramidal tippet is large, and an enlarged illustration of it is inset in the same leaf.[2] Their hood had always been the same as that of a Bachelor of Arts.

In 1656 collectors had lost for the time being their special dress, being forced to wear simply the ordinary Bachelor of Arts gown.[3] In 1822 the office, the holder of which was responsible for gathering together the Bachelors of Arts for public acts in the schools, for arranging their disputations in the schools and for collecting the proctors' fees, was abolished.[4]

In a letter of 1721 from William Bishop of Gray's Inn to Arthur Charlett, Master of University College, it is mentioned as being maintained by a certain Dr. Crowder, a contemporary, that deans of colleges should wear a proctor's hood when in Congregation, and Henry Gandy, the then Dean of Oriel, on the persuasion of Crowder wore the hood on these occasions. The outcome of this move for the revival of the wearing of proctorial dress by deans was that Dr. Haughton, the vice-chancellor in this year, explained that certainly deans used to wear such miniver hoods, but that as they were so expensive they were dispensed from wearing them. In 1721, however, it was still the custom for Bodley's librarian to wear a proctor's gown on public days.[5]

(d) Doctors of Divinity (originally called Masters of Theology)

The earliest reference to the costume of Masters of Theology in the *Statuta Antiqua* of Oxford belongs to a date previous to

---

[1] Oxf. Bodl. Libr. MS. Top. Oxon. c. 16, 9; G. V. Cox, *Recollections*, pp. 228 and 241–2.   [2] Oxf. Bodl. Libr. MS. Top. Oxon. d. 130, leaf 18.

[3] Oxf. Univ. Archives, Registrum T (1647–59), fo. 282; Oxf. Bodl. Libr. MS. Wood, F 27, fo. 73.

[4] G. V. Cox, pp. 228 and 241–2.   [5] J. Walker, iii. 162–3.

PLATE 7

Members of New College, Oxford, in a group with the Warden, *c.* 1463

PLATE 8

Philip Bisse in Oxford D.D. Convocation dress, 1612

1350 when they were ordered to have the *cappa clausa* for formal and the *pallium*, a sleeveless dress[1] worn over a full sleeved *roba*,[2] for informal occasions, furred with lamb's-wool but never with miniver.[3] At the same period the head-dress of Masters of Theology is described as the *pileus*,[4] that is, the *pileus rotundus*.[5] In this early statute monks (*religiosi*) are naturally excluded from the use of this pileus.[6] Later, at any rate by the mid-fifteenth century, the date of the Chaundler New College group (Pl. 7), a 'stalk' apex was added in order that by means of it the close-fitting *pileus* might be pulled off the head.[7] With the *cappa* a hood and 'shoulder piece' were worn. By the beginning of the fifteenth century Masters of Theology of sufficient ecclesiastical dignity had these outer garments lined with miniver, as can be seen from the inventory of the goods of Walter Skirlaw, Bishop of Durham (d. 1406), in which two of his hoods, one of miniver and one of ermine, are described.[8]

There are some good fifteenth-century examples of the dress of Masters of Theology. Consisting of a *cappa clausa* with its one large opening in front, a hood and its 'shoulder piece', a *sub-tunica* (cassock), and a 'stalk'-apexed *pileus*, it appears in the brass of Thomas Hylle, S.T.P. (1468) in the chapel of New College, Oxford.[9] This *pileus* was black for Masters of Theology as a good fifteenth-century example in the east light of the north window of Newington Church, Oxon., shows.[10]

In the painted glass in the main lights of the fifth window at Clavering, Essex, the subject of which is St. Catherine disputing with the philosophers, the latter are given the *cappa clausa* and are no doubt intended to be Masters of Theology.[11]

[1] First mentioned in a general way at Oxford in 1322 (S. Gibson, *Statuta Antiqua Universitatis Oxoniensis*, p. 126).

[2] E. C. Clarke, art. 'English Academic Costume' in *Archaeological Journal*, l (1893), 101.

[3] S. Gibson, pp. 51–52; E. C. Clarke, art. cit. l. 205; F. E. Brightman, Preface to R. T. Günther's art. 'Description of the Chapel Brasses' in *Magdalen College Register*, N.S. viii (1915), p. v.   [4] S. Gibson, p. 37.

[5] E. C. Clarke, art. 'College Caps and Doctors' Hats', in *Archaeological Journal*, lxi (1904), 33–34.   [6] S. Gibson, loc. cit.

[7] E. C. Clarke, art. cit. in op. cit., l. p. 144.

[8] *Testamenta Eboracensia*, iv (Surtees Soc. liii (1868), 322).

[9] E. T. Beaumont, *Ancient Memorial Brasses*, pp. 106 and 108; F. H. Crossley, *English Church Monuments*, p. 231.

[10] Illustrated in *Oxford Archaeological Society*, no. 84 (1938), pl. 3, no. 2.

[11] F. C. Eeles, art. 'The Clavering Glass' in *Transactions of the Essex Archaeological*

On the other hand, in the miniatures illustrating a manuscript of a collection of English theological orations of about 1475 the Masters of Theology here depicted[1] appear in undress, which consists of a *supertunica* with moderately hanging sleeves, a 'shoulder piece' with a hood close round the neck, and a black *pileus* sometimes with an apex and sometimes without one. The colouring varies in the different miniatures.[2]

As was the case with all academical costume, in the sixteenth century the dress of this degree changed considerably. During this period the full festal scarlet dress appeared, as well as the Convocation 'habit' and the undress, all of which gradually came to be opened up down the front, and took on approximately the same shape as was afterwards maintained.

Henry VIII's *Act for the Reformation of Excess of Apparel* (1533), which, while forcing all people of private standing to adopt a more sober dress, allowed those of position to use such a colour as scarlet, no doubt gave a stimulus to its use on the festal robe which Doctors of Divinity and other doctors were beginning to wear. This robe, which originated in a lay fashion—we find such a one worn by courtiers of the day with official posts such as Sir Thomas More—was similar to those of mayors and aldermen. It seems likely that it was introduced into the universities at this time, although there are no details about its use until the reign of Elizabeth, by which time its was well established.

In the later fifteenth century, when Masters of Theology gave up wearing the *cappa clausa* with one slit, they used the *cappa* with two slits as their formal dress. This was what came to be known in the course of the sixteenth century as the 'Convocation habit', and was worn over the *supertunica*, which gradually developed into the *roba* (gown). In the inventory which was made about 1508 of the goods of the late Warden of Canterbury College, who was of this degree, we read of 'a coote of cloyth in grayn made when he was doctor, also hys doctors abett of the same cloyth', which seems to indicate that such a dress was

Society, xvi (1922), pt. 2, N.S., p. 83, and fig. 1, opp. p. 77; J. D. Le Couteur, *English Mediaeval Painted Glass*, pp. 115–16, fig. 32.

[1] B.M. MS. Harl. 2887, fos. 56, 56ᵛ, and 58.

[2] For this see above, (*a*) Chancellor. Even if this is simply the result of the artist's whim, it was the cut of the dress rather than the colour which was as yet only important. The undress for this degree was the same at Cambridge at the same period.

already in being, the 'abett' being the *cappa* with two slits and the 'coote' being the *supertunica* (*roba*).[1]

The *supertunica* itself during the same period changed into a full-sleeved gown, but in the latter part of the century the gown of Doctors of Divinity, Bachelors of Divinity, and Masters of Arts, as a result of lay fashion, was given glove-sleeves.[2] When worn under the 'habit' these sleeves were pulled through its arm-holes and hung down at the sides. For Convocation dress a hood was worn with 'habit' and gown. Earlier in the century this was scarlet and lined with miniver, as is to be seen from the inventory of goods left by John West, D.D. (d. 1543),[3] but later black silk replaced the miniver. The 'habit' was by this time scarlet.[4]

In 1566, at the time of Queen Elizabeth's visit to Oxford, doctors, though described as wearing 'habits' and hoods when she arrived, wore their festal dress when they rode with her to see her on her way at the time of her departure.[5] On the occasion of Charles II's visit to Oxford in 1663, the full dress of Doctors of Divinity is described as a full-sleeved scarlet robe, faced with velvet, which means black velvet,[6] but sometimes the hoods belonging to Convocation dress were wrongly worn with the full dress robe, as at the time of the visit of Charles I in 1636.[7]

A good example of the Convocation dress at the beginning of the seventeenth century is to be seen in the portrait (1612) of Philip Bisse (1540–1613) (Pl. 8), Archdeacon of Taunton and founder of Wadham College Library.[8] He wears the scarlet habit, open some way down the front, the opening becoming of a sharp V-shape towards the waist, the hood fastened low in front, while the gown appears underneath the habit with very short glove sleeves appearing through the arm-holes.

Until the end of the fifteenth century the *pileus rotundus*

[1] The inventory is given in W. A. Pantin, *Canterbury College*, i (Inventories) (O.H.S., n.s. vi. (1947)), 84.
[2] A. Clark, *Wood*, i. 68–69.
[3] *Somerset Mediaeval Wills, 1531–58* (Somerset Record Soc. xxi, 1905), p. 76.
[4] E. C. Clarke, art. cit., l. 138.
[5] Oxf. Bodl. Libr. MS. Twyne, 17, fos. 157ᵛ, 159, and 173ᵛ.
[6] A. Clark, *Wood*, i. 494.
[7] Oxf. Bodl. Libr. MS. Twyne, 17, fo. 187.
[8] Mrs. R. L. Poole, *Oxford Portraits* (O.H.S.), iii, frontispiece (Wadham College, no. 8).

continued to be the head-dress of Doctors of Divinity as of other doctors, but by the beginning of the sixteenth century it had lost its 'stalk' apex and had begun to assume a cusped shape, doubtless arising from the necessity of a convenient grip, now that there was no longer a 'stalk', when putting it on and off.[1] By 1520 the academical *pileus* had become rigid and square at the University of Paris, and this fashion rapidly spread to the other universities of Europe.[2]

Unlike the *pileus quadratus* of the Continent the *pileus* of Oxford and Cambridge developed in a particular way un-parelleled elsewhere. Instead of taking either the form of a biretta or of a small square bonnet, it became a very large flat, shallow, square cap, loose and flagging at the corners. Under it a skull-cap was usually worn, and during the first part of the seventeenth century the upper cap and the skull-cap were joined to form one article.[3] As early as 1600 a board was intro-duced to prevent the side-pieces falling over the face, so long had they become.[4] A tump appears on top of the cap by the beginning of Charles II's reign. It is very large in Samuel Cooper's miniature (about 1663) of Gilbert Sheldon, Arch-bishop of Canterbury in the collection of the Duke of Portland. The square top was still wide in 1663, according to the engraving of Bishop Sanderson of this date,[5] but by 1674, the year of G. Edwards's costume plates of Oxford, it had become much smaller.[6]

In the Laudian statutes of 1636 we find that the scarlet Convocation habit might either be entirely closed, or have an opening down the front which was buttoned up after it had been put on. This latter form had been introduced in the early seventeenth century in order to facilitate the drawing on of it.[7]

[1] E. C. Clarke, art. cit. lxi. 36.

[2] J. Launoy, *De vera causa de secessu Brunonis*, p. 121; N. F. Robinson, art. 'The *Pileus Quadratus*' in *Transactions of St. Paul's Ecclesiological Society*, v, pt. 1 (1901), p. 2.

[3] E. C. Clarke, art. cit. lxi. 36, 38, and 42. See for a good example of this the portrait of James Warner, Bishop of Rochester, painted in 1637, at Magdalen (Mrs. R. L. Poole, op. cit. ii, pl. xxvii, no. 1, opp. p. 210).

[4] H. Norris, *Costume and Fashion*, iii, bk. II, p. 733. For heraldic representations of the square cap in England see W. Berry, *Encyclopaedia Heraldica*, iii, pl. xxix, no. 32.

[5] Oxf. Bodl. Libr. MS. Top. Oxon. c. 16, § 74.

[6] Oxf. Bodl. Libr. MS. Wood 276B, xix, 7 (*Artium Baccalaureus*).

[7] G. R. M. Ward, i. 153, n.

In the eighteenth century only this form was used, according to all the illustrations. It was laid down by Laud that the hood of a Doctor of Divinity was to be scarlet lined with black silk, and the 'habit' is to be 'turned up' (that is, faced) with it. A square cap was to be used.[1] The three costumes of this degree are shown in Loggan's plate of 1675, Nos. 26, 27, 28. The dress in each case is very full and cumbrous, the heavy dress of a slow-moving age, and the plane of the square board of the cap is tilted forward very much. In 1679 the inventory of Michael Roberts, D.D., gives the value of 'two habits (i.e. Convocation habits), two hoods, and a gown scarlet' (i.e. festal robe) as £5 the lot.[2]

To the original tump on the square cap a tassel was unofficially added during the 1730's.[3] It was given official approval in the statutes of 1770.[4]

In the statutes of the university published in 1770 Doctors of Divinity were ordered to wear, in common with other doctors, their Convocation dress on all Sundays within term, at St. Mary's in the morning, and in Lent and on Easter Sunday in the afternoon at St. Peter's-in-the-East:[5] a modification of the times and places at which this dress was to be worn from those mentioned in the Laudian statutes.[6] C. Grignion's engravings of 1770 (Pl. 11 A) which were made after drawings of academical dress by two amateur artists, Huddesford, Keeper of the Ashmolean, and Taylor for the registry to be kept there for reference, show the three Doctor of Divinity dresses as being somewhat less full than the Loggan plates.[7] It is worth noticing that the square board of the cap is larger than in Loggan, but it is still inclined forward.

In James Roberts's water-colours of 1792, the Doctor of Divinity in full dress[8] wears bands, carries his black square tasselled cap, and wears a broad black scarf as long as his dress. His scarlet robe with black velvet bell sleeves is as now, but it is

---

[1] G. R. M. Ward, i. 70–71 (*Laudian Statutes*, cap. 5).
[2] Oxf. Univ. Archives, Hypomnemata Antiquaria, B. 18—Inventories R–S, s.v. Roberts.
[3] A. D. Godley, *Oxford in the Eighteenth Century*, p. 167.
[4] G. R. M. Ward, ii, 9–10.
[5] G. R. M. Ward, ii. 11.
[6] Cf. G. R. M. Ward, i. 153.
[7] Oxf. Bodl. Libr. MS. Top. Oxon. c. 16. 19, 20, 21.
[8] 11–12.

noticeable that his broad black cincture is drawn over the scarlet robe and holds it closed. The Convocation dress consists of bands, a square cap, a long broad scarf, a full scarlet hood lined with black fastened high in front, and the scarlet habit which is so long that it sweeps the ground, so that all that can be seen of the master's gown is the gloved and key-shaped ended sleeves appearing on each side. As can be seen from a plate of the Doctor of Divinity in chapel dress (that is surplice and hood) from the back view, the shape of the hood is very full and rounded with a square liripipe (Frontispiece). The ordinary dress was cap, hood, and master's gown, with cassock, cincture, and scarf.[1]

The scarf associated academically with Oxford and Cambridge Doctors of Divinity[2] does not appear to have any connexion with the stole (στολή; *orarium*), though they (and particularly the black stole when compared to the scarf) superficially appear to be like one another. The origin of the scarf is to be found in the long piece of stuff to which the roundlet was attached, and which was later detached and hung round the neck, being held in place by means of a loop on the back of the collar of the gown. The stole was a vestment, the scarf simply a symbol of dignity and learning. This can be the more readily realized if it is remembered that until about the middle of the nineteenth century the mayor of Christchurch, Hants, wore a broad scarlet silk scarf with a narrow border of black velvet over his gown to distinguish him from the councillors.[3] In 1522 in Bishop Smyth's statutes for Brasenose it is called a 'tippet',[4] which implies that it was not regarded as anything particularly ecclesiastical.[5]

A good example of the scarf worn with his black gown by a Doctor of Divinity is the engraving of John Wythines on his brass (1615) at Battle, Sussex. In the *Spectator*[6] is a satirical

[1] Oxf. Bodl. Libr. MS. Top. Oxon. d. 58, 14–15; 17–18.

[2] M. E. C. Walcott, *Constitutions and Canons*, p. 82, n.

[3] H. Druitt, *Manual of Costume*, p. 109, n. 2.

[4] *Brasenose College Quatercentenary Monographs* (O.H.S.), ii, pt. 1, Monograph IX, p. 36.

[5] It certainly was not a debased form of amess, for the use of the amess was forbidden in 1559, and the scarf survived, being used by royal and collegiate chaplains as well as by Doctors of Divinity.

[6] No. 609, 20 Oct. 1714.

account written in 1714 of the wearing of the scarf by young clergymen who wanted to pass for Doctors of Divinity.

(e) Doctors of Canon Law

The full dress of the degree of Doctor of Canon Law was also the *cappa clausa*.[1] According to an enactment of before 1350, at lectures they might use a *pallium* instead of a *cappa clausa*, both of which were to be black, and they might have them furred with lamb's-wool, but never with miniver. They were never to use a *cappa manicata*.[2] Their head-dress in the fourteenth century was for all solemn occasions the *pileus rotundus*.[3]

A large hood furred or lined 'extending beyond the points of the shoulders' was allowed to them in the sumptuary laws of Henry IV (1403) in common with Masters of Theology and other regents, the lord chancellor, and high law officers.[4] An example of the *cappa clausa* with one slit worn by a fifteenth-century Doctor of Canon Law appears in a brass of William Hautryve (1441) in the chapel of New College, Oxford.[5]

In Chaundler's New College drawing of about 1463 (Pl. 7) the Masters of Theology and Doctors of Canon Law to the immediate right and left of the warden, two on each side, all wear the same dress, which consists of *cappa clausa* with one slit, 'shoulder piece', and *pileus*.[6]

Indeed, the dress of this degree had the same character as and followed the same development as that of the degree of Master of Theology. It did not survive the Reformation.

(f) Doctors of Civil Law

According to an illumination in the Holkham Bible (*c.* 1330), the head-dress of a Doctor of Civil Law was a red *pileus rotundus* with a blue button on top.[7] In one of the earliest clauses in the Oxford statutes concerning a distinctly academical dress (prior to 1350) doctors of this degree were ordered to wear a *pileus*.[8]

---

[1] E. C. Clarke, art. cit. l. 205; F. E. Brightman, Preface, p. v.
[2] S. Gibson, pp. 51–52 and 56–57.
[3] S. Gibson, p. 37.
[4] J. Strutt, *Dresses and Habits*, ii. 224.
[5] H. Druitt, pl. opp. p. 129.
[6] M. R. James, *The Chaundler Manuscripts*, pp. 21–22 and pls.
[7] W. O. Hassall, *The Holkham Bible Picture Book*, p. 106, pl. of fo. 19.
[8] S. Gibson, p. 37.

At the same time they were told to use a *cappa manicata*, a long garment closed in front but having long sleeves, through which the arms passed. The sleeved tabard, a garment with shorter sleeves, was soon allowed to them as a more convenient alternative.[1] Under this, as is the case with all other degrees, were worn an ordinary loose over-tunic, the *supertunica* (*roba*), and under that the *subtunica* (cassock).[2]

A fine example of the dress of a Doctor of Civil Law of about 1408 is to be seen in a miniature in a manuscript, *De Regimine Principum*,[3] in which a doctor of this degree among the courtiers of Henry IV wears a long red trailing *cappa clausa* with two side slits, a mid-blue 'shoulder piece' lined with white fur, a pointed *pileus*, and white gloves. During the fifteenth century the use of the *cappa manicata* for this degree was still maintained on occasion. It was sometimes red and sometimes blue, as in the fifth window of the main lights in Clavering Church, Essex;[4] but they wear the *cappa* with two slits in the Chaundler drawing of about 1463 (Pl. 7). They stand with the Doctors of Medicine behind the clerical doctors.[5]

The *cappa clausa* with two slits appears in a particular character in the brass of John Lowthe, a Doctor of Civil Law (d. 1427), at New College, for attached to the back of the dress on each shoulder are two hollow pendants or liripipes, the open ends being dressed with fur, and as long as the main costume. These liripipes were merely an extravagance and do not seem to have had any significance.[6] They were looked upon critically by the authorities, and in the visitation of Magdalen College by Bishop Foxe's commissary in 1507 the wearing of liripipes beyond the precincts of the college was deemed unsuitable.[7] No more is heard of this fashion. By 1529, the date of the brass of Bryan Roos, D.C.L., in Childrey Church, Berks., the *supertunica*, the outer garment when the *cappa* was not used, has become a true gown, a full-sleeved *roba*.[8]

---

[1] E. C. Clarke, art. cit. l. 139 and 206; F. E. Brightman, Preface, p. vi.

[2] F. E. Brightman, Preface, p. v.

[3] Oxf. Bodl. Libr. MS. Digby 233, fo. 1.

[4] F. C. Eeles, art. cit., p. 83 and fig. 1, opp. p. 77.

[5] M. R. James, loc. cit.

[6] H. Druitt, pp. 131–2. There was also a temporary fashion for liripipes at Cambridge. See also E. C. Clarke, art. cit. l. 188.

[7] W. M. Macray, *Register of the Members of Magdalen College, Oxford*, N.S.i, §§ 44–45, p. 55.   [8] E. C. Clarke, art. cit. l. 101.

Hoods, which were worn in conjunction with the 'shoulder piece', might be lined with rich fur or silk according to the enactment of Congregation of 1432,[1] and it is doubtless one of these silk hoods which an Oxford Doctor of Civil Law, William Poteman, Archdeacon of the East Riding (d. 1493), leaves in his will, describing it as a 'doubled' (i.e. doubled back to show the lining) silk hood, to Robert Both, late Dean of York.[2]

The changes in the dress for this degree at the end of the Middle Ages followed the same development as that of Masters of Theology in that in this case the *cappa manicata* being entirely left off, a modified form of the *cappa* with two slits became the outward garment for solemn occasions. The *roba* was used alone for informal ones, while the full-dress robe for the most out-standing ones made its appearance about the middle of the sixteenth century.

In the sixteenth century Doctors of Civil Law and other secular doctors began to wear two articles of dress directly derived from lay fashion. The first was the round velvet bonnet, the head-dress of dignity of the time of Henry VIII, which Doctors of Civil Law, Medicine, and Music wore with festal dress, although for undress they followed the Elizabethan statutes in wearing the *pileus quadratus*.[3]

The second was a black gown with a flap collar and winged sleeves, such as was worn by wealthy citizens, often decorated on the sleeves and the skirt with straight lines of black braid with usually three buttons to a line.[4] Such a gown came at this period to be used for undress by all graduates except those of the Faculties of Divinity and Arts. A good example of the winged-sleeved gown worn by a Doctor of Civil Law is to be found in the brass of Hugh Lloyd (1601) at New College.[5] In another brass (1605) also at New College, that of Hugh Barker, D.C.L., is to be found the first example of black tassels added to the buttons in the rows of braid,[6] but long after that there is proof that this winged-sleeved, flap-collared gown was worn

---

[1] S. Gibson, pp. 239–40.
[2] *Testamenta Eboracensia*, iv (Surtees Soc. liii (1868), 82).
[3] S. Gibson, pp. 525 and 540.
[4] See the full-length effigy of Sir Eubule Thelwall (1630) in Jesus College Chapel, Oxford, where it is worn not as the gown of a degree, but as a dress of dignity.
[5] H. Druitt, p. 132.
[6] Mrs. R. L. Poole, i (New Coll., no. 29).

absolutely plain by some Doctors of Civil Law, as in the case of John Favour (d. 1623) whose monumental effigy is in Halifax parish church, Yorks.[1]

In Loggan's plate of 1675 the three forms of dress are given. No. 25 is the festal dress described in 1663 on Charles II's visit to Oxford as a wide-sleeved scarlet cloth 'gown' faced with scarlet taffeta,[2] but without the taffeta on the sleeves, which are hitched up with a cord and buttons; No. 24, the Convocation dress, perhaps better illustrated in Edwards, consists of hood, 'habit', and black winged-sleeved gown; No. 23, the undress, consisted of the black gown. In these plates the round bonnet is worn only with festal dress, but in Robert Sayer's *Oxonia Illustrata* (1700), a reissue of Loggan brought up to date as to contemporary fashion, but very inferior in quality and accuracy it is worn with the undress.[3]

The undress gown as it appeared in 1710 is clearly seen in the portrait in Bodley's Library of Edmund Halley, D.C.L., the astronomer.[4] It is of black silk and decorated on sleeves and skirt with cord-braid and black tufts. Another painting in oil, in the Bodleian Law Library, second room, provides an excellent example of the festal robe in the first half of the eighteenth century. In his portrait Richard Rawlinson, D.C.L. (d. 1755), wears a scarlet cloth robe with salmon-coloured silk on the facings in front and half-way up the bell-sleeves, which are no longer held up by means of a cord because they have been reduced in size. Laud had in 1636 ordered that the silk used on the facings and hoods of Doctors of Civil Law and Doctors of Medicine should be of a colour 'intermediate' to scarlet. Hence the subsequent use of salmon-pink as the colour of these faculties.[5]

In Grignion's plates of 1770 the festal dress is shown. The bonnet is small and toque-like, while the robe has a narrow cord just below the throat, probably to keep the dress steady and the garment from riding up.[6] Among the water-colours of Roberts (1792) the full dress appears again (Frontispiece), consisting of

[1] J. Horsfall Turner, *Coats of Arms of Yorkshire*, i. 161.
[2] A. Clark, *Wood*, i. 494.
[3] Oxf. Bodl. Libr. MS. Top. Oxon. a. 36, fos. 77–78.
[4] Mrs. R. L. Poole, i, pl. xvi, no. 3, opp. p. 101.
[5] G. R. M. Ward, i. 70–71, cap. 5.
[6] Oxf. Bodl. Libr. MS. Top. Oxon. c. 16. 18.

PLATE 9

Stained glass window of an Oxford Doctor of Medicine, 1440

the small black velvet toque-bonnet, and the scarlet bell-sleeved robe, the lower part of the sleeves faced with salmon-pink silk[1] (Frontispiece). The other dresses are not given, but Thomas Uwins (1815) gives the three kinds of costume which show what they must have been like in the later eighteenth century. First, there is the festal dress consisting of a scarlet cloth robe, with sleeves and facings of pink silk, and a round black velvet bonnet; secondly, the convocation dress, which consists of the 'habit' and the hood of scarlet cloth, the habit with an opening down the front and faced with pink silk, the scarlet cloth hood being lined with pink silk, and the black gown, whose sleeves appear through the openings of the 'habit'; and the black silk gimp gown.[2] It is to be noticed that gimp has taken the place of tufts, and that the round velvet bonnet is worn instead of the square cap with the Convocation dress.

(g) Doctors of Medicine

In common with other doctors, Doctors of Medicine, had as head-dress before 1350 the *pileus rotundus*.[3] They originally wore the *cappa manicata*, but soon wore in its place except on the most formal occasions a *cappa clausa* with two slits. For undress they wore a sleeveless tabard like a *pallium*,[4] which later became shorter, with or without sleeves.[5] In 1432, again in common with other doctors, they were allowed to use silk in their hoods in summer.[6] In the Chaundler drawing of about 1463 (Pl. 7), they wear, as do the Doctors of Civil Law, who appear with them behind the Masters of Theology and Doctors of Canon Law, a *cappa clausa* with two slits, 'shoulder piece', hood, and *pileus*,[7] but in a stained glass window of about 1440 in Minster Lovell Church, Oxon., a Doctor of Medicine, holding the symbols of his profession, a bottle and staff, wears a crimson *cappa manicata* lined with miniver, and a black *pileus* (Pl. 9).

The *Act for the Reformation of Excess in Apparel* of 1533 allowed them, as other doctors, the use at all times of 'sarcenet' (silk) in the lining of their gowns, as well as satin or velvet for facings, and they were privileged enough to be able to use such colours

[1] Oxf. Bodl. Libr. MS. Top. Oxon. d. 58, 20–21.
[2] W. Combe and T. Uwins, ii. 16 and plates.
[3] S. Gibson, p. 37.
[4] F. E. Brightman, Preface, p. vi.   [5] E. C. Clarke, art. cit. l. 206.
[6] S. Gibson, pp. 239–40.   [7] Cf. M. R. James, pp. 21–22.

as scarlet, murrey, and violet,[1] proof that even yet uniformity of colour in academical dress was not assured.

There are only three undoubted examples in brasses of Doctors of Medicine wearing academical dress, and these are all Post-Reformation. They are those of Walter Bailey (1592) at New College, Richard Radcliff (1599) at St. Peter's-in-the-East, Oxford, and Anthony Aylworth (1619) at New College.[2] All wear the undress false-sleeved gown, and Aylworth also wears a hood, deep and V-shaped in front.

A fine water-colour copy, in the possession of the Royal College of Physicians, of the oil portrait formerly in the hall of the Barbers' Company, shows Sir Charles Scarburgh (1616–94), who attended Charles II in his last illness, giving an anatomy lecture. The picture was executed in 1651. Scarburgh wears a Doctor of Medicine's Convocation dress, consisting of a very high bonnet, a very large white fur hood with only a thin line of pink silk showing, a scarlet 'habit', closed in front except for a little furred slit on the chest, and a black winged sleeved gown under it.[3] The height of their bonnets seems to have been a particular feature of their dress until the end of the seventeenth century, and it appears in the portrait of Richard Hale, D.M. (1670–1728), worn with the festal robe.[4] Otherwise the dress is the same as that of Doctors of Civil Law.[5]

In the diary of Dr. Claver Morris, he mentions that in 1691, on taking this degree, he paid £2. 13s. for having velvet and tufts added to his Bachelor of Medicine gown,[6] which means that the doctor's undress gown differed from it in having extra decoration.[7]

In R. Sayer's plates (1700),[8] in those of Grignion (1770)[9]

---

[1] *Statutes of the Realm*, iii. 430–2: 24° Hen. VIII, c. 13.

[2] H. Druitt, p. 133.

[3] The picture is reproduced in R. Crawfurd, *The Last Days of Charles II*, opp. p. 52.

[4] Mrs. R. L. Poole, i, opp. p. 96, pl. xiv, no. 1 (Bodleian, no. 229).

[5] See Loggan's plate (1675). The only difference between the dress of the two degrees is that in No. 23 the Doctor of Medicine wears the round bonnet with the undress gown instead of the square cap.

[6] E. Hobhouse (ed.), *Diary of a West Country Physician*, p. 148.

[7] Cf. a plate by Edwards (1674) in Oxf. Bodl. Libr. MS. Wood 276B, xix, 4. This is still the case today, for the undress gowns of doctors of all 'lay' faculties have an extra decoration of gimp under the arms. Those of bachelors of the 'lay' faculties do not have this.   [8] Oxf. Bodl. Libr. MS. Top. Oxon. a. 36.

[9] Oxf. Bodl. Libr. MS. Top. Oxon. c. 16, 17.

(Pl. 11 B), and in the water-colours of 1792[1] the festal dress of Doctors of Medicine is exactly the same as that of Doctors of Civil Law, as were their other dresses.[2]

(h) Doctors of Music

This degree until recent times has had a surreptitious existence. It appeared at the beginning of the sixteenth century, but was never considered of much importance and was granted after the manner of a diploma to proficient musicians. At Oxford no actual regulations as to the dress of the musical degrees were ever formulated, but it seems probable that originally, as was the case at Cambridge,[3] Doctors of Music made use of the dress of those of Medicine,[4] on the rare occasions when they did appear at academical functions, as can be seen from the fact that until the nineteenth century Bachelors of Music wore blue hoods like those of Bachelors of Civil Law and Medicine.

There are no brasses or other illustrations to aid us in the earlier period, but it seems likely that the elaborate dress of Doctors of Music was adopted in late Elizabethan or early Jacobean times, at any rate before the statutes of 1636 when Laud ordered inceptors in Music at the Vesperies and Act to wear sleeved gowns with 'white wavy damask capes' and round black caps, all of silk,[5] which shows that they were to wear a hood with the festal robe.

The development of the dress was the same as that of other secular doctors, and thus by the beginning of the seventeenth century Doctors of Music wore the black tufted winged sleeved gown and the square cap for undress, and the round velvet bonnet with their full dress. Their position in the academical hierarchy was uncertain, for the degree did not carry with it membership of Convocation, since it was open to all who had passed Responsions. In fact doctors of this degree were generally regarded as infrequent visitors to functions such as Encaenia, loosely attached to the university.

---

[1] Oxf. Bodl. Libr. MS. Top. Oxon. d. 58, 23–24.
[2] W. Combe and T. Uwins, ii. 16.
[3] Cambridge Grace Books, Δ, p. 28.
[4] C. A. H. Franklyn, art. 'Dress of the Clergy' in Parson and Parish, no. 16, p. 33.
[5] G. R. M. Ward, i. 70–71, cap. 5.

They naturally had no Convocation 'habit',[1] but until recently, as Laud had ordered, wore their hood with their festal dress. Their position in the seventeenth century was so far depressed that they had no place in the procession in honour of Charles II's visit to Oxford in 1663.[2]

John Evelyn in his diary describes the Encaenia of 10 July 1669 at which the Professor of Mathematics introduced a Doctor of Music who was received with the ceremony of cap, ring, and kiss. The robe of the new doctor, he noticed, was of white damask,[3] that is, with no cherry silk on the sleeves, and its shape was the same as that of the festal robes of other doctors as is to be seen in the costume plate of Loggan (1675) where the Doctor of Music (No. 12) wears hood, festal robe, and round bonnet.

The shape of the hood changed during the seventeenth century, for in a print of him Orlando Gibbons (D.Mus. 1623) wears his tucked down in front and fastened underneath his closed robe, but William Child (D.Mus. 1663) wears his hood squarely and not tucked into the robe as in the former example. The hood had again been altered in shape by the early eighteenth century, for William Croft (D.Mus. 1713) wears in his print of that year a smaller one than Gibbons and Child, which unlike theirs is high at the throat and not square on the shoulders.[4]

In Grignion's plates of 1770 the festal dress consists of a small round bonnet, the festal robe, and a very large hood with a square-shaped liripipe;[5] while in 1792 (Frontispiece) it comprises a white damasked robe lined with cherry-red silk, with white damask bell-sleeves, over that a full hood of white damask silk lined with cherry-red silk, the hood having a long square liripipe, and a small black velvet bonnet.[6] Other good examples are Sir Joshua Reynolds's portrait of Charles Burney (D.Mus. 1769) in Bartolozzi's engraving, and J. Russell's portrait of

---

[1] L. H. D. Buxton and S. Gibson, p. 39.
[2] A. Clark, *Wood*, i. 494. As late as 1857 they were not allowed at Encaenia to sit with the other doctors, and, worse still, could not even sit with members of Convocation (*Notes and Queries*, 2nd ser. iii. 115–17, 275–7).
[3] *Diary of John Evelyn*, ed. E. S. de Beer, iii. 533; J. E. Sandys, art. cit., p. 232.
[4] Oxf. Bodl. Libr. MS. Top. Oxon. c. 16, §§ 98, 99 and 101.
[5] Oxf. Bodl. Libr. MS. Top. Oxon. c. 16, 10.
[6] Oxf. Bodl. Libr. MS. Top. Oxon. d. 58, 26–27.

T. S. Dupuis (D.Mus. 1790). Cherry-coloured facings and sleeves are not found until the 1815 plates of T. Uwins.[1]

(i) Masters of Surgery

The degree of Master of Surgery, formerly very rare, was until recent times considered as invariably associated with the degree of Doctor of Medicine, so that it was never mentioned on its own account, and is never considered in statutes, nor does it appear in costume plates.[2]

(j) Masters of Arts

In the fourteenth century the *pileus* was forbidden to Masters of Arts,[3] and it was found necessary as early as before 1350 to prevent them from assuming other articles of dress proper to doctors.[4] It was not until 1529 that we hear of a *pileus* being allowed to a candidate supplicating for this degree,[5] but they had a kind of knitted skull-cap as a protection against cold by the middle of the fifteenth century, for a *caleptra* (hure; coif) is mentioned in the will of John Shyrburn, M.A., fellow of Lincoln College, in 1452.[6] Their other dress consisted of what was originally the *cappa manicata*, but they soon gave this up as inconvenient, and took to a variety of *cappa clausa*, a shorter dress closed in front with side slits and without sleeves, the sleeves of the *supertunica*, later to become the *roba* or *toga*, passing through the arm-holes. This was their dress of dignity, and was ordered as late as 1480–8 to be worn in Congregation by regent masters in statutes in which it is referred to as the *cappa nigra*.[7] The earliest example of this costume on brasses appears in that

[1] W. Combe and T. Uwins, loc. cit.
[2] Masters of Surgery once claimed, at the period during the nineteenth century when the degree became a separate entity, to wear the scarlet dress of Doctors of Medicine, but it was considered that if they did not hold the doctor's degree they had no right to it. They came to have as their dress in the nineteenth century the black silk laced gown, and wore a plain blue hood of the same shape as that of Masters of Arts. From the fact that the hood was of navy blue it can be seen that it was derived from the old Civil Law faculty colour of blue, which in the fifteenth century Bachelors of Medicine assumed in common with Bachelors of Law as the colour of their hood (L. H. D. Buxton and S. Gibson, pp. 38–39).
[3] E. C. Clarke, art. cit. lxi. 33.
[4] S. Gibson, pp. 28 and 40.
[5] E. C. Clarke, art. cit. l. 148.
[6] H. E. Salter, *Registrum Cancellarii* (O.H.S.), i. 293.
[7] S. Gibson, p. 292.

of John Kyllingworth (1445) at Merton College, Oxford.[1]
With this was worn a *subtunica* (cassock), a 'shoulder piece'
edged with fur only at the lower edge, and a hood.[2]

During the mid-fifteenth century the *cappa clausa* with two
slits was worn less and less by masters except on the most
formal occasions, and otherwise the *roba* was used alone. This
can be well seen in the Chaundler manuscript (Pl. 7) in
which the Masters of Arts stand facing the warden with their
backs to the onlooker. The sleeved *robas* which they wear reach
to their feet and have short bell sleeves which come only to the
elbow. With this dress is worn a 'shoulder piece' and a hood
with a long, square-ended liripipe, and they still have no head-
dress;[3] but in the brass of Walter Wake, M.A. (1451), in New
College Chapel, Oxford, the bell sleeves are much fuller and
the 'shoulder piece' is completely lined with fur.[4]

It was from the *roba* which was increasingly worn as the outer
garment that the Master of Arts gown of later times developed,
gaining towards the end of the sixteenth century its rudimentary glove or bag sleeves, at first very short and which hung
down below the elbow. As late, however, as 1636, according to
the Laudian statutes, the old full-sleeved gown was still to be
worn by all inceptors in Arts,[5] as is to be seen in the fine oil-
painting attributed to J. de Critz, of the poet Richard Lovelace
at Worcester College, Oxford. Lovelace was created M.A. in
1636. At the time of Charles I's visit to Oxford in the same year
all masters were ordered to wear this type of gown,[6] and probably the Lovelace portrait was painted on this occasion. With
this gown he wears a fairly soft square cap with a tump. Good
examples of the glove-sleeved gown in the course of its earlier
development in which the sleeves reach only half-way down the
length of the dress are to be found in the monumental effigy of
an unknown clergyman (1615) at Steeple Langford, Wilts.,
and in another to another unknown clergyman (about 1630)

[1] E. C. Clarke, art. cit. l. 199.
[2] H. Druitt, p. 135.
[3] M. R. James, loc. cit.
[4] M. Stephenson, *List of Monumental Brasses*, p. 414 (New Coll. ix).
[5] G. R. M. Ward, i. 70–71, caps. 4–5.
[6] Oxf. Bodl. Libr. MS. Twyne 17, fo. 187. Not only, according to the Laudian
Codex, was the wide-sleeved Master of Arts gown to be worn on formal occasions,
but also during the year of 'necessary regency', that is the academical year after
taking the degree.

PLATE 10

a. An Oxford Master of Arts

b. An Oxford Bachelor of Arts

c. An Oxford Commoner

d. An Oxford Servitor, 1695

a–c from G. Edwards, *Omnium Ordinum Habitumque Academicorum Exemplaria*, 1674

at Bishopstone near Salisbury. In both cases the gown is peaked at the shoulders, a passing fashion.[1]

Square caps without any stiffening in them so that the corners flagged had made their appearance some years before the Reformation.[2] Masters took to them, and in 1565 the use by them of the *pileus quadratus* was given official sanction.[3]

They had been allowed silk in their hoods in 1432 in common with doctors.[4] By 1592 they had come to be worn with the lining displayed[5] and were generally preferred to the furred ones. On special occasions even as late as 1636 the old 'shoulder piece' as a kind of cape (*mantellum*) was still worn by all inceptors.[6] This did not survive the Civil War, and was after all a revival of an obsolete medieval dress which appealed to Laud; but miniver was still officially allowed in masters' hoods as late as the statutes of 1770.[7] Hoods during the early seventeenth century were very broad in front as is to be seen in the monumental effigy in St. John's College Chapel, Oxford, to Ralph Huchenson (1606).

By 1674 the sleeves of the gown had reached the length of the hem and had a key-shaped ending which was copied from the similarly shaped liripipe of the hood (Pl. 10a).[8] The gown, which in 1701 cost £4,[9] was very full and long, and the hood large but not as full and rounded as those of doctors. As can be seen in figure No. 14 of Loggan's costume plate it was worn in such a way that only the crimson lining showed. In the plates of both Edwards and Loggan the square cap has a large tump, and the plane of the square board is inclined very much forward. It remained so inclined until the last quarter of the eighteenth century.

In the oil-painting by Hogarth, *The Western Family* (about 1735), the clergyman wears a master's gown which is less full than shown in Loggan's plates and is the same as it is now,[10]

---

[1] K. A. Esdaile and S. Sitwell, *English Church Monuments*, pls. 57 and 59, opp. p. 61.

[2] J. Walker, i. 20. [3] S. Gibson, p. 386.

[4] S. Gibson, pp. 239–40.

[5] A. Clark, *Register of the University of Oxford*, ii. 231.

[6] G. R. M. Ward, i. 70–71, cap. 4.

[7] G. R. M. Ward, ii. 11.

[8] Oxf. Bodl. Libr. MS. Wood 276B, xix, 8.

[9] Oxf. Bodl. Libr. MS. Rawl. Letts. 108, fo. 279.

[10] S. Sitwell, *Conversation Pieces*, pl. 14; R. B. Becket, *Hogarth*, pl. 94.

otherwise the dress continued the same throughout the earlier eighteenth century, except that a tassel was added to the tump on the cap unofficially in the 1730's.[1] The cassock had been left off under the gown by lay masters in the previous century.

The statutes of 1770 were generally a reiteration of the Laudian *Codex*,[2] but in the engravings which Grignion made (Pl. 11) in order to illustrate the academical dress mentioned in 1770[3] there is a notable change in the Master of Arts hood. It has become narrow and deep, as have those of all non-doctors except Bachelors of Divinity. In the Roberts water-colours of 1792 the crimson hood and the gown of the master are the same as before.[4] The neck-band of the hood was of the same colour as the lining of the hood of the various degrees, at any rate until 1815.[5]

(k) Bachelors of Divinity

In the fourteenth century Bachelors of Divinity had no head-dress.[6] The best early example of the dress is to be seen in the bracket brass in Merton College Chapel representing both John Bloxham and John Wytton. Bloxham is described as a Bachelor of Divinity who died in 1387, but the brass was not executed until 1420. He wears a *supertunica* and a *cappa clausa* with two side slits such as Masters of Arts at this time wore, a white fur hood, and a 'shoulder piece', and he is bare-headed.[7]

In 1426 Bachelors of Divinity in common with Bachelors of Canon Law were allowed hoods of black cloth furred inside with budge, or of black cloth lined with black silk,[8] an enact-ment which distinguishes between a summer and winter dress, and precedes by six years the comprehensive statute (1432) already referred to.[9]

[1] A. D. Godley, loc. cit.   [2] G. R. M. Ward, pp. 9ff.
[3] Oxf. Bodl. Libr. MS. Top. Oxon. c. 16, 12, § 32.
[4] The change from the key-shaped end to the sleeves to the lunated end did not take place until after 1840, for in that year, according to N. Whittock's *Costumes of Oxford*, key-shaped ended sleeves were still worn.
[5] W. Combe and T. Uwins, loc. cit.
[6] E. C. Clarke, arts. cit. l. 147–8 and lxi. 33.
[7] Oxf. Bodl. Libr. MS. Top. Oxon. a. 36, fo. 13 (water-colour of 1792); M. Stephenson, p. 413 (Merton iii).
[8] W. A. Pantin, *English Black Monks*, ii (Camden Soc. xlvii (1933)), p. 177 (§ 172, 7).
[9] The summer variety of this hood is still worn by Bachelors of Divinity.

Collector

Doctor of Divinity in full dress

Doctor of Divinity in
Convocation dress

Doctor of Divinity in
undress

HUDDESFORD AND TAYLOR'S PLATES TO ILLUSTRATE
THE OXFORD STATUTES OF 1770

Festal dress of Doctor of Medicine

Master of Arts

Bachelor of Divinity

Bachelor of Civil Law

According to the Chaundler drawing (Pl. 7) the Bachelors of Divinity behind the doctors to the warden's left wear the *cappa clausa* with two slits.[1]

By the early sixteenth century they, like the Masters of Arts, had left off the upper dress, so that the by now full-sleeved *supertunica* appeared as the outer garment (*roba*), as is to be seen in the brass of John Spence, B.D. (1517), at Ewelme, Oxon.[2] During this century they took to a head-dress which developed in the same way as those of Doctors of Divinity, Masters of Arts, and others, finally becoming the *pileus quadratus*, a head-gear regulated by Elizabethan enactments and confirmed as their official head-covering in 1617 and 1620.[3]

The 'shoulder piece', which had long been abandoned, appears again in the Laudian *Codex* (1636) in the form of a cape, to be worn on certain occasions,[4] but the 'civil hood' mentioned in the inventory of Edward Cooper, B.D. (1640) was an ordinary lay cape to put round the shoulders in cold weather and had nothing to do with an academical hood.[5]

The development in the latter sixteenth century and early seventeenth century of the Bachelor of Divinity's gown was similar to that of the Master of Arts, and in Loggan's costume plate (figure No. 19) the two are exactly the same. With this is worn a full black hood and a square cap with a tump.

During the eighteenth century, when the hoods of all other non-doctors became narrower and deeper, that of the Bachelor of Divinity preserved the full shape. In Grignion's plates (1770) (Pl. 11 B) the dress of the Bachelor of Divinity consists of a square black tasselled cap, a gown exactly the same as that of masters, and a cassock with a sash.[6] The hood is not shown in this example, but in the water-colour by Roberts of 1792 the very large hood is made entirely of black silk, there being no difference in material between the outside and the lining,[7] but this is an eighteenth-century innovation.

---

[1] Cf. M. R. James, loc. cit.; E. C. Clarke, art. cit. l. 101, 202, and 207–8; E. T. Beaumont, *Academical Habit*, p. 27.

[2] H. Druitt, p. 135.

[3] S. Gibson, pp. 525 and 540.

[4] G. R. M. Ward, i. 70–71, cap. 4.

[5] Oxf. Univ. Archives, Hypomnemata Antiquaria, B. 11–Inventories BR–C, s.v. Cooper (Cole misunderstood this and suggested 'sable' for 'civil').

[6] Oxf. Bodl. Libr. MS. Top. Oxon. c. 16, 16.

[7] Oxf. Bodl. Libr. MS. Top. Oxon. d. 58, 29–30.

(l) Bachelors of Canon Law

Bachelors of Canon Law originally had no head-dress.[1] At first they wore the sleeveless tabard (*pallium*) over a *supertunica*,[2] but by the middle of the fifteenth century they were wearing a sleeved tabard and a 'shoulder piece' with a 'roller' hood close to the neck, as can be seen in the Chaundler drawing.[3] In 1426, as has already been noticed, in common with Bachelors of Divinity they had been allowed hoods of black cloth lined with budge fur or black cloth lined with black silk.[4] In the Chaundler drawing (Pl. 7) the group of Bachelors of Canon Law stands among the Masters of Arts, but a little below them from the warden. None has any head-dress.[5]

By the end of this century at any rate, like those of other degrees Bachelors of Canon Law had taken to wearing the *roba* (*supertunica; toga*) alone as their outer dress, for in 1507 the *toga talaris* is mentioned as their costume on the occasion of their being allowed a *typet* or *cornetum* as an alternative.[6] This may mean a robe-like garment and not merely a liripipe, in fact a *roba* whose particular features were that it had liripipes attached to it, as is to be seen in the brass of John Lowthe, D.C.L. (d. 1427). If this is so then the tendency to adopt lay fashions in academical dress was officially recognized as early as this.

The last example of the dress of this degree, which certainly did not survive Mary Tudor, appears in the painted alabaster figure in St. Aldate's Church, Oxford, of John Noble, B.Can.L. (d. 1522), who was Principal of Broadgates Hall. He wears over a *roba*, a full 'shoulder piece' which covers the shoulders and arms as far as the elbows. The hood is detached from the 'shoulder piece' in a deep V-shape. Hood and 'shoulder piece' are red.[7]

(m) Bachelors of Civil Law

The outer dress of this degree was in the fifteenth century the sleeved tabard, as can be seen in the Chaundler drawing,[8] a

---

[1] E. C. Clarke, art. cit. l. 33. [2] F. E. Brightman, Preface, p. vi.
[3] M. R. James, loc. cit.
[4] W. A. Pantin, *Black Monks*, loc. cit.
[5] M. R. James, loc. cit.; E. C. Clarke, art. cit. l. 207–8. See also the brass of Richard Wyard, B.Can.L., New Coll. Oxf. (1478) (M. Stephenson, p. 415 (New Coll. xiv)).
[6] G. Clinch, *English Costume*, pp. 250–2.
[7] T. and G. Hollis, *Monumental Effigies*, pl. St. Aldate's Ch. Oxf. effigy; Mrs. R. L. Poole, op. cit. iii (Pembroke, no. 1). [8] M. R. James, loc. cit.

dress that they wore in common with bachelors of other faculties except Divinity, who wore the *cappa clausa* with two slits at this time. They also had a 'shoulder piece', a liripiped hood, and a *roba (supertunica)* which was worn underneath the tabard. The best examples of Bachelors of Civil Law on brasses are those of John Mottesfont (1420) at Lydd, Kent,[1] and David Lloyd (1510) in the chapel of All Souls College, Oxford.[2] The colour of the dress of this degree, as was the case with all medieval academical dress at an early period, greatly varied, and might be of such as russet, tawny, or blue, but the dress of bachelors was restricted as to the fur with which it was edged, for it might only be of cheap kinds or of wool.[3] In 1490 they and all other bachelors were ordered to have their hoods lined with fur throughout.[4] They had no head-dress in the Middle Ages, and like other bachelors they did not enjoy the privilege granted to doctors and masters in 1432 of wearing silk in their hoods,[5] except Bachelors of Divinity who had been allowed silk six years before. In 1533 by Act of Parliament all bachelors were allowed a choice of a variety of inferior furs.[6]

By the beginning of the sixteenth century Bachelors of Civil Law seem to have left off their tabard, and their *roba*, which had been worn underneath the tabard as a *supertunica*, became their outer garment, full sleeved, and so remained until in Elizabethan times it was replaced by the winged-sleeved lay gown. It was at this latter period also that they came to have an official head-dress, the square cap, which they wore in common with other graduates.

Their gown had reached its present shape in 1631, as the brass of Jeremy Keyt (1631) in Woodstock Church, Oxon., shows. There is a good illustration of it in Loggan's costume plate, No. 11. Here are to be seen the black tufts in rows joined together by pieces of braid, and these are laid on the upper part of the sleeves, and on the skirt of the gown in three places, that is the sides and the back. It was long after this date that gimp took the place of tufts and cord braiding. It was probably introduced from France, for gimp appears on ordinary dress

[1] H. Druitt, p. 139.   [2] M. Stephenson, p. 410.
[3] A. Clark, *Wood*, i. 69.   [4] S. Gibson, p. 297.
[5] S. Gibson, pp. 239–40.
[6] C. Wordsworth, *Social Life at the English Universities*, pp. 489–90.

in a French print of 1694 which depicts an interior with courtiers at Versailles. It is laid on the skirt of the coat of one of the men in three places, in shape square at three sides and with a pointed top,[1] exactly as later it was placed on the Oxford winged-sleeved gowns.

The tufts are still to be seen in Overton's print, *Habitus Academici in Universitate Oxoniensi*, of 1730,[2] but in Reynolds's portrait of Sir Robert Chambers (1765) the sleeves of the Bachelor of Civil Law gown are decorated with gimp in place of tufts and cord-braid.[3] It will be noticed that a closed seam runs through the middle of the upper part of the sleeve from elbow to shoulder, and that the gimp is laid close to this and not generally over the whole sleeve as was the case later. The gown is silk, which probably was less usual a century before.

In the Grignion plates of 1770 (Pl. 11 B) the Bachelor of Civil Law wears a square cap with a tassel, a long deep hood, a silk gown with the false sleeves key-shaped at the ends, with gimp of square pattern on the sleeves, in three places on the skirt, and on the flap collar.[4]

Roberts took the Grignion figures as a basis for his water-colours of 1792. In his water-colour of this degree the dress consists of a black and tasselled square cap, a long and deep lavender-blue hood with white fur along the top edge, and a black silk gown with winged sleeves, decorated with black gimp on the upper and the middle of the lower parts of the sleeves and in three places on the skirt. The design of the gimp on the skirt is square at three sides and pointed at the top, but on the lower part of the sleeves it is round. Gimp appears on the collar.[5]

(n) *Bachelors of Medicine*

Evidence for the dress of Bachelors of Medicine in the Middle Ages does not exist in any form. All that can be said is that in common with other bachelors they wore the sleeved tabard, the *roba*, the small close hood, and the 'shoulder piece', and had

[1] P. Lacroix, *XVIIᵉ Siècle*, p. 208, fig. 70.

[2] Oxf. Bodl. Libr. G.A. Oxon., a. 72, leaf 3.

[3] R. Ingpen, *The Life of Samuel Johnson by James Boswell*, ii. 929.

[4] Oxf. Bodl. Libr. MS. Top. Oxon. c. 16, 11. These changes in the undress gown were the same for D.C.L., D.M., D.Mus., B.C.L., B.M., and B.Mus.

[5] Oxf. Bodl. Libr. MS. Top. Oxon. d. 58, 32–33.

no head-dress.[1] All subsequent enactments which involved the dress of bachelors collectively naturally applied equally to them.

In the seventeenth century their dress was exactly the same as that of Bachelors of Civil Law as Loggan's engravings show. In fact, not until 1815 was there any difference in the dress of the two degrees, in which year Bachelors of Medicine are said to have a hood, not of 'dark blue' lined with fur like that of Bachelors of Civil Law, but one of lilac silk lined with fur.[2]

(o) Bachelors of Music

The degree of Bachelor of Music was the lowliest in the university, for whereas Bachelors of Arts might be considered as potential members of Convocation, Bachelors of Music who held no Arts degree would never be. The degree is first mentioned in 1502.[3]

There were no actual regulations for the dress of this degree, but the dress of Bachelors of Civil Law and Medicine seems to have been adopted for it during the seventeenth century. The gown of Bachelors of Music was, however, never as richly decorated as those of the two above-mentioned bachelors, though of the same winged-sleeved, flap-collared shape; and thus in Loggan's costume plate (No. 7) it has no tufts, but only rows of cord-braiding with three buttons to a row. A square cap with a tump was worn in the seventeenth century. Their hood was less full than those of other degrees.

In the plate of the Bachelor of Music by Grignion (1770) (Pl. 11 c) a black silk gown is worn with gimp of a rounded pattern on the collar, on the upper half of the winged sleeves, and at the sides and in the middle of the skirt. The whole decoration is much lighter than that found on the Bachelor of Civil Law and Bachelor of Medicine gowns.[4] This lightness of decoration can again be noticed in Roberts's water-colours of 1792. The hood, which is long and deep, is of powdered blue silk and edged at the top with white fur.[5] There has always been

---

[1] E. T. Beaumont, *Academical Habit*, p. 27.
[2] W. Combe and T. Uwins, loc. cit.
[3] C. F. Abdy Williams, *Historical Account of Degrees in Music*, p. 154.
[4] Oxf. Bodl. Libr. MS. Top. Oxon. c. 16, 6.
[5] Oxf. Bodl. Libr. MS. Top. Oxon. d. 58, 35–36.

confusion about this hood's colour, resulting from the lack of legislation about it.[1]

(p) Bachelors of Arts

At a date prior to 1350 Bachelors of Arts were refused any form of head-dress, and in another university statute of about 1425 there is mention of their being refused the use of a *birretum* or even a skull-cap (*tena*).[2] In 1379 their accepted outer dress was a sleeveless tabard, according to a reference in the statutes of New College,[3] but later they wore sleeved tabards lined with fur, the sleeves at first reaching only to the elbow and later to a point behind, over a full, but tight-sleeved *roba* (*supertunica*), together with a close hood and a 'shoulder piece'. Such is the dress worn by Geoffrey Hargreve, B.A., 1447, at New College.[4] Later the sleeves began to grow pointed,[5] and by about 1463, the date of the Chaundler drawing (Pl. 7), the sleeves had become fuller still, as can be seen from studying the young-looking group of Bachelors of Arts who are standing in the middle.[6] A good example of the dress in its final stage, consisting of the tabard with full and pointed sleeves, with tight sleeved *roba* and hood and 'shoulder piece', is to be found in the brass of John Palmer (1479) at New College.[7] This tabard, which is shorter than the *roba*, is lined with fur, and its sleeves reach to the wrist in front and fall far behind to a point.[8]

By the beginning of the sixteenth century, as is the case with all other outer academical dress, the tabard was generally laid aside and the *roba*, now opened down the front, became the outer garment. It has been suggested[9] that the tabard and *roba* (or *toga*) were fused into one dress during the fifteenth century, but it seems more likely that when the tabard was left off, the *roba's* sleeves from being tight to the hand under the sleeved

---

[1] The violet colour used in recent times (L. H. D. Buxton and S. Gibson, p. 40) seems to be an uncertain compromise, no doubt reminiscent of the cherry of the Doctor of Music.

[2] S. Gibson, pp. 229-30.

[3] *Statutes of the Colleges of Oxford for the Royal Commission*, i. 45-46 (R. 23).

[4] J. G. and L. A. B. Waller, *Monumental Brasses*, no. 44.

[5] F. E. Brightman, Preface, loc. cit.

[6] M. R. James, loc. cit.

[7] H. Druitt, p. 141; E. T. Beaumont, *Academical Habit*, p. 29.

[8] H. Haines, p. lxxxiv.

[9] G. Clinch, pp. 250-1 and 253.

tabard, now became large and hanging. This process of development seems the more likely when it is considered that about 1510 the sleeves of surplices had become wide-sleeved after being tight-sleeved in the previous century.[1]

It was thus by the early sixteenth century that the wide-sleeved gown had come into being. It had during the Tudor period, as was the case with masters' gowns, a 'standing collar', that is an upright one such as is mentioned in the Ecclesiastical Canon No. 74 of the Church of England of the year 1604, in opposition to the flap collar of the lay type of gown; but in the course of the seventeenth century this collar was cut away for greater comfort and for the better fitting of the dress underneath.[2]

After the Reformation the privilege of a head-dress was extended to Bachelors of Arts, and in 1565 in common with other graduates they were ordered to wear a square cap.[3] In the Laudian statutes of 1636 they were to wear loose-sleeved gowns and square caps, and at special services miniver hoods, instead of the ordinary budge-furred ones, with the lining showing. They were also to wear 'capes' (i.e. the remnant of the old 'shoulder piece') and their hood was to be square in shape.[4]

During the Protectorate there was an influx into Oxford of Cambridge men who were eager to fill the empty sister university. Among them the Bachelors of Arts seem to have been conspicuous, and the Oxford bachelors began to copy their gowns which had large hanging sleeves, larger than their own.[5] This was checked by Vice-Chancellor Fell's statute concerning academical dress of 1666.[6] In the memorandum addressed to tailors it is said: 'Bachelours of Arts . . . to weare wide-sleeved gowns, the sleeves not reaching beyond the fingers' ends nor above an ell in compass.' They were to 'hang at length', which means fairly close to the arms. They were thus reduced to a reasonable size.

In the large plate of Edwards (1674) (Pl. 10*b*) and in figure

[1] M. H. Bloxam (*Gothic Architecture*, pp. 47 and 74) gives examples of this change in 1510.

[2] M. E. C. Walcott, p. 104; H. Druitt, p. 112, n. 3; L. H. D. Buxton and S. Gibson, p. 39.　　　　　　　　　　　　　[3] S. Gibson, p. 386.

[4] G. R. M. Ward, i. 152-3, cap. iii.

[5] A. Clark, *Wood*, i. 149.　　　　　　　[6] A. Clark, *Wood*, ii. 84-85, § 7.

No. 8 in Loggan's costume plate (1675) the large gown with full bell sleeves but with no cuff strings (a cord with a loop and button later introduced to hold back the sleeve from the arm) appears. A square cap with a tump is worn, and a large black hood with a white fur lining. A determining bachelor wore the hood with the fur fully displayed,[1] but when the degree had been taken the fur was not displayed. The first reference to the use of cuff strings appears in a letter of 1684, in which is a description of the material used in making a Bachelor of Arts gown at a cost of £3. 14s. 11d. The material consists of hair prunella, serge, a neck-loop, calico, buckram, tape (for the cuff strings), galloon, and wax-light.[2]

In 1770 the square cap's tassel was given official sanction,[3] and at the same time, besides the miniver hood, which Laud had allowed to all graduates on special occasions, but which for a long time had never been used, certainly not by Bachelors of Arts, two other bachelor's hoods were mentioned. One was the ordinary Bachelor of Arts hood bordered with a fringe of fur to be worn at the act and always afterwards, and the other was the displayed hood for determining bachelors with a piece of white wool and lamb's-skin ('wool fells') fastened to the upper edge of it.[4] Both are illustrated in Grignion's plates (Pl. 11c).[5]

The determiner's hood is full and deep, showing the ordinary fur halfway down its length, while the darker wool appears on the topmost edge. This upper piece of wool is described by a contemporary as 'a little piece of lambskin with the wool on it'.[6] The gown had no cuff strings when worn by a determining bachelor, but they were used after the degree had been taken, and were worn fastened to hold the sleeve some way up the arm.[7]

In Roberts's water-colour collection (1792) the Bachelor of Arts wears the tasselled square cap. His gown is full, and the

---

[1] D. Loggan, op. cit., No. 9. Determining bachelors were those performing the last exercises for their degree.
[2] J. R. Magrath, *The Flemings in Oxford* (O.H.S.), ii. 123.
[3] G. R. M. Ward, ii. 9–10.
[4] G. R. M. Ward, ii. 11.
[5] Oxf. Bodl. Libr. MS. Top. Oxon. c. 16, 8 and 7.
[6] V. Knox, *Essays Moral and Literary*, i. 335.
[7] Oxf. Bodl. Libr. MS. Top. Oxon. c. 16, 7 and 8.

PLATE I I C

Bachelor of Music

Bachelor of Arts with ordinary hood

'Determining' Bachelor of Arts

Student of Civil Law

Nobleman

Baronet

Commoner

Servitor or Battelar

cuff strings are used to fasten the sleeves up at the elbows, while his deep hood of black stuff is trimmed with rabbit fur at the top edge.[1] It should be noticed that only the determiner's hood was *lined* with fur. The other was merely trimmed with fur after the seventeenth century.

(q) Undergraduates

1. *Students of Civil Law, or civilians*. According to Vice-Chancellor Fell (1666) Students of Civil Law were 'persons studying the law being above four years standing in the University and being entered into the law-book'.[2] It was possible by becoming a civilian to avoid reading for a Bachelor of Arts degree, and so it was an immediate step into a higher faculty, that of Law.[3]

The civilian had a special dress, the form of which in Pre-Reformation times is to be seen in the brass of Thomas Baker (1510) at All Souls, Oxford. He wears a cloak of the pattern familiar to us from the *armelausa* of judges, but as if to show that he is a legal tyro, it is the left side that is open, while the right is closed, the opposite of theirs. There are buttons on the shoulder of the cloak on the open side. Under it he wears an open tabard with furred bell-sleeves, and under the tabard a *supertunica* with a girdle. A hood rests on his shoulders.[4] Nothing more is heard of their dress until after the middle of the seventeenth century.

In Fell's order of 1666 their costume is described as a half-sleeved gown without any decoration such as buttons on the sleeve, and a square cap.[5] In Edwards's plate of 1674[6] the gown is of black silk with a plain flap collar and plain *glove* sleeves like those of a master at that time, straight at the ends, but in Loggan's plate (figure No. 6) of 1675 the tops of these sleeves are decorated with formal square pleats. In both examples there is a large tump on the square cap.

According to the statutes of 1770 civilians were allowed to

[1] Oxf. Bodl. Libr. MS. Top. Oxon. d. 58, 47–49.
[2] A. Clark, *Wood*, ii. 84–85.
[3] This special status was not abolished until 1853 (*Notes and Queries*, 2nd ser. vi. 258[a]).
[4] H. Druitt, p. 141; E. T. Beaumont, *Ancient Memorial Brasses*, p. 110; M. Stephenson, p. 410 (All Souls, iii). I cannot agree with Stephenson, who believes that Baker is wearing ordinary civil dress with a scholar's gown.
[5] A. Clark, *Wood*, ii. 85.
[6] Oxf. Bodl. Libr. MS. Wood 276B, xix, 10.

have a tassel on their square cap,[1] and in Grignion's plate of this year (Pl. 11c) the gown is silk, very full, with a flap collar and plain false winged sleeves with some vertical braid; a gown in fact the same as that of the Bachelor of Civil Law but without the gimp.[2] This gown is the same in Roberts's water-colour of 1792, and the hood is long and deep, entirely of lavender-coloured silk and without any fur, the same in fact as that of the Bachelor of Civil Law without the fur edging.[3] A hood was worn in virtue of the wearer's belonging, even though a *studiosus*, to a senior faculty. The flap collar was removed from the gown before 1815.[4]

In the later seventeenth century many undergraduates wore this dress who had no right to it.[5] The reason for their adopting it was that they might pass for gentlemen-commoners.[6]

2. *Noblemen and gentlemen-commoners*. No doubt, as was the case in most other universities, noblemen undergraduates were allowed special privileges probably including those concerning dress, but the *Statuta Antiqua* contain no mention of a special dress for noblemen until 1490. In that year noblemen were allowed, in contradistinction to other undergraduates, to have their hoods and liripipes hanging free and not stitched down, as those of lesser birth were to wear them.[7] Probably gentlemen-commoners did not exist as a recognized body of favoured undergraduates in early times.

The Reformation no doubt caused a relaxation of discipline, for the authorities soon began to show indulgence to com-moners (those not on foundations) as regards dress, particu-larly when outside their colleges.[8] As the century advanced the universities became more fashionable and so money and social position began to have an effect on the academical world as never before. Undergraduates of social standing, whether titled or not, were openly recognized in a decree of Convocation of 1576, which allowed a special latitude in dress to peers' and

[1] G. R. M. Ward, ii. 9 ff.

[2] Oxf. Bodl. Libr. MS. Top. Oxon. c. 16, 5.

[3] Oxf. Bodl. Libr. MS. Top. Oxon. d. 58, 65–66.

[4] W. Combe and T. Uwins, ii. 17.

[5] A. Clark, *Wood*, iii. 300. The printed proclamation denouncing this practice is to be found in Bodl. MS. Wood 276A, No. ccclxxxviii, 3, Year 1689.

[6] Cf. the early nineteenth-century conversation about this in H. Coombs and A. N. Bax, *Journal of a Somerset Rector*, p. 88.

[7] S. Gibson, p. 297.

[8] S. Gibson, p. 386.

knights' sons and to the heirs of esquires,[1] while in the same year when graduates and scholars were allowed to wear ordinary hats of lay fashion while outside the university precincts but always black ones, *generosi* were granted a free choice of colour.[2] In the decrees of 1617 and 1620 when they were all ordered to wear round caps (*pilei rotundi*), the three grades of undergraduates not on foundations, noblemen, gentlemen-commoners, and commoners, are officially approved.[3]

In the Laudian statutes a stricter discipline is to be seen and only sons of peers were allowed bright colours in their dress. This refers only to sons of peers who were members of the House of Lords as distinct from those who had only a courtesy peerage, and the sons of Scottish and Irish peers, whose dress was to be black or at least dark.[4]

During the residence of Charles I's court at Oxford the observance of the Laudian statutes broke down—for instance we find gentlemen-commoners imitating court fashions, wearing velvet facings on their gowns[5]—but Fell in 1666 as vice-chancellor laid down definite rules for undergraduate dress in the tradition of Laud. In his *Orders to Tailors* he described the dress for these privileged undergraduates:

The gent.-commoner's gown to be half-sleeved, and, if they please, to have buttons not exceeding 4 doz. nor the rate of 5/- the doz. nor the bigness in the public patterns. A baronet's or knight's gown, the same as the former, only distinguished (if they please) with gold and silver buttons. Noblemen to wear (if they please) coloured gowns, of the same form with the former.[6]

The gowns of these first two orders were black.

In figure No. 5 of Loggan's plate (1675) the gentleman-commoner wears a winged-sleeved gown with a flap collar, the shoulders of the gown and the sides of the skirt being richly decorated with button and cord braiding. The cap is round and black, though gentlemen-commoners had been for some time covetous of the square cap and in 1675 were wearing it by permission of the vice-chancellor.[7] They had already in 1669

---

[1] S. Gibson, p. 404. [2] S. Gibson, loc. cit.
[3] S. Gibson, pp. 525 and 540.
[4] C. E. Mallet, *History of the University of Oxford*, ii. 333.
[5] A. Clark, *Wood*, i. 149.
[6] A. Clark, *Wood*, ii. 84–85.
[7] A. Clark, *Wood*, ii. 300.

sought to distinguish themselves from lesser undergraduates by wearing silk bonnets,[1] for although as gentlemen they were allowed a band round the bonnet to distinguish them from servitors, this could not clearly be seen because it was black; but square caps, they felt, would produce even better the necessary distinction. In 1686 this practice of wearing a square cap was well established;[2] but was forbidden and finally suppressed in 1689.[3] Another abuse, which was never effectively controlled, was the wearing by noblemen and gentlemen-commoners of ordinary lay hats about the university.[4]

In Loggan (figure No. 29) the sons of esquires and baronets wear a black winged-sleeved, flap-collared gown, decorated on the sleeves, half-way down the front, and on the skirt at the back and on each side with what in fact was silver braid of the cord and button variety. The sons of noblemen, who are illustrated in Loggan's plate as figure No. 30, wore the same dress, but the braid was gold. The round black silk bonnet worn by these orders had by 1700 come to be made of black velvet.[5]

During the eighteenth century such dress became more and more elaborate. The practice continued for peers and the sons of peers to wear gowns of any colour adorned with gold braid to which gold tufts were soon added, while baronets, their sons, and the sons of knights wore black silk gowns embellished with gold braid, and gentlemen-commoners black silk gowns decorated with black braid.[6] All wore round black velvet bonnets.[7] The wearing of gold tassels on their bonnets by noblemen made its appearance in 1738, but was not as yet countenanced by statute.[8]

The statutes of 1770, however, allowed noblemen, baronets, and gentlemen-commoners to have square black velvet caps instead of round bonnets, with tassels, gold ones for noblemen and black ones for baronets and gentlemen-commoners. Noble-

---

[1] A. Clark, *Wood*, ii. 164. [2] A. Clark, *Wood*, iii. 181.

[3] Oxf. Bodl. Libr. MS. Wood 276A, no. ccclxxxviii, 4.

[4] Oxf. Bodl. Libr. MS. Wood 276A, no. ccclxxxviii, 4.

[5] Oxf. Bodl. Libr. MS. Top. Oxon. a. 36, leaves 77–78.

[6] Certainly as early as 1721 (*Brasenose College, Quatercentenary Monographs* (O.H.S.), ii, pt. 1, xiii, p. 42).

[7] [J. R. Green], *Oxford during the Last Century*, p. 48.

[8] A. D. Godley, loc. cit., the term 'tuft-hunter' refers to this, or possibly to the gold tufts on the dress gown. The *New English Dictionary* gives a reference to the term in 1755 as being the earliest. This was at Cambridge.

men were still to have coloured gowns for formal occasions, but for undress, in common with baronets, black bell-sleeved gowns with a tippet on the left shoulder like those of proctors, but smaller.[1]

In Grignion's plates of this year, the gentleman-commoner wears the silk winged-sleeved gown decorated on the sleeves and skirt with patches of braid with tassels;[2] but the baronet's undress gown is bell-sleeved and reaches to the ground, and has a tippet fastened by two buttons to the left-hand lower corner of the yoke.[3] The nobleman's undress gown is the same.[4] The full dress of baronet and nobleman was the same in shape, both having winged sleeves and panels, and a flap collar, but whereas that of the first was black, the nobleman's was coloured, purple being particularly favoured. Tippets were not worn on the full dress[5] (Pl. 11 D).

In Roberts's water-colours of 1792[6] the nobleman in full dress[7] wears a square black velvet cap with a gold tassel, and a gown of purple brocade with winged sleeves with false panels. The gown is faced with gold braid, which also runs round the wings, and near the bottom of the false panels is a square patch of gold braid with a pointed top (Frontispiece). His undress is the same as to head-dress, but he has a black silk gown with bell sleeves and a tippet attached to the yoke.[8] The baronet in full dress[9] wears the same as the nobleman in every detail except that the gown is of black brocade, but the gentleman-commoner's full dress consists of a black silk gown with winged sleeves and false panels, with a series of black tassels joined by rows of braid on the upper arm and at the bottom of the false panelled sleeves. He wears a square black velvet cap with a black tassel.[10] In undress[11] his gown is different, for though it has the same sleeves, the middle of the wings of the sleeves is decorated with small black 'pebble' pleats formed into a square with a pointed top, of the same shape as the gold decorations on the nobleman's full dress gown.[12]

[1] G. R. M Ward, ii, loc. cit.; Oxf. Bodl. Libr. MS. Top. Oxon. c. 16, 22 and 24.   [2] Oxf. Bodl. Libr. MS. Top. Oxon. c. 16, 4.
[3] 22.   [4] 24.   [5] 23 and 25.
[6] Oxf. Bodl. Libr. MS. Top. Oxon. d. 58.   [7] 50–51.
[8] 53–54.   [9] 56–57.   [10] 60–61.   [11] 62–63.
[12] Gimp was introduced in place of tassels on the gentleman-commoner's full dress gown between 1792 and 1815 (W. Combe and T. Uwins, loc. cit.).

3. *Scholars or students.* The original dress of those under-graduates who were on foundations except at New College, was the sleeved tabard.[1] It is worn by scholars in an alchemical manuscript of 1479.[2] They were bare-headed in medieval times but had a plain black cloth hood which is referred to in a statute of 1490,[3] when they were ordered to have the liripipe of their hood stitched to it (*consutum*) and not worked into the same piece (*contextum*). The reason for this was probably that its being stitched down would prevent the liripipe's being thrown round the neck like a scarf or the hood's being worn on the head.[4] The tabard was always worn closed before the sixteenth century but in 1507 scholars of Magdalen had to be warned against wearing tabards not sewn together in front.[5]

Presumably, although there is no evidence on which to base the statement, the development of the scholar's dress thereafter was the same as that of the Bachelor of Arts, so that the outer dress (the tabard) was left off and the *tunica*, worn underneath it, became the outer dress with greatly enlarged sleeves.[6]

Scholars were at length, in 1565, granted a head-dress which was to be the square cap. At the same time they were ordered always to wear their black hood at important academical functions, but might use a little shoulder-cape instead of the hood when walking at free times.[7] In 1576, owing to great opposition to the square cap on account of its supposed Romish character, scholars as well as graduates were allowed as a con-cession to wear ordinary hats of lay fashion outside the univer-sity precincts, as long as they were black. At the same time they were forbidden to wear light-coloured gowns or gowns of rich material or decorated with lace.[8] In 1617 and 1620 the square black cap as the head-dress of scholars was insisted on for all occasions.[9]

A fine example of the scholar's dress in Elizabethan times is to be found in a brass (Pl. 12 a) in Oxford Cathedral of Henry Dow, junior student (i.e. scholar of Christ Church) (1578).

---

[1] E. C. Clarke, art. cit. l. 139–40. It is preserved in the name tabarder for open scholars of Queen's (J. Walker, ii. 49). See below, p. 97, nn. 2 and 3.
[2] Cambridge, St. John's Coll. Libr., MS. James no. 182, G. 14, fo. 96b.
[3] S. Gibson, p. 297.   [4] E. C. Clarke, art. cit. l. 88.
[5] W. M. Macray, *Register*, N.S. i, §§ 44–45, p. 55.
[6] Except at New College, see below.   [7] S. Gibson, pp. 386–7.
[8] S. Gibson, p. 404.   [9] S. Gibson, pp. 525 and 540.

PLATE 12

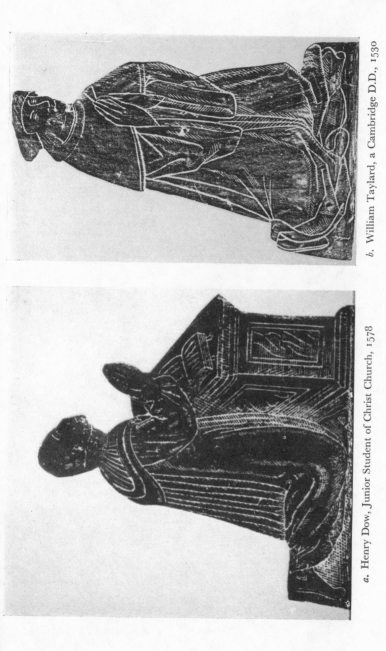

b. William Taylard, a Cambridge D.D., 1530

a. Henry Dow, Junior Student of Christ Church, 1578

He wears a long full gown with a high standing collar and large bell sleeves which hang down below his elbows behind, a ruff, and a small round and unlined hood of black cloth. Another junior student of Christ Church, John Bisshop (1588), whose brass is also in the cathedral, is similarly dressed. Such was the dress which was ordered by Laud in 1636 to be worn with a square cap by all scholars of the university.[1] All scholars thus wore the full-sleeved gown, except the scholars of New College, who clung to the medieval sleeveless serge gown, which Aubrey rightly calls a tabard, together with ruffs, both until the beginning of the Civil War.[2] They had thus kept to the clause in their foundation statutes of 1379 which ordered scholars to wear sleeveless ankle-length tabards.[3] Laud limited the use of their black hood by scholars to the occasions on which they attended the schools.[4]

In 1666 Fell in his *Orders to Tailors*[5] expected 'Foundation Men' (scholars) to wear wide-sleeved gowns, the sleeves 'not reaching beyond the fingers' ends nor above an ell in compass', exactly the same as those of Bachelors of Arts, but with this difference, that whereas the sleeves of bachelors were to hang free, those of scholars were to be held up at the wrists. In figure No. 3 of Loggan's plate, however, though the scholar on the foundation appears in a large bell-sleeved gown, the sleeves hang free and there is no sign of cuff-strings. He wears a black square cap without a tump. In 1682 on his becoming a tabarder at Queen's and so on the foundation, Henry Fleming exchanged his round commoner's cap for a square one, which cost 5s.[6] By 1700, the approximate date of Robert Sayer's *Oxonia Illustrata*,[7] the scholar's square cap had a tump, and in 1770 the use of a tassel was officially recognized,[8] but it seems from an entry in the diary of Dr. Thomas Fry, President of St. John's, that some colleges followed their own rules, and even as late as the latter year only allowed their scholars to wear a tuft or tump as an act of grace.[9]

---

[1] G. R. M. Ward, i. 152, chap. iii.
[2] Oxf. Bodl. Libr. MS. Top. Gen. c. 25, fo. 201b.
[3] *Statutes of the Colleges of Oxford for the Royal Commission*, i. 45–46, R. 23, *De habitu sociorum et scholarium de collegio*.   [4] C. E. Mallet, ii. 324.
[5] A. Clark, *Wood*, ii. 84–85.   [6] J. R. Magrath, ii. 83.
[7] Oxf. Bodl. Libr. MS. Top. Oxon. a 36, fos. 77–78.
[8] G. R. M. Ward, ii. 9 ff.   [9] MS. Diary of Dr. Thomas Fry, 5 March 1770.

In Grignion's plate of 1770 the scholar wears a full bell-sleeved gown, the sleeves tapering behind to points, hanging loose, and there are cuff-strings hanging from them (Pl. 11);[1] while in the water-colour of Roberts (1792) he wears the square black cloth cap with a black silk tassel, a black cloth gown of the same shape as that of 1770, and a black cloth hood, very narrow and flung loosely over the shoulders.[2] This hood, as has been said above, was only worn in the schools.[3]

4. *Commoners*. Although, as in other European universities, there existed at Oxford an order of undergraduates who were members of the university and paid their own way as opposed to scholars who were in receipt of pecuniary assistance and of assistance in kind and so were 'on the foundation' of their college, there does not appear to be any evidence for a particular dress worn by commoners in medieval times, no doubt because during this period they were not members of colleges, and generally living in hostels in the town, escaped a college discipline.[4]

It is not until Elizabethan times that we have any information about the costume worn by commoners, and then we find that the dress adopted for them and laid down by statute was dress entirely of lay character.

The brass of Edward Chernock, commoner, of Brasenose, who died in 1581 while still an undergraduate, which is to be seen in the church of St. Mary-the-Virgin, Oxford, sufficiently illustrates the lay character of this dress. The gown is winged-sleeved, after the style worn by Bachelors of Civil Law, but not so elaborate.

At some time between this date and 1617 the commoner's gown was altered in that the winged sleeves vanished and the panels became merely strips of stuff fastened to the back of the shoulders of the now sleeveless gown. This is to be seen in the brass of the commoner, John Pendarves of this date at St. Michael's-at-the-North-Gate, Oxford.[5] It is to be noticed that

[1] Oxf. Bodl. Libr. MS. Top. Oxon. c. 16, 2.
[2] Oxf. Bodl. Libr. MS. Top. Oxon. d. 58, 71–72.
[3] The sleeves had been shortened by 1828 (N. Whittock, *Topographical and Historical Description of Oxford*, p. 42).
[4] There are records of commoners living in college in the fourteenth and fifteenth centuries. See *Vict. Co. Hist. Oxf.* iii. 63a.
[5] E. T. Beaumont, *Academical Habit*, p. 87 and ill. opp. p. 88.

the little rib of material fastened into the shoulder of the modern commoner's gown resulted from the Jacobean fashion for padded shoulders. This appears in the Pendarves brass.

The head-dress was the round cap, the 'statute cap', which, originally of wool (though afterwards of cloth), the government in 1571 had ordered apprentices to wear.[1] At Oxford as at Cambridge it was adopted as the head-dress of undergraduates not on foundations.[2] These *pilei rotundi* of commoners are mentioned in Oxford statutes of 1617 and 1620.[3] In the Laudian statutes undergraduates not on foundations are to wear long 'square' gowns (i.e. of lay type) and round caps.[4]

In 1666 Vice-Chancellor Fell ordered that the commoner's gown should be such a one as is worn by Pendarves with a square flap collar, decorated on the strips of stuff ('streamers' or 'leading strings' as they came to be called) which hung from the shoulders, with half a dozen buttons, black and of a certain price, laid on the upper part.[5] In Loggan (1675) the commoner (No. 4) wears a gown with these buttons on the upper part of the streamers laid on in rows of three buttons, which are joined together by plain lines of braid, with the addition of tassels. The cap is round. Better illustrations of these caps appear in G. Edwards's plates of 1674 (Pl. 10 c). From these it can be seen that the cap of gentlemen-commoners had a broad band, of commoners a narrow one, while there was no band on the cap of servitors.[6] A commoner's round cap is mentioned as costing between 2s. 6d. and 3s. 6d. in the accounts of Henry Brougham of Queen's and of members of the Fleming family in 1658, 1678, 1682, and 1693.[7]

In 1770 commoners were ordered to wear the square cloth cap with a silk tassel.[8] By this time the buttons had vanished from the tops of the streamers, their place having been taken by a decoration consisting of formal pleating in large squares, which was also placed in a line below the flap collar (Pl. 11 D).[9]

[1] *Statutes of the Realm*, iv. 555 (13 Eliz. c. 19 (1571)).
[2] It is referred to by Shakespeare in *Love's Labour's Lost*, v. ii. 281, where Rosaline says: 'Well, better wits have worn plain statute-caps.'
[3] S. Gibson, pp. 525 and 540.   [4] G. R. M. Ward, i. 153, cap. iii.
[5] A. Clark, *Wood*, ii. 84–85.
[6] Oxf. Bodl. Libr. MS. Wood 276 B, xix, 9, xix, 11, and xix, 12.
[7] J. R. Magrath, p. 120 and n. 1; i. 249; ii. 68; iii. 129.
[8] G. R. M. Ward, ii. 9 ff.
[9] Oxf. Bodl. Libr. MS. Top. Oxon. c. 16, 3.

In 1792 commoners wore the black tasselled square cap, and a black cloth gown with a plain flap-collar. The gown was sleeveless, but had long thick 'streamers', which were decorated on the upper part with pleats in squares, and which were as long as the ankle-length gown.[1]

5. *Battelars and servitors*. These terms do not appear until later times, although servitors had their equivalents during the Middle Ages in all the universities of Europe. Battelars who partly supported themselves but contributed the minimum to their expenses were of a higher order than servitors, who worked their way through the university by waiting on the fellows in hall or doing all kinds of jobs for wealthy undergraduates, in fact taking the place of 'scouts' of whom there were few until the later eighteenth century.[2] In the seventeenth century servitors were referred to as 'gown-men', whereas 'cloak-men' simply meant ordinary servants whom noblemen and gentlemen-commoners sometimes brought with them to college to attend on them when in residence. They then dispensed with the aid of servitors.[3]

In Fell's *Orders to Tailors* (1666) the gowns of battelars and servitors were for the first time described.[4] They were to be the same as those of commoners but without any decoration of buttons on the 'streamers' and collar, and were thus of plain black cloth. The flap collars of the servitors were to be 'round' (that is, with a yoke), but those of battelars were to be 'square', but in Loggan's plate of 1675 their dress which appears in figures 1 and 2 is exactly the same, there being no difference in the collars, which in both cases are square. A plain low round cap is worn by both. There was an excellent drawing of a battelar or servitor by Michael Burghers of about 1695, of which copies of the engraving are at St. Edmund Hall and the Bodleian Library (Pl. 10 *d*).[5]

As time went on it became increasingly difficult to force this humble dress on either of these orders. Of servitors in 1730 Hearne writes: 'Our Servitors now . . . are generally very

---

[1] Oxf. Bodl. Libr. MS. Top. Oxon. d. 58, 68–69; and see the verses of John Skinner (1792) printed in H. Coomb and A. N. Bax, p. 315.

[2] *Brasenose College, Quatercentenary Monographs* ii, pt. 1, § xiii, p. 45.

[3] R. Magrath, i. 536–7.

[4] A. Clark, *Wood*, ii. 84–85, §§ 2 and 1.

[5] Auct. v. iii. 1 (229).

haughty and scorn to wear their proper habits, their gowns being not what properly belong to Servitors but to Battelars, and their caps (which should be Thrum [i.e. yarn] Caps or Bonnets) being what when I first came to Oxford [i.e. 1695] the Commoners wore.'[1] Hogarth's print *The Lecture* (? 1735) depicts a group of scholars, battelars, and servitors attending an Oxford lecture. The two latter wear round rigid caps with a button on top, very different from the flat bonnets of 1675,[2] and the same as the round cap of a member of a charity school[3].

In 1770 the new statutes gave battelars and servitors the square black cap but without tump or tassel,[4] and in Grignion's plates of the same year the servitor (and this was also the dress of the battelar, the two orders from about this time becoming fused) wears such a square cap and an absolutely plain black cloth gown reaching to the ground, sleeveless but with plain broad 'streamers' fixed behind the shoulders and falling the length of the gown. The gown had a plain flap collar (Pl. 11 D).[5]

(r) Notes

1. *College statutes.* Originally colleges legislated about the particular dress to be worn by their members, and the university as a body left the various foundations to their own devices beyond issuing general rules from time to time. Particularly were Queen's and New College conscious of their individual corporate systems. Thus in the foundation statutes of Queen's (1340) elaborate rules were laid down. Fellows who were Doctors of Divinity and Doctors of Canon Law, at lunch and dinner at particular times of year (*singulis anni temporibus*), in hall were to wear a *pallium* (a large sleeveless outer garment) of a purple colour as a memorial of the blood of Christ, with an opening at the neck (*scissi ad colla*), furred with black budge. The rest of the fellows were to wear a *pallium* of a quieter colour.

---

[1] T. Hearne, x. 275.

[2] J. Ireland and J. Nichols, *Hogarth's Works*, ii, pl. opp. p. 250.

[3] See the figure in Hogarth's print *First Stage of Cruelty* (1750) (ibid., pl. opp. p. 54).

[4] G. R. M. Ward, ii. 10. In the diary of Dr. Thomas Fry, President of St. John's, under date 6 March 1770, a Bible clerk is refused permission to wear a 'tuft' on his cap. This was reserved for scholars.

[5] Oxf. Bodl. Libr. MS. Top. Oxon. c. 16, 1. The same dress appears in the water-colour of this subject by James Roberts (1792) (Oxf. Bodl. Libr. MS. Top. Oxon. d. 58, 74–75).

As for the other members of the college the provost was to see that their dress conformed in colour.[1]

In the foundation statutes of New College (1379), the warden and members on the foundation were to have their dress cut from the same cloth, made up into the various shapes conformable with their various university degrees, a *cappa* for doctors, a large tabard for masters, and a less full tabard for those of lower degree. A cape or cloak (*mantellum*) was to be worn by inceptors.[2]

A college livery seems to have been used at one time at Merton, for in 1509 violet cloth, presumably for gowns, was to be given by the warden to the eighteen fellows of the college every St. John the Baptist's Day.[3]

In 1555 in the foundation statutes of St. John's it was insisted that the dress, at least of all on the foundation, should be clerkly,[4] but apart from this stipulation the character of the dress was left to the president and vice-president to decide. This seems to have been the last collegiate enactment as regards dress, and thereafter such a question was left to the university. Thus at Jesus (1571), the last of the sixteenth-century foundations, all that is mentioned about the dress of its members is that it is to be conformable with the statutes of the university and according to the discretion of the principal and vice-principal.[5] The university had already taken this matter in hand from 1565 onwards, and the way was prepared for Laud to make his all-embracing rules.

2. *Grand compounders.* One could be a grand compounder for any degree, greatly enlarged fees being paid for the privilege, for instance, £40 instead of £14 for the Master of Arts degree and £30 instead of £7 for that of Bachelor of Arts. Although the practice existed in the sixteenth century it did not become frequent until the seventeenth century. The grand compounder wearing a scarlet Convocation 'habit' (*habitus coccineus*), together

---

[1] *Statutes of the Colleges of Oxford for the Royal Commission*, i. 29.
[2] *Statutes of the Colleges of Oxford for the Royal Commission*, i. 44–45 (R. 22, *De communi annua vestium liberata*) and pp. 45–46 (R. 23, *De habitu sociorum et scholarium de collegio*).
[3] H. E. Salter, *Registrum Annalium Collegii Mertonensis* (O.H.S., 1921), p. 388.
[4] *Statutes of the Colleges of Oxford for the Royal Commission*, iii. 64, cap. 30 (*De vestitu, ornatu*).
[5] *Statutes of the Colleges of Oxford for the Royal Commission*, iii. 62, § 17.

with the gown and hood of his new degree, had his own procession, in which the vice-chancellor, the proctors, and any
members of his college who wished joined, from his college to
the Convocation House, in later times to the Sheldonian, and
back again, while the bells of St. Mary's rang. Before the seventeenth century a trumpet was blown by a *famulus* who walked
before him. He was supposed ever afterwards to wear a scarlet
'habit' with his gown and hood, but usually he obtained a
dispensation which freed him from this necessity.[1]

3. *Boots and shoes of academical significance.* In the Middle Ages
foot-gear of various shapes as befitting various degrees formed
part of academical costume.[2] *Caligae*, which were black or nearly
black boots, are mentioned in the statutes before 1350 as being
worn by regent and non-regent masters.[3] In a statute of before
1477 it is ordered that boots shall be worn by doctors, bachelors,
and inceptors in the Faculties of Theology and Canon Law,
while 'pynsons' (slippers) were to be worn by all other doctors,
masters, bachelors, and inceptors.[4]

In the seventeenth century those who took the degree of
Doctor of Divinity wore boots for the occasion,[5] while Masters
of Arts wore 'shoes and slops'.[6] In 1733 inceptors wore boots
or shoes, according to whether they were taking a divinity or
other degree, though they wore them only for the ceremony,
but after this year nothing more is heard of such a distinction.[7]
In their original form the boots (*caligae*) reached to the middle
of the leg; but the 'pynsons' were like sandals and later like
slippers. The latter appear in Latin under the various terms,
socculi, sandalia, sotularia, crepidae, and *pincernae.*[8]

4. *Gloves.* Gloves were originally regarded as betokening

[1] A. Clark, *Register of the University of Oxford,* ii (O.H.S., 1887), pt. 1, pp. 64–65;
A. Clark, *Wood,* iii. 346–7, where is to be found a full account of the ceremony in
1690. Grand-compounding virtually ended in 1821 (J. S. Reynolds, *Evangelicals at
Oxford,* p. 179), but was not formally abolished till 1857 (G. V. Cox, *Recollections,*
p. 236). There were also grand compounders at Cambridge (G. Peacock, *Observations on the Statutes of Cambridge,* app. A, p. xx and n. 3).
[2] H. C. Maxwell Lyte, *History of the University of Oxford,* p. 424.
[3] S. Gibson, pp. 58 and 288.   [4] S. Gibson, pp. 288–9; J. Walker, i. 21.
[5] Oxf. Bodl. Libr. MS. Top. Gen. c. 25, fo. 199 b.
[6] T. Hearne, xi. 229.
[7] T. Hearne, loc. cit. Until the early years of the nineteenth century an annual
formal dispensation from the necessity of inceptors using them was published
(G. V. Cox. p. 414; C. Wordsworth, p. 479).
[8] A. Clark, *Register of the University of Oxford,* ii, pt. 1, p. 87.

dignity or learning.[1] They were to be given to the vice-chancellor and proctors by new Bachelors of Civil Law at the time
of their presentation, according to a statute of 1588.[2] In 1597
incepting Doctors of Theology, Law, and Medicine were to
present gloves through the beadle of whichever faculty each
was a member to the chief officers who took part in the Act,
and to all doctors who attended if suitably dressed, and even to
those who had a reasonable excuse for absence.[3] In the plates
of G. Edwards (1674) the vice-chancellor and the Doctor
of Divinity wear gloves,[4] and there are portraits of Doctors of
Divinity wearing gloves well into the nineteenth century.

5. *The mourning gown.* The mourning gown, exactly the same
as the canonical gown of the Church of England in the seventeenth and eighteenth centuries (e.g. the figure of the cleric
with punch ladle in Hogarth's *Modern Midnight Conversation*
(1735)),[5] was an open full cloth gown with pudding sleeves,[6]
and appeared at Oxford after the Restoration. It was to be
used, as Anthony à Wood correctly used it in 1667,[7] on the
occasion of the death of a personal friend, together with gloves
which had been presented to the mourner. It was to be worn
also at the time of mourning for the death of a monarch.[8]

The wearing of it was much abused, for those who, like
commoners, were dissatisfied with their sleeveless gowns,
seized upon it with avidity, so that they might pass for graduates.
Wood complains of this more than once, as in 1675.[9] After this
the practice became so general an abuse that the authorities
took notice. One of the proctors of 1684 denounced it publicly,[10]
and it was condemned officially in 1689.[11] Even those of standing, such as members of Convocation, took to wearing mourning gowns for no good reason, as is recorded in 1680 and 1693,
with the result that those who appeared in Convocation wearing
such gowns were denied their votes.[12] After 1693 nothing is
heard of the wearing of mourning gowns in the university.

[1] S. W. Beck, *Gloves*, p. 56.   [2] A. Clark, ii, pt. 1, p. 115.
[3] A. Clark, ii, pt. 1, p. 121; S. Gibson, pp. 455–6.
[4] Oxf. Bodl. Libr. MS. Wood 276 B, xix, 2, 3.
[5] J. Ireland and J. Nichols, i, pl. opp. p. 184.
[6] D. Loggan, pl. x, no. 15.   [7] A. Clark, *Wood*, ii. 102.
[8] Ibid. iii. 133.   [9] Ibid. ii. 304.
[10] Ibid. iii. 92.   [11] Oxf. Bodl. Libr., MS. Wood 276 A, no. ccclxxxviii, 1.
[12] A. Clark, *Wood*, ii. 502; and iii. 424.

6. *Bands.* Bands originated in the falling collar of the earlier seventeenth century, but they did not become academically significant until they had been abandoned as an ordinary lay fashion after the Restoration. At the universities they then came to be regarded as an item of academical dress and all of every degree and order wear them in Loggan's plates (1675).[1] They were made of holland (i.e. linen) which was bleached, the two tongues being in the seventeenth century short and broad, but in the eighteenth century longer and narrower, descending parallel and not pointing outwards as they have often come to do in modern times.[2] Cravats were absolutely forbidden at this period, and even Charles II's bastard, the Earl of Southampton, was in 1678 refused the right to wear a cravat instead of bands,[3] but laced bands are worn by Doctors of Medicine in G. Edwards's collection (1674). In 1713, however, William Croft, D.Mus., wears an ordinary cravat probably because not a member of Convocation.[4]

In the new statutes of 1770 all are reminded always to wear bands,[5] and in Roberts's water-colours of 1792 all do so, doctors (except for Doctors of Music) and proctors wearing them with a plain stock, non-doctors and Doctors of Music over a cravat of contemporary fashion.[6] The bands worn with the cravat are very small, but are of the full length when worn with the stock.[7] Until the turn of the century bands were always worn, but by 1807 their use was becoming more and more confined to formal occasions.[8] In later times as a sign of mourning, bands with a double pleat running down the middle of each wing were worn, and still are.

7. *The surplice.* The surplice was in 1603 enjoined upon fellows and scholars on the foundation of their colleges for chapel,[9] and this was repeated in the Laudian statutes. It was very full and long with long pointed sleeves like those of the gown of a Bachelor of Arts.[10] In the later seventeenth century

---

[1] D. Loggan, op. cit., pl. x.
[2] A pair of holland bands (or more correctly 'a band') cost 1s. in 1683 (J. R. Magrath, ii. 122).   [3] J. R. Magrath, i. 245–6.
[4] Oxf. Bodl. Libr. MS. Top. Oxon. c. 16, § 101.
[5] G. R. M. Ward, ii. 12.   [6] Oxf. Bodl. Libr. MS. Top. Oxon. d. 58.
[7] For the difference between the bands of doctors and others see *The Letters of Radcliffe and James, 1755–83* (O.H.S.), p. 72.   [8] J. S. Reynolds, p. 79.
[9] M. E. C. Walcott, p. 37 (Canon 17).
[10] Oxf. Bodl. Libr. MS. Top. Oxon. d. 58, 17–18.

it was opened down the front and fastened with a button at the throat. This was for the convenience of putting it on.[1]

8. *The attempt to abolish academical dress during the Commonwealth.* While on his visit to Oxford in the summer of 1654 John Evelyn noticed that the old ceremonial was still maintained,[2] but in 1658 the most outright republicans and presbyterians were coming to the fore in the university, and as those who would have opposed the abolition of academicals, 'the antediluvian Cavaliers' who had managed to keep their fellowships 'never appeared in Convocation', it looked as though such dress was doomed. One of the proctors of that year, however, Walter Pope, stood out against this, rallied his friends to defeat the attempt in Convocation, and triumphantly succeeded in preserving gowns, hoods, and caps, and the 'distinctions of Degrees'.[3]

[1] L. H. D. Buxton and S. Gibson, p. 37.
[2] *Diary of John Evelyn*, ed. E. S. de Beer, iii. 105.
[3] W. Pope, *The Life of Seth*, pp. 34–35, 40, and 41–42.

4

II. CAMBRIDGE

(a) The Chancellor

DURING the whole of the Middle Ages and beyond them the chancellor had no special official costume, but wore the dress of whatever degree he held, nearly always that of Doctor of Divinity. Even after the Reformation when laymen began to assume this office in place of clerics, their dress as chancellor was markedly similar to the dress which their clerical predecessors wore. The three chancellor's seals which range from the late thirteenth century to 1580 show the chancellor in three stages of the development of the dress of Doctors of Divinity, and until this year the general medieval characteristics of the costume remained.

In the original seal, first used in 1291, the chancellor wears a stiff and apexed *pileus* and a *cappa clausa*,[1] while in the second seal, used from about 1420, the seated chancellor wears a small round *pileus*, a small hood close round the neck, a miniver 'shoulder piece' joined to it, and a full and loose *cappa clausa*.[2] In the third seal, which is still used today and dates from 1580, he wears a *cappa clausa*, a thick and large miniver 'shoulder piece' with all the fur showing, a hood attached to it and lying close round the neck, and a rigid and pointed *pileus* like a top-shell in shape, with flaps over the ears.[3]

A great change appears in another seal also of 1580. In this the chancellor wears the recently altered dress of Doctors of Divinity, showing the great influence of Tudor lay fashion. He appears in a festal robe with pudding-sleeves (i.e. baggy sleeves,

[1] W. H. St. J. Hope, *Seals of the University of Cambridge*, pl. ii, fig. 1; A. F .Leach, *The Schools of Medieval England*, pl. opp. p. 156.

[2] W. H. St. J. Hope, pl. ii, fig. 2.

[3] W. H. St. J. Hope, pl. iii; V. de Viriville, *Histoire de l'Instruction Publique*, p. 103.

loose at the elbow and tight at the wrist). The old *cappa* has been reduced to a shortened cape worn over the robe but under a large miniver 'shoulder piece'. This 'shoulder piece' covers the shoulders and the upper part of the arms, and thus almost entirely covers the cape. The head-dress is a *pileus quadratus*.[1]

In the early seventeenth century the chancellor's dress was entirely changed, and he at last had a true dress of office which owed nothing to the costume of a degree. It consisted of a black brocaded winged-sleeved robe with a train, the whole being decorated with gold braid. This dress is depicted in R. Harraden's *Costumes of the University of Cambridge* (1803). Such a dress, hardly academical but rather a dress of dignity, was worn also by such important officials of the realm as the lord chancellor, the lord chamberlain, and the speaker of the House of Commons.

(b) The Vice-Chacellor

As H. Rashdall[2] says, the costume of the Cambridge vice-chancellor was the *cappa clausa* dress of a doctor. The reason for this was the same as that mentioned in regard to the dress of the chancellor. The costume of both chancellor and vice-chancellor differed in no way from one another, as far as one can say owing to a complete lack of records, until the seventeenth century when, as we have seen, the chancellor began to wear his special official dress.

When that occurred the vice-chancellor continued to wear the pudding-sleeved robe with the shortened *cappa* and the large miniver hood which he had used earlier. By the end of the eighteenth century the dress was still much the same as before, for in Harraden's collection it consists of a square black cap,[3] a scarlet cloth robe with pudding-sleeves, and over this a scarlet cape, the shortened *cappa*, which now comes down square over the sleeves of the robe. The robe is edged with miniver, and a huge miniver hood, developed from the original 'shoulder piece', covering the shoulders entirely, is worn over all the other dress. The only significant changes are that both robe and cape are open right down the front as a convenience for putting them on, so that a cassock can be seen underneath, and the cape is now

---

[1] W. H. St. J. Hope, pl. ii, fig. 3.
[2] *Universities of Europe in the Middle Ages*, iii. 392.
[3] Cf. W. H. St. J. Hope, pl. ii, fig. 3.

PLATE 13

Cambridge Vice-Chancellor, 1803

square in front and longer than it had been in the sixteenth century (Pl. 13).

The vice-chancellor had worn a round black bonnet with a gold cord in 1665, according to J. W. Clark's transcript of Bedell Buck's *Book of Ceremonies*,[1] but this practice does not seem to have long survived.

(c) The Proctors

In the seal of the late thirteenth century already mentioned the two proctors standing one on each side of the chancellor wear coifs, short hoods falling down a little way behind, and sleeveless tabards open down the sides from the arms.[2] In the fifteenth century seal[3] the two proctors are bare-headed, and their sleeveless tabards, which were plain in the earlier example are pleated.

In the 1580 university seal, which is that at present in use,[4] the two proctors both carry a book of the statutes. Their gowns are full and closed with bell-shaped sleeves, while their fur-lined hoods are very large. The right-hand figure, the senior proctor, wears a large tippet on the left shoulder falling equally before and behind, but the junior proctor is without one. Both wear small turn-down collars.

In the print of Andrew Willet (d. 1621) as a proctor, he is shown wearing a gown with full bell sleeves, open in front and with silk facings, a skull-cap, a ruff, and a very square-shaped miniver hood, fastened far down in front;[5] but in D. Loggan's *Cantabrigia Illustrata* (1690) the proctor (No. 12) wears an ordinary Master of Arts gown and a Regent Master of Arts hood with the white silk lining fully displayed, but with this difference, that there is a large black square of material, a remnant of the medieval *bourrelet-chausse*, hanging behind which, attached to the main hood, lies underneath it and falls below, and is edged all round with white silk. This was the *Ad Clerum* habit, which was the less formal dress for proctors.

The formal one, the 'Congregation habit', consisted of the

---

[1] Cambridge, Univ. Libr. MS. Add. 5107, fo. 31; E. C. Clarke, art. 'College Caps and Doctors' Hats' in *Archaeological Journal*, lxi (1904), 64.

[2] W. H. St. J. Hope, pl. ii, fig. 1.

[3] W. H. St. J. Hope, pl. ii, fig. 2.

[4] W. H. St. J. Hope, pl. iii; V. de Viriville, p. 103.

[5] S. Clark, *Marrow of Ecclesiastical History*, p. 448. Four prints of this in the first state are in the Ashmolean Museum (Hope Collection).

master's gown, a black silk pleated 'shoulder piece' which covered the shoulders, known as the 'ruff', and an ordinary regent master's hood, that is with the white silk lining displayed but with no square of material attached to it.[1] A black square cap with a tuft was usually worn; but they wore in 1665 when presiding at the Act a round bonnet with a gold cord.[2]

In Harraden's plate of 1803 the proctor is shown in his *Ad Clerum* dress, consisting of a black silk master's gown (earlier it had been of cloth), a black square cap of cloth with a black silk tassel, bands, a regent-master's hood with the addition of the square of stuff which lies flat under the hood's liripipe, and a black breeches suit. The two halves of the hood are seen to be folded over one another in front, a shape which was obtained by bringing the two long ends over the shoulder, folding them, and inserting a hook and eye where the edges crossed.[3]

In T. Uwins's illustrations of Cambridge dresses of 1815 we see the proctor in 'Congregation habit' consisting of master's gown, with a cassock and sash, the ordinary regent-master's displayed hood without the square of material, and the 'ruff'. In addition was worn a black stuff tippet falling equally before and behind fastened with a button on the top of the right shoulder. It was exactly the same as that noticed as being worn by the senior proctor on the seal of 1580, but was then worn on the left shoulder.[4] According to H. Gunning, a senior esquire bedell, who in 1828 brought out an edition of Bedell Wall's *Ceremonies observed in the Senate House*, the proctors wore 'ruffs' and displayed hoods at Congregation only,[5] and the *Ad Clerum* dress, that is, the squared hood and no 'ruff' on other occasions.[6]

(d) *The Taxor*

The original function of the taxor was the taxing of halls of residence. Later his duties approximated to those of the clerks of the market at Oxford.[7] There are no early references of any kind to the dress of this official, but in the seventeenth century,

---

[1] J. R. Tanner, *Historical Register*, p. 197.
[2] E. C. Clarke, art. cit., lxi, 64.
[3] *Notes and Queries*, 2nd ser. vi. 211.
[4] W. Combe and T. Uwins, *History of the University of Cambridge*, ii. 313 and pl. at end.   [5] H. Gunning, *Ceremonies*, p. 15.
[6] H. Gunning, pp. 28, 41, 61, and 119.
[7] H. Rashdall, iii. 287.

according to Loggan's costume plate (figure No. 11), it still retained a medieval character. Over a master's gown he wore a black silk 'shoulder piece' of the same nature as the 'ruff' of proctors but not pleated, and lined with white silk. This 'shoulder piece' was so long that in front it reached to the waist and behind to the back of the knees. In 1815 taxors wore a 'squared' hood.[1]

(e) Doctors of Divinity

The earliest mention of the dress of this degree is to be found in a university statute of 1414, which in the following year was incorporated in a royal ordinance directed to the university by Henry V. From this we see that it had come to consist of the *cappa clausa* for all but informal occasions when the *pallium* might be used,[2] the *pileus*, though different from that of the lay doctors,[3] and hoods and 'shoulder pieces' lined with a fur of good quality.[4] Examples of this dress showing the *roba* or *supertunica*, the *cappa clausa* over this, the furred hood and 'shoulder piece', and the small apexed *pileus* appear on the brasses of Richard Billingford, D.D., 1442, in St. Benet's Church, Cambridge; of an unknown Doctor of Divinity, about 1490, in St. Mary's-the-Less, Cambridge; and of William Towne, D.D., 1495, in King's College, Cambridge.[5]

In 1533 the *Act for the Reformation of Excess in Apparel* regulated the dress of both the English universities. In common with other doctors, Doctors of Divinity were allowed silk linings to their gown (i.e. the *roba* worn underneath the *cappa*), and black satin linings to their *cappa*. Their outer dress might be of scarlet, murrey, or violet, and they were allowed the use of all kinds of rich fur for facings or linings, the fur or the silk being presumably used according to season.[6] That the favoured colour of the outer dress of Doctors of Divinity at Cambridge was red and the favoured fur miniver in the early sixteenth century is exemplified in the articles mentioned in the inventory of the goods of

[1] W. Combe and T. Uwins, ii. 313.

[2] Cambridge, Univ. Libr. MS. Mm. 4.47, § 147, fo. 228 (*De habitubus et insigniis Magistrorum*); J. Heywood, *Collection of Statutes*, p. 159.

[3] Cambridge, Univ. Libr. MS. Mm. 4.47, 148, fos. 229 (23) ff.

[4] Cambridge, Univ. Libr. MS. Dd. 4.35, fos. 75 ff.; *Communications, Cambridge Antiquarian Soc.*, 8vo ser. iv [1854], ¶ iii, p. 87.

[5] H. Druitt, *Manual*, p. 127; E. T. Beaumont, *Academical Habit*, pl. opp. p. 7; H. W. Macklin, *Monumental Brasses*, p. 51.

[6] C. H. Cooper, *Annals*, i. 355; C. Wordsworth, *Social Life*, p. 489.

William Melton, D.D., of Cambridge, in 1496, Chancellor of York, who died in 1528, as 'a gowne of rede scarlet, furred with menyvere and a hood';[1] and there is another example of the same dress in the will of William Elistonn, sub-Dean of York (d. 1548).[2] It was a period of rapid change in academical dress, and this can be particularly well seen in the brass (Pl. 12 b) of the Cambridge Doctor of Divinity, William Taylard, 1530, in All Saints' Church, Huntingdon. He wears a Tudor cap with side pieces, a small hood and a 'shoulder piece', and a closed roba with moderately hanging sleeves.[3]

Regents of this degree were ordered to wear a pileus quadratus in common with regents of other faculties by command of the parliamentary visitors in 1549,[4] and this order was repeated in 1559.[5]

In 1560 Doctors of Divinity in common with doctors of other faculties and Bachelors of Divinity were allowed to have silk in their hoods when they required a cooler dress, instead of having fur hoods at all seasons. The undress gown for all was to be of the 'priest's' shape (i.e. pudding-sleeved), or of the 'Turkey' variety (i.e. the 'lay' type either with falling collar and false sleeves, or with a yoke and short glove sleeves). The colours of these gowns were to be black or 'London russet', a kind of brown.[6] Here then we have the official recognition of the ordinary undress gown which during the seventeenth century developed into the familiar master's gown, in this case a 'Turkey' gown with a yoke and glove sleeves, and it is worth noticing that at the present day Doctors of Divinity at Cambridge may use a short bell-sleeved gown as an alternative to the master's.[7]

Ten years later Doctors of Divinity were affected as were others by the statute De Vestitu Scholarium,[8] which ordered that for all degrees the gown should be ankle-length, that the hood should be constantly worn, that the neck-wear should be of a

[1] Testamenta Eboracensia, v. 253 [Surtees Soc. lxxix].
[2] Testamenta Eboracensia, vi. 198 [Surtees Soc. cvi].
[3] E. R. Suffling, English Church Brasses, p. 196, fig. 127.
[4] J. D. Mullinger, Hist. Univ. of Cambridge, ii. 392, n. 1.
[5] J. Heywood, p. 241, ¶ 10.
[6] C. H. Cooper, ii. 161–2; B.M. MS. Cole xlii, fos. 290–1, i.e. Add. 5843.
[7] The pudding-sleeved gown was preserved as late as 1803 as the dress of fellows of King's. The mourning gown originated in this.
[8] J. Lamb, Documents, pp. 341–2, cap. xlvi; G. Dyer, Privileges, i. 195.

priestly character, and that the cap should be square. Those in Orders were to wear a pleated cassock with a collar.[1]

The festal robe for Doctors of Divinity is first directly mentioned in a statute of 1578, which orders that it should be used by all doctors on scarlet days.[2] In 1585 all doctors were allowed full-length facings on their gowns, and the use of silk in their hoods is confirmed,[3] and their hoods might be lined and edged with miniver. In 1588 Lord Burghley, who had been responsible as chancellor for the above enactments of 1578 and 1585, ordered Doctors of Divinity to wear scarlet cloth or black velvet scarves. At the same time he mentioned that the outside of all hoods of whatever degree was to be made of cloth, and pointed out that all graduates must wear the square cap.[4]

In Bedell Buck's book (1665), *Rules for Magna Congregatio or Black Assembly*, the scarlet days and other occasions for festal dress are mentioned.[5] By this time the various other dresses of the Doctor of Divinity had become what they have since been.

What these were can be seen from Loggan's plate in his *Cantabrigia Illustrata* (1690). No. 15 shows the undress consisting of a square black cap with a tuft, a cassock with a sash, and the Master of Arts gown; No. 16 shows the chapel dress, long full surplice with tapering sleeves and full hood; and No. 20 is the Congregation dress. This consists of the same square cap, a scarlet garment open half-way down the front, which was originally placed there to allow for the passage of the arms, the opening being edged with miniver, and over this a miniver-furred hood like a shoulder piece covering the shoulders and reaching half-way down the back.[6] The festal dress (No. 18) consists of an open bell-sleeved robe, the sleeves being folded back at the wrists, a scarf, and a square cap.

From the eighteenth century the Congregation dress was less and less worn by doctors until it came to be used only by professors when presenting candidates for degrees. The cassock

[1] Cambridge, Univ. Libr. MS. Mm. 4.51, fo. 243.
[2] C. H. Cooper, ii. 359; G. Dyer, i. 221. See also p. 118, n. 5.
[3] C. H. Cooper, ii. 410–12.
[4] H. Ellis, *Original Letters*, iii. 26, no. ccxxvi ('Ld. Treasurer Burleigh to the University of Cambridge as their Chancellor for the Reformation of Apparel', B.M. MS. Harl. 704, fo. 199).
[5] Cambridge, Univ. Libr. MS. Mm. 1.53, fo. 139; Cambridge, Univ. Libr. MS. Add. 5107, fo. 28.
[6] Cf. the dress of the chancellor and vice-chancellor.

and a broad silk cincture were worn by Doctors of Divinity with all their costumes.

There are two interesting eighteenth-century portraits showing the full dress (or festal) robe. In the portrait of Sir Thomas Gooch, Bart., Bishop of Ely, by an anonymous artist, the scarlet cloth robe is lined with white silk, and the sleeves are not held back by cord and button, as was later the case.[1] Changes are apparent in the second portrait, that of Anthony Shepherd (d. 1796) by L. F. G. van der Puyl, dated 1784. Here the cord and button on the sleeve are to be seen and the robe is lined with scarlet silk (Pl. 15).[2]

By 1803, the year of Harraden's costume book, the colour of the silk lining and the recently introduced facings of the festal robe had come to be salmon-pink, and the full round-shaped scarlet cloth hood, worn only with the chapel dress, was also lined with silk of this colour. The festal robe had by this time come to be used in Congregation instead of the proper Congregation dress. The cord and button had doubtless been introduced in order to keep the hands free of the large sleeves.

A loose plate of the full dress by William Miller (1805) is of much better quality than any in Harraden's collection. It depicts a black square cap with a tassel (the tassel was introduced at Cambridge as at Oxford during the eighteenth century), and the scarlet festal robe lined with cherry-coloured silk, which is incorrect, the long full tapering sleeves being fastened up by means of button and cord. With this is worn a black scarf. The peculiarity of the plate consists in its having in the background a group of Oxford buildings, although this is definitely a Cambridge dress.[3]

T. Uwins's plates (1815) and W. Combe's text give us once more the four dresses of the Doctor of Divinity. First, the festal dress consisted of the open scarlet cloth robe faced with pink silk shot with either pink or violet, the bell sleeves being lined with the same material of the same colour and looped up with a black button and cord. With this was worn cassock, sash, and scarf. The second dress, the Congregation dress, or dress of business, consisted of the scarlet cloth *cappa*, by this time opened

---

[1] J. W. Goodison, *Catalogue of Cambridge Portraits*, i. 24, and pl. xi, no. 27.
[2] J. W. Goodison, i. 28, and pl. xvi, no. 32.
[3] Oxford, Bodl. Libr. MS. G.A. Oxon. a.72, leaf 21.

right down the front, sleeveless and without holes for the passage for the arms, and so worn like a cloak, fastened at the neck with a bow of scarlet ribbon. It fell to the ground and was edged over three-quarters of the way down the front with white fur. The miniver hood is of the same shape as in 1690, but it is shorter at the back. The third, the undress is not illustrated, but is said to be the pudding-sleeved gown and the cassock, sash, and scarf, although the master's gown was often preferred. The fourth dress was the chapel dress, the same as before described.[1] It should be noticed that the hood worn with the chapel dress was full and rounded, of exactly the same shape as that worn by Oxford doctors.

(f) Doctors of Canon Law

The dress of this degree which existed until the ending of the study of Canon Law at the Reformation,[2] although it was revived for a short time during the reign of Mary Tudor,[3] was, as at Oxford, of the same character as that of the Doctor of Divinity. Thus in 1414 we find that Doctors of Canon Law in common with Masters of Theology and of Arts are to wear the *cappa clausa* for all formal occasions, although at the same time the more comfortable *pallium* is mentioned as also allowable, although less acceptable.[4] Their head-dress was to be the *pileus*.[5] With this was to be worn a hood of the familiar pattern with its 'shoulder piece' lined with the best kind of fur, as runs the royal order of Henry V (1415).[6]

There are no other records of the dress of this degree.

(g) Doctors of Laws (LL.D.)

The dress of Doctors of Laws was in 1414 ordered to be the *cappa manicata* edged with fur certainly, but not lined with it unless the doctors particularly wished it so.[7] They were to wear

---

[1] W. Combe and T. Uwins, ii. 312–13 and pls. at end.
[2] C. H. Cooper, i. 375.
[3] J. Romilly, *Graduati Cantabrigienses*, following p. vi.
[4] Cambridge, Univ. Libr. MS. Mm. 4.47, § 147, fo. 228 (*De Habitubus et insigniis Magistrorum*); J. Heywood, p. 159.
[5] Cambridge, Univ. Libr. MS. Mm. 4.47, § 148, fos. 229 (23) ff.
[6] Cambridge, Univ. Libr. MS. Dd. 4.35, fos. 75 ff.; *Communications, Cambridge Antiquarian Soc.*, 8vo ser. iv (1854), ¶ iii, p. 87.
[7] Cambridge, Univ. Libr. MS. Mm. 4.47, § 147, fo. 228.

this as opposed to the *cappa clausa* of those of Divinity and Canon
Law to show their inferiority of position.[1] Their head-dress was
the *pileus*.[2] In accordance with the statutes for the *studium* of
Cambridge made by Hugh de Balsham, Bishop of Ely, in 1276,[3]
incepting Doctors of Laws were to wear a red *cappa manicata*.[4] In
the same statute Doctors of Laws are granted the use of the
pallium as a secondary dress, and when later this *pallium* was dispensed with they were left with the *roba*, which had been worn
underneath it, as the outer dress, which developed into the
undress gown, which in its turn was discarded for a lay Tudor
one. The development was the same as at Oxford. A good
example of this secondary dress is to be seen in the brass of Eudo
de la Zouch, LL.D., 1414, at St. John's College, Cambridge.

In common with other doctors they were ordered to wear
silk linings in their dress according to the Act of Parliament of
1533, and the cloth of their full dress was to be of scarlet, murrey,
or violet; they were also allowed a choice of costly furs with
which to face or line it.[5] Scarlet was always favoured.[6]

In 1558/9 the square cap was enjoined for them as for others,[7]
and in 1576 we hear of insistence upon their wearing the festal
robe on suitable occasions.[8] In 1585 they were affected by
Burghley's important statutes in that they were to have full-
length facings of the same colour as the gown of such stuff as
silk. These undress gowns, by this time open, were to be of 'sad
color', and as had been enacted in 1560 were to be either false
sleeved or of the pudding-sleeved variety.[9] As laymen they took
to the first of these shapes.

As to the head-dress, we have seen that the *pileus quadratus* was
insisted upon for graduates and for those scholars on foundations in 1559, which followed the enactment of Edward VI's
visitors of 1549.[10]

[1] J. Heywood, loc. cit.
[2] Cambridge, Univ. Libr. MS. Mm. 4.47, § 148, fos. 229 (23), ff.
[3] B.M. MS. Harl. 7032, ¶ 146.
[4] Cambridge, Univ. Libr. MS. Mm. 4.47, § 147, fo. 228. This dress is worn by
the LL.D. on the extreme right in the illuminated initial of the Confirmatory
Charter of Cambridge (1291-2) in the University Archives, Cambridge.
[5] C. H. Cooper, i. 355.   [6] J. R. Tanner, p. 194.
[7] J. Heywood, p. 241, ¶ 10; J. Lamb, p. 290.
[8] C. H. Cooper, ii. 359; G. Dyer, i. 221.
[9] C. H. Cooper, ii. 161-2 and 410-12; B.M. MS. Cole xlii, fo. 29, i.e. B.M. MS.
Add. 5843.   [10] J. Heywood, p. 241, ¶10; J. D. Mullinger, ii. 392, n. 1.

For full-dress a bonnet with a small brim and a low round pleated top was worn by Doctors of Laws and other lay doctors from the middle of the sixteenth century certainly.[1] A gold cord on these bonnets is mentioned by Bedell Buck in 1665. E. C. Clarke believed that this cord was not a mere decoration but was a symbol of authority.[2] It seems more likely that these gold hat-bands or cords were simply adopted from lay fashion, for late in Elizabeth's reign gold hat-bands were considered a distinguishing feature of the lay dress of noblemen and gentlemen. In Ben Jonson's *Every Man out of his Humour* (1599) a gold cable hat-band is mentioned.[3] Doctors had some pretensions to social standing.

We can see from Loggan (1690) how the dresses of this degree had become stabilized by the later seventeenth century. The undress (No. 14) consists of the black winged-sleeved gown decorated with tassels in rows and with a flap collar much like the Oxford equivalent, and with this is worn surprisingly enough a round bonnet. The Congregation dress (No. 19) is a scarlet dress, closed in front and with holes at the sides for the passage of the arms like the Oxford Convocation habit, with a large hood lined with fur, the flat liripipe of which hangs down almost to the foot of the dress, and a round bonnet; and the festal dress (No. 17) consists of a full scarlet robe with large bell sleeves folded back a little way at the wrists, and a round bonnet. In using the bonnet in the first two instances Burghley's order, to the effect that then the square cap should be worn, was ignored.

After this time the various costumes for the degree changed little. In Uwins's coloured plates of 1815 we see, first, the festal robe of scarlet differing from the festal robe of Doctors of Divinity only in the sleeves being looped up with pink cords and buttons instead of black ones. With this is worn the round black bonnet with a gold cord, and a hood is incorrectly worn over the festal robe. Next, the Congregation dress is shown, which consists of the scarlet cloth *cappa* of the same shape as that of the

---

[1] E. C. Clarke, art. cit., lxi. 33, believed 'in fault of proof to the contrary' that the bonnet appeared at Cambridge in the fifteenth century, but there is no evidence to support him. It was introduced into academical dress from lay fashion.

[2] E. C. Clarke, art. cit., lxi. 64.

[3] J. A. Repton, art. 'Observations on the Fashions of Hats' in *Archaeologia*, xxiv (1832), 184.

Doctor of Divinity. It is faced with miniver and is worn with a scarlet hood lined with miniver of the same shape as worn in 1690. The bonnet is also worn with this dress. The undress, with which a black tasselled square cap is worn, consists of a plain black silk gown (the tufts having vanished) fastened up in front with two pieces of black ribbon to form a bow, the 'strings' of later times.[1] The arms came through a gash, of which the upper part was cut in the shape of an inverted V, from which a seam ran up to the shoulder. The sleeves hung down in square-ended false panels, and the gown had a square flap collar.[2]

(h) Doctors of Medicine

The degree of Doctor of Medicine was instituted after that of Doctor of Laws, the earliest doctorate in a secular faculty, and holders of it wore the same dress as Doctors of Laws.[3] Regents in Medicine are mentioned in 1414, when like legist regents they were ordered to wear the *cappa manicata*, edged with fur or lined with it if they so preferred,[4] but there is at this time no record of inceptors for this degree being ordered to wear a red *cappa* as inceptors in the Faculty of Laws were ordered to do.

From then on in all particulars the history of their costume is that of Doctors of Laws, and so the scarlet festal robe came to them in the sixteenth century, and at the time of Queen Elizabeth's visit to Cambridge in 1564 Doctors of 'Physic' wore this robe with a hood to match lined with miniver.[5] The first evidence that we have of the round bonnet worn by holders of this degree is the 17th century picture of a university procession by Cobbould after Bedell Stokys (1590) in the Registry at Cambridge (Pl. 14).[6]

In Loggan (1690) the dress is the same as that of Doctors of Laws,[7] and consists of the festal robe, the Congregation *cappa* dress, and the undress gown, a bonnet with a gold cord being used in the first two cases and without one in the third.

Late in the eighteenth century, however, while Doctors of Laws continued to wear for undress the plain black silk gown

---

[1] For an account of 'strings' see under § (j), the description of Loggan's illustration of a Master of Arts.   [2] W. Combe and T. Uwins, ii. 312–13.

[3] Cf. *Cambridge Grace Book Δ*, p. 28.

[4] Cambridge, Univ. Libr. MS. Mm. 4.47, § 147, fo. 228.

[5] B.M. MS. Cole xliv, fo. 382, i.e. MS. Add. 5845.

[6] E. C. Clarke, art. cit. lxi. 62.   [7] Nos. 14, 17, and 19.

PLATE 14

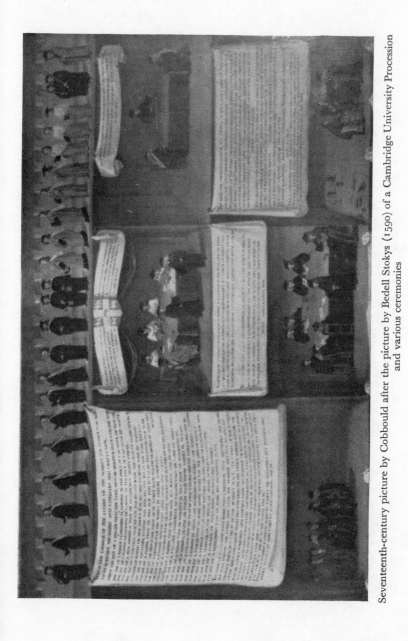

Seventeenth-century picture by Cobbould after the picture by Bedell Stokys (1590) of a Cambridge University Procession and various ceremonies

Anthony Shepherd, D.D. (d. 1796) by L. F. G. van der Puyl

(without tufts since the previous century), Doctors of Medicine had theirs worked with ornaments of black cross and bead braiding on the upper part of the false sleeve, and with plain braid on the facings and on the flap collar. The engraving of the portrait by J. Page of R. G. Clobury, M.D. (d. 1800),[1] provides a good illustration of this.[2] The change must have come about after 1780, for in John Downman's chalk drawing of Thomas Okes, M.D., of this year, Okes wears a plain silk gown exactly the same as the Doctor of Laws undress gown described above except that no 'strings' can be seen.[3]

(i) Doctors of Music

As was the case at Oxford holders of degrees in Music stood outside university affairs in an ambiguous position. The degree of Doctor of Music was instituted in the early sixteenth century. All that we know of their early dress is the statement in 1545 that an inceptor for the doctorate is to appear in the dress of a Doctor of Medicine,[4] from which we may conclude that by grace and not by right they shared the dress of the Doctors of Laws and of Medicine. This was not the case later in the century, and by 1578 when Burghley ordered the full scarlet festal dress to be worn by doctors on scarlet days,[5] they had perhaps taken to their full dress of white brocade lined with purple silk.[6] In all probability it was as a result of their inferior position as not of necessity being members even of the Black or Non-Regent Assembly, that led to their having a festal dress with no scarlet in it. In 1605 on presentation to this degree by grace, candidates wore the hood and gown of Bachelors of Arts, afterwards assuming the doctoral dress.[7]

In Loggan (No. 13) they wear the round bonnet, the brocaded robe and a hood to match.

In Harraden's plates (1803) this full dress is again shown, and consists of a white satin robe and hood, both lined with crimson silk, and a round black velvet bonnet with a gold cord and tassel. The large tapering sleeves of the robe are caught up

---

[1] Oxford, Ashmolean Museum (Hope Collection).
[2] See also W. Combe and T. Uwins, ii. 312–13.
[3] Cambridge, Fitzw. Mus., no. 1943.   [4] Cambridge Grace Book Δ, p. 28.
[5] C. H. Cooper, ii. 359; G. Dyer, i. 221.
[6] Cf. J. R. Tanner, p. 194.
[7] Cambridge, Univ. Libr. MS. Mm. 5.50 (Adam Wall MS. vol. l), fo. 68.

above the wrist with a crimson cord and button, and the robe, instead of having a yoke as do the other festal robes, has a black velvet flap collar.

Again in Uwins's plate of 1815 the full dress robe is of white damask or satin and the sleeves are lined with crimson satin, while the hood is of white damask lined with crimson satin. The bonnet is the same as in 1803. The undress is described as being the Master of Arts gown, and by grace, though not by right, the non-regent's black hood was worn with it.[1]

(j) Masters of Arts

The history of this dress is in general outline the same as that of the same degree at Oxford.[2]

In 1414 Regent Masters of Arts were ordered to use the *cappa clausa* or *pallium* during lectures and disputations and on all important occasions, but on less formal occasions they were allowed the use of the *cappa manicata*, the much more comfortable substitute.[3] They were not allowed the *pileus*, which was reserved for doctors.[4] At the same time the use of silk on their dress was granted to all masters gremial.[5]

In the following year these enactments were confirmed by the royal order of Henry V when it was added that masters both regent and non-regent were to wear, as showing their dignity, fur of good quality in their hoods.[6]

Until the middle of the fifteenth century the generally worn dress of Masters of Arts consisted of the *supertunica*, the short sleeved *cappa manicata* with pointed ends to the sleeves, a 'shoulder piece' edged with fur only at the bottom edge, and attached to it the fur-lined hood proper, without a head-dress. However, after the middle of this century the *cappa manicata* was

---

[1] W. Combe and T. Uwins, ii. 312–13.

[2] H. Druitt, p. 135.

[3] Cambridge, Univ. Libr. MS. Mm. 4.47, § 147, fo. 228 (22); J. Heywood, p 159.

[4] Cambridge, Univ. Libr. MS. Mm. 4.47, § 148, fos. 229 (23) ff.

[5] C. H. Cooper, op. cit. i. 157. Gremials were those who were permanent residents in the university and generally also associated members of it who lived in some college, hall, or hostel, but non-regent masters if resident in the town were also regarded as gremials. This distinction of dress as regards gremials was still observed in the seventeenth century (G. Peacock, *Observations on the Statutes of Cambridge*, app. A, p. xvii, n. 1).

[6] Cambridge, Univ. Libr. MS. Dd. 4.35, fos. 75 ff.; *Communications, Cambridge Antiquarian Soc.*, 8vo ser. iv. ¶ iii, p. 87.

given up by them, and the sleeveless *tabard* (a closed dress shorter than the *supertunica*, which continued to be worn underneath it), with fur-lined slits at the sides for the passage of the arms, took its place as the ordinary outer dress.[1] This dress is seen worn by a Cambridge Master of Arts in the brass of William Blakwey (d. 1521) at Little Wilbraham, Cambs.[2] Early in the sixteenth century the 'shoulder piece' was no longer worn, and the hood, much elongated, was used alone, at any rate by 1545, the date of a brass of a vice-provost in Eton College chapel.

From this time on, as was the case before, the changes in the dress, except hoods, of Cambridge masters followed the same process as at Oxford. The *roba*, developed from the *supertunica*, came into its own during the sixteenth century since the tabard had been left off. By 1589 the *roba* already had very short glove-sleeves.[3]

The head-dress of masters—they do not appear to have been allowed one until the Reformation—was the *pileus quadratus*, which was enjoined upon them in company with other graduates in 1549,[4] in 1559,[5] in 1570,[6] in 1585,[7] and in 1588.[8]

In the Elizabethan statutes we notice that the gown of masters is to be of a black, brown, or other such sombre colour, with a standing collar, the material being wool-cloth, but they might be partly faced with black silk or other material.[9] These statutes, particularly those of 1560, were a reiteration of the Act of Parliament of 1533.[10]

It is in the history of the hoods of Masters of Arts that we find the main differences from those of Oxford, but these differences

---

[1] H. Druitt, pp. 135–6; E. C. Clarke, art. 'English Academic Costume', in *Archaeological Journal*, l (1893), 202.

[2] E. C. Clarke, loc. cit. The long-sleeved gowns of the period 1450–1525 mentioned by Druitt (op. cit., pp. 136 and 137, n. 1) appear to be examples of the priestly gown such as is illustrated in J. S. Cotman, *Sepulchral Brasses of Norfolk and Suffolk*, ii, pl. xcviii).

[3] Brass of Edward Leeds, Master of Clare College, 1589, in Croxton Church, Cambs. See also for another example a brass of 1619 illustrated in J. S. Cotman, op. cit., ii, pl. xliii, brass of Henry Mason (1619), Eyke Church, Suffolk.

[4] J. D. Mullinger, ii. 392, n. 1.　　　　[5] J. Heywood, p. 241, ¶ 10.

[6] J. Lamb, p. 341.　　　　[7] E. T. Beaumont, *Academical Habit*, p. 57.

[8] E. C. Clarke, art. cit., lxi. 44–45.

[9] C. H. Cooper, ii. 161–2 and 410–12; B.M. MS. Cole xlii, fo. 290, i.e. MS. Add. 5843; C. Wordsworth, pp. 495–6.

[10] *Statutes of the Realm*, iii. 430–2—24° Hen. VIII, c. 13.

do not occur before the middle of the sixteenth century. The Act of 1533 implies that fur was used in the masters' hoods.[1]

There seems to have been no distinction between the hoods of regents and non-regents until the middle of the sixteenth century, but in 1545 'non-regent dress' is mentioned,[2] and in the statutes of Dr. Caius for his refounded Gonville Hall (1558) we notice that the hoods for regents and non-regents are to be different. In this case hoods worn by regent masters were to be lined with miniver, but those of non-regents were to be lined with silk. The colour is not mentioned, but probably lack is meant.[3] It is uncertain how long it was before the distinction between regent and non-regent hoods was accepted throughout the university, but in 1614 the black cloth hoods lined with white fur of regents and the black cloth hoods lined with black cloth of non-regents are mentioned.[4]

The practice pursued in regard to this distinction was that from the time of inception all Masters of Arts were (keeping up the fiction derived from medieval times) nominally liable to teach and were thus considered 'necessary regents', and so wore the white hood for five years after taking their degree; but after that period, unless in the meantime they had been chosen fellows or tutors, they left off the white hood and took to the black one which they henceforth always wore.[5] The use of the regent hood by all newly admitted masters is mentioned by Bedell Buck in 1665.[6] As at Oxford, in the course of the seventeenth century the use of miniver in the regent hood was gradually given up, and at Cambridge white silk was substituted for it.

In Loggan's plate (1690) the Master of Arts (No. 7) wears the square cap and gown exactly the same as those worn by the Oxford master at that time. There was one point of difference, however, although it cannot be seen here, which was that 'strings' were attached to the Cambridge gown. They consisted of two pieces of black ribbon fastened one on each side of the gown in front under the facings, and were originally used to tie up the gown.[7] 'Strings' were worn not only on masters' gowns,

---

[1] *Statutes of the Realm*, loc. cit.   [2] *Cambridge Grace Book Δ*, fo. 12 b.
[3] *Cambridge University and College Statutes*, ii. 259–60, ¶ 27 (*De Vestitu*).
[4] B.M. MS. Cole xlii, fo. 286, i.e. MS. Add. 5843.
[5] *Notes and Queries*, 2nd ser. v. 501–2.
[6] Cambridge, Univ. Libr. MS. Add. 5107, fo. 39.
[7] Cambridge, Univ. Libr. MS. Add. 2616, no. 3, fo. 144 (R. Gooch, *Collectanea*).

but on those of all other degrees. They were introduced in the sixteenth century when gowns became open. The reason for their not appearing in Loggan, Harraden, and Uwins is because from their position they could not be seen unless the wearer was in movement. The regent master (No. 8) wears a fully displayed hood with all the lining showing. It is large and descends to the liripipe in the same way as an Oxford master's hood, but has a square of material underneath the main part of the hood. On the other hand, the non-regent (No. 9) wears a plain black cloth hood which appears as a simple square of black material covering the shoulders and reaching half-way down the back.

On studying Harraden (1803) we see that at this time on informal occasions Masters of Arts wore an ordinary hat with the gown,[1] but a hat was never worn when the hood was, the square cap being then used.

By the time we reach Uwins's plates of 1815 the gown is the same as before, but the non-regent hood has become full and of the same shape as that of the regent.[2] It was silk-lined.

There were two different ways of wearing the regent hood. When worn 'squared' for ordinary occasions it appeared entirely black except for a thin edging of the white silk lining, but when 'flourished' or 'displayed' all the white showed.[3] The 'flourished' hood is thus described: 'The hood "flourished" signifies not merely that it is pendant in chance folds, but that the peaked position of the lines is folded over till it touches the flat half of the hood which covers the back; so that if the hood were applied to its original use, the frontlet of the "head gear" would be the white edging.'[4]

Masters of Surgery wore the dress of non-regents in the early nineteenth century, and presumably they did so earlier, but there is no record.

(k) Bachelors of Divinity

In the draft of regulations for the halls of Cambridge made by Hugh de Balsham, Bishop of Ely, in 1276, Bachelors of Divinity of the *studium* were expected to wear a *cappa clausa*.[5] Their dress by the fifteenth century had come to be the same as

---

[1] Cambridge, Univ. Libr. MS. Add. 2616, no. 3, fo. 144 (R. Gooch, *Collectanea*).
[2] W. Combe and T. Uwins, ii. 312–13.   [3] W. Combe and T. Uwins, loc. cit.
[4] *Notes and Queries*, 2nd ser. viii. 74–75.   [5] B.M. MS. Harl. 7032, ¶ 146.

that of Bachelors of Divinity at Oxford, and consisted of *subtunica*, *supertunica*, and a *cappa clausa* with two side slits. With this was worn a hood lined with white fur and a 'shoulder piece' similarly lined. They had no form of head-dress.[1]

What kind of fur was used on the dress can be seen from a clause in the royal statutes of 1415, in which Bachelors of Divinity in common with bachelors of other faculties were ordered to use only fur of inferior quality such as budge or lamb's-wool.[2] In 1494, however, they were allowed by grace to use silk for the lining of their hoods.[3]

In 1533 the Act of Parliament allowed them a scarlet lining to their *roba*, which had become the outside garment.[4] In common with others they began to wear the square cap in the reign of Edward VI, and this was confirmed in 1559.[5] According to the Elizabethan statutes ranging from 1560 to 1585 their gown was to be the same as that of Masters of Arts of either the 'priest's' or the 'Turkey' variety.[6]

By 1690 their dress with its square cap with a tuft, black gown, and black hood was exactly the same as that of the non-regent masters. They wore the non-regent hood in virtue of their being regarded as non-regents when they took this degree, more than five years always having elapsed from their being admitted to the master's degree before they could proceed to the degree of Bachelor of Divinity.[7]

By 1815 the hood was lined with black silk in conformity with the similar elaboration of the non-regent master's,[8] and so by a dissimilar process became the same as the Oxford Bachelor of Divinity hood except that it was less full.

(*l*) *Bachelors of Canon Law*

The last graduations in Canon Law at Cambridge took place in 1556.[9] There is no direct evidence for the dress of this degree,

[1] H. Druitt, p. 135.
[2] Cambridge, Univ. Libr. MS. Dd. 4.35, fos. 75 ff.; *Communications, Cambridge Antiquarian Soc.*, 8vo ser. iv, ¶ iii, p. 87.　　[3] *Cambridge Grace Book B*, pt. i, p. 70.
[4] C. H. Cooper, i. 355.　　　　　　　　　[5] J. Heywood, p. 241, ¶ 10.
[6] C. H. Cooper, ii. 161–2 and 410–12.
[7] Compare with this the Oxford Bachelor of Divinity hood whose black lining represented the original colour of the Faculty of Theology, whereas the Cambridge non-regent hood was simply the small clerkly hood common to all members of universities in the Middle Ages.
[8] W. Combe and T. Uwins, ii. 312–13.　　　　[9] J. Romilly, following p. vi.

and it can only be inferred that it was like that of Masters of Arts and Bachelors of Divinity.[1] In 1533 in company with masters and others of higher standing below the doctorates they were allowed a variety of furs but of secondary quality.[2]

(m) Bachelors of Laws

The dress of Bachelors of Laws was in medieval times the same as that of bachelors of the higher faculties, and followed the same changes and developments. The only departure from these principles is referred to in 1522 when Bachelors of Laws were allowed the use of silk or miniver in their hoods at the time of the disputations to complete the exercises for their degree (*tempore sue predicationis*), on condition of a certain payment to the university.[3]

The Elizabethan statutes treated them better than Masters of Arts and Bachelors of Medicine, allowing them silk or other rich stuff on their collars as well as half a yard of silk down the facings of their black or dark gowns.[4] During the seventeenth century they wore, with a Bachelor of Arts hood, a winged-sleeved gown with tufts at the top of the sleeves and four rows of button and cord braiding at the bottom of them, which appears in Loggan's costume plate as No. 6, but during the eighteenth century they seem to have taken to the plain Bachelor of Arts gown as can be seen from John Downman's chalk drawing of Charles Chadwick, LL.B. (1778).[5] By 1815, however, they had come to wear the master's gown with 'strings', and the non-regent black hood,[6] and they sometimes even attempted to assume the regent hood.[7] A tassel was added to the tump of their square cap in the middle of the eighteenth century.

(n) Bachelors of Medicine

The history and development of the dress of this degree are exactly the same as that of the Bachelor of Laws.

Apparently in Elizabethan times Bachelors of Medicine as

---

[1] Cf. E. C. Clarke, art. cit., l. 207–8; E. T. Beaumont, *Academical Habit*, p. 27.
[2] *Statutes of the Realm*, loc. cit.
[3] *Cambridge Grace Book Γ*, p. 199.
[4] C. H. Cooper, ii. 161–2; C. Wordsworth, p. 496.
[5] Cambridge, Fitzw. Mus., no. 1894.
[6] W. Combe and T. Uwins, ii. 312–13.
[7] *Notes and Queries*, 2nd ser. v. 501–2.

being practising physicians and so 'doctors' tried to affect the scarlet *cappa* (or Congregation) dress of Doctors of Medicine, for a clause in a university statute of 1570 orders them to wear a tabard, which they chose to interpret as a long over-garment such as the *cappa* was. In fact, 'tabard' was simply used loosely for 'gown'.[1]

In Loggan's 1690 plate (No. 6) they wear a winged-sleeved tufted and braided gown with a Bachelor of Arts hood, but they did not do so after the eighteenth century. Certainly by 1815 they were wearing the non-regent master's costume.[2]

The Baccalaureate of Surgery was always held in conjunction with this degree, and so there was no separate dress for it.

(o) Bachelors of Music

In 1502 an Oxford Bachelor of Music who wished to be incorporated as Bachelor of Music at Cambridge was allowed by grace to have the academical dress of this degree of any colour he wished.[3] It seems to have been the shape or cut of the habit which mattered as yet. By 1545 Bachelors of Music were wearing non-regent master's dress.[4] In Burghley's statutes of 1585 Bachelors of Music, together with Master of Arts and Bachelors of Laws and Medicine, were allowed silk or similar facings running part of the length of their gown.[5] In 1606 and 1616 there are references to the use of Bachelor of Arts dress by Bachelors of Music.[6] After this we hear no more of their dress for a long time, in fact until 1815, by which date they were wearing once more the costume of non-regent masters.[7]

(p) Bachelors of Arts

The dress of the degree of Bachelor of Arts is mentioned for the first time in the statutes of King's Hall (1380), and is to consist of a *roba* (i.e. *supertunica*) with a tabard suitable to the degree over it.[8]

In 1414, according to the university statutes, bachelors were ordered to wear a tabard on which there was to be no kind of

---

[1] Cambridge, Univ. Libr. MS. Mm. 4.51, § 3, fo. 383.
[2] W. Combe and T. Uwins, ii. 312–13.
[3] C. F. Abdy Williams, *Historical Account of Degrees in Music*, p. 154; *Cambridge Grace Book Γ*, p. 5. [4] *Cambridge Grace Book Δ*, p. 28.
[5] C. H. Cooper, ii. 410–12. [6] C. F. Abdy Williams, p. 156.
[7] W. Combe and T. Uwins, ii. 312–13. [8] T. Rymer, *Foedera*, tom. vii, p. 242 b.

adornment of fur or silk or anything of value. On their hoods they were allowed to use only budge or lamb's-wool unless of noble family when they might use rich fur.[1] They were not to have any head-covering.[2] Thus we realize that at both Oxford and Cambridge the dress of Bachelors of Arts in the Middle Ages consisted of a *supertunica*, with a sleeved tabard over it, and presumably a 'shoulder piece' and a furred hood.

There next followed the process which has been described in the account of the dress of Oxford Bachelors of Arts, the leaving off of the tabard during the latter part of the fifteenth century with the consequent enlargement of the *roba*, which now became the outer dress with full sleeves.[3]

Bachelors of Arts gained a head-dress during the sixteenth century, for they were ordered to wear the *pileus quadratus* from 1559 onwards.[4] In 1585 Burghley ordered them to wear black or brown cloth gowns with cloth facings (the gown now being open in front), a standing collar, and a hood of the same material and colour as the gown.[5] The use of budge or lamb's-wool in the hood was still enforced, and the square cap was again enjoined as the head-dress. In 1586 they were warned against wearing silk facings on their gowns.[6]

In 1690 the bachelor's dress appears in Loggan's costume plate (No. 5) as a black square cap with a tuft, a black gown with very full and long tapering sleeves exactly the same as the sleeves of the Oxford Bachelor of Arts, and a full hood with a 'displayed' lining of white fur. John Evelyn in 1680,[7] and John Byrom in 1711,[8] mention that lamb's-skin was used for the lining. According to the university statutes of 1750 the official material for the gown was 'Prunello or Prince's Stuff'.[9]

---

[1] *Communications, Cambridge Antiquarian Soc.*, 8vo ser. iv, ¶ v, p. 89.

[2] Cambridge, Univ. Libr. MS. Dd. 4.35, § 5; Cambridge, Univ. Libr. MS. Mm. 4.47, § 176, fos. 271 (65) ff. (*De penulis et pelluris Baccalaureorum*); C. H. Cooper, op. cit. i. 156–7.

[3] G. Clinch, *English Costume*, pp. 250–1 and 253. In view of the development of all other academical costumes at this time which resulted in formal outer garments being left off and the *supertunica* taking their place, the opinion of H. Druitt (pp. 135–6), that the Cambridge bachelor's gown of modern times is the original tabard, seems untenable.   [4] J. Heywood, p. 241.

[5] C. H. Cooper, ii. 410–12.

[6] Cambridge, Univ. Libr. MS. Mm. 4.56, § 1, fo. 62.

[7] *The Diary of John Evelyn*, ed. E. S. de Beer, iv. 217.

[8] J. Byrom, *Remains*, i, pt. l, p. 17 (Chetham Soc., vol. xxxii, 1854).

[9] Cambridge, Univ. Libr. MS. Mm. 4.55, § 1, fo. 126.

From 1777 to 1780 the well-known artist John Downman stayed in Cambridge and made a good income by executing chalk drawings of members of the university, especially those who had just taken degrees. Many are in the Fitzwilliam Museum, and there are three examples of Bachelor of Arts dress, one of 1777 and two of 1778.[1]

In 1803 according to Harraden the gown was generally made of bombazine and the hood was lined with lamb's-wool, while the sleeves of the gown were the same as in 1690. The black square cap, by this time with a tassel, was used.

The dress in 1815 was the same as before except for a change in the gown's sleeves, which, although retaining the same shape as before, had now a hole in the front, through which the arms passed. This was the first change made to free the hand from the cumbrous, loose sleeve. It is important also to notice that the black 'strings' were fastened on the front in a bow,[2] as they had been in 1792.[3] Later the sleeves were split open down the seam right from the shoulder, so that they hung down free of the arm, for the sake of convenience when dining.[4] Cuff-strings were never used at Cambridge.

(q) Undergraduates

1. *Students of Civil Law.* As result of the fact that originally the standing of students of Civil Law in the Faculty of Law was considered as equivalent to that of Bachelors of Arts in the Faculty of Arts, they wore the dress of Bachelors of Arts.[5]

2. *Noblemen.* According to the enactments of the Congregation of 1414, noblemen, while they were to conform in general shape to the *talaris* dress of scholars in the widest sense of the word 'scholars', were allowed silk facings to their dress like masters gremial and beneficiaries of good position.[6] At the same time they were allowed to use rich fur in their hoods if noblemen-bachelors.[7]

---

[1] Examples of those in Bachelor of Arts dress are Francis Randolph (1777) (Fitzw. Mus. no. 1819); Thomas Mantell (1778) (Fitzw. Mus. no. 1865); and Gilbert Wakefield, Porson's enemy (1778) (Fitzw. Mus. no. 1874).

[2] W. Combe and T. Uwins, ii. p. 313.

[3] J. W. Goodison, p. 105 (portrait of Philip Francis).

[4] *Notes and Queries,* 2nd ser. viii. 74–75.

[5] *Notes and Queries,* 2nd ser. x. 160–1; *Notes and Queries,* 2nd. ser. vi. 258 a.

[6] C. H. Cooper, i. 157.

[7] Cambridge, Univ. Libr. MS. Mm. 4.47, § 176, fos. 271 (65), ff.

In the statutes of Cardinal Pole (chancellor 1556–8) noblemen and their sons were allowed to wear at the university any dress they liked since they were living at their own expense,[1] but when from 1566 onwards the university under the chancellorship of Sir William Cecil, afterwards Lord Burghley, began to legislate about academical dress,[2] their costume was brought into general line with that of other undergraduates, though it was in every way richer.

In 1588 Burghley in a letter to the university ordered that, though they must conform to the wearing of a round cap, which was to be worn by those not on foundations, noblemen might have them made of black velvet.[3] This was a reiteration of the 1585 order.[4]

By 1690 their dress had become so greatly elaborated that they wore a brocaded gown with braiding and buttons at the shoulders, and with false panel sleeves reaching to the hem of the gown decorated in two places with a square of braid.[5] The round velvet cap was still worn, but as often as not an ordinary lay hat. So popular among noblemen did the wearing of ordinary hats become that their use was given official sanction, as long as they were plain, in the statutes of 1750.[6]

In 1769 the cap of all undergraduates was changed from round to square,[7] and in Harraden's plate (1803) we find the nobleman wearing a black square cap with a gold tassel. With this he wears a long pale blue gown (the full dress) edged with gold lace, a gold embroidered coronet appearing on the train of the gown. The sleeves are winged and have false panels, and the whole dress is decorated at intervals with great double knots of gold braid sewn on. The colour of this silk gown might vary according to choice. The great Cambridge benefactor Viscount Fitzwilliam wore when a nobleman of Trinity Hall (1761–4) a red silk gown embroidered with gold lace, as can be seen from his portrait (1764) painted by Joseph Wright of Derby,[8] but blue

---

[1] J. Heywood, pp. 241–3, ¶ 10; J. Lamb, pp. 245–7.
[2] C. H. Cooper, ii. 230.
[3] H. Ellis, iii. 26; E. C. Clarke, art. cit., lxi. 44–45.
[4] E. T. Beaumont, *Academical Habit*, p. 57.
[5] D. Loggan, costume plate, no. 21.
[6] Cambridge, Univ. Libr. MS. Mm. 4.55, § 1, fo. 126.
[7] C. H. Cooper, iv. 355.
[8] J. W. Goodison, i. 89 and pl. xv, no. 127.

was the favourite colour. The undress of noblemen was a full bell-sleeved black silk gown, and with this a three-cornered hat, by 1803 a top-hat, was worn.[1]

3. *Fellow-commoners*. This order was the equivalent of the Oxford gentleman-commoner (fellow-commoner, however, at Worcester), but in earlier times it was not well defined, and fellow-commoners were treated as members of the order of noblemen in the statutes of Cardinal Pole.[2] In common with them they were in 1588 allowed round black velvet caps,[3] but they were forced to conform to the Burghley statutes as regards a sober and clerical colour of dress. By 1690[4] they wore the winged-sleeved gown, braided in loop and button style at the bottom of the sleeves, on the skirt at each side, and at the back. With this gown an ordinary lay hat was worn.

In Harraden's plate of 1803 the dress consists of a black square cap with a gold tassel and a false panel-sleeved gown of black Prince's stuff. The sleeves above the arms are richly embroidered with horizontal bars of gold lace, but the panels are plain except that very near the bottom there is one horizontal row of gold braid. The shoulders of the gown are stuffed so as to form a high ridge, which is also decorated with gold braid.

A distinction had been made half a century before between two kinds of fellow-commoners. Those who were the eldest sons of baronets and the younger sons of noblemen had in 1750[5] been confirmed in their use of an ordinary hat instead of the square academical one for informal occasions, and were called 'hat fellow-commoners', but ordinary fellow-commoners had to conform to the wearing of the square cap. For formal wear both classes used the black velvet square one with a gold tassel, which we know was used in 1736, as can be seen in Hogarth's full-length portrait of this year of Thomas Western, a fellow-commoner of Clare.[6]

Fellow-commoners of Trinity were distinguished from fellow-commoners of other colleges, who had black gowns decorated

[1] Cambridge, Univ. Libr. MS. Mm. 4.55, § 1, fo. 126.
[2] J. Heywood, loc. cit.; J. Lamb, loc. cit.
[3] H. Ellis, iii. 26; C. H. Cooper, ii. 456.
[4] D. Loggan, op. cit., no. 4.
[5] Cambridge, Univ. Libr. MS. Mm. 4.55, § 1, fo. 126.
[6] R. B. Becket, *Hogarth*, p. 61 and pl. 80. According to the *New English Dictionary* the term 'tuft-hunter' was first used at Cambridge in 1755.

with gold braid,[1] by having a blue bell-sleeved gown decorated down the front on each side of the opening with a zigzag line of silver braid. They wore a blue gown in virtue of the foundation statutes of their college (1546),[2] although violet appears to have been originally intended. Fellow-commoners of Trinity wore a square black velvet cap with a silver tassel.

Two water-colours by the artist Silvester Harding provide excellent illustrations of the gown of fellow-commoners of Trinity and of those of all the other colleges. His portrait of J. T. Nottidge (1794) shows him wearing the silver-laced, light blue gown,[3] while that of Marmaduke Dayrell (about 1790), a fellow-commoner of Christ's, depicts him in the black gown decorated with gold lace.[4]

In 1815 all fellow-commoners, except those of Trinity and Emmanuel, wore a black gown of Prince's stuff with a velvet 'bridge' yoke and velvet facings down the front, and false panel sleeves, together with a square black velvet cap with a gold tassel, unless 'hat fellow-commoners' who wore a top-hat. Fellow-commoners of Trinity wore blue bell-sleeved gowns decorated with gold buttons on the sleeves, and gold lace, while those of Emmanuel had their black, velvet-faced gown decorated with gold embroidery round the shoulder-ribs, on the skirts, and on the panel-sleeves in bars and squares.[5] It thus appears that between 1803 and 1815 gold braid had been left off the gowns of fellow-commoners of all the other colleges. Trinity fellow-commoners had changed from silver to gold.

4. *Pensioners.* As opposed to Oxford the dress of under-graduates at Cambridge was generally a college and not a university affair, at any rate in later times, except as regards head-dress. King's Hall seems to have been the first Cambridge body to pay special attention to dress. In 1380 its scholars were ordered to wear a long outer garment (*roba talaris*) befitting their state of being clerks.[6]

By the middle of the next century the dress of the scholars had been somewhat elaborated, as appears from the foundation statutes of King's College (1441), in which undergraduate

---

[1] R. B. Becket, loc. cit.
[2] *Cambridge University and College Statutes*, iii. 444 and 446.
[3] J. W. Goodison, i. 108.   [4] J. W. Goodison, i. 107.
[5] W. Combe and T. Uwins, ii. 313.   [6] T. Rymer, tom. vii, p. 242b.

members were bidden to use a short tabard (as an outer dress)
and a cloth hood.[1]

In the foundation statutes of Trinity (1546) we find that a
definite livery was intended for junior members of the college,
for it was ordered that all bachelors and undergraduates of
the college were to wear gowns of a violet colour. This dress,
together with a head-dress, was to be used on all occasions,
even more particularly in public, so that everyone might be
able to admire the college's corporate qualities through such
visible symbols.[2] This use of the statutory colour, which came
to be blue, was maintained by undergraduates but not by
bachelors. It is mentioned in 1669,[3] and in 1711.[4]

Caius at the time of his refounding of Gonville Hall in 1558
had the same idea in mind when he ordered all members of his
new college to wear a *vestis*, a long gown reaching to the ankles,
with full sleeves, and a standing collar, the whole to be of black
or violet, or a colour in between the two.[5] This being so, it is
impossible to doubt that the fellows must have known this when
in 1837 the blue gown was introduced for undergraduates of
Caius.[6] Although, of course, this was according to statute, until
that year black seems always to have been used.

It is noticeable that so reactionary was Caius, who seems to
have remained faithful to the Church of Rome, that he also
ordered the *exomis* ('shoulder piece') to be worn as part of the
dress, and a *tunica* or cassock under the gown whether the
wearer was in Orders or not.[7] It is scarcely likely that such a
rule was long obeyed. Apart from these exceptional rules the
statute dress at the other colleges had become at the beginning
of Elizabeth's reign a dark coloured gown with a cloth hood to
match.

In 1549 scholars on the foundations of colleges were ordered

---

[1] *Cambridge University and College Statutes*, ii. 538–9, § 23 (*De habitu Sociorum et
Scholarium*).

[2] Cambridge, Univ. Libr. MS. Mm. 1.40 (Baker MS., vol. 29) (*Statuta Sanctae et
Ind. Trinitatis Cantabrig.*), cap. 23, fo. 159, and cap. 21, fos. 157–8; *Cambridge
University and College Statutes*, iii. 444 and 446.

[3] S. Newton, *Diary*, p. 46.

[4] J. Byrom, p. 17. It is still used.

[5] *Cambridge University and College Statutes*, ii. 258–60, ¶ 27 (*De Vestitu*).

[6] A. G. Almond (*Gowns and Gossip*, p. 14) seems unaware of this and quotes
Whibley's poem *In Cap and Gown* which mocks Caius for using Trinity blue.

[7] *Cambridge University and College Statutes*, loc. cit.

by the parliamentary visitors to wear square caps, but apart from the question of head-dress the university in the following years left the initiative with the colleges, and in 1559 the colleges were ordered to obey their several statutes.[1] By 1570 pensioners were wearing the dress of the character which remained theirs for nearly two hundred years, an ankle-length gown and a round bonnet with a band and a brim larger than that on the Oxford one. It did not originate as at Oxford in the apprentice's 'catercap', but in the ordinary lay hat of the period.[2] Black hats were again enjoined for the generality of undergraduates in 1576,[3] and the wearing of the round cloth cap by pensioners was again insisted on by Burghley in 1588.[4] In Jacobean times, when the gown was also elaborated, black velvet was added to the brim of the pensioner's bonnet which otherwise continued to be of black cloth lined with black silk on canvas.[5]

By the end of the seventeenth century the dress of pensioners varied, as can be realized by studying D. Loggan's plates. The gown worn at Trinity was violet and full-sleeved like a Bachelor of Arts gown;[6] at King's, Queens', Peterhouse, and Trinity Hall a plain black gown was worn, in shape like that used at Trinity but in every way shorter,[7] and as nearly all members of these four colleges were on the foundation it seems reasonable to suppose that the bell-sleeved gown which they wore was a natural development of the sleeved *supertunica*, a 'clerkly' dress. At all the other Cambridge colleges, with a few exceptions for special scholars, a lay type of gown (like that worn by Oxford commoners) had appeared during the sixteenth century. The majority of the members of those colleges were not on foundations, and so in those the lay type of gown prevailed.

This lay gown appears to have been worn as a prescribed dress for pensioners from about 1570,[8] and was further elaborated during Jacobean times. In Loggan's costume plate (figure No. 1)

[1] J. D. Mullinger, op. cit. ii. 392, n. 1.   [2] J. D. Mullinger, op. cit. ii. 392.
[3] C. E. Mallet, *History of the University of Oxford*, ii. 120.
[4] H. Ellis, iii. 25.   [5] C. H. Cooper, iv. 355.
[6] D. Loggan, no. 3. A miniature of John Byrom (1709), who in that year was elected to the foundation at Trinity, shows him wearing such a gown, but with the addition of large buttons like those of an overcoat (J. Byrom, op. cit., frontispiece). Buttons were sometimes used on B.A. gowns at this period (W. J. Harrison, *Life in Clare Hall, Cambridge, 1658–1713*, p. 77).   [7] D. Loggan, no. 2.
[8] J. D. Mullinger, ii. 392.

it is depicted as a long open black gown faced with black velvet half-way down the front. To these facings is joined a black velvet flap collar, and the shoulders of the gown are decorated with black velvet. Broad streamers like those on Oxford commoners' gowns hang from the shoulder to the hem, and they are decorated all the way down with small lozenges of braid. With it is worn a round bonnet bound with a cord, the bow of which hangs off at the back.

All these dresses were the same in 1803 as in 1690 except that the ordinary pensioners' gowns had lost their streamers, and all now wore the black square cap with the black silk tassel, the round cap having been abolished throughout the university in 1769 owing to an agitation against it by certain pensioners.[1] In the statutes of 1800 for the new college of Downing, the full-sleeved gown of the shape used at Trinity was to be worn by all undergraduates, but it was to be black,[2] an early indication of the change from 'curtain' to bell-sleeved gown which many colleges were to begin to adopt about thirty years later. In Harraden's book of 1803 the bell sleeves of the Trinity, Peter-house, King's, Queens', and Trinity Hall gowns had come to be split high up the arm so that the arm was free of them. A good example of the Trinity pensioner's dress before this change is provided by Silvester Harding's water-colour (1798) of Robert Rushbrooke.[3]

In 1815[4] we find that these bell sleeves have been sewn up, the seam showing vertically running the length of the upper part of the sleeve. The Trinity pensioner's gown was now dark blue with black cloth facings of 'Prince's stuff', while Peterhouse and Queens' pensioners now wore the black bell-sleeved gown with the sleeves sewn up. Pensioners of King's wore a gown of the same shape and colour but of a special thick cloth. Those of Trinity Hall also wore the type of gown of Peterhouse and Queens', but the sleeves were fastened up at the elbow with a black button and cord. All other pensioners wore black sleeveless gowns which in the course of the eighteenth century seem to have lost their streamers. These 'curtains', as they were sometimes disparagingly called, were made of 'Prince's stuff'

[1] C. H. Cooper, loc. cit.   [2] *Cambridge University and College Statutes*, iii. 645.
[3] Cambridge, Fitzw. Mus., no. 622a.
[4] W. Combe and T. Uwins, ii. 313 and pls.

and were faced in front with black velvet and had black velvet flap-collars. The square cap remained as before. Never at any time were there 'strings' on undergraduate gowns.[1]

5. *Scholars and Exhibitioners.* Under this section are mentioned only such scholars and exhibitioners whose dress did not conform with that of pensioners.

Thus scholars of King's, Rustat scholars of Jesus, Patchett scholars of St. John's, and Duchess of Somerset exhibitioners of St. John's wore a full bell-sleeved black gown of fine cloth ('costume cloth'). In all these cases the arms appear through a gash in the middle of the upper part of the sleeve. Westminster scholars of Trinity wore a black bell-sleeved gown with a violet button and loop at the bottom of the forearm seam.[2]

As members on foundations scholars and exhibitioners were ordered in 1549 to wear the square cap.[3] After 1769 they were differentiated from pensioners, who in this year began to wear a square black cap with a black tassel,[4] by continuing to have on their caps the tump without the tassel.[5]

6. *Sizars and sub-sizars.*[6] The position of sizars was originally very lowly, but had greatly improved by 1730.[7] After this they began to approach more and more the position of pensioners and so came to wear the pensioners' dress except that the square cap which they began to wear in 1769 had no tassel. At those colleges at which the 'curtain' was worn they wore a plain one with no velvet on facings or collar.[8]

Until 1769 they had worn round black cloth bonnets with a brim of prunella or silk.[9]

(r) Notes

1. *Use of the chapel dress at Cambridge.* Until the Reformation the surplice had been worn in the college chapels of the universities, but in Elizabeth's reign the question of its retention came

---

[1] The subsequent changes in the college gowns from 1828 onwards are discussed by A. G. Almond in his *Gowns and Gossip* (1925). They are illustrated in N. Whittock's *The Costume of the Members of the University of Cambridge* (? 1847) and, showing certain modern alterations, in A. G. Almond's, *College Gowns* (2nd edn., 1926).

[2] J. R. Tanner, p. 196.   [3] J. D. Mullinger, ii. 392, n. 1.

[4] C. H. Cooper, loc. cit.   [5] J. R. Tanner, loc. cit.

[6] Sizars were the equivalent of Oxford battelars and sub-sizars of Oxford servitors. They could not take their commons in hall, but had to 'size' (i.e. bespeak and eat their meals) in their own room. *Gentleman's Magazine*, lvii, pt. 2 (1787), p. 1146.   [7] T. Hearne, *Collections*, x (O.H.S., lxvii), 281.

[8] W. Combe and T. Uwins, loc. cit.   [9] C. H. Cooper, loc. cit.

under review. Elizabeth was one of those who favoured its use, but the question of the surplice was a hotly contested one all over Europe as can be realized from the quaint book, *Responsio M. Nic. Galli et M. Fla. Illyr.* which gives both sides of the argument.[1] At Cambridge there had been trouble about the wearing of the surplice,[2] but it was finally decided that it should be worn in college chapels, at any rate on saints' days, together with a hood in the case of holders of degrees.[3] This use of the surplice was again insisted on in 1603, when in canon 17 of the Church of England canons all masters, fellows, scholars, and students were to wear a surplice in chapel on Sundays and holy days, the graduates among them to appear in the hood of their degree.[4] The use of the hood was insisted upon in college chapels and in cathedral churches to prevent the wearing of the amess which had been affected particularly by members of collegiate and cathedral institutions.[5] The use of the amess had been forbidden at Cambridge in 1571.[6]

In 1643 the Long Parliament decided that anyone might, if he wished, refuse to wear the surplice in chapel.[7] As a result it was almost entirely abandoned at Cambridge, but was ordered to be worn again at the Restoration.

2. *The mourning gown.* The mourning gown at Cambridge was of the same shape as that used at Oxford, according to Loggan's costume plate, figure No. 10.[8]

We find its origin in the statutes of 1560 in which the 'sad-colored' gown of 'priest's shape' is allowed as one of the alternatives for the ordinary dress of graduates.[9]

It was not until the Restoration that members of the university began to wear it indiscriminately. Even undergraduates wore it for the same reason as at Oxford, and it was found necessary to legislate against this abuse. Thus in 1681 it was ordered that no one below the degree of Master of Arts might wear it for any reason whatever.[10]

[1] For instance in its favour, see typographical p. A5.
[2] C. H. Cooper, ii. 217.   [3] J. Lamb, p. 324; G. Dyer, i. 196.
[4] M. E. C. Walcott, *The Constitutions and Canons Ecclesiastical of the Church of England*, p. 25.
[5] M. E. C. Walcott, p. 37, Canon 25; P. Dearmer, *Ornaments of the Ministers*, p. 5.
[6] C. H. Cooper, ii. 277.   [7] C. H. Cooper, iii. 336.
[8] Cambridge, Univ. Libr. MS. Mm. 1.53.
[9] C. H. Cooper, ii. 161-2; B.M. MS. Cole xlii, fo. 290, i.e. MS. Add. 5843.
[10] Cambridge, Univ. Libr. MS. Mm. 4.56, fos. 158-9.

The gown survived as an alternative dress to the master's gown for Doctors of Divinity, as we have seen, and it was also worn by fellows of King's.[1]

3. *Academical mourning at Cambridge.* This, besides the mourning gown which drops out of view in the late seventeenth century, was indicated by wide black ribbons drawn across the square cap from corner to corner with a black rosette of ribbon in the middle where the lines of ribbon intersected.

In the case of mourning for the chancellor or a member of the royal family bows of black ribbon called 'butterflies' were worn upon the skull-piece of the cap at the back, three in the longest part of it, two on the narrowing spaces on each side, and one each side on the narrowest part.[2]

4. *'Fathers.'* At the time of introducing their pupils for degrees 'fathers' (i.e. praelectors) wore the *cappa* (Congregation) dress with a round black velvet bonnet with a gold band.[3]

LAMBETH DEGREES

The Archbishops of Canterbury and Armagh from the time of the Reformation had the right of bestowing all degrees upon persons of their choice. The recipient of the degree thus granted wore the academical dress suitable to his degree of the university of the archbishop who bestowed it.[4] There does not, however, seem to be any authority for this custom.

III. SCOTLAND

ST. ANDREWS (1411)

At St. Andrews from the first some accepted kind of academical costume was worn, and it was of the same character as that used at other European universities.[5] We have no definite evidence as to the type of dress used, for Scotland is particularly poor in illuminated manuscripts, brasses, and glass, and the fine

---

[1] Plate in R. Harraden.

[2] J. R. Tanner, p. 194. Tanner is not explicit as to the position of these bows, but Mr. A. Rutherford Almond in a letter to me of 5 Aug. 1955 says, 'I should conclude that the three at the back would be worn vertical and so with those at the sides. The two at the front I think would have to be horizontal as there would scarcely be room for them otherwise.'

[3] Cambridge, Univ. Libr. MS. Add. 5107, fo. 31.

[4] C. Wall, art., 'Lambeth Degrees', in *British Medical Journal*, ii (1935), 854 ff.

[5] R. G. Cant, *The University of St. Andrews*, pp. 19–20.

sixteenth-century university seal does not aid us.[1] However, it is not difficult to believe that, as Scotland looked to France for political and cultural leadership till the middle of the sixteenth century, it copied the dress of its universities.[2]

Hoods were early prescribed for all graduates of St. Andrews, and we know that furred hoods were associated with the degree of Bachelor of Arts and red cloth or silk hoods with that of Masters of Arts.[3] Masters and doctors wore some form of *cappa*, perhaps a *cappa manicata*, their head-dress being the *pileus*. The *pileus* preserved at the university and still used there at the doctoral ceremony[4] was probably made for the university in 1696 on the model of earlier ones.[5]

Undergraduates do not seem to have had a special dress before the foundation of St. Leonard's College (1512), the second in age of the three collegiate foundations. In the original statutes of this college the students were ordered to wear 'gown and hood', no doubt the same kind of undergraduate dress as was worn in the Middle Ages at all European Universities, consisting of a black *supertunica* of some kind and small black cloth hood.[6]

At the Reformation the link with medieval times was suddenly broken. The Kirk looked with hostility upon such memorials of the papal world as academical dress, and for the future only during periods of episcopal rule was any attention paid to it. The custom of wearing it was not interdicted, but was simply allowed to die of neglect. All that remained in use at St. Andrews of the old dress was the rector's purple robe, and this has survived to the present day.[7] A gown of lay type was, however, from this time onwards worn by Regent Masters of Arts. It is described by Thomas Kirk, an English visitor to St. Andrews in 1677, as a black gown, 'almost such as our freshmen have at Cambridge', that is like the sleeveless 'curtain'.[8] Doctors of Laws of all Scottish universities were ordered by James VI in 1610 to wear black gowns, faced in front and on the collar with back velvet.[9]

[1] H. Laing, *Ancient Scottish Seals*, i. 200–1, no. 1114.
[2] The influence of the University of Paris is mentioned in T. Baty, *Academic Colours*, pp. 6 and 26; of Louvain in *Notes and Queries*, 1st ser. iii, 329.
[3] R. G. Cant, pp. 19–20, n. 1.
[4] J. Wells, *The Oxford Degree Ceremony*, p. 30, n. 1.
[5] R. G. Cant, pp. 19, n. 1, and 20.
[6] R. G. Cant, p. 19. [7] R. G. Cant, p. 20. [8] R. G. Cant, p. 74.
[9] Anon. art. 'Scottish Legal Costume', in *Journal of Jurisprudence*, xxviii (1884), 67.

Academical head-gear was given up at the Reformation as were hoods.[1] Hoods were not revived until the 1870's. Should head-covering be needed on account of the weather when wearing an academical gown, an ordinary hat of contemporary lay fashion was worn.[2]

All undergraduates of the university, irrespective of their college, were instructed by James VI, perhaps in the latter part of his reign, to wear a scarlet gown, as were those of the other Scottish universities.[3] Scarlet was chosen to be the colour so that students, particularly at night, could be watched and tracked down by the disciplinary officers.[4] The scarlet gown of St. Andrews was made of thin stuff, and was short and sleeveless, varying slightly for primars, secondars, and termars.[5]

In the eighteenth century Doctors of Divinity wore bands and an open gown with a very broad black velvet collar reaching over the shoulders both before and behind. It was fastened at the neck like a cloak and had false panel-sleeves; but what was chiefly remarkable about the gown was that there were decorations of cloth sewn on down the front of it on each side and on the sleeves in the form of the letter gamma and the gamma reversed, as is to be seen in Raeburn's portrait of Hugh Blair, D.D., St. Andrews (1718–1800), an interesting example of the revival of the medieval *gammadium*.[6]

GLASGOW (1451)

At the time of the foundation of Glasgow College it was decided that its dress was to be modelled on that worn at the University of Bologna,[7] but Paris academical costume also had a great influence. Dress was to be of a clerical character, full-length, closed, and girt, such as is in 1482 mentioned as a dress befitting students of Arts and of Canon Law.[8] The material of the outer dress was to be of frieze (i.e. coarse woollen cloth) as at Paris.[9]

[1] *Notes and Queries*, 1st ser. iii. 329; cf. *Notes and Queries*, 7th ser. xii. 241–2.

[2] R. G. Cant, p. 119 and n. 2.

[3] R. G. Cant, p. 19 and n. 4, and p. 20.

[4] Cf. C. Innes, *Fasti Aberdonenses*, p. 372, 'The Commission on Scottish Universities, 1695'.   [5] R. G. Cant, 74 and n. 2. It was altered in 1838.

[6] See A. Cardon's engraving of the original in *The Life of Samuel Johnson*, by James Boswell, ed. R. Ingpen, ii. 661.

[7] C. Innes, *Munimenta Universitatis Glasguensis*, ii. 24.

[8] C. Innes, *Munimenta*, ii. 19.

[9] D. Murray, *The Old College of Glasgow*, p. 474.

Students on ceremonial occasions were at first ordered to wear a certain form of dress, the character of which is not explained, but later the rule was relaxed, and as long as they had a seemly dress that was deemed sufficient.[1]

As regards graduates, the furred hood was the mark of the bachelor.[2] In 1452 Masters of Arts were ordered to wear a cloth *cappa*,[3] probably a *cappa manicata*. In 1463 two masters were ordered to buy for the Faculty of Arts a magistral *cappa* and four or six hoods,[4] and in the same year Patrick Linch bequeathed to the college of Glasgow a red hood lined with miniver.[5] In 1464 the office of keeper of vestments (*Custos habituum*) was established. He was to be in charge of academical dresses and to be responsible for hiring them out for degree ceremonies, for it seems that full dresses were not owned, their cost being too great to buy them. A fund was from this time worked up and the accounts were audited in 1469.[6]

From the fact that in 1490 the bursar was appointed to purchase six hoods of blue (*blodius*) cloth 'sufficiently furred' for the common use of the Faculty of Arts both regents and students, it would seem that this was the established and recognized symbol of the mastership, and that students wore such a hood at the ceremony at which they took the master's degree,[7] for from the silence about the Bachelor of Arts degree it seems that it had already died out. This hood is supposed to have been modelled on that of Bologna.[8] Graduates wore a *pileus*.[9]

The Rector in 1469 was ordered to have at least a furred hood or one lined with taffeta, and for certain feasts he was to have a richer dress still.[10]

At the Reformation the *pileus* and *birettum* and the hood were rejected,[11] but a lay Tudor bonnet was used at the doctoral ceremony and at the time of the bestowal of the degree of Master. D. Murray[12] gives examples of two kinds of bonnet. The doctor's bonnet was black and the same as the Oxford lay doctor's bonnet; the master's bonnet, also black, was larger, was flat and

---

[1] J. Coutts, *A History of the University of Glasgow*, p. 28.
[2] J. Coutts, p. 24.   [3] C. Innes, ii. 180.
[4] C. Innes, ii. 201.   [5] C. Innes, ii. 199–200.
[6] J. Coutts, pp. 28–29.   [7] C. Innes, ii. 256; J. Coutts, pp. 28–29.
[8] *Notes and Queries*, 1st ser. iii. 329.
[9] C. Innes, loc. cit.; J. Coutts, loc. cit.   [10] C. Innes, ii. 75.
[11] D. Murray, p. 473, n. 2. Cf. R. G. Cant, p. 19, n. 1.   [12] Pl. opp. p. 308.

brimless, and had a red silk lining. Otherwise, on ordinary occasions a hat of contemporary lay fashion was worn with the gown, for the square cap was not introduced until modern times.[1] Gowns, of what shape we are not told, were worn by all regents, as Andrew Melvill, who became principal of the college of Glasgow in 1574, mentions in his *Diary* under the year 1578.[2]

In 1634 Charles I ordered students to wear their gowns in Glasgow Cathedral, in the university buildings, and even in the streets of the city.[3] According to Sir William Brereton, who visited Glasgow in 1635, students wore gowns of red, grey, or other colours as they pleased,[4] from which it appears that James VI's order about the use of the scarlet gown[5] was not strictly enforced.[6]

The visitation from the General Assembly in 1642 ordered all students to have gowns,[7] while in 1664 masters and students were instructed to wear their gowns in college and in the streets.[8]

A college enactment of 1690 ordered deans to have a 'grave decent gown' for important occasions, and the rector to have 'some marks of distinction becoming a Magistrate' on his gown, which might consist of decorations of either braid or velvet.[9] Then in 1695 the visitation of the Parliamentary Commission on Scottish Universities ordered the students of Glasgow to wear the scarlet gowns as described under St. Andrews, while regents were to continue to wear black gowns.[10]

In the eighteenth century Doctors of Medicine wore a black gown with a large flap-collar and wide bell sleeves. It was open in front, and was decorated at wide intervals down the front on each side with large square braided buttonholes to each of which was attached a tassel hanging from one side.[11]

---

[1] D. Murray, pp. 473-4.

[2] J. Melvill, *The Diary* (Bannatyne Club), p. 55; J. Melvill, *The Diary*, ed. R. Pitcairn, p. 72.

[3] J. Coutts, p. 96.

[4] W. Brereton, *Travels*, p. 117 (Chetham Soc. i).

[5] Mentioned under St. Andrews.

[6] *Notes and Queries*, 12th ser. ii. 537; *Notes and Queries*, 12th ser. iii. 59; D. Murray, op. cit., p. 476.

[7] *Notes and Queries*, 12th ser. ii. 537; D. Murray, p. 475.

[8] *Notes and Queries*, 12th ser. ii. 537.

[9] C. Innes, ii. 350.

[10] C. Innes, ii. 523; J. Coutts, p. 177; D. Murray, op. cit., p. 475.

[11] See Ridley's engraving of William Cullen, M.D. of Glasgow (1710-90).

As to undergraduate dress in the eighteenth century, John Wesley on visiting Glasgow in 1753 writes: 'They' [the undergraduates] 'wear scarlet gowns reaching only to their knees .. of coarse cloth.'[1] These gowns later reached well below the knees, and a flap collar, a cape, and short false panel sleeves were added to them.[2] Although this description is based on a nineteenth-century water-colour, it seems reasonable to suppose that the gown was then no different from what it had been in the latter part of the previous century. The thick cape was no doubt added to protect the shoulders of the wearer from rain.

ABERDEEN (1494)

In an instrument of Gavin, Bishop of Aberdeen, of 1529 there are orders addressed to Doctors of Canon Law, Medicine, and Civil Law of the University of Aberdeen concerning their dress, from which it would appear that the first two were to dress according to the use of the University of Paris, while Doctors of Civil Law were to use the dress worn by those of this degree at the University of Orléans.[3]

From the inventory of effects of the university (1542) we see that the chief features of the dress of the rector at that time were the scarlet *cappa* (*cappa lutea, vulgo* 'ane scarlat caip'), which means either a *cappa* with two slits or more likely simply a cloak, and a hood of skin and fur doubled over. Another item, which appears to have been the rector's everyday dress, was a 'French brown' *cappa* without a hood.[4] At the same time the Faculty of Arts had in its possession four *cappae rotundae*,[5] five furred hoods, a doctoral *cappa*, a small *cappa nigra*[6] without a hood, and four *epitogia* ('shoulder pieces'), three of them being red and one 'French brown'. In addition the Faculty of Arts owned four hoods, one of 'French brown', one red, and one black, and twenty-one furred Bachelor of Arts hoods.[7] These Bachelor of Arts furred hoods are again mentioned in a clause in the orders published at the time of the chancellor's visitation of 1549.[8] The

---

[1] J. Wesley, *Journal*, ii. 286.　　　[2] D. Murray, frontispiece.
[3] C. Innes, *Fasti Aberdonenses*, p. 87.　　　[4] C. Innes, *Fasti*, p. 571.
[5] This type of *cappa* was of a round cut and was in use at Paris, particularly for members of the Theological Faculty there in 1517, according to R. Goulet, *Magnificence of the University of Paris*, pp. 38 and 78.
[6] E. T. Beaumont, *Academical Habit*, pp. 20–21, calls this a sleeveless tabard.
[7] C. Innes, p. 571.　　　[8] C. Innes, pp. 269–70, § 44.

shape of these hoods, which were short and joined to the 'shoulder piece', is said to have been copied from those worn at Paris.[1]

This visitation caused a reform to be made in the shape of the *cappa*, hood, and 'shoulder piece' of Masters of Arts and Bachelors of Arts,[2] but we are not told what this was. Bursars (i.e. students with bursaries, or scholarships) in the Arts Faculty were at the same time ordered to wear hoods (i.e. no doubt the black cloth hoods) everywhere except in their own rooms and in church,[3] and students of the Faculty of Theology were warned that if they wished to be considered for the priesthood, they must wear round hoods and round clerical birettas.[4]

In post-Reformation times we find, as in the other universities of Scotland,[5] academical dress much neglected. In one of the few memorial brasses in Scotland, that which depicts Dr. Liddel (1613) in the Old, or West, Church, Aberdeen, there is no suggestion of academical dress. Liddel is depicted wearing an ordinary lay gown with winged sleeves decorated with buttons and braid; while his bonnet with ear-flaps suggests no more than the head-dress of a man of dignity of the day, in spite of what E. C. Clarke says about its academical character.[6]

If the Kirk did not interest itself in academical dress, Charles I and Laud, with their policy of episcopacy, did. In 1634 at the visitation of King's College, Aberdeen, the king commanded that all members of the college should use gowns according to their several degrees and faculties.[7] Hoods are not mentioned. They had apparently been abandoned too long to be successfully revived.

In 1641 at King's College the same spirit, which had been instilled by the king seven years before, prevailed, and students were ordered to wear gowns (*galerus, toga*) and hats in college, but they were allowed informal caps and cloaks when enjoying recreation.[8] At the same time bursars (i.e. scholars) were ordered to wear hats and gowns, and if disobedient they were as a

---

[1] *Notes and Queries*, 1st ser. iii. 329; *Notes and Queries*, 7th ser. xii. 241–2.
[2] C. Innes, p. 265, § 22.   [3] C. Innes, p. 261, § 4.
[4] C. Innes, p. 260, § 2.   [5] R. G. Cant, p. 20.
[6] E. C. Clarke, art. cit. lxi. 62. An illustration of the brass is given in C. T. Davis, art. 'Monumental Brass in the Old, or West, Church, Aberdeen', in *Archaeological Journal* li (1894), pl. opp. p. 76.
[7] C. Innes, p. 394.   [8] C. Innes, p. 233, § 11.

punishment to wear leather belts.[1] This curious punishment of having to wear a belt, which is to be considered as a sort of symbol of restraint, is again mentioned in 1659, when a bursar speaking in 'the vulgar tongue' was told to go without his gown and with a broad white leather belt.[2] In this year bursars were again ordered to use a gown and a hat at all functions.[3] Their gowns were to be black or tawny, and not red,[4] but in 1695, as we have already seen, the Commission on Scottish Universities ordered all students in all the Scottish universities to wear red gowns; while at Aberdeen as elsewhere regents and other masters were to wear black ones.[5] Even after that there seems to have been some difficulty in enforcing this, for it was found necessary in 1704 to order bursars to wear gowns.[6] Doctors of Laws continued to wear, as in 1610 they had been ordered to do in a proclamation of James VI, black gowns faced on the front and on the collar with black velvet.[7]

It has been said that the square cap was not used in Scotland until the late nineteenth century, but in J. Kay's caricature 'The Sapient Septemviri' (1786) three professors of King's College, Aberdeen, wear square black caps without tuft or tassel.[8]

From 1695 to 1860 the students of the two colleges of Aberdeen, King's (1494) and Marischal College (1593), wore slightly differing red gowns. Two water-colours of 1860[9] show what the gowns must have been like in the eighteenth century. The first shows a bajan (freshman) of King's College wearing an open red gown reaching to a little way above the knee, with a broad flap collar in two layers covering the shoulders. The sleeves have small panels, and a hole for the arm to pass through is cut above the elbow in the shape of an inverted V. There are two red buttons in front near the top of the gown. The second water-colour shows a bajan of Marischal College wearing a gown of the same length, but it is of a duller red. It is fastened high up by two red buttons, but it is open otherwise. The broad

---

[1] C. Innes, p. 237, § 45. [2] C. Innes, p. 255, § 14.
[3] C. Innes, p. 254, § 5. [4] C. Innes, loc. cit.
[5] C. Innes, p. 372. [6] R. S. Rait, *The Universities of Aberdeen*, p. 185.
[7] Anon. art. cit., *Journal of Jurisprudence*, xxviii (1884), 67.
[8] J. Kay, *A Series of Original Portraits and Caricature Etchings*, i, pl. opp. p. 76, no. xxxv.
[9] W. Johnston, *The Last Bajans of King's and Marischal Colleges*, frontispiece and pl. opp. p. 1.

PLATE 16

Dress of Bajans of King's and Marischal Colleges, Aberdeen

flap collar, which is of the same shape as that of the King's College bajan, is of purple velvet. It has large false panel-sleeves, dull red as is the rest of the gown, which fall broad, flat and square over the arms and reach only to the hips (Pl. 16).

EDINBURGH (1582)

Until 1858 when all authority was taken from the Civic Council and placed in the hands of the *Senatus Academicus*, Edinburgh was a civic college.[1]

Though as early as 1583 it was decided that undergraduates should wear gowns, this was not observed, for when in 1695 the Parliamentary Commission ordered regents of Edinburgh College to see to it that the wearing of red gowns by under-graduates was put into practice, the wording implies that, as was not the case at St. Andrews, Glasgow, and Aberdeen, Edinburgh students were not in the habit of wearing gowns.[2] But Sir William Brereton in 1635 expressly mentions that Edinburgh undergraduates wore 'coloured cloaks'.[3] This may mean either that in the interval between 1635 and 1695 they had given up wearing them, or that the commissioners wished them to wear true gowns and not cloaks.

Principals of the college had no particular dress, but being generally clergy appeared in the Geneva gown.[4] Other develop-ments belong to the nineteenth century.

In the eighteenth century the gown of Doctors of Divinity had a velvet collar, was open in front, and had large long braided buttonholes on each side, from the outer end of which hung a tassel. A clear illustration of this is to be found in the painting by D. Martin of Robert Henry (1718–90), who became a Doctor of Divinity of Edinburgh in 1774.[5] This was an adaptation of a lay fashion of the time as can be seen from the portrait by A. Carpentier of the sculptor L. F. Roubiliac. Here the loose coat which he negligently wears while busy in his studio is decorated with tassels in precisely the same way as Henry's gown.

---

[1] Anon. *Edinburgh University: A Sketch*, pp. 19 and 76–77.
[2] Anon. *Edinburgh University*, p. 4; J. Coutts, p. 179; C. Innes, *Munimenta Universitatis Glasguensis*, iii. 523; C. Innes, *Fasti*, p. 372.
[3] W. Brereton, p. 117.
[4] J. Kay, pl. opp. p. 94, no. xlii (portrait of William Robertson, principal 1762–93).
[5] There is an engraving of this portrait by J. Caldwell. Cf. p. 141, n. 11.

IV. IRELAND

TRINITY COLLEGE, DUBLIN (1591)

After several unsuccessful attempts between 1311 and 1585 to found a university in Ireland, the first stone of Trinity College, Dublin, was laid in 1591, and the first students were admitted two years later.[1]

It was from the first greatly influenced by the University of Cambridge,[2] and its academical dress was almost entirely copied from Cambridge, and in a few cases from Oxford.

Statutes about dress are few and unsatisfactory. It is first mentioned in 1637 when in the course of Charles I's statutes the provost and all graduates are ordered to wear on every feast day, presumably in chapel, a clean surplice and the hood befitting their degree.[3] Fellows, scholars, commoners (pensioners), and other students are to have gowns, which are not described, to be worn not only in college, but in the city, while boots are not to be worn and ordinary clothing is to be plain.[4] A supplement to the statutes of 1759 contains no further information, and all that is interesting in the statutes of 1760 is the reference to a custom for all recipients of degrees to pay for gloves to be distributed to the appropriate officers.[5]

The vice-chancellor's dress was copied from that of Cambridge, as can be seen from the portrait of about 1682 of Anthony Dopping in the college. As it is a portrait showing the head and shoulders only it is not as valuable for evidence as it might have been, but the red robe and the white fur 'shoulder piece' plainly appear.[6]

The 'business' (Congregation at Cambridge) dress of Doctors of Divinity, according to the portrait of William King, Archbishop of Dublin (D.D., 1689), consisted of the *cappa* costume, the same as that of a Cambridge Doctor of Divinity with a large white fur hood spread over the shoulders and a fur-lined *cappa*

---

[1] Cambridge, Univ. Libr. MS. Add. 707, fos. 2–5 and 8.
[2] For instance, the early provosts were imported from that university (J. W. Stubbs, T. K. Abbott, J. P. Mahaffy, and others, *The Book of Trinity College, Dublin*, p. 17).
[3] H. G. MacDonnell, *Chartae et Statuta*, p. 45.
[4] H. G. MacDonnell, p. 57.
[5] *The Statutes of Trinity College, Dublin*, trans. R. Bolton, p. 161.
[6] W. G. Strickland, *Pictures, Busts, and Statues in Trinity College, Dublin*, p. 13.

PLATE 17

Edmund Burke in the LL.D. Festal Dress of Trinity College, Dublin, 1795

with a wide and long opening in front.[1] The full dress was scarlet with bell-sleeves lined and faced with white silk.[2] The undress was the Master of Arts gown, the same as at Cambridge, but without 'strings'.

Doctors of Laws wore as full dress a scarlet cloth robe with salmon pink bell-sleeves, and a salmon pink hood is worn with it, incorrectly by English standards. With this costume was worn a square black cap with a black tassel, and long white bands.[3] John Hoppner's portrait of Edmund Burke (1795) (Pl. 17) shows him in this robe, but he does not wear the hood and instead of bands wears a lace fall as being an honorand.[4] There is no record of a *cappa* dress. The Master of Arts gown was worn as undress.

Doctors of Medicine wore for full dress a scarlet cloth bell-sleeved robe faced with crimson silk, and if the hood was worn it was of the same colours.[5] The head-dress was the same as for the Doctor of Laws, and the Master's gown was worn for undress.

Doctors of Music followed the Cambridge dress of that degree.[6]

The dress of a Master of Arts was the black gown, the same as the master's gown at Oxford and Cambridge and without 'strings'. The hood is given in Taylor's book as being of black silk lined with pink silk.[7] The change to dark blue lining[8] took place in the mid-nineteenth century.[9] With this the black square cap with a tassel copied from Oxford and Cambridge was worn, but no doubt it would have had a tuft and no tassel before the later eighteenth century. The shape of the master's hood was in 1850 described as being smaller in itself than those of either Oxford or Cambridge, but having a long square-ended liripipe,[10] and it had probably always been like that.

The dress of the Bachelor of Divinity and the Bachelor of

---

[1] J. W. Stubbs, T. K. Abbott, J. P. Mahaffy, and others, p. 241.

[2] W. B. S. Taylor, *History of the University of Dublin*, pl. opp. p. 530. In the nineteenth century the colour of the facings on the sleeves and the lining was changed to black (T. W. Wood, *Ecclesiastical and Academic Colours*, p. 48).

[3] W. B. S. Taylor, frontispiece.

[4] A. P. I. Samuels, *Early Life of Edmund Burke*, pl. i, opp. p. 1.

[5] T. W. Wood, p. 48. [6] T. W. Wood, loc. cit.

[7] W. B. S. Taylor, loc. cit. [8] T. W. Wood, loc. cit.

[9] It is worth noticing that at Trinity 'a pink' is the equivalent of the Oxford and Cambridge 'blue'.

[10] G. J. French, *Tippets of the Canons Ecclesiastical*, p. 6, fig. 16.

Laws was the same as the dress for these two degrees at Cambridge. That of the Bachelor of Medicine was the same as the Dublin master's dress, while the dress of the Bachelor of Music had a mid-blue silk hood trimmed with white fur. The hood of Masters of Surgery was copied from that of this degree at Oxford.[1]

In the 1820 plates the Bachelor of Arts wears the same square cap as those of all other degrees wear. His gown has very large bell sleeves slashed open as at Cambridge and his hood is trimmed with white fur.[2]

In the same series the junior fellow wears a long black plain open and sleeveless gown, but which has material covering the upper part of the arm as if the beginning of a master's sleeve. He wears bands, as do doctors and masters in these plates.[3]

The nobleman wears a square black cap with a gold tassel, and a long black gown adorned with thick gold braid and gold tassels on the sleeves, on the sides of the gown, and on the skirts. The decorations on the skirts and on the sides consist of two or three buttons from which small gold tassels hang, and these buttons have a connecting piece of braid between them; but the braiding on the sleeves is more elaborate and consists of five rows of three buttons with connecting braid between them and small gold tassels hanging from the outer buttons, while down the middle of all these a thick piece of braid runs vertically. One feature of this dress to be particularly noticed, since it is not found in the dress of Oxford or Cambridge, is that the sleeves end in front at the elbow and hang down behind the arms in little panels with one gold tassel on the lower outside corner.[4]

The dress of the fellow-commoner differs from that of the nobleman in that all the decorations, which are exactly the same in character as those on the nobleman's gown, are black instead of gold, and the sleeves in this case reach only to the elbow and stop abruptly there without the little panel.[5]

The foundation scholar wears a square black cap without a tassel and a full long black gown with bell-sleeves not slashed open. The upper part of the open gown is faced with mid-blue velvet and there is a mid-blue velvet stripe at the wrist on each of

[1] T. W. Wood, loc. cit.   [2] W. B. S. Taylor, pl. opp. p. 440.
[3] W. B. S. Taylor, pl. opp. p. 364.
[4] W. B. S. Taylor, pl. opp. p. 364.   [5] W. B. S. Taylor, pl. opp. p. 530.

the sleeves.[1] There is no illustration of the pensioner's dress, but it seems to have been (if we take into account its present appearance) the same as that of the foundation scholar except that there was no velvet on the gown, and the cap had a tassel.

In the eighteenth century sizars seem to have worn a sleeveless black stuff gown and a red cap, 'the badge of a servant'.[2] The red cap was probably round after the 'catercap' style.

[1] W. B. S. Taylor, pl. opp. p. 440.
[2] J. Forster, *Life of Goldsmith*, chap. ii.

5

I. GERMAN-SPEAKING COUNTRIES

A. GENERAL

A GERMAN professor of about 1490 wears a long and ample *supertunica* with close-fitting sleeves, and a small low hat with a turned-up brim. At his feet among the students sits second from the left a probable Bachelor of Arts, who is to be distinguished by his little low flat cap and a hood hanging behind.[1]

In a good woodcut of about 1500 showing the Emperor Maximilian I in disputation with seven professors representing the seven liberal arts we have examples of German professorial dress, particularly in that of the professor with his back full towards us. A small flat cap is worn, and the rest of the habit consists of an ample gown with openings in the glove sleeves for the arms; and a 'shoulder piece' with a very small rudimentary hood at the back of the neck. From this descends a long straight liripipe reaching nearly as far as the back of the knees.[2]

From the *Epistolae Obscurorum Virorum*, written at Erfurt and published in 1516, we learn that at this time in Germany Doctors of Theology wore black *tunicas* and large hoods with a liripipe (*nigras tunicas, et magna caputia cum liripipiis*).[3] At the same period furred *cappas* were generally associated with the dress of Doctors of Law.[4]

As to colours, during the first half of the sixteenth century, as before, persons of academical dignity in company with lawyers and schoolmasters wore a red *Sendelbinde* (*chaperon*) on the left shoulder; but Protestant members of these professions after this time discarded the *Sendelbinde*.[5] By the seventeenth

---

[1] E. Reicke, *Lehrer und Unterrichtswesen in der deutschen Vergangenheit*, p. 38, Abb. 29.
[2] E. Reicke, *Lehrer*, p. 43, Abb. 34.
[3] *Epistolae Obscurorum Virorum*, i, letter 2, p. 294; letter 26, pp. 339–40.
[4] *Epistolae Obscurorum Virorum*, i, letter 2, p. 295.
[5] F. Hottenroth, *Handbuch*, p. 597, fig. 152. 3.

century the faculty colours generally observed in Germany, though there were exceptions such as at Leipzig, Kiel, and Helmstädt, were for Theology, black; for law, red; for Medicine, blue; and for Philosophy, violet.[1] By this time the shape of the *pileus* varied at different universities.[2]

As for the academical gown it was worn closed and had a standing collar, until at the Reformation, under the much increased influence of lay fashion Protestants of academical dignity, as well as lawyers and schoolmasters of the Reformed Faith, giving up the *Sendelbinde*, took to an open black gown with a flap collar.[3] Roman Catholic lawyers continued to wear the *Sendelbinde* and the old type of closed gown.[4] The new gown was really the *Schaube*, a lay gown, which came also, but in a somewhat altered form, to be identified with the dress of the Protestant clergy.[5]

B. INDIVIDUAL UNIVERSITIES

PRAGUE (1347)

In 1367 it was ordered that at all academical Acts and on all solemn occasions Bachelors of Arts and Masters of Arts should wear a tabard or special dress suited to their standing. If they failed to do this their presence would be ignored.[6] It was found necessary to insist upon this again in 1389, when masters were particularly mentioned.[7] From these two references, and from another of 1380 of a similar character,[8] it would seem that, although other forms of *toga* were used, the tabard was the most generally accepted form of dress for graduates. Another form of dress appears in a clause of the 1380 enactment.[9] This is the *toga rugata*, a gown of many pleats or folds.[10] Candidates about to be created bachelors were especially ordered to wear this, but it was equally used by masters.[11] It was in fact some form

---

[1] A. Steger, *Dissertatio de purpura*, pp. 29–30.

[2] F. G. Struve, *De Symbolis*, p. 3a; A. Steger, p. 29; C. Biccius, *Tractatus Juridicus de Pileo*, p. 18, cap. ii. x.

[3] F. Hottenroth, p. 597, fig. 152. 3.   [4] F. Hottenroth, p. 763.

[5] M. von Boehn, *Modes and Manners*, ii. 77 and 128–9.

[6] *Monumenta historica universitatis Pragensis*, i. 9.   [7] Ibid. i. 10.

[8] Ibid. i. 54, § 21.   [9] Ibid. i. 55, § 25.

[10] *Rugata = plissée*; see H. Beaune and J. d'Arbaumont, *Les Universités de Franche-Comté*, p. xlix, n. 2.

[11] W. W. Tomek, *Geschichte der Prager Universität*, p. 37.

of tabard, or perhaps simply another name for it.[1] In 1393 the tabard is again insisted on for masters.[2]

The following was the dress at this university in the Middle Ages: for students a plain, closed, sleeved *mantellum*, i.e., a short *supertunica*; and for Bachelors and Masters of Arts a much-pleated sleeveless closed *supertunica* called a tabard or *habitus*, or *toga rugata*, the two degrees being distinguished by the fact that, whereas the bachelors had no head-dress and had plain gowns, Masters of Arts not only wore the *pileus*, but were also allowed to have their dress lined with silk and trimmed with fur.[3]

As to doctoral dress at Prague it consisted of *biretta* or *pileus* (the biretta, rigid, square and four-cornered, succeeding to the *pileus* during the sixteenth century), and the 'shoulder piece' (*epomis*), worn over the *toga*, and the doctor on his creation received the ring, the book, and the kiss.[4] The biretta and *epomis* of the Faculty of Theology were purple, and those of the later Faculty of Philosophy, created from that of Arts, violet. The insignia of Doctors of Medicine were altered in 1614 to a round black bonnet and a black shoulder scarf (*chaperon*). The wearing of all doctoral insignia was abolished by imperial decree in 1784.[5]

VIENNA (1365)

In 1389 Doctors and Bachelors of Theology were ordered to wear the *cappa clausa*,[6] while in the same year Masters of Arts were required to wear dress reaching to the ankles, and Bachelors of Arts were not to make use of any fur, but noblemen and bishops were exempt from these orders.[7] In 1458 Masters of Arts are described as wearing *pallium* (a loose *supertunica*) and biretta,[8] and in 1503 they still wore the long *pallium*.[9] In 1513 academical head-dress was forbidden to Bachelors of Arts of any condition.[10]

---

[1] W. W. Tomek, loc. cit.   [2] *Monumenta Pragensis*, i. 96, § 6.
[3] C. Meiners, art. 'Geschichte der Trachten', in *Göttingische akademische Annalen*, i (1804), 219; A. Schultz, *Deutsches Leben*, p. 215; W. W. Tomek, p. 37.
[4] *Monumenta Pragensis*, ii. 562, n.   [5] Ibid. ii. 562.
[6] R. Kink, *Geschichte der Univ. zu Wien*, ii. 95.   [7] R. Kink, ii. 193–4.
[8] i.e. the round variety, for the square one had not yet appeared.
[9] C. Meiners, art. cit. i. 220–1; *Conspectus historiae universitatis Viennensis*, ii. 68.
[10] R. Kink, ii. 318.

As to undergraduates, in 1458 they were ordered to wear *tunicas* which were short to distinguish them from graduates;[1] while in 1503 they wore with their closed *tunica* a girdle. This girdle was worn by them as a sign that they were still apprentices bound to their university, and seems to have been a mark of their dress long before this date.[2] By the early sixteenth century they had come to wear a much longer *tunica*, dark brown or black with sleeves, and a small round brown cap (*Gugel*).[3]

At the beginning of the eighteenth century the dress of the deans of the four faculties consisted of bell-sleeved gowns, open from the waist downwards, 'shoulder pieces' divided down the front and edged with plain braid, and cylindrical caps.[4] In 1703 the rector wears a closed cassock with tight sleeves, and over this a damasked 'shoulder piece' reaching to the elbows, edged along the lower edge and probably lined with miniver. He wears white bands and has a cylindrical black velvet hat with a gold hat-band (Pl. 18 *a*).[5]

In 1752 the dress of the chancellor consisted of the 'shoulder piece' (*epomis*) with a little hood attached, a black velvet gown embroidered with gold thread and trimmed with ermine, and a black velvet gimped biretta. On occasions of mourning these articles of dress were all of red velvet. The dress of the deans was by this time the same as that of the chancellor, but less richly embroidered. Their dress was also of red velvet for mourning.[6]

When in 1773 the university applied for new dress the Empress Maria Theresa refused to comply with the request, but allowed the old to be retained on the condition that it should never be worn in her court, where university officials were warned to appear only in black suits. One can see how affairs were tending, and it is not surprising to note that on 11 November 1784, the Emperor Josef II abolished the old dress which he considered to be 'a reminder of the dark days when the Papal chair claimed the sole right to establish universities'.

[1] C. Meiners, art. cit. i. 220–1. [2] *Conspectus*, ii. 68.
[3] A. Richter, *Bilder aus der deutschen Kulturgeschichte*, ii. 349; J. von Aschbach, *Geschichte der Wiener Universität*, i. 67.
[4] E. Reicke, *Der Gelehrte*, p. 102, Abb. 88.
[5] J. R. Planché, *Cyclopaedia of Costume*, ii. 325.
[6] R. Kink, i. 112–13, n. 126.

In 1792 the chancellor and deans wore black suits with a ribbon round the neck, red for the secular and purple for the clerical members, and from the ribbon hung a medal. In 1804 gold chains were acquired instead of the ribbons with more attractive medals.[1]

ERFURT (1378)

In the late fourteenth-century seal of the university the rector, seated on the left, has a small round shallow *pileus* with a button apex, a *tunica*, and a furred 'shoulder piece' quite open in front. The doctors on the right have long closed *tunicas* with short puffed sleeves and large *pilei* with the button apex.[2] During the next hundred years a change took place in the rector's dress, for in the rectorial seal of the late fifteenth century he wears a flowing *roba* with hanging sleeves. His head-dress is the same as before.[3]

COLOGNE (1385)

In the statutes of 1392 all of whatever degree are ordered to wear clerical dress, not short, decorated, or parti-coloured.[4] At the same time the dress of the rector is mentioned, from which it appears that as yet no definite costume had been given him, for he is to wear for the present an *epitogium*, that is, a large gown with a 'shoulder piece' with a miniver hood which in summer may be of silk. If he prefers he may simply wear the dress of the degree he holds as a doctor or master.[5] Two interesting points arise from this, first, that already silk was allowed as an alternative lining for the hood forty years before it was allowed at Oxford, and secondly, that the rector, like the vice-chancellors of Oxford and Cambridge, had no special official costume.

As early as 1389 the Faculties of Theology and Arts had legislated about the dress of their members. Thus Bachelors of Theology were ordered to wear a variety of *cappa clausa*, the

---

[1] R. Kink, i. 112–13, n. 126.
[2] J. G. Hagelgans, *Orbis Literatus Academicus Germanico-Europaeus*, p. 5, top large illustration.
[3] E. Gritzner, *Die Siegel deutscher Universitäten*, Taf. 6, no. 2.
[4] F. J. von Bianco, *Geschichte der Universität und der Gymnasium der Stadt Köln*, p. 406, § 7.
[5] F. J. von Bianco, p. 416, § 42.

PLATE 18

b. A Master of Theology of Ingolstadt lecturing, early sixteenth century

a. Rector Magnificus of Vienna, 1703

cappa rotunda as at Paris for all formal occasions,[1] while Masters of Theology were to wear the same dress as Masters of Arts. What this was is not mentioned, but Masters of both Theology and Arts were to wear the *birettum* while bachelors of both faculties, as was the case throughout Europe at this time, had no head-gear.[2] Very likely both these masters wore the *cappa clausa*. Bachelors of Arts were ordered to wear a hooded *epitogium* or a tabard, the hood either lined with miniver or with silk.[3] In 1393 members of the Faculty of Medicine were also allowed these alternative linings to their hoods.[4] In the re-formed statutes of the Faculty of Arts of 1457 masters were required to wear the *epitogium*.[5]

This dress, consisting of *epitogium* and cylindrical biretta, was worn by regents in 1508.[6]

In 1516 a Master of Arts is said to have been privileged to wear a gold ring and to have a silk lining to his *cappa* (*sericum sub cappa*),[7] but the latter must have been used only on formal occasions.

In the eighteenth century professors wore the *epomis* ('shoulder piece') over a black gown as at Vienna, Heidelberg, and Mainz.[8]

HEIDELBERG (1386)

In 1386 masters and bachelors of all faculties are to wear uniform *cappas* (of what kind is not stated) at all acts in the schools.[9]

In the following year there is mention of the Faculties of Arts and Theology. All that is said about the dress of Bachelors and Masters of Theology is that they are to use *cappas*,[10] but the dress of Masters of Arts is given in detail. They are to wear a dress which is a form of tabard lined with miniver or silk with two lappets (*cum duabus lingulis*), of which there are many examples in illustrations of academical and legal persons at this time throughout Europe, worn at the neck. The tabard is either to be without sleeves or with short and close-fitting

---

[1] F. J. von Bianco, p. 456.
[2] F. J. von Bianco, p. 444.
[3] F. J. von Bianco, p. 439.
[4] F. J. von Bianco, p. 490.
[5] F. J. von Bianco, p. 501.
[6] E. Reicke, *Der Lehrer*, p. 40, Abb. 31.
[7] *Epistolae Obscurorum Virorum*, ii, letter 23, p. 442.
[8] E. Winkelmann, *Urkundenbuch der Universitaet Heidelberg*, ii. 305, § 2421.
[9] E. Winkelmann, i. 5; E. F. Henderson, *Historical Documents*, p. 263.
[10] E. Winkelmann, i. 23.

sleeves, and the head-dress is to be the biretta, that is the round one.[1] Incepting masters are to wear a black *cappa* lined with miniver or silk and are to have a biretta.[2] Bachelors of Arts had apparently dress of the same cut as masters, but except by special permission were not to have linings of either miniver or silk[3] and were presumably without a head-dress.

In 1409 the Faculty of Theology made it clear that as far as the faculty was concerned bachelors and licentiates were not to wear a head-dress, and that what was done in other faculties was no concern of theirs.[4] It seems that there was at this time a love of luxury among the clergy, and in 1411 the Faculty of Theology legislated against this abuse and refused to allow Bachelors of Theology to wear a ring unless persons of dignity.[5]

By 1444 Masters of Arts had begun to wear such unseemly dress that they had to be forbidden to wear a *pallium* open right down the side or a *tunica* too long or too short, and if they continued to disobey they were to be suspended from their functions.[6]

At length in 1469/70 came the first legislation about costume addressed to the university in general, but particularly to students of all faculties. As at Oxford in 1489 the hood is ordered to be worn fastened down to the *supertunica*.[7] After this perhaps students, deprived of the head-covering which the hood had provided, tried to wear some kind of academical cap, but in common with bachelors this was forbidden them.[8]

Regular legislation about dress ended in the sixteenth century. In 1533 there is evidence that already students had taken to Spanish fashions instead of the old long *tunica*,[9] but the little cloak then mentioned came in time to have an academical significance, and in a somewhat longer form was the only particular dress which German students had in the seventeenth century.

In 1580 the chancellor and rector were both distinguished by a velvet biretta, presumably round.[10] The type of dress worn

---

[1] E. Winkelmann, i. 43.   [2] E. Winkelmann, i. 41.
[3] E. Winkelmann, i. 36.   [4] E. Winkelmann, i. 103.
[5] E. Winkelmann, i. 106.   [6] E. Winkelmann, i. 152.
[7] E. Winkelmann, i. 186; R. F. Seybolt, *Manuale Scholarium*, p. 117.
[8] E. Winkelmann, i. 198, and ii. 61, § 551.   [9] E. Winkelmann, ii. 88, § 811.
[10] A. Thorbecke, *Statuten und Reformationen der Universität Heidelberg vom 16. bis 18. Jahrhundert*, p. 184, § 60.

about this time by doctors can be seen from the print of a Doctor of Theology of this university, D. Pareus (d. 1622). He wears a gown with broad plain stuff facings sewn on flat and with a large falling fur collar. The bag sleeves of the gown have wide slits for the arms to pass through, the upper part of these openings being cut in the middle in the shape of an inverted V.[1]

As the seventeenth century progressed the wearing of academical costume was less and less observed, but the authorities at first did their best to counteract this. In 1656 professors were reminded that at lectures and academical Acts they must wear a long gown,[2] and so that there should be no excuse for not having one, in 1672 long black gowns were specially made for professors at the expense of the university, and they were requested to wear them while performing academical functions.[3] This 'professorenrock' is mentioned in 1682 as if a particular form of gown common to all professors, who wore this and not the dress of their various degrees.[4]

During the eighteenth century the 'shoulder piece' (epomis) was worn by professors and doctors as is mentioned in 1750[5] and 1774.[6] From this it seems that the use of the 'professors' gown' had died out and that professors wore the dress of the doctorate which they held. Professors and doctors wore the epomis over the black gown and had a red biretta on important occasions, but on ordinary or mourning occasions they wore the black gown alone and had a black biretta.[7] In 1795 the Professor of Theology was allowed to use a particular shape of epomis unspecified such as was used at Cologne and Mainz.[8]

The ensuing political changes which affected Heidelberg no less than other towns of Western Germany seem to have led to the abandonment of old ceremonial observances in the university, and when dress is again mentioned in 1804 it appears that there had been a complete break with the past. In this year the authorities decided to revive for professors the use of suitable dress according to the spirit of a bygone age for academical occasions.[9]

[1] S. Clark, *Marrow of Ecclesiastical History*, p. 451.
[2] E. Winkelmann, ii. 204, § 1664.   [3] A. Thorbecke, p. 253, § 10.
[4] E. Winkelmann, ii. 215, § 1745.   [5] E. Winkelmann, i. 428.
[6] E. Winkelmann, ii. 281, § 2237; 282, § 2244; 283, § 2250.
[7] E. Winkelmann, ii. 283, § 2250.
[8] E. Winkelmann, ii. 305, § 2421.   [9] E. Winkelmann, i. 454.

WÜRZBURG (1403)

The statutes make no mention of a special academical dress before 1587, but in that year there was a complete review of the whole question. As a result the following rules were drawn up. The rector was to be distinguished by a gold 'shoulder piece' (*epomis*) and the vice-rector by a red one.[1] It is to be assumed that these were to be worn over the ordinary rectorial robe, probably a purple, bell-sleeved gown.

As the university remained loyal to the Roman Catholic Church after the Reformation, the chancellor and vice-chancellor were still priests, and when they appeared at University functions were ordered to wear surplice and stole.[2]

Doctors of Theology were to wear a black woollen 'shoulder piece' on all important occasions, while when they presided at disputations or Acts they were to wear in addition to their other dress a fur 'roller' hood close round the neck. With this was to be worn a *cappa pellita duplici*, a 'shoulder piece' lined with fur. Bachelors and Licentiates of Theology were to wear a large fur hood (*cappa pellicea maioris*) except monks, who were, of course, to wear their monastic habit.[3] Bachelors were always to appear bare-headed.[4] Doctors of Theology wore a blue silk *pileus*.[5]

In 1610 professors of the Faculty of Medicine were ordered to wear at their lectures and at all solemn Acts a black gown (*toga*), a blue 'shoulder piece' (*epomis*), and a blue biretta.[6] A non-Regent Doctor of Medicine was in 1713 commanded to wear at his investiture a gown and *pileus*,[7] from which we may infer that the 'shoulder piece' was the sign of the regent; and to this may be added the fact that in 1732 only regent doctors wore gown, 'shoulder piece' and *pileus*. The two latter garments were of the colour of the faculty to which the doctor belonged.[8]

[1] F. X. von Wegele, *Geschichte der Universität Wirzburg*, ii. 155, § 70.
[2] F. X. von Wegele, ii. 160, § 70.
[3] F. X. von Wegele, ii. 175–7, § 71.
[4] F. X. von Wegele, ii. 183, § 71.
[5] F. X. von Wegele, ii. 186 and 188.
[6] F. W. von Wegele, ii. 250, § 94.
[7] F. X. von Wegele, ii. 306, § 122.
[8] L. Carlier, *In Iure academico*, p. 26 (pars. i, sect. iii, 33). In 1809 lay professors were given the title of *Rath* (councillor) and were ordered to wear the military type of costume of that office, while clerical professors were to dress according to episcopal instruction (F. X. von Wegele, ii. 512).

LEIPZIG (1409)

Doctors in 1496 wore a biretta, a very large hood, a 'shoulder piece', and some form of *supertunica* not specified. The biretta appears to have been black.[1]

Members of the Faculty of Philosophy (Arts) were in 1436 ordered to wear their *pallium* closed, but without a belt, and to have a cap (*Mütze*), a 'shoulder piece', and a hood hanging down behind.[2] This dress appears on the fifteenth-century seal of the Faculty of Philosophy.[3] It seems from this that originally masters were not allowed a head-dress of distinction like a biretta, which was reserved for doctors, but something of a less dignified nature. In 1496 masters still wore a small cap, this time called a *mitra*, which was flat,[4] but by 1499 they were wearing a black (*fuscus*) biretta.[5]

Already in 1495 the authorities had had to combat the growing fondness of members of the university for lay fashions, of which the 'little winged cape' (*caputiolus petiatus*) is especially condemned.[6]

Bachelors were to assume a simple dress to reach below the knees, and they were on no account to wear the black biretta, according to an order of 1499. This was repeated in 1507 and 1512.[7] The dress of undergraduates seems to have been almost, if not the same, as that of bachelors.[8]

In the *Dritte Statutenredaction* of 1471, with additions to 1490, is a reference to the dress of deans of the Faculty of Philosophy. These officers on their election were to wear a tabard, the symbol of their office.[9]

The particular mark of the *Rector Magnificus* in 1741 was a purple silk-cloth (*pannus sericus*) cloak-gown edged with various

[1] F. Zarncke, *Die Statutenbücher der Universität Leipzig*, pp. 18–19, § 5, *De Habitus Honestate* (1496), and p. 456, *Vierte Statutenredaction*, viii. 10; A. Schultz, p. 212.

[2] F. Zarncke, *Statutenbücher*, p. 320, § 4, *De Palleis apertis*; A. Schultz, loc. cit., where he gives the date wrongly as 1440.

[3] J. G. Hagelgans, p. 13, small seal on lower right.

[4] F. Zarncke, *Statutenbücher*, pp. 18–19, § 5.

[5] F. Zarncke, *Statutenbücher*, p. 456, *Vierte Statutenredaction*, viii, § 10.

[6] F. Zarncke, *Die Deutschen Universitäten in Mittelalter*, p. 166, quoting the *Libellus Formularis*, § 27.

[7] F. Zarncke, *Statutenbücher*, p. 470, *Vierte Statutenredaction*, xiii, § 21; p. 477, *Vierte Stat.*, xiv, § 17, *De Habitu Baccalariorum*; p. 496, *Fünfte Statutenredaction*, i, § 19.

[8] F. Zarncke, *Statutenbücher*, loc. cit.

[9] F. Zarncke, *Statutenbücher*, p. 383, *Dritte Statutenredaction*, ii, § 12.

furs and a 'shoulder piece' with a small hood attached of the same colour and material; while Doctors of Theology and of Philosophy wore a violet biretta and a violet cape (*paludamentum*), and Doctors of Law and of Medicine a purple biretta and purple cape.[1]

GREIFSWALD (1456)

In 1456 at the time of the foundation of Greifswald University, Bachelors of Arts were ordered always to appear in a hood (*caputium cucullatum*).[2]

In the university seal, struck the same year, the *Rector Magnificus* appears wearing a 'shoulder piece', a long fur robe, and a round cap with a long 'stalk' apex, and he holds a sceptre.[3] A rector of 1522 appears on the right-hand side of his seal wearing a long sleeveless pleated tabard closed in front, a 'shoulder piece' covering his chest, and a fur bonnet which he holds in his hand.[4]

On the university seal of 1692 the rector is not dressed in the style of that year but rather of the sixteenth century. He wears a *pallium* and a 'shoulder piece' in two layers, and is bareheaded.[5]

INGOLSTADT (1472)

According to the foundation statutes of the university (1472) the rector's hood and *birettum* were to be red if he was a doctor or a prelate of the highest standing, brown if a master or a prelate of lower standing, and if a priest black.[6]

There are examples in the university archives[7] of the red hood and *birettum*, and no doubt it was nearly always a doctor or a highly placed prelate who was elected rector. From these it can be seen that over a long loose cape was worn the hood and 'shoulder piece', red in colour edged with gold braid and

---

[1] A. Steger, pp. 28–29; F. G. Struve, p. 3b.
[2] J. G. L. Kosegarten, *Geschichte der Universität von Greifswald*, ii. 309 (Stats. Fac. Arts, § 109).
[3] J. G. L. Kosegarten, ii (at end), Taf. 3, no. 15.
[4] J. G. L. Kosegarten, ii (at end), Taf. 4, no. 19.
[5] E. Gritzner, Taf. 11, no. 1; J. G. Hagelgans, p. 9.
[6] C. Prantl, *Geschichte der Ludwig-Maximilians-Universität in Ingolstadt*, i. 40.
[7] As for instance in the 'Matriculation Book', University Archives D, iv, no. 4, depicting the inauguration scene of the *Rector Magnificus* in 1589.

ermine, while the *birettum* was of the same colour and similarly adorned.[1]

In 1475 scholars, bachelors, licentiates, and secular doctors are ordered to wear *cappas*, perhaps in fact the loose capes mentioned above, at all academical functions according to the practice of other universities, after which there is no legislation about dress for a considerable time.[2]

A Master of Theology, Magister Adorf, on a tombstone of 1505 wears a fairly rigid *pileus* without an apex, but with side-pieces (Pl. 18*b*). He has a *cappa manicata*, a 'shoulder piece', and a hood with a liripipe which falls behind. The man, a Master of Arts, standing on the right behind the students has a long-sleeved gown and a long and large *chaperon* (*Sendelbinde*) on his left shoulder.[3]

Here during the latter fifteenth century the practice had arisen for all graduates to wear the *birettum* (*pileus*). Doctors of the lay faculties wore red ones, Masters of Arts dark purple ones, while graduates in Orders wore black ones.[4] Towards the end of this century, the *cingulum*, or girdle, had become an acknowledged part of the dress of Masters of Arts. This was no doubt regarded by the masters as a symbol of servitude fit only for students, for they appealed for permission to dispense with them.[5] Indeed students of Ingoldstadt did wear girdles.[6] The *cingulum* seems to have been variously regarded at different universities and at different times, sometimes being forced upon undergraduates as a sign of their inferiority, sometimes refused them and given only to graduates and even doctors as a sign of dignity.

After a very long gap dress is at length mentioned in 1642 when the rector's costume is described. By this time it consisted of the same loose cape or cloak as in the fifteenth century, decorated with buttons.[7]

MAINZ (1477)

In 1629 doctors used the ring at the ceremony of their creation, and their head-dress was the biretta (*pileus*) of the colour of the faculty to which they belonged. It was black for Masters of

---

[1] C. Prantl, i. 40, n. 13.   [2] C. Prantl, ii. 62.
[3] F. Philippi, *Atlas zur Weltlichen Altertumskunde des deutscher Mittelalters*, Taf. 117.
[4] C. Meiners, art. cit., pp. 228–9.   [5] C. Meiners, art .cit., pp. 229–30.
[6] *Conspectus*, ii. 68.   [7] C. Prantl, ii. 394.

Theology, red for Doctors of Law, and blue for Doctors of Medicine and of Philosophy. All wore the same black silk damasked gown.[1] Professors were wearing the *epomis* in 1795.[2]

TÜBINGEN (1477)

At the University of Tübingen in the sixteenth century the particular mark of the Master of Arts (Philosophy) was the round violet-blue biretta, while the Master of Theology was distinguished by the square scarlet biretta, a ring, and a 'shoulder piece'.[3] In 1525 it was ordered that all Masters of Theology and of Philosophy (Arts) must wear gowns with full sleeves, as also scholars, but ordinary students of Law and Medicine might wear the sleeves or not.[4] This last is particularly interesting as being comparable to the full sleeves of Oxford scholars, while commoners are without them.

Academical dress was, however, falling rapidly out of use, and by 1543 Doctor Leonard Fuchs when taking a degree at Tübingen simply wore ordinary dress, as he writes to a friend.[5] From the short clause, *De Vestitu*, in the revised statutes of 1601 it would seem that any fixed rules as to the wearing of academical dress had been abandoned.[6]

The ducal college. From the set of plates of the ducal college of Tübingen published about 1589 it is to be seen that, while on ordinary occasions no academical dress was worn,[7] it was worn at certain times. Thus in the quaint scene of dinner in hall[8] with the duke and his suite at high table, masters sitting at a table on the right in the foreground wear full gowns and short round hoods. They are in fact dressed for an occasion, as for dining in hall at Oxford and Cambridge (Pl. 19).

WITTENBERG (1502)

Since in the statutes nothing is mentioned about dress except sumptuary rules, one is dependent in the case of Wittenberg on odd fragments of information gathered from various sources.

[1] M. Sandaeus, *Theologia Juridia*, Comment. L, pp. 676–7.
[2] E. Winkelmann, ii. 305, § 2421.
[3] K. Klüpfel and M. Eifert, *Geschichte der Universität Tübingen*, pt. 2, pp. 18–19.
[4] K. Klüpfel and M. Eifert, pt. 2, p. 27.
[5] M. von Boehn, *Die Mode, 16 Jahrh.*, p. 94.
[6] *Statuta universitatis scholasticae Studii Tubingensis*, pp. 111–12.
[7] J. S. Neyffer and L. Ditzinger, *Illustrissimi Wirtembergici ducalis novi collegii Delineato*, pl. i.   [8] Ibid., pl. ii.

PLATE 19

Scene in the Hall of the University of Tübingen, c. 1589

Among the medallions of coats of arms in the *Lutherhaus* is a portrait of Polich von Mellerstadt, first Rector of Wittenberg. He wears a round pill-box *pileus* and a white turn-down collar. Unfortunately only the head and shoulders appear.[1]

In 1702 on the occasion of the bicentenary a festival was held. An anonymous eyewitness of the grand procession of doctors describes the colours of the birettas of the doctors of the various faculties as being black for Theology, red for Law and Medicine, and violet for Philosophy.[2]

In the seventeenth century students wore a short gown (*halbgeistliche*),[3] but at the festival of 1702 they wore what might have been a cloak-gown, for it is not described as *geistlich*[4] or even *halbgeistlich*.

FRANKFURT-ON-ODER (1506)

The statutes of Frankfurt University published at the beginning of the *Notitia Universitatis Francofurtanae* (1707) contain no reference to academical dress.[5]

All the information to be found is that provided by the print of Cornelius Boutekoe. Here is to be seen the type of gown worn in the late seventeenth century by a Doctor of Medicine. It is of the bag-sleeved variety with an opening for the arm to pass through. The upper part of this opening is cut in the shape of an inverted V. The gown has black velvet facings and a flap collar.[6]

KÖNIGSBERG (1544)

On the seal of the Faculty of Law of about 1544 the Rector of Königsberg University wears a small lace collar, a short ermine 'shoulder piece', a loose-sleeved *tunica* with an opening down the front, though it is worn closed, and a bonnet broadly edged with ermine and having a short tassel.[7] The statutes contain no relevant information.

---

[1] W. Friedensburg, *Geschichte der Universität Wittenberg*, 2nd pl. at end.
[2] K. H. Schundenius, *Erinnerungen an die festlichen Tage der dritter Stiftungsfeyer der Akademie zu Wittenberg*, p. 61.
[3] W. Friedensburg, p. 35.
[4] K. H. Schundenius, p. 60.
[5] J. C. Becmann, *Notitia Universitatis Francofurtanae*.
[6] Oxford, Ashmolean Museum (Hope Collection).
[7] J. G. Hagelgans, p. 17, top right figure.

JENA (1558)

In the fine woodcut of the sixteenth century by Hans Weiditz depicting the ceremony of the bestowal of the doctoral bonnet all the doctors and the rector wear soft bonnets, open gowns, and a *Sendelbinde*, which hangs over both shoulders and descends in front like a sling.[1]

A full-length print of a late seventeenth-century *Rector Magnificus* shows his dress to perfection. His head-dress is a round tall pleated bonnet with a hat-band of gold braid. He wears a 'shoulder piece' which covers the shoulders and the arms as far as the elbow. It is fastened vertically down the front with many small buttons, embroidered with a leaf motif, and edged with ermine at the bottom. His robe is tight-sleeved and is fairly close to the body, but has a long train, and although it is open down the front the two sides are drawn together. He wears bands.[2]

In the seventeenth and eighteenth centuries the insignia of Doctors of Law were the purple *pileus*, a purple silk gown, and a gold ring.[3]

Although students of the lay faculties, as was the case at most German universities, seem to have given up the cloak-gown in the later seventeenth century, theological students continued to wear it. In a small water-colour illustration in the university *Stammbuch* for the year 1730 a theological student is depicted at his *viva* standing before the Professors of Theology. He wears a black flap-collared cloak which hangs behind him well away from his arms.[4]

HELMSTÄDT (1575)

Information about the dress worn at Helmstädt (now Helmstedt) is meagre. According to a patent of 1644 issued by the regents, the use of the *Pennalkleidung* (i.e. any dress with winged or long and hanging sleeves) was forbidden.[5]

In 1739 a purple silk *pileus* (i.e. round bonnet) was being worn not only by Doctors of Law,[6] but by doctors of all faculties.[7] Doctors throughout the period seem to have worn a cloak with

[1] E. Borkowsky, *Das alte Jena und seine Universität*, p. 29.
[2] E. Borkowsky, p. 68.
[3] P. Müller, *De Gradu Doctoris*, p. 26; A. Steger, p. 31.
[4] E. Borkowsky, p. 83, upper figure.
[5] Helmstädt Univ. Archives, *Decretum in Consistorio XI Maij, 1644*.
[6] J. G. Kipping, *Oratio de Honoribus Academicis*, p. 21; A. Steger, p. 31.
[7] F. G. Struve, p. 3b.

a flap collar fastened in front with a morse. The whole cloak was edged with braid and reached half-way down the body. This dress is exemplified in the print of the first half of the eighteenth century of J. G. Pertsch, Doctor of Law.[1]

ALTDORF (1578)

The University of Altdorf is particularly rich in pictorial information, thanks to collections of engravings of portraits of professors past and present brought out in the earlier eighteenth century. One of these collections shows the dress of regents at the time of the university's foundation. It consists of a close-fitting skull-cap like a helmet and an open flap-collared gown with cord and button braiding on the sleeves.[2]

J. C. Durrius (d. 1677), Professor of Theology, wears in a print of after 1657 a flap-collared black cloak and broad white bands.[3] This may be termed academical 'undress'.

M. Koenig (1616–99), Professor of Greek and Poetry, and librarian, wears full academical dress consisting of a black cassock with many buttons down the front, over this a full black gown with hanging bell sleeves, the gown having broad facings, and large white bands.[4]

An early eighteenth-century Professor of Medicine, J. J. Baier, wears a silk 'shoulder piece' with an opening in the middle and edged at the top and bottom with broad embroidery.[5] A dean's dress of the same period is remarkable for the plain cloth 'shoulder piece' with an opening in the middle and with a thin edging of lace.[6] The gowns of all lay professors were red.[7] Professors of Theology wore black.[8] The rector wore the same as the lay professors.

STRASSBURG (1621)

At first a gymnasium, in 1566 it became a degree granting academy, and in 1621 it gained the status of university by imperial decree.[9]

[1] Oxford, Ashmolean Museum (Hope Collection).
[2] S. J. Apin, *Vitae Professorum Philosophiae* (Altorfinae), pl. before p. 1.
[3] G. G. Zeltner, *Vitae Theologorum Altorphinorum*, p. 344.
[4] S. J. Apin, pl. opp. p. 188.
[5] J. J. Baier, *Biographiae Professorum Medicinae . . . In Academia Altorf*, frontispiece.
[6] S. J. Apin, pl. opp. p. 300.
[7] A. Tholuck, *Das akademische Leben des siebzehnten Jahrhunderts*, p. 132, § 7.
[8] C. Meiners, art. cit., p. 252.   [9] See S. d'Irsay, *Histoire des Universités*, ii. 25.

By an order of 1604 gentlemen-commoners, noblemen, licentiates, masters, and doctors were allowed the use of velvet, silk, satin, and damask in their dress, and to wear a biretta or hood, but bachelors and all other students were forbidden these.[1] Although this indulgence was granted, dress of a military type was not to be tolerated.[2]

According to the plates in the *Speculum Cornelianum* (1618), the dress of professors consisted of a round, pleated, corded bonnet and a fur-lined, fur-faced gown with a flap collar of fur. Whether the sleeves were of a bell shape or of the character of false panels seems to have been immaterial.[3]

KIEL (1665)

Kiel University was of slight importance until it came directly under Prussia in the nineteenth century. There is no reference to dress in its statutes.

Doctors of Theology wore purple *pilei* (i.e. round bonnets) and black gowns,[4] while Doctors of Law wore purple *pilei* and purple gowns.[5]

HALLE (1694)

At the time of Halle's foundation there was much opposition to the adoption of a purple robe for the *Rector Magnificus* because of that colour's original association with the papacy, the belief being that popes had first granted the use of that colour to doctors; but owing to the influence of Christian Thomasius, the jurist, it was agreed to use it in *defiance* of the pope.[6]

A. H. Francke, a Professor of Theology, wears in a print of about 1719 a cassock, white bands, an open gown with a flap collar, and a small round loose velvet bonnet, i.e. a *pileus*.[7] In 1736 a purple *pileus* was worn by the *Rector Magnificus*, a black one by Regents of Theology, and a blue one by the Dean of the Faculty of Philosophy.[8] Further than this we know nothing,

---

[1] M. Fournier, *Les Universités françaises—Les Statuts et Privilèges*, iv. 333, Order no. 2144 (1604), ¶ 10, § 11, 9.

[2] M. Fournier, iv. 34, Order no. 1992, n. 2, Latin version.

[3] J. von der Heyden, *Speculum Cornelianum*, pls. 2, 20, and 56.

[4] J. F. Mayer, *De Doctoratu Theologico*, p. 12.

[5] A. Steger, p. 31.

[6] F. Delitzsch, *Iris*, p. 88.

[7] W. von Seidlitz, *Allgemeines historisches Porträtwerk*, pt. 12, port. of Francke.

[8] C. Biccius, p. 17, cap. ii, x.

for the short and business-like statutes contain no mention of dress.

GÖTTINGEN (1737)

Göttingen was founded in the same modern and scientific spirit as Halle, and in like manner there is no mention of dress in the statutes. However, from a pictorial source one learns that in 1747 the dress of a professor consisted of an open gown with a flap collar and probably (for the picture is under half-length) bell sleeves. The collar and the facings of the gown are decorated with velvet, and on the sleeves above the elbows is a horizontal fold of velvet.[1]

ERLANGEN (1743)

At Erlangen the King of Prussia was nominally rector, while the pro-rector carried out the functions performed by a rector in the older universities.[2] The dress of the pro-rector consisted of a purple-coloured gown (*pallium*), a gold-embroidered 'shoulder piece', and a head-dress which might be according to choice either a purple biretta or a purple four-cornered cap, presumably like the English one.[3]

Regents wore on all important occasions a long and full cloth robe faced with velvet, and a biretta or a four-cornered velvet cap as they wished. Robe and cap were of the colour of the regent's faculty. All regents were doctors. Thus Doctors of Theology wore black, those of Law red-scarlet, those of Medicine dark red, and those of Philosophy violet.[4]

C. STUDENT DRESS

This is so significant a branch of this study as regards German-speaking countries that the dress of students is worth a special review.

Although true academical student dress vanished early, there are enough examples, both descriptive and pictorial, to furnish us with information as to its original character. Thus in

---

[1] W. von Seidlitz, pts. 10 and 11, port. of J. M. Gesner.
[2] G. W. A. Fikenscher, *Geschichte der Königlich Preussischen Friedrich-Alexanders-Universität zu Erlangen*, p. 431.
[3] G. W. A. Fikenscher, p. 454; F. Delitzsch, p. 88.
[4] G. W. A. Fikenscher, pp. 455 and 468.

1436 students of Leipzig wore a closed *supertunica*,[1] in 1470 Heidelberg students had to have their hood fastened on to their *supertunica* to prevent its being worn on the head,[2] and in 1489 a student is depicted in a woodcut wearing a *tunica* reaching to a little way above his ankles, and over it a loose sleeveless mantle.[3] In 1495 students of Leipzig were ordered to wear full-length hoods and not abbreviated ones, and to go bare-headed.[4] Length of dress for students of Erfurt was insisted on in the fifteenth century.[5] In 1505 students of Ingolstadt wore closed gowns with loose sleeves.[6] At Cologne in 1516 students wore plain black hoods.[7] In 1523 students in general wore open full-sleeved gowns with ordinary hats of contemporary lay fashion,[8] while at Tübingen in 1525 they were ordered, if scholars (bursars), to wear full-sleeved gowns, but if commoners, gowns with sleeves or without them as they preferred.[9] We can see exactly what this enactment meant by looking at the plates of Tübingen scenes in Neyffer and Ditzinger's late sixteenth-century book. In the scene in the hall,[10] in which the members of the university are dining, commoners, if we are to judge from the figure near the lower table standing up near a recess with a tankard in his hand, wear a long cape with a flap collar, while servitors carrying in dishes wear the same cape with the addition of 'streamers' falling from the shoulders, exactly the same as those of Oxford commoners. Other examples of the streamer-less capes of commoners are to be seen in the plate of a lecture and that of the library.[11] A Strassburg student of 1618 who appears in a print depicting 'Thaïs', the symbolical woman who lures scholars away from their work, with her devotees,[12] wears over his ordinary dress a cloak with a flap collar. The cloak is of moderate length and is drawn over the arms to below the elbow, but what is chiefly remarkable about his dress is his head-dress which is a trencher cap with a tump like the English one.

[1] F. Zarncke, *Statutenbücher*, p. 350.   [2] E. Winkelmann, i. 186.
[3] F. Philippi, Taf. 62, '*Studente, 39*' (*Des Dodes Danz*, Lübeck).
[4] R. F. Seybolt, p. 118, n. b.   [5] C. Meiners, art. cit., pp. 227–8.
[6] F. Philippi, Taf. 117.   [7] *Epistolae Obscurorum Virorum*, i, letter 39, p. 366.
[8] H. Peters, *Der Arzt in der deutschen Vergangenheit*, p. 25, Abb. 24.
[9] K. Klüpfel and M. Eifert, pt. 2, p. 27.
[10] J. S. Neyffer and L. Ditzinger, pl. ii.
[11] J. S. Neyffer and L. Ditzinger, pls. iii and iv.
[12] J. von der Heyden, pl. 56.

The story of the students' opposition to the *geistliche Kleide* begins at Leipzig as early as 1412 when it was found necessary to order students not to carry weapons. This seems to have been obeyed, for in 1440 the university felt strong enough to forbid Bachelors of Arts and students to wear a cloak or to gird their *tunica*. In the same year they were told to wear large hoosp on festive occasions.[1] This seems to have met with only slight response, for in 1458 legislation was directed against foppish dress, and the close, tight-sleeved *tunica* was still insisted on. The answer of the students to this was to ignore the order and later to rip the document off the church door and tear it up. In 1500 there was further legislation, of the success of which we hear nothing;[2] but no wonder action was necessary, for in 1482 Leipzig students had worn hats with high plumes and the rich dress of courtiers.[3] At Leipzig throughout the sixteenth century the lamentation goes up that so scandalously slack is the regard that is had to appearances that one cannot tell a doctor or a master from a shopkeeper. In 1570, it seems, not only students but doctors and masters went about armed.[4]

Throughout the fifteenth century members of the University of Vienna had been exceptionally orderly in their dress, which remained clerical and accorded with the statutes; but in 1503 a fight took place between the students and the vintners of the suburbs, and so hard pressed were members of the university that the authorities allowed the students to leave off their *tunicas*, which must have greatly impeded them in fighting, and allowed them to wear ordinary dress for the time of the emergency. After the trouble had passed the authorities realized too late that they had given away their powers of discipline, and the Faculty of Philosophy sought to repair the damage by ordering the students to resume the *tunica* and to give up their arms. Indignant at this the students refused to comply and presented their case to the Emperor Maximilian, who referred them to his Governor of Austria, and he took the side of the students.[5] For some years the students enjoyed their freedom to dress as they wished and to carry arms, until in 1516 with the help of the church authorities the regents forced them to

[1] A. Schultz, p. 210. [2] A. Schultz, p. 212.
[3] C. Meiners, art. cit., p. 232. [4] A. Schultz, pp. 213–14.
[5] C. Meiners, art. cit., pp. 238–40.

give up arms and to wear open cloaks of the colour of the faculty to which they belonged.[1]

The sixteenth century, an age of violence, contributed still further to the laying aside of students' academical dress, but this was far more widespread in the Protestant universities than in the Roman Catholic ones. There was less discipline in the Protestant bodies where the college system had entirely broken down,[2] and where there was no discipline such rules as those which entailed the wearing of academicals could least of all be enforced, especially as the students were living in lodgings spread all over university towns. In some cases the authorities themselves may have discouraged the wearing of the old dress as 'papistical'.

By 1558 the short Spanish cloak was worn generally by the students of Wittenberg,[3] and in 1562 their dress was described as consisting of a velvet bonnet, wide Spanish breeches, a jacket, and a cloak trimmed with velvet and silk,[4] a costume inspired by the modes of Spain, the great military power of the age, whose influence could be felt even in Germany.

On the other hand the authorities of certain universities opposed this military fashion. For instance, at Tübingen an ordinance of 1525 prohibited the wearing of an imitation of military dress. Students were to use not a lay hat, but a plain biretta without plumes (though noblemen-students were allowed plumes), and long dress. It appears that by this time it was too late to forbid swords, so the authorities contented themselves with ordering that short swords (which no doubt would be less dangerous) alone might be used.[5] Legislation involving the same prohibitions appeared at Ingolstadt in 1556.[6] At Heidelberg no less the wearing of military dress by students was increasing during the sixteenth century, and in 1558 it was found necessary to legislate against it.[7] At this time, however, there was an exception to this state of affairs at Prague where students seem to have worn on special occasions national costumes,[8] and there is no mention of military dress in the university statutes.

[1] C. Meiners, art. cit., p. 240.   [2] C. Meiners, art. cit., p. 245.
[3] C. Meiners, art. cit., pp. 241–2.   [4] *Leges academiae Witebergensis*, p. 24.
[5] K. Klüpfel and M. Eifert, pt. 2, p. 27.   [6] C. Prantl, ii. 225.
[7] A. Thorbecke, p. 30, § 28, iv, and p. 151, § 153, 13.
[8] V. de Viriville, *Histoire de l'Instruction Publique*, pl. opp. p. 193 (no source).

In 1572 a Leipzig student depicted in a water-colour in an album wears a black velvet cap with a red feather, a pleated lace ruff and a tight red jacket and baggy red breeches of Spanish style, while over this he has a scarlet cloak, and at his left hip a long sword with a basket-hilt.[1] In 1618 a student wears a hat with two tall plumes in front,[2] while a student of Jena of 1621 in a quaint picture of that year showing him in his study wears the ordinary lay fashion of the day.[3]

If the sixteenth century has seen the introduction into the German universities of Spanish court fashions,[4] the Thirty Years War of the following century (1618–48), when nearly every student took to arms, increased the tendency towards military dress. In 1635 a certain Professor Gerhard in an inaugural lecture mentioned the change in respect of dress which this war has brought about,[5] and Meyfart, another professor, describes the sword, feathers, boots, and spurs of the student of that time.[6] But if commoners, who could pay for it, adopted such dress, servitors were dressed in rags.[7]

All that was left of any kind of academical dress for students by this time was the short cloak with a flap collar (*Mantel*). Most universities during the greater part of the seventeenth century insisted that students should wear it on formal occasions. These black cloaks were to be seen at important functions about 1655,[8] and in 1678, or the following year, students of Jena were severely reprimanded for coming before the rector without them.[9] The University of Frankfurt-on-Oder still ordered students to wear the cloak in the presence of the chancellor in 1683,[10] and in the same year the students of Heidelberg were instructed to wear it when attending Communion.[11] Although, as we have noticed above[12] all students of Wittenberg wore the cloak in 1702 and the theological students of Jena in 1730, the diarist Veltheim was in 1696 writing as if

---

[1] R. and R. Keil, *Geschichte des Jenaischen Studentenlebens*, p. 55.

[2] F. Hottenroth, *Handbuch*, p. 763, fig. 218, no. 7.

[3] Jena Univ. Bibl., *Stammbuch*, Nr. 7, Bb. 272v—'Ein Jenaischer Student von Jahre 1621, in seinem Zimmer.'

[4] R. and R. Keil, loc. cit.

[5] A. Tholuck, p. 259.   [6] A. Tholuck, p. 134.

[7] R. and R. Keil, p. 98.   [8] C. Meiners, art. cit., p. 247.

[9] R. and R. Keil, p. 99; A. Tholuck, p. 134.

[10] C. Meiners, art. cit., pp. 247–8.

[11] E. Winkelmann, ii. 217, § 1763.   [12] See under Wittenberg and Jena.

it had been disused for years.[1] This was probably the case in most universities then.

In 1642 students of Ingolstadt were ordered to wear a *pallium* over their other dress for lectures.[2] There are no means of telling what this was like, and it is not referred to again. Although this may merely mean a cloak-gown it may have been a real gown of medieval character, still preserved in the Roman Catholic university.

In 1665 on the occasion of the opening of the University of Kiel students appeared in ridiculous (*lächerlich*) costumes,[3] and this was a foretaste of what was to come. By the beginning of the eighteenth century the state of the dress of students had grown from bad to worse. In 1702 it was found necessary to legislate against the wearing of dressing-gowns and night-caps and of smoking pipes at lectures.[4] Leipzig, Jena, and Halle were particularly noted for this kind of behaviour. At Leipzig the practice was three times condemned between 1702 and 1719,[5] at Jena it was prohibited and finally stopped in 1750,[6] but at Halle it lasted into the 1820's.[7]

On the other hand there were fashionable students who wore full-bottomed wigs and assumed red cloaks exactly the same as those cloaks used at some universities by the professors on festal occasions.[8] The days when the first student to wear a wig at Altdorf had it torn to pieces by his fellows (1671) were long since past.[9] The fop was well established, although the ordinary student probably wore dress unobtrusive enough.[10]

There is much evidence as to students' dress during the course of the eighteenth century. The plates by P. J. Leidenhoffer in J. F. Leopold's *Academia* (about 1720) provide examples of the typical student of various universities. Thus the Leipzig student wears beautiful laced clothes, the Giessen student carries a muff, but the Tübingen student is sombrely dressed. In each case the inevitable sword is to be seen. A

[1] A. Tholuck, p. 135; R. and R. Keil, p. 99.
[2] C. Prantl, ii. 403 (Caput 13, no. 2).
[3] H. Ratjen, *Geschichte der Universität zu Kiel*, p. 59 (n. 5, 'Bericht von den Processionen, Schleswig, 1665').
[4] A. Tholuck, p. 134.   [5] A. Tholuck, loc. cit.
[6] R. and R. Keil, p. 158.   [7] A. Tholuck, op. cit., loc. cit.
[8] C. Meiners, art. cit., op. cit., p. 248.
[9] C. Meiners, art. cit., op. cit., loc. cit.   [10] R. and R. Keil, op. cit., p. 156.

satirical article of 1736 on the eve of the university's incorpora-
tion, mocked both the over-rich and the over-mean dress of
the students arriving at Göttingen.[1] In the engraving above the
title of F. W. Zachariä's *Poetische Schriften* (1765) we see his
Renommist (Braggart) wearing dress of a military cut, with a
very large hat, square in shape and cocked on one side. He has
boots or gaiters reaching to the knee, a riding-whip, and a large
sword. In 1775 the student of Giessen 'does not spend much
money on his dress', writes the theological student Laukhard.
'On Sundays or on weekdays alike he wears the same dress;
a coat (*Flausch*) of thick stuff, or an overcoat (*Rock*), breeches,
and boots.'[2] The fashion for extravagant head-dress with plumes
is ridiculed in 1780.[3] K. A. Kortum in his mock heroic, *The
Jobsiad* (1784), describes his comic hero arriving home from
the university wearing 'a very large hat with a feather, breeches,
a waist-coat of yellow leather, a short cape of grey cloth, a huge
sword . . . large and pointed'; while C. J. Weber in *Demokritus*
writes that even boys at school during their last year wore carefully blacked boots, and gloves like courtiers.[4] The authorities
did nothing to put a stop to this, and at Heidelberg in 1775
foreign students were even allowed by statute to wear gold-
laced or silver-laced clothes.[5]

In the latter part of this century at Tübingen only sons of
the nobility and of officers might use powder, and it was especially forbidden to beneficiaries (holders of scholarships and
other grants of money).[6]

The French war which began in 1792 gave an impetus to
the students' associations (*Landsmannschaften*), but in the earliest
stages of the war they, as champions of liberty, supported the
revolutionary armies, the very opposite of the attitude that the
student-bodies later took. It was during the Thirty Years War
that members of most universities in Germany had divided
themselves up into military groups, according to nation, each
nation having its own uniform. Particularly noticeable features

---

[1] F. C. Neubur, art. 'Kleidung der Studirenden auf der Universität Göttingen'
in *Der Sammler*, v. Stück, pp. 33–35.
[2] Letters from Dr. A. Roth of Baden-Baden.
[3] M. Schluck, *Dissertatio de Norma Actionum Studiosorum*, p. 18.
[4] Letter from Dr. A. Roth.
[5] E. Winkelmann, op. cit. ii. 284, § 2256.
[6] M. von Boehn, *Modes and Manners*, iv. 244.

of the dress were the coloured ribbons, variously coloured for each nation, tied to the sword-hilt.[1] After the Thirty Years War these ribbons are lost sight of for a long time, but in an album in which A. B. Filzhofer collected poems, quotations, sketches, and water-colours contributed by his friends from his student days onwards is to be found a water-colour dated 1727. It depicts Altdorf students sitting at a table, one of whom wears a plain red ribbon slung across his chest.[2]

In the last decade of the eighteenth century arose a new style of military dress for students, from which was derived at the time of the War of Independence (1813) the dress of the new *Burschenschaften*, popular bodies which came into being in opposition to the old exclusive *Landsmannschaften*.[3]

In the 1790's it was at Jena that the *Landsmannschaften* particularly flourished. Here the students' everyday dress consisted of a coat of military cut and breeches, with a plumed leather helmet and a sword, while on Sundays and on festal occasions they wore a *Stürmer* dress, which consisted of a three-cornered hat decorated with braid, tassels, and coloured plumes, a gold-embroidered uniform jacket with silver or gold epaulettes, or sometimes a short jacket with facings of a different colour. At the end of the century the round coloured pill-box hat took the place of the three-cornered one.[4] Two silhouettes of 1795 (Pl. 20) show what the students' head-dress was like at Jena. One wears a helmet with a plume falling forward. The other has a cocked hat and a pig-tail.[5]

Of the student dress of Halle, where he was from 1804 to 1806, Ludwig Börne the publicist says that it consisted of such items as large boots called *Kanonen*, and leather helmets with plumes of the colours of the particular *Chore* to which the student belonged. The senior members of the corporations always wore their *Stürmer* hat and their sword.[6]

In the earlier period of the French war the authorities looked askance at all manifestations of sympathy with the new liberty. This seems to have been especially the case at the University

---

[1] R. and R. Keil, op. cit., p. 122.
[2] B.M. MS. Eg. 1425, fo. 88ᵛ (Album of A. B. Filzhofer, 1719–71).
[3] F. Paulsen, *The German Universities*, p. 372.
[4] R. and R. Keil, op. cit., p. 303.
[5] E. Borkowsky, op. cit., ills. on p. 134.
[6] R. and R. Keil, op. cit., pp. 303–4.

PLATE 20

Silhouettes showing Students' head-dress at Jena, 1795

of Würzburg, where in 1799 Bishop Georg Karl decreed that
no students were to wear the French tricolour on their collars.[1]
This Roman Catholic university continued to hold out against
the wearing of military fashions, and in 1805 the use of coloured
cockades and cords, and of masks and uniforms was forbidden.[2]
At Heidelberg in 1800 students were ordered not to wear
sansculotte dress.[3]

Certainly during the eighteenth century what little remained
of the true forms of academical dress of the German student
was destroyed. 'The recent revolutions and developments in
our own lifetime', writes C. Meiners in 1804,[4] 'have abolished
them completely.'

II. THE LOW COUNTRIES

A. HOLLAND

Until the provinces began their fight for national freedom under
William the Silent there were no universities. The first was
Leyden, founded in 1575.

LEYDEN (1575)

At Leyden until the end of the seventeenth century professors
of the university wore cloth cloaks, without sleeves and with
flap collars, of the colour of their faculty; white for Arts (Philosophy), red for Law, green for Medicine, and orange (the
national colour) for Theology.[5] The flap collar with gatherings
on the shoulder appears in the portraits of Leyden professors
in the *Academia Lugd-Batava Virorum Icones* (1613). In a series
of prints of the city of Leyden in 1625 this cloak can be seen,
particularly in the illustration of the university garden.[6] Here
a figure in the left foreground wears such a cloak, which has a
flap collar, falls over the shoulders, but leaves the arms quite
free. It falls behind in slight, wide pleats, and reaches to the
heels, but in front it is wide open and does not cover any part

---

[1] F. X. von Wegele, op. cit. ii. 450.
[2] F. X. von Wegele, op. cit. ii. 489, § 183 (h).
[3] E. Winkelmann, op. cit. ii. 323, § 2532.
[4] C. Meiners, art. cit., op. cit., p. 201.
[5] T. Baty, *Academic Colours*, p. 76.
[6] J. Meursius, *Athenae Bataviae*, p. 31.

of the body. An ordinary hat of the lay fashion of the period is worn with it. But there are examples[1] of a much shorter garment, in reality a gown with short sleeves fairly close to the arm and reaching a little way below the elbow, which at the end of the century in a somewhat altered form succeeded the cloak as academical wear. A Professor of Theology as early as 1625 was wearing a gown in preference to the cloak. This was Andreas Rivetus, Professor and Doctor of Theology, who appears in his print in the Meursius book in an open gown with a flap collar, with black silk facings down the front, and with hollow sleeves with gashes, the upper part of the gashes being cut upwards in the middle in the shape of an inverted V.[2] The lay hat was not invariably worn, for a Doctor of Medicine, Petrus Forestus, wears a round bonnet with a cord,[3] which seems to have become the formal doctoral head-dress. There is in the Rijksmuseum, Amsterdam, a painting of 1655–60 by Hendrik van der Burch of a graduation ceremony at Leyden. The picture has darkened, but it can be seen that all wear black gowns with ordinary black felt, high-crowned hats with wide brims except the new doctor who wears a small soft round black bonnet.[4]

By the late seventeenth century the cloak had been superseded by a full, wide-sleeved gown, open in front, the arm coming through a slit in the sleeve. The gown was of the appropriate faculty colour and had a square flap collar decorated with velvet.[5] J. Perizonius, Doctor of Law (d. 1710), wears such a gown in his portrait in the Senate Room of the University of Leyden.[6] The slit in the sleeve was generally given up in the earlier eighteenth century. A Doctor of Medicine, B. S. Albinus (1697–1770), wears a bell-sleeved gown with velvet facings and velvet flap collar, as is to be seen in J. J. Haid's engraving after the painting by C. de Moor.[7] A later example of this gown is to be found in the portrait of the famous classical scholar David Ruhnken of Leyden, painted by J. Pothoven in 1791.[8] There is,

---

[1] For example, J. Meursius, p. 36, 'The University Library'.

[2] J. Meursius, p. 314.   [3] J. Meursius, p. 96.

[4] W. R. Valentiner, *Pieter de Hooch, with Appendix on Hendrik van der Burch's Art*, ill. on p. 228.   [5] T. Baty, pp. 75–76.

[6] See the reproduction in A. Gudeman, *Imagenes Philologorum*, p. 14, no. 4.

[7] Oxford, Ashmolean Museum (Hope Collection).

[8] J. E. Sandys, *A History of Classical Scholarship*, ii. 458; A. Gudeman, p. 16, no. 1.

however, one notable exception to this style of gown. An engraving after J. M. Quinkhard's painting of P. van Musschenbroek (Doctor of Medicine of Leyden and professor there, 1692–1761) shows him wearing a winged-sleeved gown decorated with gimp, exactly like the Bachelor of Civil Law type of gown at Oxford.[1]

Early in the eighteenth century the colour of the Faculty of Theology was changed from orange to white and that of the Faculty of Arts from white to blue, but the colours for Law and Medicine remained the same as before. On formal occasions a stiff black velvet cylindrical cap was worn by professors.[2] White bands, some being very large and lying in double or triple layers, were worn by all regents. J. Perizonius (seventeenth century) and H. D. Gaubius, Professor of Medicine in the mid-eighteenth century, both wear very large bands which flow out in four folds to a great broadness.[3]

In 1699 the secretary of the university was given an allowance to buy a gown (*tabbaart*) for himself.[4] It is not described.

FRANEKER (1586)

In the foundation statutes of Franeker (1586) professors were advised to wear some dress befitting their dignity, and to avoid one of a military type. A gown (*toga*) was considered the best costume for them, but it does not seem to have been regarded as academical, merely a sober form of lay dress.[5]

UTRECHT (1636)

At Utrecht the faculty colours were copied from those of Leyden, but when in the early eighteenth century changes were made for the colours of Theology and Arts, Utrecht accepted the alteration of the Arts colour, but still kept the original orange for Theology.[6]

In the second half of the seventeenth century Professors of

[1] Oxford, Ashmolean Museum (Hope Collection).

[2] T. Baty, pp. 75–76.

[3] A. Gudeman, p. 12, no. 2; print of H. D. Gaubius after the portrait (1741) by H. van der Mij (Oxford, Ashmolean Museum (Hope Collection)). There are besides several examples among the portraits in the Senate Room at Leyden.

[4] Cambridge, University Library, MS. Add. 105, fo. 25ᵛ.

[5] *Statuta et Leges Fundamentales Academiae Frisiorum quae est Franequerae*, pp. 12–13, § xxxv.

[6] T. Baty, pp. 75–76.

Theology wore long black closed gowns with full hanging sleeves.[1] By 1764, as James Boswell on a visit to Utrecht noticed, professors only wore their gowns on special occasions.[2]

OTHER UNIVERSITIES

Of the other Dutch universities founded before 1801, Groningen (1614) was of no account until the nineteenth century, and there is no mention of dress in its meagre statutes. The same is the case with Harderwijk (1648).

DRESS OF STUDENTS

Sir William Brereton on his visit to Holland in 1634 found little outward sign of academical life at Leyden. Only divinity students went 'in the habit of scholars', which must mean that they wore black cloaks. Otherwise students dressed as they pleased.[3]

In 1743 an English traveller, J. Knapton, noticed that Dutch students in all the universities he visited wore 'morning gowns' (i.e. dressing gowns) and swords.[4] This was a slovenly habit introduced from Germany and should not be confused with the wearing of 'studying gowns'.[5,6]

B. BELGIUM

LOUVAIN (1426)

The constitutions of the University of Louvain were modelled on those of the universities of Paris, Vienna, and Cologne, each

[1] A. Tholuck, *Das akademische Leben des siebzehnten Jahrhunderts*, p. 134.

[2] *Boswell in Holland, 1763–4*, ed. F. A. Pottle, p. 134.

[3] W. Brereton, *Travels* (Chetham Soc. i), pp. 39–40.

[4] [J. Knapton], *Description of Holland*, pp. 334, 337, and 338.

[5] 'Studying gowns', worn by many academical persons old and young, especially in the seventeenth century, were not academical gowns. They were simply used in order to keep warm when sitting in libraries, and so on. They were long and voluminous with straight sleeves. There is a good example of this gown in the oil-painting, 'Scholar and Youth in a Library' by Caspar Netscher (1639–84) in the possession of Messrs. Thomas Agnew & Sons (reproduced in R. Edwards, *Early Conversation Pictures*, no. 37).

[6] In the early nineteenth century Dutch students copied the German students in wearing peaked caps, but whereas the latter wore *Chore* ribbons on their caps, Dutch students wore caps of the colour of the faculty to which they belonged (T. Baty, pp. 75–76).

PLATE 21

Brass of Jacob Schelewaerts of Louvain, 1483

of which had influence in various ways.[1] At first there were three faculties, those of Theology, Law, and Medicine, the last of these being a lay faculty.[2] A Faculty of Arts was formed in 1429, at which time an iron mace washed over with silver was made for it. It is still preserved. In the niches on it are figures, among them Aristotle and Boëthius, dressed as Masters of Arts. Both wear a loose, pleated *cappa rugata*, and Aristotle wears in addition a 'shoulder piece' (*epitogium*).[3]

In 1450 it was ordered that all, whether clerical or lay, should wear a long dress befitting learned men, and this was repeated in 1455 and at other times in the following years.[4]

The fine brass of Jacob Schelewaerts (d. 1483) in Bruges Cathedral[5] gives us a good idea of the academical dress of Louvain in the fifteenth century (Pl. 21). In it Schelewaerts, who was a Doctor of Theology and from 1472 to 1476 was Professor of Theology at this university, is seen giving a lecture to a class of seven. He wears a *cappa* with side slits through which his arms appear, and wears on his head a hood, under which is a skull-cap. As to his audience, not one of them are exactly pupils, but are rather senior members of the university doing him homage as a great teacher, for their faces are those of mature men, and they all have a head-dress, which no undergraduate in Europe would have been allowed. Of the three closest figures, the first (left foreground) has a *chaperon* falling scarf-wise over his left shoulder. His gown is narrow and bell sleeved, and his head-dress is a *pileus*. He is probably a Master of Arts if we are to judge by the prominence of his *chaperon*. The figure in the middle foreground with a large round *pileus* with a button on top of it and a short round hood without a liripipe is perhaps a licentiate of a higher faculty; while the figure in the right foreground who wears a *pileus*, a hood with a rounded liripipe, and a miniver 'shoulder piece' is likely to be a Bachelor of Theology, if we take into consideration the fact that he wears miniver. None below the degrees of Bachelor of Theology and

[1] P. F. X. de Ram, *Considérations sur l'histoire de l'Université de Louvain*, p. 10; P. Delannoy, *L'Université de Louvain*, p. 24.

[2] V. Andreas, *Fasti Academici Lovaniensis*, p. 241.

[3] P. F. X. de Ram, *Analectes*, no. 33, p. 28.

[4] V. Andreas, pp. 338-9.

[5] A reproduction of this brass is given in W. F. Creeny, *A Book of Fac-similes of Monumental Brasses on the Continent of Europe*, p. 44.

Master of Arts, according to medieval statutes generally, were allowed so rich a fur, and the rounded liripipe was a feature of the hood of Bachelors of Theology of Paris at this period. It was probably copied at Louvain.

It is worthy of notice that Schelewaerts, although a Doctor of Theology, wears not the *cappa clausa* but a less formal variety of *cappa*. That the *cappa clausa* was the full dress of Doctors of Theology at Louvain at this time can be seen from the fact that the four figures in the four corners of the brass representing the Four Doctors of the Church are shown wearing it. We must suppose some latitude at ordinary university functions such as lectures, while on the most solemn occasions, for Doctors of Theology at any rate, the *cappa clausa* would still be insisted on, unpopular as it was.

In 1430 it is stated that the biretta was for doctors and masters only and not for bachelors,[1] which must mean Bachelors of Arts, for bachelors of the higher faculties must have been allowed them if we compare the practice at other universities. In 1481 these birettas are described as being 'double', that is, of two parts sewn together.[2]

Nothing more is heard of dress until the middle of the sixteenth century. In 1565 the existing statutes were codified and new ones were made,[3] and it was ordered that the rector should be distinguished by a scarlet 'shoulder piece' lined with fur.[4] At the end of the century (the date is not known) students were instructed to wear as a fitting dress a *tunica* reaching to the knee, and not to go out without an over-gown and cap.[5]

A print (1606) of the *Halle*, the Cloth Hall of the city of Louvain used by the university for its assemblies, shows what the dress of the regents was at this time. It consisted of a rigid biretta with a tump, and a black gown open in front with bell sleeves reaching to the waist and black velvet facings down the front.[6] This dress was still worn in 1752 as the portrait of a Regent Doctor of Medicine, H. J. Réga (1690–1754), shows. The original oil-painting was destroyed with the Cloth Hall in 1914.[7]

[1] V. Andreas, p. 241.   [2] V. Andreas, p. 149.
[3] P. Delannoy, p. 27.   [4] P. Delannoy, p. 28.
[5] P. F. X. de Ram, *Analectes*, no. 22, p. 105, n. 1, § *De moribus scholarium*; P. Delannoy, p. 144.
[6] P. Delannoy, ill. opp. p. 192.   [7] P. Delannoy, ill. opp. p. 156.

The rector's dress in 1741 was the same as in the sixteenth century, and consisted of gown, *pileus*, and a red 'shoulder piece' edged and lined with fur.[1] In the reformed statutes for the university granted by Maria Theresa in 1755 the bonnet is mentioned as being the head-dress of the chancellor and rector.[2]

The university was dispersed in 1797.[3]

DOUAI (1560)

All the information which can be gained about dress at the University of Douai is that in the year of its foundation the rector was ordered to wear a bonnet, a *roba*, and a large 'shoulder piece' with a hood (*caputium*) attached to it.[4]

III. SWITZERLAND

The only two Swiss universities which had a prescribed dress were the University of Basel and Calvin's Academy of Geneva.

BASEL (1460)

In the year of the foundation of Basel University its members were ordered to wear a closed *pallium* of proper length, and over this on important occasions a *Schaube* (*zschupparum*), a black closed bell-sleeved gown such as was worn by the older and graver sort of citizen of the day. Over this members were to wear a 'shoulder piece' with a hood and liripipe (*capucium et lyripipiatum*). No one unless a bishop, a Doctor of Law or Medicine, a canon of the cathedral, a nobleman, or those who held the combined degree of Doctor of Philosophy and Master of Arts might wear the round red bonnet (*birettum rotundum*).[5] This *Schaube* dress, but not the 'shoulder piece', liripipe, and hood, continued to be worn after the Reformation. Felix Platter, as he mentions in his diary, wore in 1557 when he took the degree of Doctor of Medicine at Basel a *Schaube* guarded with velvet.[6] In an engraving Johann Buxtorf (1564–1629),

---

[1] A. Steger, *Dissertatio de purpura*, p. 28.
[2] *L'annuaire de l'Université de Louvain*, p. 197.
[3] P. F. X. de Ram, *Considérations*, p. 52.
[4] G. Cardon, *La Fondation de l'Université de Douai*, p. 225.
[5] W. Vischer, *Geschichte der Universität Basel*, pp. 133, n. 46, and 214. Doctors and masters were called the *Birretati*.
[6] M. von Boehn, *Modes*, ii. 155–6.

Professor of Oriental Languages at Basel, wears a plain open *Schaube* pleated at the shoulders.[1] By 1617 it had a standing collar and fairly close sleeves with turned-back cuffs, and was open in front. The doctor who wears this dress in a woodcut in a book published that year has a biretta, a rigid form of the original *birretum rotundum*.[2]

In 1465 the rector's dress was ordered to consist of a red 'shoulder piece' with hood attached made of fine cloth lined with miniver, worn over a *Schaube*, and a red bonnet double-lined with fur.[3]

GENEVA (1559)

At the Academy of Geneva at the time of its foundation all regents wore the *Schaube*; but by the seventeenth century, as is to be seen in the fine print of F. Spanheim, D.Th. (1647), this has been changed to a gown with false panel sleeves, very broad black silk facings, and a very large flap collar.[4] By the early eighteenth century all wore a flap-collared cloak without sleeves except for Doctors of Theology, who continued to wear the full gown.[5] Later in the century, however, they also took to the cloak.[6] Sumptuary rules for the dress of students were framed in 1640, 1652, and 1670.[7]

IV. SCANDINAVIA

A. DENMARK

The early statutes of the University of Copenhagen (1478) contain only one reference to dress, when it was ordered that all members of the university were to wear dark dress of seemly cut. They were at the same time forbidden to use chains and buckles. Later statutes concerned with dress are all of a sumptuary nature.[8]

---

[1] D. Herrliberger, *Schweitzerischer Ehrentempel*, pl. 2. For another good example of the *Schaube* see J. F. K. Johnstone, *Alba Amicorum*, pl. xvii (lower).

[2] L. Kunning von Basel, *Stambuch der Jungen Gesellen*, pl. 56.

[3] W. Vischer, p. 116.

[4] C. Borgeaud, *Histoire de l'Université de Genève*, i, pl. opp. p. 352.

[5] C. Borgeaud, pl. opp. p. 504 (2), portrait of Gabriel Cramer, and pl. opp. p. 530, portrait of B. Pictet (1707).

[6] C. Borgeaud, pl. opp. p. 558, portrait of J. Vernet (1785).

[7] C. Borgeaud, p. 453.

[8] H. Matzen, *Kjøbenhavns Universitets Retshistorie*, ii. 151.

The only other information which can be found is hidden away in an academical dissertation of 1694. From this it appears that at that time Doctors of Theology wore a black four-horned biretta (*quadratus cornutus*), while the birettas of doctors in the other faculties were of the same shape but purple.[1]

B. SWEDEN

There are no records about academical dress in Sweden before the eighteenth century, and it would seem that no illustrative material before this period exists. No doubt, as can be seen in such a work as the mural, 'The Gathering of the Manna', by Albert the Painter, in Härkeberga Church, Uppland (about 1480), which shows civilian dress of the time, it was the same as that worn in other parts of Europe. In Post-Reformation times it would have followed the developments of academical dress in north Europe.

Then suddenly in 1778 the existing dress of professors was abolished and instead they wore the costume of members of the Swedish Academy, which King Gustav III himself designed. It consisted of a black suit with a standing collar, a broad red sash over the right shoulder and coming down over the chest, and red rosettes at the knees and on the shoes.[2] At Uppsala in 1784 a black cloak was worn with this uniform, and a traveller of this year says that regent-doctors (i.e. professors) wore silk hats of the colour of the faculty to which they belonged. Doctors of Theology wore black hats, Doctors of Law white ones, Doctors of Medicine green, and it would appear, although the author writes that Doctors of Medicine wore hats of green *or* sky-blue silk, that the last were worn by Doctors of Philosophy, as conformable with the German practice.[3] In 1784 students' dress still consisted of a black silk flap-collared cloak, but it was worn only on very special occasions and was rapidly disappearing.[4] At Lund in the early nineteenth century a gold buckle was introduced on the front of the silk hats of Doctors of Law and of Medicine.[5] This was undoubtedly the result of a

[1] S. P. Glud, *Dissertatio de Gradu Magisterii*, p. 64.

[2] E. Bergman, *Nationella Dräkten*, p. 111, fig. 29, 'Professor C. P. Thunberg (1743–1828) I svart akademiuniform (1808)'. This dress for professors died out about 1830.   [3] W. Coxe, *Travels*, iv. 147.   [4] W. Coxe, loc. cit.

[5] D. J. Cunningham, *The Evolution of the Graduation Ceremony*, pp. 39 and 51; J. E. Sandys, art. 'Ancient University Ceremonies', in *Fasciculus*, p. 237.

late eighteenth-century lay fashion. The familiar student's cap of Scandinavian universities was introduced from Germany in the early nineteenth century.

C. FINLAND

The University of Åbo was founded in 1640. The old dress of the Rector of Åbo, revived when the university was moved to Helsingfors in 1827, was a red velvet mantle with a white silk lining. Doctors of Arts (Philosophy) and Doctors of Medicine wore a black cylindrical hat decorated with gold emblems, while Doctors of Law had red cylindrical hats similarly decorated.[1] These were also revived on the move to Helsingfors. Otherwise at Helsingfors all wore the military type of dress prescribed in 1817. The lyre motif on the cap of students was introduced at this date.[2]

D. NORWAY

No university existed in Norway before the nineteenth century.

V. HUNGARY

This section has been written with the help of a monograph specially composed for me by Dr. Csizmadia Andor, University Lecturer at Budapest University, and dated 6 June 1957.

There is no reference before the eighteenth century to any particular academical dress being worn except by students at any Hungarian university. The statutes of the three old universities, Pécs (1367), Óbuda (1389), and Pozsony (1467) are almost entirely lost, and such as remain provide no information to the purpose.

If one is to judge by the earliest portrait remaining of an academical person, that of István Huszthy, the great Hungarian jurist of the seventeenth century, and the first Professor of Law at the Bohemian Academy of Eger, it will be seen that his full dress is simply Hungarian national costume.

It is not until 1759 that we hear of any true academical dress

[1] T. Baty, p. 81.
[2] Letter from Helsinki University with information extracted from the archives, 28 Feb. 1955.

being worn by regents. In that year, as can be realized from the story of Miklós Székely, a dismissed professor, who tried to join in a procession wearing one, regents of the Law Faculty of the University of Nagyszombat (later Budapest) wore a cloak-gown.[1]

Apparently before 1784 rectors and regents wore with this black gown on important occasions a 'shoulder piece' with hood attached falling behind (*epomis*), for in that year Josef II put a stop to the wearing of all such costume in Hungary as in Austria. This dress was sold by public auction at Pest and Pozsony.[1] The members of the University of Budapest are said to have been pleased to be rid of academicals except for regents of the theological faculty. In order to satisfy the latter they were allowed to wear with their canonicals a red cincture and a ring, old symbols of the doctorate in many European countries, to distinguish them among the rest of the clergy. The full professors of the other faculties were given the title of 'royal councillor'.[3] They would thus wear a form of court dress.

The picture of the ceremony held at the opening of the University of Buda in 1780 is lost, and unfortunately the reproduction of it in *The History of Hungarian Culture*[4] is not clear enough for one to be able to see what dress was worn.

The first mention of the dress of students occurs in 1621 in the statutes of the Calvinist and Lutheran College of Sárospatak, but this was only a sumptuary measure and gives no positive information.

There is, however, a detailed description of the dress of students of the Calvinist College of Debrecen, which in 1624 György Rákóczy, the Governor of Transylvania, ordered them to wear. This consisted of an ankle-length dolman (i.e. like a cassock) fastened by means of hooks and eyes, and over that a green gown (*tóga*) with yellow facings and with an embroidered eagle on one side of the facings. The head-dress consisted of a high fur hat decorated on top with pieces of green stuff.

This remained the dress of students at Debrecen until 1774 when under the influence of Josef II it was altered. The dolman

---

[1] F. Eckhart, *The History of the Faculty of Law*, p. 22.
[2] Hungarian Public Record Office, nos. 14/127/1784 and 7235/1785 (Orders of the Council of Governor-General).
[3] T. Pauler, *The History of the Hungarian Royal University of Budapest*, i. 201.
[4] iv. 468.

remained as before, but the colour of the gown was changed from green to black, and a three-cornered hat took the place of the high one. In 1775 the gown was given up, and in summer the dolman was worn alone or with an ordinary cloak over it if the weather was bad; but in winter a short coat lined with fox fur was worn over the dolman. In 1776 the black gown was reintroduced, but was given up again in 1780 when the fox fur coat reappeared.[1] The two kinds of dress are shown in the drawings of students of 1774 and 1803 reproduced in *A History of the Royal Free Town of Debrecen.*

The dress of the *Rector Magnificus* dates only from the nineteenth century.[2]

There is no record of students of other colleges and universities wearing a particular costume.

VI. POLAND

The University of Cracow, the only old one in Poland, was recognized by the papacy in 1362, but was in a poor condition until refounded by Vladislas Jagellon, Duke of Lithuania, in 1400.[3] It consisted of three colleges, the *Jagellonicum*, commonly known as the Greater College or the College of Artists; the *Collegium Minus*; and the *Collegium juridicum.*[4]

Tabards seem to have been the ordinary dress worn by regents, for in 1429 new regent-masters of the *Jagellonicum* were ordered to procure and wear them.[5] Again in 1449 it was enacted that no one would be elected to the staff of the regent-masters of the *Jagellonicum* unless he had a tabard. This was also insisted upon in the *Collegium Minus*, where failure by regents to procure a tabard would mean a loss of salary.[6] At the end of the same year it was enacted that no one should be elected to the post of Dean of the Faculty of Arts unless he possessed a good tabard to be worn to do honour to the faculty he represented.[7] Just over a week later it was decided that it was neces-

---

[1] *History of the Royal Free Town of Debrecen,* iii. 926–7.

[2] T. Baty, p. 79.　　　　　　[3] S. d'Irsay, *Histoire des Universités,* i. 184.

[4] *Statuta nec non Liber Promotionum Jagellonica, 1402–1849,* ed. J. Muczkowski, p. 444.

[5] *Statuta antiqua Collegii Majoris,* p. 13, § 29, *De habitu magistrali* (*Archiwum do Dziejów Literatury,* i).　　　　　　[6] *Stat. ant. Coll. Maj.,* p. 17, § 43.

[7] *Statuta nec non Liber Promotionum Jagellonica,* pp. xxviii–xxix.

sary to renew the university's tabards, and allowances of cloth for these garments were voted to be given to the regents to divide amongst themselves.[1] A large hood was regarded as the particular mark of the master's degree in 1491.[2]

As to the dress of Bachelors of Arts at this time, it consisted, as we see from an inventory of the goods of Johannes de Olomucz (1490), of a yellow gown (*schuba*), lined with wolf-skin, brown *tunica*, biretta, two cassocks, and padded cloak (*puluilotega*).[3] Two points arise from this, the first being that bachelors had already come to wear the much-coveted biretta of the masters;[4] and the second, the bright colour of the *schuba*. This need not surprise us. As in all universities before the middle of the sixteenth century great latitude as to colour was allowed.[5] It was the cut rather than the colour that was considered all-important for distinguishing the different degrees. But bachelors had to be careful not to be too free with their dress, for one who continually wore a *tunica* of too good a black cloth and a gown (*palium*) with large sleeves decorated with purple was condemned to some punishment not specified in 1473.[6]

Only in the Faculty of Theology was the *cappa clausa* preserved. In the revised statutes of the Faculty of Theology (1521), Masters (Doctors) of Theology and Bachelors of Theology were ordered to wear the *cappa* on solemn occasions.[7]

By 1533 the undress of Masters (Doctors) of Theology and the dress for all occasions of doctors in the lay faculties and for Masters of Arts had come to consist of a long closed narrow-sleeved *tunica* and a round biretta.[8] The biretta of Masters of Theology was black, and red for the lay doctors.[9]

In 1537 and 1538[10] Masters of Arts were once more ordered to wear a tabard; but later in the century they had returned to the dress which they had worn in 1533. Thus in 1572 at a Convocation of the university they were forbidden to wear the

---

[1] *Statuta Jagellonica*, n. p. xxix.
[2] *Acta Rectoralia Cracoviensis*, i, § 1406 (Year 1491).
[3] *Acta*, i, § 1343 (Year 1490).   [4] Cf. *Acta*, i, § 2299 (Year 1514).
[5] Cf. *Acta*, i, § 2799 (Year 1524).
[6] *Acta*, i, § 293 (Year 1473).
[7] *Stat. ant. Coll. Maj.*, p. 81.
[8] *Acta*, i, § 3195 (Year 1533).
[9] *Acta*, i, § 3189 (Year 1533).
[10] *Acta*, ii. 27, § 88 (Year 1537) and ii. 47, § 129 (Year 1538).

dress of lay doctors, that is, a tight-sleeved *tunica*, and a doctoral *pileus* or biretta,[1] or a cap with ear-flaps (*auriculatus*), and if they continued to do so they were not to be admitted to the higher faculty to which they aspired.[2] In 1601 a new Master of Arts on taking the oaths at the time of the ceremony of his admittance was ordered to promise to wear at his public lectures a gown with side sleeves.[3] From this it may be seen that the difference in dress between lay doctors and Masters of Arts at this period was that the doctors wore a tight-sleeved *tunica* and the masters a wide-sleeved gown.

We know that by 1547 gloves had come to be considered as part of the doctoral dress.[4] In 1579 a festal dress for lay doctors is first mentioned, and reference is again made to it in the following year.[5] This festal dress—it is interesting to notice that festal dress was introduced at Oxford and Cambridge almost at the same time—consisted of a blue damask gown (*subba*, i.e. *schuba*). In 1579 it is referred to as the festal dress of doctors generally, but in 1580 it is described as worn by a Doctor of Law. In spite of this reference to an exclusive use of the blue *schuba*, the 1579 statute was no doubt observed, and all doctors used it.

Students seem to have been left to their own devices as long as their dress was modest. In the early days the authorities seem to have found nothing in the students' costume to which to take exception, but in the later fifteenth century it began to run to extravagance. In 1473, 1493, and 1533 the dress of students is mentioned only to condemn its richness or its too blatant lay character. Thus in the first of these years the wearing of a black *tunica* of very good cloth (*Astrodomensis*, Astrakhan), or a gown with sleeves decorated with purple is condemned,[6] as is the wearing of green boots;[7] while by 1533 it had become necessary to legislate against a short dress of a lay character.[8]

During the course of the sixteenth century the disturbances and changes in Europe made it more and more necessary, as

---

[1] Cf. the ceremony of the creation of doctors described as *Ad Biretti Impositionem* (*Statuta nec non Liber Promotionum Jagellonica*, footnote, pp. cxxxiv–cxxxvi).

[2] *Statuta Jagellonica*, p. lxviii.   [3] *Statuta Jagellonica*, p. lxxvii.

[4] *Acta*, ii. 139, § 326 (Year 1547).

[5] *Acta*, ii. 324, § 623 (Year 1579), and 331, § 635 (Year 1580).

[6] *Acta*, i, § 290 (Year 1473).

[7] *Acta*, i, § 1594 (Year 1493).   [8] *Acta*, i, § 3197 (Year 1533).

elsewhere, for the authorities at Cracow to keep watch over the dress of members of the university. Thus in 1537 the rector took action against tailors who cheated members of the university and encouraged them to spend their money freely in buying rich cloths. The legislators looked with particular disfavour upon the grey-blue cloth (*szupyczka*) very popular at this time.[1] There were also offences of another kind, as when in 1580 Laurencius Gadomski, a Bachelor of Arts, was punished for appearing in a *pileus*, although in 1514 this had been allowed.[2]

The Deans of the Faculty of Philosophy wore from 1601[3] until about 1778, at their installation, an *epomis* (cloak) once worn by St. Joannes Cantius (d. 1473), a former professor at Cracow. It was kept in the church of St. Anna at Cracow, and was only brought out on these special occasions.[4]

In the eighteenth century regents wore the *palliolum*, a loose and ample cloak; while an order of 1765 demanded that pro-deans should wear a purple *epomis*, a garment which was shorter and less full than the *palliolum*. Deans had a similar dress, but it was richly braided, while ex-deans were to wear black silk cloaks or mantles decorated with purple and edged with a narrow line of silver.[5]

[1] *Acta*, ii. 21, § 68 (Year 1537).
[2] *Acta*, ii. 324–5, § 625 (Year 1580). Cf. *Acta*, i, § 2299 (Year 1514).
[3] Probably earlier.
[4] *Statuta Jagellonica*, pp. lxxvii–lxxviii and 445.
[5] *Statuta Jagellonica*, p. cci.

GLOSSARY

Du Cange's *Glossarium Mediae et Infimae Latinitatis*, originally published in 1678, remains, in the Benedictine edition(10 vols., 1883–7), unsurpassed for giving exact meanings of Latin terms of dress, although even so there are some examples which leave one in doubt as to the exact nature of certain articles mentioned in medieval statutes and other manuscripts. Sometimes the same word is used in a different sense in different passages, and sometimes one finds more than one word used for the same dress. By closely comparing many passages I have sought to reach definite conclusions. J. H. Baxter and C. Johnson's *Mediaeval Latin Word-List* (1955) is most useful, but in itself is not always sufficient to solve these difficulties. Other works such as V. Gay's *Glossaire archéologique* (2 vols., 1887–1928) are not enough specialized to be of use. The terms in the list which follows are used continually throughout the book.

The writers on monumental brasses, from whom general readers usually gain their knowledge of medieval academical and legal dress, have unfortunately no systematic terminology. H. Haines in his *Manual of Monumental Brasses* (1861) did pioneer work in this way and with much success, and H. Druitt, whose *Manual of Costume as illustrated by Monumental Brasses* appeared in 1906, is on the whole a very accurate writer on this subject; but F. E. Brightman in his valuable introduction to R. T. Günther's article on the brasses in Magdalen Chapel (*Magdalen College Register*, N.S., vol. viii (1915)) rightly complained of the often inaccurate explanations of articles of dress by this class of writer. How this inaccuracy persists can be seen for instance in the old mistake about the word 'tippet' still to be found in the 1953 edition of H. W. Macklin's *Monumental Brasses*.

APEX. The point, often like a stalk or button on the top of the *Pileus*, which later reappeared on the biretta, and as a tump or tuft on the *Pileus Quadratus* (Fig. 6).

ARMELAUSA (MANTLE). An outer garment open right down one side and closed on the other. Originally a late Western Roman and Byzantine dress, it was worn (as the *manteau*) by French *Chevaliers*, and soon became the recognized full dress of judges in northern Europe (Fig. 1).

BIRETTA, BIRETTUM and other spellings. Used for the horned and rigid variety of *Pileus* (Fig. 2).

CAPPA CLAUSA. A voluminous dress, sleeveless and reaching to the feet, with one slit in the middle front for the passage of both arms, or with two side slits (Figs. 3a, b).

1. Armelausa (Mantle)

2. Biretta

Flap collar

False sleeve

7. Flap-collared, false-
sleeved gown

3a. Cappa Clausa
with one slit

3b. Cappa Clausa
with two slits

4. Chaperon

5. Hood showing
liripipe

Liripipe

6. Pileus with
apex

8. Gown with winged sleeves

9. Gown with glove
sleeves

10. Sleeved tabard showing
various features common to
medieval academical dress

'Roller' hood
attached

Shoulder
piece

Short
sleeved
tabard

Tippet

11. Gown with tippet

12. Tunica

CAPPA MANICATA. A closed dress, shorter than the cassock (*Subtunica*) with full sleeves reaching to a point behind. F. E. Brightman in his Preface to the *Magdalen College Register*, N.S., viii, p. vi, calls the *Cappa Manicata* a Chimere with long sleeves. T. A. Lacey, describing the two forms of *Cappa*, compares the *Cappa Manicata* with the ecclesiastical Chimere and the Italian *Zimarra*, but he fails to see that it is the *Cappa Clausa* with two slits with which the Chimere should be compared (T. A. Lacey, art. 'The Ecclesiastical Habit in England' in *St. Paul's Ecclesiological Society*, iv, pt. ii, pp. 128–9). N. F. Robinson realizes this. See his article in *St. Paul's Ecclesiological Society*, iv, pt. iii, pp. 189 and 192. See TABARD.

CAPPA NIGRA. This was the same as the *Cappa Clausa* with side slits.

CAPPA ROTUNDA. A full, round form of *Cappa Manicata*. Though this is not anywhere specified, it was probably cut round at the neck and shoulders.

CAPE-GOWN OR CLOAK-GOWN. A Spanish lay fashion which appeared in the sixteenth century and was soon copied throughout Europe. It had a collar with a square flap which fell behind the neck. It hung down at the back, free of the arms.

CHAPERON (CHAUSSE). 'Chaperon' is the preferable term. It was a broad band of stuff lying on one shoulder, and was originally used as a band to which a hat was fastened so that it could be thrown off the head to hang down behind. The BOURRELET was a padded cap joined to the Chaperon (Fig. 4).

COLLAR (FLAP). The square collar falling below the neck on 'lay' gowns. A sixteenth-century fashion. L. H. D. Buxton and S. Gibson (*Oxford University Ceremonies*, p. 37) are wrong in stating that it is a modern addition (Fig. 7).

COLLOBIUM. Used in some works for the Tabard (e.g. E. C. Clarke, art. in *Archaeological Journal*, l. 139–40; V. Gay, *Glossaire archéologique*, ii. 365a, S.V. TABART, XVe S.).

EPITOGIUM. In medieval manuscripts this usually means 'Shoulder Piece' but it is sometimes used for a gown with a large 'Shoulder Piece' and hood placed above it.

EPOMIS. A 'Shoulder Piece'. At Cracow the term appears to have been used for 'Cloak' (J. Muczkowski, *Statuta nec non Liber Promotionum Jagellonica*, pp. lxxvii, cci, and 445).

LIRIPIPE. The piece of material at the end of the hood used originally for pulling it on and off the head (Fig. 5).

MINIVER. A loose term for varieties of fur used in ceremonial costume. Sometimes different varieties sewn together were used at the same time, and were disguised to look like expensive fur. Marten's fur was often used.

PALLIUM. A plain, closed, and sleeveless garment which was worn over the *Supertunica* (*Roba* or *Toga*) (E. C. Clarke, art. in *Archaeological Journal*, l. 101–2; S. Gibson, *Statuta Antiqua*, pp. 39–40. Stat. of before 1350). By the fifteenth century it had come to be no different from the sleeveless

Tabard. After the Middle Ages the word *Pallium* lost the force of its particular meaning and when used meant no more than 'gown'. This has nothing to do with the ecclesiastical dress of the same name (Oxf. Bodl. Libr. MS. Rawl. B. 461 (*in fine*)).

PILEUS. Used of the round cap in its various stages of development before its squareness appeared in the sixteenth century. Although medieval legislators as often as not use BIRETTUM (particularly outside England), I employ in the earlier stages the word *Pileus* according to the above definition to avoid any confusion, the word *Birettum* being so much associated with the modern ecclesiastical hard square biretta. The biretta and the English square cap were two forms of the sixteenth-century *Birettum*. The APEX was a point or button on the top. It later reappears as a tump or tuft on the *Pileus Quadratus*.

PILEUS QUADRATUS. Used generally for the square cap, at first soft and afterwards rigid with horns, which originated at Paris about 1520. See BIRETTA and PILEUS.

ROBA. In medieval times this was the middle dress worn under such outer dress as the *Cappa*, the *Pallium*, or the *Tabard*, and above the cassock (*Subtunica*). The *Roba* or *Toga* was known as the *Supertunica*.

ROBE AND GOWN. I use the word 'Robe' only for the academical festal robe of scarlet or for the scarlet robes of judges, in the sense of a dress of particular dignity, also for such official dress as that worn by the Lord Chancellor in England. The word 'Gown' I use in its modern sense of a black outer garment. According to J. Strutt (*Dresses and Habits of the English People*, ii. 357) the word was first applied (as *Gunna*) to the *Supertunica* of certain religious orders in the thirteenth century. It was afterwards used for the upper garment of burghers and magistrates of corporate towns and cities, and lastly became a common appellation for a garment substituted for the *Supertunica*.

ROLLER' HOOD. The medieval hood proper resting upon the 'shoulder piece' and surrounding the neck. The liripipe fell over it behind (Fig. 10).

'SHOULDER PIECE.' The lower part of the medieval hood, usually of a piece with it, and covering the shoulders and chest. The 'roller' hood was the upper part (Fig. 10).

SLEEVES (GLOVE AND FALSE PANEL). Long, hanging sleeves, hollow inside, e.g. M.A. sleeves in England. Before they reached the full length of the gown in the seventeenth century they were sometimes called Bag-sleeves. These are the Glove-sleeves. The False panel Sleeves, which are of much the same character, were hanging bands of stuff, either free of the arms or hanging over them, flat and sewn up, so that they were not hollow (Figs. 7 and 9).

SLEEVES (WINGED). Usually on gowns with a flap collar. Open above the elbow in the shape of an inverted V, then cut away horizontally on each side of the elbow to meet the flat lower part of the sleeve behind (Fig. 8).

SUBTUNICA, SUPERTUNICA. E. C. Clarke (article in *Archaeological Journal*, l. 94) calls the *Subtunica* the tight tunic worn under the cassock and the *Supertunica* the cassock itself; but F. E. Brightman (Preface to *Magdalen College Register*, N.S., viii, p. iv) calls the *Subtunica* the cassock and the *Supertunica* the *Roba* or *Toga*. I believe that Brightman is right, for, as he says, one could hardly call a dress underneath the cassock a particular dress at all. See also TUNICA.

TABARD. It was long but not full, sometimes with short pointed sleeves and sometimes without sleeves (Fig. 10).

TIPPET. Only used of such pieces of material as were fastened to the shoulder of gowns and robes. These Tippets represent the remnant of the scarf which held the *Bourrelet*. Other uses of this term are incorrect (Fig. 11).

TOGA. In late medieval times this meant the same as *Roba*. From the sixteenth century the term was used loosely for 'Gown'.

TUNICA. Used of a closed, plain, often pleated outer dress, usually girded, and with close sleeves, in those cases when it cannot be called either a *Supertunica* or a *Subtunica* (Fig. 12).

CRITICAL BIBLIOGRAPHY

A. MANUSCRIPTS

Baden-Baden
Letters from Dr. A. Roth on German academical costume. 15 August 1952 and 2 September 1952.

Budapest
Monograph on the academical and legal dress of Hungary by Dr. Csizmadia Andor. 6 June 1957.

Cambridge
Fitzwilliam Museum
Maclean 173. Petrarcha, *Canzone* (probably Bolognese). Fourteenth century.
Maclean 180. Orosius, *Historiarum adversus Paganos Libri VII* (Spanish). 1442.
James 251. Bartholomaeus Anglicus, *De Proprietatibus Rerum*, French translation by Jean Corbechon (miniatures of the style of the Boucicault master). Early fifteenth century.
Chalk drawings by John Downman. 1777–80.
Water-colours by Silvester Harding. 1794–8.
St. John's College
James 182. *Alchemica* (English). 1479.
Sidney Sussex College
James 76. *Psalterium cum Canticis. c.* 1340.
University Library
Dd. 4.35 [*Universitatis Cantabrigiensis*] *De antiquis consuetudinibus* (a very important contemporary document). Fifteenth century.
Mm. 1.40. Miscellaneous transcripts including statutes of Trinity Hall, and papers on Gonville and Caius College. Eighteenth century.
Mm. 1.53. Miscellaneous papers including one on university ceremonies. Eighteenth century.
Mm. 4.47, 51, 55, 56 Transcripts of the statutes of the University of Cambridge (of great value). 1758–78.
Mm. 5.50. Customs and ceremonies of the University of Cambridge (Adam Wall MS. vol. l). Eighteenth century.
Add. 105. A description of the University of Leyden with an account of its internal government. *c.* 1700.
Add. 707. J. Barret, Historical collections concerning Trinity College, Dublin. Eighteenth–nineteenth centuries.
Add. 2616. R. Gooch, *Collectanea* (important transcriptions of sometimes lost MSS.). 1821–37.
Add. 5107. J. W. Clark, Mr. Buck's Book (the famous Bedell's Book). Nineteenth century.

Coniston, Lancs.
Collection of Mrs. R. A. Parsons. The diary of Dr. Thomas Fry. 1768–72.

Helmstedt
University Library. University Archives. *Decretum in Consistorio, xi Maij, 1644.* 1644.

Helsinki
Extracts relating to academical dress from the university archives. 28 February 1955.

Jena
University Library. Stammbuch, Nr. 7. Seventeenth century.

Karlsruhe
Badische Landesbibliothek. Cod. St. Peter, perg. 92. Life and works of Raymond Lull. *c.* 1320.

London
British Museum.
Arundel 484. *Justiniani Imperatoris Digestum vetus,* with glosses of F. Accursius (German). Thirteenth century (miniatures 1399).
Harley 2887. A collection of theological orations (English). *c.* 1475.
Harley 7032. Various papers including transcripts of: *Statuta antiqua Academiae Cantabr.; Statuta vetera Domus S. Petri Cant. (Peterhouse)*; and *Miscellanea quaedam circa domum S. Petri,* viz. de Hugone de Balsham (Baker MSS., vol. i). 1707.
Egerton 1191. Album of Sigismund Ortelius of Padua, &c. 1573–9.
Egerton 1192. Album of P. Behaim of Nuremberg. 1574–80.
Egerton 1264. Album of Georg von Holtzschuher of Giessen, Bourges, &c. 1621–4.
Egerton 1425. Album of A. B. Filzhofer. 1719–71.
Additional 5843 (Cole Collections, vol. xlii). Antiquarian matter relating to Cambridge, including royal visits. Eighteenth century.
Additional 5845 (Cole Collections, vol. xliv). Antiquarian matter relating to Cambridge, including royal visits. Eighteenth century.
Additional 25693. *Le Chappelet de Jhesus et de la Vierge Marie.* Sixteenth century.
Additional 25695. *Horae Beatae Mariae Virginis* (French). Late fifteenth century.
Additional 25885. The first part of *Ludolphi de Saxonia Carthusianorum Argentinensium Prioris, Vita Christi* (German). Fifteenth century.
Victoria and Albert Museum
Drawer 53. Diploma of Doctorate of Law of Padua granted to Quintilio Carbo (coloured engraved portrait of later date). 1627.

Malta
Valletta. Royal University Library
1343. *Costituzioni per i nuovi Studi dell' Università e per il Collegio di Educazione di Malta.* 1769.
Correspondence Reg. No. 389/54. Letter from Librarian, 12 September 1955.

Oxford

Ashmolean Museum

Hope Collection of engraved portraits. Sixteenth–eighteenth centuries.

University Archives

Hypomnemata Antiquaria B.11. Inventories BR–C. Seventeenth century.

Hypomnemata Antiquaria B.18. Inventories R–S. Seventeenth century.

Registrum A, fo. 13. Illumination of King Edward III and the university chancellor. 1375.

Registrum T. Convocation Register. 1647–59.

Bodley's Library

Digby 233. *De Regimine Principum. c.* 1408.

Douce 244. Album of R. Rhetinger (or Rechtinger). 1598–1610.

G.A. Oxon. a. 72. Various illustrations including H. Overton, *Habitus Academici in Universitate Oxoniensi*; and coloured plate of William Miller. *c.* 1730, 1805.

Top. Gen. a. 36. Miscellanies including R. Sayer, *Oxonia Illustrata. c.* 1700.

Top. Oxon. c. 16. Miscellaneous illustrations, the set used being 25 engravings of university costumes by C. Grignion after drawings by Huddesford and Taylor to illustrate the requirements contained in the statutes of 1770. 1770.

Top. Gen. c. 25. J. Aubrey, Antiquities and miscellanies (Miscellanies, pt. II). Seventeenth century.

Top. Oxon. d. 58. J. Roberts, Water-colours of the academical dresses of Oxford (this unique collection is the finest of all illustrative material). 1792.

Top. Oxon. d. 130. T. Uwins, Pencil drawings of academical dress for R. Ackermann's 'Oxford'. 1813–14.

Rawlinson D 413. Constitutions of the College of Civil Law, Bologna. Eighteenth century.

Rawlinson Letters 108, fo. 279. Letter of J. Wildgoose to T. Tanner. 1701.

Twyne 2, fos. 101–3. The colleges of Paris. Seventeenth century.

Twyne 17, fos. 147 ff. (i.e. 1–43). Oxford entertainments: royal visits to 1636. Seventeenth century.

Wood 276 A. Printed mandates of the University of Oxford. [1689].

Wood 276 B. G. Edwards, *Omnium Ordinum Habitumque Academicorum Exemplaria* (a set of 10 plates similar to those in the above work was published *c.* 1680 as *Habitus Academicorum Oxoniensium a Doctore ad Servientem* by I. Oliver, Ludgate Hill). 1674.

Wood F 27. Miscellaneous papers including note on collectors, 1656. Seventeenth century.

Paris

Bibliothèque nationale. Département des Estampes Oa 10. J. Gaignières, *Recueil des portraits des roys et reynes de France, des princes, princesses, seigneurs et dames et des personnes de toutes sortes de professions.* 1581.

Rome

Biblioteca Angelica. 569. A. da Butrio, *Commentariorum super Libro II Decretalium* (Italian). Second half fifteenth century.

Vienna
University Library: University Archives. Matriculation Book of the
University of Ingolstadt, D. IV. 1589.

B. PRINTED BOOKS

ABDY WILLIAMS, C. F., *A short Historical Account of the Degrees in Music at Oxford and Cambridge* (1894).

Acta Rectoralia almae Universitatis studii Cracoviensis, 2 vols. (vol. 1 ed. by W. Wisłocki, vol. 2 ed. by S. Estreicher), 1893–1909.

ALMOND, A. G., *Gowns and Gossip*, 1925.

—— *College Gowns*, 2nd edn., 1926.

ANCONA, P. D', and AESCHLIMANN, E., *Dictionnaire des miniaturistes*, 1949.

ANDREAS, V., *Fasti Academici Lovaniensis*, 1650. (The best work on the subject for Louvain.)

APIN, S. J., *Vitae Professorum Philosophiae* (Altorfinae), 1728. (The prints, of course, lack colour and are limited in value by being half-length.)

ARCO, R. DEL, *Memorial de la Universidad de Huesca* (Colección de Documentos de la Historia de Aragón, tom. viii). n.d. (Full documents.)

ASCHBACH, J. VON, *Geschichte der Wiener Universität*, 3 vols., 1865–88.

ASHDOWN, C. H., *British Costume during Nineteen Centuries, Civil and Ecclesiastical*, 1910.

BAIER, J. J., *Biographiae Professorum Medicinae qui in Academia Altorf unquam vixerunt*, 1728.

BARCKHAUSEN, H., *Statuts et Règlements de l'ancienne Université de Bordeaux (1441–1793)*, 1886.

BARETTI, J., *A Journey from London to Genoa, through England, Portugal, Spain, and France*, 3rd edn., 4 vols., 1770.

BATY, T., *Academic Colours*, 1934. (Contains correspondence with university registrars.)

BEAUMONT, E. T., *Ancient Memorial Brasses*, 1913.

—— *Academical Habit illustrated by Ancient Memorial Brasses* (typescript), 1928. (Not a scholarly work, but a very full one on its subject. The only copy is in the Bodleian.)

BEAUNE, H., and ARBAUMONT, J. D', *Les Universités de Franche-Comté: Dôle, Besançon*, 1870.

BECK, S. W., *Gloves: their Annals and Associations*, 1883.

BECKET, R. B., *Hogarth*, 1949.

BECMANN, J. C., *Notitia universitatis Francofurtanae*, 1707.

BERGMAN, E., *Den svenska dräkten. Nationella Dräkten: En studie Kring Gustaf III:s dräktreform 1778*, 1938.

BERRY, W., *Encyclopaedia Heraldica*, 3 vols., 1828–40.

BIANCO, F. J. VON, *Geschichte der Universität und der Gymnasien der Stadt Köln*, 1833.

BICCIUS, C., *Tractatus Juridicus De Pileo*, 1736. (An important academical dissertation.)

BISHOP, W. J., art. 'Notes on the History of Medical Costume', in *Annals of Medical History*, N.S., vol. vi, no. 3, May 1934, pp. 193–218.

BLOXAM, M. H., *Companion to Gothic Architecture*, 1882.

BOEHN, M. U. VON, *Die Mode: Menschen und Moden in 16. Jahrhundert*, 1923.

—— *Modes and Manners*, 4 vols., 1933–5.

BONANNI, P., *Ordinum religiosorum in ecclesia militanti catalogus*, 3 vols., 1722–3.

BONNEROT, J., *L'Université de Paris du moyen âge à nos jours* (1933).

BORGEAUD, C., *Histoire de l'Université de Genève*, vol. i, 1900. (Good collection of portraits.)

BORKOWSKY, E., *Das alte Jena und seine Universität*, 1908.

BOSWELL, J., *The Life of Samuel Johnson*, ed. R. Ingpen, 2 vols., 1925.

BOURMONT, A. DE, art. 'La Fondation de l'Université de Caen et son organisation au XVᵉ Siècle', in *Bulletin de la Société des Antiquaires de Normandie*, t. xii (1884), pp. 293–622.

BOXHORNIUS, M. Z., *Monumenta illustrium virorum, et Elogia*, 1638.

BRADFORD, W., *Sketches of the Country, Character and Costume in Portugal in 1808–9*, n.d.

BRAGA, T., *Historia da Universidade de Coimbra*, vols. i–iii, 1892–8. (Full documentary evidence.)

Brasenose College, Quatercentenary Monographs, vol. ii (O.H.S., vol. liii), pt. 1, 1909.

BRERETON, W., *Travels in Holland. The United Provinces England Scotland and Ireland M. DC. XXXIV–M. DC. XXXV.* Ed. E. Hawkins (The Chetham Society, vol. i), 1844. (Some account of student dress. Eyewitness.)

BRIGHTMAN, F. E., Preface to R. T. Günther's article, 'Description of the Chapel Brasses', in *Magdalen College Register* (ed. W. M. Macray), N.S., vol. viii, 1915. (A scholarly study. Very valuable for the use of a correct terminology.)

BROOKE, I., *Western European Costume*, 2 vols., 1939–40.

BROOKS, E. ST. J., *The Life of Sir Christopher Hatton*, 1946.

BRUCK, R., *Die Malereien in den Handschriften des Königreichs Sachsen*, 1906.

BURIUS, G., *Onomasticon Etymologicum*, 1751.

BUXTON, L. H. D., and GIBSON, S., *Oxford University Ceremonies*, 1935.

BYROM, J., *The Private Journals and Literary Remains*, ed. R. Parkinson, vol. i, part 1 (The Chetham Society, vol. xxxii), 1854.

CABROL, F., and LECLERCQ, H., *Dictionnaire d'archéologie chrétienne et de liturgie*, t. iii, 1911.

Calendar of Papal Registers, ed. J. A. Twemlow, *Papal Letters*, viii (1427–47), 1909.

Cambridge Grace Books: *B*, pt. 1, ed. M. Bateson, 1903; *Γ*, ed. W. G. Searle, 1908; *Δ*, ed. J. Venn, 1910.

Cambridge University and College Statutes, printed for the Royal Commission, 3 vols., 1852.

CANT, R. G., *The University of St. Andrews: a Short History*, 1946. (Contains various useful items of information.)

CARDON, G., *La Fondation de l'Université de Douai*, 1892.

CARLIER, L., *In Iure academico (Wirceburgense)*, 1732.

CARLYLE, T., *Miscellaneous Essays*, vol. ii (Chapman and Hall's Stereotype edition, 1888).

Ceremonias y costumbres usadas y guardadas en colegio mayor de S. Clemente, Bolonia, 1660.

Chartularium Studii Bononiensis, 2 vols., 1909–13. (Contains useful material.)

CLARK, A., *Register of the University of Oxford*, vol. ii, 1571–1622, pt. 1 (Introduction) (O.H.S., vol. x), 1887.

—— *The Life and Times of Anthony à Wood*, 5 vols. (O.H.S., vols. xix, xxi, xxvi, xxx, and xl), 1891–1900.

CLARK, S., *The Marrow of Ecclesiastical History*, 1675.

CLARKE, E. C., art. 'English Academic Costume', in *The Archaeological Journal*, vol. l (1893). (Generally speaking the most complete article in existence.)

——, art. 'College Caps and Doctors' Hats', in *The Archaeological Journal*, vol. lxi (1904) (A useful work. The best on the subject in spite of some faults.)

CLINCH, G., *English Costume from Prehistoric Times to the End of the Eighteenth Century*, 1909.

COLLE, F. M., *Storia scientifico-letteraria dello Studio di Padova*, vol. i, 1824.

COMBE, W., *A History of the University of Cambridge* (Ackermann), vol. ii, 1815. (Contains the costume plates by T. Uwins.)

——, *A History of the University of Oxford* (Ackermann), vol. ii, 1815. (Contains the costume plates by T. Uwins.)

Communications addressed to the Cambridge Antiquarian Society, 8vo series, vol. iv (1854), pp. 85–93. (Edition of Cambridge University Library MS. Dd. 4.35.)

Conspectus historiae universitatis Viennensis, 3 vols., 1722–5.

КОНСТАНДСКІЙ СОБОРЪ 1414–1418. *Concilium Constantiense* (Société archéologique russe), 1874.

Constituciones , Estatutos, y Privilegios de la Universidad Luliana de Mallorca, 1698.

Constituiones et statuta coll. maj. Sanctae Crucis oppidi Vallisoletani, 1727.

Constitutiones insignis Collegii S. Ildephonsi, ac per inde totius almae Complutensis academia; and *Reformacion en la Universidad de Alcalá de Henares* (2 vols. bound in 1), 1716.

COOMBS, H., and BAX, A. N. edd., *The Journal of a Somerset Rector*, 1930.

COOPER, C. H., *Annals of the University of Cambridge*, 5 vols., 1842–53. (Particularly valuable for the sixteenth century.)

CORSINI, A., *Il Costume del medico nelle pitture fiorentine del Rinascimento*, 1912.

COTMAN, J. S., *Sepulchral Brasses of Norfolk and Suffolk*, 2 vols., 1839/8.

COUTTS, J., *A History of the University of Glasgow*, 1909.

Cox, G. V., *Recollections of Oxford*, 1868.

COXE, W., *Travels into Poland, Russia, Sweden, and Denmark*, vol. iv, 1787.

CRAWFURD, R., *The Last Days of Charles II*, 1909.

CREENY, W. F., *A Book of Fac-similes of Monumental Brasses on the Continent of Europe*, 1884.

CRÉVIER, J. B. L., *Histoire de l'Université de Paris*, 7 vols., 1761. (The chief source for Paris from 1673 to 1761. Before that uncritically reliant on Du Boulay.)

CROSSLEY, F. H., *English Church Monuments*, 1921.

CUNNINGHAM, D. J., *The Evolution of the Graduation Ceremony*, 1904.

CUNNINGTON, C. W. and P., *Handbook of Mediaeval Costume*, 1952.

DAVIS, C. T., art. 'A Monumental Brass in the Old, or West, Church, Aberdeen', in *The Archaeological Journal*, vol. li (1894), and pl. opp. p. 76.

DEARMER, P., *The Ornaments of the Ministers*, revised edn., 1920.

Debrecen, The History of the Royal Free Town of, 1871.

DE CAUMONT, A., *Cours d'antiquités monumentales,* vol. vi, 1841.

DELANNOY, P., *L'Université de Louvain,* 1915. (Photographs of portraits destroyed in 1914. Only one of these is really useful for this subject.)

DELITZSCH, F., *Iris,* 1889.

DENIFLE, H., and CHATELAIN, E., *Chartularium Universitatis Parisiensis (1200–1452),* 4 vols., 1889–97.

—— and EHRLE, F., *Archiv für Literatur- und Kirchen- Geschichte des Mittelalters,* Banden iii (1887) and vi (1892). (Band iii particularly contains much information, period fourteenth century.)

DIDEROT, D., and D'ALEMBERT, J. LE R., *Encyclopédie,* 35 vols., 1751–77. (Valuable contemporary articles.)

DRUITT, H., *A Manual of Costume as illustrated by Monumental Brasses,* 1906. (A competent study.)

DUBARLE, E., *Histoire de l'Université de Paris,* 2 vols. in 1, 1844.

Dublin, The Statutes of Trinity College, trans. R. Bolton, 1760 (with a supplement, 1759). (The only systematic collection, but with little information on the subject.)

DU BOULAY, C. E., *Historia Universitatis Parisiensis,* 6 vols., 1665–73. (Much out-of-the-way information. Best for contemporary facts. In the earlier period much romancing.)

—— *Remarques sur la dignité du recteur de l'Université de Paris,* 1668.

DU CANGE, C. D., *Glossarium Mediae et Infimae Latinitatis,* 10 vols., 1883–7.

DUGDALE, W., *Origines juridiciales,* 1671.

DU MOLINET, C., *Figures des differents habits des Chanoines,* 1666.

DUPONT FERRIER, G., *Du Collège de Clermont au Lycée Louis-le-Grand (1563–1920),* 1922.

DYER, G., *Privileges of the University of Cambridge,* 1824.

Edinburgh University: a Sketch of its Life for 300 years, 1884.

EDWARDS, K., *The English Secular Cathedrals in the Middle Ages,* 1949.

EDWARDS, R., *Early Conversation Pictures,* 1954.

EELES, F. C., art. 'The Clavering Glass', in *Transactions of the Essex Archaeological Society,* vol. xvi, pt. 2 (1922).

ELLIS, H., *Original Letters illustrative of English History,* vol. iii, 1824.

Epistolae Obscurorum Virorum, ed. and trans. F. Griffin Stokes, 1909.

ESDAILE, K., and SITWELL, S., *English Church Monuments, 1510–1840,* 1946.

Estatutos da Universidade de Coimbra, 3 vols., 1772. (Pombal's reforms.)

Estatutos de la Universidad de Valladolid, 1651.

EVELYN, J., *The Diary of John Evelyn,* ed. E. S. de Beer, 5 vols., 1955.

FABRONIUS, A., *Historiae Academiae Pisanae,* 3 vols., 1791–5. (A solid work.)

FACCIOLATI, J., *Fasti Gynmasii Patavini* (2 pts. in 1 vol.), 1757.

FAVA, D., ed., *Tesori delle Biblioteche d'Italia: Emilia e Romagna,* 1932.

FÉLIBIEN, M., and LOBINEAU, G. A., *Histoire de la Ville de Paris,* 5 vols., 1725.

FERRARIO, G., *Le Costume ancien et moderne,* 1827 (various volumes). (Fine plates of the latter period.)

FIKENSCHER, G. W. A., *Geschichte der Königlich Preußischen Friedrich-Alexanders-Universität zu Erlangen,* 1795.

FORSTER, J., *The Life of Oliver Goldsmith* (Hutchinson edn., 1905).

FOURNIER, M., *Universités françaises — Les statuts et privilèges*, 4 vols., 1890–4. (Invaluable for the whole of the medieval period. It is to be regretted that it does not extend to the Revolution.)

FRANKLIN, A., *La Vie privée d'autrefois. Arts et métiers, modes, mœurs, usages des Parisiens*, vols. x–xii, 1892–3.

FRANKLYN, C. A. H., and ROGERS, F. R. S., art. 'The Dress of the Clergy', in *Parson and Parish*, 6 pts., 1951–3.

FRENCH, G. J., *The Tippets of the Canons Ecclesiastical*, 1850.

FRIEDENSBURG, W., *Geschichte der Universität Wittenberg*, 1917.

FRIEDLAENDER, E., and MALAGOLA, C., *Acta Nationis Germanicae Universitatis Bononiensis*, 1887.

FUENTE, V. DE LA, *Historia de las Universidades de Enseñanza en España*, vols. i–iv, 1884–9.

GABRIEL, A. L., *Student Life in Ave Maria College, Mediaeval Paris: A History and Chartulary of the College*, 1955.

GADAVE, R., *Les Documents sur l'histoire de l'Université de Toulouse, 1229–1789*, 1910.

GALLUS, N., and FLACIUS ILLYRICENSIS, M., *Responsio*, ?1550.

GANDILHON, R., *Sigillographie des Universités de France*, 1952.

GASPAR, C., and LYNA, F., *Bibliothèque Royale de Belgique — Principaux Manuscrits à Peintures*, vol. i (Text) and vol. i (Plates), 1937.

GERMAIN, A., art. 'L'École de Droit de Montpellier, 1160–1793', in *Académie des Sciences et Lettres de Montpellier* (Section des Lettres, vi, 1874–9).

——, art. 'Notice sur le cérémonial de l'Université de Médecine de Montpellier', in *Académie des Sciences et Lettres de Montpellier* (Section des Lettres, vi, 1874–9).

——, art. 'La Faculté des Arts et l'Ancien Collège de Montpellier, 1242–1789', in *Académie des Sciences et Lettres de Montpellier* (Section des Lettres, vii, 1882–6). (Germain's three articles are undoubtedly the best *studies* of the provincial universities. The best *sources* are to be found in Fournier.)

Gentleman's Magazine, vol. lvii, pt. 2, 1787.

GHERARDI, A., and MORELLI, C., *Statuti della Università Fiorentina*, vol. i (*Documenti di Storia Italiana*, vol. viii, 1881). (The only good collection of Florence statutes.)

GIBSON, S., *Statuta Antiqua Universitatis Oxoniensis*, 1931. (The documentary corner-stone.)

GLASSON, E. D., art. 'Les Origines du costume de la magistrature', in *Nouvelle Revue historique de Droit français et étranger*, 1884.

GLUD, S. P., *Dissertatio de Gradu Magisterii*, 1695.

GODLEY, A. D., *Oxford in the Eighteenth Century*, 1908.

GOLDONI, C., *Memoirs* (English trans.), 1926.

GOODISON, J. W., *Catalogue of Cambridge Portraits* (vol. i, The University Collection), 1955.

GOULET, R., *Compendium on the Magnificence of the University of Paris in 1517*, trans. R. B. Burke, 1928.

[GREEN, J. R.], *Oxford during the Last* (i.e. eighteenth) *Century*, n.d.

GRITZNER, E., *Die Siegel deutscher Universitäten.* (In J. Siebmachers *Wappenbuch*, Bd. i.8. Heft 1 (1904).)

GUDEMAN, A., *Imagines Philologorum*, 1911.

GUNNING, H., *Ceremonies observed in the Senate House at Cambridge*, 1828.

GYLLENE BÖCKER, *Nationalmuseum, Stockholm. Illuminierade medeltida handskrifter i dansk och svensk ägo*, 1952.

HAGELGANS, J. G., *Orbis Literatus Academicus Germanico-Europaeus*, 1737. (Perhaps the engravings leave something to be desired, but they are clearer than those of Gritzner.)

HAINES, H., *A Manual of Monumental Brasses*, 1861.

HARRADEN, R., *Costumes of the University of Cambridge* (1803). (Useful but crudely executed plates. Often wrongly dated 1805.)

HARRISON, W. J., *Life in Clare Hall, Cambridge, 1658–1713*, 1958.

HARTLEY, D. R., *Mediaeval Costume and Life*, 1931.

HASKINS, C. H., *The Rise of Universities*, 1923.

HASSALL, W. O., *The Holkham Bible Picture Book*, 1954.

HEARNE, T., *Collections*, vol. x (1728–31), ed. H. E. Salter (O.H.S., vol. lxvii (1915)) and vol. xi (1731–5), ed. H. E. Salter (O.H.S., vol. lxxii (1918)).

HENDERSON, E. F., *Select Historical Documents of the Middle Ages*, 1910.

HERMANN, H. J., *Die Italienischen Handschriften des Dugento und Trecento*, 2 vols., 1928–9. (Pictorial sources for Bologna.)

HERRLIBERGER, D., *Schweitzerischer Ehrentempel*, 1748. (Of pictorial value.)

HEYDEN, J. VON DER, *Speculum Cornelianum*, 1618; facsimile reprint, ? 1879. (Illustrative material for the early seventeenth century.)

HEYWOOD, J., *A Collection of Statutes for the University and Colleges of Cambridge*, 1840. (The fullest collection.)

HOBHOUSE, E., ed., *The Diary of a West Country Physician*, 1934.

HOLLIS, T. and G., *The Monumental Effigies of Great Britain*, 6 pts., 1840–2.

HOPE, W. H. ST. J., *The Seals of the University of Cambridge* (1883).

HOTTENROTH, F., *Handbuch der Deutschen Tracht*, 1896. (Unfortunately sources for the figures are not given.)

HURTAUT, P. T. N., and MAGNY, ., *Dictionnaire historique de la ville de Paris*, 4 vols., 1779.

INNES, C., *Fasti Aberdonenses: Selections from the Records of the University and King's College of Aberdeen, 1494–1854* (Spalding Club), 1854.

——, *Munimenta Universitatis Glasguensis, 1450–1727*, vol. ii (Maitland Club), 1854.

IRELAND, J., and NICHOLS, J., *Hogarth's Complete Works*, 3 vols., 1883.

IRSAY, S. D', *L'Histoire des Universités françaises et étrangères à nos jours*, 2 vols., 1933–5.

JAMES, M. R., *The Chaundler Manuscripts* (Roxburghe Club), 1916. (Contains account of the most important pictorial evidence of the Middle Ages.)

JAMESON, A. B., *Legends of the Monastic Orders*, 1850.

JOHNSTON, W., *The Last Bajans of King's and Marischal Colleges, 1859–60*, 1899.

JOHNSTONE, J. F. K., *The 'Alba Amicorum' of George Strachan, George Craig, and Thomas Cumming*, 1924.

JOURDAIN, C., *Histoire de l'Université de Paris au XVIIe et au XVIIIe siècles*, 2 vols., 1888.

KAY, J., *A Series of Original Portraits and Caricature Etchings*, 2 vols., 1838. (Some information to be derived from these.)

KEIL, RI. and ROBT., *Geschichte des Jenaischen Studentenlebens (1548–1858)*, 1858. (An important contribution to the study of university life, others such being by Reicke, Tholuck, and Zarncke.)

KIBRE, P., *The Nations in the Mediaeval Universities*, 1948.

KINK, R., *Geschichte der Kaiserlichen Universität zu Wien*, 2 vols., 1854.

KIPPING, J. G., *Oratio de Honoribus Academicis* (Helmstädt), 1744.

KLÜPFEL, K., and EIFERT, M., *Geschicht und Beschreibung der Stadt und Universität Tübingen*, 2 pts., 1849. (Pt. 2 deals with the university and is by Klüpfel.)

[KNAPTON, J.], *Description of Holland*, 1743.

KNOX, V., *Essays Moral and Literary*, vol. i, 1784.

KORTUM, K. A., *Jobsiade*, 1784.

KOSEGARTEN, J. G. L., *Geschichte der Universität von Greifswald*, 2 vols., 1857/6.

KUNNING VON BASEL, L., *Stambuch der Jungen Gesellen*, 1617; Facsimile reprint, ?1879.

LACROIX, P., *The Eighteenth Century, France, 1700–89. Its Institutions, Customs, and Costumes*, 1876.

——, *XVIIᵉ Siècle. Institutions, usages et costumes, France, 1590–1700*, 1880.

LAING, H., *Ancient Scottish Seals*, 2 vols., 1850–66.

LAMB, J., *Documents relating to the University of Cambridge*, 1838. (Useful but too selective.)

LAUNOY, J., *De vera causa de secessu Brunonis*, 1662.

——, *Regii Navarraei Gymnasii Parisiensis Historia*, 2 vols., 1677.

——, *Epistolae Omnes*, 1689.

LEACH, A. F., *The Schools of Medieval England*, 1916.

LE COUTEUR, J. D., *English Mediaeval Painted Glass*, 1926.

Leges academiae Witebergensis, 1607.

LÉNAUDIÈRE, P., *De Privilegiis Doctorum*, 1584. (In *Tractatus Universi Iuris*, tom. xviii.)

LENS, L. DE, *L'Université d'Angers du XVᵉ siècle à la Révolution française* (T. i. Faculté des Droits), 1880.

LEOPOLD, J. F. and LEIDENHOFFER, P. J., *Academia*, ?1720.

LOGGAN, D., *Oxonia Illustrata*, 1675. (The first of the collections of engravings.)

——, *Cantabrigia Illustrata*, 1690. (The finest pictorial evidence of the post-medieval period which we possess.)

LOISELEUR, J., art. 'L'Université d'Orléans pendant sa période de décadence' in *Mémoires de la Société d'Agriculture d'Orléans*, t. xxv, no. 3 (1885).

Louvain, L'Annuaire de l'Université de, 1847.

LOYSEAU, C., *Traité des ordres*, 1610.

LÜBKE, W., *Ecclesiastical Art in Germany during the Middle Ages*, 1870.

LYELL, J. P. R., *Early Book Illustration in Spain*, 1926. (Pictorial sources for Salamanca.)

MACALISTER, R. A. S., *Ecclesiastical Vestments*, 1896.

[MACDONNELL, H. G.], *Chartae et Statuta collegii Sacrosanctae et individuae Trinitatis reginae Elizabethae juxta Dublin*, 1844.

MACKLIN, H. W., *Monumental Brasses*, revised by C. Oman, 1953.

MACRAY, W. M., ed., *Register of the Members of Magdalen College, Oxford*, N.S., vol. i, 1894.

MAGRATH, J. R., *The Flemings in Oxford*, 3 vols. (O.H.S., vols. xliv, lxii, and lxxix), 1904–24.

MAISONNIER, J., *La Faculté de droit de l'Université de Pau (1726–93)*, 1902.

MALLET, C. E., *A History of the University of Oxford*, 3 vols., 1924–7.

MALLIOT, J., and MARTIN, P., *Recherches sur les costumes*, 3 vols., 1809. (Contains valuable information.)

MALAGOLA, C., *Statuti delle Università e dei Collegi dello Studio bolognese*, 1888. (The fullest and best collection of Bologna statutes.)

——, *Storiche sullo Studio Bolognese*, 1888.

MARRIOTT, W. B., *Vestiarium Christianum*, 1868.

MARTIN, C., *Civil Costume in England*, 1842.

MARTIN, E., *L'Université de Pont-à-Mousson (1572–1768)*, 1891.

MATZEN, H., *Kjøbenhavns Universitets Retshistorie, 1479–1879*, vol. ii, 1879.

MAXWELL LYTE, H. C., *A History of the University of Oxford from the earliest times to the year 1530*, 1886.

MAYER, J. F., *De Doctoratu Theologico*, 1699.

MEINERS, C., art. 'Kurze Geschichte der Trachten und Kleide-Gesetze auf hohen Schulen', in *Göttingische akademische Annalen*, i, 1804. (Particularly trustworthy for German student dress.)

MELVILL, J., *The Diary of Mr. James Melvill, 1556–1601* (The Bannatyne Club), 1829.

MEURSIUS, J., *Athenae Bataviae*, 1625.

MONTFAUCON, B. DE, *Les Monumens de la monarchie françoise*, 5 vols., 1729–33.

Monumenta historica universitatis Carol. Ferdinandeae Pragensis, 2 vols., 1830–2. (A much better collection than more modern ones of its kind.)

MORAZZONI, G., *La moda a Venezia nel secolo XVIII*, 1931.

MORÓNI, G., *Dizionario dell' erudizione*, s.v. Z, ciii, 1861.

MOTTA VEIGA, M. E. DA, *Esboço Historico-litterario da Faculdade de Theologia da Universidade de Coimbra*, 1872.

MÜLLER, P., *De Gradu Doctoris*, 1687.

MULLINGER, J. D., *A History of the University of Cambridge*, 3 vols., 1873–1911.

MURRAY, D., *Memories of the Old College of Glasgow*, 1927.

NADAL, J. C., *Histoire de l'Université de Valence*, 1861.

[NEUBUR, F. C.], art. 'Kleidung der Studirenden auf der Universität Göttingen', in *Der Sammler*, 1736.

NEVEUX, P., and DACIER, E., *Les Richesses des bibliothèques provinciales de France*, 1932.

NEWTON, S., *The Diary of S. Newton, Alderman of Cambridge, 1664–1717*, ed. J. E. Foster, 1890.

NEYFFER, J. S., and DITZINGER, L. *Illustrissimi Wirtembergici ducalis novi collegii Delineato*, 1626. (Valuable contemporary engravings.)

NORRIS, H., *Costume and Fashion*, 3 vols., 1924–7.

——, *Church Vestments*, 1949. (A book to be used with great caution.)

Notes and Queries, 1st series, iii. 329; 2nd series, iii. 115–17 and 275–7; v. 501–2; vi. 211 and 258a; viii. 74–75; x. 160–1; 7th series, xii. 241; 12th series, ii. 537; iii. 59.

PANTIN, W. A., *Chapters of the English Black Monks (1215–1540)*, vol. ii (Camden Society, 3rd series, vol. xlvii (1933)).

——, *Canterbury College*, vol. i (Inventories) (O.H.S., N.S., vol. vi (1947)).

PANZIROLUS, G., *De Claris legum interpretatibus*, 1721.

PARNELL, H., *The College of Vicars Choral, Wells*, 1927.

PASQUIER, E., *Les Recherches de la France*, 1621.

PATIN, G., *Lettres choisies*, 1683.

——, *Nouvelles lettres*, 2 vols., 1718.

PATINUS, C., *Lyceum Patavinum*, 1682.

PAULSEN, F., *The German Universities*, 1906.

PEACOCK, G., *Observations on the Statutes of Cambridge*, 1841.

PÉRIES, G., *La Faculté de droit dans l'ancienne Université de Paris, 1160–1793*, 1890.

PERRAULT, C., *Les Hommes illustres qui ont paru en France*, 2 vols., 1696.

PETERS, H., *Der Arzt und die Heil und die Heilkunst in der deutschen Vergangenheit (15–18. Jahrh.).* (In G. Steinhausen, *Monographien zur deutschen Kulturgeschichte*, Bd. iii, 1900.)

PHILIPPI, F., *Atlas zur Weltlichen Altertumskunde des deutscher Mittelalters*, 1924. (Some good pictorial evidence taken from woodcuts and other sources.)

PIC, P., *Guy Patin*, 1911.

PITON, C., *Le Costume civil en France du XIIIe au XIXe siècle*, n.d.

PLANCHÉ, J. R., *Cyclopaedia of Costume*, 2 vols., 1876–9.

POOLE, Mrs. R. L., *Oxford Portraits, a Catalogue*, 3 vols. (O.H.S., vols. lvii, lxxxi, and lxxxii (1911–26)).

POPE, W., *The Life of Seth [Ward]*, 1697.

PORT, C., *Les Statuts des quatre facultés de l'université d'Angers, 1464–94*, 1878.

POTTLE, F. A., ed., *Boswell in Holland, 1763–4*, 1952.

POWELL, A., *John Aubrey and his Friends*, 1948.

PRANTL, C., *Geschichte der Ludwig-Maximilians-Universität in Ingolstadt, Landshut, München*, 2 vols., 1872.

QUICHERAT, J., *L'Histoire du costume en France*, 1875. (The best study of French professional costume.)

RAIT, R. S., *The Universities of Aberdeen. A History*, 1895.

RAM, P. F. X. DE, *Analectes pour servir à l'histoire de l'Université de Louvain*, Nos. 1–43, 1838–78. (Some of the analectes are important for the purpose.)

——, *Considérations sur l'histoire de l'Université de Louvain (1425–1797)*, 1854.

RASHDALL, H., *The Universities of Europe in the Middle Ages*, ed. F. M. Powicke and A. B. Emden, 3 vols., 1936.

RATJEN, H., *Geschichte der Universität zu Kiel*, 1874.

REICKE, E., *Der Gelehrte in der deutschen Vergangenheit (15–18. Jahrh.).* (In G. Steinhausen, *Monographien zur deutschen Kulturgeschichte*, 1900.)

——, *Lehrer und Unterrichtswesen in der deutschen Vergangenheit (15–18. Jahrh.).* (In G. Steinhausen, *Monographien zur deutschen Kulturgeschichte*, Bd. ix, 1901.)

RENAN, A., *Le Costume en France*, 1890.

RENAZZI, F. M., *Storia dell' Università di Roma*, 4 vols., 1803–6. (Dry but reliable.)

REPTON, J. A., art. 'Observations on the various Fashions of Hats, Bonnets, or Coverings for the Head', in *Archaeologia*, xxiv (1832), 168–89.

REYNIER, G., *La Vie universitaire dans l'ancienne Espagne*, 1902. (Particularly important for Salamanca.)

REYNOLDS, J. S., *The Evangelicals at Oxford, 1735–1871*, 1953.

RICHTER, A., *Bilder aus der deutschen Kulturgeschichte*, 2 vols., 1882.

ROBINSON, N. F., art. 'The Black Chimere of Anglican Prelates', in *Transactions of St. Paul's Ecclesiological Society*, vol. iv (1898).

——, art. 'The *Pileus Quadratus*', in *Transactions of St. Paul's Ecclesiological Society*, vol. v, pt. 1 (1901).

ROMILLY, J., *Graduati Cantabrigienses*, 1846.

ROSENBERG, A., and TILKE, M., *The Design and Development of Costume*, 5 vols., 1925.

RYMER, T., *Foedera*, tom. vii (1373–97), 1709.

SAINT, L. B., and ARNOLD, H., *Stained Glass of the Middle Ages in England and France*, 1913.

SALMI, M., *La Miniatura Italiana*, 1956.

SALTER, H. E., ed., *Registrum Annalium Collegii Mertonensis, 1483–1521* (O.H.S., vol. lxxvi (1921)).

——, *Registrum Cancellarii*, vol. i (O.H.S., vol. xciii (1932)).

SAMUELS, A. P. I., *The Early Life and Correspondence and Writings of the Rt. Hon. Edmund Burke, LL.D.*, 1923.

SANDAEUS, M., *Theologia Juridica*, 1629.

SANDYS, J. E., *A History of Classical Scholarship*, vol. ii, 1908.

——, art. 'Ancient University Ceremonies', in *Fasciculus Ioanni Willis Clark dicatus*, 1909.

SAVIGNY, F. K. VON, *Histoire du droit romain au moyen âge*, 4 vols., trans. Guenoux, 1839.

SCAPPUS, A., *De Birreto Rubeo*, 1592.

SCHACHNER, N., *The Mediaeval Universities*, 1938.

SCHLUCK, M., *Dissertatio de Norma Actionum Studiosorum, seu von dem Burschen-Comment*, 1780.

SHULTZ, A., *Deutsches Leben in 14–15. Jahrhunderts*, 1892.

SCHUNDENIUS, K. H., *Erinnerungen an die festlichen tage der dritter stiftungsfeyer der Akademie zu Wittenberg*, 1803.

'Scottish Legal Costume', art. in *The Journal of Jurisprudence* (Edinburgh), xxviii (1884), 62 ff. and continued pp. 124 ff.

SEIDLITZ, W. VON, *Allgemeines historisches Porträtwerk*, 12 pts. (6 vols.), 1884–90.

SEYBOLT, R. F., *The 'Manuale Scholarium'*, 1921.

SITWELL, S., *Conversation Pieces*, 1936.

Somerset Mediaeval Wills, ed. F. W. Weaver (Wills, 1531–58) (Somerset Record Society, vol. xxi), 1905.

Spectator, The, Routledge edn., 4 vols., 1860.

Statuta almae universitatis Patavini gymnasii, 1570. (Good collection of documents.)

Statuta almi et perinsignis Collegii maioris Sancti Clementis Hispanorum Bononiae conditi, 1648.

Statuta almi Pisani studii sumpta ex originalibus per Iulianum Lupium, 1621–2 (*Annali delle università toscane*, tom. xxx), 1911. (Some information of value.)

Statuta antiqua Collegii Majoris (*Cracow*) (in *Archiwum do Dziejow Literatury i Oświaty w Polsce*, vol. i), 1878.

Statuta et Leges Fundamentales Academiae Frisiorum quae est Franequerae, 1647.

Statuta et privilegia almae universitatis iuristarum gymnasii Bononiensis, 1561. (The best of the old collections.)

Statuta nec non Liber Promotionum Jagellonica (*Cracow*), *1402–1849* ed. J. Muczkowski, 1849.

Statuta universitatis scholasticae Studii Tubingensis, 1602. (A good example of a valuable old collection.)

Statutes of the Colleges of Oxford, printed for the Royal Commission, 3 vols. 1853.

Statutes of the Realm, vol. iii, 1817, and vol. iv, 1819.

STEGER, A., *Dissertatio de purpura*, 1741. (An excellent monograph.)

STEPHENSON, M., *A List of Monumental Brasses in the British Isles*, 1926.

STRICKLAND, W. G., *Pictures, Busts, and Statues in Trinity College, Dublin*, 1916.

STRUTT, J., *Dresses and Habits of the English People*, 2 vols., 1796–9.

STRUVE, F. G., *De Symbolis quae in promotionibus doctorum adhibentur*, 1739.

STUBBS, J. W., ABBOT, T. K., MAHAFFY, J. P. and others, *The Book of Trinity College, Dublin, 1591–1891*, 1891.

Studia Gratiana, ed. J. Forchielli and A. M. Stickler, 3 vols., 1953–5.

SUFFLING, E. R., *English Church Brasses*, 1910.

TANNER, J. R., *The Historical Register of the University of Cambridge*, 1917.

TAYLOR, W. B. S., *A History of the University of Dublin*, 1845. (Crudely executed, but invaluable plates.)

Testamenta Eboracensia, vols. iv, v, vi (Surtees Society, vols. liii, 1868; lxxix, 1884; and cvi, 1902).

THIERS, B., *L'Histoire des Perruques*, 1777.

THOLUCK, A., *Das akademische Leben des siebzehnten Jahrhunderts*, 1853.

THORBECKE, A., *Statuten und Reformationen der Universität Heidelberg, vom 16. bis 18. Jahrhundert*, 1891. (A good example of sound editing.)

THORNDIKE, L., *University Records and Life in the Middle Ages*, 1944.

TOMASINI, J. P., *Gymnasium Patavinum*, 1654. (Good illustrations.)

TOMEK, W. W., *Geschichte der Prager Universität*, 1849.

TURNER, J. HORSFALL, *The Coats of Arms of the Nobility and Gentry of Yorkshire*, vol. i, 1911.

UWINS, T. *see* COMBE, W.

VALENTINER, W. R., *Pieter de Hooch, with appendix on Hendrik van der Burch's Art* (1931).

VECELLIO, C., *Habiti Antichi e Moderni*, 1590.

——, *Habiti Antichi et* [*sic*] *Moderni di tutto il Mondo* (1598).

VELÁZQUEZ DE FIGUEROA, V., and others, *Anales universitarios. Historia de la Universidad de Valladolid*, tom. i, 1918. (More reliable than the old collections, although these contain more information for the purpose.)

VIDAL Y DIAZ, A., *Memoria Histórica de la Universidad de Salamanca*, 1869. (Contains full statutes of Salamanca.)

VIERO, T., *Raccolta di 126 Stampe che rappresentano Figure ed Abiti di varie Nazioni*, vols. i and ii, 1783–5.

VILLANUEVA, J., *Viage Literario a las Iglesias de España*, t. xvi, 1851.

VILLAR MAIOR, J., *Exposição succinta*, 1877.

VIOLLET-LE-DUC, E. E., *Dictionnaire raisonné du mobilier français*, vol. iv, 1873.

VIRIVILLE, V. DE, *L'Histoire de l'instruction publique*, 1849.

VISCHER, W., *Geschichte der Universität Basel von der Gründing 1460 bis zur Reformation 1529*, 1860. (Important early statutes printed here.)

WALCOTT, M. E. C., *The Constitutions and Canons Ecclesiastical of the Church of England*, 1874.

WALKER, J., *Oxoniana*, 4 vols., 1808.

WALL, C., art. 'Lambeth Degrees', in the *British Medical Journal*, ii (2 Nov. 1935), 854 ff.

WALLER, J. G. and L. A. B., *A Series of Monumental Brasses from the Thirteenth to the Sixteenth Century*, 1864.

WARD, G. R. M., ed., *Oxford University Statutes* (vol. i: *Caroline Code, or Laudian Statutes, 1636*; vol. ii: *University Statutes, 1767–1850*), 2 vols., 1845–51. (A serviceable collection of modern statutes.)

WARD, R. SOMERSET, *Robespierre*, 1934.

WEBB, W. M., *The Heritage of Dress*, 1912.

WEGELE, F. X. VON, *Geschichte der Universität Wirzburg*, 1822. (One of several good examples of painstaking German scholarship, others such being by Tomek, Kink, and Bianco.)

WELLS, J., *The Oxford Degree Ceremony*, 1906. (Mediocre work.)

WESLEY, J., *The Journal of the Rev. John Wesley, A.M.*, 4 vols., 1830.

WHITE, J. B., *The Life of the Rev. Joseph Blanco White written by himself; with portions of his Correspondence*, ed. J. H. Thom, 3 vols., 1845.

WHITTOCK, N., *The Costumes of the Members of the University of Oxford* (1840).

——, *The Costumes of the Members of the University of Cambridge*, ?1847.

——, *A Topographical and Historical Description of the University and City of Oxford*, 1828.

WILKINS, D., *Concilia Magnae Britanniae et Hiberniae*, vols. i and ii, 1737.

WINKELMANN, E., *Urkundenbuch der Universitaet Heidelberg*, 2 vols. (in 1), 1886. (Excellent edition of documents.)

WOOD, T. W., *Ecclesiastical and Academic Colours* (1875).

WOODFORDE, J., *The Diary of a Country Parson*, vol. i, 1758–81, ed. J. Beresford, 1925.

WORDSWORTH, C., *Social Life at the English Universities in the Eighteenth Century*, 1874.

ZACHARIÄ, F. W., *Poetische Schriften*, 1765.

ZARNCKE, F., *Die Deutschen Universitäten in Mittelalter*, 1857.

——, *Die Statutenbücher der Universität Leipzig*, 1861. (Useful edition of statutes.)

ZELTNER, G. G., *Vitae Theologorum Altorphinorum*, 1722.

INDEX

Aberdeen, University of, 142–5.

Åbo, University of, 184.

Academical dress, origins of, 4–6; attempt to abolish at Oxford, 106; abolition of insignia of doctors at Prague, 152; abolished at Vienna, 153; abolition of academical dress at Budapest, 155.

Ad Clerum habit, 109 f.

Adorf, Magister, 161.

Agrégés (assistant professors), of all higher faculties, at Montpellier, 51; at Orléans, 52; of Law, at Paris, 46 f.; at Pau, 59; of Medicine, at Montpellier, 50; at Nancy, 58; stipendiary doctors at Bordeaux, 55.

Aix, University of, 53 f.

Albanensis, A., 22 n. 4.

Albert the Painter, 183.

Albinus, B. S., 176.

Alcalá, University of, 31 f.

Aldrovandi, U., 17.

Altdorf, University of, 165, 172, 174.

Amess (Almuce), worn by Doctors of Theology, Padua, 20; Chancellor of Oxford, 60 f.; Ecclesiastical Amess, 70 n. 7, 136.

Ancharano, P., 15.

Andreae, J., 14.

Angers, University of, 53.

Antécesseurs (professors), of all faculties, at Montpellier, 51; Orléans, 52; of Law, at Paris, 46 f.; Pau, 59; of Medicine, at Nancy, 58.

Apex, described, 190; illust., 192. For instances *see* references under *Biretta* and *Pileus*.

Aristotle, 38, 179.

Armagh, Archbishop of, 137.

Armelausa, see reference under Mantle.

Arnauld, A., 45 n. 6.

Aubrey. J., 10 n. 3, 97.

Autun, Collège de, Paris, 42.

Ave Maria College, Paris, 39.

Avignon, University of, 51 f.

Aylworth, A., 76.

Bachelors, in general, 2; at Bologna, 16 f.; Florence, 24; Coimbra, 32 f.;
Malta, 34; Montpellier, 51; Avignon, 51 f.; Angers, 53, Caen, 55; Pont-à-Mousson, 57; Oxford, 85, 103; Cambridge, 124; Trinity College, Cambridge, 132; Glasgow, 140; Prague, 151; Heidelberg, 155; Leipzig, 159; Ingolstadt, 161; Strassburg, 165 f.

Bachelors of Arts, in France, 3; Germany, 3, 150; at Vienna, 4, 152, 155; Paris, 36 f., 38, 41, 48; Oxford, 88–91, 96; Cambridge, 126–8; St. Andrews, 138; Glasgow, 140; Aberdeen, 142 f.; Trinity College, Dublin, 148; Prague, 151 f.; Heidelberg, 156; Greifswald, 160; Leipzig, 169; Cracow, 187, 189.

— of Canon Law: at Paris, 41; Oxford, 84, 103; Cambridge, 124 f.

— of Civil Law: at Oxford, 61, 84–86, 104.

— of Divinity: at Oxford, 82 f., 103; 124; Cambridge, 112, 123 f.; Trinity College, Dublin, 147 f.

— of Law(s): at Vienna, 4; Paris, 47; Toulouse, 49; Montpellier, 49; Poitiers, 54; Nantes, 56 f.; Cambridge, 123, 126; Trinity College, Dublin, 147 f.

— of Medicine: at Vienna, 4; Paris, 37, 47; Angers, 53; Oxford, 76, 86 f.; Cambridge, 125 f.; Trinity College, Dublin, 148.

— of Music: at Oxford, 87 f.; Cambridge, 126; Trinity College, Dublin, 148.

— of Philosophy: at Pont-à-Mousson, 58.

— of Surgery: at Cambridge, 126.

— of Theology: at Vienna, 4, 152; Paris, 41, 43, 46, 179; Nantes, 56; Pont-à-Mousson, 58; Cologne, 154 f.; Heidelberg, 155 f.; Würzburg, 158; Louvain, 179 f.; Cracow, 187.

Baier, J. J., 165.

Bailey, W., 76.

Bajan (freshman) at Aberdeen, 144 f.

Baker, T., 91.

Balandran, 32.

The Genesis Record

A Scientific and Devotional Commentary
on the Book of Beginnings

The Genesis Record

*A Scientific and Devotional Commentary
on the Book of Beginnings*

Henry M. Morris

Foreword by Arnold D. Ehlert

Baker Book House
Grand Rapids, Michigan

Co-published

by

Baker Book House
Grand Rapids, Michigan

and

Creation-Life Publishers
San Diego, California

Foreword

Although there are more than twenty commentaries on Genesis currently in print, there is a unique need for this one. So far as is known, this is the only commentary on the complete Book of Genesis written by a creationist scientist. Clearly, it takes such a scientist, as well as a writer with Biblical and theological acumen, to understand and expound this book of beginnings in depth.

In fact, if a Christian worker desires to develop a commentary shelf on Genesis for his library, he would do well to begin with this one. A reader usually merely consults a commentary, but this volume tempts one to read it at length. It is written as a narrative exposition rather than as a critical verse by verse analysis (although discussions of all important historical and scientific problems are woven into the narrative); hence it is difficult to lay it down.

Dr. Morris writes from the conviction that the first eleven chapters of Genesis are as truly historical as the remaining thirty-nine. This conclusion is not based simply on faith, but on many years of study of the scientific aspects of the Genesis records and of the interchange of ideas with many other scientists, both creationists and evolutionists. Since he and many of his colleagues are convinced that the earth and universe are young, rather than billions of years old, he advocates a tight chronology in expounding Genesis. In handling the account of the worldwide Noahic Flood, the author draws on his studies in hydrology and geology, in addition to his years of teaching hydraulic engineering.

The fact that Dr. Morris has not received formal theological training does not hinder him from handling the Biblical and theological implications effectively. There is evidence of wide reading and Bible study in depth. He has taught adult and college Bible classes regularly for over thirty years. One will also find many applications to the Christian life, with unusual insight into human character.

A thorough understanding of the Book of Genesis is necessary if one is to understand the rest of sacred Scripture. In this book, the reader is conducted by a capable guide through these important corridors of earth history.

Arnold D. Ehlert

Contents

APPENDIXES

INDEXES

Testimony and Introduction

I first read the wonderful Book of Genesis fifty years ago, as a small boy. My mother had given me a Bible and, not knowing any better, I began to read on page 1. The great themes of Creation, the Fall, the Deluge, and the Dispersion, along with the absorbing stories of Abraham and the other patriarchs, all made a deep impression on a little boy's mind.

I had been taught from earliest days that the Bible was God's Word, and it never occurred to me in those childhood days to doubt any of these stories. Years later, however, the evolutionary teachings in college (Rice University), combined with years of lukewarm teaching in church and Sunday school during junior and high school years, left me with many questions. Consequently, I soon became what would now be called a theistic evolutionist. The great Creation and Flood stories could hardly be taken literally any more, and the tales of the patriarchs apparently had many legendary embellishments over their hidden core of facts. I practically stopped reading the Bible altogether during those college years, though I was still fairly regular in church attendance.

I had trusted in Jesus Christ for salvation as a very small boy, however, even before starting to school, and He would never allow one of His little ones to perish (John 10:27-30; Matthew 18:10-14). After graduating from college, a combination of influences—starting to attend an evangelical church, joining the Gideons, hearing the World War II edition of Irwin Moon's *Sermons from Science,* and, most of all, starting to read the Bible again—eventually led me back to confidence in the full truth of God's Word.

Returning to Houston later to teach at Rice gave the opportunity of trying to witness to college students concerning their need for Christ. These were intelligent students, most of them majors in science and engineering, and I quickly discovered that the same old questions that had troubled me (as well as several questions I had never thought of) were also hindering many others from believing. Central to all these problems was the question of the reliability of Scripture, especially the Book of Genesis. If Genesis were not historically trustworthy, then simple logic showed that neither was the rest of the Bible, including its testimony about Christ.

Thus began a study of the scientific and historical accuracy of Genesis—a study which has engaged much of my interest for the past thirty years and more. Not only did this open numerous opportunitities for discussing questions related to Creation and early history, but also for pointing out to many the wonderful ways of God with man, especially His provision of salvation through Christ. The Bible became a living, exciting book, and God a very present help. What God planned and promised and prepared in Genesis, He accomplished and perfected in the coming of Christ, and is now, today, applying and fulfilling in the lives of those who believe His Word.

Over the years since that time, I have had many occasions to teach the Book of Genesis—I would estimate a total of eight times. Each time is more exciting and instructive than the time before. The Book of Genesis is no mere collection of myths and legends; it is the actual, factual record of real events and real people at the beginning of history. Neither is the Book of Genesis merely a tedious scientific or theological treatise; it is an intimate diary of some of the greatest and most fascinating men and women who ever walked this earth. Furthermore, all of its scientific and theological inferences are profoundly important and literally true.

I can only hope that my own studies on this book, now set down here in *The Genesis Record,* will help make Genesis as real and thrilling to others as it has become to me. I am anticipating the opportunity soon, when the Lord returns, of getting personally acquainted with Noah and Abraham and Jacob and Rebekah and the other great men and women whose records have already been such a blessing in my own life.

I should say just a few words here about this commentary and its format. A narrative style has been followed, rather than that of a critical and analytical exposition. This is because it is so important for people to sense that the Genesis narrative is real and historical. At the same time, the treatment also deals with all the important critical questions and problems. In particular, the scientific difficulties usually associated with Genesis have been discussed and, I trust, completely resolved in favor of the literal accuracy of the Genesis record. I have tried to discuss and explain all the salient material in every verse, even though the discussion is organized in terms of groups of verses rather than individual verses.

The King James text of the Book of Genesis has been inserted for easy reference. Appropriate changes are indicated in the commentary wherever necessary. Since many references are made to books of the Bible other than Genesis (completely indexed at the end of this book), the reader is encouraged to have his Bible alongside this commentary.

I want to thank Arnold D. Ehlert for reviewing the manuscript and for writing the foreword. Dr. Ehlert is a valued personal friend, as well as a man of much "book learning." After a distinguished career as Director of Libraries successively at Dallas Seminary, Fuller Seminary, and Talbot Seminary, he is now serving in this capacity at Christian Heritage College. With his Th.D. from Dallas Seminary, he is unexcelled in the evangelical world as a theological bibliographer; and I am especially honored that he would consent to write the foreword to *The Genesis Record.*

Thanks also must go to that one who gave me my first Bible. She is now (1976) 77 years old, and is still typing my book manuscripts. *The Genesis Record* is probably the longest one she has typed, but there have already been at least ten others. Very special thanks for this labor of love, therefore, go to my mother.

The book was written initially in syllabus form for my course in the Book of Genesis at Christian Heritage College. Various suggestions and contributions from my students have been very helpful. Miss Marsha Heller, a teacher in Richmond, California, edited the manuscript. Some of the material in a previous study of mine on the first eleven chapters of Genesis has been adapted and incorporated herein.[1] Many other commentaries have, of course, been helpful in the preparation of *The Genesis Record,* and these are listed in Appendix 1. Special mention should be made of the classic two-volume commentary of Leupold, which has been of more direct help than any other.[2]

---

1. Henry M. Morris, *Science, Scripture and Salvation* (Denver: Accent Books, 1971), 155 pp.
2. H. C. Leupold, *Exposition of Genesis,* vols. I, II (Columbus: Wartburg Press, 1942), 576 pp., 655 pp.

My oldest son, Henry Morris III, has been very helpful in reviewing the entire manuscript and preparing the two indexes. Although he is the only one of my children who has directly helped with this book, all six of them have continually been a source of inspiration to me in the writing of all my books through the years. Just as the Word of God was of such blessing to me as a small boy, so each of them has known and loved the Lord Jesus Christ and His Word from childhood. All are adults now and active as witnessing Christians in the Lord's work, honoring their parents and loving one another. Humanly speaking, of course, the reason for this has been the faithful instruction and unfailing love of their mother, my beloved wife. Therefore, I would like to dedicate *The Genesis Record* to my beloved wife, Mary Louise, and our six sons and daughters.

I have personally enjoyed working on *The Genesis Record* more than on any of my other books through the years. My prayer is that God will allow it to be used effectively as a faith strengthener and thanks builder, as many come to believe and understand the marvelous works of God recorded in the Book of Genesis.

Henry M. Morris
San Diego
March   1976

PART ONE

Introduction to Genesis

1

The Book of Beginnings

The Foundation of History

The Book of Genesis is probably the most important book ever written. The Bible as a whole would surely be considered (even by those who don't believe in its inspiration) as the book that has exerted the greatest influence on history of any book ever produced. The Bible, however, is actually a compilation of many books, and the Book of Genesis is the foundation of all of them.

If the Bible were somehow expurgated of the Book of Genesis (as many people today would prefer), the rest of the Bible would be incomprehensible. It would be like a building without a ground floor, or a bridge with no support. The books of the Old Testament, narrating God's dealings with the people of Israel, would be provincial and bigoted, were they not set in the context of God's developing purposes for all mankind, as laid down in the early chapters of Genesis. The New Testament, describing the execution and implementation of God's plan for man's redemption, is redundant and anachronistic, except in the light of man's desperate need for salvation, as established in the record of man's primeval history, recorded only in Genesis.

The Book of Genesis gives vital information concerning the origin of all things—and therefore the meaning of all things—which would otherwise be forever inaccessible to man. The future is bound up in the past. One's belief concerning his origin will inevitably determine his belief concerning his purpose and his destiny. A naturalistic, animalistic concept of beginnings specifies a naturalistic, animalistic program for the future. An origin at the hands of an omnipotent, holy, loving God, on the other hand, necessarily predicts a divine purpose in history and an assurance of the consummation of that purpose. A believing understanding of the Book of Genesis is therefore prerequisite to an understanding of God and His meaning to man.

The word *genesis* of course means "origin," and the Book of Genesis gives the only true and reliable account of the origin of all the basic entities of the universe and of life. These will each be discussed in an appropriate place, along with the alternative naturalistic philosophies of origins proposed by various philosophers (sometimes calling themselves scientists). At this point the foundational importance of the Book of Genesis is stressed simply by noting the fact that it does give this information. Note, for example, the following:

(1) *Origin of the universe*
The Book of Genesis stands alone in accounting for the actual creation of the basic space-mass-time continuum which constitutes our physical universe. Genesis 1:1 is unique in all literature, science, and philosophy. Every other system of cosmogony, whether in ancient religious myths or modern scientific models, starts with eternal matter or energy in some form, from which other entities were supposedly gradually derived by some process.

Only the Book of Genesis even attempts to account for the ultimate origin of matter, space, and time; and it does so uniquely in terms of special creation.

(2) *Origin of order and complexity*
Man's universal observation, both in his personal experience and in his formal study of physical and biological systems, is that orderly and complex things tend naturally to decay into disorder and simplicity. Order and complexity never arise spontaneously—they are always generated by a prior cause programmed to produce such order. The Primeval Programmer and His programmed purposes are found only in Genesis.

(3) *Origin of the solar system*
The earth, as well as the sun and moon, and even the planets and all the stars of heaven, were likewise brought into existence by the Creator, as told in Genesis. It is small wonder that modern scientific cosmogonists have been so notably un-

successful in attempting to devise naturalistic theories of the origin of the universe and the solar system.

(4) *Origin of the atmosphere and hydrosphere*
The earth is uniquely equipped with a great body of liquid water and an extensive blanket of an oxygen-nitrogen gaseous mixture, both of which are necessary for life. These have never "developed" on other planets, and are accounted for only by special creation.

(5) *Origin of life*
How living systems could have come into being from non-living chemicals is, and will undoubtedly continue to be, a total mystery to materialistic philosophers. The marvels of the reproductive process, and the almost-infinite complexity programmed into the genetic systems of plants and animals, are inexplicable except by special creation, at least if the laws of thermodynamics and probability mean anything at all. The account of the creation of "living creatures" in Genesis is the only rational explanation.

(6) *Origin of man*
Man is the most highly organized and complex entity in the universe, so far as we know, possessing not only innumerable intricate physico-chemical structures, and the marvelous capacities of life and reproduction, but also a nature which contemplates the abstract entities of beauty and love and worship, and which is capable of philosophizing about its own meaning. Man's imaginary evolutionary descent from animal ancestors is altogether illusory. The true record of his origin is given only in Genesis.

(7) *Origin of marriage*
The remarkably universal and stable institution of marriage and the home, in a monogamous, patriarchal social culture, is likewise described in Genesis as having been ordained by the Creator. Polygamy, infanticide, matriarchy, promiscuity, divorce, abortion, homosexuality, and other corruptions all developed later.

(8) *Origin of evil*
Cause-and-effect reasoning accounts for the origin of the concepts of goodness, truth, beauty, love, and such things as fundamental attributes of the Creator Himself. The origin of physical and moral evils in the universe is explained in

Genesis as a temporary intrusion into God's perfect world, allowed by Him as a concession to the principle of human freedom and responsibility, and also to manifest Himself as Redeemer as well as Creator.

(9) *Origin of language*
The gulf between the chatterings of animals and the intelligent, abstract, symbolic communication systems of man is completely unbridgeable by any evolutionary process. The Book of Genesis not only accounts for the origin of language in general, but also for the various national languages in particular.

(10) *Origin of government*
The development of organized systems of human government is described in Genesis, with man responsible not only for his own actions, but also for the maintenance of orderly social structures through systems of laws and punishments.

(11) *Origin of culture*
The Book of Genesis also describes the beginning of the main entities which we now associate with civilized cultures— such things as urbanization, metallurgy, music, argiculture, animal husbandry, writing, education, navigation, textiles, and ceramics.

(12) *Origin of nations*
All scholars today accept the essential unity of the human race. The problem, then, is how distinct nations and races could develop if all men originally were of one race and one language. Only the Book of Genesis gives an adequate answer.

(13) *Origin of religion*
There are many different religions among men, but all share the consciousness that there must be some ultimate truth and meaning toward which men should strive. Many religions take the form of an organized system of worship and conduct. The origin of this unique characteristic of man's consciousness, as well as the origin of true worship of the true God, is given in Genesis.

(14) *Origin of the chosen people*
The enigma of the Israelites—the unique nation that was without a homeland for nineteen hundred years, which gave to the world the Bible and the knowledge of the true God, through which came Christianity and which yet rejects Chris-

tianity, a nation which has contributed signally to the world's art, music, science, finance, and other products of the human mind, and which is nevertheless despised by great numbers of people—is answered only in terms of the unique origin of Israel as set forth in the Book of Genesis.

The Book of Genesis thus is in reality the foundation of all true history, as well as of true science and true philosophy. It is above all else the foundation of God's revelation, as given in the Bible. No other book of the Bible is quoted as copiously or referred to so frequently, in other books of the Bible, as is Genesis.

In the Old Testament, for example, Adam is mentioned by name in the Books of Deuteronomy, Job, and I Chronicles; and Noah is mentioned in I Chronicles, Isaiah, and Ezekiel. Abraham is mentioned by name in fifteen books of the Old Testament and eleven of the New. Jacob is named in twenty books (other than Genesis) of the Old Testament, and in at least seventeen of the New Testament. In a special sense, every mention of the people or nation of Israel is an implicit acknowledgment of the foundational authority of Genesis, since Israel was the new name given to Jacob, and his sons became the twelve tribes of Israel. Apart from the Book of Genesis, there is no explanation for Israel, nor consequently for all the rest of the Old Testament.

The New Testament is, if anything, even more dependent on Genesis than the Old. There are at least 165 passages in Genesis that are either directly quoted or clearly referred to in the New Testament. Many of these are alluded to more than once, so that there are at least two hundred quotations or allusions to Genesis in the New Testament.[1]

It is significant that the portion of Genesis which has been the object of the greatest attacks of skepticism and unbelief, the first eleven chapters, is the portion which had the greatest influence on the New Testament. Yet there exist over one hundred quotations or direct references to Genesis 1-11 in the New Testament.[1] Furthermore, every one of these eleven chapters is alluded to somewhere in the New Testament, and every one of the New Testament authors refers somewhere in his writings to Genesis 1-11. On at least six different occasions, Jesus Christ Himself quoted from or referred to something or someone in one of these chapters, including specific reference to each of the first seven chapters.

Furthermore, in not one of these many instances where the Old or New Testament refers to Genesis is there the slightest evidence

1. See Appendix 4.

that the writers regarded the events or personages as mere myths or allegories. To the contrary, they viewed Genesis as absolutely historical, true, and authoritative.

It is quite impossible, therefore, for one to reject the historicity and divine authority of the Book of Genesis without undermining, and in effect, repudiating, the authority of the entire Bible. If the first Adam is only an allegory, then by all logic, so is the second Adam. If man did not really fall into sin from his state of created innocency, there is no reason for him to need a Savior. If all things can be accounted for by natural processes of evolution, there is no reason to look forward to a future supernatural consummation of all things. If Genesis is not true, then neither are the testimonies of those prophets and apostles who believed it was true. Jesus Christ Himself becomes a false witness, either a deceiver or one who was deceived, and His testimony concerning His own omniscience and omnipotence becomes blasphemy. Faith in the gospel of Christ for one's eternal salvation is an empty mockery.

By all means, therefore, we must oppose any effort from any source to mythologize or allegorize the Genesis record. It was written as sober history, the divinely inspired account of the origin of all things. No one, therefore, can hope to attain a true and full understanding of anything, without a basic acceptance and comprehension of the origin of everything, as recorded in Genesis.

Who Wrote Genesis?

The Book of Genesis, in common with all the other books of the canonical Scriptures, was written under the inspiration of the Holy Spirit. "For the prophecy came not in old time by the will of man: but holy men of God spake as they were moved by the Holy Ghost" (II Peter 1:21). "All Scripture is given by inspiration of God, and is profitable for doctrine, for reproof, for correction, for instruction in righteousness" (II Timothy 3:16).

The question is, however, exactly who were the "holy men" who were moved by the Holy Spirit to write the marvelous words of the Book of Genesis? There have been three main suggestions, or perhaps groups of suggestions, attempting to answer this question.

1 Various Writers after Moses

Most so-called liberal theologians and commentators, along with not a few conservatives, have followed the theory that a number of unknown writers and editors, during the period of Israel's history from about the time of King Hezekiah to that of Ezra the Scribe, compiled and edited several old legends and traditions, verbally transmitted not only by their own Israeli ancestors but also by the Egyptians, Babylonians, and others, into the Book of Genesis. Presumably they then allowed the story to be circulated that these had come down from Moses, in order to invest them with the authority of their great Lawgiver. This is the "Documentary Hypothesis," and has been applied not only to Genesis but also to the other books of the Pentateuch and to Joshua, and in a lesser degree to many of the other books of the Old Testament. It is also called the "J, E, D, P Hypothesis," the letters standing for the supposed writers of the respective portions. The "Jehovist Document," supposedly dated about 850 B.C., was marked by the use of the divine name *Jehovah;* the "Elohist Document," about 750 B.C., was marked by use of the name *Elohim;* the "Deuteronomist Document," was supposed to be a further editorial emendation of the first two, dated about 620 B.C., containing especially most of the Book of Deuteronomy; and, finally, the "Priestly Document," represents supposed editorial revisions by a group of Jewish priests around 500 B.C.

Adherents of this odd idea have attempted to justify it on the basis of supposed peculiarities of language and style, references to customs and cultures, and other internal evidences which seemed to them to warrant this patchwork approach to the study of the book's compilation. No doubt their real reason, however, was their basic commitment to the evolutionary concept of man's development. The original "higher critics," as such scholars were called (to distinguish them from the scholars known as "textual critics," whose work it is to try to determine as accurately as possible, from all the old manuscripts, the original text of Scripture) were convinced that man had not evolved to the state of culture described in Genesis until much later than the time of Moses and that, in fact, Moses could not have written any part of Genesis or the rest of the Pentateuch, since writing was unknown in his day.

These higher critics maintained that some of Genesis, especially the material in the first eleven chapters, had been derived from myths of the ancient Babylonians. These evolutionary presuppositions were quite false, however; and most of them have been thoroughly repudiated by modern archaeological excavations. Today it is beyond question that writing was practiced widely, and in many forms, long before the time of Moses. This is acknowledged even by evolutionary anthropologists. One of the leaders in this field, Ralph Linton, says:

> Writing appears almost simultaneously some 5000-6000 years ago
> in Egypt, Mesopotamia, and the Indus Valley.[2]

The time of Moses, of course, was only around thirty-five hundred years ago. Similarly, archaeologists now recognize that the cultural indications in Genesis, at least from the time of Abraham onward, are exactly what would be expected of eyewitness records from those times. Dr. Nelson Glueck, generally acknowledged as the leading Palestinian archaeologist of our times, has said, for example:

> As a matter of fact, however, it may be stated categorically that
> no archaeological discovery has ever controverted a Biblical ref-
> erence. Scores of archaeological findings have been made which
> confirm in clear outline or in exact detail historical statements
> in the Bible.[3]

In the context of this statement, Glueck was speaking particularly of archaeological discoveries having to do with the general time and place of Abraham, hundreds of years before Moses.

In similar fashion, linguistic studies by numerous first-rate Biblical scholars have repeatedly shown that there is no real substance to the claims of the higher critics that the language of Genesis was much later than the time of Moses.[4]

Undoubtedly, the underlying reason for this documentary hypothesis was the evolutionary prejudice of liberal scholars, who were unwilling to concede that monotheism and a high culture could have prevailed during Moses' day.

> The higher criticism has been simply an application of an awak-
> ened critical faculty to a particular kind of material, and was
> encouraged by the achievement of this faculty to form its bold
> conclusions. If the biologists, the geologists, the astronomers,
> the anthropologists had not been at work, I venture to think that
> the higher critics would have been either non-existent or a tiny
> minority in a world of fundamentalists.[5]

Although this book is not the place for a detailed discussion of evolution and its scientific fallacies, it can certainly be said that the scientific case for evolution has been thoroughly repudiated by creationist scientists in recent years. There is much good material now

2. Ralph Linton, *The Tree of Culture* (New York: Alfred A. Knopf, 1955), p. 110.

3. Nelson Glueck, *Rivers in the Desert* (New York: Farrar, Strauss & Cudahy, 1959), p. 31.

4. Oswald T. Allis, *The Five Books of Moses* (Philadelphia: Presbyterian & Reformed, 1947).

5. F. M. Powicke, *Modern Historians and the Study of History* (London, 1955), p. 228.

available supporting scientific creationism,[6] and there is no more basis at all for the evolutionary argument for the higher critical theories.

Consequently, the documentary theory of the authorship of Genesis is not the view advocated in this commentary. While occasional reference may be made to it later, wherever appropriate by way of illustration, the concern herein is not with these details, either of textual criticism or of so-called higher criticism. The Book of Genesis is assumed, with good reason, to be authentic as to date and authorship, and to have been transmitted down through the centuries essentially intact in its original form.

2 Moses as the Author

Probably most conservative scholars in the past have accepted the view that Genesis was written by Moses. This has been the uniform tradition of both the Jewish scribes and the Christian fathers. Genesis is considered to be the first book of the Pentateuch (the others being Exodus, Leviticus, Numbers, and Deuteronomy), and all of them together taken as the Law (Hebrew, *torah*) of Moses. This general view was apparently accepted by Christ Himself: "And beginning at Moses and all the prophets, he expounded unto them in all the scriptures the things concerning himself. . . . These are the words which I spake unto you, while I was yet with you, that all things must be fulfilled, which were written in the law of Moses, and in the prophets, and in the psalms, concerning me" (Luke 24:27, 44).

Assuming that Moses was responsible for the Book of Genesis as it has come down to us, there still remains the question as to the method by which he received and transmitted it. There are three possibilities: (a) he received it all by direct revelation from God, either in the form of audible words dictated by God and transcribed by him, or else by visions given him of the great events of the past, which he then put down in his own words, as guided subconsciously by the Holy Spirit; (b) he received it all by oral traditions, passed down over the centuries from father to son, which he then collected and wrote down, again as guided by the Holy Spirit; (c) he took actual written records of the past, collected them, and brought them together into a final form, again as guided by the Holy Spirit.

Evidently any of these methods would be consistent with both the doctrine of plenary verbal inspiration and that of Mosaic authorship. However, neither of the first two methods has a parallel anywhere in

---

6. Henry M. Morris, ed., *Scientific Creationism* (El Cajon, Calif.: Creation-Life Publishers, 1974).

the canon of Scripture. "Visions and revelations of the Lord" normally have to do with prophetic revelations of the future (as in Daniel, Ezekiel, Revelation, etc.). The direct dictation method of inspiration was used mainly for promulgation of specific laws and ordinances (as in the Ten Commandments, the Book of Leviticus, etc.). The Book of Genesis, however, is entirely in the form of narrative records of historical events. Biblical parallels to Genesis are found in such books as Kings, Chronicles, Acts, and so forth. In all of these, the writer either collected previous documents and edited them (e.g., I and II Kings, I and II Chronicles), or else recorded the events which he had either seen himself or had ascertained from others who were witnesses (e.g., Luke, Acts).

It also is significant that, although the Book of Genesis is quoted from or alluded to at least two hundred times in the New Testament, as we have already noted, in none of these references is it ever stated that Moses was the actual author. This is especially significant in view of the fact that Moses is mentioned by name at least eighty times in the New Testament, approximately twenty-five of which refer to specific passages attributed to Moses in the other books of the Pentateuch.

While this evidence is not conclusive, it does favor the explanation that, while Moses actually wrote the books of Exodus, Leviticus, Numbers, and Deuteronomy, he served mainly as compiler and editor of the material in the Book of Genesis. This in no way minimizes the work of the Holy Spirit, who infallibly guided him in this process of compilation and editing, just as He later did the unknown compiler of the Book of Kings and Chronicles. It would still be appropriate to include Genesis as one of the books of Moses, since he is the human writer responsible for its present form. In fact, this explanation gives further testimony to the authenticity of the events recorded in Genesis, since we can now recognize them all as firsthand testimony.

3 Compilation of Patriarchal Records
It is suggested in this commentary, therefore, that Moses compiled and edited earlier written records that had been handed down from father to son via the line of the patriarchs listed in Genesis. That is, Adam, Noah, Shem, Terah, and others each wrote down an individual account of events which had occurred in his own lifetime, or concerning which he in some way had direct knowledge. These records were kept, possibly on tablets of stone, in such a way that they would be preserved until they finally came into Moses' possession. He then selected those that were relevant to his own purpose (as guided by the Holy Spirit), added his own explanatory editorial comments and transitional

sections, and finally compiled them into the form now known as the Book of Genesis.

It is probable that these original documents can still be recognized by the key phrase: "These are the generations of. . . ." The word "generation" is a translation of the Hebrew *toledoth,* and it means essentially "origins," or, by extension, "records of the origins." There are eleven of these divisions marked off in Genesis:

(1) "These are the generations of the heavens and of the earth" (Genesis 2:4).

(2) "This is the book of the generations of Adam (Genesis 5:1).

(3) "These are the generations of Noah" (Genesis 6:9).

(4) "Now these are the generations of the sons of Noah, Shem, Ham, and Japheth" (Genesis 10:1).

(5) "These are the generations of Shem" (Genesis 11:10).

(6) "Now these are the generations of Terah" (Genesis 11:27).

(7) "Now these are the generations of Ishmael" (Genesis 25:12).

(8) "And these are the generations of Isaac, Abraham's son" (Genesis 25:19).

(9) "Now these are the generations of Esau, who is Edom" (Genesis 36:1).

(10) "And these are the generations of Esau the father of the Edomites in Mount Seir" (Genesis 36:9).

(11) "These are the generations of Jacob" (Genesis 37:2).

Assuming that these *toledoth* divisions represent the original documents from which Genesis was collected, there is still the question whether the specific names are to be understood as subscripts or as superscripts, or some of each. Are they headings applied to the material following, or closing signatures of that which which precedes?

The weight of evidence suggests that the respective names attached to the *toledoth* represent subscripts or closing signatures. The events recorded in each division all took place *before,* not after, the death of the individuals so named, and so could in each case have been accessible to them. The main difficulty with this view is that most of the portions that would be assigned to Ishmael and to Esau under this formula hardly seem appropriate for them to have written. However, this problem can be avoided by assuming that "the generations of Ishmael" constituted a small subdivision within the broader record maintained by Isaac, and finally transmitted by him. Similarly, the "generations of Esau" may have been appropriated by Jacob in his own larger account later transmitted under the heading "the generations of Jacob."

If this explanation is correct, then the Book of Genesis can be divided into nine main subdivisions, as follows:

(1) *"The generations of the heavens and the earth"* (Genesis 1:1—2:4)

This section, describing the initial Creation and the work of the six days, has no human name attached to it, for the obvious reason that no man was present at the time to record what happened. It must either have been written directly by God Himself and then given to Adam, or else given by revelation to Adam, who then recorded it.

(2) *"The book of the generations of Adam"* (Genesis 2:4b—5:1)

This section, written by Adam, describes the Garden of Eden, the temptation and fall, and the experiences of Cain and Abel. Adam was obviously the logical one to record this particular history. The use of the word "book" makes it clear that these primeval records were actually written down, and not simply handed down by word of mouth. It also is significant in light of the beginning phrase of the New Testament: "The book of the generation of Jesus Christ" (Matthew 1:1).

(3) *"The generations of Noah"* (Genesis 5:1b—6:9)

The patriarch Noah, sometime before the actual coming of the Flood, compiled the records of the antediluvian patriarchs before him. According to the genealogies listed in Genesis 5, Noah's father, Lamech, had lived contemporaneously with every one of these patriarchs, including Adam. Noah himself had known all of them except Adam, Seth, and Enoch. Noah then also recorded his own observations of the rapid degeneracy of men in his day and God's determination to destroy them, mentioning, however, that he himself had found grace in God's eyes.

(4) *"The generations of the sons of Noah"* (Genesis 6:9b—10:1)

Shem, Ham, and Japheth evidently took the responsibility of recording the preparations for the Flood, and then describing the Flood itself. They also recorded the immediate postdiluvian

events, including Noah's prophecy concerning themselves, and
then later his death.

(5) *"The generations of Shem"* (Genesis 10:1b—11:10)
After Noah's death, and after the dispersion at Babel, it seems
that the three sons of Noah became separated, and Shem
took the responsibility of keeping the records. Accordingly,
he wrote about the confusion of languages at Babel and the
resultant scattering of the families. He also recorded the
names of the descendants of Noah down to about the time
of the scattering, in the so-called Table of Nations in Genesis
10. Presumably he more or less lost track of the descendants
of Ham and Japheth after this, even though he himself lived
five hundred years after the Flood.

(6) *"The generations of Terah"* (Genesis 11:10b—11:27)
This is a very brief document, containing only the genealogies
in the Semitic line, from Shem down to Terah and his three
sons. It is important, however, in that it gives us the only
possible basis for a chronology from the Flood to Abraham.

(7) *"The generations of Isaac"* (Genesis 11:27b—25:19)
In contrast, this is quite a long document, giving all the details of the life of Abraham, from the time of his call by
God to the time of his death, and also including events in
Isaac's life until his father died. Isaac apparently also appended to his own record the "generations of Ishmael" (Genesis 25:12), the record of his half-brother's sons, which he must
have obtained from him at the time Ishmael returned home
to help Isaac bury his father (Genesis 25:9). Isaac also included mention of the death of Ishmael, about forty-eight
years after Abraham's burial.

(8) *"The generations of Jacob"* (Genesis 25:19b—37:2)
Jacob's record, like Isaac's, is much longer than most of the
others in Genesis, giving the later events in the life of his
father Isaac and then including all his own history through
the time of his twenty-year sojourn with Laban and his
return to Canaan, with the record of the death of both his
wife Rachel and his father Isaac. As Isaac had appended
Ishmael's record of descendants to his own, so Jacob also
included two documents from his brother Esau (Genesis 36)
after his brother had joined with him in burying his father
(Genesis 35:29). It is also possible that some of this material,
in particular the eight generations of Edomite kings listed in

Genesis 36:31-39, may have been inserted later as an editorial addition by Moses.

(9) *"The generations of the Sons of Jacob"* (Genesis 37:2b—Exodus 1:1)

Although the regular formula is not used in this case, the wording in Exodus 1:1 is very similar to the others: "Now these are the names of the children of Israel, which came into Egypt. . . ." The events in the life of Joseph and his brethren, as recorded in these latter chapters of Genesis, could have originally been known only to them. Whether they wrote them down, as their fathers had done, or transmitted them orally, somehow their stories must finally have come into the possession of Moses, as is indicated by the smooth transition from the last verses of Genesis to the first verses of Exodus. The formula would be exactly repeated, in fact, if the word "names" in Exodus 1:1 were replaced by the word "generation." It would then read: "Now these are the generations of the children of Israel. . . ."

Thus it is probable that the Book of Genesis was written originally by actual eyewitnesses of the events reported therein. Probably the original narratives were recorded on tables of stone or clay, in common with the practice of early times, and then handed down from father to son, finally coming into the possession of Moses. Moses perhaps selected the appropriate sections for compilation, inserted his own editorial additions and comments, and provided smooth transitions from one document to the next, with the final result being the Book of Genesis as we have received it.

Although this theory of the authorship of Genesis cannot be rigidly proved, it does seem to fit all available facts better than any other theory. It is consistent with the doctrine of Biblical inspiration and authority, as well as with the accurate historicity of its records. Furthermore, this approach provides vivid insight into the accounts, and a more vibrant awareness of their freshness and relevance, than any other.

Principles of Interpretation

Many writers on Genesis have emphasized an allegorical approach to its meaning. This has been especially true of interpretations of the first eleven chapters. Expositors of liberal and neo-orthodox persuasion have rejected the historicity of these records, but have tried to salvage "theological" values from them by a spiritualizing interpretation. Thus, Adam is not considered to be a real person, but rather a symbolic representation of all men. The fall was not an actual act of disobedience by the first man and woman, but rather a figurative expression of the common experience of all men. And so on.

Such allegorical exegesis must, however, be rejected by serious Bible students. As already noted, the writers of the New Testament, and Jesus Christ Himself, accepted the Genesis record as literal history. It is arrogant and presumptuous for modern-day "scholars" to undertake to correct Christ and the apostles on this vital matter. There are no allegories in Genesis, unless the dreams interpreted by Joseph are so described. The symbols in these dreams, of course, represented real events, and were so interpreted by Joseph, coming to pass historically exactly as he had said.

Some might feel that Galatians 4:24, which says that these "things are an allegory," referring to the story of Hagar and Sarah, warrants an allegorizing approach to Genesis. Nothing could be further from the truth. The apostle Paul simply uses the spiritual principles by which God dealt with Abraham, his wives and sons, to illustrate eternal principles by which He deals with all men. He does make an allegorical *application,* but not an allegorical *interpretation.* Abraham and Isaac, Sarah and Hagar, were to Paul real people, as the context clearly demonstrates. The events described in Genesis really happened to these real people, and it is because of this very fact that Paul can draw his conclusions as to the spiritual implications of these events as they relate to God's plans for mankind as a whole.

Many other writers, while not rejecting the historicity of Genesis, emphasize the typological interpretations of these events rather than their actual temporal significance. The characters and experiences of Noah, Abraham, Joseph, and the others are taken as "types" of experiences in the life of Christ, or of the people of Israel, or of the Church, or of something else. Such writers are often very reverent and spiritual in their expositions, and certainly believe in the historicity of Genesis and in the verbal inspiration of Scripture. Nevertheless, they often tend to go far beyond what is actually written by indulging in such excessive typology, and there is serious question whether such interpretations are really warranted.

There is no question, of course, that some portions of Genesis are treated as types in the New Testament. The first Adam is taken as a contrasting type of the second Adam (Romans 5:12-19; I Corinthians 15:21-22, 45-47). Eve is taken as a type of the church (Ephesians 5:29-33). Abraham and Isaac are discussed as a type of the Father offering up His only-begotten Son (Hebrews 11:17-19). Perhaps other typological interpretations are occasionally justified even when not explicitly expounded as such in the New Testament. An example of this would be the experiences of Joseph, which seem to parallel those of Christ in such a detailed fashion as to be inexplicable as mere coincidence.

It should never be forgotten, however, that types must be considered only as illustrations or applications, not as doctrinal interpretations, except to the extent that the inspired New Testament writers themselves make such applications a part of their own doctrinal systems. Neither should it be forgotten that whatever value typological applications may have will depend first of all on the actual historicity of the events so utilized.

In this commentary, therefore, the emphasis will be placed primarily on the exposition of the actual events and their historical significance in terms of God's purposes for the world in general, and as principles by which He deals with individuals of all times and places. Typological illustrations will be included where appropriate, but will not constitute the primary emphasis. We wish to stress most of all the real-life truthfulness and significance of this primeval record of man's origin and early history.

Anticipation of Eternity

Genesis is important not only as a history of man's origin, but also as a prophecy of man's future. The Book of Revelation should be taken literally no less than the Book of Genesis. Paradise lost, in Genesis, becomes Paradise regained, in Revelation.

The first chapters of Genesis describe a perfect world, made for man and placed under his dominion. Had man not sinned, he would have continued to rule and develop that perfect world, for man's good and God's glory. Since God cannot be defeated in His purpose, even though sin and the curse have come in as intruders for a time, we can be sure that all God intended in the beginning will ultimately be consummated. The earth, therefore, will be restored to its original perfection, and will continue eternally. Sin and the curse will be removed, and death will be no more.

It is instructive, therefore, to compare the people and events in Genesis with those in Revelation, and to a lesser extent in other prophecies of the future. We can learn much about the original world by the study of Revelation, and much about the final world by the study of Genesis, since in a very real sense, these are essentially the same.

These worlds are not quite the same, of course, since man in the first world, though sinless, was yet untested. The first world was suited as a probational world, still somewhat tentative, though perfect and flawless for its purpose. In the final world, man, though having experienced sin and failure, has also experienced redemption and renewal. He will have been made perfect and eternal, and so, therefore, will his world be made perfect and unchanging, no longer with aspects appropriate to a probationary period, but equipped ideally and fully as man's eternal home, in the presence of God, his Creator and Savior.

For example, note the following comparisons between the original world and the final world:

Probationary World (Genesis)	*Eternal World (Revelation)*
Division of light and darkness (1:4)	No night there (21:25)
Division of land and sea (1:10)	No more sea (21:1)
Rule of sun and moon (1:16)	No need of sun or moon (21:23)
Man in a prepared Garden (2:8, 9)	Man in a prepared city (21:2)
River flowing out of Eden (2:10)	River flowing from God's throne (22:1)
Gold in the land (2:12)	Gold in the city (21:21)
Tree of life in the midst of the Garden (2:9)	Tree of life throughout the city (22:2)
Bdellium and the onyx stone (2:12)	All manner of precious stones (21:19)
God walking in the Garden (3:8)	God dwelling with His people (21:3)

A number of other similar instructive comparisons could be made. Study of each would show that the particular characteristics of the first world were suited for man in a state of probationary innocence; whereas the corresponding characteristics of the eternal world will be designed for man in a state of everlasting redemption.

Perhaps a more striking contrast can be noted between the characteristics of the world under God's curse and the eternal world renewed:

Cursed World (Genesis)	*Eternal World (Revelation)*
Cursed ground (3:17)	No more curse (22:3)

Daily sorrow	(3:17)	No more sorrow	(21:4)
Thorns and thistles	(3:18)	No more pain	(21:4)
Sweat on the face	(3:19)	Tears wiped away	(21:4)
Eating herbs of the field	(3:18)	Twelve manner of fruits	(22:2)
Returning to the dust	(3:19)	No more death	(21:4)
Evil continually	(6:5)	Nothing that defileth	(21:27)
Coats of skins	(3:21)	Fine linen, white and clean	(19:14)
Satan opposing	(3:15)	Satan banished	(20:10)
Kept from the tree of life	(3:24)	Access to the tree of life	(22:14)
Banished from the Garden	(3:23)	Free entry to the city	(22:14)
Redeemer promised	(3:15)	Redemption accomplished	(5:9, 10)

Many other similar contrasts could be noted. It is obvious how directly connected are the Books of Genesis and Revelation. Many of the personages mentioned in Genesis also reappear in Revelation. The rainbow associated with the Noahic covenant (Genesis 9:16) is seen as the crown on the head of the mighty angel (probably Christ Himself) in Revelation 10:1.

Though it is doubtful (as some have suggested) that the Beast (Revelation 13:4) is actually Nimrod returned from the grave, it does seem that many of the attitudes and attributes of the latter are expressed again in the person of the great Antichrist of the last days. Father Abraham is pictured by Christ as in a supervisory position in the abode of the dead who are saved (Luke 16:22). The witnesses of Revelation 7 are made up of twelve thousand from each of the twelve tribes of Israel, and the twelve gates of the New Jerusalem are inscribed with the names of the twelve sons of Israel. The redeemed in heaven are seen as singing the song of Moses (Revelation 15:3).

For these and many other reasons, it is evident that an understanding of Genesis is vital to an understanding of the eternal purposes of God.

PART TWO

God and the World He Made

2

The Creation of the World

(Genesis 1:1-2)

Foundation of Foundations

The first verse of the Bible is the foundational verse of the Bible. If the Book of Genesis is indeed the Bible's foundational book, as shown in chapter 1, then it is obvious that the first eleven chapters of Genesis, which deal with the whole world and with all the nations, constitute the foundation for the rest of Genesis, which deals specifically with the beginnings of the nation Israel.

By the same token, chapter 1 of Genesis is the foundational chapter of these first eleven chapters, since it summarizes the creation of the world and all things therein. Finally, Genesis 1:1 is the foundational verse of this foundational chapter, speaking of the primeval creation of the universe itself. It is the foundation of all foundations and is thus the most important verse in the Bible. It undoubtedly contains the first words ever written, and, since it is the opening statement of the world's most often printed book, these are surely the most widely read words ever written. Most people at least *start* to read the Bible and, therefore, most people have read at least these opening words in the Bible, even if they never got any farther.

It has often been pointed out that if a person really believes Genesis 1:1, he will not find it difficult to believe anything else recorded in the Bible. That is, if God really created all things, then He controls all things and can do all things.

37

Furthermore, this one verse refutes all of man's false philosophies concerning the origin and meaning of the world:

(1) It refutes *atheism,* because the universe was created by *God.*

(2) It refutes *pantheism,* for God is *transcendent* to that which He created.

(3) It refutes *polytheism,* for *one* God created all things.

(4) It refutes *materialism,* for matter had a *beginning.*

(5) It refutes *dualism,* because God was *alone* when He created.

(6) It refutes *humanism,* because God, *not man,* is the ultimate reality.

(7) It refutes *evolutionism,* because God *created* all things.

Actually all such false philosophies are merely different ways of expressing the same unbelief. Each one proposes that there is no personal, transcendent God; that ultimate reality is to be found in the eternal cosmos itself; and that the development of the universe into its present form is contingent solely on the innate properties of its own components. In essence, each of the above philosophies embraces all the others. Dualism, for example, is a summary form of polytheism, which is the popular expression of pantheism, which presupposes materialism, which functions in terms of evolutionism, which finds its consummation in humanism, which culminates in atheism.

The entire system could well be called the system of atheistic evolutionary humanism. Other philosophical ideas could also be incorporated into the same monstrous structure: naturalism, uniformitarianism, deism, agnosticism, monism, determinism, pragmatism, and others. All are arrayed in opposition to the great truth—marvelously simple, and understandable to a child, yet inexhaustibly profound—that "in the beginning, God created the heaven and the earth."

It is remarkable that, when there have been so many anti-theistic philosophies (ancient and modern) affecting untold millions of people, the book of God makes no attempt to prove that God exists. The opening verse of Genesis simply takes this fact for granted, as though it were so obvious that only a fool could say "there is no God" (Psalm 14:1).

That this fact is *not* obvious, however, is obvious in light of the contrary fact that *only in the Bible* does such a revelation appear. That is, all of the other ancient religious books and religious systems, as well as all modern philosophies, begin, not with God, but with preexisting matter or energy in some form. In the primeval chaos (of water or fire or whatever), the forces of nature (or the gods and goddesses personifying them) then begin to bring about the cosmic changes which developed the world into its present form.

In spite of the universal prevalence of such pantheistic evolutionary cosmogonies among the nations of antiquity, the inspired account in Genesis does not attempt to refute them or to prove the existence of the true God. The reason for this strange silence is, most likely, the fact that the Genesis account was written *before* any of these other systems developed. The others were developed later for the very purpose of combating and replacing the true account in Genesis. The latter had been written originally, possibly by God Himself ("the generations of the heavens and the earth") soon after the Creation, setting forth in simple narrative form the actual events of Creation Week. At that point in time, there was no need to argue about the reality of God and the Creation, since no one doubted it!

The First Verse

CHAPTER 1

IN the beginning God created the heaven and the earth.

It is vitally important, if we would ever really fully understand anything in the Bible, or in the world in general, that we first understand the teaching of Genesis 1:1. Consider, therefore, each word in this all-important declaration.

1 "God"

This first occurrence of the divine name is the Hebrew *Elohim,* the name of God which stresses His majesty and omnipotence. This is the name used throughout the first chapter of Genesis. The *im* ending is the Hebrew plural ending, so that *Elohim* can actually mean "gods," and is so translated in various passages referring to the gods of the heathen (e.g., Psalm 96:5).

However, it is clearly used here in the singular, as the mighty name of God the Creator, the first of over two thousand times where it is used in this way. Thus Elohim is a plural name with a singular meaning, a "uni-plural" noun, thereby suggesting the uni-plurality of the Godhead. God is one, yet more than one.

2 "Created"

This is the remarkable word *bara,* used always only of the work of God. Only God can create—that is, call into existence that which had no existence. He "calleth those things which be not as though they were" (Romans 4:17). "... The worlds were framed by the word of God, so that things which are seen were not made of things which do appear" (Hebrews 11:3).

Men can "make" things or "form" things, but they cannot *create* things. God also can "make" and "form" things (Hebrew *asah* and *yatsar,* respectively), and do so far more effectively and quickly than man can do. The work of creation, however, is uniquely a work of God. The work of making and forming consists of organizing already existing materials into more complex systems, whereas the act of creation is that of speaking into existence something whose materials had no previous existence, except in the mind and power of God.

The use of the word "create" here in Genesis 1:1 informs us that, at this point, the physical universe was spoken into existence by God. It had no existence prior to this primeval creative act of God. God alone is infinite and eternal. He also is omnipotent, so that it was possible for Him to call the universe into being. Although it is impossible for us to comprehend fully this concept of an eternal, transcendent God, the only alternative is the concept of an eternal, self-existing universe; and this concept is also incomprehensible. Eternal God or eternal matter—that is the choice. The latter is an impossibility if the present scientific law of cause and effect is valid, since random particles of matter could not, by themselves, generate a complex, orderly, intelligible universe, not to mention living persons capable of applying intelligence to the understanding of the complex order of the universe. A personal God is the only adequate Cause to produce such effects.

3 "Heaven"

This word is the Hebrew *shamayim* which, like *Elohim,* is a plural noun, and can be translated either "heaven" or "heavens," depending on the context and on whether it is associated with a singular or plural verb. It does not mean the *stars* of heaven, which were made only on the fourth day of Creation Week (Genesis 1:16), and which constitute the "host" of heaven, not heaven itself (Genesis 2:1).

There is a bare possibility that the Hebrew word may originally represent a compound of *sham* ("there") and *mayim* ("waters"), thus reflecting the primeval association of water with the upper reaches of the atmosphere (Genesis 1:7).

It seems, however, that the essential meaning of the word corresponds to our modern term *space,* such as when we speak of the universe as a universe of space and time. Apparently there is no other Hebrew word used in this sense in the Bible, whereas the use of "heaven" is everywhere consistent with such a concept.

Understood in this way, it can also refer either to space in general or to a particular space, just as we may speak of "outer space," "inner space," "atmospheric space," and so forth. In Genesis 1:1, the term refers to the component of space in the basic space-mass-time universe.

4 "Earth"

In like manner the term "earth" refers to the component of matter in the universe. At the time of the initial creation, there were no other planets, stars, or other material bodies in the universe; nor did any of them come into being until the fourth day. The earth itself originally had no form to it (Genesis 1:2); so this verse must speak essentially of the creation of the basic elements of matter, which thereafter were to be organized into the structured earth and later into other material bodies. The word is the Hebrew *erets* and is often also translated either "ground" or "land." Somewhat similarly to the use of "heaven," it can mean either a particular portion of earth (e.g., the "land of Canaan"—Genesis 12:5) or the earth material in general (e.g., "Let the earth bring forth grass"—Genesis 1:11).

5 "In the beginning"

Not only does the first verse of the Bible speak of the creation of space and matter, but it also notes the beginning of time. The universe is actually a continuum of space, matter, and time, no one of which can have a meaningful existence without the other two. The term *matter* is understood to include *energy,* and must function in both space and time. "Space" is measurable and accessible to sense observation only in terms of the entities that exist and the events that happen in space, and these require both matter and time. The concept *time* likewise is meaningful only in terms of entities and events existing and transpiring during time, which likewise require space and matter.

Thus, Genesis 1:1 can legitimately and incisively be paraphrased as follows: "The transcendent, omnipotent Godhead called into existence the space-mass-time universe." As noted earlier, the name Elohim suggests that God is both one God, yet more than one. Though it does not specify that God is a trinity, the fact that the product of His creative activity was a tri-universe does at least strongly suggest this possibility. A trinity, or tri-unity is not the same as a triad (in which there are three distinct and separate components comprising a system), but rather is a continuum in which each component is itself coexistent and coterminous with the whole. That is, the universe is not part space, part time, and part matter, but rather *all* space, *all* time, *all* matter, and so is a true tri-unity.

The phrase "In the beginning" is the Hebrew *bereshith,* and is properly translated in the Authorized Version. In the Greek Septuagint it is translated *en arche,* the same words used in John 1:1: "In the beginning was the Word." Although the universe had a beginning, the Word was already there and thus transcends the universe.

Some modern translators, trying to find a means of accommodating the supposedly great age of the universe, have suggested a weaker translation of *bereshith,* such as: "In the beginning of God's creating . . . ," or "When God began to create. . . ." Although Hebrew scholars recognize that this is a grammatically permissible translation, the context precludes it. The purpose is clearly to tell about the beginning of all things; whereas this kind of translation, rather than answering the question, really raises the question instead. Furthermore, the conjunction "And" connecting verses 1 and 2 clearly shows sequential action. That is, verse 1 cannot be a sort of modifying clause of verse 2, but rather is a declarative statement followed by a second declarative statement.

Neither can verse 1 as a whole be considered a title or summary of the events described in the succeeding verses of the chapter, for the same reasons. The summary, in fact, is given in Genesis 2:4: "These are the generations of the heavens and of the earth when they were created. . . ." Furthermore, Genesis 2:1 notes the termination of the work of the six days of creation by the following summary: "Thus the heavens and the earth were finished, and all the host of them." This statement clearly refers to the work of the previous six days, including the first day. However, it includes "the heavens" in this summary; and the only mention of the heavens during the six days is in Genesis 1:1, a fact which demonstrates that the summary of Genesis 2:1 embraces also the work of Genesis 1:1. In other words, the primeval creation of the heaven and the earth in the beginning was the first act of the first day of the six days, calling into existence the basic elements of the space-mass-time continuum which constitutes the physical universe.

The Date of Creation

The vital question as to exactly *when* the uniquely significant event of Genesis 1:1 took place cannot be completely settled in the present state of the art of the study of Bible chronology. Although a great number of men have labored diligently in the attempt to formulate a complete chronology of the Bible, the very fact that they all disagree with each other demonstrates that the problems are serious and the issue still unsettled. A list of the difficulties that hinder this work would include the following, among others:

(1) The uncertainty of accurate copying and transmission of the numbers originally recorded, since the Massoretic, Septuagint, and Samaritan texts all disagree in this respect

(2) The uncertainty as to whether the length of the ancient calendar year was the same as the length of our present year

(3) The possibility of missing generations in the genealogies of the Old Testament

(4) The confusing and sometimes apparently contradictory lists of the durations of the administrations of the various judges and kings of Israel and Judah

(5) The even more unsatisfactory state of the comparable secular chronologies of Egypt and Babylonia

(6) The still less satisfactory results derived from radiocarbon and other physical methods of dating

In view of the highly equivocal and contradictory data from all extra-Biblical sources, the only possibility of obtaining anything approximating an exact chronology would have to lie in the Bible itself. Biblical data essentially cluster around the following framework:

(1) Genesis 1 gives the time from the creation of the universe to the creation of man.

(2) Genesis 5 contains chronological data from the time of the first man to the great Flood.

(3) Genesis 11 summaries the chronology from the Flood to Abraham, the founder of the Hebrew nation.

(4) The historical books of the Old Testament (especially Genesis, Exodus, Numbers, Joshua, Judges, I and II Samuel, I and II Kings, I and II Chronicles) contain chronological data of the nation of Israel from the time of Abraham to the captivity.

(5) The chronology of the captivity and restoration is obtained from certain of the prophetical books (especially Isaiah, Jeremiah, and Daniel) and the postcaptivity historical books (Ezra and Nehemiah).

(6) The intertestament period chronology necessarily must depend either on secular chronology (especially the very questionable Manethan chronology of Egypt) or else the chronology implicit in the "seventy-weeks" prophecy of Daniel 9.

The best-known chronological system based on these Biblical data is that of Archbishop James Ussher (1581-1656), who computed the date of creation as 4004 B.C. In these days of the dominance of evolutionary uniformitarianism, it is fashionable to ridicule the Ussher chronology. However, Ussher was a distinguished scholar and knew a great deal more about the subject than his modern detractors do. Though Ussher made his studies before the days of Darwin, it was not done in a time of scientific ignorance.

> Nor was this belief restricted to the credulous or the excessively devout. No less a thinker than Isaac Newton accepted it implicitly, and in his detailed study of the whole question of dating, *The Chronology of Ancient Kingdoms Amended,* took the ancient Egyptians severely to task, since they had set the origins of the monarchy before 5000 B.C. ... This criticism was meant literally; for an educated man in the seventeenth or even eighteenth century, any suggestion that the human past extended back further than 6000 years was a vain and foolish speculation.[1]

To the modern mind, this Biblical chronology is absurdly too short. However, the chronologies of other ancient nations are of at least the same order of magnitude.

> Until the discovery of radiocarbon dating, therefore, there was really only one reliable way of dating events in European prehistory. ... This was by the early records of the great civilizations, which extended in some cases as far back as 3000 B.C. ... The Egyptian king lists go back to the First Dynasty of Egypt, a little before 3000 B.C. Before that, there were no written records anywhere.[2]

Thus all actual historical records agree in substance with the Bible's short chronology. A longer chronology, which of course is needed to support the modern dogma of evolution, must be based on uniformitarian extrapolation of certain present physical processes. It should be recognized, however, that all such calculations necessarily must be based on a number of unproved and, as a matter of fact, untestable assumptions. They can never be as accurate or reliable as actual historical records, of which the Bible is certainly the most accurate and reliable.

---

1. Colin Renfrew, *Before Civilization* (New York: Alfred A. Knopf Publishers, 1974), p. 21. Renfrew is Professor of Archaeology at the University of Southampton.
2. Ibid., p. 25.

Furthermore, there are many physical processes which, even with these uniformitarian assumptions, can be shown to agree in order of magnitude with the short Biblical chronology, and only a few which can be made to give a chronology long enough to support the evolutionary idea. This subject has been discussed extensively elsewhere,[3] showing that the weight of the scientific data is heavily on the side of a recent creation and chronology of history, in agreement with the Biblical record.

With such facts in mind, there is no good reason not to accept the simple literal Biblical chronology. This is not necessarily Ussher's chronology; but it will be of the same general magnitude, since Ussher did base his calculations on the Biblical data. There are many uncertainties in such calculations, as noted above. In addition to Ussher's date of 4004 B.C. for the creation, many other dates have been computed, some of which are as follows (all in years B.C.): Jewish, 3760; Septuagint, 5270; Josephus, 5555; Kepler, 3993; Melanchthon, 3964; Luther, 3961; Lightfoot, 3960; Hales, 5402; Playfair, 4008; Lipman, 3916; and others.

In addition, all the above calculations assume the completeness of the genealogies in Genesis 5 and 11. Many writers have argued that one or more gaps of unknown magnitude may be assumed in these lists, especially in Genesis 11. This possibility will be discussed later, in the commentary on these chapters. In any case, they cannot be stretched sufficiently to accommodate modern evolutionary chronology, which places the origin of modern man at about 3,000,000 B.C., rather than 4000 B.C. At the outside, it would seem impossible to insert gaps totaling more than about five thousand years in these chapters without rendering the record irrelevant and absurd. Consequently, the Bible will not support a date for the creation of man earlier than about 10,000 B.C.

As far as the creation of the universe is concerned, this took place five days earlier than the creation of man. That these were literal days, not ages of indefinite duration corresponding to the supposed geological ages, will be shown in the next chapter. That there is no gap in time of any significance before the six days of creation will be shown in the next section of this chapter.

Consequently, the account of earth history as recorded in Genesis fixes the creation of the universe at several thousand, rather than sev-

---

3. Henry M. Morris, ed., *Scientific Creationism* (San Diego: Creation Life Publishers, 1974).

eral billion, years ago. The exact date may be as long ago as 10,000 B.C., or as recently as 4000 B.C., with the probabilities (from Biblical considerations, at least) favoring the lower end of this spectrum.

The Gap Theory

A widely held opinion among fundamentalists is that the primeval creation of Genesis 1:1 may have taken place billions of years ago, with all the geological ages inserted in a tremendous time gap between Genesis 1:1 and 1:2. The latter verse is believed by these expositors to describe the condition of the earth after a great cataclysm terminated the geological ages. This cataclysm, which left the earth in darkness and covered with water, is explained as a divine judgment because of the sin of Satan in rebelling against God. Following the cataclysm, God then "re-created" the world in the six literal days described in Genesis 1:3-31.

Most popularly known as the "gap theory," this idea has also been called the "ruin-and-reconstruction theory" and the "pre-Adamic cataclysm theory." First revived in the early nineteenth century by a Scottish theologian, Thomas Chalmers, it has been widely popularized by the notes in the Scofield Reference Bible and has been taught in most of the Bible institutes and fundamentalist seminaries of the United States for the past century.

The main purpose of the gap theory has been to try to harmonize the Biblical chronology with the accepted system of geological ages which was becoming prominent in the days of Chalmers. Many fundamentalists have felt they could ignore the whole troublesome system of evolutionary geological ages by simply pigeonholing them in this "gap" and "letting the geologists have all the aeons they want."

Unfortunately this attitude has allowed the evolutionary establishment to take over the nation's school systems, news media, and most other important institutions of our society. Although very few such "gap theorists" also believe in evolution, the tendency of Bible expositors simply to ignore the whole problem, on the basis of a false sense of security stemming from the gap theory, has had this effect. The geological age system is essentially synonymous with the evolutionary system. Each geological age is identified and dated by the same fossil record which constitutes the main evidence for organic evolution. Historically, as well as logically, acceptance of the geological age system is inevitably followed, sooner or later, by acceptance of the evolutionary system.

Any theory of Biblical interpretation which accommodates the geological age system must be scrutinized very critically on this account, to ascertain whether or not it is based on sound exegesis. Not only is its motivation suspect, but also its scientific premise is fallacious. The gap theory does *not* accommodate the geological ages as it purports to do, since the system of geological ages is based completely on the assumption of uniformitarianism (the belief that physical processes have always functioned in the past essentially as they do at present), which of course precludes any worldwide cataclysm such as is required by the gap theory. As a result, no geologist accepts the gap theory, or any other theory requiring a global cataclysm, if he also accepts the geological ages. The gap theory is thus self-defeating scientifically. It attempts to accommodate the geological ages by postulating a world-wide cataclysm, but a worldwide cataclysm denies the premise on which the geological age system is based, and would indeed obliterate all the so-called evidence of the geological ages.

The geological age system depends on the supposed evolutionary succession of the fossils preserved in the evolutionary rocks of the earth's crust. A cataclysm of such dimensions as to leave the earth inundated with waters and with darkness covering the face of the deep could have been nothing less than a global explosion, blowing billions of tons of debris into the sky to blot out the sun, and all the rest of the solid earth down into the ocean. Such a disintegrative explosion would obliterate the sedimentary crust and all its fossils, and thus would leave no evidence of the "geological ages" which the gap theory is attempting to accommodate.

The gap theory is not only impossible scientifically but also destructive theologically. By accepting the geological age system, the Bible scholar is thereby accepting the fossil record which identifies these "ages." Fossils, however, are dead things! They speak clearly of a world in which suffering, disease, and death—often violent, widespread death—were universal realities. They speak of a world much like our own world, a world containing sharks and jellyfish, dragonflies and cock-roaches, turtles and crocodiles, bats and beavers—as well as dinosaurs and gliptodons and other animals now extinct. But that world—the "world that then was"—perished (II Peter 3:6). If that world existed prior to the supposed pre-Adamic cataclysm, then it existed before the sin of Satan which brought on the cataclysm. That is, suffering and death existed for a billion years before the sin of Satan and the sub-sequent sin of Adam.

The Bible says, however, that death came into the world only when Adam brought sin into the world (Romans 5:12, I Corinthians 15:21).

This fact directly contradicts the assumption in the gap theory that death prevailed for ages before Adam. Furthermore, this primeval prevalence of suffering and death even before Satan's rebellion leaves only God Himself as responsible for such a state. But the very idea that the God of order and love would directly create and use a universal system based on randomness and cruelty seems almost blasphemous. These, however, are the implications of the gap theory.

If sound Biblical exegesis requires us to accept this concept, then of course we should accept it, in spite of the above (and many other) scientific and theological problems encountered by the theory. The fact is, however, as seen in the next section, that the natural reading of Genesis 1:1-2 suggests no such idea at all.

The Second Verse

---

2 And the earth was without form, and void; and darkness *was* upon the face of the deep. And the Spirit of God moved upon the face of the waters.

Every word and phrase of Genesis 1:2, like Genesis 1:1, is vitally important to a sound understanding of God's created universe.

1 "And the earth was . . ."

It is significant that every verse in the first chapter of Genesis (except Genesis 1:1) begins with the conjunction "And" (Hebrew *waw*). This structure clearly means that each statement is sequentially and chronologically connected to the verses before and after. Each action follows directly upon the action described in the verse preceding it.

This pattern must apply to the first two verses, as well as to any other pair of verses in the chapter. Thus there seems no room for a chronological gap of any consequence between the first two verses of Genesis. The condition described in verse 2 follows immediately upon the creative act of verse 1.

Even if there were a significant time gap implied between these two verses, there is nothing whatever in the context to justify inserting the supposed ages of geology there. This device, as already noted, would generate overwhelming scientific and theological problems.

The gap theory also proposes that the word translated "was" (Hebrew *hayetha*) should really be translated "became," thus suggesting a change of state from the original perfect creation to the chaotic condition inferred from verse 2. Although such a translation is grammatically possible, it is highly unlikely in this particular context.

The verb is the regular Hebrew verb of being *(hayetha),* not the word normally used to denote a change of state *(haphak).* Although *hayetha* can also, if the context warrants, be used to introduce a change of state, it simply means "was" in 98 percent of its occurrences. That is why, in the King James and every other standard translation of the Bible, Genesis 1:2 is always translated "was," never "became." There is nothing at all *in the context of Genesis 1* to suggest that it should in this particular case be rendered "became." But even if it were to be translated "became," it would not necessarily imply a change of state. It might well refer simply to the nature assumed by the created earth in response to the divine creative fiat of Genesis 1:1.

2 "Without form and void"

This phrase is, in Hebrew, *tohu wavohu,* or *tohu waw bohu.* The gap theory suggests that these words should really be translated "ruined and desolate," or some such phrase. It would then speak of a divine cataclysmic judgment which had been visited on the earth and which had left it in a chaotic and ruined condition.

In justification of this claim, reconstructionists maintain that God, being perfect, would never create the universe in a chaotic state. Therefore, they say, such a state must have come about long after the creation itself, probably because of Satan's sin and judgment. Furthermore, they point out, Isaiah 45:18 specifically says that God created not the earth "in vain [Hebrew *tohu*], He formed it to be inhabited."

Such an interpretation of Genesis 1:2, however, is very forced and unnatural. The word *tohu* can carry various shades of meaning. It occurs twenty times in the Old Testament and is translated in the King James Version no less than ten different ways ("vanity," "confusion," "empty place," "nothing," etc.). Its proper translation depends on the specific context and the best translation in the context of Genesis 1:2 is exactly as the King James scholars rendered it: "without form."

Similarly, the context of Isaiah 45:18 (having to do with God's purpose for the land of Israel) makes the best translation there to be "in vain." Paraphrasing, the message can be read: "God created not the earth [to be] forever unformed and uninhabited, He formed it to be inhabited." The creation narrative in Genesis 1 tells the steps by which He brought form to the unformed earth and living inhabitants to its empty surface. There is certainly no contradiction with the statement in Genesis 1:2 that the initial creation was of basic elements rather than of a completed system. The initial creation was not perfect in the sense that it was complete, but it was perfect for that first stage of God's six-day plan of creation.

Likewise, the word *bohu* does not connote a desolation, but simply "emptiness." When initially created, the earth had no inhabitants; it was "void."

The essential meaning, therefore, is: "In the beginning God created the heaven and the earth [or space and matter], and the matter so created was at first unformed and uninhabited."

The created cosmos, as discussed earlier, was a tri-universe of time, space, and matter. Initially there were no stars or planets, only the basic matter component of the space-matter-time continuum. The elements which were to be formed into the planet Earth were at first only elements, not yet *formed* but nevertheless comprising the basic matter—the "dust" of the earth.

3 "Darkness upon the face of the deep"

The idea that God, being Light, could not create a world in darkness is invalid, God Himself said: "I form the light, and create darkness . . . (Isaiah 45:7). The physical universe, though created, was as yet neither formed nor *energized,* and light is a form of energy. The absence of physical light means darkness, just as the absence of form and inhabitants means a universe in elemental form, not yet completed. No evil is implied in either case, merely incompleteness.

Further information concerning this initial stage of the creation is given in the phrase "the face of the deep." The word "face" is the Hebrew *panim* and is used primarily to refer to "presence" (e.g., "in the face of danger"); in fact, it is often translated "presence." This is probably its meaning in Genesis 1:2—not "surface" but "presence." That is, wherever the "deep" was, there also was darkness.

The "deep" (Hebrew *tehom*) refers later to the waters of the ocean. Initially, however, the earth had no form; and similarly, this state must apply to the waters also. The picture presented is one of all the basic material elements sustained in a pervasive watery matrix throughout the darkness of space. The same picture is suggested in II Peter 3:5: ". . . The earth standing out of the water and in the water."

There is an important reference to the initial formless condition of this watery suspension in Proverbs 8:24, 27: "When there were no depths [same word as 'deep'], I was brought forth. . . . when he set a compass upon the face of the depth [or 'deep']." This section of Prov-

erbs 8 is a remarkable summary of the work of the Second Person of
the Godhead on each of the first three days of creation.

It was He who existed before there was an "earth" or a "deep"
(Proverbs 8:23, 24), and it was He who "set a compass upon the
face of the depth [deep]" (Proverbs 8:27). The word "compass" is
the Hebrew *chug,* which also occurs in Isaiah 40:22 (". . . He sitteth
upon the circle of the earth . . .") and Job 22:14 (". . . He walketh in
the circuit of heaven . . ."). It is thus a striking reference to the earth's
sphericity, especially referring to the shape of the ocean, the spherical
form of whose surface is everywhere the standard of measurement in
the vertical—that is, from sea level.

The fact that this "compass" had to be "set" on the face of the
deep shows that the face of the deep originally had no such sphericity—
it was formless, exactly as intimated in Genesis 1:2. Elements of matter
and molecules of water were present, but not yet energized. The force
of gravity was not yet functioning to draw such particles together into
a coherent mass with a definite form. Neither were the electromagnetic
forces yet in operation and everything was in darkness. The physical
universe had come into existence, but everything was still and dark—
no form, no motion, no light.

4 "The face of the waters"

This term is synonymous with "the face of the deep." Again the
word "face" means "presence," and the thought is that the formless
waters, like the formless earth, were essentially a "presence" rather
than a cohesive body.

Although the marvelous universe had been called into existence
by the omnipotent Creator, it had not yet been imbued with energy
and set in motion. This must await the energizing action of the Spirit
of God and the activating power of the Word of God.

5 "The Spirit of God moved"

It was noted previously that the divine name Elohim suggests that
God is both a unity and a plurality, and that the tri-universe created
by God probably reflects the tri-une nature of the Godhead. At this
point, a particular person of the Godhead, the Holy Spirit, is seen in
action.

The word "Spirit" is the Hebrew *ruach,* which is also the word for
"wind" and "breath." The context determines which is the correct
meaning in any given instance. In Genesis 1:2, there is no doubt that
the creative activity requires not a wind but the person of God Himself.
Since the universe was everywhere in need of activation, that person

of the Godhead who is both omnipresent and energizing is appropriately mentioned as working in the creation at this point.

This activity of the Holy Spirit is called that of "moving" in the presence of the waters. The word "moved" (Hebrew *rachaph*) occurs only three times in the Old Testament, the other two being translated "shake" (Jeremiah 23:9) and "fluttereth" (Deuteronomy 32:11), respectively. Some commentators relate the word particularly to the hovering of a mother hen over her chicks. In any case, the idea seems to be mainly that of a rapid back and forth motion.

In modern scientific terminology, the best translation would probably be "vibrated." If the universe is to be energized, there must be an Energizer. If it is to be set in motion, there must be a Prime Mover.

It is significant that the transmission of energy in the operations of the cosmos is in the form of waves—light waves, heat waves, sound waves, and so forth. In fact (except for the nuclear forces which are involved in the structure of matter itself), there are only two fundamental types of forces that operate on matter—the gravitational forces and the forces of the electromagnetic spectrum. All are associated with "fields" of activity and with transmission by wave motion.

Waves are typically rapid back and forth movements and they are normally produced by the vibratory motion of a wave generator of some kind. Energy cannot create itself. It is most appropriate that the first impartation of energy to the universe is described as the "vibrating" movement of the Spirit of God Himself.

As the outflowing energy from God's omnipresent Spirit began to flow outward and to permeate the cosmos, gravitational forces were activated and water and earth particles came together to form a great sphere moving through space. Other such particles would soon come together also to form sun, moon, and stars throughout the universe. There was now a "compass" on the face of the deep, and the formless earth had assumed the beautiful form of a perfect sphere. It was now ready for light and heat and other forms of enlivening energy.

There is another "moving" of the Spirit of God mentioned in the Bible. "For the prophecy came not in old time by the will of man: but holy men of God spake as they were moved by the Holy Ghost" (II Peter 1:21). Here the word "moved" is the Greek *phero,* which in fact is used in the Septuagint as the translation of "moved" in Genesis 1:2. As the Holy Spirit energized the primeval universe, to bring form and life to God's creation, so He later empowered God's prophets, to bring beauty and spiritual life to His new creation, through the energizing Word which they inscripturated.

3

The Six Days of Creation

(Genesis 1:3-2:3)

The Day-Age Theory

In this chapter, the events and divine work of Creation Week are to be examined. The first two verses of Genesis describe the creation of the basic elements of the physical universe and its initial energizing by the Spirit of God. As seen in the previous chapter, these two events were actually closely connected and were the first two events of the first day of creation.

Before the remaining events of the six days can be discussed meaningfully, however, it must be decided whether these days are to be understood as natural days or as symbolic terms for long ages. Many sincere and competent Biblical scholars have felt it so mandatory to accept the geological age system that they have prematurely settled on the so-called day-age theory as the recommended interpretation of Genesis 1. By this device, they seek more or less to equate the days of creation with the ages of evolutionary geology.

However, this theory, no less than the gap theory, encounters numerous overwhelming objections which render it invalid. In the first place, the order of creative events narrated in Genesis 1 is very different from the accepted order of fossils in the rocks representing the geological ages. A number of these contradictions will be noted in the course of the exposition.

Second, as already pointed out when discussing the gap theory, the geological ages are predicated on the fossil record, and fossils speak unequivocally of the reign of suffering and death in the world. The day-age theory, therefore, accepts as real the existence of death before sin, in direct contradiction to the Biblical teaching that death is a divine judgment on man's dominion because of man's sin (Romans 5:12). Thus it assumes that suffering and death comprise an integral part of God's work of creating and preparing the world for man; and this in effect pictures God as a sadistic ogre, not as the Biblical God of grace and love.

Finally, the Biblical record itself makes it plain that the days of creation are literal days, not long indefinite ages. This will become conclusively evident as we examine the actual wording of these verses. Even though it may occasionally be possible for the Hebrew word for "day" *(yom)* to mean an indefinite time, the specific context in Genesis 1 precludes any such meaning here.

If the reader asks himself this question: "Suppose the writer of Genesis wished to teach his readers that all things were created and made in six literal days, then what words would he use to best convey this thought?" he would have to answer that the writer would have used the actual words in Genesis 1. If he wished to convey the idea of long geological ages, however, he could surely have done it far more clearly and effectively in other words than in those which he selected. It was clearly his intent to teach creation in six literal days.

Therefore, the only proper way to interpret Genesis 1 is not to "interpret" it at all. That is, we accept the fact that it was meant to say exactly what it says. The "days" are literal days and the events described happened in just the way described. This incomparable first chapter of Scripture tells us what we could never learn any other way— the history of creation. "For in six days the Lord made heaven and earth, the sea, and all that in them is, and rested the seventh day: wherefore the Lord blessed the sabbath day, and hallowed it" (Exodus 20:11).

Genesis 1:3-5

---

3 And God said, Let there be light: and there was light.
4 And God saw the light, that *it was* good: and God divided the light from the darkness.
5 And God called the light Day, and the darkness he called Night. And the evening and the morning were the first day.

Although the earth had been created in a formless watery dispersion, existing in static darkness, God had a great and eternal purpose for it. First the Spirit of God imparted motion and form to the inert and shapeless elements, and next would come the energy of light to dispel the darkness.

Verse 3 is the first record of God speaking in the Bible. "And God said, Let there be light; and there was light." The Word of God brings light! The Father is the source of all things (verse 1), the Spirit is the energizer of all things (verse 2), the Word is the revealer of all things (verse 3).

"For God, who commanded the light to shine out of darkness, hath shined in our hearts, to give the light of the knowledge of the glory of God in the face of Jesus Christ" (II Corinthians 4:6). Jesus Christ, the living Word of God (John 1:1, 14) is the "light of the world" (John 8:12), and "in him is no darkness at all" (I John 1:5).

When light appeared, "God divided the light from the darkness." Darkness was not removed completely, so far as the earth was concerned, but only separated from the light. Furthermore, "God called the light Day, and the darkness he called Night." As though in anticipation of future misunderstanding, God carefully defined His terms! The very first time He used the word "day" (Hebrew *yom*), He defined it as the "light," to distinguish it from the "darkness" called "night."

Having separated the day and night, God had completed His first day's work. "The evening and the morning were the first day." This same formula is used at the conclusion of each of the six days; so it is obvious that the duration of each of the days, including the first, was the same. Furthermore, the "day" was the "light" time, when God did His work; the darkness was the "night" time when God did no work—nothing new took place between the "evening" and "morning" of each day. The formula may be rendered literally: "And there was evening, then morning—day one," and so on. It is clear that, beginning with the first day and continuing thereafter, there was established a cyclical succession of days and nights—periods of light and periods of darkness.

Such a cyclical light-dark arrangement clearly means that the earth was now rotating on its axis and that there was a source of light on one side of the earth corresponding to the sun, even though the sun was not yet made (Genesis 1:16). It is equally clear that the length of such days could only have been that of a normal solar day.

It should be noted that in the Hebrew Old Testament *yom* without exception never means "period." It normally means either a day (in the twenty-four-hour sense), or else the daylight portion of the twenty-four hours ("day" as distinct from "night"). It may occasionally be used in the sense of indefinite time (e.g., "in the time of the judges"), but never as a definite period of time with a specific beginning and ending. Furthermore, it is not used even in this indefinite sense except when the context clearly indicates that the literal meaning is not intended.

In the first chapter of Genesis, the termination of each day's work is noted by the formula: "And the evening and the morning were the first [or 'second,' etc.] day." Thus each "day" had distinct boundaries and was one in a series of days, both of which criteria are never present in the Old Testament writings unless literal days are intended. The writer of Genesis was trying to guard in every way possible against any of his readers deriving the notion of nonliteral days from his record.

In fact, it was necessary for him to be completely explicit on this point, since all the pagan nations of antiquity believed in some form of evolutionary cosmogony which entailed vast aeons of time before man and other living creatures developed from the primeval chaos. The writer not only defined the term "day," but emphasized that it was terminated by a literal evening and morning and that it was like every other day in the normal sequence of days. In no way can the term be legitimately applied here to anything corresponding to a geological period or any other such concept.

Returning to the significance of light as created, it is obvious that visible light is primarily meant, since it was set in contrast to darkness. At the same time, the presence of visible light waves necessarily involves the entire electromagnetic spectrum. Beyond the visible light waves are, on the one hand, ultraviolet light and all the other shortwave-length radiations and, on the other hand, infrared light and the other longwave phenomena.

In turn, setting the electromagnetic forces into operation in effect completed the energizing of the physical cosmos. All the types of force and energy which interact in the universe involve only electromagnetic, gravitational, and nuclear forces; and all of these had now been activated. Though no doubt oversimplified, this tremendous creative act of the Godhead might be summarized by saying that the nuclear forces maintaining the integrity of matter were activated by the Father when He created the elements of the space-mass-time continuum, the gravitational forces were activated by the Spirit when He brought form and motion to the initially static and formless matter, and the electromagnetic forces were activated by the Word when He called light into existence out of the darkness. Of course, God is One, and all three persons of the Godhead actually participated in all parts of the creation and continue to function in the maintenance of the universe so created.

All of this was accomplished on the first day of creation. The physical universe had been created and energized, and was ready for further shaping and furnishing in preparation for man, whose dominion it would be.

Although not mentioned in Genesis 1, it is probable that another act of creation took place on this first day. Sometime prior to the third day of creation, a multitude of angels had been created, since they were present when the "foundations of the earth" were laid—probably a reference to the establishment of solid land surfaces on the earth (Job 38:4-7). It is impossible that they could have existed before the creation of the physical universe itself, since their sphere of operation is in this universe and their very purpose is to minister to the "heirs of salvation" (Hebrews 1:14). Angels are called the "host of heaven," and so could not have been created before the existence of heaven.

Psalm 104 (verses 2-5) says that angels were made as spirits after the materialization of God's light-arrayed presence in the stretched-out heavens, but prior to the laying of the solid foundations of the land. Therefore, although angels are not mentioned as such at this point in Genesis, their spiritual presence as fascinated observers at the remaining acts of creation and formation may certainly be inferred.

A Tent to Dwell In

After the first day, the earth was no longer without form, but it was still void of inhabitants. It must next be prepared as a home for man during his probationary period. Ultimately the entire universe would be made available for man's exploration and utilization, but first he must be given the earth (Psalm 115:16), on a trial basis, and it must be made ready as a uniquely suitable planet for him to dwell on.

The earth is indeed a planet uniquely suitable for human habitation. Of special importance is its oxygen atmosphere and its hydrosphere of liquid water. Both are vital for man's existence and both are unique to the earth, so far as all evidence goes. The first essential in God's preparation of the earth was a carefully designed atmosphere and hydrosphere. "Who hath measured the waters in the hollow of his hand, and meted out heaven with the span, and comprehended the dust of the earth in a measure...? It is he that sitteth upon the circle of the earth, and the inhabitants thereof are as grasshoppers; that stretcheth out the heavens as a curtain, and spreadeth them out as a tent to dwell in" (Isaiah 40:12, 22).

Genesis 1:6-8

---

6 ¶ And God said, Let there be a firmament in the midst of the waters, and
let it divide the waters from the waters.
7 And God made the firmament, and
divided the waters which *were* under the
firmament from the waters which *were*
above the firmament: and it was so.
8 And God called the firmament Heav-
en. And the evening and the morning
were the second day.

On the first day the earth was still of dominantly watery aspect.
Other materials were in solution or suspension, presumably with the
water mainly in the liquid state. Some of these waters were to be separated from the greater mass of waters, however, and placed high above
the rotating globe, with a great space separating them from the waters
below. The lower waters would provide the water base for living flesh
and for earth processes, the upper waters would provide a sort of protective canopy ("a tent to dwell in") for earth's inhabitants, and the
space between would provide an atmospheric reservoir to maintain the
breath of life.

The power required to effect such a tremendous separation once
again came from God's spoken Word: "Let there be a firmament in
the midst of the waters. . . ."

The word "firmament" is the Hebrew *raqia,* meaning "expanse," or
"spread-out-thinness." It may well be synonymous with our modern tech-
nical term "space," practically the same as discussed earlier in connection with the meaning of "heaven." In fact, this passage specifically
says that "God called the firmament Heaven. . . ."

This statement seems to confirm the fact that "firmament" and
"heaven" are essentially synonymous terms, both meaning "space"—
either space in general or a particular region of space, depending on
context. There are three particular "heavens" mentioned in Scripture:
the atmospheric heaven (Jeremiah 4:25), the sidereal heaven (Isaiah
13:10), and the heaven of God's throne (Hebrews 9:24). Likewise the
term "firmament" is used in each of these same three ways (Genesis
1:17, 20; Ezekiel 1:22). The term "heaven of heavens" is also used
frequently (II Chronicles 2:6), referring probably to the entire universe,
the space comprising all spaces.

The firmament referred to in this particular passage is obviously
the atmosphere. Unfortunately the English word has been interpreted
by many to refer to a solid dome across the sky; consequently this idea
has been used by liberal critics as evidence of the "prescientific" out-

look of Genesis. Neither the original Hebrew word nor any of the passages in which it occurs suggest such an idea, however. A "firmament" is simply "thin, stretched-out space."

Separated by this firmament, or atmosphere, the two bodies of water henceforth were ready for their essential functions in sustaining future life on the earth. The actual process of separation was possibly implemented by converting a portion of the liquid water into the vapor state, perhaps through application of divine heat energy. The reactions so induced on the watery suspension also released the other gaseous components of the atmosphere, which became the "firmament" holding up the lighter water vapor above.

The "waters above the firmament" thus probably constituted a vast blanket of water vapor above the troposphere and possibly above the stratosphere as well, in the high-temperature region now known as the ionosphere, and extending far into space. They could not have been the clouds of water droplets which now float *in* the atmosphere, because the Scripture says they were *"above* the firmament." Furthermore, there was no "rain upon the earth" in those days (Genesis 2:5), nor any "bow in the cloud" (Genesis 9:13), both of which must have been present if these upper waters represented merely the regime of clouds which functions in the present hydrologic economy.

The concept of an antediluvian water canopy over the earth has appeared in many writings, both ancient and modern. A number of writers have visualized it as a system of rings like those of the planet Saturn, composed possibly of ice particles orbiting the earth. Others have described it as an orbiting "shell" of ice or liquid water. Some have thought of it merely as dense banks of clouds surrounding the earth, possibly analogous to the cloud cover around the planet Venus (the latter, however, is now believed to be composed of carbon dioxide rather than water).

A vapor canopy seems more likely, however, both because of the inferred manner of its formation and because it would have to be transparent in order for the heavenly bodies to "give light upon the earth" and to "be for signs, and for seasons, and for days, and years" (Genesis 1:14, 15). Water vapor, even in vast amounts, is invisible, whereas clouds, fog, and so forth, are composed of minute droplets of liquid water and are therefore opaque.

Furthermore, a vapor canopy could be more easily maintained aloft and would serve much more effectively as a marvelous sustainer of vigorous life conditions on the earth. It can be shown that such a canopy would accomplish the following services, for example:

(1) Since water vapor has the ability both to transmit incoming solar radiation and to retain and disperse much of the radiation reflected from the earth's surface, it would serve as a global greenhouse, maintaining an essentially uniformly pleasant warm temperature all over the world.

(2) With nearly uniform temperatures, great air-mass movements would be inhibited and windstorms would be unknown.

(3) With no global air circulation, the hydrologic cycle of the present world could not be implemented and there could be no rain, except directly over the bodies of water from which it might have evaporated.

(4) With no global air circulation, and therefore no turbulence or dust particles transported to the upper atmosphere, the water vapor in the canopy would have been stable and not precipitate itself.

(5) The planet would have been maintained not only at uniform temperatures but also at comfortable uniform humidities by means of daily local evaporation and condensation (like dew, or ground fog) in each day-night cycle.

(6) The combination of warm temperature and adequate moisture everywhere would be conducive later to extensive stands of lush vegetation all over the world, with no barren deserts or ice caps.

(7) A vapor canopy would also be highly effective in filtering out ultraviolet radiations, cosmic rays, and other destructive energies from outer space. These are known to be the source of both somatic and genetic mutations, which decrease the viability of the individual and the species, respectively. Thus the canopy would contribute effectively to human and animal health and longevity.

(8) Some have objected to the idea of a heavy vapor canopy because of the great increase in atmospheric pressure which it would cause at the earth's surface. Rather than being a problem, however, this effect would contribute still further to health and longevity. Modern biomedical research is increasingly proving that such "hyperbaric" pressures are very effective in combating disease and in promoting good health generally. There should be no problem in organisms living under high external pressures, provided their internal pressures had time to adjust correspondingly.

(9) Later, when needed, these upper waters would provide the reservoir from which God would send the great Flood, to save the godly remnant from the hopelessly corrupt population of that day (the content of water vapor in the present atmosphere, if all precipitated, would cover the earth only to a depth of about one inch).

Although the waters above the firmament were condensed and precipitated in the Flood, they will apparently be restored in the millennial earth and in the new earth which God will create. Psalm 148:4, 6 speaks of the "waters that be above the heavens" which, like the stars, will be established "for ever and ever."

Genesis 1:9-10

---

9 ¶ And God said, Let the waters under the heaven be gathered together unto one place, and let the dry *land* appear: and it was so.

10 And God called the dry *land* Earth; and the gathering together of the waters called he Seas: and God saw that *it was* good.

The "waters under the firmament" still constituted a shoreless ocean, in which probably all other material elements were randomly dissolved or suspended. On the third day of creation, a third act of division was accomplished by God. The light had been divided from the darkness on the first day, the waters above the firmament divided from the waters below the firmament on the second day, and now the dry land from the lower waters on the third day.

Once again, the energizing agent was the Word of God. "Let the dry land appear!" Tremendous chemical reactions got under way, as dissolved elements precipitated and combined with others to form the vast complex of minerals and rocks making up the solid earth—its crust, its mantle, and its core. The materials so formed tended in general (though with many localized exceptions due to the complex and cataclysmic energies operating) to arrange themselves isostatically, with heavier materials sinking and lighter materials "floating," and with many substances still in suspension or solution.

Great earth movements also got under way, in response to differential heating and other forces. Finally, surfaces of solid earth appeared above the waters and an intricate network of channels and reservoirs opened up in the crust to receive the waters retreating off the rising continents.

Some of these reservoirs were open directly to the waters descending from above, others were formed as great subterranean chambers within the crust itself. All were interconnected by a complex network of tubes and waterways, so that in essence they were all "gathered together unto one place."

Although in one "place," the waters had assembled in numerous distinct basins, so that God called this "gathering-together of the waters Seas" (i.e., a plural term). These were, of course, not the same as our present seas, since the antediluvian arrangement of continental and marine areas was completely changed at the time of the Flood.

Finally, these "foundation(s) of the earth" (Psalm 102:25; Job 38:4; Zechariah 12:1; Isaiah 48:13; etc.) had been perfectly laid, and "God called the dry land Earth." This name (Hebrew *eretz*) is the same as used in Genesis 1:1 and 2, showing that the formless matter originally created is the same matter as used in the finally constituted solid ground. All of this was accomplished during the first part of the third day of creation.

Genesis 1:11-13

11 And God said, Let the earth bring forth grass, the herb yielding seed, *and* the fruit tree yielding fruit after his kind, whose seed *is* in itself, upon the earth: and it was so.
12 And the earth brought forth grass, *and* herb yielding seed after his kind, and the tree yielding fruit, whose seed *was* in itself, after his kind: and God saw that *it was* good.
13 And the evening and the morning were the third day.

Not only had rocks and minerals been formed, but so had a blanket of fertile soil—sand, silt, and clay-sized particles in an ideally graded mixture, with abundant chemical nutrients and soil moisture.

Then God spoke again, this time organizing certain of the chemical elements of the earth into tremendously complex systems, each with a marvelous informational program built into its chemical structure which could henceforth specify the reproduction of other units like itself. There is no suggestion that these systems were "living," at least not in the sense that they possessed any form of consciousness; but each did have its "seed in itself" and so had the ability of reproducing its kind.

Three main orders of plant "life" are mentioned: grasses, herbs, and trees. Whether this classification corresponds to modern taxonomic nomenclature or not is irrelevant. The latter is man-made and entirely arbitrary, whereas these Biblical divisions are obvious and natural. The three are intended to cover all types of plants and these are the most obvious comprehensive categories. The term "grass" is intended to include all spreading ground-covering vegetation; "herbs" includes all bushes and shrubs; "trees" includes all large woody plants, including even fruit-bearing trees.

It is significant that these plants were made, not as seeds, but as full-grown plants whose seed was in themselves. They thus had an "appearance of age." The concept of creation of apparent age does not, of course, suggest a divine deception, but is a necessary accompaniment of genuine creation. The processes operating in Creation Week were not the processes of the present era, but were processes of "creating and making," and are thus not commensurate with present processes at all. Adam was created as a full-grown man, the trees were created as full-grown trees, and the whole universe was made as a functioning entity, complete and fully developed, right from the beginning. The "apparent age" that might be calculated in terms of present processes would undoubtedly be vastly different from the "true age" as revealed by the Creator.

In verse 11 occurs the first mention of both "seed" and "kind." Implanted in each created organism was a "seed," programmed to enable the continuing replication of that type of organism. The modern understanding of the extreme complexities of the so-called DNA molecule and the genetic code contained in it has reinforced the Biblical teaching of the stability of kinds. Each type of organism has its own unique structure of the DNA and can only specify the reproduction of that same kind. There is a tremendous amount of variational potential within each kind, facilitating the generation of distinct individuals and even of many varieties within the kind, but nevertheless precluding the evolution of new *kinds!* A great deal of "horizontal" variation is easily possible, but no "vertical" changes.

It is significant that the phrase "after his kind" occurs ten times in the first chapter of Genesis. Whatever precisely is meant by the term "kind" (Hebrew *min*), it does indicate the limitations of variation. Each organism was to reproduce after its own kind, not after some other kind. Exactly what this corresponds to in terms of the modern Linnaean classification system is a matter to be decided by future research. It will probably be found eventually that the *min* often is identical with the "species," sometimes with the "genus," and possibly once in a while with the "family." Practically never is variation possible outside the biologic family. In any case, the evolutionary dogma that all living things are interrelated by common ancestry and descent is refuted by these Biblical statements, as well as by all established scientific observations made to date.

The permanence of the created kinds is further supported by I Corinthians 15:38, 39: "But God giveth it a body as it hath pleased him, and to every seed his own body. All flesh is not the same flesh: but there is one kind of flesh of men, another flesh of beasts, another of fishes, and another of birds." The term "kind," as applied to animals at least, is somewhat amplified in Leviticus 11:13-32.

It should also be mentioned that the formation of plants, even in such complex forms as fruit trees, occurred before the creation of any form of animal life. This, of course, is quite logical, but it does flatly contradict the accepted evolutionary system, which has marine animals, both invertebrates and vertebrates, evolving hundreds of millions of years before the evolution of fruit trees and other higher plants. Furthermore, many plants require pollination by insects, but insects were not made until the sixth day of creation, which fact argues against the possibility that the days of creation could have been long ages. The idea of theistic evolution is counter to the Biblical record of creation in practically every passage.

Then, for the third time we read the phrase "God saw that it was good." This was the pronouncement after the work of bringing light to the earth (verse 4), after the work of dividing the waters and establishing the land surfaces (verse 10) and now after the development of a plant cover for the land (verse 12).

"And the evening and the morning were the third day." The terms "evening" (Hebrew *ereb*) and "morning" (Hebrew *boqer*) each occur more than one hundred times in the Old Testament, and always have the literal meaning—that is, the termination of the daily period of light and the termination of the daily period of darkness, respectively. Similarly, the occurrence of "day" modified by a numeral (e.g., "third day") is a construction occurring more than a hundred times in the Pentateuch alone, always with the literal meaning. Even though it may challenge our minds to visualize the lands and seas, and all plants, being formed in one literal day, that is exactly what the Bible says! We are not justified at all either in questioning God's power to do this or His veracity in telling us that He did.

Genesis 1:14-19

14 ¶ And God said, Let there be lights in the firmament of the heaven to divide the day from the night; and let them be for signs, and for seasons, and for days,

and years:

15 And let them be for lights in the firmament of the heaven to give light upon the earth: and it was so.

16 And God made two great lights; the greater light to rule the day, and the lesser light to rule the night: *he made* the stars also.

17 And God set them in the firmament of the heaven to give light upon the earth,

18 And to rule over the day and over the night, and to divide the light from the darkness: and God saw that *it was* good.

19 And the evening and the morning were the fourth day.

On the first day of creation, God created and energized the entire universe, the infinite sphere of divine activity and purpose. On the second day, He made the primeval hydrosphere and atmosphere for the terrestrial sphere. On the third day, He made the earth's lithosphere and plant biosphere. Finally, on the fourth day, He made the astrosphere, the "celestial sphere" of the stars and planets surrounding and illuminating the terrestrial sphere.

On the first day, He had said: "Let there be light!" (Hebrew *or*). On the fourth day, He said: "Let there be lights" (or light-givers, Hebrew *ma-or*). Intrinsic light first, then generators of light later, is both the logical and the Biblical order.

The chief purpose of both the light of the first three days and the light-givers of all later days was to "divide the light from the darkness" (verses 4, 18), and this can only mean that the two regimes were essentially identical. The duration of the days and nights was the same in each case, and the directions of light emanation on the earth from space must have been the same in each case.

In other words, light rays were impinging on the earth as it rotated on its axis during the first three days of essentially the same intensities and directions as those which would later emanate from the heavenly bodies to be emplaced on the fourth day. Light was coming during the day as though from the sun and during the night as though from the moon and stars, even though they had not yet been made.

If such a concept sounds strange, let it be remembered that it is as easy for God to create waves of light energy as to create generators to produce such waves. There was no need for such generators except to serve the additional function (after man's creation) of marking "signs and seasons, days and years."

It therefore did not take a billion years for the light from a star which is a billion light-years distant from the earth to reach the earth after the star was created. The light-trail from the star was created in transit, as it were, all the way from the star to the earth, three days before the star itself was created! As noted earlier, the universe was created "full-grown" from the beginning; God did not require millions of years to develop it into its intended usable form. The purpose of the heavenly bodies was "to give light upon the earth"; so this is what they did, right from the beginning.

Some have objected to this concept on the basis of evolutionary changes supposedly taking place in the stars. The fact is, however, no one has ever observed such changes taking place. As long as men have been observing the stars, they have always looked as they do now (allowing, of course, for the changes in orientation due to the earth's rotation, orbital revolution, and axial wobble). The only possible exception of any consequence to this statement might be the novas or supernovas that are occasionally observed in the heavens when stars apparently heat up or explode. Some of these have been observed in galaxies supposedly hundreds of thousands of light-years from the earth; the argument is, therefore, that the stellar event producing the nova or supernova must have taken place the corresponding number of hundreds of thousands of years ago.

This may constitute a minor problem, but there are several possible answers. The tremendous stellar distances commonly cited are obtained only on the basis of a number of very esoteric and questionable assumptions. Geometric methods for measuring such astronomical distances can reach only to about 330 light-years; so any greater distances are uncertain, to say the least. Furthermore, there is no assurance of the uniformity of the speed of light at such tremendous distances. There exist respectable models of relativity and space curvature, for example, which yield light motions such that light would reach the earth even from infinite distances in only a few years. Finally, there is no reason why God could not, if He had so willed, created "pulses" in the trails of some of the light waves created traversing space in the beginning. When such pulses reach the earth, they would then be interpreted as, say, novas, when they were in reality merely created bursts of energy in the light trails connecting with various stars. Though the reason for God doing such a thing is not yet clear, that in itself is no argument against it. God may have reasons for some of His acts of creation which we do not yet understand, and our ignorance is no reason for questioning His purposes. In any case, our uncertainty as to the exact reconciliation of these distant novas with a recent creation of the universe cannot offset the clear Biblical testimony to such recent creation.

The lights were set in "the firmament of heaven," but this was not the same firmament as formed on the second day. The latter is the "open firmament of heaven" where birds were to fly (verse 20). As noted above, the term "firmament" may apply to any particular region of space, as determined by context. In verse 8, we were told that "God called the firmament Heaven." Evidently "firmament" is the common term and "heaven" is the formal name for any firmament (or space) which has been designated as a particular sphere of God's creative or purposive activity.

The fact that both sun and moon are called "light-givers" does not suggest that they are of the same substance. One actually generates light, whereas the other only reflects light; but both "give light" as far as their functions relative to the earth are concerned.

It is interesting that the stars are mentioned as of only minor importance relative to the sun and moon. "He made the stars also." Even though stars are incomparably bigger than the earth, and many of them even larger than our sun, they are of much simpler structure than the earth. A star is mostly hydrogen and helium, essentially quite simple; whereas the structure of the earth is of great complexity, perfectly and uniquely designed for living creatures. Complexity and organization are much more meaningful measures of significance than mere size!

There is no need to try to correlate this simple record of the making of the stars with various modern theories of stellar and galactic evolution. It is sufficient to note that these are all at best only interesting speculations, none of which is generally accepted and all of which encounter important objections. On the other hand, there is no reason at all (other than naturalistic prejudice) not to believe that the stars were made just as they are now. No one has ever *seen* a star or galaxy evolve, or change at all.

Since the heavenly bodies were to be used to denote the "seasons" (as well as "days and years"), it is obvious that there were to be distinct seasons through the year, and this implies that the earth's axis was inclined as it is at present. Although the vapor canopy maintained a warm climate everywhere, there would still have been slight seasonal changes in temperature.

The use of the stars also "for signs" is somewhat more uncertain in meaning. Although various suggestions have been made, the most natural interpretation is that this term has reference to various star groupings which would serve both for easy visual recognition of the advancing days and years and also, by extension, for tokens of the advancing stages of God's purpose in creation. If so, however, these zodiacal "signs" were soon corrupted into pagan astrology.

The phrase "and it was so" occurs in this passage for the fourth time (out of six) in Genesis 1 (verses 7, 9, 11, 15, 24, 30). The account thus stresses that what God says, He also does. The phrase "and God said" occurs ten times (verses 3, 6, 9, 11, 14, 20, 24, 26, 28, 29). The first seven of these were each followed by a creative command beginning with the imperative word "Let ... !"

Finally the work of this fourth day of creation was also summarized by an assertion that God saw it all to be "good." There was at that time nothing on any of the stars, planets, satellites, or any other heavenly body that was out of place or indicative of conflict or catastrophe in any way.

Living Creatures

Having made the atmosphere and hydrosphere on the second day, and then the lithosphere and biosphere on the third day, God next proceeded to make animal life for the atmosphere and hydrosphere on the fifth day, and then animal life for the lithosphere and biosphere on the sixth day. All the necessities for living creatures were present on the earth by this time: light, air, water, soil, chemicals, plants, fruits, and so forth. One deficiency yet remained—the earth was still "void" of inhabitants. However, God had "formed it to be inhabited" (Isaiah 45:18); and the fifth and sixth days were to be devoted to this final work of creation.

Genesis 1:20-23

20 And God said, Let the waters bring forth abundantly the moving creature that hath life, and fowl *that* may fly above the earth in the open firmament of heaven.

21 And God created great whales, and every living creature that moveth, which the waters brought forth abundantly, after their kind, and every winged fowl after his kind: and God saw that *it was* good.

22 And God blessed them, saying, Be fruitful, and multiply, and fill the waters in the seas, and let fowl multiply in the earth.

23 And the evening and the morning were the fifth day.

The first introduction of animal life was not a fragile blob of proto-plasm that happened to come together in response to electrical discharges over a primeval ocean, as evolutionists believe. Rather, the waters suddenly swarmed *abundantly* with swarming creatures (the waters did not "bring forth," as mistranslated in the Authorized Version).

The Hebrew word *sherets,* which is rendered by "moving creature" in the Authorized Version, is actually translated "creeping thing" in the eleven other places where it occurs. It seems to be essentially synonymous with *remes,* which is also translated "creeping thing" (Genesis 1:24, etc.). As used in Genesis 1:20, however, it evidently refers to all kinds of marine animals: invertebrates, vertebrates, reptiles.

The word "life" occurs for the first time in this verse (Hebrew *nephesh*). Actually, this is the word also for "soul," and is frequently used to refer to both the soul of man and the life of animals. In the Biblical sense, plants do not have real life, or soul (or consciousness); but both animals and men do.

Along with animals for the water sphere, there also appeared animals for the air sphere: birds to fly in, literally, the "face of the firmament of heaven." The word translated "open" in the King James is *pene,* and can carry the meaning "face of." Thus it is reasonable to understand the phrase "firmament of heaven" in this verse to apply to both the troposphere (the lower region of the atmosphere) and the stratosphere. Birds fly only in the lower region—the "face" of the firmament.

Animal life was not simply "brought forth" from the earth or water, as was true for plant life. The principle of consciousness was not capable of development merely by complex organization of the basic physical elements; and so it required a new creation. God had created the physical elements of the universe on the first day and here He performed His second act of true creation. "God created great whales, and every living creature that moveth." The "living creature" is the same as the "living soul," so that this act of creation can be understood as the creation of the entity of conscious life which would henceforth be an integral part of every animate being, including man.

The first animals specifically mentioned as the product of this act of creation were the "great whales," or "great sea-monsters," as most translations render the Hebrew word *tannin.* It is significant, however, that this same word is most frequently translated "dragon." Evidently the term includes all large sea-creatures, even the monsters of the past that are now extinct. The frequent references to dragons in the Bible, as well as in the early records and traditions of most of the nations of antiquity, certainly cannot be shrugged off as mere fairy tales. Most probably they represent memories of dinosaurs handed down by tribal ancestors who encountered them before they became extinct.

The types of animals mentioned in this passage are apparently intended to include every inhabitant of the waters and atmosphere. Furthermore, each was to reproduce after its own kind. Like the various plants, the actual biochemical reproductive systems of the animals were programmed to assure the fixity of the kinds. Physically and chemically, animals are similar to plants. Modern genetics has shown that all replicating systems function in the framework of the marvelous information program in the DNA molecule. The DNA for each kind is programmed to allow for wide individual variations within the kind, but not beyond the structure of the kind itself.

In this case, God not only declared that His work was good, but also pronounced a blessing on the animals He had created. Though not an object of God's love as man would be, animals nevertheless are objects of His care and concern. Not even a sparrow would ever fall to the ground without His noticing and caring (Matthew 10:29), and He continually provides food for them (Matthew 6:26).

The blessing included both a command and a provision for the continued multiplication of the animals He had created, so that they would soon occupy all parts of the world. It is interesting that a similar command was given later to the animals emerging from the ark after the Flood (Genesis 8:17).

Once again it is obvious that the orthodox evolutionary order is not the same as the order of creation recorded here in Genesis. Evolutionary theory says that marine organisms evolved first, then land plants, later birds. Genesis says that land plants came first, then marine creatures and birds simultaneously. Furthermore, if anything, the largest sea animals were the first, again contrary to evolutionary theory.

Genesis 1:24, 25

---

24 ¶ And God said, Let the earth bring forth the living creature after his kind, cattle, and creeping thing, and beast of the earth after his kind: and it was so.

25 And God made the beast of the earth after his kind, and cattle after their kind, and every thing that creepeth upon the earth after his kind: and God saw that *it was* good.

After the creation of animal life, and its impartation to air and water creatures on the fifth day, only one day of divine work remained. Animals must be formed for the land surfaces—the lithosphere and biosphere.

It is noteworthy that the record says that God "made" (Hebrew *asah*) these land animals; whereas He was said to have "created" (*bara*) the air and sea animals. It would seem, if anything, that the land animals were of a higher order than the others and therefore they should have taken a higher category of divine activity.

The reason for this apparent anomaly undoubtedly is that the act of *creation* (verse 21) was that of "every living soul," not only of sea and air creatures. Since this "soul" principle was created on the fifth day, there was no need to mention it again on the sixth day. The formation of land creatures merely involved new types of organization of materials already in existence, including the *nephesh* as well as the physical elements. There was no intrinsic difference in the actual "making" of land animals from that of the marine animals or, for that matter, of the making of plants. All involved the same fundamental biochemical structure and reproductive mechanisms.

The land animals made during the early part of the sixth day are categorized as "cattle, creeping things, and beasts of the earth." This description is evidently intended to be comprehensive, in so far as land animals are concerned. Very likely, the term "cattle" refers to domesticable animals, "beasts of the earth" refers to large wild animals, and "creeping things" refers to all animals that crawl or creep close to the surface of the ground.

This classification has no correlation with the arbitrary system of man-made taxonomy (amphibians, reptiles, mammals, insects), but is a more natural system based on the relation of the animals to man's interests. Thus the term "beasts of the earth" includes the large mammals such as lions and elephants, and probably also the large extinct reptiles known as dinosaurs. "Creeping things" includes the insects and smaller reptiles, and probably also most amphibians and many small mammals (e.g., moles, rats; note Leviticus 11:29-31).

All three categories of land animals were made simultaneously, as is evident from the inverted order of listing in verses 24 and 25. Once again, it is obvious that there is not the slightest correlation with the imaginary evolutionary order (that is, insects, then amphibians, then reptiles, then all mammals). As a matter of fact, evolution places insects, amphibians, and land reptiles all before the birds that Genesis says were made the day before.

There was no evolutionary struggle for existence among these animals either, for "God saw that it was good." Neither could one kind evolve into a different kind, because God made each category "after his kind."

All these land animals were said to have been "brought forth" from the earth, or ground. That is, their bodies were composed of the same elements as the earth; and when they died, they would go back to the earth. They also all had "souls," because they were said to be "living creatures" (*nephesh* again). In this respect, they were like air and water animals (Genesis 1:21) and also like man (Genesis 2:7).

The Completed Creation

The world was now fully prepared for its human inhabitants, who would be given dominion over it. God did not need five billion years to prepare for man, as theistic evolutionists seem to think. In fact, He did not even need the six days that He took! The reasons for taking six days apparently were, first, to stress the orderly and logical relationships between the different components of the creation and, second, to provide a divine pattern for man's six-day work week. A regular day of rest and special fellowship with God would be essential for man's good, and God's example would be the best pattern and incentive for man to keep such a day.

Actually the formation of the land animals must have taken only a small portion of the sixth day. The second chapter of Genesis describes in fuller detail the rest of the events of the sixth day, events which are only briefly outlined here in the first chapter.

Genesis 1:26, 27

---

26 ¶ And God said, Let us make man in our image, after our likeness: and let them have dominion over the fish of the sea, and over the fowl of the air, and over the cattle, and over all the earth, and over every creeping thing that creepeth upon the earth. 27 So God created man in his *own* image, in the image of God created he him; male and female created he them.

A most intriguing picture appears in the opening verse of this section. Whereas previous acts of God have followed immediately the phrase "And God said, Let there be . . . ," in this verse God speaks, as it were, to Himself: "And God said, Let *us* make man in *our* image, after *our* likeness."

He was not speaking to the angels, because man was not going to be made in the likeness of angels but in the likeness of God. Thus God could only have been speaking to Himself; one member of the uni-plural Godhead was addressing another member or members.

This fascinating type of exchange within the Godhead appears in a number of other places in the Old Testament (e.g., Psalm 2:7; Isaiah 48:16; Psalm 45:7; Psalm 110:1). Similarly, in the New Testament, such fellowship between Christ (before His human birth) and the Father is noted in such passages as Matthew 11:27; John 8:42; John 17:24; and others.

The divine councils centering on man had first taken place long before the beginning of time (whatever is involved in the concept of *"before* time"). The Lamb had, in the determination of these councils, been slain before the foundation of the world; the names of the redeemed had been written in His book of life before the foundation of the world; and God had called those who were to be saved by His grace, before the world began (I Peter 1:20; Revelation 17:8; II Timothy 1:9).

On this sixth day, another such council took place, and the ancient plan was now formally announced, recorded, and implemented. The highest, most complex of all creatures was to be made by God and then was to be given dominion over all the rest—all the animals of the sea, air, and land. Man's body would be formed in the same way as the bodies of the animals had been formed (Genesis 1:24; 2:7). Similarly, man would have the "breath of life" like animals (Genesis 2:7; 7:22), and even have the "living soul" like animals (Genesis 1:24; 2:7). Thus, though man's structure, both physical and mental, would be far more complex than that of the animals, it would be of the same basic essence; therefore God proposed to *"make* [Hebrew *asah*] man in our image."

And yet man was to be more than simply a very complex and highly organized animal. There was to be something in man which was not only quantitatively greater, but qualitatively distinctive, something not possessed in any degree by the animals.

Man was to be in the image and likeness of God Himself! Therefore, he was also "created" *(bara)* in God's image. He was both made and created in the image of God.

This is a profound and mysterious truth, impossible to fully comprehend; therefore it is not surprising there has been much difference of opinion about its meaning. It is not sufficient merely to say that man was given a spirit, as well as a soul, unless these terms are more explicitly defined. The term "spirit" in the Old Testament is the Hebrew *ruach,* which is also commonly translated "wind" and "breath." As such, the "breath of life" (or, literally, "spirit of lives") is a possession of animals as well as man. If, however, the term is used to define that aspect of man which is like God ("the likeness of God")—an *eternal* spirit, possessed of esthetic, moral, spiritual attributes—then it may be a proper statement, at least in part. The spirit of man, like the angelic and demonic spirits, and like God Himself, is an eternal spirit; whereas the spirit of an animal ceases to exist when the body dies (Ecclesiastes 3:21) and goes back to the earth.

In any case, there can be little doubt that the "image of God" in which man was created must entail those aspects of human nature which are not shared by animals—attributes such as a moral consciousness, the ability to think abstractly, an understanding of beauty and emotion, and, above all, the capacity for worshiping and loving God. This eternal and divine dimension of man's being must be the essence of what is involved in the likeness of God. And since none of this was a part of the animal *nephesh,* the "soul," it required a new creation.

However, this does not exhaust the meaning. We must also deal with the fact that man was *made* in God's image as well. That component of man which was "made" was his body and soul. In some sense, therefore, even man's body is in God's image in a way not true of animals.

God in His omnipresence is not corporeal, however, but is Spirit (John 4:24); so how could man's body be made in God's image?

We can only say that, although God Himself may have no physical body, He designed and formed man's body to enable it to function physically in ways in which He Himself could function even without a body. God can see (Genesis 16:13), hear (Psalm 94:9), smell (Genesis 8:21), touch (Genesis 32:32), and speak (II Peter 1:18), whether or not He has actual physical eyes, ears, nose, hands, and mouth. Furthermore, whenever He has designed to appear visibly to men, He has done so in the form of a human body (Genesis 18:1, 2); and the same is true of angels (Acts 1:10). There is something about the human body, therefore, which is uniquely appropriate to God's manifestation of Himself, and (since God knows all His works from the beginning of the world—Acts 15:18), He must have designed man's body with this in mind. Accordingly, He designed it, not like the animals, but with an erect posture, with an upward gazing countenance, capable of facial expressions corresponding to emotional feelings, and with a brain and tongue capable of articulate, symbolic speech.

He knew, of course, that in the fulness of time even He would become a man. In that day, He would prepare a human body for His Son (Hebrews 10:5; Luke 1:35); and it would be "made in the likeness of men" (Philippians 2:7), just as man had been made in the likeness of God.

Both in body and in spirit, Christ was indeed Himself the image of God (Hebrews 1:3; Colossians 1:15; II Corinthians 4:4). It does not seem too much to infer that God made man in the image of that body which He would Himself one day assume. In this sense, at least, it is true that, physically as well as spiritually, man was both made and created in the image and likeness of God the Son.

It is also noteworthy that three times it is stated that God *created* man in *His* image (as well as *making* "man in *our* image"). Again it is appropriate to speak of God in both the singular and plural—God is one, and yet more than one. There is possibly a hint in this three-fold statement (as in Genesis 1:1) that God is a trinity. In a sense, man also is a trinity of body, soul, and spirit.

The word "man" is actually *adam,* and is related to "earth" (Hebrew *adamah*), since man's body was formed from the elements of the earth (Genesis 2:7). It may be noted that man was to have dominion not only over all animals but also over the earth (verse 26) from which he had been formed.

Finally, it is made clear that "man" is also a generic term, including both male and female. Both man and woman were *created* (the details of their physical formation being given in Genesis 2) in God's image, and thus both possess equally an eternal spirit capable of personal fellowship with their Creator.

Genesis 1:28-30

---

28 And God blessed them, and God said unto them, Be fruitful, and multiply, and replenish the earth, and subdue it: and have dominion over the fish of the sea, and over the fowl of the air, and over every living thing that moveth upon the earth.

29 ¶ And God said, Behold, I have given you every herb bearing seed, which *is* upon the face of all the earth, and every tree, in the which *is* the fruit of a tree yielding seed; to you it shall be for meat.

30 And to every beast of the earth, and to every fowl of the air, and to every thing that creepeth upon the earth, wherein *there is* life, *I have given* every green herb for meat: and it was so.

Having created man and woman, God pronounced a blessing on them and then gave them their basic instructions and commission. Whether He had created more than one pair of each of the animal kinds is not stated, although the seeming inference (from the use of such terms as "swarms," "abundantly," etc.) might be that many pairs of each kind were made. In any case, only one man and one woman were made, a fact made clear in Genesis 2, when the details of the formation of Adam and Eve are described.

The first command given to this first man and woman was to "be fruitful and multiply and fill the earth." The King James translation used the term "replenish," but this does not suggest the idea of *"re-filling,"* either the Old English term itself or the Hebrew word from which it is translated. The Hebrew word is *male,* and means simply "fill," "fulfill," or "be filled." Of the more than three hundred times it is used, it is translated (in KJV) by "replenish" only seven times; and even these could as well have been rendered "fill." It is certainly erroneous to use this one verse as a proof text for the gap theory, as many have done.

Man has not yet filled the earth, in accordance with God's command; nevertheless, many people today are unduly alarmed over the so-called population explosion, urging government controls of various sorts to slow down population growth. We can be sure that God's command (repeated, incidentally, after the Flood) was made in full knowledge of the earth's ability to support a large population (note Genesis 9:1), and it has never been rescinded. Even at the present level of man's technological knowledge, the earth could support a much larger population than it now holds. Obviously, it could not continue to grow indefinitely, without limit, but God no doubt has made adequate provision for such an eventuality.

For one thing, the Scriptures promise that Christ will return before man has completely destroyed his world—a prospect which, humanly speaking, seems more of an imminent danger than overpopulation. Further, there is quite a bit of evidence in the studies of animal populations that, when a given group increases in numbers to the optimum number for its own ecological niche, the population stabilizes—not because of a struggle-for-existence conflict, but by virtue of built-in psychological or physiological mechanisms which somehow slow down the reproductive activity of the population. It is possible that God would do the same with the human population.

Another possibility is that, had man not failed his probation in Eden, he would have eventually been allowed to colonize other planets as his population grew. Such ideas are speculation only, since human populations have not yet reached the optimum level even for our present decaying planet.

In addition to the command for procreation (and Genesis 2 makes it plain that this was to be within the framework of monogamous marriage), God instructed man to "subdue" the earth, and to "have dominion over . . . every living thing that moveth upon the earth." These are military terms—first conquer, and then rule. In context, however, there is no actual conflict suggested, since everything God had made was pronounced "good." The "cultural mandate," as some have called it, is clearly a very expressive figure of speech for, first, intense study of the earth (with all of its intricate processes and complex systems) and, then, utilization of this knowledge for the benefit of the earth's inhabitants, both animal and human. Here is the primeval commission to man authorizing both science and technology as man's basic enterprises relative to the earth. "Science" is man's disciplined study and understanding of the phenomena of his world. "Technology" is the implementation of this knowledge in the effective ordering and development of the earth and its resources, for the greater good of all earth's inhabitants (including such fields of human service as engineering, agriculture, medicine, and a host of other practical technologies). This twofold commission to subdue and have dominion, to conquer and rule, embraces all productive human activities. Science and technology, research and development, theory and application, study and practice, and so forth, are various ways of expressing these two concepts.

This command, therefore, established man as God's steward over the created world and all things therein. "Thou madest him to have dominion over the works of thy hands; thou hast put all things under his feet: All sheep and oxen, yea, and the beasts of the field; The fowl of the air, and the fish of the sea, and whatsoever passeth through the paths of the seas" (Psalm 8:6-8). However, as the writer of Hebrews says, commenting on this passage: "But now we see not yet all things put under him" (Hebrews 2:8). The problem is, of course, that man has failed in his stewardship. Instead of using the earth for good, under God, he has denied God and abused his stewardship. This primeval commission has never been abrogated—man is still under its obligations. The scientific and technological enterprises still comprise God's mandate to man relative to the earth and its inhabitants, and man would find himself immeasurably more productive and effective in such pursuits if he would only approach them in the reverent and believing attitude of an honest and good servant of his Maker.

After giving man his commission, God told him of the provision for his most essential need—that of food. Man had work to do, and would need a repeated renewal of energy to continue the work. This was to be provided through the marvelous digestive system and internal energy conversion apparatus designed by God as a part of man's body (as well as those of the animals). This energy supply was to be perpetually available through the fruits and herbs of the biosphere established by God on the third day of creation. The supply could not be exhausted, since these plants were designed to replicate themselves via the bearing and yielding of seed. Furthermore, as man spread out and filled the earth, his food would be available everywhere, "upon the face of all the earth." There were (primevally) no deserts or other uninhabitable regions.

The animals, too, were to obtain their food from "every green herb," a term evidently meaning all green plants, including grasses. They also had a work to do, under man's direction, even though at this late date (after millennia of fearing and dreading man in a cursed world—note Genesis 9:2) it may be difficult or impossible to determine exactly the original nature or intended functions of the different kinds of animals.

It is clear from this passage that, in the original creation, it was not intended that either man or animals should eat animal food. As far as man was concerned, this was changed at the time of the Flood (Genesis 9:3), as will be discussed later. Whether some of the antediluvians ventured to do this against God's command, we are not told, although it is a possibility (Jabal introduced cattle raising, Genesis 4:20).

As far as carnivorous animals are concerned, their desire for meat must also have been a later development, either at the time of the Curse or after the Flood. Even today, of course, such animals can and will (if they have to) live on a vegetarian diet. Whether such structures as fangs and claws were part of their original equipment, or were recessive features which only became dominant due to selection processes later, or were mutational features following the Curse, or exactly what, must await further research. The same uncertainty must prevail at this point as to how the present "balance-of-nature" arrangements developed in various environments, whereby predators keep in check the large numbers of lower animals that would otherwise take over. It is at least possible that the primeval "balances" in every environment, including the fecundity of each kind, were quite different than at present, so that predation was neither needed nor desired. The Scriptures do predict that, in the world of the future, after Christ has returned and restored the earth in part to its primeval perfection, there will be once again no predation or struggle between animals or between animals and man (note Isaiah 11:6-9; Hosea 2:18, etc.).

Genesis 1:31—2:4a

CHAPTER 2

31 And God saw every thing that he had made, and, behold, *it was* very good. And the evening and the morning were the sixth day.

THUS the heavens and the earth were finished, and all the host of them.

2 And on the seventh day God ended

his work which he had made; and he had rested from all his work which God rested on the seventh day from all his created and made. work which he had made. 4 ¶ These *are* the generations of the 3 And God blessed the seventh day, heavens and of the earth when they were and sanctified it: because that in it he created,

---

God had now completed His work but, before settling down to "rest" in contemplation of what He had produced, as it were, He first surveyed it all and pronounced the whole creation to be "very good." Six times before, He had seen that what He had made was "good"; but now that it was complete, with every part in perfect harmony with every other part, all perfectly formed and with an abundance of inhabitants, He saw with great joy that it was all (literally) *"exceedingly good."* On each previous day, the account had concluded by saying (literally) "the evening and the morning were a fifth day," and so on; but now it says, "the evening and the morning were *the* sixth day" (the definite article occurring for the first time in this formula), thus also stressing completion of the work.

This one verse is itself sufficient to refute any theory which tries to accommodate the geological ages concept in the Genesis record of creation. Everything in the universe (the next verse specifically includes all the host of heaven in its scope) was still at this time exceedingly good, in God's own omniscient judgment. There could have been nothing that was *not* good in all creation: no struggle for existence, no disease, no pollution, no physical calamities (earthquakes, floods, etc.), no imbalance or lack of harmony, no disorder, no sin and, above all, *no death!* Even Satan was still good at this point; his rebellion and fall must have come later.

Fossils, of course, speak of death—often of violent and sudden death. They also speak of disease and injuries, of storms and convulsions—in short, of a world like the present world, "the whole creation groaneth and travaileth in pain together" (Romans 8:22). Since death only "entered into the world" when sin came in through man (Romans 5:12), and since the whole creation was very good before man sinned, it is as obvious as anything could be that the fossil record now found in the sedimentary rocks of the earth's crust could only have been formed sometime *after* man sinned. The fossils could not have been deposited either before the six days of creation (as in the gap theory) or during the six days of creation (as according to the progressive creation, day-age type of theory). How could God have possibly looked upon a world of struggle and travail, and looked into the rocks to see the remains of billions of dead animals (as well as humanlike creatures), and then described it all as exceedingly good? Such a suggestion in effect makes

God out to be a monster—not the "God of all grace" (who cares for every sparrow), not the God of love and mercy (therefore too kind to create a world by such a process as suggested in the geological age concept), the God of perfect wisdom (therefore certainly able to devise a better way than that), the God of omnipotence (thus fully able to create by such a better way), and the God of infinite order (not the "author of confusion" and of wasteful inefficiency which is implied if the fossil record is indeed a record of prehuman earth history), as revealed in the Bible.

As we will see later, the cataclysmic events of the great Flood in the days of Noah are quite sufficient to account for all the phenomena of the sedimentary rocks and the fossil record. At the time of man's creation, however, the whole universe was a beautiful, perfect creation, the finest that the mind and heart of God Himself could devise for man.

This verse concludes the first chapter of Genesis but, as we have noted earlier, this first chapter should really not have been marked at this point, but in the middle of verse 4 of Genesis 2. It is there that the first *toledoth* subscript appears: "These are the generations of the heavens and of the earth when they were created." It is likely, as discussed previously, that this statement represents the subscript, or signature as it were, of the author of the section that has gone before. In this case, since there was no human author, no man having been present to observe the creation, no human name is attached as in the case of the other ten "toledoths" that occur later in Genesis. The account tells about, not the genealogical and historical records of some patriarch, but about the "genealogy" of the universe itself.

The passage in Genesis 2:1-3 is, of course, a marvelous assertive summary that God had now completed His work of creating and making all things. Four times it is emphasized that God had finished His work, and three times it is emphasized that this included *all* His work.

These points are stressed because it is vitally important for man to realize that the present processes of the cosmos are not processes of creating and making, and therefore it would forever be impossible for him to understand about the origin of things apart from divine revelation. Both the ancient pagan evolutionists and the modern "scientific" evolutionists continue over and over to repeat this same folly, trying to explain the origin and basic meaning of things in terms of a self-contained, closed universe, an attempt which is absurdly impossible.

The present processes of the universe are, without exception, processes of *conservation* and *disintegration,* as formulated in the two universal Laws of Thermodynamics. The processes of the creation period, on the other hand, were processes of *innovation* and *integration* (or "creating" and "making"), which are exactly opposite. Science can deal only with present processes, to which alone it has access. It should be completely clear to all who are not willfully ignorant that universal processes of conservation and disintegration could never produce a universe requiring almost infinite processes of innovation and integration for its production. Therefore, if we really want to *know* anything about this creation period (other than the fact that there must have been such a period, to produce the universe, a fact certainly required by the implications of the two Laws of Thermodynamics), then such knowledge can be acquired only by divine revelation. And that is exactly what we have here in this marvelous first chapter of Genesis, the divinely revealed record of the creation and formation of all things: how long it took, what the various events and divisions were, what the order of development was, the relations of the various components, and all the other data which man could never be able to determine for himself through his own scientific observations. This completion of God's work of creation is also stressed in the New Testament (Hebrews 4:3, 4, 10; 11:3; Ephesians 3:9; etc.).

The "host of heaven" mentioned in Genesis 2:1 refers primarily to the stars (Deuteronomy 4:19; Nehemiah 9:6; Jeremiah 33:22; etc.), but may well refer also to the angels (I Kings 22:19; II Chronicles 18:18; Luke 2:13; etc.), whose sphere of residence and reference may possibly be the stars.

The fact that the seventh day is not formally summarized as are the other six days at the end of each day certainly does not mean that the seventh day is still continuing, as some day-age advocates have suggested. The Scripture does not say, "He is resting on the seventh day," but rather, "He *rested* on the seventh day." Exodus 31:17 even says that "on the seventh day he rested, and was refreshed." Though His work of creation was finished, He very soon had to undertake the great work of redemption (John 4:34; 5:17; etc.). Finally, even that work was finished (John 17:4), when the Son of God, the Redeemer, on the cross shouted the mighty cry of victory: "It is finished!" Then, once again, God rested on the Sabbath Day, in Joseph's tomb, until the dawning of the first day of the new week, and new age.

second law of Thermodynamics. The processes of the creation occur, on the other hand, via processes of innovation and integration, of creation and fission—which are exactly opposite. Hence this could only with proper processes which alone, in fact, serve the result. It is completely clear to him who are not wilfully ignorant that universal processes of conservation and disintegration could never produce a life; these continual, almost anarchic processes of dissolution and integration form a production. Therefore, if we really want to know anything about this, we can never infer from the fact that they must have been such in order to produce the universe, a fact certainly required by the conditions of the two laws of thermodynamics; then such knowledge can be acquired only by divine revelation. And that is exactly what we have here in this narration, not chapter of Genesis, the divinely revealed record of the creation and formation of all things, how long it took, what the various events and durations were, what the order of development was, the relation of the various components, and all the other data which man could never be able to determine for himself through his own scientific observations. Full completion of God's work of creation is also implied in the New Testament (Hebrews 4:3, 4, 10; II Peter 3:5, etc.).

The "rest" of heaven mentioned in Genesis 2:1 refers primarily to the sky (Deuteronomy 4:19, Nehemiah 9:6, Jeremiah 33:22, etc.), but may possibly also include the earth (Haggai 2:21, 2 Chronicles 16:9, etc.). The use of the host of heaven and earth, and reference may possibly be to stars.

The fact that the seventh day is not really summarized as are the other six days, at the end of each day, suggests to some that the seventh day is still continuing. Using the six days as examples have suggested, the Scripture does not say, "He is resting in the seventh day," but rather, "He rested on the seventh day." Verse 3 plainly even says that "on the seventh day he rested and was refreshed." Though His work of creation was finished, His very Son had to undertake the great work of redemption (John 5:17). Then, finally, even that work was finished (John 17:4), when the Son of God the Redeemer, on the cross, uttered the mighty cry of victory, "It is finished." Then once again, God rested on the Sabbath Day, in Joseph's tomb, until the dawning of the first day of the new week, and new age.

4

The Creation of Man

(Genesis 2)

The Geography of Eden

The second chapter of Genesis describes in greater detail certain of the events of the sixth day of creation, especially of the formation of the first man and woman. It does not in any respect contradict the account in the first chapter, but instead is complementary to it. The vocabularies in the two chapters are somewhat different, reflecting the different emphases as well as the human authorship of the second chapter. The section from Genesis 2:4b through Genesis 5:1 was probably written originally by Adam himself, as discussed previously, and in effect represents his own perspective on the creation and the first events of human history.

In this section, the most distinctive vocabulary difference is the use of the divine name Lord *(Jehovah Elohim)* instead of God *(Elohim)*. In Genesis 4, however, Lord *(Jehovah)* is used almost exclusively (the name God occurs in 4:25).

The section begins by using a phrase that ties it back to the subscript of the previous *toledoth* ("generations") section: "in the day that the Lord God [first occurrence of the name 'Lord God'] made the earth and the heavens" (Genesis 2:4b). It has occasionally been suggested that since the word "day" has been used in this verse to denote the entire period of creation, the word therefore need not be taken literally in the rest of Genesis 1 either. This conclusion does not follow, however.

As pointed out before, the Hebrew word *yom* can, if the context justifies, be translated as "time," in a general sense. The context here perhaps *does* justify such a meaning in this case. The context in the verses of the first chapter, however, most emphatically does *not* justify such a translation there. Furthermore, it is quite possible to understand the usage even in this verse in the literal sense, as referring either to the first day of creation, when the heavens and the earth were first created, or to the seventh day when God had declared the making of the heavens and the earth to be finished.

Genesis 2:4b-6

. . . in the day that the LORD God made the earth and the heavens, 5 And every plant of the field before it was in the earth, and every herb of the field before it grew: for the LORD God had not caused it to rain upon the earth, and *there was* not a man to till the ground. 6 But there went up a mist from the earth, and watered the whole face of the ground.

As an introduction to the creation of man, the account first describes the condition of the world immediately prior to man's creation. Although, to judge from the various translations and commentaries, this passage is of uncertain meaning, a perfectly plausible translation would be somewhat as follows: "In the day that the Lord God made the earth and the heavens there was as yet no field plant in the earth and no field shrub growing, since the Lord God had not yet established rainfall on the earth and since there was as yet no man to cultivate the ground. But there were water vapors arising from the earth, which kept watering the whole face of the ground."

The original hydrologic cycle was thus drastically different from that of the present day. The present cycle, which began at the time of the great Flood, involves global and continental air mass movements, and annual and seasonal temperature changes. It is summarized quite scientifically in such Scripture passages as Ecclesiastes 1:6-7; Isaiah 55:10-11; Job 28:24-26; Job 36:26-29; Psalm 135:6-7, and others. This present cycle centers around the solar evaporation of ocean waters, transportation to the continents in the atmospheric circulation, condensation and precipitation in the form of rain and snow, and transportation back to the oceans via rivers. In the original world, however, there was no rainfall on the earth. As originally created, the earth's daily water supply came primarily from local evaporation and condensation. There was also, as noted later, a system of spring-fed rivers.

The change in temperature between daytime and nighttime apparently was adequate to energize daily evaporation from each local body of water and its condensation as dew and fog in the surrounding area each night. This arrangement was implemented on the second and third days of the creation week, prior to the formation of the plants on the latter part of the third day.

The inhibition of true rainfall was probably, as discussed in the previous chapter, accomplished by the great vapor canopy, "the waters above the firmament." Maintaining an approximately uniform temperature worldwide, no great air mass movements were possible under the canopy, and the necessary conditions for rainfall unsatisfied.

A few commentators have suggested that the "mist" was actually a river. However the word means "mist," or "fog," and is always so used.

Genesis 2:7

---

7 And the LORD God formed man *of* into his nostrils the breath of life; and the dust of the ground, and breathed   man became a living soul.

The narrative then skips the work of the fourth and fifth days of creation and proceeds immediately to man himself. This verse tells not of the *creation* of man (as in Genesis 1:27), but of the formation and energizing of his body.

God used the "dust of the ground" to make man's body, a remarkable phrase conveying the thought that the smallest particles of which the earth was composed (in modern terminology, the basic chemical elements: nitrogen, oxygen, calcium, etc.) were also to be the basic physical elements of the human body. "The first man is of the earth, earthy" (I Corinthians 15:47). This fact is not at all obvious to superficial examination (rocks seem to all appearances to be composed of totally different substances than human flesh), but it has nevertheless been verified by modern science.

Then God "breathed into his nostrils the breath of life." This statement may seem at first to be "anthropomorphic," picturing God as puffing up His cheeks and blowing air into the inert figure He had just molded. Such a notion is quite inadequate, however. Man's body had been completely formed, equipped with nostrils, lungs, and the entire breathing apparatus, as well as bones and organs and other appurtenances, but was lifeless. It must be energized. The breathing mechanism must be activated, the heart must start to pump and circulate the blood, and all the metabolic functions must begin their operations.

But life can come only from life, and the living God is the only self-existent Being, so it must ultimately come from Him. Especially to stress the unique relationship of human life to the divine life, this Scripture verse tells us that God Himself directly imparted life and breath to man.

The "breath of life" is shared in common with animals (Genesis 7:22). "Breath" is the same word (Hebrew *ruach*) as "spirit" or "wind." However, it was only to man that God *directly* (rather than at a distance, as it were, by His spoken Word) "breathed" in the "breath of life."

At this point, man became a "living soul." The "soul" is the *nephesh*, also shared by animals (Genesis 1:24), and refers to the consciousness principle, the realm of the mind and emotions. The soul was created on the fifth day; but just as man's body was tremendously more complex and capable than those of animals, so man's soul was of much higher order than the animal soul, requiring God's direct energizing for its activation.

There is an incidental refutation of the assumption of human evolution in this verse, which tells us that man became a living soul when God gave him the breath of life. However, if he had arrived at this stage by a long process of animal evolution, he already *was* a living soul! As I Corinthians 15:45 says: "The first man Adam was made a living soul. . . ." Not only did man receive his soul directly from God rather than from an animal ancestry, but Adam was the *first* man. There was *no* "pre-Adamite man," as some have suggested.

Genesis 2:8, 9

---

8 ¶ And the LORD God planted a garden eastward in E′den; and there he put the man whom he had formed.
9 And out of the ground made the LORD God to grow every tree that is pleasant to the sight, and good for food; the tree of life also in the midst of the garden, and the tree of knowledge of good and evil.

The whole world had been placed under man's dominion, and it all was good in every way. However, a particular region was prepared as a special garden spot, in which the first man was to make his own home. This region was called "Eden," from a word meaning "delight."

In the garden of Eden, God "planted" a beautiful garden, in which were growing beautiful fruit trees of every kind, each already laden with delicious fruits. This planting was done directly by God, just as He had formed man's body and breathed into his nostrils directly, not merely by an impersonal command as had been the case when plants were first made on the third day.

It seems likely that the man (*Adam* = "man") had been created somewhere in the world outside of Eden, but was able to observe God in this special work preparing this beautiful garden for his home. The garden was planted "eastward" (Adam's location at that time being somewhere west of Eden) in the land of Eden, and then God placed Adam there in the garden. Adam's first knowledge of his Creator thus would be of one who loved him and carefully and abundantly provided for him.

Verse 8 is sort of an initial summary of this completed action of the Lord's; and then verse 9 (in fact, verses 9 through 14) goes back, as it were, and gives some of the details.

Among all the lovely shrubs and trees of the garden were two specially important and beautiful trees. In particular, a tree called the "tree of life" was planted right in the center of the garden. The fruit of this tree would, if eaten regularly, have enabled even mortal, dying men to live forever (Genesis 3:22). It is noteworthy that this tree will be growing in profusion in the New Jerusalem (Revelation 22:2), for the "health" of the nations.

Exactly how a physical fruit could be of such rich nourishment as to halt the aging process in a human body is not within our limited understanding at this time. A very active field of modern scientific research is gerontology, the study of the phenomena of aging. As yet, gerontologists have no significant scientific understanding of the aging process at all, and therefore no real understanding of what systems of chemicals might be able to stop the process. Since God is the giver of life, He can give it either directly or indirectly, through whatever secondary agency He might choose. In the absence of any contextual indication that this "tree of life" was a mere symbol of something, and in the current absence of any scientific understanding of what causes aging and death at all, there is no reason not to think of this tree as a literal tree.

The same applies to the "tree of knowledge of good and evil," which also had been planted somewhere in the garden. The fruit of this tree also was "good for food and . . . pleasant to the eyes" (Genesis 3:6). Whether this fruit had some kind of toxic substance which would penetrate the blood stream and even the genetic system, upsetting the finely balanced structure which otherwise would forever have kept both the individual and the race from decay and death, may be arguable. It does seem doubtful that God would have created anything really harmful, since He pronounced everything "very good" (Genesis 1:31).

Whether there was anything harmful in the fruit itself or not, it would certainly become a tree of "knowing" evil, as soon as man disobeyed God's word concerning it. He would know evil experimentally (he already knew "good"), and the breaking of fellowship with God would cut him or anyone off from the life that has its source only in God.

Genesis 2:10-14

---

10 And a river went out of Ē'den to water the garden; and from thence it was parted, and became into four heads.

11 The name of the first is Pī'sŏn: that is it which compasseth the whole land of Hăv'ĭ-läh, where *there is* gold;

12 And the gold of that land *is* good: there *is* bdellium and the onyx stone.

13 And the name of the second river *is* Gī'hŏn: the same *is* it that compasseth the whole land of Ethiopia.

14 And the name of the third river *is* Hĭd'dē-kĕl: that *is* it which goeth toward the east of Assyria. And the fourth river *is* Eū-phrā'tēṣ.

More information is given next about the geography of Eden and the primeval water supply system. The luscious garden in Eden would require an abundance of water, probably more than could be derived from the diurnal mist. This supply of water came from a river flowing through the garden area, which would of course maintain a sufficiently high water table in the vicinity to amply nourish the roots of the trees and other plants in the garden.

The source of the river was said to be in Eden, though presumably somewhere outside the garden itself. Since there was no rainfall, the river would have to be supplied through a pressurized conduit from an underground reservoir of some kind, emerging under pressure as a sort of artesian spring. The fluid pressure, however, could not have been simple hydrostatic pressure (pressure resulting from gravitational flow of groundwater from a source area at a higher elevation), because this also would depend on rainfall.

The pressure in the subterranean reservoir could have been established either when the waters were first entrapped below the land surface and compressed by the weight of the overlying rocks (presumably on the third day of creation) or else by being heated from a deep-lying heat source. The latter is more likely, since otherwise the pressure would gradually be dissipated as the waters escaped to the surface. If there was a continuing heat source, however, as well as a continuing supply of water to the subterranean pool, then the artesian spring at the surface could be fed indefinitely.

The water coming into the pool must have flowed by gravity from one of the surface "seas," through permeable sands or channels in the rocks, down into the great water heater below. There were probably similar subterranean channels and chambers in the earth's crust all around the world. Thus the antediluvian hydrologic cycle conveyed water from the sea to the land via subterranean channels, whereas the postdiluvian cycle accomplishes this movement via the atmosphere. The prediluvian water chambers were destroyed by the upheavals at the time of the Flood; but to compensate for this loss, the concurrent precipitation of the vapor canopy permitted the circulation of the atmosphere to begin and continental rainfalls to supply the new river systems.

The water flow in the river of Eden must have been very large for, after traversing the garden, it separated into four "distributaries," each of which was a large and long river. The rivers must eventually have reached one or more of the antediluvian seas, thus completing the cycle.

The names of the four rivers are given as the Pishon, the Gihon, the Hiddekel, and the Euphrates. The Hiddekel is a name which, in the Assyrian monuments, is also given to the Tigris. The other two names are not clearly identified with any known rivers, although some writers suggest the Gihon is the Nile and the Pishon either the Ganges or Indus. These latter identifications seem impossible in view of the other geographical features described, however; and it is more likely that these were rivers of the antediluvian world which do not even exist in the present world.

The Pishon is described as encircling the whole land of Havilah, and the Gihon as encircling the land of Ethiopia (or Cush). The land of Havilah is also of uncertain geography, but Cush is associated later in Scripture with both a region of Arabia and the present land of Ethiopia. In either case, there is certainly no river encircling it. Furthermore, the Tigris (Hiddekel) is described as going eastward of Assyria, whereas the Tigris of known history was on the west side of Assyria.

In general, it is evident that the geography described in these verses does not exist in the present world, nor has it ever existed since the Flood. The rivers and countries described were antediluvian geographical features, familiar to Adam, the original author of this part of the narrative. They were all destroyed, and the topography and geography completely changed, when "the world that then was, being overflowed with water, perished" (II Peter 3:6).

This means, in turn, that the names which seem to be postdiluvian (E‘ḥi pia, Assyria, Tigris, Euphrates) were originally antediluvian names. The names were remembered by the survivors of the Flood and then given to people or places in the postdiluvian world, in memory of those earlier names of which they were somehow reminded later. Those who have tried to identify the garden of Eden as in the present Tigris-Euphrates region fail to realize that these antediluvian rivers were completely obilterated by the Flood, and have no physical connection with their counterparts in the present world.

The garden of Eden was, of course, also destroyed in the Flood, so that it is quite impossible to locate it now in terms of modern geography.

It is worth noting that the primeval land of Havilah was said to be a land rich in gold, precious stones (though the exact nature of the so-translated "onyx stone" is uncertain), and a precious gum called bdellium (likened to the miraculous substance called "manna" in Numbers 11:7). Havilah later was a name given to a son of Cush (Genesis 10:7) and a son of Joktan (Genesis 10:29), the first a descendant of Ham and the other of Shem. Evidently both these sons were named after the antediluvian Havilah (a name believed to mean "Sandland"); so it seems that this rich primeval land had made a great impression on the sons of Noah.

Since this account was written in both the past tense (verse 10, referring to the garden) and the present tense (verses 11-14, describing the rivers and regions), there is at least a hint that, when Adam wrote this account, the garden in Eden had somehow already been removed.

The Moral Choice

Adam had been created in the image of God and was to be given dominion over the entire physical and biological creation. Even the angels had been created for a ministry which was in relation to humanity and its destiny. Furthermore, the world in which Adam was to live, and specially the beautiful garden which would be his headquarters, was a perfect environment in every way. No physical, mental, or spiritual need that he might have would be withheld.

But "... unto whomsoever much is given, of him shall be much required ..." (Luke 12:48). Here the question must be raised as to the purpose of man's creation. The triune God had existed from eternity without men: why would He now create man and a space-time universe in which man would dwell?

It is impossible to answer such a question apart from divine revelation. We ourselves are a part of this creation and are therefore in no position to judge our Creator. The fact that He created man is sufficient proof in itself that He had reason to do so. What God does must be right, and must be rational, by definition. "Shall the thing formed say to him that formed it, Why hast thou made me thus?" (Romans 9:20).

Such revelation as God has given us on this subject at least assures us that God is a God of love (I John 4:16-19) and that He loves all people. Man was created at God's will and pleasure (Revelation 4:11), and He intends to demonstrate the exceeding riches of His grace on man's behalf through all the ages to come (Ephesians 2:7).

Thus there can be no doubt that God's nature of love was central to His purpose in creating men and women. In some mysterious depths of God's own nature, there seems to have been a desire for other spiritual personalities (other than within the Godhead itself) on whom He could bestow His love.

But love is a reciprocal relationship. One cannot really "love" an inanimate object, though such a term is often carelessly used. Furthermore, love which is unrequited is one of the great tragedies of human life. For love to be expressed in all its fulness there must be mutual love, each for the other; and a perfect Creator could hardly be satisfied with an imperfect love relationship.

Therefore, if God created people with the purpose of bestowing His love on them, His purpose must also have included a mutual and reciprocated love on their parts. But love, by its very nature, must be voluntary. An automaton cannot love its maker. If they are really to love God, men and women must be able to choose of their own will to love God, in response to God's love for them. An involuntary love is a contradiction in terms and there can be no such thing.

On the other hand, if Adam was free to love God on his own initiative, he was obviously free also *not* to love God. If he was able to make the right moral choice, he was necessarily able also to make a wrong moral choice. God's creation of morally free spiritual beings, "in his own image," clearly must run the risk of having them reject Him and His love. It must involve a probationary period, to allow them a free decision.

Genesis 2:15-17

---

15 And the LORD God took the man, and put him into the garden of É'den to dress it and to keep it.
16 And the LORD God commanded the man, saying, Of every tree of the garden thou mayest freely eat:
17 But of the tree of the knowledge of good and evil, thou shalt not eat of it: for in the day that thou eatest thereof thou shalt surely die.

In a sense, Adam's experience is like that of every other person. Each of us shares in God's commission to all people as His stewards over the creation; each of us lives for a time without consciousness of sin and guilt; each is on probation for a time; and, finally, each of us, like Adam, becomes guilty as a deliberate sinner against the Word of God.

On the other hand, although Adam's experience can be considered in this way as an allegory of every other person's experience, it is not *only* that, as liberals often suggest. He was actually the first man, and his experience took place literally, exactly as described. He and Eve alone, of course, entered the world by creation, rather than by birth; and they alone entered the world with sinless natures, in perfect innocence.

Before explaining to Adam the terms of his "probation," God first assigned him the specific duty of caring for his garden home. Apparently it was later, after God had formed Eve, that He gave the two of them the much broader commission to exercise dominion over the entire creation (Genesis 1:28-29). At this point, Adam was instructed merely to till the ground in the garden of Eden, to dress it and keep it. Even though there were as yet no noxious weeds, the ground was so fertile and the plant cover so luxuriant that its growth needed to be channeled and controlled.

It is noteworthy that, even in the perfect world as God made it, work was necessary for man's good. The ideal world is not one of idleness and frolic, but one of serious activity and service. Even in the new earth to come, after sin and the curse have been completely removed, Scripture says that "his servants shall serve him" (Revelation 22:3).

Adam was told to "keep" the garden. The word means actually to "guard" it. There is no thought involved of protecting it from external enemies, of which there were none, but rather that of exercising a careful and loving stewardship over it, keeping it beautiful and orderly, with every component in place and in harmonious relationship with the whole. The charge of certain latter-day evolutionary ecologists that the concept of man's dominion has led to exploitation of earth's resources is patently absurd. God's command was to *keep* the ecology, not to destroy it; and those who believe and understand the Bible have always taken it that way.

God then called Adam's attention to the abundance of His provision for his every need. He was free to eat of *any* tree of the garden (a better word, in context, than "every"), as much as he wanted. He could also eat of any "herb" he wanted (Genesis 1:29). There was not even any restriction against eating of the fruit of "the tree of life."

There was only a single minor restraint; but it would be this restraint that would test man's love for God, giving him an opportunity to reject God's word if he wished. True love is based on trust, of course; and it would have been altogether natural and appropriate for man to have been so grateful to God for all He had done for him—giving him life, a beautiful home, an abundance of good food in profuse variety, and everything he would need or want—that his own love for God would cause him gladly to follow His will in all things. Seeing so much evidence of God's love, Adam should naturally assume that any instruction coming from God would likewise evidence His love, and therefore willingly obey it.

Thus the one restriction placed by God on Adam (and, a bit later, on Eve) was singularly appropriate for its purpose. There was every reason (based on love, not fear) for man to conform to God's command, and no reason to disobey. If he did disobey, he would be without excuse. Yet he did have a choice, and so was truly a "free moral agent" before God. This was the simplest imaginable test of man's attitude toward his Creator. Would he "trust and obey" because he loved the one who had shown such love for him; or would he doubt God's goodness and resent His control, rejecting and disobeying His word on even such an apparently trivial restriction as one forbidden fruit in a whole paradise of abundant provision?

The one forbidden tree was the tree of the knowledge (or "knowing") of good and evil. It is not suggested that there was some magical substance in the fruit which would impart such knowledge to its consumers. Even less is this phrase intended to be a euphemism for sexual intercourse, as many commentators, ancient and modern, have for some reason interpreted it.

Nevertheless, eating of the fruit of this tree after it had been specifically forbidden by God would indeed give man a very real knowledge of evil. After all, "evil" can be cogently defined simply as rejection of God's will. Disobedience to His will is therefore participation in, and experimental knowledge of, evil.

Man already had knowledge of "good." All he had seen and experienced was "good." Rejection of God's word would necessarily convey knowledge of "evil" to him. Partaking of the forbidden fruit would therefore surely give Adam knowledge of good and evil, as well as the difference between them, in the most intensely real way.

Adam should have obeyed God merely as an expression of his love. But God, in grace, provided him still further incentive by giving clear warning of the necessary consequences of disobedience. Rejecting God's love would necessarily raise a barrier between man and God, and would break the sweet fellowship for which man was created. Since God was the source of life itself, real life is found only in communion and connection with the divine life. The essence of death (the opposite of life) is therefore separation from God (the opposite of fellowship with God). "In the day that thou eatest thereof, thou shalt surely die."

The primary warning is undoubtedly that of spiritual death, or separation from God. But this also entails physical death, since God is the source of physical life as well as spiritual life. Literally, the warning could be read: "Dying, thou shalt die!" The moment Adam disobeyed God, the principle of decay and death would begin to operate in his body; and, finally, this would overcome the built-in metabolic processes and he would go back to the dust from which his body was formed. Even though he continued functioning biologically for over nine hundred years, he died both spiritually and (in principle) physically the very day he rejected and disobeyed the word of God. And this same type of act is the basis and root of all sin from that day to this.

Man and the Animals

If there were any remaining question as to whether the Bible teaches that man is simply an animal, related by common ancestry and evolutionary continuity to all the other animals, the rest of this second chapter of Genesis will lay such an idea to rest. The first man and woman were unique and special creations of God, not to be compared with animals at all but rather to be contrasted with them.

The widespread belief that people evolved from apelike ancestors is not only refuted by Scripture but also by all the facts of science. The "missing links" of Darwin's day are still missing today. There have been many fossils of true human beings excavated by anthropologists and paleontologists, and many fossils of true apes. To date, however, neither any living animals nor any fossil remains have ever been found which are intermediate between men and apes, nor between men and their imaginary apelike forebears. The best candidates in recent years have been the so-called *Australopithecus* fossils. However, recent fossil evidence has indicated, according to anthropologist Richard Leakey, that *Australopithecus* was a "long-armed short-legged knuckle-walker." He thus was most likely merely an extinct ape, with an ape-sized brain (about 500 c.c.) but with teeth that had a smaller size and somewhat "humanlike" appearance because of his peculiar diet.

Furthermore, more recent finds by Dr. Leakey, as well as by Johansen and others, have proved that true humans (with a truly human skull, erect posture, etc.) existed at least as early as *Australopithecus, Homo erectus,* and all others that had previously been considered candidates for the transition between apes (or apelike creatures) and people. So far as the actual fossil evidence shows, man has always been man and the ape has always been an ape, exactly as the Bible teaches.

Genesis 2:18

---

18 ¶ And the LORD God said, *It is* not good that the man should be alone; I will   make him a help meet for him.

At the end of the six days of creation, God saw that everything He had made was "very good" (Genesis 1:31). The last act of creation, however, was that of woman; hence, prior to this final work, the creation was yet incomplete. Man, especially, was incomplete without woman; and this was *not* good (this does not mean it was evil, but only that it was unfinished and therefore imperfect). God Himself, therefore, said: "It is not good that the man should be alone."

All the animals had been made both male and female (Genesis 6:19) and had been instructed to bring forth after their kinds and to multiply on the earth (Genesis 1:22, 24). Man alone, of all God's creatures, had no such companion.

Therefore, God set about to make "an help meet for man" (literally, "a helper like man"). As He had personally formed man's body, so He would set about personally to form woman's body. Furthermore, He would do this by a remarkable method rich in symbolic meaning which neither the man nor the woman would ever forget.

Genesis 2:19, 20

---

19 And out of the ground the LORD God formed every beast of the field, and every fowl of the air; and brought *them* unto Adam to see what he would call them: and whatsoever Adam called every living creature, that *was* the name thereof.

20 And Adam gave names to all cattle, and to the fowl of the air, and to every beast of the field; but for Adam there was not found a help meet for him.

First, however, God arranged for Adam to become familiar with many of the animals by personal inspection. This was apparently for the twofold purpose of acquainting him with his responsibilities relative to the animal kingdom (Genesis 1:28) and also of emphasizing to him that, though he could exercise rulership over them, he could not have fellowship with them. There was not one among them qualified to be a helper suitable for his own needs. He was yet incomplete without such a helper, but this would require another act of creation on God's part.

Many people quibble at verse 19, professing to find a contradiction between this account of the formation of the animals and the account in the first chapter of Genesis. According to the latter, the birds were made on the fifth day and the land animals on the sixth day, all prior to Adam's creation. The second chapter, however, seems to say in this verse that these animals were only created at this time, *after* Adam's creation.

Such an interpretation, however, is alien to the context. It would in effect, charge God with first trying to find a helper for Adam by making a lot of animals and then, when this failed, finally deciding to make woman. God had just expressed His purpose to make a "help meet for man," and it is absurd to think He would set about to carry out this purpose by first making animals.

Actually, all these animals were already in existence, exactly as the first chapter of Genesis says. All this had already been recorded in chapter 1; so there was no need to go through the entire chronological record again in chapter 2. There was no need even to mention the animals, since the account was concentrating on giving details of the *later* part of the sixth day, until the point at which the animals were actually to encounter man.

When this point is reached in the narrative, verse 19 merely calls attention to the fact that God was the one who formed the animals and that their bodies had been formed out of the "ground," even as Adam's body had been formed from the dust of the ground. However, though the physical elements were the same in the bodies of both man and beast, there was still no real fellowship possible between them, as Adam would soon learn when he examined them. He had been created "in the image of God" and would require a being of like nature to himself.

As a matter of fact, it would be quite legitimate to translate verse 19 as follows: "Also out of the ground the Lord God had formed every beast of the field and every fowl of the air; and had brought them unto Adam to see what he would call them." The Hebrew conjunction *waw* can just as well be translated "also" as "and." Furthermore, the word "formed" as in the King James (Hebrew *yatsar*) can, in the context, legitimately be translated "had formed." In any case, the obvious intent of the passage is to tell us that certain of the animals, already in existence, were now brought at this time to be inspected by Adam. There is no contradiction, either real or apparent, with the "official" order of creation in Genesis 1.

It was only those animals in closest proximity and most likely as theoretical candidates for companionship to man that were actually brought to him. These included the birds of the air, the cattle (verse 20—probably the domesticable animals), and the beasts of the field, which were evidently the smaller wild animals that would live near human habitations. Those not included were the fish of the sea, the creeping things, and the beasts of the earth (Genesis 1:24), which presumably were those wild animals living at considerable distance from man and his cultivated fields.

It is not likely that all these animals actually lived in the garden of Eden, though they may have had access to it. Therefore, God must have directed them to come to Adam in some unknown fashion, so that both master and animal might learn to know each other. We have no way of knowing exactly how many "kinds" of animals appeared before Adam, but it was clearly not such a large number as to be incapable of examination within a few hours at most. It is not unreasonable to suggest that Adam could note and name about ten kinds each minute, so that in, say five hours, about three thousand kinds could be identified. Clearly, this number seems more than adequate to meet the needs of the case.

As the animals passed in review, Adam gave each a quick appraisal and an appropriate name. What language he used, and on what basis he selected names for them, there seems no way of knowing. The fact that he named them, however, indicates (as we would expect, in view

of his recent creation in human perfection by the omniscient God)
that he was a man of high intelligence and quick discernment. There
seems to have been no need for second thoughts and later changes
in those names. "Whatsoever Adam called every living creature, that
was the name thereof."

As one after another of the animals passed before him (no doubt
in pairs, male and female) Adam could not help but be impressed with
his own uniqueness—not only in intelligence and spirituality, but also
in "aloneness." Each animal had its mate, "but for Adam there was
not found an help meet for him."

There was clearly no *kinship* in any manner between man and the
animals. None was *like* him; none could provide fellowship or companionship *for* him. It is abundantly clear and certain that he had not recently *evolved from* them! If the latter were true, and his body were
still essentially an ape's body (or the body of whatever "hominid" form
may have been his immediate progenitor), it seems strange that he
could have found nothing in common with either parents or siblings.
On this point, as on many others, the notion of human evolution con-
fronts and contradicts the plain statements of Scripture.

In all the animal kingdom, there could not be found a "helper like
him." He alone, of all creatures, was really alone. And that was not
good! Before God could declare His creation "finished" and "very good,"
this all-important deficiency must be eliminated. God would provide
such a helper and companion for Adam, one "like" him, and yet different, perfectly complementing him and completing God's work.

Flesh of His Flesh

The account of the creation and formation of Eve is the despair
of theistic evolutionists. Even if one can bring himself to believe that
man evolved from an apelike ancestor and that this is what Scripture
means when it says Adam was formed from the dust of the ground,
there seems to be no way at all in which the account of Eve's unique
mode of origin can be interpreted in an evolutionary context.

To make matters worse for the evolutionist, the New Testament
explicitly confirms the historicity of this record. "For Adam was first
formed, then Eve" (I Timothy 2:13). "For the man is not of the
woman, but the woman of the man" (I Corinthians 11:8). All other
men have been born of woman, but the first woman was made from man.

It is significant that the first human institution established by God
was that of marriage. The long period of human infancy and helpless-

ness requires careful protection and training of the children by their parents. In His wisdom, God ordained that the home, built on the mutual love and respect of husband and wife, should be the basic human unit of authority and instruction.

From the authority of the father in the home there would develop, as populations grew, the patriarchal and tribal systems, and, later, still more elaborate governmental structures. Similarly, from the fundamental activity of the parents in teaching and training their children, schools and other educational institutions would eventually be established. The church also, which has the function of teaching and authority in the spiritual realm, is likewise patterned in many respects after the home.

The way in which God made the first woman is certainly not what one would naturally expect. It would seem rather that He would form her body in the same way He did Adam's—directly out of the earth itself. But instead He "built" her out of the body of Adam! Adam's life would become her life.

God must have had a good reason for "building up" Eve in this peculiar way. From the New Testament we infer that there were certain great spiritual truths which were being pictured in this symbolic action, as well as the more immediately meaningful truth that Adam and Eve were truly "one flesh" and should thus serve their Creator together in unity and singleness of heart.

Genesis 2:21, 22

---

21 And the LORD God caused a deep sleep to fall upon Adam, and he slept; and he took one of his ribs, and closed up the flesh instead thereof.

22 And the rib, which the LORD God had taken from man, made he a woman, and brought her unto the man.

Having completed His presentation of the animals to Adam, God quite probably explained to Adam what He was about to do (Adam seemed later to have understood clearly how God had formed Eve).

In any case, God put Adam into a "deep sleep" and, while Adam slept, performed a marvelous surgical operation. Since this sleep was not necessary to prevent pain (as yet, there was no knowledge of pain or suffering in the world), there must have been some profound spiritual picture in the action. It seems almost as though Adam "died" when as yet there was no death in the world, in order that he might obtain a bride to share his life.

On this side of Calvary, the Christian can hardly fail to see here God's first proclamation of the *everlasting* gospel (Revelation 14:6), telling of one who was "slain from the foundation of the world" (Revelation 13:8). Though Adam himself may not have understood this, he would at least forever be impressed with the formation of new life and perfect fellowship out of what would have seemed, except for God, to be the very cessation of life!

It is likely that the word "rib" is a poor translation. The Hebrew word *tsela* appears thirty-five times in the Old Testament and this is the only time it has been rendered "rib." Most of the time (in at least twenty of its occurrences) it means simply "side." The thought evidently is to stress that woman was made neither from Adam's head (suggesting superiority to him) nor from his feet (suggesting inferiority), but from his side, indicating equality and companionship. Probably the verse should be translated somewhat as follows: "And he took one of his sides, and closed up the [remaining] flesh in the stead of [that which he had taken]; And the side, which the Lord God had taken from man, made he a woman, and brought her unto the man."

Instead of what some have regarded as a childish and unscientific myth (pointing out that man does not have one less rib than woman, and ignoring the fact that, even if this were an actual rib, such "acquired characteristics" are never inherited!), this narrative is beautifully realistic and meaningful.

In what sense did the Lord God take one of Adam's sides? A "side" would include both flesh and bone, as well as blood, released from the opened side. Adam could later say, "This is now bone of my bones, and flesh of my flesh."

Physiologically, it is significant that *both bone and flesh,* in the human body, are sustained by blood and the marvelous blood-pumping and circulatory network designed by God. The blood carries the necessary oxygen and other chemicals from the air and the food taken in by man to maintain all the substance and functions of the body. In fact, the very "life of the flesh [literally 'soul' of the flesh] is in the blood" (Genesis 9:4; Leviticus 17:11).

These thoughts, of course, immediately remind us again of the One whose side was pierced on Calvary as He entered the "deep sleep" of death, of whose body not a bone was broken, but from whose side "forthwith came there out blood and water" (John 19:34-36). From the "life" of Adam (the blood sustaining his bones and his flesh) God made Eve, his bride. In like manner, we who constitute the "bride of Christ" (II Corinthians 11:2) have received life by His blood (John 6:54-56). Thereby we become "members of his body, of his flesh, and of his bones" (Ephesians 5:30).

Eve was thus made from Adam's side, to work alongside him in carrying out the divine commission to "fill the earth" and to "subdue" it. She not only had the same "flesh" (that is, *body*) and "life" (that is, *soul*) as' did Adam, but she also had an eternal *spirit,* as he did; but the spirit (or, better, the "image of God") was directly from God, not mediated through Adam as was her physical life. This we know from Genesis 1:27: "So God created man in his own image . . . male and female *created* he him." The "image of God," directly created by God, was given to both man and woman. As "joined unto the Lord," however, even in this dimension of life, they would become "one spirit" (I Corinthians 6:17).

Similarly, although all the descendants of Adam and Eve have inherited their physical and mental characteristics by genetic transmission, yet each individual has an eternal spirit directly from God, and thus himself is capable of personal fellowship with God. It is God who "formeth the spirit of man within him" (Zechariah 12:1) and to whose disposal each man's spirit "returns" (Ecclesiastes 12:7) when his body returns to dust.

When Adam awoke from his deep sleep, and when God had finished forming Eve, He "brought her unto the man," to be with him from that time forth. In like manner, God is now forming a bride for Christ (Acts 15:14), as it were "building up the body" (Ephesians 4:11-16). When this work is finished, God will bring His bride to the Lord Jesus and He will go to meet her, and she will be evermore joined to the Lord (John 14:2, 3; I Thessalonians 4:16, 17; Revelation 19:7-9; 21:1-4).

Genesis 2:23, 24

---

23 And Adam said, This *is* now bone of my bones, and flesh of my flesh: she shall be called Woman, because she was taken out of man.

24 Therefore shall a man leave his father and his mother, and shall cleave unto his wife: and they shall be one flesh.

When God brought Eve to Adam, the man exclaimed: "This is now bone of my bones, and flesh of my flesh: she shall be called Woman [Hebrew *isha*], because she was taken out of Man [Hebrew *ish*]." Earlier the Hebrew word *adham* had been used exclusively for "man."

Then follows the classic passage establishing the nature of marriage: "Therefore shall a man leave his father and his mother, and shall cleave unto his wife: and they shall be one flesh." Children are to be subject to their parents until the time when they are ready to establish their own homes, when as bride and groom they would leave their parents and become "one flesh" from that day forward.

The integrity and permanence of the individual home is of such great importance that God made it plain from the beginning that marriage was intended to be permanent until death. It is true, of course, that with marriage as well as with all other human activities, "God hath made man upright; but they have sought out many inventions" (Ecclesiastes 7:29). Polygamy, concubinage, polyandry, easy divorce, adultery, promiscuity, and other distortions of the marriage covenant have permeated many cultures; but, as the Lord Jesus said: "From the beginning it was not so" (Matthew 19:8).

It is significant that ethnologists and anthropologists find evidence that monogamous, permanent marriage has everywhere and in all ages been considered as the ideal and preferred form of family life. True happiness, true fulfillment, true accomplishment of God's purposes necessarily involve obedience to God's primal command. "A man shall *cleave* unto his wife: and they shall be *one* flesh."

Because of the entrance of sin into the world, it has not always been expedient for God to rigidly enforce this ideal. He has even seemed to sanction (or at least to allow) polygamy at times (e.g., Abraham, Jacob, David) and to bless the work of some who practiced it. Similarly, the Mosaic law allowed divorce and, in some cases, God even commanded divorce (Ezra 10:11).

"But from the beginning it was not so." With the full light of the gospel and the New Testament Scriptures, the believing Christian who seeks to do his Lord's will in all things will certainly desire to follow His will in this most basic and important of all earthly relationships.

This institution of monogamous marriage, home, and family as the basic medium for the propagation of the race and the training of the young is so common to human history that people seldom pause to reflect on how or why such a custom came into being. It can hardly be a product of evolution, since it is not habitual with other primates or with other mammals. The marvelous provisions for marital companionship and love, for sexual union and conception, for embryonic growth and childbirth, and for development from childhood into adulthood—all these are incalculably complex and wonderful evidences of

God's power and wisdom. As Paul says: "This is a great mystery" (Ephesians 5:32).

The blessings and joys of a true Christian home are worth all the study and prayers and effort that can be expended to attain such a home. Furthermore, God has chosen this relationship to be the picture and pattern of the relation of Christ to His Church. The classic passage is Ephesians 5:22-33. Husbands are to love their wives with a sacrificial, protecting, providing, perfecting love, even as "Christ loved the church, and gave himself for it." Wives are to "reverence" and "be submissive" to their husbands in return, even as the Church is to revere and obey Christ in all things.

As a matter of fact, the family unit ordained by God when He created man and woman is also itself a beautiful type of the heavenly family. Paul says, concerning the "Father of our Lord Jesus Christ," that it is of Him that every "family in heaven and earth is named" (Ephesians 3:15). In our human families, at least in those where God is honored and His Word is believed, the love of husband and wife, parents and children, somehow shows forth the eternal love of the Father, Son, and Holy Spirit, and the redeeming love of Christ for His Church.

We may note in passing that the Lord Jesus Christ based His own teaching on marriage on this primeval account in Genesis (Matthew 19:3-9; Mark 10:2-12). He obviously regarded it as historical, not allegorical. Furthermore, He quoted in the same context from both of the first two chapters of Genesis. "Have ye not read," He said, "that he which made them at the beginning made them male and female [quoting Genesis 1:27], And said, For this cause shall a man leave father and mother, and shall cleave to his wife: and they twain shall be one flesh?" [quoting Genesis 2:23, 24]. It seems as though the Lord Jesus was not aware of the results of modern critical analysis, which has assured us that these two chapters "contradict" each other! Those modern theologians (and there are many such today, even in certain "evangelical" circles) who regard these accounts as contradictory, and who regard Adam and Eve as merely allegorical, are thus in rebellion against these inspired testimonies of the apostle Paul and the Lord Jesus. This is no light matter.

Genesis 2:25

---

25 And they were both naked, the man and his wife, and were not ashamed.

Thus was the first marriage consummated and the first home established. Adam and Eve were truly "one flesh," each complementing the nature of the other, physically, mentally, and spiritually. Before the entrance of sin into this ideal family, the Scripture says that they were naked, but "were not ashamed."

They were alone, of course, with no other people before whom to be embarrassed, and their physiological differences had been divinely created in accord with God's purposes, so that they felt perfectly natural with each other. Any sense of shame or embarrassment would have been entirely unnatural under the circumstances.

Even more importantly, they were still innocent, with no consciousness of sin or moral guilt. God had commanded them to "be fruitful and multiply," so there was no reason for their physical union in marriage to bring guilt feelings. Later, however, their sin of rebellion against God's word did bring an awareness that the springs of human life had been poisoned, not only in themselves but also in the lives of all their future progeny. This consciousness soon made them painfully aware of their reproductive organs and they were then "ashamed." That was a later development, however. In the beginning there was no sin and therefore no shame.

5

The Fall of Man

(Genesis 3)

That Old Serpent

When God's six-day work of creation was complete, everything in the world was "very good." There was nothing out of order, no pain, no suffering, no disease, no struggle for existence, no disharmony, no sin, and—above all—no death.

But things are *not* "very good" in the world now! In the physical realm, everything tends to run down and wear out. In the living world, each animal is engaged in a perpetual struggle against other animals and against disease, as well as the universal process of aging and death. Culturally, one civilization after another seems to rise for a time, then decline and die. In the spiritual and moral realm, each individual invariably finds it easier to do wrong than right, easier to drift downward than to struggle upward. The world is full of hatred, crime, war, pollution, selfishness, corruption—evil of all kinds. Something has gone wrong with God's perfect creation.

The problem of the existence of evil in a world created by a holy, loving God is one that has exercised the minds and hearts of philosophers and theologians through the ages. If God is omnipotent and holy, why does He permit such things? How, indeed, could evil ever have appeared at all?

These questions do not have easy answers. Atheism, in fact, is largely founded on the pessimistic belief that such an evil world proves either that God is not good (condoning evil as He does) or not omnipotent (and therefore unable to correct and remove the evil). The philosophy of dualism tries to solve the problem by proposing an eternal principle of evil in the universe, as well as one of good.

But such answers as these are, of course, neither Scriptural nor do they satisfy the needs of the human heart. God *is* omnipotent and He *is* perfectly righteous. Only His own revelation, therefore, can enable us to understand the source and significance of evil in the world.

The only true and reasonable answer to this problem is found here in the third chapter of Genesis. The apostle Paul, referring to this chapter, says, "Wherefore, as by one man sin entered into the world, and death by sin; and so death passed upon all men, for that all have sinned" (Romans 5:12). Later, he says, "For the creature [actually *creation*] was made subject to vanity [or futility], not willingly, but by reason of him who hath subjected the same in hope. Because the creature [creation] itself also shall be delivered from the bondage of corruption [literally *decay*] into the glorious liberty of the children of God. For we know that the whole creation groaneth and travaileth in pain together until now" (Romans 8:20-22).

But before man could bring sin into the world, he must be persuaded to sin by an agent external to himself, since there was as yet nothing within his own nature to lead him in such a direction. We must first, therefore, consider the nature of the serpent who was the vehicle of this temptation.

Genesis 3:1

CHAPTER 3

NOW the serpent was more subtile than any beast of the field which the LORD God had made. And he said unto the woman, Yea, hath God said, Ye shall not eat of every tree of the garden?

Among the beasts of the field that had been examined and named by Adam was one whose coloration was bright and beautiful and whose movements were smooth and graceful, a most attractive animal. Furthermore, this animal, the serpent, was more clever than any of the other animals. In her innocence, the woman was dazzled and soon led astray by this subtly attractive and deceptive creature.

Before considering the difficult question associated with the capacity of the serpent to speak in human language and his remarkable ability to deceive Eve, we must first examine the nature of the evil spirit using the serpent's body. It is obvious that there is more to this event than a mere fable of a talking snake. The Bible later identifies that "old serpent" as none other than the devil himself (Revelation 12:9; 20:2), who has led an agelong angelic rebellion against God and His plans for mankind.

As noted earlier, a great host of angels (meaning "messengers") had been created (probably on the first day of creation) for a variety of ministries around God's throne. They had various ranks and positions of authority: "principalities and powers." Evidently the greatest of these created spirit-beings was one called Lucifer ("day-star").

Lucifer is spoken of in Isaiah 14:12-15. This passage is in the context of a prophetic warning to the wicked "king of Babylon," but the prophet seems to go beyond his denunciation of this earthly monarch to the malevolent spirit who had possessed and utilized the king's body and powers. The statements made in this passage could never be true of a mere earthly king. This same powerful spirit is similarly addressed in Ezekiel 28:11-19, a passage first directed at another later earthly potentate, similarly possessed, the king of Tyre. In the latter passage, he is addressed as "the anointed cherub that covereth" the very throne of God, the highest being in all of God's creation.

God had told this high angel that he had been "created" (Ezekiel 28:13, 15), and no doubt informed him that he and all the other mighty angels were to be "ministering spirits, sent forth to minister for them who shall be heirs of salvation" (Hebrews 1:14). He was perfect in his ways (Ezekiel 28:15), just as was everything else God had created (Genesis 1:31); and he continued thus for some time after man's creation. Lucifer did not sin until later since, as the Scripture says, everything in God's completed creation, even "the heavens and the earth . . . and all the host of them" (Genesis 2:1), were very good. The "host of heaven," as we have noted previously, included the angels as well as the stars.

Soon after this, however, Lucifer's "heart was lifted up" because of his beauty and he corrupted his wisdom by reason of his brightness (Ezekiel 28:17). Though God had assured him that He had created him, he somehow began to doubt God's word and deceived himself into thinking he himself could become God. ". . . I will be like the Most High," he said in his heart (Isaiah 14:14), evidently thinking that he and God were similar beings and that, therefore, he might lead a successful rebellion and overthrow Him. Perhaps, he may have reasoned, neither he nor God was really "created," but all of the angels, as well as God Himself, had just arisen by some natural process from the primeval chaos. All had somehow developed (or "evolved") out of prior materials and it was only an accident of priority of time that placed him, with all his wisdom and beauty, beneath God in the angelic hierarchy.

Lest anyone should express surprise or doubt that Satan might ever conceive such an absurd notion, he should remember that exactly the same absurdity (namely, that this complex universe has arisen by natural processes from the primeval chaos, that the universe is a self-existing, self-sustaining, self-developing entity, and that man is "god") is believed and taught as solemn fact by most of the world's intellectual leaders even today! Satan is evidently the "deceiver of the whole world" (Revelation 12:9) and has apparently deceived himself most of all, believing in all seriousness that he can exalt his own "throne above the stars of God" (Isaiah 14:13). Many other angels, possibly a third of them, followed him in his rebellion (Revelation 12:4, 9).

Because "iniquity was found in him" (Ezekiel 28:15), Satan fell "as lightning falls from heaven" (Luke 10:18). God "cast him to the ground" (Ezekiel 28:17) and ultimately he will be "brought down to hell" (Isaiah 14:15; Matthew 25:41).

It may well be possible also that one of the factors that generated Satan's resentment against God was God's plan for mankind. People were to be uniquely "in the image and likeness of God," and also were to be able to reproduce their own kind, neither of which blessings was shared by Lucifer or the angels. This may be the reason why God cast Satan to the *earth,* instead of sending him immediately to the lake of fire, to enable him to tempt man to fall as he himself had fallen.

Perhaps he believed that, by capturing man's dominion and affection, along with the allegiance of his own angels, he might even yet be able to ascend back to heaven and dethrone God. Thus Lucifer, the "day-star," became Satan, the "adversary," or "accuser," opposing and calumniating God and all His purposes. And now he became "that old serpent," entering into the body of this "most clever" of all the "beasts of the field" in order to approach Eve with his evil solicitations.

Demonic spirits evidently have the ability, under certain conditions, to indwell or "possess" either human bodies or animal bodies (Luke 8:33); and Satan on this occasion chose the serpent as the one most suitable for his purposes. There has been much speculation as to whether the serpent originally was able to stand upright (the Hebrew word, *nachash,* some maintain, originally meant "shining, upright creature").

This idea is possibly supported by the later curse (Genesis 3:14), dooming the serpent to crawl on its belly "eating" dust, and perhaps also by those structures in the snake's skeleton which have been interpreted by evolutionists as "vestigial" limbs.

There is also the unsolved question as to whether some of the Edenic animals, especially the serpent, may have originally had the ability to converse with man in some way. There is now, of course, a great gulf between the barks and grunts of animals and the intelligent, abstract, symbolic speech of man. On one occasion, God did, as it were, "open" the vocal organs of an animal, when He allowed Balaam's ass to speak (Numbers 22:28). Some modern zoologists are now claiming the ability to teach chimpanzees a rudimentary form of speech.

On the other hand, it may simply be that Eve, in her innocence, did not yet know that the animals around her in Eden were incapable of speaking and so was not alarmed when the serpent spoke to her. One's interpretation of this occurrence, in the complete absence of any further Scriptural explanation or amplification, may depend on the degree of his subconscious commitment to uniformitarianism.

Apart from uniformitarian considerations, there may really be no reason why we should not assume that, in the original creation, the serpent was a beautiful, upright animal with the ability to speak and converse with human beings. Such an interpretation would at least make the verses in this passage easier to understand, even though it may make them harder to believe. The fact that great physiological changes took place in both the plant and animal kingdoms at the time of the curse, as well as in man himself, is obvious from Genesis 3:14-19, and it is obvious also that changes of such degree are quite within the capabilities of God to produce.

In cases of doubtful meanings of Scripture, one must not be dogmatic; but, at the same time, he should not forget the cardinal rule of interpretation; the Bible was written to be *understood,* by commoner as well as scholar, and that it should therefore normally be taken literally unless the context both indicates a nonliteral meaning and also makes it clear what the true meaning is intended to be.

It is at least possible (as well as the most natural reading) that the higher animals could originally communicate directly with man, who was their master. These were possibly the same as the animals to whom Adam gave names, and over whom man was to exercise friendly dominion.

It is further possible that all these animals (other than the birds) were quadrupeds, except the serpent, who had the remarkable ability, with a strong vertebral skeleton supported by small limbs, to rear and hold himself erect when talking with Adam or Eve. After the temptation and fall, God altered the vocal equipment of the animals, including the structure of the speech centers in their brains. He did this in order to place a still greater barrier between men and animals and to prevent further use of their bodies by demonic spirits to deceive men again in this fashion. The body of the serpent, in addition, was altered even further by eliminating his ability to stand erect, eye-to-eye with man as it were.

Again it should be emphasized that the above interpretation is not intended dogmatically. The Bible is not explicit on these matters and such explanations no doubt are hard to accept by the "modern mind." Nevertheless, they are not impossible or unreasonable in the context of the original creation and, indeed, appear to follow directly from the most natural and literal reading of the passage.

In any case, the approach of Satan (through the serpent) to the woman was a masterpiece of effective subtlety. Catching her when she was alone, without Adam to counsel and warn her, probably one day when she was admiring the beautiful fruit trees in the garden, he first insinuated something which neither she nor Adam had even imagined before, namely, that it was possible for a creature to question God's Word, "Yea, hath God said?" In other words, "Did God *really* say such a thing as that!" Note the slightly mocking superior condescension to Eve's "naive" acceptance of God's command, a technique followed by Satan and his human emissaries with great success ever since.

This first suggestion that God could be questioned was accompanied by an inference that God was not quite as good and loving as they had thought. "He has not allowed you to eat the fruit of *every* tree, has He? Why do you suppose He is withholding something from you like that?"

If one studies each situation closely enough, he will find that sin always begins by questioning either the Word of God or the goodness of God, or both. This is the age-old lie of Satan, the lie with which he deceived himself in the first place, and which succeeded so well with our first parents that he has used it ever since.

Genesis 3:2, 3

2 And the woman said unto the serpent, We may eat of the fruit of the trees of the garden:
3 But of the fruit of the tree which *is* in

the midst of the garden, God hath said,   touch it, lest ye die.
Ye shall not eat of it, neither shall ye

Eve's response to the serpent's insinuations was, of course, to assure him that he was wrong. God had allowed them to eat of the fruit of the trees of the garden. It was only the one tree in the midst of the garden which was restricted to them.

However, even in the midst of her attempt to correct the serpent's implication, she revealed that his question had had a deadly effect on her. In her reply, she both added to and subtracted from God's actual words, with the effect of making Him seem less generous and more demanding than He really was. She said, "We may eat of the fruit of the trees of the garden," whereas God had said they could *freely* eat of *all* the trees. God had told them they should not partake of only one tree in the midst of the garden; but Eve said that He added, "neither shall ye touch it." God had not forbidden them to *touch* the fruit, of course; so this further supposed restriction had been purely the product of Eve's developing resentment.

It is always dangerous to alter God's Word, either by addition (as do modern cultists) or by deletion (as do modern liberals). God, being omniscient, can always be trusted to say exactly, and only, what He means (Deuteronomy 4:2; Proverbs 30:5; Revelation 22:18, 19); and finite man is inexcusable when he seeks to change God's Word. Such will lead either to divine reproof (Proverbs 30:6) or death (Revelation 22:19).

Genesis 3:4, 5

---

4 And the serpent said unto the woman,   ye eat thereof, then your eyes shall be
Ye shall not surely die: opened, and ye shall be as gods, know-
5 For God doth know that in the day   ing good and evil.

Having led Eve first to question God's authority and goodness and then both to augment and dilute His Word, Satan now was ready for the "kill." "Ye shall surely *not* die." The fact that God had warned Adam, and Adam had told Eve, that eating the fruit of this tree would result in death, was beside the point. That warning, Satan suggested, was merely because of God's fear that they would learn too much. Not content merely with altering God's Word, Satan now blatantly *denied* it, calling God a liar!

"Ye shall be as gods." This was the same temptation that had led to Satan's own downfall (Isaiah 14:13, 14), and it proved an irresistible temptation to Eve as well. In effect, of course, as soon as one begins to deny God's Word or to question His sovereign goodness, he is really setting himself up as his own god. He is deciding for himself the standards of truth and righteousness. This had been the subtle implication of Satan's probings all along; and now that Eve was properly softened to the idea, the overt assertion of imminent divinity and omniscience was more than she could resist.

The same temptation comes to us today, of course, over and over, in various guises. The fact is, we react only too often the same way as Eve, wanting to *know* (experimentally, that is) "evil," as well as the "good" we receive from God continually. The better course is to do what Eve did not do—resist the devil by maintaining faith in God's Word. "Above all, taking the shield of faith, wherewith ye shall be able to quench all the fiery darts of the wicked" (Ephesians 6:16).

In one sense, Satan's promises were true. Their eyes *were* opened, and they *did* know good and evil—but not as "gods." Satan is the great deceiver, and his deceptions are all the more effective when they are half-truths or distorted truths. God, on the other hand, is wholly Truth and only Truth (John 14:6).

In concluding this section on the temptation, it should be noted that, regardless of the "modern mind" which questions it, the New Testament writers have placed their stamp of full approval on its authority and historicity (note II Corinthians 11:3; I Timothy 2:14; John 8:44).

The First Human Sin

The next few verses are among the most important in the Bible, recording as they do the great tragedy of man's fall from his created state of innocence and fellowship with God to his present state of sinfulness and alienation. As stressed earlier, man was not created as an automaton, but as a free being with the moral ability to love God or reject God as he should choose. There was not the slightest reason why he *should* sin, but he *could* if he so desired. God had made him perfect and placed him in a perfect environment, with every need fully supplied. He did not have an inherited sin nature, as we do now; so he was fully capable of resisting any external pressure toward sin.

The tragic fact, however, is that he *did* sin, and thereby brought sin and death into the world. "Wherefore, as by one man sin entered the world, and death by sin; and so death passed upon all men, for that all have sinned" (Romans 5:12). "In Adam, all die" (I Corinthians 15:22).

Because Adam had the sentence of death imposed as an actual operational feature of his biological life, his descendants also have inherited a life principle which involves a built-in death principle. The moment a child is conceived he begins to die, and eventually the death principle wins out over the life principle and he does die.

As the tendency toward death is inherited by all men, so also is the tendency toward sin. No descendant of Adam has ever lived to an age of conscious awareness of right and wrong without actually *choosing* wrong. He has become a deliberate sinner because he has inherited a sinful nature, which leads him to sin in practice. Thus, "death passed upon all men, for that *all have sinned.*" Each person continues under the divine judgment of death, not only because of Adam's sin, but because of his own deliberate sin.

Genesis 3:6

---

6 And when the woman saw that the tree *was* good for food, and that it *was* pleasant to the eyes, and a tree to be desired to make *one* wise, she took of the fruit thereof, and did eat, and gave also unto her husband with her; and he did eat.

As Eve, having allowed her mind and emotions to be influenced by the Satanic suggestions of doubt and pride, continued to gaze at the forbidden tree, its fruit seemed to become more and more beautiful and delectable all the time. It is remarkable that the particular attributes of this fruit that seemed so tempting are the same as the overt characteristics of practically every type of temptation which man faces today.

To her, it seemed that the tree was: (1) "good for food" (that is, something appealing to the physical, bodily appetites); (2) "pleasant to the eyes" (that is, something appealing to the emotions—the esthetic senses); (3) "desired to make wise" (that is, appealing to the mind and spirit, and to one's pride of knowledge and spiritual insight).

This threefold description is perfectly parallel to the outline of I John 2:16: "For all that is in the world, the lust of the flesh, and the lust of the eyes, and the pride of life, is not of the Father, but is of the world." Temptations thus may be directed against either the body, soul, or spirit—or, as in Eve's case, against all three at once. The source of the temptation is said by James, again stressing all three aspects, to be "earthly, sensual, devilish" (James 3:15).

One day, of course, the Second Adam would come into the world, and He would also have to be tempted in all points like as we are (Hebrews 4:15). At the very beginning of His public ministry, He was "led by the Spirit into the wilderness, being forty days tempted of the devil" (Luke 4:1, 2). The temptation again was of the same threefold scope: (1) appeal to the physical appetite, offering bread when He was hungry (Luke 4:3, 4); (2) appeal to the covetous and esthetic emotional desires, offering possession of all the world and its kingdoms (Luke 4:5-8); (3) appeal to spiritual pride, offering world-wide recognition as the one of highest intellectual and spiritual eminence, under the special protection of the holy angels (Luke 4:9-12).

It is significant that the Lord Jesus overcame the wicked one (I John 2:13, 14—as we can do also) by reminding both Himself and Satan of appropriate instructions and promises in the Word of God. Instead of believing and obeying God's Word, Eve questioned, doubted, then modified and finally rejected God's Word, in favor of the temptation to body, soul, and spirit which the fruit represented to her.

As the prototype of all sinners, Eve felt impelled to lead Adam to participate in the same sin. She therefore plucked more of the fruit and brought it to her husband, urging him to eat it as well. No doubt, she used the same arguments the serpent had used, also adding the personal testimony that she had eaten the delicious fruit herself without any harmful effect.

Adam, however, "was not deceived" (I Timothy 2:14). Whether this statement by the apostle Paul means that Adam was fully aware that he was willfully defying God, or whether it simply means that Adam was not the initial one whom Satan attacked with his deception, may not be completely clear. Paul goes on to say that "the woman being deceived was in the transgression," which seems to place the main blame on her, accounting for her being cursed and made subject to man. There may even be a hint that the serpent had first tried to deceive Adam, but had been unsuccessful, and so then turned to Eve.

Many have suggested that he did this out of love for Eve, choosing to share her sin and guilt rather than leaving her to face God's judgment alone. This interpretation would be consistent with the typology, suggesting the truth that "Christ also loved the church, and gave himself for it" (Ephesians 5:25). However, this motive would almost make Adam appear noble in sinning, and the Bible never implies such a thing. His sin was deliberate, wicked, and inexcusable. In fact, it was not by Eve's sin, but by Adam's that "sin entered into the world, and death by sin." All future human beings were "in Adam" (I Corinthians 15:22) and even Eve herself had been formed "of the man" (I Corinthians 11:8). He was the true federal head of the race and it was "through the offence of the one [that] many be dead" (Romans 5:15).

Genesis 3:7

---

7 And the eyes of them both were opened, and they knew that they *were* naked; and they sewed fig leaves together, and made themselves aprons.

The serpent had promised that they would acquire wisdom and become as gods, knowing good and evil. Instead, there came over them the realization of what they had done and an awful sense of shame enveloped them. As they remembered that the divine injunction had been to "multiply and fill the earth," they realized that the very fountainhead of human life had now become corrupted by their disobedience and they became acutely aware of their nakedness. Their children would all be contaminated with the seed of rebellion, so that their feeling of guilt centered especially on their own procreative organs. The result was that they suddenly desired to hide these from each other, and from God.

Hastily they fashioned crude girdles of fig leaves and covered themselves, but of course such aprons would hardly suffice to hide the guilt of their rebellion against God. Neither will the "filthy rags" of our own self-made "righteousnesses" serve to cover our sinful hearts today (Isaiah 64:6). We need rather the "garments of salvation," the "robe of righteousness" (Isaiah 61:10) with which only God can clothe us (Genesis 3:21). We can never escape God's eye of judgment by anything that we ourselves can fashion or accomplish.

Genesis 3:8-10

---

8 And they heard the voice of the LORD God walking in the garden in the cool of the day: and Adam and his wife hid themselves from the presence of the LORD God amongst the trees of the garden.

9 And the LORD God called unto Adam, and said unto him, Where *art* thou?
10 And he said, I heard thy voice in the garden, and I was afraid, because I *was* naked; and I hid myself.

No longer did Adam and Eve enjoy the fellowship with God for which they had been created. Rather they "hid themselves," and then even made excuses for avoiding God's presence.

However, the fact that they did feel shame at what they had done showed that there was hope for their salvation. When sinners feel no guilt or shame, there is no remedy but judgment and condemnation. Scripture says they feared when they heard the "voice of the Lord God." The Word of God is given to men for guidance and comfort, but it also can be used to bring conviction of sin (Romans 3:20; II Timothy 3:16).

God was "walking in the garden in the cool of the day." The more or less offhand way in which this is stated indicates that this was a normal event, perhaps a daily appointment time at which the Lord met with them for communion and fellowship. This is no crude anthropomorphism, but a repeated, or even continual, theophany, in which the Word of God, Christ preincarnate, clothed Himself in human form in order to communicate with those whom He had created in His own image.

How long this period of fellowship between God and man had lasted, we have no way of knowing. It was at least long enough for the Satanic rebellion and expulsion to have taken place in heaven. However, it was not long enough for Adam and Eve to have begotten children. It was probably a few weeks, though it is not possible to be certain.

On this occasion, however, instead of encountering Adam waiting expectantly for the daily time of fellowship, Adam was hiding among the trees, hoping to avoid seeing the Lord God altogether. But when God called to him, Adam realized he could not do this; so he replied with the weak excuse that he was hiding because of his nakedness.

This had never been a problem before, but there is no doubt that Adam was now acutely conscious of being naked in God's presence. The fig leaf girdles were of no avail, either; and he knew it. Flagrant sin had entered Adam's body and would contaminate all future generations.

It may be noted incidentally that the shame of nudity is no artificial inhibition introduced by the conventions of civilization, as certain anthropologists and self-serving sophisticates have urged. It has its source in this primeval awareness of sin, and is only discarded when the moral conscience has been so hardened as to lose all sensitivity to sin.

It is noteworthy also that clothing is worn in heaven. The "armies . . . in heaven" are seen as "clothed in fine linen, white and clean" (Revelation 19:14), and the glorified Son of Man is pictured to John as "clothed with a garment down to the foot" (Revelation 1:13). Except for the brief period of Edenic innocence, nakedness before anyone other than one's own husband or wife is, in the Bible, considered shameful (note Genesis 9:23; Exodus 32:25; Revelation 3:18; etc.).

Genesis 3:11-13

---

11 And he said, Who told thee that thou *wast* naked? Hast thou eaten of the tree, whereof I commanded thee that thou shouldest not eat?
12 And the man said, The woman whom thou gavest *to be* with me, she gave me of the tree, and I did eat.
13 And the LORD God said unto the woman, What *is* this *that* thou hast done? And the woman said, The serpent beguiled me, and I did eat.

When Adam mentioned his nakedness he was in effect exposing his sinful disobedience, since he would not have been conscious of being naked had he not sinned. God therefore immediately pointed this out to him by asking him the direct question as to whether he had eaten of the one forbidden tree, thus giving him an opportunity to confess his sin and ask forgiveness. Whether the punishment would have been lessened in some way had Adam confessed in repentance we have no way of knowing. In view of God's nature of love and mercy, though, it does seem likely. The fact is, he did *not* confess.

So rapidly had sin pervaded the hearts of both Adam and Eve that, when God began to question them, Adam blamed his wife and Eve blamed the serpent, neither being willing to acknowledge personal guilt. In fact, Adam, by implication, cast the blame on God Himself, emphasizing that it was all because of "the woman whom *thou gavest to be with me.*" Instead of praising God for His goodness, he blamed Him for his troubles! How foolish and wicked—and how much like ourselves!

God's questions, of course, were not to obtain information, but rather to encourage Adam and Eve to acknowledge and repent of their sin. Though they were sorry they had been discovered and were no doubt fearful of the consequences, there is no indication of true repentance, but rather merely an attempt to justify themselves. Accordingly, there was no course of action for the Lord except to initiate punishment—but a punishment which would be corrective and redemptive as well as punitive.

The Bondage of Decay

The passage in Genesis 3:14-19 contains what has commonly been called the *Curse.* Actually, of course, there are several curses, or phases of the curse, involved: the curse on the animal kingdom, the curse on the serpent, the special curse on the woman, the curse on Adam and his descendants, and the curse on the very elements of the ground itself.

Since Adam had been appointed to exercise dominion over the earth, and since Adam was to begin to die, his dominion also would begin to "die." Since that time, "we know that the whole creation groaneth and travaileth in pain together until now" (Romans 8:22). This condition is called by the apostle Paul the "bondage of corruption" (or, better, *decay*). "For the creation was made subject to vanity..." (or *futility*) (Romans 8:20, 21).

In a sense the three main aspects of the curse corresponded to the three basic created entities described in Genesis 1. The physical elements of the universe were first created (Genesis 1:1), then the entity of conscious life in animals (Genesis 1:21), and finally the spiritual nature of God in man (Genesis 1:27). The other great events of Creation Week consisted of processes of forming, ordering, and organizing the created entities into various "kinds" of physical and biological "bodies" (I Corinthians 15:38-41).

Likewise the curse fell on the physical elements (Genesis 3:18), the animal kingdom (Genesis 3:14), and on mankind (Genesis 3:16, 19), because all three entities (physical, mental, spiritual) were corporate components in man's being, and man had left God.

As far as the personal aspects of the curse were concerned, God pronounced them in the same chronological order in which the specific acts of sin had been committed—first on Satan, then on Eve, then on Adam. For Adam and Eve, however, their subjection under the curse was "in hope" (Romans 8:20) of eventual redemption; for Satan it was final and irrevocable. He not only had rebelled against God in heaven, but now he had also infected mankind with his rebellion.

Genesis 3:14

---

14 And the LORD God said unto the serpent, Because thou hast done this, thou *art* cursed above all cattle, and above every beast of the field; upon thy belly shalt thou go, and dust shalt thou eat all the days of thy life:

The serpent, as an animal, was cursed "above all cattle, and above every beast of the field," not because of direct culpability on its part, but rather as a perpetual reminder to man of the instrument of his fall and of the final destruction of Satan himself. Whatever may have been its beauty and posture before, it would henceforth glide on its belly and be an object of dread and loathing by all.

It would not "eat dust" in a literal sense, of course, except in the sense that its prey would have to be consumed directly off the ground in front of it. The expression is mainly a graphic figure of speech indicating its humiliating judgment and fall.

Lest anyone complain at God's injustice, since the serpent as an animal was not to blame for Satan's corrupt possession of its body, he should remember that the "potter hath power over the clay." Each animal had been made for a specific mode of life and with specific structures appropriate to such a mode. There were many other "creeping things," and God now made the serpent to join this group, for reason of the symbolism involved; but snakes, as animals, are no more capable of resentment at this lot than are moles and worms.

It should be noted also that all other animals were brought under the curse at this time, though none of them had "sinned." The serpent was merely cursed "above all" the rest, but "every beast" henceforth had the "sentence of death" in its members. Each was a part of man's dominion and it was by man's sin that death came into the world, infecting everything in that dominion.

Genesis 3:15, 16

---

15 And I will put enmity between thee and the woman, and between thy seed and her seed; it shall bruise thy head, and thou shalt bruise his heel.
16 Unto the woman he said, I will greatly multiply thy sorrow and thy conception; in sorrow thou shalt bring forth children; and thy desire *shall be* to thy husband, and he shall rule over thee.

Though the curse was outwardly pronounced on the serpent, its real thrust was against the malevolent spirit controlling its body and its speech, "that old serpent called the Devil" (Revelation 12:9). The earth had been originally placed under man's dominion. By persuading them to follow his word instead of God's word, Satan probably believed that he had now won the allegiance of the first man and woman and therefore also of all their descendants. They would be allies of himself and his host of evil angels in their efforts to dethrone and vanquish God. Satan was now the "god of this world" (II Corinthians 4:4), and the woman especially, who was to bear the earth's future children, would readily follow him. She had already demonstrated her control over the man, who had eaten of the fruit when she told him to, even though he himself was not deceived. With the wonderful potentialities of human reproduction under his control, Satan could, as it were, in time "create" an innumerable host of obedient servants to do his bidding.

But if such thoughts as these were in Satan's mind, he was not only the deceiver of the whole world (Revelation 12:9), but he himself was deceived most of all. The woman, in the first place, would *not* become his willing ally. "I will put *enmity* between thee and the woman," God said. Neither would she rule over her husband. "Thy desire shall be to thy husband, and he shall rule over thee." Conception and childbirth would not be easy and rapid. "I will greatly multiply thy sorrow, and thy conception; in sorrow thou shalt bring forth children."

Not only would victory not be as easy as he thought, but ultimately he would be completely defeated and destroyed. "There will come One who will not be of the man's seed, and who therefore will not be under your dominion. He will be uniquely the Seed of the woman, miraculously conceived and virgin-born. Though you will succeed in grievously injuring Him, He will completely crush you and all your evil ambitions."

This great promise in Genesis 3:15 has long been known as the *Protevangelium* (the "first gospel"), promising the ultimate coming and victory of the Redeemer. It obviously entails far more than a trivial reference to the physical enmity between men and snakes, though this may be included as a sort of secondary pictorial parallel. The prophecy clearly looks forward to the time when Satan will be completely crushed beneath the feet of the woman's triumphant Seed.

But first there is seen a time of conflict and even apparent victory on the part of the serpent, who is able to "bruise the heel" of the woman's seed. This predicted conflict is reflected in the legends and mythologies of the ancients, filled as they are with tales of heroes engaged in life-and-death struggles with serpents and dragons and other monsters. The star-figures by which early peoples identified the heavenly constellations repeat the same story, especially in the so-called signs of the zodiac and their accompanying "decans." There is the picture, for example, of Hercules battling with the serpent. The constellation Virgo, with the spike of wheat in her hands, may refer to the promised "seed of the woman." The king of animals, Leo, is shown clawing the head of a great fleeing serpent. The Scorpion is illustrated as stinging the heel of the great hero Ophiuchus.

These and many similar representations in the ancient myths are most likely merely distorted remembrances of this great primeval prophecy. Mankind, from the earliest ages, has recorded its hope that some day a Savior would come who would destroy the devil and reconcile man to God.

But who, or what, is meant by the "seed"—both the "seed of the serpent" and the "seed of the woman"? The term "seed" of course has a biological connotation, but this is not strictly possible here. Neither Satan, who is a spirit, nor the woman would be able to produce actual seed; only the man was created physically to do this. These two seeds, therefore, must refer primarily to spiritual progeny.

Specifically, it appears that Satan's seed consists of those who knowingly and willfully set themselves at enmity with the seed of the woman. They partake in a very specific sense of the character of the Adversary (John 8:44; Ephesians 2:2, 3) and seek to oppose God's purposes in creation and redemption.

The "seed of the woman," on the other hand, would refer in the first place to those in the human family who are brought into right relationship with God through faith, children of the Father. The prophecy forecasts the agelong conflict between the children of the kingdom and the children of the wicked one, beginning with Cain and Abel (Matthew 13:37-40; I John 3:8-12), and continuing to the end of the age (Revelation 12:17).

There is obviously another meaning as well, in addition to the above plural and corporate meaning of the two seeds. There is one primary seed of the serpent and one primary seed of the woman. The former is the soon-coming "son of perdition" (II Thessalonians 2:3), the antichrist, to whom the Dragon gives his power and throne and authority (Revelation 13:2).

The primary seed of the woman is, of course, the Lord Jesus Christ; and it is not the seed of the serpent, but Satan himself, who battles and is destroyed by *this* Seed, according to verse 15.

There is clearly an inference of human birth here; in fact, verse 16 mentions the sorrow that would attend conception of the woman's children. It is also clearly implied that someday one would be supernaturally conceived and born of a virgin. This promised Seed would not partake of the inherited sin nature of Adam's children, but would nevertheless be a man. He would not be born under Satan's dominion as would other men, and would thus be able to engage the Serpent in mortal combat. Finally, though bruised in the conflict, He would emerge as victor, "bruising" (literally *crushing*) the Serpent's head, destroying the works of Satan and setting the captives free!

This promise is, of course, fulfilled in Jesus Christ. He appeared to be mortally wounded when He died on the cross, but He rose again and soon will return to cast the devil into the lake of fire (Revelation 20:10). And in His very dying, "bruised for our iniquities" (Isaiah 53:5), He satisfied the just requirements of God's holiness. He died for the sin of Adam, and therefore also for the sin of all who were "in Adam." "For as in Adam all die, even so in Christ shall all be made alive" (I Corinthians 15:22).

There is an implied reference to this great prophecy in Isaiah 7:14, which should read: "Therefore the Lord himself shall give you a sign: behold *the* virgin shall conceive and bear a son, and shall call his name Immanuel." The definite article before "virgin" (*ha almah* in the Hebrew text) indicates one that was previously promised. Similarly in Jeremiah 31:22: "For the Lord hath created a new thing in the earth, A woman shall compass a man." An ordinary conception would not be a *new* thing.

The great sign which John saw in heaven (Revelation 12:1-17) points to the final fulfillment of the prophecy. The woman in this passage seems to represent the chosen nation Israel in general, and Mary the mother of Jesus in a specific sense, although she may also be understood to symbolize all the true people of God. The man-child is Christ and the Dragon is that old Serpent waiting to destroy Him. But He is caught up into the heavens, and the Serpent, defeated in his attempt to destroy the true Seed, angrily continues to "make war with the remnant of her seed, which keep the commandments of God and have the testimony of Jesus Christ." Finally, the Dragon is to be bound in the abyss for a thousand years, and eventually cast into the lake of fire (Revelation 20:2, 10).

The promised Seed would one day be born of a human woman, but Satan was left in the dark as to which woman and at what time. Both he and Eve may have thought initially it would be her firstborn son. Later on, as the centuries passed, Satan continued his attacks against all the males born in the promised line, particularly those who were objects of special prophetic interest (e.g., Noah, Abraham, Jacob, David), in case one of them might be the promised Seed.

Although God's grace was manifest in this particular way toward woman—despite her being the vehicle through which Satan gained control over the world—she was nevertheless to be the subject of special judgment, though even this would be for the ultimate good of humanity. Eve shared in the curse on Adam, since she was also "of the man"; but in addition a special burden was placed on her in connection with the experience of conception and childbirth, the pain and sorrow of which would be "greatly multiplied." It had been appointed to her to be the "mother of all living" (Genesis 3:20), but now her children to all generations would suffer under the curse. Their very entrance into the world would be marked by unique suffering, serving as a perpetual reminder of the dread effects of sin.

The function of reproduction and motherhood, originally given as the joyful fruition of God's purpose in her creation, but now marred so severely by her "lust" for withheld knowledge, which conceived and brought forth sin and death (James 1:15), would thus be marked by unique suffering in its accomplishment. Furthermore, she who had acted independently of her husband in her fateful decision to taste the desired fruit, must henceforth exercise her desire only to her husband and he would bear rule over her.

The long sad record of human history has confirmed the accuracy of this prophetic judgment. Woman's lot has been one of pain, pain in many forms—physical, mental, spiritual, and *especially* in her experience of conception and birth (the emphasis is warranted in the original language). Generally speaking, man has subjugated woman with little regard for her own personal feelings and needs. In non-Christian cultures and religions, such subjugation and humiliation have been almost universal, until very recent times her husband often having even the power of life and death over her.

Such harsh "rule," of course, went far beyond God's intention. Though the husband was to be the head of the house, he was to love and cherish his wife, considering her to be "one flesh" with himself, "clinging to his wife" (Genesis 2:23, 24). Those involved in the modern "women's liberation" and other feminist movements are well justified in fighting against the injustices and cruelties long associated with male-dominated governments and customs; but they should avoid carrying such movements to anti-Biblical extremes, demanding *absolute* equality in all legal, political, cultural, and personal relationships.

It is surely true that, in the Israelite economy outlined in the Mosaic code, and even more in the Christian relationships enjoined in the New Testament, the role of the woman is eminently conducive to her highest happiness and fulfillment, as multitudes of Christian women have testified. In nominally Christian countries, of course, and even in many Christian homes and churches, the proper roles of husband and wife have often been distorted in one direction or another. This can best be corrected by simple obedience to God's revealed Word on such subjects (see Ephesians 5:22-33; Colossians 3:18-21; I Peter

3:1-7; I Corinthians 7:1-40; I Timothy 2:8-15; 3:11-12; 5:14; Titus 2:4-5; Hebrews 13:4; Matthew 19:3-12; etc.).

The special curse on woman associated with child-bearing can, in fact, be turned to a blessing for a woman yielded to the will of God. Jesus said: "A woman when she is in travail hath sorrow, because her hour is come: but as soon as she is delivered of the child, she remembereth no more the anguish, for joy that a man is born into the world" (John 16:21). Somehow, in spite of the suffering, the joy of motherhood has for most normal women been their greatest happiness.

In the experience of giving birth, women actually become a type of Christ. "When thou shalt make his soul an offering for sin, he shall see his seed. . . . He shall see of the travail of his soul, and shall be satisfied" (Isaiah 53:10, 11). "Who for the joy that was set before him endured the cross, despising the shame" (Hebrews 12:2).

Each experience of birth, therefore, can be a beautiful picture and reminder of God's promise of "deliverance" from the awful curse on man and all his dominion. The entire world, in fact, is "groaning and travailing in pain," awaiting the great delivery and birth of a new world, heir to all God's glorious purposes and promises to the first world, in "earnest expectation . . . of the manifestation of the sons of God," at which great day "the creature [creation] itself also shall be delivered from the bondage of decay into the glorious liberty of the children of God" (Romans 8:19, 21, 22).

Each "birth" day is a picture and promise of such a day. For the instructed and trusting woman, the experience of childbirth, therefore, can be—and always should be—a time of blessing, of closeness to God (and to her husband). The suffering is submerged in the rejoicing, and this in itself goes far toward mitigating the physical pain. No wonder the apostle Paul says: "Notwithstanding, she shall be saved in childbearing, if they continue in faith and love and holiness with sobriety" (I Timothy 2:15).

Genesis 3:17-19

17 And unto Adam he said, Because thou hast hearkened unto the voice of thy wife, and hast eaten of the tree, of which I commanded thee, saying, Thou shalt not eat of it: cursed *is* the ground for thy sake; in sorrow shalt thou eat *of* it all the days of thy life;
18 Thorns also and thistles shall it bring forth to thee; and thou shalt eat the herb of the field:
19 In the sweat of thy face shalt thou eat bread, till thou return unto the ground; for out of it wast thou taken: for dust thou *art,* and unto dust shalt thou return.

The full force of the curse fell on Adam, but this of course included all men and women "in Adam" (even Eve, who was "of" him), as well as his entire dominion, and indeed the "whole creation" (evidently the sidereal realms were also involved in God's judgment, but this possibly was more directly related to the prior sin of the angels who inhabited them). "Cursed is the ground [same word, actually, as *earth,* and meaning the basic material of the physical creation] for thy sake." The elements themselves, the "dust of the earth," out of which all things had been made, were brought under the bondage of decay and disintegration.

The earth which had previously cooperated readily as the man "tilled" and "dressed it" (Genesis 2:5, 15), now became reluctant to yield his food. Instead it began to yield thorns and noxious weeds, requiring toil and sweat and tears before man could "eat of it." And finally, in spite of all his struggle, death would triumph and man's body would return to the dust from which it was taken.

It seems unlikely that God actually either created or "made" thorns and thistles at this time. He did not "create" death in the direct sense, but rather withdrew that extension of His power which had maintained a "steady state" of life and order, thus allowing all things gradually to disintegrate toward disorder and death. In like manner, though there is necessarily a good deal of uncertainty on such matters, it seems more in character that God merely "allowed" certain plant structures which previously were beneficent to deteriorate into malevolent characteristics. It may be assumed (as characteristic of most "decay" processes observed today) that deterioration at first was rapid, later gradually tapering off into a much more gradual process. In terms of modern genetic knowledge, such changes probably were in the form of *mutations,* or random changes in the molecular structure of the genetic systems of the different kinds of organisms.

If deteriorative mutational changes occurred in plants, it seems reasonable and even probable that they also would occur in animals. As smoothly rounded structures deteriorated to thorns in plants, so perhaps teeth and nails designed for a herbivorous diet mutated to fangs and claws which, in combination with a progressively increasing dietary deficiency of proteins and other essentials, gradually generated carnivorous appetites in certain animals.

Similarly, bacteria and other microorganisms, designed originally to serve essential functions in soil maintenance, purification processes, and so forth, underwent mutational changes which, in many cases, proved harmful and even lethal to other organisms into which they were ingested. Parasites and viral systems may also have developed in some such way.

Not all of this was bad, however, especially in view of the changed moral climate following the fall of man. As a matter of fact, God told Adam that the curse on the ground was *"for thy sake."* It was better that suffering and death accompany sin than that rebellion be permitted to thrive unchecked in the deathless steady-state economy as originally created. With no death, men would proliferate in number and wickedness without limit. The same presumably would be true of animals and plants, as far as their numbers were concerned, and the uses to which they might be devoted by the wicked angels and men who would henceforth control them.

And so God placed the curse on man and on his whole environment, thus forcing him to recognize the seriousness of his sin, as well as his helplessness to save himself and his dominion from eventual destruction. The necessity of laboring merely to keep alive would go far toward inhibiting still further rebellion and would force him to recognize that Satan's tempting promises had been nothing but lies. Such a condition would encourage him to a state of repentance toward God, and a desire for God to provide deliverance from the evil state upon which he had fallen.

In the animal and plant kingdoms likewise, limitless proliferation would be checked by these new factors of disease, predation, parasitism, and so on. Had the Fall never taken place, animal life would no doubt have remained constant at an optimum population by divinely directed constraints on the reproductive process. Now, however, God's personal presence is to be withdrawn for a time, and it is more salutary to maintain order by means of these indirect constraints associated with the curse, adding still further to the testimony that the world was travailing in pain, awaiting its coming Redeemer.

Thus, the entire "creation was made subject to vanity." The earth began to "wax old, as doth a garment" and ultimately "shall perish" (Hebrews 1:10-12). Since all flesh is made of the earth's physical elements, it also is subject to the law of decay and death and as "grass, withereth . . . and falleth away" (I Peter 1:24). It is universal experience that *all things,* living or nonliving, eventually wear out, run down, grow old, decay, and pass into the dust.

This condition is so universal that it was formalized about a hundred years ago (by Carnot, Clausius, Kelvin, and other scientists) into a fundamental scientific law, now called the Second Law of Thermodynamics. This law states that all systems, if left to themselves, tend to become degraded or disordered. It has also been called the "law of morpholysis" (from a Greek word meaning "loosing of structure"). Physical systems, whether watches or suns, eventually wear out. Organisms grow old and die. Hereditary changes in species are caused by gene mutations (sudden random disruptions in their highly ordered genetic systems) which in many cases have resulted in deterioration or extinction of the species itself. Even apart from mutations, the deterioration of the environment has often led to species extinction.

Instead of all things being "made"—that is, organized into complex systems—as they were in Creation Week, they are now being "unmade," becoming disorganized and simple. Instead of life and growth, there comes decay and death; instead of evolution, there is degeneration.

This, then, is the true origin of the strange law of disorder and decay, the universally applicable, all-important Second Law of Thermodynamics. Herein is the secret of all that's wrong with the world. Man is a sinner and has brought God's curse on the earth.

The curse on man himself was fourfold: (1) *sorrow,* resulting from continual disappointment and futility; (2) *pain and suffering,* signified by the "thorns" which intermittently hinder man in his efforts to provide a living for his family; (3) *sweat,* or *tears,* the "strong crying" of intense struggle against a hostile environment; and finally (4) physical *death,* which would eventually triumph over all man's efforts, with the structure of his body returning to the simple elements of the earth.

But Christ, as Son of Man and second Adam, has been made the curse for us (Galatians 3:13). He was the "man of *sorrows*" (Isaiah 53:3); acquainted more with grief than any other man, He was wounded, bruised, and chastised for us (Isaiah 53:5), and indeed wore the very *thorns* of the curse as His crown (Mark 15:17); in the agony of His labor, He *sweat* as it were drops of blood (Luke 22:44), and "offered up prayers and supplications with strong crying and tears" (Hebrews 5:7). And, finally, God brought Him into the "dust of death" (Psalm 22:15).

Therefore, because He bore all the curse Himself for us, once again the dwelling of God shall someday be with men and "there shall be no more *death,* neither *sorrow,* nor *crying,* neither shall there be any more *pain*: for the former things are passed away" (Revelation 21:4). "And there shall be no more curse: but the throne of God and of the Lamb shall be in it: and his servants shall serve him" (Revelation 22:3).

Although the complete removal of the curse awaits the return of Christ to purge and renovate the earth (II Peter 3:10; Revelation 20:11; 21:1), He has already paid the price for its redemption (I Peter 1:18-20), not with "corruptible things" (which could never redeem anything under the "bondage of corruption") but with His "precious blood," by the "incorruptible word" (I Peter 1:23). In token, therefore, we can already appropriate the results of this deliverance by faith. We can be in *sorrow,* "yet always rejoicing" (II Corinthians 6:10); we can endure the *"thorn* in the flesh" with His sufficient grace and perfecting strength (II Corinthians 12:7-9). Though our labor ceases not "night and day with *tears,"* yet there is rest in Him (Acts 20:31; Matthew 11:28); and though "made conformable unto his *death,"* we know the "power of his resurrection" (Philippians 3:10).

Even the earth itself, though groaning under the curse, continually gives testimony, by His grace, of the promised deliverance. Each day that passes, the world descends into darkness, and seems, as it were, to lose its light of life; yet the sun rises and the dawn always comes, providing a continual reminder that soon "shall the Sun of righteousness arise with healing in his wings" (Malachi 4:2). Every year the earth sees the plants die and the cold winter come; but soon, once again, when we "behold the fig tree, and all the trees, when they now shoot forth," we know that "summer is now nigh at hand." In a similar manner, this encourages us to know also that "the kingdom of God is nigh at hand" (Luke 21:29-31).

Though the whole creation travails in pain and sorrow, and we can never forget the curse on the earth and our necessary toil before it will yield its bread, "nevertheless he left not himself without witness, in that he did good, and gave us rain from heaven, and fruitful seasons, filling our hearts with food and gladness" (Acts 14:17). Though pain and death may accompany birth, yet new life is ever born and hope springs eternal.

Paradise Lost

The last verses of this important third chapter of Genesis deal with man's expulsion from his home in the beautiful garden of Eden. It had been prepared by God's loving hands as the perfect home for His children, and they had rejected Him. It was no longer appropriate for them in their fallen condition. God's justice required punishment; but, even more, His love required imposition of conditions calculated pedagogically to make them realize their lost estate and seek salvation.

Genesis 3:20

---

20 And Adam called his wife's name
Eve; because she was the mother of all
living.

As God pronounced the great curse, with all its aspects and implications, He had also given the even greater promise of the coming
Redeemer. When Adam and Eve heard His proclamation of this "first
gospel," promising salvation in spite of their sin and the resulting curse,
this time they believed God's Word, instead of doubting and rejecting it.

Adam called his wife's name Eve (meaning "life") because she was
the "mother of all living." He thus indicated his faith in God's promises,
not only that they would have children but also that through this means
God would send the "seed of the woman" to bring salvation. Since true
faith in God's Word always is preceded and accompanied by repentance,
it is evident that Adam's attitude had changed toward Satan and toward
himself, as God had spoken to him. He was truly sorry for his grievous
mistake and was willing now simply to thrust himself on God's mercy
and trust Him for salvation. No doubt, Eve also experienced the same
change of heart, with also the still further reason that she now desired
to follow her husband rather than to act independently of him.

The statement that Eve "was the mother of all living" was not a
part of Adam's declaration, since at that time no children had yet been
born (had there been, they presumably would have been born in a
sinless state, but Scripture teaches that all died "in Adam"—I Corinthians 15:22). This statement was added later as an editorial explanatory
insertion, possibly by Moses. In any case, it surely refutes the idea that
there were any "pre-Adamite men" living in the world outside the
garden, as some have speculated.

Another point worth noting is that Adam and Eve were not in the
garden very long before their sin took place. God had commanded
them to "be fruitful and multiply," and in their initial state of fellowship and obedience, they would of course have set about immediately to follow this command.

In spite of their condemnation unto death, God promised they
would indeed live long enough at least to have their children and raise
them. They believed God's word and so were saved. As "the mother
of all living," Eve has become a type of our heavenly home, "Jerusalem
which is above is free, which is the mother of us all" (Galations 4:26).

Genesis 3:21

---

21 Unto Adam also and to his wife did the LORD God make coats of skins, and clothed them.

In response to their faith, God graciously provided a covering for their nakedness. Their self-made fig leaf aprons were entirely inadequate; so God made "coats of skins, and clothed them" (Genesis 3:21). Perhaps they silently and sorrowfully watched as God selected two of their animal friends, probably two sheep, and slew them there, shedding the innocent blood before their eyes. They learned, in type, that an "atonement" (or "covering") could only be provided by God and through the shedding of blood on the altar (note Leviticus 17:11). We do not know, of course, but it may well be that this experience also taught them that the woman's promised Seed must eventually shed His own blood in the awful conflict that was coming, before the full atonement could be provided. In any case, they were soon to experience the reality of this conflict in the tragic history of their first two sons.

An incidental bit of instruction from this record is that, in man's fallen state, a sense of shame relative to nakedness is entirely appropriate. Modern nudists and hedonists, despite protestations about the beauty of the human body and the "freedom" and "naturalness" of displaying it openly, should recall that God Himself took pains to provide clothing to cover the nakedness of the first man and woman.

Genesis 3:22-24

---

22 ¶ And the LORD God said, Behold, the man is become as one of us, to know good and evil: and now, lest he put forth his hand, and take also of the tree of life, and eat, and live for ever: 23 Therefore the LORD God sent him forth from the garden of E'den, to till the ground from whence he was taken. 24 So he drove out the man: and he placed at the east of the garden of E'den cherubim, and a flaming sword which turned every way, to keep the way of the tree of life.

The garden of Eden continued to exist for an unknown length of time after the departure of Adam and Eve. The tree of life still grew there, and man was driven from the garden in order to prevent him from eating of its fruit any longer. As already discussed, we have no idea what this fruit was, or by what marvelous medicinal reactions it was able to inhibit cellular decay and enable its user to continue indefinitely in perfect health; but God could certainly have endowed it with such capacity and His own testimony is that He did so. It will once again be planted along the Edenic river in the coming age when the earth is made new again (Revelation 2:7; 21:1, 5; 22:1-2).

Verse 22 gives a brief insight into the inner councils of the tri-une Godhead. As in Genesis 1:26, such a council was recorded relative to the decision to create man, so now the council decrees his expulsion from the garden and the tree of life. In both passages, the divine unity is stressed ("And the Lord God said") and also the divine plurality ("us").

The council recognized that man had "become as one of us, to know good and evil." This statement is not made in irony or ridicule, as some have thought, but in sadness. Man had once known only the goodness of God; but now he had come to know experimentally the evil inherent in rejecting God's Word, as well as the necessary spiritual and physical suffering resulting from such action, so that he did, indeed, "know good and evil." His hoped-for "godness," however, as promised by the Serpent, was indeed a pitiful caricature of what he had anticipated. He had been created in God's very image, but now that image had been gravely marred and defaced by his experience of evil.

God, moreover, had to "drive out" the man from the garden. It seems that, even though Adam and Eve were truly repentant and believing, they were extremely reluctant to leave their home for the unknown and harsh world outside. Probably they feared they would never see God again, since His own "home" seemed to be in the garden; and they desperately wanted His fellowship and protection. Also the necessity now to "till the ground from which he was taken," securing his bread by the sweat of his face, was not nearly so pleasant a prospect as freely eating all the fruit of the trees of the garden. They naturally demurred at God's command to leave; so God was forced to insist sternly that they depart.

Although a just punishment was involved, God's deeper reason was pedagogical. It would have been calamitous had they continued in a perfect environment as sinful people, especially eating of the life-tree fruit and living on indefinitely in such a condition. They and their descendants to many generations must be taught the true nature and effects of sin, and of living out of fellowship with God, so that they could eventually come to know and understand and love Him fully, as Savior, as well as Maker and Provider.

It is significant that, from Genesis 3:8 onward, the writer (presumably Adam himself, originally) uses the name "Lord God" *(Jehovah Elohim)*. God is still the omnipotent uni-plural God of creation; but He is also the eternal, unchanging Lord of grace and mercy, and, through these experiences, Adam and Eve were coming to know Him in that way also.

To "keep" (or "guard") the way of the tree of life, God placed at the east of the garden two cherubim, with a revolving swordlike flame flashing around them like lightning bolts. These creatures, apparently the highest in the angelic hierarchy, are described more fully in Ezekiel 1:4-28; 10:1-22; and Revelation 4:6-8. Satan himself had once been the "anointed cherub" (Ezekiel 28:14) on God's holy mountain.

The cherubim are always associated closely with the throne of God (note Psalm 18:10; 80:1; 99:1) and it is thus intimated that God's presence was particularly manifest there at the tree of life. Later, His presence was especially revealed over the mercy seat in the holy of holies in the tabernacle (Exodus 25:17-22; Hebrews 9:3-5), and it is significant that this mercy seat was overshadowed by two golden representations of the cherubim. It was here that once each year the high priest entered with the sacrificial blood of atonement to sprinkle over the mercy seat (see Leviticus 16; Hebrews 9:7-9; 24-28).

By analogy, it may well be that it was here, between the cherubim guarding the way to the tree of life, that God continued at intervals to meet with Adam and those of his descendants who desired to know Him.

6

The Lost World

(Genesis 4-5)

The Blood of Righteous Abel

In the great protevangelic prophecy, God had spoken of a coming conflict between the seed of the serpent and the seed of the woman. Adam and Eve were soon to experience the reality of this conflict in the tragic history of their two sons.

The story of Cain and Abel, while in every way to be understood as actual history, is also a parable of the agelong conflict of the two seeds. Cain typifies the "seed of the serpent," while Abel is a type of Christ, the "seed of the woman." In a secondary sense, Abel represents also those who, by faith, are "in Christ," and who therefore also are in a spiritual sense "seed of the woman."

It seems reasonable to infer that, after the expulsion from Eden, God had made gracious provision to continue to commune with man, even though now "at a distance," on the basis of His promise of a coming Redeemer, whose shed blood would be the price of redemption. He had shown Adam and Eve that an "atonement" required the shedding of innocent blood to provide a "covering" for the guilty. Probably at an appointed time and place, men were able to meet God, first being careful to approach Him by means of a proper offering, especially marked by the principle of substitution—the innocent for the guilty. Those who "worshiped" (that is, literally, "bowed down" to God's will) in this way thus acknowledged their own guilt and helplessness, as well as their trust in God alone for complete salvation and provision. There was nothing in such a process that would appeal to the physical or esthetic or mental appetites of man (as contrasted with Satan's appeal to Eve in Genesis 3:6); hence it would require the complete subjugation of human pride to the will of God.

Genesis 4:1, 2

CHAPTER 4

AND Adam knew Eve his wife; and she conceived, and bare Cain, and said,

I have gotten a man from the LORD. 2 And she again bare his brother Abel. And Abel was a keeper of sheep, but Cain was a tiller of the ground.

One's attitude of heart toward this matter of approaching and knowing God actually determines his destiny in eternity. If he willingly accepts God's Word, approaching Him solely on the basis of faith in God's provision, through the shed blood of the Redeemer, God's Lamb, then he is spirituallly of the heaven-born "seed of the woman" and he is restored to God's presence and fellowship. But if he continues to distort and reject God's Word, relying on his own personal merits to earn salvation, he is then in effect interposing his own will in place of God's. He is presuming to be "as gods, knowing good and evil," and consequently becomes of the serpent's seed.

This great twofold division of humanity is perfectly illustrated in the first two sons of Adam. When the first was born, Eve exclaimed: "I have gotten a man from the Lord" (literally *"with* the Lord"). This testimony of praise is itself sufficient proof that Eve was a believer in the Lord and in the truthfulness of God's promises. Though she had now experienced the suffering associated with childbirth, she had also seen God's faithfulness in giving her a son.

This is also the first use of the familiar Biblical euphemism for marital intercourse; "Adam *knew* his wife." Such an expression uniquely emphasizes both the full harmony and understanding of man and wife (*one* flesh) and also an ideal awareness of God's primeval purpose as implemented through the human capacity for sexual love and reproduction.

The name Cain means "gotten" and is obviously derived from Eve's exclamation of joyful acquisition. The practice of giving names to children associated with some specific event is frequently found in Genesis (4:25; 5:29; 17:5; 41:51; etc.) as well as other parts of the

Old Testament. It is significant that this phenomenon is found in all of the three main supposed documentary "sources" (J, E, P) of the Pentateuch, a fact which itself is strong evidence that all these so-called sources in reality constitute a consistent, unified document reporting real events.

Eve not only was thankful for a child, but also that the Lord had enabled her to beget a *man*. This seems to be a further expression of faith that her babe would grow to manhood. It is possible that she hoped this might be the promised Deliverer, even though he was not in a specific biological sense a "seed of the woman." As a matter of fact, he "was of that wicked one" (I John 3:12), and thus was the first in the long line of the Serpent's seed.

Cain's younger brother, Abel, was truly in the household of faith, however. He is the very first mentioned in the long line of men of faith recorded in Hebrews 11 (see verse 4). He is called "righteous" and a prophet (Matthew 23:35; Luke 11:50, 51).

Such testimonials from none other than the Lord Jesus can only mean that Abel was a man who believed and obeyed God's Word, with righteousness thus imputed to him. As a prophet, he must also have received God's Word by divine revelation and preached it by divine enablement. But Cain refused it and disobeyed.

Abel was Eve's second son, born some time after Cain. Some exegetes have thought the absence of a separate record of his conception implies that Abel was conceived at the same time as Cain. This is quite unlikely, however; for the record should have said so if that were the case.

The name of Abel means "vapor" or "vanity," and suggests that, by the time of Abel's birth, Eve had become thoroughly impressed with the impact of God's curse on the world. God had indeed made the creation "subject to vanity" (Romans 8:20).

As the boys grew, Cain became a farmer and Abel a shepherd. Both were honorable occupations, Cain's fruits providing food and Abel's sheep providing clothing for the family. In addition, it is probable that the sheep were to be used for sacrifice. The lesson which God had taught Adam and Eve was not to be forgotten. Atonement ("covering") required the shedding of blood.

Man was not authorized until after the Flood to use animals for food (Genesis 1:29; 2:16; 3:19; 9:3). As the population grew, Abel's sheep would no doubt have been available by trade or purchase to anyone who wished to use one for sacrifice or for clothing.

Genesis 4:3-5

---

3 And in process of time it came to pass, that Cain brought of the fruit of the ground an offering unto the LORD.
4 And Abel, he also brought of the firstlings of his flock and of the fat thereof. And the LORD had respect unto Abel and to his offering:
5 But unto Cain and to his offering he had not respect. And Cain was very wroth, and his countenance fell.

There seems to have been a regular time and place at which men were allowed to meet God. Possibly the place was at the door of entrance to the garden where the cherubim guarded the way to the tree of life (Genesis 3:24). Adam and Eve had been driven out of the garden, away from the presence of God. By God's grace, however, and in view of His promised Redeemer, He still allowed men to approach Him under certain conditions, there to hear His Word and to receive His guidance.

It seems probable that Adam and Eve had shown love to both their sons and had instructed them alike; so it is difficult to understand what caused Cain and Abel to assume different attitudes and characters. Gradually, however, these innate differences began to manifest themselves. Adam and Eve had other sons and daughters (Genesis 5:4); hence it may be that Cain and Abel had had brothers and sisters for many years prior to the events described in this chapter. They were both grown men, and their parents had been given divine instruction to multiply, so that this indeed seems more likely than not.

It is, therefore, quite probable that the offerings described in these verses were not the first ones offered by these two brothers. Rather, it must have become a regular practice, at certain definite periods of time, possibly on the Sabbath. The words in the Hebrew—literally, "at the end of the days"—seem to suggest this. Since this was the first occasion on which Cain received a rebuke, it would be inferred that his previous offerings had been acceptable to God.

The Bible does not actually say specifically whether such sacrifices had been commanded by God, or whether the practice arose merely as a spontaneous expression of thanksgiving and worship. If it was the latter, however, it is difficult to understand why God would not have been as pleased with an offering of Cain's fruits as with an offering of Abel's slain lamb. It seems more likely that God *did* give instructions, and that Cain had disobeyed. The entire occurrence can only be really understood in the context of an original revelation by God regarding the necessity of substitutionary sacrifice as a prerequisite to approaching God. Such revelation was most likely given at the time God provided coats of skins for Adam and Eve, and then banished them from His presence, providing, however, a specific means by which they could still commune with Him at certain times, on the basis of a similar sacrifice.

Adam and Eve had no doubt duly instructed their children in this provision and, for a long time, they heeded and followed it. Cain himself had probably purchased from Abel a sheep for his own sacrifice each time they came to the appointed place.

There came a time, however, when Cain began to resent this situation and finally decided to rebel against it. There seemed no good reason to him why he should be indebted to his young brother each time. His own fruits were every bit as valuable—and at least as attractive and useful to man—as were Abel's animals.

Therefore Cain, in presumption and rebellion, finally would no longer accept one of his brother's sheep, but instead brought the fruit which his own efforts had coerced from the earth God had cursed. He offered these fruits possibly in a spirit of careless unconcern for the will of God, possibly even in a spirit of pride in what he had been able to produce despite God's curse on the ground, or possibly in a spirit of rebellion against the implication that his nakedness before God required a covering which could only be provided by the shedding of blood. At any rate, his heart was not right before the Lord, and his offering was not in faith as was his brother's. Therefore, God rejected his gift.

"By faith Abel offered unto God a more excellent sacrifice than Cain, by which he obtained witness that he was righteous, God testifying of his gifts, and by it, he being dead yet speaketh" (Hebrews 11:4). Abel even offered, with the "firstlings of his flock," the "fat pieces thereof," a practice that would long afterward be incorporated into the actual Mosaic law of the peace offering: "all the fat is the Lord's" (Leviticus 3:16).

Cain's "glance" (a better rendering than "countenance") had been haughty, but now it "fell" and he became bitterly angry. Though perhaps up to this point in life, he may have seemed outwardly pious and obedient toward God, this incident finally revealed the inward pride and resentment that must have been festering in his heart for some time. The resentment was directed not only at God, but also at his brother Abel. Abel was an outward symbol of the fact that Cain's works were not adequate to get him into God's presence (since he must obtain Abel's sheep for this purpose). But Abel in addition, was a prophet, and thus quite possibly had discerned this weakness in his older brother and had been warning him about it. This situation had finally become quite intolerable for such a proud individual as Cain.

Genesis 4:6-8

6 And the LORD said unto Cain, Why art thou wroth? and why is thy countenance fallen?

7 If thou doest well, shalt thou not be accepted? and if thou doest not well, sin lieth at the door: and unto thee *shall be* his desire, and thou shalt rule over him.

8 And Cain talked with Abel his brother: and it came to pass, when they were in the field, that Cain rose up against Abel his brother, and slew him.

In spite of Cain's bitter anger, God graciously promised that he would yet be accepted if he would only "do well," which undoubtedly meant to "obey His word." If he continued in rebellion, however, "sin" (and this is the first use of the word in Scripture) was "crouching at his door." He would truly become a seed of the Serpent, using "sin" as his obedient servant (compare the similar terminology in Genesis 3:16b and 4:7) to oppose the revealed will of God.

Cain, however, rejected God's warning and elected to continue in his own way. Abel, as God's first "prophet" (see Luke 11:49-51), surely counseled urgently against this decision, as "Cain talked with Abel his brother." But the seeds of pride and envy and hatred bore their bitter fruit. The enmity of the old Serpent completely poisoned Cain's soul when God would not receive his gift, and it would not rest until Abel's blood was spilled. As they talked together out in the field, with Abel no doubt urging repentance while Cain accused God of petty favoritism and his brother of self-righteous presumption, the argument finally became so bitter "that Cain rose up against Abel his brother and slew him." "And wherefore slew he him? Because his own works were evil, and his brother's righteous" (I John 3:12). There is even a suggestion that the murder was premeditated. Although the Massoretic text does not include this, certain other ancient versions (Samaritan, Septuagint, etc.) indicate that, when Abel talked with his brother, he proposed that they go out into the field to continue the conversation, thus giving him the opportunity to murder him without being restrained by others. In any case, it is apparent that the first slight entrance of sin into the world through the mere eating of a forbidden fruit had quickly resulted in much more bitter fruit—namely, the crime of fratricide. The seed of the Serpent was quickly striking at the Seed of the woman, corrupting her first son and slaying her second, thus trying to prevent the fulfillment of the protevangelic promise right at the beginning of human history.

Genesis 4:9-12

9 ¶ And the LORD said unto Cain, Where *is* Abel thy brother? And he said, I know not: *Am* I my brother's keeper?
10 And he said, What hast thou done? the voice of thy brother's blood crieth unto me from the ground.
11 And now *art* thou cursed from the earth, which hath opened her mouth to receive thy brother's blood from thy hand.
12 When thou tillest the ground, it shall not henceforth yield unto thee her strength; a fugitive and a vagabond shalt thou be in the earth.

No sooner had the awful deed been perpetrated, than God called Cain to account. This time Cain had not gone to the place of sacrifice to seek God; rather, God had gone out into the field seeking him. God's first question was pedagogic, designed to elicit from Cain a confession; the Lord certainly was not merely seeking information about Abel's whereabouts. Instead of reacting in humility and fear of God, however, Cain boldly questioned God's right to ask such a question! "Am I my brother's keeper?" "I don't know where he is!"

This was a blatant lie, of course, although it was indeed true in one sense that Cain did not know where Abel was. Like all others who died in faith, not having received the promises, Abel was the first human inhabitant of Sheol, that place in the heart of the earth where resided the spirits of those who were to await the coming of the Savior. When God had sought out Adam after *his* sin, Adam had responded in confession and repentance, but not Cain. He compounded his wickedness by blatantly lying to God and challenging His right even to question him. Thus does long-cherished sin harden a man's heart and pervert his senses.

God, therefore, can no longer speak to Cain in mercy, but only in judgment. Cain had been able to still the hated prophesying voice of his brother, but he could not still the voice of his blood! "The voice of thy brother's blood crieth unto me from the ground." For the first time, "blood" is actually mentioned in the Bible in this verse, although its significance had been intimated several times previously. Abel, the type of the seed of the woman, was righteous before God and yet died violently at the hand of the first of the Serpent's seed. Thus, Abel's blood crying from the ground is the prototype of all the suffering inflicted on the righteous through the ages by the children of the wicked one. Its climax and fulfillment are seen in the conflict of Satan and Christ on Calvary.

This conflict had reached a tragic crescendo when those religious leaders whom Christ had said were "of your father the devil" (John 8:44; Matthew 23:15) cried out for His crucifixion, hissing: "His blood be on us, and on our children" (Matthew 27:25). Like Cain, they would see innocent blood shed rather than obey God's Word.

But the blood of Christ "speaketh better things than that of Abel" (Hebrews 12:24). The blood of animals could never really take away sin, though it might enable their skins to be used for a temporary covering. But "the blood of Jesus Christ, God's Son, cleanseth us from all sin" (I John 1:7).

This conflict between the two spiritual seeds continues today and is rapidly heading toward its final climax. The present time seemingly is one of imminent victory for Satan, but Satan's final defeat is only awaiting the approaching glorious return of Christ. Even now, we have His promise of spiritual victory in our current battle with the evil one: "And the God of peace shall bruise Satan under your feet shortly. The grace of our Lord Jesus Christ be with you. Amen" (Romans 16:20).

God's punishment of Cain is thus also a type of the ultimate crushing of the head of the Serpent, when he will be separated forever from God in the lake of fire. Cain was forever "driven out from the presence of the Lord"; likewise will all those who obey not the gospel of Christ "be punished with everlasting destruction from the presence of the Lord, and from the glory of his power" (II Thessalonians 1:9).

Furthermore, Cain could no longer produce the fruits by which he had sought to approach God. The earth would no longer yield its increase for him, and he must become a "wanderer" in the earth. In like manner, those who attempt to earn salvation by their good works find ultimately that, of themselves, they can produce only "thorns and thistles." The true "good works" are those which only God can work in us through faith (note Ephesians 2:8-10). Though God allowed Cain to live for a time in the earth, just as today He allows the "tares and the wheat," the good seed and the bad seed, to grow together until the time of harvest (Matthew 13:24-30; 36-43), yet Cain's ultimate fate, as one who had "known the way of righteousness" but had turned "from the holy commandment delivered unto them [him]" (II Peter 2:21), is condemnation.

The curse on Cain, so far as he personally was concerned, did not specifically preclude him from future repentance. However, in his future wanderings, ever moving around and trying to find some portion of ground from which he could coax a meager livelihood, he would become a byword to the antediluvians, most of whom would surely encounter him at one time or another, and thus would be a perpetual reminder to them of the sure punishment awaiting the sinner, especially the murderer. God considers human life to be very sacred, and will eventually require the blood of all those who unjustly shed blood (note Genesis 9:5; Job 16:18; Psalm 9:12; Ezekiel 3:18; etc.), unless true repentance is quickly forthcoming.

Genesis 4:13-15

---

13 And Cain said unto the LORD, My punishment *is* greater than I can bear. 14 Behold, thou hast driven me out this day from the face of the earth; and from thy face shall I be hid; and I shall be a fugitive and a vagabond in the earth; and it shall come to pass, *that* every one that findeth me shall slay me. 15 And the LORD said unto him, Therefore whosoever slayeth Cain, vengeance shall be taken on him sevenfold. And the LORD set a mark upon Cain, lest any finding him should kill him.

When Cain's punishment was pronounced, it did, indeed, seem to elicit at least a measure of sorrow for his sin, though hardly any real repentance. Actually, the word for "punishment" (Hebrew *avon*) is usually translated simply "iniquity," and so Cain's use of it does show at least that he recognized the enormity of his iniquity and the natural relation of its penalty to it. Accordingly, this may have been a sign of at least some change of heart. No longer did he blatantly question or rebuke the Lord, nor did he suggest that his punishment was undeserved; rather, he merely cried out that it was too much for him to bear.

Of course, God did spare Cain's life, not exacting the penalty of capital punishment that would later be required (Genesis 9:6). Perhaps the very reason for this mercy was God's recognition that there was at least some hope of Cain's eventual repentance. His former impudence had become a cry of fear. Specifically, he feared that, in his wretched condition, as well as in retaliation for Abel's murder, he would be in constant danger of his own life. Indeed, "the way of the transgressor is hard"!

God, therefore (partly in mercy, partly to assure that Cain would be a continuing testimony to his generation of God's warnings against sin), promised Cain that He would protect him against execution, on penalty of a sevenfold vengeance. He even gave Cain a "sign" of some kind to assure him of this protection ("sign" is the correct rendering of the Hebrew *oth,* rather than "mark"; there was no outward mark on Cain to set him apart, as some have thought).

Whatever this sign may have been, it did not give Cain the real peace that he needed. In fact, it may well have been by his constant fear of other people that he was impelled to continually move about, a fugitive and a wanderer, as God had said. God's promise to Cain, however, was widely known (see Genesis 4:24); and it did actually serve to protect him, so that he survived to found a city and become the ancestor of a large number of descendants.

The Way of Cain

The remaining portion of Genesis 4 gives a most intriguing, even tantalizing, picture of life in the antediluvian world. This is almost the only information we have about that first human civilization, which was later so completely destroyed by the great Flood that practically nothing remained to tell us about it. Archaeological excavations deal almost entirely with post-Flood deposits, so that it is only in semi-legendary recollections of the world's first "golden age," together with a very few artifacts found deep in the fossiliferous rock strata of the earth's crust, that we can now find any other clues to the nature of life in that first world.

Thus, that first mighty civilization, which once thrived over much of the earth, has been almost forgotten by the world of modern scholarship. In his researches, the ethnologist does encounter stories of a sunken Atlantis or some kind of mythological Golden Age. In recent years, a number of amazing artifacts have been brought to light by writers advocating the strange notion of ancient interplanetary astronauts. Actually, these artifacts give, instead, an insight into the remarkable technological skills of early men, some of whom may actually have been antediluvians. Such data are still quite controversial, but at least they do convey the impression that early men were far from the brutish primitives that modern evolutionists have imagined them to be.

The brief Biblical record is still the only fully reliable account we have of that first age. It leaves us in no doubt that the antediluvian world was substantially different from the one in which we now live. As already discussed, much of the earth's waters were stored "above the firmament" in the form of a vast blanket of invisible water vapor, which produced a marvelous "greenhouse effect" over the earth's entire surface. This, in turn, produced a uniformly mild, warm climate everywhere all year long, with no wind and rain storms. There were extensive land surfaces, covered with lush vegetation and an abundant animal life, all over the world.

The congenial climate, possibly augmented by hyperbaric pressures (a condition of much higher atmospheric pressure than we now have on the earth, occasioned by the weight of the vapor canopy) and the radiation-filtering effect of the canopy enabled the people of that age—and probably the animals as well—to live to much greater ages than is now possible. In recent years, it has been demonstrated in biomedical research that both the existence of such high pressures and the absence of mutation-producing radiations in the environment do contribute significantly to longevity. In addition, of course, the pristine purity of the human genetic system and its bloodstream, with so few accumulated mutant genes, together with the primeval absence of disease-producing organisms (which only gradually developed, through the outworking of the curse) from the originally created beneficent microorganisms, served also to maintain life through great age-spans.

Although we have no exact figures, it is possible to make a reasonable guess as to how rapidly the total human population developed. Since, according to the record in Genesis 5, each named patriarch lived many hundreds of years and "begat sons and daughters," it is reasonable and very conservative to assume that each family had, on the average, at least six children—three sons and three daughters. If it is further assumed that, on the average, these children grew to maturity, married, and began to have children of their own by the time their parents were eighty years old, and that the parents lived through an average of five such "generations," or four hundred years, then it can easily be calculated that the earth had acquired within its first eight hundred years (presumably approximately the lifetime of Cain, as a minimum) a population of at least one hundred and twenty thousand. It is probable that the figure was much more than this, since people lived to greater ages than assumed and probably had many more children than assumed.

In order to get this process of multiplication started, of course, at least one of Adam's sons had to marry one of Adam's daughters. Probably, in that first generation, all marriages were brother-sister marriages. In that early time, there were no mutant genes in the genetic systems of any of these children, so that no genetic harm could have resulted from close marriages. Many, many generations later, during the time of Moses, such mutations had accumulated to the point where such unions were genetically dangerous, so that incest was thenceforth prohibited in the Mosaic laws.

The ancient quibble about "Cain's wife" is thus seen to be quite trivial. Long before Cain died, there was a large population in the earth. By the time of the Deluge, 1,656 years after Creation by the Ussher chronology, even using the above conservative assumptions, the world population would have been at least seven billion people!

Not only did the population increase, but the technological and cultural level, at least of the Canaanitic civilization, seems to have been very high. Metal tools and implements of all kinds were available to produce creature comforts, as well as musical instruments to stimulate the emotional and esthetic senses. Although these and other facets of civilization can be used for good purposes, they can easily become an end in themselves and can even be used as a means of further rebellion against God. The latter seems to have been their effect, and perhaps even their purpose, among the descendants of Cain.

Genesis 4:16, 17

---

16 ¶ And Cain went out from the presence of the LORD, and dwelt in the land of Nod, on the east of É′den.
17 And Cain knew his wife; and she conceived, and bare Enoch: and he builded a city, and called the name of the city, after the name of his son, Enoch.

As Cain "went out from the presence of the Lord," presumably from somewhere near the garden of Eden where he and Abel had brought their sacrifices, he left Eden altogether, journeying eastward to "the land of Nod." Since the word "Nod" means "wandering," it is possible that this was not an actual geographical region but merely a figure of speech for Cain's perpetual manner of life from that time on.

Since the next verse mentions a city that Cain built, however, it does seem more likely that he actually dwelled for a while in a land called Nod, where his wife (presumably a sister, as noted above) bore him his firstborn son, Enoch. The name probably means "dedication" or "commencement," probably signifying to Cain that he was here starting a different life altogether from the one he had known with his parents back in Eden.

The reference to the city which Cain built possibly suggests that he was trying to defy God's prophecy that he would be a wanderer in the earth. Whatever his intent, the Hebrew verb is indefinite—"was building"—probably suggesting that, though he may have started it, he did not finish it. He moved on after a little while, perhaps leaving his son Enoch, after whom the city was named, to complete the job and to begin the true Cainite civilization.

It is interesting that one of the identifying marks which evolutionary anthropologists use to denote the emergence of a "stone age" culture into a civilized society is the development of urbanization. According to the Bible, the first such "city" (no doubt small and simple to begin with) is the city built by Cain, in the very first generation after Adam. No long, million-year development here!

Genesis 4:18-22

---

18 And unto Enoch was born Ī'răd: and Ī'răd begat Mē-hū'jā-ĕl: and Mē-hū'jā-ĕl begat Mē-thū'sā-ĕl: and Mē-thū'sā-ĕl begat Lā'mĕch.

19 ¶ And Lā'mĕch took unto him two wives: the name of the one *was* Ā'dăh, and the name of the other Zĭl'läh.

20 And Ā'dăh bare Jā'băl: he was the father of such as dwell in tents, and *of* such as have cattle.

21 And his brother's name *was* Jubal: he was the father of all such as handle the harp and organ.

22 And Zĭl'läh, she also bare Tū'băl-cāin, an instructor of every artificer in brass and iron: and the sister of Tū'băl–cāin *was* Nā'à-màh.

Here are listed the main descendants of Cain: Enoch, Irad, Mehujael, Methusael, Lamech, with Lamech's three sons, Jabal, Jubal, and Tubal-cain. Apparently Irad, Mehujael, and Methusael are listed primarily because of their membership in the line leading to Lamech, the most illustrious of Cain's descendants, and possibly also because two of the names end with *el,* the name of God, a fact which perhaps indicates that even those in the line of Cain continued to believe in God, though they were disobedient to Him.

Authorities believe Irad means "townsman," Mehujael means "God gives life," and Methusael "God's man." These are doubtful, however. Lamech may mean "conqueror."

Lamech apparently was the man who led the Cainites into open rebellion against God. He began by defying God's ordained principle of monogamy (Genesis 2:23, 24), taking two wives, Adah and Zillah. This was in the seventh generation from Adam, the same as that of godly Enoch in the Sethitic line. These were presumably attractive women (Adah means "ornament" and Zillah means "shade") and it is probable that physical lust was a prime factor in Lamech's action.

There is nothing in Scripture to indicate by what means marriages were arranged or legalized in this period. Lamech was evidently a powerful and prosperous man and it is likely that both wives entered voluntarily into this union.

A further motive may have been in anticipation of the greater number of sons a bigamous arrangement could provide. There seems to have been no organized government in those days, with society functioning on a patriarchal basis. The larger the individual clan, therefore, the more wealth and power would probably accrue to it.

In any case, bigamy was clearly contrary to God's will. Nevertheless a number of sons were born, three of whom were especially notable in the development of antediluvian civilization. Jabal ("wanderer") invented the tent, thus enabling him to carry his home with him and develop a nomadic life style. He also developed formal systems for domesticating and commercially producing other animals besides Abel's sheep. The term "cattle" here includes camels and asses (Exodus 9:3) as well as kine, goats, and perhaps others. Possibly this suggests that his contemporaries were acquiring the habit of eating meat as well as fruits and herbs, and thus had disobeyed still another of God's primal commands (Genesis 1:29). Or perhaps it means simply that he was producing them commercially for other purposes: beasts of burden, milk, skins for clothing, and so forth.

Jubal ("sound") was of markedly different bent from his brother Jabal. He had an ear for music and favored the esthetic rather than the commercial. Nevertheless he was an inventive genius, originating both stringed and wind musical instruments. These quickly appealed to the sensual Cainites, and Jubal no doubt also profited financially from his inventions.

Their half-brother Tubal-cain was evidently the inventor of metallurgy, both in bronze and iron. The meaning of his name is uncertain, but does seem etymologically to be the progenitor of the name of the Roman god Vulcan. He is said to have been "a deviser of all kinds of objects of bronze and iron," so that his was a remarkable inventive genius. The "standard of living" of the antediluvians, especially the Cainitic branch, was elevated tremendously by these talented sons of Lamech. Tubal-cain also had a notable sister, Naamah ("pleasant").

Once again, it is significant to note that the elements which modern evolutionary archaeologists and anthropologists identify as the attributes of the emergence of evolving men from the stone age into true civilization—namely, urbanization, agriculture, animal domestication, and metallurgy—all were accomplished quickly by the early descendants of Adam and did not take hundreds of thousands of years.

Musical instruments, another important aspect of modern culture, were also an early development. All of these things, in addition, confirm the necessary coexistence of a written language for formal communications. This is further intimated by use of the word "book" in Genesis 5:1. More and more modern archaeological discoveries today are verifying the high degree of technology possessed by the earliest men, thus indirectly validating this Biblical testimony.

Genesis 4:23, 24

---

23 And Lā′mĕch said unto his wives, Ā′dah and Zĭl′lah, hear my voice; ye wives of Lā′mĕch, hearken unto my speech: for I have slain a man to my wounding, and a young man to my hurt. 24 If Cain shall be avenged sevenfold, truly Lā′mĕch seventy and sevenfold.

Civilization's attempt to thwart the effects of God's curse is illustrated by the Cainitic economy as follows: (1) urban life was preferred by many, instead of "tilling the ground"; (2) nomadic life was preferred by others, instead of the settled dwelling place required for agriculture; (3) cattle raising was inaugurated, probably because men had become meat eaters instead of being content with food grown from the earth; (4) metal working and tools were developed to ease the "toil" of the curse; (5) musical instruments were devised to mitigate the "sorrow"; (6) polygamy was introduced, instead of adhering to the monogamous form of marriage; (7) metallic weapons were invented, giving those who possessed them and were skilled in their use a great advantage over other men; (8) poetic boasting, as noted here in Lamech's song and as often characteristic of human poetry and writing, asserted man's self-sufficiency and independence of God.

Cities, with their community of interrelated activities and interests, technology, animal husbandry, music, poetry, and so forth—most of these things can legitimately be regarded as a proper response to God's primeval command to subdue the earth and exercise dominion over it, provided they are regarded in this light, with man as God's steward of them for the benefit of his fellow man and for the glory of God. Unfortunately, man's history indicates, rather, that he has cultivated them primarily in rebellion against God; and this was especially true of the antediluvian civilization.

Lamech, in particular, representing the seventh generation of mankind on the Cainitic side (as Enoch did on the Sethitic side), tragically reflects the developing spirit of his age. His character is revealed by this preserved fragment of a song he had composed (the first recorded poem in history) and sung to his two wives Adah and Zillah, boasting of his prowess in combat and his determination to visit mortal retribution on anyone presuming to oppose him (there is an ancient Jewish legend that Lamech actually slew his ancestor Cain, but this is only a legend with probably no factual basis).

Now that Lamech had the advantage of possessing the metal weapons forged by his clever son, he felt safe in such boasting, though it is interesting that his audience consisted merely of his two wives! Whether he was actually so fearsome in confrontation with other men is left to speculation.

The most noteworthy aspect of Lamech's poem is its blasphemous outburst against God. In punishing his ancestor Cain, God had nevertheless issued warning against killing Cain, stating that sevenfold punishment would overtake anyone doing so. But now Lamech says in effect: "Well, if God promises a sevenfold vengeance on anyone *killing* Cain, I myself guarantee a seventy-sevenfold retribution on anyone who even *hurts* me!"

There is an interesting reference to this in the New Testament, in the contrasting attitude enjoined on us by Christ, who told Peter that he should forgive his brother not just seven times, or even seventy-seven times, but seventy times seven! (Matthew 18:22).

During this period from the Fall to the Flood, there seems to have been no organized system of laws or government for controlling human conduct. Although Adam undoubtedly instructed his children concerning the curse, as well as God's promise of a coming Redeemer and the intermediate provision for approaching Him through blood sacrifice, there was no human agency ordained to enforce standards of behavior or worship.

There were undoubtedly some, especially in the direct line of patriarchs from Adam to Noah, who heeded Adam's counsel and thus believed and obeyed God's Word. Most people, however, were content to go "in the way of Cain" (Jude 11); and with the creature comforts and advantages accruing from the rapidly developing science and technology of the day, it was not long before "the wickedness of man was great in the earth" (Genesis 6:5). Each man and each clan did whatever they wanted to do, to the extent that their strength and skills permitted. There was nothing to restrain them except, in some cases, the superior strength and skill of others. Thus, it was demonstrated long ago that men cannot simply be left to their own devices; laws and governments are absolutely necessary. Consequently, after the Flood, God formally instituted systems of human government among men (Genesis 9:6).

There is also a possible suggestion in Lamech's poem that there were other men around trying to seduce Lamech's wives, or even trying to take them from him by force, and that Adah and Zillah were not too averse to such developments. This would explain why Lamech's threats were directed especially to the hearing of his wives. In any case, this suggestion of a growing sexual laxity among the Cainites is confirmed by the condition of general lust and promiscuity implied in Genesis 6:1-4 and Matthew 24:38.

Genesis 4:25, 26

25 ¶ And Adam knew his wife again; and she bare a son, and called his name Seth: For God, *said she,* hath appointed me another seed instead of Abel, whom Cain slew.

26 And to Seth, to him also there was born a son; and he called his name E'nŏs: then began men to call upon the name of the LORD.

There is a marked change of emphasis in the record of the descendants of Adam through Seth. No more do we read of human accomplishments and boasting, but, rather, of men "calling upon the name of the Lord." If the Cainites revealed the flowering of the Serpent's seed in the life of mankind, God was still maintaining the integrity of the promised Seed of the woman.

First, He appointed to Eve "another seed instead of Abel, whom Cain slew." The name Seth means "appointed" or "substituted," and indicates that Eve had faith that it was through this son that God's promises would eventually be fulfilled. It is interesting to note that in some cases (4:25) the mother selected the name, while in others (4:26) the father did so. This probably suggests that, in all cases, there was mutual consultation between husband and wife on this important decision.

Then, in the days of Enos (meaning "mortal frailty," an implicit testimony to Seth's awareness of man's deep spiritual need), the son of Seth, it is recorded that "men began to call upon the name of Jehovah." This phrase almost certainly signifies the beginning of regular public worship of the Lord, probably replacing the previous practice of individually meeting with Him as Cain and Abel did. Perhaps it also refers to the beginning of the practice of prayer, implying that God's immediate presence was no longer accessible.

In any case, it surely denotes an act of faith on the part of those who "called upon his name." In later times, and probably even at this time, it was accompanied by the building of an altar and the offering of a sacrifice (see Genesis 12:8; 13:4; 26:25; I Kings 18:23, 24; etc.). The name of Jehovah, representing all that He is and does, promising and providing salvation to all who trust His Word, was regarded later as unutterably sacred (Exodus 20:7; Leviticus 24:16).

Before Calvary, when God Himself provided one great sacrifice for sins forever, it was needful for men, as they called on His name, again and again to offer their sacrifices, shedding the blood on the altar as atonement for their souls (Leviticus 17:11). But *since* Calvary, men need only to call in faith on the name of Jesus Christ as Lord, for eternal salvation. For "whosoever shall call on the name of the Lord shall be saved" (Joel 2:32; Acts 2:21; Romans 10:13). Jesus is not only the Christ, but He is Himself the Lord, Jehovah, the eternal "I Am." He is the *Lord Jesus Christ!* "God . . . hath given him *the* name which is above every name . . . that every tongue should confess that Jesus Christ is Lord" (Philippians 2:9-11).

Some have suggested a contradiction between Genesis 4:26 and Exodus 6:3, when God spoke to Moses concerning his forefathers and said: "But by my name Jehovah was I not known to them," as though this was the first time He was revealing Himself by this particular name. This problem is easily resolved by inserting a question mark after the declaration. "By my name Jehovah was I not known to them?" Then this becomes a rhetorical question whose obvious answer is yes. Since Hebrew sentences were not punctuated directly, the proper emphasis and divisions must be supplied by the context; and this seems quite appropriate in this case. Certainly also the patriarchs knew the Lord in terms of the character implied by the name Jehovah (self-existing, eternal, unchangeable, revealer of Himself to men), whether or not the actual name they employed, in whatever language they spoke, was the specific name Jehovah; and they could and did call on His name as so revealed.

The Line of the Promised Seed

Although the authority of God continued to be recognized among the Sethites, they were members of a fallen race no less than the Cainites. In the first verse of Genesis 5, the writer recalls again that God created man "in the likeness of God." But then, in verse 3, he says that Adam "begat a son in *his* own likeness, after *his* image, and called his name Seth." Between Adam and Seth intervened the Fall. Though Adam was *created* in God's image, Seth was *begotten* in Adam's image; he therefore partook of the fallen nature of his father (note Romans 5:12-14).

Three facts seem to be emphasized in the record of the ten antediluvian patriarchs in Genesis 5: (1) God was preserving and recording the divinely ordained line of the promised Seed, with the appropriate genealogical and chronological data; (2) God's command to "be fruitful and multiply" was being carried out, since the record recites that each one in the line "begat sons and daughters"; (3) God's curse was also in effect, since in spite of the fact that each man lived many hundreds of years, eventually "he died."

This list of names and ages of the antediluvians, which may seem dull and monotonous at first, thus becomes meaningful and exciting on closer inspection. It is from this section, telling us that men once were able to live almost a thousand years, that we deduce something of the marvelous nature of the world's primeval environment. It also indicates that men were able to father children during most of their long lives (Enoch had a son at age sixty-five, for example, and Noah at age five hundred). There is no reason to think, of course, that the men whose names are listed were the *first* born sons of their fathers. Seth, the first in the list, was the third son of Adam; and Shem was possibly the second or third son of Noah (Genesis 10:21). The recorded names are those sons who turned out to be in the line of the promised Seed.

Genesis 5:1, 2

CHAPTER 5

THIS *is* the book of the generations of Adam. In the day that God created man, in the likeness of God made he him;

2 Male and female created he them; and blessed them, and called their name Adam, in the day when they were created.

This first verse of Genesis 5 marks one of the major divisions of Genesis. It is significant that it says: "This is the *book* of the generations of Adam." The record thus was *written,* not just transmitted orally. Quite possibly, Adam himself wrote the section (chapters 2, 3, 4) which concludes with this statement and signature of Adam. Similarly Noah (note Genesis 6:9) was the probable original author of Genesis 5:1b—6:9a).

It is interesting to note that the record of Cain's descendants stops with the deeds of Lamech, who was in the seventh generation from Adam. From the chronologies of Genesis 5, it is evident that Adam died during the lifetime of Enoch, who was also in the seventh generation from Adam. This suggests that Adam still kept up with Cain and his descendants as long as he lived, even though Cain had so severely alienated himself from his family. Likewise, there was apparently still some belief in his father's God, as noted before, in Cain's own line, until about this same time.

It is also interesting to note that, while Genesis 5:1 contains the first mention of "book" (or, one might say, "Bible") in the Old Testament, the first mention of "book" in the New Testament is in Matthew 1:1, "the *book* of the generation of Jesus Christ." Thus the *first* book tells of the origins of the first Adam; the *second* book speaks of the origins of the last Adam, who is "the Lord from heaven" (I Corinthians 15:47).

It is worth mentioning again that "Adam" and "man" both translate the same Hebrew word. Whether it is being used generically, of humanity as a whole, or of the single individual Adam himself, must be determined from the context. Thus, verse 2 should probably read: "Male and female created he them; and blessed them, and called their name *man* [rather than 'Adam'], in the day when they were created."

These verses obviously refer to Genesis 1:26-28. The reason for this is clearly to tie this new section back to the first record. The first was the *toledoth* of "the heavens and the earth" (2:4), the "book of the *toledoth* of Adam" (5:1) has just been completed, and now, much later, "the *toledoth* of Noah" (6:9) is beginning to be inscribed. It was necessary for Noah's record to be identified with both of the others, as a continuation of the "official" history of the human race and specially of the line of promise. Furthermore, this brief summary then makes this section a complete record of the antediluvian patriarchs, from the date of Creation down to the birth of Shem, Ham, and Japheth. It therefore provides the chronological framework of history from Creation to the Flood.

Genesis 5:3-5

3 ¶ And Adam lived a hundred and thirty years, and begat *a son* in his own likeness, after his image; and called his name Seth:

4 And the days of Adam after he had begotten Seth were eight hundred years: and he begat sons and daughters:

5 And all the days that Adam lived were nine hundred and thirty years: and he died.

Genesis 5:5 gives Adam's obituary announcement, fulfilling the physical aspect of the death sentence pronounced on him in Genesis 3:19 and assuring all of humanity that "the wages of sin is death" (Romans 6:23). Before he died, however, he lived to the great age of 930 years, and "begat sons and daughters," probably many of each.

These latter were, it is intimated, born after Seth; and Seth was born when Adam was already 130 years old. It does seem strange that such a long period of Adam's life had elapsed before Eve began to bear other children than Cain and Abel. It may be that God deliberately withheld the "fruit of the womb" from Eve for such a long time in order to enable them to overcome their grief over the tragedy of Abel and to strengthen their life of prayer and faith (as He later did in the case of Abraham and Sarah).

It is also possible that they did have other children before Seth, but he was the one whom God revealed would be the true substitute for Abel, the son whose seed would inherit the promises. This possibility would make the previous story of Cain's exile, his wife, and his city a bit more understandable in terms of the chronology involved.

Genesis 5:6-20

---

6 And Seth lived a hundred and five years, and begat É'nŏs:
7 And Seth lived after he begat É'nŏs eight hundred and seven years, and begat sons and daughters:
8 And all the days of Seth were nine hundred and twelve years: and he died.
9 ¶ And É'nŏs lived ninety years, and begat Cā-i'năn:
10 And É'nŏs lived after he begat Cā-i'năn eight hundred and fifteen years, and begat sons and daughters:
11 And all the days of É'nŏs were nine hundred and five years: and he died.
12 ¶ And Cā-i'năn lived seventy years, and begat Mà-hā'là-lē'ĕl:
13 And Cā-i'năn lived after he begat Mà-hā'là-lē'ĕl eight hundred and forty years, and begat sons and daughters:

14 And all the days of Cā-i'năn were nine hundred and ten years: and he died.
15 ¶ And Mà-hā'là-lē'ĕl lived sixty and five years, and begat Jā'rĕd:
16 And Mà-hā'là-lē'ĕl lived after he begat Jā'rĕd eight hundred and thirty years, and begat sons and daughters:
17 And all the days of Mà-hā'là-lē'ĕl were eight hundred ninety and five years: and he died.
18 ¶ And Jā'rĕd lived a hundred sixty and two years, and he begat Enoch:
19 And Jā'rĕd lived after he begat Enoch eight hundred years, and begat sons and daughters:
20 And all the days of Jā'rĕd were nine hundred sixty and two years: and he died.

Here begins the long cyclic recital of the antediluvian patriarchs: their names, their ages at the birth of those sons who were in the line of promise, the fact that they each had sons and daughters, and finally their ages at death. In all, there were ten of the these patriarchs in the lineage, from Adam through Noah. The data are summarized in the following table.

Patriarch	Year of Birth	Age at Birth of Next Patriarch	Year of Death
Adam	1	130	930
Seth	130	105	1042
Enos	235	90	1140
Cainan	325	70	1235
Mahalaleel	395	65	1290
Zared	460	162	1422
Enoch	622	65	987*
Methuselah	687	187	1656**
Lamech	874	182	1651
Noah	1056	500	2006

* Enoch did not die, but was translated.
** Methuselah died in the very year that the Flood came.

There is no reason to think there are any "gaps" in this record, or that the years are anything other than normal years (except for the quizzical possibility that the original year was 360 days long, instead of the present 365¼). The record is perfectly natural and straightforward and is obviously intended to give both the necessary genealogical data to denote the promised lineage and also the only reliable chronological framework we have for the antediluvian period of history.

Assuming no gaps in these genealogies (a possibility which perhaps cannot be ruled out completely, but for which there is certainly no internal evidence), there was a total of 1,656 years from the Creation to the Flood. The recorded ages are somewhat larger in the Septuagint and certain other ancient versions, but most scholars believe these have been somewhat artificially elongated and that the Massoretic text preserves the original numbers.

Taking the recorded ages at face value, it is interesting to note that Adam lived until Lamech, the father of Noah, was fifty-six years old, and Noah was born only fourteen years after the death of Seth. Most likely, the oldest of the living patriarchs maintained the primary responsibility for preserving and promulgating God's Word to his contemporaries. Since both Enoch and Lamech were outlived by their fathers, there were only seven men in the line before Noah who had this responsibility. This probably explains why, in II Peter 2:5, Noah is called "eighth preacher of righteousness" in the "old world."

Occasionally critics have noted certain similarities in the names of the respective descendants of Cain and Seth, and have claimed that the two lists are therefore corrupted remnants of one original list. Such a suggestion is, of course, entirely out of order and is baldly arbitrary.

The few similarities that exist can probably be explained by the occasional contacts that the two branches of the family must have maintained with each other, and the common tendency to give children names associated with either relatives or notable events or circumstances.

The meaning of the names is somewhat obscure, but may be roughly as follows:

Seth .... "Appointed one"

Enos .... "Mortal frailty"

Cainan .... "Smith"

Mahalaleel .... "God be praised"

Jared .... "Descent"

Enoch .... "Dedication"

Methuselah .... "When he dies, judgment"

Lamech .... "Conqueror"

Noah .... "Rest"

We have already commented on the longevity of these patriarchs (averaging 912 years, except for Enoch) and possible physical reasons for it. Many writers have noted that life spans begin a slow and steady decline after the Flood, showing evidently that they were connected with the antediluvian climatological and environmental conditions. There is a partial confirmation of this condition in the well-known Babylonian list of its first ten kings as quoted by Eusebius from the Greek historian Herodotus. However, the actual ages so listed are quite astounding, running up to sixty-five thousand years each!

All in all, there is no reason whatever not to take this list in Genesis 5 as sober history in every way. The names are, of course, repeated in I Chronicles 1:1-4 and Luke 3:36-38. This confirms that they were accepted as historical by the later Biblical writers, of both Old and New Testaments.

The Amazing Case of Enoch

Just as the record of Genesis 4 gives a most striking insight into the evil character of Lamech, so the record of Genesis 5 gives a brief, but most illuminating, insight into the godly character of his contemporary, Enoch. Enoch, the seventh from Adam in Seth's line, had the same name as Cain's son. Lamech, the seventh from Adam in Cain's line, had the same name as Noah's father. But their characters were utterly different.

Enoch "walked with God" and was a prophet of God. As such,

he preached against the godlessness of his generation in fearsome, thundering words: "Behold the Lord cometh with ten thousands of his saints [or 'his holy myriads'] to execute judgment upon all, and to convince all that are ungodly among them of all their ungodly deeds which they have ungodly committed, and of all their hard speeches which ungodly sinners have spoken against him" (Jude 14, 15). It almost seems as though, when he spoke these words, Enoch had Lamech particularly in mind. This fragment probably also represents, of course, the essential content of all his prophetic burden against the blasphemous wickedness of the men of his generation.

It is remarkable that Enoch would prophesy of what we now recognize as the *second* coming of Christ even before the Flood, but this is clearly the meaning placed on it by Jude. Actually, it may be considered as an amplification and exposition of the great prophecy of Genesis 3:15, the promise of the eventual crushing of the serpent, Satan, and his seed. God "left not himself without witness," even in the days of the antediluvians. The promised "coming" in judgment had a preliminary and precursory fulfillment in the great Flood, but its final fulfillment awaits the glorious return and triumph of the Lord Jesus Christ.

The quotation in Jude seems to have been taken from one of three apocryphal books purportedly written by Enoch, but actually dating from about the first century before Christ. These books contain much interesting material and, although most of it is surely fictional, it is probable that some actual traditions of Enoch's prophecies may have been handed down in the same manner as other records which eventually reached Moses and others. At least Jude, by divine inspiration, incorporated this particular fragment as of true Enochian authorship.

Genesis 5:21-24

---

21 ¶ And Enoch lived sixty and five years, and begat Mē-thū'sē-làh:
22 And Enoch walked with God after he begat Mē-thū'sē-làh three hundred years, and begat sons and daughters:

23 And all the days of Enoch were three hundred sixty and five years:
24 And Enoch walked with God: and he *was* not; for God took him.

Enoch's "walk" with God was probably not literal in the sense in which Adam had walked with Him in the garden before the Fall. Enoch shared the fallen nature of all men and thus could not physically even "look upon God and live," unless God chose to veil His glory in theophanic revelation, as He later did on occasion to Abraham and Moses. In any case, "by faith" (Hebrews 11:5), in prayer and by obedience to His Word, Enoch maintained close fellowship and communion with God, a privilege equally possible to us today (Colossians 2:6; Galatians 5:25; II Corinthians 5:7). It is important to note that his walk with God was not such a mystical, pietistic experience as to preclude an effective family life or a strong and vocal opposition to the unbelief and wickedness of his day.

The climax of Enoch's testimony was an event all but unique in history. "By faith Enoch was translated that he should not see death, and was not found, because God had translated him" (Hebrews 11:5). This is the inspired interpretation of the phrase here in Genesis: "he was not, for God took him." Somehow, in actual physical flesh Enoch was supernaturally carried up into heaven, where presumably he still is today.

Nearly twenty-five centuries later, another prophet, Elijah, was similarly taken into heaven without dying (II Kings 2:11). It is significant that Enoch prophesied about midway between Adam and Abraham, and Elijah about midway between Abraham and Christ, and that both ministered in times of deep apostasy.

The translation of these two saints is perhaps a type of the promised translation of those who are alive and trusting in Christ when He returns in the time of the end (I Thessalonians 4:16, 17). However, the two events are not strictly parallel, since the "rapture" of the saints is to be simultaneous with resurrection and glorification; and such an experience was impossible prior to the resurrection and glorification of Christ (I Corinthians 15:22, 23, 51-53).

It is not said of Enoch, as it was said of all these other patriarchs, that "he died." Twice it is mentioned that he "walked with God," the repetition being for the purpose of explaining God's unique way of dealing with Enoch. God "took him," not in death, but in life, showing clearly even to the antediluvians that life continues beyond this present existence. The question of *where* God took him is not answered at this point, but it must have been to wherever God's presence was. Though some think the concept is crass literalism, Enoch's bodily presence (as well as, later, that of Elijah and then of the resurrected Christ) in some location in the physical heavens seems to be the only conclusion consistent with all the Biblical data on the subject. The Lord Jesus is now preparing a *place* for us (John 14:3), and someday the new Jerusalem will "come down, out of heaven" (Revelation 21:2) to the earth (and the earth, though made new, can be nothing else than this planet). Evidently there is, and always has been since creation, a real, physical place somewhere out there in the heavens, where God's temple and personal presence are centered.

One intriguing possibility to consider is that Enoch and Elijah may have been taken into heaven without dying because of a further ministry God has for them in the future—namely, that of serving as God's "two witnesses" during the coming Tribulation Period. These witnesses are also identified as the "two anointed ones, that stand by the Lord of the whole earth" in Zechariah 4:14. These anointed ones, these witnesses, are real men, not angels, as is evident from the fact that they are to be slain when they have "finished their testimony," and then resurrected (Revelation 11:7-12) and translated. But if they are men in the flesh and yet were "standing by" the Lord in the days of Zechariah, they must have been born in the world sometime before Zechariah's day. Somehow they must have been preserved against death, in heaven, for many centuries. So far as we can judge from Scripture, only Enoch and Elijah could meet such specifications.

Some have supposed that Moses and Elijah will be the two witnesses (representing "the law and the prophets"), since they were together with Christ on the Mount of Transfiguration (Matthew 17:1-4). It is very unlikely that one of these could be Moses, however, since Moses died once, and "it is appointed unto men *once* to die" (Hebrews 9:27). Enoch and Elijah have not yet died and Elijah, at least, is definitely scheduled to return to the earth to preach again (Malachi 4:5, 6; Matthew 17:11).

Some, of course, have actually died more than once (e.g., Lazarus, Dorcas); but in each of these cases, they were restored miraculously back to physical life for a season. Scripture nowhere claims this to be true of Moses, although since God Himself buried Moses (Deuteronomy 34:5, 6) and since the archangel Michael is said to have engaged in some sort of conflict with Satan about the disposition of Moses' body (Jude 9), it is perhaps possible that Moses may actually have been raised in the flesh and taken into heaven like Enoch and Elijah. This is a very tenuous supposition, however; and it is strange that, if such a thing actually happened, Scripture does not make plainer mention of it.

If Moses actually appeared in the flesh on the Mount of Transfiguration with Elijah, of course, such a resuscitation of his body must be considered a good possibility. On the other hand, that particular appearance probably was not an actual physical phenomenon, since it was plainly stated by Christ to have been a "vision" (Matthew 17:9). It was, of course, appropriate for this vision to have been of Moses and Elijah, since the purpose had to do with the Jewish Messianic kingdom of Christ and the accomplishment of "his decease at Jerusalem" (Luke 9:31). Moses and Elijah were both ministers of God in the Jewish dispensation; whereas Enoch had, of course, far antedated that period. The Tribulation Period, however, will be both the "time of Jacob's trouble" (Jeremiah 30:7) and the time of judgment of the Gentile nations; so it would likewise be more appropriate for God's two witnesses in that day to preach to both Israel and the world as a whole, as Elijah and Enoch could appropriately do.

There may even be a possibility that these same "two witnesses" were the "two men" who were "standing by" (Luke 24:4; Acts 1:10) at both the resurrection and ascension of Christ. This would correlate with the ministry of the two "anointed ones" who "stand by" the Lord (Zechariah 4:14). The fact that John calls them "angels" (John 20:12) could perhaps be explained in that case by the fact that the word "angel" simply means *messenger* and is occasionally used with reference to men (Revelation 2:1; etc.).

In any case, it does seem probable that Enoch, the amazing prophet of the antediluvian age, will yet finish his ministry of witness to a godless generation, which was once cut short by his sudden translation while he walked with God.

Genesis 5:25-27

---

25 And Mē-thū'sē-làh lived a hundred eighty and seven years, and begat Lā'mĕch:
26 And Mē-thū'sē-làh lived after he begat Lā'mĕch seven hundred eighty and two years, and begat sons and daughters:
27 And all the days of Mē-thū'sē-làh were nine hundred sixty and nine years: and he died.

A further intriguing aspect of Enoch's prophetic ministry is suggested by the name of his son Methuselah, born when Enoch was sixty-five years old (that the long ages of the patriarchs were measured in true years and not in months, as some have suggested, is obvious from the implication that such an interpretation would have made Enoch only five years old when his son was born!).

The meaning of this name is doubtful, though many scholars have said it means "man of the spear." Such a name as this, however, would hardly have been in character for Enoch to select as a name for his favorite son.

Many ancient and modern commentators have interpreted the name

Methuselah as meaning "When he dies, it shall be sent." If this suggestion is correct (and there is at least a possible basis for it), then a justifiable inference is that Enoch, the prophet of coming judgment, had received—at the time of the birth of this son—a special revelation concerning the coming judgment of the great Flood. God, however, p.omised him that it would not come as long as Methuselah lived; and Enoch gave him a name to commemorate that prophetic warning and promise. This may possibly be the significance of the fact that Methuselah lived longer (969 years) than any other man in history whose age was recorded. "God is long-suffering to usward, not willing that any should perish, but that all should come to repentance" (II Peter 3:9). As He is long-suffering toward godless men today, so He was long ago, "when once the long-suffering of God waited in the days of Noah, while the ark was a preparing" (I Peter 3:20).

Genesis 5:28-32

28 ¶ And Lā'mĕeh lived a hundred eighty and two years, and begat a son: 29 And he called his name Noah, saying, This *same* shall comfort us concerning our work and toil of our hands, because of the ground which the LORD hath cursed. 30 And Lā'mĕeh lived after he begat Noah five hundred ninety and five years, and begat sons and daughters: 31 And all the days of Lā'mĕeh were seven hundred seventy and seven years: and he died. 32 And Noah was five hundred years old: and Noah begat Shĕm, Ham, and Jā'phĕth.

Methuselah's son Lamech, like his grandfather Enoch, was a prophet of God (prophesying at least concerning his own son Noah). These are the only two antediluvian patriarchs from whom portions of their actual prophecies have been recorded in Scripture. It is also interesting that these are the only two antediluvian patriarchs who were outlived by their own fathers (Enoch was translated 435 years before Jared's death, and Methuselah outlived Lamech by five years).

For some reason also, Enoch and Lamech are the only two whose names had already been given to certain of their distant relatives in the ungodly line of Cain. It is probable that the Cainite Enoch and Lamech were both living when the Sethite Enoch and Lamech were born. One wonders whether the latter may even have been named after the former—possibly in the hope that this gesture of family affection might be a testimony which would lead them back to God. On the other hand, they may simply have been common names in the population of that day.

The antediluvian line culminates in Noah (whose name means "rest") and his three sons, Shem, Ham, and Japheth. At Noah's birth, his father Lamech prophesied of a coming time when the curse would be removed, indicating that the memory of Creation and the Fall was still fresh in the minds of at least those who had received and believed the records transmitted to them from Adam. This is strong evidence that there cannot be any large "gaps" in the genealogies of Genesis 5. It is impossible to harmonize this record with the evolutionary speculations placing man's origin at several million years ago.

Lamech (as well as Adam, Abel, and Enoch) was undoubtedly one of those in Peter's mind when he spoke of "the times of restitution [or 'restoration'] of all things, which God hath spoken by the mouth of all his holy prophets since the world began" (Acts 3:21). Noah, as the one who would by his ark preserve life as the cursed earth was being "cleansed" by the waters of the Flood, was only a precursory fulfillment of Lamech's prophecy, of course. The promised Seed was still future, but in Him and His promised coming were true "rest" and "comfort."

Lamech, like all the other patriarchs, "begat sons and daughters" in addition to Noah. It seems probable that these brothers and sisters of Noah must have perished in the Flood. Moreover, there must have been many others in the Sethite line that also perished, since it could hardly have been only the Cainites who had begun "to multiply on the earth" (Genesis 6:1). Thus, the wickedness and corruption which had become rampant had affected both branches of the human family by this time, except probably for the godly remnant in the direct line from Enoch to Noah.

It may even have affected Noah's family, though of this we cannot be sure. We are told only of his three sons who survived the Flood; but it seems rather likely that he also, like the others, "begat sons and daughters," particularly since the five-hundred-year age at which Shem, Ham, and Japheth began to be born is more than three hundred years older than the age at which any of the other named members of the patriarchal line were born. The reason for mentioning three sons by name (rather than only Shem, the next in the prophetic lineage) is that these were the ones in his family who elected to go with him into the Ark and who would, therefore, become the progenitors of the post-Flood nations.

There is no need to suppose, of course, that Shem, Ham, and Japheth were triplets, but only that Noah was five hundred years old before any of them were born. That five-hundred-year period, plus the one-hundred-year period from that time until the Flood, must have been a time of trauma and grief for godly Noah. The world was rapidly becoming unimaginably wicked and violent, and evidently his faithful preaching and witnessing seemed futile. Whether or not he saw some of his own children engulfed in this morass of evil, there is little doubt that he saw it overwhelm his brothers and sisters and other loved ones. He must often have longed and prayed that the God with whom he, like Enoch, "walked" would intervene before the entire world succumbed.

7

The Days of Noah

(Genesis 6)

The Sons of God

The first age of human history was brought to its climax and cul-
mination in the days of Noah. The sin-disease, which began so innocu-
ously when Eve was tempted to doubt the word of God, which then
began to show its true ugliness of character in the life of Cain, which
came to maturity in the godless civilization developed by his descendants,
finally descended into such a terrible morass of wickedness and corruption that only a global bath of water from the windows of heaven
could purge and cleanse the fevered earth. The characteristics of those
awful and tragic days, strange as they may seem to our enlightened
culture today, are nevertheless to be repeated in the last days of this
present age. It is urgently important, from the standpoint of both understanding past history and seeking guidance for the future, that we
understand the events which took place in the days of Noah.

Two days before Christ's crucifixion, His disciples asked Him, "What
shall be the sign of thy coming, and of the end of the age?" (Matthew
24:3). His reply pointed to a number of "signs," all of which occurring
together in *that* generation (that is, the generation which would see
the signs), would be *the* sign they had requested. These signs were
climaxed with the prophetic warning, "But as the days of Noe were,
so shall also the coming of the Son of Man be. For as in the days
that were before the flood, they were eating and drinking, marrying

163

and giving in marriage, until the day that Noe entered into the Ark, And knew not until the flood came and took them all away; so shall also the coming of the Son of Man be" (Matthew 24:37-39). Thus did Jesus not only verify the historicity of the great Flood but also encourage us to study closely the characteristics of the days before the Flood, for these would also characterize the days just before His return.

Genesis 6:1, 2

CHAPTER 6

AND it came to pass, when men began to multiply on the face of the earth, and daughters were born unto them,

2 That the sons of God saw the daughters of men that they *were* fair; and they took them wives of all which they chose.

Moral and spiritual conditions in the antediluvian world had deteriorated with the passing years, not only among the Cainites but eventually among the Sethites as well. Materialism and ungodliness abounded, except for the small remnant connected with the line of the promised Seed, along with those few who may have been influenced by the witness of such men as Enoch.

Then, in the days of Noah, a strange and terrible event took place, leading rapidly to such a tidal wave of violence and wickedness over the earth that there was no longer any remedy but utter destruction. The "sons of God" saw the "daughters of men" and took them as their wives, the children of such unions being "giants in the earth," mighty men of renown, monsters not only in size but also in wickedness (Genesis 6:1, 2, 4).

One's first reaction to this passage (and the standard interpretation of the liberals) is to think of the fairy tales of antiquity, the legends of ogres and dragons, and the myths of the gods consorting with men—and then to dismiss the entire story as legend and superstition.

On the other hand, modern Christians have often attempted to make the story more palatable intellectually by explaining the "sons of God" as Sethites and the "daughters of men" as Cainites, with their union representing the breaking down of the wall of separation between believers and unbelievers. Another possible interpretation which avoids supernaturalistic implications is that the phrase "sons of God" referred to kings and nobles, in which case the commingling so described is merely an account of royalty marrying commoners.

Neither of these naturalistic interpretations, however, explain why the progeny of such unions would be "giants" or why they would lead to universal corruption and violence. Although Scripture does teach that believers should not wed unbelievers (II Corinthians 6:14; I Corinthians 7:39), there is no intimation that this particular sin is unforgivable or more productive of general moral deterioration than other sins. Regardless of intellectual difficulties, it does seem clear that something beyond the normal and natural is described here in these verses.

The interpretation of the passage obviously turns on the meaning of the phrase "sons of God" *(bene elohim)*. In the New Testament, of course, this term is used with reference to all who have been born again through personal faith in Christ (John 1:12; Romans 8:14; etc.), and the concept of the spiritual relationship of believers to God as analogous to that of children to a father is also found in the Old Testament (Psalm 73:15; Hosea 1:10; Deuteronomy 32:5; Exodus 4:22; Isaiah 43:6). Not one of these examples, however, uses the same phrase as Genesis 6:2, 4; furthermore, in each case the meaning is not really parallel to the meaning here in Genesis. Neither the descendants of Seth nor true believers of any sort have been previously referred to in Genesis as sons of God in any kind of spiritual sense and, except for Adam himself, they could not have been sons of God in a physical sense. In context, such a meaning would be strained, to say the least, in the absence of any kind of explanation. The only obvious and natural meaning without such clarification is that these beings were sons of God, rather than of men, because they had been created, not born. Such a description, of course, would apply only to Adam (Luke 3:38) and to the angels, whom God had directly created (Psalm 148:2, 5; Psalm 104:4; Colossians 1:16).

The actual phrase *bene elohim* is used three other times, all in the very ancient book of Job (1:6; 2:1; 38:7). There is no doubt at all that, in these passages, the meaning applies exclusively to the angels. A very similar form *(bar elohim)* is used in Daniel 3:25, and also refers either to an angel or to a theophany. The term "sons of the mighty" *(bene elim)* is used in Psalm 29:1 and also Psalm 89:6, and again refers to angels. Thus, there seems no reasonable doubt that, in so far as the language itself is concerned, the intent of the writer was to convey the thought of angels—fallen angels, no doubt, since they were acting in opposition to God's will. This also was the meaning placed on the passage by the Greek translators of the Septuagint, by Josephus, by the writer of the ancient apocryphal book of Enoch, and by all the other ancient Jewish interpreters and the earliest Christian writers.

Apparently the first Christian writers to suggest the Sethite interpretation were Chrysostom and Augustine.

The reason for questioning this obvious meaning, in addition to the supernaturalistic overtones, is (for those who do not reject the idea of angels) the opinion that it would be impossible for angels to have sexual relations with human women and to father children by them. However, this objection presupposes more about angelic abilities than we know. Whenever angels have appeared visibly to men, as recorded in the Bible, they have appeared in the physical bodies of men. Those who met with Abraham, for example, actually *ate* with him (Genesis 18:8) and, later, appeared to the inhabitants of Sodom in such perfectly manlike shape that the Sodomites were attempting to take these "men" for homosexual purposes. The writer of Hebrews suggests that, on various occasions, some "have entertained angels unawares" (Hebrews 13:2).

It is true that the Lord Jesus said that "'in the resurrection they neither marry, nor are given in marriage, but are as the angels of God in heaven" (Matthew 22:30). However, this is not equivalent to saying that angels are "sexless," since people who share in the resurrection will surely retain their own personal identity, whether male or female. Furthermore, angels are always described, when they appear, as "men," and the pronoun "he" is always used in reference to them. Somehow they have been given by God the capacity of materializing themselves in masculine human form when occasion warrants, even though their bodies are not under the control of the gravitational and electromagnetic forces which limit our own bodies in this present life.

When Jesus said that the angels of God *in heaven* do not marry, this does not necessarily mean that those who have been cast *out of heaven* were incapable of doing so. It clearly was not God's will or intention that angels mix in such a way with human women, but these wicked angels were not concerned with obedience to God's will. In fact, it was probably precisely for the purpose of attempting to thwart God's will that this particular battalion of the "sons of God" engaged in this illegal invasion of the bodies of the daughters of men.

Satan had not forgotten God's prophecy that a promised Seed of the woman would one day destroy him. He had implanted his own spiritual seed in Cain and his descendants, but God had preserved the line of the true Seed through Seth. When Noah was born and Lamech was led to prophesy that "comfort" concerning the Curse would come through him (Genesis 5:29), Satan and his angels must have feared that their opportunities for victory in this cosmic conflict were in imminent danger. Desiring reinforcements for a coming battle against the hosts of heaven, and also desiring, if possible, to completely corrupt mankind before the promised Seed could accomplish Satan's defeat, they seem to have decided to utilize the marvelous power of procreation which God had given the human family and to corrupt it to their own ends. Men now were rapidly multiplying on the earth and by implanting their own "seed" in humanity, they might be able to enlist in only one generation a vast multitude as allies against God. So these "sons of God" saw the daughters of men and "took them wives [or, literally, 'women'] of all which they chose."

Some commentators have said that, since the phrase "took them wives" is the same phrase as normally used throughout the Old Testament for "taking a wife," there can be nothing involved here other than normal human marriage. Therefore, they argue, these "sons of God" must be merely male believers in the Sethite line who married good-looking women of the Cainite (or other) line with no regard to whether or not they were true believers in God. This argument, however, is weak and is hardly sufficient to overthrow the heavy weight of evidence otherwise. The word used for "wife" (Hebrew *ishah*) is commonly also used for "woman," regardless of whether or not she was a married woman. The word for "take" (Hebrew *laqach*) is a very common verb, and can have any noun as its object. Shechem, for example, "took" Dinah and lay with her, though he was not married to her (Genesis 34:2).

The fact that these creatures could take whatever women they chose further suggests a general state of profligacy which made indiscriminate sexual unions quite commonplace. This is also suggested by Christ's descriptive phrase "marrying and giving [out] in marriage" (Matthew 24:38) as characteristic of the careless attitudes of the days of Noah.

If, for the sake of argument at least, we assume that the *bene elohim* were, indeed, angels, and that angels can assume such a total human form that they actually have male reproductive systems, then a grave question would have to be posed relative to the nature of the progeny that would result from their sexual intercourse with human women. The identity of the "giants" is discussed further below, but the seriousness of this problem does have a bearing on how we should interpret these unions. Fallen angels have no possibility of salvation, but fallen men and women do have at least this possibility. What, then, would be the case with "people" who were half-angel, half-men?

This seems to be such a grotesque situation that it does appear extremely doubtful that God would have allowed it at all, even if it really were physiologically a realistic possibility. And yet, as already indicated, it does violence to the actual text of the passage if we make it mean merely that the sons of Seth began to marry the daughters of Cain. (If this were what it meant, why did not the writer simply say so, and thus avoid all this confusion?) And why the giants, and why the universal violence?

The sons of Seth were surely not all godly men; so why should they be called sons of God (remember, they all perished in the Flood)? Furthermore, Adam had many sons in addition to Cain and Seth; were they spiritual "sons of God," too? Not very likely, at this period of history. Furthermore, why stress only the union of godly men with ungodly women? What about the "daughters of God"? Were they being married to "sons of men"?

This naturalistic interpretation is so forced and awkward that it seems to do disservice to the doctrine of divine inspiration to suppose that this is really what the writer meant to say. He surely *meant* to convey to his readers the idea that, in these days of Noah, such an awful irruption of abnormality and wickedness burst forth on the earth that it could only be explained by a demoniacally supernatural cause.

Rationalistic exegetes, of course, do accept the plain meaning of the text here and agree that it speaks of angel cohabiting with human women. Then, being rationalists, they maintain that since this sort of thing is impossible, the writer of Genesis was simply drawing on the myths and legends of demigods in various religious traditions.

On the other hand, is it not possible that the Bible has the true record and these various legends of giants and demigods represent the distortions that had accrued through long centuries of verbal transmission of the tales in cultures removed from the true patriarchal transmission line?

It is significant that the Septuagint renders the phrase "sons of God" as "angels of God." This was the Old Testament version in dominant use in the Apostolic period, and thus this would be the way the phrase would have been read by Christ and His apostles. The apocryphal book of Enoch was extant then, as well, and was apparently known to the New Testament writers (Jude 14); and it intensely elaborated this angelic interpretation. As an apparent result of these facts, this interpretation is strongly implied, and probably required (as noted below) by three New Testament passages: Jude 6; II Peter 2:4-6; I Peter 3:19, 20.

Admittedly, however, there is a grave difficulty in the idea of angel-human sexual unions, not only the question of whether such a thing is possible, but even more in the theologically paradoxical and grotesque nature of the progeny of such unions. Is there any way to resolve this dilemma?

A solution seems to consist in recognizing that the children were true human children of truly human fathers and mothers, but that all were possessed and controlled by evil spirits. That is, these fallen angelic "sons of God" accomplished their purposes by something equivalent to demon possession, indwelling the bodies of human men, and then also taking (or "possessing") the bodies of the women as well. The men whose bodies they possessed were evidently thereby made so attractive to the careless and rebellious women of the age that they could take over and use any of the women they chose. The seductive beauty of the women, probably enhanced by various artificial cosmetics and allurements developed by that time, was itself sufficient to induce men to constant obsession with sex, assuring a maximum rapidity of multiplication of the population. Thus, the "sons of God" controlled not only the men whose bodies they had acquired for their own exploitation, but also the women they took to themselves in this way, and then all the children they bore.

These particular Satanic angels, therefore, compounded their original sin in following Satan in his rebellion against God by now leaving "their own habitation" and keeping not their "first estate" (literally, "principality"), "going after strange flesh" as later did the Sodomites "in like manner" (Jude 6, 7). Therefore, God no longer allows them to roam about the earth like other demons, but has confined them "in everlasting chains under darkness unto the judgment of the great day," casting them down to a special "hell" (literally, "Tartarus," not the ordinary place of departed spirits) where they are "to be reserved unto judgment" (II Peter 2:4).

This fearful phenomenon of demonic "taking" and "habitation" of human bodies has often been repeated since, though apparently never yet on the global scale which Satan attempted in the days of Noah. Many such cases of demon possession are noted in the New Testament, and missionaries still testify to its common occurrence in heathen lands today. Even in modern "Christian lands" where the influence of the gospel has until now kept it to a minimum, this form of Satanic activity is evidently rapidly increasing. Spiritism, witchcraft, and other forms of occult belief and practice—even Satanism itself—are captivating the minds and bodies of multitudes today, specially among young people.

A closely related phenomenon is the tremendous recent upsurge of interest in the "host of heaven"—in terms of astrology, the so-called chariots of the gods, the various unidentified flying objects, and their strange occupants. Although scientists quite properly have pointed out the fallacious assumptions and interpretations involved in these, there remains a stubborn residuum of scientifically inexplicable, yet apparently well-verified, phenomena attached to these highly unusual types of data.

It should not be forgotten that there do exist "principalities and powers, rulers of the darkness of this world, spiritual wickedness in the heavenly places" (Ephesians 6:12) and that Satan is "the prince of the power of the air" (Ephesians 2:2). Evil angels, as well as God's unfallen holy angels, apparently on certain occasions have the ability both to appear in material forms of various sorts (even as "ministers of righteousness"—II Corinthians 11:15) and also to inhabit and control the bodies of human beings. Furthermore, Jesus warned that, in the last days, "fearful sights and great signs shall there be from heaven" (Luke 21:11). It may be that this particular feature of the days of Noah is beginning to be repeated in the modern proliferation of this great complex of unexplained and spiritually intimidating occult phenomena, the purpose of which seems to be to gain direct Satanic control over the minds and bodies of hosts of human beings before Christ returns.

Genesis 6:3

---

3 And the LORD said, My Spirit shall not always strive with man, for that he also *is* flesh: yet his days shall be a hundred and twenty years.

This has been another difficult verse, subject to varying interpretations. When God said, "My spirit shall not always strive with man," there is a question as to whether He meant the Holy Spirit or the spirit which He had breathed into man's body, and also whether He meant mankind in general or Adam in particular (the word "man" is Adam, and Adam himself may still have been alive when God spoke those words, perhaps in the days of Enoch). The reference to "one hundred and twenty years" has been understood by some to refer to man's future longevity and by others as the time yet remaining before the coming of the Flood, in addition to the interpretation that this was simply the time remaining before Adam's death.

It does appear that the most natural reading of the passages refers to God's Holy Spirit in His ministry of "convincing the world of sin, and of righteousness, and of judgment" (John 16:8). As the moral and spiritual character of the antediluvian world degenerated, especially following the demonic takeover just described, it was apparent that the people had become so hopelessly corrupt as to be beyond reclamation. They had completely and irrevocably resisted the Spirit's witness, so that it was futile any longer for Him to "strive" with man. This word (Hebrew *doon*) is used only here and is therefore of somewhat uncertain meaning, possibly including also the idea of "judging."

The Lord emphasized that man *also* was "flesh," the "also" probably referring to the fact that he had a physical body as well as a spiritual nature. Since the witness of God's Spirit to man's spirit had been rejected, there was no purpose to be served any longer in maintaining his physical life and continued multiplication. There may also be an implicit suggestion that man had become no better than the animals: he was dominated exclusively by the "flesh"—no longer concerned with God but only with his own bodily appetites, just as the animals. God told Noah that "the end of all flesh is come before me" (6:13), and later, indeed, "all flesh died" (7:21), including both man and animals.

This striving of God's Spirit with man's fleshly appetites was later taken by the apostle Paul as a type of the conflict in the New Testament believer between his spirit (as illumined and energized by God's Spirit) and his flesh, the natural and carnal nature with which he was born (Romans 8:5; Galatians 5:16, 17).

This antediluvian witness of the Holy Spirit to man must have been accomplished by the preaching of God's Word through one of His prophets. It is known that both Enoch and Noah bore a strong witness to the people of their day, and it is possible that Methuselah and Lamech did the same.

This particular prophecy was evidently given, perhaps through Methuselah, just 120 years before the coming of the Flood. Since Enoch had already been translated, Methuselah was the oldest living patriarch at this time. Shem, Ham, and Japheth had not yet been born; and presumably God's specific commands to Noah (5:32; 6:10; 6:13-21) had not yet been given.

God has always been long-suffering, even under such awful conditions as prevailed in the days of Noah (I Peter 3:20). Though all had rejected Him, He still granted 120 years to mankind in light of the bare possibility that at least some might "come to repentance" (II Peter 3:9). This was more than adequate time even for those who were infants to grow to maturity and have abundant opportunity to accept or reject God. Those who would be born later (e.g., Shem, Ham,

Japheth, and their wives) would presumably require some very special manifestation of God's grace to have deliverance (see 6:8; 7:1).

Genesis 6:4

---

4 There were giants in the earth in those days; and also after that, when the sons of God came in unto the daughters of men, and they bare *children* to them, the same *became* mighty men which *were* of old, men of renown.

One of the most amazing facts revealed by paleontology (the study of fossilized remains of creatures which inhabited the earth in a former age) is that nearly all modern animals were once represented by larger ancestors. One thinks of the mammoths and cave bears, giant cockroaches and dragonflies, and huge reptiles like the dinosaurs. Along with them are occasionally found giant human footprints, suggesting indeed that "there were giants in the earth in those days." Not only in the Bible, but in numerous other ancient books, are preserved traditions of giants.

With such a uniform testimony from ancient tradition, and with paleontological evidence as well, it is a superficial sophistication which ignores the possibility that these data may contain primitive reflections of the real events and characters described historically here in the Genesis record.

The children of the unions of the demonically controlled men and women of this period are the ones said to have become the "giants," the mighty men of old. The word in the Hebrew is *nephilim* and comes from the verb *naphal* ("fall"). Though some commentators suggest that the word means "those who fall upon"—that is, "attackers"—the more natural and probable meaning is "those who have fallen," probably a reference to the nature of their pseudoparents, the fallen angels. The name came also to mean "giants" and was applied later to the giants seen in Canaan by the Israelite spies (Numbers 13:33). The word was so understood by the translators of Genesis into Greek, rendering the word in the Septuagint by *gigantes*.

As to why children born of demon-controlled parents should grow into giants, we can make at least a reasonable supposition, though, in the absence of Biblical revelation on the subject, it can be no more than that. Modern genetics has shown there are two basic causes of variations in physical characteristics among men, namely mutations and recombinations. In the genetic system is a tremendous number of factors for different characteristics, some dominant in a particular population, some latent or recessive. These can be "recombined" in various ways to allow an almost unlimited variation in physical features. Recombination, however, can operate only on factors which are already implicitly present in the genes. Mutations, on the other hand, can introduce new features which were not present at all, by responding to external influences whose energies effect random changes in the genetic system.

Factors for large physical stature apparently have resided from the beginning in the created gene pool of the human population. Their emergence as frequent or dominant characteristics in a specific population might result by chance in a small inbreeding population or else might result by design in the case of controlled manipulation of the genes by breeders understanding enough about the genetic process to do this. Geneticists today appear on the verge of breakthroughs which would permit exactly such "genetic engineering" as this sort of thing to be accomplished on a practical basis.

It is believed that mutations can also produce "giantism." The strange process of *cloning,* by which geneticists think they will one day be able to produce a race of carbon copies of Einstein (or "Wilt the Stilt" Chamberlain, or whatever they want) by implantation of body cells in human fertilized eggs might be still another means of doing this.

The point is that, if modern geneticists can discuss with all seriousness the imminent possibility of accomplishing such things, then it is not unlikely that knowledge of these secrets could have been available to the angelic (and demonic) hosts. Having gained essentially complete control over both minds and bodies of these antediluvian parents, these fallen "sons of God" could then, by some such genetic manipulation, cause their progeny to become a race of monsters. The latter also then would be under their control and possession as well.

The demoniacal combination of the materialism and ungodliness of the Cainitic civilization in general, with this irruption of the Serpent's seed directly into large numbers of the human race and then with the thrusting forth of hordes of the monstrous offspring of these unlawful unions, all led to conditions in the world which were finally intolerable even to a God of compassion and long-suffering.

The demon-possessed men and their progeny, along with all the other godless inhabitants of the antediluvian world, were soon to perish in the waters of the Flood. These waters are now the waters of the sea and it may well be these that are referred to in connection with the final judgment when it says that "the sea gave up the dead which were in it" (Revelation 20:13). The evil spirits who indwelt their bodies have been imprisoned in Tartarus (II Peter 2:4) and are probably "the spirits in prison which once were disobedient when the longsuffering of God waited in the days of Noah" (I Peter 3:19, 20), to whom Christ went in the Spirit after His death to proclaim His ultimate victory over their evil purposes.

There were giants "also after that," in the days of the Canaanites, and these were likewise known as, among other things, the Nephilim (Numbers 13:33). Humanly speaking, they were descended from Anak, and so were also known as the Anakim. These people were, of course, known to Moses and it was probably he who editorially inserted the phrase "and also after that" into Noah's original record here in Genesis 6:4. Moses probably also inserted the information that these were the "mighty men of old, men of renown," men whose exploits of strength and violence had made them famous in song and fable in all nations in the ages following the Flood. To rebellious men of later times, they were revered as great heroes; but in God's sight they were merely ungodly men of violence and evil.

Filled with Violence

Just as world conditions in the days before the Flood presaged a coming catastrophe, so will world conditions in the last days of *this* age foreshadow an even greater catastrophe. Some of these characteristics are summarized as follows:

(1) Preoccupation with physical appetites (Luke 17:27)

(2) Rapid advances in technology (Genesis 4:22)

(3) Grossly materialistic attitudes and interests (Luke 17:28)

(4) Uniformitarian philosophies (Hebrews 11:7)

(5) Inordinate devotion to pleasure and comfort (Genesis 4:21)

(6) No concern for God in either belief or conduct (II Peter 2:5; Jude 15)

(7) Disregard for the sacredness of the marriage relation (Matthew 24:38)

(8) Rejection of the inspired Word of God (I Peter 3:19)

(9) Population explosion (Genesis 6:1, 11)

(10) Widespread violence (Genesis 6:11, 13)

(11) Corruption throughout society (Genesis 6:12)

(12) Preoccupation with illicit sex activity (Genesis 4:19; 6:2)

(13) Widespread words and thoughts of blasphemy (Jude 15)

(14) Organized Satanic activity (Genesis 6:1-4)

(15) Promulgation of systems and movements of abnormal depravity (Genesis 6:5, 12)

These conditions prevailed in the days of Noah and they are all rapidly growing again today. There is good reason, therefore, to believe that these present times are those which immediately precede the return of the Lord Jesus Christ.

Genesis 6:5, 6

---

5 ¶ And GOD saw that the wickedness of man *was* great in the earth, and *that* every imagination of the thoughts of his heart *was* only evil continually.

6 And it repented the LORD that he had made man on the earth, and it grieved him at his heart.

The antediluvian intrigues of Satan and his angels quickly achieved astounding success, not only among the Cainites and the descendants of Adam's other sons, but even among the descendants of Seth. God had made man in His own image, to respond with a heart of love to God's love, but now "every imagination of the thoughts of his heart was only *evil* continually." Man had been told to "multiply and fill the earth" (Genesis 1:28), but now "the earth was filled with violence" (6:11). A state of anarchy and terror must have reigned. No wonder the Biblical writer (probably Noah himself), speaking in terms of the human viewpoint, said: "And it repented the Lord that he had made man on the earth, and it grieved him at his heart."

While it is true that God "is not a man, that he should repent" (I Samuel 15:29), He nevertheless seems on occasion to repent (that is, "change His mind") toward man, because man has changed in attitude toward Him. In the same situation in which the above statement was recorded, God had said: "It repenteth me that I have set up Saul to be king, for he is turned back from following me, and hath not performed my commandments" (I Samuel 15:11). Indeed, it is exactly because God does *not* repent, that He must *seem* to repent when man "changes his mind." God's attitude toward man is conditioned by man's attitude toward Him.

Although God had made a perfect world for man and had been marvelously long-suffering toward His creatures, there finally came a time when, in justice to His own holiness, He had to terminate man's boundless wickedness. Any further delay would have completely prevented the accomplishment of God's purpose in and for mankind. Man's outward wickedness had become "great in the earth," because his inward imaginations had become *completely* evil and *always* evil.

Although the evil angels had aggravated this condition, man himself was basically responsible. Demons can only control those whose minds are already so rebellious toward God or so obsessed with illicit desires as to be open to such possession. The angels did not take *all* the women, but only "all which they chose." Nevertheless, all the antediluvians had become incurably wicked, if nothing else through acquiescence in the abnormalities of those who were so possessed.

Because evil filled the thoughts of man's heart, therefore God was "grieved at his heart." Although the reasoning process does not actually center in the human heart as an organ, nor in fact does God even have a physical heart, this figure is frequently used throughout the Bible to express the deepest seat of one's emotions and decisions.

Though it is true of the natural man in general that "they are all under sin" (Romans 3:39), this description of antediluvian man in verse 5 (also in verses 11-13) can hardly be correctly applied to all men everywhere. Outward wickedness is certainly not "great" in the case of every self-righteous unbeliever, nor do any but the most depraved imagine "only evil continually." There are certainly degrees of sin, and therefore degrees of punishment, in the case of unbelievers generally. But such an awful indictment as inscribed in verse 5 surely is something grotesque and abnormal, and thus reflects a grotesque and abnormal cause. It therefore required a cataclysmic remedy, nothing less than the unique cleansing of a worldwide baptism in the waters of the great Flood. Before demonic wickedness could gain control of every man, woman, and child throughout the entire world, thus destroying God's redemptive promises, God must intervene in catastrophic judgment.

Genesis 6:7, 8

---

7 And the LORD said, I will destroy man whom I have created from the face of the earth; both man, and beast, and the creeping thing, and the fowls of the air; for it repenteth me that I have made them.

8 But Noah found grace in the eyes of the LORD.

The section called the "generations of Noah," and probably written by Noah himself, closes with these verses. Since the remedy for world-wide wickedness would have to be a worldwide Flood, all land animals would have to be destroyed as well. Thus beasts and birds and creeping things (not fish) were to be destroyed, along with man, from the face of the ground. Since the Lord had created them, as a part of man's dominion, it was His prerogative to destroy them with that dominion.

But there was to be one exception. "Noah found grace in the eyes of the Lord." It is salutary to note that the most godly and important man in the entire world at that time would close out his record with such a testimony—that he was merely a sinner saved by grace!

What a wonderful word is *grace,* here appearing for the first time in Scripture. In sovereign mercy and by the election of grace, God had prepared the heart of Noah to respond in obedient faith to His will.

Note the consistent Biblical order here. First, Noah "found grace." Then Noah was "a just man" (that is, "justified" or "declared to be righteous"). Thus he was "perfect in his generations" (or "complete," in so far as God's records are concerned), and therefore he was able to "walk with God." Salvation in any era is exactly in this way. By sovereign grace, received through faith, the believer is justified before God and declared to be complete in Him. Only as a result of, and on the basis of, this glorious gift of grace, can one then "walk" in fellowship with God, showing the genuineness of his faith by his works. Four times it is said later, for example, that Noah "did all that God commanded him" (6:22; 7:5; 7:9; 7:16).

It is noted that Noah was perfect "in his generations." Among all his contemporaries, over the many generations of a long life, he was the only one, so far as the record goes, who had "walked with God" since Enoch. He was a "preacher of righteousness" (II Peter 2:5), though apparently no one responded to his preaching. The moral pressures must have been overwhelming. The temptations of a licentious and violent society, along with the continual rejection and ridicule of those masses who were "disobedient in the days of Noah" (I Peter 3:20), were no doubt inconceivably difficult for him to bear. So far as we know, he preached hundreds of years with no converts except some in his own family.

Noah was above all a man of great faith. Among the heroes of faith recorded in Hebrews 11, it is only Noah whose description both begins and ends with the phrase "by faith" (Hebrews 11:7).

The new section of Genesis that begins at 6:9b is attributed to "the sons of Noah" (10:1). The "generations of Noah" ends at 6:9a. It is noteworthy that Noah ends with his own testimony that he had simply "found grace in the eyes of the Lord." His sons, on the other hand, began their record with a testimony concerning their father, "Noah was a just man and perfect in his generations." Noah was no doubt a sinner, being human; but he had believed God's promises and sought, by God's grace, to obey His word and follow His will. Though Satan had managed to corrupt the whole world, the one man whom he wanted most of all to destroy, was under the invulnerable protecting shield of the grace of God.

Noah's Ark

To the majority of modern intellectuals, Noah is merely a legendary character and his Ark and its animals nothing but a story for children's coloring books. That the entire account is sober and important history is a concept too naive even to consider, so they seem to think.

The later writers of the Bible did not feel that way. Isaiah certainly took Noah seriously: "For this is as the waters of Noah unto me: for as I have sworn that the waters of Noah should no more go over the earth; so have I sworn that I would not be wroth with thee, nor rebuke thee" (Isaiah 54:9). Ezekiel twice mentions Noah as one of the three most righteous men in history (Ezekiel 14:14, 20). The writer of Chronicles, as well as Luke, includes Noah in the official genealogy of Christ (I Chronicles 1:4; Luke 3:36).

In the New Testament, the apostle Peter twice mentions Noah, both times obviously regarding him as a strategic figure of history (I Peter 3:20; II Peter 2:5). Most importantly, the Lord Jesus Christ accepted the story of Noah and the ark as a real event (Matthew 24: 37-39; Luke 17:26). As pointed out already, Noah was listed as one of the greatest of all the historical men of faith, in Hebrews 11:7. Note also that the ark itself was mentioned in most of these New Testament references.

Genesis 6:9, 10

---

9 ¶ These *are* the generations of Noah: Noah was a just man *and* perfect in his generations, *and* Noah walked with God.

10 And Noah begat three sons, Shĕm, Ham, and Jā'phĕth.

As the "sons of Noah" began the record of their own "generations," they first indicated that it should be tied in to the previous record kept by their father. To do this, they began with his name and a testimony to his godly character, as we have noted previously.

They then introduced themselves, by name as Shem, Ham, and Japheth, as Noah's three sons—or at least as the three of his sons who survived the Flood. There has been much discussion about the meaning of these names, and it must be recognized that these are somewhat uncertain. Those who believe that Noah's three sons were the progenitors of three races have interpreted the names to mean: Ham, "black"; Shem, "dark"; Japheth, "fair." However, "Shem" is the usual Hebrew word for "name" or "renown," and "Japheth" is believed by most scholars to mean "enlarged" (note Genesis 9:27). There is a possibility that it means "fair," but in the sense of "beautiful," rather than "light skinned." As far as "Ham" is concerned, it may be related to the Hebrew *cham,* meaning "warm" or "hot."

Genesis 6:11-13

---

11 The earth also was corrupt before God; and the earth was filled with violence.
12 And God looked upon the earth, and, behold, it was corrupt; for all flesh had corrupted his way upon the earth.

13 And God said unto Noah, The end of all flesh is come before me; for the earth is filled with violence through them; and, behold, I will destroy them with the earth.

The narrative next proceeds to rehearse the reasons for the coming destruction. The earth was corrupt; the earth was filled with violence; all flesh had corrupted his way. The universality of human wickedness and depravity was thus repeatedly emphasized. Shem, Ham, and Japheth had all been born within the last century before the Flood, and they had lived in the midst of this corrupt society all their lives. The marvel is that they themselves somehow escaped the corruption. Had it not been for the example and teachings of their godly parents and grandparents, no doubt they also would have been inundated in the antediluvian wickedness. One factor which possibly helped was that their father probably kept them busy for many years in building the Ark and making preparations for the Flood.

God had commanded man to fill the earth. This he had done, but he also had filled it with violence. God had told man the way to walk, but now all flesh had corrupted his way. The word for "corrupt" (Hebrew *shachath*) is a very strong term, and is often translated "destroy." That is, to corrupt is to destroy! Instead of following God's way, all men, like sheep, had turned aside to their own ways (Isaiah 53:6), and thus finally had destroyed themselves.

It is interesting to take passing note that Genesis 6:12 ("And God looked upon the earth, and behold it was corrupt") marks the *middle* verse of Genesis 1—11. It is significant that, although the earth had forgotten God, God was still looking on the earth! "Neither is there any creature that is not manifest in His sight: but all things are naked and opened unto the eyes of him with whom we have to do" (Hebrews 4:13).

The term "all flesh" on occasion includes animals as well as men (note Genesis 7:21), and some writers have assumed this verse to suggest that animals had become corrupt also—suggesting that illicit unions among the animals might have produced some of the grotesque monsters (e.g., dinosaurs) found in the fossil record. However, the situation described here is obviously one of moral corruption, and since there is no suggestion in Scripture that animals can make moral judgments, there is no intimation that this particular statement ("all flesh had corrupted his way") could apply to any creature other than man.

Although animals were not morally involved in man's sinfulness, they were to participate in the judgment on man, as part of his dominion. This had been noted in verse 7.

Now God further revealed, this time directly to Noah, that the earth itself would also be destroyed. The method by which God spoke to Noah is not disclosed—whether by vision, dream, or direct theophany.

God told Noah He would destroy man *with* the earth. Those who have advocated either a local flood or a tranquil flood are forced to read this verse as God destroying man *from* the earth. However, the preposition is the Hebrew *eth,* which means "with," not "from." Like it or not, the Bible does teach that the Flood was a world-destroying cataclysm. As Peter says: "The world that then was, being overflowed with water, perished" (II Peter 3:6).

Genesis 6:14-16

14 ¶ Make thee an ark of gopher wood; rooms shalt thou make in the ark, and shalt pitch it within and without with pitch.
15 And this *is the fashion* which thou shalt make it *of:* The length of the ark *shall be* three hundred cubits, the breadth of it fifty cubits, and the height of it thirty cubits.
16 A window shalt thou make to the ark, and in a cubit shalt thou finish it above; and the door of the ark shalt thou set in the side thereof; *with* lower, second, and third *stories* shalt thou make it.

In order to preserve both human and terrestrial animal life on the earth, God instructed Noah to build a huge bargelike structure called an ark, in which the occupants would be saved from destruction in the coming Flood. According to God's instructions, the Ark was to be designed for capacity and floating stability rather than for speed or navigability. The dimensions were to be 300 cubits long, 50 cubits wide, and 30 cubits high.

The question is: how long is a cubit? The Babylonians had a royal cubit of about 19.8 inches; the Egyptians had a longer and a shorter cubit of about 20.65 and 17.6 inches, respectively; and the Hebrews apparently had a long cubit of 20.4 inches (Ezekiel 40:5) and a common cubit of about 17:5 inches. Another common cubit of antiquity was 24 inches. Most writers believe the Biblical cubit to be 18 inches.

To be very conservative, assume the cubit to have been only 17.5 inches, the shortest of all cubits, so far as is known. In that case, the Ark would have been 438 feet long, 72.9 feet wide, and 43.8 feet high. It can be shown hydrodynamically that a gigantic box of such dimensions would be exceedingly stable, almost impossible to capsize. Even in a sea of gigantic waves, the ark could be tilted through any angle up to just short of 90° and would immediately thereafter right itself again. Furthermore, it would tend to align itself parallel with the direction of major wave advance and thus be subject to minimum pitching most of the time.

With the dimensions as calculated, the total volumetric capacity of the Ark was approximately 1,400,000 cubic feet, which is equal to the volumetric capacity of 522 standard livestock cars such as used on modern American railroads. Since it is known that about 240 sheep can be transported in one stock car, a total of over 125,000 sheep could have been carried in the Ark.

A few other details of the Ark's construction are given. It was to have three stories, each ten cubits high; and each of these "decks" was to be divided into various "rooms" (literally "nests"—thus apparently each of appropriate size for the individual animals to rest in). The Ark was to be made of "gopher wood," the exact nature of which is unknown today, though apparently some type of dense, hard wood; and it was to be made waterproof and resistant to decay by impregnation with "pitch," inside and outside.

The word for "pitch" (Hebrew *kopher*) is different from that used in other places in the Old Testament. It is equivalent to the Hebrew *kaphar* ("to cover") and, in the noun form, means simply a "covering."

However, it is also the regular Hebrew word for "atonement," as in Leviticus 17:11, for example. In essence, therefore, this is the first mention of "atonement" in the Bible. Whatever the exact nature of this "pitch" may have been (probably a resinous substance of some kind, rather than a bituminous material), it sufficed as a perfect covering for the Ark, to keep out the waters of judgment, just as the blood of the Lamb provides a perfect atonement for the soul.

The Ark also had a "window" (Hebrew *tsohar*), which probably means, literally, an "opening for daylight." Although the phraseology is difficult, most authorities understand that this "window" was to consist of a one-cubit opening extending all around the Ark's circumference, near the roof, as provision for light and ventilation. Presumably there was also a parapet provided to keep out the rain.

It has also been suggested that the word "window" might refer to a low wall extending around the Ark *above* the roof, providing a sort of cistern as a means of water supply. It was obviously not the intention of the writer to record the complete specifications for the ark's construction, but only enough to assure later readers that it was quite adequate for its intended purpose.

That purpose, of course, was to "preserve life on the earth." The notion of a local flood is frivolous and harmful. The Ark was far too large and sturdily constructed to accommodate a mere regional fauna in a local flood. In fact, no ark would have been necessary at all in that type of situation. Not only the birds and mammals but also Noah and his family could have migrated to another country far more quickly and expeditiously.

Finally the Ark was to have a door in its side. There was only to be *one* door, and all must enter and leave by the same door. Once the animals started streaming into the Ark, there would be nowhere else to go but farther into the Ark. Although it is not definitely stated as such, it may be that this is also intended for instructional purposes as a type of Christ. He is the one Way (John 14:6) to the Father's house. He is the one "Door" (John 10:7-9) to the resting-place for His sheep, through which the sheep must both enter for safety and rest and go out later for service.

The word for "ark" (Hebrew *tabhah*) is not the word used later for the "ark of the covenant," but it is the word used for the ark of bulrushes in which Moses was hidden as a baby (Exodus 2:3). It seems, therefore, to be a very ancient word for a box meant to float upon water. At the time Noah began building his Ark, it must have seemed ludicrous to his antediluvian contemporaries. They had never seen any kind of flood, or even rain (Genesis 2:5), and Noah's preaching and construction work no doubt gave them much occasion for ridicule. Nevertheless, Noah had been "warned of God of things not seen as yet" (Hebrews 11:7) and, believing God's word, he proceeded steadfastly to "prepare an ark to the saving of his house." He was "moved with fear," not for his own life, but lest his own household be engulfed in the wickedness and ungodliness of the "condemned world" of his day.

The Provision of God and the Obedience of Noah

We are not told exactly when God's instructions to Noah were given, though it was obviously sometime after (probably soon after) His prophetic warning that man would have only 120 more years before judgment would come (Genesis 6:3). The work probably was going on throughout most of the century immediately preceding the Flood.

The antediluvians thus had ample warning, both through Noah's preaching (II Peter 2:5) and example, but the uniformitarian science of their day assured them such an event was impossible, and so they went on in unconcerned "eating and drinking" until the Flood came and took them all away.

Genesis 6:17

17 And, behold, I, even I, do bring a flood of waters upon the earth, to destroy all flesh, wherein *is* the breath of life, from under heaven; *and* every thing that *is* in the earth shall die.

For the first time God here tells Noah exactly what form the coming destruction would take, though it may already have been implied from His instructions concerning the Ark. It would be a mighty flood of waters *(mabbul mayim)*. The word for "flood" *(mabbul),* used here for the first time, applies only to the Noahic Flood; other floods are denoted by various other words in the original. This was *the* "mabbul," unique in all history. This word is related to an Assyrian word meaning "destruction." The phrase "a flood of waters" could thus well be translated by "the hydraulic cataclysm." Since *mabbul* is used only in Psalm 29:10, outside of Genesis 6—9, the cataclysmic activity poetically described in Psalm 29 must also refer to the Noachian Deluge.

Similarly, when the Genesis Flood is referred to in the New Testament, the Greek term *kataklusmos* is uniquely employed (Matthew 24:39; Luke 17:27; II Peter 2:5; 3:6) instead of the usual Greek word for "flood." This Flood was not to be comparable to other later *local* floods; it was to be absolutely unique in all history.

The Flood would not only destroy mankind, but also "all flesh," wherein is the breath of life, from under heaven." This phrase indicates again that animals, like men, have the "breath" (*ruach,* "spirit") of life. The phrase "under heaven" qualifies the destruction as applying to land animals only, as does also the statement "everything that is in the earth [or 'land']." The Flood would not destroy all marine species, though multitudes of marine organisms would no doubt perish in the submarine upheavals associated with the Flood. Such language, of course, is utterly inconsistent with the idea of either a local flood or a tranquil flood.

Genesis 6:18

---

18 But with thee will I establish my covenant; and thou shalt come into the ark, thou, and thy sons, and thy wife, and thy sons' wives with thee.

In this verse is the first mention of "covenant" (Hebrew *berith*) in the Bible. God promises Noah that, in response to his obedience, He will subsequently establish His covenant with him and his seed and those who accompanied him into the Ark. The details of this covenant were elaborated later, when they had all emerged from the Ark (9:9-17).

Initially, however, it was essential that Noah build and furnish the Ark, so that life could be preserved through the coming Flood. Specifically, God said that only eight people would be on board: Noah, his wife, his three sons, and their wives. God foreknew that none from that generation would be converted through Noah's preaching and so all would perish in the waters of the Flood. Of course, there were some believers (e.g., Lamech, Methuselah) who would die before the coming of the *mabbul.*

Genesis 6:19-21

---

19 And of every living thing of all flesh, two of every *sort* shalt thou bring into the ark, to keep *them* alive with thee; they shall be male and female.

20 Of fowls after their kind, and of cattle after their kind, of every creeping thing of the earth after his kind; two of every *sort* shall come unto thee, to keep *them* alive.

21 And take thou unto thee of all food that is eaten, and thou shalt gather *it* to thee; and it shall be for food for thee, and for them.

In these verses are contained the instructions for the preservation of the animals in the Ark. A male and a female of each "kind" were to be brought into the Ark, "to keep them alive." The scope was quite comprehensive: "two of every sort." God had a purpose for each created kind, so He intended that all the kinds be preserved through the Flood. In addition to this general rule, seven animals of each "clean" kind (evidently those intended for use as domestic and sacrificial animals) were to be taken on board (7:2).

Most land animals are small, of course; so this did not by any means represent an impossible task. Authorities on biological taxonomy estimate that there are less than eighteen thousand species of mammals, birds, reptiles, and amphibians living in the world today. This number might be doubled to allow for known extinct land animals (that is, those known from actual fossil records, not the imaginary transitional forms that never existed except in the minds of evolutionists). Allowing then for two of each species, there might have to be a total of about seventy-two thousand animals on the Ark—say seventy-five thousand; to allow for the five extra animals in each "clean" species.

Since, as we have already seen, the Ark could have carried as many as one hundred and twenty-five thousand sheep, and since the average size of land animals is surely less than that of a sheep, it is obvious that no more than 60 percent of its capacity would have to be used for animals. Actually, it would have been less than this, since the Biblical "kind" is probably considerably broader than that of the arbitrary "species" category of modern biology.

There were a few large animals (elephants, dinosaurs, giraffes, etc.) to be carried on the Ark, but many more small ones (mice, robins, lizards, frogs, etc.). Even the large animals were probably represented by young (therefore small) individuals, since they had to spend a year in the Ark without reproductive activity and then go out to repopulate the earth.

Thus, the specified size of the Ark seems ideally appropriate for the animals it had to carry. There was of course also ample room for the approximately one million species of insects (many of these, no doubt, could have survived outside the Ark), as well as food for the animals, for living quarters for Noah and his family, and for any other necessary purposes.

Neither was there any serious problem involved in assembling the animals. It will be recalled that the climate before the Flood was probably uniformly warm all over the earth. Furthermore, the seas, hills, and other geographical features were also more or less uniformly distributed over the globe. Consequently, animals were not ecologically isolated in different latitudes or altitudes as at present, but were more or less uniformly distributed around the world. No great distances were involved, then, when the time came for representatives of each kind to migrate to the Ark.

The Lord told Noah that the animals would "come unto thee" at the proper time, so that Noah did not have to send out hunting and trapping expeditions to get them. This was probably the first animal migration in history, as such migrations had never been necessary before, with pleasant climate and abundant food available everywhere.

Within each animal kind, however, had been placed genes which were programmed to impart such migratory instincts to their possessors. In the antediluvian populations, these had no selective value and so were not dominant. Certain individuals still possessed them, however. When the time came, these individuals, instinctively sensing the approaching storm, began to move, God somehow urging and impelling them toward the waiting Ark.

The animals on the Ark, therefore, were all individuals possessing such genes. Their descendants have inherited them and utilized the powers imparted by them as necessary in the postdiluvian world. Scientists as yet have no naturalistic explanation for the remarkable migratory and directional instincts possessed by animals, especially by birds, which enable them to adjust to the sharp latitudinal and seasonal temperature and other changes that characterize the post-Flood world. These abilities have been inherited from their ancestors on the Ark.

Another remarkable physiological mechanism possessed by most animals (possibly latent in all), as a protection against sharp temperature and other climatological changes, is the ability to suspend all bodily changes in a state of hibernation. This ability enables an animal to pass the winter in very confined quarters, with little or no food intake or bodily excretions (the phenomenon of "estimation" is a similar state of dormancy during very hot weather).

Practically the same discussion could apply to the capacity of hibernation as to that of migration. Both are remarkable abilities, instinctive abilities possessed by animals (not by man) which enable them to cope with prolonged periods of bad weather. Neither of these abilities has as yet been adequately analyzed by scientists on any kind of naturalistic basis. These were both probably latent genetic abilities possessed by some individuals in animal populations since creation, then divinely

selected and activated by God at the time of the Flood. As these animals
arrived at the Ark, partook of a good meal, and then entered the Ark,
in response to the suddenly darkened sky and the chill in the air, they
settled down for a year-long "sleep" in their respective "nests" in the
Ark. Some may have eaten part of the stored food during the year, but
perhaps much of it was to provide them all another good meal as they
left the Ark after the Flood.

Genesis 6:22

**22 Thus did Noah; according to all that
God commanded him, so did he.**

Noah was not only a man of strong faith in God's word, but of
thoroughgoing obedience to that word. The tasks God had given him
to do were monumental—extremely difficult and discouraging—and yet
Noah never questioned or complained. He simply obeyed!

This last verse of the sixth chapter succinctly summarizes a whole
century of God's "long-suffering" while Noah "preached righteousness"
to those "who were disobedient while the Ark was a preparing" (I Peter
3:20; II Peter 2:6; Luke 17:26, 27).

Not only in this verse, but three times more we are told that Noah
did all God commanded him (7:5, 9, 16). Not physically perhaps, but
spiritually, Noah indeed was a giant in the earth in those days, and the
world has perhaps never seen his equal since.

Because Naoh walked with God and was obedient in faith to His
word, God had wonderful fellowship with Noah. There are seven recorded instances in which it is said that God spoke to Noah (Genesis
6:13; 7:1; 8:15; 9:1, 8, 12, 17), each time in fellowship and blessing
to Noah and his family.

In contrast, in Psalm 29 (which, as noted earlier, deals with the
Noahic Flood), seven times the "voice of the Lord" thunders forth in
majesty and judgment before a world which had rejected Him (verses
3, 4a, 4b, 5, 7, 8, 9). These no doubt answer also to the "seven thunders" and their "voices" which, though uttered in the future judgment,
are not to be revealed in detailed content until that time (Revelation
10:3, 4).

8

The Great Flood

(Genesis 7-8)

The Last Days of the Old World

God had spoken to Noah nearly one hundred years earlier giving instructions concerning the Ark and the animals, and assuring him that the flood indeed would come on schedule. There had been no further word from heaven, but Noah had proceeded steadily and faithfully with his unique mission and ministry, obeying God's commandments without question. With all the urgency possible, he preached the coming judgment, year after year, but to no avail, so far as converts were concerned.

Finally, the Ark was completed and all the animals were assembling. The 120 years would be up in a few days, and Grandfather Methuselah, who had served the Lord longer than any man who ever lived, was on his deathbed.

Then it was, after a century of silence, that God once again spoke to Noah. Noah had indeed prepared an ark "to the saving of his house" (Hebrews 11:7).

Genesis 7:1

CHAPTER 7

AND the LORD said unto Noah, Come thou and all thy house into the ark; for thee have I seen righteous before me in this generation.

189

The Lord said to Noah: *"Come* thou and all thy house into the ark; for thee have I seen righteous before me in this generation." Because Noah had exercised faith (Hebrews 11:7) in God's word, demonstrating his faith through unwavering obedience to His commandments, God saw (accounted) him as righteous, and saved both him *and his house.* This is God's gracious provision and promise to the one who is head of the house. "Believe on the Lord Jesus Christ and thou shalt be saved, and thy house" (Acts 16:31).

It is significant, too, that the Lord said *"Come* into the Ark," not "Go." God would be in the Ark with them, and although the Flood would soon be unleashed in devastating fury, they were all safe with Him.

Though it was because of Noah's faith and obedience that God gave the promise concerning his house, each member of that household also exercised saving faith as well. Each one chose voluntarily to enter the Ark and renounce the world in which they had lived so long. Noah was undoubtedly a man of great wealth, in order to finance the building of the Ark; but he and his sons and their wives willingly left it all behind because of their faith that God would perform what He had promised. The balance between man's free choice and God's electing grace is one which man, in finite understanding, can never fathom; but both are true. God promised Noah that his family would be saved (6:18) long before they voluntarily chose to enter the Ark (7:7), but choose they did when the time arrived.

Genesis 7:2, 3

---

2 Of every clean beast thou shalt take to thee by sevens, the male and his female: and of beasts that *are* not clean by two, the male and his female.

3 Of fowls also of the air by sevens, the male and the female; to keep seed alive upon the face of all the earth.

Immediately after telling Noah the time had come, God instructed him to take seven of each clean animal, along with the pairs of all the others, onto the Ark, "to keep seed alive upon the face of all the earth." The stated purpose was, of course, valid if the Flood was to be universal, but irrelevant if the Flood were local. The clean animals included a few "beasts" and "birds," but apparently no "creeping things." It seems likely that the clean animals were those adjudged suitable for domestication and a form of fellowship with man, and thus also suitable for sacrificial offerings in atonement for man. Since no previous categorization of animals as "clean" or "unclean" is given in Genesis, it is perhaps most reasonable to believe that God allowed Noah to use his own judgment on this. The three pairs were to encourage the relatively greater numerical proliferation of the clean animals after the Flood (on a par with man, with his three surviving families) and perhaps also to allow for a greater variety of genetic factors, so that more varieties could be developed later as needed. The seventh animal in each group clearly was intended for sacrificial purposes (Genesis 8:20). Much later, the Mosaic law plainly spelled out which animals were to be regarded as clean in the Israelite system (Leviticus 11, etc.), though all such distinctions were to be removed altogether in the Christian dispensation (Acts 10:9-15; I Timothy 4:4).

Genesis 7:4, 5

---

4 For yet seven days, and I will cause it to rain upon the earth forty days and forty nights; and every living substance that I have made will I destroy from off the face of the earth.

5 And Noah did according unto all that the LORD commanded him.

God next made the rather unexpected statement that it would still be seven days before the Flood would actually come on the earth. This was no doubt primarily for all of Noah's last-minute preparations—the installation of the animals "in their stalls," feeding them, and so on, and perhaps for one last warning to the world of the ungodly. Perhaps it was also the period of mourning after the burial of Methuselah (compare Genesis 50:10).

God assured Noah, however, that after the seven days were finished a tremendous rain would pummel the earth for forty days and forty nights, until every living substance was destroyed "from off the face of the earth."

A worldwide rain lasting forty days would be quite impossible under present atmospheric conditions; so this phenomenon required an utterly different source of atmospheric waters than now obtains. This we have already seen to be the "waters above the firmament," the vast thermal blanket of invisible water vapor that maintained the greenhouse effect in the antediluvian world. These waters somehow were to condense and fall on the earth.

God also revealed that everything in the dry land that had life would be, literally, "wiped out" from the face of the ground. This was to be no small matter; the earth would be completely cleansed of its corruption in this global bath from heaven. The words translated "every living substance" are *kol yeyum,* and mean literally "all existence," or "all that grows up." This concept does not limit itself merely to everything with "the breath of life," but seems to include plants as well as animals. The ground was to be so inundated and devastated as to be made utterly barren of vegetation. The lush forests and meadows of the antediluvian world were all to be uprooted, washed away, and finally either buried in the sediments (where they would one day become coal beds of the post-Flood world) or else just decay and go back to dust.

When God had finished His instructions, Noah proceeded to do "all that God commanded him," just as he had done for over a hundred years. Here was the final test, the final break with the world he had known, thrusting himself completely on God's mercy. And so again, Noah obeyed without a shadow of hesitation.

Genesis 7:6-9

---

6 And Noah *was* six hundred years old when the flood of waters was upon the earth.

7 ¶ And Noah went in, and his sons, and his wife, and his sons' wives with him, into the ark, because of the waters of the flood.

8 Of clean beasts, and of beasts that *are* not clean, and of fowls, and of every thing that creepeth upon the earth,

9 There went in two and two unto Noah into the ark, the male and the female, as God had commanded Noah.

At this point, the authors (originally presumably the sons of Noah) pause to mark the solemnity of the occasion, denoting it in terms of Noah's age at the time. This date, in effect, terminated the antediluvian and initiated the postdiluvian age. Though the Flood had not yet begun, the entrance of Noah's family and the animals into the Ark cut them off, once and for all, from the world outside. From that moment on, the new order had begun for all those with whom God was dealing in grace.

Very solemnly, in order to emphasize that every one of God's promises and commandments were being carried out to the letter, the narrative enumerates all who entered the Ark: Noah, his sons, his wife, his sons' wives, the clean animals, the unclean beasts, the birds, and the creeping things. These were the ones concerning which God had instructed Noah, and all were now on the Ark as planned. Each kind of animal was represented by a male and female, so that the created kinds could be preserved through the Flood. Of each clean animal, there were two additional pairs and another individual for sacrificial purposes. Everything had been done as commanded.

Genesis 7:10-12

---

10 And it came to pass after seven days, that the waters of the flood were upon the earth.
11 ¶ In the six hundredth year of Noah's life, in the second month, the seventeenth day of the month, the same day were all the fountains of the great deep broken up, and the windows of heaven were opened.
12 And the rain was upon the earth forty days and forty nights.

All of these preparations were completed on the "selfsame day" (verse 13) that the Flood came. The last grace period of seven days (verse 4) was ended, and the time of judgment had arrived. The exact date, in fact, was recorded—"the second month, the seventeenth day of the month."

The dating of the coming of the Flood raises the question as to what calendar was in use then—or whether possibly the date might later have been editorially emended by Moses to correspond to the Jewish religious calendar. It is probably impossible to be sure about this; but since all Scripture is divinely inspired, there must have been some reason for recording the date with precision.

It is known that the Jewish civil year began in the late fall, as did most other ancient calendars, presumably to correspond with the agricultural harvest. The Jews, of course, had attempted to base their calendar on the date of Adam's creation. The most natural interpretation of the chronological information in the early chapters of Genesis, in the absence of any other date, would be that the measurement of time began with the Creation. In this case, the data given would lead to the simple conclusion that the Flood came on the earth 1,655 years, one month, and seventeen days after Creation. However, a calculation with this precision would depend on the assumption that in Genesis 5 each named son was born on the exact named birthday of his father, an assumption which is quite unreasonable. Consequently, it seems unlikely that the purpose of this passage was to give the exact date after Creation when the Flood came.

It is still possible, however, that the month and day as given do refer to a calendar based on the date of Creation. In that case the inference would be that Creation took place in what would now correspond to the late fall, probably October, and then the Flood came in late November or December. On the other hand, if Moses later had superimposed the Jewish religious year calendar on the dates, then Creation was probably in April, the Flood in late May or June. This matter is discussed further in connection with Genesis 8:4.

In any case, the account stresses that on a certain particular day, marking the prophesied end of the antediluvian world, on that *one day* "were all the fountains of the great deep broken up, and the windows of heaven were opened." It is clear that the geophysical implications of this event are enormous, and it is vital to both the scientific and Biblical understanding of earth history that we determine exactly what these statements mean.

We have already discussed (see on Genesis 1:6-8; 2:5, 10-14; 5:5; etc.) the fact that the antediluvian hydrologic cycle was sharply different from that of the present day. It seems to have been controlled by the two great reservoirs of water resulting from the primeval separation of the waters of the primordial "deep" (Hebrew *tehom,* Genesis 1:2) on the second day of Creation into "waters above the firmament" and "waters below the firmament," the firmament in this case consisting of the atmospheric heavens.

The "waters above the firmament" (also called "waters above the heavens" in Psalm 148:4) constituted the vast vaporous canopy which maintained the earth as a beautiful greenhouse, preventing cold temperatures and therefore preventing wind and rain storms. Being in the vapor state, it was invisible and fully transparent, but nevertheless contained vast quantities of water extending far out into space.

The "waters below the firmament" became what is referred to as "the great deep" or "the great depths" of water. This was water in the liquid state, visible especially to the first man in the form of the antediluvian seas (Genesis 1:10) and rivers (Genesis 2:10-14). These rivers were not produced by run-off from rainfall (Genesis 2:5), but emerged through controlled fountains or springs, evidently from deep-seated sources in or below the earth's crust. There is an interesting reference to the abundant supplies of water pouring forth from these fountains of the great depths in Proverbs 8:24, and probably another in Job 38:16.

Such subterranean reservoirs were apparently all interconnected with each other, as well as with the surface seas into which the rivers drained, so that the entire complex constituted one "great deep." The energy for repressurizing and recycling the waters must have come from the earth's own subterranean heat implanted there at Creation. This entire system must have been a marvelous heat engine, which would have operated with wonderful effectiveness indefinitely, as long as the earth's internal heat endured and as long as the system of reservoirs, valves, governors, and conduits maintained their structure. The details of its design were not revealed, but such a system is quite feasible hydraulically and thermodynamically, and there is no reason to question the Creator's ability to provide it for the world He had made.

When the time for the destruction of this world arrived, however, all that was required was to bring the two "deeps" together again, as they had been when first created. The waters above the firmament must be condensed and precipitated, and the waters below the crust must burst their bounds and escape again to the surface.

Exactly *how* God caused the great Flood has been the occasion of wide speculation by various writers. All sorts of catastrophes have been suggested: the sudden tilting of the earth's axis, a bombardment of the earth by asteroids or meteorites, a sudden slipping of the earth's crust, nuclear explosions detonated by extraterrestrial space travelers, gravitational and electromagnetic forces resulting from a near miss of the earth by a wandering planet or comet, and others. All are highly imaginative and, of course, completely incapable of proof.

It would be helpful to keep in mind Occam's Razor (the simplest hypothesis which explains all the data is the most likely to be correct), the Principle of Least Action (nature normally operates in such a way as to expend the minimum effort to accomplish a given result), and the theological principle of the Economy of Miracles (God has, in His omnipotence and omniscience, created a universe of high efficiency of operation and will not interfere in this operation supernaturally unless the natural principles are incapable of accomplishing His purpose in a specific situation), in attempting to explain the cause and results of the great Flood.

There is no question that God *could* have accomplished the entire event miraculously (say, by special creation of the waters of the Flood and then by special "uncreation" of them when it was over), but this would be unnecessary and therefore theologically unlikely. By the same token, although a bombardment by asteroids or a series of orbital sweeps by an "astral visitor" would not necessarily require any supernatural interposition, except providential timing, these also would be unnecessary and, therefore (at least in the complete absence of any Biblical record of such phenomena as causing the Flood) most improbable.

The Bible specifically attributes the Flood to the bursting of the fountains of the great deep and the pouring down of torrential rains from heaven. These two phenomena are sufficient in themselves (in the light of related Biblical information, as discussed above) to explain the Flood and all its effects without the necessity of resorting either to supernatural creative miracles or to providentially ordered extraterrestrial interferences of speculative nature.

The breaking up (literally "cleaving open") of the fountains of the great deep is mentioned first and so evidently was the initial action which triggered the rest. These conduits somehow all developed uncontrollable fractures on the same day. For such a remarkable worldwide phenomenon, there must have been a worldwide cause. The most likely cause would seem to have been a rapid buildup and surge of intense pressure throughout the underground system, and this in turn would presumably require a rapid rise in temperature throughout the system.

Too little is known even today about the nature of the earth's deep interior and its thermal activity to decide exactly what might have triggered such a temperature rise. Nuclear reactions involving heavy elements, a slow buildup of temperature against some sort of insulating layer in the deeper crust followed by sudden fracture of the layer when the pressures and temperatures became too great, various combinations of seismic and volcanic activity—many possibilities might be conjectured. In any case there is surely abundant evidence in the earth's crust, especially its "crystalline basement complex," of intense igneous, metamorphic, and tectonic activity in the past, just the sort of evidence one might expect to find if such a sequence of events as outlined above had actually taken place. It is also possible that some of these phenomena could have been miraculous, in the sense of providential ordering of times and circumstances (if so, however, the providential miracles so involved would at least have been intraterrestrial and directly related to the Biblical explanation, not extraterrestrial and arbitrary).

Once the postulated pressure rise caused the first "fountain" to crack open, the pressurized fluid would surge through at this point and further weaken nearby boundaries, until soon a worldwide chain reaction would develop, cleaving open all the fountains of the great deep throughout the world.

The volcanic explosions and eruptions which would have accompanied these fractures would have poured great quantities of magma up from the earth's mantle along with the waters.

Furthermore, immense quantities of volcanic dust would have been blown skyward, along with gigantic sprays of water and turbulent surges of the atmosphere. The combination of atmospheric turbulence, expanding and cooling gases, and a vast supply of dust and other particles to serve as nuclei of condensation would suffice to penetrate the upper canopy of water vapor and trigger another chain reaction there, causing its waters to begin to condense and coalesce and soon to start moving earthward as a torrential global downpour of rain.

This entire phenomenon merits much further research and analysis, but at least there is good reason to conclude that the simple statement of verse 11 provides the basic information needed to explain the physical cause of the great Flood, all of course under the providential supervision of the same God who created the earth and its lands and waters in the first place.

The phrase "windows" of heaven is very graphic, many translators rendering it by "floodgates" or "sluiceways" (though its usual meaning is simply "windows"). In any case, it certainly is intended to convey the idea of great quantities of water, formerly restrained in the sky, suddenly released to deluge the earth. The downpour continued at full intensity—exactly as God had predicted (verse 4)—for forty days and forty nights.

Genesis 7:13-16

---

13 In the selfsame day entered Noah, and Shĕm, and Ham, and Jā'phĕth, the sons of Noah, and Noah's wife, and the three wives of his sons with them, into the ark;

14 They, and every beast after his kind, and all the cattle after their kind, and every creeping thing that creepeth upon the earth after his kind, and every fowl after his kind, every bird of every sort.

15 And they went in unto Noah into the ark, two and two of all flesh, wherein *is* the breath of life.

16 And they that went in, went in male and female of all flesh, as God had commanded him: and the LORD shut him in.

Once again the writer stresses, as though he realized future generations would find such a story exceedingly difficult to believe, the great number of animals that were in the Ark—"every sort of beast after his kind": wild beasts, cattle, creeping things, birds, insects (the Hebrew phrase means literally "every kind of little bird of every kind of wings"), in fact, everything with the breath of life, male and female. Furthermore, on the very last day, after the seven days were finished, the day on which the Flood came, Noah and his family themselves entered the Ark. This evidenced their faith in the absolute accuracy of God's Word, neither fearfully rushing into the Ark ahead of time, nor presumptuously delaying past the announced time.

Once all were inside, Noah evidently being last, a remarkable thing took place. "The Lord shut him in." *How* He did this is not recorded, but somehow the door to the Ark was shut and sealed, without the help of any human hands. This provided a final assurance to the occupants that they were in the will of God and under His protection.

The old world was forever dead to them from that moment on. Their life was henceforth a new life and they were to live in a new world. The Ark of safety endured the batterings of the Flood for them, as the Flood destroyed the world of the ungodly which would otherwise soon have destroyed them. So Christ, in dying for our sins, triumphed over sin "that he might deliver us from this present evil world, according to the will of God and our Father" (Galatians 1:4).

As the waters raged over the surface, gradually rising to destroy and bury the old world, the same waters bore the Ark and its occupants far above the destruction experienced in the depth below. Thus the waters of judgment and death were also waters of cleansing and deliverance. In a "like figure" to this first great baptism, our baptismal waters now are said to "save" us (I Peter 3:20, 21), setting forth in a most striking figure the destruction of the old life and elevation to a new life, delivered from the bondage of corruption into the glorious liberty of the children of God.

Overflowed with Water

The question of the nature and historicity of the Noahic Deluge is of immense importance to Biblical Christianity. The fact of the Flood is a pivotal issue in the entire conflict between Christianity and anti-Christianity. If the principle of innate evolutionary development can fully explain the universe and all its inhabitants, as its proponents claim, then there is no need to postulate a Creator. The chief evidence for evolution is the geological record of the supposed billions of years of earth history, documented by the fossils entombed in the sedimentary rocks of the earth's crust; and there is no room in this framework of interpretation for a world-destroying Flood. Thus, if the latter has actually occurred, the assumptions of uniformity and evolution as guiding principles in interpreting earth history are thereby proved completely deceptive and false.

In its history, the earth has suffered much under the effects of the Curse. Heat and cold, floods and droughts, earthquakes and eruptions—

all kinds of physical upheavals—have disturbed its crust and the inhabitants dwelling on its surface. But immeasurably greater in magnitude and extent than all other catastrophes combined was the great Flood. In our modern age of scientific skepticism, the enormity of this great event of the past has been all but forgotten. Its testimony of the awfulness of sin and the reality of divine retribution is so disturbingly unwelcome that men have tried for ages somehow to explain it away and forget it.

Even conservative Christians, although professing belief in the divine inspiration of Scripture, have often ignored the significance of the Flood. They have been intimidated by the evolutionary geologists and paleontologists who, for over a hundred years, have insisted that all of earth history should be explained in terms of slow development over great ages by the operation of the same natural processes which now prevail, completely rejecting the concept of the universal Flood at the dawn of history. Many Christians have attempted to work out a compromise with evolutionary geology by explaining the Flood as a local flood, caused by a great overflow of the Euphrates or some other river in the Middle East. It must be settled here, therefore, first of all, that the Bible record does describe a universal, world-destroying Flood.

Genesis 7:17, 18

---

17 And the flood was forty days upon the earth; and the waters increased, and bare up the ark, and it was lifted up above the earth.

18 And the waters prevailed, and were increased greatly upon the earth; and the ark went upon the face of the waters.

In the next several verses of Genesis 7 appear a considerable number of reasons to prove that the Bible is describing a worldwide Flood, not a local flood. Some of these are as follows:

(1) The wording of the entire record, both here and throughout Genesis 6—9, could not be improved on, if the intention of the writer was to describe a universal Flood; as a description of a river overflow, it is completely misleading and exaggerated, to say the least.

(2) Expressions involving universality of the Flood and its effects occur more than thirty times in Genesis 6—9.

(3) The Flood "was [or better, 'was coming'] forty days upon the earth." A continual downpour lasting for forty days, concur-

rently with a bursting of great clefts in the crust (verses 11-12) would be impossible under present uniformitarian conditions.

(4) The Flood which came on the earth was the *mabbul,* a word used solely in connection with the Noahic Flood. The ordinary Hebrew words for a local flood are not used here at all.

(5) The water rise was quickly sufficient to "bear up the ark," indicating a depth of at least twenty feet in the earliest stages of the Flood, since the Ark was at least forty-four feet high and heavily loaded. As already noted, the Ark was far too large to accommodate a mere regional fauna and was more than adequate to house two of every species of land animal in the whole world, living or extinct.

(6) As the rains continued, the waters "prevailed," a word which means, literally, "were overwhelmingly mighty," and would be quite inappropriate in the setting of a local flood. Job 12:15 says that the waters "overturned the earth."

(7) The construction, outfitting, and stocking of the Ark, so that it "went upon the face of the waters" had all been an absurd waste of time and money if the Flood were to be only a local flood. Migration would have been a far better solution to the problem, for Noah as well as the birds and beasts.

Genesis 7:19, 20

---

19 And the waters prevailed exceedingly upon the earth; and all the high hills, that *were* under the whole heaven, were covered.

20 Fifteen cubits upward did the waters prevail; and the mountains were covered.

The record of the Flood gives every indication of being an eyewitness account, written originally by either Noah or his sons, probably the latter. As the account advances, it becomes more and more obvious that these witnesses intended to describe what they firmly believed to be a worldwide, uniquely destructive cataclysm. Some other reasons are as follows:

(8) The waters covered all the "high hills" and the "mountains" ("hills" and "mountains" are the same word in the original, the repetition being a case of Hebrew parallelism for the purpose of emphasis).

(9) The waters not only "were overwhelmingly mighty" (translated "prevailed" in verse 18) but "prevailed *exceedingly*" over the earth.

(10) All the mountains "under the whole heaven" were inundated under at least fifteen cubits of water (half the height of the Ark, probably representing its depth of submergence), telling us that the Ark could float freely over all the mountains. These would patently include at least the mountains of Ararat, the highest peak of which reaches 17,000 feet. A 17,000-foot Flood is not a *local* flood!

(11) The mountains were "covered." The Hebrew word here, *kasah,* conveys a very positive emphasis; it could well be rendered "overwhelmed," as it is translated in some instances. The waters not only inundated the mountains but eventually washed them away.

(12) A double superlative—*"all* the high mountains under *all* the heavens"—cannot possibly allow the use of the word "all" here in a "relative" sense, as sometimes maintained by proponents of the local flood theory.

Genesis 7:21-23

---

21 And all flesh died that moved upon the earth, both of fowl, and of cattle, and of beast, and of every creeping thing that creepeth upon the earth, and every man:
22 All in whose nostrils *was* the breath of life, of all that *was* in the dry *land,* died.

23 And every living substance was destroyed which was upon the face of the ground, both man, and cattle, and the creeping things, and the fowl of the heaven; and they were destroyed from the earth: and Noah only remained alive, and they that *were* with him in the ark.

---

(13) "All flesh died that moved upon the earth." In a local flood, most of the fauna can escape death by fleeing the rising waters or by swimming to dry ground if necessary (or by flying away, in the case of birds); but this would be impossible in a universal Flood.

(14) "Every man" died, in accordance with the very purpose of the Flood. In a local flood, most people escape. Furthermore, there is no longer any question that ancient man occupied the entire globe at a date (as calculated by anthropologists, at least) much earlier than the date of any supposed "local flood" cor-

responding to the event described in Genesis. A local flood would not have reached "every man."

(15) Not only did everything with "the breath of life" die (this including animals, as well as man, further confirming that animals possess the *ruach,* or "spirit" of life), but so was "every living substance destroyed." The word translated "living substance" is one word in Hebrew, *yequm,* and is simply translated "substance" in Deuteronomy 11:6. It clearly refers here to vegetation, as well as animals. In fact, God had told Noah: "I will destroy man *with the earth"* (Genesis 6:13).

(16) Only Noah and those with him in the Ark survived the Flood, so that all present men are descended from Noah's three sons (see also Genesis 9:1, 19). Likewise, all the earth's present dry-land animals came of those on the Ark (Genesis 8:17, 19; 9:10). The very purpose of God had been to destroy all other living men (Genesis 6:7) and land animals (Genesis 6:17, 7:22).

Genesis 7:24

---

24 And the waters prevailed upon the earth a hundred and fifty days.

For the third time the word "prevailed" is used (see comments on verses 18 and 20), this time indicating that the waters prevailed 150 days. It was not until after this period that the "fountains of the deep" and the "windows of heaven" were shut (8:2) and the waters began to retreat. The extreme duration of the Flood indicates still further Biblical reasons for regarding it as universal.

(17) No local flood continues to rise for 150 days.

(18) Even after the waters began to abate, and the Ark grounded on the highest of the mountains of Ararat (Genesis 8:4), it was another 2½ months before the tops of other mountains could be seen (8:5).

(19) Even after four months of receding flood waters, the dove sent out by Noah could find no dry land on which to light (8:9).

(20) It was over an entire year (7:11; 8:13) before enough land had been exposed to permit the occupants to leave the Ark.

In view of all the above considerations, it is almost inconceivable that men professing to believe the Bible could endorse the local flood theory. Nevertheless, many evangelicals have been so intimidated by the pretensions of modern scholarship that they would sooner give up "the praise of God" than "the praise of men" (John 12:43).

To the above twenty reasons may be appended the following additional Biblical reasons for believing in a worldwide flood:[1]

(21) God's promise never to send such a Flood again (Genesis 8:21; 9:11, 15) has been broken repeatedly if it were only a local or regional flood.

(22) The New Testament uses a unique term (*kataklusmos,* "cataclysm") for the Flood (Matthew 24:39; Luke 17:27; II Peter 2:5; 3:6) instead of the usual Greek word for "flood."

(23) New cosmological conditions came into being after the Flood, including sharply defined seasons (Genesis 8:22), the rainbow along with rain (Genesis 2:5; 9:13-14), and enmity between man and beasts (Genesis 9:2).

(24) Man's longevity began a long, slow decline immediately after the Flood (compare Genesis 5 and Genesis 11).

(25) Later Biblical writers accepted the universal Flood (note Job 12:15; 22:16; Psalm 29:10; 104:6-9; Isaiah 54:9; I Peter 3:20; II Peter 2:5; 3:5, 6; Hebrews 11:7).

(26) The Lord Jesus Christ accepted the historicity and universality of the Flood, even making it the climactic sign and type of of the coming worldwide judgment when He returns (Matthew 24:37-39; Luke 17:26, 27).

As will be noted in the next section, there is also strong geological evidence for the universal Flood, rather than for uniformitarianism and evolution. Regardless of any real or imagined geological difficulties, however, the Word of God teaches unequivocally that the Flood was worldwide in its extent and cataclysmic in its effects. The only course legitimately open to Bible-believing Christians is to reinterpret the geological data to conform to this Biblical revelation.

After the Deluge

The Bible unequivocally teaches that the Genesis Flood was worldwide, not local. Since the Bible is infallibly true, this means there *was*

---

1. In Appendix 5, there are listed a total of one hundred Biblical and scientific reasons for believing that the Flood was worldwide.

a worldwide Flood, whether or not modern geologists are willing to believe it. Furthermore, a worldwide Flood could not have been a tranquil flood. A worldwide tranquil flood is a contradiction in terms, comparable to a tranquil explosion. The tremendous ability of moving water to erode and transport great quantities of sediment and heavy objects of all sorts is well known to all who have ever experienced even a local flood. In fact, most modern geologists believe that the majority of geological formations were produced in local floods or other local catastrophes; so it is obvious that a worldwide flood must have had worldwide geologic effects.

Especially must this have been true in such a Flood as described in the Bible, caused by global eruptions and downpours continuing for 150 days. Such a Flood would have destroyed every earlier physiographic feature on or near the earth's surface, redepositing the eroded materials all over the world in stratified sedimentary rocks of the earth's crust.

Not only do such sedimentary rocks abound all over the world, but they give much evidence of having been formed by rapid and continuous depositional processes. Each individual stratum is a distinct sedimentary unit and, in most formations, can be shown by hydraulic analysis to have been formed within a few minutes' time. Furthermore, it can be shown that within a series of "conformable" strata, each subsequent stratum began to be deposited immediately after the preceding one. When the strata above and below a given interface are *not* conformable (such a surface is called an "unconformity" by geologists), then a significant time gap is indicated. However, since there are no *worldwide* unconformities, one can always find a place at which any given formation does grade conformably and imperceptibly into another formation above it, *without* a time gap.

The obvious conclusion from such syllogistic reasoning is that, since each unit in the geological column was formed rapidly, and since each unit was followed immediately by another unit above it, therefore the whole column was formed rapidly! Thus, the geologic evidence demands a catastrophic, rather than a uniformitarian, explanation. For example, if it is assumed (reasonably) that the average thickness of the sedimentary rocks around the world is about one mile and the average rate of deposition during flooding conditions is one inch of compacted sediment every five minutes, then it would only take 220 days to form the entire column.

The existence of fossils in these sedimentary deposits is further evidence that they were formed rapidly. Fossils are so ubiquitous and so important, in fact, that they constitute the chief means of assigning a geologic "age" to a given formation (as deduced from the presumed "stage-of-evolution" of its fossil contents). However, the preservation of fossils requires rapid burial and lithification, or else they will be destroyed by decay or scavengers.

In addition to the testimony of the sedimentary processes which formed them and the fossils contained in them, all of the different types of sedimentary rocks (and igneous and metamorphic rocks as well) give strong evidence that they could never have been produced by modern uniformitarian processes. The same is true of geologic structures such as mountains, canyons, alluvial plains, and so forth. More and more evolutionary geologists today are returning to the concept of at least local catastrophism as the explanation for all types of geological features and formations. More and more *creationist* geologists and other scientists are returning to the concept that all these local catastrophes were essentially contemporaneous and continuous, making up a complex which was nothing less than a worldwide cataclysm. Clearly, that cataclysm was the Genesis Flood.

Genesis 8:1, 2

CHAPTER 8

AND God remembered Noah, and every living thing, and all the cattle that *was* with him in the ark: and God made a wind to pass over the earth, and the waters assuaged.

2 The fountains also of the deep and the windows of heaven were stopped, and the rain from heaven was restrained.

After the Flood had "prevailed" for 150 days, utterly destroying the "world that then was" (II Peter 3:6) and leaving the remains of multitudes of dead organisms buried in its sediments or still floating in its waters, God began to bring it to a termination. He "remembered" Noah and the animals in the Ark (not, of course, that He had ever forgotten them; the term is a Hebraism for "began again to act on their behalf"), and was ready to start them on their way to the new life they would find in the new world.

Three specific actions were taken by God: He caused a wind to pass over the earth, He stopped the fountains of the deep from further eruptions, and He closed the windows of heaven from further downpours (both were essentially emptied of their waters by this time).

The nature and effects of the "wind" need discussion. This again is the word *ruach* and so could be translated either "wind" or "spirit," depending on context. Its fundamental meaning (actually it is trans-

* changed in structure by heat, pressure, chemical action etc.

limestone into marble - granite into gneiss (NTS)

lated numerous different ways) is probably something like "invisible force."

It is possible that the energizing power of God's Spirit is intended here. That is, in analogy to His work on the first day of Creation (Genesis 1:2), so now again, with waters covering the earth as in the beginning, He exerted His creative power once again to separate the lands and the waters (Genesis 1:9).

Most translators believe, however, that the context here suggests an actual wind, God using a natural force providentially to accomplish His purposes. As discussed earlier, the uniform temperatures of the antediluvian world would have precluded strong winds. With the vapor canopy gone, however, sharp temperature differentials would have been established between equator and poles, and great air movements begun. These would soon have been complicated by the earth's rotation, so that the present complex system of atmospheric circulations would finally be initiated. The early phases, in particular, would probably have been quite violent. With nothing but a shoreless ocean, these winds would generate tremendous waves and currents, and vast quantities of water would be evaporated, especially in the equatorial regions.

Wind, waves, and evaporation, however, could hardly account in themselves for more than a minor lowering of water level (unless the winds were so violent as to sweep quantities of water clear off into outer space, which seems impossible on a nonsupernatural basis). Somehow there must also be a drastic rearrangement of terrestrial topography, with continental land masses rising from the waters, and ocean basins deepening and widening to receive the waters draining off the lands.

This is, in fact, exactly what happened according to Psalm 104:6-9:

> Thou coveredst it [the earth] with the deep as with a garment: the waters stood above the mountains. At thy rebuke they fled, at the voice of thy thunder they hasted away. They go up by the mountains; they go down by the valleys [or better, according to the American Standard Version, 'the mountains go up, the valleys go down'] unto the place which thou hast founded for them. Thou hast set a bound that they may not pass over; that they turn not again to cover the earth.

The first five verses of this psalm apply to the creation period, but it is obvious that verses 6 through 9 apply to the Flood, with an allusion to God's covenant with Noah (Genesis 9:11) in verse 9. During the Flood itself, the breaking up of the "great-deep" complex of subcrustal reservoirs and conduits, the tremendous release of heat energy, and the outflow of great quantities of water and magma undoubtedly left the earth's crust in a highly unstable condition. Furthermore, the erosion of the antediluvian mountains and continents had resulted in the deposition of great quantities of sediment in the seas.

Somehow, these great subterranean caverns, no longer pressurized, collapsed and the surface elevations sank correspondingly. Since these had been mainly underneath the antediluvian continents, to serve as the storage reservoirs for their rivers, and since these continents had by this time been essentially planed off by flood erosion, this mean that they now became the bottoms of the postdiluvian ocean basins. As they collapsed and the waters began draining into them, the sedimentary strata which had been deposited during the Flood in the antediluvian seas were now left suspended above them, becoming the postdiluvian continents. This was further augmented by an actual uplift of these areas because of an isostatic readjustment. The sediments newly deposited on them were much less dense than the earlier continental cores which had now settled into the former cavernous reservoirs, and this required a lateral shifting of materials toward the new continents, thus raising them still more.

Obviously the above outline of events is oversimplified and necessarily speculative, but does seem to be the most reasonable reconstruction of what must have happened in at least a general way, so far as the Biblical and scientific information now available will allow. The great winds and waves quite possibly could have been the "straw that broke the camel's back," producing just the additional force needed to cause the collapse of the emptied caverns below, already on the verge of failure.

Genesis 8:3, 4

---

3 And the waters returned from off the earth continually: and after the end of the hundred and fifty days the waters were abated.

4 And the ark rested in the seventh month, on the seventeenth day of the month, upon the mountains of Ăr′ă-răt.

Once the crust began to move (the previous land surfaces downward to form the new ocean basins, the previous sea bottoms and their new deposits of stratified sediments upward to form the new continents), the waters began to drain off the emerging lands, "returning from off the earth continually." The expression in the Hebrew indicates a quite rapid subsidence, as would be expected under the circumstances just outlined.

As the new land surfaces rose up, they would presumably have been fairly level, except for volcanic mountains and great batholiths (massive igneous upheavals, such as in the Sierra Nevada and many other coastal ranges) which had been pushed up by the magmatic activity associated with the eruption of the fountains of the great deep. Such ranges would, in the main, tend to be peripheral to the new ocean basins, in effect outlining the previous subterranean cavernous reservoirs. Except for these, the new continents would tend to be great plateaus of flat-lying sediments dotted by volcanic cones here and there, modified in some areas by buckling and folding of the strata during the process of uplift.

Depending on topography, vast interior continental lakes would exist for a time and great rivers would form, scouring out great canyons rapidly and depositing tremendous amounts of alluvium in their lower courses. It is significant that, all over the world, interior lakes and seas show evidence of much higher water levels in the recent past. Rivers also everywhere show that they once carried much greater quantities of water and sediment than they do at present. These and related phenomena provide still further geologic evidence of a worldwide Flood several thousand years ago.

Since it is not practicable to include extensive geological discussions in a Biblical commentary, readers interested in this aspect of the subject are referred to the writer's book *The Genesis Flood* (see bibliography) for detailed treatment of such matters.

One of the volcanic mountains formed in an earlier period of the Flood is Mount Ararat, along with other similar mountains in the upland regions of what is now Armenia. The Ararat region, including Mount Ararat itself (now 17,000 feet in elevation), abounds in what is known as pillow lava, a dense lava rock formed under great depths of water. The mountain also includes certain sedimentary formations containing marine fossils.

It was apparently on this mountain that the Ark came to rest as the Flood waters began to abate after the 150 days. Other mountains have been suggested, in Iraq, Ceylon, India, and elsewhere; but the weight of evidence still favors Mount Ararat. It is true that the entire region later was known as Ararat (Jeremiah 51:27), which is the Hebrew form equivalent to the Greek *Armenia* (II Kings 19:37; Isaiah 37:38), and Scripture says only that the Ark landed somewhere in the mountains of Ararat. However, it was the highest mountain in the region by far (8:5), and such a description could apply only to the mountain presently known as Mount Ararat. Furthermore, a rather large number of reported sightings of the Ark have come from explorers or travelers on this mountain during the past century, as well as during ancient and medieval times. A number of modern expeditions have been trying (unsuccessfully so far) to relocate the Ark with an adequate documentation, something which all earlier reports have lacked. This would surely be the most important archaeological discovery of all time, if successful.

It is significant that the Ark is said to have "rested," as though it had been *laboring* for five months in accomplishing its work of saving its occupants from sin and judgment. This is the second mention of "rest" in Scripture, the first being when God rested after His work of creation (Genesis 2:2, 3; actually these are two different, though synonymous, Hebrew words). If the Ark is a true type of Christ, as previously intimated, this is most appropriate. As God "finished" His work of creation and as the Ark "finished" its mission, so Christ "finished" (John 19:30) His work of salvation.

It also was considered significant that the Ark rested on "the seventeenth day of the seventh month." In our discussion of Genesis 7:11, the reason why the exact date was given for the beginning of the Flood ("the seventeenth day of the second month") was found to be uncertain. A possible reason appears here in connection with the typological inferences. The Lord Jesus Christ rose from the dead also on "the seventeenth day of the second month." The seventh month of the Jewish civil year (and this is probably the calendar used here in Genesis 7 and 8) later was made the first month of the religious year, and the Passover was set for the fourteenth day of that month (Exodus 12:2). Christ, our Passover (I Corinthians 5:7), was slain on that day, but then rose three days later, on the seventeenth day of the seventh month of the civil calendar.

Genesis 8:5-12

5 And the waters decreased continually until the tenth month: in the tenth *month*, on the first *day* of the month, were the tops of the mountains seen.

6 ¶ And it came to pass at the end of forty days, that Noah opened the window of the ark which he had made:

7 And he sent forth a raven, which went forth to and fro, until the waters were dried up from off the earth.

8 Also he sent forth a dove from him, to see if the waters were abated from off the face of the ground.

9 But the dove found no rest for the sole of her foot, and she returned unto him into the ark; for the waters *were* on the face of the whole earth. Then he put forth his hand, and took her, and pulled her in unto him into the ark.

10 And he stayed yet other seven days; and again he sent forth the dove out of the ark.

11 And the dove came in to him in the evening, and, lo, in her mouth *was* an olive leaf plucked off: so Noah knew that the waters were abated from off the earth.

12 And he stayed yet other seven days, and sent forth the dove, which returned not again unto him any more.

Securely anchored on the earth again, Noah and the others needed only to wait until the waters receded enough for them to disembark. But this took yet another seven months, so that they were in the Ark slightly over a year—371 days altogether. After 2½ months, they could see the tops of the nearby lower mountains. Forty days later, Noah released a raven and (seven days later) a dove from the Ark. The dove returned; but the raven, a scavenger bird with no qualms about resting on unclean surfaces, stayed. A week later, Noah sent out the dove again, which returned this time with a fresh olive leaf, indicating that seedlings or cuttings from the hardy olive tree were already beginning to grow again on the mountain sides.

The frequent references to "seven days" in this narrative (7:4; 7:10; 8:10; 8:12) have suggested to some that these were Sabbath Days. However, there was not an even number of weeks between the first of these and the second of these; so this is doubtful.

The narrative is not completely clear on the chronological details, but it does seem most likely that Noah sent out the raven on the 264th day after the onset of the Flood, then the dove on the 271st day. The dove was sent out again, and returned with the olive leaf, on the 278th day.

Genesis 8:13, 14

---

13 ¶ And it came to pass in the six hundredth and first year, in the first *month,* the first *day* of the month, the waters were dried up from off the earth: and Noah removed the covering of the ark, and looked, and, behold, the face of the ground was dry.

14 And in the second month, on the seven and twentieth day of the month, was the earth dried.

Seven days later, on the 285th day, Noah sent the dove out again. This time the dove stayed away, showing that the land was sufficiently dry and vegetation sufficiently established to support bird life. Noah waited still another 29 days, to the first day of the first month (314 days after the Flood began) to remove the Ark's covering (presumably a part of the roof) and behold the dry ground for himself. He must have observed, however, that there was still much water about and a forbidding and barren landscape in general. He thus waited still another 57 days, 371 days after the Flood began, before he determined that they could leave the Ark and undertake life in the new world.

This was on the 27th day of the second month. These months were apparently 30 days in length, as is inferred from the data in

Genesis 7:11, 24 and 8:3, 4. The Flood had started on the 17th day of the second month; so they were in the Ark a total of 371 days, a period of exactly 53 weeks.

The New World

The world had not been *annihilated* by the Flood, but it was drastically changed. As the apostle Peter says, "The world that then was, being overflowed with water, perished" (II Peter 3:6). When they left the Ark that had preserved them through that year of God's awful wrath, Noah and his family truly disembarked on a new world. The Ark had provided the bridge—seemingly fragile and easily demolished—from the old cosmos through the terrible Cataclysm to the present cosmos, "the heavens and the earth which are now" (II Peter 3:7).

The lands that once had teemed with animals and people and lush vegetation had been replaced by a desolate wilderness. The air which formerly was warm and gentle now moved in stiff and sometimes violent winds, and there was a chill on the mountain slope where the Ark rested. Dark clouds rolling about the sky, which had once been perpetually and pleasantly bright, seemed to threaten more rains and a recurrence of flood conditions. At the same time, however, the earth had been purged of the wicked hordes that had made its physical beauty only a mockery, and God had granted a gracious opportunity for a new beginning for the children of Adam.

Some of the implied physical changes after the Flood are as follows:

(1) The oceans were much more extensive, since they now contained all the waters which once were "above the firmament" and in the subterranean reservoirs of the "great deep."

(2) The land areas were much less extensive than before the Flood, with a much greater portion of its surface uninhabitable for this reason.

(3) The thermal vapor blanket had been dissipated, so that strong temperature differentials were inaugurated, leading to a gradual buildup of snow and ice in the polar latitudes, rendering much of the extreme northern and southern land surfaces also essentially uninhabitable.

(4) Mountain ranges uplifted after the Flood emphasized the more rugged topography of the postdiluvian continents, with many of these regions also becoming unfit for human habitation.

(5) Winds and storms, rains and snows, were possible now, thus

rendering the total environment less congenial to man and animals than had once been the case.

(6) The environment was also more hostile because of harmful radiation from space, no longer filtered out by the vapor canopy, resulting (along with other contributing environmental factors) in gradual reduction in human longevity after the Flood.

(7) Tremendous glaciers, rivers, and lakes existed for a time, with the world only gradually approaching its present state of semiaridity.

(8) Because of the tremendous physiographic and isostatic movements generated by the collapse of the subterranean caverns and the post-Flood uplifts, the crust of the earth was in a state of general instability, reflected in recurrent volcanic and seismic activity all over the world for many centuries and continuing in some degree even to the present.

(9) The lands were barren of vegetation, until such time as plant life could be reestablished through the sprouting of seeds and cuttings buried beneath the surface.

(10) There is even a possibility that the earth's rotation speeded up by about 1.5 percent if the year was really 360 days long.

Scattered around on the land surfaces were occasional rotting carcasses and skeletons of the animals and people doomed in the waters of the Flood, a vivid reminder of the ungodliness of the antediluvian world and the fate from which God had delivered the survivors. Since the new land surfaces probably had been formed mainly from the prediluvian seas, filled with sediments and then uplifted, more such remains were buried in the sediments beneath the land surfaces.

These sediments were rapidly being lithified, through the eroded and dissolved cementing agents present in the waters that had deposited the sediments, thus becoming the great beds of fossil-bearing sedimentary rocks that are now found everywhere around the world. The fossils so preserved were not heterogeneously dispersed throughout the sediments, but were generally deposited in a certain statistical order, from the more simple marine invertebrate organisms on the bottom to complex land vertebrates near the top.

This is in the order of (1) increasing elevation of natural habitat, with fossil assemblages tending to be buried in association with the same ecological communities in which they had lived; (2) increasing

ability to flee from the encroaching Flood waters; (3) increasing resistance to hydrodynamic forces and therefore an increasing tendency
to be transported farther and deposited more slowly. Thus, in general,
at any one locality, there would be a definite tendency for similar kinds
of animals to be buried at about the same levels, and for different
kinds to be buried in order of increasing size and complexity.

This order is exactly what is commonly found in the sedimentary
rocks (with many statistical exceptions, of course, as is to be expected
of such catastrophic phenomena as were occurring during the Flood),
and thus clearly confirms the predictions based on the Flood "model"
as outlined in the Biblical record. However, it has been deplorably
misinterpreted by modern uniformitarian geologists to teach a gradual
evolution of life (from simple marine invertebrate organisms to complex land vertebrates) through long geological ages.

Evolutionists have arranged these supposed "geological ages" in
a supposed chronological order, purportedly extending vertically upward
through the "geological column" of sedimentary rocks deposited above
the crystalline rocks on the bottom. The fossils found in these rocks,
proceeding supposedly from simple to complex, comprise their best
evidence for the theory of organic evolution. Thus, if the fossiliferous
deposits are mainly records of the Flood year, instead of millions of
years of upward evolutionary struggle, the entire evolutionary system
is scientifically bankrupt. There is little wonder, therefore, that the
concept of the geological ages is defended with such fervor, and that
"flood geology" is ridiculed or ignored.

One should recognize, too, that nowhere in the world does the
so-called geological column actually occur. It is possible for *any* vertical
sequence of these "ages," or any portion of them, to exist in any given
locality. Any age may be on the bottom, any on top, and any in between. The contained fossils—rather than vertical superposition or any
other physical feature of the formation—constitute the controlling factor
in the "age" assigned it. Thus the theory of evolution is *assumed* in
building up the geological column, and then the latter is taken as the
main proof of the theory of evolution!

The fossils in this geological column, however, speak eloquently of
death, and therefore they must have been deposited after Adam's fall
and God's curse. Thus, both the Biblical and scientific data, rightly
understood, show that the earth's great fossil graveyards must for the
most part have been buried by the Flood and its after-effects. The record
in the rocks is not a testimony to evolution, but rather to God's sovereign power and judgment on sin.

Genesis 8:15-19

15 ¶ And God spake unto Noah, saying,
16 Go forth of the ark, thou, and thy wife, and thy sons, and thy sons' wives with thee.
17 Bring forth with thee every living thing that *is* with thee, of all flesh, *both* of fowl, and of cattle, and of every creeping thing that creepeth upon the earth; that they may breed abundantly in the earth, and be fruitful, and multiply upon the earth.
18 And Noah went forth, and his sons, and his wife, and his sons' wives with him:
19 Every beast, every creeping thing, and every fowl, *and* whatsoever creepeth upon the earth, after their kinds, went forth out of the ark.

A year and seventeen days earlier, God had said to Noah: "Come thou and all thy house into the ark" (Genesis 7:1). But now He said: "Go forth of the ark, thou and thy wife, and thy sons, and thy son's wives with thee." These two commands are not contradictory, but complementary, reminding us of two complementary commands of Christ. First, He said: "*Come* unto me, all ye that labor and are heavy laden, and I will give you rest" (Matthew 11:28). This command (all the more meaningful in light of the fact that "rest" was the very meaning of Noah's prophetic name) is but the preparation for His great command: "*Go ye* into all the world and preach the gospel to every creature" (Mark 16:15). The Ark had been like the great sheepfold, with Christ the door, through whom the sheep "shall go in" to be saved, but also, through whom, they shall "go out, and find pasture" (John 10:9).

The animal occupants, awakened from their long rest in the Ark, were also brought forth and instructed to "breed abundantly" and to "multiply upon the earth." They and their progeny gradually spread out from Ararat, migrating and multiplying over many generations, until they found environments and biologic communities of plants and other animals suited to their needs. Scripture is clear in insisting that "every beast, every creeping thing, and every fowl, and whatsoever creepeth upon the earth, after their kinds, went forth out of the ark." All the earth's present dry-land animals, therefore, are descendants of those that were on the Ark.

In like manner, all the present tribes and nations of men are descended from Noah's family. "These are the three sons of Noah; and of them was the whole earth overspread" (Genesis 9:19).

As both animals and men later radiated out from Mount Ararat, they found open country ahead of them. They could move west into

Asia, east into Europe, south into Africa. Some of their descendants found a land bridge across what is now the Bering Straits into the Americas. Others found a similar land bridge down the Malaysian Straits into New Guinea and perhaps into Australia. Such land bridges are known geologically to have existed during the Ice Age, when there was a considerable lowering of sea level due to the vast amounts of water stored in great ice sheets. Modern computer studies have shown, interestingly, that the geographical center of the earth's land areas is located within a short distance of Mount Ararat, a "coincidence" that can hardly be other than providential.[2]

Lack of competition permitted animal populations to multiply very rapidly; so there was much incentive for the different groups to keep pressing forward until they found an ecological niche for which they were more suited than other groups. These conditions (rapid multiplication, small inbreeding populations, rapidly changing environments) were ideal to permit rapid variation to take place in each kind (not evolution, but rather opportunity for the originally created variational potential latent in the genetic system of each kind to become expressed openly in distinct varieties). Consequently, different varieties (or even species, and perhaps genera, in some cases, as arbitrarily defined by modern taxonomists) could rapidly develop and become established in appropriate environments.

Although God had implanted genetic factors for wide-ranging adjustment and variation in each created kind (especially was this true in the case of the "clean" kinds), permitting them to adjust to many different environments, nevertheless this potential variation was limited. Never could one kind change so much that it would become a different kind; "after its kind" was the divine principle. Since the environment was so drastically different after the Flood, there were many kinds of animals, especially those that were highly specialized or unusually large, that found it difficult to adjust. Finally, after a number of generations, these became extinct. Included in this group were the dinosaurs, the pteronodons, the creodonts, the glyptodons, and other bizarre creatures of the past.

Many of these extinctions probably took place during the Ice Age. The sharp change in temperatures following the Flood, occasioned by the precipitation of the vapor canopy that had maintained the greenhouse effect over the world, led to the buildup of great thicknesses of snow and ice near the polar regions. These eventually radiated out in

2. Andrew Woods, *The Center of the Earth* (San Diego: Institute for Creation Research, 1973), 18 pp.

the form of tremendous ice sheets, covering northern Europe and reaching down into the northern third of the United States in this hemisphere. The Ice Age probably lasted several hundred or a thousand years (not several million years, as believed by evolutionary geologists) and undoubtedly had a profound effect on the earth's animal kinds.

Genesis 8:20

20 ¶ And Noah builded an altar unto the LORD; and took of every clean beast, and of every clean fowl, and offered burnt offerings on the altar.

With such a forbidding and unpromising scene before him, and with an apparently imminent danger that the great rains and upheavals might start again at any time, Noah quite properly turned his thoughts toward God. Ever since Eden, the way of access to God had been through the offering of an animal sacrifice; accordingly, Noah had taken one extra animal of each "clean" kind on the Ark for this purpose. He proceeded immediately to build an altar (possibly after descending to the lower slopes of Mount Ararat) and to offer up burnt offerings of every clean animal and every clean bird.

This is the first mention of "altar" in the Bible, and these were sacrifices of both praise and propitiation. Noah gave thanksgiving for deliverance from the corruption of the antediluvian world and preservation through the Flood, and also made intercession for his descendants in the new world, that their lives might be protected and the earth not again destroyed.

This was, no doubt, a very considerable and generous offering of animals on Noah's part. The clean animals presumably represented mainly the domesticable animals, the ones for which Noah would have the greatest need and for which he had the greatest love and compassion. In effect, he was giving to God one-seventh of all his flocks. This required no little faith, but Noah also had much for which to praise and pray, and he had long since proved himself to be a man of strong faith.

Genesis 8:21

21 And the LORD smelled a sweet savor; and the LORD said in his heart, I will not again curse the ground any more for man's sake; for the imagination of man's heart *is* evil from his youth: neither will I again smite any more every thing living, as I have done.

"And the Lord smelled a sweet savour." That is, He heard and respected the believing—though perhaps unspoken—prayer of Noah, represented by the incense rising from the smoke of the burnt offering. Generations yet unborn, including our own, have benefited from Noah's sacrifice of intercession, and God's response to it.

God first of all relieved their immediate apprehensions by promising never again to destroy all life on the earth, smiting the earth with such a devastating curse as it had just experienced. The curse of Genesis 8:21 is not primarily the Flood, but the curse of Genesis 3:17, which will prevail until the new earth of Revelation 22:3 is created. This is evident in that the language is so similar in both cases ("curse the ground for man's sake," where "man" is the same word as "Adam"). God was not removing the Curse at this time (though Noah had brought comfort concerning the ground which the Lord had cursed—Genesis 5:29), but rather promising that there would never again be a worldwide judgment on man's dominion, such as the Edenic law of death or the Noahic visitation of death, both of which had affected the entire earth. God would *neither* curse the ground again with an additional curse to the one pronounced in Eden, *nor* again destroy everything living, as He had done with the Flood.

The reason for this promise at first seems strange: "for the imagination of man's heart is evil from his youth." This would seem to be justification for smiting the earth, rather than for promising not to do so, except for the great paradox of the love and grace of God. Here is a testimony both to what theologians call original sin and universal depravity, and also to God's redeeming mercy. Because man is helpless to save himself—his very thoughts born and nurtured in sin— he desperately needs the grace of God. On the basis of an atoning sacrifice, God's salvation and blessing are received by faith. Thus, for the very reason that man is completely unable to save himself, *therefore* God saves him! Truly, He is the God of all grace! Noah had "found grace in the eyes of the Lord" (Genesis 6:8) and, through his faithful obedience and his believing sacrifice, so have multitudes of his descendants. He did, indeed, "comfort us concerning our work and toil of our hands, because of the ground which the Lord hath cursed" (Genesis 5:29).

Although there would never again be a worldwide judgment on either the ground or on all men living, as long as the earth continued in its present form, there would, of course, be a perpetual testimony to both, easily seen by all men yet to come. The testimony of the Curse is found in the structure of the basic laws of science, the laws of thermodynamics. The testimony of the Flood is seen everywhere in the structure of the rocks of the earth's crustal surface, the worldwide fossil graveyard, and the universal evidence of catastrophism. Man's perverse and depraved nature has somehow distorted both into a system of evolution and uniformity. As Peter says, he is "willfully ignorant" (II Peter 3:5). Nevertheless the evidence is there, everywhere, for all who have eyes to see. "God is longsuffering to usward, not willing that any should perish, but that all should come to repentance" (II Peter 3:9).

Genesis 8:22

---

22 While the earth remaineth, seed-time and harvest, and cold and heat, and summer and winter, and day and night shall not cease.

The duration of God's gracious promise to Noah would be "as long as the earth remaineth." Someday, however, "the day of the Lord will come." At that time, "the earth also and the works that are therein shall be burned up" (II Peter 3:10). Then the very elements will disintegrate and all the effects of the Curse on these elements removed before they are brought together again (Revelation 21:1-5; 22:3; Romans 8:21). The fossils in the rocks, along with the other worldwide witnesses of the cataclysmic Flood, will also disintegrate and disappear.

Until that day, however, uniformity in physical processes can be counted on. Most of the earth's natural processes depend, in one way or another, on the constancy of the earth's rotation and its solar orbital revolution, controlling all diurnal and annual cycles, especially the new hydrologic and climatologic cycles.

The earth's physical features had been vastly changed by the Flood and its physical processes modified in various ways. The present hydrologic cycle was gradually established, with the energy of the solar radiation serving to draw up water by evaporation from the oceans and then to move it inland by the winds, whence it can condense into clouds and fall to the ground as rain or snow, finally to run off through the rivers or groundwater channels back to the ocean again. This present hydrologic cycle marvelously provides for the maintenance of life on the present earth in many different ways. Its ministry is often mentioned in the Bible, and always with remarkable scientific accuracy (for example, note Psalm 33:7; 135:7; Ecclesiastes 1:6, 7; Job 26:8; 36:27, 28; Isaiah 55:10).

Although the new hydrologic cycle would produce rains, and sometimes floods, God assured Noah that there would never again be a worldwide flood which would destroy all life on the land. In fact, He assured him that a regular order of nature, with a fixed sequence of seasons and a fixed cycle of day and night, would prevail from that time on. Thus, that regularity of nature which modern scientists have formalized as their "principle of uniformity" was instituted by God after the Flood. The seasons, heat and cold, day and night, are now controlled primarily by the sun, which actually supplies all the energy for the earth's physical processes. The earth's orbital revolution about the sun, its axial rotation and inclination, and its marvelous atmosphere also help establish these constants of nature, which in turn control most other geological processes. Thus the promised uniformity of the seasons and the daily cycle implies the essential uniformity of all other natural processes. It is, of course, only these *present* processes which modern scientists can actually observe, describe, and analyze. The present —not the past or the future—is the proper domain of true science.

9

The New World

(Genesis 9)

The Establishment of Human Government

In the ninth chapter of Genesis, following God's resolution "in his heart" (Genesis 8:21) not to destroy the earth again with a further curse in spite of the fact that every "imagination of man's heart" is evil, God spoke again openly to Noah. The first seventeen verses of this chapter contain a detailed quotation of God's own words, given to Noah in response to his believing sacrifice after leaving the Ark. These verses contain the basic provision for human governments among men, exercised on behalf of God. They also contain the great Noahic covenant with post-Flood man, which is still in effect as far as God is concerned, though thousands of years have passed since it was made.

Genesis 9:1, 2

CHAPTER 9

AND God blessed Noah and his sons, and said unto them, Be fruitful, and multiply, and replenish the earth. 2 And the fear of you and the dread of you shall be upon every beast of the earth, and upon every fowl of the air, upon all that moveth *upon* the earth, and upon all the fishes of the sea; into your hand are they delivered.

These verses constitute essentially a renewal (with slight modifications) of the original divine mandate given to man by God in Genesis 1:26-28. Just as Adam and Eve had been told to "be fruitful, and multiply, and fill the earth" (not "refill the earth," as the King James Version misleadingly suggests), so Noah and his three sons were now commanded once again to multiply rapidly and *fill* the earth. It was God's design that mankind should quickly spread over the entire habitable earth, in order to exercise proper dominion over it, under His sovereignty.

Actually, the specific command to "have dominion over the earth and subdue it," as given to Adam (Genesis 1:28) is omitted here, possibly an intimation that, despite the destruction of many of his hosts in the Flood, Satan still retained at least proximate dominion on the earth (I John 5:19). Thus, man no longer was to exercise *direct* authority over the animal creation, as had apparently once been his prerogative; rather, there was to be fear manifest by animals, rather than obedience and understanding. The word "dread" in the King James could better be rendered "terror." If it were otherwise, the animals, since they would be multiplying much more rapidly than man, might quickly have exterminated mankind.

It is significant that the animals that were to be characterized by fear of man included the "beast of the earth, the fowl of the air, all that 'crawls upon the ground,' and the fish of the sea." The "cattle," however, seem not to have been included in this category. The domesticated animals, which apparently are those meant by this latter term, would not shun man's presence and company; but all the others, in so far as possible and normal, would seek to flee at the approach of man. They were delivered into man's hand, in the sense that he was free to do as he would with them, though, of course, always as a responsible steward under God's jurisdiction.

Genesis 9:3, 4

---

3 Every moving thing that liveth shall be meat for you; even as the green herb have I given you all things.

4 But flesh with the life thereof, *which is* the blood thereof, shall ye not eat.

Furthermore, animals were for the first time authorized for use as food (although quite possibly this had been done before the Flood without authorization). The reason for this change is not obvious; perhaps the more rigorous environment in the new world required the animal protein in meats for man's sustenance to a degree not normally available in other foods. Possibly the Lord also desired thus to show the great gulf between man and the animals, anticipating the dangers implicit in the evil doctrine of the evolutionary continuity of life of all flesh, which ultimately equates man with the animals and denies the Creator, in whose image man alone was made. The fact is, that doctrine had already begun to make its appearance in the early forms of paganism and polytheism.

Apparently no restrictions as to which animals man could eat were made at this point, though in the special economy of Israel only a few animals were later denominated by God as "clean" for this purpose. Mankind in general, both before the call of Israel and after the formation of the Church, incorporating believers of every nation, was free to partake as freely of "every moving thing that liveth" as he had been previously free to partake of every green herb (Genesis 1:29, 30). Obviously, of course, he was also free to refrain from eating any creature or any herb which he did not want.

But with this permission, there was also the restriction: "flesh with the life thereof, which is the blood thereof, shall ye not eat." The flesh was given for meat, but the *life* of the flesh was given for sacrifice. "For the life of the flesh is in the blood; and I have given it to you upon the altar to make an atonement for your souls: for it is the blood that maketh an atonement for the soul" (Leviticus 17:11). The words "life" and "soul" in these verses are the same word (Hebrew *nephesh*). The blood, of course, performs the physiological function of conveying the necessary chemicals from the air and food to sustain and renew the physical flesh, and particularly to maintain the consciousness and the ordinary thought processes of the brain. All of this complex of marvelous operations is called the "life" or the "soul," the consciousness which distinguishes animal life from plant life. The "life" of an animal, spilled on a sacrificial altar, was accepted by God in substitutionary death for the life of a guilty sinner, who deserved to die but who was permitted to live because of the sacrifice, whose blood "covered" his sins.

The blood of animals could only figuratively cover sins, of course. The reality represented by the figure was the sacrifice of the Lamb of God, Jesus Christ, who "now once in the end of the world hath appeared to put away sin by the sacrifice of himself" (Hebrews 9:26).

Genesis 9:5, 6

---

5 And surely your blood of your lives will I require: at the hand of every beast will I require it, and at the hand of man; at the hand of every man's brother will I require the life of man.

6 Whoso sheddeth man's blood, by man shall his blood be shed: for in the image of God made he man.

Thus the blood of animals, representing their life, was sacred and not to be eaten, since it was accepted in sacrifice in substitution for the life of man. Also involved was the simple matter of reverence to the life principle, as a specially created entity by God (Genesis 1:21), not merely something to satisfy man's appetite. There is also a possible divine warning here against the pagan notion that drinking the blood of a slain enemy, either animal or human, would allow the life characteristics of that creature to be incorporated in the life of its vanquisher.

Man's blood, representing *his* life, was even more sacred than that of animals, for "in the image of God made he man." Though animals shared the possession of a soul and body with man, it was only man who had an eternal spirit, the image of God. Neither beast nor man was therefore permitted to spill man's blood. From any animal or any man who shed human blood, God would require satisfaction; and that would be nothing less than the very blood of their own lives.

The word "require" is a judicial term, God here appearing as a judge who exacts a strict and severe penalty for infraction of a sacred law. If a beast kills a man, the beast must be put to death (note also Exodus 21:28). If a man kills another man (willfully and culpably, it is assumed), then he also must be put to death by "every man's brother." The latter phrase is not intended to initiate family revenge slayings, of course, but rather to stress that all men are responsible to see that this justice is executed. At the time these words were first spoken, all men indeed were literal brothers; for only the three sons of Noah were living at the time, other than Noah himself. Since all future people would be descended from these three men and their wives, in a very real sense all men *are* brothers, because all were once in the loins of these three brothers. This is in essence a command to establish a formal system of human government, in order to assure that justice is carried out, especially in the case of murder.

The authority to execute this judgment of God on a murderer was thus delegated to man. "Whoso sheddeth man's blood, by man shall his blood be shed: for in the image of God made he man." The anarchistic conditions that had developed before the Flood—men slaying whom they would and defending themselves as they could—were not to be permitted to recur. Before the Flood, there was evidently no formal arrangement of human government, save perhaps the patriarchal authority of the father. There was no formal mechanism for the punishment of crime, or of crime prevention, even for the capital crime of murder, as evident in the individual histories of Cain and Lamech. Evidently each person was able to act quite independently of all restraints except those of his own conscience and self-interest. This eventuallly led to a universal state of violence and anarchy. To prevent the development of similar conditions after the Flood, God established the institution of human government, including especially the authority for capital punishment.

It is clear, of course, that the authority for capital punishment implies also the authority to establish laws governing those human activities and personal relationships which if unregulated could soon lead to murder (e.g., robbery, adultery, usurpation of property boundaries). Thus, this simple instruction to Noah is the fundamental basis for all human legal and governmental institutions.

The instruction here given in no way refers merely to vengeance; the emphasis is rather on justice and on careful recognition of the sacredness of the divine image in man, marred by sin though it be. Obviously some means of impartial verification of guilt prior to execution of the judgment is assumed, though no formal legal system is here outlined. Evidently the particular *form* of government might vary with time and place; but the *fact* of human government, exercised under God, is clearly established.

The modern "liberal" objections to capital punishment are insufficient to warrant setting aside this decree of God. The prohibition in the Ten Commandments against killing plainly applies only to murder, not to judicial executions; in fact, the Mosaic laws themselves established capital punishment as the penalty not only for murder but also for breaking any one of the Ten Commandments (note Hebrews 10:28).

Similarly, the Christian dispensation in no way sets aside these provisions of the Noahic covenant. The eating of meat (I Timothy 4:3, 4), the abstinence from blood (Acts 15:19, 20), and the authority of the governmental "sword" (Romans 13:4; Acts 25:11) are reaffirmed in the New Testament, by way of emphasizing to the early Christians that these were not merely a part of the Jewish law, but were integral components in God's original covenant with *all* men. Christ, in fact, seemed almost to echo God's words to Noah when He said: "All they that take the sword shall perish with the sword" (Matthew 26:52).

The above observations are not to suggest that there is never to be an exception to the punishment of execution for the crime of murder. With God, justice may be tempered with mercy, especially in response to genuine repentance. Though David, for example, was guilty of the capital crimes of adultery and murder in the case of Bathsheba and Uriah, God forgave him when he repented. And so David, rather than dying by the sword or by stoning, as he may strictly have deserved, "died in a good old age, full of days, riches, and honour" (I Chronicles 29:28). Although the woman taken in adultery was guilty by the Mosaic law of a crime punishable by death (Leviticus 20:10; Deuteronomy 22:22), the Lord Jesus, seeing her heart of repentance, was moved to forgive her and to see that she was set free (John 8:3-11). In like manner, a judge (or the particular governmental structure as established) is no doubt warranted in taking such mitigating factors as may exist in a given situation into consideration in determining a sentence, even though he would also be fully warranted in carrying out the strict legal penalty of capital punishment. The essential point is that man is hereby given the responsibility of human government and that this responsibility entails first of all the recognition of the sacredness of human life and the recognition of capital punishment as the just and legal penalty for murder.

The Hebrew word *shaphak* is interesting. It is translated "sheddeth" here in Genesis 9:6, where it is used for the first time in Scripture. It is often translated also as "poured out" or "poured forth" or "shed forth." It is frequently used of the "pouring out" of the wrath of God (Psalm 69:24), but also of the pouring out of His Spirit (Joel 2:28). Many times it refers to the pouring out of the blood of the animal sacrifices at the base of the altar (Leviticus 4:30). It is the word used prophetically by Christ on the cross, when He cried: "I am poured out like water" (Psalm 22:14).

Its first mention, here in Genesis 9:6, thus stresses not only the sacredness of human life, but also points us forward to the One who was most perfectly and eternally "in the image of God," and whose blood would be shed judicially, though utterly unjustly, by human governmental authority—but who, in the marvelous counsels of God, thereby "made his soul an offering for sin" (Isaiah 53:10).

Genesis 9:7

---

7 And you, be ye fruitful, and multiply;
bring forth abundantly in the earth, and
multiply therein.

In concluding these commands, God repeated His injunction to multiply in the earth. Literally, man was to "bring forth in swarms." As a matter of fact, in perhaps a little over four thousand years, man's population has increased from eight people to almost four billion. This amounts to an average of 2.5 children per family, or an increase of ½ percent annually.

The Rainbow Covenant

God's covenant with Noah involved a number of elements, several of which have just been discussed, as far as the responsibilities of Noah and his descendants were concerned. However, the word itself is first used in verse 9, in connection with God's promise not to send the *mabbul* again to destroy the earth, so that the emphasis is on God's promises rather than man's obligations. As a matter of fact, man's obedience to these commands was not a condition determining whether God would keep His part of the bargain. God promised unconditionally— evidently as a result of Noah's faith and his sacrificial offerings—that He would never again send a worldwide flood, or destroy all flesh, as long as the earth remained. Furthermore, God graciously gave Noah and his descendants a beautiful "sign" that He would keep His word.

As His assurance that, despite the clouds in the sky, and the prospects of more rain, and perhaps occasional *local* floods in the future, there would never again be a *universal* flood, God established the rainbow. The "bow in the cloud" (verse 13), of course, requires both sunlight and "the cloud"—that is, liquid water droplets in the air— before it can form. Before the Flood, the upper air contained only invisible water *vapor,* and therefore no rainbow was possible. With the new hydrological cycle following the Flood, the former vapor canopy is gone; and it is physically impossible now for enough water ever to be raised into the atmosphere to cause a universal flood. When a storm has done its worst and the clouds are finally exhausted of most of their water, then there always appears a rainbow, and so God would have us remember again His promise after the great Flood.

Genesis 9:8-10

---

8 ¶ And God spake unto Noah, and to his sons with him, saying,
9 And I, behold, I establish my covenant with you, and with your seed after you;

10 And with every living creature that *is* with you, of the fowl, of the cattle, and of every beast of the earth with you; from all that go out of the ark, to every beast of the earth.

There apparently was a pause in God's communication with Noah and his sons after He finished giving His instructions to them concerning the future responsibilities of them and their offspring. Then, once again

He began speaking, this time to convey the gracious promises of His rainbow covenant.

There are many important covenants in Scripture—with Moses, with the nation of Israel, with David, and, especially, the "new covenant" (Hebrews 8:8). However, in these verses is the first use of the actual word (except for its promise, in Genesis 6:18). Presumably, then, this was the *first* covenant. Some writers do speak of an Edenic covenant and an Adamic covenant, but the word itself (Hebrew *berith*) was not used in connection with God's dealings with Adam. The protevangelic promise of Genesis 3:15 might be understood as such a covenant, but Scripture itself does not use that term in connection with it.

It is significant that the Noahic covenant was not only with Noah and his descendants, but also with the animals going out of the Ark and their descendants. Even though animals do not possess an eternal soul and spirit, as men do, they are God's creatures; and He is concerned about them (note Matthew 6:26; 10:29; Jonah 4:11). It is perhaps especially significant that the wild beasts are mentioned twice by God, as though to emphasize that even that portion of the animal kingdom which might superficially seem to be of least concern to the Creator is also under His providential care. Floods may be especially destructive to those animals which can neither fly nor depend on man for assistance, and so God makes a special point that these will never have to fear another worldwide flood.

Note the description of those animals with whom His covenant was made: "all that go out of the Ark." Here is another incidental reference to the universality of the Flood, since otherwise all land animals surviving a mere local flood would not have come under the terms of God's covenant.

Genesis 9:11, 12

---

11 And I will establish my covenant with you; neither shall all flesh be cut off any more by the waters of a flood; neither shall there any more be a flood to destroy the earth.

12 And God said, This *is* the token of the covenant which I make between me and you, and every living creature that *is* with you, for perpetual generations:

In this verse again God employs the term "covenant," as had been done in Genesis 6:18, as well as here in verses 9, 11, 12, 13, 15, 16, and 17—a total of no less than eight times! Evidently, God regarded it as important that "perpetual generations" should continually remember this tremendous unconditional covenant which He made with all men right at the very beginning of this age. The tragedy is, that though all men admire the beautiful rainbow, few any longer associate it with God's promise; nor do many even believe that there ever was such a Flood!

Nevertheless, God did make His promise that never would *the* "mabbul" come again (the definite article before "Flood" is justified in the original). Here also is another verse that indicates the *earth,* as well as man, had been destroyed by the Flood. It is obvious, of course, that if the Flood were only a local flood, then the great promise in this verse is meaningless. There have been many destructive local floods throughout history.

God not only made His covenant with man, but also proceeded to tell him that He will give a perpetual token, or sign, by which he is to be reminded perpetually of this covenant. The word for "token" (Hebrew *oth*) is the same word translated "sign" in Genesis 1:14 in connection with the purpose of the heavenly bodies, and translated "mark" in connection with God's protection of Cain (Genesis 4:15).

Genesis 9:13-17

---

13 I do set my bow in the cloud, and it shall be for a token of a covenant between me and the earth.
14 And it shall come to pass, when I bring a cloud over the earth, that the bow shall be seen in the cloud:
15 And I will remember my covenant, which *is* between me and you and every living creature of all flesh; and the waters shall no more become a flood to destroy all flesh.
16 And the bow shall be in the cloud; and I will look upon it, that I may remember the everlasting covenant between God and every living creature of all flesh that *is* upon the earth.
17 And God said unto Noah, This *is* the token of the covenant, which I have established between me and all flesh that *is* upon the earth.

For the "token of the covenant," God established the beautiful rainbow in the clouds. Just as the fossil-bearing rocks of the earth's crust would continually remind us that God once destroyed the earth with a Flood, so the rainbow after the rain would remind us that He will never do so again. In fact, regardless of the latter-day threats of thermonuclear bombs, death rays, germ warfare, pollution of the atmosphere and hydrosphere, and other fearful things, we have His promise that, at least until the end of the millennium—"while the earth remaineth"— He will never again "smite any more everything living" (Genesis 8:21, 22).

It is not only that man himself would see the rainbow. God also would "look upon it," whenever He would "bring a cloud over the earth," and would "remember his covenant." This was peculiarly "my bow," according to the Lord, probably referring to the fact that it had just now been formed as a result of the great Flood which He had brought on the earth. Some writers, of uniformitarian tendencies, can hardly believe that this was the first time the rainbow appeared; and so they explain this by saying that God just now invested the rainbow with this symbolic meaning, even though it had been in existence for millions of years before. Such an interpretation, of course, makes God out to be quite puerile in His dealings with man. The prior existence of rain and the rainbow, of course, is really a part of the local flood theory, which has already been shown to be impossible.

In these verses, the Lord seems to be repeating, over and over in various ways, His great promise and covenant with all flesh. Such repetition was no doubt of great comfort and assurance to those who had been through such traumatic experiences during the awful year of the Flood and who, apart from God's promise, would have had little hope for the future. But the same Lord who had seen them safely through the Flood would also protect and provide for them in the future; and in the months and years to come, they would often remember these promises. There would be many devastating local floods, continuing earthquakes and volcanism, cold winters and even a long Ice Age, and many other disturbances in the physical earth, all a part of the "residual catastrophism" resulting from the upheavals of the great Flood. But over and over again, after a period of such storms and convulsions, they would see the beautiful rainbow traversing the heavens, and remember that God was still on His throne and the world was safe from destruction.

Furthermore, they had His word that His covenant was an everlasting covenant. It was valid for them and for their children to "perpetual generations," until God's great promised time of consummation and restoration of all things. The rainbow, spanning from one end of heaven to the other, would remind them that God's promises were from eternity to eternity, from beginning to end.

The rainbow thus demonstrates most gloriously the grace of God. The pure white light from the unapproachable holiness of His throne (I Timothy 6:16) is refracted, as it were, through the glory clouds surrounding His presence (I Kings 8:10, 11), breaking into all the glorious colors of God's creation. In wrath, He remembers mercy. The glory follows the sufferings; and where sin abounded, grace did much more abound!

The rainbow reappears only three more times in Scripture. Once, in Ezekiel 1:28, the rainbow is seen surrounding the throne of God as He prepares to visit judgment on His people Israel. Again, the rainbow is seen around His throne just before the coming Great Tribulation, in Revelation 4:3. In both these cases, the picture is one of imminent judgment and suffering, but only *limited* judgment and suffering, with God's grace ruling over all.

Finally, when the mighty angel of Revelation 10:1, who can be none other than the Lord Jesus Christ Himself, comes to claim dominion over the world, which He had created but which had long been under the dominion of the wicked one, He is accompanied by the same "seven thunders" of judgment which apparently had once cried forth at the time of the Flood (Revelation 10:3, 4, compared with Psalm 29:3-10). And instead of a crown of thorns, which once He wore as He bore the Curse for us, the Word says there will be *"the rainbow upon his head."* The definite article is in the original: *the* rainbow. This can hardly refer to any other rainbow than to "my bow," the token of the *everlasting* covenant between God and all flesh (Genesis 10:16, with Revelation 10:6).

Forevermore, it is in this glorious apparel that we will see our Lord Jesus Christ "crowned with glory and honour, that he by the grace of God should taste death for every man" (Hebrews 2:9).

The Sons of Noah

The so-called race question has certainly been one of the most important issues of our time. The same is true for the issue of nationalism versus internationalism. The existence of distinctive races and nations and languages is obviously a fact of modern life, in spite of the efforts of many modern sociologists and politicians to break down all racial and national barriers. The problems created by these issues often seem almost insurmountable.

The true origin of the world's various races and nations, and the events associated with it, must be clearly understood and placed in right perspective before these problems can ever be adequately resolved. The Genesis record gives us the only fully reliable account of these matters, and it is thus urgently important that we understand and believe what it says.

In the world today there seem to be several major "races" (three to six or more, depending on the particular system of classification), perhaps 150 or so nations of some significance, and well over 3,000 tribal languages and dialects. Yet this diversity of peoples and tongues must have come from a common ancestor, because all of these are true men, capable of physical interrelationships, capable of learning and education, and even capable of spiritual fellowship with the Creator, through faith in Christ. The origin of races and nations is still a mystery to most scientists, determined as they are to explain man and his cultures in an evolutionary framework. There are numerous contradictory theories on these matters among anthropologists and ethnologists, but the only fully reliable record of the true origin of races, nations, and languages is found here in Genesis 9 through 11.

Genesis 9:18, 19

---

18 ¶ And the sons of Noah, that went forth of the ark, were Shĕm, and Ham, and Jā'phĕth: and Ham *is* the father of Cā'nǎan.

19 These *are* the three sons of Noah: and of them was the whole earth overspread.

Although the "sons of Noah" have been referred to several times throughout the Flood narrative, they are here actually once again identified by name. Although, when listed, their names are usually given in the order "Shem, Ham, and Japheth" (Genesis 5:32; 6:10; 7:13; 9:18), it is not certain as to what chronological order actually applies to them. In any case, it was from these three, and their wives, that "the whole earth was overspread." Scripture is quite explicit in teaching that all men now living in the world are descended from Noah through his three sons (see also Genesis 10:32; Acts 17:26). All the physical characteristics of the different nations and tribes must, therefore, have been present in the genetic constitutions of these six people who came through the Flood in the Ark. Somehow, by the regular mechanisms of genetics—variation, recombination—all the various groups of nations and tribes must have developed from this beginning.

It is interesting that in this summary verse, Ham is identified particularly as the one of Noah's sons who was the father of Canaan. Canaan, in reality, seems to have been Ham's youngest son (Genesis 10:6), and was no more prominent in history than his other sons. Presumably, he is singled out for special mention because of his being the ancestor of the Canaanites, who were the wicked inhabitants of the land promised to Abraham and to the children of Israel, at the time when Moses was later editing this narrative and leading his people there.

Genesis 9:20, 21

---

20 And Noah began *to be* a husband-man, and he planted a vineyard:
21 And he drank of the wine, and was drunken; and he was uncovered within his tent.

Noah and his family, according to ancient traditions at least, lived for a goodly number of years after the Flood on the lower slopes on the northern side of Mount Ararat. Although Noah lived for three hundred years after the Flood, he never had any other sons. Shem, Ham, and Japheth lived near him and soon began to raise families of their own.

All three of these sons had been born after Noah was 500 years old (Genesis 5:32) and before he was, say, 575 years old (since they were all grown and married before his 600th year, when the Flood came). The Adamic nature was, of course, still a part of the Noahic heredity. This fact, coupled with the terrible moral environment of the antediluvian world, was bound to leave Noah and his sons still subject to Satanic temptation. Ham, especially, seems to have been secretly rebellious and carnally minded, even though a real believer in God. The tragic story of Noah's drunkenness and the sudden unveiling of Ham's rebellious heart provides graphic evidence that, despite the cleansing judgment of the Flood, man was still a sinner and Satan still "the spirit that now worketh in the sons of disobedience" (Ephesians 2:2). But the behavior of Shem and Japheth, as well as that of Ham, in this time of sudden family crisis, provides the clue to their characters and the occasion for Noah's remarkable prophecy.

The first time "wine" is mentioned in the Bible occurs here in connection with the drunkenness and shame of Noah. Undoubtedly the nature of wine was well known to the antediluvians, and there is no intimation in Scripture that Noah was not fully cognizant of what he was doing when he made and drank his wine. Scripture does not hesitate to call attention to the failures of even the most saintly of men. Noah, having stood strong against the attacks of evil men for hundreds of years, remaining steadfast in the face of such opposition and discouragement as few men have ever faced, now let down his guard, as it were, when it seemed that all would be peace and victory from now on. After everything he had been through, what harm could there be in a little relaxation and a little provision for the comforts of the flesh?

But Scripture warns: "Be sober, be vigilant; because your adversary the devil, as a roaring lion, walketh about, seeking whom he may devour" (I Peter 5:8). Satan had been unable to corrupt the family of Noah before the Flood, although he had succeeded with all other families; and he now seized his opportunity. The formation of intoxicating wine from the pure, healthful juice of grapes is a perfect symbol of corruption and decay. The process of fermentation is a decay process and the effect of drinking the alcoholic product of this decay is likewise, in several respects, a "breaking down," both physically and morally. It is essentially the same process as that of "leavening," which is everywhere in Scripture symbolic of corruption.

Noah doubtless had no intention of drinking to excess, but he did. The artificial heat induced by the wine impelled him to throw off his clothing and finally he lay down in his tent in a drunken sleep. Noah cannot be excused for this on the basis of his ignorance that the new wine would decay into intoxicating wine (some writers have suggested that the different atmospheric conditions before the Flood somehow inhibited the decay process, but there seems to be no reasonable scientific basis for this idea), but this seems to have been his only significant moral lapse in a long life of faithful obedience to God under the most difficult of circumstances.

Genesis 9:22, 23

---

22 And Ham, the father of Cā′năan, saw the nakedness of his father, and told his two brethren without.
23 And Shĕm and Jā′phĕth took a garment, and laid *it* upon both their shoulders, and went backward, and covered the nakedness of their father; and their faces *were* backward, and they saw not their father's nakedness.

As Noah lay sleeping on his couch, his robe fallen on the floor where he had dropped it when he, only half-aware of what he was doing, threw it off, Ham chanced to enter his tent.

This event took place probably many decades after the Flood, because Canaan, the youngest of Ham's four sons, was at least sufficiently mature for the bent of his character to be well known to his grandfather Noah. Ham, along with Shem and Japheth, had undoubtedly each established his own independent residence at some distance from that of Noah, but maintained contact with him by occasional visits.

Noah thought he was alone while he was savoring the wine he had made, and thus had no idea that anyone would see him that day. If he had been anticipating such a visit, he would certainly have been more careful. But he was *not* careful, and Satan seized on this rare opportunity, implanting somehow within Ham's mind the desire to call unexpectedly on his father at that particular time.

As Ham entered the tent, he was surprised to see his father lying there, naked and in a drunken sleep. But he did more than see him. The word "saw," in this context implies "gazed at"—evidently with satisfaction.

Some commentators have interpreted this account as Ham experiencing homosexual lust and perhaps even a homosexual act on his father (because of the phrase "done to him" in verse 24). The passage does not say this, however, and therefore such an interpretation is unwarranted. Ham was a believer, after all, and had entered the Ark voluntarily to escape the moral corruption in the old world.

A much more probable interpretation of Ham's actions here is that they expressed a long-hidden resentment of his father's authority and moral rectitude. There was apparently a carnal and rebellious bent to Ham's nature, thus far restrained by the spiritual strength and patriarchal authority of his father.

Now, however, beholding the evidence of his father's human weakness before his very eyes, he rejoiced, no doubt feeling a sense of release from all the inhibitions which had until now suppressed his own desires and ambitions. Thinking his brothers would share his satisfaction, he hastened to find them and tell them the savory news. Literally, the text means "he told with delight."

Shem and Japheth, however, reacted quite differently than Ham. They did rush to Noah's tent, but not to revel in his weakness and shame. Instead, they refused even to look at their father. Doing what they could to help him, they covered him with the garment he had discarded. Apparently they did not rebuke Ham verbally, but their actions were a stronger rebuke than anything they could have said.

Ham's sin was not so much one of immoral lust or prurient pleasure in what he saw, though there may have been an element of this present. Rather it was one of rebellion against his father's authority, plus resentment against the entire moral standard that had been taught and enforced by Noah in his family for well over a hundred years. Fundamentally, his act revealed an attitude of resentment against God Himself, a character trait which was bound to crop out explosively some day, if not in Ham, then in his children.

Genesis 9:24

---

24 And Noah awoke from his wine, and
knew what his younger son had done
unto him.

Eventually Noah awakened "from his wine"—that is, from his wine stupor. He noticed the robe that had been placed on him. Obviously, someone had placed it there. Perhaps he vaguely remembered throwing it off the evening before; but in any case, it was not on him in the same fashion as if he had merely lain on the couch fully clothed to take a nap.

He must have inquired, first from his wife (if she was still living) and then from his sons, until he learned fully what had transpired. As ashamed as he must have been of his own moral lapse, he realized that the sin of Ham was far greater, since it revealed a heart of rebellion and unbelief—not only against his father but also against his father's God. Similarly, the act of Shem and Japheth plainly testified of both their respect for their father and their own reverential faith in the Lord.

The Noahic Prophecy

With the deepest hearts of his own sons thus laid bare before him, Noah was moved to make the great prophetic declaration of verses 25-27. To some extent the insight thus revealed concerning the future was no doubt based on the insight he had gained into the character of his sons. Knowing them, and their children, he could foresee the future course their descendants would necessarily tend to follow, because of their respective genetic inheritances, as well as from the teachings and examples set by their fathers. More importantly, of course, he spoke in the Spirit, prophesying as the Spirit gave utterance. He first of all had to take proper note of what "his younger son had done unto him." It is probable, though not certain, that the adjective "younger" here actually means "youngest," Ham being Noah's youngest son and Japheth the "eldest" (Genesis 10:21).

It is significant that, as the great prophecy of Genesis 3:15-19 was given as a result of the fall of Adam, this prophecy was given as a result of the fall of Noah.

The parallel between the two situations is striking. Both Adam and Noah were commanded to fill the earth and exercise control over it. Each of them is actually the ancestor of all men in the present world. Each sinned by partaking of a fruit—Noah of the fruit of the vine and

Adam of the fruit of the tree of knowledge. As a result, each became naked and then was provided with a covering by someone else. Finally the prophecy resulted in a curse which has affected mankind ever since. Along with the curse, however, there were also the blessing and anticipation of ultimate salvation.

According to Acts 17:26, God has a specific time and place and purpose for each nation throughout the ages. Although each race and nation were to contribute to the corporate life of mankind as a whole, the overriding purpose of every national entity was "that they should seek the Lord" (Acts 17:27). The basic outline of the function of each of the three major streams of nations is given in the remarkable prophecy of Noah in Genesis 9:25-27.

Genesis 9:25

---

25 And he said, Cursed *be* Cā′năan; a servant of servants shall he be unto his brethren.

Noah's prophetic words were directed first toward Ham (in the person of his son Canaan), then Shem, then Japheth, the order probably representing order of age from youngest to eldest, as noted above. Because of the seriousness of his offense, Ham received first attention.

While he could gladly pronounce a blessing on his sons Shem and Japheth, Noah could not bring himself to pronounce a curse directly on his other son, Ham, though he knew prophetically that such a curse would be the lot of his descendants. Thus he said instead, as it were: "Cursed is [not 'be'] Canaan, since he, along with his older brothers [Cush, Mizraim, and Phut], has inherited the carnal and materialistic nature of his father Ham."

It has long been argued whether this curse applies only to Canaan or to all the descendants of Ham. The difficulty with applying it only to Canaan is threefold: first, the prophecy seems intended to be symmetrical and worldwide, applying to all Noah's descendants; second, if it deals solely with Canaan, it has been fulfilled only very sporadically and imperfectly. The descendants of Canaan included, for example, the Phoenicians and Hittites, who constituted two of the greatest nations of antiquity for a long time. It is true that even these, as well as the other Canaanites, were eventually subjugated or destroyed by their enemies; but the same fate befell many of the descendants of Shem and Japheth as well.

Finally, it was the sin of Ham (not Canaan) that had served as the occasion for his father's curse, and it would have been inappropriate for Noah thus to single out only one of Ham's four sons as bearing the burden of the curse. Therefore, it seems necessary to understand this as a Hamitic, rather than Canaanitic, curse, with Canaan mentioned specifically in order to stress that the terms of the prophecy extended to all of Ham's sons, even his youngest. In the context of the immediate situation, it may also have been a reaction to Noah's hurt; that is, as Noah's youngest son had brought grief to his own heart, so he especially singled out Ham's youngest son in his prophecy.

Assuming, however, that the curse did apply to the Hamitic peoples in general, what was its meaning and how has it been fulfilled? "A servant of servants shall he be to his brethren" can hardly mean "a slave of slaves," because such a situation has never occurred among the descendants of any of Ham's four sons, including Canaan. The descendants of Ham included the Sumerians, the Egyptians, the Ethiopians, and other great nations of the past; and there is a good possibility they include some of the great Asiatic nations of the present as well.

Unfortunately, there have been some interpreters who have applied the Hamitic curse specifically to the Negro peoples, using it to justify keeping the black man in economic servitude or even slavery. It is obvious, however, that the prophecy applies not only to black Africans but also to all other descendants of Ham (most of whom are *not* blacks), and no more of the Hamitic peoples have experienced such servitude during their history than the non-Hamitic peoples.

If "servant of servants" does not mean "lowest slave," then what does it mean? Although the word "servant" is used frequently in the Old Testament, this is the only place where "servant of servants" occurs. In the next two verses, Noah predicted that Canaan would be both "servant" to Shem and "servant" to Japheth. In other words, the nations descended from Ham would be servants not only to one other nation or one other group of nations, but to *all* other nations. This unique and worldwide "service" is probably in part what is meant by the superlative "servant of servants."

It might be objected, however, that the Hamitic nations have never been under worldwide subjugation to the Japhetic and Semitic nations (neither, for that matter, have the Canaanites alone). In answer to this objection, it may be noted that a servant is not necessarily a slave. In fact, the word is used much more often to refer to one who has the position of "steward," a very honorable position in a household, rather than to one who is a slave.

This, in fact, is the first mention of the word "servant" in the Bible and, as such, undoubtedly has special significance. In a sense, it may be prophetic of Christ, who was in the fullest degree made to be a servant of servants for all the world, bearing the curse for us (Philippians 2:6-8; Galatians 3:10, 13).

There is one other possibility, which does seem to fit all the facts of the case. If "servant" in this case means "steward," then the prediction becomes one of material service to mankind. Man in general is God's steward over the physical world and its processes, as well as its living creatures. Because of man's sin, the ground had already come under God's "curse" (Genesis 3:17); and man was from then on to develop and utilize its resources for the sustenance of life "in the sweat of his face." However, man still had the responsibility of subduing and exercising dominion over the earth and its creatures (Genesis 1:28; Psalm 8:6-9), a responsibility which demanded first of all that he seek to *understand* his dominion. This would require intellectual effort, research, knowledge, and everything that is involved in the term "science," as well as "philosophy."

The greatest of man's responsibilities, however, was to fill the earth, not only with physical descendants (Genesis 1:28; 9:1) but "with the knowledge of the Lord" (Isaiah 11:9; Habakkuk 2:14). He was to teach men to "call upon the name of the Lord" (Genesis 4:26), preserving and transmitting the promises of God until the coming of the world's Redeemer.

Mankind thus had three fundamental types of duties to perform as God's steward over the world: (1) *spiritual*—receiving, preserving, and teaching the knowledge of the word of God; (2) *intellectual*—expanding and teaching the knowledge of the world of God; and (3) *physical*—providing the material means for man's bodily needs and comforts, thus enabling him to fulfill his intellectual and spiritual functions more effectively. These three duties correspond, in fact, to the tripartite nature of man: spirit, soul, and body.

Every person has, to some degree, all three capacities, but in each person one usually dominates. That is, some people are dominated by physical considerations, some by intellectual, some by spiritual. The same generalization applies to nations: some have historically been primarily motivated by religious considerations, some by philosophical and scientific thinking, others by materialistic (or so-called practical) pursuits.

It is therefore very significant that these first three progenitors of

all modern nations were recognized by their father to have characteristics representing these three emphases. Shem was mainly motivated by spiritual considerations, Japheth by intellectual, and Ham by
physical; and the same would be true (in a very general way, of course)
of the nations descending from them, by reasons of both genetic inheritance and parental example.

Each was regarded as God's servant—Shem in spiritual service
and Japheth in intellectual service. Ham, responsible for physical service,
was thus a "servant of servants," serving both Shem and Japheth, who
were also servants. He would provide the physical means (food, clothing,
shelter, weapons, machinery, transportation, technological inventions, and
equipment of all kinds) which would enable his brothers to carry out
their spiritual and mental responsibilities toward mankind and toward
God. In this way, Ham also would be serving God.

Since, however, Ham would be concerned more directly than the
others with the "ground which the Lord hath cursed" (Genesis 5:29),
the great Curse would be felt more directly by him than by the others.
In this sense, the Hamitic responsibility was itself a "curse," even though
his duties were absolutely necessary for the accomplishment of God's
purposes in mankind. This prediction by Noah was, of course, a Spirit-
inspired prophecy (not an imprecation born of Noah's resentment),
appropriate to the nature of Ham and his sons, and concerned, as it
has shown itself to be, mainly with physical considerations.

Assuming (as will be discussed more completely in the next chapter)
that we can identify fairly well the Semitic nations (Jews, Arabs, Syrians,
Assyrians, Babylonians, Persians, etc.) and the Japhetic nations (Indo-
Europeans), then by process of elimination all others are Hamitic. The
Hamites, in general, have been largely unconcerned with either science,
philosophy, or theology, and have been occupied largely with material
pursuits. They have often been great inventors and technologists, as
well as hard laborers on farms and hard fighters in battle.

Descendants of Ham included the Egyptians and Sumerians, who
founded the first two great empires of antiquity, as well as other great
nations such as the Phoenicians, Hittites, and Canaanites. The modern
African tribes and the Mongol tribes (including today the Chinese and
Japanese), as well as the American Indians and the South Sea Islanders,
are probably dominantly Hamitic in origin.

Among the many ways in which the Hamites have been the great
"servants" of mankind are the following:

(1) They were the original explorers and settlers of practically all parts of the world, following the dispersion at Babel.

(2) They were the first cultivators of most of the basic food staples of the world, such as potatoes, corn, beans, cereals, and others, as well as the first ones to domesticate most animals.

(3) They developed most of the basic types of structural forms and building tools and materials.

(4) They were the first to develop most of the usual fabrics for clothing and the various sewing and weaving devices.

(5) They discovered and invented a wide variety of medicines and surgical practices and instruments.

(6) They invented most of the concepts of basic practical mathematics, as well as surveying and navigation.

(7) The machinery of commerce and trade—money, banks, postal systems, and so forth—was developed by them.

(8) They developed paper, ink, block printing, movable type, and other accouterments of writing and communication.

If one traces back far enough, he will find that practically every other basic device or system needed for man's physical sustenance or convenience originated with one of the Hamitic peoples.[1] Truly they have been the "servants" of mankind in a most amazing way.

Yet the prophecy had an obverse side as well. The Hamites have usually been able to go only so far with their explorations and inventions, and no farther. The Japhethites and Semites have, sooner or later, taken over their territories and their inventions, and then developed and utilized them to their own advantage in accomplishing their own "service" to mankind. Sometimes the Hamites, especially the Negroes, have even become actual slaves to the others. Possessed of a genetic character concerned mainly with mundane, practical matters, they have often eventually been displaced by the intellectual and philosophical acumen of the Japhethites and the religious zeal of the Semites.

These very general and broad national and racial characteristics obviously admit of many exceptions on an individual genetic basis. Furthermore, it is obvious that the prophecy is a divine description of future facts, in no way needing the deliberate assistance of the Semites or Japhethites for its accomplishment. Neither Negroes nor any other Hamitic people is intended to be forcibly subjugated on

---

1. Arthur C. Custance, *Noah's Three Sons* (Grand Rapids: Zondervan Publishing House, 1975), 368 pp.

the basis of this Noahic declaration. The prophecy would be fulfilled because of innate genetics and divine leading, not by virtue of any artificial constraints imposed by man.

Genesis 9:26

26 And he said, Blessed *be* the LORD God of Shĕm; and Cā'năan shall be his servant.

Having predicted Ham's primary relationship to the cursed ground, along with his material responsibilities to mankind, Noah turned his attention to his next son, Shem. Not only by his action of filial respect, but apparently also by a character of life closely observed by his father, Shem had long indicated his love for the Lord God and his faith in God's promises.

Noah therefore knew that God's spiritual blessings would especially rest on Shem, and so exclaimed: "Blessed be Jehovah, the God of Shem!" Shem knew the Lord personally, in his covenant relationship, and so knew Him by the name Jehovah. This strongly implies, even though it is not explicitly stated, that it was through Shem that God's greatest blessing for mankind, the promised Seed of the woman, would eventually come into the world. Shem would not be prevented from transmitting God's spiritual blessings to mankind through future opposition by Canaan and the other sons of Ham, for indeed Canaan would be his "servant," helping him to accomplish it.

Genesis 9:27

27 God shall enlarge Jā'phĕth, and he shall dwell in the tents of Shĕm; and Cā'năan shall be his servant.

Finally coming to Japheth, Noah prophesied that Japheth would be "enlarged" and that the Hamites would also be of service to him in this function. *Pathah,* the Hebrew word used here, is not the usual word for "enlarged" and is so translated only in this one instance. It apparently does not refer to a geographical enlargement, for which the Hebrew *rachab* would have been suited (actually both Semites and Hamites have spread geographically as far as the Japhethites).

The word is usually translated "entice" or "persuade." However, in the particular form in which it occurs in this verse, it occurs only this once; and translators have been unanimous in rendering it "be enlarged." It is apparently derived from the word "to make open" (Hebrew *pathach*).

It seems most probable, putting all this together, that the thought here is one of *mental* enlargement. If one is "persuaded" or "enticed," his previous opinions have been altered, he has changed his mind, or "opened" his mind. Japheth was an open-minded man, and so would be his descendants. The Japhethites would be intellectually curious, explorers in the world of thought, as Ham would be in the physical realm and Shem in the spiritual.

Not only would Japheth be intellectually enlarged, but he would also "dwell in the tents of Shem." This is a common figure of speech meaning "have fellowship with him." Thus "dwell in the tents of wickedness" (Psalm 84:10) means "live in wickedness, out of fellowship with God." Japheth would not literally live in the same tents (same word as "tabernacles") with Shem, but he would come to share in Shem's inheritance— that is, his spiritual blessings, which constituted the essence of Shem's inheritance as prophesied by Noah. Though Shem would be the means of mankind's receiving God's great spiritual promises, Japheth also would appropriate these blessings to himself by enjoying fellowship with Shem. As Shem and Japheth had unitedly shown respect to their father and their father's God, so they would unitedly worship "the Lord God of Shem." The Hamites, on the other hand, by implication would not do so, but would presumably follow other gods of their own devising. Nevertheless, Ham's "service" would contribute to the purpose of the true God for all men.

Although Noah's threefold prophecy has been abundantly fulfilled in general and in principle throughout history, it surely allows for individual exceptions. That is, a particular descendant of Ham may be very spiritually minded and become a fruitful servant of the true God. A particular descendant of Japheth may be dull of mind while skilled in technological devices. A particular Semite may be an atheist.

In general, however, it has been true throughout history that the Semites have been dominated by religious motivations centered in monotheism (the Jews, the Moslems, the Zoroastrians, etc.). The Japhethites (especially the Greeks, Romans, and later the other Europeans and the Americans) have stressed science and philosophy in their development. The Hamites (Egyptians, Phoenicians, Sumerians, Orientals, Africans, etc.) have been the great pioneers that opened up the world to settlement, to cultivation, and to technology.

Each stream of nations has influenced the others, of course, and there has been much mixing of peoples from different tribes and nations; so there may well be many apparent exceptions to the general trends. But it is possible to discern these general trends, and they do follow the prophetic pattern outlined thousands of years ago by father Noah. The Semites have been predominant in theology, the Japhethites in science and philosophy, the Hamites in technology.

Note that these three streams of nations are *not* three "races." Though some have thought of the Semites, Japhethites, and Hamites as three races (say, the dusky, the white, and the black races—or the Mongoloid, Caucasian, and Negroid), this is not what the Bible teaches, nor is it what modern anthropology and human genetics teach. There are dusky and black people found among all three groups of nations. The Bible does not use the word "race" nor does it acknowledge such a concept. The modern concept of "race" is based on evolutionary thinking. To the evolutionist, a race is a subspecies in the process of evolving into a new species, and this idea is the basis of modern racism. The actual original descendants of Shem, Ham, and Japheth are identified in Genesis 10, as discussed in the next chapter.

Genesis 9:28, 29

---

28 ¶ And Noah lived after the flood three hundred and fifty years.

29 And all the days of Noah were nine hundred and fifty years: and he died.

These verses conclude the ninth chapter of Genesis as well as the story of Noah. Noah himself was not greatly affected by the changed atmospheric conditions following the Flood, as were his descendants, and so lived another 350 years, dying at the advanced age of 950, having lived longer than any of his ancestors except Jared (962) and Methuselah (969).

If there are no gaps in the genealogies of Genesis 11, this means that Noah continued living until Abraham was about fifty-eight years old. On the other hand, as indicated in the next chapter, there is at least a possibility that some gaps of uncertain duration may exist in these genealogies. It is at least likely, however, that Noah lived until after the dispersion of the nations at Babel.

10

God and the Nations

(Genesis 10-11)

The Table of Nations

Even higher critics have often admitted that the tenth chapter of Genesis is a remarkably accurate historical document. There is no comparable catalog of ancient nations available from any other source. It is unparalleled in its antiquity and comprehensiveness.

Dr. William F. Albright, universally acknowledged as the world's leading authority on the archaeology of the Near East, though himself not a believer in the infallibility of Scripture, said concerning this Table of Nations:

> It stands absolutely alone in ancient literature, without a remote parallel, even among the Greeks, where we find the closest approach to a distribution of peoples in genealogical framework. . . . The Table of Nations remains an astonishingly accurate document.[1]

Here is the one link between the historic nations of antiquity and the prehistoric times of Noah and the antediluvians. The grandsons and great-grandsons of Noah are listed, each of whom is identified with the city or country established by his descendants. There is nothing in any other ancient writing discovered by archaeologists which is at all comparable in scope and accuracy. It gives every appearance of being a sort of family record, kept by a venerable patriarch of the family as long as he remained alive and could keep in touch with his descendants.

---

1. "Recent Discoveries in Bible Lands"—article appended to Robert Young's *Analytical Concordance to the Bible* (New York: Funk and Wagnalls, 1936), p. 25.

245

Shem, as the one of Noah's sons most interested in God's promise of the coming Seed, would be the logical one to keep such a record. He lived for 502 years after the Flood (Genesis 11:10, 11), which would have encompassed the entire period included in the Table of Nations. It is significant that the sons of Ham and Japheth are given only to the third generation after the Flood, whereas Shem's descendants extend to the sixth, indicating perhaps that he lost touch with the other branches of the family after the Dispersion. His signature is attached in the subscript at Genesis 11:10, after he had written of the events at Babel.

It has been possible in many cases to identify the names in Genesis 10 with nations and peoples known to antiquity, especially as revealed by archaeology. Thus this chapter provides the link between recorded history and the period of "prehistory" which is, except for the Bible, preserved only in ancient traditions.

Genesis 10:1

CHAPTER 10

NOW these *are* the generations of the sons of Noah; Shĕm, Ham, and Jā'phĕth: and unto them were sons born after the flood.

The first part of this verse is probably the signature subscript of the previous section beginning at Genesis 6:9. "These are the generations of the sons of Noah." Probably the three sons went their separate ways after the traumatic experience of Genesis 9:20-27, coming together again only to share in the burial ceremonies for their father Noah and to conclude their "generations" with the record of his death. Shem had apparently taken over the task of recording the genealogies of the three families in the meantime and continued until the time of the confusion of languages at Babel, after which he seems to have lost touch with the Hamites and Japhethites.

Genesis 10:2-4

---

2 The sons of Jā'phĕth; Gō'mĕr, and Mā'gŏg, and Măd'ā-ī, and Jā'văn, and Tū'băl, and Mē'shĕeh, and Tī'răs.
3 And the sons of Gō'mĕr; Ăsh'kĕ-năz, and Rī'phăth, and Tō-gär'măh.
4 And the sons of Jā'văn; Ē-lī'shăh, and Tär'shĭsh, Kĭt'tĭm, and Dō'dà-nĭm.

Assuming Shem to have been the original compiler of this Table of Nations, it is appropriate that he would begin with the family of the older brother, Japheth, then proceed to that of Ham, and finally conclude with his own. It is noteworthy also that only the sons in the various families are mentioned by name, although it is probable that there were as many daughters as there were sons.

Japheth's seven sons are listed as Gomer, Magog, Madai, Javan, Tubal, Meshech, and Tiras. Allowing for the gradual modifications in form that always occur in such names with the passage of time, and noting pertinent references in both Scripture and early secular historical writings and on excavated archaeological monuments, we can trace most of these names and recognize them as ancestors of the Indo-European peoples.

The name of Japheth himself, for example, is found in the literature as Iapetos, the legendary father of the Greeks, and Iyapeti, the reputed ancestor of the Aryans in India. The first son, Gomer, is generally identified (by Herodotus, Plutarch, and other ancient writers) with the district of Cimmeria, north of the Black Sea, a name surviving to the present in the form Crimea. One branch of the descendants of Gomer eventually moved westward, with the name probably being preserved both in Germany and Cambria (Wales).

Three of Gomer's sons are identified as Ashkenaz, Riphath, and Togarmah. The Jews identified Ashkenaz with Germany and, to this day, German Jews are called the Ashkenazi. Some ethnologists think the name Ashkenaz has also been preserved under the names Scandia and Saxon, as colonists from Germany made their way into Denmark and its northern islands and to the western shores of the continent. Other descendants of Ashkenaz remained in a region of Armenia which, according to Strabo, was called Sakasene.

Another son of Gomer was Riphath, whom Josephus identifies as the ancestor of the Paphlagonians. Another possibility is the Carpathians. There is even a slight possibility that the name Europe was originally a corruption of Riphath.

A third son of Gomer, Togarmah, is almost certainly the ancestor of the ancient people known as Armenians. The Armenian traditions themselves claim this. Some have also claimed (e.g., the Jewish Targums) that Germany was derived from Togarmah. Turkey and Turkestan also have a possible etymological connection with Togarmah.

Returning to Japheth, we find his second son, Magog, listed. This name can mean "the place of Gog," and so quite possibly referred to Georgia, a region near the Black Sea still known by that name. Josephus says that Magog (or Gog) was the ancestor of the Scythians, who also originally inhabited the Black Sea area.

Magog is commonly associated in the Bible with two other sons of Japheth—Meshech and Tubal (especially Ezekiel 38:2). Meshech clearly is preserved in the name Muskovi (the former name of Russia) and Moscow. Tubal is known in the Assyrian monuments as the Tibareni, and probably has been preserved in the modern Russian city of Tobolsk. In Ezekiel 38:2 they are associated with "Rosh,"[2] a name from which modern "Russia" was derived. Generally speaking, therefore, these three sons of Japheth—Magog, Meshech, Tubal—can be considered as the progenitors of the modern Russian peoples.

Madai, according to all authorities, is the ancestor of the Medes. They settled in what is now Persia and perhaps were in part (along with the Semitic Elamites) ancestors of the Persians as well. It was evidently through this group of Japhethites that the Aryans developed, who later migrated into India to become the progenitors of the Indian peoples.

It is also well established that the name Javan is the original form of Ionia, which was the same as Greece. The same word is translated "Javan" in some Old Testament passages, "Greece" in others. Both Japheth and his son Javan are considered to be the original founders of the Greeks.

Javan is listed as the father of Elishah, Tarshish, Kittim, and Dodanim. "Hellas" is a form of "Elishah," which came to be applied to Greece as a whole (note Hellespont, Hellenists, etc.). The *Iliad* mentions the Eilesian people; the Tell el Amarna tablets and the Ugaritic tablets mention the Alasians, people apparently from Cyprus.

Tarshish has been variously identified with Tartessos in Spain and with Carthage in North Africa. Both of these, however, were Phoenician cities and the Phoenicians were Canaanites. It is possible that the descendants of Tarshish may have been early settlers of Spain and North Africa, but that the Phoenicians were later more prominent in their development.

Kittim is almost certainly a reference to Cyprus and possibly, to some extent, to the Greek mainland as well. It is just possible that the term "Ma-Kittim" (the land of Kittim) may have given rise to the name Macedonia.

Dodanim is the same, evidently, as Rodanim (I Chronicles 1:7).

---

2. Translated "chief" in the King James Version.

His name is probably preserved today in the geographical names Dardanelles and Rhodes.

The last-named son of Japheth, Tiras, became the ancestor of the Thracians, according to Josephus. There is also a possibility that Tiras gave rise to the Etruscans of Italy.

Genesis 10:5

---

5 By these were the isles of the Gĕn⸗ tĭlĕṣ divided in their lands; every one after his tongue, after their families, in their nations.

Although some of the above identifications are uncertain, they do seem reasonable. In any case, there is enough clear identification to recognize that the descendants of Japheth spread all over Europe, with one major branch heading eastward into Persia and India.

It is especially to the descendants of Japheth that the term "Gentiles" was applied. The islands, coastlands, and other regions to which they spread were "divided" to these different groups, a development which took place at Babel. This reference thus indicates that chapter 10 of Genesis was written after the Dispersion. This is further proved by the fact that they were so divided "after their tongues." The Japhethites, as noted earlier, were of an intellectual and philosophical turn of mind. This fact later made Europe the center of the development of philosophy and science.

Genesis 10:6

---

6 ¶ And the sons of Ham; Cŭsh, and Mĭz′rā-ĭm, and Phŭt, and Cā′nǎan.

The account next proceeds to the sons of Ham, whose descendants are given in somewhat more detail than those of Japheth. The grandsons of Japheth are listed for only two of his sons (Gomer and Javan), but those of three of Ham's sons are given (Cush, Mizraim, and Canaan). For that matter, the sons of only two of Shem's five sons are listed (Aram and Arphaxad). Why these were selected, omitting the sons of so many others (five of Japheth's sons, one of Ham's, three of Shem's), is not clear. Perhaps these were the only ones of whom the writer still had information at the time he compiled his lists; this may explain why he would be selective in this way. It is an incidental confirmation of the Semitic authorship of this section to note that at least some of Shem's descendants are listed to the fifth generation after Shem. Japheth's descendants are given in two cases to the second generation and Ham's, in two cases, to the third.

The writer perhaps also assumed that the names so listed were sufficient to establish the origin of all the major tribes and nations after the Disperson, and therefore it was unnecessary to list any others. One other possibility is that the names listed in Genesis 10 were the families actually living in Babel at that fateful time when the tongues were changed. The reference to different "tongues" (verses 5, 20, and 31) shows, at least, that those whose names are listed either participated in the Dispersion themselves or else were directly affected by it in the development of their own families.

The sons of Ham were Cush (probably the same as Kish), Mizraim, Phut, and Canaan. "Cush" is the same in the Bible as "Ethiopia," and is usually so translated. The Cushites apparently first migrated southward into Arabia, and then crossed the Red Sea into the land now known as Ethiopia. The Tell el Amarna tablets call this land "Kashi."

Mizraim is the ancestor of the Egyptians, and is the customary name for Egypt in the Bible. Egypt is also called "the land of Ham" (Psalm 105:23, etc.), suggesting that Ham accompanied his son Mizraim in the original settlement of the Nile Valley. Since "Mizraim" is a plural form, this may not have been the exact form of his name originally; and some writers have suggested that the semi-legendary founder of Egypt's first dynasty, Menes, was the same as Mizraim.

Phut, in the Bible, is the same as Libya, applied to the region of North Africa west of Egypt. This identification was confirmed by Josephus. Canaan is, of course, the ancestor of the Canaanites and gave his name to the land of Canaan.

Genesis 10:7

7 And the sons of Cŭsh; Sē'bȧ, and Hăv'ĭ-läh, and Săb'tȧh, and Rā'ȧ-mȧh, and Săb'tē-ẹhȧ: and the sons of Rā'ȧ-mȧh; Shē'bȧ, and Dē'dȧn.

Five of the sons of Cush are listed: Seba, Havilah, Sabtah, Raamah, and Sabtechah. Seba was one of those who migrated from southwestern Arabia across the Red Sea, into the region now known as the Sudan, giving his name to the Sabeans (Isaiah 45:14). There is uncertainty as to the exact relationship between the people descended from Seba and those from several men named Sheba (Genesis 10:7; 10:28; 25:3). People called Sabeans are known in both Arabia and Africa. Josephus identifies "Saba" as the city of "Meroe," in upper Egypt.

Havilah, Sabtah, and Sabtechah all seem to have been located in Arabia. Another "Havilah" was a Semite, son of Joktan (Genesis 10:29). Sabtah has been identified with the ancient city of Sabatah in Arabia.

Raamah also settled in Arabia, but is specially mentioned as the father of Sheba and Dedan. He is the only one of the sons of Cush whose own sons' names are listed. Presumably, in their day, Sheba and Dedan were unusually well known, a presumption which may account for the fact that, later, two of Abraham's grandsons through Keturah were apparently named after them.

Genesis 10:8, 9

---

8 And Cūsh begat Nimrod: he began to be a mighty one in the earth.
9 He was a mighty hunter before the LORD: wherefore it is said, Even as Nimrod the mighty hunter before the LORD.

Although Cush and all his other sons moved south and west into Arabia and Africa, his most illustrious son settled in the Tigris-Euphrates valley, apparently remaining there even after the rest of the three Noahic families had been compelled, by the confusion of tongues, to move away. Nimrod was apparently the youngest son of Cush, and perhaps felt something of a moral kinship with his Uncle Canaan, who had been the youngest son of Ham and the special designee of the Noahic curse.

Cush, as Ham's oldest son, had apparently resented this curse more and more as the years passed by. By the time Nimrod was born, the resentment had become so strong that he gave his son a name meaning "Let us rebel!" The inference is that Cush trained Nimrod from childhood to be a leader in a planned and organized rebellion against God's purposes for mankind. Had God destined them to perpetual servitude to the descendants of Shem and Japheth? Oh, no! They would rule instead! And so Cush, perhaps encouraged by Ham and his other sons, began to train Nimrod to struggle for the ascendancy among men.

Thus Nimrod "began to be a mighty one in the earth," and he soon had all the Hamites—and possibly many of the Semites and

Japhethites—under his influence and leadership. They finally settled in the fertile plain of Shinar (a name probably later identified as Sumer) and began to build a great complex of cities, with "the beginning of his kingdom at Babel."

Nimrod became a "mighty tyrant in the face of Jehovah." He was a "hunter" in the sense that he was implacable in searching out and persuading men to obey his will. The Jerusalem Targum says:

> He was powerful in hunting and in wickedness before the Lord, for he was a hunter of the sons of men, and he said to them, "Depart from the judgment of the Lord, and adhere to the judgment of Nimrod!" Therefore is it said: "As Nimrod the strong one, strong in hunting, and in wickedness before the Lord."

The reference to Nimrod's hunting prowess suggests that wild beasts were thought to be a real source of danger at the time and that Nimrod acquired a hero's reputation by protecting the population against them. Skill at hunting game animals for food for his family would hardly be so unusual as to warrant making his name a proverb to the generations to come, as the text indicates. However, in the context of the first century or two after the Flood, it is probable that there was a great proliferation of animal populations. Before the Flood, with lush vegetation everywhere, there was an abundance of food for the animals; but the post-Flood world was very different and many of the larger animals particularly may have found it difficult to survive after a time. The fossil record, in both the Flood sediments and the post-Flood (Ice Age) deposits, indicates that there were tremendous animals living at the time that might well have been feared as a potentially serious danger to mankind in the early centuries after the Flood, until they became extinct. Consequently a strong man who could hunt and slay such great animals would assume the role of hero and benefactor to mankind and would easily acquire a great following.

That there was probably no genuine danger to mankind from the animals, however, is evident from God's promise to put the "fear and dread" of man on all of them (Genesis 9:2), so that the deliberate hunting and slaughter of them was "against the Lord" (verse 9, literally). It was by this means, however, that Nimrod apparently acquired his great reputation and rose to a position as world leader of the time.

Genesis 10:10-12

---

10 And the beginning of his kingdom was Bā′běl, and Ĕr′ĕch, and Ăc′căd, and Căl′něh, in the land of Shī′när.

11 Out of that land went forth Ăṣsh′ŭr,

and builded Nĭn′ē-vĕh, and the city
Rē-hō′bŏth, and Cā′läh,

12 And Rē′sĕn between Nĭn′ē-vĕh
and Cā′läh: the same *is* a great city.

Nimrod was a man of great ability and energy and was evidently the leader of the group that built Babel (Genesis 11:4, 8, 9), which then formed the capital city of the region over which he became king. Though God had instructed man to establish human governmental systems, He could hardly have intended them to assume the form developed by Nimrod—a great empire comprising a complex of cities centered at Babylon.

These cities included Erech, Accad, and Calneh in Shinar. Erech (also called Uruk) is one hundred miles southeast of Babylon, and was the legendary home of Gilgamesh, hero of the Babylonian flood story. Its excavation yielded examples of very ancient writing, long antedating the time of Abraham. Accad was immediately north of Babylon. Also spelled Akkad and Agade in the monuments, the city gave its name to the Akkadian empire, essentially synonymous with the Sumerian empire. Calneh has apparently not yet been identified; but all were in the land of Shinar, presumably equivalent to Sumer, and identified in later Scriptures (e.g., Daniel 1:2) as Babylonia.

From Babel, Nimrod also "went forth into Assyria" (better than "went forth Asshur"), where he built Nineveh, Rehoboth, Resen, and Calah. Nineveh was situated on the upper Tigris River as Babylon was on the Euphrates. Nineveh was roughly two hundred miles north of Babylon and later was the capital of the great Assyrian empire. Both Babylonia and Assyria were subsequently conquered by Semites, but the Hamite Nimrod was the founder and first emperor of both of them. Nineveh's two satellite cities, Rehoboth and Resen, have not been definitely identified.

Calah, however, has been excavated, on the Tigris about twenty miles south of Nineveh. It is still called "Nimrud," after its founder. Resen was said to be between Nineveh and Calah, so that the entire complex of cities was called "a great city," that is, a large metropolitan area. The Assyrian legends speak of "Ninus" as the founder of Nineveh. This is evidently a form of "Nimrod."

Genesis 10:13, 14

13 And Mĭz′rā-ĭm begat Lū′dĭm, and Ăn′ă-mĭm, and Lē-hā′bĭm, and Năph-tū′hĭm,

14 And Păth-rŭ′sĭm, and Căs′lū-hĭm, (out of whom came Phĭ-lĭs′tĭm,) and Căph′tō-rĭm.

The sons of Mizraim (the founder of Egypt) are next listed. All are shown as the names of peoples, with the plural "im" ending. Unfortunately, most of these (Ludim, Anamim, Lehabim, Naphtuhim) have not yet been identified. They were evidently important tribes in or near Egypt at the time of the writing of Genesis 10. Perhaps they later moved south and west into other parts of Africa.

The Pathrusim dwelt in Pathros, or Upper Egypt. The text says that the Philistines, well known in later Biblical history, came out of the Casluhim, who are otherwise unknown. Another group, the Caphtorim, are also identified, in the Bible, with the Philistines (Amos 9:7; Jeremiah 47:4). Secular writings generally place the origin of the Philistines on the island of Crete, and identify Caphtor as Crete. It seems probable that these two sons of Mizraim, ancestors of the Casluhim and Caphtorim, kept their families together, later migrating to Crete and still later, in successive waves, to the eastern shore of the Mediterranean to the land later known as Philistia.

Genesis 10:15

---

15 ❡ And Cā'năan begat Sī'dŏn his firstborn, and Heth,

Ham's youngest son, Canaan, was very prolific, having eleven sons and an unknown number of daughters. The eldest was Sidon, the progenitor of the Phoenicians. This was written long before the founding of Tyre, the sister city of Sidon.

Heth is undoubtedly ancestor of the Hittites (Genesis 23:10), who ruled a great empire centered in Asia Minor for over eight hundred years, apparently migrating there originally from the home of their brothers in Canaan.

Hittites were present in the land of Canaan during the time of Abraham (Genesis 15:19-21), and apparently reached the heights of their power in Asia Minor sometime later. They were still a great power at the time of Solomon a thousand years later (II Chronicles 1:17).

There is some evidence that, when the Hittite empire finally crumbled, the remnant of the people fled eastward. The Cuneiform monuments record the name of the Hittites as "Khittae," and this may well have been modified later to "Cathay" as they settled again in the Far East. Archaeologists have noted a number of similarities between the Hittites and the Mongoloids. Both are known, for example, to have pioneered in the art of smelting and casting iron and in the breeding and training of horses.

Genesis 10:16-18

---

16 And the Jĕb'ū-ṣīte, and the Ăm'ō-rīte, and the Gīr'gȧ-sīte, 17 And the Hī'vīte, and the Ärk'īte, and the Sī'nīte, 18 And the Är'văd-īte, and the Zĕm'ȧ-rīte, and the Hā'măth-īte: and afterward were the families of the Cā'năan-ītes spread abroad.

The other nine sons of Canaan were the progenitors of the Canaanite tribes that inhabited the land when the Israelites arrived. The Jebusites, apparently descended from a man named Jebus, were early inhabitants of Jerusalem (Joshua 15:63). The Amorites were one of the most prominent tribes, with their name sometimes used as representative of all the Canaanites (Genesis 15:16). The Amarna letters call all these tribes the "Amurru."

Although the Girgasites are mentioned frequently in the Bible, their location has not been determined. The Hivites are also frequently mentioned, and some of their cities have been identified archaeologically all the way from Sidon to Jerusalem. The Arkites seem to have been centered in the region around Tell Arka in Syria. The Arvadites lived in Arvad, a port city of the Phoenicians, and the Zemarites about six miles south of Arvad in a town identified in the Amarna letters as Sumur and still known today as Sumra. The Hamathites are associated with the prominent Syrian city Hamath, mentioned frequently in later Biblical history.

The Sinites are intriguing. It is possible that they may have been an insignificant Canaanite tribe, but the similarity of the name to other Biblical names (e.g., the wilderness of Sin, Mount Sinai, Sinim) suggests that their influence may have been greater than commonly realized.

The tendency of many early tribes toward ancestor worship and actual deification of ancestors may be reflected in the frequent use of the name "Sin" in connection with the ancient pantheon of deities. One of the most important Assyrian gods was "Sin." The particular son of Canaan named Sin, thus, may have been prominent enough in his time not only to give his name to a wide region in the land of Canaan but also to exert great influence in the Sumerian-Assyrian homeland of the Canaanites. The deified "Sin" was said in the monuments found in Ur to have established "laws and justice" among men.

The Biblical mention of a people in the Far East named "Sinim" (Isaiah 49:12), together with references in ancient secular histories to people in the Far East called "Sinae," at least suggests the possibility that some of Sin's descendants migrated eastward, while others went south into the land of Canaan. It is significant that the Chinese people have always been identified by the prefix "Sino-" (e.g., Sino-Japanese War; Sinology, the study of Chinese history). The name "Sin" is frequently encountered in Chinese names in the form "Siang" or its equivalent.

The evidence is tenuous but, of all the names in the Table of Nations, it does seem that two sons of Canaan, Heth (Hittites = Khittae = Cathay) and Sin (Sinites = Sinim = China), are the most likely to have become ancestors of the Oriental peoples. Since it seems reasonable that divine inspiration would include in such a table information concerning the ancestry of all the major streams of human development, it is reasonable to conclude that the Mongoloid peoples (and therefore also the American Indians) have come mostly from the Hamitic line.

After naming the tribes descended from Canaan, the Bible makes the significant statement that "afterward were the families of the Canaanites spread abroad." The Hittites spread to Asia Minor and perhaps the Sinites to China. The others may well have spread out as well. It is only of the Canaanites that this statement is made, suggesting thereby that these tribes eventually spread out more than any of the others. Perhaps this is seen best in their spread north and east into Asia and then ultimately (via the Bering Sea land bridge which existed during the Ice Age) into North and South America.

Genesis 10:19, 20

---

19 And the border of the Cā'năan-ītes was from Sī'dŏn, as thou comest to Gē'rär, unto Gā'zà; as thou goest unto Sŏd'ŏm, and Gō-mŏr'ràh, and Ăd'màh, and Zē-bō'ĭm, even unto Lā'shà.
20 These *are* the sons of Ham, after their families, after their tongues, in their countries, *and* in their nations.

The dimensions of the Canaanite boundaries, at the time of the compiling of the Table of Nations (or perhaps as inserted later by Moses in order to identify them to his own generation), were from Sidon on the northern coast in Phoenicia down almost to Gerar, as far as

Gaza (in Philistia) on the southern coast, then east and south to the
Dead Sea and the four "cities of the plain," Sodom and Gomorrah,
Admah and Zeboim. These had not been destroyed at the time this
passage was written. The location of Lasha was presumably to mark
the northeastern boundary, but this has not yet been identified. It was
not a very extensive region, but it was from there that "the Canaanites
spread abroad."

The record of Ham's descendants is then summarized, as Japheth's
had been, by the statement that these were grouped by "families, tongues,
countries, and nations." This tells us that Genesis 10 was written after
the Tower of Babel incident; before, there were no 'tongues," but
only *one* tongue. Furthermore, it suggests that this division by "tongues"
had been made to correspond to "families," that each such division
presupposed there would be a "country" (or "land") where the family
could live and work, and, finally, that such family groups would indeed
become "nations."

The Days of Peleg

After listing the main nations descended from elder brother Japheth
and other brother Ham, Shem then proceeds to his own family, which
he knew from Noah's prophecy (9:26) would be the one chosen to
transmit the knowledge of the true God and His promises to later
generations. He lists his own descendants to the fifth generation in some
cases, whereas Ham's genealogy extends to only the third generation
and Japheth's to only the second.

Shem probably lost touch with many of his relatives, especially after
the confusion of languages and the great dispersion. If this took place
shortly before Peleg (Shem's great-great-grandson) was born, as seems
most plausible, it is easy to understand why this would have been the
case. In all likelihood, Shem himself did not migrate to Babel, as so
many of his father's family did. He perhaps remained near Noah until
his father's death, long after the events at Babel, and then eventually
settled near the family of Peleg for his final years.

Genesis 10:21

---

21 ¶ Unto Shĕm also, the father of all   Jā′phĕth the elder, even to him were
the children of Ē′bĕr, the brother of *children* born.

It is interesting that Shem is identified first as "the father of all
the children of Eber" and "the brother of Japheth the elder." In the

day and place in which this was written, the children of Eber were presumably well known; so this reference would have lent additional interest to the account.

It is from "Eber" that the term "Hebrew" has apparently been derived. Abraham, for example, was called a Hebrew (Genesis 14:13), indicating that he was of the children of Eber. This term obviously, therefore, is applied in these early Scriptures to a much larger group of peoples than to only the descendants of Abraham. There is some indication that the people described in certain archaeological monuments as "the Habiru" were not the Israelites, but other tribal descendants of Eber.

Shem is also identified (or identifies himself) as "the brother of Japheth the elder," making no such reference to his other brother, Ham. Perhaps this is because he was associated more directly with Japheth in his father's prophecy (9:27), or perhaps it was a token of courtesy to his elder brother.

Some of the later versions reject the Authorized Version rendering at this point, and translate the phrase as "Shem, the elder brother of Japheth." However, the Masoretic text favors the Authorized Version translation, and this also fits better in the entire context. Shem was born ninety-seven years before the Flood (compare Genesis 5:32 and 11:10), whereas Noah begat the first of his three sons one hundred years before the Flood (Genesis 5:32 with 7:11).

Genesis 10:22

---

22 The children of Shĕm; Ē′lăm, and Ăssh′ŭr, and Ăr-phăx′ăd, and Lŭd, and Ă′răm.

Five children of Shem are listed: Elam, Asshur, Arphaxad, Lud, and Aram. Elam is the ancestor of the Elamites, well known in both Scripture and the monuments. Chedorlaomer, king of Elam, was the apparent leader of the confederacy which invaded Canaan during the days of Abram (Genesis 14:4, 5). The ancient city of Susa, or Shushan, east of Mesopotamia, was their capital. The Elamites apparently later merged with others, especially the Medes (descendants of Madai and thus of Japheth), to form the Persian empire.

Asshur was evidently the founder of the Assyrians. However, as noted in Genesis 10:11, Nimrod and his followers later invaded the land of Asshur and there founded Nineveh (later to become the capital) and a number of other cities. Consequently, the Assyrian people and culture were a mixture of both Semitic racial stock and Hamitic (Babylonian) culture, language, and religion.

Little is known of Arphaxad except that he was in the direct line leading to Abraham. A region known as Arrapachitis in Assyria may stem from his name.

Lud probably was the ancestor of the Lydians, in Asia Minor, at least according to Josephus. A similar name, however (Ludim—Genesis 10:13), is listed as Hamitic in descent.

The fifth son was Aram, father of the Aramaeans, the same as the Syrians. These people also became a great nation, even finally seeing their Aramaic language adopted as almost a *lingua franca* for the leading nations of the ancient world, including Assyria and Babylonia. Some of the Old Testament (portions of Daniel and Ezra) was apparently originally written in Aramaic, and it was a common spoken language among the Jews at the time of Christ.

Genesis 10:23, 24

---

23 And the children of Ā′răm; Ŭz, and Hŭl, and Gē′thĕr, and Măsh.

24 And Ăr-phăx′ăd begat Sā′lăh; and Sā′lăh begat Ē′bĕr.

Four sons of Aram are listed, even though none of the children of three of Shem's sons are named. Probably the children of Aram had more direct contact with the descendants of Abraham than the others in the early days. Little is known of these four. Uz evidently gave his name to a region in Arabia which later was Job's homeland (Job 1:1; Jeremiah 25:20). The others (Hul, Gether, Mash) are essentially unknown at this late date, but evidently were important in the days from Shem to Moses.

The most important son of Shem (even though nothing is known of him personally) was Arphaxad, since he was in the line of the promised Seed. Even though, presumably, he may have had more than one son, only Salah is listed, apparently for the same reason. Similarly, of Salah's sons, only Eber is listed. The significance of Eber's name has already been briefly discussed.

Genesis 10:25

---

25 And unto Ē'bĕr were born two sons: the name of one *was* Pē'lĕg; for in his days was the earth divided; and his brother's name *was* Jŏk'tăn.

This is the most intriguing verse in the Semitic section of the Table of Nations. Eber had two sons, Peleg and Joktan, of whom Peleg was the one to be in the chosen line. More about Joktan is given in verses 26 through 30.

Peleg—or rather, the event associated with his name—is of more interest today. "In his days was the earth divided."

Evidently this was a most memorable event, and Eber named his son in commemoration of it. The name Peleg means "division." There is the possibility that Peleg is the ancestor of a people known as the Pelasgians, but this seems the only possible item of distinction or interest that can knowingly be attributed to Peleg himself. The big question concerns the meaning of the indicated division of the earth.

The most obvious interpretation of this verse is that the division was the division of the peoples at the Tower of Babel, as discussed in Genesis 11. It is significant that some such division is mentioned here in Genesis 10:5 ("By these were the isles of the Gentiles divided in their lands; every one after his tongue, after their families, in their nations") and Genesis 10:32 (". . . by these were the nations divided in the earth after the flood"). These verses seem clearly to refer to a linguistic and geographic division, rather than to an actual splitting of the continents. This is especially clear in verse 5, where the division is specifically "after his *tongue.*"

Nimrod, as Noah's great-grandson through Ham, was in the same generation as Eber, Noah's great-grandson through Shem. Thus, it is reasonable to infer that the division at Babel took place when both Nimrod and Eber were mature men. If Peleg was born soon after the Dispersion, it is not surprising that Eber would commemorate such a momentous event in the name of his son. Otherwise, it is difficult to understand why the writer would take the trouble to note the meaning of "Peleg," since this was not done in the case of the other names in the Table of Nations.

It is true that the word used for "divided" (Hebrew *palag*) in the verse associated with Peleg (10:25) is different from the word for "divided" (Hebrew *parad*) in verses 5 and 32, and this may possibly mean that two different types of division are in view. However, Hebrew authorities indicate the two words are essentially synonymous.

If it is ever actually proved that the earth once was a single land mass that somehow split apart, with the segments gradually drifting away to form the present continents, then indeed this verse might be understood to refer to such an event. At present, the question of continental drift is still open among scientists; and creationist scientists have pointed to a number of unresolved physical difficulties with the whole idea.

In any case, it is not at all necessary to postulate continental drifting in order to account for the populations now found in remote parts of the globe. Migrations undoubtedly took place across the former land bridges at the Bering Strait and the Malaysian Strait, when the sea level was much lower than it now is, during the centuries following the Flood when much of the earth's water was frozen in the great continental ice sheets of the Glacial Epoch. Furthermore, early man knew how to construct seagoing vessels (their ancestors had, after all, constructed the Ark!) and could easily have traveled from continent to continent by water, as much evidence from antiquity in fact indicates he did.

It is just possible, however, that the great store of energy beneath the earth's crust, much of which was released when the "fountains of the deep" were "broken up" at the time of the Flood, provided the tremendous force needed to move continents apart, and that a further release of this energy took place in connection with the Tower of Babel.

If this happened, then the rate of separation would have been rapid at first, gradually slowing down to the imperceptible present-day movements.

Although the question is still unsettled, it seems most likely that the division referred to in this passage was simply the geographic division resulting directly from the confusion of tongues at Babel. If something more was involved, especially such a catastrophic event as a tectonic splitting-up of the land mass, it does seem strange that the account of the judgment at Babel in Genesis 11 does not mention it.

Genesis 10:26-30

---

26 And Jŏk′tăn begat Ăl-mō′dăd, and Shĕ′lĕph, and Hā′zär-mā′vĕth, and Jĕ′răh,

27 And Hȧ-dō′răm, and Ū′zăl, and Dĭk′läh,

28 And Ō′băl, and Ȧ-bĭm′ā-ĕl, and

Shē'bà,
29 And Ō'phĭr, and Hăv'ĭ-läh, and Jō'băb: all these *were* the sons of Jŏk'tăn.

30 And their dwelling was from Mē'shà, as thou goest unto Sē'phär, a mount of the east.

These verses list the thirteen sons of Joktan, Peleg's brother. The names are mostly known from this passage alone, but indications are that all settled in Arabia. Two of the names—Ophir, associated with a region famous for its gold, and Sheba, possibly associated with the Sabaeans (although another Sheba is listed as a grandson of Cush, and another as a son of Abraham)—were definitely located in Arabia.

The fact that all of Joktan's sons are listed, and none of Peleg's, may suggest that Shem (the probable author of this section) was living near Joktan at the time and so was more familiar with the names of his sons than of those of his other fifth-generation descendants. In any case, these names were more prominent in the day in which this was written than they have been in later times.

Genesis 10:31

---

31 These *are* the sons of Shĕm, after their families, after their tongues, in their lands, after their nations.

A summary verse is included here for Shem, as it had been for Japheth (verse 5) and Ham (verse 20). Once again it is mentioned that they involved distinct family units, distinct languages (therefore, subsequent to Babel), distinct regions, and, finally, actual nations. A total of twenty-six such "nations" is listed as coming from Shem, as compared with thirty listed from Ham (not including the Philistines, as apparently referred to in an editorial insertion by Moses in verse 14) and only fourteen from Japheth. Thus a total of seventy such primeval nations is listed here by Shem in his original Table of the Nations.

Genesis 10:32

---

32 These *are* the families of the sons of Noah, after their generations, in their nations: and by these were the nations divided in the earth after the flood.

After the nations have been listed individually as Japhetic, Hamitic, or Semitic in derivation, a final summary verse is appended, emphasizing again that these were the original inhabitants of the entire post-Flood world. The term "generations" (Hebrew *toledoth*) is used here, the same word used by the original writers of Genesis to mark its major divisions (2:4; 5:1; 6:9; 11:10; 11:27; etc.). Evidently, there were definite genealogical records available to Shem—either in written form or by oral communication from his brothers or their descendants—from which he compiled the Table. It may be possible that he obtained it in part when he and his brothers got together at the time of Noah's death, a reunion which may be inferred from the signature of "the sons of Noah" to the *toledoth* terminating with Noah's death (9:29—10:1).

One remarkable feature of the Table of Nations may be noted in closing this section. As stated above, there are seventy of these "families of the sons of Noah" mentioned by name, and it was "by these that the nations were divided in the earth after the flood." There may well have been others, as the listings seem quite uneven in a number of cases; but for some reason only these seventy are listed. There is at least a possibility that the number was selected because of its symbolic significance.

More likely, however, it was the fact that seventy nations were listed here that led the later Jewish writers to attach such significance to it. This is the same number as the number of the children of Israel that came into Egypt from Canaan (Genesis 46:27). Later (Deuteronomy 10:22), when Israel had multiplied and was returning out of Egypt and was itself a nation—in fact, God's chosen nation—Moses exhorted the people to "Remember the days of old .... When the Most High divided to the nations their inheritance, when he separated the sons of Adam, he set the bounds of the people according to the number of the children of Israel" (Deuteronomy 32:7, 8).

The number seventy has ever since been peculiarly associated with the nation Israel. Thus "seventy weeks were determined upon thy people" (Daniel 9:24), and Israel's history can be understood within a remarkable framework of successive cycles of seventy "weeks" of years.[3] Israel was led by seventy elders (Numbers 11:16, 25) and later there were seventy members of the Jewish Sanhedrin. Seventy scholars translated the Old Testament into Greek to produce the Septuagint version of Scripture. Moses also wrote that man's allotted life span was seventy years (Psalm 90:10). The Babylonian captivity lasted seventy years; and Jerusalem and Herod's temple were destroyed by the Romans about seventy years after Herod's attempt to murder Jesus, the Jewish Messiah, in His infancy.

3. Henry M. Morris, *Many Infallible Proofs* (San Diego: Creation-Life Publishers, 1974), pp. 321-324.

The Tower of Babel

The eleventh chapter of Genesis tells of an event of almost equal importance to that of the great Flood. The Flood was worldwide in its effects, and so was the confusion of tongues of worldwide impact—at least as far as man was concerned.

Although the curtain had now been drawn, as it were, on his activities, there can be little doubt that Satan was still energetically working behind the scenes. He pressed his advantage, gained when he capitalized so effectively on the fatal weakness in Ham's character, and soon gained the allegiance of the Hamites in general and of Nimrod in particular.

Romans 1:18-32 graphically describes the resulting moral and spiritual deterioration of Nimrod and his followers. Willfully leaving the knowledge and worship of the true God and *Creator,* they began instead to worship the *creation.* This soon led to pantheism and polytheism and idolatry. How much of this new system of religion came by direct communication with Satan himself we do not know, but there is abundant evidence that all forms of paganism have come originally from the ancient Babylonian religion. The essential identity of the various gods and goddesses of Rome, Greece, India, Egypt, and other nations with the original pantheon of the Babylonians is well established. Nimrod himself was apparently later deified as the chief god ("Merodach," or "Marduk") of Babylon.

These pagan deities were also identified with the stars and planets— the "host of heaven"—with sun-worshiping occupying a central place. This system was formalized in the zodiac, with its numerous constellations—a most remarkable construction which seems to have been the common possession of all the nations of antiquity. And behind this facade of images (both on the star charts of the heavens, and in their stone and metallic representations in the temples) of "men and birds and four-footed beasts and creeping things" lurked a real "host of the heavens," the angelic and demonic hosts of Lucifer, the "day-star."

Many of these rebel angels had already been "cast down to hell" (or Tartarus) and delivered into chains of darkness, to be reserved unto judgment (II Peter 2:4), because of their participation in the attempt to corrupt the human race in the days of Noah (Genesis 6:1-4); but a great host remained at liberty to actively oppose the work of God and the people of God (Ephesians 6:12). The main thrust of the work of Satan and his hosts has always been that of *deception.* He is the one "which deceiveth the whole world" (Revelation 12:9) into worshiping something or someone other than the true God of creation (see also Revelation 13:14, 15).

Satan is notoriously a corrupter, rather than an innovator. Hence it is probable that the system of paganism, with its astrological emblems and complex mythology and mysteries, represents a primeval distortion of God's true revelation concerning His creation and promised redemption of the universe. Thus, the zodiac system of constellations may originally have been devised by the antediluvian patriarchs as a means of indelibly impressing the divine promises on the consciousness of mankind through marking them on the very heavens themselves. If so, the subsequent system of astrology is a gross corruption of the original evangelical significance of the heavenly bodies, created originally to serve in part for "signs and seasons." In any case, as they were interpreted by Nimrod and his followers, they soon led not only to astrology but also to spiritism and all the other evils of paganism and idolatry.

Furthermore, the development of this system of idolatry and Satan-worship was accompanied by an attempt to unify all mankind under one government. That government was not to be a system of theocracy as implied by God to Noah when He committed to man the responsibility of human government, but rather a dictatorship under Nimrod, the rebel. As later developments indicated, Nimrod not only set up a military dictatorship but also established a priestly oligarchy, in which he himself was chief priest and later the chief object of worship. There is some indication that the queen Semiramis, a familiar name in the ancient traditions, was Nimrod's wife, and that she was also an active leader of the conspiracy.

Not only has the original Babylonian religious system served as the source of all the world's non-Christian religions (Babylon, according to Revelation 17:5, was the "mother of harlots and abominations of the earth"), but it has also infiltrated and corrupted Christendom to an alarming degree. This has taken place not only in terms of outward ritualism and idolatry but also in the more insidious philosophy of evolutionary pantheistic humanism which permeates its educational and political centers.[4]

It had been God's command to the sons of Noah that they "be fruitful and multiply and fill the earth" (Genesis 9:1). In order that this might be accomplished in an orderly manner, God had ordained the principle of human government (9:6). This evidently was to be implemented through subdividing the future population into workable and controllable social units or nations. Each organized national group

---

4. Henry M. Morris, *The Troubled Waters of Evolution* (San Diego: Creation-Life Publishers, 1975), pp. 25-76.

would thus contribute in its own way to the corporate life of mankind as a whole, even as each individual family unit would contribute to its own nation. The diligence with which each man would make the contribution of which he was capable would be reflected in the material rewards accruing to him and his family as a result. Similarly, those nations which contributed significantly to the benefit of mankind as a whole would be recognized and rewarded correspondingly on a national level. Such recognition and reward is clearly the most effective incentive to diligence and faithfulness in service. This principle seems to be deeply ingrained in human nature and is endorsed by God Himself (I Corinthians 3:14; Revelation 22:12).

If any individual (or group) should attempt to gain advantage over another by dishonest methods, however, he would be penalized by the governmental authority established under God for this very purpose. Such a social structure ought to have been most conducive to the development of a strong sense of both individual and corporate responsibility to God. It also ought to have encouraged the greatest appreciation of God's grace, which was manifest in His providential maintenance of the physical conditions for life (Genesis 8:21, 22) and His promise of ultimate redemption and salvation.

But, as it turned out, men in general refused to submit willingly to this arrangement; so God had to bring it about by special intervention. As men began to multiply, they preferred to live together in one unit, instead of separating into many units.

Genesis 11: 1, 2

CHAPTER 11

AND the whole earth was of one language, and of one speech.

2 And it came to pass, as they journeyed from the east, that they found a plain in the land of Shī'när; and they dwelt there.

As the people migrated eastward (or southward) from the forbidding region of Ararat, they finally came to Shinar and the fertile Mesopotamian plain, where they decided to settle and build a city. Perhaps the region reminded them of their antediluvian home, and they thought they might even be able to restore the conditions of Eden itself, for they named the rivers Tigris and Euphrates after two of the streams that had once flowed from the Garden.

The immediate descendants of Noah, of course, all spoke the same language, the same as had been spoken by men in the antediluvian period. It is probable that this was a Semitic language (perhaps even Hebrew), since the proper names of men and places in the pre-Babel period all have meanings only in Hebrew and its cognate languages. Also, it seems unlikely that Shem participated in the Babel rebellion; so it is probable that his own language was not affected by the resulting confusion of tongues. Consequently, his family would have continued speaking the same language they had always spoken.

This faculty of human speech and language is truly one of the most amazing attributes of mankind. The evolutionist is utterly unable to explain the unbridgeable gulf between the chatterings of animals and human language. The unique and fundamental essence of speech in the very nature of man is underscored in the revelation of God to man through His *Word*. Christ Himself is the *living* Word! "God has *spoken* to us by his Son" (Hebrews 1:2). It is not too much to say that this was the very reason man was created able to speak and to hear; that is, in order that there might first be communication between God and man and, secondarily, between man and man. But when men began to prostitute this divine gift in order to cooperate in rebellion against their Maker, in a most appropriate judgment God confused their tongues and thereby forced them to separate from each other.

The whole population was said originally to have been "of one language and one speech" (or, literally, "of one lip and one set of words," apparently a reference to one phonology and one vocabulary). This was evidently the same as the common language spoken by the antediluvians. In all likelihood, this vocabulary also included a written language, although the various tribes had to develop new systems of writing later, after the confusion of tongues.

As the people migrated away from the Ararat region, they came "from the east" to the plain of Shinar, according to the Authorized Version. Since Shinar is southeast of Ararat, this may suggest they had first traveled to the far southeast, perhaps into the region of modern Persia or Afghanistan, and then later headed westward into Mesopotamia.

However, the phrase in the Hebrew is of uncertain meaning, and most expositors think it should be translated "eastward." In any case, the people apparently were not satisfied with any region where they stayed until they finally reached the fertile Tigris-Euphrates plain, and there they settled down. The population soon grew to the point where not all their attention had to be given merely to food production, and it became possible to develop an urban community.

Genesis 11:3

---

3 And they said one to another, Go to, thoroughly. And they had brick for let us make brick, and burn them stone, and slime had they for mortar.

By this time, Nimrod had evidently attained to the leadership of the people (see discussion under Genesis 10:8-10). Undoubtedly he recognized that their new status, with time for specialization and activities other than mere survival, would provide the opportunity for either of two future courses of action: (1) systematic colonization and development of all parts of the earth, each with its own local government, in accordance with God's command (Genesis 1:28; 9:1); or (2) establishment of a strongly centralized society which, with controls over resources and occupations, would soon be able to produce a self-sufficient civilization capable of similarly controlling the entire world.

The latter alternative clearly would better serve the purpose of Nimrod and his fellow rebels (and, of course, of the invisible Satanic conspiracy as well). A self-sufficient society, integrated under a powerful and brilliant leader, would be a society no longer dependent on God. And this was Nimrod's aim.

The implication in this verse is that, soon after establishing the settlement at Babel, Nimrod called a council of the family leaders of the community. After discussion of the various issues and alternatives, a formal decision was made. "Go to [Hebrew *yahab,* usually translated 'give,' probably signifying the pronouncement of the decision], we shall begin, first of all, to develop a brick-making industry." Good building stones were not conveniently accessible on the river plains, and timber was not durable enough for the permanent structures they had in mind. The clay soil, however, was highly suitable for strong bricks, after proper heat treatment in a kiln.

The more common manner of construction in antiquity was apparently to use stone, with a clay mortar. When bricks were used, as in Egypt and Assyria, they were only sun-dried. The Babylonian construction was stronger and more enduring, so the writer called special attention to it. Furnace-treated bricks were used instead of stone, and bitumen instead of mortar. This "slime" was probably tarry material from the abundant asphalt pits in the Tigris-Euphrates valley. Archaeology has revealed that this type of kiln-fired brick and asphalt construction was common in ancient Babylon.

Genesis 11:4

---

4 And they said, Go to, let us build us   a name, lest we be scattered abroad
a city, and a tower, whose top *may*   upon the face of the whole earth.
reach unto heaven; and let us make us

Having made this decision, which in itself indicated they intended
to erect a permanent community of strong buildings at Babel, and perhaps even after the brick industry had been established and was soundly
developing (as suggested by the introduction of a new sentence), they
again took counsel together and made an official declaration. "Go to,
the decision is that we will build a city, especially a great tower unto
heaven." ·

This would be no naturally growing, haphazard accumulation of
dwellings and business places. This would be a carefully planned urban
center, each component designed for maximum permanence and utility,
contributing to the optimum efficiency of the entire complex.

The great tower would dominate the city, both architecturally and
culturally. It would serve as the focal point of the political and religious
life of the population, and would be a symbol of their unity and strength.

Perhaps there was a minority that felt uncomfortable about these
grandiose plans, recalling that God had not given any such instructions,
and urging Nimrod that it was most important to get about the business
of colonizing the entire earth and developing its resources in a manner
that would glorify God, not man. It would seem that Noah and Shem,
at least, would not have endorsed these plans; and it seems likely that
their influence would still carry some weight with these first Babylonians.

It may even have been that Nimrod's colonizing expeditions to Assyria
(Genesis 10:11, 12) were an attempt to satisfy this minority opinion,
although, since Asshur was already there with his own settlement, it
may be more likely that this was an invasion for the very purpose of
thwarting *independent* expansion.

In any case, the collectivist and centrist position prevailed, and the
great construction project got under way. The builders were not concerned with God's plans; they intended to "make *us* a name." In fact,
they deliberately acknowledged their purpose to be contrary to God's
command: "Lest *we* be scattered abroad upon the face of the whole
earth." Not only the awareness of God's will, but the basic human drives
of curiosity and independence of spirit might impel many among them

to want to explore and develop the unknown regions in other parts of the world, if there were not a strong unifying and binding influence tying them to one location.

Even their fear and admiration of their great leader Nimrod might not suffice to keep them together. Nimrod must have realized that they needed a strong *religious* motivation as well, a motivation powerful enough to overcome their knowledge that God had indeed commanded them to fill the whole earth.

The tower was designed to satisfy that need as well. The tower was not designed *to reach* to heaven (except possibly in a figurative sense—that is, to reach the spiritual resources available in the heavens). The words "to reach" are not in the original. They would build a "tower *unto* heaven"—in other words, a tower dedicated to heaven and its angelic host.

Quite likely, this project was originally presented to the people in the guise of true spirituality. The tower in its lofty grandeur would symbolize the might and majesty of the true God of heaven. A great temple at its apex would provide a center and an altar where men could offer their sacrifices and worship God. The signs of the zodiac would be emblazoned on the ornate ceiling and walls of the temple, signifying the great story of creation and redemption, as told by the antediluvian patriarchs.

The impressive beauty and sacred purpose of the tower would, in the reasonings of the people, surely please God and more than compensate for the fact that the entire project was contrary to God's commandment and would glorify human achievement rather than recognize human frailty and divine salvation. But "to obey is better than sacrifice" (I Samuel 15:22). Cain's offering of the luscious fruit produced by his own hands was not acceptable to the Lord; no more acceptable would be Nimrod's magnificent tower.

Nimrod, at least, was well aware of what he was doing, however deceived the people themselves may have been. When the tower was completed (verse 8 suggests they were still building the city when the confusion of tongues took place, but evidently the tower was already in use), Nimrod no doubt instituted religious services there. It was only a short time, however, before the ostensible worship of the Creator was corrupted into the worship of the "creature" (Romans 1:21-23, 25). The grandeur of the tower and the ornateness of its designs and furnishings appealed to the flesh, and soon it was felt that additional "aids to worship" would be helpful. Not only paintings on the walls, but three-dimensional representations of the "men and birds and four-footed beasts and creeping things" began to be constructed, not only in the temple but along the streets and in the homes.

These figures, which had once been designed only as symbolic representations on the heavens of the coming Redeemer and of God's great plan of salvation, now began to take on the aspect of actual spiritual entities. The Virgin, whose sign among the stars once reminded men of the promised Seed of the woman, began to assume the proportions of an actual Queen of Heaven; and Leo, the great sidereal lion at the other end of the zodiac, became a great spiritual King of Heaven. Soon the stars, the physical "host of heaven," were invested with the personalities of the angels, the invisible spiritual heavenly host.

In acknowledging and worshiping these angelic spirits, the people no doubt felt very pious and religious; for they were merely recognizing the immanence of the omnipresent God of heaven throughout His creation. There were specific angels (and stars) concerned with every aspect of human life and terrestrial processes. In paying due reverence to these, they were, so they believed, thereby worshiping God. Furthermore God, through these same spirits (and their respective stars), would in response provide protection and provision and guidance in their own lives.

But this system soon became so complicated that it required a specially devoted class of men and women to dedicate their lives to its study and interpretation, so that they might guide the people in their devotions and sacrifices and in the ordering of their lives. Furthermore, as the preoccupation of both priests and people with specific localized spirits (or local representations of the great universal Spirit) increased, so did their awareness of the great "Father of spirits" (Hebrews 12:9) decrease. As the consciousness of God's personal nearness receded, so did their concern to obey Him. But also, this absence of true spiritual communion left a spiritual vacuum in their souls which could only be satisfied by some other kind of personal spiritual communion.

This vacuum was soon to be filled. There were, indeed, a host of angels in the heavenly places, but vast numbers of these were fallen angels, under the hierarchical control of Satan. God's holy angels were, no doubt, appalled at these developments in Babel and would have abhorred and repudiated any worship accorded to them by human beings (whose servants they had been created to be); but no such inhibition hindered the rebellious angels—the evil spirits, or demons. They reveled in it and encouraged it; for all this was in accord with the desire of Lucifer, their master, to become God himself.

As they had done before the Flood, these evil spirits began to control the minds and bodies of those human beings who were open to such possession and guidance, especially those of the priests and priestesses who had become devoted to this system of worship. To the innermost circle of these initiates, demonic revelations were given. To some, perhaps especially to Nimrod (and his wife Semiramis), Satan revealed the entire conspiracy against God.

From some such beginning soon emerged the entire complex of human "religion"—an evolutionary pantheism, promulgated via a system of astrology and idolatrous polytheism, empowered by occultic spiritism and demonism.

Genesis 11:5, 6

---

5 And the LORD came down to see the city and the tower, which the children of men builded.
6 And the LORD said, Behold, the people *is* one, and they have all one language; and this they begin to do: and now nothing will be restrained from them, which they have imagined to do.

Normally the Lord allows men and nations to pursue their own ways without supernatural interference on His part. Man is free and responsible; and though he will eventually suffer the consequences of his evil deeds, God is long-suffering. Therefore ungodliness often seems to thrive without hindrance in the affairs of men.

But there have been a few occasions on which the accomplishment of God's very purposes for the world became so endangered that divine intervention was required. The antediluvian corruption was one such instance, the rebellion at Babel another.

How long it was after the construction of the Tower of Babel before God "came down to see the city and the tower, which the children of men builded" we are not told. It would have been in accord with His nature to have waited as long as possible, in hopes that the godly minority there (if there were such) would prevail and the people would repent. They did not repent, however, and God finally "came down." This "anthropomorphic expression" does not suggest that God was not always fully aware of what was going on, but only that He now was officially and judicially taking the situation under direct observation and consideration, it having become so flagrant that there was danger (as in the days of Noah) that the truth of God's revelation might be completely obliterated if it were allowed to continue.

The problem, in the Lord's own judgment, lay in the *unity* of the people, a unity which was made possible only by a common language. The decision by practically the entire population to construct an autonomous, man-centered civilization, in direct defiance of God's command, could finally be ignored no longer.

Furthermore, with Nimrod's presumed knowledge of the Satanic mysteries and his access to demonic powers, literally nothing which he might decide to do in the future would be beyond his reach. The conditions of the antediluvian world might be repeated and this God would not allow, even though He had promised Noah He would never again send a worldwide flood. Incidentally, the naive opinion of some commentators that the building of the tower was as a potential haven from some future flood is obviously erroneous. Nimrod was no foolish simpleton in a fairy tale, imagining he could escape a global flood by building a tower that reached to heaven. His purpose was not to thwart another diluvial judgment but to dethrone the very Judge Himself! He had, indeed, practically unified all men (most of them perhaps unwittingly) in his Satanic partnership, and no doubt had other plans in mind once the human population was completely involved in his conspiracy. Satan had surely promised him the rulership of the world—perhaps even of the whole galaxy—once his heavenly rebellion was successful and God had been dethroned.

Genesis 11:7

---

7 Go to, let us go down, and there confound their language, that they may not understand one another's speech.

But as Nimrod and his cohorts had held a council of conspiracy and aggression on earth, so God now called a "council," as it were, in heaven, to institute formal action to prevent the accomplishment of Nimrod's plans. Such a divine council is indicated by the plural pronoun in verse 7, "let us." At least the three persons of the Godhead were involved, as in the primeval councils in Genesis 1:26 and 3:22, and perhaps also certain of the holy angels.

"Go to," said the Lord, in a sense mocking the foolish decisions of Nimrod's conclaves. Shall "the kings of the earth set themselves, and the rulers take counsel together against the Lord?" (Psalm 2:2). Only if they desire to bring down God's wrath on their heads. "The Lord shall have them in derision."

Men had proved unwilling to obey God's simple instructions to fill the earth, dividing into many separate, but parallel, governmental units. They preferred to remain together under one great centralized and highly regimented government, and this union had quickly led to a vast unified anti-God religious philosophy as well. The key was their ability to cooperate and organize together, and this depended on their ability to formulate and implement complex plans. Basic to everything was their ability to communicate with each other. They were all "of one lip and one vocabulary," speaking with the same sounds and formulating thoughts in the same way.

The decision of the heavenly council, therefore, was to "confound their language [or ability to make the same sounds with their lips], that they may not understand one another's speech [even though their thoughts are still the same]."

Genesis 11:8, 9

---

8 So the LORD scattered them abroad from thence upon the face of all the earth: and they left off to build the city. 9 Therefore is the name of it called Bā′bĕl; because the LORD did there confound the language of all the earth: and from thence did the LORD scatter them abroad upon the face of all the earth.

It was by this expedient of confusing their languages that God forced the "children of men [or, literally, 'Adam']" to cease in their further building of the city and to scatter abroad "upon the face of all the earth." It is not hard to imagine the surprised confusion that quickly spread through Babel. Presumably individual members of each family group could still understand each other, but otherwise everyone else was talking nonsense. Various ones thought others were mocking them. Foremen became irritated when their crews would not obey their orders, and workmen imagined their bosses were making sport of them and trying to make them look bad. In the palace itself, mighty Nimrod found it impossible to get servants to carry out his commands, and then became furious when those he instructed to punish them wouldn't do it.

Loud, incoherent arguments erupted throughout the city, and full-fledged chaos eventually reigned. Finally there was nothing to do but separate, with only individual family units remaining intact. No further urban cooperation between families was possible; so each family group had to learn how to meet its own needs directly. Eventually, if not immediately, each family became a tribe and moved away from Babel to work out its own manner of life, as God had intended them to do in the first place.

As the population grew (and this was a rapid process as longevity was still high and it was advantageous for each family to have many children), geographic expansion likewise was rapid. The stronger and more industrious and intelligent tribes took and held the more favorable regions. With resulting greater resources, they soon became great nations. The weaker and less ambitious families were pushed further and further away from the great centers of civilization, being forced to colonize new regions altogether, before they could set about to establish their own particular culture.

This process of migration and cultural development did not require long ages, as evolutionists imagine. Rather, the entire world was inhabited within a few generations at most. Increasingly in recent years has archaeology been confirming that civilization appeared more or less contemporaneously in all parts of the world, only a few millennia ago.

A similar pattern of cultural development seems to have occurred over and over again. As a tribe migrated to an unexplored region, it would find a suitable location (most commonly on a high elevation for protection, but near a spring or river, with fertile alluvial plains, for water and food supply) and then try to establish a village. Although members of the tribe certainly knew many useful arts, such as agriculture, animal husbandry, ceramics, metallurgy, and so on, they could not use them right away. Veins of metal had to be discovered, mined, and smeltered; suitable clay muds had to be found for making bricks and pottery; animals had to be bred; and crops had to be planted. All of this might take several years. In the meantime, the tribe had to survive by hunting, fishing, and gathering fruits and nuts. Temporary homes had to be built of stone, if available, or timber, or even in caves.

Remains of these original occupation sites naturally suggest to evolutionists a "stone age culture," but actually they reflect only a very temporary situation. As soon as materials for ceramics and metals could be found, the "stone age" at the site was succeeded by a "bronze age" or "iron age." The "village economy" was quickly succeeded by "urbanization" as the population increased and suitable building materials were developed.

Not infrequently, particularly if the site was especially desirable, a subsequent invasion by a stronger tribe would drive out or destroy the occupants, and a distinctively different culture would succeed the original on that site. Some of the tribes grew rapidly and developed strong nations. Others grew slowly, then stagnated, deteriorated, and finally died out.

As each family and tribal unit migrated away from Babel, not only did they each develop a distinctive culture, but also they each developed distinctive physical and biological characteristics. Since they could communicate only with members of their own family unit, there was no further possibility of marrying outside the family. Hence it was necessary to establish new families composed of very close relatives, for several generations at least. It is well established genetically that variations take place very quickly in a small inbreeding population, but only very slowly in a large interbreeding population. In the latter, only the dominant genes will find common expression in the outward physical characteristics of the population, reflecting more or less average characteristics, even though the genetic factors for specifically distinctive characteristics are latent in the gene pool of the population. In a small population, however, the particular suite of genes that may be present in its members, though recessive in the larger population, will have opportunity to become openly expressed and even dominant under these circumstances. Thus, in a very few generations of such inbreeding, distinctive characteristics of skin color, height, hair texture, facial features, temperament, environmental adjustment, and others, could come to be associated with particular tribes and nations.

Since earth's population was still relatively young and since, before the Flood, there had been a minimum of environmental radiations to produce genetic mutations, there was as yet no genetic danger from inbreeding. After many further centuries had elapsed, however, the accumulation of mutations and the associated danger of congenital defects had become sufficiently serious to cause God to declare incestuous marriages illegal (Leviticus 18:6-14).

It is true that the above sequence of post-Babel events is not actually recorded in Scripture, but it does seem to fit all the real data in science as well as in the Bible. It is a striking commentary on the importance of human language to note that worldwide migrations and the development of distinct tribes and nations—even their distinctive physical characteristics—were a direct result of the divine imposition of different languages.

As time went on, of course, people found they could, by diligent effort, learn each other's languages. The confounding of languages applied only to the phonologies, not to the underlying thought processes which are part of man's uniqueness. Mankind was still one *kind,* even though he now was divided into "tongues, in their lands, after their nations" (Genesis 10:31). Eventually this would permit a degree of intermarriage and mixing of nations, but the institution of distinct nations became permanent.

The nature of the miracle by which God confused the tongues is unknown, by virtue of the very fact that it was a miracle. The entity of language is, indeed, itself a miracle; there is absolutely no way in which the grunts and barks of animals could ever have evolved by natural processes into the articulate, symbolic, abstract language of humans. A mighty miracle of creation was required to endow man with this capacity. Likewise, another miracle of creation was required to create many new such phonologies all at once (presumably leaving the old intact, in the brain-nerve-tongue complex of those who did not participate in the Babel rebellion).

This multiplicity of tongues, however, was not God's original purpose for man, even though He did want mankind divided into different national units throughout the world. Accordingly, God has promised that eventually, in a future day when all nations will follow His will in obedience to His Word, "then will I turn to the people [literally, 'the peoples'—that is, all the nations] a pure language, that they may all call upon the name of the Lord, to serve him with one consent" (Zephaniah 3:9), even though there will still be distinct nations (note Zechariah 14:9, 16-19; Isaiah 2:2; Micah 4:2; Psalm 72:17; Revelation 21:24-26; etc.). A foregleam of this miraculous future elimination of the language barrier occurred with the coming of the Holy Spirit on the day of Pentecost, with His miraculous gift of tongues to the first disciples, enabling them to declare the wonderful works of God in many languages (Acts 2:6-11).

As the family units gradually packed their goods and departed from Babel, the last memory of the place was one of a loud "babble" of angry and incoherent noises pouring from the lips of those who had once been their friends and fellow citizens. "Therefore is the name of it called Babel, because the Lord did there confound the language of all the earth."

The word "confound" is the Hebrew *balal,* which means "mingle" or "mix" (usually translated "mingled"), and thus, by extension, "confusion." The meaning in this particular context is clarified by its purpose as stated in verse 7: "that they may not understand one another's speech." Apparently, in the mind of Shem or Moses, whoever originally wrote verse 9, the name "Babel" was connected with this word "balal." The name thus meant "confusion." It is not unlikely that the very sounds emanating from the confused throngs at Babel (like the unintelligible babblings of babies) became the name of the city in the minds of those who left it. The English word "babble" is not so much a word as it is an example of onomatopoeia—that is, a word formed to imitate an actual sound, and thus basically understandable in all languages. Thus, in the ages following, the very name Babylon would come to mean to all peoples "the city of babbling, or confusion."

It was later that those who remained in Babel tried to upgrade its meaning by claiming it meant "Bab-el," the "gate of God." Its true nature, however, is revealed by both the original record in Genesis 11 and the very sound of its name!

Babylon has ever since been a source and center of confusion in matters religious as well as linguistic. The complex religious system established there was apparently carried into all the nations by those who were scattered from it. Evidently in most families there was at least one member who had been thoroughly indoctrinated (possibly Nimrod had required each family to dedicate one of its members to become a priest or priestess in the temple worship system), and these naturally tended to become the spiritual leaders of the various tribes. Thus it is that astrology and polytheistic pantheism—basically evolutionism—became the established religion of all the nations of the ancient world. The Babylonian pantheon, with its array of heavenly gods and goddesses, was equivalent to the corresponding pantheon in Assyria, Egypt, Greece, India, and others. All followed the astrological emblems of the zodiac and all were idolaters. Furthermore, every one of these religious systems in one way or another communed with the evil spirits who were associated with the idols.

To some degree, however, all nations retained awareness of the true God of heaven as they scattered around the world, even though He receded more and more from their consciousness as time went on. They retained their corrupted traditions of the Deluge and, to a lesser extent, of the Dispersion. Their vague recollections of God's promised Redeemer were distorted into various systems of animal and even human sacrifices, to gain favor with the spiritual beings who seemed to govern their daily lives. Eventually these spirits were more and more identified simply with the forces of nature in a closed-system universe.

The Generations of Terah

For almost two centuries after the Dispersion at Babel (or longer, depending on whether there are gaps in the genealogies), almost nothing is revealed about the further history of mankind. The tribes were migrating and cultures developing, as described in the last section, with knowledge of the true God receding further and further from man's consciousness. In the far north, a great ice sheet was advancing over the continent; in the south, regions that are now deserts (Sahara, Arabia, etc.) were enjoying a pluvial period, with abundant water resources able to support developing civilizations throughout the world.

Though these events were of great importance in world history, they are passed over in silence in Scripture, since nothing of consequence was happening in revelational history. God was no longer working directly with and through mankind as a whole, since they all had rebelled against Him; yet the time was not yet propitious for Him to begin to prepare a special nation to receive and transmit His Word to the other nations. The latter must first be established in the world, and then a suitable man chosen and trained to found that special nation.

Nevertheless, the line of the promised Seed was being preserved, the records of the patriarchs were being protected, and God's plan was on schedule. In this section of the pre-Abrahamic records of Scripture, the patriarchal genealogies and chronology from the Flood down to the call of Abraham are preserved. Thus, in spite of its apparent lesser interest, it is really a very important passage of Scripture.

Genesis 11:10, 11

---

10 ⁋ These *are* the generations of Shĕm: Shĕm *was* a hundred years old, and begat Är-phăx'ăd two years after the flood:

11 And Shĕm lived after he begat Är-phăx'ăd five hundred years, and begat sons and daughters.

At this point, the "generations of Shem" are concluded. Shem had apparently kept the record from Genesis 10:1 through 11:9, covering the descendants of Ham and Japheth through the third generation after the Flood and some of his own descendants through the sixth. His record included the account of the confusion of tongues and the Dispersion, which apparently occurred in the fourth generation after the Flood, shortly before the birth of Peleg.

The account was then taken up by Terah, who was in the ninth generation after the Flood, assuming no gaps in those genealogical records. However, again assuming no gaps, the figures in this chapter indicate that Shem lived until after Terah's death, so that Terah had ample opportunity to talk with Shem and get the records from him. Even Noah lived until Terah was 128 years old.

Even if there are gaps in the genealogies (for example, at the time of Peleg, as seems possible—see discussion below), it is still likely that the days of Terah overlapped those of Shem to some extent. If there are no gaps, Shem lived until 278 years after Terah's birth, so that a gap of over two centuries would have been possible without preventing their being contemporaries.

As noted earlier, it seems possible that, sometime after the Dispersion, Shem may have moved southward into Arabia to live among the sons of Joktan (as suggested by the history of their names in Genesis 10:26-30), and so lost direct contact with the descendants of Joktan's brother Peleg. Perhaps Shem thought at the time that it was through Joktan the promised Seed would come. If so, he was wrong, because as it turned out, it was Peleg's descendant Terah who was destined to keep the next set of "generations" and who would be in the promised line. One can realistically suppose that, many years later, Shem somehow came in contact with young Terah and realized this was the man to whom he should entrust the sacred records from Adam through Noah, as well as those of his brothers and himself.

Terah, therefore, seems to have been the one who kept the brief, but important, record from Genesis 11:10 through 11:27a. Apparently, the only thing which he (or better, the Holy Spirit) judged worthy of recording during this period was the family genealogical record.

He began by tying his own record back to that of Shem, using Shem's name as the progenitor of his own line. "Shem was a hundred years old, and begat Arphaxad two years after the flood." Evidently, therefore, Shem was ninety-seven when the Flood began and ninety-eight a year later when it ended. Perhaps two of Arphaxad's brothers, Elam and Asshur, were born in the two years immediately after the Flood (their names are listed before Arphaxad's in Genesis 10:22). However, the purpose here is not to give all the names in the various families but only the direct line from Shem to Terah.

Shem lived another five hundred years after Arphaxad's birth, begetting other sons (listed in Genesis 10:22) and daughters (not listed). Each of the patriarchs presumably had as many daughters as sons, even though their names are not given.

Genesis 11:12-17

---

12 And Är-phăx′ăd lived five and thirty years, and begat Sā′läh:

13 And Är-phăx′ăd lived after he begat Sā′läh four hundred and three years,

and begat sons and daughters.
14 And Sā′lăh lived thirty years, and begat Ē′bĕr:
15 And Sā′lăh lived after he begat Ē′bĕr four hundred and three years, and begat sons and daughters.

16 And Ē′bĕr lived four and thirty years, and begat Pē′lĕg:
17 And Ē′bĕr lived after he begat Pē′lĕg four hundred and thirty years, and begat sons and daughters.

These verses give the genealogy from Arphaxad to Peleg, "in whose days the earth was divided" (Genesis 10:25), whereas verses 18 through 25 give it from Peleg to Terah. This entire section is much like the passage in Genesis 5:6-27, except that, there, the typical formula includes a statement concerning the total age of the patriarch and the fact that he finally died. In Genesis 11, the same information can be gleaned by adding the years the patriarch lived both before and after the birth of his son as listed.

It is obvious, in comparing Genesis 5 and 11, that patriarchal longevity began to decline immediately after the Flood. Noah lived 950 years (about the same as his antediluvian forebears), but Shem lived only 600 years, Arphaxad 438 years, Salah 433 years, and Eber 464 years. A still sharper decline took place after Peleg, as noted below.

It seems evident that this decline must have been triggered by the Flood. The radiation-filtering vapor canopy had been dissipated, and both genetic and somatic mutations must have increased significantly, though it would no doubt take a number of generations before the effect of mutations in the genetic system would have caused a significant impact on hereditary longevity. The increase in somatic (body cell) mutations, however, would have caused immediate acceleration of the aging process. Other factors might have included the more rugged environment, inadequate nourishment in the food, inbreeding, or greater stress of living.

It is worth noting that Luke (3:36) inserts the name of Cainan between Arphaxad and Salah in this genealogy. This name is found in some manuscripts of the Septuagint, and Luke may have used them in the compilation of his own record. If this name Cainan should really be included here, then another generation should be inserted in each appropriate place in the foregoing discussion.

However, the name is not included in the genealogical record in I Chronicles 1:18, nor is Cainan given as a son of Arphaxad in Genesis 10:24. The Masoretic scribes, who compiled the present Hebrew text, were no doubt familiar with the Septuagint text; but they nevertheless did not include this name. The unsettled question is whether the Septuagint text had somehow added the name Cainan where it shouldn't be, or whether the other texts (as sorted out by the Masoretes) had inadvertently omitted it, in both Genesis and I Chronicles. In view of the known fastidiousness with which the Hebrew copyists maintained the accuracy of their copies, it is difficult to understand how they would make such an obvious error as this. Furthermore, the name Cainan is not found in any of the other ancient versions of the Old Testament, such as the Samaritan, the Vulgate, or others.

On the other hand, why would the Septuagint translators arbitrarily add Cainan to the record? One possibility stems from the fact that the same name is found in Genesis 5:9 as the son of Enos. There are no other names in Genesis 5 which are also found in Genesis 11, and it would not be too difficult for a careless scribe to copy "Cainan" inadvertently from Luke 3:37 as he was copying Luke 3:36, thus getting two Cainans into the list. It is known that the New Testament copyists were often much less careful in this work than had been the Old Testament scribes.

The oldest Septuagint manuscripts do not include Cainan in their listings in Genesis 11; so it is altogether possible that later copiers of the Septuagint (who also were not as meticulous as those who copied the Hebrew text) inserted Cainan into their manuscripts on the basis of certain copies of Luke's Gospel to which they then had access. This is the conclusion of those scholars who have devoted the most intense amount of study to this particular problem.

Although the question is not settled, the weight of evidence does seem to be in favor of the Hebrew text as it stands. Cainan's name should not be included, and its insertion in Luke 3:36 is most likely a copyist's error.

Adding up the numbers in these verses, therefore, the record indicates that Peleg was born 101 years after the Flood. This probably was the year of the Babel Dispersion.

Some may doubt that a single century would be a long enough period of time for the population to grow from the eight survivors of the Flood to the substantial number of people that were involved in building Babel and its tower. However, there is no doubt that the population would have increased rapidly in that first century. It was to the advantage of all concerned (as well as in accordance with God's command) for each family to attempt to have as many children as possible. Shem, Ham, and Japheth had a total of sixteen listed sons (there may well have been others not listed, and even Noah may have had other unnamed children after the Flood) and presumably at least as many daughters. Thus the first generation after the Flood had at least 32 people, an increase of 533 percent over their original six parents. Assuming this proportion remained the same (and this is a conservative assumption), then the second generation had 171 people and the third 912, making a total of at least 1,120 mature adults at the time of the Dispersion at Babel.

Many of the young men of the fourth generation also would be old enough to help in the work. Furthermore, it is quite possible that each family had many more children than the numbers calculated above. A growth rate of only 8 percent annually would produce a population of nine thousand in only one hundred years. As noted previously, there is indication that the names in the Table of Nations do not constitute a complete listing, but only a specially selected listing of those families that originated from the three sons of Noah.

Thus it is easily possible for the earth to have had a population of many thousands at the time of the Dispersion, only one century after the Flood; but even if there were only several hundred, these could well have constructed the great tower over a period of several years. Many large structures of antiquity (the pyramids, Stonehenge, the Mesopotamian ziggurats which apparently copied the original Tower of Babel, among others) indicate that ancient men possessed remarkable engineering and construction capabilities.

Therefore, there seems no good reason why we should not take the record from Shem to Peleg as we actually have it, as a literal and complete genealogy and chronology for the period from the Flood to the Dispersion.

Genesis 11:18-25

18 And Pĕ′lĕg lived thirty years, and begat Rē′ū:
19 And Pĕ′lĕg lived after he begat Rē′ū two hundred and nine years, and begat sons and daughters.
20 And Rē′ū lived two and thirty years, and begat Sĕ′rŭg:
21 And Rē′ū lived after he begat Sĕ′rŭg two hundred and seven years, and begat sons and daughters.

22 And Sĕ′rŭg lived thirty years, and begat Nā′hŏr:
23 And Sĕ′rŭg lived after he begat Nā′hŏr two hundred years, and begat sons and daughters.
24 And Nā′hŏr lived nine and twenty years, and begat Tē′rȧh:
25 And Nā′hŏr lived after he begat Tē′rȧh a hundred and nineteen years, and begat sons and daughters.

If there is no great problem with respect to the development of a sufficient population to build the Tower of Babel, there is still less difficulty in understanding how there could have been an adequate population at the time of Abraham. According to the record, when Abram was seventy-five years old (Genesis 12:4), it had been 367 years since the Flood, and thus about 267 years since the Dispersion.

Assuming the record of Noah's grandsons was complete, we have noted that there was probably an increase of 533 percent in the first generation after the Flood. If a generation was thirty-three years (there had been three grown generations a century after the Flood), there would then have been eleven such generations by the time Abram went to Canaan. In the genealogical listing from Shem, Abram is ninth from Shem. However, his seventy-fifth year would have allowed two more normal generations, even though he himself had no children at the time. Evidently, it is reasonable to assume eleven generations since the Flood at this stage in world history.

If each such generation were to experience a 500 percent increase, slightly less than did the first generation (and this certainly was not impossible or unreasonable in those early days), then the world population at this time could have been at least 300 million people! Of course, it is more likely that this rate of increase fell off as time went on, but at least it is clear that the world population in Abraham's time could have easily been large enough to account for all the evidences of civilization at that time throughout the world.

It is not necessary, therefore, to assume gaps in these genealogical lists in order to account for the widespread evidence of population and civilization at the time of Abraham. On the other hand, we must recognize at least the possibility that some slight gaps may exist. The term "begat" refers sometimes to a descendant rather than to an immediate son, though this of course is the exception.[5]

A more cogent argument for a genealogical gap in this chapter is in connection with Peleg. The longevity of the post-Peleg patriarchs was only half that of the pre-Peleg patriarchs (438, 433, and 464 years for the three before Peleg, then suddenly down to 239 years for Peleg, and 239 and 230 years for the two after Peleg). The apparent suddenness of this drop suggests that a gap of unknown duration may have intervened, during which life spans were gradually declining.

There are difficulties with this suggestion, however. There seems to be no reason why the writer should be so careful to give precise chronological data for each of the links in the chain unless the chain itself is intact and complete. There is no indication in the record that the

---

5. See the discussion on this possibility in chapter 11, pp. 306-310.

writer was conscious of any gaps in his record. Furthermore, the writers in I Chronicles 1:25 and Luke 3:35 give no hint of a gap at this point (or at any other point in the genealogy, for that matter). Except for the sudden drop in longevity, there is no evidence of any genealogical gap here.

As far as the drop in longevity is concerned, it was apparently just before Peleg's birth that the Dispersion took place, as we have seen. This was an extremely traumatic experience for the entire human race, and it is not surprising that it would have severe physical effects on mankind in general. In addition to the difficulty of mere survival under the new conditions of living in small tribal communities, the effects of the genetic mutations that had been accumulating for several generations since the Flood were much aggravated by the necessity of close inbreeding. In general, it does not seem at all necessary to assume a gap in the genealogy in order to account for the drop in longevity at this time.

The only real reason for wanting to stretch the chronology here, therefore, is to deal with the opinion of archaeologists that early civilizations must be dated earlier than the Ussher chronology (which is based on the assumption of complete genealogical lists in Genesis 5 and 11) will allow. This opinion, however, is based mainly on uniformitarian methods of dating, especially the radiocarbon method; and one should not base his Biblical exegesis on some latter-day scientific theory. There are no actual, indisputable written historical records in Egypt, Sumeria, or any other ancient nations, which force the insertion of any gaps in these genealogies. The uniformitarian premises in radiocarbon and other dating methods have been seriously questioned in recent years, and there is no firm evidence that the Flood needs to be dated significantly earlier than about 2350 B.C., which is the traditional Ussher date.

The question may be unsettled, so that the possibility of one or more gaps in Genesis 11 does exist; but they could not be legitimately stretched in any case to fit the evolutionary chronology of human origins. The latter places the origin of true man at no less than a million years ago. The 222 years listed from the Flood to the birth of Terah can hardly be stretched this much. There are only eight possible locations for gaps from Shem to Terah, and this would mean an average gap of 125,000 years between each adjacent pair of names. This, of course, is absurd, and should be dismissed out of hand.

The actual names of the patriarchs from Peleg to Terah were not given in Genesis 10, so are found here for the first time. The names, in order, are Peleg, Reu, Serug, Nahor, and Terah. Each presumably had other sons and daughters not listed.

Genesis 11:26-28

---

26 And Tĕ′răh lived seventy years, and begat Abram, Nā′hŏr, and Hā′răn.
27 ¶ Now these *are* the generations of Tĕ′răh: Tĕ′răh begat Abram, Nā′hŏr, and Hā′răn; and Hā′răn begat Lot.
28 And Hā′răn died before his father Tĕ′răh in the land of his nativity, in Ûr of the Chăl′dēeṣ.

It is interesting that the genealogical lists in both Genesis 5 and 11 close with a patriarch whose three sons are all listed by name. Shem, Ham, and Japheth were sons of Noah; and Abram, Nahor, and Haran were sons of Terah. Similarly, in both cases, the father's age is given presumably to correspond to the birth of the first of his three sons: five hundred in Noah's case and seventy in Terah's case. It almost seems as though Terah deliberately patterned his own formula directly after that of his ancestor Noah. Perhaps he knew (by revelation) that a new dispensation would begin with his sons, just as had been the case with Noah's sons.

In any case, Terah knew somehow that he had been chosen to keep the patriarchal records received from Shem, and he had completed his assignment with verse 27. "These are the generations of Terah."

The next writer, presumably Isaac (Genesis 25:19), picked up the narrative at verse 27b, by tying his record back to that of Terah, giving the names of his three sons again. Terah apparently lived until Isaac was thirty-five years old (Genesis 11:26, 32; 21:5), assuming Abram was Terah's oldest son, born when he was seventy years of age. It is conceivable that Terah could somehow have transmitted his records directly to Isaac. It is more likely, however, that Abram took them all with him when he left his father in Haran (Genesis 12:4), especially in view of the fact that Terah seems to have become an idolater in his later years (Joshua 24:2, 3).

In addition to Abram, Terah was father of Nahor and Haran, both of whose names are associated with cities in Mesopotamia (Genesis 24:10; 28:10). Nahor was named after his grandfather (11:24). His brother Haran died when he was less than 135 years of age (11:26, 28, 32), while his father was still living, apparently while visiting his father back home in Ur. He left one son, Lot, who soon became attached to his Uncle Abram.

Genesis 11:29, 30

---

29 And Abram and Nā'hŏr took them wives: the name of Abram's wife *was* Sā'raï; and the name of Nā'hŏr's wife, Mĭl'càh, the daughter of Hā'răn, the father of Mĭl'càh, and the father of Ĭs'càh.
30 But Sā'raï was barren; she *had* no child.

The name of Lot's mother is not given, but the wives of both Abram and Nahor are introduced at this point, because of their importance in connection with later events and possibly also because Haran died prior to the time his two brothers married.

Nahor, in fact, married his niece, Milcah, daughter of Haran. As Abram seems to have become Lot's guardian when Haran died, it may have been that Nahor similarly took care of Milcah. As she grew into womanhood, then, he took her to be his wife.

Haran also had another daughter, Iscah, of whom nothing further is said. Jewish tradition identified her with Sarai, Abram's wife, but this is unlikely. Sarai was later acknowledged to be Abram's sister (Genesis 20:12), not his niece. Evidently, Sarai was also a daughter of Terah, but Terah had more than one wife, so she was only a half-sister of Abram.

Such close marriages were later forbidden in the Mosaic law; but, as we have seen, at this early date they were not particularly dangerous from a genetic point of view, and so were not uncommon. In fact, to preserve the spiritual purity of the patriarchal families at this time, it seems necessary to have sacrificed to some extent the genetic purity, thereby guarding insofar as possible against the introduction of idolatry into godly homes.

Note is made of Sarai's barrenness at this time, so that Abram, unlike Haran and Nahor (Genesis 22:20-24), had no children in either Ur or Mesopotamia. The child of promise must be born in the land of promise.

Genesis 11:31, 32

---

31 And Tē'ràh took Abram his son, and Lot the son of Hā'răn his son's son, and Sā'raï his daughter-in-law, his son Abram's wife; and they went forth with them from Ûr of the Ĉhăl'dēeş, to go into the land of Cā'năan; and they came unto Hā'răn, and dwelt there.
32 And the days of Tē'ràh were two hundred and five years: and Tē'ràh died in Hā'răn.

It was apparently soon after Haran's death, and the marriage of Abram, that Terah decided to leave Ur of the Chaldees. The archaeologist's spade has shown Ur to have been a great city, with a high civilization (including· a great library) even before Abram's time; but it was also a very idolatrous and wicked city.

This passage suggests that Terah himself may have received some kind of command from the Lord to go to the land of Canaan. If so, he only obeyed in part. He left Ur all right; but instead of striking directly westward across the desert to Canaan, he moved northwest up the Mesopotamian valley, finally reaching Haran.

Haran was apparently the settlement that had been established by Terah's son Haran, or to which at least his name had become attached. Ur was in the lower reaches of the Euphrates, on the Persian Gulf. Originally, before the millennia of delta deposits that have since formed downstream, it was actually a great seaport. Haran was perhaps six hundred miles northwest, whereas Canaan was about the same distance due west.

It may be that Terah needed to go to the city of Haran to settle his son's affairs, following Haran's premature death while visiting his father in Ur, and thus was justified in traveling to Canaan by way of Haran. In traveling up the Euphrates valley, the party would have to pass through, or near, the great city of Babylon and many of the other great cities of Chaldea. They would have surely been reminded of the terrible judgment on mankind that had taken place at Babylon two centuries previously.

On the other hand, an even stronger impression may have been made on them by the evident prosperity of the whole country. Haran was located on an important trade route coming up from Canaan and Syria, and had quickly become an important city (still in existence today, as a matter of fact). All of these considerations, in addition to his increasing age (Terah was probably well past a hundred years old by this time, since he was seventy when his first son was born, and all three sons were now mature men—Haran in fact with three children of his own), led Terah to keep putting off going on to Canaan. Finally he settled permanently in Haran, where he died at the age of 205 years.

When they left Ur, Terah took Abram and Sarai with him, as well as his grandson Lot. Nahor stayed behind in Ur, apparently with Lot's sister Milcah (who became Nahor's wife) and possibly his other sister, Iscah, as well. Later on, however, Nahor must have brought his own family on up to Haran, or to the nearby city of Nahor (Genesis

22:20-24; 24:10, 15; 27:43; 28:2; 29:4), so that the family probably was reunited for a while.

There is a problem in reconciling verse 32, which speaks of Terah's death in Haran at the age of 205, and Genesis 12:4, which says Abram left Haran when he was seventy-five years old, with Acts 7:4, where Stephen says that Abram waited until his father was dead before he left Haran. Genesis 11:26 says that Terah "lived seventy years and begat Abram, Nahor, and Haran." If Abram was Terah's firstborn son, as this verse may imply, then Terah was only 145 years of age when Abram left Haran, living there another sixty years before he died.

There is a possibility that Abram was *not* the first son, with his name being first listed only because of his later importance. In this case, if Abram were born only after Terah was 130 years old, and if their migration from Ur took place, say, thirty years or so later, then Terah could have died in Haran before Abram reached his seventy-fifth birthday.

The problem with this proposed solution is why, if Abram himself were born when his father was 130 years old, it should have taken a special miracle for Abram to become a father when he was only one hundred years old!

Another possibility is that Stephen simply made a mistake of interpretation in his speech. The doctrine of inspiration would apply in this case not to Stephen's speech but to Luke's accurate recording of Stephen's speech. It does seem unlikely, however, that a good Bible student like Stephen, familiar as he was with the Mosaic writings, would make such an obvious error as this.

The most likely solution of the problem is that Stephen was referring to Terah's becoming "dead" as far as God's will for his life was concerned. Stephen also noted that Abram received God's call originally while he was still in Mesopotamia (Acts 7:2, 3), as might indeed be inferred from the fact that Abram decided to take his own family along and go with Terah in his journey toward Canaan.

Perhaps God appeared to *both* Terah and Abram in Ur, and they both set out to Canaan together, father and son. Terah, however, delayed long in Haran and it eventually became apparent to Abram that his father no longer intended to go on to Canaan. The prosperity and comfort at Haran were too great a temptation for him. Eventually Terah even began to get involved in the Chaldean idolatries, which were part and parcel of both the trade and the culture of the region (Joshua 24:2, 14, 15).

It was at this point that Terah was, for all practical purposes, "dead" to God's will and plan for his life. God therefore renewed His call, but this time to Abram alone.

It was this sort of situation that the Lord Jesus Christ encountered one day when He called one to follow Him. That disciple, however, said, "Lord, suffer me first to go and bury my father." Jesus answered, "Follow me, and let the dead bury their dead" (Matthew 8:21, 22).

Terah was "dead," though he would not actually be ready for burial for perhaps another threescore years. This record is a sad commentary on the end of a venerable and once godly patriarch, one who had even been used to record a part of Scripture. In like manner, it is also a sober warning to any in later times who would allow ease or comfort to hinder them from following Christ.

Terah became a "castaway" (I Corinthians 9:27), presumably still saved but no longer useful to the Lord, trying to hold on to the world and its idolatries while still believing in God and hoping to retain His blessing.

But God had turned to Abram. "Get thee out ... from thy father's house" (Genesis 12:1). His father must delay the inauguration of God's plan for a new nation no longer. What Terah might have been, his son became—a blessing to all the families of the earth.

PART THREE

The Chosen Nation

11

The Call of Abraham

(Genesis 12-13)

A New Nation

Until the time of the Dispersion, and for some time after, God had
been dealing with mankind as a whole. The postdiluvian world had
begun with Noah and his sons, and they all had shared in the knowledge
of the true God and His laws and purposes. It had not been long, however, before rebellion had again entered the human family, finally becoming almost as serious as in the days before the Flood. God once
again had to intervene on a drastic scale, this time confusing human
tongues and forcing men to separate into different tribes and nations.
The judgment of the Dispersion did not cause mankind to return to God,
however. Most of the resulting nations continued in their rebellious ways,
worshiping the host of heaven and descending into ever deeper moral
degradation.

There were a few here and there who retained some knowledge of
the true God, even among those who practiced polytheism. There were
apparently even a few (as illustrated by Job, Melchizedek, and others)
who genuinely loved God and tried as best they could to maintain a
form of true spiritual worship among their own families and communities. But such were few and scattered, with the result that there
was real danger that, in a generation or so, knowledge of God would
vanish from the earth.

Or at least this is the way it might have seemed from the human point of view. God, however, cannot fail, and He will never "leave himself without witness" (Acts 14:17). Accordingly, at this point in history, two thousand years or more since He had first created man, God undertook a completely new approach toward mankind. He began to prepare a new nation, one which would be responsible for carrying God's revelation to other men and through whom the Redeemer could finally come into the world to work out God's plan of salvation. For this purpose, He chose a man named Abram, a descendant of Shem and a son of Terah—the two men who, since the Flood, had kept the records of God's dealings with the world.

Abram had gone from Ur, in the land of the Chaldees, to Haran with his father Terah. While he was in Haran, God renewed His call to Abram (given earlier while he was still in Ur, according to Stephen, in Acts 7:2, 3) to go into the land of Canaan to establish the new nation. It is probable (in view of Christ's rebuke of the man who wanted first to bury his father before he could follow Him, as recorded in Matthew 8:21, 22) that Abram should not have waited this long. According to Joshua 24:2, even Terah had begun to worship other gods while still in Chaldea, and it is possible that some of this culture had begun to rub off on Abram and Sarai. In any case, God did call him once again, and this time Abram obeyed without further delay.

Genesis 12:1-3

CHAPTER 12

NOW the Lord had said unto Abram, Get thee out of thy country, and from thy kindred, and from thy father's house, unto a land that I will show thee:
2 And I will make of thee a great nation, and I will bless thee, and make thy name great; and thou shalt be a blessing:
3 And I will bless them that bless thee, and curse him that curseth thee: and in thee shall all families of the earth be blessed.

God's calls are not always easy to follow. He stressed the difficulties first of all, telling Abram he would have to leave his home and family and go into a strange land, a land which even at that time had become notorious for its wickedness, the land settled by the descendants of Canaan, the cursed son of Ham. At the same time, God also made to Abram a wonderful promise. He told him He would establish a great nation through him, a nation through which someday all other nations would be blessed.

This promise has justifiably been regarded as one of the first promises of the coming Savior, who would bring salvation to all nations.

God had long ago made it clear that the Savior would be born into the human family ("seed of the woman," as promised in Genesis 3:15), and now it becomes clear to Abram that it would be accomplished through his own family.

God also promised protection, saying He would bless those that bless Abram and curse those that curse him. This was an unconditional promise, assuming only that Abram would migrate to Canaan as God had told him. Although this promise was made specifically to Abram, it may also have applied in a secondary and broader sense to his descendants, the Jewish nation, which has certainly been blessed and protected in a marvelous way through the centuries.

Genesis 12:4-9

4 So Abram departed, as the LORD had spoken unto him; and Lot went with him: and Abram *was* seventy and five years old when he departed out of Hā′răn.

5 And Abram took Sā′raī his wife, and Lot his brother's son, and all their substance that they had gathered, and the souls that they had gotten in Hā′răn; and they went forth to go into the land of Cā′năan; and into the land of Cā′năan they came.

6 ¶ And Abram passed through the land unto the place of Sī′chĕm, unto the plain of Mō′rĕh. And the Cā′năan-īte *was* then in the land.

7 And the LORD appeared unto Abram, and said, Unto thy seed will I give this land: and there builded he an altar unto the LORD, who appeared unto him.

8 And he removed from thence unto a mountain on the east of Beth-el, and pitched his tent, *having* Beth-el on the west, and Hā′ī on the east: and there he builded an altar unto the LORD, and called upon the name of the LORD.

9 And Abram journeyed, going on still toward the south.

When Abram left Haran, his wife Sarai accompanied him. Abram was seventy-five years old at this time, and Sarai ten years younger. The aging process at this time was still much slower than it is in our own day, so that Sarai was still considered a very beautiful woman (verse 11). Abram's nephew, Lot, also decided to accompany them, because his own father, Haran, had died even before Terah's death. Abram was evidently a fairly prosperous rancher or businessman at this time, because he had considerable wealth and a number of servants, all of which he took with him to Canaan.

It was a long journey to Canaan, approximately four hundred miles to the southwest of Haran. The testimony of Hebrews 11:8 tells us that "by faith, Abraham, when he was called to go out into a place which he should after receive for an inheritance, obeyed; and he went out, not knowing whither he went." Abram knew where he was going in general, but not where he would settle in particular. Trade routes from Haran down into Damascus and the Canaanite countries were already established at this time. As he entered Canaan, he stopped for a time at Sichem (or Shechem) near the center of the land, where he built an altar unto the Lord. This was near a well-known landmark of the time, the oak or terebinth grove (a more likely translation of the Hebrew word than "plain") belonging to a Canaanite named Moreh.

At this point, God "appeared unto him." This is the first time in Scripture where we read of an actual appearance of God. God had "walked" and spoken with Adam, Enoch, and Noah, and perhaps He also had been visible in some way to them, but Scripture does not say so. Here, however, there must have been an actual visible manifestation— a theophany—and, therefore, we must understand this as a preincarnate appearance of Christ (John 1:18).

The Lord here confirmed His promise to Abram, adding the specific promise that his seed would inherit this land, though at the time he owned none of it (Acts 7:5). Abram continued traveling, then stopped for a time at a mountain east of Bethel, about thirty-five miles farther south of Shechem. Here he built another altar and again called on God for guidance and help. Then he continued on, going still farther south, toward the Negev, finally traveling the entire length of the land of Canaan.

Although the Bible doesn't say so specifically, we receive the impression that Abram at this time was living more or less as a nomad, moving with his flocks and herds wherever he could find water and pasture and wherever the inhabitants of the land were not too numerous. Although God had promised him the land, as well as a seed to inherit the land, this was not yet the time for the fulfillment of these promises; hence Abram was still forced to live by faith. God did, nevertheless, lead him day by day, so that neither he nor those with him lacked daily bread, guidance, and protection.

Such experiences are not unique to Abram, but are common to all those who seek to follow God's will. The promise often seems long delayed, and the believer must simply continue following day by day, trusting God and knowing that His timing is always right. In the meantime, until the opening of the larger door and the accomplishment of His specific and ultimate will in our lives, there are daily opportunities for service and witness wherever we are, and in whatever circumstances. There is still a testing time, when God must teach us patience and submission; and such a training often is long and slow. "He that is faithful in that which is least is faithful also in much" (Luke 16:10).

Abraham in Egypt

Genesis 12:10

---

10 ¶ And there was a famine in the land: and Abram went down into Egypt to sojourn there; for the famine *was* grievous in the land.

At this time, a particularly severe trial of Abram's faith took place. A grievous famine developed in the land (Genesis 12:10), and it looked as though the land could no longer sustain him and his family and flocks. God's promise had not changed, however, and Abram needed to learn to trust God not only when all his needs were being supplied freely but also when it appeared that suffering and privation were imminent. But Abram was not yet equal to this test, and he soon yielded to the temptation to take matters into his own hand. God had told him to go to Canaan, where He would bless him, but now it seemed that Canaan was no longer able to support him. On the other hand, the land of Egypt was prosperous; so he finally made the decision (evidently without calling on God for guidance) to move to Egypt. Although the Bible doesn't say so, it is possible that this decision was reached in part because of the complaining of his wife and nephew, who had never been accustomed to hardship and whose faith was not yet as strong as that of Abram. In any case, they all headed "down into Egypt to sojourn there."

Genesis 12:11-16

---

11 And it came to pass, when he was come near to enter into Egypt, that he said unto Sā′raī his wife, Behold now, I know that thou *art* a fair woman to look upon:
12 Therefore it shall come to pass, when the Egyptians shall see thee, that they shall say, This *is* his wife: and they will kill me, but they will save thee alive.
13 Say, I pray thee, thou *art* my sister: that it may be well with me for thy sake; and my soul shall live because of thee.
14 ¶ And it came to pass, that, when Abram was come into Egypt, the Egyptians beheld the woman that she *was* very fair.
15 The princes also of Phā′raōh saw her, and commended her before Phā′raōh: and the woman was taken into Phā′raōh's house.
16 And he entreated Abram well for her sake: and he had sheep, and oxen, and he asses, and menservants, and maidservants, and she asses, and camels.

It often seems at first that a compromise between the methods of the world and God's will and promises works out very well. Following the criteria of the practical world system will often prove profitable because of the pragmatic nature of that system. Christians who follow this path may easily misinterpret the prosperity that follows such a compromise as a confirmation that this was, after all, God's leading; and they may become quite satisfied with the situation. Until, that is, God finally has to deal with them in chastisement, forcing them out of the compromising position back into the walk of true faith.

This chastisement may take various forms. Perhaps the most painful —at least to one who truly loves God and desires to witness effectively for Him—is to find that his compromise has destroyed his testimony. The worldly men with whose standards he has compromised, rather than being drawn to God through him, are used by God to rebuke him.

This is what happened to Abram. As he entered the mighty land of Egypt, he became aware of an unforeseen danger. The Egyptians, like the Canaanites, were descendants of Ham (through Mizraim, rather than Canaan) and were also polytheistic, cruel, and immoral. Polygamy and sexual promiscuity were common. As they entered Egypt, Abram probably noted the admiring glances being directed by the inhabitants toward his beautiful wife, Sarai, and he realized that it was not at all beyond them to decide to kill him and his servants in order to have Sarai for themselves.

He was suddenly confronted with a decision he had not anticipated and for which he was not prepared. How often this happens to a believer when he falls in with an ungodly company! If Abram openly acknowledged Sarai to be his wife, he reasoned, he would probably be killed and she would be taken by the Egyptians into who-knows-what circumstances of moral degradation. If he said she was one of his servants, his own life might be spared; but she herself would probably be taken and defiled in perhaps even greater ways. The best solution would be to call her his sister. Actually, he reasoned, this was really true, because she *was* his half-sister (Genesis 20:12). This was still in the early centuries after the Flood, and close marriages were still common and often necessary.

If Sarai were recognized as his sister, both she and Abram would be treated with respect and his life would not be endangered. It is true that this might mean she would be approached by the Egyptians for sexual purposes, but that would be true also if Abram were killed for her sake; so this seemed the best of a bad bargain.

Sarai no doubt saw it in this light also, and so she went along with the half-truth. No doubt she wished she had never encouraged Abram to move to Egypt, but it was too late.

Actually, it turned out better than they had hoped. Instead of becoming involved with the ordinary Egyptians, Sarai came to the attention of Pharaoh himself. She was seen by Pharaoh's princes, and they "commended" her to Pharaoh as a prime candidate to become one of his wives!

The word used here is the Hebrew *hallal,* meaning "to praise." This is the first occurrence of this word in the Bible and, in accordance with the principle of first mention, as it applies to important Biblical words, it seems to have a special significance here. Nearly always, it is used in reference to praising God; but here first of all it is used in reference to praising a godly woman. One of the very purposes of man's creation is that he might offer the response of praise to God, and this in fact will be a dominant activity in the eternal ages to come. An unsaved man, however, being alienated from God, is not able to praise Him. He cannot even see or know Him until he comes to Him in repentant and believing faith. Those who have been redeemed become His witnesses, and unsaved men can only learn of God through their testimony. Jesus said: "Let your light so shine before men, that they may see your good works, and glorify your Father which is in heaven" (Matthew 5:16).

The first use of *hallal* in this connection, therefore, seems to be reminding us that unsaved men will only come to praise God if they have first been constrained to praise those who manifest God to them. Pharaoh's princes could see something unique in Sarai, not only her physical beauty, but also an "adorning" with a meek and quiet spirit, an inner beauty (I Peter 3:3-6). Rather than taking her for themselves, they were constrained to "praise" her to Pharaoh himself. Pharaoh then sent for her, and she was taken into his house. Rather than defiling her, however, he began to consider her for marriage. Furthermore, rather than Abram's being murdered for Sarai's sake, as he had feared, he was lavished with presents from Pharaoh, with flocks and herds and servants in abundance.

Genesis 12:17-20

---

17 And the LORD plagued Phă'raōh and his house with great plagues, because of Să'raī, Abram's wife.
18 And Phă'raōh called Abram, and said, What *is* this *that* thou hast done unto me? why didst thou not tell me that she *was* thy wife?

19 Why saidst thou, She *is* my sister? so I might have taken her to me to wife: now therefore behold thy wife, take *her,* and go thy way.
20 And Phă'raōh commanded *his* men concerning him: and they sent him away, and his wife, and all that he had.

Abram's compromise seemed to be working out very well. Sarai was still safe, and he himself not only was alive but was prospering. But what would happen when Pharaoh actually decided to take Sarai as his wife? Would both Abram and Sarai still continue the deception to that point? Having involved themselves so deeply, what else could they do? It had been God's intention to bring the promised Seed into the world through them, and this development would certainly prevent that from happening. No doubt both of them spent many sleepless hours and were driven to much prayer, far into the night, on many nights. Abram and Sarai loved each other, and surely wished many times they had never left Canaan, famine or no famine, in spite of their apparent prosperity in Egypt. But what could they do now?

They themselves were helpless to change the situation, but God was not! "The Lord plagued Pharaoh and his house with great plagues because of Sarai Abram's wife." Whether God actually spoke to Pharaoh, or whether he found it out by talking to Lot or to one of Abram's servants, the king of Egypt soon came to realize that Sarai was already married, that the great attractiveness which he had seen in her was because of her relation to the true God, and that she and her husband were under the special protection of that God.

Pharaoh now feared to harm either Sarai or Abram; but he did sharply rebuke Abram, and no doubt Sarai also. He lost all respect and affection for them, and of course was not attracted to their God, even though he had to recognize that God was with them and that he could not harm them. The only thing he could do was tell them to leave his country, which they did, taking all the possessions they had acquired in Egypt.

As they journeyed back home, it must have been largely in embarrassed silence. Outwardly, of course, everything had gone well. They had not only escaped the Canaanite famine, but had come out of Egypt with increased goods. Sarai was still with Abram and neither had been injured in any way. If they had been worldly people, no doubt they would have been very self-satisfied. But they were not. They had suffered a deep rebuke. They who had testified to others about God's power and faithfulness, who had followed God's call into a strange land and had enjoyed His protection for many years, now had lost their testimony.

The Egyptians had at first been greatly impressed by them and might well have been won to faith in God through them. Instead, their fearfulness and compromise had caused the house of Pharaoh to suffer greatly, and the Egyptians had finally come to despise them. Even Abram's own servants must have been disgusted.

They should never have gone into Egypt in the first place. The Lord surely could have supplied their needs in Canaan, even in time of famine. But once in Egypt, they should have been careful to maintain a good testimony at all costs. God could have protected them there, too, without such a degrading compromise. After all, He *did* protect them and provide for them, even in spite of their compromise.

It is easy, of course, for us to be critical of Abram as we read these things. But it is very doubtful, if we had been in his shoes, that we would have chosen differently. We also engage in similar expediencies, and we rationalize them, as he did. We also need to learn the same lesson he learned and often we have to learn it in the same way, by being rebuked by the very unbelievers we would like to win to Christ. "Wherefore let him that thinketh he standeth take heed lest he fall. There hath no temptation taken you but such as is common to man: but God is faithful, who will not suffer you to be tempted above that ye are able; but will with the temptation also make a way to escape, that ye may be able to bear it" (I Corinthians 10:12, 13).

Lot's Sad Choice

Genesis 13:1-4

CHAPTER 13

AND Abram went up out of Egypt, he, and his wife, and all that he had, and Lot with him, into the south.

2 And Abram *was* very rich in cattle, in silver, and in gold.

3 And he went on his journeys from the south even to Beth-el, unto the place where his tent had been at the beginning, between Beth-el and Hā'i;

4 Unto the place of the altar, which he had made there at the first: and there Abram called on the name of the LORD.

As they traveled up from Egypt into the Negev, they did not stop until they once again reached Bethel, the last place where Abram had built an altar and called on the name of the Lord. It was there he had last been in sweet fellowship with God; and he evidently felt constrained to return, there to confess his sins and seek full restoration to God's favor. When he arrived at "the place of the altar," there, as in earlier and happier days, "Abram called on the name of the Lord" (Genesis 13:4). Since God promises to forgive our sins when we confess them (I John 1:9), Abram was no doubt restored there to full fellowship and joy of the Lord.

Genesis 13:5-11

---

5 ¶ And Lot also, which went with Abram, had flocks, and herds, and tents.

6 And the land was not able to bear them, that they might dwell together: for their substance was great, so that they could not dwell together.

7 And there was a strife between the herdmen of Abram's cattle and the herdmen of Lot's cattle: and the Cā′năan-īte and the Pĕr′ĭz-zīte dwelt then in the land.

8 And Abram said unto Lot, Let there be no strife, I pray thee, between me and thee, and between my herdmen and thy herdmen; for we *be* brethren.

9 *Is* not the whole land before thee? separate thyself, I pray thee, from me: if *thou wilt take* the left hand, then I will go to the right; or if *thou depart* to the right hand, then I will go to the left.

10 And Lot lifted up his eyes, and beheld all the plain of Jordan, that it *was* well watered every where, before the LORD destroyed Sŏd′ŏm and Gō-mŏr′rȧh, *even* as the garden of the LORD, like the land of Egypt, as thou comest unto Zō′ȧr.

11 Then Lot chose him all the plain of Jordan; and Lot journeyed east: and they separated themselves the one from the other.

Although Abram and Sarai were restored to the fellowship of the Lord, the experience had left scars on Lot and their servants, as they also had gone to Egypt and watched the events there. They no longer felt the reverent admiration they once had felt for Abram, and began to be self-seeking on their own behalf. This situation no doubt was also aggravated by the great wealth they had observed in Egypt, including the considerable portion of it with which they themselves had returned. Consequently, there began to be serious friction between the servants of Lot and those of Abram and, no doubt, to some extent also between Lot and Abram. The saddest thing about this, of course, was that this was a bad testimony to the Canaanites around them, just as they had already compromised their testimony to the Egyptians. Material possessions of God's people, especially if they have been acquired by worldly methods, often lead to such problems.

Under such circumstances, the best solution often will be for the believers so affected simply to separate from each other. Continued contact under such conditions, even with good intentions, will only generate increased friction. Sometimes, even a church split is advisable, so that each of the two factions can then follow its own preferred methods and witness to those in the neighborhood, instead of destroying the entire ministry by continued bickering.

This was the solution proposed by Abram. Rather than seeking to perpetuate a forced and artificial union, he saw that it would be better to have a complete geographical break with Lot and his herdsmen. There was still at that time plenty of open land in Canaan; so there was no reason for them to strive over the same land. Likewise, there is more than enough work to be done by two (separate churches or student groups, or other Christian organizations) working apart; so there is no reason for them to argue over which has priority in a given field. Far better to separate, with each working to reach as many as possible in different areas, than to continue debating with each other in the same area.

Abram had learned that God could take care of his needs no matter where he was, so that he offered Lot the choice of fields. As the older man and the leader of the clan, Abram by all rights should have had priority; but he graciously offered it to Lot. Instead of deferring to Abram, as he should have done, Lot seized the opportunity to his own advantage (as he thought). He had been infected with the luxury and excitement of Egypt, and was no longer content to be a "stranger and pilgrim in the land" (Hebrews 11:13). He looked down to the plain of the Jordan River, as it flows into the Salt Sea, where there were five prosperous, exciting cities, and decided that was where he would like to be.

The region of these cities now is almost unbearably hot and desolate, but in those early days there was still abundant rainfall in the region. The temperature, also, was much more pleasant than now, probably because of the lingering effects of the great Ice Age far to the north. According to verse 10, the Jordanian plain was "as the garden of the Lord."

If Abram had in his possession the "book of the generations of Adam," as has been suggested in chapter 1, then Lot no doubt had read about the beauties of the Garden of Eden. As a youngster with his father Haran in Ur in the land of Babylonia, he had known the luxuries of the Mesopotamian region. More recently he had been with Abram along the Nile in Egypt. As he "lifted up his eyes, and beheld all the plain of Jordan," it seemed to him "like the land of Egypt." Though he no doubt knew something of the wickedness of these cities, just as he had observed the pagan worlds of Sumeria and Egypt, he nevertheless decided that was what he wanted. Perhaps he also, like many believers today who make similar choices, rationalized that he could be a witness for the Lord there, while at the same time enjoying the creature comforts they offered.

That was what Lot saw, as he lifted up his eyes. Abram, on the other hand, "looked for a city which hath foundations, whose builder and maker is God" (Hebrews 11:10). So Lot journeyed east, down toward the plain; and Abram headed back up into the hill country of Canaan.

Genesis 13:12, 13

---

12 Abram dwelt in the land of Cā'năan, and Lot dwelt in the cities of the plain, and pitched *his* tent toward Sŏd'ŏm.

13 But the men of Sŏd'ŏm *were* wicked and sinners before the LORD exceedingly.

At that time, the land of Canaan was sparsely inhabited, with most of the settlements concentrated along the seacoast, along the northern plain of Esdraelon, and here along the Jordanian plain. Abram had the more rugged hill and desert country almost to himself, in what is now termed the Negev (usually translated simply as "the south," in the King James Version).

Lot didn't move into Sodom immediately, probably having some reservations about living in a city where it was known that the inhabitants were "wicked and sinners before the Lord exceedingly"; so he only "pitched his tent toward Sodom." He dwelled "in the cities of the plain"—not actually within the cities, since he still lived in his tent, but in their orbit, as it were, near enough to enjoy their advantages but not yet actually a part of their life. Christians today often follow the same path, hoping to have both the spiritual blessings of a separated walk with God and the carnal advantages of fellowship with the world. Sooner or later, however, one has to decide which it will be. He cannot have it both ways. Neither God nor the world will allow it. Lot first "pitched his tent toward Sodom," but soon he "dwelt in Sodom" (Genesis 14:12), and finally "sat in the gate of Sodom" (Genesis 19:1) as one of its business leaders. Thus began the tragedy which would ultimately destroy him and his family.

Genesis 13:14-18

---

14 ¶ And the LORD said unto Abram, after that Lot was separated from him, Lift up now thine eyes, and look from the place where thou art northward, and southward, and eastward, and westward:

15 For all the land which thou seest, to thee will I give it, and to thy seed for ever.

16 And I will make thy seed as the dust of the earth: so that if a man can number the dust of the earth, *then* shall thy seed also be numbered.

17 Arise, walk through the land in the length of it and in the breadth of it; for I will give it unto thee.

18 Then Abram removed *his* tent, and came and dwelt in the plain of Măm'rē, which *is* in Hē'brŏn, and built there an altar unto the LORD.

What was a sad mistake for Lot, however, was a good move for

Abram. He could now once again devote his full attention to serving God and walking in His good will. When Abram was more or less settled in Canaan, God once again spoke to him, as He had several years before in Shechem. Abram had learned a hard lesson, and had learned it well; and now God in grace once again confirmed His covenant with Abram to give him the land. God told him that, as far as he could see in every direction, probably from lofty Mount Hebron, the land would belong to him and his seed forever. God even told him to walk through the length and breadth of the land, as a conqueror claiming his territory, as though in faith taking possession.

Abram never actually owned the land himself, however, during his lifetime. Nor, for most of human history, have his descendants actually owned the land, especially those of the promised seed, Isaac. The Israeli nation has currently regained possession of this region, but whether they can hold on to it remains to be seen. Thus, this promise must either be taken in a spiritual sense (applying it to a spiritual land of promise, as so interpreted by many expositors) or else ascribed to a time yet future. Since God promised the land to Abram and his seed *forever,* this can ultimately, if taken literally, be fulfilled only in the new earth of Revelation 21. It will quite probably be fulfilled precursively, however, during the coming millennial age.

God also assured Abram again that He would make him a great nation, with his seed numbering "as the dust of the earth." The descendants of Abram today include not only the Jews but also the Arabs, and the number indeed is great. Once again, though, for the promise to be strictly literal, there must be a future fulfillment. During the Millennium, according to Revelation 20:8, earth's population will be "as the sand of the sea." Since it would be physically impossible to have as many people on earth as there are grains of sand (say, perhaps a billion billion), this expression evidently is a figure of speech for a number too great for actual enumeration. In any case, it does seem probable that its ultimate fulfillment is in the future.

Although the term may itself be a figure of speech, there is no reason to doubt the reality of its promised literal fulfillment. God does not break His word, nor change His mind, and this promise was given unconditionally. Abram would surely have taken it literally, as he had no basis for interpreting it otherwise. He was promised a nation that would bless other nations. It would, thus, be an actual nation, living among other actual nations, and physically descended from Abram.

At the same time, the New Testament makes it clear that Abram's "seed" was Christ Himself (Galatians 3:16), and that Abram is "father of all them that believe" (Romans 4:11), so that he also has a spiritual seed. It is evidently not a case of either this or that, but of both! The Jewish nation is to be eternally blessed as a nation, chosen of God in Abram. Likewise, the Christian Church, genuine believers in Christ from all nations, is itself a "holy nation" (I Peter 2:9), "Abraham's seed, and heirs according to the promise" (Galatians 3:29). Abram indeed was to be the "father of many nations" (Genesis 17:5).

After this marvelous experience and revelation from God, quite possibly accompanied by another theophany, Abram pulled up his tent again and descended from the mountain into the plain of Mamre (or the terebinth "grove of Mamre," as rendered by the newer versions) near Hebron. Hebron, of course, was not yet in existence as a city by that name (Numbers 13:22), so this reference to Hebron should be understood as an editorial insertion by Moses into Isaac's "generations" document to identify the location to future readers. The same will be found true of a number of other localities mentioned in Genesis.

Here in Mamre (so named after an Amorite chieftain who had settled there earlier—see Genesis 14:13), Abram built another altar. This was to be his home for some time now, and he wanted a place where his family and servants could meet for formal worship of God. Here also was where God had spoken to him, and so the place was especially dear to him. He had built similar altars at Shechem and at Bethel.

It is interesting to note in passing that all the places mentioned in these chapters—Shechem, Bethel, Sodom, Haran, Ur, and others—have been shown by modern archaeological excavations to have been real cities in existence at the time of Abram, answering in every way to the descriptions of them in Genesis.

The World of Abraham

Before closing this chapter, it is well to digress briefly to describe the age in which Abraham lived. A hundred years ago, it was common for skeptics to question whether he had ever lived at all. The evolutionary and higher critical theories were holding sway, and men assumed Abraham was only a legendary hero of the Jews, comparable to Romulus and Remus in Rome.

Only those who are ignorant of modern archaeology hold such views today. Whether one believes in the Biblical record of the divine call and purpose for Abraham or not, few would question that he actually existed. Nor do men seriously question any more the substantial accuracy of the Genesis descriptions of the world of his day. As just noted, most of the places mentioned in these chapters of Genesis, though hidden under the sands for millennia of time, have in recent years been unearthed and their culture again revealed.

It is significant that these excavations do not show primitive, half-bestial cultures, newly evolved from an animal ancestry, but a high civilization, exactly as suggested in Genesis.

For example, Abraham's boyhood home in Ur was known only by its mention in the Bible, until it began to be excavated in the nineteenth century. Now it is known that it was a great and prosperous city, though highly idolatrous, exactly as Genesis suggests. The Euphrates River was adjacent to the city, and it contained numerous canals. Its skyline was dominated by one of the greatest of the Babylonian ziggurats, but there were also numerous other impressive buildings. Excavations have yielded a wealth of jewelry and art objects, with beautiful vessels of gold and silver. More significantly, Ur has yielded a vast library of books, business documents, and other written materials. Not only did the "intelligentsia" of Ur know how to read and write long before the time of Abraham, but so did even the ordinary citizens. When Abraham lived there, Ur had already begun to decline somewhat from a former glory.

Haran also has been excavated, and, as a matter of fact, is still in existence as a town today. Although it has the same name as Abraham's brother, the latter died in Ur. The nearby town of Nahor may well have been named after Abraham's other brother, or more likely, after his grandfather. This town also has been explored archaeologically.

Egypt during the time of Abraham was a great empire, and had been so for a long time. There is considerable uncertainty about the exact chronology, but most conservative scholars place Abraham no later than Egypt's twelfth dynasty. Considering that it is believed the greatest pyramids were constructed during the fourth dynasty, it seems likely that the pyramids had already been standing for a long time when Abraham entered Egypt.

The Canaanite towns of Shechem and Bethel, as well as others mentioned later in Genesis, such as Salem, Gerar, and Beersheba, have also been confirmed by archaeology. In fact, it can be said that nothing in these chapters has been proved wrong through archaeological investigation, and that a great many of their implications have been substantiated. We can read the Book of Genesis, especially from chapter 12 onward, in full confidence that it is giving us a true and accurate picture of the world of those days. It could only have been written by men who actually lived in those days—either Abraham and Isaac or at least men who were their contemporaries.

As far as the exact chronology is concerned, however, there is still considerable uncertainty. The Ussher chronology, of course, is based on the assumption that the genealogies given in Genesis 11, as well as the other chronological information given later in the Bible, are complete and correct. In general, this would seem to be a sound approach, in view of both the doctrine of verbal inspiration of the Bible and the highly uncertain status of ancient secular histories. There is certainly no reason to regard the chronologies of Manetho, Herodotus, Berosus, and other ancient historians as more trustworthy than those in the Bible. These were all written much later than Genesis, and quite likely contain many errors. That genealogical gaps are not necessary has been shown in chapter 10.

On the other hand, the strictly Biblical approach also raises problems. For example, according to Genesis 11, Abraham was born only 292 years after the Flood and migrated into Canaan 367 years after the Flood. If Peleg, in whose "days the earth was divided" (Genesis 10:25), and whose name means "division," was so named because of the division of the nations at the Tower of Babel, as seems likely, then the Dispersion took place about 101 years after the Flood, and Abram's trip to Canaan took place only 266 years after the Dispersion.

In Abraham's time, however, Ur was already an old city, many dynasties of Egypt had come and gone, and other indications of lengthy histories prior to that time abound. Many conservative scholars feel that a period of less than three centuries does not seem long enough to allow the world to have reached the state of settlement and culture indicated in Genesis at the time of Abraham.

Even more problematical are the interesting chronological comparisons presented by the records of longevity in Genesis 11. If there are no gaps in these chronologies, then Shem was still living at the time of Abraham, since he did not die until 502 years after the Flood. As a matter of fact, Abraham died thirty-five years before Shem! Even Noah lived 350 years after the Flood (Genesis 9:28), so that Abraham was fifty-eight years old when Noah died.

Now none of these situations are impossible, but they do seem strange. Other difficulties with the strict-chronology interpretation of Genesis 11 have been discussed in detail elsewhere.[1]

---

1. John C. Whitcomb, Jr. and Henry M. Morris, *The Genesis Flood* (Philadelphia: Presbyterian and Reformed Publishing Company, 1961), pp. 474-489.

Furthermore, there are a number of other places in the Bible where it is evident that the term "begat" does not necessarily denote a direct father-son relationship. The best known is Matthew 1:8, where it says that "Joram begat Uzziah." Comparison with II Chronicles 21—26 shows that Joram begat Ahaziah, who begat Joash, who begat Amaziah, who begat Uzziah. Thus, three generations are omitted. The term "begat" in Matthew 1:8 obviously refers to ancestry rather than immediate generation. It is at least conceivable that a similar meaning may be attached in some of the cases (not all, by any means) in Genesis 11.

If so, then it is impossible to assign a definite date to the Flood or to the Dispersion by use of Biblical data only. Also, in view of the very unsatisfactory state of the non-Biblical chronological data, it seems there is little hope of arriving at a sure chronology for these years. We must apparently leave this as an open question.

If one feels strongly that Genesis 11 was indeed intended to give a complete chronology from the Flood to Abraham (perhaps as supplemented by the insertion of Cainan between the names of Arphaxad and Salah, as noted in Luke 3:36), then he may justifiably say that there is no real *proof,* either in archaeology or the Bible, to the contrary. It seems unlikely, but certainly not impossible, that the world could have developed to the point of maturity implied in Genesis 12—13 in less than three centuries, and that most of the postdiluvian patriarchs of Genesis 11 were still living at that time.

There is also considerable uncertainty, though not as much, concerning the post-Abrahamic chronology, due mainly to the unsatisfactory state of Egyptian chronology as interpreted from the Manetho dynastic lists and the so-called Sothic cycle. Some writers (notably Velikovsky and his followers) have proposed a drastic reduction in Egyptian history, amounting to perhaps six hundred to eight hundred years.

Most conservative scholars, however, follow a modified Ussher chronology for this period, which would place Abraham's career at around 2000 B.C. The traditional Ussher chronology places his birth at 1,948 years after the Creation, or 2056 B.C. A modified chronology developed by Edwin R. Thiele has been widely accepted in recent decades, according to which Abraham's birth is placed at 2167 B.C.[2] If Thiele's analysis is correct, this would place the Flood (assuming no gaps in Genesis 11) at 2459 B.C. and the Dispersion at about 2358 B.C. If gaps are allowed, however, these dates might conceivably be increased by, say,

---

2. Edwin R. Thiele, *The Mysterious Numbers of the Hebrew Kings* (Chicago: University of Chicago Press), 1951.

up to about one thousand years or more (possibly five thousand years at the very outside).

Although chronological questions are still unsettled, there is no reason to question the accuracy of the names and events reported in Genesis. It seems that almost every new archaeological discovery adds further support to the Bible. Sodom and Gomorrah, and the other cities of the plain, have now been definitely identified. Archaeology has confirmed the fertility and productivity of the region during Abraham's time, as well as the desolation after that, showing clearly that the description in Genesis 13 could only have been written at that time, and not (as the higher critics allege) many centuries after. The world of Abraham was a very real world, and fits precisely the specifications set forth in the Book of Genesis.

12

The Abrahamic Covenant

(Genesis 14-17)

The Northeastern Kings

Abram apparently lived in comparative quiet and security in Mamre for several years after Lot departed from him. Archaeology has confirmed that, during those early years of Abram in Canaan, all the lands from Syria through Sinai were peaceful and fruitful. Then, however, the calm was broken, and broken severely, as a great northeastern confederation of kings swept through the land, devastating everything in their path. This was a new and serious danger and, humanly speaking, could easily have destroyed Abram and his possessions and left God's promise utterly broken.

God's promises are not breakable, however! Furthermore, rather than panic and compromise as in Egypt, Abram this time passed the test and gained a great victory.

Genesis 14:1-4

CHAPTER 14

AND it came to pass in the days of Ăm′rȧ-phĕl king of Shī′när, Är′ĭ-ŏeh king of Ĕl-lā′sär, Ĉhĕd′ŏr-lā-ō′mĕr king of Ē′lăm, and Tī′dăl king of nations;
2 *That these* made war with Bē′rȧ king of Sŏd′ŏm, and with Bĭr′shȧ king of Gŏ-mŏr′rȧh, Shī′năb king of Ăd′mȧh, and Shĕm-ē′bĕr king of Zē-bôī′ĭm, and the king of Bē′lȧ, which is Zō′ȧr.
3 All these were joined together in the vale of Sĭd′dĭm, which is the salt sea.
4 Twelve years they served Ĉhĕd′ŏr-lā-ō′mĕr, and in the thirteenth year they rebelled.

The confederacy consisted of the kings of Shinar (Babylonia), Ellasar (the leading tribe in southern Babylonia), Elam (the original kingdom of Persia), and Goiim (translated "nations," but probably a tribe of northeastern Babylonia).

At this time, of course, kingdoms were still small, probably not much more than city-states; so these invading armies were not comparable to those that invaded Palestine in later times. Nevertheless they were fierce and cruel and could well have destroyed all the inhabitants. Archaeology has revealed, as is well known, that such invasions and destructions were common all through the Middle East, as each tribe sought to obtain for itself the most desirable lands and mineral resources. This particular invasion probably had as its goal the rich metal deposits of the region.

At one time, Amraphel was identified by many writers as Hammurabi, the great king of Babylon. However, it has now become generally settled that Hammurabi did not come on the scene until many years later. Neither have the other kings yet been definitely identified archaeologically. According to Genesis 14:4, 5, Chederlaomer, king of Elam, was the acknowledged leader of the group.

Because of the difficulty in identifying the kings, and also because their invasion route did not seem to follow the usual trade routes through the region, scholars at one time thought this whole story to be fictitious. In recent years, however, further exploration has unequivocally confirmed its historicity. Dr. Nelson Glueck, the leading Palestinian archaeologist of modern times, has said:

> Centuries earlier, another civilization of high achievement had flourished between the 21st and 19th centuries B.C., till it was savagely liquidated by the kings of the East. According to the Biblical statements, which have been borne out by archaeological evidence, they gutted every city and village at the end of that period from Ashtaroth-Karnaim in southern Syria through all of Trans-Jordan and the Negev to Kadesh-Barnea in Sinai (Genesis 14:1-7).[1]

According to the Bible, this confederacy had come earlier into the region and had placed the local kings under tribute. These included the five city-states of the Jordanian plain and southern Dead Sea area: Sodom, Gomorrah, Admah, Zeboim, and Zoar. This area was called the "vale of Siddim," meaning "fields," probably because of the high fertility and extensive agriculture at the time. Evidently Moses added the editorial explanation, "which is the Salt Sea," for later readers.

---

1. Nelson Glueck, *Rivers in the Desert* (New York: Farrar, Strauss, and Cudahy, 1959), p. 11.

Quite possibly the Salt Sea (which came to be known as the Dead Sea in the second century A.D. and was sometimes also called the Asphalt Sea by early writers) was not originally salty when it first began to fill up after the post-Flood topographic upheavals. Centuries of salt-laden tributary inflows, combined with heavy evaporation and no outlet, gradually made it salty. Another unusual characteristic is indicated in verse 10: "And the vale of Siddim was full of slimepits." As a rich source of bitumen, this may also have been one of the attractions of the area to the invading kings.

After the cities of the plain had been under tribute for twelve years, "in the thirteenth year they rebelled" (verse 4). This is the first occurrence in the Bible of the number "thirteen," and it is interesting that it should be associated with rebellion (as it often seems to be throughout the rest of Scripture).

Genesis 14:5-12

---

5 And in the fourteenth year came Chĕd'ŏr-lā-ō'mĕr, and the kings that *were* with him, and smote the Rĕph'ā-ĭm in Ăsh'tē-rŏth Kär-nā'ĭm, and the Zū'zĭm in Ham, and the Ē'mĭm in Shā'vĕh Kĭr'ĭ-a-thā'ĭm,

6 And the Hō'rītes in their mount Sē'ĭr, unto Ēl-pā'răn, which *is* by the wilderness.

7 And they returned, and came to Ĕn-mĭsh'păt, which *is* Kā'dĕsh, and smote all the country of the Ăm'ā-lĕk-ītes, and also the Ăm'ō-rītes, that dwelt in Hăz'ē-zŏn-tā'mär.

8 And there went out the king of Sŏd'ŏm, and the king of Gō-mŏr'răh, and the king of Ăd'măh, and the king of Zē-bŏï'ĭm, and the king of Bē'lā, (the same is Zō'ăr;) and they joined battle with them in the vale of Sĭd'dĭm;

9 With Chĕd'ŏr-lā-ō'mĕr the king of Ē'lăm, and with Tĭ'dăl king of nations, and Ăm'rā-phĕl king of Shī'när, and Ăr'ĭ-ŏch king of Ēl-lā'sär; four kings with five.

10 And the vale of Sĭd'dĭm *was full of* slime pits; and the kings of Sŏd'ŏm and Gō-mŏr'răh fled, and fell there; and they that remained fled to the mountain.

11 And they took all the goods of Sŏd'ŏm and Gō-mŏr'răh, and all their victuals, and went their way.

12 And they took Lot, Abram's brother's son, who dwelt in Sŏd'ŏm, and his goods, and departed.

The result of this ill-considered rebellion was that it precipitated Chedorlaomer's destructive invasion. Apparently, he not only directed his bitterness against the Jordanian cities, but against all others in the region.

> The rebellion of the small kings of the cities on the east side of the Dead Sea against what must have been the extortionate rule of absentee suzerains was brutally crushed. This comparatively minor insurrection was thereupon utilized as a pretext to settle old scores and to raid and ravage with unleashed ferocity for as much booty as could possibly be won. An old order was crumbling. From southern Syria to central Sinai, their fury raged. A punitive expedition

developed into an orgy of annihilation. I found that every village in their path had been plundered and left in ruins, and the country-side laid waste. The population had been wiped out or led away into captivity. For hundreds of years thereafter, the entire area was like an abandoned cemetery, hideously unkempt, with all its monuments shattered and strewn in pieces on the ground.[2]

The invasion of the northeastern kings first crushed all the tribes north, east, and then west of the Salt Sea before it reached the five cities on the southern shores, against which the invasion had been mounted in the first place. The purpose of these preliminary battles was no doubt to eliminate the possibility of an attack from the rear while they were occupied with the five kings.

Some of the tribes and places named are interesting, though not all have yet been identified archaeologically. The Rephaim, Zuzim, and Emim are first mentioned as located in Ashteroth Karnaim, Ham, and Shaveh, respectively. The Zuzim are probably the same as the Zam-zummim (Deuteronomy 2:20), who are said to have been giants, "a people great, and many, and tall." The same description was applied to the Emim (Deuteronomy 2:10), whose name meant "the terrible ones." The Rephaim ("strong ones") and the Zamzummim ("powerful ones") were possibly tribes of the Anakim ("giants"), who were de-scended from Anak, the son of Arba (Joshua 15:13). Arba, in turn, was one of the children of Heth (Heth was also ancestor of the Hit-tites), from whom Abraham later purchased land in Hebron (Genesis 23:19, 20). Hebron had earlier been known as Kirjath-Arba ("the city of Arbah"—Genesis 35:27).

It is also significant that the "sons of Anak" were identified with the "giants" (Hebrew *nephilim*—Numbers 13:33), which is the same word as that used for the "giants" of Genesis 6:4. The word *nephilim,* although translated "giants" in the Septuagint, actually means "fallen ones" (or possibly "those who fall upon"), and was associated in ante-diluvian days with the illicit activity of the fallen angels in their pos-session and corruption of the antediluvian women (see the comments on this subject in chapter VII). Although it is well not to be dogmatic on this subject, it seems possible to infer from the above references that, soon after the Flood, another unusually intense demonic invasion of earth took place, probably in connection with the rebellion at Babel, and that certain Canaanite tribes in particular subsequently became so demon controlled that a race of monsters was again produced, as in the days before the Flood. Finally, Moses and Joshua were instructed

---

2. Ibid., pp. 72-73.

by God to utterly exterminate these tribes, just as God had destroyed the antediluvians.

The theory that these references to the Rephaim and others may have occult implications is strengthened when it is noted that the same word (i.e., *rephaim*) is also used as the term for the spirits of certain of the wicked dead (see Job 26:25; Proverbs 2:18; 9:18; 21:16; Isaiah 14:9 and 26:14).

At the time of the invasion described here in Genesis 14, there were evidently considerable numbers of these demon-energized tribes living in Canaan. Somehow, evidently, Abram had managed to coexist with them in peace. At this time they were apparently scattered in pockets throughout the land of Canaan, rather than all living at one place. The fact that the invading kings could defeat them gives some indication of the numbers and strength of the armies from the east.

Glueck identifies Ashtaroth Karnaim, where the kings encountered the Rephaim, as two adjacent sites in southern Syria, Tell Ashtarah and Sheikh Sa'ad, which was called Carnaim in New Testament times. The name Ashtaroth, of course, comes from the name of the moon goddess, Astarte (Greek), equivalent to the Babylonian Ishtar and the Canaanite Ashtaroth, the goddess of sensual love, whose worship was one of the sources of the gross immorality of the Canaanites.

After defeating the Rephaim, Chedorlaomer smote the Horites in Mount Seir. These are now known to have been the same as the Hurrians, well known to archaeologists as one of the leading tribes of the ancient Middle East. They possessed Mount Seir, which later became the country of the Edomites (Deuteronomy 2:22; Genesis 36:20). The kings went on to El-Paran, in the southern wilderness, and then returned to Kadesh, on the western side of the Salt Sea, where they smote the inhabitants of the region that would later belong to the Amalekites (Amalek was a grandson of Esau). They also defeated a contingent of the Amorites, who were probably the dominant tribe in Canaan at this time.

After thus routing all who might stand in their way, the eastern confederacy then turned its full attention to the rebellious kings of the five cities of the south. They joined battle with them in the Vale of Siddim, decisively defeating them, so that the "kings of Sodom and Gomorrah fled," possibly hiding in the asphalt pits, with many of their followers fleeing to the mountains.

Chedorlaomer's armies then gathered up all the possessions of the vanquished cities, including the women and children and servants, as well as many captured soldiers, and headed north again. Unfortunately for them, however, they also took Lot and his family captive as well. Lot was living in Sodom proper by this time. In spite of his carnality, Lot was a "righteous man" (II Peter 2:8), as well as nephew of Abram, who had received God's call; so God would not allow Lot to be carried off by Chedorlaomer.

Genesis 14:13-16

---

13 ¶ And there came one that had escaped, and told Abram the Hebrew; for he dwelt in the plain of Măm′rē the Ăm′ō-rīte, brother of Ĕsh′cŏl, and brother of Ā′nĕr: and these *were* confederate with Abram.

14 And when Abram heard that his brother was taken captive, he armed his trained *servants*, born in his own house, three hundred and eighteen, and pursued *them* unto Dan.

15 And he divided himself against them, he and his servants, by night, and smote them, and pursued them unto Hō′băh, which *is* on the left hand of Damascus.

16 And he brought back all the goods, and also brought again his brother Lot, and his goods, and the women also, and the people.

Although, as Glueck's excavations revealed, the invading armies destroyed the cities as they marched, many of the inhabitants escaped and fled, later settling in new locations. One of those that escaped, presumably an Amorite, came to warn those of his tribe who were living near Abram by the grove of Mamre. Mamre, and his brothers, Eshcol and Aner, were "confederate with Abram."

Verse 13 contains the first mention of the name "Hebrew," applying it to Abram. Although its origin is uncertain, most scholars assume it is derived from the name of Eber, great-grandson of Shem and a distant ancestor of Abram. The term "habiru" has been found in a number of archaeological texts from soon after the time of Abram, but does not seem to apply exclusively to the children of Israel. It is apparently used in such a way as to suggest simply any moving tribe—as, of course, was true of the Israelites for a time after they left Egypt. Even so, it still might refer to descendants of Eber, since his son Joktan seems to have been ancestor of many tribes in Arabia, and Abram himself had many other nomadic descendants besides the Israelites.

The term "Hebrew" as applied here to Abram has also been translated by others as "the man from beyond the river [that is, the Euphrates]." Possibly both interpretations have a measure of truth in them. In any case, its first mention here is mainly to clearly distinguish Abram from the other inhabitants of Canaan, even though he had entered into an economic and political pact with some of them.

Abram by this time was practically a king, or at least a tribal chieftain. From his retinue, he was able to gather 318 men, all of them trained in his own household, to pursue the kings and to rescue Lot. It seems probable also that a number of the Amorites went with him.

In any case, their total numbers were surely no match for those invading armies who had already overwhelmed many armies much larger than the contingent following Abram. The odds were no doubt quite comparable to Gideon's 300 battling later against 135,000 Midianites (Judges 6:7; 8:10). But God was with them, as He was with Gideon; and that was more than enough. Quite probably, the returning armies were relaxing and enjoying the spoils of war, and the idea of a sudden nighttime attack was absolutely the remotest thought from their minds at this time. Abram suddenly attacked them from different directions at once, and they soon became utterly demoralized. They fled, but Abram pursued them all the way to north of Damascus, recapturing Lot, as well as all the other captives and booty they had taken. Those of the invading armies that had not been slain no doubt straggled back to their homelands as best they could, amazed at this unexpected end to what had been until then a mighty wave of conquest. Small wonder that no mention of this battle has yet been found on any of the Babylonian or Elamite inscriptions; ancient kings were accustomed to recounting only their victories. Defeats usually left them either dead or in slavery. Abram himself would not boast of such a victory, because he well knew that it had come from the Lord, and not from his own exploits.

Melchizedek

Genesis 14:17-24

---

17 ¶ And the king of Sŏd′om went out to meet him, after his return from the slaughter of Ĉhĕd′ŏr-lā-ō′mĕr and of the kings that *were* with him, at the valley of Shā′vĕh, which *is* the king's dale.

18 And Mĕl-chĭz′ē-dĕk king of Sā′lĕm brought forth bread and wine: and he *was* the priest of the most high God.

19 And he blessed him, and said, Blessed be Abram of the most high God, possessor of heaven and earth:

20 And blessed be the most high God, which hath delivered thine enemies into thy hand. And he gave him tithes of all.

21 And the king of Sŏd′om said unto Abram, Give me the persons, and take the goods to thyself.

22 And Abram said to the king of Sŏd′om, I have lifted up mine hand unto the LORD, the most high God, the possessor of heaven and earth,

23 That I will not *take* from a thread even to a shoe-latchet, and that I will not take any thing that *is* thine, lest thou shouldest say, I have made Abram rich:

24 Save only that which the young men have eaten, and the portion of the men which went with me, Ā′nĕr, Ĕsh′cŏl, and Măm′rē; let them take their portion.

In Genesis 14:17-24, we have one of the most intriguing stories in the Bible, that of Abram's encounter with Melchizedek, king of Salem, and "the priest of the most high God." This fascinating individual is referred to nine hundred years later by King David (Psalm 110:4) and one thousand years later than that by the writer of the Epistle to the Hebrews (5:6, 10; 6:20; 7:1-21), where he is mentioned by name no less than nine times!

There is no question that Melchizedek must at least be a marvelous type of Christ. The passage in Hebrews draws many analogies between the two to this effect. But that fact in itself hardly explains the remarkable things revealed about him.

His name means "King of Righteousness" (Hebrews 7:2), and his title "King of Salem" means also "King of Peace." For an individual to have such a name in such a place as Canaan, filled with wickedness and demonism as it was, is sufficiently remarkable in itself. All indications, however, show that his name was appropriate. He is the first priest mentioned in the Bible (and this is also the first mention of "peace"), and he obviously had a unique relation to the true God. He used the name *El Elyon* (the "most high God") to stress the absolute superiority of God to the multitude of gods and goddesses worshiped in Canaan. He also identified God as "the possessor of heaven and earth," thus referring back to Genesis 1. Abram gladly recognized Melchizedek as representing the same God who had called him to Canaan, and he "gave him tithes of all." Melchizedek had brought bread and wine and, assuming this was meant for the refreshment of the weary fighters and travelers, it would have required a very large amount. Either Melchizedek had great resources or, possibly, the bread and wine were intended for ceremonial purposes only, as a thank-offering to God.

Certain questions suggest themselves. How was it that a man like Melchizedek could become king of a city in a land settled by idolatrous descendants of Canaan, and how could he come to be recognized as the priest of the one true God? If Salem, his city, is actually the same as Jerusalem, as most scholars are convinced, then both the Bible and archaeology indicate it to have been inhabited at this time by the Jebusites, one of the Canaanite tribes from whom it was eventually taken by David (II Samuel 5:7). There is no reason to suppose the Jebusites were different in their paganism from the other Canaanites; so it hardly seems likely that Melchizedek could have been a Jebusite. But how otherwise could he have become king of Jerusalem?

Furthermore, how did he come to be recognized as God's priest, especially by Abram? Abram had been called to go to Canaan to establish a new nation that would be true to God. Abram recognized Melchizedek as his spiritual superior, giving a tithe to him; so why was not Melchizedek himself chosen to establish such a nation? The priesthood which he represented was later acclaimed as superior to the Aaronic priesthood established in Abram. Melchizedek also recognized himself as superior to Abram, because he gave him his blessing, though he recognized also that God had already blessed Abram in giving him a miraculous victory.

Such questions as these do not seem to be answered by the usual interpretation that Melchizedek was simply a local chieftain who was chosen, because of his dramatic appearance in the Genesis narrative at this point, to be a type of Christ. The problems are compounded when we find the Holy Spirit, almost a millennium later, through King David, speaking of "my Lord" (Hebrew *adonai*) as "a priest for ever after the order of Melchizedek" (Psalm 110:1, 4). Melchizedek was not alone as a non-Levitical priest; there was an "order" of Melchizedek, and this order was an *eternal* order!

The commentary in Hebrews adds the information that Melchizedek was "without father, without mother, without descent [i.e., 'genealogy'], having neither beginning of days, nor end of life; but made like unto the Son of God; abideth a priest continually" (Hebrews 7:3). The same writer strongly stresses the superiority of Melchizedek to Abram, as well as to the Levitical priests who descended from Abram. He also notes again the fact that it was witnessed of Melchizedek (that is, in Psalm 110:4) that he did not die.

The usual interpretation of these amazing statements is that they refer to the fact that Melchizedek appears on the scene suddenly, and then disappears again as suddenly. There is no genealogy listed, no record of his parents or children, no record of birth or death.

This is no doubt the naturalistic interpretation. But one who believes in *verbal* inspiration cannot help wondering why, in this case, the Holy Spirit did not say that Melchizedek was "without a *record* of father or mother, or of genealogy, or of birth or death." Could He not foresee that stating it in the way He did, leaving out the simple word "record," or some equivalent, would easily and naturally lead readers to a misunderstanding of Melchizedek's true nature? Instead of this, however, He seemed to aggravate the misunderstanding by saying, literally, that Melchizedek was "made like unto the Son of God" and that he "remains a priest for ever" (Hebrews 7:3).

Although there is no doubt that the great majority of sound, conservative commentators, both on Genesis and Hebrews, consider Melchizedek to be an ordinary man who was used as merely a *type* of Christ, it does seem that this interpretation cannot adequately answer all the above questions and does not do real justice to the exalted language of the three passages dealing with Melchizedek.

There is an ancient Hebrew tradition, which of course would not have been affected by the passage in the Book of Hebrews, that Melchizedek was actually the patriarch Shem, still alive during Abram's day. Assuming there are no gaps in the genealogies of Genesis 11, Shem would have lived until thirty-five years after Abraham's death, so that this would be possible. The name Melchizedek would, in this case, be regarded as a title rather than as an actual name. It does not seem unreasonable to imagine that, after the Dispersion at Babel, Shem might have moved, under divine guidance, to the place where God would one day establish His temple. As the custodian of the patriarchal records, he could then have transmitted them to Isaac after Abraham's death. This would also help explain why there was no document entitled "the generations of Abraham." Terah, according to Genesis 11:32, continued to live in Haran for sixty years after Abram had left for Canaan, and therefore also was still alive at this time. Isaac was thirty-five years old when Terah died and forty-five when Shem died, again assuming no gaps in the genealogies.

One could then interpret the eternal priesthood as referring to the order of Melchizedek, rather than to Melchizedek himself. That is, the line of the promised Seed, from Adam through Shem to Judah and finally to Christ, would represent the priestly order of those who, in their generations, were God's representatives manward and man's intercessors Godward. The first "priest" in this order, Adam, had neither father nor mother, nor was he born. The last, Christ Himself, had no descendants, nor does He have an end of life.

This interpretation of the words, however, seems at least as strained as the previous one. Adam did have a "beginning of days," even though he had neither birth nor ancestral genealogy. Furthermore, the description in Hebrews does seem intended to apply to Melchizedek directly, rather than to the priesthood of which he was a member.

There have been a few other interpretations, which seem even more unrealistic. One idea is that Melchizedek was the "unfallen Adam" from some other planet, sent to this planet to observe the progress of God's work of redemption for the fallen race of our Adam. Another is that Melchizedek was actually an angel, or possibly a specially created being of some kind. Comment on such ideas hardly seems necessary, but there have actually been serious advocates of each of these views.

The one other possibility is that   Melchizedek was not only a *type* of Christ, but was actually Christ Himself, in one of His preincarnate appearances. Although this interpretation is not without its own difficulties, it does seem to harmonize most naturally with the doctrine of verbal inspiration and the principle of literal interpretation. The only person of whom the statements in Hebrews 7:3 could be literally true as they stand, without addition of other words supposedly implied, would have to be none other than the Second Person of the Godhead.

An objection has been put forth that it would be tautological to say that Melchizedek was made *"like unto* the Son of God," if actually he *was* the Son of God. However, this is quite parallel to the case in Daniel 3:25, where one was seen in the fiery furnace whose form also was *"like* the Son of God." There is also a sense in which the Word of God was made to be the Son of God when He became flesh, so that until then, in any of His preincarnate appearances, He was only temporarily made *like* the Son of God, as He would one day become permanently.

A similar objection is to the effect that Melchizedek was said to be a man (Hebrews 7:4), which would not be true if he were Christ preincarnate. However, there are numerous cases in which the theophanic appearance is said to be that of a man, one of which was likewise to Abram (Genesis 18:2, 22; 19:1, 24), when there were three "men" who spoke and ate with him, two of whom turned out to be angels and one the Lord Himself.

The question cannot be said to be settled completely by such considerations; otherwise, the identity of Melchizedek would have been agreed on by Bible scholars long ago. The student should consider the evidences for each possibility on their own merits. However, it does seem that the most Christ-honoring interpretation, the one most consistent with Biblical literalism, and the one with the fewest difficulties is the recognition of Melchizedek as a glorious manifestation to Abram of God incarnate, the eternal priestly Mediator between man and God.

Abram gave a tenth of "all" to Melchizedek. This is the first mention of tithing in the Bible. It is normally assumed that this refers to a tithe of the spoils of the battle, but Scripture does not actually say so. It is possible that Abram, overwhelmed by the presence and blessing of Melchizedek, really did give him a tenth of *all* that he had.

As far as the actual spoils of battle were concerned, the king of Sodom (who had in the meantime reappeared from the slimepits where he had fled from the armies of the four kings) recognized that their recovery was due entirely to Abram, and told him to take all the goods, returning only the people who were captives back to their homes. Abram, however, knew that the victory was not due to him, but to God, and would not take any of the goods. Apparently his experience in Egypt had completely changed his attitude toward being enriched by goods received from pagan idolaters, and he had promised the same God represented by Melchizedek that he would never again take a gift of so much as a shoe latchet from such sources. His confederates from the Amorites were under no such compunction, and Abram acknowledged that they had a right to a share for what they had done, but he himself would not touch the spoils.

This tremendous test of faith, courage, generosity, and love was passed with flying colors by Abram. Accordingly, it set the scene for the greatest experience with God, and revelation from God, which he had yet received.

The Word of the Lord

Genesis 15:1

CHAPTER 15

AFTER these things the word of the LORD came unto Abram in a vision, saying, Fear not, Abram: I *am* thy shield, *and* thy exceeding great reward.

One of the grandest concepts of human thought is that of the Word. Man is distinguished from the animals primarily by his ability to formulate and communicate ideas. His capacity for intelligible, abstract, symbolic language, both written and spoken, is unique in the world of living creatures.

The source of such a remarkable ability can only be divine creation. As a matter of fact, the very purpose of language is that God might communicate His will to man and man might respond in praise to God. Since man was created for fellowship with God, and since fellowship requires communication, it is essential that the Creator somehow speak to man.

God's Word to man, therefore, is of unique importance; there is nothing else comparable in all God's creation. "Thou hast magnified thy word above all thy name" (Psalm 138:2).

The concept of the Word of God includes both the written Word, Holy Scripture, and the living Word, God the Second Person. After the Word was made flesh, in the person of Jesus Christ, and after He died and rose again, He proclaimed: "I am Alpha and Omega, the beginning and the ending" (Revelation 1:8). He is the sum of all that can be communicated. Alpha and Omega are, of course, the first and last letters of the Greek alphabet, the language chosen by God in which to inscripturate His new covenant with man. This proclamation seals the oneness of the written and living Words.

It should also be remembered that, prior to His incarnation, the Word often appeared to man in what is called a theophany, a preincarnate appearance of Christ. It is most significant that the first time the word "word" appears in the Bible, it refers not to the words of men, but to the Word of the Lord, manifesting a marvelous claim and promise to Abram.[3]

"After these things the word of the Lord came unto Abram in a vision, saying, Fear not, Abram: I am thy shield, and thy exceeding great reward" (Genesis 15:1). Not only does this remarkable verse contain the first mention of "word," but it also introduces for the first time in Scripture the words "vision," "shield," and "reward." Even more significantly, this is the first of the great "I am's" of Scripture.

Many of the great claims of Christ began with the words "I am." "I am the light of the world." "I am the way, the truth, and the life." "I am the door." Last of all, He said: "I am the Alpha and Omega," and then "I am the root and the offspring of David, and the bright and morning star" (Revelation 22:13, 16). In fact, His very name is "I am that I am" (Exodus 3:14).

Jesus said to the Jews: "Your father Abraham rejoiced to see my day: and he saw it, and was glad" (John 8:56). When they questioned how Abraham could have seen Him, He simply answered: "Before Abraham was, I am", (John 8:58). They recognized this claim as a claim to be God Himself, and immediately tried to stone Jesus. But, in truth Abram *had* seen Him! It was probably this very occasion to which Jesus referred, when He first identified Himself to Abram as the self-existing God, the One who was able and willing to supply every need in time and eternity.

---

3. The Hebrew word *dabar* carries a number of different meanings; in Genesis 11:1, for example, it means "speech" or "vocabulary." This verse (15:1) is the first occurrence of its most common meaning, "word."

Perhaps, after the great excitement of the battle and victory, and the marvelous experience with Melchizedek, and then after everyone had gone and Abram was alone, a spiritual reaction began to set in. God's promise of a seed was still not fulfilled, and he was still in the midst of a dangerous and wicked country. Abram began to be a bit doubtful and fearful of what the future might hold.

"Fear not!" came the word of the Lord. This is not the first time the word "fear" occurs in Scripture, but it is the first time "fear *not*" occurs. Once before, "the voice of the Lord God" is mentioned, and it was that voice that caused Adam to "fear" (Genesis 3:10). This points up the striking contrasts between Adam and Abram. Adam was the father of all men; Abram is the "father of all them that *believe*" (Romans 4:11). Adam had a fig leaf, but Abram had a *shield*. Adam received a curse, Abram a *reward*.

For the believer, Christ is both protection from all harm and provision of all needs. He provides our "shield of faith" (Ephesians 6:16)— indeed the "whole armour of God," so that we can "be strong in the Lord, and in the power of his might" (Ephesians 6:10, 11). He is also our "exceeding great [literally 'abundant'] reward." We need not be enriched with the wealth of the kings of the East, because "he is able to do exceeding abundantly above all that we ask or think, according to the power that worketh in us" (Ephesians 3:20). "Say ye not, A confederacy, to all them to whom this people shall say, A confederacy; neither fear ye their fear, nor be afraid. Sanctify the Lord of hosts himself; and let him be your fear, and let him be your dread" (Isaiah 8:12, 13).

Genesis 15:2-7

2 And Abram said, Lord GOD, what wilt thou give me, seeing I go childless, and the steward of my house *is* this Ĕl′ĭ-ē′zĕr of Damascus?
3 And Abram said, Behold, to me thou hast given no seed: and, lo, one born in my house is mine heir.
4 And, behold, the word of the LORD *came* unto him, saying, This shall not be thine heir; but he that shall come forth out of thine own bowels shall be thine heir.
5 And he brought him forth abroad, and said, Look now toward heaven, and tell the stars, if thou be able to number them: and he said unto him, So shall thy seed be.
6 And he believed in the LORD; and he counted it to him for righteousness.
7 And he said unto him, I *am* the LORD that brought thee out of Ûr of the Chăl′-dēeṣ, to give thee this land to inherit it.

This was not a dream, but a vision. Abram was awake, and the vision continued all day and into the night, as the Word of the Lord appeared to him. Abram expressed to God the reason for his concern, that he still had no seed. Were he and Sarai to die, all his house would go to his steward Eliezer, not even one of his own people. Lot had returned to Sodom, apparently well content there and, so far as the record goes, had not even shown any particular appreciation to Abram for saving his life.

Once again, therefore, the Lord renewed His promise. Before, He had said Abram's seed would be as the dust of the earth. Now, He says they will be as the stars of heaven. Not only does this imply a great number, but perhaps also that the sphere of activity of the promised seed in the eternal ages will be both on earth and in heaven.

Now, once again we have a first mention, this time of the word "believe." Abram "believed God and he counted [or 'imputed'] it to him for righteousness" (Genesis 15:6). Here is the great principle of true salvation, set forth for the first time in the Bible. Not by works do men attain or manifest righteousness, but by faith. Because they believe in the Word of God, He credits them with perfect righteousness and therefore enables sinful men to be made fit for the fellowship of a holy God. In this verse is also the first occurrence of "imputed" (Hebrew *chashad*) and the first occurrence of "righteousness" (except in the name "Melchizedek"; also, a similar word, though not the same, was applied to Noah, in Genesis 6:9, translated "just"). The whole vocabulary is new, because here is a new covenant. In Noah's case, "grace" comes before "righteousness"; in Abram's case, "faith" comes before "righteousness." The one stresses God's sovereignty, the other man's responsibility. Both are true and necessary. "By grace are ye saved through faith. . . . For we are his workmanship, created in Christ Jesus unto good works" (Ephesians 2:8, 10).

This wonderful verse, Genesis 15:6, is quoted in three epistles of the New Testament (Romans 4:3; Galatians 3:6; James 2:23); and in each it is stressed that Abraham was a type of all who would ever be saved, the principle always being that of salvation through faith unto righteousness.

Genesis 15:8-11

---

8 And he said, Lord GOD, whereby shall I know that I shall inherit it?
9 And he said unto him, Take me a heifer of three years old, and a she goat of three years old, and a ram of three years old, and a turtledove, and a young pigeon.
10 And he took unto him all these, and divided them in the midst, and laid each piece one against another: but the birds

divided he not.
11 And when the fowls came down **upon the carcasses, Abram drove them**
away.

God then renewed His promise also to give Abram the land. Abram responded by asking for a sign. By this time, Abram surely believed; so this request was not made in doubt. It was, rather, an inquiry, seeking fuller explanation and assurance as to details. God in grace granted his request, by means of a most remarkable ceremony.

The ceremony not only confirmed the promise, but was highly instructive. The provision of imputed righteousness and full salvation is altogether God's gift of grace to man, but it would be highly costly to God. The curse of sin can be removed only by sacrifice, in the shedding of blood. Abram had known and practiced this, but now God stressed its necessary connection with His promise. One each of the five acceptable sacrificial animals (cow, sheep, goat, pigeon, dove) was to be slain by Abram and laid on the altar. The slain animals were placed in two rows, one bird in each, along with a half-portion of each of the other animals. This arrangement was evidently intended to conform to the custom of the day, when a covenant was made between two parties; each would pass between the two rows, as a sign that he was bound by the terms of the contract. The intimation perhaps was that, if he broke it, the substitutionary death of the animals would no longer be efficacious and he himself (or possibly his cattle) would be subject to death. Following this, presumably, the animals would either be roasted and eaten or else simply consumed by fire.

After Abram made the preparations, however, nothing happened during the rest of the day, and finally the sun went down. The delay possibly symbolized the fact that, although God's covenant would be sure, its accomplishment would take a long time. In the first place, Abram himself would have to wait many years for the promised seed. Even then, it would still be many long centuries before the seed would become a great nation and possess the promised land, and many millennia before the ultimate fulfillment would take place, with all nations being blessed through the nation of Abram's seed.

During the wait, as could be expected, Abram had to drive off the birds of prey that tried to devour the carcasses. This experience no doubt symbolized the attempts of Satan to thwart the plans of God, plus the need for alertness in the believer in order that the enemy not succeed.

Genesis 15:12-21

---

12 And when the sun was going down, a deep sleep fell upon Abram; and, lo, a horror of great darkness fell upon him.

13 And he said unto Abram, Know of a surety that thy seed shall be a stranger in a land *that is* not theirs, and shall serve them; and they shall afflict them four hundred years;

14 And also that nation, whom they shall serve, will I judge: and afterward shall they come out with great substance.

15 And thou shalt go to thy fathers in peace; thou shalt be buried in a good old age.

16 But in the fourth generation they shall come hither again: for the iniquity of the Ăm'ō-rītes *is* not yet full.

17 And it came to pass, that, when the sun went down, and it was dark, behold a smoking furnace, and a burning lamp that passed between those pieces.

18 In that same day the LORD made a covenant with Abram, saying, Unto thy seed have I given this land, from the river of Egypt unto the great river, the river Eū-phrā'tēṣ:

19 The Kē'nītes, and the Kē'nĭz-zītes, and the Kăd'mŏn-ītes,

20 And the Hĭt'tītes, and the Pĕr'ĭz-zītes, and the Rĕph'ā-ĭm,

21 And the Ăm'ō-rītes, and the Cā'nāan-ītes, and the Gĭr'gā-shītes, and the Jĕb'ū-ṣītes.

Finally, however, the vision took a new turn. As darkness descended, Abram fell into a deep sleep, with "an horror of great darkness upon him." This could only symbolize death itself, from which Abram was to be delivered by God's covenantal grace. In the case of the nation sired by Abram, it also symbolized their long tribulation in Egypt before they could inherit the promised land. Perhaps ultimately it also symbolized, as Adam's "deep sleep" had symbolized, the death of Christ and the glory that would follow.

God said they would be in an alien land 400 years, a round number which was later seen to be exactly 430 years (Exodus 12:40). This was indicated to be equivalent to "four generations," perhaps since men were still living to be one hundred years of age and older as a general rule at that time. That is, among those leaving Egypt after the captivity would be old men whose great-grandfathers had been among the seventy Israelites who entered Egypt.

Galatians 3:17, however, suggests that the 430-year period was from the time of the covenant with Abraham until the giving of the Law on Mount Sinai. This, in turn, suggests that Genesis 15:13 can be interpreted: "Thy seed shall be a stranger in a land that is not theirs, and shall serve them; and [all the people among whom they dwell, both Canaanites and Egyptians] shall afflict them four hundred years." Similarly, Exodus 12:40 can be understood as follows: "Now the sojourning of the children of Israel, who dwelt in Egypt, was [altogether, that is, from the time of the covenant until they left Egypt] four hundred and thirty years."

If this is the intended meaning, then the actual sojourn in Egypt itself would only be approximately 215 years, taking the entry of Abram into Canaan as the effective date of God's covenant promise. This interpretation is also supported by the Septuagint translation of Exodus 12:40, which substitutes the words "in the land of Egypt and the land of Canaan" for the words "in Egypt." In this case, the "four generations" could refer to the 215 years, rather than the four hundred years.

The reason for the delay, God said, was that "the iniquity of the Amorites is not yet full." Just as God delayed the judgment of the Flood for 120 years, so here He waited four hundred years. "God is not willing that any should perish" (II Peter 3:9).

Then, when it was dark, a smoking firepot and flaming torch, representing God's presence in the covenantal relation with Abram, passed between the two parts of the sacrifice. Only God passed through, not Abram, denoting an unconditional promise on God's part, not dependent on Abram's fulfilling his part of the contract, since he had no such part. It was all of God, in response to Abram's believing faith. In order for God to keep His covenant, there must first be suffering, with glory then to follow. This is suggested by the furnace and the lamp.

The covenant, already made, is now expounded. The land which God will give Abram is from the Nile to the Euphrates, the land then occupied by Canaanites, represented by the ten tribes named. For a very brief time, under Solomon (I Kings 8:65) and possibly again under Jeroboam II (II Kings 14:25), the children of Israel ruled all this territory, as a token of the final and permanent possession they will have in the future.

Ishmael and the Arabs

In spite of God's promise and Abram's faith, however, he still had to wait many years before Isaac would be born. God would demonstrate His omnipotence by waiting until it was humanly impossible for Abram and Sarai to have a child before He would miraculously fulfill His word. In the meantime, Abram and Sarai, realizing what was happening in the aging of their bodies, began to feel that they must somehow intervene to help God out in the accomplishment of His promise. This is an all-too-common experience for believers. "God helps those who help themselves," as the motto goes. Failing to see God work as soon as we think He should, we begin to feel that He is waiting for us to do "our part" before He will do His. We then devise various plans and programs to get it done, only to find it is all in vain, and in fact we probably do more harm than good. This was now the unhappy experience of Abram and Sarai.

Genesis 16:1-4

CHAPTER 16

N OW Sā'raī, Abram's wife, bare him no children: and she had a handmaid, an Egyptian, whose name *was* Hā'gàr.

2 And Sā'raī said unto Abram, Behold now, the LORD hath restrained me from bearing: I pray thee, go in unto my maid; it may be that I may obtain children by her. And Abram hearkened to the voice of Sā'raī.

3 And Sā'raī, Abram's wife, took Hā'gàr her maid the Egyptian, after Abram had dwelt ten years in the land of Cā'năan, and gave her to her husband Abram to be his wife.

4 ¶ And he went in unto Hā'gàr, and she conceived: and when she saw that she had conceived, her mistress was despised in her eyes.

It was Sarai whose faith first weakened. She felt so keenly the shame of her own barrenness, and seeing no other naturalistic solution, she made a decision which must have been extremely distasteful to her. Just as Abram had once been willing to share her with other men, as the least of the evils he confronted, so now she felt it necessary to share her husband with another woman, as the only solution to their problem.

By this time, Abram was eighty-five years old, and Sarai seventy-five (note Genesis 16:16). Her maid, Hagar (an Egyptian girl, perhaps acquired during their stay in Egypt), was, in effect, her own personal property. Thus any children that she might bear to Abram would legally belong to Sarai, in accordance with the customs of the day. Abram "hearkened to the voice of Sarai," and this turned out to be a serious mistake, just as it had for Adam long ago (Genesis 3:17). He had still not fully learned that we must "through faith and patience inherit the promises" (Hebrews 6:12). Scripture enjoins us: "Cast not away therefore your confidence, which hath great recompense of reward. For ye have need of patience, that, after ye have done the will of God, ye might receive the promise" (Hebrews 10:35, 36).

Abram went in to Hagar, who quickly conceived. Hagar was only a second-choice wife, but had proved more fruitful than Abram's true wife, and therefore she soon became disdainful of her mistress.

However worthy and unselfish may have been the motives of Abram and Sarai, and perhaps even of Hagar, in carrying out this plan, it was bound to create problems. God's creative purpose included only monogamous marriage, and anything else was bound to generate problems. There are many instances recorded of polygamous marriages in the Bible, which God allowed because of mitigating circumstances at the time (e.g., Jacob, Moses, David), but none of a *happy* polygamous marriage.

Genesis 16:5-16

---

5 And Sā′raī said unto Abram, My wrong *be* upon thee: I have given my maid into thy bosom; and when she saw that she had conceived, I was despised in her eyes: the LORD judge between me and thee.

6 But Abram said unto Sā′raī, Behold, thy maid *is* in thy hand; do to her as it pleaseth thee. And when Sā′raī dealt hardly with her, she fled from her face.

7 ¶ And the angel of the LORD found her by a fountain of water in the wilderness, by the fountain in the way to Shur.

8 And he said, Hā′gār, Sā′raī′s maid, whence camest thou? and whither wilt thou go? And she said, I flee from the face of my mistress Sā′raī.

9 And the angel of the LORD said unto her, Return to thy mistress, and submit thyself under her hands.

10 And the angel of the LORD said unto her, I will multiply thy seed exceedingly, that it shall not be numbered for multitude.

11 And the angel of the LORD said unto her, Behold, thou *art* with child, and shalt bear a son, and shalt call his name Ĭsh′mā-ĕl; because the LORD hath heard thy affliction.

12 And he will be a wild man; his hand *will be* against every man, and every man′s hand against him: and he shall dwell in the presence of all his brethren.

13 And she called the name of the LORD that spake unto her, Thou God seest me: for she said, Have I also here looked after him that seeth me?

14 Wherefore the well was called Bē′ĕr-lā-haī′-rôi: behold, *it is* between Kā′dĕsh and Bē′rĕd.

15 ¶ And Hā′gār bare Abram a son: and Abram called his son′s name, which Hā′gār bare, Ĭsh′mā-ĕl.

16 And Abram *was* fourscore and six years old, when Hā′gār bare Ĭsh′mā-ĕl to Abram.

The situation eventually became almost unbearable for Sarai. In response to her complaining, Abram allowed her finally to deal so harshly with Hagar as to cause her to run away.

That Hagar was perhaps less blameworthy than the others in this unhappy situation is indicated by the way the Lord dealt with her. Hagar had started home to Egypt, but the journey through the wilderness was bound to be too much for her. Consequently, the "angel of the Lord" met her and constrained her to return to Abram. This is the first occurrence of this phrase in the Bible, and the context indicates (verse 13) that this "angel" was indeed God Himself, that is, another preincarnate appearance of the Messiah.

The Lord addressed Hagar by name. Though He had called Abram and had given him special promises for a special work, He is interested in every individual, including Hagar and the child she would bear. It had not been God′s will for this union between Abram and Hagar to take place; but now that it had, He would make a gracious promise to their descendants. He promised Hagar a son, and even gave her the name for him, Ishmael, promising him also an abundant progeny.

Ishmael (meaning "God hears") would, by his name, always remind his mother how the God of Abram (not her old gods in Egypt, to which she had started to return) had met her need. She even named the well where the Angel of Jehovah had spoken to her "the well of the Living One who seeth me" (Beer-lahai-roi), and called God by the name El Roi ("the God who sees").

God also foretold the nature of her son, that he would be, literally, "a wild ass of a man," one who would be perpetually in conflict with others, dwelling "against the face of his brethren." The long history of the Arab peoples, who are descended from Ishmael, is an obvious commentary on the fulfillment of this ancient prophecy, seen most vividly at present in the current Israeli-Arab hostilities.

After this experience, Hagar did return to Hebron, to Abram and Sarai, no doubt telling them about her experience with God. No doubt there was a time of repentance and thanksgiving on the part of all three of them, and they resolved to live together as amicably as the situation would permit, and by God's help. When the child was born, Abram, in obedience to the revelation received by Hagar, named him Ishmael and raised him as his son. This was the right and necessary thing for Abram to do at this point.

An Everlasting Covenant

The next thirteen years are passed over in silence, so far as the record of Scripture goes. It would have been easy to forget God's covenant promise. Abram was prospering financially, Ishmael was growing into young manhood, the land was at peace, and Abram had apparently given up all hope that he and Sarai would have a son of their own.

God had not forgotten, however, and in the fulness of time, He would bring it to pass. As the time drew near, it was important that the promise should be refreshed in their hearts and minds. On four earlier occasions, God had spoken His covenant to Abram (Genesis 12:1-3; 12:7; 13:14-17; 15:5-21), although He used the term "covenant" (Hebrew *berith*) only once (15:18, outlining the boundaries of the promised land). Here in chapter 17, however, God uses the term "covenant" no less than thirteen times! The adjectives attached to the word are significant. Nine times it is called "*my* covenant," three times it is called "an everlasting covenant," and once it is called "the covenant betwixt me and you." In every case, God Himself was speaking. In Genesis 15:18, it had been stated simply that "the Lord made a covenant with Abram."

Genesis 17:1-8

CHAPTER 17

AND when Abram was ninety years old and nine, the LORD appeared to Abram, and said unto him, I *am* the Almighty God; walk before me, and be thou perfect.

2 And I will make my covenant between me and thee, and will multiply thee exceedingly.

3 And Abram fell on his face: and God talked with him, saying,

4 As for me, behold, my covenant *is* with thee, and thou shalt be a father of many nations.

5 Neither shall thy name any more be called Abram, but thy name shall be Abraham; for a father of many nations have I made thee.

6 And I will make thee exceeding fruitful, and I will make nations of thee, and kings shall come out of thee.

7 And I will establish my covenant between me and thee and thy seed after thee in their generations, for an everlasting covenant, to be a God unto thee and to thy seed after thee.

8 And I will give unto thee, and to thy seed after thee, the land wherein thou art a stranger, all the land of Cā'nǎan, for an everlasting possession; and I will be their God.

When God appeared once again, Abram was ninety-nine years old. He and Sarai were now past the age for children. God revealed Himself this time to Abram by a new name, *El Shaddai,* meaning "Almighty God," thus stressing His omnipotence. God had already made His covenant with Abram; He was now ready to put it into force.

First, He admonished Abram to be careful to walk in fellowship with Him (as occasionally in the past he had forgotten to do), and to be wholly dedicated to performing the will of God (the word is translated "perfect," but means, simply, "whole"). These admonitions were not stated as conditions of the covenant, however, but simply as commands.

God again promised to make Abram a father of many nations, and then changed his name to Abraham ("father of a multitude") instead of Abram ("exalted father") in token thereof. God stressed also that His covenant was not only with Abraham, but with "thy seed after thee," as an everlasting covenant. Specifically He said that Canaan would be an *everlasting* possession; so it is clear no action on the part of Abraham's descendants can ever *permanently* sever the land from them.

"I will be their God." Though many have gone astray, and the history of Abraham's seed has been long and sad, there has always been at least a remnant in every generation that continues to worship and obey the God of Abraham. God is, of course, the God of all men, whether they acknowledge Him or not; but He undertook here to be in a special and unique way the God of Abraham's seed. This promise no doubt applied primarily to those who are his seed according to the flesh, but also encompassed the spiritual seed of Abraham, who is the father of all them that believe.

Genesis 17:9-14

---

9 ⁊ And God said unto Abraham, Thou shalt keep my covenant therefore, thou, and thy seed after thee in their generations.
10 This *is* my covenant, which ye shall keep, between me and you and thy seed after thee; Every man child among you shall be circumcised.
11 And ye shall circumcise the flesh of your foreskin; and it shall be a token of the covenant betwixt me and you.
12 And he that is eight days old shall be circumcised among you, every man child in your generations, he that is born in the house, or bought with money of any stranger, which *is* not of thy seed.
13 He that is born in thy house, and he that is bought with thy money, must needs be circumcised: and my covenant shall be in your flesh for an everlasting covenant.
14 And the uncircumcised man child whose flesh of his foreskin is not circumcised, that soul shall be cut off from his people; he hath broken my covenant.

God here established a visible seal and sign of His covenant relation with Abraham's physical seed. Those males who would participate in the covenant not only must be descended from Abraham in the line of promise through Isaac (verse 19), but also must be circumcised. This requirement was to apply not only to all male children born into the family, but also to those coming into the household as servants, along with any children born to them. This aspect of the covenant also was to be "everlasting" (verse 13).

At first, this requirement of circumcision seems very strange. To some extent, no doubt, sanitary and health reasons were involved. If the nation so formed was indeed to endure and to be a witness for God through all generations to come, then it must be physically strong and clean. There is some medical evidence that this practice has indeed contributed to the long-lasting vigor of the Jewish race.

However, if this is a factor, it can be only incidental. God does not imply such a purpose; rather, circumcision was commanded strictly as a *sign* of the covenant. It thus must symbolize in some distinct way the purpose and results of the Abrahamic covenant.

The emphasis of the covenant, of course, was on the promised *seed,* and on the abundance of progeny which would accrue to Abraham. The male sexual organ is the remarkable, divinely created vehicle for the transmission of this seed from one generation to another. The circumcision ("cutting round") of this channel would thus picture its complete enclosure within God's protective and productive will.

Furthermore, it was primarily a sign only to the individual concerned, his parents, and his wife. It was not a sign to be shown to people in general, but was uniquely personal. To his parents it would confirm that they had been faithful in transmitting the seed to the son with whom God had blessed their union, and that they were trying to follow God's will in training him. To his wife, it would give assurance that he indeed was a descendant of Abraham, to whom she could joyfully submit in the marriage relation, in faith that God would bless their home and their children. To the man himself, it would be a daily testimony that he and his family were consecrated to the God of Abraham and that they shared in his calling and ministry to the world.

That which is most sacred, of course, can be most debauched. God's first command to man, after both the Creation and the Flood (Genesis 1:28; 9:1), had been to "be fruitful and multiply." The sexual act and the reproductive process are uniquely joyful and dynamic, enjoying the full blessing of God, when carried out according to His revealed purpose, in the union of a man and woman who love Him and believe His Word. On the other hand, in any other context they can become vehicles of sin and corruption of the worst sort. Satan has again and again led man into sexual debauchery, corrupting the marriage institution in every conceivable way in order to thwart God's purpose for man and his redemption.

Recognition of this fact yields still another symbolic meaning of the act of circumcision. The "cutting" of the foreskin spoke of a surgical removal, a complete separation, from the sins of the flesh so widely prevalent in the world around them, such sins largely centered in the misuse of the male organ in adultery, fornication, and sodomy. As it directly, therefore, symbolized to the Jewish man that he was a member of an elect nation, a peculiar people, distinctly holy before God, in relation to sexual conduct, so it came indirectly to speak of holiness in every phase of life (note Deuteronomy 10:16; 30:6, etc.).

To one who refused to submit to circumcision, there was no other concession to be shown. His refusal would demonstrate his overt unwillingness to follow God, and he must therefore "be cut off from his people." This penalty normally meant that he would be exiled from Israel and from any inheritance in it. In some instances where this phrase appears in Scripture, however, it may actually have reference to capital punishment.

Genesis 17:15-27

15 ¶ And God said unto Abraham, As for Sā′raī thy wife, thou shalt not call her name Sā′raī, but Sarah *shall* her name *be*.

16 And I will bless her, and give thee a son also of her: yea, I will bless her, and she shall be *a mother* of nations; kings of people shall be of her.

17 Then Abraham fell upon his face, and laughed, and said in his heart, Shall *a child* be born unto him that is a hundred years old? and shall Sarah, that is ninety years old, bear?

18 And Abraham said unto God, O that Ĭsh′mā-ĕl might live before thee!

19 And God said, Sarah thy wife shall bear thee a son indeed; and thou shalt call his name Isaac: and I will establish my covenant with him for an everlasting covenant, *and* with his seed after him.

20 And as for Ĭsh′mā-ĕl, I have heard thee: Behold, I have blessed him, and will make him fruitful, and will multiply him exceedingly; twelve princes shall he beget, and I will make him a great nation.

21 But my covenant will I establish with Isaac, which Sarah shall bear unto thee at this set time in the next year.

22 And he left off talking with him, and God went up from Abraham.

23 ¶ And Abraham took Ĭsh′mā-ĕl his son, and all that were born in his house, and all that were bought with his money, every male among the men of Abraham's house; and circumcised the flesh of their foreskin in the selfsame day, as God had said unto him.

24 And Abraham *was* ninety years old and nine, when he was circumcised in the flesh of his foreskin.

25 And Ĭsh′mā-ĕl his son *was* thirteen years old, when he was circumcised in the flesh of his foreskin.

26 In the selfsame day was Abraham circumcised, and Ĭsh′mā-ĕl his son.

27 And all the men of his house, born in the house, and bought with money of the stranger, were circumcised with him.

After the instructions concerning circumcision, God also gave Sarai a slightly changed name, Sarah (meaning "princess"). For the first time, God now said specifically that Sarah would be the mother of the promised seed. As the mother of kings, therefore, it was appropriate for her to be called "princess." Twice, God said: "I will bless her." She had been barren all her life, and was now ninety years old; so it would take a very special blessing for her yet to have a son. When God said she would be a "mother of nations," He apparently meant Judah, Israel, and Edom.

Abraham was so elated at God's promise that he laughed with joy and surprise. That it was not a laugh of doubt is evident from the fact that God gave him no rebuke, as He later did Sarah when she laughed (Genesis 18:13). The questions which Abraham asked likewise were not in doubt, but in wonder and happy amazement.

Then he remembered Ishmael, and it seemed as though God's new promise would cut Ishmael altogether out of His favor. He therefore interceded for Ishmael, desiring God to bless him as well.

Yes, God assuredly would bless Ishmael, too; but first He emphasized again to Abraham that His *covenant* was with Isaac alone, and with his seed. In recognition of Abraham's joy, God told him to name his son Isaac (meaning "laughter"). He also gave him the glad news that Isaac would be born in only one year. Evidently the miracle was performed on Sarah's body at the time God later repeated this promise in Sarah's hearing (Genesis 18:14).

As far as Ishmael was concerned, God promised that he would beget twelve princes and would be a great nation. These twelve princes are later listed in "the generations of Ishmael" (Genesis 25:12-16).

God, having completed the revelation of His covenant promises to Abraham and given him the visible sign and seal of them, then "went up," presumably back to heaven.

Abraham immediately set about to implement the sign of the covenant on the males in his own household. This was done, not only on himself and his son Ishmael, but also on his entire retinue, both those purchased as servants and those that had been born while their parents were in service to him. Even though Ishmael was not to inherit the promises with Isaac, Abraham rightly desired to have him included among those receiving the spiritual blessings that would stem from the fulfillment of those promises.

All this was done on the same day God had spoken to him. This required a particular act of faith on Abraham's part, since it no doubt incapacitated all the males in his community for several days, thus leaving his home and possessions with no protection at all (save God!). One can imagine there may have been a great many questions from his household that day—and quite possibly some resistance. Nevertheless, finally all submitted and this in itself must have been a testimony to the effectiveness of Abraham's influence and esteem in his own household. By this time at least, everyone knew that God was with Abraham; and if this was what God asked of them, they, along with Abraham, would obey.

13

Fire from Heaven

(Genesis 18-20)

Angels Unaware

Soon after the marvelous theophany and covenant described in Genesis 17, Abraham had another visit from God. This, however, was not an appearance of God in His glory, but rather was in the form of a man and two friends traveling through Hebron in the heat of the day. The context of Genesis 18 and 19 makes it clear that the other two men were angels, who later were sent to Sodom and Gomorrah to bring God's judgment on those wicked cities. The leader of the three men could have been none other than God Himself and, therefore, Christ in His preincarnate state (John 1:18).

Genesis 18:1-8

CHAPTER 18

AND the LORD appeared unto him in the plains of Măm′rē: and he sat in the tent door in the heat of the day;

2 And he lifted up his eyes and looked, and, lo, three men stood by him: and when he saw *them*, he ran to meet them from the tent door, and bowed himself toward the ground,

3 And said, My Lord, if now I have found favor in thy sight, pass not away, I pray thee, from thy servant:

4 Let a little water, I pray you, be fetched, and wash your feet, and rest yourselves under the tree:

5 And I will fetch a morsel of bread, and comfort ye your hearts; after that ye shall pass on: for therefore are ye come to your servant. And they said, So do, as thou hast said.

6 And Abraham hastened into the tent unto Sarah, and said, Make ready quickly three measures of fine meal, knead *it*, and make cakes upon the hearth.

7 And Abraham ran unto the herd, and fetched a calf tender and good, and gave *it* unto a young man; and he hasted to dress it.

8 And he took butter, and milk, and the calf which he had dressed, and set *it* before them; and he stood by them under the tree, and they did eat.

The first verse of the chapter makes it plain that this was an actual appearance of God, whereas the second verse indicates that the appearance was in the form of the three men. Abraham was sitting in his tent door when the men appeared. There is no indication that they had been riding, or even walking; as Abraham looked up, there they were.

Abraham had apparently been praying and meditating, and there can be little doubt as to what was occupying his thoughts. Though there was nothing in the outward appearance of the three strangers to suggest they had come from heaven, Abraham somehow sensed that they were very special visitors, to be used by God in some way to answer his prayers. His whole manner suggests an urgency about his conversation with them and, although it was no doubt the custom of men in the East to be very hospitable toward guests, there is clearly an element of more than normal hospitality here. First, he ran to meet them, and then "bowed himself toward the ground." The phrase "bowed himself" is actually the Hebrew *shachah,* the usual word for "worship." This, in fact, is the first use of this word in Scripture. Although it is often also used to describe bowing down in obeisance before men, the fact that it is used first in connection with worshiping God in human appearance seems significant as setting the standard for its primary meaning throughout Scripture.

Abraham then urged the men to rest themselves while he fetched water to wash their feet and had a meal prepared for them. He addressed the spokesman as "my Lord" (Hebrew *Adonai*), which is one of the divine names. However, the same name is also used as a title of respect for men, so this does not in itself prove that Abraham recognized him yet as God. However, he also said: "For therefore are ye come to your servant," which seems to indicate that he did at least recognize that their visit was in some way providential.

Abraham went inside the tent to get Sarah started on the making of bread, then hastened out to the herd to fetch a calf, and had a servant quickly prepare it. One senses not only that Abraham was exhibiting genuine hospitality, but also that he was in a hurry to get these amenities taken care of, that he might the sooner learn what the providential message of the visitors might be.

After the meal was prepared, Abraham stood by while they ate, in order to be available to serve them as they might have need. According to Hebrews 13:2, the record of this incident had as one of its purposes that we ourselves might learn to be given to hospitality. "Be not forgetful to entertain strangers: for thereby some have entertained angels unawares."

It might seem strange that angels would actually partake physically of human food. It certainly is not necessary for them to do so for their own sustenance. Nevertheless it is evidently possible for them to do so, in connection with their service as "messengers" (actual meaning of the word "angels") from God to man. In order to communicate to man, they frequently appear in Scripture as men. This appearance is not a ghostlike, unsubstantial appearance, but in every way physical and real. There is no way of explaining this phenomenon on a naturalistic level. Angels are "spirits" (Hebrews 1:14), but evidently God allows them to be "clothed" in human form when occasion requires. It is possibly somewhat analogous to the resurrection body of the Lord Jesus, who, when He appeared to the disciples, "did eat before them" (Luke 24:43). The Lord also taught that, in the resurrection, we ourselves shall be "as the angels of God in heaven" (Matthew 22:30); and there is indication that the activities in the New Jerusalem include eating (Revelation 22:2, 14).

Also, as Abraham stood by them, he was no doubt in eager anticipation of learning why they had come. He had been thinking of God's promise of a son for him and Sarah, and somehow must have sensed that their visit was in some mysterious way connected with this promise.

Genesis 18:9-15

9 ¶ And they said unto him, Where is Sarah thy wife? And he said, Behold, in the tent.

10 And he said, I will certainly return unto thee according to the time of life; and, lo, Sarah thy wife shall have a son. And Sarah heard *it* in the tent door, which *was* behind him.

11 Now Abraham and Sarah *were* old *and* well stricken in age; *and* it ceased to be with Sarah after the manner of women.

12 Therefore Sarah laughed within herself, saying, After I am waxed old shall I have pleasure, my lord being old also?

13 And the LORD said unto Abraham, Wherefore did Sarah laugh, saying, Shall I of a surety bear a child, which am old?

14 Is any thing too hard for the LORD? At the time appointed I will return unto thee, according to the time of life, and Sarah shall have a son.

15 Then Sarah denied, saying, I laughed not; for she was afraid. And he said, Nay; but thou didst laugh.

If, indeed, this is what Abraham was thinking, he was perfectly correct. When the men had finished eating, they immediately asked the whereabouts of Sarah. She was inside the tent, behind the flap which separated her own compartment from the rest of the tent, so that she could hear what they were saying, even though she could not see them.

Verse 9 says that "they" asked him about Sarah, but verse 10 says that "he," evidently the leader of the three men, the Lord Himself, did the speaking from then on. He stated that Sarah would indeed have a son, just as the Lord had promised Abraham probably several weeks before. He said, literally, "I will surely return unto thee when the season lives." This might refer either to the return of the same season of the year in the following year, or to the reviving of Sarah's bodily functions when the Lord returned. "It had ceased to be with Sarah after the manner of women." She had passed her "change of life," but her "season" for child-bearing was to be revived, all the more miraculously since her womb had been barren even when she was young. This marvelous promise would require a miracle of physical regeneration, and therefore the presence of the Lord.

When Sarah heard this promise, she "laughed within herself," not a laugh of joy as earlier with Abraham (17:17), but a cynical laugh, knowing that it was impossible for her and her husband any longer to enjoy the pleasures of sexual relations or of child-bearing. It should be remembered, however, that she did not yet know who these visitors were, and it surely seemed outlandish for a strange man to come and make such a promise to her husband.

On the other hand, it seems certain that Abraham must have told her earlier about God's great promise (17:19), even if she had not been present at the theophany. She must have found it difficult to believe, even coming from God. Without a doubt, her faith needed to be strengthened, if indeed she was ever going to "receive strength to conceive seed, and be delivered of a child when she was past age" (Hebrews 11:11).

One thing that helped strengthen her faith was the Lord's question: "Wherefore did Sarah laugh?" The man could neither see her behind the tent flap nor hear her laugh, since she only laughed within herself. She must quickly have realized that this indeed was either an angel or God Himself, in order for Him to know these things. That being the case, maybe He would indeed be able to fulfill this miraculous promise after all.

In embarrassment, she called out, denying that she had laughed.

The Lord insisted, correctly, that she had, even though Abraham had not heard her. The Lord also repeated the promise.

Verse 14 is one of the mountain-peak verses of the Bible. "Is anything too hard for the Lord?" To ask the question is to answer it. "With God, all things are possible" (Matthew 19:26). He who created all things surely controls all things. He who enacted the laws of nature can change them if He wills.

The adjective "hard" is the same as "wonderful," the same word describing the coming Messiah in Isaiah 9:6. This was indeed a wonderful miracle, but God specializes in things thought impossible, and He Himself is Wonderful!

Genesis 18:16-22

---

16 ¶ And the men rose up from thence, and looked toward Sŏd'ŏm: and Abraham went with them to bring them on the way.

17 And the LORD said, Shall I hide from Abraham that thing which I do;

18 Seeing that Abraham shall surely become a great and mighty nation, and all the nations of the earth shall be blessed in him?

19 For I know him, that he will command his children and his household after him, and they shall keep the way of the LORD, to do justice and judgment; that the LORD may bring upon Abraham that which he hath spoken of him.

20 And the LORD said, Because the cry of Sŏd'ŏm and Gō-mŏr'răh is great, and because their sin is very grievous,

21 I will go down now, and see whether they have done altogether according to the cry of it, which is come unto me; and if not, I will know.

22 And the men turned their faces from thence, and went toward Sŏd'ŏm: but Abraham stood yet before the LORD.

After the message had been given concerning Sarah, it became apparent that the three men had another mission to perform as well. They faced south toward Sodom, and two of the men, the two angels, set out in that direction. The Lord, however, remained behind to engage Abraham in another, most remarkable, conversation.

Although the iniquity of the Amorites was not yet full, the sin of Sodom and Gomorrah, and probably also the other three cities of the plain, had become very grievous. The long-suffering of the Lord had been about exhausted in their case, and the time of their judgment was drawing nigh.

Their sin was particularly inexcusable in that they, more than any of the other cities in the land of Canaan, had seen the power of the Lord. They had been wonderfully delivered from a horrible fate at the hand of the kings of the East through Abraham's divinely empowered rescue, and had heard the testimony of Melchizedek. Even Lot must have witnessed to them in some degree, although his compromising position kept him from being effective in his testimony. God had given them a special opportunity to know Him, and they had rejected Him and fallen into even grosser wickedness than before.

As Abraham accompanied the men a short distance toward Sodom, he must have overheard the Lord speaking, as it were, to Himself, and yet no doubt intending that Abraham should hear His words. The Lord wanted Abraham to know His intentions toward Sodom and Gomorrah. After all, Lot and his family were there. Furthermore, as the "friend of God" (James 2:23), Abraham needed to know the reason for the terrible destruction the cities were about to undergo. He would need to explain it to his children, and they to all their descendants. The desolate region of Sodom would, in the centuries to come, be a perpetual warning to Israel that, although God is gracious and merciful and long-suffering, He is also a God of wrath (Jude 7), and He will not spare when the time of His judgment comes.

God gives a striking testimony to Abraham's character: "I know him, that he will command his children and his household after him, and they shall keep the way of the Lord, to do justice and judgment." The verb "know" conveys the thought that God knew him as an intimate friend. He could trust him with the information He was to give, and could know that he would use it faithfully as a vehicle of instruction to his descendants.

God did not actually say, in so many words, that He intended to destroy Sodom and Gomorrah. He merely said that the "outcry" over their wickedness was great, and that He intended to "go down" and ascertain the situation right on the spot. In the same way, He earlier had "come down" to Babel, to see the rebellion there. It was not, of course, that God could not know the full facts without actually going down into the city, since He is omniscient. He no doubt did this for appearance' sake, that men might know directly that God had actually seen the full situation before He acted in judgment. ·

These verses surely speak to our own times as well. The modern world, America in particular, has had the witness of the Christian gospel for a long time. But mankind has rejected it, and is descending into a morass of corruption and wickedness even greater than that of the pagan world before Christ. He has assured mankind, through His Word, that they will soon be coming to judgment. Until then, His people have the responsibility of intercessory prayer for lost men, and of a consistent spiritual witness to them, warning them of the wrath to come.

In particular, as was true of Abraham, it is especially vital that believers command their children to keep the way of the Lord.

As the Lord was talking with Abraham, the two men walking with them departed and headed down toward Sodom. Abraham, however, having sensed what the Lord planned to do to Sodom and Gomorrah, instead of heading back toward his own home, felt constrained to remain in His presence and to make intercession for those in the cities who might not have participated in their wickedness.

Genesis 18:23-33

23 ¶ And Abraham drew near, and said, Wilt thou also destroy the righteous with the wicked?
24 Peradventure there be fifty righteous within the city: wilt thou also destroy and not spare the place for the fifty righteous that *are* therein?
25 That be far from thee to do after this manner, to slay the righteous with the wicked; and that the righteous should be as the wicked, that be far from thee: Shall not the Judge of all the earth do right?
26 And the LORD said, If I find in Sŏd'ŏm fifty righteous within the city, then I will spare all the place for their sakes.
27 And Abraham answered and said, Behold now, I have taken upon me to speak unto the Lord, which *am but* dust and ashes:
28 Peradventure there shall lack five of the fifty righteous: wilt thou destroy all the city for *lack of* five? And he said, If I find there forty and five, I will not destroy *it.*
29 And he spake unto him yet again, and said, Peradventure there shall be forty found there. And he said, I will not do *it* for forty's sake.
30 And he said *unto him,* Oh let not the Lord be angry, and I will speak: Peradventure there shall thirty be found there. And he said, I will not do *it,* if I find thirty there.
31 And he said, Behold now, I have taken upon me to speak unto the Lord: Peradventure there shall be twenty found there. And he said, I will not destroy *it* for twenty's sake.
32 And he said, Oh let not the Lord be angry, and I will speak yet but this once: Peradventure ten shall be found there. And he said, I will not destroy *it* for ten's sake.
33 And the LORD went his way, as soon as he had left communing with Abraham: and Abraham returned unto his place.

In this section of the chapter is found the most remarkable example of intercessory prayer in the Bible. Abraham naturally was particularly concerned about Lot and his family, but no doubt also knew many of the other people in the cities, having saved them several years previously from the northeastern kings. Though he was well aware of the depravity of their practices, he was concerned for them and hoped against hope that they might still turn to God.

Abraham prayed first that the city might be spared if there were fifty righteous people found in it, then forty-five, then forty, then thirty, then twenty, and finally only ten. Each time God agreed to his request, so that if only ten righteous people could have been found in Sodom, God would not have destroyed the city.

Several important principles become evident from a study of this amazing dialogue. First, God does not want to bring judgment on any city or on any person. He does respond to the prayer of those who intercede, if there is any basis at all within the framework of His holiness and justice to enable Him to do so. Second, the remarkable influence which even a tiny minority may have for good is noteworthy. Only ten godly people in the corrupt city of Sodom would have been enough to spare it the awful destruction to be experienced shortly. Let no one think that his ministry is useless, regardless how small a number he may be able to reach for the Lord. Third, Abraham's prayer was highly reverent—never presumptuous at all—yet persistent and definite. This is the first example of an intercessory prayer recorded in the Bible, and almost certainly is included in such detail in order to serve as our prototype for all such prayers. Note also that the prayer continually recognized, and indeed appealed to, the righteous character and the loving-kindness of God as the basis for making the request. "Shall not the judge of all the earth do right? Wilt thou destroy the righteous with the wicked? That be far from thee!" To be heard and answered, our prayers must likewise be in conformity with the revealed will and character of God, as well as reverent, specific, and persevering.

It should be noted that Abraham recognized that God was not only the God whom he had followed from Ur into Canaan and who had promised to build a great nation through him, but that He was still the "judge of all the earth." Abraham's concept of God was certainly not that of a tribal god, as many liberal critics have taught.

Although Sodom is the specific city referred to in the dialogue, and no doubt was the chief city of the five, it should not be forgotten that all five cities of the plain were intended to be the subjects of the imminent destruction. Later, in response to Lot's request, the small city of Zoar was spared, but otherwise "God destroyed the cities of the plain" (Genesis 19:29; note also Deuteronomy 29:23).

Abraham thought he knew of at least ten righteous people in Sodom. There dwelt Lot and his wife, their two sons (Genesis 19:12), two married daughters and their husbands (Genesis 19:14), and two unmarried daughters (Genesis 19:8), a total of ten. Since these were in one city, perhaps Abraham inferred there would be the same number in each of the other four cities; so he interceded with God to spare the cities if He could find fifty righteous people living in them. When God agreed, Abraham continued to pray, first for forty-five, then forty, then thirty, then twenty, until the number was reduced to ten, the size of Lot's family.

There is no way of knowing whether God would have spared the city for, say, only four people—the number that actually were taken by the angels out of the city before the fire fell. Abraham may not have been close enough in fellowship to Lot for many years to realize that his own family members were largely unregenerate and were themselves part of the problem in Sodom. Or perhaps he did know this, and felt that his prayer would become totally selfish, focusing only on Lot himself, if he carried it any further. At any rate, Abraham assuredly did know that the "judge of all the earth would do right," and left it at this point in His hands.

Lot in the Gates of Sodom

The scene now shifts to Sodom itself, the chief and representative city of the five cities of the plain. It was to Sodom that Lot and his family gradually migrated, drawn like moths to a flame. He first "pitched his tent toward Sodom" (Genesis 13:12), then "dwelt in Sodom" (Genesis 14:12), and finally "sat in the gate of Sodom" (Genesis 19:1). The "gate" of the city was the place where the business and commercial activities centered, and also where the judicial councils took place. Evidently Lot himself was now some kind of magistrate of the place, for this seems to be the meaning of the term "sitting in the gate." It is possible, however, that it refers simply to the apparent fact that he liked to sit at the city gate, where he could participate easily in the trade and conversation that thrived there.

In any case, Lot presents to us a rather disheartening picture. Here is a man who had participated in one of the highest callings ever given by God to men, one who had been at hand to experience with Abraham marvelous revelations and deliverances from God, and yet who now was right at home in the midst of the life of one of the most wicked cities that ever disgraced the earth.

He was well aware of its wickedness, even before he went there. The New Testament tells us, in fact, that "that righteous man dwelling among them, in seeing and hearing, vexed his righteous soul from day to day with their unlawful deeds" (II Peter 2:8). There is no indication, however, that he tried to witness to them in any way, in order to turn them back to God and away from their sins. It is more likely that he tended to congratulate himself that he could do so well, commercially and politically, as a godly man living among an ungodly crowd.

What a perfect picture Lot exhibits of a modern-day carnal Christian! He thinks he has the best of both worlds—the eternal benefit of knowing the Lord as Savior, but also all the temporal benefits that result from worldly influence and possessions, together with acceptance by and fellowship with men of the world. Their gross wickedness may vex his soul a bit, and he may not wish to enter into quite *all* of their activities, but in general he gets along with them just fine, and is quite pleased with himself that he does. A day of reckoning will come, however.

Genesis 19:1-3

CHAPTER 19

AND there came two angels to Sŏd'ŏm at even; and Lot sat in the gate of Sŏd'ŏm: and Lot seeing *them* rose up to meet them; and he bowed himself with his face toward the ground; 2 And he said, Behold now, my lords, turn in, I pray you, into your servant's house, and tarry all night, and wash your feet, and ye shall rise up early, and go on your ways. And they said, Nay; but we will abide in the street all night. 3 And he pressed upon them greatly; and they turned in unto him, and entered into his house; and he made them a feast, and did bake unleavened bread, and they did eat.

As Lot was sitting in the gate, the two angels (the Hebrew expression includes the definite article) that had left Abraham neared the city at dusk. Lot immediately greeted them and invited them to his home. Possibly this invitation was simply the common hospitable gesture of the East (although none of the others at the gate issued such an invitation). Possibly, as a chief magistrate, this was his duty (although the later behavior of the townsmen indicated far less respect for him than would normally be given an official). Probably we should give him the benefit of the doubt, and assume that, since he was aware of the treatment generally received by strangers in this vile city, he would try to shield them from such abuse by taking them quickly into his own home. Although they, through the customary polite gesture, declined at first, saying they would spend the night in the street (obviously a perilous choice in that place), Lot urged them, and they finally yielded to his insistence.

When the men entered his home, Lot prepared them a feast. It is significant, however, that the only ingredient of this feast which is specifically mentioned is "unleavened bread." The fact that Lot baked it, rather than his wife, may suggest that his wife did not at all welcome these strangers in her house. In any case, this is the first mention of *leaven* in the Bible, and is in accord with all of its later usages. In

Scripture, leaven is generally symbolic of evil doctrine or practice corrupting God's people. The next time it is mentioned is in connection with the institution of the Passover feast, when God's people were told to observe the feast without leaven, and in fact to put away all leaven out of their houses (Exodus 12:15). It is noteworthy that, when it is first mentioned, its absence is symbolically associated with the spiritual fellowship between a remnant of believers and their God, in the midst of an utterly corrupt society. Leaven, of course, being involved with the fermentation process, is a perfect symbol of decay and corruption, and it is important that spiritual fellowship not be contaminated with it.

Genesis 19:4-11

---

4 ¶ But before they lay down, the men of the city, *even* the men of Sŏd'ŏm, compassed the house round, both old and young, all the people from every quarter:

5 And they called unto Lot, and said unto him, Where *are* the men which came in to thee this night? bring them out unto us, that we may know them.

6 And Lot went out at the door unto them, and shut the door after him,

7 And said, I pray you, brethren, do not so wickedly.

8 Behold now, I have two daughters which have not known man; let me, I pray you, bring them out unto you, and do ye to them as *is* good in your eyes: only unto these men do nothing; for therefore came they under the shadow of my roof.

9 And they said, Stand back. And they said *again*, This one *fellow* came in to sojourn, and he will needs be a judge: now will we deal worse with thee than with them. And they pressed sore upon the man, *even* Lot, and came near to break the door.

10 But the men put forth their hand, and pulled Lot into the house to them, and shut to the door.

11 And they smote the men that *were* at the door of the house with blindness, both small and great: so that they wearied themselves to find the door.

The scene depicted in these verses is almost unbelievable in its revelation of the depravity of the Sodomites. The intent of an occasional degenerate to commit homosexual rape is disgusting enough, even though sodomy is increasingly being accepted and promoted in our present day; but here we have a case in which all "the men of the city . . . both old and young, all the people, from every quarter" surrounded Lot's house with the intention to commit this crime against his guests. If they had carried out their desires, especially in view of the resistance which they would no doubt have encountered, the orgy would certainly have culminated in murder as well, at least if those whom they sought to abuse had been ordinary men.

The fact that the old men as well as the young were driven by these lusts, and that, rather than practicing them in secret, they shouted their desires aloud in the streets, adds still another dimension to the enormity of the thing. No wonder God had told Abraham that "the cry of Sodom and Gomorrah is great, and their sin is very grievous" (18:20). In these modern days, after two thousand years of Christian teaching to which the Sodomites never had access, what must God think of the current revival of homosexuality, manifest in "gay liberation" movements and political organizations, and even "gay" religious societies, not only among liberals, but even among some evangelicals?

A burning commentary on this is given by the apostle Paul in Romans 1:26, 27: "For this cause God gave them up unto vile affections: for even their women did change the natural use into that which is against nature: and likewise also the men, leaving the natural use of the woman, burned in their lust one toward another; men with men working that which is unseemly, and receiving in themselves that recompense of their error which was meet." This descent into degeneracy, both ancient and modern, is caused first of all by a rejection of God as Creator and Sovereign, equating ultimate reality and responsibility with the natural world (Romans 1:21-25). In whatever specific form this type of philosophy may appear in a given generation, it is fundamentally nothing but evolutionary naturalism and humanism. No matter how impressive may be its scientific and philosophic trappings, underneath it is rebellion against the Creator, and it always leads sooner or later to gross moral depravity.

Returning to the events at Sodom, we are amazed to see Lot in desperation making an almost unbelievable attempt to save his guests, offering the mob his two virgin daughters to abuse however they would, if they would only leave the men alone. Lot acknowledged that the men had accepted his hospitality for protection against this very thing, but his proposal only infuriated the mob even more.

It is hard for us to understand, even with all allowance for the exaggerated customs of hospitality which presumably were practiced at the time, how Lot could offer to sacrifice his daughters in this way. He was no doubt in a confused state of mind in the emergency situation thrust on him, but he did not lack personal courage, as his willingness to shield the men with his own body attested. The very fact that he had two virgin daughters, in such a place, is itself testimony to the fact that he still had some influence, both over his own family and over the men of the city.

There is a possibility that Lot had come to recognize, or at least to suspect, the real identity of his visitors. This is intimated perhaps by his preparation of the unleavened bread. If he did suspect, perhaps this might explain why he felt he must go to any lengths to protect them, even the sacrifice of his own children.

Whatever the reason for this strange proposal, it did not deter the Sodomites in the least. It only angered them, and made Lot himself the object of their passion. Lot had for some time thought he was at home among the people of the city, even "sitting in the gate." Now, however, he quickly learned that they had never really accepted him. He had no influence over them whatever under these present conditions, and they resented even the very fact that he had judged their intended action to be morally wrong. This is almost inevitably the ultimate outcome of a compromising relation between carnal Christians and the world.

As it finally became apparent that no possible stratagem would solve the problem for Lot, the angels themselves intervened. The situation had become so hopeless that even Lot must have realized there was no remedy except divine judgment. Evidently the door could not be opened from outside (archaeology has revealed that the doors to the houses of this period did have strong hinges and were exceptionally heavy and sturdy); so the men opened the door to pull Lot inside, and then shut it again.

They then struck the men outside with blindness—a particular type of blindness mentioned elsewhere in the Bible only in II Kings 6:18, when God smote the vast Syrian army with blindness in order to save Elisha. Evidently, this blindness did not leave its victims sightless, but rather was a blindness of confusion, so that they could see but could not identify where they were. Somehow they were unable to find the door to break it in.

Genesis 19:12-14

12 ¶ And the men said unto Lot, Hast thou here any besides? son-in-law, and thy sons, and thy daughters, and whatsoever thou hast in the city, bring *them* out of this place: 13 For we will destroy this place, because the cry of them is waxen great before the face of the LORD; and the LORD hath sent us to destroy it.

14 And Lot went out, and spake unto his sons-in-law, which married his daughters, and said, Up, get you out of this place; for the LORD will destroy this city. But he seemed as one that mocked unto his sons-in-law.

If Lot had not known before, he certainly now realized that these men were really angels, sent from God to judge and destroy the cities of the plain. In an atmosphere of emergency, the angels offered to spare Lot and his family, including even the men of Sodom that had married some of his daughters. The angels told him plainly, however, that his family would have to leave the city altogether, because it was about to be destroyed.

Lot then went out again to find his daughters and their husbands, to carry them the warning. (Evidently the men outside his door had either departed or were still too confused to recognize him.) However, he had long since lost any influence with them, and they simply ridiculed him, completely refusing to take his warning seriously. So far as the record goes, he didn't even bother to warn his own sons, presumably because they were so deeply involved in the Sodomite wickedness by this time that he knew it would be useless. This is a deeply sobering example of the deadly results that a father's compromise with the world system may have on his own children.

Genesis 19:15-23

---

15 ¶ And when the morning arose, then the angels hastened Lot, saying, Arise, take thy wife, and thy two daughters, which are here; lest thou be consumed in the iniquity of the city.

16 And while he lingered, the men laid hold upon his hand, and upon the hand of his wife, and upon the hand of his two daughters; the LORD being merciful unto him: and they brought him forth, and set him without the city.

17 ¶ And it came to pass, when they had brought them forth abroad, that he said, Escape for thy life; look not behind thee, neither stay thou in all the plain; escape to the mountain, lest thou be consumed.

18 And Lot said unto them, Oh, not so, my Lord:

19 Behold now, thy servant hath found grace in thy sight, and thou hast magnified thy mercy, which thou hast showed unto me in saving my life; and I cannot escape to the mountain, lest some evil take me, and I die:

20 Behold now, this city *is* near to flee unto, and it *is* a little one: O, let me escape thither, (*is* it not a little one?) and my soul shall live.

21 And he said unto him, See, I have accepted thee concerning this thing also, that I will not overthrow this city, for the which thou hast spoken.

22 Haste thee, escape thither; for I cannot do any thing till thou be come thither. Therefore the name of the city was called Zō′är.

23 ¶ The sun was risen upon the earth when Lot entered into Zō′är.

Fortunately, however, Lot still did have some influence on his wife and two unmarried daughters. Also, of course, they had seen at first hand the events of the evening, and they knew that these visitors were fully able to carry out the destruction which they had pronounced on the city. Accordingly, they went with Lot when the angels urged them early the next morning. Even so, they all held back somewhat, still clinging to the wistful hope that they would not really have to give up all the physical comforts of their home in Sodom.

In spite of their reluctance, however, "the Lord being merciful unto him," the angels insisted that they leave, actually pulling them by the hand! They made it plain that the destruction would come early in the morning, after the city was fully awake and aware of what was happening, but before any of the inhabitants would be leaving the city for work in the fields or other purposes, and before any strangers might come into the city. The angels stressed the urgency of their leaving without any delay, without even looking behind them. They would have to flee to the mountains as rapidly as they could, if they were to escape the judgment about to overwhelm the five cities and the plain they controlled. The spiritual lesson is obvious. A believer must flee the world, not looking back with regrets or longing, lest he himself be injured or destroyed in its overthrow.

Again, however, Lot tries to compromise. The angels would spare his life but, instead of being content with that, he beseeches them to allow him to move into one of the smaller cities, Zoar, and to spare that one city. Presumably, of the five cities, Zoar was the smallest and least contaminated by the wickedness of Sodom. Lot said he was afraid that he could not survive in the mountains (though, if the Lord had spared him through the destruction of Sodom, one would think he could trust God to keep him in the place where He told him to flee). It is pitiful the way Lot begs for the opportunity to continue to be at least somewhat comfortable in the world, stressing that Zoar was such a small city (the name itself means "small place") that it couldn't hurt too much to spare it. Also, it was not far distant, so the journey would not be nearly so arduous. Lot's carnality, in spite of his spirituality (which was so uncomfortable to him), kept manifesting itself at every turn.

In remarkable grace and long-suffering, through His angelic agent, God granted Lot this presumptuous request. He spared Zoar, for Lot's sake. But all of this delay had wasted valuable time, and they needed to hasten. Possibly, Lot's wife had been partially responsible for Lot's delaying tactics. She didn't want to leave in the first place, and no doubt would much rather have moved to Zoar than to an unknown life in the mountains. As they rushed to Zoar, it does seem likely that she lagged behind, still resentful of having to leave her home and friends in Sodom.

Remember Lot's Wife

It might help at this point to discuss briefly the geography of the region, as archaeology has revealed it. The Dead Sea is the lowest spot on the earth's surface, 1,286 feet below sea level. The Jordan River empties into it, and it has no outlet. The intense heat evaporates great quantities of water, so that the salinity of the sea continues to increase. It is about 40 miles long by 10 miles wide, and is divided into two parts which are connected by a narrow strait. The southern segment, about 10 miles long, is only about 10 to 20 feet deep, whereas the northern segment is very deep, up to 1,400 feet in places.

It is possible that, at the time of Abraham, the southern segment was the fertile plain which seemed so attractive to Lot. It has since been submerged by water because of the silting up of the bed of the sea in the northern segment, causing the water level to rise. It is probable that this is what the verses in Genesis 14:3, 8, 10 speak of as the "Vale of Siddim." Many archaeologists have believed that the five cities (except Zoar, which is apparently still in existence, called by the same name) were also on this plain, and that their remains are now covered by the waters of the Dead Sea.

On the other hand, archaeological explorations within the past decade have shown that, at the time of Abraham, there were five large cities on the eastern side of this southern portion of the Dead Sea which, in many respects, do seem to answer to the descriptions of the five cities of the plain. If these are indeed the cities of Lot's time, as now seems likely, then Sodom was the southernmost, with Gomorrah, Zoar, Admah, and Zeboim in order proceeding northward. Each city was located along one of the fresh-water streams coming down from the eastern hills into the Vale of Siddim and on into the sea. Each was situated on a high outspur overlooking its "wadi," so that it could control the river and its water below. The five cities were apparently very prosperous and supported a very large population (the tombs that have been uncovered indicate probably over a million individuals had been buried in them).

The word "Siddim" seems to mean "cultivated fields," indicative of the extensive agricultural system developed on them by the five-nation confederacy. The heat and fertile soil, combined with reliable irrigation, made the whole region one of tremendous agricultural productivity. It was this that so attracted Lot that he chose to live there instead of on the western uplands with Abraham. The people in Sodom and the other four cities presumably worked the fields down in the plain during the day, and then went back up to their much cooler homes during the evening.

The prosperity of the region which so impressed Lot was probably also the cause of the extreme wickedness of the cities. With all their material needs taken care of, and with an abundance of leisure time, the people developed a moral laxity which soon became gross corruption, until finally God could endure it no longer.

Genesis 19:24-29

---

24 Then the LORD rained upon Sŏd'ŏm and upon Gō-mŏr'ràh brimstone and fire from the LORD out of heaven;
25 And he overthrew those cities, and all the plain, and all the inhabitants of the cities, and that which grew upon the ground.
26 ¶ But his wife looked back from behind him, and she became a pillar of salt.
27 ¶ And Abraham gat up early in the morning to the place where he stood before the LORD:
28 And he looked toward Sŏd'ŏm and Gō-mŏr'ràh, and toward all the land of the plain, and beheld, and, lo, the smoke of the country went up as the smoke of a furnace.
29 ¶ And it came to pass, when God destroyed the cities of the plain, that God remembered Abraham, and sent Lot out of the midst of the overthrow, when he overthrew the cities in the which Lot dwelt.

As Lot and his family fled the city and reached Zoar, "the Lord rained upon Sodom and upon Gomorrah brimstone and fire from the Lord out of heaven." This verse seems to note that two persons of the Godhead were participating. "The LORD" (evidently the one manifested to Abraham) called down the judgment, but it came from "the LORD" out of heaven. This is the first mention of "fire" in the Bible, and of course speaks clearly of divine judgment on man's sin. "Even as Sodom and Gomorrah, and the cities about them in like manner, giving themselves over to fornication, and going after strange flesh, are set forth for an example, suffering the vengeance of eternal fire" (Jude 7).

Exactly what was this fire that descended from God out of heaven? The word "brimstone," of course, is usually associated with sulphur, but is also used for any inflammable substance. It has been suggested by many that the catastrophe was actually a volcanic eruption, as there is much evidence of past volcanism in the area. A more likely possibility is that a great earthquake took place in association with a violent electrical storm. The "overthrow," in verse 25, might well refer to such an event.

The region at present is one of the most unusual on earth, not only because of its great depth below sea level and the uniquely high salt content of its Dead Sea, but also because of the strange rock formations and unusual geologic structure. At the southwest corner of the sea is a great mountain of rock salt, seven hundred feet high and five miles long, known as Jebel Usdum (meaning, in Arabic, "Mount of Sodom"). Other salt deposits abound in the region. To uniformitarians, salt deposits are interpreted in terms of slow evaporation of saline waters over millions of years, and the deposits in this region are usually so interpreted as well. On the other hand, these great beds of rock salt are by no means comparable to the salt deposits actually being formed in this way in the Dead Sea itself. It is clear that some altogether different mode of origin must account for them, and evidence has accumulated in recent years that such deposits have resulted from massive precipitation from magmas and waters ascending from depths below the earth. They are volcanic, not lacustrine, phenomena.

Many other evidences of volcanism abound there, such as rocks formed from lava and volcanic ash. On the other hand, the results of archaeological investigations do not support the hypothesis that these volcanic phenomena occurred as recently as the time of Abraham and the cities of the plain. More likely, they occurred during the closing phases of the great Flood and the uplifts in the centuries immediately following it.

In these postdiluvian uplifts, however, one of the most important lines of movement evidently took place through this region. The Jordan Valley, the Dead Sea, the Gulf of Aqaba, the Red Sea, all lie along the "Great Rift," which continues on through the Upper Nile Valley and into southern Africa. This has been a very active region ever since, subject to repeated earthquakes. Furthermore, in the volcanism accompanying the earlier tectonic activity, not only had massive concentrations of salt been deposited, but also organic materials from the Flood had been converted into oil, asphalt, and natural gas, along with considerable quantities of free sulphur. The reference in Genesis 14:10 to the many asphalt pits in the Vale of Siddim, as well as the fact that the Jewish historian, Josephus, spoke of the Dead Sea as the "Asphalt Sea," is further evidence of the remarkably combustible character once possessed by the whole area.

It seems possible, therefore, that God triggered an earthquake along the great fault at this time, which released and exposed to the atmosphere vast quantities of combustible hydrocarbons and sulphur. At the same time, God sent "fire from heaven," which ignited the mixture in a great explosion and devastating fire. To Abraham, watching afar off with great concern ever since his intercessory prayer before the Lord, it seemed as though "the smoke of the country went up as the smoke of a furnace."

The "fire and brimstone" that fell from heaven possibly refers to the burning gas and sulphur that were blown into the air in the explosion and then fell back to the earth throughout the region. The most likely naturalistic explanation for the ignition of these materials probably would be that of a simultaneous electrical storm, in which case the lightning itself could also be described as "fire from heaven." Similar terminology is used in Job 1:16, Ezekiel 38:22, and elsewhere, for what probably are also violent atmospheric phenomena.

Since natural physical phenomena, divinely timed, do seem adequate to explain the destruction of Sodom and Gomorrah, perhaps we should interpret the story in this way. We do not want to exclude the possibility, however, that a specially created divine fire was sent supernaturally from heaven to ignite the region. The Bible does record other such things, as in the days of Gideon (Judges 6:21), Elijah (I Kings 18:38), and others. It is interesting that the word for "brimstone" in the New Testament is the Greek *theion,* meaning literally "God's fire." The personal connection of God and the two angelic messengers with Sodom's destruction in itself tends to suggest that the "rain of brimstone and fire from the Lord out of heaven" was actually supernatural. There is certainly no reason for us to question either God's ability or the appropriateness of a true creative miracle in this situation.

The very strange reference to Lot's wife also requires discussion. According to verse 26, she "looked back from behind him [i.e., she was already behind Lot], and she became a pillar of salt." There are today many pillars of salt in the region, and a number of these have from time to time been called "Lot's wife" by the Arabs. Though it is possible that this transmutation may have been sudden and miraculous, since with God all things are possible, such an event would seem out of character in the Bible. When God intervenes in nature miraculously, there is always an appropriate reason and the phenomena of the miracle correspond in an appropriate way to that reason.

Consequently, it seems probable that this brief statement (not referring to either God or angels, but containing only a matter-of-fact summary of an event), simply records a natural calamity that overtook this woman as she very reluctantly followed her husband and daughters out of Sodom.

When the Lord Jesus Christ, talking of the events to occur near the time of His second coming, referred by way of illustration to the event, He said: "Remember Lot's wife. Whosoever shall seek to save his life shall lose it; and whosoever shall lose his life shall preserve it" (Luke 17:32, 33). The implication is that Lot's wife was seeking to hang on to her life in Sodom, and that, consequently, she lost her life in its destruction. The word "looked back" has the connotation of "looking intently." It might possibly be rendered "lagged back," or maybe even "returned back." In any case, she was not with her husband and daughters, so that only she perished. One possibility is that the explosions in the region threw great quantities of its salt deposits into the air, and that some of these fell on her and buried her under a great pile of salt. Another is that she was buried by volcanic ash or other materials and that, gradually, over the following years, her body became petrified, "becoming salt" in fashion similar to that experienced by the inhabitants of Pompeii and Herculaneum when they were buried by the eruption of Mount Vesuvius.

Whatever the exact process may have been, the important teaching associated with Lot's wife, as emphasized by the Lord Jesus Christ, is the real peril entertained by professing believers who seek to hang on to things of the world. Whether Lot's wife was a true believer or not, Scripture does not say. Although it is possible that Lot had met and married her in Sodom, it seems more likely that she had been with him while he was still with Abraham twenty years before. They had had at least six children, two of whom we know were married. In any case, she was thoroughly imbued with the attitudes of Sodom, and was so unhappy at having to leave (even after seeing the unspeakable behavior of its inhabitants the previous evening, which had almost resulted in the death of her husband and probably her two unmarried daughters) that she remained far enough behind to be trapped and to die in the catastrophe that overwhelmed the doomed city.

Even Lot was spared only because "God remembered Abraham and sent Lot out of the midst of the overthrow, when he overthrew the cities in which Lot dwelt" (verse 29). The word "overthrow," as noted previously, suggests an earthquake. In the New Testament, Peter likewise refers to an "overthrow." "For if God . . . turning the cities of Sodom and Gomorrah into ashes condemned them with an overthrow, making them an example unto those that after should live ungodly; And delivered just Lot, vexed with the filthy conversation of the wicked: (For that righteous man dwelling among them, in seeing and hearing, vexed his righteous soul from day to day with their unlawful deeds;) The Lord knoweth how to deliver the godly out of temptations, and to reserve the unjust unto the day of judgment to be punished" (II Peter 2:4-9).

In this incisive commentary on Lot's tragic story, the word "overthrow" is the Greek *katastrophe*. In verb form, it is used to describe the action of Jesus when He "overthrew the tables of the moneychangers" (Matthew 21:12). It seems to refer to a complete physical upheaval. However, it refers only to a *regional,* not a worldwide, catastrophe. Now contrast this word with the word Peter uses in the same passage to describe the Flood of Noah (II Peter 2:5), when he speaks of God "bringing in the flood [Greek *kataklusmos*] upon the world of the ungodly." The destruction of Sodom and the cities of the plain was a regional *catastrophe;* the Flood was a worldwide *cataclysm.*

Genesis 19:30-38

30 ¶ And Lot went up out of Zō'ár, and dwelt in the mountain, and his two daughters with him; for he feared to dwell in Zō'ár: and he dwelt in a cave, he and his two daughters.
31 And the firstborn said unto the younger, Our father *is* old, and *there is* not a man in the earth to come in unto us after the manner of all the earth:
32 Come, let us make our father drink wine, and we will lie with him, that we may preserve seed of our father.
33 And they made their father drink wine that night: and the firstborn went in, and lay with her father; and he perceived not when she lay down, nor when she arose.
34 And it came to pass on the morrow, that the firstborn said unto the younger, Behold, I lay yesternight with my father: let us make him drink wine this night also; and go thou in, *and* lie with him, that we may preserve seed of our father.
35 And they made their father drink wine that night also: and the younger arose, and lay with him; and he perceived not when she lay down, nor when she arose.
36 Thus were both the daughters of Lot with child by their father.
37 And the firstborn bare a son, and called his name Mō'ăb: the same *is* the father of the Mō'ăb-ītes unto this day.
38 And the younger, she also bare a son, and called his name Bĕn'-ăm'mĭ: the same *is* the father of the children of Ammon unto this day.

Lot and his daughters apparently didn't stay long in Zoar. After losing the rest of their family in Sodom, the city no longer had the attraction for them it once did. The inhabitants of Zoar no doubt resented Lot as the only one who had not perished in the destruction of their sister city, and who seemed somehow therefore a participant in its destruction. Since Sodom and Gomorrah were south of them, and Admah and Zeboim north of them, they were right in the middle of the devastation. Continuing earth tremors and fires around them probably made it a most unpleasant place in which to live. The fertile plains had been destroyed, and the prosperity of the city had vanished. Although the angels had told Lot to go to the mountains, he had demurred. Now he realized that this instruction was best after all; so he and his daughters left Zoar. With all of their possessions gone, they had to live in a cave. It was a miserable existence, after the years of luxurious living in Sodom, but at least their lives were spared. One wonders why Lot didn't return to Abraham, but possibly his pride was in the way. The Dead Sea region, of course, abounds with caves in the nearby mountains, which have served many people as residences. (The Dead Sea Scrolls were, of course, found in such caves.)

It is interesting to note that, despite the loss of their possessions, they had managed to bring along a stock of wine! This itself now becomes a further vehicle for Lot's degradation. His daughters, on successive nights, encouraged him to drink himself into a stupor (no doubt justifying himself by his feelings of loneliness and self-pity) and then to have sexual intercourse with them.

In partial defense of their actions, we may note that they were not motivated simply by physical lust, although certainly their surroundings in Sodom had been most conducive to its full expression. They were, nevertheless, still virgins (Genesis 19:8), so at least their father's moral standards had influenced them to some degree. They had kept themselves pure for their future husbands, but now it suddenly seemed that they would never have husbands at all. The worst of it was that, now that their brothers, their sisters, and their mother had perished, neither they nor their father would leave any descendants. In view of both God's primeval command to be fruitful and the universal belief that barrenness therefore was a disgrace, this situation seemed intolerable to them. It perhaps was further aggravated by their fear that, with neither husbands nor sons, there would be no one to provide for them as they grew older. Unaccustomed to walking by faith in God to meet their needs, they reasoned that the only possible way out of the intolerable situation was that of incest with their father.

They knew that their father would not willingly consent to such a thing, however. As far as their own moral scruples were concerned, they perhaps reasoned that this would not be as bad as the proposal that their father had made concerning them to the Sodomites. Also, as noted before, there were as yet no actual Scriptural ordinances against incest, and close marriages were not uncommon (e.g., Abram and his half-sister Sarai); so this could not have seemed as serious a crime to them as it would to us today. Evidently they decided it was the only thing to do under the circumstances (except to trust God, an idea which apparently never occurred to them at all), and so proceeded to get their father drunk and to go through with it.

Scripture does not tell us how Lot felt about this matter when he finally learned about it. In fact, it tells us absolutely nothing else about Lot. Presumably, however, he did act as a father to the two sons that were born of his two daughters, since they did grow to maturity and, in fact, became the ancestors of two nations.

The son of the older daughter was named Moab (meaning "from the father"), and was the progenitor of the Moabites. The younger daughter's son was named Benammi (meaning "son of my people"), and from him were descended the Ammonites.

The Moabites and the Ammonites were frequently at war with Israel in later years. They lived mostly in the mountainous regions east of the Dead Sea. Although they were generally idolaters, not all of them were evil. Ruth, for example, was a Moabite woman and, as the wife of Boaz, became one of the ancestors of Jesus. Naamah, an Ammonite woman, was one of Solomon's wives and the mother of King Rehoboam, who also was in the ancestral line leading to Jesus. Although God in later years judged the Moabites and Ammonites severely, there is some indication that they may be revived in the last days (Jeremiah 48:47; 49:6). These people, along with the Edomites and others, have today long since been essentially amalgamated with the Arabs, descendants of Ishmael. Whether they will ever again be identified as distinct nations or (as seems more likely) will simply share in the future destiny of the Arabic peoples, only the future will reveal.

Sarah and the Philistines

In many respects, Genesis 20 is one of the most difficult chapters in the Bible to understand. The narrative is simple enough, of course; but how could Abraham and Sarah, at this time, repeat the very same sin they had committed many years ago in Egypt? It might be understandable that, in those days when their faith had not yet really been tested and God's faithfulness fully confirmed, they could have fallen into such a trap; but how could they do it again? They had, over and over again, seen many wonderful answers to prayer, many miraculous proofs of God's care and protection. Their faith had stood many tests, and God had never failed them. And now, finally, they were about to have their long-promised son! Sarah may even have been actually pregnant with Isaac, and it would only be a few months more. This is what the Bible records, however, so it must have happened, just this way.

Genesis 20:1, 2

CHAPTER 20

AND Abraham journeyed from thence toward the south country, and dwelt between Kā′děsh and Shŭr, and sojourned in Gē′rär.

2 And Abraham said of Sarah his wife, She *is* my sister: and Ȧ-bĭm′ē-lěch king of Gē′rär sent, and took Sarah.

For some unknown reason, Abraham at this time decided to take a trip down through the Negev and into Gerar, the capital city at that time of the land of the Philistines, near the Egyptian border. This was a prosperous city, as revealed by archaeological excavations there, and it may be that Abraham had some kind of business dealings in mind. The city controlled a lucrative caravan route and Abraham by this time was a wealthy and powerful chieftain.

The Philistines were Hamitic peoples (Genesis 10:14) who apparently settled at various times along the seacoast, coming probably from Crete. The name of Palestine was derived from their name. Though most of them did not arrive until many centuries later, apparently early contingents of them had settled there by the time of Abraham. The archaeological monuments indicate that, although their ancestor was Ham's son, Mizraim, who also was the progenitor of the Egyptians, there had been considerable intermixing with descendants of Japheth in the Philistine ancestry. In any case, they did not worship the true God, though they may at this time still have retained some slight knowledge of His existence.

Abraham knew little about them, evidently, but as he entered their land he saw enough to realize they were an ungodly people. The old fears he and Sarah had experienced in Egypt suddenly returned, and they agreed once again that Sarah would be presented as his sister, rather than his wife, for the same reasons as before.

It is hard to understand how they could have forgotten the rebuke this course of action had procured for them in Egypt. In spite of their sin, God had taken care of them there, and surely they knew by this time He would protect them without their again resorting to such a shameful ruse. It seems, however, that they had long ago agreed on this as a settled policy in such circumstances (verse 13), and somehow the stress of the immediate situation confronting them caught them unaware. And so, sad to say, they found themselves repeating the same old lie. Once they had committed themselves to it, they were rapidly impelled by circumstances to continue, like it or no.

Sarah was ninety years old, and it is perhaps surprising that she would still be physically attractive to a heathen king. However, she had in some measure been physically rejuvenated, in order to conceive, bear, and nurse Isaac, and possibly this manifested itself in renewed beauty as well. Or possibly Abimelech (evidently a standard name for Philistine kings, like Pharaoh in Egypt) viewed union with her as of political value, since Abraham was a powerful and rich chieftain. Abimelech already had a harem and, as considered customary in those days, kings had a right to take any woman they might choose into their harems, whether for personal or political motives. At any rate, he sent for Sarah and had her brought into his harem.

Genesis 20:3-8

---

3 But God came to Ȧ-bĭm'ē-lĕch in a dream by night, and said to him, Behold, thou *art but* a dead man, for the woman which thou hast taken; for she *is* a man's wife.

4 But Ȧ-bĭm'ē-lĕch had not come near her: and he said, LORD, wilt thou slay also a righteous nation?

5 Said he not unto me, She *is* my sister? and she, even she herself said, He *is* my brother: in the integrity of my heart and innocency of my hands have I done this.

6 And God said unto him in a dream,

Yea, I know that thou didst this in the integrity of thy heart; for I also withheld thee from sinning against me: therefore suffered I thee not to touch her.

7 Now therefore restore the man *his* wife; for he *is* a prophet, and he shall pray for thee, and thou shalt live: and if thou restore *her* not, know thou that thou shalt surely die, thou, and all that *are* thine.

8 Therefore Ȧ-bĭm'ē-lĕch rose early in the morning, and called all his servants, and told all these things in their ears: and the men were sore afraid.

Regardless of their mistake, however, God would not allow His promise to Abraham and Sarah to be broken. Before Abimelech had touched Sarah, God struck him with some kind of lethal infirmity (verses 3, 17), evidently of such nature as to prevent his coming in to her (verse 6). Furthermore, He "closed up the wombs" (verse 18) of the others in his harem and household. It may even be that the plague was about to be imposed on the entire nation, or at least Abimelech feared that it might (verse 4).

God then appeared to Abimelech in a dream, to explain the significance of what was happening to him. He informed him that Sarah was Abraham's wife and, furthermore, that Abraham was a special prophet of God. If he were to touch Sarah, or harm either of them, he and all his house—perhaps all his land—would die.

Abimelech may or may not have known anything about the true God before, but he certainly became aware of His power now. Abimelech and all his servants were "sore afraid" (verse 8). He protested to God that he didn't know Sarah's real identity and that he had taken her into his household innocently. God acknowledged his relative integrity in the matter (certainly not genuine integrity in God's economy, but only in accord with the customs of the day), then instructed him immediately to restore Sarah to Abraham, and to ask Abraham to pray for his healing.

Genesis 20:9-18

9 Then Ă-bĭm'ē-lĕch called Abraham, and said unto him, What hast thou done unto us? and what have I offended thee, that thou hast brought on me and on my kingdom a great sin? thou hast done deeds unto me that ought not to be done.

10 And Ă-bĭm'ē-lĕch said unto Abraham, What sawest thou, that thou hast done this thing?

11 And Abraham said, Because I thought, Surely the fear of God *is* not in this place; and they will slay me for my wife's sake.

12 And yet indeed *she is* my sister; she *is* the daughter of my father, but not the daughter of my mother; and she became my wife.

13 And it came to pass, when God caused me to wander from my father's house, that I said unto her, This *is* thy kindness which thou shalt show unto me; at every place whither we shall come, say of me, He *is* my brother.

14 And Ă-bĭm'ē-lĕch took sheep, and oxen, and menservants, and womenservants, and gave *them* unto Abraham, and restored him Sarah his wife.

15 And Ă-bĭm'ē-lĕch said, Behold, my land *is* before thee: dwell where it pleaseth thee.

16 And unto Sarah he said, Behold, I have given thy brother a thousand *pieces* of silver: behold, he *is* to thee a covering of the eyes, unto all that *are* with thee, and with all *other:* thus she was reproved.

17 ¶ So Abraham prayed unto God: and God healed Ă-bĭm'ē-lĕch, and his wife, and his maidservants; and they bare *children.*

18 For the LORD had fast closed up all the wombs of the house of Ă-bĭm'ē-lĕch, because of Sarah, Abraham's wife.

Abimelech quickly sent for Abraham, not really in repentance for taking his "sister" away from him, but rather in fear that his God would destroy him and his land if he didn't. Before he asked Abraham to pray for him, as God had instructed him, he first delivered Abraham and Sarah a stinging rebuke for their deception, which had almost resulted in such calamity to his nation.

There is no indication that God Himself rebuked Abraham, though certainly He was not pleased with what he had done. No doubt God knew that Abimelech's rebuke was enough. If indeed Abraham and Sarah had allowed the experience in Egypt to grow cold in their remembrance, this new, almost identical, experience in Gerar brought it all back to them in a flood of bitterness and shame.

Abraham gave the excuse that, since the Philistines had no fear of God, they might otherwise have slain him and taken his wife anyway. Abimelech did not deny this, so possibly the fear was well grounded, as far as Abimelech's own intentions were concerned. Perhaps it was partially for this reason that God sharply chastised Abimelech and his people, and did not openly rebuke Abraham.

In any event, Abimelech did restore Sarah to Abraham and, once again, God had protected her in the harem of a heathen king. In addition, Abimelech gave Abraham a large gift of sheep and oxen and servants, as well as freedom to dwell anywhere in his land. He also gave him a thousand pieces of silver.

Abraham had refused to take the spoil of battle when he had defeated the four-king confederation. He had also been most generous in giving Lot the choice of the best lands. It seems odd at first that he would now accept these gifts from Abimelech. Probably it was not cupidity on his part but rather his recognition that to refuse would offend Abimelech further.

Abimelech was told Abraham was a prophet not that Abraham might predict the future, but so he might pray for him. This is the first occurrence of the word in the Bible, and shows that "prophecy" is not primarily prediction, but rather speaking the words of God, as inspired by Him. Note the instruction in Psalm 105:15: "Touch not mine anointed, and do my prophets no harm."

Abimelech also "reproved" Sarah (verse 16) for her part in the deception, saying that Abraham should be "to thee a covering of the eyes, unto all that are with thee, and with all other." It is not completely clear what these words mean, but most likely they were intended to stress to Sarah that, since Abraham was her husband and also God's prophet, she had no need to fear the lustful attentions of other men. He himself was a sufficient veil over her eyes to prevent other men from looking on her in this way.

The final outcome of this distasteful experience seems to have been that Abraham finally learned the full lesson of faith. Never again do we read of him questioning God or His guardianship.

14

The Child of Promise

(Genesis 21-23)

The Birth of Isaac

Finally, after twenty-five years in the land of Canaan, waiting for the fulfillment of God's promise, Abraham's faith was rewarded. The apostle Paul has a beautiful commentary on this: "(As it is written, I have made thee a father of many nations,) before him whom he believed, even God, who quickeneth the dead, and calleth those things which be not as though they were. Who against hope believed in hope, that he might become the father of many nations; according to that which was spoken, So shall thy seed be. And being not weak in faith, he considered not his own body now dead, when he was about an hundred years old, neither yet the deadness of Sarah's womb: He staggered not at the promise of God through unbelief; but was strong in faith, giving glory to God; And being fully persuaded that, what he had promised, he was able also to perform. And therefore it was imputed to him for righteousness" (Romans 4:17-22).

Abraham, therefore, is offered throughout the New Testament as the prototype of those who are justified by faith. The apostle Paul stresses that this imputed righteousness was received by Abraham even before he was circumcised (Romans 4:9-12) and long before the Mosaic law was given (Galatians 3:16-18), so that salvation depends neither on the ritual nor the moral law, but only on God's grace received through faith. Abraham is called "the father of all them that believe"

(Romans 4:11) and "the father of us all" (Romans 4:16). Further, Scripture assures us that "they which are of faith, the same are the children of Abraham," and that "they which be of faith are blessed with faithful Abraham" (Galatians 3:7, 9).

Sarah also, though of doubtful mind for a time, became strong in faith. "Through faith also Sara herself received strength to conceive seed, and was delivered of a child when she was past age, because she judged him faithful who had promised" (Hebrews 11:11). It is important to note that the faith of Abraham and Sarah was not simply an attitude of faith for faith's sake. Rather they were able to believe because they had full confidence in the word of God. Abraham was persuaded that, what God had promised, He would perform. Sarah judged Him faithful who had promised. In the same way today, we are saved on the basis of faith in the sure promises of God's Word.

Genesis 21:1-8

CHAPTER 21

AND the LORD visited Sarah as he had said, and the LORD did unto Sarah as he had spoken.

2 For Sarah conceived, and bare Abraham a son in his old age, at the set time of which God had spoken to him.

3 And Abraham called the name of his son that was born unto him, whom Sarah bare to him, Isaac.

4 And Abraham circumcised his son Isaac being eight days old, as God had commanded him.

5 And Abraham was a hundred years old, when his son Isaac was born unto him.

6 ¶ And Sarah said, God hath made me to laugh, *so that* all that hear will laugh with me.

7 And she said, Who would have said unto Abraham, that Sarah should have given children suck? for I have borne *him* a son in his old age.

8 And the child grew, and was weaned: and Abraham made a great feast the *same* day that Isaac was weaned.

The first verse of Genesis 21 emphasizes that God keeps His word. "The Lord visited Sarah *as he had said;* and the Lord did unto Sarah *as he had spoken.*" Furthermore, His promise was fulfilled on schedule (God's schedule, not man's!). Sarah "bare Abraham a son in his old age, *at the set time* of which God had spoken to him" (verse 2). Like Abraham, we often become impatient waiting for God to work; but, like Abraham, we should learn to "be strong in faith, giving glory to God; and being fully persuaded that, what he had promised, he is able also to perform."

The bodies of Abraham and Sarah had been miraculously rejuvenated, their ages being one hundred and ninety years old, respectively (Genesis 17:17; 21:5). Sarah was "young" enough again, not only to have a child, but to nurse him (verse 7); Abraham was "young" enough again not only to father Isaac, but also six other sons of his wife Keturah, after Sarah died (Genesis 25:2)! When God miraculously heals, it is not a partial healing, but a complete and instant restoration.

The name chosen for their son of promise was an unusual name, Isaac, meaning "laughter." It was an appropriate name, however, for every time they would speak his name, they would remember how they had laughed at God's promise (Genesis 17:17; 18:12), a laugh of amazement in Abraham's case, and of doubt in Sarah's case. They would also remember the great joy they shared when Isaac was finally born (verse 6).

When Isaac was eight days old, Abraham circumcised him, as God had long ago commanded (Genesis 17:12), making sure that Isaac was under the terms of God's covenant. It is doubtful that ever a son was born who was more loved than Isaac. His father and mother carefully taught him in the ways of righteousness (Genesis 18:19), and, no doubt, rehearsed over and over again all the great promises of God that centered in him. So far as the record goes, Isaac was an intelligent, handsome, and obedient son, fulfilling in every way his parents' hopes and dreams.

Sarah nursed him, in accordance with the custom of the times, until probably two or three years of age. The day of his weaning was marked by a great feast, also in accord with custom. To the feast were probably invited not only all of Abraham's considerable retinue of servants, but also many of the people of the land. Abraham was still dwelling in the land of the Philistines (Genesis 21:34), who had already been made painfully aware of the power of God. Now, however, they could share with Abraham the knowledge of the fulfilled promises of God.

Genesis 21:9-21

---

9 ¶ And Sarah saw the son of Hā′gàr the Egyptian, which she had borne unto Abraham, mocking.

10 Wherefore she said unto Abraham, Cast out this bondwoman and her son: for the son of this bondwoman shall not be heir with my son, *even* with Isaac.

11 And the thing was very grievous in Abraham's sight because of his son.

12 ¶ And God said unto Abraham, Let it not be grievous in thy sight because of the lad, and because of thy bondwoman; in all that Sarah hath said unto thee, hearken unto her voice; for in Isaac shall thy seed be called.

13 And also of the son of the bondwoman will I make a nation, because he *is* thy seed.

14 And Abraham rose up early in the morning, and took bread, and a bottle of water, and gave *it* unto Hā′gàr, putting *it* on her shoulder, and the child, and sent her away: and she departed, and wandered in the wilderness of Bē′ĕr–shē′bà.

15 And the water was spent in the

bottle, and she cast the child under one of the shrubs.

16 And she went, and sat her down over against *him* a good way off, as it were a bowshot: for she said, Let me not see the death of the child. And she sat over against *him*, and lifted up her voice, and wept.

17 And God heard the voice of the lad; and the angel of God called to Hā′gắr out of heaven, and said unto her, What aileth thee, Hā′gắr? fear not; for God hath heard the voice of the lad where he *is*.

18 Arise, lift up the lad, and hold him in thine hand; for I will make him a great nation.

19 And God opened her eyes, and she saw a well of water; and she went, and filled the bottle with water, and gave the lad drink.

20 And God was with the lad; and he grew, and dwelt in the wilderness, and became an archer.

21 And he dwelt in the wilderness of Pā′răn: and his mother took him a wife out of the land of Egypt.

Almost forgotten, apparently, were Hagar and Ishmael. Ishmael was now about sixteen years old (Genesis 16:16; 21:5), and for a long time had been an only son. It was neither his fault nor his mother's that his birth had been a sort of accident, contrived due to a temporary lapse of faith on the part of Abraham and Sarah; so it is easy to understand his resentment at the unusual attention devoted to Isaac. God had also promised his mother and father that *he* would be blessed (Genesis 16:12; 17:20). Even though it was not right, it at least is understandable that he would make fun of his little half-brother, especially on the day of the great feast, where so much attention was being showered on him.

Sarah, however, could not endure his mocking. She had resented Ishmael and Hagar ever since Abraham had gone in to Hagar, even though it was at her own insistence that he do so. She could see that the rivalry between Ishmael and Isaac could only grow worse as time went on, since only Isaac was destined to share in the covenant promises and his father's inheritance. No doubt this was a weakness in Sarah's character. Though she had attained a strong faith in God, she was still human, and could simply not bring herself to love and care for Ishmael as she would her own son. Accordingly, she began to pressure Abraham to send them away. She called Hagar "this bondwoman" and Ishmael "the son of this bondwoman," harsh words for her personal maid of over twenty years and for a loved son of her own husband. She insisted that Ishmael not be allowed to share in Abraham's inheritance, all of it going only to *"my* son, Isaac."

Abraham was a kind and generous man, as well as a loving father. He had even interceded on one very important occasion with God on behalf of Ishmael (Genesis 17:18). Sarah's attitude was a source of grief to him, and it was creating a real problem in the home. He simply did not know how to work it out.

Again, however, God spoke to Abraham. Though Sarah's attitude was wrong in one way, she really was acting in consistency with God's own promises and plans. It really was *not* possible for the two families to exist together, and Abraham should follow Sarah's request, even though it would go against his own personal feelings and would no doubt seem harsh to others around them. Sometimes it is necessary for God's people, if they are truly going to be in the will of God and to enjoy the fulness of His blessing, to separate completely from those who might be a source of friction and carnality, even though such separation will be difficult and will give others (who don't understand the spiritual issues involved) occasion to criticize and ridicule.

God, therefore, instructed Abraham to send Hagar and Ishmael away. Isaac was the son of promise, and He had never intended Ishmael to share in these promises in any way. Nevertheless, He assured Abraham that He would take care of Ishmael. He need not fear that Ishmael and Hagar would die if not cared for in Abraham's home. To the contrary, Ishmael would live and also become a nation.

This conflict between Sarah and Hagar, between Isaac and Ishmael, has been appropriated in the New Testament as an illustration (Paul calls it an allegory) of the continuing conflict between law and grace, between the flesh and the spirit. In Galatians 4:22-31, the apostle Paul develops this contrast at considerable length. Those who are born after the flesh, he says, are the spiritual descendants of Hagar, great in number but nevertheless under the Law, and they seek salvation through the impossible task of making sinful flesh keep the Law of God. The Law speaks of the Mosaic covenant, a conditional covenant, given on Mount Sinai in Arabia (where Ishmael dwelt), and centered in the earthly Jerusalem.

Those who are to share in God's heavenly promises, however, centered in the heavenly Jerusalem (now being prepared by Christ and destined some day to come down out of heaven to the new earth), are the children of faith, like Isaac. The Law can never give life; but God's promise, received by faith, does give eternal life. These children of faith are not in bondage to the Mosaic covenant, whose terms are impossible to obey, but are under the Abrahamic covenant, given unconditionally and appropriated solely by faith in the promises. Though those after the flesh ridicule and persecute those after the spirit, it is the latter who will ultimately receive the blessing. They are *free,* not in bondage, as Sarah was a freewoman and Hagar a bondwoman. There must be a separation between those who are in bondage and those who are free in Christ.

The next morning after God spoke to him, therefore, Abraham sent Hagar and Ishmael away, with bread and a bottle of water. In view of Abraham's wealth, this might seem a niggardly arrangement, and we can only surmise that Abraham knew with certainty that God, as He had promised, would take care of them. He realized that, apart from God, no matter how much he gave them, it would not be enough; but *with* God, they could not lack. Quite possibly, he knew it would be for their own good if they would quickly learn they must depend on God, and no longer on Abraham, to supply their needs. However, the food and drink was no doubt enough to enable them to reach another settlement at least, had they not become lost en route.

Archaeology has revealed that there were numerous settlements at this time in the vicinity of what later was known as Beersheba, and it seems that Hagar and Ishmael set out in this direction. However, they lost their way. After wandering for some time, the water was exhausted, and soon Ishmael was at the point of death. Either Hagar was more accustomed to desert life than he or else, possibly, he had given most of the water to his mother. He finally fell down, unable to continue, and Hagar moved him under a shrub to give him a little shade from the heat. Unable to help him further, and not wanting to see him die, she went a "bowshot" away, sat down, and began to weep and pray. Ishmael apparently also was praying. God had allowed them to come to the point where they could no longer endure in their own strength and would have to depend on Him. And that, apparently, was His purpose all along—that they, like Abraham, might learn to trust Him.

God heard them, and the "angel of God" (the same divine personage, undoubtedly the preincarnate Christ, who had come to Hagar's help once before in the desert, before Ishmael was born) called to her out of heaven. He assured Hagar He had heard their prayers and that, as He had promised long ago, He would take care of them and make Ishmael a great nation.

It is more than coincidental that, in Genesis 16:7, this divine being is called "the angel of Jehovah." Here he is called "the angel of Elohim." The reason for the change is that Jehovah is God's covenant name, and Hagar was in the first instance still under the roof and protection of Abraham. Now, however, she has become a "stranger to the covenant of promise," and therefore the name of God which is used is the name associated with creation and power, rather than redemption.

God is the God of all men, however, whether or not they are embraced in His particular covenant with Abraham, and He was graciously concerned with Ishmael and his mother. He provided water for them immediately, from a well which He had either just created or which, if it already was there, they had been unable before to see. Then, apparently rather than going on to an uncertain reception in an unknown town, they decided to remain where God had met with them and promised to care for them, there in the "wilderness of Paran," a desert region in what is now the Sinai peninsula. Hagar, in fact, became so identified with Mount Sinai that Paul could say "this Hagar is Mount Sinai in Arabia" (Galatians 4:25).

Ishmael provided for himself and his mother by becoming an archer. Eventually, he married a wife, obtained by his mother for him from her people back in the land of Egypt. According to Genesis 25:13-15, he finally had twelve sons, and thus the "great nation" God promised him had begun.

Genesis 21:22-34

22 ¶ And it came to pass at that time, that Ā-bǐm′ē-lĕch and Phi′chŏl the chief captain of his host spake unto Abraham, saying, God *is* with thee in all that thou doest:

23 Now therefore swear unto me here by God, that thou wilt not deal falsely with me, nor with my son, nor with my son's son: *but* according to the kindness that I have done unto thee, thou shalt do unto me, and to the land wherein thou hast sojourned.

24 And Abraham said, I will swear.

25 And Abraham reproved Ā-bǐm′ē-lĕch because of a well of water, which Ā-bǐm′ē-lĕch's servants had violently taken away.

26 And Ā-bǐm′ē-lĕch said, I wot not who hath done this thing: neither didst thou tell me, neither yet heard I *of it,* but to-day.

27 And Abraham took sheep and oxen, and gave them unto Ā-bǐm′ē-lĕch; and both of them made a covenant.

28 And Abraham set seven ewe lambs of the flock by themselves.

29 And Ā-bǐm′ē-lĕch said unto Abraham, What *mean* these seven ewe lambs which thou hast set by themselves?

30 And he said, For *these* seven ewe lambs shalt thou take of my hand, that they may be a witness unto me, that I have digged this well.

31 Wherefore he called that place Bē′ĕr-shē′bà; because there they sware both of them.

32 Thus they made a covenant at Bē′ĕr-shē′bà: then Ā-bǐm′ē-lĕch rose up, and Phi′chŏl the chief captain of his host, and they returned into the land of the Phǐ-lǐs′tǐnĕs.

33 ¶ And *Abraham* planted a grove in Bē′ĕr-shē′bà, and called there on the name of the LORD, the everlasting God.

34 And Abraham sojourned in the Phǐ-lǐs′tǐnĕş' land many days.

The last portion of chapter 21 records an incident between Abraham and Abimelech, presumably the same king whom Abraham had encountered before in Gerar. Abimelech, well aware of God's blessing on Abraham, wished to enter into a nonaggression pact with him. Taking his army chief of staff with him, he reminded Abraham that he had dealt kindly with him and had allowed him to dwell in his land. In return, he wanted Abraham to promise that he would not try to injure him or his people.

Abraham was quite willing to make such a treaty. However, one bone of contention had developed, and Abraham used this occasion as the means to get that problem cleared up. Abraham had dug a well at Beersheba and, although Beersheba was not in the country of Abimelech, some of Abimelech's servants had raided the area and had captured the well from Abraham's servants. The foray had not been known to Abimelech and he quickly agreed to return the well to Abraham. In return, Abraham gave sheep and oxen to Abimelech, thus giving him back at least a portion of the gift Abimelech had pressed on him earlier (Genesis 20:14). Also, Abraham selected seven ewe lambs, and indicated to Abimelech that these (the number seven representing completeness, sealing the covenant, and symbolizing Abraham's permanent right to the well) were to be a special witness. Both men agreed fully to the treaty, and the place was therefore named Beersheba, which can mean both "well of the oath" and "well of the seven."

Abimelech and his captain then returned to their own country. Before going back to his own home in the Philistines' land, however, Abraham planted a grove of trees (probably tamarisk trees) near the well, and there called on the name of "Jehovah, El-Olam," meaning "Jehovah is the eternal God." Though he had made a covenant with an earthly king, in order to avoid attack, he recognized that God Himself had made an eternal covenant with him, to give him and his seed all this land for ever. He would eventually come back to Beersheba to dwell (Genesis 22:19); but for the present he went back to the place where he had been living in the land of the Philistines, where he continued to live for many years, until, in fact, Isaac was a grown man.

Sacrifice of the Beloved

The next bit of chronological information we have is that Sarah died when she was 127 years old (Genesis 23:1). When Isaac was weaned, she was ninety-two or ninety-three. Thus, the events of the latter part of chapter 21 and all the events of chapter 22 occurred during the intervening period, giving all we know from Scripture of a period approximately thirty-five years in length. Since Genesis 21:34 mentions "many days" and Genesis 22:1 is introduced by the phrase "after these things," the inference at least is that the narrative of Genesis 22 took place many years after the birth of Isaac. Isaac was no longer a little child, but was certainly at least in his teens, and quite possibly twenty-five or thirty years old. He was thirty-seven when his mother died. While it is true that he is called a "lad" (verses 5, 12), the Hebrew word (*naar*) is very flexible in meaning. Most frequently it is translated either as "servant" or as "young man." In fact, the same word is used here in Genesis 22:5 in connection with the "young men" that went with Abraham and Isaac. Since exactly the same word is used, in the same verse, for the two servants and for Isaac, it is clear that the meaning in Isaac's case should also be "young man."

Evidently the intervening years had been happy ones. Isaac was growing and in every way was a joy to Abraham and Sarah. He had been worth waiting for, an heir deserving both of Abraham's patriarchal responsibilities and of God's covenant promises. They no doubt rejoiced and praised God daily for the abundance of His blessings.

Genesis 22:1, 2

CHAPTER 22

AND it came to pass after these things, that God did tempt Abraham, and said unto him, Abraham: and he said, Behold, *here* I *am*.

2 And he said, Take now thy son, thine only *son* Isaac, whom thou lovest, and get thee into the land of Mō-rī′áh; and offer him there for a burnt offering upon one of the mountains which I will tell thee of.

Then, suddenly, the blow fell! Abraham had not heard from God directly for many long years. He seemed to have become silent. Nevertheless, Abraham continued to love and trust Him, knowing that He had wonderfully kept His promises.

But when God broke His silence, He did not speak as He had done in former days. Instead, He seemed to speak in judgment and even cruelty. It seemed as though every word was calculated to hurt Abraham as deeply as possible. "Abraham," He said, "I want you to take your son, your only son, Isaac, your beloved son." Each word was like a knife sinking deeper and deeper. "Take him, Abraham, and travel with him for three days into the land of Moriah, to a certain mountain there. Then, when you are there, you are to offer up Isaac on the mountain as a sacrifice, as an offering made by fire to the Lord."

"But, Lord," Abraham may have thought, "that doesn't sound like you. You promised to make of Isaac a great nation, and he is not yet even married! True, the gods of the nations around us are sometimes worshiped by the sacrifice of sons and daughters [a fact abundantly verified by archaeological research], and I certainly love you as much as these people love their own false gods; but this type of thing surely is not pleasing to you. What will happen to all your promises if you make me do this thing? And what about Sarah? Why, this will literally bring her down to the grave with grief!"

Whether Abraham actually thought such things or not, Scripture does not say. All we are told is that he obeyed God, with no questions asked.

Now, of course, God did not really intend that Abraham should slay Isaac. As a matter of fact, God's words were simply to "offer" Isaac for an offering; nothing was said about slaying him, though this is naturally the connotation that Abraham would have to place on the words. Likewise, we are commanded to present our own bodies as *living* sacrifices to God (Romans 12:1), dead to the things of the world, and alive and dedicated wholly to the service of Christ.

Perhaps Abraham and Sarah had come to love Isaac *too* much. There was a danger they might forget God by too much attention to God's promises. God did not want Isaac slain, but He did want Abraham's full love. Therefore, "God did test Abraham."

This is the first occurrence in the Bible of the word translated "tempt" (Hebrew *nasah*). It does not, of course, mean "tempt to do evil" (note James 1:13). It means "test" or "try" and, in fact, most of the time is translated "prove." Jesus, for example, was "tempted," but this does not mean He could have sinned. Rather, He was "proved," or "approved," so everyone could see that, in spite of the greatest tests to which He could conceivably be subjected, He would stand spotless and blameless. The engineer may know full well that his design will stand the stress and strain to which it is subjected, because he knows it has been designed properly. Nevertheless, the construction specifications will require that it be tested—not to assure the engineer, but to assure the public, that it will stand.

So it was with Abraham. God knew what Abraham would do; but Abraham and Sarah, and all around them must know, that the Lord Himself meant more to Abraham than even Isaac did.

Another word is mentioned in these verses for the first time, and this in many ways is the most important word in the Bible. It is the word "love." Love is the greatest of the gifts (I Corinthians 13:13) and, indeed, God Himself *is* love (I John 4:8). We have frequently in these pages referred to the "principle of first mention," pointing out that, when an important word or concept occurs for the first time in the Bible, usually in the Book of Genesis, the context in which it occurs sets the pattern for its primary usage and development all through the rest of Scripture. If this principle really means anything (and, in terms both of the doctrine of verbal inspiration and of numerous clear examples, it assuredly does), then it should certainly apply in a distinctive way to the word "love."

With this in mind, it does seem strange, at first, that "love" is first mentioned, not in connection with the love of a man for his wife, of a mother for her children, of brotherly love, of love for country, or even of man's love for God. Instead, it is used of the love of a father for his son. "Thy son, whom thou lovest." Furthermore, it is used in connection with the sacrificial offering of that only, and beloved, son. The deep love of a father for his only son (yet a father who is willing to slay him) is thus inferred to be representative of the most complete and meaningful concept of the very word "love" itself.

This might seem enigmatic until it is realized that in Abraham and Isaac God is giving us a beautiful picture of God the Father and God the Son. That Isaac is a type of Christ is confirmed by Galatians 3:16, and that the experience of Abraham and Isaac on Mount Moriah is a type of the offering of Christ on Mount Calvary is confirmed by the terminology in Hebrews 11:17-19. Although excessive typological interpretations in Genesis are to be avoided, in this case there is clear Scriptural warrant for such an interpretation.

This first mention of "love" in Scripture, therefore, calls attention to the fact that the love of a godly father for his only son is a miniature picture of the love existing among the persons of the Holy Trinity, and in particular the love of the Father for the Son. This love, of course, existed long before the world was created, from eternity past. Therefore, this love must be the root and foundation of all other types of love. The love of man and woman, the love of mother for child—indeed all love—has its source in God's love.

Jesus, in His incarnation, referred to this primeval heavenly love: "Father, I will that they also, whom thou hast given me, be with me where I am; that they may behold my glory, which thou hast given me: for thou lovedst me before the foundation of the world" (John 17:24).

And now we note a most remarkable and beautiful evidence of divine planning in the very structure of Scripture. The first mention of "love" in the Old Testament is this record of the love of an earthly father for his only son, a love which was to suffer the most intense anguish of soul because he would have to offer up that beloved son as a burnt offering. This, however, is recognized as a type of God the Father sacrificing His only-begotten and much-beloved Son.

If the Old Testament presents the type, the New Testament portrays the antitype, or prototype. There are, of course, four "portraits" of Christ in the New Testament. Three of these—Matthew, Mark, and Luke—are known as the "Synoptic Gospels." The Gospel of John stands essentially alone, picturing Christ especially as the Son of God, and emphasizing especially the love of God. Jesus is spoken of as the Son of God the Father as often in the Gospel of John as in all the other three Gospels combined. Similarly, the word "love" is used in the Gospel of John more than it is used in all the three other Gospels combined.

Now it is thrilling to see that the first occurrence of "love" in the New Testament is in the clearest possible expression of the love of God the Father for His Son. It is found in Matthew 3:17: "And lo a voice from heaven, saying, This is my beloved Son, in whom I am well pleased."

But that is not all! The first occurrence of "love" in Mark's Gospel is in Mark 1:11: "And there came a voice from heaven, saying, Thou art my beloved Son, in whom I am well pleased." Similarly, the first occurrence of "love" in Luke is likewise at the baptism of Jesus: "And the Holy Ghost descended in a bodily shape like a dove upon him, and a voice from heaven, which said, Thou art my beloved Son; in thee I am well pleased" (Luke 3:22).

Thus, three times over, as it were, as we enter the New Testament to learn of the love of God in its fulness, we are introduced to it by the great voice from heaven acclaiming Jesus as His beloved Son. If Abraham loved his son, how much greater is God's love for *His* Son!

But now, as we look into the Gospel of God's love and God's Son, the record of the "beloved disciple" John, we are silenced in awe when we come to read the first verse in John containing "love." What is the verse? Why, what else could it be?

> For God so loved the world, that he gave his only begotten Son, that whosoever believeth in him should not perish, but have everlasting life (John 3:16).

Three times God shouts His love for His Son from the very heavens. But then, He tells us that He loved *us* (yes, *us*!) so much that He was willing to sacrifice His only and beloved Son, in order that we might be saved. This is far beyond our understanding, of course. We can only believe and rejoice and give thanks. "In this was manifested the love of God toward us, because that God sent his only begotten Son into the world that we might live through him. Herein is love, not that we loved God, but that he loved us, and sent his Son to be the propitiation for our sins. Beloved, if God so loved us, we ought also to love one another" (I John 4:9-11).

Genesis 22:3-8

---

3 ¶ And Abraham rose up early in the morning, and saddled his ass, and took two of his young men with him, and Isaac his son, and clave the wood for the burnt offering, and rose up, and went unto the place of which God had told him.

4 Then on the third day Abraham lifted up his eyes, and saw the place afar off.

5 And Abraham said unto his young men, Abide ye here with the ass; and I and the lad will go yonder and worship, and come again to you.

6 And Abraham took the wood of the burnt offering, and laid *it* upon Isaac his son; and he took the fire in his hand, and a knife; and they went both of them together.

7 And Isaac spake unto Abraham his father, and said, My father: and he said, Here *am* I, my son. And he said, Behold the fire and the wood: but where *is* the lamb for a burnt offering?

8 And Abraham said, My son, God will provide himself a lamb for a burnt offering: so they went both of them together.

Whatever may have been the questions and protests in Abraham's heart, he obeyed God's commandment without any outward reluctance. Scripture stresses that he did not even delay; he arose early in the morning, taking Isaac and two servants, and departed for Moriah. He did not tell Isaac his intentions, and it is probable he did not tell Sarah. He knew what a shock it would be to her, and realized that this must be between himself and God. He also cut the wood with which to burn the offering, and carried it along as well, not knowing whether there would be any available at the destination, and not seeking any escape at all from the task he had to do.

Because of his age, Abraham rode on an ass. Evidently the two young men carried the wood, and perhaps food and water for the journey. Isaac and the other two young men walked. The journey took them two full days and part of the third. Moriah was near Jerusalem (that is, where Jerusalem would be) and Abraham's home was in the south, evidently not too far from Beersheba. The total distance was thus about thirty miles.

Why would God tell Abraham to go so far, and to just this spot? There is no explanation in the text; but there must have been a reason, since God is not capricious. The answer can only be that God knew this would be the place where later His temple would be built (II Chronicles 3:1). Abraham's sacrifice of Isaac was to foreshadow all the sacrifices that would later be offered in this place, which in turn were types and shadows of the one great Sacrifice that would be offered one day nearby, when the Father would offer the Son as the Savior of the world.

As the mountain came in view on the third day, Abraham realized that the rest of the way must be traveled by himself and his son alone. He got off the ass, left it with the young men, put the wood on Isaac's strong back, took the fire which the young men had apparently carried all the way from their home, and then he and Isaac walked side by side toward the place of sacrifice.

No doubt the two servants hesitated, and wanted to go with them. Abraham replied that he and Isaac were going to worship (thus satisfying them that this was somehow a private matter between father and son), and then would return to them.

This promise of Abraham speaks volumes. He was not lying to the men; he really believed that both he and Isaac would return. Even though God had, as he thought, told him to slay Isaac, and even though he fully intended to obey, yet he knew they would both come back. He had learned beyond any further question that God's word was true and His promises sure. God had told him that Isaac would become a great nation, in whom all other nations would be blessed, and this could not come to pass with Isaac dead. Therefore, Isaac must live! Abraham had learned to trust God so fully that he believed He could even raise the dead. As the writer of Hebrews said: "By faith Abraham, when he was tried, offered up Isaac: and he that had received the promises offered up his only begotten son, Of whom it was said, that in Isaac shall thy seed be called: Accounting that God was able to raise him up, even from the dead; from whence also he received him in a figure" (Hebrews 11:17-19).

In a figure (or "type") Abraham's only-begotten son was raised from the dead. The antitype can, of course, be nothing else than the resurrection of Jesus, the Son of God, from the dead, after He offered Himself up to the Father as a sacrifice for the sins of the world.

But what about Abraham's statement that he and Isaac were going to worship? Could such an act as killing his own son be considered worshiping? Yes, this was a supreme act of worship. The word "worship," as we have noted earlier, means simply "bow down," and is often so translated. Singing hymns and giving testimonies, hearing a preacher and enjoying Christian fellowship is not worshiping, although we speak of such activities as a "worship service." To worship God is simply to bow down to His will, recognizing and acknowledging that His will is best. What He does is right, by definition, whether we understand it now or not. His will may involve waiting and suffering, even dying; but if it is His will, then we must bow down to it and accept it with thanksgiving. It is then, and only then, that we *worship* God. Abraham and Isaac indeed *were* going to worship God. Not understanding, but believing, they were willing to do His will. Somehow they knew that even such a command as this, in the eternal counsels of God, was for their good.

This submission to God's will in an ultimate act of worship pictures beautifully the work of Christ. "Father, if it be possible, let this cup pass from me," He had prayed; "nevertheless not as I will, but as thou wilt" (Matthew 26:39). "Though he were a Son, yet learned he obedience by the things which he suffered" (Hebrews 5:8).

It is remarkable that, in the New Testament, we never read of Jesus worshiping God, though He taught others to do so. Though He, of course, claimed to be the Son of God, it seems that His favorite designation of Himself was as the "Son of Man," a term which He used eighty times. The first such time was when He said: "The foxes have holes, and the birds of the air have nests; but the Son of man hath not where to lay his head" (Matthew 8:20). The word translated "lay his head" is the same in the Greek as "bow his head." He had no place to worship, in other words.

But He had left heaven itself for the very purpose of doing the will of the Father. "Wherefore when he cometh into the world, he saith, Sacrifice and offering thou wouldst not, but a body hast thou prepared me. . . . Then said I, Lo, I come (in the volume of the book it is written of me,) to do thy will, O God. . . . By the which will we are sanctified through the offering of the body of Jesus Christ once for all" (Hebrews 10:5, 7, 10). "And being found in fashion as a man, he humbled himself, and became obedient unto death, even the death of the cross" (Philippians 2:8).

As He took a long journey from His home and the Father (though, as He said, "He that sent me is with me: the Father hath not left me alone"—John 8:29), He eventually arrived at the cross. There, on the cross, He finally found a place to lay His head. He cried out, "It is finished: and he bowed his head, and gave up the ghost" (John 19:30). At the last, He did have a place to lay His head—to bow His head—to worship God. He had submitted perfectly and completed fully the will of the Father.

As Abraham and Isaac walked alone toward the mountain, Scripture records the fact that "they went both of them together" (verses 6, 8). The two men could accompany them to within sight of Mount Moriah, but they could not go all the way, just as the two men accompanied Christ to the place of death, even dying on crosses of their own. But they could not join Him in the awful experience of hell itself, separation from the presence of the Father as He was "made sin, who knew no sin" (II Corinthians 5:21).

The double record of their fellowship in the approach toward the place of sacrifice must be intentional. The writer would have us know beyond question that Abraham was not compelling his son to go; instead, Isaac willingly accompanied his father. We must remember that Isaac was a grown man, no doubt much stronger than his father, and could easily have escaped had he wished. He certainly could have guessed his father's intentions; he was well aware of the human sacrifices practiced by the pagan tribes of the area. He knew they were going to offer a burnt offering because they had wood and fire and a knife, but there was no lamb. "Where is the lamb?" he asked. "God will himself provide the lamb," his father said. "So they went both of them together."

God did not force His Son to die on the cross. "Therefore doth my Father love me, because I lay down my life, that I might take it again. No man taketh it from me, but I lay it down of myself. I have power to lay it down, and I have power to take it again. This commandment have I received of my Father" (John 10:17, 18). It was the Father's will, and the Son willingly obeyed. And, because they went both of them together, lost sinners can be forgiven and receive everlasting life.

Genesis 22:9-14

9 And they came to the place which God had told him of; and Abraham built an altar there, and laid the wood in order, and bound Isaac his son, and laid him on the altar upon the wood.
10 And Abraham stretched forth his hand, and took the knife to slay his son.
11 And the Angel of the LORD called unto him out of heaven, and said, Abraham, Abraham: and he said, Here *am* I.
12 And he said, Lay not thine hand upon the lad, neither do thou any thing unto him: for now I know that thou fearest God, seeing thou hast not withheld thy son, thine only *son*, from me.
13 And Abraham lifted up his eyes, and looked, and behold behind *him* a ram caught in a thicket by his horns: and Abraham went and took the ram, and offered him up for a burnt offering in the stead of his son.
14 And Abraham called the name of that place Jehovah-ji'rĕh: as it is said *to* this day, In the mount of the LORD it shall be seen.

Finally they came to the place. For three days they had been coming, and those three days must have been agony for them. Both father and son were fully set to do God's will, from the moment they started out. Thus, for all practical purposes, Isaac had been dead three days. The three days of apparent death obviously correspond to the three days during which Christ was actually dead. The wood was on Isaac's back; Christ's back was bound against the wood of the cross. "Where is the lamb for the burnt offering?" The answer echoes back across the centuries: "Behold the Lamb of God, which taketh away the sin of the world" (John 1:29).

Abraham built an altar there on Mount Moriah. He had built altars before—at Sichem, at Bethel, at Hebron, at Beersheba—but none of these would do. For the true sacrifice, not of an animal but of his only son, the altar must be on Mount Moriah. There is no substitute for Calvary, where the Lamb of God must be offered up in sacrifice for the salvation of a lost world.

If Isaac had had the least doubts before about his father's intentions, they were all removed now, as his father bound him and laid him on the altar on the wood. As he gazed up into his father's eyes, no doubt flowing full with tears, he saw the uplifted knife in his hand.

Never was such a loving father or obedient son put to such a test as this. Abraham obeyed God, because he believed God. "Was not Abraham our father justified by works, when he had offered Isaac his son upon the altar? Seest thou how faith wrought with his works, and by works was faith made perfect? And the Scripture was fulfilled which saith, Abraham believed God, and it was imputed unto him for righteousness: and he was called the Friend of God. Ye see then how that by works a man is justified, and not by faith only" (James 2:21-24). He had received righteousness imputed by faith, but that faith was tested by works. "God did test Abraham," and Abraham passed the test.

As the knife was about to descend, the angel of Jehovah called him and told him not to harm his son. Abraham had demonstrated that he believed God, and loved God, and trusted God so much that he would not withhold even his only son from Him. "He that spared not his own Son, but delivered him up for us all, how shall he not with him also freely give us all things?" (Romans 8:32).

Note that the "angel of the Lord" commended Abraham because "thou hast not withheld thy son, thine only son, from me" (verse 12). It is evident here that this "angel of the Lord" is claiming to be none other than the Lord Himself.

"God will provide himself a lamb," Abraham had told Isaac. And now God did exactly that, except that it was a ram, rather than a lamb. The complete fulfillment must await the true Lamb, the Lamb of God. The ram was offered up on the altar as a burnt offering in substitution for his son, thus adding the teaching of substitutionary sacrifice to the type.

Abraham named the location Jehovah-jireh, which means "the Lord will provide," or, alternatively, "the Lord will appear." There is a difference of opinion among Hebrew scholars on this particular translation, the issue turning on certain vowel points. Perhaps both meanings are appropriate, with the former probably being preferable if a choice must be made. Apparently Moses made an editorial insertion here, calling attention to the fact that, even in his day, men still pointed to that mountain, saying that "in the mountain of the Lord, provision will be made," a wonderful prophecy of faith that, in the fulness of time, God would provide the Lamb to die for man's sins, just as He had provided a ram to take Isaac's place on the altar.

Sand and Stars

After Abraham had completed the work of offering the ram on the altar as a burnt offering, the angel of the Lord spoke to him again from heaven. God had given him his final examination, as it were, and Abraham had passed the test perfectly. There was no longer any question that he and his seed would be qualified to serve as God's channel of blessing for mankind; therefore God was ready to fully implement His great plan through them. As far as the record goes, this is the last time God would speak personally to Abraham, so He summed up all His previous promises and enlarged on them.

Genesis 22:15-19

---

15 ¶ And the Angel of the LORD called unto Abraham out of heaven the second time,

16 And said, By myself have I sworn, saith the LORD, for because thou hast done this thing, and hast not withheld thy son, thine only *son,*

17 That in blessing I will bless thee, and in multiplying I will multiply thy seed as the stars of the heaven, and as the sand which *is* upon the seashore; and thy seed shall possess the gate of his enemies;

18 And in thy seed shall all the nations of the earth be blessed; because thou hast obeyed my voice.

19 So Abraham returned unto his young men, and they rose up and went together to Bē'ĕr–shē'bà; and Abraham dwelt at Bē'ĕr–shē'bà.

To emphasize as strongly as possible that His word would be accomplished, God made an oath to Abraham, swearing by His own name. "For when God made promise to Abraham, because he could swear by no greater, he swore by himself, Saying, Surely blessing I will bless thee, and multiplying I will multiply thee. And so, after he had patiently endured, he obtained the promise. For men verily swear by the greater: and an oath for confirmation is to them an end of all strife. Wherein God, willing more abundantly to shew unto the heirs of promise the immutability of his counsel, confirmed it by an oath: That by two immutable things, in which it was impossible for God to lie, we might have a strong consolation, who have fled for refuge to lay hold upon the hope set before us" (Hebrews 6:13-18).

Jesus said: "He that loveth son or daughter more than me is not worthy of me" (Matthew 10:37). God told Abraham: "Because thou hast done this thing, and hast not withheld thy son, thine only son," therefore He would: (1) bless Abraham himself abundantly; (2) make his descendants as innumerable as the stars of heaven or as the sand by the sea; (3) cause his descendants to prevail against their enemies; (4) cause all other nations of the earth likewise to be blessed in Abraham's seed. All of these blessings were promised to Abraham because "thou hast obeyed my voice." This is the first occurrence of the word "obey" in the Bible, and it stresses that obedience belongs to God first of all, and that obedience to God results in rich blessing.

Three times in this promise, God used the word "seed." At that time, Abraham had only one seed, Isaac, but that seed was to be multiplied and to bring blessing to all. Nevertheless, the fact that God stressed the word in the singular, rather than plural, was significant in that it would be through the Abrahamic nation that the world's Savior would one day come. "Now to Abraham and his seed were the promises made. He saith not, And to seeds, as of many; but as of one, And to thy seed, which is Christ" (Galatians 3:16). And, surely, rich blessings have indeed come through Christ. "Blessed be the God and Father of our Lord Jesus Christ, who hath blessed us with all spiritual blessings in heavenly places in Christ" (Ephesians 1:3).

It is instructive to note God's comparison of Abraham's seed to the sand and to the stars. He had said once before (Genesis 15:5) that his seed would be as numerous as the stars of heaven. However, to the naked eye, one can only count approximately three thousand, at the most. Consequently, God's promise might not at first have seemed overly impressive, since three thousand descendants would not make a very large nation. Now, however, God says in effect that there are as many stars as there are grains of sand on the seashore. He had earlier told Abraham his seed would be "as the dust of the earth" in number (Genesis 13:16).

Abraham recognized that God was saying his descendants would be impossible to count, but it did sound as though He were making an "unscientific" comparison when He likened the stars to the sand. In our modern day of giant telescopes, however, we know that such a comparison is very appropriate. No one knows the exact number of the stars but it can be roughly estimated, for the observable universe at least, as approximately 10^{25}. Since there are approximately 10^{15} square feet of area on the earth's surface, and approximately 10 million grains of sand in a cubic foot of sand, if we assume that there is an average of 1,000 feet of unconsolidated sediments around the surface of the earth (probably deeper than this on the ocean bottom, but shallower on the land surfaces), then the number of sand-sized particles would also be calculated as 10^{25}. Although such a calculation may well be considerably in error, it at least shows that the stars and the sand are of about the same order of magnitude in number. This fact could not have been discovered by men without the telescope; so it constitutes one of the many remarkable examples of modern scientific truth found in the pages of the Bible long before scientists could have learned them by the scientific method.

After their "mountain-top experience," Abraham and Isaac returned to the young men, as he had promised, and headed back home. At this time they went to Beersheba, where Abraham from that time on made his home, where he had last "called on the name of the Lord."

Genesis 22:20-24

---

20 ¶ And it came to pass after these things, that it was told Abraham, saying, Behold, Mĭl′cȧh, she hath also borne children unto thy brother Nā′hŏr;
21 Huz his firstborn, and Bŭz his brother, and Kĕm′ū-ĕl the father of Ā′rȧm,
22 And €hē′sĕd, and Hā′zō, and Pĭl′-dȧsh, and Jĭd′lȧph, and Bē-thū′ĕl.
23 And Bē-thū′ĕl begat Rē-bĕk′ȧh: these eight Mĭl′cȧh did bear to Nā′hŏr, Abraham's brother.
24 And his concubine, whose name was Reṳ′mȧh, she bare also Tē′bȧh, and Gā′hȧm, and Thā′hȧsh, and Mā′ȧ-ehȧh.

This section represents a sort of parenthesis in the narrative, showing that Abraham and Sarah had not lost all ties with their original home. Abraham's brother Nahor still lived back in Mesopotamia, possibly in the city known as Nahor, and he had not seen him, so far as we know, for sixty years or so. He and Sarah doubtless frequently wondered what had happened to him. His other brother, Haran, had died while they all still lived in Ur.

Abraham often must have wondered where he could find a wife for his son. If Isaac was to be the father of the great nation as promised, the choice of a proper wife was all-important. There seemed to be no candidate among their neighbors, the Amorites and Hittites, and Abraham longed for Isaac to have a bride from his own people. He may even have sent back for information from home about them. More likely, a traveling caravan providentially brought them such information. In any case, "it was told Abraham" one day about the family of his brother Nahor. Nahor had married his niece, a girl named Milcah, and he also had a concubine named Reumah. Milcah had had eight sons and Reumah four. Probably they also had daughters whose names are not mentioned.

Isaac, however, having been born so late in Abraham's life, was more the age of Nahor's grandchildren than of his own cousins. The grandchildren of Nahor may have been very numerous, but only two are mentioned: Aram, son of Kemuel, and Rebekah, the daughter of Nahor's youngest son, Bethuel. The reason Rebekah is mentioned in the narrative (which is a part of "the generations of Isaac," it will be remembered) is of course that she was later to be the one chosen as Isaac's wife.

For the record, Isaac did inscribe the names of the twelve sons of Nahor. Nothing else is known about them, unless Huz is identical with Uz, in whose land Job lived (Job 1:1). Also Buz conceivably could have been an ancestor of Job's friend Elihu (Job 32:2), and Aram could have been the ancestor of the Aramaeans. It is more likely, however, that these men themselves had been named after their ancestral kin. Aram is named as a son of Shem, and Uz as a son of Aram (Genesis 10:22, 23), and it is much more likely that these are the names referred to in Job. Other indications in the Book of Job seem to indicate that Job lived even earlier than Abraham.

The Death of Sarah

After the traumatic experience on Mount Moriah, very little is reported concerning the life of Abraham, and nothing more about Sarah, until her death. As noted before, Isaac was thirty-seven years old when Sarah died, but we are not told how old he was when he and his father took the journey to the mountain; consequently, there is no knowledge of how much time elapsed after that before Sarah's death. Some have suggested that the experience was such a shock to her system that she died soon afterward. This is only supposition, and is unlikely. Sarah was a woman of strong faith at this time and, even if she had known what was happening, she would most likely have reacted in much the same way as her husband.

Genesis 23:1, 2

CHAPTER 23

AND Sarah was a hundred and seven and twenty years old: *these were* the years of the life of Sarah.

2 And Sarah died in Kĭr'jăth-är'bá; the same *is* Hē'brŏn in the land of Cā́năan: and Abraham came to mourn for Sarah, and to weep for her.

By the time of Sarah's death, the family had apparently moved from Beersheba back to Hebron, which was also known as Kirjath-Arba (the "city of Arba," the father of the Anakims), where they had lived many years earlier.

Sarah died in Hebron, still in Canaan, the land to which they had migrated, and she died without seeing the fulfillment of the promises (Hebrews 11:13), although she had seen the fulfillment of God's promise that she would have a son. Sarah died at the age of 127, there in Hebron, and it is significant that she is the only woman in all Scripture whose age at the time of death is given. By any reckoning, she is one of the outstanding women in the Bible. Peter's reference to her (I Peter 3:5, 6) indicates that, as Abraham was considered father of those who believe, so Sarah was considered mother of all believing women. "For after this manner in the old time the holy women also, who trusted in God, adorned themselves, being in subjection to their own husbands: Even as Sarah obeyed Abraham, calling him lord: whose daughters ye are [or better, 'have become'], as long as ye do well, and are not afraid with any amazement [or, 'with hysterical fears']."

Evidently Abraham was not present at the time of her decease, because it says that he "came to mourn for Sarah, and to weep for her." Possibly this suggests that her death was mercifully quick and easy; if she had been suffering a terminal illness, it is almost certain Abraham would have been at home. He loved Sarah dearly, and it must have grieved him greatly that he was not with her when she died.

Genesis 23:3-9

---

3 ¶ And Abraham stood up from before his dead, and spake unto the sons of Heth, saying,

4 I *am* a stranger and a sojourner with you: give me a possession of a buryingplace with you, that I may bury my dead out of my sight.

5 And the children of Heth answered Abraham, saying unto him,

6 Hear us, my lord: thou *art* a mighty prince among us: in the choice of our sepulchres bury thy dead; none of us shall withhold from thee his sepulchre, but that thou mayest bury thy dead.

7 And Abraham stood up, and bowed himself to the people of the land, *even*

to the children of Heth.

8 And he communed with them, saying, If it be your mind that I should bury my dead out of my sight, hear me, and entreat for me to Ĕ′phrŏn the son of Zō′här,

9 That he may give me the cave of Măeh-pē′lăh, which he hath, which *is* in the end of his field; for as much money as it is worth he shall give it me for a possession of a buryingplace amongst you.

Sarah was the first in the patriarchal family line to die in the land of Canaan. Rather than taking her back to her homeland for burial, Abraham (and, no doubt, Sarah as well, for they had probably discussed this matter between themselves earlier) desired that she remain in Canaan, as a testimony to both the people of the land and their own descendants, that Canaan was to be their home from then on.

It is touching to note that, at least so far as the record goes, Abraham did not yet own any of the land himself, and so had to purchase hurriedly a plot of ground for a burying place. The only purchase of property he ever made in the land of Canaan was for a grave. The altars and wells which belonged to him were his by result of building them himself, and probably were on land which he was only using, or leasing. Though he had many possessions, he himself had no certain dwelling place. "By faith, he sojourned in the land of promise, as in a strange country, dwelling in tabernacles" (Hebrews 11:9). He lived in different places, presumably paying some form of rental for the land and pastures used.

But he would not have a rented grave! Although the Hittites offered to let him use one of their sepulchers, he must have one of his own. No doubt, he knew that it would also be used by subsequent generations of his family, because he truly believed this would be their land forever, as God had said. Although all the land was his, by divine promise, yet he graciously offered to purchase the plot he needed for Sarah's grave.

While still mourning beside Sarah's body, Abraham rose and set about the task of purchasing land for his sepulcher. He knew the plot he wanted—a field containing a suitable cave, with trees around it, and within sight of their home in Mamre (verse 17). It belonged to a prominent Hittite named Ephron. In accordance with the exaggerated formalities of purchasing and selling that have long been practiced in the East, Abraham first asked for someone to mediate between him and Ephron, to transmit his request to be allowed to purchase the land. Although it is difficult to distinguish how much of the Hittite response was sincere and how much mere custom, it does seem significant that they called Abraham "a mighty prince [literally 'prince of God'] among us" (verse 6).

Abraham himself was obviously sincere in his offer, as well as respectful and humble before the Hittites. He did not haggle, as they perhaps expected him to, nor would he accept their offer to let him use their sepulchers or to give him their land. Almost certainly, these offers were merely opening gestures of politeness which they expected no one to take seriously.

Twice the record says that "Abraham bowed down himself before the people of the land" (verses 7, 12). His manner of dealing with people of the world is surely a noble example for believers today to follow. An attitude of superiority, no less than an attitude of begging for worldly favors, is inappropriate in such relations.

Genesis 23:10-18

10 And E'phrŏn dwelt among the children of Heth: and E'phrŏn the Hĭt'tite answered Abraham in the audience of the children of Heth, *even* of all that went in at the gate of his city, saying,

11 Nay, my lord, hear me: the field give I thee, and the cave that *is* therein, I give it thee; in the presence of the sons of my people give I it thee: bury thy dead.

12 And Abraham bowed down himself before the people of the land.

13 And he spake unto E'phrŏn in the audience of the people of the land, saying, But if thou *wilt give it,* I pray thee, hear me: I will give thee money for the field; take *it* of me, and I will bury my dead there.

14 And E'phrŏn answered Abraham, saying unto him,

15 My lord, hearken unto me: the land *is worth* four hundred shekels of silver; what *is* that betwixt me and thee? bury therefore thy dead.

16 And Abraham hearkened unto E'phrŏn; and Abraham weighed to E'phrŏn the silver, which he had named in the audience of the sons of Heth, four hundred shekels of silver, current *money* with the merchant.

17 ¶ And the field of E'phrŏn, which *was* in Măch-pē'lăh, which *was* before Măm'rē, the field, and the cave which *was* therein, and all the trees that *were* in the field, that *were* in all the borders round about, were made sure

18 Unto Abraham for a possession in the presence of the children of Heth, before all that went in at the gate of his city.

Once Ephron had been contacted, he and Abraham transacted their business openly before all, in the gate of the city. The record says that all this was done "in the audience of the children of Heth."

Ephron at first protested that he would give the field to Abraham. Abraham, of course, insisted that he in turn must give Ephron an appropriate gift of money in appreciation. Ephron then suggested a price, no doubt considerably more than the field was worth. Rather than haggling, however, as soon as he had been able to extract a price quotation from Ephron, Abraham immediately accepted the offer (no doubt surprising Ephron and all the Hittites).

Abraham weighed out the silver (evidently he had brought it with him to the city), full measure. In those days, before the regular use of coins, prices were quoted and paid in terms of weights, in this case four hundred shekels of silver. The transaction was duly noted and recorded, the purchased land carefully identified and measured, and the silver acknowledged as fully negotiable with the merchants of the area.

One of the Bible's "contradictions" has been noted between this passage and Stephen's statement in Acts 7:16: "[Our fathers were] carried over into Shechem, and laid in the sepulchre that Abraham bought for a sum of money of the sons of Emmor [presumably the same as Hamor] of Shechem." Genesis 50:13, however, says that the sons of Jacob "buried him in the cave of the field of Machpelah, which Abraham bought with the field for a possession of a burying place of Ephron the Hittite, before Mamre." Joshua 24:32 says: "And the bones of Joseph, which the children of Israel brought up out of Egypt, buried they in Shechem, in a parcel of ground which Jacob bought of the sons of Hamor the father of Shechem for an hundred pieces of silver: and it became the inheritance of the children of Joseph." This particular transaction had been recorded in Genesis 33:19.

There are several possible explanations for this apparent discrepancy. One reasonable possibility is as follows. There are two different burying places—one purchased by Abraham in Mamre, one by Jacob in Shechem, two locations about forty miles apart. Sarah was the first to be buried in the cave of Machpelah in Mamre, but later there followed Abraham (Genesis 25:9), Isaac (35:27, 29), Leah and Rebekah (49:30, 31), and finally Jacob (50:13). Jacob purchased the plot in Shechem, not for a sepulcher, but for an altar (Genesis 33:20). Jacob later gave it to Joseph, and his descendants eventually buried him there, presumably along with the others of "the fathers" whom they had brought up from Egypt (Joshua 24:32; Acts 7:15, 16).

As far as Stephen's statement that Abraham had purchased the field in Shechem is concerned, Abraham lived another thirty-eight years after Sarah died (Genesis 17:17; 23:1; 25:7). During that period he met and married Keturah and had six more sons. It seems plausible that he might have purchased a second parcel of ground for use by his second family, in the region near Shechem, where he had built his first altar in Canaan (Genesis 12:6, 7). When Abraham died, however, he was buried with Sarah in Mamre. Keturah and her sons may not have retained possession of the Shechem property, selling it or losing it somehow to the Hivites who had become the chief inhabitants of the region. Then, about eighty-five years after Abraham's death, when Jacob came to the Shechem area, knowing that this tract had once belonged to his grandfather, he purchased it back again. As Abraham had built an altar there, so Jacob then did the same. While the Bible does not specifically record such a series of transactions, they do seem quite plausible, and they do suffice to reconcile the apparent discrepancies. In any case, those who heard Stephen speak were certainly familiar with all these passages of Genesis, and they did not seem to notice such an obvious "mistake" in Stephen's recollection of these events. Presumably they were familiar, by means of tradition, either with this or some other adequate explanation of the contradiction.

Genesis 23:19, 20

19 And after this, Abraham buried Sarah his wife in the cave of the field of Măch-pē′lȧh before Măm′rē: the same *is* Hē′brȯn in the land of Cā′nǎan.

20 And the field, and the cave that *is* therein, were made sure unto Abraham for a possession of a buryingplace by the sons of Heth.

Once the purchase had been consummated, Abraham proceeded with the burial of Sarah. The field and the cave had been "made sure"; the bodies of the patriarchs and their wives would rest in the promised land until the day of resurrection. Years later, Moses would editorially insert the explanation, for the readers of his day, that Mamre was the same as the city they had heard of as Hebron, in their future home in Canaan.

15

Isaac and Rebekah

(Genesis 24-26)

Search for a Bride

Genesis 24 is the longest chapter in the Book of Genesis, and it tells a story that has charmed and enthralled readers for generation after generation. Entire books have been written around this one chapter.

Not only is it a heart-warming love story, but it chronicles a very important episode in the history of man's redemption. Since Isaac is a type of Christ, according to the New Testament, it is not surprising that there are many fascinating parallels between the story of Isaac's search for a bride, through the ministry of his father's trusted servant, and the sending forth of the Holy Spirit to take out of the Gentiles a people for His name (Acts 15:14), a bride for Christ (II Corinthians 11:2). Of greater importance than the symbolism is the fact that the bride selected for Isaac had to be chosen with particular care, since she would be the mother of the multitude of nations which God had promised would come through Abraham's seed, through which the promised Savior would come, and in which all nations of the earth would be blessed. Though perhaps no other marriage has ever been more important than this one, all marriages—in fact the very institution of marriage—are of special concern to God. For this reason, Christian young people (and their parents) would do well to study carefully the principles guiding the preparations for this marriage as they contemplate their own.

CHAPTER 24

AND Abraham was old, *and* well stricken in age: and the LORD had blessed Abraham in all things.

2 And Abraham said unto his eldest servant of his house, that ruled over all that he had, Put, I pray thee, thy hand under my thigh:

3 And I will make thee swear by the LORD, the God of heaven, and the God of the earth, that thou shalt not take a wife unto my son of the daughters of the Cā'nǎan-ites, among whom I dwell:

4 But thou shalt go unto my country, and to my kindred, and take a wife unto my son Isaac.

5 And the servant said unto him, Peradventure the woman will not be willing to follow me unto this land: must I needs bring thy son again unto the land from whence thou camest?

6 And Abraham said unto him, Beware thou that thou bring not my son thither again.

7 ¶ The LORD God of heaven, which took me from my father's house, and from the land of my kindred, and which spake unto me, and that sware unto me, saying, Unto thy seed will I give this land; he shall send his angel before thee, and thou shalt take a wife unto my son from thence.

8 And if the woman will not be willing to follow thee, then thou shalt be clear from this my oath: only bring not my son thither again.

9 And the servant put his hand under the thigh of Abraham his master, and sware to him concerning that matter.

At this point, Sarah had died and Abraham was very old. Isaac himself was forty years old by this time (Genesis 25:20), which means Abraham was 140. It was certainly time for him to get married and to begin his own family. God "had blessed Abraham in all things," both material and spiritual, and he felt his responsibility in this matter most keenly. It is significant, also, that even though Isaac was forty years old, he firmly trusted his father's judgment in such an important decision as that of his wife-to-be.

Isaac realized, as did his father, that no suitable wife could be found among the Canaanite peoples where they lived. It was profoundly important that both Isaac and his wife be completely united in their faith in their covenant God, in order to properly instruct their children in this faith. His wife must not even be a recent convert. She must be one who had been instructed concerning God from her youth, and who had loved and served Him all her life. To find such a girl, if there were any such anywhere, Abraham must search among his own people. She must be a virgin, one who loved her own family but who at the same time would not insist on staying near them, because she would have to make her home in the land of Canaan.

Abraham knew there must be such a girl somewhere, because he trusted God to provide the promised seed through Isaac; and for this Isaac must have the right woman for a wife. He had recently learned about the family of his brother Nahor, and had even learned that Nahor had a young granddaughter named Rebekah (Genesis 22:20, 23).

Abraham was too old to make the long trip back to Mesopotamia himself, for it was over five hundred miles. Also, it was customary, especially among wealthy families, for such arrangements to be made through intermediaries. He was adamant in insisting that Isaac not go (verses 6, 8), probably because he had learned by then that the heir of God's promises should stay in the promised land. As a matter of fact, during all his life, Isaac never left Canaan at all (Genesis 26:2, 3). If Isaac had gone in search of a bride, there might have been too great a temptation for him to stay with her among her own people, rather than to return to Canaan. She must be willing to come to him. Also, to reach Haran and Nahor from the Hebron-Beersheba region, one would have to cross the land of Moriah, and it would be too traumatic (as well as inconsistent with the typological symbolism) for Isaac or his father to visit the scene of the awful sacrifice again. "So Christ was *once* offered to bear [literally, 'offer up'] the sins of many; and unto them that look for him shall he appear the second time without sin unto salvation" (Hebrews 9:28).

Therefore, Abraham sent his servant on the mission. This man was the steward of all his house, the oldest and most trusted one of his servants. If Eliezer was still living (Genesis 15:2), then he doubtless was the man. However, this event took place over fifty years after Eliezer's name had been mentioned, so he may well have been dead by this time. The reason the servant's name is not mentioned is probably that he was going in the name of Isaac, not his own name. When the Father sent the Holy Spirit to obtain a bride for His Son, Jesus said: "But the Comforter, which is the Holy Ghost, whom the Father will send in my name, he shall teach you all things, and bring all things to your remembrance, whatsoever I have said unto you . . . for he shall not speak of himself; but whatsoever he shall hear, that shall he speak: and he will show you things to come. He shall glorify me: for he shall receive of mine, and shall show it unto you" (John 14:26; 16:13, 14).

Abraham placed his servant under a firm oath that he would follow his instructions in every detail. He was not to take a wife from among the Canaanites (though a marriage with a daughter of one of the regional kings or chieftains might have had important temporal advantages), but only from among his own people (though these were few and far away); and he must not take Isaac along with him (though this, no doubt, would have made it much easier to obtain a desirable bride).

The sign and seal of the oath was a strange one. The servant was to "put his hand under the thigh of Abraham," while making the promise. The only other occasion on which a similar procedure was used was the time Jacob asked Joseph to put his hand under his thigh and promise he would not bury him in Egypt (Genesis 47:29). The exact meaning of this phrase is obscure. The word "thigh" (Hebrew *yarekh*) is frequently also translated "side" or "shaft." On two important occasions, it refers to the loins. For example, in Genesis 46:26, it obviously refers to the procreative system: "All the souls that came with Jacob into Egypt, which came out of his *loins*. . . ."

All the ancient Jewish commentators understood this promise to be a euphemism for placing the hand under the male genital organ, and to have a symbolic meaning akin to that of circumcision (see comments on Genesis 17:9-14), so far as the patriarchs were concerned. It was a most solemn oath, in any event, and clearly was related to God's promise in connection with both the promised land and the promised seed.

The oath was taken in "the name of Jehovah, the God of heaven, and the God of the earth." Abraham surely had no "limited" view of God, as critics used to claim. Furthermore, he assured his servant that "the Lord God of heaven" would "send his angel before thee." He need not fear that he would not find the right woman, nor that she would be unwilling to come with him. However, to ease his mind, Abraham assured him he would be free from the obligation of his oath if he failed in his attempt, so long as he followed the instructions.

Genesis 24:10-14

10 ¶ And the servant took ten camels of the camels of his master, and departed; for all the goods of his master *were* in his hand: and he arose, and went to Měs'ŏ-pō-tā'mǐ-à, unto the city of Nā'hŏr.
11 And he made his camels to kneel down without the city by a well of water at the time of the evening, *even* the time that women go out to draw *water*.
12 And he said, O LORD God of my master Abraham, I pray thee, send me good speed this day, and show kindness unto my master Abraham.
13 Behold, I stand *here* by the well of water; and the daughters of the men of the city come out to draw water:
14 And let it come to pass, that the damsel to whom I shall say, Let down thy pitcher, I pray thee, that I may drink; and she shall say, Drink, and I will give thy camels drink also: *let the same be* she *that* thou hast appointed for thy servant Isaac; and thereby shall I know that thou hast showed kindness unto my master.

The servant immediately set out to equip a caravan for the journey and for the accomplishment of his mission. This required taking provisions for the long trip, a large quantity of his master's goods (or "valuables") as presents for the prospective bride and her family, and enough attendants (Genesis 24:59) for protection and other needs of the journey. When everything was ready, they immediately headed north for the long trip to Mesopotamia and the city of Nahor. There is a possibility that the Mesopotamia ("land of the two rivers") spoken of here does not refer to the Tigris and Euphrates, but rather the Euphrates and Chaboras Rivers, which would more nearly agree with the probable location of Nahor.

The long trek is passed over in silence, although the servant and his attendants must have traversed interesting country and perhaps encountered various difficulties and dangers. No doubt their journey was bathed in prayer daily, as they well knew its importance. However, the narrative emphasizes Isaac and Rebekah rather than the servant, and so nothing further is mentioned until the party actually arrived at the city of Nahor. It is significant that no time was wasted in futile searching for a bride elsewhere. Abraham had learned where Nahor and his family lived, and was sure that it would be from among them that Isaac's wife must come.

The caravan halted at the edge of the city by the well. The camels were made to kneel down to rest, and the entire party stopped to ascertain how God would lead them next. Abraham's servant knew that the women of the place would come out to the wells to draw water for their households in the early evening, and this seemed the best place to meet them.

While they were waiting he himself also knelt down, not to rest, but to pray. God had protected them on the journey, but now the real work was at hand. How was he to know which girl he should choose for his master? He knew some of the qualities she must have, of course. She must be from Abraham's people, she must be a godly, virtuous maiden and, hopefully, fair to look upon. But suppose there should be several who would fit these specifications, then how would he know which was the right one?

In addition, he may have reasoned, she should be strong and healthy, because she would have to make a long trip with the caravan and then would have to assume charge of a large household of servants and to bear and raise children. She should be an industrious girl, harboring no delusions of a life of ease and idleness just because Isaac had great possessions. Finally, she should be gracious and considerate, of sensitive and compassionate spirit, because these attributes would be most desirable in coping with her many responsibilities among her servants and the people of the land.

But how could Abraham's servant determine quickly which of the girls that would soon be arriving would have such qualities? It would be necessary for him to make the first approach toward conversation, and the obvious thing would be for him to ask her for a drink of water from her pitcher. However, almost any girl, out of common courtesy, would agree to such a request as that; so that act alone would not be sufficient. If, however, she would then, on her own initiative, offer to help in some further way, going a second mile as it were, this would definitely be a good sign. Perhaps the most severe test would be whether she was willing not only to give him some water, and perhaps even his attendants, but also his ten camels. Surely, if she would do this, without grumbling, it would go far toward proving that she was the kind of wife Abraham was seeking for his son.

But this would be a most unreasonable thing to expect. Drawing enough water to satisfy the thirst of ten large and tired camels would be a hard and wearisome task, to say the least. He couldn't really ask a girl to do such a thing. Nevertheless, if she would do it voluntarily, it would be a strong indication that she was the right one.

Accordingly, he decided to pray to this specific end. He knew, as did Abraham, that he had followed the Lord's leading to this point. Now, surely, he could trust God to show him the right woman, and what better indication could there be than this? Unreasonable as it might at first seem, therefore, it was really a most appropriate request.

This is a marvelous example of specific, believing prayer, an example that we can profitably follow today. It was not a presumptuous prayer; the servant knew he was following the Lord to this point, and his motives were only to do that which would honor God and accomplish the mission that the Lord, through his master, had entrusted to him. He needed definite guidance, not general direction, at this point. Therefore, he prayed quite specifically—a reasonable request, but one which would be most unlikely to come to pass without the Lord's definite intervention. Today, if we similarly meet the conditions, we can similarly expect specific answers to definite prayer.

Genesis 24:15-27

15 ¶ And it came to pass, before he had done speaking, that, behold, Rē-bĕk′ah came out, who was born to Bē-thū′ĕl, son of Mĭl′cah, the wife of Nā′hŏr, Abraham's brother, with her pitcher upon her shoulder.

16 And the damsel *was* very fair to look upon, a virgin, neither had any man known her: and she went down to the well, and filled her pitcher, and came up.

17 And the servant ran to meet her, and said, Let me, I pray thee, drink a little

water of thy pitcher.

18 And she said, Drink, my lord: and she hasted, and let down her pitcher upon her hand, and gave him drink.

19 And when she had done giving him drink, she said, I will draw *water* for thy camels also, until they have done drinking.

20 And she hasted, and emptied her pitcher into the trough, and ran again unto the well to draw *water,* and drew for all his camels.

21 And the man wondering at her held his peace, to wit whether the LORD had made his journey prosperous or not.

22 And it came to pass, as the camels had done drinking, that the man took a golden earring of half a shekel weight, and two bracelets for her hands of ten *shekels* weight of gold;

23 And said, Whose daughter *art* thou? tell me, I pray thee: is there room *in* thy father's house for us to lodge in?

24 And she said unto him, I *am* the daughter of Bē-thū′ĕl the son of Mĭl′căh, which she bare unto Nā′hŏr.

25 She said moreover unto him, We have both straw and provender enough, and room to lodge in.

26 And the man bowed down his head, and worshipped the LORD.

27 And he said, Blessed *be* the LORD God of my master Abraham, who hath not left destitute my master of his mercy and his truth: I *being* in the way, the LORD led me to the house of my master's brethren.

It would probably be a long time, the servant may have thought, before a maiden would be found who would accede to such a rigorous request as this. But not so! "And it shall come to pass, that before they call, I will answer; and while they are yet speaking, I will hear" (Isaiah 65:24). Before there was any possibility of being distracted by other girls coming to the well—indeed, before he was done speaking—Rebekah arrived, ready to draw water.

This in itself says something for Rebekah's character. The daily duty of drawing water for their families was hardly an enjoyable activity for the young girls of the town. It was a hard, though necessary, chore; and probably most of them dawdled as long as they could, or as long as their parents would let them, before actually getting to the task. But not Rebekah! She was the first one there.

When the servant saw her coming, immediately after he had risen from prayer, his heart was thrilled. The girl coming was exceedingly fair to look upon, and obviously a virgin. So he ran to apply the test he had proposed to the Lord. She hastened to give him a drink of water, as he asked. As he was drinking, she looked up beyond him and saw his camels. She must have been a girl who loved animals (as many girls today love horses); and she could not help but observe that they were dusty and tired from a long journey, as well as very thirsty. Though it would be a long, hard task, descending and ascending the stairs to the well many times, carrying a heavy pitcher of water, nevertheless, she immediately insisted on drawing water for all his camels.

One can imagine the thrilling shiver that ran up the servant's spine! God not only had immediately sent a girl who made the generous offer he had prayed for, but she was a beautiful girl, obviously kind, energetic, strong, and hospitable. God was doing "exceedingly abundantly above all" he had asked or thought (Ephesians 3:20). He did not yet know who she was, of course; so he "held his peace" until she had finished with the camels, watching her silently in wonder.

In appreciation for her generous service, the man then took three golden rings (one for the nose—not earring, as in the King James translation—and two for the hands), all very valuable, and gave them to Rebekah. In like manner, many a believer has found that generosity with possessions and service, offered in the name of Christ, is always more than amply repaid. We can never "outgive" God.

Now he was ready to ask the all-important question. "Whose daughter art thou?" When he learned that this lovely and gracious young woman was none other than Rebekah herself, about whom they had learned back in Hebron, Isaac's second cousin, he was almost overcome with emotion. He had to stop immediately, bow down and worship the Lord, in audible thanksgiving to the God who had so richly answered his prayer and the prayer of his master Abraham. God, who had so showered Abraham with His loving-kindness and truth all his life long, was still doing so!

"I being in the way, the Lord led me." The servant was actively following the Lord, and therefore the Lord directed his steps. "The steps of a good man are ordered by the Lord: and he delighteth in his way" (Psalm 37:23). "In all thy ways acknowledge him, and he shall direct thy paths" (Proverbs 3:6). The Lord leads along the path, a step at a time; but before He can lead us *along* the path, we must be *on* the path. When a man is doing God's will, as best he knows it, and is willing to do His further will even before he knows it, then he will know His will as soon as he needs to (John 7:17; Romans 12:2).

The servant had also asked Rebekah whether there was room at her home for himself and his fellow servants to spend the night. This also may have seemed a presumptuous request, to think that her family might take as overnight guests a company of complete strangers. There was something about the servant, however, that made Rebekah know him to be a godly man and one whom her family could trust. With her generous nature, she immediately assured him there was ample room, not only for the men, but also plenty of "straw and provender" for the camels. Again, an evidence of God's leading!

Genesis 24:28-33

---

28 And the damsel ran, and told *them of* her mother's house these things.

29 ¶ And Rē-bĕk'ăh had a brother, and his name *was* Lā'băn: and Lā'băn ran out unto the man, unto the well.

30 And it came to pass, when he saw the earring, and bracelets upon his sister's hands, and when he heard the words of Rē-bĕk'ăh his sister, saying, Thus spake the man unto me, that he came unto the man; and, behold, he stood by the camels at the well.

31 And he said, Come in, thou blessed of the LORD; wherefore standest thou without? for I have prepared the house, and room for the camels.

32 ¶ And the man came into the house: and he ungirded his camels, and gave straw and provender for the camels, and water to wash his feet, and the men's feet that *were* with him.

33 And there was set *meat* before him to eat: but he said, I will not eat, until I have told mine errand. And he said, Speak on.

Rebekah, of course, had to run to ask her father Bethuel and her brother Laban whether it would indeed be all right for them to stay the night with them. Not only had the courteous stranger given her a beautiful ring and bracelets, but the most exciting thing was that, as he prayed, she had heard him mention Abraham, her almost legendary relative in far-off Canaan, as his master. She sensed that there was something very important about his presence in Nahor, and she was eagerly anticipating what he would tell her family.

Rebekah went first to her mother, to whom she perhaps felt closer than to her father. This was no doubt partially because her father had a concubine, as well as his wife; and in a polygamous marriage there is naturally a closer tie between a girl and her own mother than between her and her father, other things being equal. More likely, however, Bethuel may have been an invalid at this time, so that her mother (note the phrase "her mother's house" in verse 28) and her brother Laban had to handle many of the responsibilities and decisions of the household.

Abraham's servant waited by the well while Rebekah went to tell the family. Laban being the senior active male in the house, it was his place to go welcome the servant. Scripture indicates he hurried out to do this, proving to be a very gracious and generous host. In the light of later insight into his character, gained in the accounts of Jacob's dealings with him, it may be possible that there was an underlying element of greed in his attitude. No doubt he had heard about Abraham and his wealth from travelers, just as Abraham had heard about him, and this report was also supported by the valuable-laden caravan that had just arrived.

In any case, the record does say that "when he saw the earring [or 'nose ring'] and bracelets," then he said: "Come in, thou blessed of the Lord." The servant was still standing patiently over the camels by the well, but at Laban's assurance that he had already prepared the house and a place for the camels, he came into the house.

After the camels were taken care of, and both the servant and his men had washed their feet, a necessary amenity after the long journey, the family invited him into the dining area for a meal they had prepared. Though he no doubt was hungry, and it would have been pleasant to relax and enjoy a good meal and fellowship with his master's relatives, the Lord's leading had been so marvelous to this point that he simply could wait no longer to ask the one final question, and to find whether Rebekah would indeed accept the offer of marriage and return with him to Isaac. Though it was customary to leave business until after the meal, Rebekah and her family were equally anxious to know what he had come for (one even supposes they may have guessed!), and were glad to postpone dinner for this purpose. They told him, by all means, to go ahead. Expectantly they awaited his words.

Genesis 24:34-49

34 And he said, I *am* Abraham's servant.

35 And the LORD hath blessed my master greatly, and he is become great: and he hath given him flocks, and herds, and silver, and gold, and menservants, and maidservants, and camels, and asses.

36 And Sarah my master's wife bare a son to my master when she was old: and unto him hath he given all that he hath.

37 And my master made me swear, saying, Thou shalt not take a wife to my son of the daughters of the Cā'năan-ītes, in whose land I dwell:

38 But thou shalt go unto my father's house, and to my kindred, and take a wife unto my son.

39 And I said unto my master, Peradventure the woman will not follow me.

40 And he said unto me, The LORD, before whom I walk, will send his angel with thee, and prosper thy way; and thou shalt take a wife for my son of my kindred, and of my father's house:

41 Then shalt thou be clear from *this* my oath, when thou comest to my kindred; and if they give not thee *one*, thou shalt be clear from my oath.

42 And I came this day unto the well, and said, O LORD God of my master Abraham, if now thou do prosper my way which I go:

43 Behold, I stand by the well of water; and it shall come to pass, that when the virgin cometh forth to draw *water*, and I say to her, Give me, I pray thee, a little water of thy pitcher to drink;

44 And she say to me, Both drink thou, and I will also draw for thy camels: *let* the same *be* the woman whom the LORD hath appointed out for my master's son.

45 And before I had done speaking in mine heart, behold, Rĕ-bĕk'ăh came forth with her pitcher on her shoulder; and she went down unto the well, and drew *water:* and I said unto her, Let me drink, I pray thee.

46 And she made haste, and let down her pitcher from her *shoulder,* and said, Drink, and I will give thy camels drink also: so I drank, and she made the camels drink also.

47 And I asked her, and said, Whose daughter *art* thou? And she said, The daughter of Bē-thū'ĕl, Nā'hŏr's son, whom Mĭl'càh bare unto him: and I put the earring upon her face, and the brace-

lets upon her hands.
48 And I bowed down my head, and
worshipped the LORD, and blessed the
LORD God of my master Abraham,
which had led me in the right way to
take my master's brother's daughter

unto his son.
49 And now, if ye will deal kindly and
truly with my master, tell me: and if not,
tell me; that I may turn to the right hand,
or to the left.

In these verses, we have the servant's testimony concerning Abraham
and Isaac. Though it is largely a repetition of what has already been
covered in the narrative, it is thrilling to hear it, as it were, through
the ears of Rebekah, who was learning these great things for the first
time. Since he was making a proposal of marriage, it was of course proper
to give a clear statement of his master's financial status, which he did
most impressively, ascribing all the credit for Abraham's wealth to God
rather than to his business acumen. He also noted that Isaac had been
made sole heir of all this wealth and its attendant responsibility. He
mentioned, too, the fact of Isaac's miraculous birth, coming at such
a time that he was approximately the same age as Rebekah.

He next recounted the whole thrilling story of his mission, and
the details of how the Lord had led him to Rebekah, and Rebekah
to him. Truly, the Lord "had led him in the right way," and the others
were bound to catch his own enthusiasm and thanksgiving as he testified so gratefully and happily. Abraham's Lord is still our Lord, and
He does still lead His people in the right way; the servant is a splendid
example of how the recipient of God's guidance and blessing should
share that good news with others.

After he had given the testimony as clearly and persuasively as he
knew how, it was time for a definite decision. Would Rebekah come,
or no? And would her family allow her to go? Actually, the servant
did not even have to ask the actual question as to whether Rebekah
would marry Isaac. The facts of God's leading, as narrated, were so
clear that the question was self-evident.

The typological teaching here seems so clear that it should not be
passed over. The servant is like the Holy Spirit, who is in the world
seeking a Bride for Christ. The Bride is to be made up of individuals
who receive Him as Lord and Savior, and who therefore will be brought
unto Him in regeneration by the Spirit. As the Holy Spirit (through
human witnesses, through Scripture, through circumstances) witnesses
to the hearts of individuals concerning the glories of Christ, their need
of Him, and the joys to be found in His presence, they are confronted
with the greatest decision of their lives. They cannot ignore Him; they
must say either yes or no. If they are united to Him, they must leave
the things of the world behind them and submit fully to Him. Many

reject the invitation and are separated forever from Him. "But as many as received him, to them gave he power to become the children of God, even to them that believe on his name" (John 1:12).

Genesis 24:50-61

---

50 Then Lā'băn and Bē-thū'ĕl answered and said, The thing proceedeth from the LORD: we cannot speak unto thee bad or good.

51 Behold, Rē-bĕk'ăh *is* before thee; take *her,* and go, and let her be thy master's son's wife, as the LORD hath spoken.

52 And it came to pass, that, when Abraham's servant heard their words, he worshipped the LORD, *bowing himself* to the earth.

53 And the servant brought forth jewels of silver, and jewels of gold, and raiment, and gave *them* to Rē-bĕk'ăh: he gave also to her brother and to her mother precious things.

54 And they did eat and drink, he and the men that *were* with him, and tarried all night; and they rose up in the morning, and he said, Send me away unto my master.

55 And her brother and her mother said, Let the damsel abide with us *a*

few days, at the least ten; after that she shall go.

56 And he said unto them, Hinder me not, seeing the LORD hath prospered my way; send me away that I may go to my master.

57 And they said, We will call the damsel, and inquire at her mouth.

58 And they called Rē-bĕk'ăh, and said unto her, Wilt thou go with this man? And she said, I will go.

59 And they sent away Rē-bĕk'ăh their sister, and her nurse, and Abraham's servant, and his men.

60 And they blessed Rē-bĕk'ăh, and said unto her, Thou *art* our sister; be thou *the mother* of thousands of millions, and let thy seed possess the gate of those which hate them.

61 ¶ And Rē-bĕk'ăh arose, and her damsels, and they rode upon the camels, and followed the man: and the servant took Rē-bĕk'ăh, and went his way.

After such a testimony, there could be no doubt that God had led the servant to select Rebekah as Isaac's bride. Both her father and her brother, Bethuel and Laban, immediately acknowledged that regardless of their personal feelings in the matter, God had spoken and they must accept His decision. As far as they were concerned, Rebekah was free to go.

There seems to be a hint, at least, that as far as their own desires were concerned, they were not completely happy to have Rebekah go so far from home. They loved her and realized her absence would leave a deep void in their lives. Furthermore, they had not seen Abram and Sarai since they left home; so naturally they realized they would likely never see Rebekah again either. Christian parents who have seen their children go off to the mission field can understand something of what may have been going through their minds. Knowing how much they will miss their children, such parents nevertheless are happy the Lord has chosen them to serve Him in this way and are willing, though with reluctance, to let them go.

It seems strange at first that the question was not directed to Rebekah, nor did the reply come from her. It was proper, surely, for the father's permission to be sought, as well as the brother's in this case, but were the arrangements to be made altogether without the bride's participation? A more likely suggestion is that it was so obvious to all that Rebekah wanted to go that it was unnecessary even to ask! She had heard enough about Isaac from the servant, and was sure that, if the Lord had led him to her, He also would lead her to him. It is not at all unlikely that she herself had been wondering who her husband would be, and perhaps had even been praying for God to lead the right one to her. In any case, she was anxious to go!

When the consent was given, the last proof of God's leading had been established. As Abraham would have done had he been present, his representative spontaneously prostrated himself to the ground and worshiped the Lord.

Immediately the servant went to his store of valuables, and began to lavish gifts of jewelry and beautiful raiment on Rebekah. The bride of a prince must be provided with new clothing and adornments furnished by the father of the prince. Similarly, the one who is to be the Bride of Christ can no longer be dressed in the "filthy rags" of his own "righteousness" (Isaiah 64:6), but must be "arrayed in fine linen, clean and white" (Revelation 19:8).

He also gave valuable gifts to Laban and Bethuel's wife. He did not slight Bethuel himself, since the gifts to Rebekah's mother were, in effect, gifts to her father. It is also possible that, because of infirmities, Bethuel was no longer able to receive and use anything of his own.

All the members of the caravan's entourage then, finally, were able to eat their meal and settle down to rest for the night. One suspects, however, that there were at least a few who didn't sleep much that night!

When they arose in the morning, the servant surprised everyone by requesting an immediate departure. Rebekah's mother and brother, quite naturally, demurred. They had willingly agreed that she could go, but did it have to be so sudden? Only half a day had passed since the stranger had arrived, and here he was preparing to take a loved family member away forever with hardly time even to say good-bye. They felt that a minimum of ten days would be necessary for her to make adequate preparations and for them to adjust to the idea of her departure.

The servant had good reasons, however, regardless of how insensitive his request may have seemed. The Lord had clearly indicated His leading; therefore, there should be no delay in following His will. Delay would only give opportunity for the flesh to find reasons for rethinking the decision, and possibly changing it. Also, Abraham (not to mention Isaac) was anxiously awaiting word, and the servant needed to get back to him as soon as possible. Anyway, Rebekah's mother and brother would really be no more ready for her to leave ten days hence than they were at that moment. It would be just as hard, if not even harder, to say good-bye later, than right then, before there was much time to think about it. Better to remember her as she had been, than as she would be during a ten-day period of strain and possible misunderstandings.

After the servant's reference to the Lord's leading, Laban and Bethuel's wife decided to leave the decision up to Rebekah. It didn't take her long to make up her mind. She was ready to go immediately!

Her decision was right. One should not go ahead of the Lord's will, but neither should he lag behind, once that will is known. This rule is most important in connection with the greatest decision of all— whether to accept Christ or not. Once the Holy Spirit has taught a person about Christ, and he understands the implications of the gospel, he should accept Him and follow Him immediately. Delay can only be dangerous. "Behold, now is the accepted time; behold, now is the day of salvation" (II Corinthians 6:2).

Rebekah took her nurse with her, as well as her maids; evidently her own family was not exactly poverty-stricken! The family then bestowed a blessing on Rebekah, with prayers for a billionfold progeny, and said their good-byes. The traveling party then mounted their camels and started out to meet Isaac.

Genesis 24:62-67

---

62 And Isaac came from the way of the well Lâ-haï′-rôi; for he dwelt in the south country.

63 And Isaac went out to meditate in the field at the eventide: and he lifted up his eyes, and saw, and, behold, the camels *were* coming.

64 And Rē-běk′áh lifted up her eyes, and when she saw Isaac, she lighted off the camel.

65 For she *had* said unto the servant, What man *is* this that walketh in the field to meet us? And the servant *had* said, It *is* my master: therefore she took a veil, and covered herself.

66 And the servant told Isaac all things that he had done.

67 And Isaac brought her into his mother Sarah's tent, and took Rē-běk′áh, and she became his wife; and he loved her: and Isaac was comforted after his mother's *death*.

The long trip home is again passed over without any record in the narrative. No doubt, much of the time was occupied with discussion about Isaac. Rebekah wanted to learn everything she could about him, and about his father, and about God's plan for them. The servant was a good teacher as well as protector, as they made their way through the land of the Canaanites down into the Negev, where Isaac lived.

In type, of course, the servant is the Holy Comforter, the Paraclete ("one called alongside of"), who accompanies the Church through the world's wilderness, teaching her the things of Christ and showing things to come, until finally He presents her to Christ at the end of the journey.

Isaac is, as we have seen, a type of Christ, awaiting union with His bride when she comes to Him, and in the meantime preparing a place for her (John 14:3) as she approaches. Rebekah represents the Church, the chaste Bride (II Corinthians 11:2), who is preparing to meet her heavenly Bridegroom (John 3:29; Romans 7:4). There are various ways in which Rebekah foreshadows the Christian believer. For example: (1) her marriage was planned long before she knew about it (Ephesians 1:3, 4); (2) she was necessary for the accomplishment and completion of God's purpose (Ephesians 1:23); (3) she was to share the glory of the son (John 17:22, 23); (4) she learned of the son through his emissary and her paraclete; (5) she immediately left all, to go to the son, loving him before she saw him, and rejoicing with unspeakable joy (I Peter 1:8); (6) she journeyed through the wilderness to meet him, guided by the servant (I Peter 1:3-9); (7) she was loved by, and finally united forever to, the son (Ephesians 5:26, 27; Revelation 19:7; I Thessalonians 4:17).

Isaac, like Christ, (1) was promised long before his coming (Luke 1:70); (2) finally appeared, at the appointed time (Galatians 4:4); (3) was conceived and born miraculously (Luke 1:35); (4) was assigned an appropriate name by God before his birth (Matthew 1:21); (5) was offered up in sacrifice by his father (I John 2:2); (6) was himself obedient unto death (Philippians 2:8); (7) was brought back from the dead (Ephesians 1:19-23) to be the head of a great nation and to bless all peoples.

In the Genesis account, Isaac had last been seen at the place of sacrifice (Genesis 22:13, 16). Though his name was frequently on the lips of Abraham, the servant, Rebekah, and others in the narrative, Isaac himself does not appear again until he goes out to meet Rebekah. This, also, is appropriate in the type, corresponding to the going forth of Christ to meet His Bride at the end of the age (I Thessalonians 4:16, 17).

Isaac had apparently made preparation to set up his own tent near Hagar's well, the well Lahai-roi (Genesis 16:14; 25:11) far in the Negev, the south country, where Hagar had first discovered "the well of the living-and-seeing One." One evening he "went out to meditate in the field at the eventide," evidently as he was returning to his father from the site of his prospective home. The "meditation" certainly included prayer, and it is permissible to infer from this, both that Isaac was a deeply spiritual man, to whom prayer and meditation were habitual, and also that one of the main thoughts that occupied his meditations was his coming bride.

It was then, as he rose from prayer and looked up, he saw the caravan approaching and, instinctively, he must have known his bride was in it. It was his father's company, he recognized, but more people were coming than had left many weeks earlier.

Rebekah saw him at about the same time, and also instinctively knew it was Isaac. When she asked the servant, and he had confirmed it, she literally "fell off" the camel to meet him (the Hebrew verb is *naphal,* which the King James translation renders "lighted off").

She quickly put on a "veil," actually a garment which covered both face and body, as this was the proper way, in accord with the custom, to first meet her husband-to-be. Isaac, outwardly calm but inwardly eager with anticipation, listened patiently as the servant made the appropriate introductions, and then recounted how the Lord had led him so plainly and clearly to Rebekah, and how Rebekah had consented to come.

What a meeting it must have been! And what a glorious meeting there will one day be "in the air," when our Lord "descends from heaven" and we are "caught up to meet him" (I Thessalonians 4:16, 17).

Isaac first took Rebekah into Sarah's tent, vacant for the three years since his mother's death, until the formalities of the marriage ceremony could be arranged. Then he married her, and took her into his own tent at Lahai-roi (25:11). He quickly learned to love her, and she him. When God leads in a marriage, true love, both physical and spiritual, is assured. Isaac had loved his mother dearly and missed her greatly; but now, with Rebekah, he "was comforted after his mother's death." A man who truly loves and honors his father and mother will, when the time comes for marriage (Genesis 2:24), likewise love and honor his wife.

Sons of Abraham

When God heals, He heals completely, restoring the injured member or diseased organ back to full soundness again. In order to father a son in his old age, Abraham's reproductive system had to be rejuvenated. The one-hundred-year-old man became as a man of thirty or forty again, in that respect at least. He had been eighty-six when Ishmael was born, so presumably his rejuvenation restored his full procreative power for a period of perhaps fifty years after Isaac's birth.

Abraham was 140 years old when Isaac married Rebekah, and evidently his ability to father children continued for another ten years or so after that. When Isaac married, and he and Rebekah moved south to Lahai-roi, Abraham was left alone, and no doubt soon became lonely. Finally, he decided to remarry.

Genesis 25:1-4

CHAPTER 25

THEN again Abraham took a wife, and her name *was* Kĕ-tu̱′räh.
2 And she bare him Zĭm′rän, and Jŏk′shän, and Mē′dän, and Mĭd′ĭ-än, and Ĭsh′bäk, and Shu̱′äh.
3 And Jŏk′shän begat Shē′bä, and Dē′dän. And the sons of Dē′dän were Ăs̱-shu̱′rĭm, and Lē-tū′shĭm, and Lē-ŭm′mĭm.
4 And the sons of Mĭd′ĭ-än; Ē′phäh, and Ē′phēr, and Hā′nŏch, and Ȧ-bĭ′däh, and Ĕl-dā′äh. All these *were* the children of Kĕ-tu̱′räh.

"Then again Abraham took a wife, and her name was Keturah." Some commentators argue that Keturah was a concubine (as she is called in I Chronicles 1:32) whom Abraham had taken long before Sarah died. This seems very unlikely, however, not only because of the very wording of this verse, but also because Abraham loved Sarah alone, consenting to go in even to Hagar only very reluctantly.

There is no indication as to Keturah's home or background. Her name has been interpreted to mean "covered with incense," but this seems to offer no clue. It does seem unlikely that Abraham would marry a Canaanite woman, in view of his great concern that Isaac not do so. Scripture is silent on the matter, however, so we don't know. She did surely understand when Abraham married her, that although she and any children of the marriage would be adequately provided for, only Isaac would have the inheritance.

Remarkably enough, Abraham and Keturah did have six sons.

Abraham lived for thirty-five years after Isaac's marriage, but it is probable Keturah's sons were born within the first ten years or so of the marriage. It is certainly possible that one of the reasons Abraham married Keturah was the prophecy (Genesis 17:4) that he would be a father of many nations. Undoubtedly he sought and followed God's will in connection with this late marriage.

Of Keturah's six sons, the descendants of Zimran, Ishbak, Shuah, and Medan have not been satisfactorily identified. Jokshan is identified primarily by his two sons, Sheba and Dedan, who are mentioned on a number of occasions later in the Bible. On the other hand, two other men named Sheba and Dedan are listed in Genesis 10:7 as grandsons of Cush. Another Sheba was a grandson of Eber (Genesis 10:28). It is difficult to distinguish one from the other in the later references.

The other son of Keturah was Midian, and his descendants are mentioned frequently in the Old Testament. The Midianites, on various occasions, seem to have been allied with the Ishmaelites (Genesis 37:25, 27, 28, 36), the Moabites (Numbers 25:1, 6-15), and the Amalekites (Judges 6:3).

Genesis 25:5, 6

---

5 ¶ And Abraham gave all that he had unto Isaac.
6 But unto the sons of the concubines, which Abraham had, Abraham gave gifts, and sent them away from Isaac his son, while he yet lived, eastward, unto the east country.

The few intimations of the names of the sons of Keturah that have appeared in the archaeological inscriptions do seem to confirm the statement of verse 6 that they were sent by Abraham into the east country, which would mean into Arabia. Through millennia of migrations and intermarriages, it seems likely that all of these peoples, together with the descendants of Ishmael, Lot, and Esau, along with earlier descendants of Shem and, in some cases, Ham, have gradually merged and become the modern-day Arabic peoples.

Before he died, Abraham endowed all the sons of Keturah, as well as Ishmael, the son of Hagar (Keturah and Hagar are both called "concubines" at this time, to distinguish them from his primary wife, Sarah), with "gifts," no doubt a reference to an adequate provision for each to have a reasonable start on his own flocks and herds. The bulk of his inheritance, however, he gave to Isaac.

Genesis 25:7-11

7 And these *are* the days of the years of Abraham's life which he lived, a hundred threescore and fifteen years.

8 Then Abraham gave up the ghost, and died in a good old age, an old man, and full *of years;* and was gathered to his people.

9 And his sons Isaac and Ĭsh'mā-ĕl buried him in the cave of Măch-pē'läh, in the field of E'phrŏn the son of Zō'här the Hĭt'tĭte, which *is* before Măm're;

10 The field which Abraham purchased of the sons of Heth: there was Abraham buried, and Sarah his wife.

11 ¶ And it came to pass after the death of Abraham, that God blessed his son Isaac; and Isaac dwelt by the well Lā-haï'–rôi.

In these verses is recorded the end of the remarkable life of Abraham. He died at what even then was the advanced age of 175. He was "gathered to his people," which (since none of his ancestors were buried in the cave of Machpelah, where he was buried) can not refer simply to his death and burial, and therefore must refer to life after death, with those who before him had died in faith. The location of such departed spirits was, nineteen hundred years later, actually called "Abraham's bosom" (Luke 16:22).

He was buried, where Sarah was also buried, in the cave of Machpelah, near Mamre, with Isaac and Ishmael both officiating. Their earlier estrangement had evidently been healed, possibly because of their father's death.

Isaac was now the only surviving link in the Messianic line. He was Abraham's heir and, as God had blessed Abraham, so He now began to prosper Isaac.

Genesis 25:12-18

12 ¶ Now these *are* the generations of Ĭsh'mā-ĕl, Abraham's son, whom Hā'gär the Egyptian, Sarah's handmaid, bare unto Abraham:

13 And these *are* the names of the sons of Ĭsh'mā-ĕl, by their names, according to their generations: the firstborn of Ĭsh'mā-ĕl, Nē-bā'jŏth; and Kē'där, and Ăd'bē-ĕl, and Mĭb'säm,

14 And Mĭsh'mä, and Dū'mäh, and Măs'sä,

15 Hā'där, and Tē'mä, Jē'tŭr, Nā'phĭsh, and Kĕd'ē-mäh:

16 These *are* the sons of Ĭsh'mā-ĕl, and these *are* their names, by their towns, and by their castles; twelve princes according to their nations.

17 And these *are* the years of the life of Ĭsh'mā-ĕl, a hundred and thirty and seven years: and he gave up the ghost and died, and was gathered unto his people.

18 And they dwelt from Hăv'ĭ-läh unto Shŭr, that *is* before Egypt, as thou goest toward Assyria: *and* he died in the presence of all his brethren.

This section contains "the generations of Ishmael." As noted in chapter 1, it may be that Ishmael had kept this record, and that Isaac incorporated it into his own "generations" record (Genesis 25:19).

The most plausible explanation is that Isaac acquired Ishmael's record at the time they were together for their father's funeral. Ishmael at that time was ninety years old. His own twelve sons were grown, and they had become prolific and powerful enough to have settled towns and strongholds of their own, and to be called princes, as God had promised (Genesis 17:20).

As in the case of Keturah's sons, the specific sons of Ishmael have been hard to identify archaeologically, although there is little doubt that most or all of them settled in the general regions of central and north central Arabia. His eldest son, Nebaioth, has been suggested by some authorities as the ancestor of the Nabateans, a prominent tribe who later lived in the same region as the Edomites. Kedar (who is associated with Nebaioth in Isaiah 60:7) evidently had many descendants, and his name is often used in Scripture as essentially synonymous with all the Arabs (Isaiah 21:17; Jeremiah 49:28; Ezekiel 27:21, etc.). Jetur seems to have given his name to Ituraea, mentioned in Luke 3:1. Certain Assyrian inscriptions have tentatively been tied in with the names of Adbeel, Massa, Nebaioth, and Kedar. Dumah is named in Isaiah 21:11 as "calling out of Seir," which was the home of the Edomites. There is a town in northern Arabia named Dumath al-Jandel, which may have some ancestral connection with Dumah. Similarly, Tema may be identified with the town of Teyma, in Arabia. Apparently nothing is known about Mibsam, Mishma, Hadar, Naphish, and Kedemah.

Isaac, after inserting Ishmael's "generations" in his own record, then also later recorded Ishmael's death. He died at the age of 137, fifty-eight years before Isaac died. Scripture says that Ishmael, like Abraham, was "gathered unto his people." This suggests that, though not sharing in the material aspects of the Abrahamic covenant, Ishmael was a believer in the God of Abraham and shared in the spiritual blessings of all who die in the true faith.

Though his sons have been difficult to identify precisely in secular references, Scripture does tell us that they "dwelt from Havilah unto Shur, that is before Egypt, as thou goest toward Assyria," and this places them generally in northern Arabia, along the main caravan route between Egypt and Assyria. Shur is the wilderness just east of the border of Egypt, and Havilah (meaning "sandy") probably refers to all the sandy desert area of northern Arabia.

Ishmael "died" (literally "fell") in the presence of (possibly better rendered "to the east of") all his brethren. He apparently was something of a "loner," as had been predicted (Genesis 16:12).

The Birthright

The next major section of Genesis actually begins in the middle of chapter 25, and in the middle of verse 19. As discussed in chapter 1, it is probable that the statement "And these are the generations of Isaac" is actually the signature terminating the records beginning in Genesis 11:27, dealing with the life of Abraham and the early portion of the life of Isaac. This record was kept and transmitted by Isaac. The next section, beginning in 25:19b and continuing through 37:2a, was probably recorded by Jacob. It begins with a general statement of Isaac's background, continues through his life following marriage, and then narrates the experiences of Jacob until the time when Joseph was sold into Egypt.

Genesis 25:19-23

19 ¶ And these *are* the generations of Isaac, Abraham's son: Abraham begat Isaac:

20 And Isaac was forty years old when he took Rē-bĕk'áh to wife, the daughter of Bē-thū'ĕl the Syrian of Pā'dăn–ā'răm, the sister to Lā'băn the Syrian.

21 And Isaac entreated the LORD for his wife, because she *was* barren: and the LORD was entreated of him, and Rē-bĕk'áh his wife conceived.

22 And the children struggled together within her; and she said, If *it be* so, why *am* I thus? And she went to inquire of the LORD.

23 And the LORD said unto her, Two nations *are* in thy womb, and two manner of people shall be separated from thy bowels; and *the one* people shall be stronger than *the other* people; and the elder shall serve the younger.

Isaac was forty years old when he was married to Rebekah, and it would be another twenty years (Genesis 25:20, 26) before they would have any children. Like Abraham and Sarah, they had to wait many years and to make it a matter of special prayer, before God sent them a son. Rebekah was from Syria (Hebrew *Aram*) and her relatives are said to be Syrians. Aram was a son of Shem, so the Aramaeans, or Syrians, were Semites. She had lived in Padan-aram ("the plain of Aram"), where the towns of Haran and Nahor were settled, and to which her family had migrated.

Isaac well knew God's promises concerning the seed that would come through him, but perhaps he took them too much for granted. Twenty years of barrenness, however, finally drove him to prayer that he and Rebekah might have a child. It does seem that God desires us to pray for the supply of our needs and His blessings, even though He has already promised to send them (Matthew 6:11; 7:11; Philippians 4:19; II Peter 1:4).

In any case, when Isaac prayed for his wife, God answered, and she finally conceived—not one son, but twin sons! Note Ephesians 3:20 again.

However, a problem soon developed. Within the very womb, there began to be a conflict between the two boys. Rebekah was feeling more than normal fetal movements; an actual struggle was taking place in her womb, and Rebekah seemed to realize that this was a portent of something significant.

There is much we do not yet understand concerning the growth of the embryo. Present-day abortionists seem to feel that an embryo is not really a person until its birth, even though live births can take place any time over a period of several months before and after the normal gestation period. It is true we cannot remember anything connected with our life before birth, but neither do we remember anything for several years after birth. A new-born babe does have feelings, however, and can exhibit anger, as well as contentment, so why should this not also be true for the period prior to birth? The few references in the Bible that discuss embryonic development and attitudes at least intimate that this is so (Psalm 139:14-16; Ecclesiastes 11:5; Luke 1:44, etc.). Babies can surely fight with each other, if they are given opportunity, very soon *after* they are born. What is to prevent their doing so *before* they are born? Thus, there is no reason not to take this passage quite literally.

Rebekah was so puzzled and disturbed by this situation, which apparently neither Isaac nor her nurse, nor anyone else, was able to explain, that she finally, in desperation, called on the Lord for an answer. Marvelously, the Lord did give her an answer! Whether through a prophet, or dream, or theophany, we are not told, but in some way God spoke to her, so clearly that she could never forget the remarkable revelation which she received.

The twins in her womb were of two utterly different and antagonistic temperaments. The nations which they would establish would inherit these tendencies. The struggle which had begun in her womb would continue throughout their lives and throughout the histories of their respective nations.

Which, then, would prevail? The Lord was most specific in His reply: "The elder shall serve the younger." The younger son would become stronger than the older, and would finally prevail. Since one of the two must carry on the Messianic line and must inherit the promises of the Abrahamic covenant, it is crystal clear that God here told Rebekah that His covenant would be with the younger son, not the older. The younger must therefore receive the father's inheritance and blessing, as Isaac had from Abraham (in Isaac's case, also, this had been true, as Ishmael, the elder son, did not share in either the covenant or the inheritance).

Men normally have felt that the first-born son should receive the greater honor and inheritance, but God does not necessarily work in such ways. In the Messianic line, it is significant that neither Seth, Isaac, Jacob, Judah, nor David were first-born sons; and it is not certain if any of the others were.

There was surely no reason why God could not select the younger if He so willed. God is sovereign, and we do well not to question His choice. "And not only this, but when Rebekah also had conceived by one, even by our father Isaac; (For the children being not yet born, neither having done any good or evil, that the purpose of God according to election might stand, not of works, but of him that calleth;) It was said unto her, The elder shall serve the younger. As it is written, Jacob have I loved [see Malachi 1:1-3], but Esau have I hated" (Romans 9:10-13).

God is sovereign, and can do as He wills, but He is not capricious and always has reason for what He does. He knew the younger would be (as Abraham was) qualified spiritually and morally to transmit the seed and the covenant promises, whereas the older would not be so qualified. Therefore, though most men would have made a different selection, God loved and chose Jacob, and hated and rejected Esau.

No doubt, Rebekah told all this to her husband Isaac; and later, when the time was appropriate, she told it to Jacob and perhaps even to Esau. As time went on, however, Isaac and Esau began to reject and to forget this decision of the Lord, even trying to thwart it. Strange it is, and a sad commentary on the spiritual discernment of most believers even today, that they tend to favor Esau rather than Jacob, just as Isaac did.

Genesis 25:24-26

24 ¶ And when her days to be delivered were fulfilled, behold, *there were* twins in her womb.

25 And the first came out red, all over like a hairy garment; and they called his name E'sau.

26 And after that came his brother out, and his hand took hold on Ḗ'saŭ's heel; and his name was called Jacob: and

Isaac *was* threescore years old when she bare them.

When the twins were born, the first one to emerge from the womb was red and hairy, the second evidently light and smooth. Apparently they were still struggling even as they were born, because the second was hanging on with his hand to the heel of the first, as though trying to pull him back.

The strikingly unusual appearance of the two boys is reflected in the names given them. The first was named Esau, which means "hairy." He was obviously a rugged, strong child. The second was named Jacob, which means "heel-catcher" (perhaps also, by extension, "supplanter"). With respect to Jacob's odd name, the prophet Hosea seems to interpret it as an evidence of strength and power with God. "He took his brother by the heel in the womb, and by his strength he had power with God" (Hosea 12:3).

Though, to the natural eye, Esau appeared the stronger and more attractive, Jacob was tenaciously "following on his heels," and would one day overtake and replace him, not only in the eyes of God but even in the world of men.

Genesis 25:27-34

---

27 And the boys grew: and Ḗ'saŭ was a cunning hunter, a man of the field; and Jacob *was* a plain man, dwelling in tents.

28 And Isaac loved Ḗ'saŭ, because he did eat of *his* venison: but Rḗ-bĕk'åh loved Jacob.

29 ¶ And Jacob sod pottage: and Ḗ'saŭ came from the field, and he *was* faint:

30 And Ḗ'saŭ said to Jacob, Feed me, I pray thee, with that same red *pottage;* for I *am* faint: therefore was his name

called Ḗ'dŏm.

31 And Jacob said, Sell me this day thy birthright.

32 And Ḗ'saŭ said, Behold, I *am* at the point to die: and what profit shall this birthright do to me?

33 And Jacob said, Swear to me this day; and he sware unto him: and he sold his birthright unto Jacob.

34 Then Jacob gave Ḗ'saŭ bread and pottage of lentils; and he did eat and drink, and rose up, and went his way. Thus Ḗ'saŭ despised *his* birthright.

As the boys grew, the difference in their characters, which God could see in the womb, began to be apparent in their respective interests and activities. Esau, the rugged outdoor type, spent his time out in the fields and became a cunning hunter. Jacob stayed home with his family, "dwelling in tents," thus evidently occupying most of his time caring for the flocks and herds of his father.

For some reason, most people think the attributes of Esau commendable, those of Jacob distasteful. Exactly the opposite is the truth of the matter.

What, for example, is good about being a "cunning hunter"? Esau's family was not in the least endangered by wild beasts, nor did they, with their extensive flocks and herds, have any need to slaughter deer and other wild animals for food. That there was no overpopulation of animals that needed thinning-out for the sake of a balanced ecology is obvious from the fact that Esau had to become a *cunning* hunter to find them. The only other hunter mentioned in the Bible is "Nimrod the mighty hunter before [literally 'against'] the Lord" (Genesis 10:9). One Biblical hunter was a rebel against God, the other was a sportsman unconcerned with God. Esau preferred playing out in the field, even long after he was a grown man, to working for his family and serving the Lord. He also was a "fornicator" (Hebrews 12:16) and profane person. Such a man as this was in no way qualified to inherit God's covenant promises, with all the spiritual responsibilities attached to them.

Jacob, on the other hand, was a "plain man, dwelling in tents." Just like Abraham and Isaac, he "sojourned in the land of promise, as in a strange country, dwelling in tabernacles" (Hebrews 11:9). He did this because he was a man of faith, to whom God's plans and promises meant far more than physical pleasure.

The translators have done Jacob a disservice by calling him a "plain" man, or a "quiet" man. The Hebrew word is *tam,* which means "perfect" or "complete" or possibly "mature." It is exactly the same word God used to describe Job when He called him "a *perfect* and an upright man, one that feareth God, and escheweth evil" (Job 1:8).

Jacob had learned of God's promises from his mother and father, and no doubt also knew of God's word that he, not Esau, was to be the inheritor of those promises. He took them with all seriousness and desired to see God's will accomplished. He was a "mature" person, not a carnal, immature playboy like his brother. Rebekah also, who had been attracted to Isaac in the first place because of her desire to follow God's will, had a strong desire to fulfill this part of His will as well. She and Jacob were of kindred minds, spiritually, and so "Rebekah loved Jacob."

Unfortunately for the cause of family harmony and spiritual growth, Isaac became partial to Esau, and indeed encouraged him in his irresponsible activities, for the highly unworthy reason that "he did eat of his venison." Eating venison might have seemed exciting in some way to Isaac, possibly because he was proud of the athletic prowess of his son, but it could hardly have been solely because of its delectable taste. Rebekah, in fact, could prepare goat meat in such a way that he couldn't tell it from venison.

In any case, he began soon to be so partial to Esau (probably feeling guilty that Jacob's concern for God had in recent years begun to exceed his own) that both Jacob and Rebekah could sense that he was likely to give Esau the blessing in spite of the fact God had appointed Jacob. They realized this would be tragic, as Esau was neither interested in God's promises nor qualified to administer them or transmit them to his own children.

If Isaac wished to favor Esau, he of course had the example of custom to justify him. The eldest son customarily received a double portion in the division of the inheritance (Deuteronomy 21:17) and the right to lead the household (Genesis 27:29). The eldest son, of course, also had sober responsibilities. If he was to rule over the household, then he had to provide for the household, both materially and spiritually. In fact, in this particular family, the spiritual responsibilities were paramount (Genesis 18:19). In particular, there was the responsibility of building and officiating at the altar (Genesis 22:9; 26:25; 35:1; etc.), as well as the transmission of God's word and His promises.

The right of primogeniture may have been a custom at this time, but it was not yet a Biblical law. In any case, the father had the privilege of transferring it from the eldest son to another, more deserving, son (I Chronicles 5:1, 2).

As far as Esau was concerned, the only aspect of the birthright which appealed to him was the double inheritance. He cared nothing for the spiritual aspects—he was a profane person! On the other hand, Jacob longed to have the spiritual privileges and patriarchal blessings; the material inheritance was only incidental. He knew his father should have transferred the birthright to him, but Isaac kept putting it off, and now it began to seem that he would never do it. The birthright was often on Jacob's mind, and he knew that Esau neither wanted it nor would honor it. No doubt, the two brothers had often discussed this very thing.

Then, one day, Esau suddenly appeared from one of his excursions in the field, making a great to-do about being faint from hunger and begging Jacob for some food. Jacob at the time was boiling a pot of red lentils, and the aroma was overpoweringly tempting to Esau.

Jacob was evidently preparing it either for his own or his parents' dinner, and it would have been a matter of only a few minutes for Esau to fix himself something to eat. Jacob was more than ever disgusted with the carnality and irresponsibility of his brother and was more horrified all the time at the thought that his father would actually trust the birthright to a man like Esau.

Well, perhaps if his father insisted on giving the birthright to Esau, then Esau himself might be willing to sell it to Jacob. Jacob therefore made him a proposition, perhaps initially in jest or in disgust, not really expecting Esau to accept it. Would Esau sell his birthright in return for a good meal of red lentils? Probably to his amazement, Jacob heard him agree to the absurd transaction!

Esau lamented that he would one day die anyway, and the birthright would not profit him then. Furthermore, it would be a long time before Isaac died, and maybe he would decide eventually to give it to Jacob anyway. A good hunter knows that a bird in the hand is worth two in the bush. This way he would at least get a good meal out of it. "Let us eat and drink, for tomorrow we shall die" (Isaiah 22:13).

When he saw Esau was really serious, Jacob realized that the birthright really didn't mean anything at all to his brother, and that alone was enough to convince him that he should go ahead and consummate this contract. He therefore asked Esau to bind his agreement with a formal oath, which he readily agreed to do. Even if Isaac now gave the birthright to Esau, he would never interfere with a contract between the two brothers sealed in this way. The birthright now would go to Jacob, as God had instructed his parents in the first place.

Esau then sat down and enjoyed his meal, apparently not giving the birthright a further thought.

Why do people so often consider Jacob the culprit in this transaction? Scripture does not offer one word of condemnation or criticism of Jacob. Instead, it condemns Esau unequivocally. "Thus Esau despised his birthright" (Genesis 25:34). "Lest there be any fornicator, or profane person, as Esau, who for one morsel of meat sold his birthright. For ye know how that afterward, when he would have inherited the blessing, he was rejected" (Hebrews 12:16, 17).

This experience with the red lentils, in fact, was closely associated with his very name after that. People from then on often called him Edom (meaning "red"), so that, whenever he heard his name, he was forced to remember that he had sold his birthright for a mess of red pottage!

Jacob, of course, should have been willing to let God work out this problem. God would certainly have overruled the situation even if Isaac had not been willing to give Jacob the birthright as God had instructed him. However, Jacob's sin was not a sin of greed or blackmail, but rather one of lack of faith. He so strongly wanted to see God's purposes advanced that he felt he must help them along by his own actions. This sin, of course, is one of which even the most devoted Christian workers often become guilty. Abraham and Isaac themselves suffered far greater lapses of faith than this.

God could easily forgive this sin of Jacob since he meant it for good, and it did accomplish God's purpose relative to the birthright. On the other hand, it also led to an increasing estrangement from his father and brother. Instead of winning them, he had alienated them. How much better it would have been to resort only to secret prayer about the matter, rather than overt action, and then wait for God to work it out. And how much we ourselves, so quick to criticize Jacob, need to learn the same lesson.

Isaac Versus the Philistines

Sometime after the two boys had grown to manhood, and Isaac himself was at least eighty years old, he and Rebekah encountered a severe test of faith and obedience. We do not have as much information concerning Isaac's life as we do for that of his father, so we do not know whether he had many earlier trials or not. Except for the experience on Mount Moriah, and his problem with Jacob and Esau, he seems to have led a peaceful and comfortable life up to this point.

But any true child of God must go through repeated testings and refinings. "Wherein ye greatly rejoice, though now for a season, if need be, ye are in heaviness through manifold temptations: That the trial [or *proof*] of your faith . . . though it be tried with fire, might be found unto praise and honour and glory at the appearing of Jesus Christ" (I Peter 1:6, 7).

Though there is no statement to this effect, there may also be a possibility that God now allowed these trials to come into Isaac's life because of the character weakness showing up in his preferential bias toward Esau.

Genesis 26:1-5

CHAPTER 26

AND there was a famine in the land, besides the first famine that was in the days of Abraham. And Isaac went unto Å-bĭm'ē-lĕch king of the Phĭ-lĭs'tĭneş unto Gē'rär.

2 And the LORD appeared unto him, and said, Go not down into Egypt; dwell in the land which I shall tell thee of.

3 Sojourn in this land, and I will be with thee, and will bless thee; for unto thee, and unto thy seed, I will give all these countries, and I will perform the oath which I sware unto Abraham thy father;

4 And I will make thy seed to multiply as the stars of heaven, and will give unto thy seed all these countries; and in thy seed shall all the nations of the earth be blessed:

5 Because that Abraham obeyed my voice, and kept my charge, my commandments, my statutes, and my laws.

First, conditions of famine developed in the land where Isaac was living, presumably still near the well Lahai-roi. This seems to have been the first famine in that place in over a hundred years (the other being early in Abram's sojourn there), so that it truly had been a land of plenty. Isaac had never experienced such a thing, and it was beginning to be disastrous for his flocks and herds.

Apparently it was not so bad over near the seacoast, in the Philistines' land, so he decided to move to Gerar. He was evidently even considering going farther, all the way into Egypt, when the Lord stopped him.

So far as the record goes, this is the first time God had appeared to Isaac since he was on Mount Moriah with his father Abraham, probably fifty or more years earlier. The Lord had spoken to Rebekah just before her twins were born, but this is the first time He had spoken to Isaac.

The Lord had not forgotten His covenant concerning Isaac, however; and so He at this time repeated it to Isaac, in much the same words Isaac had heard Him speak to Abraham so long ago. "Do not leave this land to go to Egypt," God said, in effect, "but live where I lead you in this land, and I will bless you with all the blessings I promised your father."

He again told Isaac He would give his descendants all the countries of the promised land, would give him an innumerable progeny, and bless all nations through him. However, God pointed out that He would do these things because of Abraham's faithfulness and obedience, with no mention of Isaac's. One senses in this a backhanded rebuke to Isaac, along with a plea for him to manifest the same characteristics as his father.

God said that Abraham "kept my charge, my commandments, my statutes, and my laws." Presumably these were not at the time codified in written form as they were later through Moses. Nevertheless, God's "word is settled forever in heaven" (Psalm 119:89), and even the Gentiles "show the work of the law written in their hearts" (Romans 2:15). What Abraham heard from God, he obeyed explicitly; what he did not actually hear, he followed through an enlightened conscience and obedient heart.

Genesis 26:6-11

6 ¶ And Isaac dwelt in Gĕ'rär.

7 And the men of the place asked *him* of his wife; and he said, She *is* my sister: for he feared to say, *She is* my wife; lest, *said he,* the men of the place should kill me for Rē-bĕk'áh; because she *was* fair to look upon.

8 And it came to pass, when he had been there a long time, that Á-bĭm'ē-lĕch king of the Phĭ-lĭs'tĭnes looked out at a window, and saw, and, behold, Isaac *was* sporting with Rē-bĕk'áh his wife.

9 And Á-bĭm'ē-lĕch called Isaac, and said, Behold, of a surety she *is* thy wife: and how saidst thou, She *is* my sister? And Isaac said unto him, Because I said, Lest I die for her.

10 And Á-bĭm'ē-lĕch said, What *is* this thou hast done unto us? one of the people might lightly have lain with thy wife, and thou shouldest have brought guiltiness upon us.

11 And Á-bĭm'ē-lĕch charged all *his* people, saying, He that toucheth this man or his wife shall surely be put to death.

Isaac therefore stayed in Gerar, which was a part of Canaan but which had been controlled for some time by a colony of Philistines. At this time, the main body of the Philistines still lived on the island of Crete, not actually moving en masse to "Palestine" until centuries later. The king, or "Abimelech," of this colony was hardly the same one encountered by Abraham nearly a century earlier, but no doubt he had heard of Abraham and his traumatic experience in Philistia on that earlier occasion.

Isaac knew about it also, but the memory had grown dim by this time, and he suddenly found himself repeating the same lie Abraham had used, and for the same reason. "Rebekah? Oh, yes, she is my sister." Rebekah, though she must have been at least sixty years old by this time, was still a very beautiful and desirable woman, and quickly attracted much attention from the Philistine men. Isaac, like Abraham, began to be afraid he might be murdered on her account. Perhaps he may have reasoned that, even though Abraham had been embarrassed through this type of deception, he had at least come out of it alive and so had Sarah; so maybe it was the best course of action to follow. Anyway, maybe they wouldn't discover the deception this time.

In fact, they didn't for a long time. Though some of Abimelech's men evidently desired Rebekah, Isaac was a wealthy and respected friend of King Abimelech, and they were hesitant to follow too bold a course in pursuing his "sister." The absence of any mention of Jacob and Esau in this narrative may suggest they remained back in the Negev looking after the possessions which Isaac couldn't bring with him to Gerar. Otherwise, the presence of two grown sons would have made it especially difficult to pass off their mother as his sister.

Isaac's tent was pitched not too far from the house of Abimelech himself, which was probably on the highest eminence in the community. Abimelech could see down into the women's quarters of the tent from his window and, one day, perhaps not too much to his surprise, he saw Isaac making love to Rebekah. He had probably suspected it for some time, but now he knew she was really Isaac's wife.

When he confronted Isaac with this evidence, Isaac had to admit what he had done and why he had done it. Abimelech rebuked Isaac, and protested that he and his people had much higher standards of morality than Isaac had given them credit for. Adultery with his wife, which conceivably might have ensued, would have involved his whole nation in guilt before God.

One wonders about this surprising moral sensitivity on the part of a Philistine king. If his people were really so concerned about their morality, it seems strange that Isaac would have been so fearful of them. Either he was a poor judge of character or else the Philistine men were somehow constrained to follow a different standard with respect to Isaac and Rebekah than with others. Perhaps they had heard of the similar experience with Abraham long ago, when the nation almost died as that earlier Abimelech took Sarah into his harem. In some way, at any rate, God kept the men away from Rebekah. Then, surprisingly, Abimelech, instead of taking vengeance on Isaac for his deception, pronounced a potential capital penalty for any of his subjects who harmed either Isaac or Rebekah.

Genesis 26:12-16

---

12 Then Isaac sowed in that land, and received in the same year a hundred-fold: and the LORD blessed him.

13 And the man waxed great, and went forward, and grew until he became very great:

14 For he had possession of flocks, and possession of herds, and great store of servants: and the Phĭ-lĭs′tĭneş envied him.

15 For all the wells which his father's servants had digged in the days of Abraham his father, the Phĭ-lĭs′tĭneş had stopped them, and filled them with earth.

16 And Å-bĭm′ē-lĕeh said unto Isaac, Go from us; for thou art much mightier than we.

Isaac seems to have learned well the lesson of trusting God through this experience. For a while longer, he stayed in Gerar, and he prospered greatly.

Until this time, he and his father seem to have been solely occupied with raising animals. Now, however, he acquired some land, possibly by a rental agreement, on which to plant and raise crops. Perhaps the famine had persuaded him that he needed a more reliable source of food for his flocks and herds. At any rate, he began to practice agriculture, and it proved highly successful.

In verse 12 occurs the first mention of seed-sowing in the Bible, along with the information that the Lord blessed it with a hundredfold increase. Seed-sowing is frequently used in the New Testament as symbolic of witnessing; and it is noteworthy that the first mention is in the familiar parable of the sower, in which the good seed likewise brought forth a hundredfold (Matthew 13:23).

Isaac at this point prospered so greatly that his power began to eclipse even that of Abimelech and the Philistines. His herds and flocks, the richness of his crops, the increasing number of his servants, became so great that the envy of the Philistines, already vexed because of Abimelech's protection of him, finally led to retaliation.

An adequate supply of water was, of course, absolutely necessary for Isaac's operations; and this was obtained from the many wells dug by Abraham, his father, in the Philistine country. The Philistines decided to plug up all these wells and to force him out of their country. Abimelech himself called on Isaac to depart from their land, since he had become more powerful than his own nation.

Genesis 26:17-22

---

17 ⁋ And Isaac departed thence, and pitched his tent in the valley of Gĕ'rär, and dwelt there.

18 And Isaac digged again the wells of water, which they had digged in the days of Abraham his father; for the Phī-lĭs'tĭneş had stopped them after the death of Abraham: and he called their names after the names by which his father had called them.

19 And Isaac's servants digged in the valley, and found there a well of springing water.

20 And the herdmen of Gĕ'rär did strive with Isaac's herdmen, saying, The water *is* ours: and he called the name of the well E'sĕk; because they strove with him.

21 And they digged another well, and strove for that also: and he called the name of it Sĭt'näh.

22 And he removed from thence, and digged another well; and for that they strove not: and he called the name of it Rē-hō'bŏth; and he said, For now the LORD hath made room for us, and we shall be fruitful in the land.

Isaac could have resisted this demand, since the earlier Abimelech had given his father the right to dwell anywhere in the land he might choose (Genesis 20:15), and since the wells belonged to Abraham by right of construction. Also he might well have been able to defeat the Philistine colonists in battle, if it had come to that (26:16), since he now had ample manpower.

Nevertheless, he realized such resistance would still further alienate the Philistines, and he chose to let them have their way. He moved away, therefore, from the capital, going east and farther up the valley of Gerar. Here there were other wells which Abraham had constructed, but these had already been plugged up when Abraham died. Evidently the Philistine settlers were not yet numerous or prosperous enough themselves to need them, but wanted to discourage others from settling there in the meantime, as they were trying to maintain a claim to the land themselves. Isaac embarked on a program of reopening these wells; no one else was using this part of the land, so he thought the Philistines would not object. To emphasize his right to the wells by way of inheritance, he used the same names Abraham had given them.

In addition, his servants dug another well, evidently lower in the valley, and this turned out to be an artesian well, a well of "living water." The Philistine herdsmen, however, claimed this water should belong to them, evidently on the ground that Isaac no longer had the right to dig new wells in their country. Rather than argue the point, Isaac instructed his own herdsmen to let them have the well and to dig another farther up the valley. He gave the first well the ironic name of Esek (the "Quarrel Well"). They proceeded to dig the second well, but the men of Gerar followed them there and demanded that well also.

Isaac then named it Sitnah (the "Hatred Well") and again gave it to them. He moved much farther away this time, beyond any region to which the Philistines had any reasonable claim. Finally, this time the men from Gerar no longer followed him; so the new well he dug was called Rehoboth ("the Well of Ample Room"). Isaac left some of his flocks and herds in this location, with their herdsmen, while he himself went on still farther.

Genesis 26:23-25

---

23 And he went up from thence to Bē'ĕr–shē'bȧ.

24 And the LORD appeared unto him the same night, and said, I *am* the God of Abraham thy father: fear not, for I *am* with thee, and will bless thee, and

multiply thy seed for my servant Abraham's sake.

25 And he builded an altar there, and called upon the name of the LORD, and pitched his tent there: and there Isaac's servants digged a well.

Years ago, Abraham had made a covenant with the Philistines at Beersheba ("the Well of the Covenant," or "Well of the Seven") and had built an altar there (Genesis 21:32-34). There, too, Isaac himself had lived after the sacrifice on Mount Moriah (22:19). After all the bitter experiences of recent years in Gerar, Isaac apparently felt the need to return to the place where he had been in the closest fellowship to the Lord, perhaps to find again real joy in his walk with God.

And, sure enough, God graciously met him the very first night he was back in Beersheba. God had spoken to him once before, as he was leaving the land, but he had failed to stay as close to Him as he should have there in Philistia. Now God graciously met him and assured him once again that he need not fear the Philistines or any others, for God was with him and would keep His promises, for Abraham's sake. There Isaac built an altar of his own—apparently the only one he ever built—and worshiped the Lord, pitching his tent and instructing his servants to reopen Abraham's well.

Genesis 26:26-33

---

26 ¶ Then Ȧ-bĭm'ē-lĕch went to him from Gē'rär, and Ȧ-hŭz'zăth one of his friends, and Phī'chŏl the chief captain of his army.

27 And Isaac said unto them, Wherefore come ye to me, seeing ye hate me, and have sent me away from you?

28 And they said, We saw certainly that the LORD was with thee: and we said, Let there be now an oath betwixt us, *even* betwixt us and thee, and let us make a covenant with thee;

29 That thou wilt do us no hurt, as we have not touched thee, and as we have done unto thee nothing but good, and have sent thee away in peace: thou *art* now the blessed of the LORD.

30 And he made them a feast, and they did eat and drink.

31 And they rose up betimes in the morning, and sware one to another: and Isaac sent them away, and they departed from him in peace.

32 And it came to pass the same day, that Isaac's servants came, and told him concerning the well which they had digged, and said unto him, We have found water.

33 And he called it Shē'bah: therefore the name of the city *is* Bē'ēr-shē'bȧ unto this day.

While the well-digging was under way at Beersheba, a delegation of the Philistines again appeared—this time none less than King Abimelech himself, along with his chief captain Phichol (probably a title, like Abimelech, rather than a proper name) and another man. But in contrast, this time they were on a mission of peace, possibly because

Isaac's policy of nonresistance had finally shamed them. Also, they knew Jehovah was blessing Isaac and that he was growing stronger all the time. Now that he was out of their land, they decided it was the policy of wisdom to stay on good terms with him.

They reminded him that they had not harmed him or Rebekah (a good thing for them they hadn't!) and that he had prospered greatly in their land; so hopefully he wouldn't hold their recent frictions too much against them. They proposed a mutual nonaggression treaty, somewhat like the one Abraham and the earlier Abimelech had made on this same spot nearly a century before.

Isaac was quite agreeable, especially after his recent encounter with God. They engaged in a ceremonial feast that night in token of their covenant and sealed it the next morning with a solemn oath.

As they were departing, no doubt quite self-satisfied at accomplishing their mission, Isaac's servants came to him with the happy news that the well they were digging had struck a good supply of water. It was appropriate that the well be called "the Well of the Oath" (Beersheba), not only because of the pact signed that day, but also because of the similar covenant and name assigned the place by Abraham long ago. No doubt also Isaac had in mind God's great covenant, which He had confirmed to him here.

Genesis 26:34, 35

These last two verses of the chapter, dealing with Esau's wives, are best discussed in context with Genesis 27, which deals with the conflict between Jacob and Esau. The absence of any mention of the two sons during the time of Isaac's stay in Gerar suggests that they had stayed back home either in Mamre or Lahai-roi, but now the family was reunited for a while.

16

The Mystery of Jacob and Esau

(Genesis 27-28)

How Could God Love Jacob?

One of the most intriguing questions associated with Genesis and with the establishment of God's chosen people, the children of Israel, is how God could bless and use such a person as Jacob for the accomplishment of His divine purposes for mankind. Jacob seems so obviously to be a sly schemer, a liar and deceiver, a "supplanter," a man intent only on acquiring money by whatever means he can devise. He is shrewd, crafty, covetous, with no ethical scruples except those dictated by his own self-interest. Even granting His covenant obligations to Abraham and Isaac, why would God choose Jacob instead of Esau? Esau seems a much more admirable character—a strong, virile, outdoor man, surely much more suited to be the founding father and head of a new nation than a man like Jacob.

Sad to say, it is just such caricatures of Jacob and Esau, and the Jews in general, as sketched in the above paragraph, that have caused tremendous waves of anti-Semitism and persecution to be visited against the Jews down through the centuries. Somehow even Christians have been caught up in the fever of anti-Semitic feeling on many occasions for reasons like this. Many pastors and Bible teachers who outwardly would deny strongly that they are anti-Jewish, nevertheless seem to let their hidden feelings on the subject come out when dealing with Jacob.

It should not be thought that, when we defend Jacob, we thereby are condoning lying and deception. However, one paramount consideration must be kept in mind in trying to understand and apply these passages in the Book of Genesis. There is never a single instance *in the Bible* of criticism of Jacob (except on the lips of Esau and Laban, both of whom are unworthy witnesses). Every time God spoke to Jacob, it was in a message of blessing and promise, never one of rebuke or chastisement. If we would be faithful Bible expositors, therefore, we must be guided by what God has actually said, not what we think He should have said. "For my thoughts are not your thoughts, neither are your ways my ways, saith the Lord" (Isaiah 55:8).

We suggest, therefore, that such an attitude as commonly expressed by Bible expositors relative to Jacob is entirely out of line. When, for example, Dr. Scofield, in his reference Bible, heads certain passages in Genesis by titles such as "The stolen blessing" and "Jacob reaps the harvest of his evil years," he is pronouncing moral judgments of his own which are not at all founded on the actual Biblical statements concerning Jacob.

God's judgment concerning Jacob is given in Genesis 32:28: "As a prince hast thou power with God and with men, and hast prevailed." "Was not Esau Jacob's brother? saith the Lord: yet I loved Jacob and I hated Esau" (Malachi 1:2, 3).

We have already discussed at some length, in chapter 15, God's decision to establish the Messianic line and promises through Jacob, rather than Esau, even before the two boys were born. This decision was clearly conveyed to Rebekah and Isaac; but the latter nevertheless favored Esau, resolving to give him both the birthright benefits and the patriarchal responsibilities and blessings associated with God's promise to Abraham. As the boys grew, their characters soon proved that God's decision had been eminently wise. "Jacob was a plain [literally 'perfect,' or 'complete'] man" (Genesis 25:27). Esau, on the other hand, "despised his birthright" (Genesis 25:34).

Genesis 26:34, 35

---

34 ¶ And E'saû was forty years old when he took to wife Judith the daughter of Bē-ē'rī the Hit'tite, and Băsh'ē-māth the daughter of E'lŏn the Hit'tite: 35 Which were a grief of mind unto Isaac and to Rē-bĕk'áh.

The carnality of Esau's character is further confirmed in these two verses. Knowing well how cautious God had been in selecting a wife for his own father, a selection which carefully guarded the integrity of the line of the promised seed, Esau nevertheless proceeded to take a Hittite woman for his wife. No doubt also knowing that God's will for the marriage relationship was monogamy, he compounded the insult to God and took still another Hittite woman for a second wife. He was both presumptuous and utterly unconcerned about God's promised blessings associated with the patriarchal line.

Esau was forty years old when he married these two women; so it was hardly a matter of youthful indiscretion. It was a deliberate choice and was certainly made against the counsel of his parents, as well as against God's will, as he well knew. These wives "were a grief of mind unto Isaac and to Rebekah," probably not only because they were "daughters of Canaan" (Genesis 28:8) and because Abraham had so carefully avoided taking one of "the daughters of the Canaanites" (Genesis 24:3) as a wife for Esau's father, but probably also because they were idolaters and ungodly in life style as well. They no doubt still further alienated Esau from concern for God's promises and purposes, as well as His standards of holiness.

Genesis 27:1-5

CHAPTER 27

AND it came to pass, that when Isaac was old, and his eyes were dim, so that he could not see, he called É'saù his eldest son, and said unto him, My son: and he said unto him, Behold, *here am* I.

2 And he said, Behold now, I am old, I know not the day of my death:

3 Now therefore take, I pray thee, thy weapons, thy quiver and thy bow, and go out to the field, and take me *some* venison;

4 And make me savory meat, such as I love, and bring *it* to me, that I may eat; that my soul may bless thee before I die.

5 And Rē-bĕk'ăh heard when Isaac spake to É'saù his son. And É'saù went to the field to hunt *for* venison, *and* to bring *it.*

But in spite of all this—in spite of God's instruction concerning Jacob before he was born, in spite of the plainly obvious superiority of Jacob's character and spiritual discernment and convictions over those of Esau, in spite of Jacob's further legalization of his claim to the patriarchal blessing through his purchase of the birthright from Esau, confirmed by Esau's solemn oath, in spite of Esau's obvious indifference to his spiritual heritage and to the will of God—in spite of all this, Isaac nevertheless determined that he was going to give the blessing to Esau.

And evidently, Isaac's deliberate intent to thwart the purpose of God was motivated primarily by his personal love of Esau, and that was "because he did eat of his venison" (Genesis 25:28). It is hard indeed to comprehend how such favoritism, on the part of such a presumably spiritual man as Isaac, could have been based on such a carnal and unworthy motive. Perhaps this tended to crystallize in Isaac's mind the contrast between himself—introspective and nonaggressive—and Esau, rough, strong, bold man that he was. Esau represented the secret desires of his own heart, which he could enjoy vicariously through his son's exploits.

Whatever the reason, Isaac did decide to give the blessing, which rightly would have gone to Jacob, to Esau instead. He was quite old by this time, so that his eyes could no longer see. His age was definitely over one hundred (since he had been sixty years old when Jacob and Esau were born, and the sons were forty years old when Esau married his Hittite wives). He may have been considerably older, since Jacob was 130 years old at the time Joseph was about thirty-nine (Genesis 47:9; 41:46; 41:53; 45:11), and since Joseph was born about eighteen years or so after Jacob left his mother and father (Genesis 31:38; 30:25). Consequently, Jacob may have been about seventy-five and Isaac 135 at this particular time. Everyone involved in this episode was thus quite mature, though Jacob and Esau at least were still quite vigorous and, gerontologically speaking, relatively "young" men in terms of the aging process as it existed in those days. As a matter of fact, even Isaac was not as near death as he seems to have feared, since he lived to be 180 before he died (Genesis 35:28).

It was customary to mark solemn occasions by some kind of feast, and since Isaac had resolved to bless Esau, it seemed appropriate that the solemnities should be marked by a feast provided by Esau's skill at hunting. Isaac therefore so instructed Esau, and he set forth to hunt and slay a deer from which he could prepare him "savoury meat, such as I love." It is a sad thing for a believer to be so ruled by his appetite that he actually "loves" his food and bases important decisions on its availability. But Isaac is not the last one of whom this is true.

It is significant that Isaac was not doing this with Rebekah's knowledge. She only happened to overhear the conversation. This secretive nature of Isaac's plans can only be explained on the assumption that he was ashamed of what he was doing, knowing that Rebekah would not approve but hoping that he would get it accomplished before she could interfere.

---

6 ¶ And Rē-bĕk′àh spake unto Jacob her son, saying, Behold, I heard thy father speak unto E′saŭ thy brother, saying,

7 Bring me venison, and make me savory meat, that I may eat, and bless thee before the LORD before my death.

8 Now therefore, my son, obey my voice according to that which I command thee.

9 Go now to the flock, and fetch me from thence two good kids of the goats; and I will make them savory meat for thy father, such as he loveth:

10 And thou shalt bring *it* to thy father, that he may eat, and that he may bless thee before his death.

Rebekah, as soon as she learned of Isaac's plans, acted immediately to prevent his carrying them out. Though she must have been very hesitant, as a good and faithful wife, to do anything but follow her husband's wishes, she evidently felt that, in this case, God's will must override her husband's will. She may have failed to understand, and perhaps had inadequate faith, to realize that God's will would be accomplished whether or not men cooperated in its accomplishment. Isaac's blessing of Esau could not possibly overrule what God had long ago decreed, but Rebekah seems to have been afraid that it might, and so she resolved to see that Jacob would receive what was rightfully his regardless of any consequence.

She quickly conceived an audacious plan to make Isaac pronounce his blessing on Jacob even while intending to bless Esau. Since Isaac was blind, she would have Jacob pretend to be Esau. Fearing that Jacob would demur from such a plan, she invoked her right to filial obedience: "Obey my voice according to that which I command thee." Jacob must quickly prepare two kids from the flock, and she would cook them, fixing them in such a way that Isaac could not distinguish them from venison. This in itself shows that Isaac's love for venison was at least partially based on his admiration for Esau's skill at hunting; the taste of the meat itself could be duplicated by Rebekah's culinary skills, so that the actual killing of wild game was not at all necessary to satisfy his taste preferences.

Rebekah told Jacob that after she had prepared the food, he must take it to his father in Esau's name, so that his father would pronounce the blessing intended for Esau on Jacob. Rebekah appears to have had a most naive faith in the magical power of the words themselves in order to believe that God's true blessing was dependent to this degree on their actually being pronounced by Isaac.

There is, however, one other possible explanation of her adoption of such a strategy, an explanation which should at least be considered.

Perhaps she intended to use this means to call Isaac's attention to his presumptuous determination to thwart God's will. He had not heeded her previous pleadings on Jacob's (and God's) behalf. Perhaps he could be brought to see the enormity of his error if he were forced to bless Jacob in spite of himself. Rebekah knew she was taking a terrible risk of permanently alienating both Isaac and Esau by this scheme, since it would only be a matter of a few hours at most before it would be discovered, and she knew that Jacob also would realize this. Isaac knew that Rebekah loved him, and he loved her. If he could be made to realize that God's will was so important that Rebekah (and Jacob, as well) was willing to sacrifice even his own love for it, then perhaps the shock would be the means of bringing him back to his senses and get him to realize his error. Perhaps also it would spare Isaac the almost certain wrathful retribution of God if he were to carry out his own plan.

Since all this turned out to be the actual result of Rebekah's strategy, as we will see, can we not at least give Rebekah (as well as Jacob) the benefit of the doubt, and assume that this was really her purpose? Once again, we should remember that God did not rebuke either Rebekah or Jacob for this plan, but instead seemed to honor it, at least in its results.

Genesis 27:11-17

---

11 And Jacob said to Rē-bĕk′ăh his mother, Behold, E′saŭ my brother *is* a hairy man, and I *am* a smooth man:

12 My father peradventure will feel me, and I shall seem to him as a deceiver; and I shall bring a curse upon me, and not a blessing.

13 And his mother said unto him, Upon me *be* thy curse, my son: only obey my voice, and go fetch me *them*.

14 And he went, and fetched, and brought *them* to his mother: and his mother made savory meat, such as his father loved.

15 And Rē-bĕk′ăh took goodly raiment of her eldest son E′saŭ, which *were* with her in the house, and put them upon Jacob her younger son:

16 And she put the skins of the kids of the goats upon his hands, and upon the smooth of his neck:

17 And she gave the savory meat and the bread, which she had prepared, into the hand of her son Jacob.

Jacob, indeed, did demur at first from his mother's plan. Though he knew the blessing should go to him, and not to Esau, he did not wish to deceive his father. Furthermore, even though his father was blind, his sense of touch was still sound; so he could easily distinguish Jacob's smooth skin from Esau's hairy skin. His father, in anger, would then curse him instead of bless him; and that would make matters worse than ever. Rebekah, however, somehow confident the plan would work out for good, again insisted that he, as a good son, simply obey her command. If, perchance, Isaac did find out, she would explain that it was all her own idea and that Jacob was merely obeying her. If any curse was involved, she would receive it herself, taking full responsibility.

Jacob, therefore, proceeded to follow her instructions, selecting and killing two kids of the goats, dressing them and bringing them to his mother. Rebekah then began to prepare the meat and, while the meat was roasting, she prepared the skins in such a way as to simulate the skin of a hairy man. In some way, she fastened these skins on Jacob's hands and neck, then had him dress in some of Esau's clothing, with the "smell of a field" on them. Thus, Jacob would both feel and smell like Esau when he came into his father's presence. All of this no doubt took a considerable amount of time, and they did not know how soon Esau would be successful in his hunting and would be returning home. It was clearly a very tense situation and, once they had started on this plan of action, they were in such a hurry that there was no time to stop and think much about it. Rebekah, indeed, had always been a woman of quick decision and action, as is evident from the time she first made her choice to follow Abraham's servant and marry Isaac. Probably, also, she and Jacob had often discussed the whole problem, and perhaps she had foreseen this development and already decided what she must do if the time should ever come.

Jacob's fear that his father would think him a "deceiver" needs a little clarification. The word actually means "mocker," and seems to suggest that discovery of the plan by his father would make him seem to be mocking his father's blindness. This was Jacob's concern, rather than that his father would think him a liar.

There is also a possibility that the "goodly raiment of her eldest son Esau, which were with her in the house," were special garments associated with the priestly functions of the head of the house. It would have been appropriate for the recipient of the father's commission, centering as it did in the transfer of Isaac's patriarchal commission to his son, to be so clothed. If so, it would appear that Rebekah had kept these particular garments in her own house for this purpose, since Esau quite probably lived elsewhere with his two wives. This, in any event, was an interpretation of the ancient Hebrew commentators. In this case, we would also have to assume that Esau nevertheless had worn them occasionally while in the fields, in order for the pleasant "smell of a field" to be on them.

Jacob, then, no doubt with considerable hesitation, took the meat, along with bread his mother had baked, into the presence of his father. His hands would feel like Esau's hands, his clothing would smell like Esau's clothing, and his meal would taste like Esau's venison. Thus, the senses of touch, smell, and taste would be taken care of; and the sense of sight was not a problem, since Isaac could not see. However, the sense of hearing was still a problem, since Jacob would have to speak, and his voice was not Esau's voice.

Genesis 27:18-25

18 ¶ And he came unto his father, and said, My father: and he said, Here *am* I; who *art* thou, my son?

19 And Jacob said unto his father, I *am* E'sau thy firstborn; I have done according as thou badest me: arise, I pray thee, sit and eat of my venison, that thy soul may bless me.

20 And Isaac said unto his son, How *is* it that thou hast found *it* so quickly, my son? And he said, Because the LORD thy God brought *it* to me.

21 And Isaac said unto Jacob, Come near, I pray thee, that I may feel thee, my son, whether thou *be* my very son E'sau or not.

22 And Jacob went near unto Isaac his father; and he felt him, and said, The voice *is* Jacob's voice, but the hands *are* the hands of E'sau.

23 And he discerned him not, because his hands were hairy, as his brother E'sau's hands: so he blessed him.

24 And he said, *Art* thou my very son E'sau? And he said, I *am*.

25 And he said, Bring *it* near to me, and I will eat of my son's venison, that my soul may bless thee. And he brought *it* near to him, and he did eat: and he brought him wine, and he drank.

When Jacob entered and spoke to his father, he no doubt tried to speak as nearly like Esau as he could. Being brothers, there was certainly some similarity in their two voices. Isaac was expecting Esau, and he could no doubt smell the dinner; so his presumption was that it was Esau. Nevertheless, the voice didn't seem quite normal; so he asked directly which of his two sons it was.

Jacob had surely hoped that Isaac would not question him at all, but now there was apparently nothing he could do except to be as persuasive in the deception as possible. He identified himself by name as Esau, assuring his father that he had taken and prepared the venison his father loved and that he was ready to receive the blessing. Isaac was strangely uncomfortable; the voice sounded like Jacob's and perhaps he felt a twinge of conscience in that he was preparing to give Jacob's blessing to Esau.

He asked his son to come close, so that he could feel his hands, and thereby satisfy himself that this indeed was Esau. Rebekah's preparations were good, and the skins of the goats on Jacob's hands did seem indeed like the hands of Esau. Nevertheless Isaac asked him point-blank: "Art thou my very son Esau?" And Jacob said, "I am."

Isaac finally was assured that it was Esau, and therefore partook of the meal and prepared to give his blessing to him. When he said "that my soul may bless thee," it should be noted that the word "soul" is the Hebrew *nephesh,* and refers to the mind and heart, or the consciousness, of man. It is an emphatic way of saying "I," stressing the deep conviction of the person regarding the action undertaken.

The problem that many have with Jacob's character, of course, focuses especially on this passage. Several of his statements were openly and intentionally false. One of them, when he claimed that God had brought him the game unusually quickly, seemed actually to be associating God's own name with a lie. This would certainly seem to be taking God's name in vain, in addition to the sin of lying.

Why is it that God did not rebuke Jacob and cause Isaac to withhold the blessing from him? Or, even after Isaac had blessed him, why did God later confirm the blessing? (Genesis 28:13-15). The rebuke was solely for Esau, and the repentance was Isaac's, not Jacob's.

It would seem that the only way of understanding this situation is to conclude that, whatever may have been wrong with the stratagem and deception of Jacob and Rebekah, the sin of Esau and Isaac was infinitely more grievous. God does not approve of lying, and Jacob and Rebekah well knew this. They were sensitive and spiritual people; but they had decided that, as bad as deception might be in God's sight, it had become necessary in this case in order to prevent a much worse sin, that of blasphemously presuming to convey the most holy of God's promises to a man who neither wanted it nor would honor it, and to do so directly in the face of God's commandment against it. Such an eventuality surely would have incurred God's most severe judgment on both Isaac and Esau, and this they felt they must prevent at all costs.

A somewhat parallel situation is found in Exodus 1:15-20. The Hebrew midwives deliberately disobeyed the king of Egypt (this also normally is a sin—note Romans 13:2 and I Peter 2:13) and blatantly lied to him, because to do otherwise would have been cowardly and cruel, resulting in the death of large numbers of male infants. Furthermore, Scripture says: "Therefore God dealt well with the midwives" (Exodus 1:20). There is no way of understanding this passage except that God was pleased with this particular deception practiced by these Hebrew women.

Another instance of God's blessing on a lie was His preservation of Rahab and her family because she hid the two Israelite spies and told the king of Jericho they were not there (Joshua 2:3-6; 6:25).

There are a number of other instances in the Bible in which godly men, in order to accomplish the will of God and to glorify Him, had to break one or another of His commandments, at least in the form in which, for purposes of simplicity and everyday use, they are normally expressed.

We have to recognize this fact, in order to do full justice to Scripture as God has revealed it to us. At the same time, we must emphasize strongly the fact that such instances as these constitute rare exceptions to the rule, and can only be justified by very special and unusual circumstances. The one overriding criterion seems to be that such an exception can at best be warranted only when a still greater principle, associated with the greater revealed purposes of God, will be sacrificed by legalistic adherence to the letter of the law.

Furthermore, the examples given in Scripture never indicate that such actions were in order to gain some temporal advantage for those practicing them. Both Rahab and the Hebrew midwives risked their lives by their deceptions. They would seem to have been much better off, temporally speaking, to tell the truth; but this would have resulted in death to God's people.

Similarly, Jacob and Rebekah, in order to do what they thought was necessary to accomplish God's will, and to spare Isaac and Esau God's judgment for opposing His will, were willing to risk the wrath and hatred of their own loved ones, and Jacob even to risk his life at the hands of his angry brother. Their action was hardly for any temporal advantage it might have given them because, to all appearances at least, there could be none.

While it is true that the Bible does not explicitly place this interpretation on these events, it is also true that it does not explicitly place any other interpretation on them, and it certainly does not preclude this interpretation. In view of the events that followed, as well as of God's further dealings with all concerned, it does seem to be the interpretation which is most consistent with all the recorded facts. In any case, the very fact that it is a possible and plausible interpretation does make it feasible to see Jacob and Rebekah in a much more favorable light than most have been willing to consider. This in itself is a good reason for favoring it.

The Blessing and the Tears

After the festive meal had been finished (Jacob and Rebekah no doubt waiting on pins and needles, as it were, lest Esau should return before the blessing had been given), Isaac beckoned to Jacob to come near and kiss him. Isaac, because of the solemn nature of what he was intending to do (conveying God's covenant promises and blessings to his son, who in turn would be responsible for their transmission and implementation in his own family, until the ultimate promised Seed would come), was no doubt "in the Spirit" as he began to pronounce the blessing. God also, who had made His solemn covenant with Abraham, and who had renewed it with Isaac, certainly was present on this occasion. What would have happened had it indeed been Esau standing there, rather than Jacob, we can only surmise; but it surely seems likely that it would have resulted in tragedy for both father and son. God's solemn promises and covenants are not to be dispensed as trifles, subject to the whim and preference of the individual.

Genesis 27:26-29

26 And his father Isaac said unto him, Come near now, and kiss me, my son. 27 And he came near, and kissed him: and he smelled the smell of his raiment, and blessed him, and said, See, the smell of my son *is* as the smell of a field which the LORD hath blessed: 28 Therefore God give thee of the dew of heaven, and the fatness of the earth, and plenty of corn and wine: 29 Let people serve thee, and nations bow down to thee: be lord over thy brethren, and let thy mother's sons bow down to thee: cursed *be* every one that curseth thee, and blessed *be* he that blesseth thee.

That this blessing was definitely the same as the blessing given to Abraham and Isaac is clear from the words spoken by Isaac at its climax. First, however, Isaac referred to the material aspects of life which so occupied Esau and which had apparently increasingly concerned Isaac. He did, of course, recognize that these also were gifts of God, and so invoked God's material blessings on his son. There is nothing in his words to suggest, however, that this also involved an actual bequeathal of his own property. The latter was a transaction more associated with the birthright, which Jacob had also secured by direct purchase as well as by God's instruction.

Then, however, Isaac got to the heart of the matter, as he repeated God's own promise to Abram: "Cursed be every one that curseth thee, and blessed be he that blesseth thee" (note Genesis 12:3). At the same time, note his awful presumption in saying to, as he thought, Esau: "Be lord over thy brethren, and let thy mother's sons bow down to thee." This is in direct opposition to God's statement: "The elder shall serve the younger" (Genesis 25:23).

In any case, he did pronounce the blessing; and he did so under the inspiration of God, even though he himself was trying to thwart the will of God as he was speaking. Just so, many years later, the prophet Balaam was forced to bless Israel even against his will (Numbers 23:11, 12). In Jesus' day, likewise, the high priest spoke prophetically of the meaning of Jesus' death, though he himself did not understand the real import of what he was saying (John 11:49-52). The blessing which, by God's command, should have gone to Jacob was indeed pronounced by his father on Jacob.

Genesis 27:30-33

---

30 ¶ And it came to pass, as soon as Isaac had made an end of blessing Jacob, and Jacob was yet scarce gone out from the presence of Isaac his father, that E′saū his brother came in from his hunting.

31 And he also had made savory meat, and brought it unto his father, and said unto his father, Let my father arise, and eat of his son's venison, that thy soul may bless me.

32 And Isaac his father said unto him, Who *art* thou? And he said, I *am* thy son, thy firstborn, E′saū.

33 And Isaac trembled very exceedingly, and said, Who? where *is* he that hath taken venison, and brought *it* me, and I have eaten of all before thou camest, and have blessed him? yea, *and* he shall be blessed.

The fine timing of God's counsel, as well as a capsule commentary on the urgency of the drama from Jacob's standpoint, is shown by the immediate arrival of Esau on the scene, just as Jacob left Isaac's presence. He had a meal of fine venison prepared for his father and was all set to receive Isaac's blessing. Though he had despised his birthright enough to sell it to Jacob, and though he had no real interest in the spiritual aspects of the blessing, he did understand enough about it to realize it would include political and military superiority for himself and his children. In addition, he did have enough confidence in the God of his father to realize that God's word in this respect would be fulfilled. This feature of the blessing he wanted, most earnestly.

When he approached his father with the venison, however, he was surprised to hear his father asking, "Who art thou?" "Why, Esau, of course, your oldest son!" His father had sent him on the errand. Why was he surprised when he completed it?

Then it began to dawn on Isaac what had happened. He answered haltingly: "But if you are Esau, who was it who has just brought me venison and received my blessing?" Who, indeed! The truth suddenly came home to Isaac like a mighty blast of icy wind. In spite of all his intentions, God had overruled, and he had blessed Jacob instead of

Esau. Furthermore, he realized that he had been deceived by his beloved wife and his faithful son, in order to prevent him from doing what he knew he had no right to do. God had spoken through him in spite of himself; so he told Esau: "Therefore, Jacob indeed shall receive the blessing." This was clearly the will of God, and there was nothing he could do to change that! He had tried to do so, but God had stopped him.

As the impact of these thoughts came over him, "Isaac trembled very exceedingly." Hebrew scholars tell us the original language is extremely graphic, something like "Isaac trembled most excessively with a great trembling." Emotions of all sorts overwhelmed him. Anger with Jacob, concern over Esau, grief over Rebekah's act, resentment at having his own plans thwarted—all these contributed to his trembling. But far more than any of these, he quickly came to see that God Himself had spoken to him in judgment, and that he had incurred great peril to himself in so ignoring the will of God. He had betrayed the trust of his father Abraham and had practically destroyed his own home, all because of a carnal appetite and adulation of his son's physical exploits. These thoughts (and who knows what others) flooded upon him. Indeed, it was enough to make a man exceedingly quake and shake.

Genesis 27:34-40

---

34 And when Ē'saū heard the words of his father, he cried with a great and exceeding bitter cry, and said unto his father, Bless me, *even* me also, O my father.

35 And he said, Thy brother came with subtilty, and hath taken away thy blessing.

36 And he said, Is not he rightly named Jacob? for he hath supplanted me these two times: he took away my birthright; and, behold, now he hath taken away my blessing. And he said, Hast thou not reserved a blessing for me?

37 And Isaac answered and said unto Ē'saū, Behold, I have made him thy lord, and all his brethren have I given to him for servants; and with corn and wine have I sustained him: and what shall I do now unto thee, my son?

38 And Ē'saū said unto his father, Hast thou but one blessing, my father? bless me, *even* me also, O my father. And Ē'saū lifted up his voice, and wept.

39 And Isaac his father answered and said unto him, Behold, thy dwelling shall be the fatness of the earth, and of the dew of heaven from above;

40 And by thy sword shalt thou live, and shalt serve thy brother: and it shall come to pass when thou shalt have the dominion, that thou shalt break his yoke from off thy neck.

Esau was momentarily stunned as he watched the spectacle. Then, as the truth dawned upon him as well, he also gave vent to his emotions. He "cried with a great and exceeding bitter cry." But perhaps his father could bless him anyway, he suddenly thought. Since he hadn't really intended to bless Jacob, why couldn't he simply retract his words and bless his older son as he had intended? Surely no human tribunal would enforce a contract acquired by deception; so why should Isaac, and why should God?

But Isaac could not change it even if he wanted to, and he realized this now. Hardly knowing how to explain all this to Esau, he simply blamed Jacob for a clever deception which robbed Esau of his intended blessing. Esau bitterly recalled that Jacob had already "taken away" his birthright (forgetting that, at the time, he had despised it); and now, he complained, he had likewise taken away his blessing. Whether Esau, like Isaac and Rebekah, knew about God's decree concerning himself and Jacob Scripture does not say, although it does not seem likely that such an important matter could or would have been kept secret from him by his mother for perhaps seventy-five years.

He commented on the relevance of Jacob's very name to the situation. It will be recalled that he was named "Jacob" because, as he was born, he was holding his brother by the heel. The name means something like "heel-gripper" and, therefore, by extension, "one who trips another by the heel." If someone overtakes another by tripping him up by the heel, then he will supplant him in the race. By this kind of etymology, "Jacob" came to mean "supplanter." Esau noted that he had lived up to his name by twice overtaking and tripping him, first in the matter of the birthright and now in the blessing. His anger and frustration were very bitter.

It must have been a strange sight, to see such a strong man as Esau screaming like a woman and weeping like a baby; but that is how he reacted. Agonizingly, he begged his father for a blessing of some kind for himself, hoping that somehow God, through his father's intercession, could be persuaded to change His mind.

But the portion of the blessing in which Esau was most interested, that of political superiority, had been given irrevocably to Jacob, and all Esau's crying could not change the situation. The sad commentary in Hebrews refers to his pleading in these words: "Lest there be any fornicator, or profane person, as Esau, who for one morsel of meat sold his birthright. For ye know how that afterward, when he would have inherited the blessing, he was rejected: for he found no place of repentance, though he sought it carefully with tears" (Hebrews 12:16, 17). That is, he wept in seeking the blessing, but there was no way of changing God's mind.

Isaac did finally, no doubt as God led him, make a prophecy concerning Esau. Esau (meaning his descendants) would, in contrast to Jacob, dwell in a region away from the fertile and well-watered places of the earth. The King James translation is apparently not quite correct at this point: the words "away from" should be inserted ("thy dwelling shall be away from the fatness of the earth"). This was fulfilled by the very nature of the rugged region that came to be known as the land of Edom. The Edomites would generally live in violence and in subjection to Israel. However, whenever he would "shake himself" (not "have dominion," as in the King James Version), he would be able to loosen the yoke. The Edomites remained essentially independent, however, until David's time. They were subjugated permanently after that, in spite of frequent rebellions and temporary partial freedom. Finally, Edom disappeared completely as a nation. Esau's long life of immorality and indifference to spiritual things, in spite of being born to one of the most privileged heritages possible, had finally caught up with him, and it was too late even for regrets.

The unhappy story of Esau has been repeated time without number throughout Christian history. How often do we hear of a young man (or young woman), brought up in a Christian home and in a Bible-teaching church, who rebels against the instruction and discipline there received in order to participate in the pleasures of worldly acquaintances, selling his birthright, as it were, for a mess of pottage! Perhaps it is also often the case that this carnal attitude has been unconsciously developed in the child by the overindulgent pride and adulation of his parents, as seems to have been true with Isaac and Esau. The Christian parent is commanded to "bring them up in the nurture [that is, 'discipline'] and admonition of the Lord" (Ephesians 6:4).

Genesis 27:41-46

41 ¶ And Ē'saū hated Jacob because of the blessing wherewith his father blessed him: and Ē'saū said in his heart, The days of mourning for my father are at hand; then will I slay my brother Jacob.

42 And these words of Ē'saū her elder son were told to Rē-běk'áh: and she sent and called Jacob her younger son, and said unto him, Behold, thy brother Ē'saū, as touching thee, doth comfort himself, *purposing* to kill thee.

43 Now therefore, my son, obey my voice; and arise, flee thou to Lā'bǎn my brother to Hā'rǎn;

44 And tarry with him a few days, until thy brother's fury turn away;

45 Until thy brother's anger turn away from thee, and he forget *that* which thou hast done to him: then I will send, and fetch thee from thence: why should I be deprived also of you both in one day?

46 And Rē-běk'áh said to Isaac, I am weary of my life because of the daughters of Heth: if Jacob take a wife of the daughters of Heth, such as these *which are* of the daughters of the land, what good shall my life do me?

Esau had suddenly changed from an indifferent, carefree sportsman into a bitter, vindictive neurotic. The thought of Jacob exercising dominion over *him,* who had always been idolized for his strength and prowess, was more than he could bear. He resolved to murder his brother as soon as his father died, evidently assuming that his father was indeed at the point of death (Genesis 27:2) and that probably his decease would even be hastened by the traumatic events of the day.

Uttered in the hearing of some of the servants, his threatening words were brought to his mother's attention. Again showing herself to be a woman of quick decision, she called Jacob and instructed him to leave the house "for a few days," in order to visit her brother Laban in Haran. Knowing Esau's nature, she assumed his anger would pass away quickly and he would soon return to his carefree ways.

However, her "few days" turned out to be over twenty years! So far as the record goes, she never saw Jacob again after that day. Her stratagem did indeed prove costly to her, but it would have been worse had Esau actually slain Jacob. He would probably in turn have been put to death in some fashion, or at least would have become permanently alienated from the family. In that way, she would really have lost both her sons. She, no doubt, had counted all these costs, and believed the issue was vital enough to require her to do what she did. As a matter of fact, later events proved that she was correct. Esau did soon forget his anger, and he did prosper quite adequately in a material sense, which was really all he cared about (Genesis 33:1, 4, 9). Isaac repented and gave Jacob his sincere blessing, instructing him to marry a woman of their own people, not a Canaanite, as Esau had done (Genesis 28:1-4). Rebekah was never able, however, to "send and fetch" Jacob from Laban, as she had planned—for what reason we are not told. We do not know when Rebekah died; all we know about later events concerning her has to do with her burial in the cave of Machpelah, along with Abraham, Sarah, and Isaac (Genesis 49:30, 31).

The last verse of this chapter, noting Rebekah's request of Isaac to send Jacob away for a wife, really belongs with the discussion of chapter 28.

The Flight of Jacob

Esau's hatred might well have led quickly either to murder or to such family conflict as would destroy the house of Isaac and Rebekah. Even though Jacob was confident he had received only what God wanted him to have, and therefore he would be entitled to stand and fight for what was his, both he and his mother realized it would be best for him to leave home for a while. It would be far better, of course, if he could leave in his father's good will, rather than simply run away.

As a matter of fact, Isaac should have tried to find the right kind of woman to be Jacob's wife long before this. As Abraham had carefully made provision to locate and bring Rebekah to Isaac, so Isaac should have done for Jacob. Even Esau should have secured a wife from his parents' people; but Isaac's negligence in this matter had led to Esau's presumptuous union with two Canaanite women, with the result that Esau had been further alienated from God, and life around them had become almost intolerable for Rebekah.

Now that the blessing had actually been pronounced, and it had become clear even to Isaac that Jacob was the choice of God to perpetuate the line of the promised Seed, there was no excuse to delay any longer in this matter of finding a proper wife. This fact, combined with the immediate danger of fratricide, was more than enough reason for Isaac to send Jacob back to Haran to seek a wife. Finally, Rebekah's personal desire for Jacob to have a wife from her own people, one with whom she could have fellowship rather than continual friction, as with Esau's Hittite wives, impelled her to insist to Isaac that her life would no longer be worth living if Jacob could not have such a godly wife.

Genesis 28:1-5

CHAPTER 28

AND Isaac called Jacob, and blessed him, and charged him, and said unto him, Thou shalt not take a wife of the daughters of Cā'năan.

2 Arise, go to Pā'dăn-ā'răm, to the house of Bē-thū'ĕl thy mother's father; and take thee a wife from thence of the daughters of Lā'băn thy mother's brother.

3 And God Almighty bless thee, and make thee fruitful, and multiply thee, that thou mayest be a multitude of people;

4 And give thee the blessing of Abraham, to thee, and to thy seed with thee; that thou mayest inherit the land wherein thou art a stranger, which God gave unto Abraham.

5 And Isaac sent away Jacob: and he went to Pā'dăn-ā'răm unto Lā'băn, son of Bē-thū'ĕl the Syrian, the brother of Rē-bĕk'ăh, Jacob's and E'saū's mother.

Rebekah's counsel quickly convinced Isaac, still shaken from the recent events, and no longer in any mood to try to delay or thwart God's purposes. He called Jacob, and gave him strict instruction not to marry a Canaanite woman, almost in the same words that Abraham had used long ago concerning his own marriage (Genesis 24:3). Rather, he was to go back to Rebekah's family in Padan-aram, and there take a wife from among his own cousins, the daughters of his mother's brother.

Then, in order that neither Rebekah nor Jacob could have any more doubt that he now fully desired and intended that Jacob should have the full blessing, Isaac repeated the blessing in terms much more like those which he himself had received from God (Genesis 26:3-5).

That is, he specifically invoked on Jacob the blessing of Abraham, as well as the promise that he would be the father of a great multitude, and his seed would possess the land of promise. Then Isaac sent him away, and Jacob started out on the long journey. So far as Isaac and Rebekah knew, he would be able to find a wife who believed in Jehovah only among their own kin; and this consideration far outweighed any genetic problems that might be involved in such a close marriage. Besides, the race was still young enough that the danger of accumulated mutational defects was minimal.

Genesis 28:6-9

6 ¶ When E′saŭ saw that Isaac had blessed Jacob, and sent him away to Pā′dăn-ā′răm, to take him a wife from thence; and that as he blessed him he gave him a charge, saying, Thou shalt not take a wife of the daughters of Cā′năan;
7 And that Jacob obeyed his father and his mother, and was gone to Pā′dăn-ā′răm;
8 And E′saŭ seeing that the daughters of Cā′năan pleased not Isaac his father;
9 Then went E′saŭ unto Ish′mā-ĕl, and took unto the wives which he had Mā′hă-lăth the daughter of Ish′mā-ĕl Abraham's son, the sister of Nē-bā′jŏth, to be his wife.

Esau perhaps thought until this point that he still had the full backing of Isaac; but now, knowing that Isaac had again blessed Jacob, much more specifically this time, and without any question of deception, he realized that he himself was on dangerous ground. The fact that Isaac had sent Jacob far away to find a wife from Rebekah's people emphasized to Esau that his father, as well as his mother, was highly displeased with Esau's choice of wives.

In a belated attempt to partially correct this situation, Esau went to the home of his Uncle Ishmael (Ishmael himself was already dead at this time) and secured one of his daughters, Mahalath (probably the same as Bashemath in Genesis 36:3), as another wife. This was a rather pathetic attempt, a closing of the barn door after the horse was gone. Esau had been spiritually blind and stubborn about this all-important issue of an appropriate wife for many years; but, now that it was too late, he made a last desperate attempt to regain the favor of his parents and of God. But even in this attempt, he still was wrong, because Ishmael and his descendants had already been cast out by God, so far as the national promises were concerned. It may be true, of course, that Ishmael's family had been taught many of the personal and moral standards of the true faith of Jehovah, so that Mahalath probably would get along better with Isaac and Rebekah than Judith and Bashemath, his Hittite wives.

There is an apparent contradiction between the names of Esau's wives in Genesis 26:34 and 28:9 and in the summary of Esau's generations in Genesis 36:2, 3. The probable resolution of this problem is discussed in chapter XVIII, in the comments on Genesis 36.

In any case, this action on Esau's part, even though it dealt only superficially with the real problem, probably does indicate that he realized his troubles were not all of Jacob's doing. He himself had, by his indifference to spiritual matters and by his carnal desires, been the underlying reason for God's choice of Jacob. It was likely at this point that his hatred of Jacob began to soften to regret. Jacob, however, did not know about these developments, and so did not return to see Esau again for over twenty years.

As to why God allowed these developments, resulting in Jacob's prolonged absence from home (rather than, as in Isaac's case, the dispatch of a servant to find a wife for him), it can be said that Jacob's role in establshing the tribes of Israel required the strengthening of his character through a long period of forced dependence on God alone. He had spent many decades in a rather restrictive family situation, dominated in many respects by his mother but also affected seriously by his brother's worldliness and his father's weakness. It was essential that he get out on his own if his character and faith were ever to be built into the stature which his role in God's economy would require. Though it is one of God's commandments that young people honor their parents, the time must also come when a man must "leave his father and his mother" if he is to fulfill God's will for his own life, especially when he takes a wife (Genesis 2:24).

Stairway to Heaven

As Jacob started out on the long road northward, all he had to go on were the promises implicit in God's blessing. He was alone and traveling light, hastening to escape the wrath of his brother. He had no caravan to sustain him, not even a tent under which he could rest. There were no armed servants to protect him against beasts or bandits, and he was not a huntsman like Esau, experienced in living off the land by his skill with spear and bow. Rebekah no doubt had packed such food and other supplies as he could carry on his back, and presumably he had money with which to purchase the necessaries as he traveled, but otherwise he was alone in a strange and dangerous country. Except for God, that is!

Genesis 28:10, 11

---

10 ⸿ And Jacob went out from Bē'ĕr-shē'bā, and went toward Hā'răn.
11 And he lighted upon a certain place, and tarried there all night, because the sun was set; and he took of the stones of that place, and put *them for* his pillows, and lay down in that place to sleep.

So far as the record goes, Jacob had spent most of his life to date in the family home in Beersheba (Genesis 22:19; 26:33; 28:10). It was five hundred miles to Haran and, even though he no doubt had either a camel or ass to ride on, it would be many weeks before he could hope to reach his destination. The region around the town of Haran was called Padan-aram (meaning, probably, the "field of Aram," Aram having come essentially to mean the land of Syria).

When Jacob arrived at Bethel, he had one of the most remarkable dreams any man ever experienced. Bethel is about seventy miles north of Beersheba, and it seems likely that it took Jacob at least two—possibly three—days to get this far. The first two or three days of his trip are passed over in silence. Whatever adventures he might have had were of trivial importance compared to this experience. Scripture says that he "lighted upon a certain place," and it sounds almost as if he simply happened on it by chance. However, God does not "throw dice," as Einstein once said; He does not lead His people by chance. To the contrary, God led Jacob to this place, whether Jacob knew it or not. "O Lord, I know that the way of man is not in himself: it is not in man that walketh to direct his steps" (Jeremiah 10:23).

It was near Bethel that Abraham had built an altar (Genesis 12:8; 13:3, 4), and this was a place to which Jacob would later return (Genesis 35:1). Bethel would become to him a lifelong memorial of God's promises to him and of His ability to fulfill those promises. The word *Bethel* itself means "the house of God." Though it was to have many such sacred connotations and memories, apostasy eventually developed there, over a thousand years later, and it had to be destroyed (I Kings 12:28-33; II Kings 23:15-17).

As Jacob arrived at Bethel, Scripture does not say whether he realized this place had been important to Abraham. The remains of Abraham's altar might still have been standing there. Possibly Jacob used some of the very stones for a pillow as he slept that night. At any rate, it was at this time and in this place that God chose to make Himself personally known to Jacob, as He had been known to Abraham and, in earlier and happier days, to Isaac.

Genesis 28:12-15

12 And he dreamed, and behold a ladder set up on the earth, and the top of it reached to heaven: and behold the angels of God ascending and descending on it.
13 And, behold, the LORD stood above it, and said, I *am* the LORD God of Abraham thy father, and the God of Isaac: the land whereon thou liest, to thee will I give it, and to thy seed;
14 And thy seed shall be as the dust of the earth; and thou shalt spread abroad to the west, and to the east, and to the north, and to the south: and in thee and in thy seed shall all the families of the earth be blessed.
15 And, behold, I *am* with thee, and will keep thee in all *places* whither thou goest, and will bring thee again into this land; for I will not leave thee, until I have done *that* which I have spoken to thee of.

Jacob had known and believed God's promises practically all his life. No doubt he worshiped the Lord and prayed frequently to Him. Never before, however, had God actually appeared and spoken to him, as He had to Abraham and Isaac. It was on this occasion, as Jacob slept on the stones of Bethel, that God once again came down in a theophany, the first of about eight which Jacob would experience during his lifetime.

This theophany was in the form of a dream. Though not the only way—or even the usual way—in which God had appeared to men in these ancient times, such a means was certainly used on many occasions. This does not mean, of course, that any supernatural significance is normally to be ascribed to dreams. It is only that, when Scripture so indicates, God has used this means, as well as various other means, to speak to man. "God at sundry times and in divers manners spake in time past unto the fathers by the prophets" (Hebrews 1:1).

The dominant feature of Jacob's dream was a mighty ladder, reaching from the earth far up into the sky and even into the very heaven of God's presence itself. The ladder was wide as well as high, so that streams of heavenly angels could be seen going both up and down the ladder simultaneously.

It is obvious that this was no ordinary ladder. The word is the Hebrew *sullam,* and is used only this one time in the Bible. Whatever its exact form may have been, it clearly pictured to Jacob the interrelationships of earth and heaven. It showed there was intense interest in heaven concerning what took place on earth, with multitudes of mighty ministers of God coming down to earth to carry out God's commands, then returning to report concerning the earth and to receive further instructions. Though they are normally invisible to human eyes, Scripture teaches that there does indeed exist "an innumerable company of angels" (Hebrews 12:22), that these are mighty beings, "angels that excel in strength, that do his commandments, hearkening unto the voice of his word" (Psalm 103:20), and that their main function is to serve as "ministering spirits, sent forth to minister for them who shall be heirs of salvation" (Hebrews 1:14). They take very special interest in God's people and in the working out of their salvation and growth in grace (Luke 15:10; I Corinthians 4:9; Ephesians 3:10; I Peter 1:12; Psalm 34:7; Psalm 91:11; etc.).

In the accomplishment of their ministries on behalf of the heirs of salvation, there is frequent occasion for liaison between earth and heaven (II Kings 6:17; II Chronicles 18:18, 19; Job 1:6; 2:1; Daniel 9:21-23; 10:10-13; Mark 1:13; Luke 22:43; Acts 12:11; 27:23; etc.). Angels have the ability to "fly swiftly" (Daniel 9:21) between earth and heaven. Regardless of the exact location of God's throne in the physical universe, or what limitations are experienced by their peculiar spirit-bodies in accomplishing such translocation, angels therefore do move back and forth, up and down, between God and man, as they carry out their assignments from God on behalf of men.

This activity of communication and implementation of God's commands was pictured to Jacob as he viewed the ladder in his dream. Perhaps he had often wondered about the accessibility of God and whether or not He really was as concerned with the affairs of men as Abraham and Isaac had taught. He had no doubt read of the far-off days of Adam and the Garden of Eden, and knew that man's sins had separated him from God's presence. He also knew that God had promised a Deliverer who would come someday to bring God and man together again, bridging the great gulf between earth and heaven. He realized, too, that the very blessing he had sought so desperately from his father was closely associated with this promise, and that it would somehow come to pass through his own seed. Nevertheless, although he believed all these things, he himself had never seen God or heard His voice. He surely must have longed for some kind of personal assurance that God was really there and that He was truly concerned for man's salvation, even though well over two thousand years had come and gone since Adam sinned. It is not unlikely that, often as he traveled, and especially that night as his head lay on the stone pillow, he had prayed to God for some such assurance.

In any case, God did appear to him that night. Finally he could know beyond any question that God cared for him, that there were multitudes of angels who were actively working toward man's redemption and for his own personal protection and guidance, and that there was indeed a bridge between heaven and earth by which God could come down to man and man could be brought to God. The great promises of God, even those centered in himself, would surely be performed.

There is not, of course, a literal staircase to heaven, on which angels ascend and descend. This was only a dream, but it was a dream symbolizing a marvelous reality. Though earth is surely separated by a vast, seemingly impassable gulf of space from the heaven of God's presence, signifying man's separation from God's holiness, a bridge *has* been built to span the gulf. That magnificent Ladder could only be built by God Himself. As a matter of fact, it *is* God Himself.

Almost two thousand years in the future from Jacob's day, a devout Israelite named Nathanael was meditating on the things of God, and quite probably was reading in Scripture this very account of Jacob's dream, wondering himself how it would ever be possible for there to be a reconciliation between man and God, how there could ever be a real ladder from earth to heaven. He knew that, somehow, all these promises were centered in the promised Messiah; but would Messiah ever come?

As he was meditating and praying about these matters under his fig tree, a dear friend of his suddenly appeared. Philip, knowing Nathanael's great interest in these spiritual matters, excitedly told him of Jesus and urged him to come meet the One who was indeed the Messiah! Nathanael was skeptical at first, but Jesus soon convinced him, telling him things about himself and his activities which He could only have known supernaturally. And it was then that Jesus made the tremendous claim and promise, referring to Jacob's dream: "Verily, verily, I say unto you, Hereafter ye shall see heaven open, and the angels of God ascending and descending upon the Son of man" (John 1:51).

In other words, the Lord Jesus Christ claimed that He Himself was Jacob's Ladder, the one means by which one could go from earth to heaven. He is the Way, He is the one Mediator, between man and God. All the infinite ministries and activities of the mighty angels depend on Him. He is none other than God, the Creator, the Sustainer, and the Redeemer of all things.

Though in past ages angels had frequently traveled from heaven to earth and back again, at the time when Jesus spoke these words, "no man [had] ascended up to heaven, but he that came down from heaven, even the Son of man which is in heaven" (John 3:13). The preincarnate Christ had on occasion come down to speak to man, as was true on this very occasion as Jacob slept, and sometimes such theophanies were in the "appearance" of men. But now, finally, God had actually *become* man and had entered the earthly sphere to redeem man, as He had promised. After His crucifixion and descent into Hades, Jesus rose from the dead and opened the way henceforth into the presence of God. "When he ascended up on high, he led captivity captive, and gave gifts unto men. (Now that he ascended, what is it but that he also descended first into the lower parts of the earth? He that descended is the same also that ascended up far above all heavens, that he might fill all things)" (Ephesians 4:8-10).

From that time on, whenever a believer died, his spirit would enter directly into heaven "to be with Christ" (Philippians 1:23), "to be present with the Lord" (II Corinthians 5:8). Angels would accompany him up the ladder (Luke 16:22) from earth to heaven. When the Lord finally comes to earth again, to complete His work of reconciliation, He "shall be revealed from heaven with his mighty angels" (II Thessalonians 1:7). Quite literally, at that time, the angels will be "descending upon the Son of man."

Jacob may not have understood the full New Testament import of his remarkable dream, but he surely could understand that there was communication between man and God, and that God would provide the means by which man could be restored to God. As far as his own personal situation was concerned, he learned beyond any further question that God would care for him and that, regardless of future circumstances, God would lead him and fulfill all His promises to him.

As Jacob marveled at the ladder in his dream, he saw God Himself standing above the ladder and heard Him speak words of blessing, repeating all the promises He had made to Abraham and Isaac concerning the Seed and the land. Regarding his own immediate situation, God promised Jacob that He would be with him wherever he would go, protecting him, and then one day bringing him back to the land he was leaving.

It should be noted again that God did not offer a single word of rebuke to Jacob, but only of blessing and promise. Bible teachers who have been quick to rebuke Jacob should realize that they have pronounced a moral judgment which God Himself did not make and which, therefore, should not be made. Their analysis and exposition of

Jacob's character and actions should be built on God's evaluation, not on one associated with naturalistic prejudices.

Genesis 28:16-22

---

16 ¶ And Jacob awaked out of his sleep, and he said, Surely the LORD is in this place; and I knew *it* not.

17 And he was afraid, and said, How dreadful *is* this place! this *is* none other but the house of God, and this *is* the gate of heaven.

18 And Jacob rose up early in the morning, and took the stone that he had put *for* his pillows, and set it up *for* a pillar, and poured oil upon the top of it.

19 And he called the name of that place Beth-el: but the name of that city *was* *called* Luz at the first.

20 And Jacob vowed a vow, saying, If God will be with me, and will keep me in this way that I go, and will give me bread to eat, and raiment to put on,

21 So that I come again to my father's house in peace; then shall the LORD be my God:

22 And this stone, which I have set *for* a pillar, shall be God's house: and of all that thou shalt give me I will surely give the tenth unto thee.

After God had finished speaking, Jacob awoke, in awe. He had actually met God in this place. Perhaps he realized that Abraham also had long ago worshiped God here, but Abraham had never seen such a remarkable revelation as this. The great God of creation, the God of heaven and earth, ruling an infinite multitude of mighty angels, was also interested in him! This God was Jehovah, the God of Abraham and Isaac, and this very place was where God, in the vision, had installed the great ladder symbolizing His redemptive promise.

Jacob of course knew the doctrine of the omnipresence of God, and therefore he realized that God was here, as well as everywhere. But He was also here in a special way, a particular presence. Here He had been actually seen and heard; here He met with His people. This place should be called the House of God, Bethel, though it had formerly been called Luz. And so it *was* always called Bethel after that. As the House of God, it was also the Gate to Heaven, through which God could come to man and into which man must enter to go to God.

Jacob had been well instructed in the essential importance of the sacrificial altar, and the necessity of the substitutionary death of an animal to cover the sins of a believing and repentant sinner. Since the altar (like the ladder in the dream) represented the means by which man could approach God, it was appropriate that the now invisible dream be commemorated by a visible altar. Accordingly, Jacob resolved to build such an altar on the spot, beginning with a single pillar, as soon as the sun rose the next morning.

It is not very likely that, after such a dream, Jacob could sleep any more that night. He must have spent the balance of the night in meditation and prayer, still in wondering awe at what he had experienced.

Early in the morning, Jacob rose and hastened to set up the pillar. The central support stone was the stone he had used for a pillow the night before. He had no animal to sacrifice, but he did make a drink-offering of oil he was carrying, thus also "anointing" the pillar, dedicating it to the truth of God's promises.

After receiving such marvelous assurances and benedictions from God, Jacob naturally wanted to respond in some kind of dedication, not only of the altar he would build, but also—more importantly—of his own life. After anointing the pillar, he rehearsed God's gracious promise of the night before—God's promise to be with him wherever he would go, providing all his material needs and someday bringing him back home again in peace. Therefore, said Jacob (and this was not just making a bargain, as some have suggested, but rather an expression of gratitude and love), "then shall Jehovah be my God, and this place will always be a place of remembrance wherein to worship God." Furthermore, although he had no possessions at the time, Jacob believed that God would indeed supply them, and he voluntarily promised to restore one-tenth of everything to God. It would be impossible for him to give a tithe to God of the promised land of his descendants or any of those greater blessings of the future, but the immediate blessings would be physical and visible to Jacob himself, and of these he would certainly give a tenth to God.

So far as any record goes, there was no written law at this time concerning the giving of tithes to God. Abraham had given tithes to Melchizedek, and Jacob probably had this example in mind. Exactly how he would give the tithe, and to whom, we are not told. Possibly there would be some expense in building and maintaining a suitable altar, and perhaps he also meant he would offer up as sacrifices on this altar one-tenth of all the fruits and flocks that would come into his possession. It is probable, of course, that he was referring to his eventual return home to the promised land. At that time he would give this tithe to God, a tithe of everything he had obtained in the interim. He finally did return to this spot and actually built an altar there (Genesis 35:3, 7).

Jacob's vow, therefore, was given in appreciation of God's promise, not because of legal compulsion or as a means of assuring God's blessings. God's promise had been unconditional and hence did not require the payment of tithes to keep it in force. It is legitimate, in the Hebrew, to read Jacob's statement in this way: *"Since* [instead of 'if'] God will be with me, and will keep me . . . then shall Jehovah be my God . . . and of all that thou givest me I will surely give the tenth to thee."

Later, tithing would become a definite obligation of the Mosaic Law (Leviticus 27:30; Numbers 18:21, 24; etc.), and it actually was a political law among many ancient kingdoms (a form of taxation, that is). But so far as both Abraham and Jacob were concerned, it was purely voluntary, as an expression of their thanksgiving to God.

This motive, of course, should be that which constrains Christians today to tithe their possessions and incomes. There is no law requiring tithing as a condition of salvation, or even of God's blessing in material things. Tithing is to be rather an expression of love and concern for the Lord and His service. Neither is there a legalistic specification of exactly one-tenth to be set aside for God. It is convenient to think in decimal fractions, and the principle of proportionate giving is taught in the New Testament (I Corinthians 16:2). The Christian can conveniently think in terms of "tithes." That is, how many tithes can he return to the Lord in gratitude for God's blessings—one tithe, two tithes, 1½ tithes, or whatever? Many have been able to follow the practice of "double tithing," for example, with real joy. Everything Jacob received (and everything a believer receives today) is by the Lord's grace, and it is the Christian's privilege to seek to utilize as much as possible for the Lord's work. Jacob voluntarily (with much less knowledge and with much less blessing than we have today) undertook to give one tithe to the Lord. It is likely that, in by far the majority of cases, a present-day Christian can and should give much more. But it should be done cheerfully and gratefully, not grudgingly or of necessity (II Corinthians 9:7).

17

Jacob and Laban

(Genesis 29-31)

Jacob's Love Life

In the next three chapters of Genesis is found the record of Jacob's twenty long years away from the land of Canaan and his home. It will be recalled that he was probably close to seventy-five years old when he left home, so that he was almost ninety-five when he came back. However, in terms of normal aging and life spans today, these figures could be cut almost in half to correspond to equivalent situations in our own time. Even so, he was still well along in years to be leaving home for the first time and to be looking for a wife.

Many writers on Genesis treat this period of Jacob's life as though it were a punishment for his treatment of his brother. Actually, however, they were for the most part very happy and prosperous years, with no more troubles and problems than are normally encountered by a believer seeking to follow the Lord. He did receive some rather shabby treatment at the hand of his Uncle Laban. On the other hand, Laban did give him a job, permitted him to marry his daughters, and made it possible for Jacob to build up extensive holdings of his own.

Genesis 29:1-6

CHAPTER 29

THEN Jacob went on his journey, and came into the land of the people of the east.

2 And he looked, and behold a well in the field, and, lo, there *were* three flocks

of sheep lying by it; for out of that well they watered the flocks: and a great stone *was* upon the well's mouth.

3 And thither were all the flocks gathered: and they rolled the stone from the well's mouth, and watered the sheep, and put the stone again upon the well's mouth in his place.

4 And Jacob said unto them, My brethren, whence *be* ye? And they said, Of Hā'răn *are* we.

5 And he said unto them, Know ye Lā'băn the son of Nā'hŏr? And they said, We know *him*.

6 And he said unto them, *Is* he well? And they said, *He is* well: and, behold, Rachel his daughter cometh with the sheep.

After Jacob left Bethel, the rest of his long journey is passed over in silence. He may have spent some time at Bethel, naturally loath to leave a place where God had spoken to him so wonderfully. Finally, however, he "went on his journey," or, more literally, "lifted up his feet," continuing northward into Syria, then eastward across the Euphrates through the "land of the children of the East." As he neared his goal, the town of Haran in Mesopotamia, the Lord guided him providentially to the very well where the flocks of sheep belonging to his relatives were watered. He spotted the well through the rather unusual circumstance that, although it was still fairly early in the afternoon, there were already three flocks of sheep lying near the well waiting to be watered. There seems to have been a local regulation regarding the well stipulating that its stone covering only be removed at a certain time in the evening, at which time all the flocks of the vicinity were to be watered in turn, in order of arrival. Those that arrived first would get through first; hence, there were some that would come to "get in line" quite early.

The shepherds tending the flocks were apparently either women or young lads, the latter being the case with the three flocks Jacob first saw. The stone on the well was too large for any one or two of them to move; it was easier therefore to have the well opened by several helping each other once a day. This type of well was apparently not a well of flowing water, but rather of stored water.

Jacob was somewhat perplexed by the fact that the sheep and shepherds were simply resting by the well so early in the day. Before he questioned them about this matter, however, he first greeted them in a friendly manner, asking where they were from. Like Abraham's servant as he searched for a bride for Isaac, Jacob was amazed and thankful to learn they were from Haran and that they knew Laban quite well. Furthermore, they informed him that Laban was still in good health. Not only that, but his daughter, Rachel, was the shepherdess who kept his flocks and she would be coming shortly to this very well to provide water for the sheep she was tending.

It is interesting to note that both Jacob and the young shepherds still spoke the same language. The language of Haran was Aramaic, or Chaldee, and was evidently a language well known to Abraham, and therefore also to Isaac and Jacob. The means by which these patriarchs communicated with the Canaanites, and even with the Egyptians, in the course of their travels, is never mentioned. Their languages were certainly quite different. Evidently they either spoke through interpreters or else they themselves were good linguists and had learned several languages. As far as the immediate family of Abraham was concerned, however, it is reasonable that they all had continued to speak Aramaic, as well as Hebrew.

Genesis 29:7-12

7 And he said, Lo, *it is* yet high day, neither *is it* time that the cattle should be gathered together: water ye the sheep, and go *and* feed *them.*

8 And they said, We cannot, until all the flocks be gathered together, and *till* they roll the stone from the well's mouth; then we water the sheep.

9 ¶ And while he yet spake with them, Rachel came with her father's sheep: for she kept them.

10 And it came to pass, when Jacob saw Rachel the daughter of La'băn his mother's brother, and the sheep of La'băn his mother's brother, that Jacob went near, and rolled the stone from the well's mouth, and watered the flock of La'băn his mother's brother.

11 And Jacob kissed Rachel, and lifted up his voice, and wept.

12 And Jacob told Rachel that he *was* her father's brother, and that he *was* Rē-běk'ăh's son: and she ran and told her father.

When Jacob had learned this most welcome and intriguing bit of information, he no doubt could hardly wait to meet Rachel. This might be the very woman he was seeking! It would be better, however, if their meeting could take place after the shepherd lads had left the well. He urged them, therefore, to hurry and water the flocks and then get back out to the pasture lands to feed them while there was still plenty of daylight left. He was puzzled, and perhaps a bit critical, of the apparent indifference of the boys to the welfare of their flocks (he would certainly never have wasted time like this when he was keeping his own father's flocks); but probably his main motive was simply that he wanted to be alone with Rachel when she came.

The shepherd boys replied, however (no doubt as curious about Jacob as they were unconcerned about their sheep), that they could not do this. It was necessary that they remain until all the flocks could be taken care of at once, when there were enough of them present to roll the stone from the well's mouth.

While this discussion was taking place, Rachel arrived with her father's flock. The phrase, "for she kept them," actually says, "for she was a shepherdess," thus calling attention to the fact that it was somewhat unusual for a woman to do this kind of work. Laban did indeed have sons (Genesis 31:1), as well as two daughters, and these sons did tend his flocks (Genesis 30:35). Evidently at this time they were either too young or else Laban had so many flocks and herds, in different regions, that it took his whole family to care for them.

When Jacob saw Rachel, there is no doubt that he was thrilled beyond words. She was a beautiful woman (Genesis 29:17), in addition to being industrious and strong enough to shepherd her father's sheep. In a reaction generated partly by the lackadaisical attitude of the boys toward the stone on the well and partly by his desire to make an immediate good impression on Rachel, Jacob impulsively ran to the well and single-handedly rolled away the stone. He was older and stronger than the shepherd boys, of course, but his unusual strength and energy at this time were no doubt largely generated by his joy at finding his beautiful cousin.

After removing the stone, Jacob quickly proceeded to give water to all of Rachel's sheep. Three times in verse 10 mention is made of "Laban his mother's brother"; so it was not solely of Rachel that Jacob was thinking. No doubt he had often heard his mother speak fondly of Laban, and it was to Laban that he would look for help in finding not only a wife but also a means of livelihood in this land, until such time as he could safely return home.

One receives the impression in reading the narrative here that with Jacob it was a case of love at first sight. Before even introducing himself, Jacob went up to Rachel, after watering the sheep, and proceeded to kiss her, so overcome by emotion was he. This was not intended as a kiss of personal love, of course, but rather simply a kiss of greeting; but even this was practiced only by relatives or close friends, so that it must surely have startled Rachel. She was even more shocked when she saw this strong man begin to weep and cry in a loud voice!

Then, however, he managed to control his emotions long enough to tell her who he was. He was her cousin, the son of her father's beloved sister. No doubt Rachel had also heard much from Laban about the beautiful Rebekah, who had left home so long ago under such remarkable circumstances, and she had often wondered about what had happened to her.

Now it was Rachel's turn to be emotional! When she learned who Jacob was, she immediately ran as fast as she could to tell her father the glad news. Rebekah had left her brother almost one hundred years before, on almost a moment's notice; and so far as the record goes, he had never seen her since. Whether or not it had been possible to communicate occasionally through traveling caravans we do not know, but there is no doubt that Laban also was overjoyed at this news from his sister and at the opportunity of meeting his nephew.

Genesis 29:13-19

---

13 And it came to pass, when Lā′băn heard the tidings of Jacob his sister's son, that he ran to meet him, and embraced him, and kissed him, and brought him to his house. And he told Lā′băn all these things.

14 And Lā′băn said to him, Surely thou *art* my bone and my flesh. And he abode with him the space of a month.

15 ¶ And Lā′băn said unto Jacob, Because thou *art* my brother, shouldest thou therefore serve me for nought? tell me, what *shall* thy wages *be*?

16 And Lā′băn had two daughters: the name of the elder *was* Lē′ăh, and the name of the younger *was* Rachel.

17 Lē′ăh *was* tender eyed; but Rachel was beautiful and well-favored.

18 And Jacob loved Rachel; and said, I will serve thee seven years for Rachel thy younger daughter.

19 And Lā′băn said, *It is* better that I give her to thee, than that I should give her to another man: abide with me.

Jacob remained behind, probably to shepherd Rachel's sheep while she was gone. When Laban heard the surprising news, he also was so excited that he ran out from the house to meet Jacob coming along with the sheep. After embracing him, Laban brought Jacob home with him and, no doubt, the whole family talked with Jacob far into the night as he told them all the news about Isaac and Rebekah and the events that had transpired since Rebekah left home.

Laban insisted that Jacob stay in the home with them, as one of the family. It is interesting that he used the term "my bone and my flesh," no doubt an unintentional and prescientific (but no less truly scientific) recognition of genetic controls specifying that Jacob's physical characteristics must be closely like those of Laban. Both Isaac and Rebekah were close relatives of Laban and their son would be like him as well.

Jacob was industrious and wanted to make himself useful to Laban, so he soon began to help with the family business, primarily handling the flocks. This all kept him frequently near Rachel, and his love for her grew. He soon knew beyond any doubt that this was the woman he wanted for his wife.

After he had been there a month, Laban offered to employ him as a regular salaried employee. Jacob immediately proposed that, if Laban would give him his daughter, it would be worth seven years of service, as far as he was concerned.

Laban had found that Jacob was a willing and able worker and, furthermore, he realized that he would eventually come into a substantial inheritance. He had surely observed by this time Jacob's evident affection for Rachel, and recognized there would be many advantages to having him as a son-in-law. He wanted to bind Jacob to him in some way, and rather craftily let Jacob himself name the terms, anticipating that, because of Jacob's desire for Rachel, he would get a better bargain this way. Seven years of free service, by a man who was an exceptional worker, was surely a fine windfall for Laban, especially in view of the fact that he would have been happy to have Jacob marry into the family regardless.

Laban, therefore, immediately agreed to Jacob's offer. Whether, at this time, he already was planning the later deception he practiced on Jacob (in giving him Leah instead of Rachel) we do not know; but it is quite possible. He may have been hoping Leah would also find a husband in the meantime.

Both of his daughters were apparently well beyond the age at which women usually married, and Laban may have become quite concerned about finding a husband for Leah, the older sister. According to Laban's later explanation (verse 26), it was contrary to strong custom for the younger to wed before the older; and since Leah had been unable to find a husband, both she and Rachel had remained unmarried. Laban certainly should have explained this to Jacob at the time of his proposal, but he kept it to himself, not wishing to lose the opportunity to have Jacob work for him and to get him into the family.

Rachel was beautiful in both face and form, much more so than Leah apparently, and much more desirable. Since they were sisters, however, there must have been a considerable family resemblance between them, so that Leah could not have been too homely. The only specific weakness that is mentioned is that she was "tender-eyed." This does not necessarily mean "weak-eyed," however, as some have interpreted it; it could mean that she did not have eyes as dark and lustrous as those of Rachel, or it might even refer figuratively to Leah as a woman of compassion. It is not clear why she had been unable to find a husband; quite possibly it was because none of the eligible men of Haran were acceptable to her father.

Genesis 29:20-24

20 And Jacob served seven years for Rachel; and they seemed unto him *but* a few days, for the love he had to her.

21 ¶ And Jacob said unto Lā′băn, Give *me* my wife, for my days are fulfilled, that I may go in unto her.

22 And Lā′băn gathered together all the men of the place, and made a feast.

23 And it came to pass in the evening, that he took Lē′àh his daughter, and brought her to him; and he went in unto her.

24 And Lā′băn gave unto his daughter Lē′àh Zĭl′pàh his maid *for* a handmaid.

Jacob gladly served his seven years for Rachel, and the joyful anticipation of having her for his wife made the time pass quickly. He knew this was the woman God had chosen for him, that she would fulfill every requirement to be the mother of the nation God had promised, and furthermore he loved her deeply. A God-ordained marriage and the genuine love of husband and wife in such a marriage are surely among the greatest joys available to God's people in this life.

When the time was up, however, Laban seemed not to notice at all. No doubt, Laban was reluctant to face the prospect of losing Jacob's services after his marriage, so he said nothing. Jacob finally had to remind him that he had kept his part of the agreement, and now he wanted to take his bride.

At this time, if not earlier, Laban devised one of the most mendacious schemes imaginable, resolving to substitute Leah for Rachel on the wedding night. Then, he could extract still another seven-year period of free service from Jacob, as well as solve the problem of getting a husband for Leah at the same time. He felt reasonably certain, knowing Jacob's honorable character, that he would not cast out Leah once he had gone in to her; and if Jacob should actually refuse to work another seven years as he would demand, then at worst it would not be too difficult to find another husband for Rachel. Even if Jacob decided to elope with Rachel (a practically unthinkable development in terms of the customs of the land), Laban still would not have lost anything. So it was worth a try.

It was the custom to have a great festive week after a wedding, beginning with a banquet on the nuptial night, with many male guests invited. At the proper time, when the wedding formalities had been observed, Laban presented his daughter to Jacob as his wife.

Although Leah was veiled, Jacob never questioned that it was really Rachel. The two sisters were no doubt sufficiently alike in stature and general mien, probably even in tone of voice, that the deception was fairly easy to accomplish on the unsuspecting Jacob. When he took her into his chambers and into his bed, it was dark, and no doubt much of the conversation that night was in whispers and in brief words of love. Probably also Leah had been arrayed in Rachel's clothing and perfumes. It was not until the morning that Jacob actually saw he had been grievously deceived.

Genesis 29:25-30

---

25 And it came to pass, that in the morning, behold, it *was* Lē'ăh: and he said to Lā'băn, What *is* this thou hast done unto me? did not I serve with thee

for Rachel? wherefore then hast thou beguiled me?

26 And Lā′băn said, It must not be so done in our country, to give the younger before the firstborn.

27 Fulfil her week, and we will give thee this also for the service which thou shalt serve with me yet seven other years.

28 And Jacob did so, and fulfilled her week: and he gave him Rachel his daughter to wife also.

29 And Lā′băn gave to Rachel his daughter Bĭl′hăh his handmaid to be her maid.

30 And he went in also unto Rachel, and he loved also Rachel more than Lē′ăh, and served with him yet seven other years.

There is much left unsaid in this brief account. Where was Rachel while all this was going on? Whether she had simply been persuaded, or commanded, by her father to go along with this stratagem, or whether she had to be forcibly detained in the women's quarters during the evening and long night, we are not told. In any case, it must have been a most difficult night for her, likely one of real mental agony.

It could not have been easy for Leah, either. Though she earnestly wanted a husband, and quite probably had harbored a secret love for Jacob, she knew that he really loved Rachel and that, as he made love to her on their wedding night, he was really in his own heart making love to Rachel. Scripture does not tell us what the feelings between the two sisters may have been; no doubt Leah was somewhat jealous of Rachel, but there is no reason to think she would have relished hurting her sister in such a way. She was, of course, being obedient to her father in going through with this deception, but she surely realized it was wrong and cruel. Unless she wanted Jacob so badly herself that all other considerations were forgotten, it may have been a very difficult night for her, too.

As far as Jacob was concerned, when he discovered the deception, he could hardly fail to have been initially angry and bitter, both with Leah and Laban. However, he must certainly also have been quickly struck with the similarity of this situation to the deception he himself had played on Isaac and Esau. Isaac had thought Jacob was Esau, and so gave him the blessing. Now Jacob had thought Leah was Rachel, and had taken her to wife. In both cases, the deception had been commanded by a parent and in both cases the purpose of the deception was to acquire something desperately desired. Jacob had been sure the end justified the means in his case, but perhaps Leah and Laban also felt the same way in their case.

Such considerations no doubt contributed to a lessening of Jacob's anger. He may even have recognized his situation as providential, in view of the remarkably similar circumstances. Accordingly, so far as the record goes, at least, he did not berate Leah for her part in the affair. It is not unlikely that his experience with her during the night had engendered a certain amount of love for her, in spite of her deception, especially as he suddenly realized that she had herself been in love with him all along. At any rate, though he still wanted Rachel, he could not bring himself to hurt Leah any more.

At the first opportunity, he confronted Laban with a demand for an explanation. Laban responded with his rehearsed answer that the older sister must always be the first to wed. Then, he proposed his new bargain. If Jacob would fulfill Leah's wedding week, Laban would then give him Rachel also, provided Jacob serve Laban another seven years.

This seems like an utterly unreasonable proposition. Jacob could well have demanded Rachel without any further service (though whether he could have enforced such a demand is doubtful). Out of respect to Leah, apparently (if Rachel was worth seven years of service, was not her older sister also worth as much?), Jacob consented.

He therefore fulfilled Leah's week, and then Laban finally gave Rachel to him. Jacob was thus more or less forced to become a bigamist. In light of the times, however, this was not as serious a corruption of the marriage relation as it would be in the Christian dispensation. Polygamy was quite common; Jacob's own brother had two wives, and his grandfather had taken Hagar as well as Sarah as his wife. Nevertheless, many problems did develop later in Jacob's home and family because of it, thus showing again that monogamy is the better way. Even today, although "parallel" polygamy is illegal in Western nations, a "serial" type of polygamy is commonly practiced as a result of frequent divorces. Today, however, as well as in Jacob's time, such multiple marriages normally involve much heartache and serious family problems.

Mention is made here (verses 24 and 29) of the two maids that Laban gave Leah and Rachel, Zilpah and Bilhah, respectively. They too were destined to play an important role in Jacob's home and family life.

Jacob continued in service to Laban for the seven additional years on which he had agreed. He did not have to wait all this time for Rachel, however, but went in to her as soon as Leah's festive week was finished. This is clear from verse 30, which indicates that he went in to Rachel first, and then served Laban another seven years. Rachel was his true love, of course, and he could hardly avoid showing this. Nevertheless, he did learn to love Leah also, even though he loved Rachel "more than Leah."

The Sons of Jacob

Whereas Abraham and Isaac had only had one son each to whom the promises were given, all the sons of Jacob were to share in the promises. Only one would be the progenitor of the Messiah, but all would be the "children of Israel" and would constitute the promised nation, the chosen people. Therefore, a detailed account is given in the latter part of chapter 29 and the first half of chapter 30 concerning the birth of Jacob's twelve sons and one daughter.

Genesis 29:31-35

---

31 ¶ And when the LORD saw that Lē'áh *was* hated, he opened her womb: but Rachel *was* barren.

32 And Lē'áh conceived, and bare a son; and she called his name Reuben: for she said, Surely the LORD hath looked upon my affliction; now therefore my husband will love me.

33 And she conceived again, and bare a son; and said, Because the LORD hath heard that I *was* hated, he hath therefore given me this *son* also: and she called his name Simeon.

34 And she conceived again, and bare a son; and said, Now this time will my husband be joined unto me, because I have borne him three sons: therefore was his name called Levi.

35 And she conceived again, and bare a son; and she said, Now will I praise the LORD: therefore she called his name Judah; and left bearing.

That God was concerned for Leah, as well as Jacob and Rachel, is indicated in verse 31. Rachel, like Sarah and Rebekah before her, was "barren" for a time, until the Lord answered her prayers for a son. In the meantime, though, since Jacob was so partial to Rachel (he did not, of course, "hate" Leah, as the literal meaning of the word would suggest; he only loved Rachel more, and so "slighted" Leah), God opened Leah's womb first and gave her, in fairly rapid succession, four sons.

Jacob, of course, was anxious to establish his family and so, when he saw that Leah was more productive than Rachel in this respect, he spent more and more of his time with her, and less with Rachel than he originally did. Each of her sons was named by Leah in accordance with her feelings at the time. Her first-born was named Reuben, meaning "Behold, a son!" Her second was Simeon, "Hearing," in thanksgiving for the fact that God had heard her prayers. The next was Levi, meaning "Attachment," expressing her confidence that three sons would thus ensure Jacob's permanent attachment to her. Then came Judah, whom she called simply "Praise," as a token of her praise to Jehovah.

Apparently these four sons were born in rapid succession, probably within the space of four years or less. Leah's fruitfulness did, indeed, cause Jacob to love her more than before, though Rachel always remained his first love. Leah seems to have been a godly woman, who spent much time in prayer concerning her marriage and her children. She acknowledged that her sons were given by the Lord in response to her prayers and her difficult position in the home. The fourth of her sons, Judah, was the only one whose name did not reflect her own personal situation, his name being a simple expression of praise to God. It is perhaps significant that this is the one through whom God intended one day to bring the Messiah into the world.

Genesis 30:1-8

CHAPTER 30

AND when Rachel saw that she bare Jacob no children, Rachel envied her sister; and said unto Jacob, Give me children, or else I die.

2 And Jacob's anger was kindled against Rachel; and he said, *Am* I in God's stead, who hath withheld from thee the fruit of the womb?

3 And she said, Behold my maid Bĭl′hȧh, go in unto her; and she shall bear upon my knees, that I may also have children by her.

4 And she gave him Bĭl′hȧh her handmaid to wife: and Jacob went in unto her.

5 And Bĭl′hȧh conceived, and bare Jacob a son.

6 And Rachel said, God hath judged me, and hath also heard my voice, and hath given me a son: therefore called she his name Dan.

7 And Bĭl′hȧh Rachel's maid conceived again, and bare Jacob a second son.

8 And Rachel said, With great wrestlings have I wrestled with my sister, and I have prevailed: and she called his name Năph′tȧ-lī.

Rachel, of course, could hardly have been unmoved by the fact that her sister (who, no doubt, had been somewhat the object of her own resentment for many years, since she had been forced to wait for her own marriage until Leah could find a husband) had been blessed with four sons while she remained barren. She could also see Jacob's love gradually shifting from her to Leah because of this. Her envy finally surfaced in a petulant outburst to her husband: "Give me children, or else I die."

Possibly she felt that, if Jacob would spend more time in her own bed, and not so much with Leah, she would be more likely to conceive. Otherwise her remonstrance was merely an emotional exclamation, since she certainly realized that it was not Jacob who was sterile. Jacob himself no doubt had been deeply disappointed also in the fact that Rachel had not been able to produce children, since it was she whom he had loved and had chosen to be the mother of the seed God had promised in the first place.

Her outburst, as could be expected, angered him. He struck back at her with a strong suggestion that there was something wrong in her own life, since God had not judged her worthy of being blessed with children. This interchange of angry words, between a husband and wife who really loved each other very much, possibly points up the dangers to believers' fellowship with the Lord and with each other which may appear when too many worldly considerations come into their relationship. It certainly is a commentary on the frictions that necessarily appear when God's ideal of monogamous marriage is not followed.

In desperation, Rachel decided to resort to the expedient that had been followed by Sarah long ago—that of having a child through her maid. How much better it would have been for husband and wife to have prayed together about the matter, trusting the Lord to answer in His own good time and will, rather than descending to such an expedient as this. Surely they both knew about the unhappy results of Sarah's venture down this route. Of course, in their defense, it should be observed that this device was an accepted social custom of the day. In fact, it is quite possible that it was for this very purpose—as a guard against barrenness—that Laban gave each of his daughters a personal maid. Humanly speaking, it was an understandable and perhaps somewhat justifiable expedient. Spiritually, however, it can only be regarded as a testimony of their lack of faith in God's promises at this juncture.

In any case, Rachel prevailed on Jacob to "go in unto Bilhah," a euphemism for having sexual intercourse with her, with, of course, the firm understanding that any fruit of this union would be regarded legally and morally as her own, rather than Bilhah's. It is not clear whether or not the statement "she shall bear upon my knees, that I may also have children by her" is to be taken literally, though as a symbolic gesture of proxy childbirth, the maid may well have been actually delivered of the child while lying on the lap of her mistress. In any case, Bilhah was immediately successful, and she bore Jacob a son, whom Rachel named Dan, meaning "Justice," testifying through this name that God had heard her prayer and justified her in her husband's sight.

Pleased with the quick success of this procedure, Rachel had Jacob continue to lie with Bilhah, now regarded as an actual wife of Jacob, though only a second-class wife (more like a concubine), and she soon became pregnant with a second son. This one Rachel named Naphtali, which means "Wrestlings." This unusual name was a reference to her long-continued rivalry with her sister. She felt she had now finally prevailed in this rivalry, and Jacob would be fully restored in his love for her instead of for Leah.

Genesis 30:9-13

---

9 When Lē'áh saw that she had left bearing, she took Zĭl'páh her maid, and gave her Jacob to wife.

10 And Zĭl'páh Lē'áh's maid bare Jacob a son.

11 And Lē'áh said, A troop cometh: and she called his name Gad.

12 And Zĭl'páh Lē'áh's maid bare Jacob a second son.

13 And Lē'áh said, Happy am I, for the daughters will call me blessed: and she called his name Ăsh'ĕr.

Leah, however, was not yet ready to accept defeat. Though she herself had stopped bearing, she also had a maid, and she reasoned that what had worked for Rachel would work for her too. Therefore she prevailed upon Jacob to take Zilpah, her maid, also as his wife, that she might have additional children by her.

Our own culture today is so different that it is difficult for us to understand the attitude of mind which would give Leah and Rachel vicarious satisfaction when their husband would have sexual relations with their respective maids. The matter of productivity was apparently of such overriding concern that the question of physical jealousy of their maids did not enter much into it. Perhaps they also reasoned that, the more sons they had, either directly or by proxy, the more security they would have in old age. As far as Jacob was concerned, he seems to have been rather pliant, going indiscriminately to whichever bed was most conveniently available at the time. Perhaps, virile as he was, he rather enjoyed the sexual variety which this household rivalry afforded him. It also served the purpose of producing a large family quite rapidly, and this would be important in the future accomplishment of God's promises regarding the nation which would come from him. Much of his indiscriminate moving about from bed to bed, however, was simply due to his desire to keep peace in his family, insofar as possible, by not favoring either wife in excess.

Leah's maid, Zilpah, also had two sons in quick succession, once Jacob had gone in to her. Leah named them Gad and Asher, meaning "Fortunate" and "Happy," respectively. The King James translation here ("a troop cometh") seems to be in error. The name "Gad" was associated with a pagan god of luck, but Leah used the word, no doubt, merely as an expression of her good fortune, sent to her by God, in the form of a fifth son. Then, when she had a sixth one, she truly was overjoyed. She, who had been despised as unmarriageable for so long, now would be acknowledged as unusually blessed, even by those young women who once had made her the object of their sneering gossip.

Genesis 30:14-16

14 ¶ And Reuben went in the days of wheat harvest, and found mandrakes in the field, and brought them unto his mother Lē′ăh. Then Rachel said to Lē′ăh, Give me, I pray thee, of thy son's mandrakes.

15 And she said unto her, *Is it* a small matter that thou hast taken my husband? and wouldest thou take away my son's mandrakes also? And Rachel said, Therefore he shall lie with thee to-night for thy son's mandrakes.

16 And Jacob came out of the field in the evening, and Lē′ăh went out to meet him, and said, Thou must come in unto me; for surely I have hired thee with my son's mandrakes. And he lay with her that night.

Jacob now had eight sons, and presumably from six to eight years had elapsed since his marriage. The eldest son, Reuben, was thus probably about seven years old by this time. He was at least old enough to play by himself in the field. One day during the season of wheat harvest (there is no indication that Laban himself was a wheat farmer, but it was during the time when neighbors at least were harvesting) Reuben chanced to discover mandrakes growing in the field. He recognized them as a fruit prized by his mother and by other women as well, so he plucked them and brought them home to Leah.

The mandrake is a small orange-colored berrylike fruit, much esteemed in ancient times as an aphrodisiac and inducer of fertility. It has been called the "love-apple" and, in Western countries, the "May-apple." It has also been used as a narcotic and emetic, especially its large roots. It was no doubt because of its supposed value in promoting fertility that both Leah and Rachel desired it.

When Rachel saw what Reuben had brought his mother, she wanted them herself, hoping that they might solve her problem of barrenness. Leah demurred, however, no doubt realizing plainly what Rachel was thinking. It had apparently been some time since Jacob had actually made love to her, as he had been spending his nights with the two maids and with Rachel, whom he still loved most of all. Leah had thought after her first four sons were born that Jacob's love for her was assured, but now Rachel was more in favor again.

Rachel, badly wanting the mandrakes, finally acquired them from Leah by making a bargain which must have been unpleasant for her. She agreed to insist that Jacob lie with Leah that night, hoping that, later, when she would be with Jacob, the mandrakes would enable her to become pregnant.

Leah eagerly met Jacob that evening immediately as he returned from the field. Before he had a chance to go to Rachel, or to Bilhah or Zilpah, she told him of her agreement with Rachel. She had no doubt also made herself as attractive as possible for Jacob, so that he quite willingly accepted her invitation and returned to her bed that night. He must have been somewhat amused, and possibly flattered, by this odd bargaining for his favors engaged in by the two sisters. He was quite willing to go in unto Leah, especially in view of her own eagerness to have him do so; but even if he had not been willing, he would no doubt have done so to keep peace in the family.

Genesis 30:17-21

---

17 And God hearkened unto Lē′ăh, and she conceived, and bare Jacob the fifth son.

18 And Lē′ăh said, God hath given me my hire, because I have given my maiden to my husband: and she called his name Ĭs′să-ehär.

19 And Lē′ăh conceived again, and bare Jacob the sixth son.

20 And Lē′ăh said, God hath endued me *with* a good dowry; now will my husband dwell with me, because I have borne him six sons: and she called his name Zĕb′ū-lŭn.

21 And afterward she bare a daughter, and called her name Dinah.

Leah had also been praying about the situation. The only time when Jacob had really shown much love for her was after she had borne him his first four sons. Even the two sons by her maid, Zilpah, had not regained his love and attention in recent years. She earnestly desired to have a son of her own again, and prayed to that end. God, in grace, heard her prayer, and once again Leah conceived. She took this as a reward from the Lord for being willing to share Jacob with her own maid. Accordingly, she named her own fifth son Issachar, meaning "Reward."

This development did, indeed, cause Jacob's attentions to turn again to Leah, and so he continued to spend much time with her. She soon had another son, whom she named Zebulun, meaning "Dwelling." This, she said, was in testimony of God's gracious gift to her, assuring her that her husband now would be willing to dwell with her.

Jacob now had ten sons. No mention is made of any daughters up to this point, and it does seem statistically unlikely that there would have been ten sons, by four different wives, with no daughters. Such oddities do happen, however, and in this case there is the all-important added factor of divine providence. It was now time for the promised nation to get under way, and this required a large family of sons.

At this point, Jacob's first daughter was born to Leah. Later Jacob had other daughters (Genesis 37:35; 46:7, 15), but the only one whose name and whose mother's name is given is Dinah, meaning "Judgment." Any father who has had several sons before his first daughter is born can testify what a real joy a little girl can be in a household. Dinah's brothers also loved her very much—even too much, as later developments proved (chapter 34).

Genesis 30:22-24

---

22 ¶ And God remembered Rachel, and God hearkened to her, and opened her womb.

23 And she conceived, and bare a son;

and said, God hath taken away my
reproach:

24 And she called his name Joseph;

and said, The LORD shall add to me another son.

Finally, after many years, the Lord answered Rachel's prayers, and she also conceived. This was not due to the mandrakes, of course, which had in any case been eaten several years previously, but due to the power of God. Rachel, though once rather proud of her beauty and desirability, had by now been sufficiently humbled. Sterility was considered to be a divine reproach, so it was an occasion of great joy and thankfulness for Rachel when God finally took away her reproach. The name she chose for her son when he was born, Joseph, can be derived both from "Taken Away" and "May He Add," thus indicating both her thanksgiving and her faith that God would give her yet another son.

Spotted and Speckled

By this time, Jacob had more than fulfilled his contract with Laban. He had agreed to serve with him seven more years, and more than that period of time must have elapsed by the time his four wives had borne him eleven or twelve children. He was with Laban a total of twenty years altogether (Genesis 31:38), including the fourteen years he had served for Leah and Rachel. Since the first seven years had been prior to his two marriages, all of his eleven sons and one daughter must have been born during a thirteen-year period at most. It is possible that Leah was pregnant with Judah and Bilhah with Dan at the same time, Bilhah with Naphtali and Zilpah with Gad at the same time, and Leah with Zebulun and Rachel with Joseph at the same time. Dinah may have been born after Joseph. If so, the entire sequence of sons from Reuben to Joseph could possibly have been born within a period of eight or nine years. In any case, by the time Joseph was born, all of Jacob's obligations to Laban were more than settled.

Jacob now had a large family, and his work had been highly productive on Laban's behalf, but he still had nothing of his own. He was also anxious to go home again, although he had apparently heard nothing from his family. Increasingly, therefore, he became restless and dissatisfied with his current situation.

Genesis 30:25-28

---

25 ¶ And it came to pass, when Rachel had borne Joseph, that Jacob said unto Lā'băn, Send me away, that I may go unto mine own place, and to my country.

26 Give *me* my wives and my children, for whom I have served thee, and let me go: for thou knowest my service which I have done thee.
27 And Lā'băn said unto him, I pray thee, if I have found favor in thine eyes, tarry: *for* I have learned by experience that the LORD hath blessed me for thy sake.
28 And he said, Appoint me thy wages, and I will give *it*.

Finally, Jacob went to Laban and announced his decision to return to his home. He intended, further, to take his wives and all his children with him. He reminded Laban that he had more than lived up to his part of the bargain, so that he had no further moral or legal claim on him or his family.

Laban, however, was very reluctant to see him go. He had prospered greatly because of Jacob's abilities and faithfulness, and he was willing to make almost any bargain that would keep him working for him. Laban even acknowledged that the Lord was with Jacob, and that it was of the Lord that he had profited so much through Jacob. Once before, he had gotten the better bargain by letting Jacob name his own wages; so now he made the same proposition again. Jacob had merely to name his price, and Laban assured him he would meet it, if Jacob would only keep working for him.

He had no other daughters to offer Jacob, of course; so this time the arrangement would have to be one of an actual payment of money or property. Laban's offer seemed generous, but later developments showed he did not actually intend to let Jacob leave with anything.

The phrase "learned by experience" (verse 27) is interesting. It represents the Hebrew word *nachash,* and means literally "learned by enchantments." Laban had been somewhat perplexed by the fact that Jacob's care of his flocks had resulted in such a great increase in his own wealth. Accordingly, he had in some way either carried out certain divination practices of his own, or else consulted some kind of soothsayer or oracle, seeking the secret. Laban, it becomes clear, though related to Abraham and knowing about Jehovah, had become to some degree a pagan mystic. At any rate, God so overruled his enchantments that, even through them, he had gotten the message that Jacob was under the special care of Jehovah and that it was because of this that God had blessed his service.

Genesis 30:29-34

29 And he said unto him, Thou knowest how I have served thee, and how thy cattle was with me.
30 For *it was* little which thou hadst before I *came,* and it is *now* increased unto a multitude; and the LORD hath

blessed thee since my coming: and now, when shall I provide for mine own house also?

31 And he said, What shall I give thee? And Jacob said, Thou shalt not give me any thing: if thou wilt do this thing for me, I will again feed *and* keep thy flock.

32 I will pass through all thy flock to-day, removing from thence all the speckled and spotted cattle, and all the brown cattle among the sheep, and the spotted and speckled among the goats: and *of such* shall be my hire.

33 So shall my righteousness answer for me in time to come, when it shall come for my hire before thy face: every one that *is* not speckled and spotted among the goats, and brown among the sheep, that shall be counted stolen with me.

34 And Lā'băn said, Behold, I would it might be according to thy word.

Jacob had apparently through the years said little about all this, simply keeping his agreement with Laban to the best of his ability. Laban, on his part, had evidently never before admitted openly to Jacob that he knew it was because of Jacob and Jacob's God that he had prospered so much in recent years. Jacob, therefore, took this opportunity to give his own testimony to this effect, indicating to Laban that he well knew all this, but had until now refrained from using it to his own advantage. He had been completely responsible for Laban's flocks for over fourteen years, and a relatively small number of animals had become a great multitude under his care. This blessing had, indeed, come from Jehovah, though Jacob had done his part by faithful and industrious service.

Now, however, it was reasonable that he (Jacob), having fulfilled all his commitments to Laban, should begin to provide for his own family. Laban again, therefore, asked what he could give him to make him stay.

Jacob did not wish Laban to "give" him anything. He had learned that God would supply what He wanted him to have, and he did not wish to be indebted in any way to a man whom he had come to know as a self-seeking, deceptive, ungodly schemer. He therefore made a proposition to Laban which would give God the opportunity to bless Jacob materially also, as He had Laban through Jacob. This plan would bring blessing to Jacob without taking anything belonging to Laban. Though Laban had doubtless expected Jacob to ask for a certain number of animals to begin his own flocks and herds, and would have been willing (at least outwardly) to give him whatever he would ask, Jacob would not take anything of Laban's which then existed. Instead, he agreed to shepherd and supervise Laban's flocks, exactly as he had been doing, and his pay would consist of those animals yet unborn that would be less desirable to Laban because of their markings. It would thus be entirely up to God as to how many animals would become Jacob's.

Jacob agreed that none of the solid-color animals would be taken into his own flocks. If any should be found by Laban in Jacob's flocks, Laban would have the right to take them out. Only those future animals that would be born speckled or striped or spotted, or abnormally colored in some way, would become Jacob's wages. The dominant color traits in Laban's flocks and herds were evidently white among the sheep, black among the goats, and brown among the cattle. Most of the animals were of these colors, but there were a few that were spotted and speckled among the cattle and goats, and brown among the sheep. It was of such as these that Jacob's pay would be.

However, Jacob further proposed that, not only would none of these living speckled animals be taken by him, but they would not even be used for breeding purposes. He would separate them into a separate flock, and keep them away from the normal-colored animals. Only such spotted and speckled animals as would be born in the future from the normal-colored animals would become his. Since the solid-colored animals were by far the more numerous, and since it was much less likely that they would bear striped and speckled offspring than those animals that were already striped and speckled—or brown among the sheep—this arrangement clearly was highly favorable to Laban and of very doubtful value to Jacob. Indeed, it was an act of pure faith on his part. He had put himself entirely at God's mercy. It would be up to the Lord to indicate, by a very unlikely set of circumstances, whether Jacob should prosper personally or not.

Laban, who was willing to make a far more generous outlay than this to keep Jacob, immediately jumped at the chance to seal such a bargain. He would lose nothing that now belonged to him, and it appeared very unlikely that Jacob would acquire any future animals by this process either. He had no breeding stock of his own, and none of the animals from which his pay was to come would be likely to produce spotted and speckled progeny of their own without a spotted and speckled population with which to interbreed.

Although Jacob had given Laban no reason whatever to mistrust him, it is hard for men who are themselves dishonest to trust anyone else. The deal was so unbelievably good from Laban's point of view that he felt there must be some catch to it. Perhaps, while alone with the flocks in the fields, Jacob would bring together the flocks with the normal colorings and those that were spotted, in order to increase his chances that some of the lambs and kids would be off-color.

Genesis 30:35, 36

35 And he removed that day the he goats that were ring-streaked and spotted, and all the she goats that were speckled and spotted, *and* every one that had *some* white in it, and all the brown among the sheep, and gave *them* into the hand of his sons.

36 And he set three days' journey betwixt himself and Jacob: and Jacob fed the rest of Lā′băn's flocks.

With some such thoughts as these in his mind, Laban decided not to trust Jacob to keep the two sets of flocks separate. He himself, probably aided by his sons, went through the flocks, culling out all the striped and spotted goats, the brown sheep, and other odd-colored animals, and put them into a separate flock, thus assuring himself that Jacob would not leave any of them in the main flock. Then, to make it quite impossible in the future for there to be any mixing, he gave the speckled flock into the hands of his sons, and told them always to keep them at least three days' journey away from the main body of animals which would be tended by Jacob.

Genesis 30:37-43

37 ¶ And Jacob took him rods of green poplar, and of the hazel and chestnut tree; and pilled white streaks in them, and made the white appear which *was* in the rods.

38 And he set the rods which he had pilled before the flocks in the gutters in the watering troughs when the flocks came to drink, that they should conceive when they came to drink.

39 And the flocks conceived before the rods, and brought forth cattle ring-streaked, speckled, and spotted.

40 And Jacob did separate the lambs, and set the faces of the flocks toward the ring-streaked, and all the brown in the flock of Lā′băn; and he put his own flocks by themselves, and put them not unto Lā′băn's cattle.

41 And it came to pass, whensoever the stronger cattle did conceive, that Jacob laid the rods before the eyes of the cattle in the gutters, that they might conceive among the rods.

42 But when the cattle were feeble, he put *them* not in: so the feebler were Lā′băn's, and the stronger Jacob's.

43 And the man increased exceedingly, and had much cattle, and maidservants, and menservants, and camels, and asses.

Jacob knew a great deal about sheep and goats and cattle, however— much more than Laban. He had kept his father's flocks for decades, and now had been in charge of Laban's for over fourteen years. As a very observant and intelligent man he had apparently learned something of what we now call Mendelian genetics, simply by long-continued observation of generation after generation of these animals. He knew that, even though a species of animal may have certain "dominant" traits (such as the white color in this type of sheep), there are, in each generation, certain individual animals that manifest one or more "recessive" traits (such as the brown color among the sheep). Furthermore, actual physical vigor and usefulness for man's needs are quite independent of this matter of coloration. He believed that he could simply trust God to increase the statistical proportion of animals in future generations of Laban's flocks that would appear with these recessive traits. He knew, furthermore, that if he would then use these for future breeding in the flock, this would increase their numbers still more. A certain proportion of the solid-color animals he knew would be "homozygous" and, if mated with other homozygous animals, would bear only solid-color offspring. The "heterozygous" animals, which did contain in some proportion the genes for off-colored progeny, would be the ones which would have to supply his own future flocks; but by selective breeding he could eventually develop a flock of predominantly spotted and speckled animals.

Many commentators have suggested that Jacob deceived Laban by making this bargain, and that he used unfair means to increase the proportion of spotted and striped animals. It should not be forgotten, however, that Jacob was given the opportunity by Laban to set his own wages, and Jacob could well have requested a significant portion of Laban's existing flocks. Whatever advantages his own knowledge of animal genetics might have given him would have been immensely augmented by a larger, more varied, flock to start with. He made the bargain as difficult for himself, and as generous to Laban, as it could possibly have been. There is no basis at all for any criticism of Jacob's conduct in this regard.

Critics not only raise questions about Jacob's ethics, but also about his knowledge of science. His actions in peeling white stripes in rods from trees of poplar, hazel, and chestnut (or, perhaps more likely, storax, almond, and plane trees), and placing them in the cattle watering troughs, have been attacked as showing his belief in the outmoded ideas of prenatal influence. The idea is that Jacob supposed, by making the animals look at striped rods at the time of conception, he could induce them to bring forth striped offspring. The doctrine of prenatal influence is, of course, believed by modern zoologists to be nothing but an old wives' tale.

It should not be overlooked, however, that Jacob was over ninety years old at this time, that he was a very intelligent and careful observer, and that he had spent most of his long life raising and studying cattle, sheep, and goats. He would have been most unlikely to have been taken in by a groundless superstition.

There is a great deal, even today, that scientists have not been able to work out concerning the transmission of hereditary factors. In a certain population, there are multitudes of different characteristics which may appear in different individual animals of that species. The variational potential in the DNA molecular structure is tremendous. Exactly what it is that determines the actual characteristics a particular individual may have, out of all the potential characteristics that are theoretically available in the gene pool, is not yet known in any significant degree. It may be that Jacob had learned certain things about these animals which modern biologists have not yet even approached.

There are, indeed, certain factors which can become prenatal influences, and which can determine to some degree the physical characteristics of the progeny. Though it is surely very unlikely that an external image can be transmitted through the visual apparatus to the brain and thence in some way as a signal to the DNA structure to specify certain characteristics to be triggered in the embryo, it is nevertheless true that certain chemicals can and do have a significant prenatal influence if they can reach the embryo or, prior to conception, the DNA in the germ cells. It is possible that certain chemicals in the wood of these trees—peeled rods of which were actually in the water which the flocks came to drink—were capable somehow of affecting the animals. If nothing else, water treated thus may have served as an aphrodisiac and fertility promoter among the cattle. At least one such chemical substance found in these trees has been used for such a purpose in both ancient and modern times.

Further, whether or not the sense of sight can actually "mark" the embryo in some way, there is no doubt that what one sees may have a strong effect on certain physiologic mechanisms in his body. The phenomenon of blushing, the nauseous reactions produced by viewing gruesome sights, and the effect of pornographic pictures in stimulating the sexual apparatus are typical cases in point. The mere sight of the striped rods may have served simply as an aphrodisiac to the cattle when they came to drink. This in fact seems indicated by verse 38, in which the word translated "conceive" in the King James Version is actually the Hebrew *yacham,* meaning "to be hot." That is, the verse may be read: "And he set the rods which he peeled before the flocks in the gutters in the watering troughs when the flocks came to drink, that they should become hot [or 'in heat'] when they came to drink." In some way not understood (but apparently confirmed by many practical animal raisers since), the sight of white-streaked rods seems to stimulate these animals to sexual activity.

All things considered, it seems most likely that this is what Jacob had in mind. He wanted to speed up the reproduction process and to induce the animals to have as many offspring as possible in the shortest time possible. This would presumably benefit Laban even more than himself since most of the animals should be of the normal type; but statistically, he knew that a certain proportion would be spotted. The more animals born, the sooner there would be some with the characteristics he was looking for.

When the animals did conceive and bear, Jacob was possibly quite surprised to note that a larger proportion than he had expected were ring-streaked, speckled, and spotted. He placed these animals in a group by themselves, after they were weaned, no doubt, and thus had the beginning of a flock of his own.

The bulk of the animals, which were Laban's, were made by Jacob to face toward the separate flock of speckled and spotted lambs, but were kept separate from them. The reason for having them thus oriented is not clear; perhaps it was to make a subconscious impression on them that stripes and speckles were a mark of distinction in the flock, so as to make preparations for and augment the aphrodisiac influences of the striped rods. It is possible that, as a symbolic gesture, he had them face toward the three-days-distant flock of Laban's ring-streaked cattle. Though they could not see them, this might have symbolized Jacob's confidence that Laban's pure-color flock would eventually produce a new ring-streaked flock for himself.

A further measure was taken by Jacob to ensure that the flocks so produced would be composed of strong animals. He divided the flocks into two shifts, composed of stronger and weaker animals, respectively. He used the rods in the troughs when the stronger animals drank, but not when the weaker ones came there. Thus the stronger animals were stimulated to mate, and the others were not. This measure, likewise, to the extent it would be effective, constituted a sound practice of animal husbandry, and should have been of as great benefit to Laban as to Jacob. It would ensure that, statistically at least, most of the newborn lambs and kids, whether solid color or spotted, would be sturdy and healthy. However, there continued to be produced an abnormally large proportion of spotted and speckled young. This meant that a greater and greater percentage of the animals in Jacob's flock were strong animals, and an increasing percentage in Laban's were weaker animals.

It was not until later that Jacob came to understand the providential intervention that caused the unusual percentage of streaked and spotted animals to be born (see Genesis 32:10). In the meantime, within the space of only a few years—perhaps four or five—Jacob's flock had grown so large, and he had prospered from it so greatly, that he had to employ many servants, both male and female, and had purchased many camels and asses. He had quickly become a very prosperous rancher. He had done so, not by any dishonest manipulation of his own, but by means of sound practices of animal breeding which, by all normal standards, should have been of even greater benefit to Laban than to himself. The God of his fathers, however, had intervened in a marvelous and mysterious way.

Genesis 31:1-3

CHAPTER 31

AND he heard the words of Lā′băn's sons, saying, Jacob hath taken away all that *was* our father's; and of *that* which *was* our father's hath he gotten all this glory.

2 And Jacob beheld the countenance of Lā′băn, and, behold, it *was* not toward him as before.

3 And the LORD said unto Jacob, Return unto the land of thy fathers, and to thy kindred; and I will be with thee.

By this time, Laban and his sons were becoming greatly concerned. What had seemed like an extremely good contract at the time they made it had taken a most surprising and distressing turn. Jacob had kept his part of the bargain faithfully, but somehow his flock was prospering and theirs was suffering. Laban's sons, in particular, who could see their inheritance slipping away from them (Laban was an old man by this time, no doubt), became unreasonably bitter, accusing Jacob of a thieving appropriation of their father's wealth. Laban also was most distressed. Before this time, Jacob had been the cause of great prosperity to him; now, however, things were working out altogether differently. Laban now would have been glad for Jacob to leave, but how could he annul his agreement with Jacob? Also (most importantly), how could he prevent his taking the flocks he had acquired? These were developments he had not foreseen.

Jacob himself heard about these charges and he realized what Laban was thinking. He knew he couldn't stay much longer in Haran, but he had made a contract to keep Laban's flocks and he hesitated to be the first to break it. He no doubt suspected that Laban did not intend to honor it and would probably take his flocks from him by force, but Laban had not yet made any overt move to do this, and he could not discern the intent of Laban's heart.

God could do this, however. And so again God spoke to Jacob in a dream, telling him that the time had come for him to leave Laban and return to his home in Canaan. Just as God had been close to him at all times in Haran, so would He be as he returned home. It was now time for Jacob to begin the establishment of the promised nation in the promised land.

Genesis 31:4-9

4 And Jacob sent and called Rachel and Lē′ăh to the field unto his flock,

5 And said unto them, I see your father's countenance, that it *is* not toward me as before; but the God of my father hath been with me.

6 And ye know that with all my power I have served your father.

7 And your father hath deceived me, and changed my wages ten times; but God suffered him not to hurt me.

8 If he said thus, The speckled shall be thy wages; then all the cattle bare speckled: and if he said thus, The ring-streaked shall be thy hire; then bare all the cattle ring-streaked.

9 Thus God hath taken away the cattle of your father, and given *them* to me.

In obedience, Jacob prepared to depart. However, he must first explain the situation to Leah and Rachel. There was a possibility that, not understanding the whole situation, they would not want to leave their home.

Knowing that he would not be allowed by Laban to leave openly with his flocks and family, Jacob realized he would have to leave unannounced. He knew that Laban would, if he could, take all his possessions from him before he would allow him to leave (Genesis 31:42). Of course, Jacob could, and perhaps should, have trusted God to overrule Laban's plotting and to force Laban to let him go. On the other hand, he probably reasoned that, since Laban would surely not let him go willingly, some form of severe judgment by God would be necessary to force him to do so, and Jacob did not want that to happen, for Leah's and Rachel's sake. It seemed to be the best thing for all concerned if he would just slip away quietly.

To secretly inform his wives about his plans, he had to send for them to come out into the fields where he was keeping the flocks. He had evidently said little to them before about what had been happening the past few years, out of respect for their love for their father. But now he had to present the complete picture to them.

He told them their father no longer felt toward him as he formerly did, because of his increasing prosperity. He recounted numerous instances when Laban had deceived him and when he had changed his wages for no reason except to hinder Jacob's increase in wealth. (Evidently Laban had frequently altered his original agreement with Jacob.) When he saw the cattle were producing speckled cattle, he would tell Jacob he had decided only the striped would be his wages. Then, when the cattle would produce striped offspring, he would change it again. In every case, however, the Lord had kept blessing Jacob. No matter what Laban had tried to do to him, God had protected and prospered him. During all this time, Jacob had continued to serve Laban to the very best of his ability, trying to keep his own word and to be a good testimony to all concerned. Jacob also knew Leah and Rachel were aware of this, and they could hardly fail to have been deeply impressed with the way the Lord was miraculously prospering their husband in spite of all their father could do to prevent it. Jacob made no claim that it was by his own ability or ingenuity that he had acquired such wealth; he gave all the credit to the Lord, as indeed he should have done, because his prosperity was entirely due to the Lord.

Genesis 31:10-13

---

10 And it came to pass at the time that the cattle conceived, that I lifted up mine eyes, and saw in a dream, and, behold, the rams which leaped upon the

cattle *were* ring-streaked, speckled, and grizzled.

11 And the angel of God spake unto me in a dream, *saying,* Jacob: and I said, Here *am* I.

12 And he said, Lift up now thine eyes, and see, all the rams which leap upon the cattle *are* ring-streaked, speckled, and grizzled: for I have seen all that Lā'băn doeth unto thee.

13 I *am* the God of Beth-el, where thou anointedst the pillar, *and* where thou vowedst a vow unto me: now arise, get thee out from this land, and return unto the land of thy kindred.

Jacob then explained how it was that the newborn cattle all happened to correspond so remarkably to the specifications in his contract with Laban for the animals he would receive for his hire. God had shown it to him in a dream. At the time the animals were in heat and mating by the water troughs, he saw in his dream that the male animals which impregnated the females were all "ring-streaked, speckled, and grizzled."

The actual animals that mated, however, were not ring-streaked, speckled, and spotted at all, but were animals in the solid-color flock belonging to Laban. The meaning of the dream, quite plainly, is that these animals were heterozygous, rather than homozygous, carrying the particular genes for streaks, spots, and speckles, even though their own coats were all solid color. God could see into the gene structure, though Jacob could not, and He knew the true nature of the animals. Jacob had learned from experience that a certain small proportion of the descendants of even pure-colored animals would be off-colored; but he had no way of knowing which ones, or of controlling them. God knew which ones, and could control them, however. The homozygous animals, which could produce only progeny colored like themseslves, were restrained from mating by supernatural means imposed by God Himself, or by His angel. No doubt some of the mated heterozygous animals also produced solid-colored offspring, so that Laban's flock increased too; but the proportion of these was not nearly so great as previous experience would have indicated.

God also revealed in the dream, through His angel, that the reason He had done this was His awareness of what Laban was attempting to do to Jacob. He reminded Jacob that He had spoken to him at Bethel, twenty years before. In the vow, made at that time, when he had set up and anointed a pillar in commemoration of God's promise, Jacob had contemplated someday returning to his father's house in peace. Now the time had come, and God told him to be on his way, returning to his homeland. God had certainly taken care of him in the past, prospering him in a marvelous way, despite many obstacles, just as He had promised.

Heading for Home

Jacob, after his heartfelt rehearsal of the situation to his wives, was relieved to hear them both assure him they would gladly go with him. They knew their life was with Jacob. Their father no longer was concerned about their future; whatever inheritance they might once have had would not now go to them but to their brothers. They had watched closely, though silently, the actions of their father and brothers in contrast with those of Jacob, and they could well understand why God had blessed Jacob. They both loved him, and they realized it was to their own best interests, as well as those of their children, for them all to leave their father's home and go with Jacob to his own land.

Genesis 31:14-16

---

14 And Rachel and Lē′áh answered and said unto him, *Is there* yet any portion or inheritance for us in our father's house? 15 Are we not counted of him strangers? for he hath sold us, and hath quite devoured also our money. 16 For all the riches which God hath taken from our father, that *is* ours, and our children's: now then, whatsoever God hath said unto thee, do.

Rachel and Leah revealed in their words here that they had long resented the way their father had essentially "sold" them to Jacob. He had treated them as "strangers" or "foreigners," rather than as his own daughters. The exorbitant price which Jacob had paid for them—fourteen years of free service to Laban—made them love Jacob but resent their father. Rather than treating this payment like a dowry, to provide a financial base for his daughters' future well-being and security, as should have been done, he had "devoured" it all himself, using it probably to build up his own holdings, and had given nothing to them personally. They rightly felt that, since their husband had been responsible for the great prosperity of their father, and since this was in effect what Jacob had given in order to marry them, these possessions by all rights should have come to them. Instead, Laban had made it clear that they would receive none of his riches. Consequently, they felt justified in interpreting God's dealings with Laban, in causing his flocks to gradually become those of Jacob, as simply taking what had rightly belonged to them and their children and restoring it to them. Though their decision was not based on the same high spiritual considerations as that of Jacob, they nevertheless realized it was of God, and therefore had confidence that, whatever God had told Jacob to do, was the thing that should be done. They were ready to go.

Genesis 31:17-21

---

17 ¶ Then Jacob rose up, and set his sons and his wives upon camels;

18 And he carried away all his cattle, and all his goods which he had gotten, the cattle of his getting, which he had gotten in Pā′dăn-ā′răm, for to go to Isaac his father in the land of Cā′năan.

19 And Lā′băn went to shear his sheep: and Rachel had stolen the images that were her father's.

20 And Jacob stole away unawares to Lā′băn the Syrian, in that he told him not that he fled.

21 So he fled with all that he had; and he rose up, and passed over the river, and set his face *toward* the mount Gĭl′ē-ăd.

Jacob lost no time in preparing to depart. Laban was away shearing his sheep; so it was a good time to leave, before anyone knew what was happening. Jacob herded together all his flocks, which had become his through his agreement with Laban, as well as his other possessions. He had camels for his wives and children to ride on. His servants of course assisted in all the preparations and in shepherding the flocks (Genesis 32:3, 5, etc.). The entire assemblage, when ready, must have made quite a large caravan. Quite a contrast to the way he had arrived in Haran! The statement that he "carried away all his cattle" could better be rendered "he drove away all his cattle," indicating something of the urgency of the rapid departure.

The momentous nature of this event is indicated by the formal statement of verse 18. Jacob was now leaving Padan-aram, or Mesopotamia, to go back to Canaan and to Isaac his father. The time had come for him to take over the patriarchal responsibility associated with God's promises. He possessed both the birthright and the blessing; and they entailed great responsibilities, as well as privileges, which it was now time to fulfill.

An apparently minor matter, but nevertheless quite serious, is mentioned almost in passing. Rachel, before leaving, and quite unknown to Jacob, had slipped into Laban's tent and stolen his "images" (literally, *teraphim,* or small idol figurines used in divination and as household deities supposed to bring good luck to the owner). Their use frequently cropped up in later Israelite history, but was definitely idolatrous and contrary to the true faith of Jehovah. It has already been noted that Laban had become an idolater, though he did know about Jehovah in a general way, and Rachel seems to have been influenced somewhat by him in this regard. Though she trusted Jacob's God, she also was reluctant to completely give up her previous superstitions, and she thought that taking these images along would in some way help them on the long journey and in the new home to which they were going. Her attitude was little different from that of many a new Christian today, happy to know the Lord but not yet willing to enter a life of separation from the world.

It is also possible, as implied in some of the Nuzu tablets excavated around 1930, that the teraphim were associated with the inheritance and property rights of their owner. If so, Rachel may have stolen them with the thought that possessing them would somehow help validate the legitimacy of her husband's title to the flocks he had acquired while serving Laban and represent the inheritance she had a right to expect.

Jacob then left before Laban knew anything about his plans. He and his party forded the River Euphrates (the river is sufficiently shallow at certain points near its source for this) and headed for Mount Gilead, far to the southwest. Mount Gilead is actually a mountainous region east of the Jordan River. Its northern edges are nearly three hundred miles from Haran; so a long journey stretched ahead of them. It is possible, of course, that Jacob had already worked his flocks around to the south as far as possible so as to have the advantage of a head start when he was ready to leave. If the three-days' journey which typically separated him from Laban's flocks was oriented in such a way as to place Jacob's flocks a three-days' journey southwest of Laban's home (the sheep-shearing would probably have taken place not too far from there), then Jacob and his flocks would have already been about eighty or ninety miles on their way when their flight began in earnest. A day's journey was usually reckoned at about thirty miles, for men traveling unencumbered. However, once they began moving the flocks along, they would be able to make only fifteen or twenty miles a day. Thus, once they started driving the cattle, it would take them probably ten days or so to reach the Mount Gilead region.

Genesis 31:22-24

---

22 And it was told Lā′băn on the third day, that Jacob was fled.
23 And he took his brethren with him, and pursued after him seven days' journey; and they overtook him in the mount Gĭl′ē-ăd.
24 And God came to Lā′băn the Syrian in a dream by night, and said unto him, Take heed that thou speak not to Jacob either good or bad.

Laban and his retinue were busy with the sheep-shearing, not only with the actual work itself, but also with the festivities which accompanied this annual event. Word did not reach them that Jacob and his family had departed until after they had already been on the trail for three days. Laban no doubt was furious, as were his sons, but they could not drop everything at the sheep-shearing immediately (this particular chore Jacob had no doubt taken care of on his own sheep ahead of time, in order to take advantage of Laban's preoccupation with this essential work while Jacob was fleeing). By the time they were ready to pursue Jacob, probably another day or so had elapsed.

As soon as they could leave, Laban and his men started the pursuit, and pushed it as hard as they could. In fact, they covered the entire three hundred miles in only seven days, an indication of the fast, hard traveling they did. Laban and his sons had no intention of letting Jacob take all his flocks to Canaan, and were resolved to take them from Jacob by whatever force was necessary. Quite likely they also intended to slay Jacob, especially if he tried to resist them.

They finally overtook Jacob's caravan in the mountains of Gilead, probably soon after they had entered them. Knowing that there was no possibility of his escaping them now, they made camp for the night, in order to be rested for whatever might be required in the way of combat the next day.

But that night, Laban had a dream! In the dream, God spoke to him, giving him a sober warning against doing injury to Jacob in any way. He was not even to speak to him, if the intent of the conversation was to induce him to return or to reproach him for leaving. God made it plain to him that Jacob was under His protection and was following His directions. Though Laban did not know the Lord in any personal way, he did know enough about Him to know he had better do what He said.

Genesis 31:25-30

---

25 ¶ Then Lā′băn overtook Jacob. Now Jacob had pitched his tent in the mount: and Lā′băn with his brethren pitched in the mount of Gĭl′ē-ăd.

26 And Lā′băn said to Jacob, What hast thou done, that thou hast stolen away unawares to me, and carried away my daughters, as captives *taken* with the sword?

27 Wherefore didst thou flee away secretly, and steal away from me; and didst not tell me, that I might have sent thee away with mirth, and with songs, with tabret, and with harp?

28 And hast not suffered me to kiss my sons and my daughters? thou hast now done foolishly in *so* doing.

29 It is in the power of my hand to do you hurt: but the God of your father spake unto me yesternight, saying, Take thou heed that thou speak not to Jacob either good or bad.

30 And now, *though* thou wouldest needs be gone, because thou sore longedst after thy father's house, *yet* wherefore hast thou stolen my gods?

The next morning, Laban broke camp early and overtook Jacob before his party got under way. As they rode into camp, the atmosphere must have been very tense. No one knew what Laban would attempt, but Jacob no doubt had full confidence that God would fulfill His promise to be with him. Laban, on his part, was not only still angry and bitter, but now also frustrated, because God had barred him from carrying out his intentions.

He immediately blurted out, when he met Jacob, a hypocritical speech of feigned concern over Jacob's secret snatching-away of his daughters and grandchildren, without giving Laban an opportunity even to kiss them good-bye. He complained that he would have sent them away joyously with great festivities of music and laughter, had Jacob not slipped away unannounced. Jacob, as well as Leah and Rachel, and no doubt the whole company, all knew Laban was lying; but Laban was afraid to say what was really on his mind, in view of God's warning.

He then boasted that he was well able to do Jacob harm (though, in view of his dream, he knew this was an empty threat). Noting that his speech seemed to have produced neither fear nor sorrow in the hearts of Jacob and his daughters, he decided he had better tell them exactly why it was that he was *not* going to try to hurt Jacob, even though it was obvious, from the intense way in which he had pursued them, that he had fully intended to do so. He then told of his dream, and of God's warning.

Recognizing there was no point in carrying this particular line of conversation further, he abruptly changed the subject. Trying to justify his actions in some measure, he told Jacob that he realized he wanted to return to his father's house, and that this was good enough reason for him to leave Haran. Why, however, had he stolen his teraphim? Laban was obviously trying now to excuse his pursuit of Jacob on this ground, though it was hardly likely that he would have borne the cost and trouble of such a long and difficult adventure merely to recover two small figurines, which would have been much cheaper, and just as efficacious in whatever magical power Laban may have thought they possessed, to replace locally. Anyway, Laban knew Jacob well enough to know that Jacob, of all people, would never have taken his "gods"; Jacob would have had nothing whatever to do with them, even if they really did (as some have suggested) represent the inheritance rights of their owner.

Genesis 31:31, 32

---

31 And Jacob answered and said to Lā′băn, Because I was afraid: for I said, Peradventure thou wouldest take by force thy daughters from me.

32 With whomsoever thou findest thy gods, let him not live: before our brethren discern thou what *is* thine with me, and take *it* to thee. For Jacob knew not that Rachel had stolen them.

Before answering Laban's charge of theft of the teraphim, Jacob felt it good, for the record, to tell Laban, and all the assemblage, exactly *why* he had left suddenly and secretly. Laban had asked the question and, even though Jacob knew that Laban knew the real answer already, perhaps there were others among the family or servants who had not seen the full picture. Jacob said that, if he had proposed departing openly, he was afraid (and with good reason) that Laban would try to take his daughters (and their children, of course) back from him by force. Jacob would certainly have fought (and, furthermore, God would have fought for him as well) Laban in this eventuality, and no telling what damage might have been done. So it was far better for him to take his family and possessions away quietly and with no advance notice.

As far as Laban's images were concerned, Jacob knew nothing of them, and was angry at the very thought. If, by chance, someone in his employ (he certainly had no reason to suspect anyone in his own family, least of all Rachel, his beloved wife) had taken them, thus embarrassing him and giving Laban an excuse for chasing him, Laban could feel free to take him and exact whatever penalty the law of the times would warrant (the laws of Hammurabi, for instance, cite the theft of temple gods as a capital crime). Furthermore, if Laban found anything that really belonged to him (Jacob had been most scrupulous on this point, as he gathered up his belongings for the flight), he was welcome to take it back.

Genesis 31:33-35

---

33 And Lā′băn went into Jacob's tent, and into Lē′ăh's tent, and into the two maidservants' tents; but he found *them* not. Then went he out of Lē′ăh's tent, and entered into Rachel's tent. 34 Now Rachel had taken the images, and put them in the camel's furniture, and sat upon them. And Lā′băn searched all the tent, but found *them* not. 35 And she said to her father, Let it not displease my lord that I cannot rise up before thee; for the custom of women *is* upon me. And he searched, but found not the images.

Laban proceeded to search the camp. Although it is not mentioned, presumably he searched throughout the entire caravan, but most definitely he searched Jacob's tent. Then, supposing that Jacob might have hidden something in one of his wives' tents, he looked through the tents of Leah, Bilhah, and Zilpah, and finally through Rachel's tent. If not the gods, he was hoping earnestly he might be able to find something Jacob had stolen, thus giving him warrant to complain to God that His protection of Jacob was unjustified, and perhaps to justify himself in taking back all his flocks, as he no doubt still desired to do.

Rachel had hidden the images in the saddle-and-basket assemblage used on her camel. This "furniture" was now in her tent, having been placed there the previous night as they made camp. Rachel was sitting on this equipment (perhaps her skirts even hid it) as Laban entered the tent. She excused herself for not rising by saying she was not feeling well (due to her menstrual period). This was probably a legitimate excuse, at the time, or Jacob himself might have suspected she was concealing something. Consequently, Laban found nothing in her tent either.

What Jacob would have done had Laban discovered the images in Rachel's tent we do not know. Would he have actually handed Rachel over for execution as he had offered? And would Laban have carried out such a penalty against his own daughter? Rachel, by what she probably thought at the time was only a "little" sin, had indeed placed her husband, her father, and herself in a most difficult situation. She was no doubt fearful for her own life, as well as for that of Jacob, and felt it was altogether out of the question at this point simply to confess what she had done and ask forgiveness. Her best alternative was exactly the strategy she used. God allowed it to succeed, knowing that Jacob himself was innocent in the matter and that its discovery would have fallen hardest of all on Jacob. Laban would have charged him with theft and lying, even though Laban knew well enough that Jacob would never have taken the images.

Genesis 31:36-42

---

36 ⁋ And Jacob was wroth, and chode with Lā′băn: and Jacob answered and said to Lā′băn, What *is* my trespass? what *is* my sin, that thou hast so hotly pursued after me?

37 Whereas thou hast searched all my stuff, what hast thou found of all thy household stuff? set *it* here before my brethren and thy brethren, that they may judge betwixt us both.

38 This twenty years *have* I *been* with thee; thy ewes and thy she goats have not cast their young, and the rams of thy flock have I not eaten.

39 That which was torn *of beasts* I brought not unto thee; I bare the loss of it; of my hand didst thou require it, *whether* stolen by day, or stolen by night.

40 *Thus* I was; in the day the drought consumed me, and the frost by night; and my sleep departed from mine eyes.

41 Thus have I been twenty years in thy house: I served thee fourteen years for thy two daughters, and six years for thy cattle; and thou hast changed my wages ten times.

42 Except the God of my father, the God of Abraham, and the fear of Isaac, had been with me, surely thou hadst sent me away now empty. God hath seen mine affliction and the labor of my hands, and rebuked *thee* yesternight.

Jacob, still of course completely unsuspecting that Rachel had the images, lost his temper at this point, bursting forth in a heated protest at Laban's attitudes and actions, which he had suffered in silence for so many years. All the pent-up emotion which he had restrained for so long poured forth in a tirade against Laban, especially as climaxed by this last thoroughly unreasonable and unwarranted charge that he had stolen Laban's "gods." He called for Laban, before all his kinsmen and servants, to set forth explicitly exactly what charges he wished to bring against Jacob, that could justify such a hot pursuit to catch him before he could reach his own home with what was in every way rightfully his. Jacob challenged him to allow all his kinsmen to be the judge of such charges and to render a just verdict. Laban could only maintain an embarrassed silence as Jacob spoke.

Once having begun his impassioned protest, Jacob could hardly restrain himself. He had waited so long to express his resentment at Laban's treatment, and now he had to get it completely off his chest. He reminded Laban of his faithful service for twenty years, fourteen of which had been simply for the privilege of marrying his daughters. He did not mention Laban's deception (probably for Leah's sake), which had doubled the length of service in return for a wife he didn't want in the first place. Six years he had served him "in relation to his cattle"; that is, the cattle were not a price paid by Laban, but rather the result of God's blessings on his labors. Because of Jacob's faithful attention to the cattle when they were young, none had ever been lost by miscarriage—a frequent occurrence under less careful shepherds. Jacob had never even used any of Laban's animals for his own food while caring for them, although this was considered the right of every shepherd.

Furthermore, in a day when wild animals were a real danger to the flocks, Jacob had himself borne the cost of any losses due to this cause. It was customary that, when a shepherd brought a torn animal to his master, this was regarded as evidence that he had defended the sheep and had driven the beast away, that he had done all he could to save it; under these circumstances, the master bore the loss, rather than the shepherd. Jacob, however, had borne all the losses himself, evidently by replacing lost animals from Laban's flocks with animals from his own flocks.

He had given faithful service in the highest degree, through intense heat and intense cold, often spending sleepless nights in caring for the flocks. With all of this, Laban had no less than ten times changed his agreement with Jacob as to his payment, each time trying to prevent Jacob from prospering and trying to secure all the gains for himself. And finally, Laban was fully intending to send Jacob away completely empty-handed—if indeed he would even spare his life.

Jacob concluded with a testimony that God had been with him, and that He had seen his diligent labor as well as the unscrupulous way in which Laban had dealt with him. Jacob's increasing prosperity had been due to the Lord's blessings, and now God had confirmed all this by His sharp rebuke to Laban the night before. Jacob pointed out that the God who had protected and intervened for him was the God who had led Abraham away from Haran in the first place and (lest Laban should suggest that he also served the God of Abraham) was the God whom Isaac (who had never set foot in Haran) had served with reverential fear.

Genesis 31:43-47

---

43 ⸿ And Lā′băn answered and said unto Jacob, *These* daughters *are* my daughters, and *these* children *are* my children, and *these* cattle *are* my cattle, and all that thou seest *is* mine: and what can I do this day unto these my daughters, or unto their children which they have borne?

44 Now therefore come thou, let us make a covenant, I and thou; and let it be for a witness between me and thee.

45 And Jacob took a stone, and set it up *for* a pillar.

46 And Jacob said unto his brethren, Gather stones; and they took stones, and made a heap: and they did eat there upon the heap.

47 And Lā′băn called it Jē′gär–sā′hă-dū′thà: but Jacob called it Găl′e-ĕd.

When Laban finally had opportunity to reply to Jacob's outburst, he could not say anything at all by way of denial of his claims and charges. He tried to divert attention from Jacob's embarrassing facts by changing the subject. How could Jacob suppose that he would do anything to hurt his daughters or his grandchildren? Further, all of Jacob's cattle had come from Laban's flocks; so why wasn't Jacob grateful that he had made a way for Jacob to acquire them?

Though he realized he was in the wrong, a self-seeking hypocrite such as Laban cannot bring himself to repent or to make public acknowledgment of his guilt. He must try by whatever means he can muster to shift the blame away from himself, or at least to shift the attention away from his own culpability to whatever real or imagined grievances he can find in others.

He therefore proposed a formal covenant between himself and Jacob. Though Laban had proposed the covenant, Jacob knew such a covenant should be commemorated by a pillar; so he and his sons performed the actual work of gathering the stones and setting up the pillar and the heap of stones supporting it. The pillar was called by Laban "The Heap of Testimony" in the Aramaic or Chaldaic language of his ancestors. Jacob called it "The Heap of Witness" in the Hebrew language which had been in use by Abraham and Isaac, and perhaps by the patriarchal line back at least to the time of Eber (Genesis 10:25), whose name it commemorated. Abraham and his descendants of course continued to understand and speak the Aramaic language and, after the Babylonian captivity, in fact adopted it again as a common language among the people.

Genesis 31:48-53

---

48 And Lā'băn said, This heap *is* a witness between me and thee this day. Therefore was the name of it called Găl'ē-ĕd,

49 And Mĭz'päh; for he said, The LORD watch between me and thee, when we are absent one from another.

50 If thou shalt afflict my daughters, or if thou shalt take *other* wives beside my daughters, no man *is* with us; see, God *is* witness betwixt me and thee.

51 And Lā'băn said to Jacob, Behold this heap, and behold *this* pillar, which I have cast betwixt me and thee;

52 This heap *be* witness, and *this* pillar *be* witness, that I will not pass over this heap to thee, and that thou shalt not pass over this heap and this pillar unto me, for harm.

53 The God of Abraham, and the God of Nā'hŏr, the God of *their* father, judge betwixt us. And Jacob sware by the fear of his father Isaac.

Laban, continuing this diversionary tactic, took the initiative in proposing the terms of the covenant after the pillar was erected. Implying that Jacob was the one not to be trusted, he demanded certain restrictions on his activities. Jacob must not afflict his daughters (Jacob had always treated them with kindness and consideration, and Laban had no cause to think that he ever would do otherwise); neither must he ever take any wives other than Laban's daughters (Jacob had only wanted Rachel in the first place, but had been forced into a bigamous relationship by Laban's own deception); finally, after Jacob had become strong in the land of Canaan (as Laban realized he inevitably would, under God's blessing), he must not come back to Haran bent on revenge against Laban (Laban knew Jacob was not a vindictive man and would never think of such a thing, but he got a measure of vicarious satisfaction by imputing his own base motives to Jacob in this way). In return, Laban would promise not to come any farther into Canaan to hurt Jacob (he no doubt would have, if he could, but knew God would not allow it; so he might as well appear noble by promising this restraint).

Laban then also called the heap of stones "Mizpah" (meaning "watchtower"), denoting it as a sort of sentry guarding the boundary between Laban's sphere of activities and Jacob's sphere of activities. Laban even invoked the name of Jacob's God, saying, "May Jehovah watch between me and you, when we cannot see each other." He implied that Jacob was the one who needed watching, and this was Jehovah's responsibility. Laban's own "god" would not need to do anything, since Laban was a man of his word! Laban even took the credit for building the pillar and the heap (verse 51), though it had been done at Jacob's initiative and by his labor. Laban's hypocrisy and self-righteous sanctimoniousness would be almost unbelievable, were they not so typical of many superficially religious moralists of the present day.

It is sad and strange that Laban's hypocritical and suspicious statement (verse 49) has been so often appropriated in the present day by Christians as the so-called "Mizpah Benediction." It was not intended by Laban as a blessing in any sense at all.

Laban concluded his wordy proposal by invoking the names of "the God of Abraham and the God of Nahor, the God of their father." The word used here, of course, is "Elohim," which is basically a plural noun and can be used, when justified in the context, to mean "gods." This was most probably Laban's intent. The "God of Nahor" was probably Laban's idol. The term "God of their father" probably referred to both "gods," or else perhaps was an attempt to try to identify Laban's "god" with the true God of Abraham.

Jacob, rather than trying to clear up Laban's theological confusion, simply made his own oath in the name of the God who had been the "Fear of his father Isaac."

Genesis 31:54, 55

---

54 Then Jacob offered sacrifice upon the mount, and called his brethren to eat bread: and they did eat bread, and tarried all night in the mount.
55 And early in the morning Lā′bǎn rose up, and kissed his sons and his daughters, and blessed them: and Lā′bǎn departed, and returned unto his place.

Most of the day had been spent by now, so they prepared to pass another night in their respective camps in the mountains of Gilead. Jacob, in thanksgiving for God's final deliverance from Laban, offered sacrifices that evening there on the mountain. He and his family, along probably with the servants that were with them, then ate a happy meal together, no doubt spending much time in praise and testimony and prayer before retiring for the night. Laban came back early in the morning from his own camp, somewhat softened in attitude. He did not altogether lack affection for his own family, so he wanted to kiss his grandsons and daughters good-bye, and to give them his fatherly blessing. He knew that they must have come to resent him by now (at the very least), and he was probably feeling a measure of remorse. He could not bring himself to apologize to Jacob, or to give *him* any words of blessing, but he did at least want to leave his daughters and grandsons on a note of affection.

After this was done, Laban immediately departed and went home to his own place. No further mention is made of him or his sons in Scripture, and it probably is merciful of the Lord not to say more about them. Laban is an unfortunate example of a worldly, covetous man, one who knows about the true God and to whom a thorough witness has been given. He had seen the reality of God in the life of Jacob, along with the power of God in His blessing and protection of Jacob. He himself had even enjoyed many of the blessings of God through his relationship to Jacob. Nevertheless, he continued in idolatry and covetousness, seeking material gain for himself to the exclusion of all other considerations. Rather than seeking to follow the truth of God's plan as witnessed by Jacob, he merely resented and coveted the blessing of God on Jacob. He finally ended up with neither. His life constitutes a sober warning to a great host of semireligious but fundamentally self-worshiping and self-seeking men and women today.

18

Jacob in Canaan

(Genesis 32-36)

Wrestling with God

Jacob's two great enemies and opponents were Laban and Esau—one outside the promised land, one within. One might say they typify the believer's struggles against the world and the flesh.

As Jacob entered the lands promised to his fathers, through the mountains of Gilead, having triumphed over Laban and separated from him at the Mizpah monument, he knew he must soon confront another—perhaps even more serious—problem. His mother had told him she would send for him as soon as the wrath of Esau had cooled (Genesis 27:45), but, so far as the record goes, he had never heard from her during all the twenty long years spent in Padan-aram. Either, therefore, his mother was ill or deceased, and hence unable to call him back home, or else Esau was still threatening vengeance. Neither did Jacob know the state of his father Isaac, although there is a possibility that he had at least heard that he was still alive (Genesis 31:18). At best, he knew he was facing a very uncertain—and possibly dangerous—reception when he returned to Canaan.

Genesis 32: 1, 2

CHAPTER 32

AND Jacob went on his way, and the angels of God met him.

2 And when Jacob saw them, he said, This *is* God's host: and he called the name of that place Mā′hȧ-nā′ïm.

It was appropriate, and a testimony of God's loving grace, that just at this time Jacob once again saw some of the angels of God, as he had in his dream at Bethel many years before (Genesis 28:12). Humanly speaking, Jacob was almost helpless, with only a small band of servants to fight for him and his family if opposition were encountered. Laban's band could easily have destroyed them, apart from God; and he had every reason to think that Esau likewise would have, by this time, a much larger body of fighting men than he did. Consequently, Jacob had to depend solely on the Lord.

But when he saw the angels, he knew there was ample protection. He exclaimed, when he saw them, "This is God's army!"; and he called the place by the name "Mahanaim," a name which means "Two Hosts." By this act Jacob was testifying that he was being guarded not only by his own small host, but also by God's infinitely more numerous and powerful host.

Scripture seems to imply that it was only Jacob, not all his company, who saw the angels. Because of his faithful obedience to God's call, God "opened his eyes," just as He did on another occasion when Elisha and his servant seemed all alone against overwhelming odds (II Kings 6:16, 17). Though invisible under normal conditions, God's angelic hosts are none the less real and powerful. They are "mighty angels" (II Thessalonians 1:7), that "excel in strength" and "do his commandments" (Psalm 103:20), and they are "sent forth to minister for them who shall be heirs of salvation" (Hebrews 1:14).

It was appropriate that Jacob should see them just at this time, as he left the land of Mesopotamia behind him and entered the land of Canaan, the great Mizpah sentinel guarding the boundary between them as it were. As God had led and protected him in Haran, so He would in Canaan. Many a believer in days since has felt the comforting and protecting presence of God's holy angels, even though he could not see them. The God of Jacob changes not, and He has said: "I will never leave thee, nor forsake thee. So that we may confidently and boldly say, The Lord is my helper, and I will not fear what man shall do unto me" (Hebrews 13:5, 6).

Genesis 32:3-8

---

3 And Jacob sent messengers before him to Ē′saū his brother unto the land of Sē′ĭr, the country of Ē′dŏm.

4 And he commanded them, saying, Thus shall ye speak unto my lord Ē′saū; Thy servant Jacob saith thus, I have so-

journed with Lā'băn, and stayed there until now:

5 And I have oxen, and asses, flocks, and menservants, and womenservants: and I have sent to tell my lord, that I may find grace in thy sight.

6 ¶ And the messengers returned to Jacob, saying, We came to thy brother E'saŭ, and also he cometh to meet thee,

and four hundred men with him.

7 Then Jacob was greatly afraid and distressed: and he divided the people that *was* with him, and the flocks, and herds, and the camels, into two bands;

8 And said, If E'saŭ come to the one company, and smite it, then the other company which is left shall escape.

Not knowing what to expect, Jacob decided it would be expedient to send a delegation ahead of him to interview Esau. He had learned that Esau lived in the region south of the Dead Sea, in the "land of Seir," so named after a Horite chieftain who had apparently formerly inhabited the area (Genesis 36:20). It had also come to be known as the "field of Edom," after Esau's own nickname (Genesis 25:30).

Jacob instructed his servants precisely how to address Esau, acknowledging Esau as Jacob's "lord," in whose sight he desired to find favor. Esau had especially hated Jacob because of his gaining what Esau judged to be political advantage through Isaac's blessing, so that Jacob desired to emphasize that it was not political sovereignty in which he was interested, being quite content to regard Esau as his master in that regard. He wished to indicate further that he had no desire to claim any of Esau's possessions, since he had acquired ample goods for himself through his sojourn with their Uncle Laban.

Esau, on his part, had apparently heard that Jacob was migrating back to Canaan. Though his anger against Jacob had long since cooled, he himself did not know what Jacob's intentions might be. For all he knew, Jacob might be coming with a large body of fighting men to claim his promised boundaries and possessions and to subjugate Esau. When he learned of Jacob's approach toward Canaan, he therefore assembled an army of his own and marched forward to meet Jacob, prepared for whatever eventuality might come. He was able to commandeer a force of no less than four hundred men, probably men whom he had used in conquering the region of Seir where he now lived.

Jacob's messengers met Esau much sooner than they had expected, well northward of Seir, en route to meet Jacob. They immediately returned and informed Jacob concerning the close proximity of Esau's band.

Jacob naturally jumped to the conclusion that Esau still intended to make good his threat to kill him, and he seems to have temporarily forgotten the encouragement he had received by the sight of the angels at Mahanaim. He knew his own small body of servants could not cope with four hundred armed men led by Esau. Following a custom often followed by endangered caravans, he divided his company into two divisions, hoping to give one a chance to escape while Esau's army was busy subduing the other. He realized they would require God's protection, and he fully intended to call on the Lord. But he also realized it was wise, as well as in keeping with God's will, for him to take what natural precautions were open to him as quickly as possible, after which he could pray in good faith, knowing that he had done all he could and the Lord would have to take over the rest of the way.

Genesis 32:9-12

---

9 ¶ And Jacob said, O God of my father Abraham, and God of my father Isaac, the LORD which saidst unto me, Return unto thy country, and to thy kindred, and I will deal well with thee:

10 I am not worthy of the least of all the mercies, and of all the truth, which thou hast showed unto thy servant; for with my staff I passed over this Jordan; and now I am become two bands.

11 Deliver me, I pray thee, from the hand of my brother, from the hand of E'sau: for I fear him, lest he will come and smite me, *and* the mother with the children.

12 And thou saidst, I will surely do thee good, and make thy seed as the sand of the sea, which cannot be numbered for multitude.

These verses record Jacob's prayer under what he had full reason to believe were desperate and, humanly speaking, almost hopeless circumstances. In many respects, it is a fine pattern of prayer for believers under similar circumstances, when, after doing all they know how to do, and trying as well as they know how to follow the Lord's guidance, they are still confronted with what seem to be insurmountable problems. Jacob "reminded" God of His promises, thanked Him for His previous blessings and leading, acknowledged his own unworthiness, and then thrust himself on God for deliverance.

Jacob, in his prayer, acknowledged God as both "Elohim" (the God of power who had so marvelously blessed and protected Abraham and Isaac) and "Jehovah" (the Lord who is faithful in His covenant promises, the merciful, redeeming One). Jacob was confident that he had been following God's leading in returning to his home country, and he was well aware how greatly God had prospered him since he left there twenty years before. He knew he was right in calling on God now for protection, not only for himself, but even more for his wives and children. For all he knew, Esau, in order to prevent the fulfillment of God's promises concerning the multiplication of Jacob's seed, might well decide to slay all his family as well. He did not pray boastfully, however, but humbly, knowing that God's blessings on him were because of His grace, not because of Jacob's personal merits. The same, of course, is true of every believer who has likewise received divine blessing. Above all, it is important to note that Jacob based his prayer on God's word. God had made certain promises; therefore, Jacob could confidently claim those promises and take his stand on them, calling on God to show Himself strong in fulfilling them. No prayer can be truly efficacious unless it, likewise, is in harmony with God's revealed Word.

Genesis 32:13-20

13 ¶ And he lodged there that same night; and took of that which came to his hand a present for E'saŭ his brother;

14 Two hundred she goats and twenty he goats, two hundred ewes and twenty rams,

15 Thirty milch camels with their colts, forty kine and ten bulls, twenty she asses and ten foals.

16 And he delivered *them* into the hand of his servants, every drove by themselves; and said unto his servants, Pass over before me, and put a space betwixt drove and drove.

17 And he commanded the foremost, saying, When E'saŭ my brother meeteth thee, and asketh thee, saying, Whose *art* thou? and whither goest thou? and whose *are* these before thee?

18 Then thou shalt say, *They be* thy servant Jacob's; it *is* a present sent unto my lord E'saŭ: and, behold, also he *is* behind us.

19 And so commanded he the second, and the third, and all that followed the droves, saying, On this manner shall ye speak unto E'saŭ, when ye find him.

20 And say ye moreover, Behold, thy servant Jacob *is* behind us. For he said, I will appease him with the present that goeth before me, and afterward I will see his face; peradventure he will accept of me.

After rising from his prayer, he decided it would be proper to send a substantial gift to Esau. This would clearly show he was not coming with the intention of plundering his brother's possessions, but that he desired to live at peace with him and to share God's blessings with him.

The gift which he sent was very large, amounting to a total of 580 animals, a fact which in itself is a striking commentary on the degree to which God had blessed Jacob in material possessions. His animals included goats and sheep, cattle, camels, and asses, and he designated some of each for Esau. He had little time to assemble them; so he took merely of "that which came to his hand," dividing them apparently into five separate droves; first the goats, then the sheep, then the camels, then the cattle, then the asses. He told his servants to keep a good distance between the respective droves, so that in effect Esau would receive five separate gifts at different times.

He instructed the servants in command of each drove to tell Esau that the animals were a gift from Jacob, who was following along behind them.

Each shepherd was to follow his herd, rather than lead it, in order to impress Esau first of all with the herd, then the message that the herd was a gift for him.

These gifts should not be regarded as a bribe on Jacob's part, but rather as an expression of good will and conciliation. Regardless of Esau's intentions, Jacob had good reason to believe God would protect him, as He had promised. God had turned Laban back, and He could do the same with Esau; furthermore, the angels at Mahanaim had given Jacob further assurance. Most importantly, a battle would result in suffering and death for many, possibly even Esau himself; and it would be much better if the brothers could be united in peace in their latter years. Giving such a generous present, especially coming in successive waves as it did, would be the best outward gesture Jacob could make toward this end. He hoped that, when he finally met Esau face to face, he would be able to tell by his countenance whether Esau would accept him in this spirit or not.

Genesis 32:21-23

---

21 So went the present over before him; and himself lodged that night in the company.
22 And he rose up that night, and took his two wives, and his two women-servants, and his eleven sons, and passed over the ford Jăb′bŏk.
23 And he took them, and sent them over the brook, and sent over that he had.

After dispatching the droves, Jacob remained behind with his family and the rest of his company to spend the night in the encampment by the river Jabbok, a stream which flows west into the Jordan, entering it about halfway between the Sea of Galilee and the Dead Sea. They were at first north of the Jabbok, while of course Esau was approaching from the south. During the night, he decided to move his entire company across the river to the south side. The river was fordable at that point, and Jacob wished to have the somewhat troublesome business of herding all the animals across the stream completed before Esau reached him. By this action, he obviously indicated that it was certainly not his intention to retreat before a possible attack by Esau.

Having done everything he could, Jacob then decided to spend the rest of the night in prayer. Though the text does not say so specifically, the implication is that Jacob returned to the northern bank of the Jabbok in order to be completely alone. He knew Esau would not arrive until the next morning, at least; so his family would be safe for the night with the other servants.

Genesis 32:24-32

---

24 ¶ And Jacob was left alone; and there wrestled a man with him until the breaking of the day.

25 And when he saw that he prevailed not against him, he touched the hollow of his thigh; and the hollow of Jacob's thigh was out of joint, as he wrestled with him.

26 And he said, Let me go, for the day breaketh. And he said, I will not let thee go, except thou bless me.

27 And he said unto him, What *is* thy name? And he said, Jacob.

28 And he said, Thy name shall be called no more Jacob, but Iṣ'rā-ĕl: for as a prince hast thou power with God and with men, and hast prevailed.

29 And Jacob asked *him,* and said, Tell *me,* I pray thee, thy name. And he said, Wherefore *is* it *that* thou dost ask after my name? And he blessed him there.

30 And Jacob called the name of the place Pē-nī'ĕl: for I have seen God face to face, and my life is preserved.

31 And as he passed over Pē-nū'ĕl the sun rose upon him, and he halted upon his thigh.

32 Therefore the children of Iṣ'rā-ĕl eat not *of* the sinew which shrank, which *is* upon the hollow of the thigh, unto this day; because he touched the hollow of Jacob's thigh in the sinew that shrank.

It is significant that the name Jabbok means "Wrestler," a name evidently given to it later in commemoration of Jacob's amazing experience that night. This section is indeed one of the most difficult to understand in the Bible. Did he actually wrestle with a man, or with an angel, or is the entire description simply an allegory of the spiritual battle through which he passed that night? Interpretations of this passage have been many and fanciful.

There seems to be no question, however, that the writer of the passage (originally Jacob, probably) intended it to be taken literally. As far as the mysterious wrestler is concerned, he was in the form of a man, but angels often assumed such forms in those days. Angels had actually eaten a meal with Abraham, and two of them had been the objects of the depraved sexual lusts of the Sodomites; so there is no doubt that angels can take on the physical structure of men in every detail when there is proper occasion for them to do so. That this was, indeed, an angel is indicated in a commentary by Hosea on this passage. "[Jacob] took his brother by the heel in the womb, and by his strength he had power with God: Yea, he had power over the angel, and prevailed: he wept, and made supplication to him: he found him in Bethel, and there he spake with us; Even the Lord God of hosts; the Lord is his memorial" (Hosea 12:3-5).

Apparently in Jacob's evaluation, his combatant was more than even an angel. It was none other than *the* Angel, the pre-incarnate Christ, because, according to Jacob's testimony, he had "seen God face to face."

This experience must, therefore, have been an exceedingly important event in the history of man's redemption. Jacob, whom God had chosen to be the father of the children of Israel, through whom He would finally come into the world not only in the form of man but as the very Son of Man, was facing the greatest opposition to the accomplishment of his divinely ordered mission. If Esau were to be victorious here, all of God's plans and promises would be defeated, and the world would never have a Savior.

It was essential that Jacob receive both understanding and assurance concerning the supreme importance of his mission. He must learn clearly, as he began the establishment of the chosen nation, that God was all-sufficient and that he had been prepared by God to accomplish this incomparable task. He must know fully his own weakness, but even more he must know the power of God and his right to claim that power.

Little did he dream, as he began to pray that night, that his agony of soul as he cried to God for strength and deliverance would soon become an actual physical battle, and with none other than God Himself. As he earnestly wrestled in prayer, it was as though he sensed that God was really present with him and was declining to grant his request, perhaps because of Jacob's remaining fears and doubts, perhaps also because of his greater immediate concern for physical protection rather than for the fulfillment of God's purposes.

As he felt more and more this conflict, he cried the more earnestly to God, seeing ever more clearly that it was not the immediate dangers that should be the burden of his prayers, but rather the accomplishment of God's will for all men everywhere. God's presence and purpose became more and more real to him until, suddenly, He *was* real! His uplifted arms were actually clinging to God Himself, God in human form. Jacob felt that, if he ever let go, it would mean that God had left him, with prayer unanswered; and so he clung desperately, pleading all the while for His blessing. God in grace allowed him to hang on, seeing that Jacob's faith and understanding were growing as he clung.

As the day began to break, Jacob was still holding on, refusing to let go until God would give him full and final assurance of permanent blessing. According to Hosea's commentary, this "wrestling" on Jacob's part involved weeping and supplication, as well as physical tenacity. Hosea compared Jacob's holding to the Angel with his tenacity in holding onto his brother's heel as he was born, both testifying of his great desire to be the recipient of God's greatest blessings and responsibilities.

When God saw that He could not prevail against Jacob, He finally gave him the blessing he sought. This, of course, does not suggest that God was weaker than Jacob, but does show that God desires men to persist in prayer and that He delights to yield to such prayers. "Shall not God avenge his own elect, which cry day and night unto him, though he bear long with them?" (Luke 18:7). "Men ought always to pray, and not to faint" (Luke 18:1). There indeed is such a thing as prevailing prayer, when the request conforms to the will and the word of God; and Jacob's experience symbolizes all such prayers.

To remind Jacob perpetually of the experience, the Angel imposed a physical injury on him, which evidently consisted of a slight dislocation of the ball-and-socket joint in the thigh. This would inhibit Jacob from any undue presumption against God, since he would know that God really only *allowed* him to prevail; but at the same time it would never let him forget that God indeed had promised in this most unique encounter to bless him forever.

Before He pronounced the blessing, the Angel, to show the transition between Jacob's time of preparation and his time of fulfillment, called attention to his name, Jacob, by asking him to state it. He is no longer to be the "Supplanter," but the "Prevailer." The name "Israel," which Jacob received that night, and which has continued to be the name of his descendants for thirty-seven hundred years, means "One Who Fights Victoriously with God." It has also been rendered "A Prince with God," since it is derived from the two words *Sarah-El* with the word *sarah* meaning "fight, or rule, as a prince." It is the word which, in this verse, is translated "as a prince hast thou power."

The name Israel is God's permanent testimony to the character and power of Jacob, a considerably different testimony than has been afforded to him by numerous commentators through the years. One is justified in accepting God's testimony rather than man's!

Jacob then, after the Angel had asked his name, felt he must also ask the Angel's name. He well realized he had been experiencing a unique encounter with the divine presence, but never had he met God in this form before. He had seen and heard God in dreams and visions, but here was an actual physical person with whom he had been struggling. Was this actually Jehovah, the God of his fathers, to whom he had so often prayed? From what He had said, and from what Jacob had sensed, it must be. And yet, could God actually assume a physical human body?

The Angel responded by a rhetorical question. "Why do you ask my name?" Jacob already knew who it was. He had been earnestly praying to Jehovah, and Jehovah had answered his prayer in this most remarkable way, an experience neither he nor his children could ever forget. Then the Lord—for it was He—gave Jacob a divine blessing, probably (though the text does not actually say) recalling and reaffirming all the great promises which were to be centered in Israel, culminating finally in the actual entrance of God into the human family (as prefigured by this physical appearance of God to Jacob), when Messiah would come.

When the Lord had departed, and the sun had risen, Jacob found he had to limp because of his thigh. This was no mere dream he had experienced, but an actual physical struggle; and he would carry the resulting injury with him as a token of it all his life. The later editor (Moses, presumably) recorded that, because of this, the children of Israel had adopted the practice of not eating that particular muscle (probably the portion of the hindquarter containing the sciatic nerve) when eating meat. God did not command such a practice, of course, but it did indicate the importance of this event in the minds of those who practiced it.

Jacob named the place "Peniel," meaning "The Face of God." Jacob marveled greatly that he had actually been allowed to see and touch God, and that he had survived to tell the experience. This would have been utterly impossible, had not God veiled Himself in human form, of course (Exodus 33:20; I Timothy 6:16).

The name of the place, as given by Jacob, was not forgotten. Though slightly changed in form, to Penuel, it continued to be known by that name until at least the days of the divided kingdom (I Kings 12:25).

After such an encounter, Jacob was now fully prepared to meet Esau, and then to enter the promised land to establish the foundations for the nation Israel. As the sun rose, though forced to limp because of the crippled thigh, he passed over Penuel, and presumably also the Jabbok River, to rejoin his family and to await the coming of Esau.

Encounter with Esau

Although Jacob's servants had reported back to him that Esau was coming, there is no indication that they had actually talked with Esau. It is not even certain that Esau had seen them; they may have been so alarmed when they unexpectedly came upon Esau's large band that they rushed back to Jacob without even stopping to make their presence known to Esau. In any case, Esau may not have known Jacob's intentions until he began to encounter the droves of animals Jacob later began sending along as presents for Esau. Whatever his uncertainties may have been, they soon began to dissipate as the several shepherds accompanying the droves reported to him concerning Jacob; so he probably was looking forward to a reunion with his brother. Jacob, however, did not yet know what Esau would do. All he knew was that he was coming toward him with a large band of armed men, and that the last thing he had ever heard about Esau was that twenty years before he had planned to kill him.

Genesis 33:1-7

CHAPTER 33

AND Jacob lifted up his eyes, and looked, and, behold, Ê′saū came, and with him four hundred men. And he divided the children unto Lē′ăh, and unto Rachel, and unto the two handmaids.

2 And he put the handmaids and their children foremost, and Lē′ăh and her children after, and Rachel and Joseph hindermost.

3 And he passed over before them, and bowed himself to the ground seven times, until he came near to his brother.

4 And Ê′saū ran to meet him, and embraced him, and fell on his neck, and kissed him: and they wept.

5 And he lifted up his eyes, and saw the women and the children, and said, Who *are* those with thee? And he said, The children which God hath graciously given thy servant.

6 Then the handmaidens came near, they and their children, and they bowed themselves.

7 And Lē′ăh also with her children came near, and bowed themselves: and after came Joseph near and Rachel, and they bowed themselves.

No sooner had Jacob returned to his family after his night of prayer than he saw Esau and his army approaching in the distance. As one final precaution, Jacob arranged his wives and children in appropriate order, the two handmaids and their children first, then Leah and her children, then Rachel and Joseph. Presumably the purpose was to give the maximum possible protection to those he loved the most, but at least a secondary purpose was to have them meet Esau in climactic order. Jacob then proceeded ahead of them all to meet his brother.

As was customary in those days (the Tell el Amarna tablets record that one approaching a king always bowed seven times in so doing), Jacob bowed low before Esau seven times as he came near him. This was not intended as an acknowledgment of servility on Jacob's part, but as a token of respect and recognition of Esau as ruler of the region.

Then an amazing thing happened! Esau could restrain himself no longer and ran forward to Jacob, hugging and kissing him in a free display of joyful reunion and reconciliation. He had long since realized that Jacob had properly been entitled to the birthright and blessing, and that God had chosen Jacob to be the inheritor of the promises, and he was reconciled to this fact. Now, finding that Jacob no longer held any bitterness in his heart toward him, but that he earnestly desired to regain their lost fellowship, Esau was overjoyed.

As for Jacob, this sudden outburst of affection and gladness, instead of the bitter encounter he had been dreading for twenty years, was too wonderful for words. For some time, neither brother could speak a word. "They wept." God had indeed worked mightily, both to accomplish His own will, and to do so in a way which brought joy and blessing to all concerned.

Finally, noticing all the children and their mothers who had come up to them, Esau spoke, asking Jacob what relation these were to him. Jacob then gave his testimony concerning the large family with which God had blessed him since he had last seen his brother. Each of his wives and their children then came up to be introduced to their uncle and brother-in-law, in the order Jacob had assigned to them, each showing full and proper respect.

Genesis 33:8-11

---

8 And he said, What *meanest* thou by all this drove which I met? And he said, *These are* to find grace in the sight of my lord.

9 And E'sau said, I have enough, my brother; keep that thou hast unto thyself.

10 And Jacob said, Nay, I pray thee, if now I have found grace in thy sight, then receive my present at my hand: for therefore I have seen thy face, as though I had seen the face of God, and thou wast pleased with me.

11 Take, I pray thee, my blessing that is brought to thee; because God hath dealt graciously with me, and because I have enough. And he urged him, and he took *it*.

After seeing the family, Esau viewed the large flocks and herds of animals in the band that was still with Jacob (one had been sent away when he had divided them into two bands—Genesis 32:7, 8). This reminded him of the five droves that had met him as he approached Jacob the previous day. Though the shepherds had told Esau they were meant as a present for him, he felt it proper that he should inquire more specifically about them from Jacob himself. It seemed out of proportion that he should receive such a large gift. Jacob, however, assured him that they were indeed intended as a present, in hopes that he would be found acceptable to Esau.

Although Esau greatly appreciated Jacob's generosity, especially since it showed that he was not in any way desirous of acquiring Esau's property for himself, he felt it was unnecessary to accept it. He himself had great wealth by now, and he was more than happy to be reunited with his brother without his favor having to be "purchased" by a gift of this magnitude. He therefore demurred, urging Jacob to keep the animals for himself and his family.

Jacob, however, insisted. In accordance with oriental customs, which have continued to be practiced for thousands of years, the most certain way for one who desires reconciliation to be assured of it is to have his proffered gift accepted by the one whose favor he seeks. In seeing Esau's countenance beaming with joy at the reunion, Jacob felt that this was a token of God's most direct blessing. God had worked in Esau's heart as well as his own. It would be a great personal favor if Esau would accept his gift, even though Jacob knew that Esau did not need it in any material sense.

In the Authorized Version, both Esau and Jacob are reported as saying, "I have enough" (9, 11). However, the Hebrew words are different. Actually, Esau said, "I have much [*rab*]," whereas Jacob said, "I have everything [*kol*]." Esau may quite likely have had more actual possessions than Jacob by this time, though Jacob had also been greatly blessed materially; but Jacob knew that, in the Lord, he had an inexhaustible resource. God had blessed him beyond measure, most of all now in this joyful meeting with his long-estranged twin brother.

Esau, realizing the sincerity of Jacob's motives, and also desiring that there be no question that he also earnestly desired full reconciliation with his brother, finally agreed to accept the gift.

Genesis 33:12-17

---

12 And he said, Let us take our journey, and let us go, and I will go before thee.

13 And he said unto him, My lord knoweth that the children *are* tender, and the flocks and herds with young *are* with me; and if men should overdrive them one day, all the flock will die.

14 Let my lord, I pray thee, pass over before his servant; and I will lead on softly, according as the cattle that goeth before me and the children be able to endure, until I come unto my lord unto Sē'ïr.

15 And Ē'saù said, Let me now leave with thee *some* of the folk that *are* with me. And he said, What needeth it? let me find grace in the sight of my lord.

16 ¶ So Ē'saù returned that day on his way unto Sē'ïr.

17 And Jacob journeyed to Sŭc'cŏth, and built him a house, and made booths for his cattle: therefore the name of the place is called Sŭc'cŏth.

No doubt, the two brothers then spent some considerable time in telling each other all that had happened since they had separated so long ago. Esau also had a large family and great possessions (Genesis 36:1-8), and he had undergone many experiences, which he shared with Jacob. Jacob told all about Laban and Padan-aram, and how God had led him through the years. Jacob was anxious to hear also about his mother and father, no doubt, and probably Esau told him about them, but for some reason no further mention is made in Genesis concerning either Rebekah or Isaac except in connection with their deaths and burials (Genesis 35:27-29; 49:31). Quite probably, Rebekah had died by this time and

Isaac was not only blind but completely incapacitated with age. Isaac died at the age of 180, and was probably about 153 when Jacob returned to Canaan.

Isaac was presumably living in Hebron, where he later died, and Esau assumed Jacob would be journeying on southward in that direction. He offered to accompany him, with the two companies traveling together. Jacob, however, declined the offer, not because he did not trust Esau, but because he knew it would be impracticable. Esau's band of armed men would be impatient with the slow pace they would have to follow, desiring to get back home as soon as possible. Jacob's company, on the other hand, would have to travel very slowly. They had already been under great strain in escaping from Laban, and now that the anticipated danger from Esau had also been removed, they would want to take it very easy for a time.

Jacob assured Esau that they would follow on behind, and would eventually see him again back in his own land of Seir. Jacob's children were all young, the oldest probably not more than twelve or so; and the animals were all but exhausted from their long trek, many of them even nursing their young.

Esau then offered to leave at least a portion of his men with Jacob for protection, but Jacob assured him that even this was not necessary. His one concern had been Esau himself; now that this fear had been removed, Jacob was fully confident there would be no further obstacles in his way, and his company would be perfectly safe. Though he did not say so, Jacob no doubt also realized that he should remain separate and independent from Esau, as far as the future accomplishment of God's plans for his children was concerned; and it would be better to establish such a separation from the beginning. It was a great blessing and answer to prayer to be reconciled to his brother, but they were still of different natures and had different ways of life. They could, and no doubt did, continue to see each other frequently; but they must each live their own separate lives and accomplish their own independent purposes.

Esau therefore agreed to Jacob's request, and headed on back to Seir. Jacob also planned to continue south, but went much more slowly, actually stopping for considerable intervals at both Succoth and Shechem. Succoth (meaning "booths") is probably the same place mentioned later in the time of Joshua (Joshua 13:27) and Gideon (Judges 8:5-16). It was still east of the Jordan and probably north of the Jabbok, in a plain where there was pasture for the flocks and where they could rest awhile to regain their strength. It seemed a good place to stay temporarily; so Jacob built crude reed-grass huts for the cattle and a simple house for himself, until they were ready to continue on across the Jordan into Canaan proper.

Genesis 33:18-20

---

18 ⁋ And Jacob came to Shā′lĕm, a city of Shē′chĕm, which *is* in the land of Cā′năan, when he came from Pā′dăn-ā′răm; and pitched his tent before the city.

19 And he bought a parcel of a field, where he had spread his tent, at the hand of the children of Hā′mŏr, Shē′chĕm's father, for a hundred pieces of money.

20 And he erected there an altar, and called it Ĕl′-Ē-lō′hĕ-Ĭṣ′rā-ĕl.

Jacob probably stayed longer in Succoth than he had originally anticipated, but eventually moved on. All of his company finally pulled up stakes and headed westward across the Jordan River. After crossing the Jordan, they came to a valley near the city of Shechem, and there Jacob pitched his tent. This was not very far from Succoth, but it was definitely in the land of Canaan and, actually, it was the place where God had first appeared to Abram as he entered the land (Genesis 12:6, 7).

The King James translation says that "Jacob came to Shalem, a city of Shechem," but most translators believe that *Shalem* (meaning "peace") should not be considered a proper name here. That is, the verse may mean that "Jacob came in peace to the city of Shechem." If so, the verse may be regarded as a fulfillment of God's promise in Genesis 28:15 and 31:3. This interpretation is strengthened by the formal nature of the verse, mentioning Jacob's coming back into Canaan from Padan-aram.

This was the first spot in Canaan proper where Jacob set up an encampment. Expecting that some day in the future his seed would inherit the whole land, he desired to purchase a portion right here, which would serve as a token of his confidence in God's future fulfillment of the complete promise. He would make this his first "capital." Furthermore, the plain was fertile and would make an excellent place for pasturing the flocks. He would also dig a well here, in order to have an independent water supply. The well is not mentioned in Genesis but is referred to in the New Testament (John 4:6). Shechem was a prominent city throughout Biblical history, located on Mount Gerizim in what later became the territory of the tribe of Ephraim. It was very close to the future city of Samaria, which became the capital of the northern kingdom of Israel.

When Jacob arrived there, the city was controlled by the Hivites, a Canaanite tribe, whose chieftain was a man named Hamor. Hamor had a son named Shechem, possibly named after the city in which they lived.

(It is possible also that the city was later named after Shechem, with these early references to the city's name being later editorial insertions for the benefit of readers in Moses' day.)

Jacob arrived peacefully at Shechem, and the Shechemites apparently welcomed him, thinking that the addition of such a prosperous man to their own community would add to their own prosperity. He soon arranged to purchase from Hamor and his sons a substantial tract of property for a goodly price, a hundred pieces of silver. Much later, Jacob's favorite son, Joseph, would be buried on this same spot (Joshua 24:32).

Jacob rightly considered this acquisition of his first property in Canaan as an important milestone in his life. Accordingly, he wanted first of all to build an altar there, dedicating it to "El-elohe-Israel," saying in effect that his God was the true and mighty God. "God was the God of Israel." It is significant that, in naming the altar, he used (for the first time, as far as the record indicates) his new name "Israel." There, in the center of an idolatrous land, he had established a new center of worship of the true God.

Dinah and the Canaanites

Jacob and his family must actually have spent several years living in either Succoth or Shechem or both. The events described in chapter 34 presuppose that Leah's youngest child, Dinah (Genesis 30:21), must have been at least in her teens, which means that her older brothers, especially Reuben, Simeon, and Levi, must have been in their twenties. When they first moved to Succoth, Reuben was probably about twelve years old, so that the family must have lived at least ten years in Succoth and Shechem, mainly the latter. Though the text does not mention it, it seems likely that Jacob must have visited Isaac and Esau on various occasions during this period. Since Jacob at this time was the key personage involved in God's plans, rather than either Isaac or Esau, evidently the writer felt it was unnecessary to include purely personal matters of this sort.

Genesis 34:1-4

CHAPTER 34

AND Dinah the daughter of Lē′ăh, which she bare unto Jacob, went out to see the daughters of the land.

2 And when Shē′chĕm the son of Hā′mŏr the Hī′vīte, prince of the country, saw her, he took her, and lay with her, and defiled her.

3 And his soul clave unto Dinah the daughter of Jacob, and he loved the damsel, and spake kindly unto the damsel.

4 And Shē′chĕm spake unto his father Hā′mŏr, saying, Get me this damsel to wife.

Living so close to an ungodly city as his family was, however, soon began to foster serious perils of a sort Jacob had not anticipated. As his children grew into their teens and then into adulthood, the low moral environment around them began to have its deadly effect. Living in a polygamous home, with four different wives and mothers, made it very difficult to maintain consistent and unified spiritual instruction, though no doubt Jacob made a serious and partially successful attempt to teach his children about God's great promises and the noble calling that had been committed to them.

Young people need companionship with others of their own age, of course, and this was bound to be true of those in Jacob's household. His eleven sons probably had enough fellowship just among themselves to satisfy these needs, but Dinah was the only daughter, at least for some time, and she must have longed for the opportunity to be with other girls her own age. Evidently the problem of finding suitable wives and husbands for his children had not yet become serious, since they were not really old enough; but Jacob and his wives must have been concerned about this. It probably would have been impossible to insist on mates being obtained from their own people, as Abraham and Isaac had done, since there were too many in the family and too few (if any, in fact, considering Laban's lapse into idolatry) from whom they could choose. They would sooner or later be forced to find mates for their children from the people of the lands where they were living, and it would be better if these people could first be won to faith in the true God through their testimony to them.

The immediate problem, however, was the need for teen-age feminine companions for Dinah. She had probably met some of the Shechemite girls and gotten to know them. This was good in a way; but it also raised problems, since their standards were quite different from those Jacob and Leah had tried to teach her. Whether she had become a bit rebellious against these standards is not mentioned, but it is possible, in view of the circumstances. In any case, Dinah, being now and then in the company of the Shechemite girls, could hardly have failed also to come to the attention of some of the Shechemite young men. She must have seemed particularly attractive, being of a different nationality, as well as possessed of a grace and charm which was not shared by girls raised in an atmosphere of idolatry and lasciviousness such as characterized most Canaanite communities.

Dinah soon came to be desired by young Shechem, the son of Hamor, the city's chieftain. Unattached young women were considered fair game in cities of the time, in which promiscuity was not only common but, in fact, a part of the very religious system itself. It seems likely that Dinah must have been warned about such dangers by her parents, but perhaps she felt she could look out for herself and resented their overprotective attitude. To what extent she may actually have encouraged Shechem, who must have seemed a rather glamorous figure to a young girl like Dinah, is not stated. In any case, it was only a matter of time until she had been seduced by Shechem while she was visiting some of her girl friends in the city. Shechem may or may not have actually forced her, but in view of her age it was at least a case of what today would be called "statutory" rape.

With Shechem, however, it was not merely a case of a routine conquest, as no doubt often was true in such a place, for he really had fallen in love with Dinah and wanted her to become his wife. After he had seduced her, he did not cast her aside, but tried to comfort her and assure her that he loved her and would marry her. In fact, he took her into his own house (verse 26) and kept her there.

Marriage was not as easily accomplished as a simple sexual adventure, however. In those days, even among pagans, marriage had to be arranged by the parents. Consequently, Shechem asked his father to take the necessary steps with Dinah's father to obtain Dinah as his wife. It is an interesting commentary on the Shechemite culture to note that Hamor apparently thought nothing about the moral implications of what his son had done. He neither rebuked Shechem nor apologized in any way to Jacob or Dinah's brothers. For a young man to lie with a young woman, even by force, was apparently such a common thing in Canaanite towns that no one gave it a second thought.

Genesis 34:5-17

5 And Jacob heard that he had defiled Dinah his daughter: now his sons were with his cattle in the field: and Jacob held his peace until they were come.

6 ¶ And Hā'mŏr the father of Shē'chĕm went out unto Jacob to commune with him.

7 And the sons of Jacob came out of the field when they heard *it:* and the men were grieved, and they were very wroth, because he had wrought folly in Ĭṣ'rā-ĕl in lying with Jacob's daughter; which thing ought not to be done.

8 And Hā'mŏr communed with them, saying, The soul of my son Shē'chĕm longeth for your daughter: I pray you give her him to wife.

9 And make ye marriages with us, *and* give your daughters unto us, and take our daughters unto you.

10 And ye shall dwell with us: and the land shall be before you; dwell and trade ye therein, and get you possessions therein.

11 And Shē'chĕm said unto her father and unto her brethren, Let me find grace in your eyes, and what ye shall say unto me I will give.

12 Ask me never so much dowry and gift, and I will give according as ye shall say unto me: but give me the damsel to wife.

13 And the sons of Jacob answered Shē'chĕm and Hā'mŏr his father deceitfully, and said, because he had defiled Dinah their sister:

14 And they said unto them, We cannot do this thing, to give our sister to one that is uncircumcised; for that *were* a reproach unto us:

15 But in this will we consent unto you: If ye will be as we *be*, that every male of you be circumcised;

16 Then will we give our daughters unto you, and we will take your daughters to us, and we will dwell with you, and we will become one people.

17 But if ye will not hearken unto us, to be circumcised; then will we take our daughter, and we will be gone.

Word quickly reached Jacob concerning what had happened to Dinah, probably by way of some of her girl friends in the town. Jacob no doubt was grief-stricken and angry, but decided not to do anything without first consulting Dinah's brothers, who were still out in the field with the cattle. He probably regretted settling down so close to a place like Shechem, where it would be almost impossible not to have his children subjected to bad influences. On the other hand, where else in Canaan would it have been any better? He needed to pray and trust God more, he must have felt, and to do more to help his children live victoriously in a pagan world. But what to do about the immediate situation was the problem, and he didn't know the answer.

While Jacob was waiting for his sons to come home, Hamor appeared at his house, with the proposal that Dinah be given as Shechem's wife. No word of apology or sympathy was offered, nor any suggestion that his son be punished in any way. He merely suggested a proposition of marriage. As this interchange between Jacob and Hamor was taking place, the sons of Jacob came bursting into the room. They also had heard the story by now, and were grieved and bitterly angry. Dinah had been the only and beloved sister in a large family of boys, and they had all been taught the sacredness of the marriage relation. Even though they had been raised in a polygamous household, at least Jacob had not sought women other than his wives, and his wives had been faithful to him. They all knew of God's purpose to raise up a holy nation through their family, and that the maintenance of national integrity and purity was essential to assure God's continued blessing on them. Not only did they resent the affair for Dinah's sake, but because Shechem had "wrought folly in Israel," disrupting that national purity which they had regarded as so vital. Their use of the generic name of Israel in this connection indicates that they must have had a substantial comprehension and recognition of the deeper values and implications of this event.

Their anger apparently made little impression on Hamor, however, as he continued urging them to accept his proposition. Not only was he proposing that Shechem take Dinah, but suddenly he began to make a much broader suggestion, namely, that there should be general intermarrying between the people of Israel and those of Shechem.

Although he didn't say so openly, he was thinking that, since his own people were far more numerous than those of Israel, this would be a fine way of quickly assimilating them and taking over their possessions (verse 23). Shechem himself, who had evidently come with his father but had remained discreetly silent to this point, then eagerly offered to pay Jacob and his sons whatever they would require in the way of a dowry and other gifts. Though he obviously really did love Dinah, and was more interested in having her than in his father's concern for full amalgamation with the Israelites, he did not seem to feel any pangs of conscience for what he had done to her, or for the terrible offense to her family.

Quite possibly it was this matter-of-fact, businesslike attitude of Hamor and Shechem that infuriated Dinah's brothers beyond limit. Here these men were making a monetary offer for their beloved sister, just as though she were nothing but a harlot (verse 31) whose body could be purchased for the asking!

From this point on, the sons of Jacob did all the talking with Hamor. Jacob was apparently so distressed that he left the room altogether, or at least was unable to discuss the subject further. Whether these "sons of Jacob" were only Simeon and Levi, or whether Reuben and Judah (and perhaps others) were also involved, is not stated. Later it was Simeon and Levi who took revenge on the Shechemites, but there is a possibility that some of the others participated in the plot which here began to develop.

While Hamor and Shechem were talking, the "sons of Jacob" devised a plan of vengeance which involved both blasphemy and murder, as well as deception and cruelty. Such a shocking plan was justified in their own minds because of what they considered to be intolerable sin against their sister and against their name.

Not content to take vengeance against Shechem only, they felt (and no doubt correctly) that in a sense the whole city was guilty and deserved judgment, just as God had judged Sodom and Gomorrah in the days of their great-grandfather. No one in the city had protested Shechem's behavior toward their sister; no one had tried to protect her and, in fact, they had seemed rather pleased with Shechem's conquest of the beautiful young foreign girl. They would have done the same if they had been able, but Shechem, as their prince, had first priority and they derived vicarious pleasure from his sexual exploits.

Not content, however, to leave the city's judgment—if such it deserved —in the hands of God as in the time of Sodom, Simeon and Levi in particular resolved to take it into their own hands. Pretending to go along with Hamor's proposition that there should be general intermarriage between the two peoples, with consequent commercial advantage to both, they said that the only problem was a religious one. It was their religious conviction that every male in their own nation should be circumcised. If indeed they were from that time on to be one people, then the Shechemites also would need to be circumcised. Otherwise, they would have to take Dinah back and keep the two peoples completely segregated in the future. Whether the other brothers knew about the murderous plan or not, the Bible is not clear; but it was Simeon and Levi who carried it out.

Genesis 34:18-24

18 And their words pleased Hā'mŏr and Shĕ'ehĕm Hā'mŏr's son.

19 And the young man deferred not to do the thing, because he had delight in Jacob's daughter: and he *was* more honorable than all the house of his father.

20 ¶ And Hā'mŏr and Shĕ'ehĕm his son came unto the gate of their city, and communed with the men of their city, saying,

21 These men *are* peaceable with us; therefore let them dwell in the land, and trade therein; for the land, behold, *it is* large enough for them; let us take their daughters to us for wives, and let us give them our daughters.

22 Only herein will the men consent unto us for to dwell with us, to be one people, if every male among us be circumcised, as they *are* circumcised.

23 *Shall* not their cattle and their substance and every beast of theirs *be* ours? only let us consent unto them, and they will dwell with us.

24 And unto Hā'mŏr and unto Shĕ'ehĕm his son hearkened all that went out of the gate of his city; and every male was circumcised, all that went out of the gate of his city.

The unsuspecting Shechemites readily agreed to this proposition, beginning first of all with Shechem himself, who had no hesitation in submitting himself to the surgical rite, out of love for Dinah. There were certain other nations, besides the Israelites, who practiced circumcision in early times, so that the terms of the agreement did not sound too strange or offensive to the men of Shechem. Hamor gathered them all together at the city's gate, and laid the whole proposition before them, stressing that they would eventually own all the property of the Israelites as well as have access to their women. The men of Shechem were easily persuaded by such inducements. They would be willing to go along with this peculiar religious notion to gain such wealth especially since there was nothing in their own carnal religion that precluded it.

Shechem's example further encouraged them. He was held in considerable esteem among them. Verse 19 says, literally, that "he was more honored than any in his father's house." Finally, they all agreed to the terms and consented to be circumcised. The day was set; all other work was stopped, and all the men, from Hamor and Shechem on down, allowed themselves to be circumcised.

In the meantime, the Bible is silent concerning the natural question as to what Jacob thought about this arrangement. He would certainly not have approved of the overt plan, that of amalgamating the people of Shechem and his own family, because he well knew that God had called them to be a separate people. Neither could he have approved the covert plan of Simeon and Levi, because he later bitterly rebuked them when he learned what they had done. We therefore must assume that he had participated in none of these conversations. In his grief and uncertainty, he had evidently left the room while Hamor was talking with his sons, thus completely abdicating his responsibilities as father at this point and leaving everything up to them. This was a serious mistake on his part, and Levi and Simeon took full advantage of their father's uncharacteristic weakness. Jacob must simply have isolated himself until he learned later about the terrible act of vengeance that had been carried out in his name.

It also seems a little odd that neither Reuben nor Judah took part in the affair. Reuben, especially, as Dinah's oldest brother, should have taken charge if Jacob didn't. Later developments show that both Reuben and Judah were much less disposed toward bloodshed than the rest of their brothers (Genesis 37:21, 26), and it may be that they demurred after they saw what Simeon and Levi were really planning—though not to the extent of doing anything to prevent them from carrying out their strategy. There is, of course, the possibility that they were simply away at the time. Probably Jacob's other sons were still too young to take an active part in the plot.

In any case, Simeon and Levi took the lead. Though they were right and, to some extent, spiritually motivated in their zeal for the good name of their sister and their family, and in their rejection of the proposal that the Israelites allow their distinctiveness to be corrupted by unions with the wicked and idolatrous people of Shechem, they were utterly wrong in taking the law into their own hands in such a cruel way. God would one day have to judge these Canaanites for just such sins, but "the iniquity of the Amorites was not yet full," and they should have been willing to leave the matter to their father's disposition of it. He in turn then should have relied on God for proper wisdom in dealing with it. But Jacob, in his grief, had turned away from facing the problem, and Simeon and Levi felt they could not leave the crime unpunished.

The two brothers decided that nothing but the death of all the men of the city would atone for such a crime, but the two of them (even if aided by such servants as they might be able to command) would of course be no match for the much larger number of Shechemites. They probably realized, too, that they could not merely slay Shechem himself, as his fellow townsmen would immediately come after them and probably kill all the Israelites. They could see no solution but to get the entire city so incapacitated, by having them all submit to circumcision, that they would be unable to defend themselves. Even though this involved a blasphemous corruption of the holy meaning of circumcision, they proceeded with this ruse, only too successfully.

Genesis 34:25-29

25 ¶ And it came to pass on the third day, when they were sore, that two of the sons of Jacob, Simeon and Levi, Dinah's brethren, took each man his sword, and came upon the city boldly, and slew all the males.

26 And they slew Hā'mŏr and Shĕ'chĕm his son with the edge of the sword, and took Dinah out of Shĕ'chĕm's house, and went out.

27 The sons of Jacob came upon the slain, and spoiled the city, because they had defiled their sister.

28 They took their sheep, and their oxen, and their asses, and that which *was* in the city, and that which *was* in the field,

29 And all their wealth, and all their little ones, and their wives took they captive, and spoiled even all that *was* in the house.

Simeon and Levi knew that the painful and crippling effects of the circumcision surgery were greatest on the third day. On that day, the two brothers (possibly assisted by their servants) proceeded boldly into the city, going from one house to the next, putting every male to the sword, until they had slain them all. When they came to the house of Shechem, they killed him also, and took Dinah out of his house back home with them.

After the deed was done, perhaps assisted now by some of Jacob's other sons, they took all the women and children captive, probably making slaves out of them, and also took all the animals of the Shechemites plus their other possessions as spoils. In effect, Simeon and Levi had waged a two-man war against the city of Shechem and had come out completely victorious, in their own estimation at least. Perhaps they even considered their victory to be evidence of God's blessing on their stratagem, and their cruelty actually to be holy zeal in defending their faith from corruption by pagan idolaters.

They were young men, not yet seasoned in judgment, and they had surely been grievously provoked, not only by the actual rape of their sister, but also (and even more) by the moral indifference of the Shechemites themselves to the crime. Though such considerations can hardly justify their blasphemous treachery and murder, it is clear that much of the real blame must lie with Jacob. Not only had he, who had once been so strong in the Lord, allowed conditions to develop in his household which could lead to such things, but, when the crisis came and serious decisions had to be made, he went off by himself and refused to face the problem until it was too late. Probably the first he knew about his sons' deed was when he saw them bringing back their captives and the spoils from the Shechemite houses and fields. Dinah was also back home, no doubt in a state of mind approaching shock from what she had seen and experienced. Jacob must have been aghast with the enormity of what had happened so suddenly to disrupt the peace of his life and that of his family.

Genesis 34:30, 31

---

30 And Jacob said to Simeon and Levi, Ye have troubled me to make me to stink among the inhabitants of the land, among the Cā'năan-ītes and the Pĕr'ĭz-zītes: and I *being* few in number, they shall gather themselves together against me, and slay me; and I shall be destroyed, I and my house.

31 And they said, Should he deal with our sister as with a harlot?

When Jacob finally did put in his appearance again, it was merely to complain to Levi and Simeon about what they had done. He had left the matter in their hands, but now was appalled at what they had done with it. He had tried to live peaceably with the Shechemites, perhaps even hoping that his altar, and the testimony that he and his family had borne to them, would influence them someday to follow Jehovah. But now, whatever testimony his family might have had was gone. Instead of being a witness for truth and love, their name would become associated with deception and cruelty. They had become an actual stench to the other Canaanites in the land, with their vaunted moral purity becoming an excuse for murder and pillage rather than an example of God's holiness and mercy.

Furthermore, Jacob continued, they were vastly outnumbered in the land, and when the news of this massacre circulated among the other Canaanite tribes in the region, it would not be long before they would all converge on Jacob and destroy him and his whole family. God had delivered them from Laban and from Esau, both with relatively small bands of followers, when Jacob's cause was right. But how could they expect divine protection from the great host of ungodly Canaanites surrounding them when they themselves were in the wrong?

Jacob's complaint was silenced, however, by one question from Simeon and Levi. He was complaining about the action they had taken, but what had *he* done? Had he forgotten that his daughter had been raped by the very prince of the city of Shechem and that, to add insult to injury, his father Hamor had actually sought to *purchase* Dinah, as though she were nothing but a harlot? And then they had dared to propose to unite with the Israelites in one great mixed multitude which would inevitably have destroyed them and their high calling. Was all of this of no concern to Jacob? If he had known of a better way of dealing with the problem, why had he not said so? Where was *Israel,* the strong prince who had power with God, when action was needed?

Jacob could say nothing in reply. He had indeed failed, and now was in desperate need of revival in his own soul, as well as of a fresh word of guidance from the Lord. Though Scripture does not explicitly say so, it seems most likely that Jacob did quickly go to his altar and there cry to God for forgiveness and for instruction. And God, who is gracious and long-suffering, answered him once again.

Return to Bethel

Jacob had been too long at Shechem. God had not really intended that he stay there, but it had been a convenient place to settle. Furthermore, Jacob knew that there were remnants of Laban's idolatry among his family, as well as certain infiltrating influences of the Shechemites, and he had failed to deal decisively with these corrupting tendencies in his own household. He had perhaps become a bit smug and confident in his own spirituality, as he had seen God's great power exercised so frequently on his behalf, and felt that he and his family were more secure than they really were, in such an ungodly land. He was in critical need of a fresh revelation of God and His holy purposes.

Genesis 35:1-4

CHAPTER 35

AND God said unto Jacob, Arise, go up to Beth-el, and dwell there: and make there an altar unto God, that appeared unto thee when thou fleddest from the face of E'saū thy brother.

2 Then Jacob said unto his household, and to all that *were* with him, Put away the strange gods that *are* among you, and be clean, and change your garments:

3 And let us arise, and go up to Beth-el; and I will make there an altar unto God, who answered me in the day of my distress, and was with me in the way which I went.

4 And they gave unto Jacob all the strange gods which *were* in their hand, and *all their* earrings which *were* in their ears; and Jacob hid them under the oak which *was* by Shē'chĕm.

It was at this critical point in Jacob's life that God once again spoke to him in grace rather than judgment. Quite probably, Jacob's grief over the events of those days led him to go to God in confession and prayer, seeking wisdom for the future and forgiveness for his negligence during the decade spent at Shechem. When God answered him, it was to instruct Jacob to move away from Shechem and to go up to Bethel, which was about fifteen miles south of Shechem but one thousand feet higher in elevation.

For some strange reason, though Bethel must have held uniquely powerful memories for Jacob (it was there God had first spoken to him, from the top of the heavenly ladder, when he fled from Esau, as recorded in Genesis 28:12-15), and though he had lived so close to it for about ten years, he had evidently never returned to see it again. This is all the more strange in view of the fact that Bethel is located almost directly between Shechem and Hebron, and Jacob certainly must have journeyed to Hebron on one or more occasions during this period to see his father Isaac. It almost seems that he had deliberately avoided Bethel. If this is so, it is probably because he knew he had not completely followed God's will, nor had he fully kept the promise he had made to the Lord at Bethel. God had surely fulfilled His promise in bringing Jacob safely back to his father's house and in supplying all his needs; but Jacob had never built "God's house" on the pillar he had erected at Bethel (Jacob had even named the place "The House of God"), nor had he fully made the Lord the God of his own entire household. There was still some use of idols among his servants and evidently even among his own family. Jacob had no doubt been faithful in teaching his wives and children about Jehovah and His promises, but he had been negligent in insisting that they discard completely their images and amulets. They were trying, like so many professing Christian people today, to worship God while at the same time hanging on to some of the superstitions and practices of the world around them. The many years of Shechemite influence, especially during the critical teen-age years of most of his children, had made matters worse, and climaxed finally in the awful events associated with the seduction and rape of Dinah and the resultant massacre of the Shechemite males by Simeon and Levi. Then, the sacking and looting of the city had probably brought still more images and other objects of pagan worship into their possession. All of this would have to be put away now, and a fresh start made, if God was going to bless them again.

God reminded Jacob of his encounter with Him at Bethel, and of his promises there, and commanded him immediately to move on to Bethel. With a broken and repentant heart, Jacob did what he should have done long ago: he required his family and servants to abandon all remnants of idolatry; discard their images, earrings, and other amulets; put away their "foreign gods" and even the garments they had been wearing; then wash themselves clean and put on fresh clothing symbolic of the pure worship of Jehovah. The recent traumatic experiences had so shaken them, as had their awareness of the very real dangers they now faced from the other people of the land, that they yielded to Jacob's commands. All these remnants of their "old life" were buried under the "oak" at Shechem, quite possibly the same terebinth tree that had been noted by Abram (Genesis 12:6) as he entered Canaan.

Jacob told his household they were finally going back to Bethel (no doubt he had often told his wives and children of his experience at Bethel, and they had probably wondered why he had not returned there sooner), where he was resolved to build a sanctuary for the worship of God, centered especially around a sacrificial altar, in recognition of God's faithfulness to him through the years.

Genesis 35:5-8

---

5 And they journeyed: and the terror of God was upon the cities that *were* round about them, and they did not pursue after the sons of Jacob.

6 ¶ So Jacob came to Lŭz which *is* in the land of Cā′năan, that *is,* Beth-el, he and all the people that *were* with him.

7 And he built there an altar, and called the place Ĕl′–bĕth′–ĕl; because there God appeared unto him, when he fled from the face of his brother.

8 But Deborah Rē-bĕk′ăh's nurse died, and she was buried beneath Beth-el under an oak: and the name of it was called Ăl′lŏn–băch′ŭth.

As Jacob had surmised (34:30), the cities around them would be seeking vengeance on them for their slaughter of the Shechemites, and would be almost certain to pursue them as they were apparently trying to escape. In some way, however, God prevented this. The surrounding Canaanite tribes were far superior to them numerically, but nevertheless became so fearful of them that they refrained from attacking them. They did realize, of course, that the Israelites worshiped Jehovah, and that this worship was of a higher moral and ethical nature than their own degraded religious practices, and they somehow sensed therefore that Jehovah was far more powerful than their own gods. Unfortunately, the testimony of the Israelites had induced fear of Jehovah, rather than love of Jehovah, in their hearts. But it did at least serve to prevent their attacking them, as they surely must have intended.

Jacob and his company therefore arrived safely at the little community of Luz, which he had renamed Bethel, and he immediately proceeded to build the altar and its associated house of worship there. He had named the place Bethel, and now he named the altar El-Bethel ("The Strong God of the House of God").

At this point, the writer notes that it was at this time and place that Deborah, Rebekah's nurse, died. She was very old by now, and the experiences of the recent days proved too much for her. She was well loved and revered by the family, and there was sincere grief at her departing, as indicated by their naming the place of her burial "The Oak of Weeping."

Jacob had known Deborah all his life. She had come with Rebekah from Mesopotamia when Rebekah had left to marry Isaac (Genesis 24:59), and no doubt had cared for Jacob from the time he was born. She had not, of course, accompanied him when he fled from Esau to Haran, but she, as well as his mother, must have grieved to see him go. The record does not say when she rejoined Jacob, but it was probably on the occasion of one of his visits to Isaac while he was living at Shechem. In fact, her presence in Jacob's household is one of the reasons we are confident that he did visit his father during those years. Furthermore, the fact that she was now with Jacob is proof that Rebekah herself was dead at this time. Probably, when Jacob returned to Hebron and found that his mother was dead, and that Deborah really was not needed any longer in his father's home, he urged her to come live with his own family. Possibly she served as a sort of "senior advisor" to his other servants, as well as a "grandmother" to his children. It must have grieved her greatly to see the things that took place at Shechem. In addition to that burden, the arduous trip up to Bethel was too much for her aged body, and she died.

Genesis 35:9-15

---

9 ⁋ And God appeared unto Jacob again, when he came out of Pā'dăn-ā'răm, and blessed him.

10 And God said unto him, Thy name *is* Jacob: thy name shall not be called any more Jacob, but Ĭṣ'rā-ĕl shall be thy name; and he called his name Ĭṣ'rā-ĕl.

11 And God said unto him, I *am* God Almighty: be fruitful and multiply; a nation and a company of nations shall be of thee, and kings shall come out of thy loins;

12 And the land which I gave Abraham and Isaac, to thee I will give it, and to thy seed after thee will I give the land.

13 And God went up from him in the place where he talked with him.

14 And Jacob set up a pillar in the place where he talked with him, *even* a pillar of stone: and he poured a drink offering thereon, and he poured oil thereon.

15 And Jacob called the name of the place where God spake with him, Beth-el.

It was here at Bethel, however, that God once again appeared to Jacob, renewing the promises made thirty years before at the same spot. God identified Himself as "God Almighty" (Hebrew *El Shaddai*). God had revealed Himself by this name to Abram (Genesis 17:1) and to Isaac (Genesis 28:3), and now to Jacob. The name is related to the Hebrew word for "breast" *(shad)*, and conveys the idea of God as the One who nourishes and provides, who is strong enough to meet every need.

Once again God promised Jacob that he and his seed, which would be a great multitude, would possess this land, as He had promised also to Abraham and Isaac. Furthermore, though he would be a "nation," he would also be a "company of nations," no doubt a reference to the continuing distinctiveness of the twelve tribes of Israel.

God also reaffirmed and reimpressed on Jacob that he now had a new name, *Israel*. He was a prevailing and powerful prince of God! He should therefore live and comport himself as one who possessed such a high calling.

And so, of course, should it be with us today. As those who have been made "joint-heirs with Christ" (Romans 8:17) of "all things" (Hebrews 1:2), we have a noble calling and therefore great responsibilities. The strongest incentive to holy living is the comprehension of our holy calling. "I therefore, the prisoner of the Lord, beseech you that ye walk worthy of the vocation wherewith ye are called" (Ephesians 4:1).

After God had appeared and spoken to Jacob there at Bethel, He "went up," as it were, up the heavenly ladder back into the heavens. Just as he had done thirty years previously when God spoke with him at Bethel, Jacob erected another stone pillar in commemoration of the event. As he had done on the earlier occasion, he anointed the stone with oil, symbolic of consecration. This act is here called, for the first time in Scripture, a "drink-offering." Later, such drink-offerings, though not a primary part of the Levitical sacrificial offerings, were offered frequently as auxiliary gifts of devotion and consecration, and it was no doubt with such a motive that Jacob so acted here. Jacob then, this time in the company of all his family and followers, in recognition of God's unique presence in this place, once again called the name of the place Bethel, the "House of God."

Genesis 35:16-20

16 ¶ And they journeyed from Beth-el; and there was but a little way to come to Ĕph'răth: and Rachel travailed, and she had hard labor.

17 And it came to pass, when she was in hard labor, that the midwife said unto her, Fear not; thou shalt have this son also.

18 And it came to pass, as her soul was in departing, (for she died,) that she called his name Bĕn-ō'nī: but his father called him Benjamin.

19 And Rachel died, and was buried in the way to Ĕph'răth, which *is* Bethlehem.

20 And Jacob set a pillar upon her grave: that *is* the pillar of Rachel's grave unto this day.

After completing his pilgrimage to Bethel, and dwelling there long enough to build the altar, and probably a sanctuary of worship, Jacob moved on south, probably intending to move all the way back to Hebron with his father Isaac. When they had almost reached Ephrath, the region around Bethlehem, another notable event, both joyful and tragic, occurred. Previous to this pilgrimage, after years of barrenness, Jacob's beloved wife Rachel had finally borne a son, before they left Laban and the region of Haran (Genesis 30:22-25). She had named him Joseph and had, at the time, expressed faith that God would give her still another son. That, however, had been nearly fifteen years before, and her faith had not yet been rewarded. No doubt she had continued to pray about it, and God finally answered. Rachel must have been well along in years by now, as Jacob was certainly 105 years old or more by this time. Finally, however, she became pregnant again. Jacob's other wives had long since ceased bearing children, so Rachel gave birth to Jacob's twelfth and last son.

Possibly the baby was born prematurely, as they were still en route to Ephrath when the birth pains began. This time, perhaps because of her age, the birth was very difficult. She was assisted by an older servant acting as midwife, and, as the child was born, the midwife assured her that it was a son, in answer to her prayers.

It cost Rachel her life, however. Before she died, in grief she named the child Benoni, meaning "Son of Sorrow." Her husband, Jacob, though no doubt also experiencing real anguish of soul as he saw Rachel leaving him, realized that it would be an unhealthy burden for his son to carry such a name through life; so he renamed him Benjamin after Rachel's death and burial. The name Benjamin means "Son of the Right Hand," thus signifying a particularly honored position in the family.

Rachel was buried nearby, on the way to Bethlehem, in the Ephrath area. Perhaps this experience of travail and birth, in Bethlehem Ephratah, can be considered as a type of the later birth of the promised Seed (see Micah 5:2). Jacob erected a marker over Rachel's grave which, according to what seems to be an editorial insertion here, could still be seen in Moses' day.

Genesis 35:21-26

21 ¶ And Ĭṣ'rā-ĕl journeyed, and spread his tent beyond the tower of Ē'där.

22 And it came to pass, when Ĭṣ'rā-ĕl dwelt in that land, that Reuben went and lay with Bĭl'häh his father's concubine: and Ĭṣ'rā-ĕl heard *it*. Now the sons of Jacob were twelve:

23 The sons of Lē'áh; Reuben, Jacob's firstborn, and Simeon, and Levi, and Judah, and Ĭs'sá-chär, and Zĕb'ŭ-lŭn:

24 The sons of Rachel; Joseph, and Benjamin:

25 And the sons of Bĭl'häh, Rachel's

handmaid; Dan, and Năph'tà-lī: the sons of Jacob, which were born to
  26 And the sons of Zĭl'pàh, Lē'àh's   him in Pā'dăn–ā'răm.
handmaid; Gad, and Ăsh'ēr. These *are*

Jacob then continued on south for a while, stopping again near the "tower of Edar," a location apparently quite near Jerusalem. While they were camped here, a most unfortunate and disgusting event took place. Jacob's oldest son, Reuben, was now probably about thirty years old. He was presumably a virile young man, but he was unmarried and evidently there was little opportunity for him to find a wife or even to meet any prospective girl friends, except possibly the servant girls in Jacob's household. These, however, were off limits to him in view of his position as eldest son and their position as servants. The Canaanites around them also avoided them, and the experiences at Shechem had made them all very wary of any contacts with the people of the land.

No details are given concerning events leading up to the affair, but somehow Reuben began to associate intimately with Bilhah, Rachel's maid. She was much older than Reuben, of course, and it was clearly a very abnormal situation, whether or not there were as yet any actual laws in effect against this type of incest. Bilhah was actually the mother of two of Reuben's younger brothers, Dan and Naphtali. There is no indication, and it seems unlikely, that Reuben was guilty of rape; and it also seems unlikely that it could have been a simple matter of seduction on his part, since Bilhah was certainly sufficiently mature not to have submitted to a sudden infatuation. A possible suggestion is that, after Rachel's death, Bilhah wanted to take Rachel's place in Jacob's affections and attentions. When he failed to respond, she may have reacted by consorting with Reuben, his oldest son, in a way that was unhealthy and dangerous. With both of them seeking a physical outlet, one thing led to another until they actually began to have intercourse together. When Jacob learned of it, as he was sure to do, he no doubt put a stop to it; but at the time he apparently took no punitive action against either party. In time, however, it cost Reuben his birthright (Genesis 49:3, 4), as Jacob never forgot it. No matter what the temptations and mitigating circumstances may have been, such an act as this could not be excused.

At this point, the writer (presumably Jacob, or possibly Moses, by an editorial insertion) felt it appropriate to recapitulate the names of the sons of Jacob, because they were to become the twelve tribes of the children of Israel. His family was returning finally to the home from which Jacob had gone out long before, and these were the grandsons whom he would present to his father, Isaac, as evidence that God was fulfilling His promises to both of them.

Genesis 35:27-29

---

27 ⁋ And Jacob came unto Isaac his father unto Măm′rē, unto the city of Är′bå, which *is* Hē′brŏn, where Abraham and Isaac sojourned.

28 And the days of Isaac were a hundred and fourscore years.

29 And Isaac gave up the ghost, and died, and was gathered unto his people, *being* old and full of days: and his sons Ē′saŭ and Jacob buried him.

Finally Jacob came home. He had, as we have noted, no doubt visited Isaac, and Esau as well, while he was living at Shechem, but now his entire household had come home with him. Isaac was very old at this time, not only blind but surely very feeble as well, possibly even senile, since nothing is said about his welcoming Jacob and his grandsons, but in any case, Jacob was home again. Isaac was still living at Hebron, where Abraham also had lived.

At the age of 180, Isaac died. This must actually have been about 25 years after Jacob came back from Padan-aram, since Isaac had probably been about 135 years old or so when Jacob left home. Actually, Isaac must have still been living at the time Joseph was sold into Egypt, but the writer found it appropriate to mention his death at this point. Mention of the fact that he "was gathered unto his people" is evidence that although nothing much is said about it in this part of the Bible, the patriarchs did believe in life after death. Isaac's spirit, no doubt, was transported to Sheol, where the spirits of Abraham, Shem, Noah and others who had died in faith were resting and awaiting the coming redemption and resurrection.

It is noteworthy that Esau and Jacob were still in fellowship with each other, these many years after their first reunion, as the two once-alienated brothers came together to participate with each other in the burial ceremonies for their father. Issaac was buried in the same sepulchre with Rebekah, and with Abraham and Sarah, in the cave in the field which Abraham had purchased in Mamre (Genesis 49:29-31).

The Generations of Esau

Chapter 36 of Genesis closes that long section of the book which seems originally to have been written by Jacob. As discussed in chapter 1, the divisions of Genesis are noted by the phrase "These are the generations of. . . ." There is good reason to think that this statement in each case marks the signature of the man who first wrote the material preceding the statement, beginning with the first verse following the previous reference to the "generations" (Hebrew *toledoth,* meaning "historical records"). If this assumption is correct, the portion of Genesis from 25:19b through 37:2a was written by Jacob, with later editorial insertions by Moses, who brought all the patriarchal records together in the present Book of Genesis.

However, to complete his own record, Jacob seems to have obtained from Esau the records of Esau's family and then incorporated them into his own records before finally attaching his (Jacob's) signature to the completed work. At least this seems to be a plausible explanation of how these "generations of Esau" came to be included in a book which is primarily concerned with the story of Israel and the line of the promised Seed. In any case, this particular chapter is occupied exclusively with Esau and his descendants.

By the time Isaac died, when Jacob and Esau spent some time together in connection with Isaac's burial, Esau and Jacob were each 120 years old (Genesis 25:26; 35:28). Esau had been married for eighty years (Genesis 26:34), whereas Jacob had been married less than forty. Esau, consequently, had at least a full generation of descendants more than Jacob, and this fact is reflected in the extensive list of names given in this chapter. The most likely time for Jacob to have acquired a copy of Esau's records would seem to have been on the occasion of Isaac's burial. It is on such occasions that children take more interest than usual in such matters as family records. It is also probable that Moses later augmented these original records with additional data that had come into his possession. By Moses' time, the descendants of Esau (by then known as the Edomites) were a nation of considerable concern to the Israelites.

Genesis 36:1-8

CHAPTER 36

NOW these *are* the generations of E'saŭ, who *is* E'dŏm.

2 E'saŭ took his wives of the daughters of Cā'năan; Ā'dăh the daughter of E'lŏn the Hĭt'tĭte, and Ả-hŏl'ĭ-bā'măh the daughter of Ả'năh the daughter of Zĭb'-ē-ŏn the Hī'vĭte;

3 And Băsh'ē-măth Ĭsh'mā-ĕl's daughter, sister of Nē-bā'jŏth.

4 And Ā'dăh bare to E'saŭ Ĕl'ĭ-phăz, and Băsh'ē-măth bare Reŭ'ĕl;

5 And Ả-hŏl'ĭ-bā'măh bare Jē'ŭsh, and Jā'ȧ-lăm, and Kō'răh: these *are* the sons of E'saŭ, which were born unto him in the land of Cā'năan.

6 And E'saŭ took his wives, and his sons, and his daughters, and all the persons of his house, and his cattle, and all his beasts, and all his substance, which he had got in the land of Cā'năan; and went into the country from the face of his brother Jacob.

7 For their riches were more than that they might dwell together; and the land wherein they were strangers could not bear them because of their cattle.

8 Thus dwelt E'saŭ in mount Sē'ĭr: E'saŭ *is* E'dŏm.

A difficulty occurs right at the beginning of these lists, because of the apparent contradiction between the names of Esau's wives as given here (36:2) and as given in Genesis 26:34 and 28:9. The names as they are given are outlined below.

Genesis 26:34 ... Judith, daughter of Beeri
　　　　　　　　Bashemath, daughter of Elon

Genesis 28:9 .... Mahalath, daughter of Ishmael

Genesis 36:2 .... Aholibamah, daughter of Anah
　　　　　　　　Adah, daughter of Elon

Genesis 36:3 .... Bashemath, daughter of Ishmael

Comparison of the names above indicates that, probably, Judith is the same as Aholibamah; Bashemath, daughter of Elon, is the same as Adah; and Bashemath, daughter of Ishmael, is the same as Mahalath. That it was not uncommon for one person to have two names is well known. The women were probably known by the first set of names early in their lives (when Jacob had known them, as recorded in his "generations"), and by the second set of names later, at the time Esau wrote them down in his "generations." It is possible that the women were given new names at the time of marriage, and the first set of names corresponded to their unmarried, given, names. Similarly, Beeri must have been the same man as Anah.

Aholibamah is also said to have been the "daughter" of Zibeon, but since she is clearly the daughter of Anah (verse 25), she must have been the daughter of Zibeon in the sense of being his descendant, probably his granddaughter. The fathers of Esau's first two wives were said to be Hittites (Genesis 26:34), but one of them here (verse 2) is said to be a Hivite and also (verse 20) a Horite (the same people known to archaeologists as Hurrians). All three groups were scattered throughout Canaan, and were Canaanite tribes; so there was undoubtedly much intermarriage among them, and the names were frequently used interchangeably.

Esau had five sons and an unknown number of daughters, as well as many servants and much cattle. After realizing that Jacob was destined to be the heir of Isaac and to possess the land of Canaan, he realized there would not be room enough for both of them, so began to move southward into the mountainous regions southeast of the Dead Sea. Both he and Isaac, and Jacob when he returned, were still "strangers" (foreigners) in these lands, owning little property of their own but pasturing their flocks and herds wherever there was room for them.

The region into which Esau (also known as Edom) migrated had previously been settled by the descendants of Seir, and the central range of mountains had come to be known as Mount Seir. To some extent the children of Esau had subjugated the Horites (equivalent to Horims, or Hurrians) by force (Deuteronomy 2:12, 22), but perhaps to an even greater extent had essentially assimilated them through intermarriage, so that the people eventually known as Edomites were a mixture of Semitic (through Isaac and Esau) and Canaanitic (through Seir) inheritance.

Genesis 36:9-19

9 ¶ And these *are* the generations of E′saū the father of the E′dŏm-ītes in mount Sē′ĭr:

10 These *are* the names of E′saū's sons; Ĕl′ĭ-phăz the son of A′dăh the wife of E′saū, Reṵ′ĕl the son of Băsh′ē-măth the wife of E′saū.

11 And the sons of Ĕl′ĭ-phăz were Tē′măn, Ō′măr, Zē′phō, and Gā′tăm, and Kē′năz.

12 And Tĭm′nȧ was concubine to Ĕl′ĭphăz E′saū's son; and she bare to Ĕl′ĭphăz Ăm′ȧ-lĕk: these *were* the sons of A′dăh E′saū's wife.

13 And these *are* the sons of Reṵ′ĕl; Nā′hăth, and Zē′răh, Shăm′măh, and Mĭz′zăh: these were the sons of Băsh′ē-măth E′saū's wife.

14 ¶ And these were the sons of A-hŏl′ĭ-bā′măh, the daughter of A′nȧh the daughter of Zĭb′ē-ŏn, E′saū's wife: and she bare to E′saū Jē′ŭsh, and Jā′ȧ-lăm, and Kō′răh.

15 ¶ These *were* dukes of the sons of E′saū: the sons of Ĕl′ĭ-phăz the firstborn *son* of E′saū; duke Tē′măn, duke Ō′măr, duke Zē′phō, duke Kē′năz,

16 Duke Kō′răh, duke Gā′tăm, *and* duke Ăm′ȧ-lĕk: these *are* the dukes *that came* of Ĕl′ĭ-phăz in the land of E′dŏm: these *were* the sons of A′dăh.

17 ¶ And these *are* the sons of Reṵ′ĕl E′saū's son; duke Nā′hăth, duke Zē′răh, duke Shăm′măh, duke Mĭz′zăh: these *are* the dukes *that came* of Reṵ′ĕl in the land of E′dŏm: these *are* the sons of Băsh′ē-măth E′saū's wife.

18 ¶ And these *are* the sons of A-hŏl′ĭ-bā′măh E′saū's wife; duke Jē′ŭsh, duke Jā′ȧ-lăm, duke Kō′răh: these *were* the dukes *that came* of A-hŏl′ĭ-bā′măh the daughter of A′năh, E′saū's wife.

19 These *are* the sons of E′saū, who *is* E′dŏm, and these *are* their dukes.

These verses give the names of the sons and grandsons of Esau, all of whom had risen to considerable prominence in the land of Edom, as "dukes," or chieftains, by the time of Isaac's death, when presumably these records came to Jacob's hand. A total of eleven such grandsons are listed, seven from Eliphaz and four from Reuel (sons of Adah and Bashemath, respectively). On the same level with them are listed the three sons of Aholibamah, making fourteen such "dukes" altogether.

Esau's daughters (verse 6) had no doubt also married Horite men, as presumably also his granddaughters. The listing of Korah as one of the dukes in the family of Eliphaz (when he is not listed in verse 11 as one of Eliphaz' natural sons) is probably best explained by assuming he was Eliphaz' son-in-law. It is interesting that the name of Eliphaz' concubine, Timna, is given, whereas that of his wife is not given. Probably this is because of the future prominence of her son, Amalek, who became the ancestor of the notorious Amalekites, the inveterate enemies of Israel in later years. The mention of Amalekites at the time of Abram (Genesis 14:7) is presumably an editorial addition by Moses to identify the region as it was known in his day. There is also a cryptic reference to the Amalekites as the "first of the nations" (Numbers 24:20), but this probably is a reference to the fact that they were the first nation to oppose the entrance of Israel into the promised land after their deliverance from Egypt (Exodus 17:8). The fact that Amalek was not of the same mother as the other sons of Eliphaz may have led to discrimination against him in the family, which in turn forced him to live in a separate region and to develop finally his own nation. The Amalekites in general lived west of the rest of the Edomites.

Genesis 36:20-30

20 ¶ These *are* the sons of Sē'ĭr the Hō'rīte, who inhabited the land; Lō'tăn, and Shō'băl, and Zĭb'ē-ŏn, and Ā'năh,

21 And Dĭ'shŏn, and Ē'zĕr, and Dĭ'shăn: these *are* the dukes of the Hō'rītes, the children of Sē'ĭr in the land of Ē'dŏm.

22 And the children of Lō'tăn were Hō'rī and Hē'măm; and Lō'tăn's sister *was* Tĭm'nă.

23 And the children of Shō'băl *were* these; Ăl'văn, and Măn'ă-hăth, and Ē'băl, Shē'phō, and Ō'năm.

24 And these *are* the children of Zĭb'ē-ŏn; both Ā'jăh, and Ā'năh: this *was that* Ā'năh that found the mules in the wilderness, as he fed the asses of Zĭb'ē-ŏn his father.

25 And the children of Ā'năh *were* these; Dĭ'shŏn, and Ă-hŏl'ĭ-bā'măh the daughter of Ā'năh.

26 And these *are* the children of Dĭ'shŏn; Hĕm'dăn, and Ĕsh'băn, and Ĭth'răn, and Chē'răn.

27 The children of Ē'zĕr *are* these; Bĭl'hăn, and Zā'ă-văn, and Ā'kăn.

28 The children of Dĭ'shăn *are* these; Ŭz, and Ā'răn.

29 These *are* the dukes *that came* of the Hō'rītes; duke Lō'tăn, duke Shō'băl, duke Zĭb'ē-ŏn, duke Ā'năh,

30 Duke Dĭ'shŏn, duke Ē'zĕr, duke Dĭ'shăn: these *are* the dukes *that came* of Hō'rī, among their dukes in the land of Sē'ĭr.

This section of the "generations of Esau" lists the prominent descendants of Seir, and is included no doubt because of the fact that these people became so closely associated with the descendants of Esau by intermarriage that the two groups finally were one people, the Edomites. The Hurrian patriarch Seir evidently was the pioneer settler of the region. His seven sons each became prominent chieftains in the land. In turn, they are listed as having nineteen sons of their own. The sons of Seir were evidently approximately contemporaneous with the generation of Isaac, since Esau married the daughter (Aholibamah) of one of them (Anah). In addition to their nineteen sons, only this one daughter is mentioned, obviously for this reason.

There is one daughter of Seir himself mentioned also, namely Timna, the sister of Lotan. The fact that she is named as sister to only one of Seir's sons shows, of course, that polygamy was practiced among the Horites. She is probably mentioned because she was concubine to Esau's son Eliphaz, as noted above. Presumably Eliphaz was Esau's eldest son, and Timna was a daughter of Seir's old age, since Timna was of the same generation as Isaac, Eliphaz' grandfather. Timna was thus probably considerably older than her "husband," another fact (in addition to her status as concubine rather than wife) which would have tended to make her son Amalek an outcast among his brothers.

One of Seir's sons, Zibeon, is mentioned as having two sons, one of whom was Anah (verse 24), probably named after his uncle (verse 25). The former Anah has often been confused with the other Anah, but it is clear from verse 25 that he could not have been the same as the father of Aholibamah, Esau's wife. The latter Anah was obviously a son of Seir (verse 20), not of Zibeon. However, Anah the son of Zibeon is mentioned as of special importance because of his finding "mules in the wilderness" while he was feeding the asses of his father Zibeon. This is the first mention of mules in the Bible, and may have been noteworthy for that reason. (A mule, of course, is the usually sterile hybrid animal produced by a cross between a male donkey and a female horse.)

However, this is not the usual Hebrew word for mules, and "mule" may or may not be its meaning. The word is *yēmim,* and occurs only this one time in the Bible. Neither does it seem to occur in other known Hebrew writings, so that its meaning is unknown. The Latin Vulgate translates it as "warm springs"; but this is very doubtful, since it does not relate to any of the several other Hebrew words for springs. Jewish writers for the most part have understood it to refer to mules, but the question is unsettled at this time.

Some commentators have, on the basis of the idea that the word had reference to a spring that Anah discovered, identified Anah with Beeri the Hittite (Genesis 26:34), since *be'er* is the Hebrew word for "well." However, this obviously very strained identification is impossible, since this would make Aholibamah to be the daughter of Anah the son of Zibeon rather than of Anah the son of Seir (verses 20, 25). The Zibeon who was the grandfather of Aholibamah (verses 2, 14) was therefore most likely her maternal grandfather. This may be another reason why this Zibeon is identified as "the Hivite," rather than as a "Horite." It is possible that Seir's son Zibeon (verse 20) was named after him.

Genesis 36:31-39

31 ¶ And these *are* the kings that reigned in the land of Ē'dŏm, before there reigned any king over the children of Iṣ'rā-ĕl.

32 And Bē'lȧ the son of Bē'ŏr reigned in Ē'dŏm: and the name of his city *was* Dĭn'hȧ-băh.

33 And Bē'lȧ died, and Jō'băb the son of Zē'rȧh of Bŏz'rȧh reigned in his stead.

34 And Jō'băb died, and Hū'shăm of the land of Tĕm'ȧ-nī reigned in his stead.

35 And Hū'shăm died, and Hā'dăd the son of Bē'dăd, who smote Mĭd'ĭ-ăn in the field of Mō'ăb, reigned in his stead: and the name of his city *was* Ā'vĭth.

36 And Hā'dăd died, and Săm'lȧh of Măs'rē-kȧh reigned in his stead.

37 And Săm'lȧh died, and Saul of Rē-hō'bŏth *by* the river reigned in his stead.

38 And Saul died, and Bā'ăl-hā'năn the son of Ăch'bŏr reigned in his stead.

39 And Bā'ăl-hā'năn the son of Ăch'-bŏr died, and Hā'dȧr reigned in his stead: and the name of his city *was* Pā'ū; and his wife's name *was* Mē-hĕt'ȧ-bĕl, the daughter of Mā'trĕd, the daughter of Mĕz'ā-hăb.

The balance of this chapter in Genesis seems most likely to have been added later by Moses, who appended it to the basic "generations of Esau" document which Jacob had transmitted. The names are those of kings and chieftains in Edom long after the time of Esau and continuing to about the time of Moses.

If we assume this section to be an insertion of Moses, it is interesting to see that he began by stating these kings of the Edomites reigned long before there was any king in Israel. Of course, the Israelites had no kings even in Moses' time, but Moses did know prophetically that they eventually *would* have kings (Deuteronomy 17:14-20). He quite possibly wished to include this reference to the kings to which their sister nation had submitted by way of a warning against the desire of the children of Israel to have kings.

None of the names in this list can with confidence be identified with similar names found in other connections in the Bible. It is interesting that the Edomite kings never became a family dynasty. When each king died, another unrelated individual acceded to the throne, probably by force of arms. Altogether, eight such kings are listed. The fact that each king died is also noted, except in the case of the last one, Hadar, who thus probably was still alive at the time Moses wrote. Three of them are listed as having a particular city of their own; there was evidently no permanent capital city in Edom, any more than a permanent dynasty.

The fourth king in the list, Hadad (besides the first and the last on the list, the only one to establish a city of his own), is especially notable apparently because of his victory over the Midianites in the "field of Moab." Since the Midianites lived south of Edom, and the Moabites north of Edom, it seems probable that the Midianites during this period had swept northward through Edom (or perhaps around to the east of Edom's mountains) on a mission of conquest into Moab, and that Hadad had taken his own army into Moab to defeat them. This is the only military exploit mentioned for any of these Edomite kings.

Genesis 36:40-43

---

40 And these *are* the names of the dukes *that came* of Ē′saù, according to their families, after their places, by their names; duke Tĭm′nàh, duke Ăl̓-vàh, duke Jē′thĕth,
41 Duke Ă-hŏl̓ĭ-bā′màh, duke Ē′làh, duke Pĭ′nŏn,

42 Duke Kē′năz, duke Tē′măn, duke Mĭb′zär,
43 Duke Măg′dĭ-ĕl, duke Ĭ′răm: these *be* the dukes of Ē′dŏm, according to their habitations in the land of their possession: he *is* Ē′saù the father of the Ē′dŏm-ĭtes.

These last verses of the chapter give the names of the more important dukes, or chieftains, descended from Esau — eleven in all. These names do not seem to be listed chronologically, but geographically; and they do not seem to have any necessary connection with any of the names listed previously in the chapter. Probably they refer to the main "dukedoms" of the country of Edom. The identification of the names with "families" and "places" is noted in verse 40. Thus, one can understand this section as saying essentially that "these are the names of the dukedoms of Esau . . . namely, the duke of Timnah, the duke of Alvah, the duke of Jetheth, [etc.]."

It is interesting that most of these "generations of Esau," including the material from about 36:15 through 36:43 (most of it, at least), have been incorporated in the genealogical lists of I Chronicles 1:35-54. Not only Moses, but the much later chronicler, considered them important enough to include in the genealogical records of Israel. It was vital that there be a perpetual distinction between the descendants of Jacob and Esau, but the Holy Spirit perhaps would assure us by the inclusion of these names in the inspired Word that God is forever concerned about every single individual.

19

The Testing of Joseph

(Genesis 37-39)

The Coat of Many Colors

We come now to one of the most interesting sections in the Bible, the fascinating story of Joseph and his experiences in Egypt. The events in Genesis 37 actually took place some years prior to Isaac's death, as recorded in Genesis 35:29. However, the record of Isaac's death (and the parenthetical record of Esau's descendants) seems to have been the concluding sections in the narrative kept and transmitted by Jacob. The story of Joseph's life must have been originally written down by the sons of Jacob, especially by Joseph himself. This is probably indicated by the reference in Exodus 1:1, terminating this account, to the "names of the children of Israel, which came into Egypt." This is essentially equivalent to the standard formula which would have said: "Now these are the generatiions of the children of Israel, which came into Egypt." This section, however, probably more than those preceding, had been subject to Moses' editorial emendations, in view of his more immediate connection to it. Hence the standard formula was slightly modified to indicate that this particular record was not as directly received and transmitted by him as had been those of the patriarchs earlier than Joseph and his brothers.

At this time Jacob and his family were dwelling near Isaac in Hebron (Genesis 35:27; 37:14). In fact, the narrative begins within about two years after they had reached Hebron, since Joseph was seventeen years old at this time (Genesis 37:2), and he had been about fifteen at the time of his mother's death shortly before they reached Hebron.

Genesis 37:1, 2a

CHAPTER 37

AND Jacob dwelt in the land wherein his father was a stranger, in the land of Cā'năan.

2 These *are* the generations of Jacob.

This, we believe, constitutes the concluding statement and the signature of Jacob's long record, beginning with Genesis 25:19b. Although he had trusted for years in God's promise that he would inherit the land, the same as God had promised Abraham and Isaac, he, like they, continued to live as a "foreigner" in the land of Canaan. They did not yet own the land, only certain very small portions that they had purchased. Nevertheless, God had indeed blessed them materially with great possessions, and they believed that the complete promise would surely be fulfilled in God's own time. "By faith [Abraham] sojourned in the land of promise, as in a strange country, dwelling in tabernacles with Isaac and Jacob, the heirs with him of the same promise. . . . These all died in faith, not having received the promises, but having seen them afar off, and were persuaded of them, and embraced them, and confessed that they were strangers and pilgrims on the earth" (Hebrews 11:9, 13).

Genesis 37:2b-4

Joseph, *being* seventeen years old, was feeding the flock with his brethren; and the lad *was* with the sons of Bĭl'hăh, and with the sons of Zĭl'păh, his father's wives: and Joseph brought unto his father their evil report.

3 Now Ĭş'rā-ĕl loved Joseph more than all his children, because he *was* the son of his old age: and he made him a coat of *many* colors.

4 And when his brethren saw that their father loved him more than all his brethren, they hated him, and could not speak peaceably unto him.

Here we begin the actual story of Joseph. Though he was a great man, Joseph hardly attained the spiritual stature of Abraham, Isaac, and Jacob. God never actually appeared to him, as He had to them, nor were the covenant promises given to him in any special way. In fact, of the sons of Jacob it was Judah, not he, through whom God would fulfill the coming of the Savior in times to come. His personal character, while morally pure, was marred by spiritual pride to a degree which his brothers finally found impossible to tolerate.

Many commentators have considered Joseph to be an almost perfect type of Christ. Though a number of interesting parallels can be noted, it should not be forgotten that the New Testament nowhere speaks of Joseph as a type of Christ. In view of the dangers inherent in allegorical interpretation, it is generally safest to avoid spiritualizing, allegorizing, and typological interpretations in general except where there is explicit Biblical warrant. Since such does not exist in the case of the narrative of Joseph, it seems best not to try to view Joseph in any special way as a type of Christ. His story is intensely interesting and instructive without that sort of embellishment.

Joseph's oldest brothers (Reuben, Simeon, Levi, Judah) were mature men by this time and apparently had duties in the family which kept them generally away from Joseph. Leah's other two (considerably younger) sons, Issachar and Zebulun, were also either with them or with their mother. Joseph stayed more with the sons of Bilhah and Zilpah (Dan, Naphtali, Gad, and Asher), who were nearer his own age, and so they had similar duties. Perhaps all five were still in process of learning the arts of shepherding and animal husbandry. Benjamin, of course, was still quite young, and was home with Jacob.

Jacob had already been rather bitterly disappointed in the behavior of his three oldest sons. Now Joseph began to bring him disturbing reports about his four sons by the two handmaids also. No doubt the reports were true, and Jacob needed to know them, but it is questionable whether Joseph should have become a talebearer in this way. In any case, he certainly did not endear himself to his brothers by so doing.

Joseph had probably been somewhat spoiled by his father, since he was born in his old age and also was the firstborn son of his favorite wife. Joseph's moral standards and spiritual interests, however, were clearly superior to those of his brothers, possibly because Jacob had taken more time to teach him such things (especially since the tragic experiences at Shechem and Edar). Jacob recognized Joseph's leadership capabilities by placing him in charge of the work of shepherding the flock, even though he was younger than the four brothers he was working with. The phrase "feeding the flock" actually connotes that he was "shepherd over the flock" (verse 2). His authority was also indicated by the "coat of colors" which his father made for him. The word "colors" (Hebrew *passim*) is uncertain in meaning, and newer translations often render it "long sleeves." In any case, it seems clear that the intent of this special garment was as a symbol of his authority and favored position in the family. Whether Jacob was wise in thus favoring Joseph is questionable, but he may well have had good reason to believe he was the one who could best be trusted with such authority, at least among these five.

Whatever may have been the merits of Jacob's decision, it certainly did not please the other brothers, increasing their resentment rather than improving their behavior. Joseph's abilities, no less than his moral standards, were much superior to those of the others. He was to Jacob as "a son of old age," or a "wise son," with intelligence beyond his years. Joseph could hardly help realizing his superiority, especially since his father also saw and utilized it. This was not properly conducive to humility on his part, to say the least.

Genesis 37:5-8

---

5 ¶ And Joseph dreamed a dream, and he told *it* his brethren: and they hated him yet the more.

6 And he said unto them, Hear, I pray you, this dream which I have dreamed:

7 For, behold, we *were* binding sheaves in the field, and, lo, my sheaf arose, and also stood upright; and, behold, your sheaves stood round about, and made obeisance to my sheaf.

8 And his brethren said to him, Shalt thou indeed reign over us? or shalt thou indeed have dominion over us? And they hated him yet the more for his dreams, and for his words.

At this time, Joseph had a remarkable dream. Scripture does not say whether this dream came from the Lord (although its later fulfillment makes this likely) or whether it was only an expression of Joseph's subconscious feelings and ambitions, or both. Just as his brothers resented him, so he no doubt longed for them to recognize and appreciate him, a desire which naturally tended to express itself more and more openly in his self-assertive conversations with them. In any case, even if the dream came from the Lord, it was for his own encouragement, not for their edification, and he was very unwise to insist on telling it to them.

Tell it to them he did, however, with the predictable result that his brothers hated him more than ever, not only because of his words but because they saw that even his subconscious thoughts centered on his desire for pre-eminence among them. The dream had to do with a field of corn, in which he and his brothers were going about the work of binding the corn in sheaves. The sheaf which he had bound suddenly rose and stood up, while the sheaves which his brothers had bound surrounded Joseph's sheaf and bowed down to it.

The meaning of the dream, at least as Joseph was understanding it, was quite obvious, and his brothers (probably all ten of his older brothers had heard it by now from him) fiercely resented it. They assured him in no uncertain terms that he would never have dominion over *them!*

Genesis 37:9-11

---

9 ¶ And he dreamed yet another dream, and told it his brethren, and said, Behold, I have dreamed a dream more; and, behold, the sun and the moon and the eleven stars made obeisance to me. 10 And he told *it* to his father, and to his brethren: and his father rebuked him, and said unto him, What *is* this dream that thou hast dreamed? Shall I and thy mother and thy brethren indeed come to bow down ourselves to thee to the earth? 11 And his brethren envied him; but his father observed the saying.

But then Joseph had still another dream, and this time, it was not only his brothers, but also his mother and father, who were bowing down to him! Though his mother was dead, she was represented in his dream in this way, or perhaps he could have interpreted the moon in his dream to represent Leah. In any case, he understood that he was to be pre-eminent over his entire family.

Once again, even assuming the dream came from the Lord, he was foolish and even arrogant to tell it, not only to his brothers this time but also to his father. The dream was intended for Joseph's own comfort, if for anything, and was not to be used as a club with which to intimidate his family. This time, even his father rebuked him. Jacob, who had known the Lord more intimately than anyone of his generation, had difficulty believing that this dream was anything but the product of Joseph's egocentric subconscious.

Regardless of whether Joseph should have reported the dream or not, it does seem likely that it really was sent from God. As unlikely as it may have seemed at the time, it eventually was fulfilled. Furthermore, almost the same symbols appeared in the visions of the apostle John (Revelation 12:1), again probably representing Israel and the twelve tribes. Though Jacob had felt he should rebuke Joseph for dreaming such things and for interpreting them as prophetic of his own future pre-eminence, he wondered in his heart whether Joseph might be right after all. He had himself observed and acknowledged that Joseph by his actions was more promising than his brothers. As far as the latter were concerned, however, they now not only hated but envied him.

Genesis 37:12-14

---

12 ¶ And his brethren went to feed their father's flock in Shĕ′chĕm.

13 And Iṣ′rä-ĕl said unto Joseph, Do not thy brethren feed *the flock* in Shĕ′chĕm? come, and I will send thee unto them. And he said to him, Here *am I.*

14 And he said to him, Go, I pray thee, see whether it be well with thy brethren, and well with the flocks; and bring me word again. So he sent him out of the vale of Hĕ′brŏn, and he came to Shĕ′chĕm.

An unusual, even strange, development took place at this time. Jacob and his sons were living at Hebron, at least fifty miles south of their old home in Shechem. Presumably there was adequate pasturage around Hebron, especially since Esau had moved away. For some reason, however, the older brothers decided to take the flocks back up to Shechem to feed. Perhaps they were reacting in anger against Joseph and Jacob's apparent favoritism. Perhaps they were somewhat homesick. Their father still owned property there (Genesis 33:19; John 4:5), and there was even an altar which he had built at that place. Even though they had left the area in fear of the inhabitants of the land after the massacre of the Shechemites, God had protected them. In addition, they were bold men; so they had apparently lost whatever hesitation they might have had in going back.

It is doubtful that Jacob would have agreed to this. Possibly they left without asking him because he had turned over most of the business affairs of the family to them by now. So they may simply have left word to be conveyed to him after they were gone. It would have taken several days for them to get there, and evidently a long period of time went by without his hearing from them; consequently he finally became quite concerned about them. What if the Canaanites and Perizzites of the region had indeed attacked them (Genesis 34:30)?

All ten of the sons of Israel (leaving only Joseph and Benjamin at home) had apparently gone to Shechem with the flocks. Finally, Jacob became so concerned about them that he decided to send Joseph to see how they were. He knew he could depend on Joseph for a reliable and truthful investigation and report, but he must have had some misgivings about sending him because of the length of the journey and the dangers of the land. As far as Joseph's brothers were concerned, at this time neither Joseph nor Jacob suspected the intense enmity which they carried for Joseph; otherwise Jacob surely would not have sent him. Even at that, Jacob's decision was put to Joseph in the form of a request, rather than a command. Joseph was quite willing to go, however. He was to locate his brothers, see how they and their flocks were doing, and then report back to his father.

Genesis 37:15-17

---

15 ¶ And a certain man found him, and, behold, *he was* wandering in the field: and the man asked him, saying, What seekest thou?

16 And he said, I seek my brethren: tell me, I pray thee, where they feed *their flocks.*

17 And the man said, They are departed hence; for I heard them say, Let us go to Dō'thăn. And Joseph went after his brethren, and found them in Dō'thăn.

Joseph no doubt made better time to Hebron than his brothers had done, since he was not encumbered by the flocks. However, it would have taken him at least two days to make the fifty miles. When he arrived at Shechem, he was dismayed to find they were not there. He roamed around the area, trying to find some clue as to what might have happened to them; but Shechem was apparently still in ruins and no one seemed to be around.

Finally, however, he met a man who could give him the information he desired. As the man scrutinized him, he could tell he was looking for something, and so questioned Joseph. Joseph knew that his brothers were well known (indeed notorious!) to the people of the vicinity; so there would be no doubt that, if his brothers and their extensive flocks had been there, this man would know about it. Joseph therefore confidently asked him where his brothers were feeding their flocks. Sure enough, the man had overheard them saying they planned to go on northward to Dothan. What the occasion of this decision may have been we are not told, but probably it was because of the good water supply and excellent pasturage there. They were in no mood to return home, and so had just kept on going farther away.

Rejected by His Brethren

Dothan was about twenty miles north of Shechem; so it took Joseph at least another day to reach there. The word "Dothan" is believed to mean "two cisterns," and was presumably so named because of two storage wells there. One of these cisterns was dry at the time Joseph's brothers were there, and it was into this well that they later decided to place him. Possibly both wells were dry, so that the men were perhaps frustrated at this point anyway, not finding water after they had led their flocks so far from home. Students who stress the typological aspects of this narrative suggest that the brothers represent the nation of Israel, wandering far from the Father's house while searching for greener pastures out in the world, but finding none. "For my people have committed two evils; they have forsaken me the fountain of living waters, and hewed them out cisterns, broken cisterns, that can hold no water" (Jeremiah 2:13).

In the further development of this type, Joseph is believed to represent the Lord Jesus Christ, who was sent from the Father to the chosen people, but who was rejected and slain by them. "He was in the world, and the world was made by him, and the world knew him not. He came unto his own, and his own received him not" (John 1:10, 11).

Genesis 37:18-22

---

18 And when they saw him afar off, even before he came near unto them, they conspired against him to slay him.
19 And they said one to another, Behold, this dreamer cometh.
20 Come now therefore, and let us slay him, and cast him into some pit, and we will say, Some evil beast hath devoured him; and we shall see what will become of his dreams.

21 And Reuben heard *it*, and he delivered him out of their hands; and said, Let us not kill him.
22 And Reuben said unto them, Shed no blood, *but* cast him into this pit that *is* in the wilderness, and lay no hand upon him; that he might rid him out of their hands, to deliver him to his father again.

Whether Joseph's experiences were divinely intended to foreshadow those of Christ, Scripture does not actually say. In any case, Joseph's own experiences were very real and harrowing. He had incurred the murderous hatred of his brothers, and as he approached them in Dothan, he little realized the awful deed they were about to plan. Though it would be a terrible and bitter experience for him, in the providence of God it would work together for good. He himself, with his serious personal problem of pride and arrogance, needed to learn humility and patience before his remarkable gifts of intellectual brilliance and political leadership could be put to God's use. His brothers, also, before they could be brought to genuine repentance and spiritual maturity, as necessary for the founders of the tribes of Israel, must be taught the awful consequences of sin and must themselves be brought low in confession and humiliation. Then, the nation which would come from their loins must also be prepared by suffering and divine deliverance to believe and trust God and His promises, as well as to obey His laws. All of this, in the providence of God, would be the ultimate outcome of the traumatic experience Joseph was about to undergo as he approached his brothers in Dothan.

They saw him coming a great way off, recognizing him by his colorful coat, which, as usual, he was wearing in pride of his position. They had been, no doubt, fretting about Joseph and his presumptuous dreams and boasts ever since they had left Hebron; in fact, it may very well have been because of him that they had left in the first place. What should have been a spirit of brotherly love and patient teaching of their younger brother had turned into a bitter spirit of jealousy and revenge. He was only their half-brother anyway. In view of their own background in a polygamous home, where there was bound to be a certain amount of feuding among the different families, combined with the low moral standards of the people with whom they had been in contact all their lives, it is not too surprising that they finally came to such a desperate decision as to do away with the problem which he had posed to them by actually doing away with him!

They were far from home and paternal restraint. As they saw him coming, they said sarcastically to each other: "Look yonder, here comes that specialist in dreams!" The Hebrew word for "dreamer" implies one who is a master at dreaming, perhaps suggesting that he is good for nothing else. They had no doubt previously been muttering about Joseph, and their anger had built to the point where they had actually discussed getting rid of him somehow. Now, here he was, giving them the perfect opportunity. They could slay him, throw him into one of the empty cisterns, and then report back to their father that he had been killed by a wild animal. That would be the end of his dreams!

Apparently this plan was hatched mainly by the younger brothers, perhaps supported by Simeon and Levi, since neither Reuben nor Judah would go along with it. Reuben, of all the brothers, would seem to have the most cause to resent Joseph, since Jacob obviously intended to give Joseph the birthright instead of him, the oldest son. His defense of Joseph is, therefore, the more commendable. Though he had lost his right of primogeniture through his incestuous relation with Bilhah, he must have truly repented of his deed, and tried henceforth as best he could under the circumstances to exercise the moral leadership which his firstborn position in the family should have elicited.

Reuben intended, if possible, to help Joseph escape back to his father, but he knew the murderous intent of the other brothers would not allow this immediately. He therefore persuaded them not to slay him right then, at least, but to catch him and throw him into the pit alive, perhaps letting him die of thirst rather than shedding his blood. They well knew God's primeval command against the shedding of human blood (Genesis 9:6). Though Simeon and Levi may have felt justified in shedding blood in the matter of the Shechemites, they realized that there was no such justification in this case; furthermore, Joseph was their father's son, even though he had made himself personally so obnoxious to them. Reuben was thus able to persuade them against the overt act of fratricide.

Joseph evidently realized that Reuben was really trying to save him; probably Reuben actually whispered words to this effect as they later cast him into the pit. Years later, Joseph indicated he remembered this by holding Simeon (the next oldest of the sons), rather than Reuben, captive in his prison (Genesis 42:24).

Genesis 37:23-28

23 ¶ And it came to pass, when Joseph was come unto his brethren, that they stripped Joseph out of his coat, *his* coat of *many* colors that *was* on him;
24 And they took him, and cast him into a pit: and the pit *was* empty, *there was* no water in it.
25 And they sat down to eat bread: and they lifted up their eyes and looked, and, behold, a company of Ĭsh′mā-ĕl-ītes came from Gĭl′ē-ăd, with their camels bearing spicery and balm and myrrh, going to carry *it* down to Egypt.

26 And Judah said unto his brethren, What profit *is it* if we slay our brother, and conceal his blood?
27 Come, and let us sell him to the Ĭsh′mā-ĕl-ītes, and let not our hand be upon him; for he *is* our brother *and* our flesh: and his brethren were content.
28 Then there passed by Mĭd′ĭ-ăn-ītes merchantmen; and they drew and lifted up Joseph out of the pit, and sold Joseph to the Ĭsh′mā-ĕl-ītes for twenty *pieces* of silver: and they brought Joseph into Egypt.

Having decided what they were going to do, the brothers laid hands on Joseph as soon as he reached them. The first thing they did was to strip off the resented coat of many colors (or long-sleeved coat, if that is what it was), his vaunted symbol of prestige. Then they threw him, probably violently, down into the dry well.

Reuben had persuaded them not to kill Joseph, doing this by craft rather than by overt moral leadership as, in his position of the eldest, he should have exercised. Probably he had forfeited much of his authority in his brothers' eyes by his sin with Bilhah, so that they had no great respect for him anymore. Simeon was, on the other hand, a strong-minded moral zealot, as the affair at Shechem had demonstrated; and he no doubt was the chief voice among the brothers on this occasion. After they had thrown Joseph into the cistern, they probably discussed at some length what to do with him. It was mealtime; so they sat down to eat while they were discussing it.

In the meantime, Reuben had left them, possibly distressed at the whole situation and not wanting to argue with them further. Perhaps he was intending, after they had left the locality, to come back by himself and free Joseph. Or he might have gone to take care of the flocks, since the others had apparently forgotten them. In any case, he was absent.

As they were eating, they saw other visitors coming in the distance—a caravan following the regular nearby trade route from the mountains of Gilead down into Egypt. Gilead was a plateau region east of the Jordan and extending down from about the Sea of Galilee to the Dead Sea. It was in that area that Laban and Jacob had had their confrontation some years before. It was a lushly forested region, specially known for its balms and spices.

The men in the caravan are called both Ishmaelites (verse 25) and Midianites (verse 28). This is not a contradiction; both Ishmael and Midian were sons of Abraham (Genesis 16:15; 25:2), and their respective descendants were often together. The two names were often used interchangeably (note, e.g., Judges 8:24, 26). Quite likely both groups were present in this caravan.

With Reuben gone, and most of the brothers still arguing that they should at least abandon Joseph to die in the pit even if they didn't actually shed his blood, Judah felt it was now his responsibility to save his life. He was the fourth oldest of the children of Israel, but the three older ones had already really forfeited their right to leadership. With his older brothers Simeon and Levi, however, joining with the rest who wanted to see Joseph dead, he really had little chance of saving him. At least, so it seemed.

Seeing the Ishmaelites, however, gave Judah an idea. Why not sell Joseph to them as a slave, whom they in turn could sell in Egypt? That way, Joseph would be removed from any further influence in the family—which was what the brothers wanted most—and still his life would be spared and they would not be guilty of murder. After all, he *was* their brother, and that should count for something. On top of that, they could actually make a financial profit for themselves.

With these arguments he convinced his brothers to sell Joseph into bondage, rather than to leave him to die in the pit. Probably they thought also that, even though the pit was in the wilderness (verse 22), there might still be some chance that some passer-by would rescue Joseph, in which case they would be entertaining the grave risk that he would return home and tell his father what they had done. Sending him as a slave into Egypt was clearly the best way of handling the whole problem.

When the Midianites reached them, they therefore hailed them and told them their proposition. After bargaining a bit, they settled on a price of twenty pieces of silver as Joseph's price. All this time, Joseph had been pleading with his brothers in "anguish of soul" (Genesis 42:21) from the bottom of the pit, but they would not listen. The deal was struck, Joseph was drawn up out of the pit, delivered over to the Midianites, and then carried by them down into Egypt. The price paid for Joseph was later fixed as the price of dedication for a young man or boy (Leviticus 27:5). The price of a mature slave was set at thirty pieces of silver (Exodus 21:32).

Genesis 37:29-33

---

29 ¶ And Reuben returned unto the pit; and, behold, Joseph *was* not in the pit; and he rent his clothes.

30 And he returned unto his brethren, and said, The child *is* not; and I, whither shall I go?

31 And they took Joseph's coat, and killed a kid of the goats, and dipped the coat in the blood;

32 And they sent the coat of *many* colors, and they brought *it* to their father; and said, This have we found: know now whether it *be* thy son's coat or no.

33 And he knew it, and said, *It is* my son's coat; an evil beast hath devoured him; Joseph is without doubt rent in pieces.

Evidently the brothers then left the vicinity of the pit and went about their business. Reuben, knowing they were gone, came back secretly, intending to free Joseph. To his surprise and dismay, Joseph was not there. He "rent his garments," a conventional way of expressing grief in those days. He then rushed to catch up with his brothers to tell them about Joseph's disappearance, only to find out what they had done with him. He realized he would be held responsible by his father, and was confused and disturbed over what he should do. It would be impossible now to rescue Joseph, and he certainly would be unable to tell his father what had really transpired.

They all finally settled on a convenient lie. They would lead their father to think Joseph had been slain by a wild beast, as they had originally intended to say anyway (verse 20). They would not overtly tell a lie, however; they would simply let their father deduce this from the evidence. They dipped Joseph's coat in the blood of a slain kid of the goats, and then had it brought to their father when they finally returned home. They said they had "found it" (not saying *where* they had found it), and wanted him to tell them whether he thought it might be Joseph's coat. Jacob, of course, immediately recognized it. But, rather than questioning his sons more carefully, in grief he jumped to the conclusion that Joseph had been slain by an animal and torn in pieces. (He evidently didn't stop to notice that the cloak was not torn in pieces.)

Genesis 37:34-36

---

34 And Jacob rent his clothes, and put sackcloth upon his loins, and mourned for his son many days.

35 And all his sons and all his daughters rose up to comfort him; but he refused to be comforted; and he said, For I will go down into the grave unto my son mourning. Thus his father wept for him.

36 And the Mĭd'ĭ-ăn-ites sold him into Egypt unto Pŏt'ĭ-phảr, an officer of Phả'raōh's, *and* captain of the guard.

Jacob was so grief-stricken that he tore his clothing, donned sackcloth (coarse garments something like a gunnysack), and went into a protracted period of great mourning. He had lost Rachel only a few years before; and now he had lost her first, and his favorite, son, the one to whom he had intended conveying the birthright and who would be the best equipped to carry on the responsibilities of spiritual leadership in the family and the nation which they would establish.

Jacob continued mourning for so many days that finally his sons became seriously concerned and tried to "comfort" him (a sharp commentary on their hypocrisy). His daughters also tried to comfort him. This is the first mention of any daughters besides Dinah, though they are also mentioned in Genesis 46:7, 15, so that he must have had at least one other daughter by this time. No one could comfort him, however, so great was his loss. He said that he would continue to mourn until he actually died and went to his son in *Sheol* (translated "the grave," but really referring to the place of departed spirits).

In the meantime, the caravan of Ishmaelites had arrived in Egypt. There they sold Joseph, who was obviously a healthy and intelligent young man, to a prominent Egyptian official named Potiphar. Potiphar is called an "officer," but the Hebrew word is *saris,* meaning "eunuch," which fact is no doubt partially explanatory of his wife's later attempt to seduce Joseph. His office was the rather unsavory duty of captain of the "guard," or, more literally, the "slaughterers" or "executioners" for Pharaoh, the king of Egypt. It was a drastically different household into which Joseph came, in comparison to that which he had left. For a long time, he was no doubt intensely homesick and bitterly resentful of what his brothers had done to him. Time and events, however, would eventually ameliorate both his homesickness and resentment.

Judah

The time that elapsed between the events of Genesis 37, when Joseph was sent into Egypt, and those of chapter 47, which describe the coming of Jacob into Egypt, was about twenty-two years (Genesis 37:2; 41:46; 41:53; 45:6). It is strange and sad that almost the only information we have concerning Joseph's family back in Canaan during that period (except concerning their trips down into Egypt to buy corn) is the tale of Judah's shameful experience with Tamar, as recorded in Genesis 38. Jacob during this time was apparently so occupied with his grief that he did little useful work; and the ten brothers were busy with their own affairs, doing their jobs and raising their families. The only one of them who had shown any spiritual promise at all (not counting Benjamin, who had been just a child when Joseph was sold into slavery) was Judah. Apparently the writer of this part of the record did not deem it worthwhile to include further information concerning the other brothers, in view of their atrocious behavior toward Joseph. Reuben, though not participating in the crime, had already lost his right to leadership.

Judah, however, seemed to have some sense of moral and spiritual responsibility. Consequently, now that Joseph was gone, Jacob probably had decided to convey to him the patriarchal leadership he had once intended for Joseph. This chapter in Genesis, however, which almost seems to have been inserted parenthetically, shows that even Judah could behave very selfishly and carnally.

Genesis 38:1-5

CHAPTER 38

AND it came to pass at that time, that Judah went down from his brethren, and turned in to a certain Ă-dŭl-lăm-īte, whose name *was* Hī'răh.

2 And Judah saw there a daughter of a certain Cā'năan-īte, whose name *was* Shŭ'à; and he took her, and went in unto her.

3 And she conceived, and bare a son; and he called his name Ẽr.

4 And she conceived again, and bare a son; and she called his name Õ'năn.

5 And she yet again conceived, and bare a son; and called his name Shẽ'lăh: and he was at Chẽ'zĭb, when she bare him.

"At that time," Scripture says, Judah decided to leave his brothers and move his tent somewhere else. This seems to tie Judah's move to the events surrounding Joseph's sale into slavery, and may well have been occasioned by it. Judah was possibly so disturbed by his brothers' actions, and his father's resulting grief, that he resolved to get away from the entire situation. He did not, however, abdicate his family duties and responsibilities, as we find him later going with the rest of his brothers down into Egypt to buy grain. He evidently simply wanted to get away by himself for a while, perhaps to think things over with respect to the future, especially if, as seems at least possible, Jacob had begun to tell him something concerning his future role as leader of the nation and ancestor of the Messiah.

Actually, he did not go far away from the family headquarters, and certainly not beyond the circuit within which they took their flocks for pasture. Adullam, where he went, was not nearly so far away as Shechem or Dothan. Adullam was a small, and long established, Canaanite settlement about eight miles northwest of the family home. Judah also was evidently looking for a wife. He realized it would be essentially impossible for him or his brothers to find a wife among Laban's people, as Isaac and Jacob had been able to do, since they were now as far gone in idolatry as the rest of the world. Esau's family also was now a mixture of Semitic and Canaanitic stock, as was Ishmael's. God could lead Judah to a suitable bride anywhere, of course, and she could be taught to know and serve the true God, in order to be a proper mother for the kingly line which would come through him.

Judah had become friendly with an Adullamite named Hirah, and decided to live near him. He soon became acquainted with others in the community, including an attractive young daughter of a Canaanite named Shua. Since Judah was evidently looking for a wife, he decided (much too quickly, as it turned out) that this woman was the one he was looking for. There is no indication that he consulted his father, Jacob, in the matter, nor even the girl's father, Shua. He apparently simply married her on his own initiative. Since Judah was destined to be the ancester of the Messiah, he should have been much more cautious in selecting the proper wife. Shua's daughter, though physically attractive to him, was a true Canaanite, not only in parentage but in character, and was evidently unwilling to be converted to the worship of Jehovah. It is true that the Bible does not say this, but the inference is justified in view of the fact that all three of her sons were rejected by God from carrying on Judah's patriarchal line. Two of them, at least, were notoriously wicked, and it is likely that their characters largely reflected their mother's character and teaching.

Evidently her three sons were born in fairly rapid succession. They were named Er (meaning "watcher," so named by Judah), Onan (meaning "strong," named by his mother), and Shelah (also named by his mother, the meaning of the name being uncertain). It is interesting to note this apparent increasing dominance by the mother in the family. By the time of Shelah's birth, they had moved to Chezib, evidently a small town near Adullam.

Genesis 38:6-10

---

6 And Judah took a wife for Ĕr his firstborn, whose name *was* Tā'màr.

7 And Ĕr, Judah's firstborn, was wicked in the sight of the LORD; and the LORD slew him.

8 And Judah said unto Ō'năn, Go in unto thy brother's wife, and marry her, and raise up seed to thy brother.

9 And Ō'năn knew that the seed should not be his; and it came to pass, when he went in unto his brother's wife, that he spilled *it* on the ground, lest that he should give seed to his brother.

10 And the thing which he did displeased the LORD: wherefore he slew him also.

As Er grew into his late teens, Judah was anxious to obtain a wife for his oldest son. Though he had relied on his own judgment in selecting *his* wife, apparently he realized by now he had not made the best choice, and he resolved not to let Er make the same mistake he had made. Judah realized that, since he was Jacob's spiritual heir, it was important that his own heir have the right kind of wife. Knowing the weak and sinful character of his sons as he must have by this time, he probably felt it was all the more important that a wife be selected for his oldest son who would be a good influence on her husband, as well as on her chidren.

He finally found Tamar, a girl he apparently judged suitable for such needs. Though nothing is said about her background, we believe the above inferences are warranted from all the recorded circumstances. As things later developed, Tamar was indeed to be the mother of the messianic line from Judah; so we must assume that God Himself, in the long view, must have participated in this choice. Tamar must therefore have been the most suitable woman for this purpose in her generation, regardless of her questionable actions. Judah made the necessary arrangements, and Er was married to Tamar, evidently while he was still a very young man, probably in his teens.

It seems, however, that Er was a rebellious son, and he probably bitterly resented this arrangement of his father. Tamar was not at all the kind of wife he wanted; in fact, he probably was not yet willing to be married to anyone. Though his father had certainly discussed the matter with him, and explained his reasons, Er was not in the least interested in exercising spiritual leadership in the family, and had every intention to follow his mother's Canaanite religion rather than to worship Jehovah.

Once again, it is true that the Bible does not give these details; so we cannot be overly dogmatic in reading such things between the lines. All that Scripture says is that Er was "wicked in the eyes of the Lord." The most natural inference, however, is that Er's wickedness somehow had to do with his position as Judah's "firstborn" in relation to his presumed spiritual responsibilities. In view of Onan's specific sin, which later resulted in *his* death also, it seems most probable that Er's sin had to do with his refusal to consummate the marriage with Tamar as arranged for him by his father.

Judah wanted Tamar as a wife for his son in order that she might produce a son herself, to carry on the Judaic line. Er, however, rebelled against this intention, not wanting to have a wife and son who would follow Jehovah. Consequently he refused to "go in unto" Tamar. For this overt rebellion against God's purpose in Israel, "the Lord slew him." Exactly how the Lord put him to death we are not told, but it was in some way which clearly tied his death to his own wickedness against God.

It was already a custom in those days that, if a man died without children, his next younger brother should marry his wife and "raise up seed to his brother." The first son from such a marriage would then be recognized legally as the son and heir of the dead brother. This was the so-called Levirate marriage, which later was incorporated as a part of the Mosaic law (Deuteronomy 25:5-10; Matthew 22:24). Judah had an obligation to Tamar, having contracted with her and her father to marry his son, and no doubt had told her something about the spiritual responsibilities and privileges this would entail. Tamar was agreeable, even anxious, to fulfill her own duties in this arrangement, but had been thwarted by Er's rebellion against it and his subsequent death.

The obvious step to be taken, therefore, was to enforce the Levirate (a word from the Latin *levir,* meaning "brother-in-law") regulation, which was a common part of the legal codes of the nations even before Moses, and to have Tamar marry Judah's second son, Onan. Accordingly, this was done.

Onan, however, was of the same mind as his brother in this matter. No doubt he was supported in this attitude, perhaps encouraged in it in the first place, by his mother. At the same time, he was aware of the fate which had taken his brother, and so was torn between fear of disobeying his father's God and his antipathy toward the idea of being the father of Tamar's son. He especially disliked the idea of fathering a son who would not be reckoned as his.

In his indecisiveness, he did go ahead and marry Tamar and actually "went in unto his brother's wife." At the last moment, however, he changed his mind and "spilled the seed on the ground." As a result, the Lord was greatly displeased, and slew Onan also.

It should be noted that it was not the overt act of spilling the seed on the ground that occasioned Onan's death, but rather his rebellion against his duty to give Tamar a son. The term "onanism" has come to be applied to masturbation; but it is clear that God's judgment was not visited on Onan either for practicing masturbation, or for so-called coitus interruptus, or for involuntary nocturnal emissions (which, physically speaking, involve the same phenomenon), but rather for his *motive* in thus refusing to consummate the marital act with Tamar. The Bible is silent with respect to the moral connotations of such practices as the above, or even with respect to birth control measures in general, though it does condemn adultery, homosexuality, incest, and sodomy in no uncertain terms. As far as sexual practices which are not explicitly either approved or condemned in the Bible are concerned, they should be evaluated in the light of those principles which Scripture sets forth regarding "doubtful things" in general (e.g., Romans 14:1-4, 13-16, 21-23; I Corinthians 10:31; Colossians 3:17).

Genesis 38: 11, 12

---

11 Then said Judah to Tā′mȧr his daughter-in-law, Remain a widow at thy father's house, till Shē′lȧh my son be grown: for he said, Lest peradventure he die also, as his brethren *did*. And Tā′mȧr went and dwelt in her father's house.

12 ¶ And in process of time the daughter of Shụ′ȧ Judah's wife died; and Judah was comforted, and went up unto his sheepshearers to Tĭm′năth, he and his friend Hī′rȧh the Ȧ-dŭl′lăm-īte.

One can imagine Judah's dismay at these developments. Two of his sons were already dead, without issue, while still in their teens. He had one other son, Shelah, and the proper thing to do would be to have him now marry Tamar. However, Judah was reluctant to have Shelah die also, and he evidently feared that Shelah's attitude would be the same as had been Er's and Onan's. Shelah certainly would not *want* to marry Tamar, and his mother would no doubt resist it vehemently.

Still, Judah did have a serious obligation to Tamar, and he did want a grandson who would carry on his family line and patriarchal leadership. Not knowing what to do, he simply deferred his decision for a time. Shelah was not really quite old enough to get married anyway; so he told Tamar to wait for a while until Shelah was older. In the meantime, Judah sent Tamar back to her father's home, thinking perhaps that her presence in his own household was too great a source of irritation to his wife and his one remaining son. He may have more or less decided that he would, by sending her away, cause her to forget the whole matter, in which case he would not have to make Shelah marry her. As things later developed, of course, Shelah did not marry Tamar. That he did marry someone, however, is evident, in that he became the ancestor of the Shelanites, in the tribe of Judah (Numbers 26:20).

Sometime after Tamar left, still another tragedy struck the household of Judah. His own wife died. She must still have been a relatively young woman, because Judah could hardly have been more than forty; and so it seems likely that her death may also have been in the nature of a judgment from the Lord, reflecting her own responsibility in the training of Er and Onan and their resulting attitudes of bitter rebellion against God.

Judah's grief was not overmuch, however. His home life with her had hardly been a happy one. After a suitable period of mourning, "Judah was comforted." He quickly got back into the routine of his business life, taking care of his flocks and herds. They were at the time being pastured up near Timnath (same as "Timnah"), a town a few miles from Adullam. The time of sheep-shearing was usually a time of festivity and merrymaking, so Judah decided to go up to Timnath for the occasion, taking his friend Hirah along with him. He had seemingly forgotten all about Tamar and his commitment to her, even though by this time Shelah was old enough to marry her. Possibly he even took Shelah along with him and Hirah, since Shelah's mother was now dead, and he was old enough to participate in the shearing operations and also to enjoy the accompanying festivities.

Genesis 38:13-19

---

13 And it was told Tā'mȧr, saying, Behold, thy father-in-law goeth up to Tĭm'nȧth to shear his sheep.

14 And she put her widow's garments off from her, and covered her with a veil, and wrapped herself, and sat in an open place, which *is* by the way to Tĭm'nȧth; for she saw that Shē'lȧh was grown, and she was not given unto him to wife.

15 When Judah saw her, he thought her *to be* a harlot; because she had covered her face.

16 And he turned unto her by the way, and said, Go to, I pray thee, let me come in unto thee; (for he knew not that she *was* his daughter-in-law:) and she said, What wilt thou give me, that thou mayest come in unto me?

17 And he said, I will send *thee* a kid from the flock. And she said, Wilt thou give *me* a pledge, till thou send *it*?

18 And he said, What pledge shall I give thee? And she said, Thy signet, and thy bracelets, and thy staff that *is* in thine hand. And he gave *it* her, and came in unto her, and she conceived by him.

19 And she arose, and went away, and laid by her veil from her, and put on the garments of her widowhood.

Tamar had not forgotten Judah and Shelah, however. It had not been her fault that Er and Onan had died; she had been willing and anxious to fulfill her contracted responsibilities as wife and mother. She was being treated as though it was her fault, however, and her life back in her father's household was undoubtedly quite unhappy. She had left there once, intending to follow Judah's God, but now she was forced to go back into a pagan home. Under the circumstances, her father could not have been very pleased to have her back again either.

Furthermore, it was evident by this time that Judah did not intend to keep his agreement with her regarding Shelah. Whether or not she would ever have any other hope of marriage and children, in view of her particular experiences, which would be almost certain to be interpreted with superstitious fear by any prospective Canaanite husbands, we do not know. Anyway, it seems most likely that, having been converted through Judah to faith in God's covenant promises, she truly longed to play the part in God's plan which Judah had promised her.

Finally, she became desperate and decided that, if she was ever going to become the mother of the Judaic line as Judah had promised her, it would have to be accomplished outside of an actual marriage relationship with Judah's son. She would have to arrange for Shelah, or perhaps even Judah himself, to have intercourse with her without realizing it, since he would never do so intentionally.

Whether she considered Shelah in such plans may be questioned. It is probable that she deliberately chose Judah himself. She was considerably older than Shelah, and it was actually Judah with whom she had made her agreement anyhow. He had been responsible for her decision to come into the family of the household of faith, the nation of Israel. She admired Judah, and perhaps even loved him. She began, therefore, to watch for an opportunity to get him to make love to her.

Such an opportunity came when she learned he had gone to join his sheepshearers in Timnath. She took off her widow's clothing and put on the attire of a temple prostitute. This included a veil, which would prevent her being recognized. She then seated herself by the wayside in a spot where she knew Judah would encounter her, near Timnath. She hoped that, when he saw her, he would employ her "services" as a prostitute, and thus give her the long-awaited opportunity to become the mother of his successors in the Judaic line.

It is difficult for us properly to evaluate the moral implications of this device of Tamar. Under normal circumstances, Scripture condemns harlotry in vigorous terms. In the Mosaic law, the penalty for adultery was death by stoning (Deuteronomy 22:20-24); if the daughter of a priest became a harlot, she was to be put to the flames (Leviticus 21:9). In a sense, Tamar was betrothed to Shelah and this would make her guilty of adultery. In reality, however, it was her father-in-law himself who was preventing her from actually marrying Shelah. This circumstance, in effect, had therefore freed her from that engagement. She was, in her view, merely trying to assure the fulfillment of the essence of the marriage covenant which Judah had made with her in the first place.

Considering her Canaanite background, in which promiscuity was practically a way of life, one should not condemn her actions too severely. Even the profession of temple prostitute was considered respectable. It is known that in many such ancient religious systems, all the women of the community were expected to devote themselves on occasion to this practice, as an actual votive offering to their pagan gods and goddesses. That she was actually posing as such a temple prostitute, rather than as a common harlot, is evident from the fact that the word used to describe her later by the Canaanite men themselves (Hebrew *cedesha,* meaning "one set apart," as used in verses 21 and 22) was the word used for this purpose.

Furthermore, her motive in so doing was neither lust nor money, but rather ensuring her place in the covenant family, for which she had so longed but which it seemed was about to be denied her. She was surely no ordinary harlot. It must also be recognized that the Biblical record itself does not condemn or criticize her. Indeed, her decision and her action at this point did accomplish exactly what she intended, for she became the mother of the ancestor of King David and, eventually, of the Messiah. God is not bound by human stratagems, of course; but one would be justified in concluding that God placed His approval on Tamar's action in this case, at least if we are to judge by the result which God allowed to be accomplished by it.

We cannot judge Judah's actions so charitably, however. In fact, he later acknowledged that he had sinned (verse 26). It is perhaps understandable, though hardly excusable, that he would desire a woman on this occasion. He had suffered for many years with an unhappy marriage and a wife who probably loved neither him nor his religion. The fact that he had only the three sons, and these early in his marriage, suggests that he may not have been able to have marital relations with his wife for a long time. Now that his wife was dead, the sheep-shearing accomplished, and the general hilarity of the festivities stirring his passions, the sight of the beautifully attired woman by the wayside was more than he could resist. He must have known quite well that sex outside of marriage was not pleasing to the God whom he was trying, however poorly, to serve, but he (like many others since) was a rather weak and carnal believer, and he justified himself on the basis of all his other trials and tribulations and his own immediate physical needs, which could be satisfied in no other way, so he thought.

Therefore he turned aside to Tamar and struck up a bargain with her for her favors. He agreed to send her a kid from his flock in payment. In the meantime, until he could return to his flock and obtain a kid, he would leave with her a "pledge" in the form of his signet, his bracelets, and his staff. These items probably were, respectively, his seal, the cords by which the seal was strapped to his arms, and a rod with his own particular insignia attached to its head. In any case, they were items which were particularly his, and thus would be identified with him and no other.

He then "came in unto her, and she conceived by him." Her purpose was accomplished, and she certainly did not wish to continue in this distasteful role as a prostitute. As soon as he left, she returned home and dressed herself in her widow's garments.

Genesis 38:20-23

---

20 And Judah sent the kid by the hand of his friend the Ă-dŭl'lăm-ite, to receive *his* pledge from the woman's hand: but he found her not.

21 Then he asked the men of that place, saying, Where *is* the harlot, that *was* openly by the wayside? And they said, There was no harlot in this *place*.

22 And he returned to Judah, and said, I cannot find her; and also the men of the place said, *that* there was no harlot in this *place*.

23 And Judah said, Let her take *it* to her, lest we be shamed: behold, I sent this kid, and thou hast not found her.

After Judah went home, he obtained a kid from his flock, as he had pledged, and asked his friend Hirah the Adullamite to take it to her and bring back the personal items he had left with her to secure his pledge. Possibly he was somewhat ashamed of what he had done, and did not want to face the woman again or to be seen talking to her. Hirah the Canaanite had no such compunction.

However, search and inquire as he would, Hirah could find neither the woman nor anyone who remembered ever seeing her there. The men who were regularly in the area assured him that there was no prostitute who frequented that place. Mystified, Hirah finally had to return to Judah with his mission unfulfilled.

Judah decided to let the matter drop there, not wanting to advertise what he had done any more than necessary. He had tried to fulfill his agreement to pay the woman with a kid of the flock; but since she was no longer where he could reach her, he felt that should be the end of the matter. As far as the tokens he had left with her were concerned, she could keep them if she wished, though it was difficult to see how they could be of any value to her. Little did he know!

Genesis 38:24-26

24 ⁋ And it came to pass about three months after, that it was told Judah, saying, Tā'mär thy daughter-in-law hath played the harlot; and also, behold, she *is* with child by whoredom. And Judah said, Bring her forth, and let her be burnt.
25 When she *was* brought forth she sent to her father-in-law, saying, By the man, whose these *are, am* I with child: and she said, Discern, I pray thee, whose *are* these, the signet, and bracelets, and staff.
26 And Judah acknowledged *them,* and said, She hath been more righteous than I; because that I gave her not to Shē'läh my son. And he knew her again no more.

It was some three months later when Judah heard a bit of shocking news. His daughter-in-law, Tamar, was pregnant! He was righteously indignant. Not only had she somehow been the occasion of the death of two of his sons, but here she had disgraced their memory, and his own name as well, by an adulterous intrigue with some nameless lover. She had, as it were, "played the harlot." What an ingrate she must be, to repay his kindness and love to her with such behavior as this!

Even though she was living back in her own father's home, she was still under Judah's authority, nominally engaged to his son Shelah. The penalty for adultery in such a case, even in an ungodly society like that of Canaan, was death, as may be observed in the Code of Hammurabi and other ancient codes. In all such systems there seems to have been a double standard, with much more severe penalties being imposed on the woman than on the man, evidently on the basis of the shame attached to a man having some other man's child born in his family.

Consequently, Judah immediately judged Tamar to be guilty of a capital crime and ordered her to be burned. It may be, also, that he was subconsciously happy at this unexpected opportunity to solve the vexatious problem of how to avoid marrying Shelah to Tamar. In the process of interrogating her as to the other guilty party, however, Judah suddenly experienced an even greater shock. He himself—self-righteous Judah!—had been the adulterer responsible for her condition. There was no doubt about it, because she brought forth his seal and cord and staff to prove it. Tamar did know enough about Judah that she had confidence he would treat her fairly, once he saw the full truth of the situation. The mystery of the vanishing harlot was solved, and he immediately realized not only what she had done, but why she had done it. No longer could he be angry, but only repentant and compassionate. She had been more righteous than he. Rather than slaying her and her unborn child, he would care for them as his own. He could no longer give her to Shelah, nor would it be right for him to live with her as husband and wife, but he would at least acknowledge her son as his heir.

Genesis 38:27-30

27 ¶ And it came to pass in the time of her travail, that, behold, twins *were* in her womb.

28 And it came to pass, when she travailed, that *the one* put out *his* hand: and the midwife took and bound upon his hand a scarlet thread, saying, This came out first.

29 And it came to pass, as he drew back his hand, that, behold, his brother came out: and she said, How hast thou broken forth? *this* breach *be* upon thee: therefore his name was called Phā'rēz.

30 And afterward came out his brother, that had the scarlet thread upon his hand: and his name was called Zā'ràh.

As it turned out, Tamar, instead of bearing one son, was to be the mother of two sons. The entire situation was, in many respects, similar to the birth of Jacob and Esau, with an apparent conflict between the two sons even before birth. There seemed almost to be a contest between the two as to which would have the honor of being firstborn.

The midwife attending the birth first saw a tiny hand emerge and, in order to keep the twins distinct, assuming this one would be born first, she tied a scarlet thread on his hand. But then, surprisingly, his hand drew back, and the other twin forged ahead and came out first. The latter was named Pharez, meaning "breaking-through," in token of the manner of his birth. The other was named Zerah, meaning "rising." It was he on whose hand had been tied the scarlet thread.

There is another interesting parallel between the birth of Rebekah's twin boys and those of Tamar. In the former case, the firstborn came out with a reddish color, which (along with the red pottage for which he sold his birthright) occasioned his nickname, Edom. His twin brother, Jacob, held on to his heel as he emerged, and, even though he was not firstborn, was the one chosen to receive the covenant promises. In the case of Tamar's twins, the one that apparently was to be firstborn was likewise marked with a scarlet color, but replaced by his brother who was the one destined to inherit the promises.

Incidentally, there is no connection between the scarlet thread (Hebrew *shani*) of Zerah and the line of scarlet thread (Hebrew *chut*) used by Rahab (Joshua 2:18, 21). The two words are quite different, even though some commentators have attempted to find parallel typological teachings in the two stories.

Both brothers, as well as Judah's other living son, Shelah, eventually became ancestors of large families in the tribe of Judah. It was Pharez, however, who was the ancestor of David, and eventually of Jesus Christ.

Tamar, therefore, had the distinction of being one of the few women whose names are listed in the official genealogy of Jesus (Matthew 1:3). The others were Rahab, Ruth, and the one who had been wife of Uriah, that is, Bathsheba (Matthew 1:5, 6). It is remarkable that all four of these women were non-Jews who had been won by other witnesses to the true faith of Jehovah. Tamar was a Canaanite, Rahab a native of Jericho and thus presumably also a Canaanite, Ruth was a Moabitess, and Bathsheba probably a Hittite (at least by marriage to Uriah, if not by birth). Each of the four came into the family of Judah and Israel by morally dubious means. Tamar posed as a prostitute in order to become pregnant by Judah, Rahab was a harlot by profession until she married Salmon after the Israelites captured Jericho, Ruth persuaded Boaz to marry her by the questionable device of spending the night with him as he slept intoxicated on the threshing floor, and Bathsheba became wife of King David by first committing adultery with him. Yet in spite of the apparently unsavory past of these women, each one became a strong and faithful believer in God; and God signally honored them by placing them in the genealogical line of the Messiah. The one who was, in her early life, probably the most irreligious and carnal of all of them, Rahab, has actually been included by the Holy Spirit in the great catalog of the heroes of faith in the New Testament (Hebrews 11:31). What a marvelous testimony to God's grace, and the truth that God forgives past sins and brings new life!

Potiphar's Wife

The narrative now returns to Joseph, upon whom it centers throughout most of the rest of the Book of Genesis. Chapter 37 had closed with a brief mention of the fact that he had been sold by the Midianites who purchased him from his brothers as a slave to an Egyptian officer named Potiphar. The first verse of this chapter refers to these men as Ishmaelites, indicating again that the two terms were essentially synonymous.

The Egypt into which Joseph entered was, of course, a very ancient nation already. It was a highly civilized and organized empire, yet one which was polytheistic and immoral in its faith and practice. Egyptologists have never come to full agreement about Egyptian chronology, though it is largely upon this chronology that much of the dating of ancient history depends. The records of Manetho, an Egyptian priest of the third century B.C., constitute the most complete set of king lists. Manetho listed thirty-one dynasties (ruling families), giving the years of reign of each king within each dynasty. It is not clear, however, how many of these may have been contemporary dynasties in Upper and Lower Egypt, and how many ruled over the entire kingdom. The first pharaoh (meaning "Great House") was Menes, who was evidently the first to unite the two divisions of Egypt. The actual date of Menes' reign has been variously estimated, all the way from 5500 B.C. (Petrie) to 2000 B.C. (Sharpe). Probably the majority of Egyptologists date Menes at about 3100 B.C., but a vigorous group of modern writers who have studied outside the usual tradition have offered strong arguments favoring a reduction of the entire Egyptian chronological framework by several hundred years (Velikovsky,[1] Courville,[2] etc.). The question as to the number and duration of successive Egyptian dynasties thus has to be regarded as still unsetted at this time, and therefore also the particular pharaoh and date of Joseph's sojourn in Egypt.

Probably most scholars believe that this was during the reign of the Hyksos kings in Egypt. They were foreign invaders, probably at least partially of Semitic stock, who came from the East and conquered Egypt, according to the standard chronology, about 1720 B.C. They were also called the "Shepherd Kings." Many believe that it was because of their Semitic origin that the rulers of Egypt in Joseph's day treated the children of Israel so well when Jacob and his family moved to Egypt. The Hyksos were expelled from Egypt prior to Moses' time, so that the pharaoh of the new dynasty "knew not Joseph," and soon began to persecute these Hebrew "relatives" of the Hyksos. While this general background and its inferences may be correct, they should not be regarded as firmly established.

Genesis 39:1-6

CHAPTER 39

AND Joseph was brought down to Egypt; and Pŏt'i-phăr, an officer of Phä'raōh, captain of the guard, an Egyptian, bought him of the hands of the Ish'mā-ĕl-ītes, which had brought him down thither.

2 And the LORD was with Joseph, and he was a prosperous man; and he was in the house of his master the Egyptian.

3 And his master saw that the LORD was with him, and that the LORD made all that he did to prosper in his hand.

4 And Joseph found grace in his sight, and he served him: and he made him overseer over his house, and all *that* he had he put into his hand.

1. Immanuel Velikovsky, *Ages in Chaos* (New York: Macmillan, 1952), 350 pp.
2. Donovan Courville, *The Exodus Problem* (Loma Linda, Calif.: Crest Challenge Books, 1971), 2 vols., 687 pp.

5 And it came to pass from the time *that* he had made him overseer in his house, and over all that he had, that the Lord blessed the Egyptian's house for Joseph's sake; and the blessing of the Lord was upon all that he had in the house, and in the field.

6 And he left all that he had in Joseph's hand; and he knew not aught he had, save the bread which he did eat. And Joseph was a goodly person, and well-favored.

Potiphar, to whom Joseph was sold, was captain of Pharaoh's bodyguard, and also probably in charge of political executions ordered by Pharaoh. He is also called an "officer" of Pharaoh, the Hebrew word being *saris,* meaning "eunuch," or "chamberlain." It was evidently customary in ancient pagan countries, beginning with Sumeria, to require prominent officers associated closely with the king's court to be castrated, perhaps to ensure full-hearted devotion to the duties required of them and to minimize the possibility of their taking over the kingdom by military coup to establish a dynasty of their own. Since Potiphar was a married man, it would seem either that Potiphar had consented to such an operation after he was married in order to acquire his high office or else that his wife had married him for political or financial reasons rather than for normal marital relations. In either case, it is perhaps understandable, though hardly justifiable, that she would be prone to adulterous episodes from time to time.

Joseph was a highly intelligent and personable young man, and Potiphar soon recognized his abilities, placing more and more responsibilities on him. Though Joseph did have a natural problem with personal pride, and it was probably in part because of this that God allowed him to pass through so many difficult and humiliating experiences, he was indeed of high moral integrity and industry, and the Lord therefore prospered his work for Potiphar in an extraordinary way. It is not unusual that unbelieving employers, though themselves indifferent to God, recognize that earnest Christians make the best employees and hence desire to have them in their organizations. Honesty, integrity, faithfulness, sobriety, and similar characteristics are genuine assets to an employer; and such are the fruits of Christian faith and obedience.

It may even be that, because of these attributes, the employee will occasionally have opportunity to give a word of testimony to his "boss" as to the true source of the blessing that attends his activities. This seems to have been the case with Joseph and Potiphar, since "his master saw that the Lord was with him, and that the Lord made all that he did to prosper in his hand." More and more responsibility did Potiphar turn over to Joseph, until everything in his household and business affairs was under Joseph's oversight.

Just as the Lord made everything Joseph did "to prosper in his hand," so will it be with Christ in His exaltation: "He shall see his seed, he shall prolong his days, and the pleasure of the Lord shall prosper in his hand" (Isaiah 53:10). It is a beautiful token of God's grace that He often blesses even the masters (or, in modern parlance, the employers or supervisors) of those servants who are faithful to Him.

It is interesting that three times (verses 1, 2, 5) Potiphar is specifically called an "Egyptian." Since Joseph was in Egypt, this would seem unnecessary, even tautological, except on the supposition that Pharaoh and most of the rulers of Egypt were themselves *not* Egyptians, as would indeed be the case if this was the time of the Hyksos dynasties.

Potiphar eventually came to trust Joseph so implicitly that he no longer even bothered to check up on his own business. He knew that he would prosper more by completely forgetting it all than by checking the records, offering suggestions of his own, and so forth.

In addition to his assets of mind and character, Joseph was of handsome physique and countenance. A similar statement was made much later relative to young David (I Samuel 16:12), whom God also selected for a high calling and special service. On the other hand, even in the same context, Scripture makes it clear that it is not such outward features that matter with the Lord (I Samuel 16:7), but the attitude of the heart. Absalom, for example, was also of handsome appearance (II Samuel 14:25), but his heart was vindictive and filled with personal ambition and rebellion, and he came to a bitter end.

Genesis 39:7-10

---

7 ⁋ And it came to pass after these things, that his master's wife cast her eyes upon Joseph; and she said, Lie with me.
8 But he refused, and said unto his master's wife, Behold, my master wotteth not what *is* with me in the house, and he hath committed all that he hath to my hand;

9 *There is* none greater in this house than I; neither hath he kept back any thing from me but thee, because thou *art* his wife: how then can I do this great wickedness, and sin against God?
10 And it came to pass, as she spake to Joseph day by day, that he hearkened not unto her, to lie by her, *or* to be with her.

Although adultery was subject to severe legal penalties in Egypt, it apparently was often tacitly condoned and was not uncommon. Especially in such situations as in Potiphar's household, where a wife was married to a husband who had been made a eunuch, it may have been regarded as almost something to be expected. Though nothing is said explicitly to this effect, one gets the impression that this was not the first of his wife's amorous adventures. In any case, as Joseph became more and more important around the household, and more and more on his own, he gradually became more and more attractive to this woman.

Joseph certainly would have behaved politely and considerately toward his master's wife, but he soon must have realized she was taking more interest in him personally than was fitting. There is no indication that he encouraged her in any way—quite the contrary in fact. Finally she impatiently decided that, since a subtle seduction was not proving effective, she would try overwhelming him with a bold invitation to her bedroom!

Now Joseph was a virile and active young man, and this invitation must have both flattered and tempted him. Her husband was gone, none of the other servants were around (and, even if they should find out, they would probably think nothing of it), and she was an attractive and eagerly available woman. Sexual dalliances were common in such circumstances and, even in his own family, Joseph had no doubt seen examples of his brothers' indifference to high moral standards. Furthermore, in view of his knowledge of the unsatisfactory nature of her marital relations with Potiphar, he might even have justified it as an act of service to meet her own needs.

With such an array of rationalizations easily at hand, it would have been natural to yield to her invitation. But with Joseph there was one consideration which overshadowed all others. He knew that such actions were contrary to God's revealed will. Even though the Mosaic laws were not yet written, there was enough primeval knowledge concerning God's purposes for mankind available for him to know beyond question that adultery and fornication were wrong in God's sight. He knew from the account of man's creation that God had ordained the permanence and sanctity of marriage, and that none of man's convenient excuses for breaking this ordinance were justified in God's economy.

In rejecting her invitation, Joseph tried not to offend her. It was not that she herself was unattractive or undesirable, nor that he was condemning her as immoral for making such a proposal, but that there were greater considerations which must take precedence. His master, and her husband, trusted him fully; it would be a terrible betrayal of his trust for Joseph to take the one thing he had kept from him, his own wife. Even more importantly, such an action would be a great sin against God Himself! Even though neither her husband nor the other servants should ever find out, God would know. "The eyes of the Lord are in every place, beholding the evil and the good" (Proverbs 15:3). All sin, and especially sin against the integrity of God's first institution, that of marriage, must fundamentally be a sin against God.

Therefore Joseph refused her invitation, strong though the temptation may have been. Potiphar's wife, however, was not persuaded by Joseph's good and proper reasoning, but continued day after day trying to attract him to her bed. Joseph not only continued to refuse, but began to avoid her altogether, trying not even "to be with her."

Genesis 39:11-15

---

11 And it came to pass about this time, that *Joseph* went into the house to do his business; and *there was* none of the men of the house there within.
12 And she caught him by his garment, saying, Lie with me: and he left his garment in her hand, and fled, and got him out.
13 And it came to pass, when she saw that he had left his garment in her hand, and was fled forth,
14 That she called unto the men of her house, and spake unto them, saying, See, he hath brought in a Hebrew unto us to mock us; he came in unto me to lie with me, and I cried with a loud voice:
15 And it came to pass, when he heard that I lifted up my voice and cried, that he left his garment with me, and fled, and got him out.

The situation came to a climax one day when Potiphar's wife apparently determined that she would actually pull Joseph to her side by force. The time was opportune, since everyone was gone. Possibly if she could once get him intimately close to her, his resistance would be overcome and he would be impelled by passion to continue all the way. She felt that, if she could really have him completely just one time, then he would keep on coming back to her whenever she wished.

Joseph, however, realizing the danger of the situation, especially the spiritual implications if he should yield, pulled himself away from her arms and rushed out of the room and even out of the house. She had been in the process of pulling his clothing off him (her own had probably already been removed when she came up to him) when he realized what she was doing and immediately fled. However, she clung to the garment as he fled, partially unclothed, from her presence.

At that point, the passionate desire of Potiphar's wife suddenly turned into the rage of a woman scorned. Knowing that her desire for Joseph was now completely impossible of fulfillment, her only thought was to humiliate him as deeply as possible for his rejection of her. Joseph's garment (Hebrew *beged,* apparently a sort of long cloak or robe) was still in her hand. She knew it would be interpreted as evidence incriminating her unless she quickly took the initiative by accusing Joseph.

Accordingly she began to make a loud outcry, calling for the men servants to come help her. She cleverly appealed to their latent jealousy of Joseph and resentment of Potiphar, by suggesting it was her husband's fault for bringing in an outsider ("an Hebrew") who would come in and endanger all the women of the household ("to mock us"). Now, sure enough, this man, elevated so quickly above all the other servants, had actually attempted to rape the very mistress of the household! She had only saved herself by screaming so loudly that he was frightened away, leaving his shed garment in his haste.

Nothing is said, however, about whether the servants believed her tale. The chances are that they knew her, as well as Joseph, too well for that. In their position, however, they could hardly challenge her story. Joseph probably went to his own quarters to await the outcome.

Genesis 39:16-20

---

16 And she laid up his garment by her, until his lord came home.
17 And she spake unto him according to these words, saying, The Hebrew servant, which thou hast brought unto us, came in unto me to mock me:
18 And it came to pass, as I lifted up my voice and cried, that he left his garment with me, and fled out.

19 And it came to pass, when his master heard the words of his wife, which she spake unto him, saying, After this manner did thy servant to me; that his wrath was kindled.
20 And Joseph's master took him, and put him into the prison, a place where the king's prisoners *were* bound: and he was there in the prison.

When Potiphar returned home, his wife repeated her story to him, embellishing it with the same prejudicial words and lies which she had used with the servants. In effect, she seemed to place the blame on Potiphar himself for giving a foreign slave such authority and freedom around the house that he would try to take advantage of his own faithful and long-suffering wife!

On hearing this story, Potiphar's "wrath was kindled." If his wife's story were true, he indeed would be fully justified in his wrath and in taking severe retaliation on Joseph. The severest penalty of the law (capital punishment) would be appropriate.

It may be significant, however, that Scripture does not say that his "wrath was kindled against Joseph." Furthermore, rather than having Joseph slain, he merely put him in that part of the prison reserved for political, rather than criminal, prisoners. It almost seems that Potiphar also knew both his wife and Joseph too well to really believe he had heard the whole story.

There is no indication that Joseph made any effort to defend himself from these charges. Though they were utterly untrue, and he was being punished unjustly, he still kept quiet. Perhaps it was partly because he felt sorry for Potiphar's wife, knowing something of the difficult aspects of her own life which led her to behave as she did. Possibly also he realized that the political realities of the situation would not permit Potiphar to take a servant's word against that of his wife, even if Potiphar had good reason to doubt his wife. In any case, whatever the reason, Joseph opened not his mouth, thus demonstrating one of the most difficult —because most Christlike—traits of character for a Christian to develop (note Isaiah 53:7; I Peter 2:19-23).

Among other things occasioning Potiphar's anger, no doubt, was his realization that he would now have to lose the services of one who had proved extremely profitable to him. Nevertheless, for appearance' sake, he did have Joseph put into the prison, where he apparently remained for a long while. It is noteworthy that this was the same prison over which Potiphar himself was in charge (Genesis 40:3); so it may be that Potiphar hoped he would one day be able to bring Joseph back to resume his previous duties. On the other hand, the prison was not necessarily a comfortable country-club type of prison. The king's political prisoners were not normally favored, but, if anything, were treated more severely than others. Psalm 105:18 says that Joseph's "feet they hurt with fetters: he was laid in iron."

Genesis 39:21-23

---

21 ¶ But the LORD was with Joseph, and showed him mercy, and gave him favor in the sight of the keeper of the prison.
22 And the keeper of the prison committed to Joseph's hand all the prisoners that *were* in the prison; and whatsoever they did there, he was the doer *of it*.
23 The keeper of the prison looked not to any thing *that was* under his hand; because the LORD was with him, and *that* which he did, the LORD made *it* to prosper.

Once again, however, God began to bless Joseph. He had allowed him to be unjustly accused and punished, no doubt for purposes of developing his character for the great work He had for him to do in the future, but He would still acknowledge His approval of Joseph by blessing and prospering him in those difficult circumstances.

The overseer of the prison, just as Potiphar had done, soon could see that Joseph was an unusually capable and reliable individual. Probably he knew about his accomplishments for Potiphar. Therefore, this prison governor, exactly as Potiphar had done, soon placed all the prisoners and affairs of the prison in Joseph's charge. Joseph continued to bear a good testimony for the Lord, and the Lord confirmed Joseph's testimony by clearly showing that He was with him. Again, as in Potiphar's home, so now in the prison of which he was manager, everything prospered under Joseph's hand. Both experiences were prophetic and preparatory for what he would later acomplish as governor of all Egypt.

20

The Exaltation of Joseph

(Genesis 40-41)

The Butler and the Baker

Joseph was seventeen years old when he was sent down into Egypt and thirty years old when he appeared before Pharaoh and was placed in charge of Egypt's grain conservation program (Genesis 37:2; 41:46). Consequently, he must have spent a total of thirteen years in Potiphar's house and then in Potiphar's prison. This was a long time for a proud, intelligent young man to have to "waste" in servitude and in prison. In God's planning, however, it was not wasted at all, but was a necessary preparation for the great position of leadership and deliverance to which He would call Joseph. Young people often feel they should be promoted to positions of leadership in the Lord's work—especially those who feel they have spiritual gifts as evangelists or teachers—almost as soon as they become witnessing Christians and begin to acquire a rudimentary knowledge of the Bible. They tend to become impatient with what they regard as irrelevant attitudes and programs of their churches and Christian training institutes. They would rather develop new methods of their own and get immediately out into the active ministry (supported financially, of course, by those same outdated churches and Christians whose methods they regard as anachronistic).

To all such impatient Christians, the story of Joseph will prove salutary. He thought himself ready for leadership at seventeen; the Lord had to chastise him and put him through a rigorous training program before he was finally ready at thirty! Israel's greatest king, David, was likewise thirty years old when he finally became king (II Samuel 5:4), even though he had been anointed when only a youth (I Samuel 16:11-13). Those who were trained from childhood to enter the Levitical service of the Lord around the tabernacle were nevertheless permitted to enter that service only when they reached thirty years of age (Numbers 4:46, 47).

The apostle Paul, though he had received outstanding training prior to his conversion, had to be sent for three years into the desert (Galatians 1:15-18) for special full-time training before he was ready to enter his own ministry for the Lord. Likewise, the twelve apostles received over three years of full-time training from the Lord Jesus Himself before they were equipped to go out in fulfillment of His great commission. It seems as though, based on the examples in Scripture, a young Christian needs at least the equivalent of three years of full-time study in the Word and should be roughly thirty years of age before he is fully ready to assume the responsibilities of Christian leadership in the service of Christ.

For that matter, even Jesus Himself did not enter on His own public ministry until He was "about thirty years of age" (Luke 3:23), devoting His prior experience to the all-important purpose of "increasing in wisdom and stature, and in favor with God and man" (Luke 2:52). A ministry of, say, forty years' duration, with proper intellectual and spiritual preparation, will, in the long run, be far more fruitful than fifty years of effort built on an inadequate foundation.

Joseph was faithful in whatever came to him during those otherwise frustrating thirteen years, and no doubt was diligent in pondering the ways of the Lord, until the time finally arrived when God judged him properly seasoned and ready for the great work he would accomplish for his people and for the world.

Genesis 40:1-4

CHAPTER 40

AND it came to pass after these things, *that* the butler of the king of Egypt and *his* baker had offended their lord the king of Egypt.

2 And Phā'raōh was wroth against two *of* his officers, against the chief of the butlers, and against the chief of the bakers.

3 And he put them in ward in the house of the captain of the guard, into the prison, the place where Joseph *was* bound.

4 And the captain of the guard charged Joseph with them, and he served them: and they continued a season in ward.

Joseph probably spent at least several years in Potiphar's prison, but only one event during that time is recorded, and that because it later led directly to Joseph's being summoned to appear before Pharaoh. This is the account of the peculiar experience of the butler and the baker.

The chief butler of Pharaoh was the overseer of his vineyards and wine cellar, as well as his personal cupbearer, responsible to see that all drinks served the king were both safe and of best quality. Likewise the chief baker was responsible for the food which Pharaoh ate. It is said that both of these men were "officers," but again the word used is (as in the case of Potiphar) actually the Hebrew word for "eunuchs." Some writers have suggested that this word may have come to be synonymous with any official, whether or not he was a true eunuch, but this suggestion is not based on any direct evidence. It therefore seems likely that Pharaoh required all those officers who were to have close personal contact with him and who were directly responsible for important court functions to be made eunuchs.

In some way, these two men had offended (literally "sinned against") Pharaoh, and so were thrown into the same prison where Joseph was. Verse 3 says they were imprisoned in "the house of the captain of the guard." This was Potiphar's title (Genesis 39:1), from which it is known that this was the prison over which Potiphar had jurisdiction. It is indicative of the high esteem in which Joseph was held by both Potiphar and the governor of the prison that he was even placed in charge of these two high officials of Pharaoh's court.

The record does not say for what offense the butler and baker had been imprisoned. What follows in the chapter would seem to indicate that they were both suspected of a possible capital offense, but that it was unclear whether one or both of them were guilty. In view of their responsibilities for the king's food and drink, and since no others apparently had been put in ward for the same offense, the presumption would be that the crime had something to do with Pharaoh's table. Possibly a cache of poison had been discovered, under such circumstances that it appeared destined to reach Pharaoh by way of either his food or drink. When questioned about it, no doubt both the baker and butler had denied any responsibility for it; so Pharaoh, to be safe, threw them both into jail. However, since their guilt or innocence was not yet established, they were apparently treated fairly well for the time being. Joseph had the responsibility of seeing their needs were met. At the same time he was accountable for their security. Apparently an investigation into the problem which led to their imprisonment was proceeding in Pharaoh's court, quite possibly under the direction of Potiphar himself (whose position would roughly correspond to that of chief of the security police); so the two men spent quite some time in jail. Joseph got to know them rather well, becoming friends with them while they waited there for the disposition of their case.

Genesis 40:5-8

---

5 ¶ And they dreamed a dream both of them, each man his dream in one night, each man according to the interpretation of his dream, the butler and the baker of the king of Egypt, which *were* bound in the prison.

6 And Joseph came in unto them in the morning, and looked upon them, and, behold, they *were* sad.

7 And he asked Phā'raōh's officers that *were* with him in the ward of his lord's house, saying, Wherefore look ye *so* sadly to-day?

8 And they said unto him, We have dreamed a dream, and *there is* no interpreter of it. And Joseph said unto them, *Do* not interpretations *belong* to God? tell me *them*, I pray you.

Probably the police investigation finally had come across firm evidence as to which of the two men was guilty, and the king was preparing to render a verdict. Then, one night, both the butler and the baker had a dream, and each man's dream was so unusual and made such an impression on him that he could not get it out of his mind. Both dreams seemed to have a mysterious symbolic significance, and both the butler and the baker believed that the gods had sent them some kind of message. Men of all times and places, of course, have tended to regard dreams as having special significance on occasion. As a matter of fact, dreams sometimes have proved to have such significance. A number of instances in the Bible, especially here in the Book of Genesis, are of this sort.

Modern-day psychologists such as Freud have also devoted much study to dreams and have tended to regard them as reflective of the subconscious desires and frustrations of the individual's own experience. From a scientific point of view, dreams are to a large degree still not understood, either as to cause or significance. To what extent they might be capable of control by external spiritual beings, whether angelic or demonic, is an unsettled question, but there do seem to be enough documented cases of precognitive dreams on record to warrant the belief that, at least under certain undefined circumstances, such powers, with their own limited knowledge of future events, do have the capability occasionally of controlling the brain cells of sleeping individuals in such a way as to cause a sort of pre-enactment of these events in their minds.

It is not evident in the case of the butler and baker as to exactly what the cause of their strange dreams may have been. Perhaps their own consciences, innocent in the one case and guilty in the other, caused them

subconsciously to realize what their futures would be, and these thoughts
were then reflected in their dreams. More likely, however, God Himself,
possibly through angelic agents, led them to dream as they did, in order
to give Joseph the opportunity to come to Pharaoh's attention. This was
the main ultimate outcome of the dreams, and so God's overruling providence at least used them in this way. They were not the kind of dreams,
however, that had been experienced by Abraham and Jacob, in which God
had directly spoken; and they are not recorded in Scripture as having been
directly instigated by God. Consequently, this matter must remain indefinite.

In any case, the dreams made such an impression on the men that
Joseph noticed their preoccupation the next morning. When he made
inquiry as to what was wrong, they both told him of their conviction that
their dreams had meaning, but that they did not know how to interpret
them. Had they been at liberty, they would probably have contacted
some astrologer or other professional occultist for his interpretation.
Joseph, however, had had experience with certain dreams of his own, and
something about the situation seemed to suggest to him that God Himself
had a message through these dreams. Since only God could really know
the future (because He controlled it), only He could give truly effective
meaning to dreams which ostensibly bore on the future. Joseph therefore
suggested that the two men tell him their dreams, and he would seek to
learn the divine message intended by them.

Genesis 40:9-15

---

9 And the chief butler told his dream to Joseph, and said to him, In my dream, behold, a vine *was* before me;
10 And in the vine *were* three branches: and it *was* as though it budded, *and* her blossoms shot forth; and the clusters thereof brought forth ripe grapes:
11 And Phä′raōh's cup *was* in my hand: and I took the grapes, and pressed them into Phä′raōh's cup, and I gave the cup into Phä′raōh's hand.
12 And Joseph said unto him, This *is* the interpretation of it: The three branches *are* three days:

13 Yet within three days shall Phä′raōh lift up thine head, and restore thee unto thy place; and thou shalt deliver Phä′raōh's cup into his hand, after the former manner when thou wast his butler.
14 But think on me when it shall be well with thee, and show kindness, I pray thee, unto me, and make mention of me unto Phä′raōh, and bring me out of this house:
15 For indeed I was stolen away out of the land of the Hebrews: and here also have I done nothing that they should put me into the dungeon.

In these verses, the chief butler reports his dream and receives Joseph's
interpretation. Probably he spoke first because, even though he was
curious about the meaning of his dream, he was confident of his own
innocence and therefore was not hesitant to hear its significance. In his

dream, there had been a vine with three branches, so ordered that its "threeness" was a prominent feature. As he dreamed, he observed the branches budding, then blossoming, and finally bearing luscious bunches of grapes. The grapes were immediately ready for plucking, so the butler dreamed that he picked them and then pressed the grape juice from them into Pharaoh's cup, which had mysteriously appeared in his hand.

Straightway (the butler dreamed) he gave the cup to Pharaoh, in accord with his responsibilities as chief butler. All of these events clearly manifested the butler's confidence that he had faithfully carried out his duties, along with his hope that he would be able to carry them out again. The quick succession of events probably denoted to him that there had been no opportunity, either through his negligence or his direct guilt, for anything alien to be introduced into the cup. He knew in his heart that he was blameless of Pharaoh's charges, and this fact seemed to reflect itself in his dream.

He might himself have interpreted his own dream to mean that he would again one day serve as Pharaoh's butler. The three branches, however, seemed to have some significance also, and this he had no way of interpreting. Joseph, presumably by divine revelation, was able to inform him that the three branches represented three days, and that this meant that in three days he would be released from prison and restored to his former office.

This must indeed have been a message of joy to the butler. He would be exonerated and, since the security investigation would have revealed his full loyalty to Pharaoh in a way that nothing else could, he would probably be even more highly regarded than ever. Joseph knew, however, that there would be one difference; he would have his memories of time spent in prison, which he had never had before. Joseph therefore requested that, when he should have opportunity, he remember him, and how well he had been treated by Joseph and, especially, the manner in which Joseph had been able to give him the meaning of his dream. Joseph also was innocent of any crime, just as the butler had been. He had been taken into slavery out of the land of the Hebrews, in the first place, and so was in Egypt not for some nefarious purpose of subversion or espionage, as his place in a political prison might have suggested, but because he had been stolen from his own people. (Note that he makes no mention of his brothers' part in this affair, no doubt being ashamed of this for the sake of the family name.) Furthermore, even in his servitude he had been faithful and had done nothing whatever to warrant imprisonment. Therefore, in view of the similarity of his case to that of the butler, both being innocent of wrongdoing, he requested that the butler, once he was back in a position of influence at the court, intercede for him with Pharaoh. The butler no doubt promised to do this, but unfortunately soon forgot.

Genesis 40:16-19

---

16 When the chief baker saw that the interpretation was good, he said unto Joseph, I also *was* in my dream, and, behold, *I had* three white baskets on my head:
17 And in the uppermost basket *there was* of all manner of bakemeats for Phā'raōh; and the birds did eat them out of the basket upon my head.

18 And Joseph answered and said, This *is* the interpretation thereof: The three baskets *are* three days:
19 Yet within three days shall Phā'raōh lift up thy head from off thee, and shall hang thee on a tree; and the birds shall eat thy flesh from off thee.

The chief baker also had a dream, but he was much less comfortable about his. Nevertheless, when he heard the favorable interpretation given by Joseph to the dream of his colleague, he hoped that this dream likewise might forecast a favorable outcome in his own case, and so asked Joseph to interpret his as well.

In his dream, he was carrying baskets of baked goods on his head to Pharaoh. Again there was a distinctive "threeness" about the dream, for there were three baskets. In the uppermost, exposed, basket, there were all kinds of "goodies," such as he hoped he would be able again to prepare for Pharaoh. Unlike the butler, however, he never had opportunity actually to present them to Pharaoh. There was a time lapse between the baking and the serving in his case, affording opportunity for alien creatures to befoul them and to steal the good food. He had failed to provide protection against this, as the duties of his office required.

In Egypt, birds were sacred and so were protected; therefore they were often a nuisance. Such experiences as the one the baker dreamed about were not uncommon in Egypt, for this reason. Nevertheless, the possibility that such could happen in the case of food intended for the king himself would surely indicate a serious lapse of proper care—whether intentional or accidental—on the part of the chief baker. It may well be that the baker realized his own culpability, and his dream to some extent reflected his awareness of guilt.

In any case, Joseph (no doubt after hesitation and prayer) informed him that the interpretation of his dream was entirely different from that of the butler. The three baskets again represented three days, but instead of being elevated back to his office at that time, his very head would be removed from his body and his body then hanged on a' tree. Instead of the birds eating Pharaoh's bread, they would eat the baker's flesh. The baker had been found guilty, and would pay with his life.

A number of typological meanings have suggested themselves to various interpreters of these verses. The contrast between the butler and baker has been suggested as parallel to the conflict between the saved and the lost, or to that between the spirit and the flesh. The butler, with his grape juice, is associated with the redeeming blood; the baker, with his bakemeats, is identified with those who present their own works for salvation. The three-day period is tied in with the three days Christ spent in the grave.

The reader may judge whether these or other typological applications of this passage have merit. They seem strained, at best, and of course have no specific New Testament warrant.

Genesis 40:20-23

20 ¶ And it came to pass the third day, *which was* Phā′raōh's birthday, that he made a feast unto all his servants: and he lifted up the head of the chief butler and of the chief baker among his servants.
21 And he restored the chief butler unto his butlership again; and he gave the cup into Phā′raōh's hand:
22 But he hanged the chief baker: as Joseph had interpreted to them.
23 Yet did not the chief butler remember Joseph, but forgat him.

The interpretation of the dreams came to pass exactly as Joseph had said. Apparently Pharaoh had delayed announcing the findings of his investigation and his resultant verdict until the date of his own birthday, which was, as it turned out, the third day after the two dreams.

It was customary for the king to give a banquet for his servants on his birthday, and this would be the ideal occasion to announce to all concerned the fate of these two most prominent of the servants. One might speculate that whatever plot had been laid against Pharaoh might have been intended to be consummated on this occasion; if so, this would lend peculiar significance to its exposure and punishment at this time.

At any event, as the festivities were in progress, Pharaoh called for the butler and baker to be brought to him out of the prison. In the sight and hearing of all the other servants, Pharaoh then pronounced the chief butler innocent of all charges, and restored him back to his high office. In great joy, the butler immediately, as a symbol of his gratitude and faithfulness, took the cup himself, filled it with the choicest wine, and offered it to Pharaoh.

But then when Pharaoh turned to his former chief baker, his countenance was severe. Here was the culprit, guilty as charged, and the penalty was death. He was then removed to a tree outside the palace, where all could see his fate and be thereby warned; and there he was hanged.

These outcomes were exactly as Joseph had predicted, and both the butler and baker must have been amazed and impressed by his prophetic knowledge, much greater and more specific than shown by any of the wise men and magicians of Egypt. Nevertheless, in the joy and excitement of his restoration and the subsequent press of duties, catching up on everything that had been delayed while he was in prison, the chief butler gradually let Joseph and his promise to him slip from his mind. Actually two full years (Genesis 41:1) were to lapse before he would remember and bring Joseph to Pharaoh's attention.

Pharaoh's Dream

As Joseph continued to languish in prison, especially after his experience with the chief butler which had seemed to offer some promise of his possible release, he must have become at least partly discouraged. The butler had forgotten him and, even though Potiphar most likely knew he was innocent of the charge for which he had been placed in prison, the politics of the situation kept him from taking the initiative to set him free. Joseph no doubt longed to see his father and younger brother again, even though the rest of his brothers had treated him so shamefully.

Many a Christian, under much less discouragement than Joseph endured, has simply quit trying, perhaps even becoming embittered against God. However discouraged he may have been, however, Joseph continued to believe in God and to trust Him. He did not even have such a Scripture verse as Romans 8:28 to comfort him, though the realities of that verse are beautifully illustrated in Joseph's life. He knew God had spoken to him and through him, and that God and His promises were real. In good time, he would understand why God was allowing him to go through these difficult experiences. In the meantime, he no doubt made good use of his time in studying such material as came to his hand, and in prayer and rehearsing such portions of God's Word as had been available to him under the earlier instruction of his father.

The time soon would come, on God's calendar, for Joseph's exaltation. Once again, dreams would play an important part in his life. In earlier years, dreams had given certain insights concerning his future relating to his own family. Later, other dreams had been associated with the careers of certain important court officials. This time, the dreams would be those of Pharaoh himself, and would have to do with important developments that would affect the land of Egypt and, in fact, the entire Near East.

Genesis 41:1-7

CHAPTER 41

AND it came to pass at the end of two full years, that Phā′raōh dreamed: and, behold, he stood by the river.

2 And, behold, there came up out of the river seven well-favored kine and fat-fleshed; and they fed in a meadow.

3 And, behold, seven other kine came up after them out of the river, ill-favored and lean-fleshed; and stood by the *other* kine upon the brink of the river.

4 And the ill-favored and lean-fleshed kine did eat up the seven well-favored and fat kine. So Phā′raōh awoke.

5 And he slept and dreamed the second time: and, behold, seven ears of corn came up upon one stalk, rank and good.

6 And, behold, seven thin ears and blasted with the east wind sprung up after them.

7 And the seven thin ears devoured the seven rank and full ears. And Phā′raōh awoke, and, behold, *it was* a dream.

The significant dreams in Joseph's experience seemed to come in pairs. First, he had two dreams himself; then two related dreams were experienced by the butler and baker; and now, Pharaoh, king of Egypt, had two dreams. These dreams occurred two full years after Joseph's interpretation of the dreams of the butler and baker.

One night Pharaoh was dreaming, apparently at first more or less without any particular theme, but then suddenly the dream became very vivid and impressive. He was standing by the River Nile when he saw, most amazingly, seven beautifully healthy, fat-fleshed cows coming up out of the river, and then grazing among the reeds along the flood plain. The cows must have impressed Pharaoh especially in a religious sense, because the cow was the emblem of Isis, the revered Egyptian goddess of fertility. In the Egyptian "Book of the Dead," the chief scripture of ancient Egypt, the god of vegetation and the nether world, Osiris, is represented as a great bull accompanied by seven cows.

As Pharaoh watched the seven well-favored cows, perhaps speaking to him of the great prosperity of the land over which he ruled, he saw seven ugly and thin-fleshed cows emerge from the river and stand beside the seven well-favored cows. Then, strangely and unexpectedly, the lean cows turned to the fat cows and proceded to eat them up! Such a thing could happen only in a dream, and it was so startling that Pharaoh woke up. After wondering what it might have meant, he soon became drowsy and fell asleep again.

Soon he was dreaming again, another dream as sharp and strange as the first. This time, he was out gazing at a grain field, such as was common throughout the fertile plains of Egypt. As he gazed, he saw a stalk of grain growing up. On the stalk, seven ears of grain (not "corn," in the modern American sense of "maize," but a form of wheat) grew plump and full. Again, Pharaoh must have been impressed with the richness of Egypt, known to all as the granary of the ancient world.

But then the same fate that had overtaken the fat cattle in his earlier dream befell the plump ears. Seven thin ears of grain, blasted and withered with Egypt's bitter east wind, came up. The violent winds from the eastern wilderness would wither almost any growing plant, and these ears of grain were hardened and thin, utterly inedible. A sight even stranger than that of cattle turning carnivorous and cannibalistic then passed before Pharaoh's startled gaze, as the thin ears swallowed up the plump ears. The word used in the case of the cattle *(akal)* indicates the lean cattle actually chewed up the fat cattle. In the case of the grain the word is *bala,* indicating a process of swallowing, or engulfing.

In any case, the repetition of the same theme with different figures greatly impressed Pharaoh. Awake again, he tossed and turned on his bed, wondering what strange meaning was behind his extraordinary dreams. The dreams had been so vivid that, in spite of the physical impossibility of the events he had observed, he had actually been surprised to find on awakening that he was only dreaming.

Genesis 41:8-13

---

8 And it came to pass in the morning that his spirit was troubled; and he sent and called for all the magicians of Egypt, and all the wise men thereof: and Pha'raōh told them his dream; but *there was* none that could interpret them unto Pha'raōh.

9 ¶ Then spake the chief butler unto Pha'raōh, saying, I do remember my faults this day:

10 Pha'raōh was wroth with his servants, and put me in ward in the captain of the guard's house, *both* me and the chief baker:

11 And we dreamed a dream in one night, I and he; we dreamed each man according to the interpretation of his dream.

12 And *there was* there with us a young man, a Hebrew, servant to the captain of the guard; and we told him, and he interpreted to us our dreams; to each man according to his dream he did interpret.

13 And it came to pass, as he interpreted to us, so it was; me he restored unto mine office, and him he hanged.

As soon as it was morning, Pharaoh sent for the most famous magicians and wise men of Egypt to interpret his dreams. He sensed that there was something ominous about the dreams, for had not the very symbols of the gods and the prosperity of the land of Egypt been destroyed before his eyes?

The fact is, however, the occultists of Egypt were helpless to understand the dreams. Great as their powers may have been (and the experience of Moses several centuries later with a similar group of Egyptian magicians indicated they were quite considerable—see Exodus 7:11, 22; 8:7), they were not able to interpret these dreams. Certain fortunetellers and necromancers have, throughout history, professed to be able to understand dreams and foretell future events. On occasion, they have made profound impressions on their contemporaries through seeming success in such endeavors. To whatever extent they have really been able to do this, it is likely that ability to communicate with demons has contributed to such successes. Demonic spirits, who as fallen angels almost certainly are associated with Satan in his rebellion against God, have some limited ability to control future events—and, therefore, to predict those events they can control. Furthermore, they utilize this power on behalf of their human intermediaries, whose occult abilities can in turn be used to turn the hearts of men away from the true God toward Satan.

In this case, Pharaoh's dreams had not been generated by evil spirits, and therefore those spirits were not able to understand their implications. One after another, the wise men and magicians had to confess, shamefacedly, that they could not explain the dreams, although they no doubt recognized, as did Pharaoh, that the dreams were significant and that they presaged some serious crisis coming on the land of Egypt.

And then it was that the chief butler finally remembered Joseph! Knowing how remarkably Joseph had been able to interpret his own dream and that of the baker, with results which had been precisely fulfilled, he should long ago have called Pharaoh's attention to such an unusual and potentially valuable man. But he had been simply too busy and had forgotten. Confessing his sins to Pharaoh, he recounted the two-year-old story to him. He reminded him how both he and the chief baker had been imprisoned in Potiphar's prison, and then told Pharaoh about their dreams while in prison. The young man of the Hebrews, Potiphar's servant, had been the only one able to give them an interpretation of their dreams. Furthermore, his interpretations had been meticulously correct. Three days later, exactly as he had predicted, the butler had been restored and the baker hanged. Here was a man who had greater insight into the future than all the sages and interpreters of the land of Egypt. If Pharaoh really wanted to know the meaning of his dreams, he should by all means send for this young man, Joseph.

Genesis 41:14-16

14 ¶ Then Phā'raōh sent and called Joseph, and they brought him hastily out of the dungeon: and he shaved *himself,* and changed his raiment, and came in unto Phā'raōh.
15 And Phā'raōh said unto Joseph, I have dreamed a dream, and *there is* none that can interpret it: and I have heard say of thee, *that* thou canst understand a dream to interpret it.
16 And Joseph answered Phā'raōh, saying, *It is* not in me: God shall give Phā'raōh an answer of peace.

As the butler had recommended, Pharaoh sent for Joseph. Though he might have normally scorned to seek help from a Hebrew, and especially from a Hebrew in jail, he now had nowhere else to turn, and he simply had to know what his dreams meant.

The Egyptians, according to Herodotus, had extreme care for cleanliness, and thus the men would let their hair and beard grow only during periods of mourning. Joseph, therefore, had to allow himself to be shaved and also to be arrayed in clothing suitable for an appearance at court. All of this was done in haste, as Pharaoh was anxiously waiting.

Finally, Joseph stood before Pharaoh, an impecunious young foreigner, a slave for thirteen years, in the presence of probably the most powerful monarch in the world! Joseph, however, was there because of God's providence; and his God was the very Creator of the world, before whom Pharaoh himself was but dust. (Note Psalm 119:46.)

Pharaoh proceeded immediately to tell Joseph his problem. He had dreamed a dream which he knew must be of great significance, but he had been unable to find an interpreter. Then, to his surprise and joy, he had heard marvelous reports about Joseph, to the effect that he could be told any dream and then correctly interpret it.

Joseph might well have felt very flattered, to be so addressed by none other than Pharaoh himself. Furthermore, he might have been tempted to bargain with Pharaoh. He was possessed of a unique ability, and this ability was in very high demand right at that moment. He could at least have extracted a promise for his freedom, and perhaps a considerable fee, in return for granting Pharaoh's request.

Instead, however, he quickly confessed that he himself had no prophetic ability at all. If he had been successful at the understanding of dreams, it had been solely because of God, in whom he believed and who had delivered to him the meaning. Literally, his answer was that such insights were "altogether apart from me." Lest Pharaoh be too quickly dismayed, however, Joseph assured him that God Himself would indeed grant Pharaoh the meaning of the dreams. Indeed, He had sent him the dreams for the very purpose of preparing him for the future. God intended to give Pharaoh an "answer of peace," that is, an answer which, in spite of the great troubles that were surely coming on the land of Egypt, would enable him to be prepared for them and to endure them in peace.

Joseph exhibited by this answer a great growth in spiritual maturity since the time of his own dreams back in Canaan. Then, he had antagonized his family by calling attention to his own superiority. Now, however, he won the confidence and respect of a heathen king and court by denying his own ability and giving full credit to the Lord. His years of slavery and imprisonment had indeed taught him humility and patience. Instead of calling attention to the failures of the other wise men and stressing his own powers, he acted with utmost courtesy and restraint, and directed all praise to God alone.

Genesis 41:17-24

---

17 And Phā′raōh said unto Joseph, In my dream, behold, I stood upon the bank of the river:

18 And, behold, there came up out of the river seven kine, fat-fleshed and well-favored; and they fed in a meadow:

19 And, behold, seven other kine came up after them, poor and very ill-favored and lean-fleshed, such as I never saw in all the land of Egypt for badness:

20 And the lean and the ill-favored kine did eat up the first seven fat kine:

21 And when they had eaten them up, it could not be known that they had eaten them; but they *were* still ill-favored, as at the beginning. So I awoke.

22 And I saw in my dream, and, behold, seven ears came up in one stalk, full and good:

23 And, behold, seven ears, withered, thin, *and* blasted with the east wind, sprung up after them:

24 And the thin ears devoured the seven good ears: and I told *this* unto the magicians; but *there was* none that could declare *it* to me.

Pharaoh then proceeded to tell Joseph the details of both his dreams, recounting the peculiar story of the triumph of the lean cows over the fat cows, and the thin ears over the full ears. A few details were added which were not recorded earlier. The thin cattle were worse than any Pharaoh had ever seen in Egypt and, even after they had eaten the fat cattle, they looked no better than before. The dream had indeed made a deep and fearful impression on Pharaoh.

Pharaoh then repeated once again that he had tried diligently to find someone who could explain the dreams, but quite unsuccessfully. The gods of Egypt, and their spokesmen, seemed helpless to interpret the dreams and therefore must likewise be helpless to deal with the serious problems that seemed to be suggested by the dreams.

Genesis 41:25-32

---

25 ¶ And Joseph said unto Phā′raōh, The dream of Phā′raōh *is* one: God hath showed Phā′raōh what he *is* about to do.

26 The seven good kine *are* seven years; and the seven good ears *are* seven years: the dream *is* one.

27 And the seven thin and ill-favored kine that came up after them *are* seven years; and the seven empty ears blasted with the east wind shall be seven years of famine.

28 This *is* the thing which I have spoken unto Phā′raōh: What God *is* about to do he showeth unto Phā′raōh.

29 Behold, there come seven years of great plenty throughout all the land of

Egypt:
30 And there shall arise after them seven years of famine; and all the plenty shall be forgotten in the land of Egypt; and the famine shall consume the land; 31 And the plenty shall not be known in the land by reason of that famine following; for it *shall be* very grievous. 32 And for that the dream was doubled unto Phā'raōh twice; *it is* because the thing *is* established by God, and God will shortly bring it to pass.

Whether Joseph paused for a while for meditation and prayer concerning Pharaoh's dreams is not stated in the text. In any case, God somehow gave to him infallible knowledge concerning their correct interpretation. Certain implications of the dreams were, of course, almost self-evident: Egypt's great prosperity in grain and cattle was surely going to be interrupted somehow. The "seven-ness" of the dreams, however, only Joseph could correctly interpret. This number represented a period of time, just as the "three-ness" of the dreams of the butler and baker had represented three days. In this case, however, there were seven years represented by the respective groups of seven.

The fact that the dream had been given to Pharaoh twice (just as Joseph's much earlier dream had been repeated to him twice, with different figures) was explained by him to constitute firm assurance that God would indeed fulfill its predictions, and would do so beginning very soon. It is noteworthy that Joseph insisted, not less than four times, that all of this had come from God (verses 16, 25, 28, 32). God had sent the dream, God had given the interpretation, and God would bring it all to pass.

The seven healthy cattle, as well as the seven full ears of grain, represented seven wonderful years of full productivity and prosperity that were coming on the land of Egypt. The seven ugly cattle, as well as the seven thin ears, on the other hand, represented seven bitter years of famine that would follow on the years of plenty. The bad years, furthermore, would be so bad that the years of prosperity would be altogether forgotten. The famine would, Joseph said, "consume the land," and "be very grievous."

Finally, Joseph stressed that the fulfillment of the double dream would not be long in coming. It would begin very shortly, and Pharaoh should not be in any doubt about that.

As an interesting and significant aside in this account, it is observed that the two names for God are used quite selectively. Whenever Joseph was speaking to Egyptians about God, he used the name *Elohim* ("God"), as is befitting for those to whom God could be known only as mighty Creator and Sovereign (note Genesis 39:9; 40:8; 41:16, 25, 28, 32). Whenever the inspired writer of the narrative made comment about God's dealing with Joseph, however, he used the covenant name, *Jehovah*

("LORD"), as this was the redemptive name by which He had made Himself specially known to the people of His peculiar promises (note Genesis 39:2, 3, 5, 21, 23). There is thus always a clear spiritual reason for the various uses of the two divine names. They are not, as the higher critics have alleged, indications of separate documentary sources.

Once Joseph had given the interpretation, everything seemed perfectly clear, both to Pharaoh and his courtiers, including those who had previously been unable to explain the dreams. The interpretation was so obvious and forceful that no one could doubt its validity, and they must even have wondered why they themselves had not been able to see it sooner. God, however, had ordained even their own ignorance on these matters as a necessary part of the great plan He was now preparing to implement through Joseph and the children of Israel. "O the depth of the riches both of the wisdom and knowledge of God! how unsearchable are his judgments, and his ways past finding out! For who hath known the mind of the Lord? or who hath been his counsellor?" (Romans 11:33, 34).

Second in the Kingdom

Pharaoh's mysterious and disturbing dreams had been interpreted, and there could be no doubt that they had been explained correctly. Therefore, great trouble was ahead for the land of Egypt. As this fact began to intrude on Pharaoh's consciousness, he pondered what, if anything, he as leader of the country might be able to do about it. His people were accustomed to prosperity, with meat and bread in abundance. In fact, they provided food for export to many other countries as well. How, then, would they react under famine conditions? Would they blame him? Would they lose faith in their gods? Would revolution follow? Especially if this Pharaoh was, as most modern scholars think, a member of the hated Hyksos dynasties, thoughts such as these must have troubled him.

God, however, had not brought all these things to pass for the purpose of embarrassing or dethroning the king of Egypt. As a matter of fact, his own control over the country was destined to be strengthened by these events; but the underlying purpose of it all had to do rather with God's plan for Israel. Even Pharaoh and his great empire were like "a drop of a bucket" (Isaiah 40:15) in relation to God's eternal purposes, which at this point were centered in Joseph. Therefore, not only did God give Joseph the true interpretation of the dreams, but also an effective plan of action for Pharaoh.

Genesis 41:33-36

---

33 Now therefore let Phā′raōh look out a man discreet and wise, and set him over the land of Egypt.

34 Let Phā′raōh do *this*, and let him appoint officers over the land, and take up the fifth part of the land of Egypt in the seven plenteous years.

35 And let them gather all the food of those good years that come, and lay up corn under the hand of Phā′raōh, and let them keep food in the cities.

36 And that food shall be for store to the land against the seven years of famine, which shall be in the land of Egypt; that the land perish not through the famine.

Joseph continued speaking, after he had explained the events which God had revealed were coming on the land, to instruct Pharaoh in how he should prepare to meet the coming crisis. Instead of living every year on that year's abundance, as the Egyptians had grown accustomed to doing, they would need to implement a sound program of savings—not of money but of grain.

Unfortunately, the people themselves could not be relied on to store up for the coming years of famine. Human nature being what it is, most people will spend all they earn, and more, for their immediate needs, both real and imagined. The few individuals who would indeed save for the future would be tempted to profiteer when opportunity came. Besides, the need was going to be so great that nothing less than a centrally administered plan could really be effective on a national basis.

On the other hand, a central bureaucracy could easily lead to despotism and cruelty, especially if all available food supplies were in the hands of a self-seeking dictator. The key to the success of such a plan, and the survival of the nation, would be the chief administrator. The right man would be a deliverer; the wrong man could become a tyrant.

Therefore, Joseph's first recommendation was for Pharaoh to find the right man, a man who was possessed of both keen intellect and true wisdom, a man who could with confidence be placed over the whole land of Egypt to plan its future food production and distribution systems.

Then, this chief administrator should be provided with a corps of capable and trustworthy deputies to administer his plan. It would be necessary to levy a "double tithe" on the produce of Egypt during the years of plenty. It has been shown by historians that tithing was practiced in ancient Egypt and other nations, as a form of taxes or tribute to the king; but a 20 percent levy would be very unusual, and might well be resisted, especially if enacted by an unpopular sovereign. Thus, the chief administrator of this plan would have to be skilled in diplomacy and persuasion, as well as be of unquestioned integrity himself, in order to overcome the natural reluctance of the people to such a tax. Of course, resistance would be minimized in times of prosperity; so the plan could work if it was properly carried out.

The food which was gathered in this manner should, Joseph advised, then be preserved in large storehouses constructed for this purpose. The 80 percent that the people would have left would be more than adequate to meet all their needs, as well as the need for exports, during the seven plenteous years, and the rest would probably have been wasted anyhow. The food should be kept stored and guarded in depositories in key cities throughout the land, in order to have food available in the years of famine which would eventually come.

There is also a possibility that the grain was acquired by purchase, rather than by taxation. Scripture is not explicit on this point. In this case, the money must itself have come through taxes, so the effect would be the same. Because of the abundance, the price would have been low. However it was done, no one would have to suffer hardship, if it were handled judiciously and fairly. The key to it all would be to select the right administrator.

There is no indication in Joseph's words that he was trying to suggest himself as the administrator. Such a thought could hardly have even crossed his mind. He was not only a foreigner but a prisoner, and had never held a political office of any sort. He had neither training nor experience for such a position, and was only thirty years old. Though God had prepared Joseph for this moment, he himself had no inkling of it.

Genesis 41:37-44

---

37 ¶ And the thing was good in the eyes of Phā'raōh, and in the eyes of all his servants.

38 And Phā'raōh said unto his servants, Can we find *such a one* as this *is,* a man in whom the Spirit of God *is?*

39 And Phā'raōh said unto Joseph, Forasmuch as God hath showed thee all this, *there is* none so discreet and wise as thou *art:*

40 Thou shalt be over my house, and according unto thy word shall all my people be ruled: only in the throne will I be greater than thou.

41 And Phā'raōh said unto Joseph, See, I have set thee over all the land of Egypt.

42 And Phā'raōh took off his ring from his hand, and put it upon Joseph's hand, and arrayed him in vestures of fine linen, and put a gold chain about his neck;

43 And he made him to ride in the second chariot which he had; and they cried before him, Bow the knee: and he made him *ruler* over all the land of Egypt.

44 And Phā'raōh said unto Joseph, I *am* Phā'raōh, and without thee shall no man lift up his hand or foot in all the land of Egypt.

Pharaoh and his advisors were amazed and impressed, not only with Joseph's ability to interpret the dreams, but also with his wise counsel and, no doubt, also with his whole aspect and character. They immediately recognized that Joseph's plan was exactly the plan which they should implement. Even though Joseph had been completely unknown to them only a few hours earlier, it was transparently clear that here was a man of unique qualities, ideally suited to administer the plan he had formulated and proposed.

They also recognized that he was a man of unique spiritual attributes and that, indeed, this was the real reason for his other abilities. Though they could hardly have understood the doctrine of the Holy Spirit and the filling of the Spirit, nevertheless they acknowledged that in Joseph dwelt the Spirit of God (Hebrew *ruach Elohim*). He had indeed "professed a good profession before many witnesses" (I Timothy 6:12). With all his brilliant insights, moreover, he was deeply humble, giving complete credit to God.

With no hesitation, therefore, Pharaoh acknowledged that none other than Joseph was truly qualified to fill the post he had described. God was clearly with him. Even though Pharaoh and his courtiers were pagans and polytheists, they did apparently, at this stage in history, still retain enough knowledge of the true God of heaven that they recognized Joseph as one who really knew Him.

Pharaoh therefore immediately appointed Joseph over his entire kingdom, second only in authority to himself. He would have full power to carry out his plan, and to enact and implement all necessary policies and regulations. Absolute obedience to Joseph would be required of all Pharaoh's subjects.

This was a truly amazing development. An unknown alien prisoner suddenly elevated over the entire land of Egypt! The necessity for Joseph's long period of suffering and humiliation, learning patience and trust, is now clearly seen. Any other man so suddenly exalted would almost certainly have quickly been filled with heady pride, and would sooner or later have been ruined by success.

Joseph was properly tempered and mellowed, however. He knew that God had prepared him and that He would continue to strengthen and guide him. Though he had not sought or anticipated such responsibilities, he was prepared to assume them when God called him.

Immediately, Pharaoh set in motion Joseph's formal investiture into his office. He gave Joseph his signet ring, possession of which enabled its owner to place his seal and signature on official documents of state. He was clad in fine linen robes, the finest in Egypt. A golden chain, emblematic of his authority, was placed around his neck.

A royal procession of state was organized, with Joseph riding immediately behind Pharaoh in a chariot only slightly less ornate than that of Pharaoh himself, thus indicating to the entire populace that Joseph was now second in command in the kingdom. As he rode, men accompanying his chariot cried out to the people along the way to bow the knee to him.

Pharaoh of course made it plain that he was still the first ruler in the kingdom, but except for him, everyone in the land of Egypt must obey all Joseph commanded them to do. No one, in fact, could "move hand or foot" without Joseph's concurrence, a figure of speech, of course, but nevertheless indicative of his absolute authority.

Was there ever a more sudden and complete change of condition in a man's estate? It is perhaps in this more than in anything else that many expositors have seen in Joseph a type of Christ. The Lord Jesus "made himself of no reputation, and took upon him the form of a servant, and was made in the likeness of men." But, then, after humbling Himself still further and becoming obedient even unto the death of the cross, "God also hath highly exalted him, and given him a name which is above every name: That at the name of Jesus every knee should bow" (Philippians 2:7-10).

The Sons of Joseph

With such a tremendous shift of his fortunes, Joseph must have felt an unusual twinge of homesickness, desiring to share his joyful news with his father. This is suggested later by the names which he gave his sons when they were born. He could hardly fail to recall his own dreams and their prophetic suggestions. Even though they had been the direct occasion of his brothers' hatred and his resultant sale into slavery in Egypt, he could now begin to see the fulfillment of them. Though his family had not yet "made obeisance" to him (Genesis 37:7, 9), all the land of Egypt had done so. Besides, he now held a higher position, humanly speaking at least, than anyone in his family had ever held before. Of course, he was careful to attribute all this to God, rather than to his own efforts and abilities.

As far as the Egyptians were concerned, in spite of the high esteem in which he was now held, there was still one problem. Joseph was not an Egyptian, and this would inevitably be a hindering factor in the effectiveness with which he could carry out his duties.

Genesis 41:45, 46

---

45 And Phā'raōh called Joseph's name Zăph'năth–pā'à-nē'ăh; and he gave him to wife Ăs'ē-năth the daughter of Pōt'ĭ–phē'răh priest of Ŏn. And Joseph went out over *all* the land of Egypt.

46 ⁋ And Joseph *was* thirty years old when he stood before Phā'raōh king of Egypt. And Joseph went out from the presence of Phā'raōh, and went throughout all the land of Egypt.

Because of Joseph's alien background, Pharaoh decided to confer, insofar as possible, Egyptian citizenship and social status on Joseph, making it easier for him to be accepted as second ruler by the Egyptian people. He first gave him an Egyptian name, Zaphnath-paaneah, the exact meaning of which is somewhat doubtful. It has been variously interpreted as "Abundance of Life," "Savior of the World," "Revealer of Secrets," "God's Word Speaking Life," "Furnisher of Sustenance," and so on. This variety of possible names at least indicates that Pharaoh probably conferred a name on him which was expressive of his unique contribution to Egypt at this time in her history. Of course, all the above names can also be taken as descriptive of Christ Himself, of whom Joseph is presumed by many to be a type.

Pharaoh next obtained a suitable wife for Joseph—suitable in the eyes of the Egyptians, that is. The girl chosen was the daughter of an Egyptian priest. Nothing is said about her except her name and parentage. We can only assume that Joseph, dedicated as he was to the Lord, would not have consented to marry her unless he was satisfied that she would leave her own pagan beliefs to follow Jehovah. She was to be the mother of Joseph's children, and the problems encountered in his own home background would have caused him to understand fully how essential it would be for him and his wife to have one mind in the training of their children to follow the Lord.

The girl's name was Asenath, which apparently indicates something like "Dedicated to Neith," Neith being the Egyptian equivalent of the goddess Minerva. Thus there is little doubt that she had been brought up in the polytheistic Egyptian religion. Her father, Potipherah (meaning essentially the same thing as Potiphar, "given by Ra, the sun-god"), was actually a prominent priest in this religious system, located at the temple at On (probably the same as Heliopolis, a city specially devoted to the sun-god). Of course, as we have noted before, some knowledge of the true God had continued into the Egypt of Abraham's day and into the time of Joseph as well; so it may be that it was not as difficult for Asenath to transfer her faith from Ra to Jehovah as we might at first suppose.

In any case, Joseph did marry her and, from all evidence, did find her to be a suitable and faithful mother for his children. So far as the record goes, at least, Joseph never married any wife other than Asenath.

After these arrangements had been consummated, Joseph immediately proceeded to get to work on the project with which he had been entrusted. The first thing he had to do, of course, was to go "out over all the land of Egypt." He needed to have firsthand knowledge of the resources and people, and this could only be acquired by a survey region by region.

It is at this point that the record indicates Joseph had reached the age of thirty. Thus he had been gone from his home for thirteen years (Genesis 37:2). He was still quite a young man, but was now mature enough to assume and carry out these great responsibilities. After his initial survey, the text again mentions that he "went throughout all the land of Egypt," probably indicating a much more detailed, unit-by-unit survey of the agriculture and other productive occupations of the Egyptians. He was then able to organize, with his assistants, a comprehensive program of conservation during the good years ahead.

Genesis 41:47-49

---

47 And in the seven plenteous years the earth brought forth by handfuls.

48 And he gathered up all the food of the seven years, which were in the land of Egypt, and laid up the food in the cities: the food of the field, which *was* round about every city, laid he up in the same.

49 And Joseph gathered corn as the sand of the sea, very much, until he left numbering; for *it was* without number.

Just as Joseph had predicted, Egypt began to experience productivity and prosperity greater than she had ever known. Seven long years of abundance were enjoyed by the people, as the "earth brought forth by handfuls." The word here is *gomets,* and personifies the earth as bestowing her bounty "with full hands." Joseph began to implement his plan, gathering up the 20 percent levy of grain throughout the land, and then installing it in the strategic storehouses that had been erected for the purpose. Perhaps in order to further assure the people that the food he was collecting was really for their own future use, he stored the grain from the fields around each city in the storehouse for that city. The levy was exacted fairly and equally everywhere, and then stored up at such points all through the land, so that no one could complain of discrimination or profiteering.

As the years moved along, the crops continued to be so abundant, and the resulting portion collected by Joseph so vast, that it finally became unnecessary, if not impossible, to keep precise records. The grains of corn were like the grains of sand in the sea, so numerous were they: quite impossible to count except possibly in units of filled storehouses. God had truly blessed the land, as He had said.

Genesis 41:50-52

---

50 And unto Joseph were born two sons, before the years of famine came: which Ăs′ē-năth the daughter of Pŏt′ĭphē′răh priest of Ŏn bare unto him.

51 And Joseph called the name of the firstborn Mănăs′sĕh: For God, *said he,* hath made me forget all my toil, and all my father's house.

52 And the name of the second called he Ē′phrā-ĭm: For God hath caused me to be fruitful in the land of my affliction.

It was during this seven-year period of prosperity that two sons were born to Joseph and Asenath. These two sons were, of course, destined to give their names to two of the most prominent tribes of Israel.

The boys were named by Joseph in recognition of his unusual experiences. The first was named Manasseh, meaning "Forgetting," and signifying that God had caused Joseph to forget all the long years of suffering and rejection he had endured—not in the sense that he had no memory of them, of course, but rather that the bitterness had been removed. Joseph could now see, as he later told his brothers (Genesis 50:20), that all of his troubles had been allowed by God for his own good and for his family's ultimate deliverance.

His second son was named Ephraim ("Doubly Fruitful") in thankfulness for the manner in which God had so richly blessed him and prospered him, in the very land where he had been unjustly afflicted for so many years.

It is thus that God typically deals with believers, particularly those whom He has called to special service and fruit-bearing. First the testing, then the triumph. Thus it was also with the Lord Jesus Christ. "It is a faithful saying: For if we be dead with him, we shall also live with him: If we suffer, we shall also reign with him" (II Timothy 2:11, 12). "For I reckon that the sufferings of this present time are not worthy to be compared with the glory which shall be revealed in us" (Romans 8:18). Even if one's entire life is spent in suffering and rejection, in the name of Christ, he can have confidence that all is in preparation for a great work for the Lord in the ages to come, following the resurrection. "And God shall wipe away all tears from their eyes. . . . And there shall be no more curse: but the throne of God and of the Lamb shall be in it; and his servants shall serve him . . . and they shall reign for ever and ever" (Revelation 21:4; 22:3, 5).

Genesis 41:53-57

---

53 ¶ And the seven years of plenteousness, that was in the land of Egypt, were ended.

54 And the seven years of dearth began to come, according as Joseph had said: and the dearth was in all lands; but in all the land of Egypt there was bread.

55 And when all the land of Egypt was famished, the people cried to Phā'raōh for bread: and Phā'raōh said unto all the Egyptians, Go unto Joseph; what he saith to you, do.

56 And the famine was over all the face of the earth: and Joseph opened all the storehouses, and sold unto the Egyptians; and the famine waxed sore in the land of Egypt.

57 And all countries came into Egypt to Joseph for to buy *corn;* because that the famine was *so* sore in all lands.

Finally, exactly as Joseph had said, the years of plenty came to an end. The people had grown accustomed to having all they needed, with much surplus left over, and probably were taken quite by surprise that such prosperity could not be regarded as a permanent right which they had somehow acquired by virtue of being residents of Egypt. When one has grown used to a certain high standard of living, he considers anything less a severe imposition, even though most of the people in the world have had to be content with a much lower level of life-quality, as it is called, than anything he can imagine. Certain ominous signs today, for example, seem to suggest that Americans will soon have to give up many of the creature comforts which they have come to regard as rights and necessities; and such deprivations, if they come, will undoubtedly be considered impossibly traumatic by most of us.

The story of Joseph in Egypt, if nothing else, should warn us that the blessings of prosperity come from the Lord and can as easily be removed by the Lord, as He wills. It should also teach us the value of saving a portion of what comes to hand, not only by depositing it in the bank account against a future rainy day, but even more by devoting it to the service of Christ, where it can never be lost. "If therefore ye have not been faithful in the unrighteous mammon, who will commit to your trust the true riches?" (Luke 16:11).

Had not Joseph prepared against the day of adversity, not only for himself but for the whole land, no doubt most of the people would soon have been reduced to abject poverty and even starvation. The years of famine came, and the meager supplies of most people quickly were exhausted. As a matter of fact, the famine came on all the nations in that part of the world; but none of them had made provision for it, as had been done in Egypt. Eventually the famine was due to affect even the land of Canaan and the family of Jacob.

Of all the lands affected by the famine, it soon appeared that only Egypt had any reserves of bread. In Egypt itself, individual stocks of food were finally exhausted, and the land was yielding only the minimum of new crops, if any. The physical causes of the famine are not stated, but it is probable that the Nile was running low because of droughts in the highlands, so that the annual inundations which nourished the productive areas of Egypt no longer occurred. In Canaan and Syria, the rains had evidently failed for some reason.

When the people began to be concerned, naturally their first reaction was to complain to Pharaoh. It is the government's responsibility to provide food for us, they reasoned, though they could hardly have expected Pharaoh to decree an increase in the flow of water in the Nile!

In this case, however, thanks to Joseph, the government really was able to help them. Pharaoh simply sent proclamations throughout the land announcing that food was available, and that they could obtain it by dealing with Joseph's food administration. Joseph in turn waited as long as possible, the better to conserve the grain which was available,. and then finally opened up the storehouses to allow the people to purchase grain.

Advocates of welfarism may wonder why Joseph did not simply give the food to the people instead of making them buy it. Joseph instead maintained strict control over the supplies, in order to prevent looting and waste, knowing that even the vast supplies that had been accumulated would have to be carefully husbanded to last through seven long years of famine. He then sold them for a reasonable price and on an equitable basis to all who were in need of grain. Had it been given away, it would have rewarded indolence and shortsightedness. Furthermore, the grain had been acquired by lawful and fair means, by devoting most of the government's taxing and buying power to it for seven years. To give it away would have meant bankrupting and probably destroying the government. It was thus perfectly right and proper for the grain to be sold, not given as a handout, to all who could afford to pay. It is reasonable to assume that special provision was made for those who were truly in poverty and unable to buy. Quite likely, they were employed on useful government service or construction of one form or another, in order to earn the necessary cash or credit to buy the supplies they needed. The people could hardly be taxed in significant amounts during the years of famine, since they were producing little; so the income from the sale of grain in effect had to take the place of taxes during those years.

As the famine wore on in other lands as well, news reached them about the Egyptian storehouses; and they began to send caravans and missions down to Egypt to buy corn. Eventually this situation would lead to the migration of Jacob and his family to Egypt. This, of course, was the ultimate purpose, in God's economy, of the entire series of events.

It is remarkable that the 20 percent of the produce during the seven years of plenty sufficed to meet all needs, not only for the Egyptians but also for those delegations from other lands, during the seven years of famine. The population thus got by on only one-fourth of what had been available during the seven good years. These proportions constitute a remarkable testimony to both the overwhelming abundance which God had provided during the first seven years and also to the exceptional efficiency of Joseph's management of the gradually dwindling stores of grain during the last seven years. People can, when they have to, get by quite well on far less than they are accustomed to during good times. God has graciously promised to supply all our needs (Philippians 4:19), but not necessarily all our wants.

By the time the famine came, Joseph had been in Egypt twenty years. He had never received any word from his family during all that time. For all he knew, his father might well be dead. Joseph must often have longed to see him, and even his brothers (time and God's providential dealings had considerably reduced his bitterness over what they had done to him). Probably, since coming to power in Egypt, he must have considered taking a trip (well protected by soldiers) back into Canaan to look up the family again; but, if so, he had presumably been hindered from it by the pressure of the business activities for which he was responsible. In any case, it would not be much longer now (though he did not know this) before God would be sending his relatives down to him in Egypt.

21

Joseph and His Brothers

(Genesis 42-45)

Famine in the Land

Genesis 39, 40, and 41 have concentrated on the experiences of Joseph in Egypt during the twenty-year period following his exile. He had spent a total of thirteen years in Potiphar's house and in the prison, and then another seven years as the second in command in the land of Egypt. Back at his boyhood home in the land of Canaan, except for the experiences of Judah as described in Genesis 38, Scripture does not tell us what had been happening to Jacob and his other sons during this interval. They had, by this time, all established their own homes and families. Benjamin himself was about twenty-three years old.

Joseph's ten older brothers had been living with a guilty secret for all those twenty years. They must often have thought of Joseph, and what they had done to him; and they must have wondered what had happened to him, down in the land of Egypt. Jacob himself had never stopped grieving over Joseph, though he continued to fulfill his responsibilities as head of his large clan.

The family was now beginning to go through hard times. The famine which had settled on Egypt had also affected Canaan and the other lands of the region. Their business was predominantly cattle and sheep raising, rather than agriculture, but the drought had seriously damaged the entire economy. Furthermore, even though they still had great wealth, money could not buy grain if there was no grain to be bought.

Genesis 42:1-4

CHAPTER 42

NOW when Jacob saw that there was corn in Egypt, Jacob said unto his sons, Why do ye look one upon another? 2 And he said, Behold, I have heard that there is corn in Egypt: get you down thither, and buy for us from thence; that we may live, and not die.

3 ¶ And Joseph's ten brethren went down to buy corn in Egypt.

4 But Benjamin, Joseph's brother, Jacob sent not with his brethren; for he said, Lest peradventure mischief befall him.

It soon became known throughout Canaan, however, that there was an abundance of grain in Egypt. Delegations were traveling southward to purchase grain there and bringing it home with them. It began to be obvious that Jacob also would have to send his sons down to Egypt, and they were aware of this. However, they were reluctant to go, no doubt because of their guilty consciences concerning Joseph and their fear that they might run into him there. To Jacob's suggestion that they go there to buy corn, they responded merely by "looking one upon another," each trying to see what the other might have been thinking.

Jacob finally insisted that they go, each to bring back food for his own family and servants; for they had now reached the point where there was imminent danger of death by starvation. It was not expedient for Jacob himself to try to migrate to Egypt, as Abraham had done in an earlier famine, because his holdings and retinue were quite large by this time.

It apparently would not have been acceptable to the Egyptians to deal with servants; so the ten brothers themselves had to go. The youngest son, Benjamin, stayed home, mainly because Jacob did not want to take a chance on anything happening to him on the long and dangerous trip. Jacob dearly missed both Rachel and Joseph, and Benjamin was Rachel's only remaining son. Jacob therefore would not allow Benjamin to accompany them.

Genesis 42:5-9

---

5 And the sons of Ĭş′rā-ĕl came to buy corn among those that came: for the famine was in the land of Cā′năan.

6 And Joseph *was* the governor over the land, *and* he *it was* that sold to all the people of the land: and Joseph's brethren came, and bowed down themselves before him *with* their faces to the earth.

7 And Joseph saw his brethren, and he knew them, but made himself strange unto them, and spake roughly unto them; and he said unto them, Whence come ye? And they said, From the land of Cā′năan to buy food.

8 And Joseph knew his brethren, but they knew not him.

9 And Joseph remembered the dreams

which he dreamed of them, and said   nakedness of the land ye are come.
unto them, Ye *are* spies; to see the

The ten sons of Israel then equipped a donkey caravan and headed for Egypt. They were not unique in this respect. Many other caravans were entering Egypt in those days on a similar mission, as the famine had become severe everywhere.

They had no inkling that Joseph would turn out to be the one from whom they would have to purchase the grain, of course. Joseph was governor, or "ruler," over the land; and he apparently maintained close personal supervision over his stores of grain, realizing how critical these were to the survival of Egypt during the long years of famine ahead of them. Apparently, everyone coming into Egypt from foreign lands to buy grain had to obtain a direct permit from Joseph before he would be allowed to do so. It might well be that, under cloak of such a purchasing mission, outsiders might enter the land for subversive purposes. Foreign kings might covet Egypt's wealth and desire to infiltrate and sabotage and possibly invade and plunder the land. It was up to Joseph to carefully screen all such alien travelers to be sure of their purposes.

As a matter of fact, as more and more delegations had been arriving in Egypt from the land of Canaan, Joseph may well have anticipated that, sooner or later, someone from his own family would have to show up. He knew they would soon need grain, and would have to buy it from Egypt.

By this time, he was more anxious for reconciliation with his brothers than for vengeance. At the same time, he did not know how they would feel toward him, nor did he know whether his father was still alive. It is not unreasonable to suppose that he had a real concern lest the family break up after Jacob's death. He knew much about God's plans for the nation of Israel, as his father had taught him these things while he was yet a boy; but he also knew of the sinful practices and the factionalism and selfishness among his brothers. If indeed his father was dead, or should soon die, there might be a very real danger that the family members would descend to bitter quarreling over the inheritance, and finally would be scattered. In that event, God's plans and promises for Israel, confirming His promises to Abraham and Isaac, would be defeated. Joseph knew that, unless there had been some drastic changes in his brothers since he had left home, only he himself was very concerned about such matters. Therefore, he longed to be able to do something which would restore close family ties and a distinct family unity and sense of purpose. As he had been elevated to such prominence in Egypt, he must have realized that somehow this was for the very accomplishment of God's plans for his family. And so he often thought and planned what he would do if and when his brothers should ever arrive in Egypt.

Joseph was, therefore, not very surprised when one day they appeared before him, even though they themselves did not recognize him. They had not changed in appearance as much as he had, of course. He had been a lad of seventeen when they last saw him; now he was about thirty-eight. Furthermore, he was not dressed as a slave, but as a king. Also, he spoke to them through an interpreter (verse 23), and so they did not even know he could speak their language.

As did everyone who came into Joseph's presence, except Pharaoh himself (Genesis 41:43), they had to bow down before him. They did not realize, of course, that in so doing they were making the very dream come true for which they had hated him (Genesis 37:7, 8). The word "bowed down" in verse 6 is the same as "make obeisance" in 37:7.

Joseph, evidently in accordance with his predetermined plan, did not make himself known to his brothers at this time. He wanted first of all to determine their true attitudes and then to set events in motion which would finally bring them to a true attitude of repentance and unity toward God and among themselves. Therefore, he acted harshly and as though he were very suspicious of their motives in coming into Egypt. When they told him they had come from Canaan simply to buy food, he replied by accusing them of being spies, using a food-purchasing mission as a cover for finding those parts of Egypt which might be vulnerable to invasion. As he saw them bowing and fearfully protesting that he had misunderstood them, he could not help but recall the dreams he had had long ago, which were now coming to pass before his eyes.

Genesis 42:10-13

---

10 And they said unto him, Nay, my lord, but to buy food are thy servants come.
11 We *are* all one man's sons; we *are* true *men;* thy servants are no spies.
12 And he said unto them, Nay, but to see the nakedness of the land ye are come.
13 And they said, Thy servants *are* twelve brethren, the sons of one man in the land of Cā'năan; and, behold, the youngest *is* this day with our father, and one *is* not.

As his brothers continued to insist that they had come merely to buy food, they began to volunteer more information about themselves. They were all brothers, who lived and worked with their father back in the land of Canaan. One brother was back home with their father and one was dead. They did not know Joseph was dead, of course, but that was what they had implied to their father, and so for many years that had been their stock answer to anyone who questioned them about Joseph. Their reason for mentioning their family relationship was to convince this governor that they were not spies. No foreign king would have sent ten brothers on a spy mission, especially if they were his own sons. It should be obvious that their only reason for coming to Egypt was to get food for their families.

Logical as this argument may have been, Joseph kept insisting that they were spies, professing to doubt their story about family connections. Exactly who was acting as spokesman is not said; evidently the brothers were speaking and protesting more or less together. Their claim that they were sons of one man did at least suggest to this governor that they were not all sons of the same mother.

Genesis 42:14-17

---

14 And Joseph said unto them, That *is it* that I spake unto you, saying, Ye *are* spies:
15 Hereby ye shall be proved: By the life of Phā'raōh ye shall not go forth hence, except your youngest brother come hither.
16 Send one of you, and let him fetch your brother, and ye shall be kept in prison, that your words may be proved, whether *there be any* truth in you: or else by the life of Phā'raōh surely ye *are* spies.
17 And he put them all together into ward three days.

Joseph surely, all the time they had been talking, had been wondering about Benjamin, who obviously was not with them. Could they have possibly resented Benjamin, as they did him, since they two had the same mother and were their father's favorites? Now they had just said Benjamin was still at home, but they had also said Joseph was dead. Since they had lied in the one case, perhaps they also had in the other. Therefore he felt he must test them further. Before he could really accept them and proceed to a reconciliation he would have to know the truth about his younger brother.

At this point he proposed that he would test the validity of their story about being brothers by having them send for their younger brother. In the meantime, he would continue to assume they were spies, and keep them all in prison until their story could be verified. Joseph may have reasoned also that, as they had once spurned their brother's pleas, so now theirs should be spurned. As they had sent him away into slavery and imprisonment, so now it would be good for them to have a similar experience.

All the while, Joseph maintained his appearance as a harsh and stubborn Egyptian official, even taking an oath "by the life of Pharaoh" that he would keep the men in prison as spies until they could demonstrate the veracity of their story by bringing their younger brother there. The brothers obviously were dismayed, because they realized that, even if one of them did return with Benjamin, there would be nothing to prevent this suspicious Egyptian ruler from throwing him into prison too. They realized that they could very well spend the rest of their lives here in an Egyptian prison. Furthermore, they could not help but realize that, if such proved to be the case, it would be divine justice, since that was the fate to which they had long ago consigned their hated younger brother.

Genesis 42:18-23

18 And Joseph said unto them the third day, This do, and live; *for* I fear God:

19 If ye *be* true *men,* let one of your brethren be bound in the house of your prison: go ye, carry corn for the famine of your houses:

20 But bring your youngest brother unto me; so shall your words be verified, and ye shall not die. And they did so.

21 ¶ And they said one to another. We *are* verily guilty concerning our brother, in that we saw the anguish of his soul, when he besought us, and we would not hear; therefore is this distress come upon us.

22 And Reuben answered them, saying, Spake I not unto you, saying, Do not sin against the child; and ye would not hear? therefore, behold, also his blood is required.

23 And they knew not that Joseph understood *them;* for he spake unto them by an interpreter.

After three days, Joseph summoned them again and told them it would not be necessary for all of them to remain there. He did not really wish to cause his father, and the rest of the household back in Canaan, any more grief than necessary. Besides, he felt that three days in prison would be enough to cause all of them to begin at least to have a change of heart from their earlier behavior and attitudes. It is interesting that he told them that his change to a more considerate course of action was because "I fear God." Since he was apparently an Egyptian, here was a testimony to these children of Israel that it was possible for a high official who lived in an idolatrous land still to know the true God and to have his behavior influenced accordingly.

Joseph then told them it would be sufficient for only one of them to be kept in prison while the rest of them returned home. The one brother would also be released when they returned to Egypt with their younger brother. In the meantime, they could proceed to carry the food, which they said they had come to acquire, back to their households.

Joseph was sure they would come back, because he knew the famine

would persist many years. The brothers also realized they would possibly
have to return, even if they should decide it expedient to abandon the
brother who would be held hostage. But at least they could go home for
the present, and take the urgently needed food back with them. If and
when they returned, however, they had better have their younger brother
with them, or the governor would decide they had been spies after all
and would put every one of them to death.

By this time, their emotions and consciences were surely in considerable turmoil. Their minds were now well exercised in remembering what
they had done to their younger brother, and in sensing that all of this was
a very appropriate punishment. When Joseph gave them this ultimatum,
they all with apparently one voice acknowledged to each other (not
realizing that Joseph could understand what they were saying) that this
distress had come on them because they had sinned against their brother.

It is noteworthy that, although there are many sins recorded in the
Book of Genesis, both of God's people and of others, this is the only
time in which the guilty ones actually make a confession of sin. These
ten brothers had gone through a truly traumatic experience the past
few days, and it had stirred their consciences to the depths. Not only
had they conspired to slay, and then, changing their minds, to sell, their
brother, but they had ignored his anguished pleadings to spare him. They
realized fully that they were now receiving what they had long deserved,
and so their bitterness was directed against themselves, not against the
governor.

Joseph perhaps had held Reuben, as the oldest brother, chiefly responsible for what his brothers had done to him. Now, however, he
heard Reuben reminding the others that he had tried to persuade them
not to carry out their crime. But Reuben, unstable and weak as he was,
had never been willing to tell his father the truth or later to set in motion any attempt to rescue Joseph. He was not quite as guilty as the
others, but neither was he innocent. He, like the others, assumed that
most likely Joseph had died in Egypt, and they were all therefore guilty
of his blood. Now it seemed as though their own blood would sooner or
later be required in payment.

None of them, of course, had any idea that Joseph could understand
what they were saying. He had been careful to carry out his conversations
with them through an interpreter. This, incidentally, provides a clue to
the otherwise somewhat enigmatic fact that, in spite of the confusion of
tongues that had taken place at Babel, all through the Book of Genesis
we read about people of different nations apparently freely conversing
with each other. This reference makes it obvious that, in most cases at

least, such conversations were carried out through interpreters. In those days, as in ours, people were able to learn foreign languages; and evidently there were linguistic specialists who actually made a profession of working as translators and interpreters. Apparently this was so common that ordinarily it is not even mentioned except when, as here, it has a vital bearing on the narrative. Joseph himself had evidently learned the Egyptian language while he was a servant in Potiphar's house.

Genesis 42:24-26

24 And he turned himself about from them, and wept; and returned to them again, and communed with them, and took from them Simeon, and bound him before their eyes.

25 ¶ Then Joseph commanded to fill their sacks with corn, and to restore every man's money into his sack, and to give them provision for the way: and thus did he unto them.

26 And they laded their asses with the corn, and departed thence.

As Joseph heard them, he realized his prayers had been answered. They had actually come to the point of confession and repentance of their sin. He himself became so overcome by his emotions that he had to make a hasty exit from their presence, lest they should see him weeping. After regaining control of himself, he returned and resumed his instructions to them. One of them must stay bound in prison while the others went home. Joseph, having heard that Reuben had at least partially tried to prevent their crime, realized that Simeon must have been chiefly responsible. Therefore, he had his guard take Simeon, and put him in bonds before their eyes. Simeon was next oldest to Reuben, and had long manifested a cruel nature. He needed the instruction of a time in prison and chains more than any of the others. The nine other brothers must have noticed with some surprise the apparent coincidence that the governor would place in prison the one among them who had been most responsible for their heinous act and therefore for the retribution that now seemed to be overtaking them. They possibly regarded this as further evidence of God's overruling justice.

Joseph then gave orders—in the Egyptian language, of course—that the sacks should be filled with grain and the men sent on their way. He also told his servants to restore the money they had paid for the grain into their respective sacks, realizing what embarrassment and concern this would cause them, but also knowing that it would further awaken their consciences. He also gave them provisions for the trip. The brothers then quickly loaded the sacks and other provisions on their asses, and departed, no doubt relieved that they had been given at least a temporary respite from punishment. Obviously, they were anxious to get home. Apparently they were not overly grieved at having to leave Simeon, since they later seemed in no hurry to go back to Egypt to get him. Simeon was hardly the best loved among them, for obvious reasons.

Genesis 42:27-35

27 And as one of them opened his sack to give his ass provender in the inn, he espied his money; for, behold, it *was* in his sack's mouth.

28 And he said unto his brethren, My money is restored; and, lo, *it is* even in my sack: and their heart failed *them,* and they were afraid, saying one to another, What *is* this *that* God hath done unto us?

29 ¶ And they came unto Jacob their father unto the land of Cā'năan, and told him all that befell unto them; saying,

30 The man, *who is* the lord of the land, spake roughly to us, and took us for spies of the country.

31 And we said unto him, We *are* true *men;* we are no spies:

32 We *be* twelve brethren, sons of our father; one *is* not, and the youngest *is* this day with our father in the land of Cā'năan.

33 And the man, the lord of the country, said unto us, Hereby shall I know that ye *are* true *men;* leave one of your brethren *here* with me, and take *food* for the famine of your households, and be gone:

34 And bring your youngest brother unto me: then shall I know that ye *are* no spies, but *that* ye *are* true *men:* so will I deliver you your brother, and ye shall traffic in the land.

35 ¶ And it came to pass as they emptied their sacks, that, behold, every man's bundle of money *was* in his sack: and when *both* they and their father saw the bundles of money, they were afraid.

Their journey back home must have been over a distance of about 250 miles or more. Presumably Jacob was still living in Hebron, and Joseph's headquarters were possibly at or near the city of Memphis, which is about ten miles south of the present city of Cairo. Thus, the journey would take them probably about three weeks.

Somewhere along the way, their extra provisions were used up, and one of them opened his sack to get grain for his ass. He was dismayed to find some money there on top of the grain. His brothers were likewise afraid when he told them what he had found. It apparently did not occur to them at the time that money would be found in all the sacks. They knew they had paid for the grain, but now it was obvious that somehow not all the price had been paid, and this was real grounds for alarm. When the time would come that they had to go back to Egypt, the governor would have still a further charge to bring against them. They attributed this development also to the Lord's judgment on them, having already become keenly aware of the apparent relation between their own predicament and the one they had inflicted on Joseph.

Apparently they were already near home by the time they had to dip into this sack; so they soon reached their father and proceeded to tell him the whole story. In spite of Jacob's advanced age, he was still very much the dominant figure in the family. None of his sons questioned his authority or ability.

When they told Jacob about the governor's demand that they bring Benjamin down the next time they came, they realized he would be greatly displeased and distressed; but of course it was necessary to tell him. If they wished to continue buying grain in Egypt, and if they wished to recover Simeon, they would have to do it.

After they had told the story, they proceeded to empty their sacks of grain into the storehouse. Now they were shocked to find, in each man's sack, the bundle of money which he supposedly had paid for the grain. They had come out of Egypt not only with a large supply of food, but had done so without paying for it! They realized they would all be subject to the charge of theft when they returned. Up until this point, Jacob had apparently taken their bad news with relative calm; but now both he and his sons were greatly alarmed.

Genesis 42:36-38

---

36 And Jacob their father said unto them, Me have ye bereaved *of my children:* Joseph *is* not, and Simeon *is* not, and ye will take Benjamin *away:* all these things are against me.

37 And Reuben spake unto his father, saying, Slay my two sons, if I bring him not to thee: deliver him into my hand, and I will bring him to thee again.

38 And he said, My son shall not go down with you; for his brother is dead, and he is left alone: if mischief befall him by the way in the which ye go, then shall ye bring down my gray hairs with sorrow to the grave.

Jacob accused his nine sons (more truly than he knew) of having been responsible for the loss of two of his children, Joseph and Simeon, and now surely they were going to cause the loss of Benjamin also, which was more than he could bear. And not only this, but even if they went into Egypt with Benjamin as the man had instructed them, they could all be charged with robbery, and maybe none of them would be allowed to return! Jacob would lose his entire family, and then how could God's plans for Israel ever be accomplished? No wonder he was upset; before he could really think through the situation and regain his trust and faith in God, he cried out that everything was against him.

Quite the contrary, however, in reality. Not only were all things not working against him but, as a matter of fact, all things were working together for good (see Romans 8:28). So it often is with God's people.

Even when all the circumstances seem negative, God is working positively, on behalf of those who are the called according to His purpose. There is never just cause to fear that God has let things get out of control. He has higher purposes related to our eternal future, for which He is preparing us through such difficulties.

Upset by his father's distress, Reuben (typically concerned, and meaning well, but nevertheless confused and unstable) rashly promised that he would be responsible for Benjamin if Jacob would let him go with them. If anything happened to him, he assured his father, then Jacob could slay his (Reuben's) own two sons in punishment. Exactly what satisfaction he thought his father could get out of killing two of his grandsons, after already losing his sons, is hardly clear. Reuben simply spoke without thinking. He perhaps was trying to appear noble to his father, who had long since been badly disappointed in this eldest son of his; but he only succeeded in looking still more foolish.

Jacob simply refused altogether to consider letting Benjamin go down to Egypt. He had grieved so bitterly over Joseph that he was not willing even to think about allowing Benjamin to risk his life. If anything would happen to Benjamin, Jacob felt that he himself could not survive. He would go down to the grave (actually *Sheol,* the place of departed spirits) if he no longer had Benjamin at least to remind him of Rachel and Joseph. And there the matter stood for the time being.

Joseph and Benjamin

Joseph's brothers had experienced a measure of repentance during their traumatic experience in Egypt, but there was still much to be accomplished in their hearts by God's Spirit before they would be truly prepared and unified spiritually to serve as the fathers and founders of the twelve tribes of Israel. They must yet have to confront Joseph himself, learn to undergo the utter confusion and helplessness into which sin leads, and finally experience the joy of forgiveness in grace, together with restoration to fellowship and unity. They must learn true faith in God and His purposes, as well as obedience to God's commands.

To accomplish these things, another trip down to Egypt was necessary. The famine continued longer than anyone could have anticipated, and the abundant supplies which they had brought back on their first trip finally were nearly exhausted. Nevertheless, they kept putting off a second trip (Genesis 43:10) because of their certainty that it would prove disastrous unless Benjamin were with them and because of Jacob's adamant refusal to let him go.

Genesis 43:1-5

CHAPTER 43

AND the famine *was* sore in the land. 2 And it came to pass, when they had eaten up the corn which they had brought out of Egypt, their father said unto them, Go again, buy us a little food.
3 And Judah spake unto him, saying, The man did solemnly protest unto us, saying, Ye shall not see my face, except your brother *be* with you.
4 If thou wilt send our brother with us, we will go down and buy thee food:
5 But if thou wilt not send *him,* we will not go down: for the man said unto us, Ye shall not see my face, except your brother *be* with you.

Finally, however, the famine became so grievous that their grain supply was fully exhausted, and they had to do something. Jacob again instructed his sons to go back to Egypt to buy "a little food." Evidently he could hope only that they would be able to get a small amount, since the Egyptians were carefully rationing all foreign sales; but any amount was better than none.

By this time, Judah seems to have taken over as spokesman for the brothers. Evidently no one paid much attention to Reuben any more, Simeon was in prison in Egypt, and Levi was apparently also regarded now with some disfavor because of his association with Simeon, probably in the matter of Joseph's sale as well as in the case of the Shechemite slaughter. Judah urged Jacob to recognize that they would be quite unable to buy even a little food, and probably would not even be allowed to leave Egypt, unless they took Benjamin with them. "The man" would not even talk to them without Benjamin; he would simply assume they had lied to him before about having another brother, and so would assume they were spies and either have them imprisoned or slain. Though he was properly respectful of his father, Judah insisted that they could not go back to Egypt without their youngest brother. With him, however, they would be willing to make another trip there, even though they certainly were not overjoyed at the prospect.

Genesis 43:6-10

6 And Ĭş′rā-ĕl said, Wherefore dealt ye *so* ill with me, *as* to tell the man whether ye had yet a brother?
7 And they said, The man asked us straitly of our state, and of our kindred, saying, *Is* your father yet alive? have ye *another* brother? and we told him according to the tenor of these words: Could we certainly know that he would say, Bring your brother down?
8 And Judah said unto Ĭş′rā-ĕl his father, Send the lad with me, and we will arise and go; that we may live, and not die, both we, and thou, *and* also our little ones.
9 I will be surety for him; of my hand shalt thou require him: if I bring him not unto thee, and set him before thee, then

let me bear the blame for ever: now we had returned this second time.
10 For except we had lingered, surely

It is interesting that, at this point in the narrative, the name Israel begins to be used instead of Jacob. This name had not been used since Genesis 37:13. It seems that, as long as Jacob seemed completely broken and defeated by virtue of Joseph's apparent death, his old name, Jacob, is used (note Genesis 37:34; 42:1, 4, 29, 36). Now, for the first time, he begins to consider the possibility of allowing Benjamin to go. His faith is in process of revival, and so he is called Israel again.

First, however, he rebuked his sons for even mentioning that they had a younger brother; that was no affair of the Egyptians, so why did they bring it up? Several of the brothers apparently spoke this time, all insisting that they only told the governor about their family because he had questioned them so closely, asking them specifically whether their father were alive and whether they had any other brother. They had no way of anticipating that he would insist that they bring their brother to Egypt.

Judah then spoke up again, promising that he himself would be surety for Benjamin. He put the matter kindly, but bluntly. This was really their only possible course of action. If they didn't follow through on it, not only would Benjamin die, but all of them, including Jacob's grandchildren. Death by starvation was becoming a very real possibility, so severe was the food shortage. Quite likely they had heard reports of others starving in Canaan and nearby lands, and it now had become a very present danger in their own families. There was no time to waste any more. Judah would do everything possible to assure Benjamin's safety. He personally could be held accountable if Benjamin did not return. He concluded by reminding Jacob that, if they had not procrastinated so long, they could already have made the trip to Egypt and back twice over.

Genesis 43:11-14

---

11 And their father Ĭṣ′rā-ĕl said unto them, If *it must be* so now, do this; take of the best fruits in the land in your vessels, and carry down the man a present, a little balm, and a little honey, spices and myrrh, nuts and almonds:
12 And take double money in your hand; and the money that was brought again in the mouth of your sacks, carry *it* again in your hand; peradventure it *was* an oversight.
13 Take also your brother, and arise, go again unto the man:
14 And God Almighty give you mercy before the man, that he may send away your other brother, and Benjamin. If I be bereaved *of my children*, I am bereaved.

Jacob (now called Israel again) recognized that Judah was speaking sensibly and that he himself had been behaving rather carnally and selfishly, thus endangering his whole family. Benjamin himself was apparently not afraid to go to Egypt; evidently this attitude had been Jacob's only. Even though he was now willing to let him go, he felt it would be wise to do everything possible to appease "the man" there in Egypt. Both Israel and his sons seem to speak of this stubborn Egyptian official only as "the man." Evidently they were never informed of his name (Zaphnath-paaneah) or else were reluctant to use it for some reason. Accordingly (as he had done in the case of his reunion with Esau), Israel prepared a gift for the man. He would send him some of the best fruits of the land which they had managed to save up during the famine. Hopefully, the man would realize how difficult such things were to obtain during those days, and he might appreciate them the more. This would at least help show their good intentions. The gift included balm, myrrh, and spices (the same articles mentioned in Genesis 37:25 as being carried into Egypt by the Midianite tradesmen, and thus apparently considered by the Egyptians as valuable imports), as well as nuts (probably pistachios) and almonds, neither of which were produced in Egypt, and honey (probably grape "honey," a thick syrup boiled down from fresh grape juice, which also was not produced in Egypt).

Besides these items, Israel reminded them to take back the bundles of money which had been restored in their sacks on the first trip, and which evidently they had left undisturbed since, as well as "double money" to pay for the new purchase of grain. They could hope that the Egyptians, realizing that the money had been placed in their sacks by mistake, would not hold them accountable, especially since they were bringing it back again. Possibly the "double money" term refers to the original money plus the new money, in equal amounts. It is interesting to note also that, since there were ten brothers involved in these two purchases, in effect there were twenty bundles of money involved. It seems possible that the brothers themselves may have noted the ironical connection between the facts that they had sold their brother for twenty pieces of silver (Genesis 37:28) into Egypt, and that now they were having to pay into the treasuries of Egypt not merely twenty pieces of money but twenty bundles of money. The words "silver" and "money" are the same in the original (Hebrew *keseph*).

Finally, Israel told them to take their brother Benjamin with them to the man down in Egypt, expressing the prayerful hope and confidence that God Almighty *(El Shaddai)*, who had been the God of the Abrahamic covenant (Genesis 17:1), would overrule in the heart of the man and constrain him to return both Benjamin and Simeon to them again. If not,

Israel was content to leave the matter with God. If he was to be deprived of his children, then it would have to be that way. Israel's faith seems to have become strong again, and he spoke at this time with the same spirit as that of Job: "The Lord gave, and the Lord hath taken away; blessed be the name of the Lord" (Job 1:21). Having done everything that he could do, humanly speaking, he now simply had to trust the Lord to work things out according to His own good will.

Genesis 43:15-23

15 ¶ And the men took that present, and they took double money in their hand, and Benjamin; and rose up, and went down to Egypt, and stood before Joseph.

16 And when Joseph saw Benjamin with them, he said to the ruler of his house, Bring *these* men home, and slay, and make ready; for *these* men shall dine with me at noon.

17 And the man did as Joseph bade; and the man brought the men into Joseph's house.

18 And the men were afraid, because they were brought into Joseph's house; and they said, Because of the money that was returned in our sacks at the first time are we brought in; that he may seek occasion against us, and fall upon us, and take us for bondmen, and our asses.

19 And they came near to the steward of Joseph's house, and they communed with him at the door of the house,

20 And said, O sir, we came indeed down at the first time to buy food:

21 And it came to pass, when we came to the inn, that we opened our sacks, and, behold, *every* man's money *was* in the mouth of his sack, our money in full weight: and we have brought it again in our hand.

22 And other money have we brought down in our hands to buy food: we cannot tell who put our money in our sacks.

23 And he said, Peace *be* to you, fear not: your God, and the God of your father, hath given you treasure in your sacks: I had your money. And he brought Simeon out unto them.

So they started out on the long trip back down to Egypt, taking the gift and the double money, and also taking Benjamin, come what may. When their arrival was announced to Joseph, he immediately had them brought into his presence. One can imagine his emotion as he saw Benjamin, his beloved younger brother, for the first time in over twenty years. He had been only a little child then; so it was practically like seeing him for the very first time. Joseph was quickly assured that his brothers had done nothing harmful to Benjamin; he was in quite good health and apparently was well regarded by his brothers. This fact, combined with their previous acknowledgment of guilt concerning their crime against Joseph, convinced Joseph that a full reconciliation with them was indeed a real possibility.

Joseph therefore quickly gave instructions to prepare a dinner at noon for the men, at which he would join them. Although his steward may well have thought such an order to be unusual, he did as he was told without question. The animal was slain and prepared for the meal, and then the men from Canaan were brought to Joseph's house.

The ten brothers, who had been so apprehensive about merely seeing this man again, hardly knew what to make of this invitation. He had been so harsh with them, and here he was inviting them to dine with him! Surely, it must be some strange, sadistic device for mocking them. After they were gathered in the dining hall, unarmed and unprepared to offer any resistance, he would probably have his guardsmen fall on them, make slaves out of them and beasts of burden out of their asses.

Since they had brought Benjamin with them, as they had been instructed, the only remaining excuse the man could have for taking such action would be the money that had been found in their sacks when they returned home after their first trip to Egypt. Accordingly, before they entered Joseph's house, they tried to explain to Joseph's steward that they had really not stolen the money; it had somehow been placed in their sacks by someone other than themselves, and they had now brought it back again, along with additional money to buy new supplies. They stressed that they were honest men, as indeed all the facts so far available indicated.

Their fear must have changed to surprise and wonder when the steward replied that he had indeed received their money, and their account was fully settled. It must therefore have been "your God and the God of your father" who had placed the money in the sacks! He assured them they could set their minds fully at ease on this matter. It almost seems that the steward himself acknowledged their God to be the true God. Perhaps Joseph had told him about God, and in this way he had come to have faith in Him. He realized, of course, that the money had not appeared miraculously in their sacks, as his words might have sounded, but that it was because of God that Joseph had ordered their money restored. Then, to their further surprise, Simeon was brought out of the place of his imprisonment, set free to join them at the meal. More at ease now, but no doubt still with some trepidation, they entered Joseph's house.

Genesis 43:24-31

24 And the man brought the men into Joseph's house, and gave *them* water, and they washed their feet; and he gave their asses provender.

25 And they made ready the present against Joseph came at noon: for they heard that they should eat bread there.

26 ¶ And when Joseph came home, they brought him the present which *was* in their hand into the house, and bowed themselves to him to the earth.

27 And he asked them of *their* welfare,

and said, *Is* your father well, the old man of whom ye spake? *Is* he yet alive?

28 And they answered, Thy servant our father *is* in good health, he *is* yet alive. And they bowed down their heads, and made obeisance.

29 And he lifted up his eyes, and saw his brother Benjamin, his mother's son, and said, *Is* this your younger brother, of whom ye spake unto me? And he said, God be gracious unto thee, my son.

30 And Joseph made haste; for his bowels did yearn upon his brother: and he sought *where* to weep; and he entered into *his* chamber, and wept there.

31 And he washed his face, and went out, and refrained himself, and said, Set on bread.

The steward proceeded to make them comfortable, treating them as honored guests. Water was provided with which to wash their feet, and even their animals were fed. They knew now that they were indeed to be honored dinner guests of the very man they had feared even to meet again, and so excitedly made preparations to present him the gift they had brought from Canaan.

Finally, Joseph arrived. Making proper obeisance, they gave him their present. Once again, Joseph's dream was fulfilled as he saw his brothers bowing down before him.

Though no doubt emotionally stirred almost beyond control, Joseph tried to appear as casual as possible, as he asked them first about their own welfare (literally "peace") and then about their father. He was overjoyed to learn that Israel was still alive and well. Again they bowed down as an expression of appreciation for his interest in them and their families.

But then Joseph turned to Benjamin, his own brother, the only other son of his beloved mother. Hardly able to contain himself any longer, he yet managed to inquire formally whether this was indeed the younger brother of whom the men had spoken. Without waiting for a reply, however, he blurted out: "God be gracious unto thee, my son." It was a part of his disguise before them that he affected to be much older than Benjamin (and, indeed, he was quite a bit older, though hardly old enough to be his father).

With this, he could no longer hide his emotions; so he hastily left the room before they could see him weeping. So copiously did the tears of happiness and emotion flow that he had to wash his face before he could reenter the room. He was finally able to keep his feelings under control, and gave instructions to begin the meal.

Genesis 43:32-34

---

32 And they set on for him by himself, and for them by themselves, and for the Egyptians, which did eat with him, by themselves: because the Egyptians

might not eat bread with the Hebrews; for that *is* an abomination unto the Egyptians.

33 And they sat before him, the firstborn according to his birthright, and the youngest according to his youth: and the men marveled one at another.

34 And he took *and sent* messes unto them from before him: but Benjamin's mess was five times so much as any of theirs. And they drank, and were merry with him.

Herodotus and other ancient writers have commented on the exclusiveness of the Egyptians. In keeping with their segregation practices, three separate tables had to be set: one for the Hebrews, one for the Egyptian guests, and one for Joseph himself—the last table because of his high position. In particular, the Egyptians abhorred the thought of eating at the same table with Hebrews. They were of a different race, a different language, a different religion. Of course the Egyptians knew that Joseph was a Hebrew and that he worshiped the Hebrews' God; this had been clearly expressed by Joseph when he first met Pharaoh and was appointed to his position. Nevertheless, as far as social customs were concerned, he now had an Egyptian name, an Egyptian wife, and in general lived in the manner of the Egyptian rulers. He therefore could not eat directly with his brothers without giving undue offense to the Egyptian guests who were present.

After they were assigned to seats at their table, the eleven brothers noted a remarkable thing. They had been seated in order of age, from the eldest through the youngest. If this were a mere coincidence, it was indeed marvelous. One can easily show (merely by multiplying together all the numbers from one through eleven) that there are no less than 39,917,000 different orders in which eleven individuals could have been seated! Thus, for the servants to select the *one* correct order by chance was almost impossible. The odds were 40 million to one against it.

Evidently, this man knew a great deal more about their family than they had realized; or else he had some kind of supernatural power. They had no answer, and could only wonder about it.

Then the waiters, on Joseph's orders, did another odd thing. They gave Benjamin five times as much as they gave the other men. This statement does not refer to the whole meal, however, but rather to portions sent from the head table, as a gift of honor. Thus Joseph deliberately honored Benjamin five times as much as the others. The reason for this was not simply to endear himself to Benjamin but more likely to ascertain whether the other brothers would manifest resentment toward Benjamin as they had toward Joseph. Apparently it did not bother them, and this was another very good sign to Joseph. They all ate and drank merrily together throughout the meal, with no suggestion of jealousy or other unpleasantness. Joseph was now almost fully satisfied with their attitudes.

The Plea of Judah

The elation of the brothers must have been great. This man, whom they had feared so greatly, had turned out to be a most congenial host. Rather than being cast into prison or worse, they had been honored guests at the table of a great Egyptian ruler. Now they would be able to return to their father with an abundant supply of grain, with both Benjamin and Simeon accompanying them.

The shock of seeing all this suddenly change for the bad again, and into apparently a hopeless situation, must have struck them with double force, following their time of relief and self-congratulation as it did. But there was one more test that Joseph must apply to them (and, though Joseph was the man responsible, it can better be regarded as a final examination that God Himself was placing on them, to ascertain whether they were truly fit to become the ancestors of His chosen people). They had already shown real sorrow for their sin against Joseph, had confessed it as sin, and had also shown themselves to be honest, God-fearing men— men who respected and loved their father, as well as industrious and courageous men. Furthermore, they had shown no resentment against Benjamin, as Joseph had feared might be the case.

But he still was not sure what their attitude might be if forced to make a choice between their own personal welfare and that of Benjamin and their father. Accordingly, Joseph planned one further test before he could completely accept and forgive them.

Genesis 44:1-3

CHAPTER 44

AND he commanded the steward of his house, saying, Fill the men's sacks *with* food, as much as they can carry, and put every man's money in his sack's mouth.

2 And put my cup, the silver cup, in the sack's mouth of the youngest, and his corn money. And he did according to the word that Joseph had spoken.

3 As soon as the morning was light, the men were sent away, they and their asses.

While the brothers were resting that evening for the return journey next day, Joseph had his steward load their sacks with food, as much as the sacks would hold and they could carry. He knew that, when they saw this, they would be still further elated (also, of course, Joseph really wanted to send as much food home as possible). In addition, however, he instructed the steward to return their money once again, in the mouth of each sack. This would have the twofold effect of renewing their sense of guilt and also of reinforcing the steward's earlier statement that God was somehow working on their behalf.

Then, as the most important part of the test, Joseph told the steward to place his own personal drinking cup, made of silver and beautifully ornamented, in Benjamin's sack. This of course was calculated to make it appear that Benjamin, carried away with youthful avarice in such an elegant palace, had actually stolen the cup and was trying to carry it home with him.

The next morning at dawn, the brothers found their asses loaded and ready to go. After making proper expressions of gratitude and farewell, they set out on the journey for home, no doubt excitedly talking about the happy turn of events.

Genesis 44:4-6

4 *And* when they were gone out of the city, *and* not *yet* far off, Joseph said unto his steward, Up, follow after the men; and when thou dost overtake them, say unto them, Wherefore have ye rewarded evil for good?

5 *Is* not this *it* in which my lord drinketh, and whereby indeed he divineth? ye have done evil in so doing.

6 ¶ And he overtook them, and he spake unto them these same words.

Almost immediately after they had left, however, and were just beyond the city limits, Joseph sent the steward after them, instructing him carefully what to say and do. First, he was to remind them of how well they had been treated, and then he was to accuse them of returning evil for good. He was to point out that it was "this" in which his master drank, and with which he was able to practice divination. The use of the pronoun, without reference to any antecedent, would indicate that he believed they all knew full well what it was they had stolen. Joseph had a well-deserved reputation for prophetic insight, and the brothers themselves had noted with wonder how Joseph had been able to have them seated at the table in order of their respective ages. The inference seems to be that the Egyptians attributed his powers to his cup of divination, and that this may well have been an object coveted by many. And now, here, these ungrateful foreigners had presumed to steal this remarkable cup for their own use!

It may seem strange that a man like Joseph, knowing the true God as he did, would have used such a cup of divination. That it was a very unusual cup is indicated by the fact that the word (Hebrew *gabia*) has only three usages in Scripture: in the sense used here, for the "bowls" on the golden candlestick in the tabernacle (Exodus 25:31, 33, 34; 37:17, 19, 20), and for the "pots" full of wine used to tempt the Rechabites (Jeremiah 35:5). It is known that the Egyptians used such cups, as did other ancient peoples, for the purpose of predicting, professing to see tokens of future events in the reflections of water in the cup or in the arrangements assumed by small particles of gold or silver in it. They believed that the spirits who knew future events would act on the cup's contents in such a way as to form these messages.

Of course, it is possible that God Himself, through His holy angels, could do similar things if He so chose, and this might conceivably be the means through which God had spoken to Joseph to enable him to interpret dreams and to make other prophecies. Such a conclusion seems very unlikely, however, especially in view of such Biblical warnings against the practice of any form of divination as found, for example, in Deuteronomy 18:9-12.

It is more probable that Joseph, in his preliminary dealings with his brothers, was still simply adapting his image to that expected of an Egyptian leader who had priestly functions as well as political. Such a man, particularly a man who was known to have the remarkable abilities of a prophet, might be expected by those who did not know better to be a practitioner of the occult arts of Egypt. In charging the children of Israel with stealing his divining cup, Joseph was implicitly suggesting that they, as professed worshipers of the true God, had actually descended to stealing the implements of worship of a heathen pantheon, perhaps because they believed their own God no longer capable of providing for them.

Such a charge and its implications caused great dismay to the men when they heard it. They were being accused of the compound sin of ingratitude, theft, and apostasy. They were honest men who believed in only the one true God, and it was unthinkable that they could commit such sins. It hurt them grievously to be accused in this fashion, especially in such a way as to suggest that the steward had no doubt about their guilt and that he was sure they also were well aware of it.

Genesis 44:7-10

7 And they said unto him, Wherefore saith my lord these words? God forbid that thy servants should do according to this thing:

8 Behold, the money, which we found in our sacks' mouths, we brought again unto thee out of the land of Cā'nǎan: how then should we steal out of thy lord's house silver or gold?

9 With whomsoever of thy servants it be found, both let him die, and we also will be my lord's bondmen.

10 And he said, Now also *let* it *be* according unto your words: he with whom it is found shall be my servant; and ye shall be blameless.

The brothers responded to his charge with an earnest denial that they could have done any such thing. They had already shown their honesty by returning the silver which had been placed in their bags' mouths on the first trip; why should they steal anything this time? So confident of their innocence were they that they offered to become Joseph's slaves if his cup were found among them, with the one actually guilty of the theft even forfeiting his life.

This was a rather rash promise, of course; but they were so shocked by the sudden change in fortunes, as well as so sure of their own innocence, that they spoke without really thinking. Joseph's servant immediately took them at their word, knowing of course what the outcome would be. He did say, however, that he would not hold them all guilty, but only the one who actually stole the cup. The guilty man would be made a slave, as they had said, but the rest could go home blameless.

Genesis 44:11-13

---

11 Then they speedily took down every man his sack to the ground, and opened every man his sack.

12 And he searched, *and* began at the eldest, and left at the youngest: and the cup was found in Benjamin's sack.

13 Then they rent their clothes, and laded every man his ass, and returned to the city.

Speedily every man's sack was opened, starting with Reuben and going on down to the youngest. As the sacks were opened, they must have seen their returned money, but no mention is made of it, either by the servant or by the brothers. Perhaps, since the same thing had already happened once before, they merely assumed, especially in their fretful state of mind, that the money was no more a problem this time than it had proved the first time, and so ignored it. As sack after sack was emptied without disclosing the cup, they must have felt more and more vindicated and resentful. But then, in the very last sack, that of Benjamin, there was the missing cup!

The older brothers of course had had no reason to think Benjamin would have stolen the cup; he was neither a covetous man nor an idolater, and he could hardly have been so foolish, despite his youth, as to take such a risk as this. Nevertheless, there was the evidence!

His older brothers might have reasoned that there was no cause for them and their families to suffer for Benjamin's crime. Besides, here they had an unexpected opportunity to be rid of him just as they had gotten rid of Joseph long ago. No doubt Jacob would take the news with grief, and it might even cause his death, but after all he could not live much longer anyhow, and they would all be better off with this favorite son of his not around to receive an undue share of the inheritance.

They *could* have reasoned in such a way, and it was to test them in this regard that Joseph arranged this entire experience. For if they still felt resentment against Jacob and Benjamin in any degree, it would show up under circumstances like these. Even though they might not take overt action against Benjamin, as they had with Joseph, they might well allow events to take their course without interference if such events would remove Benjamin, and especially if their trying to save him would turn out to be costly to themselves.

The final evidence, however, that their characters had indeed really been transformed by this time, was that, to a man, they were willing to stand by Benjamin no matter what! They all "rent their clothes" in grief, but immediately turned around and went back to Joseph's city. Benjamin no doubt protested his innocence, and they no doubt believed him; but whether he was guilty or not, they would take their place with him. For— one very important thing—they loved their father too much to face him with the news that Benjamin, like Joseph, was gone. If Benjamin were to be enslaved or die, probably their father would die too. And in that event they no longer desired to return home or even live. This decision on their part speaks volumes about the change in character that had taken place in their lives the past twenty years, and especially in the recent period associated with the famine and their experiences in Egypt.

Genesis 44:14-16

---

14 ¶ And Judah and his brethren came to Joseph's house; for he *was* yet there: and they fell before him on the ground.

15 And Joseph said unto them, What deed *is* this that ye have done? wot ye not that such a man as I can certainly divine?

16 And Judah said, What shall we say unto my lord? what shall we speak? or how shall we clear ourselves? God hath found out the iniquity of thy servants: behold, we *are* my lord's servants, both we, and *he* also with whom the cup is found.

Joseph had remained at his house until the steward could bring back word of their reaction. He was no doubt moved with joy and thanksgiving when he saw all of them coming, instead of Benjamin only. However, he still needed to hear from their own lips their thoughts and feelings. As they came before him, once again they all prostrated themselves.

Joseph opened the interview with a formal charge and inquiry as to why they had done such a thing. Furthermore, how could they expect to get away with such a foolish crime? Surely they knew by now that he had the ability of divination. This statement, incidentally, calls attention to the fact that he did not really depend on this cup for his prophetic powers. He could "divine" who had stolen the cup even without having it. In their ears, this would suggest to them (still not knowing that he was anything except a heathen Egyptian) that perhaps, after all, he had a source of inspiration which was entirely beyond the occult abilities of the Egyptian magicians, and therefore that he must really have some knowledge of their own God, the only true God.

Judah was clearly the spokesman for the brothers from this time on. He felt quite helpless; he saw the evidence of Benjamin's guilt was overwhelming, and there was really no way he could prove his innocence. It is significant that, even though Benjamin was the only one charged, Judah acknowledged that all were equally involved. If Benjamin was guilty, so were they all. Furthermore, he confessed their recognition that they all deserved punishment. Even though they were innocent in this particular situation, they were verily guilty sinners, and "God hath found out the iniquity" of them all. He and his brothers were deeply burdened with the enormity of their deed in selling Joseph into bondage twenty years ago; now, it was only fitting that they themselves should also become slaves in Egypt for the rest of their days.

Genesis 44:17-24

---

17 And he said, God forbid that I should do so: *but* the man in whose hand the cup is found, he shall be my servant; and as for you, get you up in peace unto your father.

18 ¶ Then Judah came near unto him, and said, O my lord, let thy servant, I pray thee, speak a word in my lord's ears, and let not thine anger burn against thy servant: for thou *art* even as Phā'raōh.

19 My lord asked his servants, saying, Have ye a father, or a brother?

20 And we said unto my lord, We have a father, an old man, and a child of his old age, a little one; and his brother is dead, and he alone is left of his mother, and his father loveth him.

21 And thou saidst unto thy servants, Bring him down unto me, that I may set mine eyes upon him.

22 And we said unto my lord, The lad cannot leave his father: for *if* he should leave his father, *his father* would die.

23 And thou saidst unto thy servants, Except your youngest brother come down with you, ye shall see my face no more.

24 And it came to pass when we came up unto thy servant my father, we told him the words of my lord.

Joseph, however, tested them one time further by repeating the offer of his steward. Since only the one man was guilty of the theft, only he need stay in bondage. The rest were free to return safely and in peace to their father.

His mention of their father stirred their hearts deeply, because they realized keenly what would happen to him if they returned without Benjamin. They would rather not go back at all than to see the bitter and hopeless grief of their beloved father. Judah therefore spoke again, this time at considerable length, pleading for mercy for Benjamin.

Judah recounted to Joseph all the events that had led up to this confrontation. He spoke very respectfully, but very earnestly and intensely. In this remarkable plea, Judah clearly demonstrated that, whatever may have been his earlier weaknesses, whether resentment of Joseph (though it will be recalled that he at the time had saved Joseph's life from his other brothers) or the lusts of the flesh (which had showed up especially in his dealings with Tamar), he now was a strong man of godly character and compassion. He acknowledged that Joseph had full authority, even as Pharaoh, to do with them as he pleased, and that all he could do was to plead for mercy. He reminded Joseph that he had shown real interest in their personal affairs, asking about their father and younger brother, and how Joseph had then insisted that they bring Benjamin down to Egypt with them, even though their father would be in danger of death if they did so. He was pleading, therefore, not only for Benjamin, but also for his father's life.

Genesis 44:25-31

---

25 And our father said, Go again, *and* buy us a little food.

26 And we said, We cannot go down: if our youngest brother be with us, then will we go down: for we may not see the man's face, except our youngest brother *be* with us.

27 And thy servant my father said unto us, Ye know that my wife bare me two *sons:*

28 And the one went out from me, and I said, Surely he is torn in pieces; and I saw him not since:

29 And if ye take this also from me, and mischief befall him, ye shall bring down my gray hairs with sorrow to the grave.

30 Now therefore when I come to thy servant my father, and the lad *be* not with us; seeing that his life is bound up in the lad's life;

31 It shall come to pass, when he seeth that the lad *is* not *with us,* that he will die: and thy servants shall bring down the gray hairs of thy servant our father with sorrow to the grave.

Judah next told how his father had finally given consent for Benjamin to go, knowing that there was no other alternative. Then, he told of his father's final plea, reminding his other sons how his beloved wife Rachel had given him only two sons. The first one had gone away on an errand years ago and he had never seen him since. He assumed he had met a terrible fate, being "torn in pieces." If Benjamin now were likewise not to return home, he had said it would "bring down my gray hairs with sorrow to Sheol."

Judah assured Joseph that the very life of his father was so intimately bound up with Benjamin's life that he (Judah) simply could not bear to go back home without him. He knew that when his father saw them returning without Benjamin, the very shock would kill him.

Genesis 44:32-34

32 For thy servant became surety for the lad unto my father, saying, If I bring him not unto thee, then I shall bear the blame to my father for ever. 33 Now therefore, I pray thee, let thy servant abide instead of the lad a bond- man to my lord; and let the lad go up with his brethren. 34 For how shall I go up to my father, and the lad *be* not with me? lest peradventure I see the evil that shall come on my father.

Finally, Judah came to the climax of his plea. Even though he was confident Benjamin could not be guilty of the theft, he could not argue Benjamin's innocence, for there was clear evidence against him, and no contrary evidence at hand. But, assuming that Benjamin was guilty and that, therefore, he deserved punishment, would it not be possible that Judah himself might bear his punishment in substitution? He would claim the bag in which the cup had been found as his own, and Benjamin could take Judah's. Though Judah was innocent, he desired so keenly to see Benjamin spared, for his father's sake, that he was willing to be pronounced guilty in his stead and to suffer the punishment which otherwise would be meted out to Benjamin.

Judah had promised Israel he would be surety for Benjamin, perhaps not fully realizing at the time how near this promise would come to fulfillment. He was willing to follow through, however, bearing the blame forever if Benjamin could only return to his father. Judah's intense love for his father is exhibited most of all in his final plea: "How shall I go up to my father, and the lad be not with me? How can I see the evil that shall come on my father?"

In this willingness to give his own life in place of his brother's, for the sake of his father, Judah becomes a beautiful type of Christ, more fully and realistically than even Joseph himself, who is often taken by Bible expositors as a type of Christ. "Hereby perceive we the love of God, because he laid down his life for us: and we ought to lay down our lives for the brethren" (I John 3:16).

In fact, although Scripture does not say this in so many words, the problem as to why Judah, rather than Joseph, was selected to be the ancestor of the Messiah probably has its solution right here. Judah, in his willingness to sacrifice himself, the innocent for the guilty, had become the most Christlike of all his brothers.

They Will See Him

No longer could there be the least doubt in Joseph's mind that his brothers were completely changed men. He had subjected them to the most severe tests, and they had passed with flying colors. The testing itself had been a means of spiritual growth for them; they were more conscious than ever of the leading of God and their responsibility to Him. They were more aware than they had ever been of their own unworthiness and of God's mercy. Finally, their troubles had brought them all closer together, and now they were of one mind, loving one another and their father as they had never done before.

And then, with Judah making such a strong plea that Joseph allow him to take Benjamin's punishment, so that Benjamin could go home free, Joseph could no longer control his emotions. Not only did the brothers not resent Benjamin, they were even willing to share his sufferings, and, in Judah's case at least, to die for him.

Genesis 45:1-3

CHAPTER 45

THEN Joseph could not refrain himself before all them that stood by him; and he cried, Cause every man to go out from me. And there stood no man with him, while Joseph made himself known unto his brethren.

2 And he wept aloud: and the Egyptians and the house of Phā'raōh heard.

3 And Joseph said unto his brethren, I *am* Joseph; doth my father yet live? And his brethren could not answer him; for they were troubled at his presence.

At this point, Joseph, in a sudden sweep of emotion, dramatically cried for all his servants to leave the room. What was about to transpire would not be appropriate for anyone not in the family to see. He wanted to be alone with these men from Canaan. Though the servants may not have understood what he was doing, and may even have wondered whether he would be safe alone with them, he was so insistent that they left in haste, as he commanded.

When Joseph was alone with his brothers, he cried out to them that he was their brother Joseph, the one they thought was dead. He was sobbing and crying out so loudly that those whom he had dismissed from the room could not help but overhear, and they in turn soon carried the news to Pharaoh's house (verses 2, 16).

No longer speaking through an interpreter, he announced to them, in their own language: "I am Joseph!" It was like a lightning bolt! Words not only failed the brothers, they fail expositors who would try to describe this indescribable scene. Perhaps the most dramatic confrontation and reunion in all literature, it is far more than literature. This was the event which established the miracle nation of the children of Israel. This was the founding of that unique people through whom would be given to the world the Scriptures and of whom one day the Savior would come.

Had this scene not occurred, the children of Israel would soon have scattered and merged with the other peoples of the Middle East—the Ishmaelites and Edomites and Canaanites. This meeting had been a long time in preparation, but God had a long-range goal, and He "worketh all things after the counsel of his own will" (Ephesians 1:11).

Joseph immediately followed up his traumatic announcement, lest his brothers go into shock, with a question showing his loving concern: "Is my father still living?" They had, of course, discussed their father previously; but now the question was different, coming from a loving son instead of a brusque Egyptian official. He wanted to hear, not the mere recital of facts concerning an unknown stranger, but such intimate details concerning his father's welfare as could only be conveyed from one family member to another. If their sense of guilt had been strong before, it must now have been literally overpowering, and Joseph wished to set their minds at ease by transforming the interview quickly into a personal council of family members.

Nevertheless, the eleven brothers were completely speechless. They were "troubled" at his presence, according to the Authorized Version; but the actual Hebrew word *(bahal)* also means "amazed" or "frightened," or even "terrified."

There is, of course, a great similarity here to another dramatic confrontation that will come at the end of this age, when the Lord Jesus Christ returns to meet His brothers of the house of Israel, those who rejected Him and even urged His crucifixion when He first came to them. "And I will pour upon the house of David, and upon the inhabitants of Jerusalem, the spirit of grace and of supplications: and they shall look upon me whom they have pierced, and they shall mourn for him, as one mourneth for his only son, and shall be in bitterness for him, as one that is in bitterness for his firstborn" (Zechariah 12:10). It is largely because of this striking parallel that many have taken Joseph to be a type of Christ.

Genesis 45:4-8

---

4 And Joseph said unto his brethren, Come near to me, I pray you. And they came near. And he said, I *am* Joseph your brother, whom ye sold into Egypt.
5 Now therefore be not grieved, nor angry with yourselves, that ye sold me hither: for God did send me before you to preserve life.
6 For these two years *hath* the famine *been* in the land: and yet *there are* five years, in the which *there shall* neither *be* earing nor harvest.
7 And God sent me before you to preserve you a posterity in the earth, and to save your lives by a great deliverance.
8 So now *it was* not you *that* sent me hither, but God: and he hath made me a father to Phā'raōh, and lord of all his house, and a ruler throughout all the land of Egypt.

Joseph gradually put their minds at ease, proving that he no longer was resentful against them and was not planning to take revenge on them for what they had done to him. He urged them to come near, so he could tell them what had happened when they sold him into Egypt.

He had long since learned that God had allowed them to do this for His own good purposes. The Lord had worked all these seemingly unplanned circumstances out in such a way that Joseph had been placed in Egypt to preserve life through the great famine, not only of those in Egypt but especially of those of their own household. He wanted to preserve in Israel "a posterity in the earth, and to save your lives by a great deliverance."

Therefore, they need no longer be afraid, or angry with themselves. They had already personally been brought to full repentance, and the whole bitter problem between themselves and Joseph could be forgotten.

The word "posterity" is actually the regular word for "remnant." Possibly the reference was to the preservation of Joseph himself as the remnant, to whom the others could gather for the preservation of their lives when the crisis came. The famine which had brought them down into Egypt, and which had been devastating the lands for two whole years now, actually would continue for another five years. Had God not led in this special way, the entire population might have perished.

Joseph kept emphasizing, as strongly as he could, that all of this had been planned of God. He wanted his brothers to recognize this also, that they might understand with greater appreciation how God was working on their behalf in order that He might fulfill His great promises to their fathers. So, far from being an insignificant family in the land of Canaan, they were the objects of the special solicitude of the God of all the earth. To fulfill His plans for them, He had even made Joseph a "father" to Pharaoh, advising him on all decisions, as well as lord of his household and ruler over the land of Egypt. Joseph, as usual, gave all the glory to God, and he wanted his brothers to do the same.

Genesis 45:9-15

---

9 Haste ye, and go up to my father, and say unto him, Thus saith thy son Joseph, God hath made me lord of all Egypt: come down unto me, tarry not:

10 And thou shalt dwell in the land of Gŏ′shĕn, and thou shalt be near unto me, thou, and thy children, and thy children's children, and thy flocks, and thy herds, and all that thou hast:

11 And there will I nourish thee; for yet *there are* five years of famine; lest thou, and thy household, and all that thou hast, come to poverty.

12 And, behold, your eyes see, and the eyes of my brother Benjamin, that *it is* my mouth that speaketh unto you.

13 And ye shall tell my father of all my glory in Egypt, and of all that ye have seen; and ye shall haste and bring down my father hither.

14 And he fell upon his brother Benjamin's neck, and wept; and Benjamin wept upon his neck.

15 Moreover he kissed all his brethren, and wept upon them: and after that his brethren talked with him.

Now, however, they must hurry back and share the news with their father. Furthermore, Joseph instructed them to say that he wanted the entire family to move down to Egypt with him. He would arrange for them to have adequate room for all their households, as well as their flocks and herds, in the land of Goshen, a fertile region in northeastern Egypt. The district was about nine hundred square miles in area, and would be ideal for their needs.

Joseph also emphasized again that there were five years of famine yet coming. Unless they were near to him, where he could channel adequate supplies to them, they could not even be sure of survival through the bleak years ahead. At the very least, they would come to poverty. God had providentially arranged for Joseph to be "lord of all Egypt" just at the time when Israel and his sons would be facing this otherwise desolate future. Joseph was insistent that they make no delay in getting back to their father, and that he in turn not delay in moving his entire household to Egypt. He would have to move eventually anyway, being forced out by the famine, so the sooner the better. Joseph was eager to see his father, but knew that his own responsibilities in Egypt would preclude his going after him himself.

The brothers had apparently remained silent during these revelations and instructions. They could still hardly believe their eyes and ears, even though their fears were gradually being allayed. Joseph again assured them that it was really he that they were seeing and hearing. He was speaking to them in their own language, and speaking of things which no one but Joseph could know. Even Benjamin, to whom all this must have been a complete surprise, could see and hear that it was Joseph. He had been only a child when Joseph presumably had been slain by a wild animal, so that he hardly remembered him, except for what his father had related about him. The experiences of this day would long be vivid to Benjamin. The shock of having Joseph's cup found in his sack, the uncertainty as to what terrible fate might await him, Judah's impassioned defense and offer to substitute for him, and now suddenly finding that his own older brother was still alive and was ruler of Egypt! There had never been such a day in all his life. Indeed he *would* tell his father what he had seen and heard that day!

Joseph urged them, too, to tell his father about his authority in the land, so that Israel would not be hesitant to migrate down into Egypt. Joseph was well able to care for the entire establishment. And again he urged them to make all haste.

Finally, there was no longer any remaining doubt as to his identity or his intentions. Joseph and Benjamin embraced each other, weeping. Then, one after the other, Joseph kissed and wept over each of his other brothers. Each was forgiven, and every wall of fear and shame was broken down.

Surely there was a time of blessed fellowship and joy in that household all the rest of the day and on into the night. Joseph recounted everything that had happened to him in Egypt, and how the Lord had worked so mysteriously and yet so mightily. Quite probably he called in his wife and his two sons and introduced them. For their part, his brothers told him all the news from home, about their own families, and everything that had transpired the past twenty-two years. It was a day to remember.

Genesis 45:16-20

16 ⁋ And the fame thereof was heard in Phā′raōh's house, saying, Joseph's brethren are come: and it pleased Phā′raōh well, and his servants.

17 And Phā′raōh said unto Joseph, Say unto thy brethren, This do ye; lade your beasts, and go, get you unto the land of Cā′nǎan;

18 And take your father and your households, and come unto me: and I will give you the good of the land of Egypt, and ye shall eat the fat of the land.

19 Now thou art commanded, this do ye; take you wagons out of the land of Egypt for your little ones, and for your wives, and bring your father, and come.

20 Also regard not your stuff; for the good of all the land of Egypt *is* yours.

It was naturally only a very brief time before news such as this would reach the ears of Pharaoh. The servants who had overheard so much in Joseph's house could hardly be expected to keep glad news like this to themselves. Joseph was greatly esteemed in Egypt, by everyone from Pharaoh on down. He in fact had been Egypt's deliverer, and the whole nation was grateful.

The family of such a great man as Joseph must also be a very unusual family, Pharaoh must have thought, and therefore he gladly joined Joseph in the invitation to them all to move to Egypt. They themselves would be a fine addition to the nation, and also this would give the Egyptians an opportunity to show Joseph their appreciation of what he had done for them. Pharaoh was no doubt also pleased to learn that Joseph, who had first come to his attention as a prisoner and slave, actually came from such a noble and prosperous family.

Pharaoh instructed Joseph to tell his brothers to return to Canaan, and to bring their father and all their households into Egypt, promising that they would receive the good things of Egypt and eat the "fat" (that is, the best food) of the land. Pharaoh so insisted that they come to Egypt that he actually "commanded" them to do this. He even gave them wagons with which they could bring their wives and children and their father, in order to make the journey as easy as possible for them. These "wagons" were essentially carts, usually on two wooden wheels, drawn by oxen or horses. This is the first mention of wagons in the Bible and suggests that they were essentially unique to Egypt at that time.

Pharaoh further instructed them not to try to pack up all their "stuff," or "vessels" (Hebrew *keli*). He would give them all the utensils and miscellaneous household items they would need, when they reached Egypt.

Genesis 45:21-24

21 And the children of Ĭṣ'rā-ĕl did so: and Joseph gave them wagons, according to the commandment of Phā'raōh, and gave them provision for the way. 22 To all of them he gave each man changes of raiment; but to Benjamin he gave three hundred *pieces* of silver, and five changes of raiment.

23 And to his father he sent after this manner; ten asses laden with the good things of Egypt, and ten she asses laden with corn and bread and meat for his father by the way. 24 So he sent his brethren away, and they departed: and he said unto them, See that ye fall not out by the way.

Joseph proceeded, in accord with Pharaoh's command, to equip his brothers with wagons and provisions for the journey. As a special gesture, he outfitted each of his brothers with at least two "changes of garments," a term probably referring to Egyptian clothing for special occasions. Benjamin received a very special gift, five changes of garments and three hundred pieces (probably shekels) of silver. To Jacob, his father, he sent ten asses loaded with the "good things of Egypt," thus reciprocating for Jacob's much more modest gift of the "best fruits" of Canaan (Genesis 43:11), as well as ten she-asses with food for Jacob's coming journey down into Egypt.

As Joseph sent his brothers away, he wished them well and admonished them to "fall not out by the way." This word (Hebrew *ragaz*) is translated "fall out" only this once. Its more common meaning is "be troubled." Thus, Joseph was telling them not to let doubts or fears arise again to trouble them after they had left him. Every one of his promises was genuine, and he wanted them all to move down to Egypt with minimum delay.

Genesis 45:25-28

---

25 ¶ And they went up out of Egypt, and came into the land of Cā'năan unto Jacob their father,
26 And told him, saying, Joseph *is* yet alive, and he *is* governor over all the land of Egypt. And Jacob's heart fainted, for he believed them not.
27 And they told him all the words of Joseph, which he had said unto them: and when he saw the wagons which Joseph had sent to carry him, the spirit of Jacob their father revived.
28 And Iş'rā-ĕl said, *It is* enough; Joseph my son *is* yet alive: I will go and see him before I die.

Presumably they heeded Joseph's admonition, for they came back to Canaan and to their father without anything worth recording happening along the way. Quickly they gave Jacob the glad news that Joseph was yet alive and that he was the very man they had so greatly feared. Jacob could hardly believe what he was hearing. Scripture says his heart almost stopped beating, but this is probably a figure of speech. It all seemed so amazing it simply couldn't be true. And yet, there out in front of the house were the laden donkeys, the wagons, and there was Benjamin with his unique gift brought back from Egypt. As his sons kept talking, telling him all about Joseph and what he had said to tell his father about moving to Egypt, Jacob gradually realized this was really happening and Joseph truly was alive! Once again, Jacob's faith and spiritual strength returned. He had been deprived of Benjamin for several long weeks, and had almost despaired of seeing him again; but now Benjamin was back, and also, he was actually going to see Joseph again!

It is noteworthy that, as this change in attitude came over Jacob, the narrative, which had been calling him by his old name, Jacob (verses 25, 26, 27), suddenly begins calling him Israel again (verse 28). As the full realization of all he was hearing flooded in on him, his joy was beyond measure. No comment is made on what his sons must have told him about how Joseph got to Egypt in the first place. He knew they had repented and Joseph had forgiven them, and that was enough for now. Neither did he comment on Joseph's wealth or high position in Egypt. One thing, and one thing only, concerned him. He would be able to see Joseph again. That was enough!

Many great writers and literary critics have commented on the exquisite beauty and dramatic perfection of this millennia-old story of Joseph and his brothers. There is nothing comparable to it in all the world of literature. It is too perfect to have been imagined; it must have really happened and it must originally have been written by an eyewitness, or at least by one who heard it from the lips of those who were there.

Furthermore, there is no greater example in the Bible of God's gracious watch and care over His own. A multiplicity of seemingly accidental and unrelated events—events which seemed to be ugly and difficult at the time—is gradually woven together by an unseen divine hand into a glorious tapestry in which every portion is ideally situated in its proper and unique place. To believers going through sufferings and reverses, undeserved and unexplained, the story of Joseph has always given assurance of ultimate understanding, with the believer discovering a greater good and God receiving a greater glory than could ever have been possible without them.

22

Israel in Egypt

(Genesis 46-50)

The Children of Israel

As Jacob prepared to go to Egypt, he was in a quandary. He was eager to see Joseph again, and he also knew that the famine conditions in Canaan required some type of positive action if he and his clan were to escape impoverishment and probable death by starvation. God seemed clearly to be leading him to migrate to Egypt, through the providential circumstances surrounding Joseph and his elevation to power in Egypt.

At the same time, he knew that Canaan was the land God had promised Abraham and Isaac, for this had been confirmed to him. They had lived for many years in Canaan and now he was uncomfortable at the thought of leaving it. Until now, each time he had made an important move, God had spoken to him directly. When he left his parents to go to Haran, God had appeared to him at Bethel (Genesis 28:13-15); when he had been with Laban long enough, God instructed him to return to Canaan (Genesis 31:3); even when he left Shechem, God had appeared to him (Genesis 35:1, 9-12). Naturally, therefore, he was reluctant to make such a drastic move as this without direct confirmation from God that he should do so. After all, God was quite able to break the famine and supply their needs right there in Canaan, if it was His will to do so. He had often provided miraculously before.

Genesis 46:1-4

CHAPTER 46

AND Iṣ'rā-ĕl took his journey with all that he had, and came to Bē'ēr-shē'bà, and offered sacrifices unto the God of his father Isaac.

2 And God spake unto Iṣ'rā-ĕl in the visions of the night, and said, Jacob, Jacob. And he said, Here *am* I.

3 And he said, I *am* God, the God of thy father: fear not to go down into Egypt; for I will there make of thee a great nation.

4 I will go down with thee into Egypt; and I will also surely bring thee up *again:* and Joseph shall put his hand upon thine eyes.

Nevertheless, Israel did start out on the journey, taking all of his flocks and possessions, along with his family and servants. All the circumstances indicated that was what he should do; and so he went out, trusting the Lord somehow to shut this door if it were not His will for them to move. When God, through circumstances, appears to be leading a child of His into some new place of witness, this is the proper course to follow. Assuming there is no Scripture to the contrary, one should proceed according to his best judgment, and at the same time continue in prayer for guidance. He can have confidence then that the Lord will either bless the decision or else overrule and redirect.

On his way out of Canaan Israel had in mind to stop by the old altar at Beersheba, where he had lived with his father Isaac(Genesis 28:10). Beersheba, of course, was near the southern boundary of the land, and would, so to speak, be the "point of no return." There, at Beersheba, he offered sacrifices, thinking especially of Isaac and God's promises to his father.

That night, once again, God appeared to him in a vision, for the eighth and last time, so far as the record goes (Genesis 28:13; 31:3; 31:11; 32:1; 32:30; 35:1; 35:9; 46:2). It is interesting to note that the narrative says that "God spoke unto Israel," but that He called him "Jacob." In the rest of the Book of Genesis, it seems that the two names are used indiscriminately and interchangeably (cf. Genesis 46:8 and 46:27; 47:27 and 47:28; 49:1, 2, 28, 33).

There at Beersheba, God set Jacob's mind at ease about going down to Egypt. Identifying Himself as indeed the God of his father Isaac, He also assured Jacob that He (*El,* the strong Creator and Sovereign of all men) would protect him and bless him in Egypt, even as He had in Canaan.

Furthermore, God promised that He would bring him back up out of Egypt, when it was time to do so. This promise, as applied to Jacob personally, was only fulfilled after his death (Genesis 49:29; 50:4-8), but it found its more complete fulfillment in the lives of his descendants, in the days of Moses and Joshua.

God's purpose in leading him to Egypt was that He might there make of him "a great nation." Although the foundation of the nation had been established in the twelve sons of Israel, especially now that they had become unified in God's will, their own descendants would need the discipline of living for a period in Egypt before they were really ready to assume their role in God's economy.

Although Egypt was, if anything, even more polytheistic in its religion than Canaan, there was not the danger of assimilation that perpetually confronted them in Canaan. The Egyptians felt themselves racially superior and were reluctant to mix and intermarry with foreigners, especially shepherds (Genesis 43:32; 46:34), a fact which has been clearly confirmed by students of Egyptian antiquities. Also, these people were culturally and intellectually the most advanced nation of the world at the time, so there was much of future value the children of Israel could learn in Egypt.

Thus, although they could profit much, both financially and culturally by associating with the Egyptians, they would be forced to dwell apart by themselves, developing their own peculiar culture, and in particular, learning to center their lives around the God of heaven and earth rather than the gods of the nations. All of this would forge them into a distinct and unique people, ready to receive and promulgate the laws of God and the great plan of God.

Last of all, God assured him that he would see Joseph again. Furthermore, when Jacob's time to die would come, it would be his beloved son, Joseph himself, who would perform the sacred duty of "laying his hand upon thine eyes," that is, of closing his eyes in death for his burial.

Genesis 46:5-7

---

5 And Jacob rose up from Bē′ĕr–shē′bȧ: and the sons of Ĭṣ′rȧ-ĕl carried Jacob their father, and their little ones, and their wives, in the wagons which Phā′raōh had sent to carry him.

6 And they took their cattle, and their goods, which they had gotten in the land of Cā′năan, and came into Egypt, Jacob, and all his seed with him:

7 His sons, and his sons' sons with him, his daughters, and his sons' daughters, and all his seed brought he with him into Egypt.

No longer hesitant, therefore, Jacob immediately migrated to Egypt, taking all his cattle and other possessions, as well as his sons and grandsons. He evidently also had daughters (verse 7) and granddaughters, even though Dinah is the only daughter whose name or birth is specifically mentioned (Genesis 30:21), and Serah, daughter of Asher, the only granddaughter (verse 17).

The women and children were carried in the wagons, as was Jacob himself, the younger men apparently riding on asses.

The word "daughters" (verse 7) cannot refer to his sons' wives, as those who are enumerated are said to be his seed. Evidently neither the daughters-in-law nor any of the servants are included in the various numerical totals given in this chapter.

Genesis 46:8-15

8 ¶ And these *are* the names of the children of Ĭṣ'rā-ĕl, which came into Egypt, Jacob and his sons: Reuben, Jacob's firstborn.

9 And the sons of Reuben; Hā'nŏch, and Phăl'lṳ, and Hĕz'rŏn, and Cär'mī.

10 ¶ And the sons of Simeon; Jē-mū'ĕl, and Jā'mĭn, and Ō'hăd, and Jā'chĭn, and Zō'här, and Shā'ŭl the son of a Cā'năan-ĭt-ĭsh woman.

11 ¶ And the sons of Levi; Gĕr'shŏn, Kō'hăth, and Mĕ-rā'rī.

12 ¶ And the sons of Judah; Ĕr, and Ō'năn, and Shē'läh, and Phā'rēz, and Zā'räh: but Ĕr and Ō'năn died in the land of Cā'năan. And the sons of Phā'rēz were Hĕz'rŏn and Hā'mŭl.

13 ¶ And the sons of Ĭs'sà-chär; Tō'là, and Phū'väh, and Jōb, and Shĭm'rŏn.

14 ¶ And the sons of Zĕb'ū-lŭn; Sĕ'rĕd, and É'lŏn, and Jäh'lē-ĕl.

15 These *be* the sons of Lē'äh, which she bare unto Jacob in Pā'dăn-ā'răm, with his daughter Dinah: all the souls of his sons and his daughters *were* thirty and three.

The lists that follow give the names of Jacob's sons and grandsons who went with him into Egypt. First the family of Leah is given. These names are as below:

Reuben	Simeon	Levi	Judah	Issachar	Zebulun
Hanoch	Jemuel	Gershon	Er	Tola	Sered
Phallu	Jamin	Kohath	Onan	Phuvah	Elon
Hezron	Ohad	Merari	Shelah	Job	Jahleel
Carmi	Jachin		Pharez	Shimron	
	Zohar		Zarah		
	Shaul				

These names total thirty-one. However, Er and Onan died in Canaan, leaving only twenty-nine of Leah's sons and grandsons who went to Egypt. Presumably, therefore, Leah also had four daughters or granddaughters, making a total of thirty-three (verse 15). One of these was, of course, Dinah, whose unique contribution to Israel's history (chapter 34) warrants her name being given.

The two sons of Pharez, Hezron and Hamul, are also mentioned by name (verse 12), even though they could hardly have been born in Canaan. Pharez himself was born after his brother Shelah was a grown man (Genesis 38:14, 29). Since Judah could not have been more than about forty-seven at this time, Pharez was still only a boy. The names of his sons are evidently included to point out that, so far as Judah's inheritance was to be reckoned, they had taken the place of Er and Onan, who had died in Canaan.

It is also noted that Simeon's son Shaul was the "son of a Canaanitish woman" (verse 10). This suggests that the wives of Jacob's other sons (with the exception of Tamar) were not women of the Canaanites. Probably the other sons of Israel had married women who were descendants of Ishmael or Esau, or possibly of Keturah.

It is worth noting also that one of the sons of Levi, Kohath, was to become Moses' ancestor. One of the grandsons of Judah, namely Hezron, was destined to be in the lineage of Christ.

Genesis 46:16-18

---

16 ¶ And the sons of Gad; Zĭph'ĭ-ŏn, and Hăg'gī, Shŭ'nī, and Ĕz'bŏn, Ē'rī, and Ăr'ō-dĭ, and Ä-rē'lī.
17 ¶ And the sons of Ăsh'ẽr; Jĭm'năh, and Ĭsh'ū-ăh, and Ĭs'ū-ī, and Bē-rī'ăh, and Sē'răh their sister: and the sons of Bē-rī'ăh; Hē'bẽr, and Măl'chĭ-ĕl.
18 These *are* the sons of Zĭl'păh, whom Lä'băn gave to Lē'ăh his daughter; and these she bare unto Jacob, *even* sixteen souls.

Here are listed the names of the sons and grandsons of Zilpah, Leah's maid:

Gad		Asher
Ziphion	Eri	Jimnah
Haggi	Arodi	Ishuah
Shuni	Areli	Isui
Ezbon		Beriah

In addition, a daughter of Asher, Serah by name, and two sons of Beriah (therefore great-grandsons of Jacob)—Heber and Malchiel—are listed. These are presumably included in the list because they were the only great-grandsons of Zilpah that had been born prior to the move into Egypt. All of these names total sixteen (verse 18).

Genesis 46:19-22

---

19 The sons of Rachel Jacob's wife; Joseph, and Benjamin.
20 ¶ And unto Joseph in the land of Egypt were born Mà-nàs'sĕh and Ē'phrā-ĭm, which Ăs'ē-năth the daughter of Pŏt'ĭ-phē'răh priest of Ŏn bare unto him.

21 ¶ And the sons of Benjamin *were* Bē'lăh, and Bē'ehĕr, and Ăsh'bĕl, Gē'rà, and Nā'à-măn, Ē'hī, and Rŏsh, Mŭp'pĭm, and Hŭp'pĭm, and Ărd.
22 These *are* the sons of Rachel, which were born to Jacob: all the souls *were* fourteen.

Next are given the names of the descendants of Rachel. These names add up to fourteen, as shown below:

Joseph	Benjamin			
Manasseh	Belah	Naaman	Muppim	
Ephraim	Becher	Ehi	Huppim	
	Ashbel	Rosh	Ard	
	Gera			

Genesis 46:23-25

---

23 ¶ And the sons of Dan; Hū'shĭm.
24 ¶ And the sons of Năph'tà-lī; Jäh'zē-ĕl, and Gū'nī, and Jē'zĕr, and Shĭl'lĕm.

25 These *are* the sons of Bĭl'hàh, which Lā'băn gave unto Rachel his daughter, and she bare these unto Jacob: all the souls *were* seven.

Last of all are given the names of the sons and grandsons of Rachel's maid, Bilhah:

Dan		Naphtali		
Hushim	Jahzeel	Guni	Jezer	Shillem

There are seven names in this list.

Genesis 46:26, 27

---

26 All the souls that came with Jacob into Egypt, which came out of his loins, besides Jacob's sons' wives, all the souls *were* threescore and six;
27 And the sons of Joseph, which were borne him in Egypt, *were* two souls: all the souls of the house of Jacob, which came into Egypt, *were* threescore and ten.

These four families, as listed, add up to seventy names. This number does not include any of the wives of Jacob's sons and grandsons (nor the husbands of his daughters and granddaughters), but only those who were of his own seed. Of these, however, only sixty-six actually "came with Jacob into Egypt," since Joseph, Manasseh, and Ephraim were already there when he came.

The number seventy seems to have been associated in a particular way with the nation of Israel ever since the time when these seventy apparently became its official founders. (Note Deuteronomy 32:8, which suggests that this number was tied to the seventy other nations of the world first established by God, as listed in Genesis 10. Also, see the discussion in Chapter 10 on the Table of Nations.) There were seventy "elders" (Numbers 11:16), seventy years of captivity (II Chronicles 36:21), seventy "weeks" determined on the people of Israel to finish the transgression (Daniel 9:24), seventy translators of the Septuagint translation of the Old Testament into Greek, seventy members of the Sanhedrin in the days of Christ, and seventy "witnesses" to Israel sent by Christ (Luke 10:1).

Even though the ten sons of Benjamin may not actually have been born in Canaan, they are listed in order to make this roll of founders parallel and complete, since all of Jacob's grandsons were to be reckoned among these founders. They were in the loins of Benjamin, at least, and so in that sense actually did go down into Egypt with Jacob. As a matter of fact, it is possible that they all could have been born while Benjamin was still in Canaan. Though Benjamin was not more than twenty-five at this time, at the most, it is conceivable that he could have married while in his teens and then his wife, or wives, could have borne him ten sons (including multiple births) within this relatively brief period. In view of their father's example, as well as that of Uncle Esau, some of Jacob's sons may well have had more than one wife (Simeon certainly did).

The seventy original Israelites, summing up, included Jacob and his twelve sons, fifty-one grandsons, two great-grandsons, one daughter (Dinah), one granddaughter (Serah), one other unnamed daughter of Leah, and one unnamed granddaughter of Leah (verse 7 indicates Jacob had more than one daughter and more than one granddaughter). It is unusual—though certainly such things are known to happen occasionally—for one sex to be so predominant in a family throughout two generations. It seems probable that, in this case, providential intervention actively produced an abnormally large percentage of males in order to provide a foundation for rapid enlargement of the Israeli nation (females marrying outside the family would have to be reckoned outside the developing nation). It may also be that other daughters existed but had married and so did not migrate to Egypt.

There are certain minor difficulties in interpreting these numbers and lists of names. The difference between the totals of sixty-six and seventy in these two verses seems to require that Jacob, as well as Joseph and his two sons, be included among the seventy founders of Israel. The sixty-six were those who "came with Jacob into Egypt." The problem, however, is that the totals of verses 15, 18, 22, and 25, which also add to seventy, do not include Jacob himself, but only "his sons and daughters." Though the exact solution of this problem is not clear, one possibility is that one of the number, possibly an unnamed granddaughter of Leah, may have died during or shortly after the migration. In that case, though she was counted as one of the thirty-three descendants of Leah who made the trip to Egypt, she was not considered as one of the "official" seventy who established the nation in Egypt.

Another problem is that Stephen's speech in Acts 7:14 says that there were seventy-five of Jacob's kindred who were called into Egypt. This addition of five to the total in Genesis is usually explained by noting that Stephen referred to the Septuagint translation, which for some reason had added five of Joseph's descendants through Ephraim and Manasseh to the list of Genesis 46. Perhaps a better suggestion is to include in the term "kindred" five relatives who were not actually of the seed of Jacob and who were therefore not included in the total of Genesis 46:27. It is possible that only five of the living wives of Joseph's brothers would consent to leave their homelands and move to Egypt.

Genesis 46:28-30

---

28 ¶ And he sent Judah before him unto Joseph, to direct his face unto Gō'shĕn; and they came into the land of Gō'shĕn.

29 And Joseph made ready his chariot, and went up to meet Ĭş'rā-ĕl his father, to Gō'shĕn, and presented himself unto him; and he fell on his neck, and wept on his neck a good while.

30 And Ĭş'rā-ĕl said unto Joseph, Now let me die, since I have seen thy face, because thou *art* yet alive.

As the Israelites approached Egypt, they knew they would be stopping in Goshen, according to Joseph's instruction (Genesis 45:10), whereas Joseph's headquarters were located farther south and west. Therefore Jacob sent Judah (now fully recognized as the leader among Jacob's sons) on ahead to tell Joseph to meet them in Goshen, and to direct them exactly where to go.

As soon as he heard his father was coming, Joseph hitched up his chariot and went up to Goshen to meet him. When they finally met, for the first time in over twenty-two years, the joy was almost unbearable. No words could be spoken at all; Joseph could merely fling his arms around Israel's neck, where he wept "a good while."

When he could finally manage to speak, Israel could merely sob that he was now able to die happy and in peace. His beloved son was still alive, and he had seen his face!

Genesis 46:31-34

---

31 And Joseph said unto his brethren, and unto his father's house, I will go up, and show Phā'raōh, and say unto him, My brethren, and my father's house, which *were* in the land of Cā'nǎan, are come unto me;

32 And the men *are* shepherds, for their trade hath been to feed cattle; and they have brought their flocks, and their herds, and all that they have.

33 And it shall come to pass, when Phā'raōh shall call you, and shall say, What *is* your occupation?

34 That ye shall say, Thy servants' trade hath been about cattle from our youth even until now, both we, *and* also our fathers: that ye may dwell in the land of Gō'shĕn; for every shepherd *is* an abomination unto the Egyptians.

After the emotion-charged greetings were finished, it was necessary to get down to the practical business of designating a home for the Israelites. Joseph had selected Goshen as the most suitable location, a land which was quite fertile, essentially unsettled by the Egyptians and adjacent to Canaan. Pharaoh knew they were coming (Genesis 45:17-20), but evidently had not made a formal commitment as to geographical location.

The Egyptian people, according to both the Bible and secular historians, despised the profession of sheepherding. Up to this point, apparently, Pharaoh had not been apprised of the fact that the Israelites kept flocks and herds. For this reason, it would be better for them to keep more or less segregated from the Egyptians.

Joseph instructed his brothers to stress this aspect of their activities to Pharaoh, as he also would himself, in order to encourage him to designate Goshen as their home. Otherwise, there might be many—perhaps even Pharaoh himself—who would prefer to see the Israelites mix with the Egyptians, the better to encourage intermarriage and eventual assimilation.

Prosperity in Egypt

It has often been suggested that, since the Pharaoh of Joseph's time was one of the "shepherd kings" of the Hyksos dynasties, he himself was more favorably disposed toward Joseph's family than other Egyptians would have been. This is uncertain at best, especially since Egyptian chronology is still unsettled. An increasing number of writers today are favoring a revision of this chronology which would place the Hyksos considerably later than Joseph's time. Others question whether the Hyksos were shepherds at all. At present, this controversy has not been resolved.

Genesis 47:1-6

CHAPTER 47

THEN Joseph came and told Phā′-raōh, and said, My father and my brethren, and their flocks, and their herds, and all that they have, are come out of the land of Cā′nȧan; and, behold, they *are* in the land of Gō′shĕn.

2 And he took some of his brethren, *even* five men, and presented them unto Phā′raōh.

3 And Phā′raōh said unto his brethren, What *is* your occupation? And they said unto Phā′raōh, Thy servants *are* shepherds, both we, *and* also our fathers.

4 They said moreover unto Phā′raōh, For to sojourn in the land are we come; for thy servants have no pasture for their flocks; for the famine *is* sore in the land of Cā′nȧan: now therefore, we pray thee, let thy servants dwell in the land of Gō′shĕn.

5 And Phā′raōh spake unto Joseph, saying, Thy father and thy brethren are come unto thee:

6 The land of Egypt *is* before thee; in the best of the land make thy father and brethren to dwell; in the land of Gō′shĕn let them dwell: and if thou knowest *any* men of activity among them, then make them rulers over my cattle.

In any case, although Joseph was second in power in the kingdom, he could not make a decision to assign a large area of fertile land to a foreign tribe without the specific approval of Pharaoh. Having settled them down in Goshen tentatively at least, he then took five of his brothers with him to Pharaoh's court.

He first made a formal announcement to Pharaoh that his family and their possessions—calling special attention to their flocks and herds—had come to Egypt, as Pharaoh had invited them to do. He also said they were, for the time being, in the land of Goshen, awaiting Pharaoh's pleasure.

When Joseph presented his brothers to Pharaoh, he naturally asked their business, to see how they might best fit into the Egyptian economy. As Joseph had instructed them, they announced boldly, though respectfully, that they and their fathers had always been shepherds. They also mentioned that they had come only to "sojourn" in the land, because of the famine in Canaan. They had no intention of laying permanent claim to any of Egypt. Since Goshen had good pasture land for their flocks, they requested permission to live there.

As Joseph had anticipated, this was the best solution from Pharaoh's point of view also. He first acknowledged to Joseph that he recognized his family had arrived and that he fully remembered his invitation. Graciously he offered to let them dwell anywhere in Egypt Joseph might choose; then, more specifically, he indicated his approval of Goshen.

Though shepherds were "an abomination to the Egyptians," Pharaoh did have extensive herds of cattle of his own. He therefore offered to employ any of the Israelite clan who were competent to do so to assume charge over his cattle and those that handled them.

Genesis 47:7-10

---

7 And Joseph brought in Jacob his father, and set him before Phā′raōh: and Jacob blessed Phā′raōh.

8 And Phā′raōh said unto Jacob, How old *art* thou?

9 And Jacob said unto Phā′raōh, The days of the years of my pilgrimage *are* a hundred and thirty years: few and evil have the days of the years of my life been, and have not attained unto the days of the years of the life of my fathers in the days of their pilgrimage.

10 And Jacob blessed Phā′raōh, and went out from before Phā′raōh.

After all this was decided, and the family was permanently fixed in Goshen, Joseph on a convenient day brought Jacob himself to meet Pharaoh. It must have been quite a meeting, earth's greatest king encountering the man chosen by God to lead His people in that day. Though Pharaoh was the more wealthy and powerful, Jacob clearly was the superior, for he "blessed Pharaoh." Melchizedek had blessed Abraham (Genesis 14:19), thus showing his superiority to Abraham, for "the less is blessed of the better" (Hebrews 7:7).

A reading of the passage suggests that Pharaoh indeed sensed this, in Jacob's presence. He seemed subconsciously to recognize he was speaking to a man of unusual spiritual depth and perception, a man who had known and walked with God for many years.

It is probable that Scripture records only a small portion of the actual conversation of Jacob with Pharaoh. The one item of discussion which was incorporated into the inspired account has to do with Jacob's advanced age. Jacob replied to Pharaoh's inquiry on this point by stressing that, although he was indeed 130 years old, his days had been relatively few compared to his father and grandfather. Abraham had died at 175 and Isaac at 180, respectively (Genesis 25:7; 35:28). Although he did live another seventeen years (Genesis 47:28), he realized he could never hope to live as long as they had. Longevity of mankind was still, at that time, gradually decreasing from what it had been in antediluvian days. Also, no doubt, the many hardships and sorrows in Jacob's life had taken their toll on his health.

Not only had his days been "few," they had also been "evil" or "difficult." Jacob was not complaining, for he knew God had blessed and sustained him through it all. He was merely stating fact. He also mentioned that both he and his fathers had been "pilgrims" all their lives. Though they had settled in Canaan and had purchased a few small tracts of ground, they had been semi-nomads with never a truly permanent home. They "confessed that they were strangers and pilgrims on the earth" (Hebrews 11:13).

Before concluding their conversation, Jacob once again "blessed Pharaoh," no doubt praying for him and invoking God's blessing on him and his family. Then Jacob "went out from before Pharaoh." Possibly he never saw him again. At any rate, in addition to the continuing witness of Joseph, this pagan emperor had been the recipient of the testimony and the object of the prayers of the greatest man of his generation. Whether he was ever converted to trust the true God must be left for eternity to reveal.

Genesis 47:11, 12

---

11 ¶ And Joseph placed his father and his brethren, and gave them a possession in the land of Egypt, in the best of the land, in the land of Răm′ē-sĕş, as Phā′raōh had commanded.

12 And Joseph nourished his father, and his brethren, and all his father's household, with bread, according to *their* families.

Having received the king's official approval, Joseph completed the formalities of deeding a portion of the land of Goshen to his father and his family. He selected a tract in the best part of this land, as Pharaoh had authorized, a region known as Rameses. The storehouse cities Pithom and Raamses (Exodus 1:11) were later to be built in this area.

This region seems to have been bordered on the west by the Nile, since the Israelites "did eat fish freely in Egypt" (Numbers 11:5). According to Psalm 78:12, their property must have included "the field of Zoan," which was on one of the outlet channels of the Nile fairly near the sea. In general it was close to Egypt's northeast corner, more or less isolated from the bulk of the Egyptian population, which tended to concentrate more to the south and west.

Joseph saw to it that his family had enough food. He had to ration it out, even to them, because of the years of famine he knew were still coming. Since they were obviously most concerned about the little children, each family's allocation was in proportion to the number of children in the family.

Genesis 47:13-21

13 ¶ And *there was* no bread in all the land; for the famine *was* very sore, so that the land of Egypt and *all* the land of Cā́nǎan fainted by reason of the famine.

14 And Joseph gathered up all the money that was found in the land of Egypt, and in the land of Cā́nǎan, for the corn which they bought: and Joseph brought the money into Phā́raōh's house.

15 And when money failed in the land of Egypt, and in the land of Cā́nǎan, all the Egyptians came unto Joseph, and said, Give us bread: for why should we die in thy presence? for the money faileth.

16 And Joseph said, Give your cattle; and I will give you for your cattle, if money fail.

17 And they brought their cattle unto Joseph: and Joseph gave them bread *in exchange* for horses, and for the flocks, and for the cattle of the herds, and for the asses; and he fed them with bread for all their cattle for that year.

18 When that year was ended, they came unto him the second year, and said unto him, We will not hide *it* from my lord, how that our money is spent; my lord also hath our herds of cattle; there is not aught left in the sight of my lord, but our bodies, and our lands:

19 Wherefore shall we die before thine eyes, both we and our land? buy us and our land for bread, and we and our land will be servants unto Phā́raōh: and give *us* seed, that we may live, and not die, that the land be not desolate.

20 And Joseph bought all the land of Egypt for Phā́raōh; for the Egyptians sold every man his field, because the famine prevailed over them: so the land became Phā́raōh's.

21 And as for the people, he removed them to cities from *one* end of the borders of Egypt even to the *other* end thereof.

As the days wore on, the famine continued. No relief was in sight and the people had to continue to buy their grain from Joseph's storehouse. Though Joseph presumably asked a fair price for the grain, it was only a matter of time until they had spent all their savings on food. For reasons already discussed, it would have been wrong simply to give away the grain; so Joseph worked out a barter system, allowing them to exchange their horses, cattle, and other animals for food.

This kept the people going another year, but finally all their animals were gone too. Both the money and animals became the property of Pharaoh, or, in effect, owned by the central government. This arrangement actually benefited both the people and the animals, since they would have been unable to keep the animals alive during the famine.

When they reached this state, the people came to Joseph with a new proposal of their own. Evidently some sort of meeting had been held and spokesmen elected to contract with Joseph on their behalf. They had nothing left which might be marketable except their own lands and their own labor.

The people therefore desired to dedicate themselves and their land for service to Pharaoh in return for food on a regular basis, as well as seed with which to sow their lands. They knew the famine would be over eventually, and they should at least do whatever they could with the land from year to year so that it would eventually be able to yield good crops again, but now they no longer had enough even to purchase seed.

Some people have felt that this was a scheme of Joseph not only to get wealth but also to enslave the people. However, it was their proposal, not Joseph's, and whatever gain was involved accrued to Pharaoh, not to Joseph. It is true that it created what amounted to a feudalistic economy, but the alternative—that of placing everyone on a dole system —would have destroyed personal and national morale, would have bankrupted the government, and probably would have culminated in social anarchy. The stores of food would soon have been depleted and mass starvation would have followed.

The people had learned to trust Joseph. He had always charged them a fair price and, even though they had used up all their money and marketable possessions, they still had their self-respect.

Joseph agreed to their terms, and so title to most of the property in Egypt passed to the state. In order to expedite distribution of grain and seed, and to best utilize the labor purchased in this manner, Joseph relocated many of the people, moving them nearer the various cities where the storehouses were situated. Presumably these people were employed in some form of productive work. The system certainly left something to be desired in terms of human freedom; but a centralized bureaucracy is preferable to mass starvation and anarchy, especially when the bureaucracy is administered intelligently and unselfishly, as it was by Joseph.

Genesis 47:22-26

22 Only the land of the priests bought he not; for the priests had a portion *assigned them* of Phā'raōh, and did eat their portion which Phā'raōh gave them: wherefore they sold not their lands.

23 Then Joseph said unto the people,

Behold, I have bought you this day and your land for Phā'raōh: lo, *here is* seed for you, and ye shall sow the land.

24 And it shall come to pass in the increase, that ye shall give the fifth *part* unto Phā'raōh, and four parts shall be

your own, for seed of the field, and for
your food, and for them of your households, and for food for your little ones.
25 And they said, Thou hast saved
our lives: let us find grace in the sight
of my lord, and we will be Phā'raōh's

servants.
26 And Joseph made it a law over the
land of Egypt unto this day, *that* Phā-
raōh should have the fifth *part;* except
the land of the priests only, *which* became not Phā'raōh's.

There was one noteworthy exception to these arrangements, however. The priests who administered the Egyptian religious system had extensive land holdings of their own, and they did not turn any of these over to Pharaoh. In effect, Egypt had an official state religion, and the members of its hierarchy were essentially state employees. Thus, they received an ample allocation of grain for their own needs in return for their services, and it was unnecessary for them to sell their lands.

Scripture stresses that this exception came about on orders of Pharaoh himself. Their portion of grain was that "which Pharaoh gave them." This suggests that Joseph did not agree with this exception, but was overruled by Pharaoh. He knew well that the religious system was false and harmful and that, in the long run, the concentration of greater power and wealth in the hands of the priests would be inimical to the best interests of the Egyptian people. Pharaoh, however, was somehow persuaded that the government had to support its religious leaders.

As far as the rest of the people were concerned, Joseph fulfilled his part of the contract with them, providing seed for their lands and food for their households. Since the title to the lands now belonged to Pharaoh, it was agreed that the people would continue to work their own lands, using seed furnished by the government, and that they could keep for their own use 80 percent of what they produced, with 20 percent going to Pharaoh.

In effect, this amounted to a permanent annual income tax of 20 percent of gross income. This is not excessive in terms of present-day standards, especially since these farmers had no rent to pay, no cost of investment or upkeep, in fact nothing except their own personal expenses. Pharaoh and the governmental bureaucracy administered by Joseph financed all government functions on the 20 percent. Presumably, a similar and equitable arrangement was provided for those with specific occupations other than farming, including Joseph's brothers.

It is noteworthy that there was little, if any, complaining about these terms. To the contrary, the citizens were grateful to Joseph for saving their lives, recognizing that they were being treated fairly and generously and that there could really be no other plan which would work as well under the circumstances. They only desired to continue to "find grace," or favor, in the eyes of Joseph, so that the arrangement would remain in operation.

As a matter of fact, it seemed to work so well that it continued to remain in force "unto this day"—that is, until at least the time of Moses.

Genesis 47:27-31

---

27 ¶ And Ĭṣ'rā-ĕl dwelt in the land of Egypt, in the country of Gō'shĕn; and they had possessions therein, and grew, and multiplied exceedingly.

28 And Jacob lived in the land of Egypt seventeen years: so the whole age of Jacob was a hundred forty and seven years.

29 And the time drew nigh that Ĭṣ'rā-ĕl must die: and he called his son Joseph, and said unto him, If now I have found grace in thy sight, put, I pray thee, thy hand under my thigh, and deal kindly and truly with me; bury me not, I pray thee, in Egypt:

30 But I will lie with my fathers, and thou shalt carry me out of Egypt, and bury me in their buryingplace. And he said, I will do as thou hast said.

31 And he said, Swear unto me. And he sware unto him. And Ĭṣ'rā-ĕl bowed himself upon the bed's head.

Eventually the famine diminished in intensity. The river began to bring its water and fertile soil again, and the land began to prosper once more.

Joseph's family came into Egypt a little more than two years after the famine began (Genesis 45:11), and so were there during the last five years of the famine. Even during the famine, however, they began to prosper in Egypt. Their main occupation was sheep and cattle raising. Goshen was in the Nile delta region and provided good pasturage, with the result that their flocks and herds multiplied and thrived.

Also, their own numbers rapidly multiplied. With an initial number of five people (Jacob and his four wives), they had already become a clan of, say, one hundred people (that is, the seventy mentioned in Genesis 46:27 plus the wives of the sons and grandsons who accompanied them into Egypt). This growth had taken place in approximately fifty years, representing an average increase of over 6 percent each year. With a population of one hundred when they entered Egypt and over two million when they left (the census of Numbers 1:46 counted over 600,000 men older than twenty years of age), this large growth rate must have continued. A growth of 5 percent annually, for example, would increase the population from one hundred to two million in only 215 years.

That such an increase is not unreasonable under favorable conditions is evident by considering what could have happened merely during the seventeen years Jacob lived in Egypt. An increase of 5 percent per year for seventeen years would increase the clan from one hundred people to 220. This could easily have been accomplished by each of the fifty-one grandsons who entered Egypt marrying and having an average of two children during the period.

Whatever the precise numbers may have been, the record does say that they "multiplied exceedingly." After seventeen years, when Jacob was 147 years old, the time finally came when he must die.

Jacob called Joseph to his side one day, when he knew he could not last much longer, and asked him to promise that he would bury him back in Canaan, where his parents and grandparents were buried. The solemnity of this request was stressed by Jacob's insistence that Joseph put his hand "under my thigh" while making this promise. This was the same symbolic gesture by which Abraham had made his servant swear when he sent him out to find a bride for Isaac (see the discussion of Genesis 24:2 in chapter 15), and denoted how important it was that the line of the promised Seed possess the promised land. Jacob wanted even his burial to be a testimony to his faith in God's promises.

Joseph took a solemn oath that he would indeed do as his father asked. In gratitude for this assurance, Israel, who evidently had been sitting up in bed, bowed himself against the bed's head and offered a prayer of worship and thanksgiving to God. This was, according to Hebrews 11:21, a true act of faith on Jacob's part. In this reference in Hebrews, the "bed's head" is called "the top of his staff," following the Septuagint translation. It may be that Jacob supported himself by both his staff and the bed's headboard, as he was very old and feeble by this time. It took all his remaining strength to raise himself and to utter the prophetic words of chapters 48 and 49, but he received both his strength and his inspiration by faith, still trusting in the absolute certainty that, though he himself would not live to see it, God would give his seed the land of Canaan and that, someday, all nations would be blessed through him.

The Last Days of Jacob

Even after Jacob had discussed his forthcoming burial with Joseph, he still continued to live for a time. Joseph, in the meantime, had to go about his regular duties and responsibilities. The other sons, likewise, with their increasing numbers and activities, were very busy. Jacob no longer could be active as head of the clan and was completely bedridden. Nevertheless, his mind and heart were still active. Alone on his bed, he must frequently have reminisced, recalling the marvelous events of his long walk with the Lord.

Also, he thought often of the future. He knew God's promises centered in his twelve sons and their descendants. Someday, through one of these tribes, the Savior would come. As he meditated and prayed, the Lord gradually revealed to him something of the future of each of the twelve tribes. This future, of course, would be to some extent related to their own tribal characteristics, and these, in turn, somewhat to the character of the particular son of Jacob from whom they had been inherited. "Like father, like son." With the deep insight into personality and character which only comes through much experience, a close walk with the Lord, and long periods of thought and prayer, Jacob could foresee with good probability the course the different tribes would take in history. His own insights were further supplemented by the direct illumination of the Holy Spirit, so that he could, with perfect accuracy and confidence, predict their futures.

Many of his thoughts, no doubt, were directed toward Joseph and his two sons. Joseph's influence would continue to be strong among the Israelites. His strength of character, his spiritual convictions and discernment, and his qualities of leadership would be inherited by his descendants through many generations. Nevertheless, the more he thought about it, the more he realized that Judah was also a man of tremendous strength of character and might well be more qualified in the long run to lead the nation than Joseph. Though Judah had made serious mistakes in his younger days, in recent years he had become the obvious leader in the family. In addition, his willingness to give his own life to save his father and his brothers had revealed a depth of spirituality and love which not even Joseph possessed. The loss of his own two sons, and then his traumatic experience with Tamar, had so shaken him that he had literally become a new man. He had been a wonderful father to Tamar's two sons, and Pharez, especially, had shown signs of being a worthy successor to his father.

Genesis 48:1-4

CHAPTER 48

AND it came to pass after these things, that *one* told Joseph, Behold, thy father *is* sick: and he took with him his two sons, Mà-năs′sĕh and É′phrā-ĭm.

2 And *one* told Jacob, and said, Behold, thy son Joseph cometh unto thee: and Ĭṣ′rā-ĕl strengthened himself, and sat upon the bed.

3 And Jacob said unto Joseph, God Almighty appeared unto me at Lŭz in the land of Cā′nằan, and blessed me,

4 And said unto me, Behold, I will make thee fruitful, and multiply thee, and I will make of thee a multitude of people; and will give this land to thy seed after thee *for* an everlasting possession.

Little of the above is explicitly stated in Scripture, of course, but the prophetic words uttered by Jacob in Genesis 48 and 49 seem to suggest some such background. Then, one day, Jacob could feel his strength rapidly slipping away, and he knew that his time truly was almost gone. An attendant who had been charged with caring for him immediately sent word to Joseph, telling him that he had better come to his father, before it was too late.

Joseph dropped what he was doing and rushed to his father's bedside. For some reason, he called his two sons, Manasseh and Ephraim, and took them with him. Possibly, he also sent word to his eleven brothers, telling them that they should come too.

When his attendant told him Joseph was coming, Israel summoned what strength he still had and managed to sit up on the side of the bed, to greet him when he arrived. Knowing his time was short, he indulged in no small talk. He immediately rehearsed to Joseph for the last time what he no doubt had often discussed before, how God Almighty had first appeared to him at Luz, whose name he had therefore changed to Bethel. There God had confirmed to him the promises made to Abraham and Isaac: he would become a multitude of people, and the good land of Canaan would be given to his seed for an everlasting possession. Actually, God had appeared to Jacob at Bethel twice (Genesis 28:10-19 and 35:6-13), and Jacob probably had both of these occasions in mind when he said God appeared to him there. It was on the second occasion that these specific promises had been made.

Genesis 48:5-7

---

5 ¶ And now thy two sons, Ē'phrā-ĭm and Má-năs'sĕh, which were born unto thee in the land of Egypt, before I came unto thee into Egypt, *are* mine; as Reuben and Simeon, they shall be mine.
6 And thy issue, which thou begettest after them, shall be thine, *and* shall be called after the name of their brethren in their inheritance.
7 And as for me, when I came from Pā'dăn, Rachel died by me in the land of Cā'năan, in the way, when yet *there was* but a little way to come unto Ēph'răth: and I buried her there in the way of Ēph'răth; the same *is* Beth-lehem.

In the accomplishment of these promises, it would be necessary for the twelve sons of Jacob to understand their individual and corporate roles in the development of God's plans for the nation of which they were to be progenitors. Jacob first of all desired that Joseph be recognized in a special way, partly because of all he had done for the family, but probably primarily because he was the firstborn son of his wife Rachel.

Jacob had fully intended, in the beginning, that Rachel be his only wife; in that case, Joseph would indeed have been the firstborn. It had been by Laban's deception, not by Jacob's choice, that things had developed differently. It was appropriate, therefore, that Joseph be regarded as, in a peculiar sense, Jacob's firstborn.

As discussed in the case of Esau and Jacob, it was customary that the oldest son receive a double portion of the inheritance; but the father, as head of the family, could change this arrangement if the situation, in his opinion, warranted such a change. Jacob, therefore, was perfectly within his rights to transfer this birthright from Reuben (who had clearly shown, through both his incestuous relation with Bilhah and general weakness of character, that he was not really fit for such a responsibility) to Joseph, who should have been the firstborn and who had shown beyond question that he was indeed fit for the responsibility. "[Reuben] was the firstborn; but forasmuch as he defiled his father's bed, his birthright was given unto the sons of Joseph the son of Israel" (I Chronicles 5:1). Jacob decided it would be most effective to convey this double inheritance directly to Joseph's two sons, rather than to Joseph himself. This he would do by adopting them as his own sons, so that they would each be equal in rank to Reuben and Simeon, the two who were firstborn chronologically, and to his other sons. As far as the division of the inheritance (especially the future division of the land of Canaan when they would return to inhabit the land promised them for an inheritance), both Ephraim and Manasseh, therefore, would be counted as two of Jacob's sons. Their sons, in turn, would then be accounted as though they were actual sons of Joseph. The resulting tribes, moreover, would be called the tribe of Ephraim and the tribe of Manasseh, and would be equal in fraternal rank to any of the other eleven tribes.

By way of further explanation as to what some might have seen as favoritism, Jacob recalled his great love for Rachel and how she had died prematurely in giving birth to Benjamin, near Ephrath and Bethlehem. Jacob had hoped, otherwise, to have yet other sons from Rachel, but this hope had perished in his grief at her death and burial there in Canaan. In every way, therefore, it was appropriate and fair that Joseph receive the assignment of the double portion customary for the firstborn.

Jacob also recognized the possibility that Joseph might yet have other sons besides Ephraim and Manasseh (though, so far as the record goes, he never did). If so, they would share in the inheritance of Ephraim and Manasseh, and would be assigned to either of these two tribes. Joseph would receive a double portion, but only a double portion.

Genesis 48:8-12

8 And Ĭṣ'rā-ĕl beheld Joseph's sons, and said, Who *are* these?

9 And Joseph said unto his father, They *are* my sons, whom God hath given me in this *place*. And he said, Bring them, I pray thee, unto me, and I will bless them.

10 Now the eyes of Ĭṣ'rā-ĕl were dim for age, *so that* he could not see. And he brought them near unto him; and he kissed them, and embraced them.

11 And Ĭṣ'rā-ĕl said unto Joseph, I had not thought to see thy face: and, lo, God hath showed me also thy seed.

12 And Joseph brought them out from between his knees, and he bowed himself with his face to the earth.

At this point, Jacob saw that Joseph had not come in alone. His eyes were dim with age, so that he could not recognize faces, though he apparently still could vaguely discern shadows and shapes. He asked Joseph who was with him, and Joseph told him they were his two sons whom God had given him in Egypt and about whom Jacob had just been speaking. Jacob, recognizing their presence as fitting, and indeed providential, told Joseph to have them come forward so he could bless them and pray for them. Ephraim and Manasseh were, of course, young men by this time. Joseph had married when he was about thirty years old, and he was now about fifty-six.

When the two sons approached their grandfather, Israel embraced and kissed them, tearfully expressing thanksgiving that God had allowed him to see not only Joseph again, but even Joseph's sons. Joseph, then, in order to acknowledge his father's blessing on himself and his two sons, and also to express his love and reverence for his father, fell down before him to the ground, first moving his two sons away from where they were standing beside Jacob's knees, near the edge of the bed.

It is noteworthy that Joseph, even in his exalted position as second ruler in the kingdom, still found it appropriate to bow down before his father. Long ago, he had dreamed a dream, which he had understood at the time to signify that someday his father and mother, as well as his brothers, would do obeisance to him (Genesis 37:9, 10). That dream had come to pass, as far as his brothers were concerned, but not so far as his parents were concerned. This is one reason for questioning whether the dream in its entirety, or at least that specific interpretation of it, had really been inspired by God. To some degree it may have been influenced by Joseph's subconscious desires and opinion of himself at the time. In any case, at this point he clearly recognized the pre-eminence of his father.

Genesis 48:13-16

---

13 And Joseph took them both, Ē'phrā-im in his right hand toward Ĭṣ'rā-ĕl's left hand, and Mȧ-năs'sĕh in his left hand toward Ĭṣ'rā-ĕl's right hand, and brought *them* near unto him.
14 And Ĭṣ'rā-ĕl stretched out his right hand, and laid *it* upon Ē'phrā-ĭm's head, who *was* the younger, and his left hand upon Mȧ-năs'sĕh's head, guiding his hands wittingly; for Mȧ-năs'sĕh *was* the firstborn.

15 ¶ And he blessed Joseph, and said, God, before whom my fathers Abraham and Isaac did walk, the God which fed me all my life long unto this day,
16 The Angel which redeemed me from all evil, bless the lads; and let my name be named on them, and the name of my fathers Abraham and Isaac; and let them grow into a multitude in the midst of the earth.

Rising, Joseph then brought his sons back in front of Jacob, that he might pronounce his blessing on them. Since Manasseh was the older, he guided him toward his father's right hand, and Ephraim toward his left. Jacob, however, crossed his right hand over to Ephraim, and placed his left hand on Manasseh.

First, Jacob invoked a general blessing on Joseph and his sons. He prayed—perhaps not realizing fully the significance of what he was doing, but nevertheless guided by inspiration—to the Triune God. "God before whom my fathers, Abraham and Isaac, did walk" answers to the Father. "The God which fed me all my life long unto this day," that is, "the One who daily led me and provided my needs," speaks of the ministry of the Holy Spirit. "The Angel which redeemed me from all evil" must surely correspond to the saving work of the Son of God.

There are two significant "first mentions" in these verses. The word "fed me" is equivalent to "shepherded me" (Hebrew *raah*). The word itself does not occur here for the first time, but its use in connection with God does. That is, this is the first of many references in the Bible to God as our Shepherd.

Also, the word "redeem" (Hebrew *goel*) is used here for the first time in the Bible, and it is significant that it occurs as a description of the work of the great Angel of Jehovah, none other than the preincarnate Christ. The God of his fathers had surely provided for Jacob and protected him marvelously through the years, just as He had promised when He first spoke to him (Genesis 28:15); and Jacob knew he could call on Him in faith to bless his sons, specifically those two on whose heads his hands rested, in the same ways. He then prayed especially that God would let "my name be named on them"—that is, Jacob's character, for which his name stood—and also let them "grow into a multitude" in the midst of the land.

Genesis 48:17-20

17 And when Joseph saw that his father laid his right hand upon the head of E'phrā-ĭm, it displeased him: and he held up his father's hand, to remove it from E'phrā-ĭm's head unto Mȧ-năs'sĕh's head.

18 And Joseph said unto his father, Not so, my father: for this *is* the first-born; put thy right hand upon his head.

19 And his father refused, and said, I know *it*, my son, I know *it:* he also shall become a people, and he also shall be great: but truly his younger brother shall be greater than he, and his seed shall become a multitude of nations.

20 And he blessed them that day, saying, In thee shall Ĭṣ'rā-ĕl bless, saying, God make thee as E'phrā-ĭm and as Mȧ-năs'sĕh: and he set E'phrā-ĭm before Mȧ-năs'sĕh.

At this point, Joseph noted that Jacob's right hand was on Ephraim and his left hand on Manasseh. Thinking he had made a mistake, and wanting to correct it before Jacob pronounced specific benedictions on the two by individual name, Joseph reached for Jacob's hands to interchange them. He was a little displeased, too, for evidently he had fully intended that Manasseh have the birthright in his own family. He interrupted his father's prayer to tell him to place his right hand on Manasseh.

It is worth noting again how often God bypassed the oldest son in favor of a younger: Isaac instead of Ishmael, Jacob instead of Esau, Joseph instead of Reuben, and now Ephraim instead of Manasseh. The rule is not invariable, of course. The point is that God's choice is for spiritual reasons, not chronological.

In any case, Jacob well knew what he was doing. His decision was not arbitrary but was based on prophetic knowledge of the futures of the tribes that would begin with these two young men. Israel assured Joseph that Manasseh would indeed become a great people, but that nevertheless Ephraim would become greater, a veritable "multitude" of peoples. Ephraim, of course, eventually became the dominant tribe in the northern kingdom, after the division in the days of Jeroboam (I Kings 12:19, 25).

Genesis 48: 21, 22

21 And Ĭṣ'rā-ĕl said unto Joseph, Behold, I die; but God shall be with you, and bring you again unto the land of your fathers.

22 Moreover I have given to thee one portion above thy brethren, which I took out of the hand of the Ăm'ō-rīte with my sword and with my bow.

Jacob concluded his benediction by promising Joseph that God would be with him and bring even him again back to the land of his fathers.

Joseph did indeed return there to bury his father (Genesis 50:7), and eventually he himself would be buried there, but Jacob had primary reference to the return of his descendants to inhabit the land. He then mentioned a very special tract of ground, which he himself had conquered from the Amorites. This was apparently not a large tract, and is nowhere else referred to (except possibly John 4:5), but represented to Jacob a token that God would eventually give his descendants all the land. Of this tract, he deeded to Joseph a double portion.

Prophecies of the Twelve Tribes

One of the most fascinating and most difficult portions of Genesis is chapter 49, in which Jacob gives his last words concerning his sons and the twelve tribes that would descend from them. This valedictory of Jacob can be considered as both a blessing and guide for his sons themselves and a prophecy concerning future developments in the nation, extending all the way to "the last days." In some respects it is like the prophecy of Noah concerning his three sons (Genesis 9:24-27), stemming from the actual behavior and character of his sons and yet also outlining the general future of the three streams of nations of which they were to become forebears. Both in terms of genetic theory and of the course of history, it is true that each distinctive population group—nation, tribe, and so on—tends to manifest a particular character of its own (industrious or slothful, puritanical or licentious, peaceful or aggressive, philosophical or mechanical), and that this character is the product of its history and, ultimately, of its original founders. Such general characteristics, of course, do not preclude many individual exceptions in the particular population, but it does usually seem possible to define in general terms at least the dominant nature of such a group.

This proved to be true in Israel. Though Israel was God's chosen nation, partaking as it had throughout history of the energy, intelligence, morality, and faith of its fathers (Abraham, Isaac, and Jacob), there was nevertheless a wide range of variability on an individual basis in the divinely intended optimal character. Each of Jacob's twelve sons had distinctive characteristics of his own, even though they all shared to some degree the basic character of their father. This phenomenon, of course, is true in any family.

Because of the tremendous importance of this particular family in God's economy, however, God gave their father on his deathbed a profound prophetic glimpse of their future. To those sons who needed correction, the awesome nature of his words would have served as sober warning and, hopefully, as encouragement to correction. Also, of course, the fulfillment of his prophecies in the centuries and millennia that followed serves as strong proof of the divine origin of the nation and of the Scriptures which came through them.

It is not clear whether these words were spoken on a later occasion than that of Jacob's blessing of Ephraim and Manasseh, or immediately following. The latter seems the more likely, in view of Jacob's imminent death when Joseph was called. Quite probably, word was also sent to Joseph's brothers, and they came as quickly as they could, arriving at intervals during Jacob's interview with Joseph and his sons, probably even hearing what Jacob said to them, as he surely intended the brothers also to know about his decision on the birthright. In that case, by the time he had finished speaking to Joseph, his other sons were also present.

Genesis 49:1, 2

CHAPTER 49

AND Jacob called unto his sons, and said, Gather yourselves together, that I may tell you *that* which shall befall you in the last days.

2 Gather yourselves together, and hear, ye sons of Jacob; and hearken unto Is'rā-ĕl your father.

Jacob then called all his sons to gather near the bed, where he was still sitting on the side, that he might tell each of them what would happen to them, and to their respective tribes, in the future. Calling them "ye sons of Jacob," he urged them to listen to "Israel your father."

The discourse that follows is no ordinary conversation. It is in poetic form, and thus abounds in imagery. Its very tone manifests that, though Jacob is speaking, he is speaking "in the Spirit." He is in full possession of his faculties, even though at the point of death, noting many events which had been carried in his memory for many years, and yet speaking in a manner very different from his normal mode of speech, in poetry and symbol and prophecy. The twelve brothers could hardly fail to be soberly and indelibly impressed with the memory and importance of their father's words.

Almost unconsciously, as the brothers entered the room, they gathered by their own subfamily groupings, in a circular position around the bed. As Jacob's dim eyes gradually recognized them, he proceeded to speak to each one in turn, around the circle.

Genesis 49:3, 4

---

3 ¶ Reuben, thou *art* my firstborn, my might, and the beginning of my strength, the excellency of dignity, and the excellency of power:

4 Unstable as water, thou shalt not excel; because thou wentest up to thy father's bed; then defiledst thou *it:* he went up to my couch.

Reuben, his eldest, had naturally taken his place closest to his father, on one side of the bed. Always wanting his father's favor, and yet realizing he had forfeited his right to it, Reuben is somewhat a pathetic individual. As in the case with any firstborn son, Reuben had at one time been the pride and joy of his father. The firstborn is often called in Scripture, as Jacob did here, the "beginning of his father's strength" (Deuteronomy 21:17; Psalm 78:51, etc.), testifying to the dignity and power of his father.

Unfortunately, the firstborn does not always live up to his promise and his father's hopes. Reuben had turned out to be weak and unstable, as well as lustful. Worst of all had been his act of adultery and incest with Bilhah. Though Israel had apparently said little about it at the time (Genesis 35:22), he had never forgotten. Consequently, now, at the end, he had to make it clear that, for this reason if for nothing else, Reuben's right of primogeniture had been withdrawn. He would never "excel," or, literally, have anything special to contribute or leave to the benefit of posterity.

In the history of Israel, the tribe of Reuben never furnished a leader of any kind for the nation as a whole. In the later journeys to the promised land, the Reubenites were the first tribe to ask for a place to settle, not waiting to cross the Jordan with the others (Numbers 32). They participated in the erection of an unauthorized place of worship (Joshua 22:10-34). During the later wars with the Canaanites, in the days of Deborah and Barak, the tribe of Reuben failed to answer the call to arms (Judges 5:15, 16). Jacob's prophecy concerning Reuben has continued to be fulfilled ever since. Never has Reuben excelled in anything.

Genesis 49:5-7

---

5 ¶ Simeon and Levi *are* brethren; instruments of cruelty *are in* their habitations.

6 O my soul, come not thou into their secret; unto their assembly, mine honor, be not thou united: for in their anger they slew a man, and in their self-will they digged down a wall.

> 7 Cursed *be* their anger, for *it was* fierce; and their wrath, for it was cruel: I will divide them in Jacob, and scatter them in Iş'rā-ĕl.

The next two oldest sons were Simeon and Levi. As always, they were together there before Jacob, the closest companions among all the brothers. As Reuben had manifested weakness and lust, these two had manifested anger and cruelty. These hot-tempered men had caused great embarrassment, as well as danger, to the whole family when they had slain all the Shechemites because of the rape of their sister Dinah by one of them. Apparently this was not the only example of their violent natures, though it was the most extreme. Jacob said that "implements of violence" were their very "habitation" (however, this word, *makerah,* is used only here, and its meaning is uncertain). With deep emotion, Israel dissociated himself from their motives and actions. They may have tried to justify their slaughter of the Shechemites on the basis of righteous retribution, but Israel cursed their cruel anger and fierce wrath. It was bald anger and self-will which impelled them to kill men and to "dig down a wall" (or, as most translations, "hamstring an ox"), to wantonly destroy property. As a result of these attitudes, Jacob said, "I will divide them in Jacob and scatter them in Israel." It would, in fact, be for their own good that they would not be allowed to band together, but rather would be dispersed.

This prophecy was fulfilled in different ways in the case of each brother. Simeon was given an inheritance "within the inheritance of the children of Judah" (Joshua 19:1), but some of the sons of Simeon were captured and dwelled in some of the lands of the Edomites and Amalekites, outside of Canaan (I Chronicles 4:39-43). In the days of the divided kingdom, many of the Simeonites left Israel to join Judah (II Chronicles 15:9). Apparently they were eventually either mostly assimilated by Judah or scattered outside of Israel altogether, and little is heard of them after the days of King Asa.

As far as Levi is concerned, his descendants never had an inheritance of their own in the land, but only cities scattered throughout all the other tribes (Joshua 21:1-3). However, the Levites largely redeemed themselves by their stand against idolatry in the days of Moses (Exodus 32:26), although even in this they had opportunity to exercise the capacity for rugged vengeance which had been evidenced in their father (Exodus 32:27, 28). Moses himself was, of course, a descendant of Levi, and the Levites were chosen to be the priestly tribe among the Israelites. Their zeal was better utilized in this function than had they been allowed to develop a tribal enclave of their own.

Genesis 49:8-12

---

8 ¶ Judah, thou *art he* whom thy brethren shall praise: thy hand *shall be* in the neck of thine enemies; thy father's children shall bow down before thee.

9 Judah *is* a lion's whelp: from the prey, my son, thou art gone up: he stooped down, he couched as a lion, and as an old lion; who shall rouse him up?

10 The sceptre shall not depart from Judah, nor a lawgiver from between his feet, until Shī'lōh come; and unto him *shall* the gathering of the people *be*.

11 Binding his foal unto the vine, and his ass's colt unto the choice vine; he washed his garments in wine, and his clothes in the blood of grapes:

12 His eyes *shall be* red with wine, and his teeth white with milk.

Israel had little that was good to prophesy concerning his first three sons, but Judah was different. His very name meant "Praise," and he would become the object of his brothers' praise. He would be the leader among the tribes; he would defeat their enemies and would become, as the lion is king of beasts, the one before whom all his family would bow down. As Joseph was to receive the double inheritance of the first-born, so Judah would receive the patriarchal dominion and responsibility of the firstborn. He was as strong as a young lion that has overwhelmed and eaten its prey, as secure as a mature lion resting in its den, whom no one would dare to rouse.

Not only would Judah's tribe be strong and courageous, but his land would be productive and fruitful. Vines would grow so abundantly that even the asses would be tethered to them. So full would be his wine presses that whoever trod in them would appear to have actually bathed in the juice of the grapes, and his eyes would be fiery with wine. (Whether this implies drunkenness, or perhaps the good health associated generally with good food, including the grape sugar of the unfermented "blood of the grape," may not be clear; but the rest of the context of Judah's blessing here would seem out of place if the Judaeans were to become alcoholics.) The land would also be rich with milk, which would make for strong and white teeth.

It is obvious throughout the rest of Scripture that Judah did indeed become the leading tribe, but it was not until the days of King David. The earlier leaders were from other tribes: Moses from Levi, Joshua from Ephraim, Gideon from Manasseh, Samson from Dan, Samuel from Ephraim, and Saul from Benjamin. There was really no way for Jacob to foretell Judah's pre-eminence and prosperity except by divine inspiration. Judah did not actually receive the "sceptre" of leadership for over 640 years after Jacob's prophecy. Once David became king, however, Judah was the dominant tribe from then on.

The most important aspect of Israel's prophecy concerning Judah is in verse 10. Here, Jacob assured him that the scepter would never depart from him, nor a lawgiver from between his feet, until the coming of "Shiloh." The scepter (Hebrew *shebet*), which is mentioned for the first time in Scripture at this point, is, of course, the symbol of rulership. "Lawgiver" (Hebrew *chaqaq*), which also occurs first here, is a little uncertain, but seems to mean "the one who decrees." The phrase "between his feet" probably has reference to Judah's seed.

The key word is "Shiloh." This was the name of a town that was later built near Bethel. For a while during the period of the judges, the tabernacle was set up there; but it never was a very important town and was later destroyed by the Philistines. It is obvious that the prophecy cannot refer to this town, though it is perhaps possible that the town itself was originally named in commemoration of the prophecy and the One to whom it referred.

The context makes it certain that Shiloh is intended to be the name or title of a person. It is "unto *him* that peoples shall gather." The form of the word is related to the word for "peace" *(shalom)*, and probably it means "The One Who Brings Peace." In any case, it was accepted, by both certain ancient Jewish commentators and the early church, as prophetic of the promised Messiah, although its use as a specific title of Messiah dates from the Reformation. Another possibility, suggested by the Septuagint, is based on slight changes in pointing, making the word really to be "whose it is." This thought would correspond to Ezekiel 21:27: "until he come whose right it is."

It does seem most reasonable that, in such a prophetic valedictory as this, Jacob would make it clear which son would transmit the promised Seed. The promise of a personal Messiah began in the Garden of Eden, as expressed by God in Genesis 3:15. Through all the ages, men have looked for the coming Savior, and this was certainly true of Jacob. By all means, he would be expected to indicate something of that hope in his prophecy. This promise to Judah must indeed be Jacob's specific reference to that hope. When the Promised One would come, then indeed there would be peace and rest, and all peoples would gather to Him. Centuries later, Isaiah seemed to have these prophecies in mind, when he first spoke of the coming "Son of the Virgin" (Isaiah 7:14), and then elaborated by saying that His name would be "Prince of Peace" (Isaiah 9:6). The "gathering of the peoples," of which Jacob prophesies, corresponds clearly to God's messianic promise to Abraham, Isaac, and Jacob that through their coming Seed "shall all familiess of the earth be blessed" (Genesis 12:3; 22:18; 26:4; 28:14, etc.).

The New Testament clearly identifies the Lord Jesus Christ with this prophecy concerning Judah, calling Him "the Lion of the tribe of Judah" (Revelation 5:5). Micah also seems to refer to this prophecy when, just after saying that the coming Savior would be born in Bethlehem, in Judah, and that He would be "great unto the ends of the earth," he says: "And this man shall be the Peace" (Micah 5:2-5).

Also in favor of this rendering of the passage is the fact that it has been fulfilled. Once the tribe of Judah, under King David, attained leadership over the nation, the scepter (that is, the position of leadership in the nation) never departed from Judah until after Christ came. The kingdom was divided, and later all the tribes were taken into captivity; but as far as Israel itself was concerned, Judah was always the dominant tribe. Even during the captivity, Daniel, of the nation of Judah, was the greatest among the Israelites, and in fact became the third ruler in the kingdom of Babylon.

After the captivity, those who returned were primarily from the tribes of Judah and Benjamin, along with many Levites, as the other ten tribes had been scattered by the Assyrians. Although many from the ten tribes did manage to return to the land, Judah was essentially from then on synonymous with Israel as a whole. This condition continued, of course, until the actual coming and crucifixion of Jesus Christ, the promised Messiah. Soon after, Jerusalem was destroyed and the Jews (a name derived from Judah) were dispersed into the nations. Since then, even the genealogies have been lost, so that the tribal distinctives have all been fused and blurred among the Jews as a whole. This did not happen, however (that is, the scepter did not pass from Judah), until Shiloh came— just as Jacob had predicted! This fact, incidentally, confirms that the Messiah *did come,* and that He must have come sometime before A.D. 70, since the scepter passed from Judah about that time.

Genesis 49:13-15

---

13 ¶ Zĕb'ū-lŭn shall dwell at the haven of the sea; and he *shall be* for a haven of ships; and his border *shall be* unto Zi'dŏn.

14 ¶ Ĭs'sà-chär *is* a strong ass couching down between two burdens:

15 And he saw that rest *was* good, and the land that *it was* pleasant; and bowed his shoulder to bear, and became a servant unto tribute.

After speaking to Judah, Jacob turned to Leah's two other sons, who apparently were standing together next to Judah. Nothing is said in the narrative portions of Genesis about the actions of these two sons; so all we know about their behavior is whatever describes the behavior of Joseph's brothers as a whole. Only in Jacob's words in this passage do we get any clue to their individual characteristics. About Zebulun, the only thing mentioned is that he would dwell "toward the seashore" (not *at* the sea, as in the King James Version). He also said that Zebulun would be for a haven of ships, with his northern border facing toward the ancient and great seaport of Zidon. The tract actually assigned Zebulun by Joshua was "up toward the sea" (Joshua 19:11) and "reached to the river that is before Jokneam." The precise borders of Zebulun are difficult to decipher, so that exactly how this prophecy was fulfilled may require further study. It is usually assumed that Zebulun was located between the Sea of Galilee and the Mediterranean, but whether its borders actually reached either or both these seas is not known. Matthew 4:13 suggests that its border extended to Capernaum, on the shore of Galilee. In any case, it was a region in which much of Christ's public ministry took place (Matthew 4:15, 16).

Jacob compared Issachar to a strong ass "bowing down beneath a double burden" (or, as some translations, "settled down between the sheepfolds"). Though the precise translation may be obscure, the meaning seems to be that Issachar was strong, but docile and lazy. He would enjoy the good land assigned him but would not strive for it. Therefore, eventually he would be pressed into servitude and the mere bearing of burdens for his masters. Historically, Issachar had rich lands and rich crops, which attracted marauders and captors. Again, however, there is little specific information.

Genesis 49:16-21

---

16 ⁋ Dan shall judge his people, as one of the tribes of Iṣ'rā-ĕl.

17 Dan shall be a serpent by the way, an adder in the path, that biteth the horse heels, so that his rider shall fall backward.

18 I have waited for thy salvation, O LORD.

19 ⁋ Gad, a troop shall overcome him: but he shall overcome at the last.

20 ⁋ Out of Ăsh'ẽr his bread *shall be* fat, and he shall yield royal dainties.

21 ⁋ Năph'tà-lī *is* a hind let loose: he giveth goodly words.

Next listed are the four sons of the two handmaids. They are not listed in chronological order, Naphtali appearing fourth rather than second; so it seems likely Jacob simply dealt with them in the order in which they happened to be standing around the bedside. Again, as in the case of Zebulun and Issachar, nothing specific is mentioned about any of them in the narratives of Genesis, so that the only clues to their individual characters are here in Jacob's prophecies.

Since there might have been some question as to whether these sons of the concubines would actually share in the inheritance, Jacob assured the first one of them, Dan, that he would indeed "judge his people, as one of the tribes of Israel." But then he compared Dan to a venomous snake that would defeat a mounted soldier by striking at the heel of his horse. Probably the primary reference has to do with the fact that the tribe of Dan, while apparently unimpressive (it occupied the smallest area of any of the tribes, along the northern seacoast, apparently vulnerable to attack), nevertheless was a dangerous adversary, well able to protect Israel's northern boundary against invaders.

On the other hand, the reference to the serpent may also refer symbolically to the fact that it was the Danites who introduced idolatry into the land of Israel on a regular official basis (Judges 18:30, 31). It was also in Dan that Jeroboam, who led the rebellion that culminated in the divided kingdom, set up one of his two golden calves (I Kings 12:28-30). It may be that this is why Dan is not listed among the tribes in Revelation 7:4-8 (note Deuteronomy 29:16-21).

This latter interpretation is strengthened by the fact that Jacob, immediately after his reference to the serpent, must have thought of the one whom the serpent throughout Scripture typifies—that old Serpent, the Devil. Thinking of the Serpent and his enmity against God's people, Jacob would naturally also think of God's primeval promise of the coming Seed whose heel would be bitten by the Serpent, but who would in turn finally crush his head and bring the long-awaited salvation (Genesis 3:15). It was in reference to this Messianic promise that he had just spoken to Judah. It is natural, therefore, that right at this point, he would cry out: "I have waited for thy salvation, O Lord!" It would not be too imaginative to suggest that, in Jacob's mind, this Salvation for which he was waiting was actually a person. The word itself is the Hebrew *yeshuah,* which is none other than the name "Jesus!" This becomes even the more significant when it is realized that here we have the first mention of the word "salvation" in the Bible.

Of Gad, Jacob prophesied that, although invading troops might assault his home, he (whose name itself meant "troop") would in turn repel them and press on the heel (instead of "at the last," as in King James) of the enemy. Gad's realm was east of the Jordan, on the edge of the kingdom of the Ammonites and other desert peoples, and thus was especially open to attack. However, the Gadites were well able to fight (I Chronicles 5:18; 12:8, etc.).

His brother Asher was to have and enjoy rich food and royal delicacies.

As it turned out, Asher's lot fell on the rich northern seacoast north of Mount Carmel, all the way to Tyre and Zidon (Joshua 19:24-31). However, they failed even to take possession of the Tyre-Sidon region, and the tribe soon became insignificant, possibly deteriorating because of their love of ease and proximity to the Phoenicians.

Naphtali, the brother of Dan, is described as "a hind let loose." That is, his descendants would be known for swiftness, as warriors fleet of foot. They would also be known as composers of eloquent speech and beautiful literature. Evidently, Naphtali himself was of this temperament, although nothing specifically is said about him in Scripture. The best known of his descendants was Barak, who, with Deborah, won a mighty victory over Jabin and Sisera of the Canaanites (Judges 4:6, 15) mainly with men from his own tribe and that of Zebulun (Judges 4:10; 5:18). The prediction regarding "goodly words" was, no doubt, fulfilled in measure by the victory song of Deborah and Barak (Judges 5:1-31).

Genesis 49:22-26

---

22 ¶ Joseph *is* a fruitful bough, *even* a fruitful bough by a well; *whose* branches run over the wall:

23 The archers have sorely grieved him, and shot *at him,* and hated him:

24 But his bow abode in strength, and the arms of his hands were made strong by the hands of the mighty *God* of Jacob; (from thence *is* the shepherd, the stone of Ĭṣ′rā-ĕl;)

25 *Even* by the God of thy father, who shall help thee; and by the Almighty, who shall bless thee with blessings of heaven above, blessings of the deep that lieth under, blessings of the breasts, and of the womb:

26 The blessings of thy father have prevailed above the blessings of my progenitors unto the utmost bound of the everlasting hills: they shall be on the head of Joseph, and on the crown of the head of him that was separate from his brethren.

Finally, Jacob turned to Joseph and Benjamin. To Joseph he pronounced a blessing comparable only to that of Judah. Using expressive figures of speech, he compared his favorite son to a bough from a fruitful vine, with an abundant supply of water and with branches climbing over the wall, in this way predicting that his tribe (actually the twofold tribe, Ephraim and Manasseh) would be strong and numerous. He also compared him to a man beset by enemy archers who had tried to destroy him as a hated foe, but nevertheless one whose own bow was strong and steady, and whose hands were made strong by the strong God who had strengthened his father Jacob. This description applied directly to Joseph himself and to his triumph over the enmity of his brothers, but it also was prophetic of the experience of Joseph's descendants.

The one who had strengthened Joseph's hand, and who would be likewise the strength of his tribe, is said to be both the Shepherd and the Stone of Israel. Although there had been a reference to the shepherding work of the Lord in Jacob's words to Ephraim and Manasseh (Genesis 48:15), this is the first time where God is actually called the Shepherd. Likewise, this is the first time when God is called either the Stone or the Rock. God thus would both nourish and protect Joseph. Jacob also stressed again that this God was the same God as his God, the God of his fathers. He assured Joseph that God would bless him with blessings of rain from the heavens, and with water from the deep, the water flowing through the pores of the ground beneath his feet. The "deep" *(tehom)* is a term referring to waters on or under the earth's surface. He also promised an abundance of healthful progeny, of both man and animal.

Israel also gave testimony that he himself had received greater blessing than his own fathers, with a large number of sons and with fruitful lands "unto the utmost bound of the everlasting hills," that is, "to the very boundaries marked by the surrounding ancient hills." No hill, of course, could really be everlasting. The Hebrew word is *olam,* and is often translated "ancient." The duration implied by this word depends on the context, and can actually mean either "old" or "eternal," depending on what it modifies. The hills bounding the fertile fields of Ephraim and Manasseh were, of course, much older than the tribes inhabiting them, but actually dated back only to the great Flood. All of these blessings which Jacob had experienced would likewise be showered on Joseph and his descendants. He was the one "separate from" (Hebrew *nazir,* same as the word later used for "Nazirite") his brothers, and thus marked out for special distinction and service.

These prophecies were fulfilled in the later histories of the tribes of Ephraim and Manasseh, especially the former. Many of Israel's leaders were from these tribes. Joshua, Deborah, and Samuel were from Ephraim; and Gideon and Jephthah were from Manasseh. Both tribes were strong in war, and their lands were fertile and productive. Jeroboam, an Ephraimite, led the rebellion which produced the divided kingdom; and the northern kingdom came to be called alternatively by the names Israel and Ephraim, as the southern kingdom was called by the name Judah.

It is prophetically significant that Jacob's blessing centered especially on Joseph and Judah, and that these two eventually became the two dominant divisions of Israel. It is further significant that only physical blessings were promised Joseph, whereas the spiritual blessing of being the ancestor of Messiah was promised Judah, in addition to physical blessings and political leadership.

Genesis 49:27, 28

27 ¶ Benjamin shall raven *as* a wolf: in the morning he shall devour the prey, and at night he shall divide the spoil. 28 ¶ All these *are* the twelve tribes of Ĭş'rā-ĕl: and this *is it* that their father spake unto them, and blessed them; every one according to his blessing he blessed them.

The final son was Benjamin, and Jacob prophesied that he would become as a ravening wolf, devouring the prey and dividing the spoil. This seems like a strange forecast for a son whom Jacob specially loved. It was both a promise and a warning. The tribe of Benjamin would be bold and strong, successful in warfare, but at the same time it might become cruel and voracious. Both attributes were later evident in the tribe, as is demonstrated by the strange story in Judges 20, which almost cost the Benjamites their very identity as one of the twelve tribes. Moreover, the first king of Israel was Saul, a Benjamite, whose character quite precisely corresponded to Jacob's prophecy.

Jacob thus concluded his blessings on his sons, calling them prophetically the "twelve tribes of Israel." Even though some of the predictions hardly sounded like blessings, they were intended indirectly to serve as such, through warning his sons and their children of those traits and tendencies against which they needed especially to guard. The children of Israel must have read and meditated on these sayings of Jacob many times during the ensuing centuries, particularly during their bondage in Egypt and their wanderings in the wilderness. Clearly, they should have proved (and probably did prove) very salutary to them.

Genesis 49:29-33

29 And he charged them, and said unto them, I am to be gathered unto my people: bury me with my fathers in the cave that *is* in the field of E'phrŏn the Hĭt'tite, 30 In the cave that *is* in the field of Măch-pē'làh, which *is* before Măm'rē, in the land of Cā'năan, which Abraham bought with the field of E'phrŏn the Hĭt-tite for a possession of a buryingplace. 31 There they buried Abraham and Sarah his wife; there they buried Isaac and Rē-bĕk'àh his wife; and there I buried Lē'àh. 32 The purchase of the field and of the cave that *is* therein *was* from the children of Heth. 33 And when Jacob had made an end of commanding his sons, he gathered up his feet into the bed, and yielded up the ghost, and was gathered unto his people.

The promise Jacob had extracted from Joseph he now asked from all his sons, that they would bury him with his fathers back in Canaan, in the cave which Abraham had purchased years ago for that purpose. Jacob had buried his first wife, Leah, there, and his parents and grandparents were also buried there. It was to be a testimony, to all the generations to come, that Abraham, Isaac, and Jacob had faith in God's promise that He would give the land to their seed.

With this last request, Jacob summoned all his remaining strength to pull his feet back up into the bed, to lie back down, and then to give up his spirit to be "gathered unto his people"—not merely to be buried with their bodies, but to join them in their life beyond the grave, awaiting the coming of Messiah and the great resurrection day.

A Coffin in Egypt

In the last chapter of Genesis we have the record of the burial of Jacob. No other burial in the Bible is accorded so long and detailed an account, a fact which indicates the importance placed on Jacob by God in His plan of redemptive history.

In a practical way, it emphasizes that, when a believer dies, it is appropriate that his body be treated with all due honor, and that it be buried in such a way as to give testimony that the one who died believed in the future resurrection of the body and the fulfillment of all God's promises. (It is significant that nowhere in Scripture is there an example of a believer's body being disposed of by cremation or by any means other than burial.)

Genesis 50:1-3

CHAPTER 50

AND Joseph fell upon his father's face, and wept upon him, and kissed him.

2 And Joseph commanded his servants the physicians to embalm his father: and the physicians embalmed Ĭş'rā-ĕl.

3 And forty days were fulfilled for him; for so are fulfilled the days of those which are embalmed: and the Egyptians mourned for him threescore and ten days.

When Jacob's spirit left his body, and was taken by the angels "unto his people," presumably to "Abraham's bosom" (Luke 16:22), Joseph fell down on his father, kissing him and weeping. Even though one may believe confidently in a future life, as Joseph no doubt did, and knows he will someday be reunited with a departed loved one, it is natural and proper that he feel and express a keen sense of sorrow and bereavement. Death is the great enemy, and will one day be purged completely (Revelation 21:4), so there will be no more sorrow or crying. For the present, however, death causes sorrow.

Nevertheless, we "sorrow not, even as others which have no hope" (I Thessalonians 4:13). After a little while, Joseph controlled his tears, and proceeded with the necessary duties for the dead. As God had promised Jacob, Joseph "closed [Jacob's] eyes in death" (Genesis 46:4), and Jacob died content (Genesis 45:28; 46:30).

Nothing is said about the reaction of the other sons when their father died. However, there is no doubt they all loved him dearly, even if not quite so intensely as Joseph did.

It was customary in Egypt to embalm the dead, using an elaborate process of alteration and treatment of the body which ensured that its mummified remains would be preserved almost indefinitely. Joseph had his personal physicians undertake this process with his father's body, a process which lasted forty days.

It was also customary in Egypt to have approximately a seventy-day period of mourning, especially for a person of national importance, as Jacob had come to be recognized. Not only because he was Joseph's father, but because he had come to be honored in his own right by the Egyptians as a true man of God during the seventeen years he had lived in their country, the Egyptians themselves joined in the mourning for Jacob.

Genesis 50:4-6

---

4 And when the days of his mourning were past, Joseph spake unto the house of Phā'raōh, saying, If now I have found grace in your eyes, speak, I pray you, in the ears of Phā'raōh, saying,
5 My father made me swear, saying, Lo, I die: in my grave which I have digged for me in the land of Cā'năan, there shalt thou bury me. Now therefore let me go up, I pray thee, and bury my father, and I will come again.
6 And Phā'raōh said, Go up, and bury thy father, according as he made thee swear.

After the seventy-day period was over, Joseph and his brothers determined to set about obeying their father's request that he be buried not in Egypt but in Canaan. This would perhaps be easier promised than accomplished. Since the famine was long past, this might be an excellent time for all of them to return to Canaan to live. However, the Israelites had proved to be highly productive components of the Egyptian economy, and there might be real resistance to their leaving. Joseph especially was considered indispensable by Pharaoh and his courtiers.

Accordingly, Joseph (very diplomatically) first gained the support of Pharaoh's officers for his request, and then asked *them* to convey it to

Pharaoh. He assured them the Israelites would all return after the burial was accomplished. Also, he appealed to their strong sense of respect for the dead by pointing out that his father had made them swear a solemn oath to bury him in the grave which he had dug for that purpose back in his homeland of Canaan. (The cave where Jacob's fathers were buried, of course, did not require digging, but each patriarch did have to dig the graves inside the cave for his personal burials.)

Pharaoh could see that the request was well intentioned and reasonable, especially in view of the oath, and so readily granted permission. Evidently he also gave orders that it should be recognized as an official Egyptian state funeral, with all due honors accorded to the dead.

Genesis 50:7-9

---

7 ¶ And Joseph went up to bury his father: and with him went up all the servants of Pha'raōh, the elders of his house, and all the elders of the land of Egypt,

8 And all the house of Joseph, and his brethren, and his father's house: only their little ones, and their flocks, and their herds, they left in the land of Gō'shĕn.

9 And there went up with him both chariots and horsemen: and it was a very great company.

And so the funeral procession consisted not only of Joseph and his brothers and their households (only the little ones remained behind in Goshen, as well as the flocks and herds—a fact which assured any Egyptian who might be skeptical that they would, indeed, return), but also the servants and elders of Pharaoh's household, and all the elders of the land of Egypt. There were many cavalrymen for protection, as well as chariots (probably really "wagons") for transportation of food and supplies. It constituted a tremendous caravan and funeral procession, wending its way up from Egypt, skirting the Red Sea, heading across the Sinai desert, south of the Dead Sea, and then up its eastern shores to the Jordan River.

Genesis 50:10, 11

---

10 And they came to the threshing-floor of Ā'tăd, which *is* beyond Jordan; and there they mourned with a great and very sore lamentation: and he made a mourning for his father seven days.

11 And when the inhabitants of the land, the Cā'năan-ītes, saw the mourning in the floor of Ā'tăd, they said, This *is* a grievous mourning to the Egyptians: wherefore the name of it was called Ā'bĕl-mĭz'rā-im, which *is* beyond Jordan.

The caravan seems to have stopped just east of the Jordan, at the site known as "the threshing floor of Atad," Atad presumably being a man's name. There the whole assemblage carried out a formal seven-day period of mourning. To all appearances it was an official Egyptian mourning ceremony, and was the object of much attention and discussion by the Canaanites of the area. The latter, in fact, gave the place the name Abel-mizraim ("Meadow of the Egyptians") as a result. They may have wondered what a great body of Egyptians was doing there, instead of carrying out their funeral in Egypt; however, there is some evidence that Egypt actually controlled this region in those days.

Genesis 50:12-14

12 And his sons did unto him according as he commanded them:

13 For his sons carried him into the land of Cā'năan, and buried him in the cave of the field of Măeh-pē'lăh, which Abraham bought with the field for a possession of a buryingplace of E'phrŏn the Hĭt'tĭte, before Măm're.

14 ¶ And Joseph returned into Egypt, he, and his brethren, and all that went up with him to bury his father, after he had buried his father.

When the mourning was finished, Jacob's sons took his body across Jordan, into Canaan, and to the cave of Machpelah near Mamre. There they buried him, as he had commanded, giving testimony not only of love for their father but also of faith in God's promises concerning the land, which someday would go to their seed for an everlasting possession.

Finally, Joseph and his brothers returned to Egypt. God had led them into Egypt, and there they knew they must stay until He told them it was time to return. They probably realized, because of God's word to Abraham (Genesis 15:13-16), that they would be there a long time.

Genesis 50:15-21

15 ¶ And when Joseph's brethren saw that their father was dead, they said, Joseph will peradventure hate us, and will certainly requite us all the evil which we did unto him.

16 And they sent a messenger unto Joseph, saying, Thy father did command before he died, saying,

17 So shall ye say unto Joseph, Forgive, I pray thee now, the trespass of thy brethren, and their sin; for they did unto thee evil: and now, we pray thee, forgive the trespass of the servants of the God of thy father. And Joseph wept when they spake unto him.

18 And his brethren also went and fell down before his face; and they said, Behold, we be thy servants.

19 And Joseph said unto them, Fear not: for am I in the place of God?

20 But as for you, ye thought evil against me; but God meant it unto good, to bring to pass, as it is this day, to save much people alive.

21 Now therefore fear ye not: I will nourish you, and your little ones. And he comforted them, and spake kindly unto them.

It is understandable that, after Jacob was gone, the ten brothers who had sold Joseph into slavery would be afraid he might finally take vengeance on them. Even though he had assured them that he would take care of them and their families and that he regarded his sale into Egypt as providential (Genesis 45:4-11), their sense of guilt was still so strong that they could not really believe he had forgiven them.

Actually, they had never made a full confession of their sin to Joseph, although they had shown by their actions that they were sorry. Joseph, of course, had given no indication that he held any grudge, but he may have wondered why they still were silent. A combination of pride and fear seemed to inhibit them from saying anything further as long as Jacob was living. They assumed that, for Jacob's sake, Joseph would not do anything to them. Now that Jacob was no longer a restraining influence, however, their fear and guilt complex suddenly returned.

Consequently they decided to send word to Joseph (presumably by either Judah or Benjamin) to remind him that Jacob had urged him to forgive them. This time, their message did include a clear and definite confession of sin and plea for forgiveness.

There is no previous statement in Genesis telling of this command of Jacob to Joseph. However, there is no reason to question that he had given such a commandment, nor any doubt that Joseph had every intention of following it. Jacob had undoubtedly expressed himself directly in this vein to Joseph, and the brothers knew he had. Nevertheless, they still felt it would be in order to remind Joseph of it.

Although Joseph had no thought of punishing them, their confession and plea did touch him deeply. He was no doubt thankful for their sakes that they had done this, since it testified further that their repentance was genuine and complete. Quite possibly Jacob himself had urged them to make a full confession. It was significant, too, that they called themselves "the servants of the God of thy father." They had all by this time apparently become sincere in their understanding of God's special calling for them.

Joseph's brothers did not stop with this message of confession, but quickly followed it up by coming directly into his presence with an offer to become his slaves. As they had sent him into slavery, so they now would volunteer to be slaves themselves. Sincere confession of sin against someone always includes restitution, and they were willing to do this the best way they knew how.

Joseph, of course, responded by assuring them again of his full forgiveness. Even though their intentions had been evil, God had ordained it all for good. "Surely the wrath of man shall praise thee: the remainder of wrath shalt thou restrain" (Psalm 76:10).

Even if Joseph had still harbored a personal resentment against his brothers, he would have feared to take vengeance. God had so clearly used their deed to accomplish His own good purpose to preserve life through the famine that Joseph knew it would be bold presumption on his part were he now to punish them for that same deed. If they still deserved any punishment, God Himself could take care of it. "Vengeance is mine; I will repay, saith the Lord" (Romans 12:19). In the meantime, Joseph assured them he would see that they and their children were. protected and nourished, speaking (literally) "to their hearts."

Genesis 50:22, 23

---

22 ❡ And Joseph dwelt in Egypt, he, and his father's house: and Joseph lived a hundred and ten years.
23 And Joseph saw E'phrā-ĭm's chil-dren of the third *generation:* the chil-dren also of Mā'chĭr the son of Mă-năs'sĕh were brought up upon Joseph's knees.

Jacob died when Joseph was fifty-six years old (Genesis 41:46, 53; 45:6; 47:28). Joseph continued to live for another fifty-four years after that, finally dying at the age of 110.

This was considerably younger than the age at which Abraham (175), Isaac (180), and Jacob (147) had died. Man's longevity was still declining after the Flood.

Joseph did live to know some of his great-grandchildren. His older son, Manasseh, seems to have had two sons of his own, Machir and Asriel (Numbers 26:29-31; I Chronicles 7:14), and possibly others, but apparently only the children of Machir were born while Joseph was still able to enjoy them. These included Gilead, the ancestor of the Gileadites (Numbers 26:29).

Joseph also saw the "children of the third generation" of his younger son, Ephraim. It is not clear, however, whether this expression means Ephraim's children (the third generation from Joseph) or Ephraim's grandchildren (third generation from Ephraim). In any case, Joseph could see that he would have a numerous progeny, in accord with God's promises (Genesis 48:19, 20).

Genesis 50:24-26

---

24 And Joseph said unto his brethren, I die; and God will surely visit you, and bring you out of this land unto the land which he sware to Abraham, to Isaac, and to Jacob.

25 And Joseph took an oath of the chil-dren of Ĭş'rā-ĕl, saying, God will surely visit you, and ye shall carry up my bones from hence.

26 So Joseph died, *being* a hundred and ten years old: and they embalmed him, and he was put in a coffin in Egypt.

How many of Joseph's brothers were still alive at his death is not stated. It is likely that his younger brother Benjamin was still living and quite possibly others were too. When Joseph knew he was about to die, he called these brothers (and possibly his nephews as well, to whom the Biblical term "brethren" might be applied) and reminded them—in case they were in danger of forgetting—that God intended some day that all the children of Israel return to Canaan, where He would finally give them the promised land, as He had sworn to their forefathers.

Joseph then asked his brothers, the children of Israel, to promise that they would bury him in Canaan as they had buried Jacob there. They took an oath to do this, an oath finally fulfilled by their heirs (Exodus 13:19; Joshua 24:32).

Joseph realized, now that he was dying, it would be impossible for his brothers to organize an expedition (as he had done for Jacob) to bury him in Canaan right after his death. However, he fully believed that they would someday all move back to Canaan, and it would be at that time that he wanted them to take his bones with them. For this confidence and faith, he was mentioned in the "faith" chapter of Hebrews (Hebrews 11:22).

Joseph then died and his body, like that of Jacob (verse 2), was embalmed and placed in a coffin (or wooden mummy case) in Egypt. In that way, it could be seen by his descendants and those of his brothers, serving as a perpetual reminder of God's promise to them—and therefore also as a reminder of God's purpose—that they would all someday return to Canaan.

With this record of the death of their brother and deliverer—clearly coupled with the hope and promise of a future deliverance—the Book of Genesis ends. The groundwork is laid and the transition is natural to the opening verses of the Book of Exodus, when God would raise up a new prophet and leader in His servant Moses.

Appendixes

APPENDIX 1
ANNOTATED BIBLIOGRAPHY
RECOMMENDED BOOKS FOR FURTHER READING

This bibliography is not intended to be an exhaustive list of works dealing with the Book of Genesis. Such a list would constitute a volume in itself. Its intent is to provide the user of this commentary with a brief list of especially helpful additional study books dealing with Genesis or important topics treated in Genesis. All of the recommended books are written from the perspective of sound Biblical faith and are of sufficiently recent date as to be generally available for purchase or in libraries.

Commentaries on Genesis (Conservative)

Atkinson, Basil F. C. *Genesis*. London: Henry E. Walter, Ltd., 1954. 446 pp.

Written by a librarian at Cambridge University. Highly devotional in tone, and excessively typological in approach, but with many helpful insights.

Candlish, Robert S. *Commentary on Genesis*. 2 vols. Grand Rapids: Zondervan Publishing House, n.d. 479, 381 pp.

This is a reprint of a commentary originally published in 1863. Except for certain concessions to evolutionary chronology in the early chapters of Genesis, a helpful treatment. Devotional emphasis.

Carroll, B. H. *The Book of Genesis*. New York: Fleming H. Revell Co., 1913. 451 pp.

An excellent commentary by a great Southern Baptist preacher and teacher. Postmillennial.

Davis John. *Paradise to Prison*. Grand Rapids: Baker Book House, 1975. 363 pp.

An excellent new commentary by a professor at Grace Seminary. Conservative and scholarly throughout. Contains very extensive bibliography.

Green, William Henry. *The Unity of the Book of Genesis*. New York: Charles Scribner's Sons, 1895. 593 pp.

A thorough refutation of the documentary theory as applied to Genesis. Never answered.

Keil, C. F. *The Pentateuch,* vol. I. Grand Rapids: Wm. B. Eerdmans Publishing Co., n.d. 414 pp.

A reprint of the classic Keil and Delitzsch commentary, originally published in 1875. Solidly conservative and sound exposition.

Lange, John Peter. *Genesis.* (Grand Rapids: Zondervan Publishing House, n.d. 673 pp.

Originally published as a part of Lange's *Commentary on the Holy Scriptures* in 1864, a classic reference set. Influenced somewhat by uniformitarian geological considerations.

Leupold, Herbert C. *Exposition of Genesis.* 2 vols. Grand Rapids: Baker Book House, 1949. 576 pp., 644 pp.

Originally published in 1942 by Wartburg Press, Columbus, Ohio, this is the most extensive modern conservative commentary on Genesis, and the one of most help to the author in the preparation of this present volume. Deals effectively with the various critical expositions and interpretations throughout Genesis.

Mackintosh, C. H. *Notes on the Book of Genesis.* New York: Loizeaux Brothers. 334 pp.

Standard text on the typological and dispensational approach to the study of Genesis. Highly devotional in tone.

Parker, Joseph. *Genesis.* Chicago: Moody Press, 1951. 378 pp. Reprinted with Parker's well-known *People's Bible.*

Eloquent sermons on the major passages of Genesis.

Pink, Arthur W. *Gleanings in Genesis.* Chicago: Moody Press, 1922. 412 pp.

Widely used devotional commentary on selected sections in Genesis. Excessively typological.

Thomas, W. H. Griffith. *Genesis: A Devotional Commentary.* Grand Rapids: Wm. B. Eerdmans Publishing Co., 1946. 507 pp.

Eloquent devotional expositions on important passages. Unfortunately advocates day-age and local-flood theories.

Whitelaw, Thomas. *Genesis.* Grand Rapids: Wm. B. Eerdmans Publishing Co., 1950. 644 pp.

Volume I of *The Pulpit Commentary.* Reprinted from the original 1882 edition. Argues against the higher critical approach in interpreting Genesis.

Supplementary Studies (Creationism, Archaeology, etc.)

Adam, Ben. *The Origin of Heathendom.* Minneapolis: Bethany Fellowship, 1963. 128 pp.

An illuminating study of the Satanic origins of paganism and of the significance of the Tower of Babel.

Allis, Oswald T. *The Five Books of Moses.* Nutley, N.J.: Presbyterian and Reformed Publishing Co., 1949. 319 pp.

One of the outstanding defenses of the Mosaic authorship of the Pentateuch against the documentary hypothesis and other critical theories.

Barton, George A. *Archaeology and the Bible.* Philadelphia: American Sunday School Union, 1941. 745 pp.

Though not always theologically conservative and no longer fully up to date, still probably the most complete compilation of source material on Biblical archaeology available in one volume.

Custance, Arthur C. *Noah's Three Sons.* Grand Rapids: Zondervan Publishing House, 1975. 368 pp.

An important analysis of the Semitic, Japhetic, and Hamitic contributions to civilization and world history.

————. *Genesis and Early Man.* Grand Rapids: Zondervan Publishing House, 1975. 331 pp.

Evidence of man's unique origin and nature. Written by a Ph.D. anthropologist with remarkable, new insights.

Custer, Stewart, ed. *Focus on Genesis.* Greenville, S.C.: Bob Jones University Press, 1968. 180 pp.

About a dozen topical discussions on important questions related to Genesis by the members of the graduate faculty of Bob Jones University. Very helpful.

Morris, Henry M., ed. *Scientific Creationism.* San Diego: Creation-Life Publishers, 1974. 277 pp.

The most comprehensive and up-to-date reference handbook available covering all major aspects of the scientific evidence for creationism and catastrophism.

————. *Biblical Cosmology and Modern Science.* Nutley, N.J.: Craig Press, 1970, 146 pp.

Scientific and Biblical expositions of many aspects of origins—cosmology, demography, sedimentology, and eschatology. Includes extensive critiques of day-age, gap, and allegorical theories of Genesis.

————. *The Troubled Waters of Evolution.* San Diego: Creation-Life Publishers, 1975. 207 pp.

The historical background and modern widespread influence of the evolutionary philosophy. Survey of the modern revival of creationism.

Pfeiffer, Charles F. *The Biblical World*. Grand Rapids: Baker Book House, 1966. 612 pp.

Thorough discussion of the geography and archaeology of the Biblical lands.

Pfeiffer, Charles F.; Vos, Howard F.; and Rea, John, eds. *Wycliffe Bible Encyclopedia*. 2 vols. Chicago: Moody Press, 1975. 1,851 pp.

The most up-to-date Bible encyclopedia available. Deals with all important names and places in Genesis.

Unger, Merrill F. *Archaeology and the Old Testament*. Grand Rapids, Zondervan Publishing House, 1954. 339 pp.

One of the best treatments of archaeological discoveries bearing on the Old Testament, especially Genesis.

Whitcomb, John C., and Morris, Henry M. *The Genesis Flood*. Nutley, N.J.: Presbyterian and Reformed Publishing Co., 1961. 518 pp.

The definitive text in the field of scientific Biblical creationism and catastrophism. The most extensive, fully documented treatment available on the Biblical and scientific implications of Creation and the Flood.

Whitcomb, John C. *The Early Earth*. Grand Rapids: Baker Book House, 1972. 144 pp.

Studies of the origin and nature of man, the gap theory, the antediluvian world, and other topics from the Book of Genesis.

————. *The World That Perished*. Grand Rapids: Baker Book House, 1973. 155 pp.

A sequel to *The Genesis Flood*, with refutations of criticisms and further evidences of a young earth and Biblical catastrophism.

Wiseman, P. J. *New Discoveries in Babylonia About Genesis*. London: Marshall, Morgan, and Scott, 1946. 143 pp.

Archaeological and linguistic evidence of the antiquity of writing and of the pre-Mosaic authorship and the Mosaic editorship of the documents of the Book of Genesis.

APPENDIX 2

CHRONOLOGY OF THE PATRIARCHS[1] IN GENESIS

Name	Year of Birth[2]	Age at Birth of Son (Years)	Age at Death (Years)	Year of Death[2]
Adam	0	130	930	930
Seth	130	105	912	1042
Enos	235	90	905	1140
Cainan	325	70	910	1235
Mahalaleel	395	65	895	1290
Jared	460	162	962	1422
Enoch	622	65	365[3]	987[3]
Methuselah	687	187	969	1656
Lamech	874	182	777	1651
Noah	1056	502	950	2006
Shem	1558	100	600	2158
Arphaxad	1658	35	438	2096
Salah	1693	30	433	2126
Eber	1723	34	464	2187
Peleg	1757	30	239	1996
Reu	1787	32	239	2026
Serug	1819	30	230	2049
Nahor	1849	29	148	1997
Terah	1878	70	205	2083
Abraham	1948	100	175	2123
Isaac	2048	60	180	2228
Jacob	2108	—	147	2255

1. Assuming no gaps in the lists of Genesis 5 and 11.
2. In years after the Creation.
3. Time of translation.

APPENDIX 3
CHRONOLOGY OF IMPORTANT EVENTS IN GENESIS

Event	Years after Creation[1]
The Creation	0
Birth of Seth	130
Death of Adam	930
Translation of Enoch	987
Birth of Noah	1056
Birth of Japheth	1556
Coming of the Flood and Death of Methuselah	1656
Birth of Arphaxad after the Flood	1658
Confusion of Tongues	1757
Birth of Abraham	1948
Death of Noah	2006
Migration of Abraham to Canaan	2023
Birth of Ishmael	2033
Birth of Isaac	2048
Death of Terah	2083
Death of Sarah	2085
Marriage of Isaac and Rebekah	2088
Birth of Jacob and Esau	2108
Death of Abraham	2123
Marriage of Esau	2148
Death of Shem	2158
Flight of Jacob from Esau	2181
Death of Eber	2187
Marriage of Jacob to Leah and Rachel	2188
Birth of Reuben	2189
Birth of Judah	2192
Birth of Joseph	2198
Return of Jacob to Canaan	2201
Slaughter of the Shechemites	2212
Birth of Benjamin and Death of Rachel	2213
Sale of Joseph by His Brothers	2214
Death of Isaac	2228
Elevation of Joseph by Pharaoh	2228
Birth of Pharez, Son of Judah and Tamar	2232
Migration of Israel to Egypt	2237
Death of Jacob	2255
Death of Joseph	2308

1. Assuming no gaps in the genealogical lists in Genesis 5 and 11.

APPENDIX 4

QUOTATIONS FROM OR ALLUSIONS TO GENESIS IN THE NEW TESTAMENT

Reference Number	Genesis Reference	Topic	New Testament Reference
1.	1:1	God in the beginning	John 1:1
2.	1:1	Beginning of the world	II Timothy 1:9
3.	1:1	Beginning of the world	Titus 1:2
4.	1:1	Creation of universe	Hebrews 11:3
5.	1:1	Earth and heaven in the beginning	Hebrews 1:10
6.	1:3-5	Light out of darkness	II Corinthians 4:6
7.	1:5-7	Earth out of water and in water	II Peter 3:4-5
8.	1:11	Every seed his own body	I Corinthians 15:38-39
9.	1:11-12	Earth bringing forth herbs	Hebrews 6:7
10.	1:26-27	Made male and female	Mark 10:6-7
11.	1:26-27	Made in image of God	Colossians 3:10
12.	1:27	In the image of God	I Corinthians 11:7
13.	1:29-31	All creatures good	I Timothy 4:4
14.	1:31	All things made by God	Acts 17:24
15.	2:1	All that in them is	Acts 14:25
16.	2:1	All things created in heaven and earth	Revelation 10:6
17.	2:1	First heaven and first earth	Revelation 21:1
18.	2:1-3	All things created	Colossians 1:16
19.	2:1	Works finished	Hebrews 4:3
20.	2:2	Rest on the seventh day	Hebrews 4:4
21.	2:3	Ceased from His works	Hebrews 4:10
22.	2:3	Created all things	Ephesians 3:9
23.	2:3	World made by Him	John 1:10
24.	2:3	Created all things	Revelation 4:11
25.	2:4	Creation which God created	Mark 13:19
26.	2:4	He that made heaven and earth	Revelation 14:7
27.	2:4-6	Things that were made	Romans 1:20
28.	2:7	Adam a living soul	I Corinthians 15:45
29.	2:7	Man formed	I Timothy 2:13
30.	2:9	Tree of life in paradise	Revelation 2:7
31.	2:9	Fruit of tree of life	Revelation 22:14
32.	2:17	Death by sin	Romans 5:12
33.	2:18	Woman for the man	I Corinthians 11:9
34.	2:22	Woman of the man	I Corinthians 11:8
35.	2:23	Bone of his bone	Ephesians 5:30
36.	2:24	Leave father and mother	Ephesians 5:31
37.	2:24	One flesh	I Corinthians 6:16
38.	2:24	Cleave to his wife	Matthew 19:5
39.	2:24	One flesh	Mark 10:8
40.	3:1	That old serpent	Revelation 20:2

Reference Number	Genesis Reference	Topic	New Testament Reference
41.	3:1	Subtlety of serpent	II Corinthians 11:3
42.	3:4	Father of lies	John 8:44
43.	3:6	Woman deceived	I Timothy 2:14
44.	3:13	Serpent beguiled Eve	II Corinthians 11:3
45.	3:14	Devil sinneth from the beginning	I John 3:8
46.	3:15	Made of a woman	Galatians 4:4
47.	3:15	Satan bruised under foot	Romans 16:20
48.	3:15	Enmity with the woman	Revelation 12:13-17
49.	3:15	That old serpent	Revelation 12:9
50.	3:15	Treading on serpents	Luke 10: 19
51.	3:16	Saved in child-bearing	I Timothy 2:15
52.	3:16	Woman under obedience	I Corinthians 14:34
53.	3:16	Sorrow in travail	John 16:20
54.	3:16	Man the head of the woman	I Corinthians 11:3
55.	3:17	No more curse	Revelation 22:3
56.	3:18	Thorns and briers	Hebrews 6:8
57.	3:18-19	Bondage of corruption	Romans 8:21-22
58.	3:18-19	No more death, sorrow, pain	Revelation 21:4
59.	3:19	Work for your own bread	II Thessalonians 3:12
60.	3:19	By man came death	I Corinthians 15:21
61.	3:20	Mother of us all	Galatians 4:26
62.	3:22	Fruit of tree of life	Revelation 22
63.	3:23	Man from the earth	I Corinthians 15:47
64.	4:3-5	Abel a more excellent sacrifice	Hebrews 11:4
65.	4:4	Righteous Abel	Matthew 23:35
66.	4:8	Cain slew his brother	I John 3:12
67.	4:10	Blood of Abel	Hebrews 12:24
68.	4:11	Blood of Abel	Luke 11:51
69.	4:16	The way of Cain	Jude 11
70.	4:26	Prophets since the world began	Luke 1:70
71.	5:1	Book of the generations	Matthew 1:1
72.	5:1	Similitude of God	James 5:9
73.	5:2	Created male and female	Matthew 19:4
74.	5:2	Beginning of the creation of God	Revelation 3:14
75.	5:4	Death reigned from Adam	Romans 5:14-19
76.	5:5	In Adam all die	I Corinthians 15:22
77.	5:3-6	Adam to Enos	Luke 3:38
78.	5:12-21	Cainan to Methuselah	Luke 3:37
79.	5:18	Enoch, seventh from Adam	Jude 14
80.	5:24	Enoch translated	Hebrews 11:5
81.	5:28-32	Lamech to Shem	Luke 3:36
82.	5:29	Subjected to curse in hope	Romans 8:20

Reference Number	Genesis Reference	Topic	New Testament Reference
83.	6:2	Angels that sinned	II Peter 2:4
84.	6:3	Spirit striving with flesh	Galatians 5:17
85.	6:4	Angels left their habitation	Jude 6
86.	6:4	Marrying wives	Luke 17:27
87.	6:5	Days of Noah	Matthew 24:37
88.	6:12-13	The days of Noah	Luke 17:26
89.	6:13	God spared not old world	II Peter 2:5
90.	6:14-16	Ark preparing	I Peter 3:20
91.	7:1	Saving of his house	Hebrews 11:7
92.	7:13-16	Noah entered the ark	Matthew 24:38
93.	7:17-18	The flood came	Matthew 24:39
94.	7:19-20	Overflowed with water	II Peter 3:6
95.	8:21	Sweet savour	Philippians 4:18
96.	8:22	Fruitful seasons	Acts 14:15
97.	9:2	All things subjected to man	Hebrews 2:7-8
98.	9:3	Everything meat for you	I Timothy 4:3
99.	9:4	Blood not to be eaten	Acts 15:20
100.	9:6	Life for life	Matthew 26:52
101.	10:8-11	Babylon, the mother of abominations	Revelation 17:5
102.	10:32	All nations on face of earth	Acts 17:26
103.	11:4-5	That great city	Revelation 17:18
104.	11:10-13	Shem to Cainan	Luke 3:36
105.	11:14-20	Salah to Serug	Luke 3:35
106.	11:22-26	Nahor to Abraham	Luke 3:34
107.	11:31	Abraham dwelt in Haran	Acts 7:4
108.	12:1	Abraham to leave his kindred	Acts 7:3
109.	12:3	All families of earth to be blessed	Acts 3:25
110.	12:3	All nations blessed	Galatians 3:8
111.	12:4	Abraham went out	Hebrews 11:8
112.	12:5	From Haran to Canaan	Acts 7:4
113.	12:7	Unborn seed given the land	Acts 7:5
114.	13:15	Promise to the seed	Galatians 3:16
115.	14:18	Melchizedek met Abraham	Hebrews 7:1
116.	14:19	Abraham blessed of Melchizedek	Hebrews 7:6-7
117.	14:20	Tithes to Melchizedek	Hebrews 7:4-5
118.	15:5	So shall thy seed be	Romans 4:18
119.	15:5	Seed as the stars	Hebrews 11:12
120.	15:6	Faith counted for righteousness	Romans 4:3, 5, 9, 22
121.	15:6	Abraham believed God	Galatians 3:6
122.	15:6	Imputed righteousness	James 2:23
123.	15:13	Afflicted 400 years	Acts 7:6

Reference Number	Genesis Reference	Topic	New Testament Reference
124.	15:14	Nation to be judged	Acts 7:7
125.	15:16	Iniquity to be filled up	I Thessalonians 2:16
126.	16:1	No children	Acts 7:5
127.	16:15	A son by Hagar	Galatians 4:22
128.	17:5	Father of many nations	Romans 4:17
129.	17:7	With Abram's seed forever	Luke 1:55
130.	17:8	Oath sworn to Abraham	Luke 1:73
131.	17:10	Circumcision of the fathers	John 7:22
132.	17:11	Sign of circumcision	Romans 4:11
133.	17:13	Covenant of circumcision	Acts 7:8
134.	17:17	Abraham and Sarah past age	Romans 4:19
135.	18:2	Angels unawares	Hebrews 13:2
136.	18:10, 14	Sarah to bear at appointed time	Romans 9:9
137.	18:12	Sarah called Abraham "lord"	I Peter 3:6
138.	18:20	Sin of Sodom and Gomorrah	Matthew 10:15
139.	19:1-3	Entertaining angels	Hebrews 13:2
140.	19:5	Going after strange flesh	Jude 7
141.	19:9	Lot dwelling among wicked	II Peter 2:7-8
142.	19:24	Fire and brimstone from heaven	Luke 17:29
143.	19:25	Judgment on Sodom	Luke 10:12
144.	19:26	Lot's wife	Luke 17:32
145.	21:1	Promise fulfilled	Galatians 4:23
146.	21:2	Sarah conceived seed	Hebrews 11:11
147.	21:3	Abraham begat Isaac	Matthew 1:2
148.	21:4	Isaac the son of Abraham	Luke 3:34
149.	21:9	Son of promise persecuted	Galatians 4:29
150.	21:10	Bondwoman cast out	Galatians 4:30
151.	21:12	Isaac the seed of promise	Galatians 4:28
152.	21:13	Seed of Abraham	Romans 9:7
153.	21:13	Isaac the seed called	Hebrews 11:18
154.	21:14	Hagar in the wilderness	Galatians 4:24-25
155.	22:1-3	Abraham offered up Isaac	Hebrews 11:17
156.	22:5	Accounting God could raise him up	Hebrews 11:19
157.	22:9	Isaac on the altar	James 2:21
158.	22:16	God swearing by Himself	Hebrews 6:13
159.	22:17	Blessing and multiplying	Hebrews 6:14
160.	22:17	As the sand and stars	Hebrews 11:12
161.	22:18	Heir of all nations of earth	Romans 4:13
162.	23:4	Stranger and sojourner	Hebrews 11:9
163.	23:16-20	Sepulcher bought	Acts 7:6
164.	25:21	Rebekah conceived	Romans 9:10
165.	25:23	Elder to serve the younger	Romans 9:12

Reference Number	Genesis Reference	Topic	New Testament Reference
166.	25:25-26	Jacob and Esau	Romans 9:13
167.	25:33	Birthright despised	Hebrews 12:16
168.	26:3	Blessing of Abraham	Galatians 4:14
169.	26:4-5	Covenant confirmed	Galatians 4:17
170.	27:27-29, 39-40	Isaac blessed Jacob and Esau	Hebrews 11:20
171.	27:34, 38	No place of repentance	Hebrews 12:17
172.	28:12	Angels descending	John 1:51
173.	28:15	Never leave thee	Hebrews 13:5
174.	29:35	Judah, son of Jacob	Luke 3:33
175.	30:13	Called blessed	Luke 1:48
176.	30:23	Reproach taken away	Luke 1:25
177.	31:42	God of Abraham, Isaac, and Jacob	Matthew 22:32
178.	32:12	Seed as the sand	Hebrews 11:12
179.	33:19	Jacob's parcel of ground	John 4:5
180.	35:16-17	Rachel weeping	Matthew 2:18
181.	37:28	Joseph sold into Egypt	Acts 7:9
182.	38:29	Judah begat Pharez	Matthew 1:3
183.	39:2, 23	The Lord with Joseph	Acts 7:9
184.	41:41-44	Joseph exalted	Acts 7:10
185.	41:54	Dearth in Egypt	Acts 7:11
186.	42:1-2	Corn in Egypt	Acts 7:12
187.	42:5	Famine in Canaan	Acts 7:11
188.	42:13	Twelve brethren	Acts 7:8
189.	45:1-4	Joseph revealed to his brethren	Acts 7:13
190.	45:9-11	Joseph sending for Jacob	Acts 7:14
191.	46:5-6	Jacob going to Egypt	Acts 7:15
192.	46:26-27	Seventy-five souls	Acts 7:14
193.	47:9	Strangers and pilgrims	Hebrews 11:13
194.	47:31	Leaning on top of staff	Hebrews 11:21
195.	48:13-20	Jacob blessed sons of Joseph	Hebrews 11:21
196.	49:9-10	Lion of tribe of Judah	Revelation 5:5
197.	49:10	Lord sprang from Judah	Hebrews 7:14
198.	49:11	Washed garments in blood	Revelation 7:14
199.	49:29-30	Jacob buried in Canaan	Acts 7:16
200.	50:24-26	Death of Joseph	Hebrews 11:22

Observations

1. The references listed above do not include references to "Israel" as a nation, or to "Judah," "Benjamin," and so forth, as tribes, even though such names are first encountered in Genesis.

2. The references listed do not include verses in which there is merely a similarity in wording (e.g., John 2:5 with Genesis 41:55) unless there is evidence that

the New Testament writer consciously was incorporating the Genesis phraseology into his own writings.

3. All books of the New Testament except Philemon, II John, and III John contain allusions to Genesis.

4. Of the fifty chapters in Genesis, only seven (chapters 20, 24, 34, 36, 40, 43, 44) are not quoted or cited in the New Testament.

5. More than half of the two hundred New Testament allusions to Genesis are found in the first eleven chapters of Genesis.

6. Sixty-three of the allusions are to the first three chapters of Genesis.

7. Fourteen of the allusions are from the "Flood chapters" (6, 7, 8).

8. Fifty-eight references are related to Abraham.

9. None of the two hundred New Testament references to Genesis are explicitly ascribed to Moses as their author, indicating a probable recognition that he was editor and compiler, rather than author.

10. Twenty-five of the references were directly from Christ Himself (from chapters 1, 2, 3, 4, 5, 6, 7, 9, 17, 18, 19, 28, and 31).

APPENDIX 5
The Universality of the Deluge

Central to the question of the historicity of the early chapters of Genesis is the question whether the Noahic Flood was global or only regional. A world-wide Flood would have cataclysmically changed the entire surface of the globe, including any fossil-bearing sedimentary rocks that may have been formed prior to that time. Consequently, the earth's present fossiliferous sediments must date largely from the time of their deposition in the waters of the great Flood.

On the other hand, the modern evolutionary system of earth history denies any such global cataclysm and is based on the assumption of uniformitarianism. The sedimentary rocks and their fossil contents have been interpreted as evidence of a vast series of evolutionary ages extending over billions of years of time, deposited slowly and generally uniformly over the earth as living organisms gradually evolved into higher and higher forms during those ages.

The "day-age theory" is the attempt by Bible expositors to accommodate these evolutionary ages *within* the framework of the six days of creation. The "gap theory" is the attempt by other expositors to accommodate them *outside* the framework of the six days of creation. Both such theories, if consistent, are associated with the "local flood theory," since a universal Flood would have destroyed the sedimentary framework of the geological ages. That is, a universal Flood precludes the historicity of the geological ages, and vice versa.

If the Genesis Flood actually was worldwide, then the strained exegesis associated with the day-age and gap theories becomes unnecessary and harmful. In the tabulation below, therefore, are listed one hundred reasons why the Flood should be accepted as a true global cataclysm.

From the Genesis Record

	Genesis Reference	Argument
1.	1:7	Water above the atmosphere must have been global in extent.
2.	2:5	No rain on the earth must have been worldwide condition.
3.	2:6	Earth mist watered the whole face of the ground.
4.	2:10-14	Edenic geography no longer in existence.
5.	4:22	High civilization at dawn of history not continuous with present world.
6.	5:5, etc.	Longevity of antediluvian patriarchs indicates distinctive biosphere.
7.	6:1	Man had multiplied on the face of the earth.
8.	6:2	Demonic-human unions coextensive with mankind.
9.	6:5	Universal evil inexplicable in postdiluvian society.
10.	6:6-7	Repentance of God extended to the whole animal creation.
11.	6:11	Earth was filled with violence and corruption before God.
12.	6:12	All flesh was corrupted (possibly including animals).
13.	6:13	God decided to destroy both man and the earth.
14.	6:15	Ark too large for regional fauna.

	Genesis Reference	Argument
15.	6:17	Everything with the breath of life to die.
16.	6:19	Purpose of ark was to keep two of every sort alive.
17.	6:20	Animals of all kinds migrated to the ark.
18.	6:21	All kinds of edible food taken on the ark.
19.	7:4	Every living substance on the ground to be destroyed.
20.	7:10	"The flood" (Hebrew *mabbul*) applies solely to Noah's Flood.
21.	7:11	All the fountains of the great deep cleaved open in one day.
22.	7:11	The "sluiceways from the floodgates" of heaven were opened.
23.	7:12	Rain poured continuously for forty days and forty nights.
24.	7:18	The waters prevailed and increased greatly.
25.	7:19	High hills under the whole heaven were covered.
26.	7:20	Waters fifteen cubits above highest mountains.
27.	7:21	Every man died on the earth.
28.	7:22	All flesh with the breath of life in the dry land died.
29.	7:23	Every living substance destroyed off the face of the ground.
30.	7:24	Waters at maximum height for five months.
31.	8:2	Fountains of deep open for five months.
32.	8:2	Windows of heaven open for five months.
33.	8:4	Ark floated over 17,000-ft. mountains for five months.
34.	8:5	Water receded 2-1/2 months before mountain tops seen.
35.	8:9	Dove found no suitable ground even after four months of recession.
36.	8:11	Plants began budding after nine months of the Flood.
37.	8:14	Occupants were in the ark over a year.
38.	8:19	All kinds of present nonmarine animals came from the ark.
39.	8:21	God smote all things living only once.
40.	8:22	Present uniformity of nature dates from the end of the Flood.
41.	9:1	Earth was to be filled with descendants of Noah.
42.	9:2	Changed relation between man and animals followed the Flood.
43.	9:3	Man permitted animal food after Flood.
44.	9:6	Institution of human government dates from Flood.
45.	9:10	God's covenant made with every living creature.
46.	9:11	The Flood promised by God never to come again on the earth.
47.	9:13	Rainbow placed in sky after the Flood.
48.	9:19	Whole earth overspread by the sons of Noah.
49.	11:1	Whole earth of one language after the Flood.
50.	11:9	All men lived in one place after the Flood.

From Other Biblical Writers

51.	Job 12:15	The waters overturned the earth.
52.	Psalm 29:10	The Flood testified God as eternal king.
53.	Psalm 104:8	Flood terminated by crustal tectonics.
54.	Isaiah 55:9	Waters of Noah went over the earth.

	Genesis Reference	*Argument*
55.	Matthew 24:37	The days of Noah like those when Christ comes.
56.	Matthew 24:39	The Flood took them all away.
57.	Luke 17:27	The Flood destroyed them all.
58.	Hebrews 11:7	Noah warned of things never seen before.
59.	Hebrews 11:7	Noah condemned the world by his faith.
60.	I Peter 3:20	Only eight souls saved on the ark through the Flood.
61.	II Peter 2:5	God spared not the old world (Greek *kosmos*).
62.	II Peter 2:5	God brought the Flood on the world of the ungodly.
63.	II Peter 2:5	The "flood" (Greek *kataklusmos*) applied solely to Noah's Flood.
64.	II Peter 3:6	The world that then was, perished by the watery cataclysm.

From Non-Biblical Evidence

	Argument
65.	Worldwide distribution of Flood traditions.
66.	Origin of civilization near Ararat-Babylon region in post-Flood time.
67.	Convergence of population growth statistics on date of Flood.
68.	Dating of oldest living things at post-Flood time.
69.	Worldwide occurrence of water-laid sediments and sedimentary rocks.
70.	Recent uplift of major mountain ranges.
71.	Marine fossils on crests of mountains.
72.	Evidence of former worldwide warm climate.
73.	Necessity of catastrophic burial and rapid lithification of fossil deposits.
74.	Recent origin of many datable geological processes.
75.	Worldwide distribution of all types of fossils.
76.	Uniform physical appearance of rocks from different "ages."
77.	Frequent mixing of fossils from different "ages."
78.	Near-random deposition of formational sequences.
79.	Equivalence of total organic material in present world and fossil world.
80.	Wide distribution of recent volcanic rocks.
81.	Evidence of recent water bodies in present desert areas.
82.	Worldwide occurrence of raised shore lines and river terraces.
83.	Evidence of recent drastic rise in sea level.
84.	Universal occurrence of rivers in valleys too large for the present stream.
85.	Sudden extinction of dinosaurs and other prehistoric animals.
86.	Rapid onset of glacial period.
87.	Existence of polystrate fossils.
88.	Preservation of tracks and other ephemeral markings throughout geologic column.
89.	Worldwide occurrence of sedimentary fossil "graveyards" in rocks of all "ages."

	Argument
90.	Absence of any physical evidence of chronologic boundary between rocks of successive "ages."
91.	Occurrence of all rock types (shale, limestone, granite, etc.) in all "ages."
92.	Parallel of supposed evolutionary sequence through different "ages" with modern ecological zonation in the one present age.
93.	Lack of correlation of most radiometric "ages" with assumed paleontologic "ages."
94.	Absence of meteorites in geologic column.
95.	Absence of hail imprints in geologic column, despite abundance of fossil ripple-marks and raindrop imprints.
96.	Evidence of man's existence during earliest of geologic "ages" (e.g., human footprints in Cambrian, Carboniferous, and Cretaceous formations).
97.	Similar structural features (rifts, faults, folds, thrusts, etc.) in rocks of all "ages."
98.	Absence of evidence of drainage systems in sediments of any "ages" except the most recent.
99.	Hydraulic evidence of rapid deposition of each stratum and of continuous formation of every sequence of strata, with no worldwide time gap between any formation and another above it.
100.	Numerous modern sightings of probable remains of Noah's ark at about 15,000 feet elevation in ice cap on Mount Ararat.

APPENDIX 6
"First Mentions" of Important Biblical Words in Genesis

Word	Text	Word	Text
Altar	8:20	Light	1:3
Angel	16:7	Love	22:2
Atonement (= pitch)	6:14	Make	1:7
Believe	15:6	Man	1:26
Bless	1:22	Mercy	19:16
Blood	4:10	Obey	22:18
Book	5:1	Peace (= Salem)	14:18
Choose	6:2	Perfect (= complete)	6:9
City	4:17	Power (= strength)	4:12
Clothe	3:21	Praise (= commend)	12:15
Command	2:16	Pray	20:7
Complete	6:9	Prophet	20:7
Conception	3:16	Redeem	48:16
Covenant	6:18	Rest	2:1
Create	1:1	Reward	15:1
Curse	3:14	Righteous (= just)	6:9
Darkness	1:2	Righteousness	15:6
Day	1:5	Salvation	49:18
Die	2:17	Sanctify	2:3
Door	4:7	Say	1:3
Drunken	9:21	Science (= knowledge)	2:17
Everlasting (= forever)	3:22	See	1:4
Evil	2:9	Seed	1:11
Faith	15:6	Send	3:23
Fear (= afraid)	3:10	Shed (= pour out)	9:6
Fear not	15:1	Shield	15:1
Fire	19:24	Sign	1:14
Forever	3:22	Sin	4:7
Fruit	1:11	Sorrow	3:16
Give	1:29	Soul	1:21
Glory	31:1	Sow	26:12
Good	1:4	Speak (= say)	1:3
Grace	6:9	Strength	4:12
Hear	3:8	Tempt	22:1
Heart	6:5	Tithe	14:20
Holy (= sanctified)	2:3	Truth	24:27
House	7:1	Vision	15:1
I am	15:1	Will	24:5
Impute (= count)	15:6	Wine	9:21
Just	6:9	Woman	2:22
Kingdom	10:10	Word	15:1
Knowledge	2:17	Work	2:2
Law	26:5	Worship (= bow down)	18:2
Life	2:7		

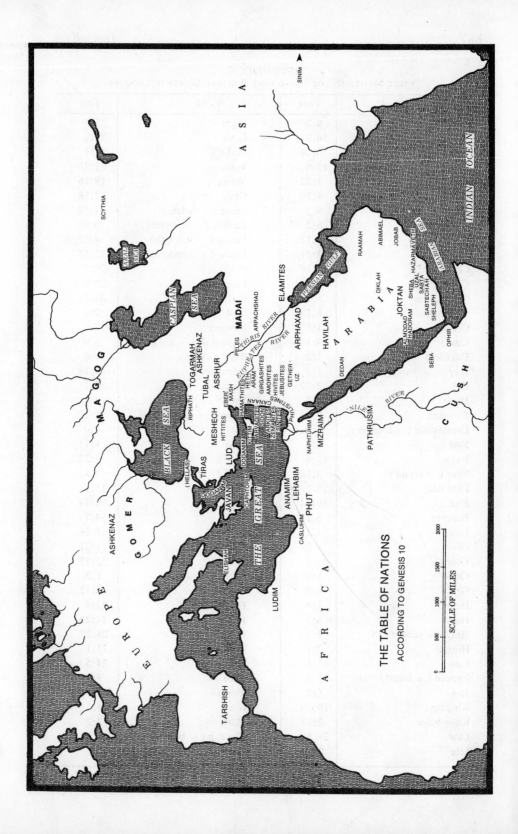

THE TABLE OF NATIONS
ACCORDING TO GENESIS 10

SCALE OF MILES

0   500   1000   1500   2000

POST-DILUVIAN WORLD

"CENTER OF EARTH" ★

CASPIAN SEA

Persian Gulf

Tigris

Babel

SHINAR

Ur

Euphrates

Padan-aram

Haran

Nahor

MT. ARARAT

BLACK SEA

Damascus

Kadesh

El-paran

Midian

Beer-lahai-roi

Goshen

Succoth

On

Memphis (Noph)

EGYPT

Nile River

Thebes (No)

MEDITERRANEAN SEA

RED SEA

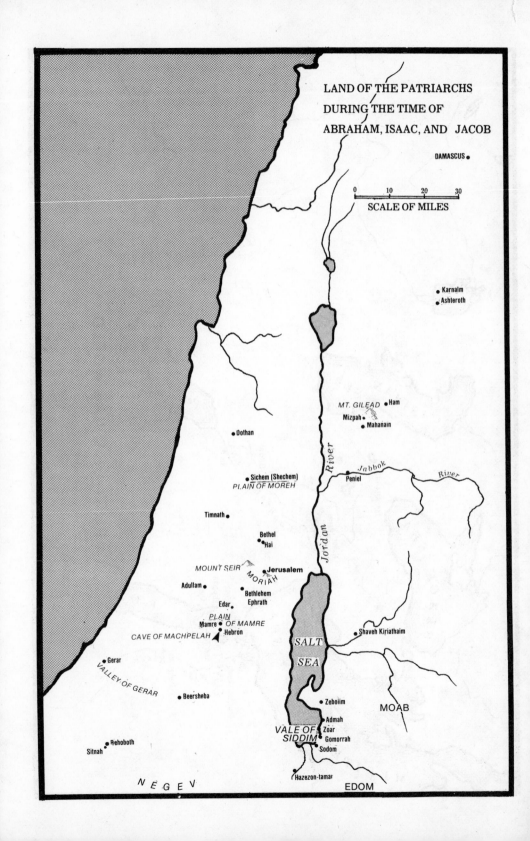

LAND OF THE PATRIARCHS
DURING THE TIME OF
ABRAHAM, ISAAC, AND JACOB

DAMASCUS •

0   10   20   30
SCALE OF MILES

• Karnaim
• Ashteroth

MT. GILEAD • Ham
Mizpah •
• Mahanaim

• Dothan

Jabbok   *River*

• Sichem (Shechem)
PLAIN OF MOREH   Peniel •

River

• Timnath

Bethel •
Hai •

MOUNT SEIR   **Jerusalem**
                MORIAH

Adullam •

Edar •   Bethlehem
        Ephrath

        PLAIN
Mamre • *OF MAMRE*
CAVE OF MACHPELAH ▶ Hebron •

        • Shaveh Kiriathaim

Jordan

SALT
SEA

• Gerar
VALLEY OF GERAR

• Beersheba   **MOAB**

        • Zeboiim
        Admah
VALE OF   Zoar
SIDDIM   Gomorrah
        Sodom

• Rehoboth
Sitnah •

N E G E V   • Hazezon-tamar

        EDOM

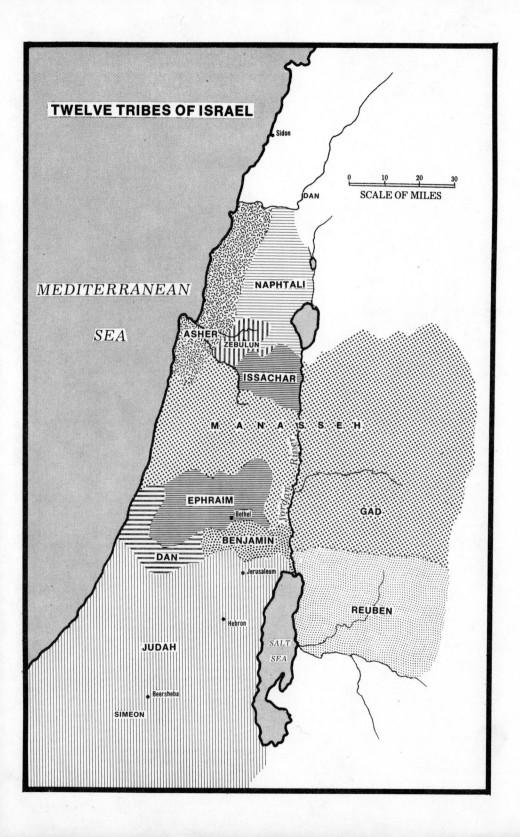

Indexes

Indexes

INDEX OF SUBJECTS

INDEX OF SCRIPTURE REFERENCES

OLD TESTAMENT

707

New Testament